The Changing School Scene. Challenge to Psychology
by Leah Gold Fein

Troubled Children: Their Families, Schools, and Treatments
by Leonore R. Love and Jaques W. Kaswan

Research Strategies in Psychotherapy
by Edward S. Bordin

The Volunteer Subject
by Robert Rosenthal and Ralph L. Rosnow

Innovations in Client-Centered Therapy
by David A. Wexler and Laura North Rice

The Rorschach: A Comprehensive System
by John E. Exner

Theory and Practice in Behavior Therapy
by Aubrey J. Yates

Principles of Psychotherapy
by Irving B. Weiner

Psychoactive Drugs and Social Judgment: Theory and Research
edited by Kenneth Hammond and C. R. B. Joyce

Clinical Methods in Psychology
edited by Irving B. Weiner

Human Resources for Troubled Children
by Werner I. Halpern and Stanley Kissel

Hyperactivity
by Dorothea M. Ross and Sheila A. Ross

Heroin Addiction: Theory, Research, and Treatment
by Jerome J. Platt and Christina Labate

Children's Rights and the Mental Health Profession
edited by Gerald P. Koocher

The Role of the Father in Child Development
edited by Michael E. Lamb

Handbook of Behavioral Assessment
edited by Anthony R. Ciminero, Karen S. Calhoun, and Henry E. Adams

Counseling and Psychotherapy: A Behavioral Approach
by E. Lakin Phillips

Dimensions of Personality
edited by Harvey London and John E. Exner, Jr.

The Mental Health Industry: A Cultural Phenomenon
by Peter A. Magaro, Robert Gripp, David McDowell, and Ivan W. Miller III

Nonverbal Communication: The State of the Art
by Robert G. Harper, Arthur N. Wiens, and Joseph D. Matarazzo

Alcoholism and Treatment
by David J. Armor, J. Michael Polich, and Harriet B. Stambul

A Biodevelopmental Approach to Clinical Child Psychology: Cognitive Controls and Cognitive Control Theory
by Sebastiano Santostefano

Handbook of Infant Development
edited by Joy D. Osofsky

HANDBOOK OF
INFANT DEVELOPMENT

HANDBOOK OF
INFANT DEVELOPMENT

Edited by

JOY D. OSOFSKY

The Menninger Foundation

and

University of Kansas

A WILEY-INTERSCIENCE PUBLICATION

JOHN WILEY & SONS, New York ● Chichester ● Brisbane ● Toronto

Library of Congress Cataloging in Publication Data
Main entry under title:

Handbook of infant development.

   (Wiley series on personality processes)
   "A Wiley-Interscience publication."
   Includes indexes.
   1. Infant psychology—Addresses, essays, lectures.
2. Parent and child—Addresses, essays, lectures.
I. Osofsky, Joy D.
BF723.I6H32   155.4'22 78–17605
ISBN 0–471–65703–4

Printed in the United States of America

10 9 8 7 6 5 4 3 2

iv

Contributors

DR. HEIDELISE ALS, Child Development Unit, Children's Hospital Medical Center, Boston.

DR. LEILA BECKWITH, Department of Pediatrics, University of California at Los Angeles.

DR. E. KUNO BELLER, Department of Psychology, Temple University.

DR. KATHLEEN M. BERG, Department of Psychology, University of Florida.

DR. W. KEITH BERG, Department of Psychology, University of Florida.

DR. YVONNE BRACKBILL, Department of Psychology, University of Florida.

DR. T. BERRY BRAZELTON, Child Development Unit, Children's Hospital Medical Center, Boston.

DR. PATRICK J. CAVANAUGH, Department of Psychology, University of Kentucky.

DR. LESLIE B. COHEN, Department of Psychology, University of Illinois, Champaign.

MS. KAREN CONNORS, Department of Psychology, Temple University.

DR. JUDY S. DeLOACHE, Department of Psychology, University of Illinois, Champaign.

DR. DOROTHY H. EICHORN, Institute of Human Development, University of California, Berkeley.

DR. GERALD GRATCH, Department of Psychology, University of Houston.

DR. FRANCES DEGEN HOROWITZ, Department of Human Development, University of Kansas.

DR. DOROTHY S. HUNTINGTON, Peninsula Hospital and Medical Center, Burlingame, California.

DR. JEROME KAGAN, Department of Psychology, Harvard University.

DR. JOHN H. KENNELL, Rainbow Babies and Children's Hospital, Cleveland.

DR. MARSHALL H. KLAUS, Rainbow Babies and Children's Hospital, Cleveland.

DR. CLAIRE B. KOPP, Division of Child Development, Department of Pediatrics, School of Medicine, University of California, Los Angeles.

DR. ANNELIESE F. KORNER, Department of Psychiatry, Stanford University Medical School.

DR. BARRY M. LESTER, Child Development Unit, Children's Hospital Medical Center, Boston.

DR. MICHAEL LEWIS, Institute for Study of Human Development, Educational Testing Service, Princeton, New Jersey.

DR. ROBERT B. McCALL, The Boys Town Center for the Study of Youth Development, Boys Town, Nebraska.

DR. EDWARD C. MUELLER, Department of Psychology, Boston University.

DR. JOY D. OSOFSKY, The Menninger Foundation, Topeka, Kansas and Department of Human Development, University of Kansas.

DR. ROSS D. PARKE, Department of Psychology, University of Illinois, Champaign.

DR. ARTHUR H. PARMELEE, Department of Pediatrics, University of California, Los Angeles.

DR. STEPHEN W. PORGES, Department of Psychology, University of Illinois, Champaign.

DR. SALLY PROVENCE, Child Study Center, Yale University.

DR. JUDY F. ROSENBLITH, Department of Psychology, Wheaton College, Norton, Massachusetts.

DR. HENRY L. ROSETT, Department of Psychiatry, Boston University School of Medicine.

DR. GENE P. SACKETT, Regional Primate Research Center, University of Washington.

DR. ARNOLD J. SAMEROFF, Department of Psychology, University of Rochester.

DR. LOUIS W. SANDER, Department of Psychiatry, University of Colorado Medical Center, Denver.

DR. PATRICIA A. SELF, Department of Psychology, University of Oklahoma.

DR. ALBERT J. SOLNIT, Child Study Center, Yale University.

DR. ALAN L. SROUFE, Institute of Child Development, University of Minnesota.

DR. MARK D. STARR, Institute for Study of Human Development, Educational Testing Service, Princeton, New Jersey.

DR. MARK S. STRAUSS, Department of Psychology, University of Illinois, Champaign.

DR. EDWARD TRONICK, Department of Psychology, University of Massachusetts, Amherst.

DR. DEBORAH VANDELL, Department of Psychology, Boston University.

DR. DIANA K. VOOS, Rainbow Babies and Children's Hospital, Cleveland.

DR. RAYMOND K. YANG, Department of Child and Family Development, University of Georgia.

DR. LEON J. YARROW, National Institute of Child Health & Human Development, Bethesda, Maryland.

Series Preface

This series of books is addressed to behavioral scientists interested in the nature of human personality. Its scope should prove pertinent to personality theorists and researchers as well as to clinicians concerned with applying an understanding of personality processes to the amelioration of emotional difficulties in living. To this end, the series provides a scholarly integration of theoretical formulations, empirical data, and practical recommendations.

Six major aspects of studying and learning about human personality can be designated: personality theory, personality structure and dynamics, personality development, personality assessment, personality change, and personality adjustment. In exploring these aspects of personality, the books in the series discuss a number of distinct but related subject areas: the nature and implications of various theories of personality; personality characteristics that account for consistencies and variations in human behavior; the emergence of personality processes in children and adolescents; the use of interviewing and testing procedures to evaluate individual differences in personality; efforts to modify personality styles through psychotherapy, counseling, behavior therapy, and other methods of influence; and patterns of abnormal personality functioning that impair individual competence.

IRVING B. WEINER

Case Western Reserve University
Cleveland, Ohio

Preface

The idea for the *Handbook of Infant Development,* which was conceived in 1975, developed from a recognized need for a comprehensive volume for teachers, researchers, and scholars that would bring together current developments in the field of infancy. In teaching infancy to graduate students over the years, my colleagues throughout the country and I have found the need for a comprehensive book that would integrate the diverse areas we cover. I have therefore developed a volume that contains both factually oriented reviews of the literature and thoughtful considerations of the major conceptual issues of the moment. The contributors to this volume have managed, through dedication and hard work, to present the most progressive perspectives on the field of infancy as it exists at the present time, and I am very grateful for their efforts.

In the *Handbook,* an attempt has been made to present a compilation of new ideas, conceptualizations, and research in the area of infancy. A broad range of subject matter is included; theoretical, methodological, conceptual, intervention, and clinical issues are considered from multiple points of view. The range, breadth, and depth of the material reflect the enormous growth that has occurred in the field of infancy over the past few years. Yet, it is recognized that in spite of the length of this book and the attempt to be comprehensive and thorough, some areas have been either omitted or not covered thoroughly—a shortcoming difficult to overcome in such a rapidly growing field. As it stands, however, I believe that the *Handbook of Infant Development* will add a great deal of information to the existing literature in the field.

The book is organized into six sections, each of which covers a different aspect of infant development. To provide an introductory perspective, Dr. Jerome Kagan presents an overview of the field of human infancy that sets the stage for the material discussed in the volume. In this chapter, he offers an historical perspective on human infancy as well as a current look at present and future directions.

Part One deals with newborn and early infant behavior. Drs. Claire Kopp and Arthur Parmelee discuss prenatal and perinatal influences which appear to play a crucial role in the behavior of the developing infant. Dr. Yvonne Brackbill in her chapter reviews the effects of obstetrical medication on newborn and infant behavior. Behavioral assessment of the newborn is discussed in an overview chapter by Drs. Patricia Self and Frances Horowitz, and assessment of the infant is discussed by Dr. Raymond Yang. These overview chapters are followed by more specific chapters reviewing work done with two widely used measures for the assessment of newborns. The first, by Drs. T. Barry Brazelton, Heidelise Als, Edward Tronick, and Barry Lester, describes the Brazelton

Neonatal Behavior Assessment Scale, and the second, by Dr. Judy Rosenblith, reviews the Graham-Rosenblith Behavioral Test for Neonates.

Part Two deals with developmental perspectives in infancy. These chapters cover important behavioral developments that take place during the first 2 years of life. The first chapter, by Dr. Dorothy Eichorn, examines physical development and maturation. The second, by Drs. Keith Berg and Kathleen Berg, covers psychophysiological development in infancy and the influence of psychophysiological factors on infant state, sensory function, and attention. The third chapter, by Drs. Arnold Sameroff and Patrick Cavanaugh, covers the vast field of learning in infancy. Drs. Leslie Cohen, Judy DeLoache, and Mark Strauss discuss the complex area of infant visual perception. The fifth chapter, by Dr. Gerald Gratch, handles the development of language and thought in infancy. Finally, Dr. Alan Sroufe covers the many parameters of socioemotional development. To provide a comprehensive and integrative view of many of the complex developmental issues, these chapters include extensive reference bibliographies, which I believe should be very useful to the reader.

Part Three deals with the area of parent-infant and infant-infant relationships. Parent-infant interaction is divided into two chapters. The first, by Dr. Joy Osofsky and Ms. Karen Connors, considers mother-infant interaction, and the second, by Dr. Ross Parke, deals with father-infant interaction. Infant-infant interaction, a very new and exciting perspective on early infant development, is presented in a chapter by Drs. Edward Mueller and Deborah Vandell. Finally, Dr. Gene Sackett discusses some of the complex methodological and data analysis issues in interactional research in his chapter on analysis of behavioral interaction research.

Part Four deals with the general issue of continuity and change and the relationship of early and later behavior. There has been considerable controversy in this area in the past few years; some researchers who have done longitudinal work and have carefully considered these issues feel that investigators may not always conceptualize the right questions. Drs. Michael Lewis and Mark Starr examine the general issue of developmental continuity. Dr. Leila Beckwith presents material on the prediction of emotional and social behavior over time. Dr. Robert McCall discusses the development of intellectual functioning in infancy and the question of predictability of later I.Q. Finally, Dr. Stephen Porges considers developmental and methodological issues that are of concern in designing infancy research dealing with continuity and change.

Part Five, presenting a broad perspective on research, theory, and possible applications of work in the area of infancy, deals with some clinical issues, applications, and interventions. Dr. Anneliese Korner provides a thoughtful overview of conceptual issues that are important for understanding infancy. Drs. John Kennell, Diana Voos, and Marshall Klaus report on their interesting and important research and conceptual thinking on parent-infant bonding. Drs. Albert Solnit and Sally Provence consider vulnerability and risk in early childhood. Drs. Henry Rosett and Louis Sander deal with available data concerning the effects of maternal drinking on newborn behavior. Dr. Dorothy Huntington discusses supportive programs for infants and parents. Finally, Dr. E. Kuno Beller reviews early intervention programs. All the chapters in this section present research, conceptual, and theoretical issues and deal with application and implications for early infant development.

The concluding chapter, by Dr. Leon Yarrow, considers historical perspectives and future directions for the study of infant development. He also discusses some interesting ideas about the present standing and the future of the field from the perspectives of research, application, and intervention.

The *Handbook of Infant Development* considers crucial issues in the area of infancy today. The various perspectives presented in the book provide a new and different look at the field. I believe that many teachers and researchers will find it an important and useful resource.

JOY D. OSOFSKY

Topeka, Kansas
April 1978

Acknowledgments

When I originally planned this volume, I was teaching at Temple University, and I would like to thank the members of the Department of Psychology for their encouragement and support. Dr. Willis Overton, Chairman of the Developmental Division and both colleague and friend, was particularly helpful and supportive during the early stages of this volume. My colleagues in the Department of Clinical Psychology at The Menninger Foundation have offered continuing support. I particularly want to thank Dr. Sydney Smith, former Director of Clinical Psychology, and Dr. Martin Leichtman, Director of Psychology at the Children's Division of The Menninger Foundation, for their help. My editors at Wiley-Interscience, Mr. Walter Maytham and Mr. Peter Peirce, have worked closely with me to help make the idea of this volume a reality, and I appreciate their efforts. I also appreciate the efforts of the production department, especially Priscilla Taguer, who have helped a great deal during the final stages of preparation of the book.

I want to express sincere thanks to the contributors to this volume. Without their efforts and excellent chapters, the *Handbook* could not have become a reality.

Finally, I want to give special thanks to my family. My husband, Dr. Howard Osofsky, has always been confident that my projects would be successfully completed and has been by my side throughout. Hari, my daughter, has helped me both to see and to understand firsthand the area of infant and child development and to become a more sensitive observer. Finally, my infant son, Justin, born at about the same time as the book went to press, is enabling me to reexperience some of the fascinating discoveries of infancy.

J.D.O.

Contents

HANDBOOK OF
INFANT DEVELOPMENT

CHAPTER 1

Overview: Perspectives on Human Infancy[1]

Jerome Kagan

Each generation of parents holds a set of beliefs regarding the essential nature of the infant, the human qualities valued by the local community, an informal theory which stipulates the experiences and supernatural interventions that can enhance or retard the child's acquisition of those qualities, and a subjective estimate of the likelihood that the child will eventually command the valued characteristics should the family make the necessary investment of emotional and material resources. Prior to the changes in attitudes that followed the second world war, the Japanese parent regarded the infant as untamed and autonomous (Caudill and Weinstein, 1969). Since both child and adult have to be capable of entering into deeply dependent relations with others—the feeling of *amae* (Akita, 1970)—the mother's task is to draw the baby into an intimately dependent relation on her through quiet, conscientious nurturance. By contrast, the modern American mother projects dependence and helplessness on her infant. Since she realizes that relentless autonomy will be required of the adolescent, she promotes independence in her young child. Thus while the distressed Japanese infant is attended with short delay, the American baby is often allowed to cry for a few minutes, presumably to prepare him for more serious future frustrations.

The Rajput mother of northern India assumes a less active attitude than either the Japanese or American. Since the Rajput hold a fatalistic belief in control of the future by supernatural powers, and since the occupational future of the child is relatively certain— the boy will be a farmer and the girl will be a farmer's wife—there is little motivation to intrude into the infant's life. Hence for most of the first 2 years the child is a passive observer of experience (Minturn and Hitchcock, 1963).

Plato's suggestions to Athenian caretakers contain a particularly nice example of the relation between the conception of the ideal and the local theory of development. Since 4th-century Greeks regarded the harmonious coordination of mind and body as a central ideal, Plato advised mothers to keep their infants in motion and to rock them to sleep rhythmically (Jaeger, 1944). The early exposure to rhythmic experience presumably sensitized the infant, making it easier for the adolescent to master difficult motor coordinations. The unstated dynamic hypothesis that seems to lie behind the advice is probably not much different from the one held by American parents. If one asked American parents what practices they should initiate with their infant so that the adolescent would appreciate music, the modal reply would probably be, "Play good music to them." The assumption

[1]The research reported in this paper was supported in part by grants from NICHD, The Carnegie Corporation of New York, The Spencer Foundation, Office of Child Development, and the Foundation for Child Development. The paper was prepared while the author was a Belding Scholar of the Foundation for Child Development.

made by both Plato and the contemporary parent reduces to: In order to promote an affinity and preparedness for a competence in later childhood, expose the infant to some reasonable representation of the relevant experience in the hope that it will prime the infant.

Plato's home-grown theory of the origin of adolescent sulkiness or aggression was also not much different from our own. A baby who was coddled became a sulky adolescent; one that was bullied became misanthropic. Since there is no support for either statement, then or now, the fact that Plato and child advisors 2400 years later make the same assumptions says more about how the adult mind works than it does about the development of a child. It is easy, however, to surmise how adults might come to that conclusion. Parents who respond every time a baby cries tend, on the average, to have more irritable babies, at least temporarily. The contemporary association between adult practice and infant attribute has been noted by many. But that fact is not sufficient to assume that the relation noted in infancy would persist indefinitely. Such a prejudice ignores the fact that with maturity the child becomes aware of the standards of his culture and begins to relinquish habits that his family dislikes. Since sulkiness is not generally admired, the child is capable of relinquishing the habit, as he gives up his earlier dispositions to soil his clothes and spill his cereal. But since the best guess about the future is the present, if there is no other information, Plato's prophecy was reasonable (Jaeger, 1944).

Freedom from fear was the second ideal of the paideia of 4th-century Greece. Since adolescents were to be resistant to apprehension, Plato suggested that the baby be exposed to events that would help him conquer early fears—an ancient example of desensitization theory, which is also held by the Gusii of Kenya (LeVine and LeVine, 1963). But many 19th-century Europeans held the opposite belief. Dr. P. Chavasse, a pediatrician who wrote popular books of advice, warned parents that if adults told the young child frightening stories, he would become timid and "continue so for the remainder of his life" (Chavasse, 1869, p. 169). Chavasse's conviction that fright was physically and psychologically dangerous has a parallel in the contemporary belief of many descendants of Mayan culture living in northwest Guatemala. *Susto*—best translated as fear—can produce serious illness. Indeed, if an adult becomes unexpectedly frightened, it is believed that the heart can tear away from the thoracic cavity, rise to the throat, and choke the afflicted person. Infants are usually restricted during most of their 1st year in order to avoid chance encounter with people or objects that might provoke fear. The wary attitude toward fear held by 19th-century Europeans was a specific instance of a more general concern with any source of excessive excitement in the child. Excessive use of mind could cause an excessive amount of blood to flow to the brain, and produce an inflammation that might lead to insanity or idiocy: "How proud a mother is at having her precocious child; how little is she aware that precocity is frequently an indication of disease" (Chavasse, 1869, p. 361). Since reality is a continuous monitor of parental apprehensions, local health conditions exert a major influence on the hierarchy of parental concerns.

Among the majority of isolated subsistence farming communities in the world, the period of infancy is one in which illness and death are common and supernatural forces—the evil eye, divine powers, polluted caretakers—believed to be the efficient causes of catastrophe. Relative to American parents there is less concern with accelerating mental and motor development, for the major task of infancy is to survive it. Preoccupation with the infant's health was also characteristic of 18th and 19th-century Europe. Most professional advice focused on the health of both mother and wet nurse, especially the quality of their breast milk. The introduction of sterile water, pasteurized milk, vaccinations, and uniformly better medical care muted these worries and replaced them with apprehension over the child's psychological growth. Modern parents assume that most of the serious problems of infancy are primarily psychological in nature and are mediated by the actions of caretakers. Hence Americans regard a rejecting attitude and failure to play with the infant with the same alarm as 18th-century English pediatricians regarded poor quality of mother's milk or unclean nipples. The facts of everyday life monitor the foci of adult concern—be it physical health, psychological retardation, excessive fearfulness, or intellectual precocity—while the history of the culture influences both the local theory used to explain distress states and the rituals to be initiated in order to prevent and alleviate symptoms and hasten the child's protected movement toward maturity.

A METAPHOR FOR INFANCY: THE DARWINIAN HERITAGE

As adults in each society hold a local theory about the nature of the young child—the Japanese assume he is autonomous, the Rajput that he is pure, the Mayan that he is vulnerable to losing his vital spirit, the American that he is helpless—so too have investigators held presuppositions about the essence of infancy. The suppositions were often influenced by a dominant scientific paradigm which had explicit implications for the human psyche and contained an implicit metaphor for infancy.

A good example from recent history is contained in the essays on the infant that followed the publication of Darwin's theory of evolution. Darwin reclassified the human infant as a member of the category "animal" by positing a continuum in evolution. Since animal behavior was regarded as instinctive, inflexible, and therefore resistant to change, a paradox was created. How was it possible for man to be varied in custom and habit—so flexible and progressive—if he were such a close relative of creatures whose behavior appeared to be excessively stereotyped and rigid. One way to resolve the dilemma was to award a special function to what seemed to be the more prolonged period of infant helplessness in humans as compared with animals. Since most 19th-century scholars assumed that all qualities of living things had a purpose, it was reasonable to ask about the purpose of man's prolonged infancy. John Fiske, among others, argued that infancy was a period of maximal plasticity—the time when adults were to teach children skills and ideas they would carry with them throughout life.

In a lecture at Harvard in 1871, Fiske noted that man's power to control his environment and to enhance progress had to be due to his educability—a potential Fiske believed animals lacked. How then to explain why man was so educable? Following popular rules of inference, Fiske looked for other major differences between man and animal; and of the many candidates he could have selected—language, the opposable thumb, upright stature, an omnivorous diet, sexual behavior throughout the year—he selected the prolongation of infancy. The logic of the argument consisted of two premises and a conclusion. Nature had to have an intended purpose for the initial 3 years of human incompetence and dependence. Since the most likely purpose was to educate the child, it must be the case that the child is maximally malleable to training during that early period. That conclusion was congruent with a deep belief in continuity of character from infancy to later childhood, it served to keep parents self conscious about their actions with their babies, and it was an argument for building good schools. It also provided an experiential explanation for individual differences in adult success—which was attractive to a democratic and egalitarian society (Fiske, 1883).

Many writers would state, with the casualness characteristic of a remark about the weather, that the obvious purpose of the long period of infant helplessness was to render the infant malleable to experience and receptive to being sculpted by the parents. At the turn of the century, Millicent Washburn Shinn (1900) had anticipated Hebb's (1949) hypothesis that with phylogeny the period of early learning was extended in the service of producing a more complex organism:

Nothing is so helpless as the human baby and that helplessness is our glory for it means that the activities of the race have become too many, too complex, too infrequently repeated to become fixed in the nervous structure before birth; hence the long period after birth before the child comes to full human powers. It is a maxim of biology that while an organism is thus immature and plastic it may learn, it may change, it may rise to higher development and thus to infancy we owe the rank of the human race. [Shinn, 1900, p. 33]

The infant's helplessness was a gift to our species, a sign of the child's preparedness to be tutored, and an invitation to parents to begin to shape the plastic creature nature awarded them. There are of course no sound empirical or theoretical reasons for assuming a necessary relation between the prolonged period of instrumental incompetence in humans and a special receptivity to environmental intrusions. Animal behavior is extremely vulnerable to experience—monkeys placed in black boxes for 6 months emerge with bizarre habits, and human infants growing up in a variety of environmental contexts display the same developmental milestones in the same sequence. But Fiske's principles seemed intuitively correct and effectively resolved the paradox created by Darwinian theory.

Early investigations of the infant were influenced in a major way by evolutionary theory and the much older idea—promoted by Bentham—that the purposes of a child's actions were to maximize pleasure and to avoid pain. Since man was on a biological continuum with animals, Haeckel coined a catchy, although almost unpronounceable, phrase: ontogeny recapitulates phylogeny—a principle that provided a guide to observers of the infant. The child revealed what we inherited from our primate ancestors; watching the baby in the protective quiet of the sunlit nursery was a way to observe the wild panorama of evolution. The energetic flailing of arms, facial frown, and piercing cry were directly traceable to our untamed chimpanzee progenitors.

Reports published before and around the turn of the century consisted of naturalistic observations of sequences of motor behavior as well as patterns of vocalization, crying, smiling, and laughing which presumably reflected states of fear, anger, and pleasure. The affects of loneliness, sadness, and pride were generally ignored, for it was fear and anger that announced man's kinship with animals. Further, although the 19th-century metaphor for the infant was incompetence, the metaphor for the 3-year-old was selfishness. In a book that was popular during the last 15 years of the 19th century, the author suggested that the child naturally developed egoism, narcissism, and individualism:

If we wish to understand the meaning of the actions of little children and to direct their wills in a useful and progressive manner, we must bear in mind that all their tendencies, whatever they may be, begin and end with egoism. [Perez, 1888, p. 290]

Perez ignored the 3-year-old who kissed his mother, played with his baby sibling, or offered restitution to a child he had just struck—behaviors that did not seem egoistic. Perez advised that egoism must be tamed through moral training by parents. Central to this training was insistence on obedience and an encouragement of the reflective judgment necessary to control passion, aggression, and narcissism. The assumption that the will of the young child had to be tamed was popular with many 19th-century parents who probably would not quarrel with the statement that "the right of the parent is to command, the duty of the child is to obey. Authority belongs to the one, submission to the other . . . ." In infancy the control of the parent is absolute—that is, it is exercised without any due respect to the wishes of the child (McLaughlin, 1975, p. 22).

And at least one upper-class parent—the Reverend Francis Wayland—was not reluctant to starve his 15-month-old son into obedience when the infant refused a piece of bread from his generous father (McLaughlin, 1975).

By contrast, American parents regard spontaneity and autonomy, rather than control and obedience, as the central traits to promote, and would regard the behavior of Reverend Wayland—the fourth president of Brown University—as an instance of child abuse. We encourage the emotional expressiveness the 19th century wanted to curb because parents believe that free access to affect and autonomous posture toward others will be adaptive when today's infants become tomorrow's young adults.

INITIAL STUDIES

The joint influence of the evolutionary doctrine, which awarded the infant a maturational sequence of fixed action patterns, and the assumption of malleability to tutoring, which laid emphasis on learning, led to two movements in the early study of the infant. One group, led by Shirley, Halverson, Gesell, Irwin, Dennis, McGraw, Pratt, and Bayley, studied the maturation of the young infant's locomotor and instrumental competences and dominated American child psychology during the early decades of the 20th century. The second group, led by John Watson, was less active empirically (it was not until the 1950s that rigorous studies of infant conditioning and learning were initiated) but had strong theoretical force.

Then a significant event occurred which had little to do with infancy and which, in the opinion of some, was probably unfortunate. Binet's original test, invented during the first decade of the 20th century, was standardized as the Stanford-Binet Intelligence Test, and psychologists began to promote the idea, which was latent in the society, that infants inherit differing amounts of an entity called intelligence. That seemingly innocuous premise motivated developmental psychologists to study this hypothetical quality during the first years of life. As a result, scales of infant intelligence were developed. Nancy Bayley in California and Arnold Gesell in New Haven were among the leaders of this movement, and their scales of development, along with those of Psyche Cattell and Charlotte Buhler, became popular. Bayley did most of her important work between 1933 and 1945, Gesell between 1922 and 1946. Although Bayley (1935) did not make any strong theoretical statements about the meaning of the development quotient, Gesell did, and his writing articulated a controversy that had been partially veiled—the degree to which maturation or learning controlled development. Gesell assumed that the developmental quotient reflected the child's differential rate of growth at the moment of testing. There was no constraint on that statement. The quotient did not refer to a specific domain of development but rather to the whole child—in anticipation of Spearman's g. Although Gesell acknowledged that the concept of constancy of development rate seemed naive and unsophisticated, he argued that, considering the state of methodology, it was serviceable. Pragmatic considerations took priority over good sense.

It is not surprising that much interest was generated by the new infant intelligence tests. The historical events that produced an industrialized technology helped to make intellectual skill the *sine qua non* for psychological survival and one's vocation the most critical component of the definition of self—more central than family, clan, ethnicity, religion, or place of residence.

"What do you do?" is one of the first questions one asks of another on an airplane or at a party, and the brief answer—a word or two—places the respondent in a category that defines his status, power, intelligence, and economic potential in a way that almost parallels the power of caste in India. A large proportion of American parents want their children to be white collar professionals, and they recognize that an education of quality is the most important prerequisite to attaining that goal. An education of quality, in turn, rests on acquiring the skills and values that permit good academic performance during the first 12 years of school. If that goal is attained, entrance into a good college and professional school will be easier. The intellectual competence of a child is, therefore, a more salient source of uncertainty for the average American parent than the child's health, character, physical prowess, or virtue. Contemporary scientists study the effect of prematurity, prenatal stress, perinatal trauma, or early malnutrition on intellectual functioning—rarely on motivation, temperament, or physical endurance. Advice to mothers emphasizes rituals and the purchase of toys that are supposed to promote precocious growth of cognitive skills, rather than interventions that might affect cooperativeness, honesty, vitality, or empathy. From the Enlightenment, and in an accelerated fashion since the Industrial Revolution, we have needed an increasing number of technically trained adults. And when a society requires a role to be filled, it awards those who can assume the position all the secular prizes it commands and invents instruments to monitor the degree to which its youth are acquiring the critical role-defining qualities. These assessments are done regularly so that every one knows who is likely to make steady progress toward the goal and who might drop along the way. Hence it is not surprising that during the early decades of this century, tests of infant intelligence were developed, while tests of infant empathy, strength, sociability, or irritability were not. The latter qualities did not seem to bear any relation to the final goal; the former did.

The invention of intelligence tests for infants made profound assumptions about the nature of mind which few parents appreciate and which, as it turns out, may be questionable. The major assumption is that the entity we call "intelligence" in adults is a context-free quality that is carried from infancy to adulthood. Intelligence was regarded the way we view a species' distinctive morphological characteristics. We examine the newborn bird or lizard and predict that the adult will resemble the infant pattern. Because we are prone to materialize psychological qualities, we treat mental competence the way we treat the structures of morphology. Even though there is no phenotypic relation between sitting at 6 months and reading at 10 years, it had been assumed that the child who sat a month or two earlier than most had a quality of psychological precocity that applied to all future abilities. That assumption has guided a great deal of research on infants for over five decades despite the fact that existing data do not reveal a strong correlation between scores on infant development scales and indices of intellectual precocity or retardation during later childhood (Lewis and McGurk, 1972). Indeed, Super (1976) has shown that even the behaviors like sitting and walking, which have been regarded by many as maturational and, therefore, immune from tutoring, are modified in a significant way by parental encouragement and opportunities for practice. Hence infant intelligence tests, like those for children and adults, also seem to be culturally biased. One example of the bias is seen in a comparison of Chinese and Caucasian American infants participating in a longitudinal study. Working-class Chinese parents living in Boston are less likely than Caucasians to talk and interact with their infant in an affectively excited way. And 1-year-old Chinese children are markedly less vocal than Caucasians in free play, to laboratory presentations of visual and auditory stimuli, and on relevant Bayley Scale items. But at 2½ years of age there was no ethnic difference in performance on tests measuring short-term memory for locations or comprehension of linguistic concepts. The quiet infant does not necessarily become a less intellectually competent child (Kagan, 1976b).

The isolated Indians of San Marcos la Laguna, who live in the highlands of northwest Guatemala, do not assume the baby possesses a unitary mental ability that is stable over time. A purely intellectual component of talent does not become important until adolescence. Before that time, the child displays his level of talent by demonstrating the normative expectations for his age, which means talking and walking by the time he is 3 years old, being willing and able to do simple chores by 8 years of age, and incorporating the work ethnic by age 15. The Indians share David Wechsler's understanding that intelligence is not a quality of a child; it is doing what is expected and required by the culture at the right time in development.

INFLUENCE OF FREUDIAN THEORY

Although study of the development of mental and motor competence dominated child psychology during the first three decades of the century, beneath the surface lay an uneasiness that was based in part on the political philosophy of the two major Protestant nations in the Western community. America and England wanted to believe in the eventual attainment of an egalitarian society where, if conditions of early life were optimal, all citizens potentially could attain dignity and participate effectively in the society. Indeed, almost two centuries earlier, during the years just prior to the American Revolution, journalists and statesmen wrote impassioned essays stressing the importance of early family treatment and proper education in the prevention of crime and the safeguarding of democracy. Despotism could be eliminated if all children were well nurtured and properly educated—a conviction not unlike Plato's assumption that if one knew what was good, immorality was impossible. From America's birth until the present a majority has believed that the correct pattern of experiences at home and school would guarantee a harmonious society. This view, which was in accord with the doctrine of infant malleability, invited each generation of parents to project onto the infant their political hopes for the future. Every infant was a fresh canvas and the community was ready to receive a psychological theory that would make social experience the major steward of growth.

Hence when psychoanalytic theory was introduced to the United States during the third and fourth decades of this century, the academy gave it a warm reception. Until that time the infant was seen as a socially isolated organism impelled by inevitable maturational forces. Psychoanalytic theory placed the child in a social matrix in which the parents' actions became a central determinant of the child's development and a phenomenon to study in its own right. It is possible that one reason psychoanalytic theory was more popular in the United States than in continental Europe was that America wanted to believe in the infant's susceptibility to adult influence. American parents were ready to celebrate a theory of development that made the family primary and treated infancy as the optimal time to mold the child—as Shinn and Fiske insisted several decades earlier.

Freud also implied that the family had a prophylactic force. Although Freud was as concerned with the creation of healthy, mature adults as he was with the avoidance of psychological distress, those who promoted Freudian theory in the 1940s and 1950s subtly shifted the emphasis to the latter issue. Since the infant was vulnerable to trauma and anxiety, caretakers had to be thoughtful about their behavior if they were to avoid deviant emotional growth and the accompanying susceptibility to the disquiet and defensive maneuvers that became known as neurotic disorder. The promotion of independence and instrumental skills in an incompetent organism was subordinated, temporarily, to the prevention of emotional distress and psychic impotence. The former attitude puts parents on the offensive; the latter on the defensive.

The Freudian era peaked in America from 1940 to 1960 under the intellectual leadership of Anna Freud, Ribble, Kris, Wolf, Spitz, Escalona, Greenacre, Klein, Bowlby, and a host of others who complicated the existing metaphor for infancy. Vulnerability to anxiety was added to the quality of malleability. The glowing optimism contained in Shinn's description of her child suddenly became ingenuous. Raising a baby was a serious and difficult mission with many shoals to avoid. Each child was a potential phobic, obsessive, depressive, or, in the extreme, schizophrenic, and parents were warned about the potentially dangerous practices they had regarded as innocuous. The prevention of psychological pathology had replaced earlier worry over physical disease. And in both periods mothers had the responsibility of taking all necessary precautions—for in addition to a belief in the infant's vulnerability to experience, the West also had an implacable faith in adult effectance: parents can prevent future pathology if they act properly.

Psychoanalytic theory led to reformulations of old phenomena in social terms. The fears of infancy, which had been seen as maturationally inevitable, were renamed as separation and stranger anxiety. The new adjectives implied social causation. One of the most significant constructions wrought by psychoanalytic theory was the introduction of ideas of maternal acceptance and rejection. Parents have always been ready to accept the notion that they should care for their children, for they realized that attention to the child's physical needs was necessary for his survival. Typically, parental concerns focused on protection from illness, provision of food, providing opportunities for instrumental mastery, and the tutoring of good habits. But it was less common for parents to brood about whether their child sensed that he was loved. Those who used psychoanalytic theory as a scaffold for theorizing—Erikson, Klein, Bowlby, and Ainsworth are examples— suggested the child required psychic security and freedom from anxiety, and an affectionate maternal attitude toward the infant was the single most significant factor determining whether the infant attained those precious states.

Since this idea could not have been promoted so successfully if American families were not prepared to believe it, why were many middle-class Americans friendly to the notion that a mother's love was the most important ingredient in her young child's development? Perez attributed an innate narcissism to the young child; 20th-century parents attributed insecurity to their children. We all seek an explanation for our moments of personal anguish. The principles of modern science, while eliminating gods, witches, supernatural forces, and the stares of pregnant women as possible causes of private unhappiness, awarded material social experiences causal power. Since 20th-century American society was fond of an ideology that insisted that each person was responsible for his own salvation—his successes and failures—the individual could not easily assign the blame for his anguish to luck, employers, rivals, or social conditions, even though the latter has recently come to be an increasingly popular explanation of misfortune. Each has to accept responsibility for failure at work or love, but he needs a little help. It is too painful to assume total blame for unmet promises, tense encounters, and dark moments of unworthiness.

Help came in the form of a belief in psychological continuity—a thick connection between the public events of early childhood and the private experiences of adulthood. This assumption was seized as a clue to the puzzle, and the blame was shared with the family of rearing. The troubled adolescent and young adult guessed that his parents may not have valued him as a young child. (The fact that the adult had not made any instrumental contribution to the family may have helped him reach that decision, for the child is of minimal economic value in the modern Western family.) The perception of fall was regarded, therefore, as partly due to a rejection that wound its way back to infancy. Psychiatrists in the clinic and psychologists in the academy awarded this interpretation scientific respectability by ascribing a special sixth sense to the infant—the capability of discerning whether his mother loved him. In a society characterized by increasing depersonalization and few groups or institutions with which to identify, the adult was left with only two sources of meaningful emotional relationships—a love object in adulthood and parents during childhood. These relationships became fountains of vitality or origins of distress. Recall Goldmund's advice to Narcissus: "But how will you die when your time comes, Narcissus, since you have no mother? Without a mother one cannot love. Without a mother one cannot die" (Hesse, *Narcissus and Goldmund,* 1930).

History had created a natural experiment by isolating family relations from other candidates for explanation. Fate, illness, or transcendental forces had been eliminated as determinants of adult ego strength or fragility, leaving, it seemed, only one cause— namely, an emotionally supporting relation to a love object. "I was rejected by my parents" became a rationalization for distress and incompetence.

Psychoanalytic theory provided considerable impetus to this idea. Perhaps the key essays, written by René Spitz, appeared during the 1940s in *The Psychoanalytic Study of the Child* (Spitz, 1945, 1946). Spitz visited poorly staffed orphanages in South America where infants were apathetic and mortality was high. Spitz concluded that the lack of a close affectionate relationship with a specific caretaker was the primary cause of both the anomalous psychological appearance of the infants and their illness, rather than the lack of variety in experience and poor health conditions in the institution. Guatemalan Indian children living in San Marcos la Laguna, who are rarely out of their mothers' sight and are nursed on demand, also display extreme apathy and high mortality—40% during the first 2 years. But these infants have a very close psychological relation with their mothers and the symptoms seem due to poor nutrition, high rate of infection, and lack of experiential variety in their daily lives. A close emotional relationship to the mother does not provide complete protection against apathy, temporary cognitive retardation, or poor physical health.

Maternal love—dyadic, intense, and devoted—became the vital force that created knights or, in its absence, produced idiocy, madness, and violence. As late as 1960 many psychiatrists and psychologists contended that autism, a rare syndrome characterized by mutism and odd stereotypic behaviors, was a profound defense to cope with the recognition that one was not loved by one's mother. The 19th century made quality of mother's milk either tonic or toxin; the 20th century continued to award the mother mysterious power, but invested that power in her attitudes and actions.

It is possible that the child's belief in his value in the eyes of his parents assumes a prominence in our culture that it may not have had in earlier periods or may not have in other contemporary societies. Its significance is reflected in the fact that many American children are uncertain over whether they are valued by their family, and parents are eager to communicate to their children that they love them. Second, unhappiness, failure, and symptoms in adolescence and adulthood are often explained as being due to absence of parental love during infancy and early childhood. But prior to the 17th century it is difficult to find Western writers referring to the importance of the love relationship between parent and child when they discussed the conditions that promoted optimal development. The child needed a good education, faith in a divine being, and parents who provided physical care and were both consistently firm in their discipline and appropriate role models.

But by the end of the 17th century, explicit recognition of the significance of the love relation between adult and child was emerging, and by the middle of the 18th century books of advice to parents began to emphasize the importance of parental displays of love and affection toward the child (Ryerson, 1959). Locke advised parents to love their children, and tutors to encourage their tutees to feel affection for them. The increasing emphasis on the love relation between socializing adults and children was paralleled by an emerging self-consciousness about the child's individualism and personal motives. The concept of the child was being differentiated as an entity separate from the family. Unquestioned loyalty and acquiescence to God and family were losing their moral force to narcissism. Rousseau predicted the mood of the 20th century when he wrote, ''The only natural passion to man is the love of himself.'' Pestallozzi agreed that self-conscious awareness of individual ego was innate: ''Consciousness of your own personality is the first object of Nature.'' And from the beginning of the 18th century until the present time there has been an increasing emphasis on the importance of the child developing an articulated, autonomous, and confident ego.

The spread of that ideal is correlated with the award of formative power to parental love. It is possible that the coincidence has theoretical substance, and reflects the introduction of a folk theory that confidence, independence, and a drive for accomplishment required a belief in one's value and potency. These attributes were acquired through parental actions that communicated to the child that he was regarded as a precious entity. When obedience to and interdependence on the family defined the ideal, parents were advised to be firm and aloof. When autonomy and achievement were required parents were advised to be intimate and loving. The question we cannot resolve is whether the folk theory is empirically valid or merely believed to be correct by the community. The research data, although fragile, do not provide much support for the empirical claim when social class is controlled. Indeed, American middle-class mothers who were hypercritical and not tender with their young daughters but urged precocious intellectual and social development produced more autonomous, independent, and achieving young women than mothers who were gentler and more affectionate (Kagan and Moss, 1962). Since the essayists who promoted this belief had no knowledge of the historical or empirical accuracy of their prediction, they may have been reflecting a cultural presupposition.

The power that modern Western society attributes to parental love—or its absence—has an analog in theories of illness held by non-Western communities. (By illness, we mean consciousness of a source of physical disability or psychological discomfort, not the physical locus or cause of dysfunction.) The possible causes of illness include spirits, loss of soul, sorcery, sin, accident, God, witchcraft, or failure to live a meritorious life. Rarely are the actions or attitudes of one's family considered to be a possible source of illness. By contrast, contemporary Western society assumes the family can be a primary cause of a small set of illnesses that we normally call psychiatric—depression, phobias, obsessions, autism, schizophrenia, criminality, and, in the infant, failure to thrive. Although phobias, depression, and madness are noted in non-Western societies, it is the modern West that believes that the family's practices toward the young child—excessive rejection, restriction, or aloof authoritarianism—can produce these symptoms.

Modern parents are convinced that if the child believes he is loved he will be free of the major source of future psychic distress. As the child grows to adolescence, he learns of scientific theories that articulate his unformed premises about parental rejection and psychic illness. He learns that a person must feel loved in order to be psychically healthy. Occasions of personal anguish in adulthood are interpreted as the delayed product of lack of parental love during childhood rather than the wrong zodiac sign, being born on the wrong day, or invasion by evil spirits. Our books, magazines, and television dramas all announce the healing and prophylactic power of parental love, and the toxicity that follows closely on its absence.

American adults seek out psychiatrists, new love objects, or peers who, it is hoped, will love them and dissolve their anguish. This faith in love is not unlike the faith in the curative power of the white powder or incantations of a shaman. If the person believes in the curative power of the ritual—be it love or white powder—he feels less anguish after participating in the ritual. As no one would quarrel with the real power of prayer or powder to alleviate disquiet, we do not quarrel with the healing power of love. Both are real and not metaphysical events. But their potency depends on a prior belief in their effectiveness.

Let us ask, therefore, whether lack of parental affection in childhood does make a serious contribution to future psychic illness. Is that proposition valid? It is not easy to answer that question for reasons that are not strictly empirical. When we ask does temperature contribute to the probability of snowfall, we only need gather easily obtained objective data to answer the query. But in the case of the contribution of parental rejection to psychic illness we are in difficulty because we are asking, "Does a mental state in the child (the belief that one is not favored) make a contribution to a future mental state (fearfulness or hostility)." That question takes two different forms.

The first form of the question is private and is concerned only with the person's belief about the validity of the functional relation. If a person believes that a set of experiences (or mental states) influences a future state, he will act as if it were so. The second form of the question is scientific and asks if there is an empirical relation between the child's perception of favor or disfavor and adult sequellae. At present that question has not been answered satisfactorily because parental rejection is not a specific set of actions by parents but a belief held by the child. The only way to exit from this frustrating position is to determine if there is any lawful relation in a culture between the actions and communications of parents and the child's belief that he is not favored. There are no data to the writer's knowledge that have demonstrated unequivocally a relation between specific parental actions and the child's belief in his favor, even in our culture. Working-class American parents punish and restrict the child much more than middle-class parents, yet there is no evidence to indicate a class difference in perception of parental favor. When we look at other cultures we note that Kipsigis mothers have older siblings care for their young children while Israeli mothers on kibbutzim use hired metaplot. There is no evidence to lead one to believe that one group of children feels more in parental favor than another. We are tempted, therefore, to suggest that each child constructs a theory of what actions imply parental disfavor. The content of the theory is based on very local conditions and will not necessarily generalize to other communities in any detail.

What seems relatively unique to modern Western society is the popularity of the thought that one might *not* be valued by one's family. Historical events have been responsible for introducing this as a major node of apprehension and, therefore, of illness—as it has been responsible for new apprehensions over nuclear waste, racial violence, and municipal defaults. Mayan villages are apprehensive about not having enough food, slanderous gossip, and the actions of gods. A society can create a new source of distress by introducing a new belief, as we created new hazards to lungs by inventing cars and factories, or hazards to viscera by introducing carcinogens into bread and water. Distress has to be viewed as responsive to the introduction of new, and in some cases unique, events.

How did the idea of parental love and rejection come to assume such prominence? We are not talking about the emotional investment that a parent feels toward a child but rather the belief that a child's perception of the favor in which he is held can exert a profound influence on his present and future states. These are two quite different notions. There are many possibilities and too little evidence to favor any one of them.

One argument takes its force from the fact that, by the middle of the 18th century, both infant mortality rates and fertility rates began to decline dramatically. The former was due, of course, to better conditions of health. It has been suggested that the decline in births was due to a lifting of the fatalistic attitude of the 15th and 16th centuries and the emergence of a mood of personal efficacy (Plumb, 1975). The 18th-century adult was beginning to sense he could alter the conditions of his life and affect his future. Hence adults tried to control the sizes of their families. As parents recognized the adaptive value of a more individualistic and autonomous attitude, they would have promoted this set of qualities in their children. Obedience and dependence require firm and consistent discipline and grow best in a mind convinced of its frailties and inadequacy. Autonomy, boldness, and achievement require an illusion of potency and value. Additionally, individual accomplishment became more highly prized and a greater possibility for more children. Hence parents would have begun to identify with the abilities and successes of their children in order to share vicariously in their victories (Plumb, 1975). It may be that the 18th century sensed, unconsciously of course, that these qualities—autonomy, independence, and achievement—are nurtured best in an atmosphere in which children sensed they were objects of intrinsic worth. The society was receptive to the hypothesis that parental favor was a good way to encourage this new spirit in the child.

It is also possible that when families moved from rural areas to the city it became somewhat more likely that the child would be outside the supervisory influence of a member of the family for short periods of the day. Hence it became necessary to use the threat of withdrawal of favor as a source of disciplinary control. When the child is continually surrounded by adults or older siblings, each of whom is within several hundred yards of his action, his mischievousness is constrained. When he is alone the policeman must be symbolic, and the society may have discovered that parental love and its potential withdrawal can play the supervisory role at a distance. Perhaps both of these factors, and others, complemented each other in promoting the attitude of parental love to a position of prominence and persuading the society that a child's psychic well being depended on his believing he was held in esteem by his family.

These speculations regarding the formative influences of the mother's practices were not the reasons for the gradual decline in the persuasiveness of psychoanalytic propositions. Rather, the cause lay with the failure of empirical attempts to verify theoretical predictions and the reemergence of cognitive theory.

The original psychoanalytic variables of interest—duration of nursing, severity of weaning, and age of toilet training—are no longer of interest today. By the late 1940s (see Orlansky, 1949; Caldwell, 1964) the research record was not in accord with prediction. Some concluded that the theory was incorrect; others, that it was difficult to investigate psychoanalytic propositions. Whatever the reason, the failure to confirm led to a restlessness and receptivity to a new paradigm which was being written by Piaget and is reflected today in the cognitive focus of modern research on the infant and young child.

Quantification of parental practices surrounding feeding, weaning, and toilet training were replaced by observations of parental talking, playing, and encouragement of cognitive development. But despite the change in content, the centrality of adult-infant interaction was retained, and recent research results point to the importance of the mutual and reciprocal relation between infant and parent. Thus psychoanalytic theory deserves extraordinary credit for pointing the empiricist's nose toward social experience as a monitor of development.

THE MODERN PERIOD

The extraordinary scientific interest in human infants during the last 10 years owes its vitality to many independent forces, each with its own special questions and presuppositions about the young child. The uniformly reliable relations among social class, reproductive risk, and difficulty in mastering academic skills have led many clinicians to the view that 3 to 10% of American newborns suffer from some degree of impairment of central nervous system functioning due either to pre- or perinatal trauma or infection. These insults, though difficult to diagnose, are assumed to contribute to later cognitive deficiency. Since early detection of these children, perhaps during the 1st year, could lead to early rehabilitation, many investigators are trying to develop such diagnostic instruments.

The crest of interest in developmental psycholinguistics, fueled by Chomsky's assertions of innate speech mechanisms, has catalyzed elegant studies of speech perception in the young infant, with the preliminary suggestion that the very young infant processes consonants with a discreteness that implies special structures for this purpose in the left temporal lobe.

But the two most sturdy supports for the zealous study of the young child come from ethology and the attempt to integrate classic behaviorism and psychoanalytic theory into a modern statement of the importance of the role of social experience on development (Bowlby, 1969). Both are concerned with the effective stimulus event that recruits the infant's attention and subsequently either releases species-specific responses or serves as a conditioned cue for a modification of an existing behavior. It was inevitable that the West's friendly attitude toward a mechanical causality between events—in preference to coherence among events—when combined with the methodological principles of stimulus-response psychology, would lead psychologists to inquire about the essential stimulus conditions that released the universal responses of sustained attention, babbling, smiling, and crying. Additionally, those who were curious about the cognitive functioning of the infant were searching for objective ways to probe the infant's mind. The experiments of Robert Fantz, published in the mid-1950s, provided a methodology that satisfied both needs, for he found that, with remarkably simple methods, one can infer the characteristics of events that recruit prolonged attention from infants, and he raised the possibility that one could infer something about mental processes from these objective data. In the 20 years since those first experiments our knowledge of perceptual dynamics in the infant has gone from almost total ignorance to a few tentative principles.

Determinants of Attention

The newborn's attention is attracted and maintained by changes in physical parameters. Hence in the visual mode, contour and movement have the greatest power to attract and to maintain prolonged attention, with the number of stimulus elements possibly playing an independent role (Fantz, 1965; Fantz and Fagan, 1975; Haith, 1966; Karmel, 1969; Karmel et al., 1974; Kessen et al., 1970, 1972). However, we still do not know how the infant transduces contour information into cognitive structure, nor do we have access to the differential salience of different stimulus qualities or patterns of dimensions. For example, there is at present no theory or set of hypotheses that could predict the outcome of the following experiment:

Ten-month-olds were initially exposed to a pair of large, open circles (outlined in black), each containing two horizontally placed smaller black circles—akin to a minimally schematic face with a pair of black eyes. After 15 seconds of exposure to this pair of identical events one of them was replaced with one of 10 different transformations on the pair of internal circles. The transformations included changing(1) the shape of the internal circular figures (to triangles or squares), (2) the placement of the internal circles (vertical, oblique, or asymmetrical arrangement; placing the circles outside the larger circular frame), (3) increasing the size of the two circles, or (4) increasing the number of circles to three.

The transformations that included the two larger circles and the two vertically oriented circles were studied far longer than any of the other eight transformations. Since the two larger circles had less total contour than the three circles, the infant's attention is not simply a function of amount of contour or number of elements, even though these qualities do exert some control over the child's behavior.

Although the powerful influence of contour and movement on visual attention of the newborn does not vanish, by 6 to 10 weeks of age or even earlier, each becomes subordinate to a more psychological dimension—namely, discrepancy between the event and the infant's schema.

There has been considerable debate as to whether the relation between duration of sustained attention and degree of stimulus-schema discrepancy is curvilinear or linear. Careful examination of the evidence (McCall and McGhee, unpublished; McCall et al., 1977) suggests, tentatively, that when new nonredundant elements are added to an old event (adding color to an achromatic event or a new figure to an existing pattern) the relation between attention and degree of change is more likely to be linear. But when the transformation involves a rearrangement of an existing dimension into a new pattern, the curvilinear function is more likely (Kagan, 1974; Zelazo et al., 1973; Kinney and Kagan, 1976; McCall et al., 1977; Hopkins et al., 1976).

In a recent ingenious study McCall et al. (1977) separated the stimulus qualities of the original and discrepant stimulus from the magnitude of discrepancy between them and found the curvilinear function for two quite different classes of events. Hence by the infant's 2nd to 3rd month the salience of an event is determined by both its physical and informational properties (Bond, 1972; Cohen et al., 1971 Cornell, 1975; Kagan, 1971, 1972, 1974; Lewis and Goldberg, 1969).

The capacity to react to a discrepancy requires positing an ability to recognize an event in the immediate field as related to past experience. Although most investigators have made the delay between familiarization of the standard and encounter with a novel or transformed event relatively short—a few seconds—Super (1972) has shown that 10-week-olds seem to recognize an event following a 24-hour delay. The more central point is that the reliable reactivity to discrepant experience seems to be due primarily to a change in psychological function—a capacity to form an articulated schema for an event and to recognize a transformation of the original experience—rather than to the growth of a new psychological structure. We say this even though the new competence permits the establishment of new structures. If the child recognizes an event as discrepant, the attempt at assimilation is likely to produce change in the existing schemata. Thus structural alterations follow the emergence of the new competence.

The Emergence of Recall Capacity and the Activation of Relational Structures

Every coherent set of investigations has two agenda; the first is to discern and explain the regularities among a set of phenomena. The more disguised mission is to affirm or, less often, to contradict the usually unstated and always unproven presuppositions that fuel the daily coding of observations and charting of graphs. Piaget's extraordinary contributions have revealed new unsuspected regularities. But a far more profound influence of his work was to persuade many that the older conception of the infant as a passive recipient of external influence—as a helpless victim of the chance pairings of events outside his control—was a less useful model than one in which the child and infant were regarded as active in the selection and manipulation of information and action. That alteration in perspective, which is probably now held by a majority of developmental psychologists, is not unlike the experience of putting on a pair of anisekonic lenses. The world suddenly looks dramatically different. Piagetian ideas contain their own set of presuppositions, however, and the one most relevant for the infant concerns the issue of whether the major changes are to be attributed to alterations in structure or process. Although Piaget's conceptualization of the later stages emphasizes the primacy of function, his description of the sensorimotor stage seems to give greater weight to structural victories. This bias is seen in the competence he calls object permanence, which emerges toward the end of the 1st year of life. The 9-month-old child is said to possess a new cognitive structure—namely, the idea that objects retain their permanence even though they are out of sight:

> The practical schema of the object is the substantial permanence attributed to sensory pictures. It is the belief that what is seen corresponds to something which continues to exist even when one does not perceive it. [Piaget, 1967, p. 13.]

Investigators studying quite different aspects of this period of development also treat the biological changes as a function of a change in psychological structure. Ainsworth, for example, explains the emergence of separation anxiety at 8 to 12 months—the time when object permanence appears—as a sign that the child is attached to his caretaker (Ainsworth and Wittig, 1969: Ainsworth and Bell, 1970). Attachment is defined as an emotional bond to the caretaker, and therefore as a psychological structure. But recent studies of this period suggest that perhaps these phenomena, as well as others, are primarily the product of a change in the ability to retrieve a schema for an event that is not in the immediate field—the capacity to recall stored information.

That assumption helps to explain why a large set of phenotypically diverse phenomena emerge between 8 and 12 months of age, while a structural interpretation seems less able to encompass all in one scheme. Although temporal covariation among manifestly different phenomena does not necessarily imply a common mechanism, the scientist's affection for parsimony invites an attempt to invent a unitary process.

Increased Attentiveness and Reactivity to Discrepant Events

Toward the end of the 1st year the infant frequently displays more prolonged attention to a variety of discrepant events than he did when he was 6 or 7 months old. If a transformation of an interestng event—social as well as nonsocial—is shown to infants from 3 to 30 months of age in either a cross-sectional or longitudinal design, there is often, but not always, a U-shaped relation between age and fixation time to the transformation, with a trough appearing between 7 and 9 months (Kagan, 1976) for American as well as rural Mexican (Finley et al., 1972) and Guatemalan children (Sellers et al., 1972).

There is also a U-shaped function relating age to the likelihood of the child's reaching for an audible object in total darkness (Bower, 1974). There is a high probability of reaching in the dark at 4 months which declines precipitously at 6 or 7 months, only to increase again through 11 months. This function, obtained with sighted children, is not different from the one observed in blind infants (Fraiberg, 1968).

Inhibition to a Discrepant Event

Prior to 8 months the infant reaches almost at once to a novel object that is presented after repeated presentation of a familiarized standard, while a 12-month-old shows an obvious delay (Parry, 1973) before reaching for the novel object. The capacity for motor inhibition to an unexpected event is not new, for newborns will inhibit both limb movement and sucking to a sudden onset of stimulation, but not to a change in psychological information.

Apprehension to Discrepant Experience

An important change that occurs at this time is a dramatic increase in the likelihood of wariness and crying to an event whose major characteristic is that it is a discrepant transformation of earlier or immediately past experience. Scarr and Salapatek (1970) exposed infants 2 to 23 months of age to six different discrepant (or novel) events—stranger approaching the child, a visual cliff, a jack-in-the-box, a mechanical dog that moved, facial masks, and a loud noise. Infants younger than 7 months rarely showed any behavioral signs of wariness toward any of these events. The peak display of wariness usually occurred between 11 and 18 months for most of these episodes—loud noise was least likely to evoke wariness—and then declined.

The effect of the appearance of a stranger on the child has been investigated many times in the last 20 years, and the consensus from these studies is in accord with the data summarized by Scarr and Salapatek. Inhibition, facial wariness, or overt distress is rare prior to 7 months and grows dramatically between that time and the end of the 1st year (Bronson, 1972; Morgan and Ricciuti, 1969; Schaffer, 1966, 1974; Spitz, 1950; Stevens, 1971; Tennes and Lampl, 1969).

Separation Anxiety

Finally, the likelihood that the child will fret, cry, or show inhibition of play when his mother or primary caretaker leaves him in an unfamiliar setting or with an unfamiliar person emerges at 8 or 9 months, rises to a peak at 13 to 15 months, and then declines until it is improbable by 3 years of age. The same growth function has been found for American children raised totally at home as well as those attending a day care center, for Israeli infants living in an infant house on a kibbutz, for Indian children living in a Guatemalan village, for children in Antigua, Guatemala, and , finally, for Bushmen children living with groups on the Kalahari Desert (Fox, 1975; Kearsley et al., 1975; Kotelchuck et al., 1975; Lester et al., 1974; Maccoby and Feldman, 1972; Kagan, 1976).

AN INTERPRETATION

It is difficult to interpret these phenomena, which occur between 8 and 13 months, as a function of a change in psychological structure. We believe that one element necessary to these behavioral changes is a qualitative increase in the ability to retrieve schema of prior events, a growth in what contemporary psychologists would call memory capacity. The most persuasive support for that idea comes from studies showing that an 8-month-old child will make an error in the "A not B" procedure if the delay between hiding of the object and the child's reaching for it is long (say 7 seconds) but not if it is 3 seconds or less. The child of 10 months will not make the error under any reasonable delay. We suggest that the child shows increased attention to the transformation and return trials of an original, familiarized event because he is able to retrieve the schema for the original standard and compare it with his present experience. He reaches for the hidden toy that makes a sound because he can actively generate a schema for objects that, in the past, have made sounds.

Now let us apply this notion to separation anxiety. Following maternal departure, the child generates from memory the schema of her presence and compares it with the present, attempting to resolve the inconsistency. This process is important but not sufficient to bear the burden of explanation because the child does not display fear in other situations where he generates a schema of a past event, as when no object is found under a cloth after the child watched an adult place one there. Moreover, the 1-year-old compares past with present all through the day in a myriad of contexts and does not usually show fear. Thus the new memory competence is necessary but insufficient.

An additional factor must be posited, and we suggest that it is the ability to generate anticipations of the future—representations of possible events. Anticipating the mother's absence as she rises is not the same competence as retrieving a past event and comparing it with the present. If the 1-year-old anticipates an unpleasant event, like pain or danger, because he experienced them in the past, he is likely to cry. Some would say he has acquired a conditioned anxiety reaction. Although this has been a popular and intuitively reasonable explanation of separation protest, it is not completely satisfying because it strains the imagination to assume that, all over the world, infants between 9 and 13 months of age, even those who are with their mothers most of the day, suddenly expect an unpleasant event when their mother leaves them, independent of the frequency of past distress when the mother was absent. Children whose mothers leave them very often do not show separation anxiety earlier or with more intensity than those who are with their mothers more or less continually. Even though we do not favor an explanation based on the anticipation of actual unpleasant past experiences when the mother was absent, we believe that the 1-year-old has a capacity to try to anticipate the future. He attempts to predict what might happen following an unusual event. Inability to generate a substantive prediction combined with the inability to resolve the inconsistency between the schema of her earlier presence and her absence produces uncertainty and fear. A dynamic, as opposed to a static, event is much more likely to elicit apprehension, for events like a jack-in-the-box or the mother walking to the door are more likely to evoke questions like, "What am I to do?" or "What will it do to me?" It is likely that if the child does not have a behavior to issue to deal with the uncertainty, distress is most likely to occur. If he has a response, distress will be buffered (Littenberg et al., 1971; Rheingold and Eckerman, 1970).

In sum, the distress that follows separation is a product of several new competences—

the new ability to retrieve a past schema and to compare it with the present in order to resolve the inconsistency, and the ability to attempt to predict possibilities. Failure to resolve the inconsistency or to make a prediction produces uncertainty. And if the child has no response to the state of uncertainty, crying is likely to occur.

It will take additional research to verify these hypotheses but, if validated, they have implications for our suppositions about developmental change. They imply that we should give as much attention to the introduction of new psychological processes as we do to new structures. This conclusion has epistemological implications. Although it is easy to appreciate how earlier structures might be incorporated into later ones, it is a bit more difficult to understand how earlier functions might be incorporated into later ones. Thus a greater emphasis on developmental changes in function is likely to lead to less emphasis on continuity and a greater emphasis on discontinuity in development. It is of interest to note that recently investigators have also noted the relevance of memory for performance on the concrete operational tasks, primarily conservation and class inclusion (Rybash et al., 1975).

This discussion provides a nice example of one of the basic uses of empirical science. Careful empirical work on a delimited aspect of nature occasionally provides a fresh view of a much larger mural. Whether the object of study be peas, fruit flies, horseshoe crabs, or infants, nature occasionally hides a prize deep within one of her possessions. If one is sufficiently gentle, careful, and persistent, she allows it to be possessed.

The metaphor for the infant implied by these recent observations is that of thinker—a creature with a small trunk and oversized head in the posutre of Rodin's famous statue. Modern parents are attracted to this view, for they seem less concerned with protecting their innocent and vulnerable organism from harm or anxiety than they are with pushing him toward precocious intellectual growth.

CONTEMPORARY THEMES

The Renaissance of Biological Determinism

The major theoretical tension in contemporary studies of the young child is not unlike that of the 1930s when the differential influence of maturation and experience was being debated. There is, however, a difference. We appreciate that a given experience does not have the same effect on all children and that the power of experience depends on the developmental status of the child. We must integrate that knowledge with the fact that maturation closely monitors the first phases of cognitive and affective development. One way to synthesize these ideas is to assume that the form of the growth function for basic social and affective systems is maturational, but that the time of emergence of each, as well as the special quality of the emerging competence, is influenced by experience (Kagan et al, 1975). This interactionist view is at the heart of Piagetian theory and is, of course, a confirmation of Hunt's statement in *Intelligence and Experience,* which was a harbinger of the mood that has dominated the last decade of infant study (Hunt, 1961).

We are returning to a more tolerant attitude (perhaps too tolerant) toward heredity's contribution to individual variation—a view that was subdued for a few decades by both behaviorism and psychoanalytic theory. The renaissance of biological determinism is due partly to the elegant methodology and exciting discoveries in microbiology and genetics, and partly to the psychologists' failure to document a strong relation between measurements of environmental experience and behavioral outcomes. We need a rationalization for what appears to be a failure of environmental intervention efforts to rehabilitate the academically retarded child from economically deprived families as well as children in other categories of risk. There is at the moment a feeling of pessimism, hopefully temporary, over the power of constructive experience to produce the form of child we desire. Sex, class, and ethnic differences in cognitive ability and school achievement, which used to be regarded as due to acquired motives and knowledge, are now viewed by many as partly under genetic control. Such a view resolves some of the uncertainty generated by our poor rehabilitation record.

There are subtle behavioral differences among Chinese, Caucasian, and Black infants. Chinese infants are a little less active, less vocal, and less irritable than Caucasians (Freedman, 1974; Kagan, 1976b). But it is proper to maintain a posture of caution toward this initial evidence. Initial reports by Geber (1958) stated that African precocity in early motor development was probably genetic in origin. However, a recent more careful analysis in a small Kipsigis village in Kenya found that the African infants were only precocious to the Caucasians on a few motor items, like sitting and walking, and were not precocious for crawling and creeping. The items on which they were advanced were precisely the ones that African mothers tutored and encouraged (Super, 1976). Hence, the African precocity, which seemed biological in origin may well be experiential. Similarly, although 1-year-old Chinese infants smile and vocalize less often to human masks and dynamic visual sequences than 1-year-old Caucasian children, there is no ethnic difference in vocalization and smiling to these same episodes at 3½ months of age. Hence the Caucasian affectivity may be influenced by home experience.

A second node of inquiry that leans on biological constructs is a renewed interest in temperament—the dispositions of passivity, activity, and irritability which affect the child's commerce with his world. Study of individual differences in temperament has several origins. The first is the recognition, after many years of work, that individual differences in cognitive functioning in infancy are not preserved for very long. Not only is the developmental quotient at 6 or 12 months not predictive of IQ, grades, or achievement test scores at 6 years, but individual differences in specific cognitive dimensions like attentiveness to events or age of walking are not predictive of theoretically related dimensions a few years later. Since this realization violates the strong belief in continuity from infancy to later childhood, it is natural that some would search for another set of attributes that might be the source of the continuity so many want to believe is there. The work of Thomas et al. (1970), which has been extremely influential, implies that temperamental qualities like irritability and irregularity place an infant at risk for psychiatric treatment when he is 5 years old.

Another reason for examining temperament is that babies act on their caretakers. Irritable infants provoke their mothers to tend to them more often and, in the extreme, to abuse them. Happy babies, who play alone for long periods of time, do not experience as much maternal intrusion as more demanding ones. A third reason for the probing of temperament comes from a small number of studies that imply a genetic component to responses like smiling and tempo of play. Indeed, in one extensive longitudinal study of infants across the period 4 through 27 months, the most stable variables were smiling and tempo of play (Kagan, 1971). The increasing popularity of biological determinism gains support from the emergence of methodologies to study electrocortical responses in infants, particularly EEG and evoked potential, as well as a practical concern with the sequelae of biological trauma surrounding birth. Anoxia, toxemia, and prematurity are believed to affect the integrity of the central nervous system. Anomalous psychological development in children with histories of early biological insult invites a physiological rather than a psychological explanation for the later variation.

Finally, there are new voices warning of the biological limitations on the doctrine of a completely malleable infant whose early experiences can be arranged to avoid all future catastrophe. Each organism inherits a set of species-specific behaviors and a maturational program that dictates the appropriate time of their appearances. Ontogeny does not recapitulate phylogeny; rather, ontogeny transcribes each species genome. Such a view contains a subtle hint of discontinuity among species, and among stages of development, where before we exaggerated the continuities. Piagetian theory, which is at a crest of popularity, awards primacy to the inevitable maturation of cognitive systems whose manifestations will emerge under almost any reasonable set of environmental circumstances. Ethologists, biologists, and behavioral geneticists warn us that experience cannot accomplish any psychological goal. The work of Seligman (1975) and Garcia et al. (1966) emphasize the biologically based preparedness each organism brings to every encounter (Seligman and Hager, 1972). Child psychologists working in other cultural settings note that despite dramatic differences in contexts of rearing and forms of child socialization practices, all children show stranger and separation anxiety, all learn a language, all can analyze pictures, and generally boys engage in more rough and tumble and aggressive play than girls whether their home is in rural Massachusetts or northern India. Experience seems to play its part in arranging the variations in timing and in quality of expression—a range that can be enormous—while biology composes the order of the themes.

CONTINUITY

Recently published data have led some psychologists to question the older assumptions about the long-term effect of early experience on future behavior. For the first time in the modern history of child psychology one senses the beginning of skepticism toward the strong form of the continuity assumption. The belief in psychological continuity within an individual life led, during the 1930s, to the initiation of several long-term longitudinal studies whose goal was to document the continuity that many investigators were sure had to be present. The twin assumptions that the infant is malleable to experience and that early structures persist for decades, which were seen as necessarily correlated, are now regarded as independent. If the young child is malleable in his current environment, then a change in context might alter the profiles produced by the prior context. The 19th-century commitment to the malleability of the infant is being taken seriously, for the young child seems to have an extraordinary capacity for change, given new adaptation demands. That insight was disguised in the past, perhaps because we implicitly assumed that the average child's environment would—or could—not change. In a more stable America, most children remained in the same family context and neighborhood until it was time to embark on adult responsibilities. The continuity of behavior noted by relatives and friends was attributed to forces within the child rather than to the environmental context in which he played out his roles. If a small marble placed in a trough on an incline rolled unerringly in a straight line, one would not credit the marble with the capacity to maintain continuous linear movement. We did not apply that principle to development but concluded instead that the child had a mysterious power to sustain his psychological direction without the help of a guiding track.

The results of the first longitudinal studies, which were published during the last 15 years, provide surprisingly fragile evidence for strong forms of continuity from infancy forward. The Fels study, which involved Caucasian families from southwest Ohio, provided frail support for the notion that infant traits like fearfulness, anger, motoricity, or dependency predicted theoretically relevant dispositions in adolescence or early adulthood. It was not until preadolescence that consistent predictive validity from childhood to adulthood appeared (Kagan and Moss, 1962).

It is still not clear whether there is any strong continuity from the period of infancy to later childhood, but the burden of proof has shifted from those who deny continuity to those who claim it is present. What does seem clear is that the child does not carry a "quality" through development that is independent of the context in which he lives. If there is continuity from infancy to adolescence it is likely to appear under conditions where the environment promotes or maintains the infant's particular qualities. For example, some 4-month-old babies babble a lot, while some are relatively quiet, and this seems to be a biologically based disposition. If a babbling baby is born to middle-class well-educated parents, 2 years later that child is more talkative than a quiet 4-month-old born to parents of the same social class. But a highly vocal 4-month-old born to lower- or working-class parents, who generally do not encourage early vocalization, was not any more talkative than a low-vocal infant (Kagan, 1971). Infants' qualities are not permanent attributes. They are continually subject to environmental pressures.

A principle that seems to emerge from the longitudinal studies is best termed "growth toward health." The child tries to grow toward adaptation, if the environment will permit him. The mistaken assumption made by the early investigators was that a node of pathology in infancy was like a blemish and, like Lady Macbeth's bloody hands, could not be wiped clean. The data do not support that pessimistic view. Dispositions that are maladaptive or pathological can be outgrown, while adaptive characteristics are more likely to be retained. Macfarlane (1963, 1964) reports that many children and adolescents who showed pathology lost it as they found better environmental niches and opportunities that permitted old anxieties to be resolved. This generalization is also supported by the early studies of Wayne Dennis (1938) who restricted a pair of twin 2-year-old infants for most of the 1st year. After they returned to a normal environment they eventually began to display a growth function that was normative.

The knowledge available at present does not indicate that the differences among 2-year-olds place profound constraints on the psychological structures of the adolescent and adult. The direction in which the young twig is bent does not seem to predict the orientation of the adult tree, at least in any way that is discernible.

Recent advances in embryology are consonant with those conclusions. Oppenheimer (1967) has argued that the three assumptions of preformation, unity of type, and recapitulation held by early 19th-century biologists obstructed progress in embryology. The latter two have a direct analog to the issue of continuity in psychological development. Like the 19th-century embryologist who assumed the existence of an abstract type—with little variation—for each species, many child psychologists assumed that a competence, habit, process, or state of organization existed in the abstract, independent of context. We describe infants and young children as attentive, irritable, or in the sensorimotor stage, subduing the obvious variation in that quality that is monitored by context and occasion. The growth rate of an Amblystoma embryo varies with slight changes in acidity and temperature. There is no construct "growth rate for Amblystoma," only growth rates under particular conditions. Similarly there is no psychological entity such as attentiveness or memory independent of classes of task contexts.

The doctrine of recapitulation, which posited a long thread of continuity from hydra to man, assumed that the early development of a form at one level of evolutionary complexity reflected the development of more primitive forms. The influence of recapitulation doctrine is seen in developmental psychology in both Freudian and Piagetian theory. Both theories assume that the structures of an early stage make a contribution to the structures of a later one. Unity of type and recapitulation have not been useful ideas in modern embryology. Since embryology is a reasonably good model for developmental psychology, it may be useful to take a lesson from our sister science and examine our commitments to these axioms.

The major conceptual advance over the last decade is seen in the increasing acceptance of the interaction of biological and experiential variables. A traumatic event during infancy seems to make a difference primarily for children from economically poor environments, not for those in more secure homes. Disease or trauma in infancy seems to affect the children in poverty more seriously than those in more affluent circumstances. We seem to be in a period of synthesis between Gesell's thesis that maturation controls most of development and Watson's pronouncement that experience has all the power. One form of that synthetic statement is that maturational forces direct the basic growth function for many psychological systems that emerge during the first 2 years—reaction to discrepancy, activation of relational structures, object permanence, and stranger and separation fears. But experience determines the age at which these competences appear or disappear and, during the period of their emergence, the intensity and frequency of their display.

The analogy to age of menarche is compelling. Most females inherit the capacity for reproductive fertility, which will appear somewhere between 10 and 18 years of age. The age at which it appears and the regularity of menstruation will be a function of health, nutrition, and pattern of earlier diseases. Onset of language provides an even better analogy. All children, save a few, inherit a tendency to speak, so long as they are exposed to language. But the appearance of the first word and the rate of growth of length of utterance will vary with exposure to adult language. Middle-class American children speak by 1 year; isolated children in San Marcos on Lake Atitlan, who do not experience as much verbal interaction with adults, do not utter their first words until they are over 2 years old. The new trend in child development is providing an empirical basis for the old maxim that experience and the child's biology interact in producing individual growth patterns.

BIBLIOGRAPHY

Ainsworth, M. D. S., and Wittig, B. A. Attachment and exploratory behavior of one year olds in a strange situation. In B. M. Foss (ed.), *Determinants of Infant Behavior,* Vol. 4. London: Methuen, 1969.

Ainsworth, M. D. S., and Bell, S. M. Attachment, exploration and separation illustrated by the behavior of one year olds in a strange situation. *Child Development,* 1970, **41,** 49–67.

Akita, G. The other Ito: a political failure. In A. M. Craig and D. H. Shively (eds.), *Personality in Japanese History.* Berkeley: University of California Press, 1970, 335–372.

Bayley, N. The development of motor abilities during the first three years. *Monographs of the Society for Research in Child Development,* 1935, **1,** (Serial No. 1).

Bond, E. K. Perception of form by the human infant. *Psychological Bulletin,* 1972, **77,** 225–245.

Bower, T. G. R. *Development in Infancy*. San Francisco: Freeman, 1974.

Bowlby, J. *Attachment and Loss,* Vol. 1. New York: Basic, 1969.

Bronson, G. W. Infants' reactions to unfamiliar persons and novel objects. *Monographs of the Society for Research in Child Development,* 1972, **37** (3, Serial No. 148).

Caldwell, B. M. The effects of infant care. In M. L. Hoffman and L. W. Hoffman (eds.), *Review of Child Development Research,* Vol. 1. New York: Russell Sage Foundation, 1964, 9–88.

Caudill, W., and Weinstein, H. Maternal care and infant behavior in Japan and America. *Psychiatry,* 1969, **32,** 12–43.

Chavasse, P. H. *Advice to a Mother on the Management of her Children*. Philadelphia: Lippincott, 1869.

Cohen, L. B., Gelber, E. R., and Lazar, M. A. Infant habituation and generalization to differing degrees of novelty. *Journal of Experimental Child Psychology,* 1971, **11,** 379–389.

Cornell, E. H. Infants' visual attention to pattern arrangement and orientation. *Child Development,* 1975, **46,** 229–232.

Dennis, W. Infant development under conditions of restricted practice and minimum social stimulation. *Journal of Genetic Psychology,* 1938, **53,** 149–158.

Fantz, R. L. Visual perception from birth as shown by pattern selectivity. *Annals of the New York Academy of Sciences,* 1965, **18,** 793–814.

Fantz, R. L., and Fagan, J. F. Visual attention to size and number of pattern details by term and pre-term infants during the first six months. *Child Development,* 1975, **46,** 3–18.

Finley, G. E., Kagan, J., and Layne, O. Development of young children's attention to normal and distorted stimuli. *Developmental Psychology,* 1972, **6,** 288–292.

Fiske, J. *The Meaning of Infancy*. Boston: Houghton Mifflin, 1883.

Fox, N. Separation distress in kibbutz reared childen. Unpublished manuscript, Harvard University, 1975.

Fraiberg, S. Parallel and divergent patterns in blind and sighted infants. *Psychoanalytic Study of the Child,* 1968, **23,** 264–299.

Freedman, D. G. *Human Infancy: An Evolutionary Perspective*. Hillsdale, N. J.: Erlbaum, 1974.

Garcia, J., McGowan, B., and Green, K. F. Biological constraints on conditioning: Learning with prolonged delay or reinforcements. *Psychonomic Science,* 1966, **5,** 121–122.

Geber, M. The psychomotor development of African children in the first year and the influence of maternal behavior. *Journal of Social Psychology,* 1958, **47,** 185–195.

Haith, M. M. The response of the human newborn to visual movement. *Journal of Experimental Child Psychology,* 1966, **3,** 235–243.

Hebb, D. O. *The Organization of Behavior*. New York: Wiley, 1949.

Hopkins, J. R. Zelazo, P. R., Jacobson, S. W., and Kagan, J. Infant reactivity to stimulus schema discrepancy. *Genetic Psychology Monographs,* 1976, **93,** 27–62.

Hunt, J. McV. *Intelligence and Experience*. New York: Ronald, 1961.

Jaeger, W. *The Paideia: The Ideals of Greek Culture,* Vol. 3. New York: Oxford University, 1944.

Kagan, J. *Change and Continuity in Infancy*. New York: Wiley, 1971.

Kagan, J. Do infants think? *Scientific American,* 1972, **226** (3), 74–83.

Kagan, J. Discrepancy, temperament, and infant distress. In M. Lewis and L. Rosenblum (eds.), *The Origins of Fear*. New York: Wiley, 1974, 229–248.

Kagan, J. Emergent themes in human development. *American Scientist,* 1976a, **64,** 186–196.

Kagan, J. The effect of day care on the infant and young child. Paper delivered at meeting of the American Association for the Advancement of Science, Boston, February 19, 1976b.

Kagan, J., and Moss, H. A. *Birth to Maturity*. New York: Wiley, 1962.

Kagan, J., Kearsley, R. B., and Zelazo, P. R. The emergence of initial apprehension to unfamiliar peers. In M. Lewis and L. A. Rosenblum (eds.), *Friendship and Peer Relations*. New York: Wiley, 1975, 187–206.

Karmel, B. Z. The effect of age, complexity and amount of contour on pattern preferences in human infants. *Journal of Experimental Child Psychology,* 1969, **7,** 339–354.

Karmel, B. Z., Hoffman, R. F., and Fegy, M. J. Processing of contour information by human infants evidenced by pattern dependent evoked potentials. *Child Development,* 1974, **45,** 39–48.

Kearsley, R. B., Zelazo, P. R., Kagan, J., and Hartmann, R. Differences in separation protest between day care and home reared infants. *Journal of Pediatrics,* 1975, **55,** 171–175.

Kessen, W., Haith, M. M., and Salapatek, P. H. Infancy. In P. H. Mussen (ed.), *Carmichael's Manual of Child Psychology,* 3rd ed. New York: Wiley, 1970.

Kessen, W., Salapatek, P. H., and Haith, M. The visual response of the human newborn to linear contour. *Journal of Experimental Child Psychology,* 1972, **13,** 19–20.

Kinney, D. K., and Kagan, J. Infant attention to auditory discrepancy. *Child Development,* 1976, **47,** 155–164.

Kotelchuck, M., Zelazo, P. R., Kagan, J., and Spelke, E. Infant reactions to parental separations when left with familiar and unfamiliar adults. *Journal of Genetic Psychology* 1975, **126,** 255–262.

Lester, B. M., Kotelchuck, M., Spelke, E., Sellers, M. J., and Klein, R. E. Separation protest in Guatemalan infants: Cross cultural and cognitive findings. *Developmental Psychology,* 1974, **10,** 79–85.

LeVine, R. A., and LeVine, B. B. Nyansongo: a Gusii community in Kenya. In B. B. Whiting (ed.), *Six Cultures: Studies of Child Rearing*. New York: Wiley, 1963, 15–202.

Lewis, M., and Goldberg, S. The acquisition and violation of expectancy: An experimental paradigm. *Journal of Experimental Child Psychology,* 1969, **7,** 70–80.

Lewis, M. A., and McGurk, H. Evaluation of infant intelligence. *Science,* 1972, **170,** 1174–1177.

Littenberg, R., Tulkin, S., and Kagan, J. Cognitive components of separation anxiety. *Developmental Psychology,* 1971, **4,** 387–388.

Maccoby, E. E., and Feldman, S. S. Mother-attachment and stranger reactions in the third year of life. *Monographs of the Society for Research in Child Development,* 1972, **37** (146).

Macfarlane, J. W. From infancy to adulthood. *Childhood Education,* 1963, **39,** 336–342.

Macfarlane, J. W. Perspectives on personality consistency and change from the guidance study. *Vita Humana,* 1964, **7,** 115–126.

McCall, R. B., Kennedy, C. B., and Appelbaum, M. I. Magnitude of discrepancy and the direction of attention in infants. *Child Development,* 1977, **48,** 772–785.

McCall, R. B., and McGhee, P. E. The discrepancy hypothesis and affect in infants. Unpublished.

McLoughlin, W. G. Evangelical childrearing in the age of Jackson: Francis Wayland's view on when and how to subdue the willfulness of children. *Journal of Social History,* 1975, **9,** 21–39.

Minturn, L., and Hitchcock, J. T. The Rajputs of Khalapur, India. In B. B. Whiting (ed.), *Six Cultures: Studies of Child Rearing*. New York: Wiley, 1963, 207–361.

Morgan, G. A., and Ricciuti, H. N. Infants' responses to strangers during the first year. In B. M. Foss (ed.), *Determinants of Infant Behavior,* Vol. 4. London: Methuen, 1969.

Oppenheimer, J. *Essays in the history of embryology and biology*. Cambridge, Mass.: MIT Press, 1967.

Orlansky, H. Infant care and personality. *Psychological Bulletin,* 1949, **46,** 1–48.

Parry, M. H. Infant wariness and stimulus discrepancy. *Journal of Experimental Child Psychology,* 1973, **16,** 377–387.

Perez, B. *The First Three Years of Childhood.* New York: Kellogg, 1888. Reprinted, New York: Arno, 1975.

Piaget, J. *Six Psychological Studies.* New York: Random House, 1967.

Plumb, J. H. The New world of children in 18th century England. *Past and Present,* 1975, **67,** 64–95.

Rheingold, H. L., and Eckerman, C. O. The infant separates himself from his mother. *Science,* 1970, **168,** 78–90.

Rybash, J. M., Roodin, P. A., and Sullivan, L. F. The effects of a memory aid on three types of conservation judgments. *Journal of Experimental Child Psychology,* 1975, **19,** 358–370.

Ryerson, A. Medical advice on child rearing 1550–1900. Unpublished Ph.D. dissertation, Harvard Graduate School of Education, 1959.

Scarr, S., and Salapatek, P. Patterns of fear development during infancy. *Merrill Palmer Quarterly,* 1970, **16,** 53–90.

Schaffer, H. R. The onset of fear of strangers and the incongruity hypothesis. *Journal of Child Psychology and Psychiatry,* 1966, **7,** 95–106.

Schaffer, H. R. Cognitive components of the infant's response to strangeness. In M. Lewis and L. A. Rosenblum (eds.), *The Origins of Fear.* New York: Wiley, 1974, 11–24.

Seligman, M. E. P. *Helpnessness.* San Francisco: Freeman, 1975.

Seligman, M. E. P., and Hager, J. C. (eds.). *Biological Boundaries of Learning.* New York: Appleton-Century-Crofts, 1972.

Sellers, M. J., Klein, R. E., Kagan, J., and Minton, C. Developmental determinants of attention: a cross cultural replication. *Developmental Psychology,* 1972, **6,** 185.

Shinn, M. W. *The Biography of a Baby.* New York: Houghton Mifflin, 1900. Reprinted, New York: Arno, 1975.

Spitz, R. A. Hospitalism: An inquiry into the genesis of psychiatric conditions in early childhood. In A. Freud et al. (eds.), *The Psychoanalytic Study of the Child,* Vol. 1. New York: International Universities Press, 1945, 53–74.

Spitz, R. A. Hospitalism: A follow-up report on investigations described in Volume 1, 1945. In A. Freud et al. (eds.), *The Psychoanalytic Study of the Child,* Vol. 2. New York: International Universities Press, 1946, 113–117.

Spitz, R. A. Anxiety in infancy: a study of its manifestation in the first year of life. *International Journal of Psychoanalysis,* 1950, **31,** 138–143.

Stevens, A. G. Attachment behavior, separation anxiety and stranger anxiety in polymatrically reared infants. In H. R. Schaffer (ed.), *The Origins of Human Social Relations.* New York: Academic, 1971.

Super, C. M. Environmental effects on motor development. *Developmental Medicine and Child Neurology,* 1976, **18,** 561–567.

Super, C. M. Long term memory in infants. Unpublished doctoral dissertation, Harvard University, 1972.

Super, C. M., Kagan, J., Morrison, F. J., Haith, M. M., and Weiffenbach, J. Discrepancy and attention in the 5 month infant. *Genetic Psychology Monographs,* 1972, **85,** 305–331.

Tennes, K. H., and Lampl, E. E. Stranger and separation anxiety in infancy. *Journal of Nervous and Mental Disease,* 1969, **139,** 247–254.

Thomas, A., Chess, S., and Birch, H. G. The origins of personality. *Scientific American,* 1970, **223,** 102–109.

Zelazo, P. R., Hopkins, J. R., Jacobson, S., and Kagan, J. Psychological reactivity to discrepant events: support for the curvilinear hypothesis. *Cognition,* 1973, **2,** 385–393.

PART ONE

Factors Influencing Newborn and Early Infant Behaviors

CHAPTER 2

Prenatal and Perinatal Influences on Infant Behavior[1]

Claire B. Kopp
Arthur H. Parmelee

The literature concerned with "developmental risk" subsequent to prenatal and perinatal stress is so extensive, diverse, and fragmented that focus and organizational perspective is required. Our focus is on research aimed at determining the implications of *early developmental risk,* as exemplified by developmental delay, neurologic sequelae, or other indices of atypical or deviant development. Although primarily concentrating on data pertaining to the first 2 years of life, it will also be necessary to discuss findings obtained with older children.

We will show that despite a rich body of literature, a well-developed conceptual model of risk does not exist. Moreover, we will suggest that the type of research that has characterized much of the literature is not well suited to developing such a model; therefore, new directions and strategies are required.

The organization of the chapter is as follows. To orient the reader we first define terminology frequently found in the literature and discuss current epidemiologic considerations. In this section we also include a brief discussion on the nature of risk conditions with emphasis placed on prenatal factors, as these are the current leading causes of moderate to severe impairment. This discussion is followed by our introduction of an organizational scheme used to put the extensive amount of research into perspective. Next, relying on this perspective as appropriate, we review literature devoted to specific risk conditions; we note the cause and nature of their influence, and their impact on developmental outcome in general and on infant behavior. Finally, in the last section, we propose a change in research focus and other research strategies. The objective is to move closer to formulation of a model of developmental risk.

INTRODUCTION

The terms intrauterine and extrauterine provide a broad and convenient conceptual framework for the study of the origins and changes in structure and function that charac-

[1]Writing of this chapter was supported in part by Public Health Service Grant No. MC-R-060396-01-0 from the Bureau of Community Health Services, Maternal and Child Health, by Public Health Sevice Contract No. 1-HD-3-2776 from the National Institute of Child Health and Human Development, and Public Health Service Grant HD-04612. Appriciation is extended to Barbara K. Keogh for reading several drafts and providing insightful critiques, and to Marian Sigman and Cathryn Trowbridge for helpful comments.

terize early life. Development, though, is neither immune to insult nor to the timing of an insult; thus, a more precise terminology is required. An approach common to the study of etiological factors contributing to human developmental problems has been to characterize onset of risk in terms of three major time periods; *prenatal, perinatal,* and *postnatal.* Prenatal, the time prior to birth, encompasses two sub-periods; the *embryonic* period refers to the stage of structural development, while *fetal* life concerns maturation of these structures. Perinatal, generally subsumes the birth or *natal* period as well as the first 3 to 4 weeks of extrauterine life. Postnatal refers to subsequent time periods. A structural malformation observed at the time of birth is considered to have its origins in the embryonic period; birth trauma is considered a natal risk event; an infectious disease acquired at 6 months of age is considered postnatal.

This system has two marked advantages. First, it can be used to classify the implications of risk onset in association with an attained structural or functional level of development. For example, an insult occurring at the time organs are being formed may have one set of consequences, whereas a risk event occurring to a structurally complete though immature organism may have a different set of implications. Secondly, the system permits measurement of the effectiveness of health and social services provided for mothers and infants. Thus mortality and morbidity can be studied in relation to prenatal, perinatal, and postnatal care. Historical trends and continuing sources of concern can be pinpointed.

Among the most positive consequences of technology are advances made in prevention and amelioration of diseases of infancy and childhood. It is sobering, indeed, to consider the illnesses that plagued many of the young, even as recently as two generations ago, and to know these are now rare occurrences in many societies. Paralleling this trend has been the reduced incidence of severely handicapping conditions stemming from postnatal illness or disease. However, these achievements need to be considered in the face of problems that still exist. Among the poor, the deprived, and the neglected, in our own country and elsewhere, the rate of postnatal mortality and morbidity is higher than found in more affluent circumstances (Birch and Gussow, 1970; Williams and Jelliffe, 1972). Moreover, while the sequelae of adverse perinatal events is declining dramatically, particularly since 1965 (Gold, 1974; Hagberg, 1975), it is still too high. Problems remain in relation to mortality of nonwhite infants (Driscoll, 1975), and morbidity of children reared under inadequate care-giving situations (Sameroff and Chandler, 1975; Tizard, 1974). However, *the* current, leading cause of *severe* impairment, among rich and poor, stems from prenatal factors (Hagberg, 1975), and these conditions may be the most difficult to ameliorate.

There are numerous prenatal contributors to developmental problems; the list is extensive and has increased appreciably in the last decades (Wilson, 1973). It was not that man in earlier times considered prenatal life immune to influence. Indeed, for some 5000 years real and mystical ideas about prenatal influences had been expressed (Stubbe, 1972). Rather, it was that the nature of reproduction and types of influence were poorly understood (Hickey, 1953). However, with contributions from modern genetics and embryology, and with incontestable evidence accumulated as a consequence of radiation warfare, ingestion of drugs, and other unfortunate catastrophes, have come an appreciation of fetal vulnerability. Factors causing impairment may include mutant genes, aberrant chromosomes, radiation, chemicals, drugs, infections, metabolic and endocrine disturbances, physical trauma, placental dysfunction, and others (Wilson, 1973). Also implicated are individual differences in vulnerability, and multifactorial conditions such as genetic predisposition in interaction with subtle environmental influences (Carter, 1974). Multifactorial events are considered by Fraser (1965) the most difficult to analyze, the most difficult to prevent, yet probably, as a major cause of problems in humans, the most important of all prenatal influences. To use Fraser's terminology, multifactorial events consist of "a lot of little things . . . a group of biological vulnerabilities each of which when considered alone would hardly be noticed, . . . but acting together, and particularly in the presence of a few minor environmental stresses . . . " lead to adverse sequelae.

Vulnerability of the prenatal organism is determined by the character of the disruptive agent and developmental status at the time of disruption. Whereas mutant genes and aberrant chromosomes begin to exert an influence early in prenatal life, harmful agents, drugs, and infections can be operative any time during prenatal life. Their effects, though, must be considered in relation to embryonic and fetal development. In the early weeks of intrauterine life, structural components of the embryo are differentiated and then formed into recognizable organ entities. At 12 weeks of prenatal life the human organism, now called a fetus, is structurally complete, and further prenatal development will consist of cell growth and functional maturity. In the first days of prenatal life, susceptibility to teratogenic agents is minimal, reaches a peak during differentiation and early organogenesis, and declines thereafter. The impact of interfering agents occurring during organogenesis results in gross structural defects, whereas a later influence may result in growth retardation of the fetus and/or functional disturbances (Wilson, 1973). It is not difficult to appreciate that outcomes subsequent to adverse prenatal influences vary from death (in intrauterine life, at birth, or later) to malformation which may be evident at birth, to growth retardation in the form of a very underweight newborn, to subtle functional deficits, or to no adverse sequelae (Wilson, 1973).

The magnitude of deleterious consequences can best be measured by examining statistics concerning severe developmental problems. It has been estimated that somewhat less than 1% of the population shows moderate to severe problems in the years before schooling (Dingman and Tarjan, 1960; Kushlick and Blunden, 1974; Mercer, 1973). How much less depends on the place of sampling, the risk criteria, and the assessments used; nonetheless, in an analysis of prevalence rates of severe mental retardation Abramowicz and Richardson (1975) found a consistently stable rate of 3 to 5 per 1000. Taking this one step further, Hagberg (1975) estimates that 85 to 90% of severe intellectual and neurological problems stem from prenatal causes. Indeed, a sobering figure!

Although the numbers, fortunately, are fewer, perinatal and postnatal factors obviously contribute to developmental problems. Natal and perinatal causes of morbidity are disorders of delivery, neonatal infections, asphyxia, hypoglycemia, prematurity, cardiac and respiratory difficulties, and a host of other conditions. Many of these perinatal events have their origins in prenatal factors. Thus, an infant born prior to his term date and underweight for his gestational age was subject to some type of prenatal risk condition that affected intrauterine nutrition. Similarly, a full-term infant, showing signs of distress during the birth process, may have experienced an antepartum hemorrhage. In either case the infant's ability to withstand stresses of the perinatal period depend on the integrity of his system, which may have been compromised by prenatal events. What is the range of consequences?

The range of outcome is wide. First of all, mortality can occur, though this has shown a 25% decline between 1965 and 1972 (Gold, 1974). However, it is important to recognize that while these deaths are classified as "perinatal," almost all had their origins in deleterious prenatal events (Driscoll, 1975); a substantial number of deaths occur to infants with congenital malformations or chromosome defects. At the more positive, other end of the continuum are the *many* infants, less stressed, who not only survive but give every evidence of normal development. What about the "middle-range" of children who continue to show problems? In some cases there is severe, long-term damage; in others, milder forms of retardation are evident. While mild intellectual deficits may stem from perinatal events, more likely contributors relate to adverse social and economic factors (Birch et al., 1970; Broman et al., 1975; Sameroff and Chandler, 1975).

Turning now to postnatal factors, in industrialized nations we know that the contribution of postnatal illness, disease, and accidents to severe developmental sequelae is relatively small. While expanded preventive services and care (particularly for the poor) will reduce the numbers somewhat, it is unlikely that additional major reductions will occur (Hagberg, 1975). In contrast to the relatively optimistic picture found in affluent nations, the rates of mortality and morbidity observed in poorer, developing nations, particularly for infants under 1 year of age, are unconscionably high. Postnatal disease, infections, malnutrition, and poverty are common, but it is difficult to sort out the exact contributions of adverse postnatal factors to impairment, as stressful prenatal and perinatal conditions surely are contributing factors that lead to more vulnerable infants.

Finally, we want to comment upon postnatal conditions associated with less severe sequelae. Mild retardation, constituting one of the largest categories of handicapping conditions found among children and adults, stems in large part from deleterious social and cultural conditions (Tarjan, 1970). However, it has been suggested that subtle prenatal and perinatal nonoptimal conditions, in interaction with deleterious postnatal factors, contribute to some of these observed functional deficits (Birch and Gussow, 1970).

In summary, in this introduction we have mentioned terminology frequently used to study onset and risk factors contributing to developmental problems. Adverse prenatal events have been emphasized, as they are viewed as the current leading cause of severe intellectual and neurological sequelae. Perinatal events have been discussed briefly, and their tie to prenatal hazards has been considered. Finally, we have mentioned current postnatal health concerns.

Much of the preceding discussion has been generic, as broadly defined diagnostic categories and group trends were examined. In the following section we become more specific as we turn to types of research that characterize the literature on developmental outcome subsequent to prenatal or perinatal stress.

RESEARCH ON DEVELOPMENTAL RISK

Two major themes are highlighted in the literature on risk conditions: one focuses on follow-up, the other on descriptions of group differences. Though somewhat arbitrary and oversimplified, we will use these themes to organize the research into manageable dimensions. As will be evident, the categories are not mutually exclusive.

Research that can be classified as follow-up (or outcome) generally starts with a group of infants identified by symptoms, physical signs, diagnostic entities, and so forth. Development is monitored from early life to a later period. Implicitly or explicitly, the researcher seeks to determine the effects of the diagnostic condition on development—the diagnostic condition being the independent variable, and outcome, however measured, the dependent variable. In some instances environmental conditions such as social class, maternal education, or other parameters may be assessed and entered as additional variables influencing outcome. Outcome, usually defined by culturally accepted standards of "normal" and "deviant," is most often measured by developmental examinations and intelligence-test measures. Neurologic, behavioral, personality, speech, and school achievement indices also may be employed. Maintaining longitudinal follow-up groups is expensive, and therefore use of comparison groups is rare; instead, the subject group's performance is contrasted with known standardization data or inferred clinical norms. However, most subject groups are followed into the school years, and occasionally into adolescence. Indeed, in our culture, one of the major tests of the impact of a prenatal or perinatal condition on the developing child is the proportion of children who need special types of education.

Outcome research, representing both prenatal and perinatal factors, accounts for a considerable portion of the developmental risk literature. A partial listing, showing the diversity of follow-up studies, includes research on (1) children who suffered anoxia in the neonatal period (Corah et al., 1965; Graham et al., 1962; Graham, et al., 1957), (2) those who had been born pre-term (Douglas, 1960; Drillien, 1964; Francis-Williams and Davies, 1974; Harper and Wiener, 1965; Hunt, 1976; Knobloch et al., 1956; Philippe and Lezine, 1974; Rubin et al., 1973; Weiner et al., 1965; Wiener et al., 1968), (3) infants who showed neurologic signs in the newborn period (Parmelee et al., 1970; Prechtl, 1965), (4) children whose mothers had been diagnosed as having rubella in pregnancy (Chess, 1974), (5) children born with congenital malformations due to teratogenic effects of thalidomide (Decarie, 1969; Decarie and O'Neill, 1974), (6) children born with defects of the spinal cord (Diller et al., 1969; Hunt and Holmes, 1975; Laurence, 1966; Laurence and Tew, 1967; Tew and Laurence, 1974), (7) children born with Down's syndrome (Carr, 1975; Dicks-Mireaux, 1972; Share et al., 1964), and (8) children showing indications of phenylketonuria (Baumeister, 1967; Berman et al., 1966; Lonsdale and Foust, 1970; Steinhausen, 1974). In addition to these studies are others where outcome has been monitored as a function of a particular symptom, or cluster of symptoms, found in the perinatal period. These might include presence of apnea, levels of blood glucose concentration, respiratory distress, and other untoward events. In these cases, the follow-up time is usually shorter than in the group of studies listed above.

A recent and encouraging subcategory of follow-up research involves evaluation of *specific* interventions administered to prenatally and/or perinatally stressed infants. For example, as neonatal intensive care units began to be established in the mid 1960s, tests of their effectiveness were made. Similarly, initiation of phototherapy, surgical interventions, changes in dietary intake for pre-terms, introduction of parents into intensive care nurseries, provision of "sensory stimulation" to pre-terms, and so forth, also were evaluated. In some interventions studies, control groups are part of the design; in others, more recently obtained data are contrasted with research findings generated from earlier time periods. Social and environmental factors may be measured, but often they are not. Dependent variables frequently include assessment of the incidence of mortality or neurologic sequelae, sensory disorders, cerebral palsy, and developmental status. Exemplars of research monitoring medical-based interventions include studies by Alden et al. (1972), Carrier et al. (1972), Mawdsley et al. (1967), Davies and Tizard (1975), and Hagberg et al. (1973). Examples of research on social and other nonmedical types of interventions include studies by Leiderman et al. (1973) and Barnard (1973).

In contrast, to the first groups of studies, another distinct category emerges around research aimed at studying behavior that differs for infants considered to be "at risk" contrasted to "nonrisk" samples. In many studies, performance may be examined solely because infants hold class membership in a diagnostic group and not necessarily because they show developmental deviance. In this research category, focus and research strategies differ considerably from those used in follow-up studies. First, there is considerable emphasis directed towards examination of *diverse* kinds of behavior, including studies of neurologic organization, psychophysiologic responses, sleep, and, more recently, attention, object exploration, memory, and so forth; standardized examinations are used infrequently. Secondly, heavy reliance is placed on cross-sectional or short-term longitudinal studies; indeed, cross-sectional studies of neonates represent a considerable portion of this research. Third, use of control or contrast groups is the rule rather than the exception. In general, data derived from these studies have been reported in terms of similarities and differences observed in behavior of the risk group and the contrast group; some "within-group" comparisons have been made of sex differences, social class factors, or degree of developmental deviance.

Exemplifying this research are studies made in the neonatal period of electroencephalographic characteristics, sensory functioning, neurologic organization, and visual fixation of pre-terms as contrasted to full-terms (Dreyfus-Brisac, 1966; Engel, 1965; Howard et al., 1976; Kopp et al., 1975; Miranda, 1970; Parmelee, et al., 1969; Saint-Anne Dargassies, 1966), of attention or object exploration of pre-terms and full terms in later infancy (Fantz and Fagan, 1975; Kopp, 1976; Sigman, 1976; Sigman and Parmelee, 1974), of attention, memory, and cognitive development of Down's syndrome infants (Miranda, 1970; Miranda and Fantz, 1973, 1974), of behavioral characteristics of intrauterine growth-retarded infants (Als et al., 1976), and of developmental patterns of blind and sighted infants (Fraiberg, 1975).

Using an "outcome" and group-difference classification scheme has allowed us to obtain an idea of the scope and perspective of the literature on developmental risk during early life. However, we require more than information about scope. Ideally we would like sufficient knowledge to permit inferences to be made about the specific and individual effects of prenatal and perinatal conditions during infancy, and later childhood.

Such information would allow us to answer a variety of questions: What specific constraints or limitations do hazardous conditions have on potential for growth and change? What limitations may be overcome or attenuated by environmental influences? Which psychological and social processes seem most affected by adverse factors? Why do some infants, seemingly impaired during the first years of life, show normal intellectual skills in childhood? Conversely, why do some infants who seem only minimally delayed in infancy show intellectual impairment in later years? Which psychological processes are most involved when developmental risk is discontinuous? What similarities and differences in psychological and social mechanisms underlie development of the mildly impaired versus the moderately or severely impaired infant? Which are the most appropriate ways to identify infants for continuing developmental risk?

As we review the literature on developmental risk it will be readily apparent that our present ability to answer most of these questions is severely limited. We will find that the implications of prenatal and perinatal influences are very complex; thus, we are pressed to find the hows and whys of the processes underlying development, rather than solely focusing on test scores or measurements of group differences made at only one time period.

A realistic appraisal of our current position is that we cannot discuss developmental risk in other than the most general terms. We have neither a cohesive body of knowledge to draw upon nor even a single prenatal or perinatal event studied in sufficient depth to provide answers to the questions we have posed.

REVIEW OF STUDIES

While in some ways the preceding may sound bleak, there is a wealth of information currently available in the literature on developmental risk. In this section we discuss some of the findings, but also point to some of the gaps in our knowledge. It will be evident that hints for future research directions can be found within the current literature.

Since the number of prenatal, perinatal, and early postnatal conditions that affect the infant are numerous, and since it is neither desirable nor feasible to review all, we have chosen to focus on exemplars of conditions that often are viewed as hazardous, and sources of developmental risk. Our emphasis is on prenatal conditions, as their contribution to morbidity is high; however, we also include discussion of a perinatal factor. The diagnostic groupings include a gene-based condition, chromosomal aberration, congenital malformation of the nervous system, intrauterine growth retardation, and pre-term birth.

Our orientation will be to provide some background information on each condition, focusing on the nature of the condition, its point of onset, and incidence rates when known. Outcome data for older children will be examined within each condition. Then data on infancy, both of follow-up type and relating to group differences, will be explored for developmental implications. If data are available on the link between infant behaviors and later development, these also will be examined. It will soon be apparent that the data base for each condition is quite different and, moreover, in some conditions is extremely limited; yet, we have included the diagnostic category if only to point out the limitations of our knowledge.

In essence, we are looking for information that indicates the specific implications of a risk event on early development.

REVIEW OF PRENATAL AND PERINATAL INFLUENCES

Gene-Based Disorders

The consequences of gene defects vary considerably, and depend on whether the mutant gene is on an autosomal or a sex-linked chromosome (location) and whether its dosage is single (heterozygous) or double (homozygous) (McKusick, 1969). Infants with a recognized autosomal dominant syndrome have inherited mutant genes from only *one* affected parent; as such, the dosage they receive is single (heterozygous). In general, these infants will be less severely affected than those with diagnosed autosomal recessive conditions; in the latter conditions, mutant genes are inherited from *both* parents, and thus the dosage is double (homozygous). Autosomal dominant gene mutations usually do not involve developmental delay and mental retardation, for those few mutations that are very serious are also life-threatening. Since reproduction in these circumstances is often impossible, the mutant gene tends to disappear from the gene pool (McKusick, 1969). In contrast, mental retardation and severe developmental problems are manifest in a number of autosomal recessive conditions; these mutant genes often directly affect biochemical reactions which impinge on functions of the brain, such as amino acid patterns, enzyme production, metabolic pathways, accumulation of substrate material, and amount of metabolites. While the brain may be affected, the individual's life is not necessarily threatened. Not all autosomal recessive conditions result in mental retardation; in a listing of 61 autosomal syndromes by Nora and Fraser (1974), one-third are associated with mental retardation. These include galactosemia, maple syrup urine disease, Hurler's syndrome, genetic thyroid defects, and phenylketonuria. As the latter exemplifies many of the characteristics of the group of gene-based disorders, it will be reviewed in some detail.

Phenylketonuria

Phenylketonuria (PKU) has been the focus of many studies; in its untreated condition it is associated with developmental delay, mental retardation, behavioral problems, and neurophysiological signs. When treated, the child's intellect is often in the normal range. We will use PKU as an example of an autosomal recessive gene-based disorder, with recognition that its characteristics do not mirror exactly the features of other gene-based disorders.

Phenylketonuria is a disease manifested by disturbance of amino acid metabolism. In PKU, an enzyme responsible for converting phenylalanine to tyrosine is insufficient. Consequently, biochemical dysfunction occurs, which leads to an excessive build-up of amino acid phenylalanine, an essential dietary amino acid related to the formation of body protein. This results in further biochemical, physiologic, and pathologic effects, which contribute to irreversible changes in the central nervous system leading to mental retardation. Although the exact reason for brain malfunction is unknown, one explanation offered is that an immature brain exposed to abnormal amino acid patterns does not grow normally. Indeed, small brains as well as defective patterns of myelination have been observed in pathological analyses made of brains of PKU patients (Knox, 1972).

The incidence of infants with PKU varies from 1 in 12,000 (Smith and Wolff, 1974) to 1 in 19,000 (Hsia and Holtzman, 1973), but the diagnosis of PKU cannot be made on the basis of visual inspection. Laboratory measurement of blood phenylalanine must be made; tests made the first day after birth may not give the same results as ones made 8 days after birth, which appears to be the peak time in rise of phenylalanine levels; 5 to 10% of cases may be missed by screening in the newborn nursery (Cedarbaum, 1976).

There is no clear relationship between level of phenylalanine in serum and mental retardation, but diets low in phenylalanine limit its build-up, and thus can influence the course of intellectual development. Infants with PKU seem to be most vulnerable for retardation during the first months of life; if therapeutic diets are initiated after 6 months of age there is often impairment.

DEVELOPMENTAL EFFECTS OF PKU

The infant born with PKU looks normal and acts as expected for a month or two after birth. Then a pattern of listless behavior, apathy, irritability, and delayed development is apparent (Koch, et al., 1964; Knox, 1972). Toward the end of the 1st year of life a drop in developmental abilities is noted, with continued, though less sharp, declines occurring until age 3. By this time severe retardation often is observed, with essentially no further declines (Knox, 1972). Neurological abnormalities, abnormal electroencephalograms, and emotional disturbances are also clinical features of the syndrome (Paine, 1957). Fortunately, under current programs, most cases of PKU are detected early so that severe features of the disease are now seen very infrequently. While the preceding seems clearcut, there have been reports that atypical phenylalanine levels were not always associated with retardation (Hsia, et al., 1968)—that is, in the past, individuals were detected who fell within the diagnostic criteria for clinical signs of PKU, who were untreated, and were asymptomatic or mildly retarded. Thus, the range of intellectual abilities of untreated PKU probably was more extensive than first realized.

In general, studies of treated PKU children indicate that early dietary restrictions alter the biochemical abnormality associated with a build-up of phenylalanine, and there is attainment of, at least, average intellectual abilities (Baumeister, 1967; Berman et al., 1966; Koch et al., 1967; Knox, 1972; Lonsdale and Foust, 1970; Sibinga and Friedman, 1972; Steinhausen, 1974). However, the IQ of treated PKU children seems to be lower than that of their siblings, suggesting a residual effect (Berman et al., 1966; Berman and Ford, 1970; Dodson et al., 1976; Smith and Wolff, 1974). As with other biological conditions, the outcome is also dependent on factors within the environment (Sibinga & Friedman, 1972).

How effective is the therapeutic regime on other aspects of the child's functioning? Treated children have been noted to demonstrate learning problems and emotional disturbances (Siegel et al., 1968). However, it is difficult to isolate the etiology of these problems, as they could be metabolic or psychosocial in origin. Parents of children with PKU are under enormous pressure; they can be anxious about dietary control, implications of genetic disease, fragility of their child, and so forth (Sutherland et al., 1966; Wood et al., 1967). Overprotection and rejection are two responses observed. Whatever the cause, emotional problems are noted early in life. For example, Lonsdale and Foust (1970) followed nine PKU infants who had dietary treatment initiated no later than 30 days after birth. The authors state that dietary management was carefully supervised, and growth and developmental measures were monitored often. Eight of the nine children tested between 6 and 25 months of age showed IQ scores between 91 and 117. Four children manifested neurologic signs such as irritability and tremors; however, neurological signs have been noted in early stages of untreated PKU, only to disappear later (Czochanska and Losiowski, 1972). Four children, including two in the neurologic group, had emotional problems serious enough for the authors to comment about their presence.

Information on the effect of treatment on other behaviors is provided in a recent study by Steinhausen (1974). He compared 45 PKU children, 22 of whom had been treated from the 1st month of life, 6 from the 2nd month of life, and 17 after the 6th month of life. Assessments were made for the first group of children between the ages of 1.1 and 5.7 years, for the second group between 2.2 and 8.10 years, and the last group between 2.3 and 12.9 years. Measures that were used included the Columbia Mental Maturity Scale (German revision), the Vineland Social Maturity Scale (German revision), the Lincoln-Oseretsky Motor scale, and the Denver Developmental Screening Test, which is an amalgam of items from various developmental examinations. Each subject was tested twice during an interval of 10 to 12 months. The author hypothesized that late-treated PKU infants would show developmental compensation while being treated with the diet but would still evidence developmental retardation, whereas infants treated early would demonstrate normal development.

Outcome measures revealed no major differences between the early treated groups, but significant differences between early and late-treated children. On all measures the early treated groups maintained normal levels of development, whereas, as expected, the late-treated group showed partial compensation but remained below age-level functioning. The author also reported another observation of interest: The early treated sample showed abnormal motor development at their first testing period but not at their second. Although Steinhausen suggested this might have been an artifact of sample size and statistical analyses, we should note that motor signs evident at the first testing period may have been due to transient neurological residuals. It has not been uncommon to find neurological impairment in early testing periods of infants who experienced perinatal stress which was not evident at later evaluations. It is possible that these instances represent recovery or development of compensating mechanisms; if so, one wonders if the processes that are involved could be the same for infants with PKU and infants who experienced perinatal stress.

Taken together, both the Lonsdale and Foust and Steinhausen studies permit conclusions to be made about treated PKU infants; both sets of data show a range of normal functioning subsequent to initiation of special diets early in life. As might be expected, these outcome data confirm previous findings. On the basis of these and many other studies on PKU, one could conclude that a straightforward interpretation is warranted regarding the implications of the disease under conditions of nontreatment versus treatment. Unfortunately, neither diagnosis, treatment, nor outcome have been without controversy and unresolved issues.

We have not delved into the issue of diagnosis of PKU, an area fraught with controversy but beyond the realm of this chapter. The interested reader is directed to a recently published analysis of screening programs, with a strong emphasis on PKU programs (National Academy of Sciences, 1975).

This topic aside, there remain numerous questions about the mechanisms underlying the emotional and behavioral findings observed with PKU infants and children. Both could be attributed to residuals of biochemical imbalance of the brain, but it is important to include the possible contributions made by parental apprehensions. Consider the situation that befalls most parents of PKU children. First, they must believe that the diet prescribed by the physician is appropriate for their child (too high a level of phenylalanine in the system and mental retardation may occur, too low a level and lethargy and poor physical growth due to nutritional deprivation may result) and, second, they must monitor the diet carefully for at least the first few years of life. Under these circumstances it would be difficult for parental anxieties not to be translated to the young child and subsequently manifested by increased emotionality.

Another question relates to the precursors of learning problems that may be observed with school-aged PKU children. Are these, in fact, related to emotionality found in infancy, that become attenuated or emphasized by the child's milieu? It would seem that promising areas of further research may center on determining parent response and perceptions to child characteristics, analyses of modes of parent-infant interaction, and searching for subtle indicators of cognitive problems in infancy.

Chromosome-Based Disorders

Incidence figures related to chromosomal abnormality are couched in "approximations"; however, chromosomal aberrations, even allowing for imprecision, are not rare. Between 3 and 6% of known conceptions show evidence of an embryo with abnormal chromosomes; of these 90% will be aborted subsequently (Ford, 1973; Jacobs, 1972). About half of chromosomally atypical abortuses have an additional autosome, while many of the remaining are sex-chromosome-related (Jacobs, 1972). Many chromosomal variants are so lethal they are rarely seen in surviving newborns; nonetheless, approximately 1% of live neonates show chromosomal aberration of one or another kind (Ford, 1973; McKusick, 1969). There are, however, some chromosomal errors that are not associated with obvious syndromes (DeMeyer, 1975).

It is hypothesized that one of the reasons chromosomal anomalies may lead to mental retardation is due to imbalance of genetic material created by either excessive or depleted amounts of chromosome (Ford, 1973; Hirshhorn, 1973). Clinical conditions associated with excess chromosomal material are commonly found in the trisomies. These are autosomal chromosomal aberrations where the individual has three chromosomes rather than two of a particular numerical pair; thus the individual has 47 chromosomes, rather than 46. Trisomy 21 (Down's syndrome), trisomy 13 (Patau's syndrome), and trisomy 18 (Edward's syndrome) are representative of this diagnostic condition. The most common of these is Down's syndrome; the others, fortunately rare, are associated with very severe malformations, severe intellectual deficit, and relatively early mortality.

The majority of trisomies seem to derive from imperfect meiosis. In this process of cell division there is duplication and then division of chromosomes. It is during meiosis that a chromosome may break off or an error can occur in division so that two chromosomes do not separate from each other. Hirschhorn (1973) estimates that imperfect meiosis may account for 70% of individuals affected by the three trisomies: 21, 13, and 18. Moreover, cells in meiosis seem to be particularly sensitive to viral influences, x-rays, and chemicals (Hirschhorn, 1973).

Other types of autosomal aberrations may occur due to structural changes in the chromosome, but the phenotypes from all these conditions are very similar. Therefore we will focus on one of the most common anomalies and the source of considerable investigation, using it as a prototype of prenatal influence of chromosomal origin.

Down's Syndrome

Down's syndrome occurs with a relative frequency of 1 in 500 to 700 cases (Hirshhorn, 1973; Thompson and Thompson, 1973); however, incidence increases dramatically with the age of the mother. Thus, the rate for a woman under 30 is 1 in 1500 and for a woman past 45 years, 1 in 65 (Smith and Wilson, 1973). It is thought that there are neither ethnic differences (Kashgarion and Rendtorff, 1969) nor sex differences in incidence (Thompson and Thompson, 1973).

Down's syndrome is associated with a group of chromosomal aberrations, the most common of which is trisomy 21. Other forms include translocation, in which a portion of chromosome 21 breaks off and becomes attached to another chromosome, and mosaicism, which involves one normal cell line and an abnormal cell line with an extra chromosome 21.

Among individuals with Down's syndrome there often is phenotypic similarity in physical characteristics and growth patterns due, in part, to timing of the stress, with the organism "insulted" or "impaired" soon after conception. It is, indeed, physical characteristics that often permit diagnosis in the neonatal period. Pre-term birth with concomitant reduction in birth weight are typical of Down's syndrome neonates, particularly males (Reisman, 1970). After birth the rate of growth continues to be slow, with shortness of stature common. Other atypical growth patterns as well as physical anomalies are frequently observed, including small nose, chin, and ears; poor development of teeth; and squint, nystagmus, and myopia. Musculoskeletal anomalies such as short and broad extremities, poor balance, nonelastic skin, and curvature of digits are also noted (Penrose and Smith, 1966). Hypotonicity, so characteristic of Down's syndrome, often leads to description of infants being quiet and contented. Serious and life-threatening characteristics of Down's syndrome infants and children involve cardiovascular defects and problems with respiration which, until recently, led to early and high mortality rates (Smith and Wilson, 1973).

Limitation in intellectual functioning is another characteristic of Down's syndrome; still, within this group, abilities vary: intelligence quotients may range from 20 to 70 (Smith and Wilson, 1973; Koch and de la Cruz, 1975), and occasionally, they may be in the 80s in cases of partial translocation (Rosecrans, 1971). In general, language and conceptualization skills required for abstraction are most impaired, while skills related to accomplishment of simple tasks, rote skills, and noncomplex language are less involved (Cornwell, 1974; Lenneberg et al., 1962).

For a long time it was assumed that a chromosomal condition such as Down's syndrome was relatively immutable to environmental influences. However, the seminal research of Stedman and Eichorn (1964) demonstrated the impact of supportive environments upon intellectual functioning. Later research corroborates these findings; infants reared in a supportive institutional setting given special intervention programs demonstrate gains in development (Bayley et al., 1971), and infants reared in homes tend to do better than those placed in routine foster placements (Carr, 1975). Recently, a number of programs have been initiated with Down's syndrome infants living at home, with the goal of reducing intellectual deficits even further (Bidder et al., 1975; Connolly and Russell, 1976; Hayden and Haring, 1976; Rynders and Horrobin, 1975). Since these programs are relatively new, it will be some time before their impact can be evaluated.

On face value it would seem that Down's syndrome, with its known associated degrees of intellectual impairment, should also be associated with relative continuity of developmental status from infancy to childhood. That is, correlation coefficients obtained from sensorimotor scores and intelligence test data should be moderately high. Actually this is only partially true. While overall prediction for Down's syndrome children does appear to be more successful than for other groups of atypical children (Share et al., 1964) or normal children (Bayley, 1949), it appears to be problematic before age 2 (Carr, 1975). In a recent study, Carr noted prediction to 48 months for infants less than 10 months of age was poor; while it was somewhat better for infants past 10 months of age, it was most accurate for children between 2 and 4 years of age.

In addition to the explanations usually advanced to explain low predictive ability from sensorimotor to childhood status (McCall et al., 1972), there is one that may be operating for Down's syndrome children: the level of developmental abilities found in early life, and that observed somewhat later. The young infant often shows a developmental quotient in the high 70s or 80s; he does not appear too dissimilar from the normal infant in terms of sensorimotor skills, albeit his rate of development is slower. In contrast, the level of abilities, and the type of skills that the Down's syndrome school-age child can perform, is markedly disparate from that of his age-mate normal peer; that is reflected by IQ differences, which may be 50 or more points. The group scores are higher in infancy and lower in childhood—which represents some diminution or decline in abilities. Thus prediction can be uncertain because the end-points of decline can vary.

The issue of developmental declines in Down's syndrome has provoked much discussion. These declines have been attributed to inability of Down's syndrome children to keep pace with rapid conceptual growth of middle childhood, to reflect poor environmental conditions, to be a manifestation of dissimilarity of skills measured during infancy and childhood, to indicate test artifact, and to signify biologically based deterioration. There is, as yet, no conclusive evidence supporting a single factor or a cluster of conditions. Although it was once thought that declines appeared as the child shifted from sensorimotor to language-based interactions, two recent studies show that declines begin to be observed in infancy.

For example, Carr (1975) followed the development of home-reared and foster-reared Down's syndrome infants from early infancy until 4 years of age. Carr's data showed a decline that was readily apparent at 10 months of age. Though the downward slope was steeper for foster-reared children than for home-reared, the general slope of mental development was similar for both groups. The mean developmental quotient of home-reared infants decreased approximately 30 points from 6 weeks of age to 10 months. For the group as a whole, declines also were noted in the 2nd year of life, but these were less than half that observed during the 1st year. Examination of varied skills subsumed in developmental and intelligence tests did not elicit any single item or cluster of items that contributed to overall decline. Carr could not state that general deterioration was a factor in decline, but suggested instead that full impairment became increasingly evident as the child was exposed to more sophisticated cognitive demands.

The issue of declines has been addressed in another recent study. Dicks-Mireaux (1972), pursuing a slightly different statistical course than Carr (1975), focused on trend analyses of scores. Using a sample of pure trisomies, a group of Down's syndrome infants were followed from approximately 10 weeks to 78 weeks of age. Their development was compared to that of normal infants tested cross-sectionally. Five age periods—16, 28, 40, 52, and 78 weeks—were chosen for test administration of Gesell schedules. Examination of developmental quotients showed each group exhibiting a downward trend in scores; among the normal group it was slight (though marked with some irregularity), but for the Down's syndrome sample there was less irregularity but a much steeper decline, reaching its maximum at 52 weeks of age.

In order to examine trends in the data, Dicks-Mireaux used covariance and regression equations of mental age over chronological age. Statistical support was found for a strong linear relationship for development of the normal group of infants, whereas a curvilinear relationship was observed for data derived from the Down's syndrome group.[2] Dicks-Mireaux reached three conclusions: Down's syndrome infants show a steady rate of development, it is slower than normal, and there is "progressive deterioration" in the rate of longitudinal development.

Both of these follow-up studies provide important information about the development of Down's syndrome infants. Although the underlying basis of developmental declines has yet to be explained, evidence clearly places their occurrence in the last part of the 1st year of life. Given that these data indicate a widening divergence of abilities during infancy, is it possible to find evidence of underlying mechanisms? Promising possibilities are reflected in data from two laboratories which show that Down's syndrome infants have difficulty processing information in the 1st year of life.

Seminal studies of aspects of visually mediated perception, attention, and memory in Down's syndrome infants have emanated from Fantz' laboratory at Case Western Reserve University (Miranda and Fantz, 1973; Miranda and Fantz, 1974; Fantz et al., 1975; Miranda, 1976). He and his associates, Fagan and Miranda, using paradigms of visual preferences and visual recognition memory demonstrated that Down's syndrome infants acquire, store, and retrieve certain kinds of information during the 1st year of life. Using cross-sectional and longitudinal home-reared samples, their data indicated that young

---

[2]We note, though, that our interpretation of the trends depicted graphically by Dicks-Mireaux indicate that the slope for the Down's syndrome infants starts to move away from a linear trend about 40 weeks of age, thus supporting Carr's findings of a somewhat earlier decline.

Down's syndrome infants showed preferences for patterns with elements, angles, and contours, demonstrated selective looking at novel versus familiar patterns, and showed decreases in fixation time over age. Many of these abilities were observed at ages comparable to those of normal infants. Nonetheless, the Case group infers that many early preference capabilities are relatively simple and undemanding, and can be explained on the basis of maturational and experiential factors which presumably are not severely constrained by chromosomal stress. Significantly greater group differences were obtained in the second part of the 1st year of life. Normal infants were capable of making differential responses to novel stimuli involving additional elements, shadings, or patterns, whereas the Down's syndrome infants encountered difficulties, and their performance frequently lagged 2 to 4 months behind the normal sample. In the recognition memory studies the Down's syndrome sample appeared to have the most problems with stimuli that had relatively complex elemental arrangements. Fantz and his associates interpret these findings as signifying cognitive limitations of Down's syndrome infants. Their interpretation seems justified, although more corroborating studies are required.

The work from Fantz' laboratory is important on two counts: first, because of the initial findings with Down's syndrome infants and, secondly, because of the conceptualization the researchers brought to the study of developmentally deviant infants. They explored the *range of capabilities* of this group by examining performance on information-processing tasks using multiple-stimulus conditions and by investigating abilities at several age periods. This systematic and cohesive approach allows initial interpretations to be made using a solid data base, and permits a refined definition of group similarities and group differences.

Another series of impressive studies also provide insights into the ways that Down's syndrome infants handle information. Sroufe and his associates (Cicchetti and Sroufe, 1976; Sroufe and Waters, 1976; Sroufe, 1977) have several thoughtful papers and studies on the relationship of affect and cognition in early life. Initially, Sroufe postulated that changes in affect would be tied to availability of cognitive schemas. With samples of normal infants, he found intrusive stimuli evoked a greater number of affective responses in the first few months of life, whereas subtle and cognitively based stimuli elicited more affective responses in the latter part of the 1st year. In describing factors evoking affective responses, he noted that infants progress from smiling and laughing to intrusive stimulation, then to stimulation mediated by active attention, somewhat later to smiling and laughing to stimulus content, and still later toward more active involvement in producing their own stimulus condition.

Although a cognitive-affective link was evident for normal infants, Cicchetti and Sroufe (1976) pursued a further test of this theory by examining the relationship in Down's syndrome infants. Using a longitudinal sample (followed from 4 through 18 months) of Down's syndrome infants, composed mainly of cytogenetically classified trisomies with a small number of mosaics and translocations, they observed that the appearance of affective expressions were delayed several months. However, the sequence found for normal infants was essentially replicated in the Down's syndrome sample. Nonetheless, at the end-point of the study, inspection of the data shows that the percentage of Down's syndrome infants responding to all affective stimuli was lower than that of the normal infants. We interpret this to indicate delay, and also a more limited range of behavior available for the Down's syndrome infants. Thus there is limitation in their overall informational repertoire.

Cicchetti and Sroufe noted differences between normal and Down's syndrome samples in affective expression. For example, with respect to the latter, smiling was a frequent affective response, whereas laughter was a rare occurrence, particularly for the more hypotonic infants. Stimuli that might elicit laughter in normal infants often evoked only a smile in Down's syndrome infants. Cicchetti and Sroufe hypothesized that the latter required a long time for processing information, and, thus, a build-up of tension required for strong affective responses did not occur.

As with normal infants, the authors also found clear positive relationships between signs of affective expression and cognitive development. Infants responding to more complex social and visual affective stimuli scored higher on the Bayley mental scale and the Uzgiris-Hunt series. Cichetti and Sroufe also examined the nature of individual differences in responsiveness. The most hypotonic infants were among the most retarded on all measures, whereas the least hypotonic, who were also the mosaics, were among the highest-performing infants.

Given a relationship between pleasurable affect and cognition, it should be possible to find a similar trend with affective signs indicating fear. In an investigation of "impending collision" in which shadow casters projected images that either seemed to approach the infant or move away from him, Cicchetti and Mans (1976) found that both Down's syndrome and normal infants responded at 4 months with blinks and at 8 and 12 months with emergence of protective arm movements and withdrawal. However, at 8 months, normal infants demonstrated fear, which increased appreciably at 12 months. In contrast, Down's syndrome infants rarely demonstrated fear; those who did were generally older. In this study as well, the authors looked for and found a relationship between affect and cognitive development: Down's syndrome children who evinced fear responses had higher developmental quotients.

The findings from Fantz' and Sroufe's laboratories, analyzed in conjunction with the research of Carr (1975) and Dicks-Mireaux (1972), are tantalizing. The former show that Down's Syndrome infants have difficulty handling some kinds of information during the 1st year of life; the latter show developmental quotients of Down's Syndrome and normals diverging by the last part of the 1st year. It is not unwarranted to conclude that difficulties with processing of incoming stimuli and recognition memory are, in part, mediating developmental declines. Moreover, it is reasonable to conclude that the scores diverge as sharply as they do because by the end of the 1st year of life normal infants show a surge in cognitive understanding (Kagan, 1972; Piaget, 1952, 1954), while Down's syndrome infants do not. The latter not only evidence delay, they probably "lose" increasing amounts of information. Early demonstrations of cognitive difficulties may, in fact, initiate a cumulative build-up of problems in information processing. Though more research is needed to support our assumptions, the studies emerging with Down's syndrome infants demonstrate promising approaches.

We conclude with two points: First, the findings being generated with Down's syndrome infants are exciting and intriguing, but whether they can be generalized to other groups of atypical infants remains to be determined. The developmental constraints imposed by a chromosomal condition may have some unique qualities, which differ from others that do not have chromosomal basis.

Second, we want to emphasize that research on Down's syndrome represents a special category. It is one of the few instances where outcome data and group-difference data can be linked by more than a slender thread. Perhaps this is due to the nature of the developmental impairment; nonetheless, the studies provide a welcome addition to the literature on developmental risk.

Congenital Malformations of the Central Nervous System

When an infant is born with any kind of anatomic abnormality, external or internal, he is considered to have a congenital malformation (Moore, 1973). Many malformations consist of variants of the musculoskeletal system—for example, club foot and cleft palate—are not life threatening, and often are amenable to surgical correction. There are, however, a group of congenital malformations related to the central nervous system (CNS) that either may be incompatible with life or result in severe physical and/or intellectual impairment. Among these is spina bifida, a term used to describe a number of conditions that have in common a lesion or separation of vertebrae elements (Brocklehurst, 1976). Serious spina bifida lesions include spina bifida aperta or cystica (exposure of neural tissue and open spinal canal), meningomyelocele (herniation of malformed spinal tissue and meninges), meningocele (herniation of meninges but not neural tissue), encephalocele (herniation of a portion of brain through a defect in the skull), and anencephaly (absence of most of the cortex). Spina bifida often may be accompanied by hydrocephalus, an abnormal accumulation of cerebro-spinal fluid. Among other malformations of the CNS are hydranencephaly (partial or complete absence of hemispheres) and holotelencephaly (absence of portion of brain and fusion of hemispheres). These conditions, as well as anencephaly, lead to death in a matter of days or weeks, whereas infants born with other forms of spina bifida may live for many years (Lemire et at., 1975). They may, however, show varying degrees of neurologic impairment, paralysis, sphincter-control impairment, and loss of sensation. Retardation is associated with cranial meningocele and encephalocele, whereas infants with other forms of spina bifida are considered to have potentially normal intelligence (Laurence and Weeks, 1971).

The incidence of CNS malformation varies; Laurence and Weeks (1971) estimate a spina bifida incidence of 1.5 per 1000 to 4.2 per 1000 depending on geographic locale; anencephaly may occur 1 per 1000 births, and encephalocele may be evident in 1 per 2000 births. These conditions, then, do not represent rare, isolated occurrences but instead point to a biologic hazard facing several thousand infants born each year.

Genetic and environmental factors have been implicated as causal agents in all forms of malformation. Anomalies noted with chromosomal conditions have been cited in a previous section; however, many similar anomalies can be observed without evidence of chromosome abnormality. Mutant genes, drugs, chemical agents, x-rays, and viruses are among other factors with a known association to malformation. Increasing prominence is being given to multifactorial causal agents—the interaction of genetic and environmental influences. Carter (1971, 1974), for example, suggests that malformations that show clear preponderance of sex and ethnic differences in incidence, which persist even after migration to other geographic locales, must have a strong genetic bias. Clearly, environmental factors can also be implicated, for some ethnic groups show higher incidence in one locale than in another. Moreover, social class, diet, and climatic conditions also have a documented association with incidence. Carter and others suggest that there may be a genetic "threshold" for certain biologic conditions, but this threshold level may be affected when genetic predisposition is combined or added to environmental factors.

Malformations of the CNS occur early in embryonic life. Given that the system sustains an insult so early when structures are in the process of formation, there is a commonly held expectation that development will be seriously compromised. We will examine this expectation in the following sections as we review available data on infants and children.

Development of Children with Spina Bifida Cystica

Of all the conditions focused upon in this chapter, the least amount of infancy data exists for the spina bifida group. Despite the scarcity of data, we shall discuss this group of children to point out both the complexity of problems subsumed under the term spina bifida as well as the heterogeneity of outcomes that may result from this condition.

Among the problems observed with spina bifida are trunk and lower-limb paralysis, upper-extremity incoordination, structural deformity, incontinence, emotional problems, social isolation, and intellectual impairment. Recurrent infections of one or another kind are relatively common. Much energy has been directed toward improving the quality of life for these children. Various types of surgery have been performed on lesions, and to reduce the effects of hydrocephalus when it accompanies spina bifida; several types of interventions have been used to improve bladder and bowel control. It is hardly surprising to find that research is often of a monitoring nature, focusing on outcome subsequent to interventions.

Developmental outcome of viable infants with spina bifida must be viewed in the context of changing medical attitudes and intervention practices. Prior to the early 20th century, active treatment of lesions was minimal; therefore, a very high mortality rate occurred not only due to spina bifida lesions but also to infections and complications of hydrocephalus (Laurence, 1964; Laurence, 1966). Interest in surgical repair of open lesions and remediation of advancing hydrocephalus developed later. However, use of newer techniques varied; in some medical facilities all infants were given surgical intervention in the neonatal period, while in others selection was based on a "waiting period" of a couple of months used in conjunction with medical screening. Thus infants who survived the first month or two were assessed for extensiveness of lesions and extent of hydrocephalus. If the prognosis seemed favorable, then surgery was indicated. Lastly, some facilities intervened selectively in the newborn period, using criteria based on the severity of the neonate's condition. The combination of paraplegia. hydrocephalus, spinal deformity, other congenital malformations, and poor neurological state were (and are) considered indicative of poor prognosis. A consideration of these factors in conjunction with ethical and social factors can lead to a decision to withhold interventions (Brocklehurst, 1976; Milhorat, 1972). Most untreated cases die very early in life.

Over the years, a sample of "untreated" surviving children have been followed by Laurence and his associates (Laurence, 1966; Laurence and Tew, 1967; Tew and Laurence, 1972). In general, those children who had meningoceles showed only a small number of mental or physical problems, whereas at least half of the children with encephaloceles and myeloceles have had severe physical impairments and retardation. That the two are not always associated is attested to by a male in the sample who has major physical disability along with an IQ of 144. Among educational problems noted with the children, who now are of school age, are difficulties with arithmetic, emotionality, poor motivation, and perseveration in language. In this sample, intellectual outcome for females is less favorable than for males, which may reflect fewer social and educational opportunities for them.

Although interventions have increased the number of surviving infants, there is no clear consensus that the incidence of severe mental and physical sequelae has been altered considerably. In some studies the percentage of children who show moderate to severe intellectual problems is as low as 20%, in others it is as high as 40%. Most sequelae are found with children with high lesions, or spina bifida combined with hydrocephalus, or those who experience infections—for example, meningitis (Brocklehurst, 1976; Diller et al., 1969; Hunt and Holmes, 1975; Liedhom et al., 1974; Lorber, 1971). However, as Lorber (1971) notes, discussions of outcome based on a single variable—for example, intelligence—does not always provide a sufficient picture of the child with spina bifida. Complicating factors can be numerous. In a large sample of surviving children with myelomeningocele, Lorber delineated 5 groups according to a combination of physical and intellectual characteristics. In his sample, he found 12% with severe physical handicap and profound mental retardation, 21% with severe physical handicap and moderate retardation, 49% with severe physical handicap and normal intelligence, 15% with moderate physical handicap and mild retardation or normal intelligence, and 3% with no impairment. Intelligence, the ability to cope, and family support are probably major factors in long-term outcome (Monsen, 1976).

No discussion of spina bifida could be complete without mention of the impact of spina bifida on the family of the child, as well as on the child himself. From the time of first diagnosis, with all of its attendant crises and stresses, there can follow a succession of illnesses and hospitalizations, and extended periods of time where parents must provide care for the child's routine daily living activities. In addition, specialized care is required for a child who is retarded. These stresses are superimposed on the minor and major crises associated with child-rearing in general (Drotar et al., 1975; Roskies, 1972). Yet, few conclusions can be reached from empirical data regarding the abilities of families to adapt to this difficult situation. On the one hand, there are reports of family breakdown, disharmony, and vulnerability to stress; on the other, there are reports that families find ways of coping, with rates of discord and divorce being not unlike those of other groups (Dorner, 1975; Freeston, 1971; Hunt, 1973; Kolin et al., 1971; Tew et al., 1974; Walker et al., 1971). Of interest, is the fact that the research has not addressed the issue of supportive versus nonsupportive caregiving relative to long-range consequences for the child with spina bifida. We presume this gap reflects the need to first address family problems, which are perceived to be overwhelming.

Turning now to infancy, it may be helpful to consider the nature of early life for infants with spina bifida. We do this to point out that the condition not only directly affects the integrity of the organism but has indirect effects as well. For example, the infant may experience considerable immobility directly due to the spinal lesion itself, or indirectly because of surgery and recurrent hospitalizations. In either case, the range of experiences for infants can be considerably less than that of physically normal children. Moreover, repeated hospitalizations force frequent separations from caregivers, and frequent illnesses, whether treated at home or in hospital, may lead to apathy and low levels of arousal. The infant's ability to attend to the environment and to explore it with whatever means he has available may be compromised for a long period of time. That spina bifida infants can be disadvantaged is undeniable; yet, despite this, a substantial number of them develop intellectual skills comparable to that of their normal peers—they adapt and cope. Again, we point to the lack of research exploring the why and how of adaptive mechanisms. In the absence of this type of data, we turn to followup studies.

In a recently reported study, Fishman and Palkes (1974) discussed the development of 31 children; 21 had myelomeningocele and hydrocephalus, 7 had hydrocephalus, and 3 had encephalocele with hydrocephalus. All the children with hydrocephalus received surgical intervention to relieve excess accumulation of cerebral spinal fluid. The children were followed from 6 months of age until they were 5 years old, using as age-appropriate, the Cattell, Vineland Social Maturity Scale, a language scale, and the Stanford Binet. Of the sample, 21 had sufficient test data for analysis. Three important findings emerged.

First, the percentage of severe intellectual impairment, though still too high, is less than one might expect from children with such serious involvements. (No data were given on physical handicaps). Examination of 18-month Cattell scores showed 3 children with scores equal to or below 65 (65, 46, 44), 6 with scores between 72 and 84, and 12 between 88 and 106 (overall $\overline{X}$ = 80.2). The authors did not present the means and ranges for developmental data obtained earlier. Nonetheless, they probably were not too dissimilar; the correlation coefficients for the 6-to-18-month Cattell relationship was 0.63, and for the 12-to-18-month Cattell it was 0.87.

Second, with the exception of the lowest-scoring infants, there are *variable,* and unexplained, patterns of change and stability in developmental scores. Infants with the lowest scores at 18 months remained at essentially the same level of impairment at 5 years of age; however, one child in the intermediate range showed a gain of 19 points, while the rest remained at about the same level of functioning. A somewhat different pattern emerged for those children who attained scores of 88 or above on the 18-month Cattell. Of this group, 6 children showed a mean increase in scores that averaged 28 points (range 9 to 39 points), one child's score decreased by 12 points, and the rest of the children stayed at approximately the same level. In the absence of explanations we can only surmise possible explanations for change, such as caregiving factors, the child's ability to seek new experiences, and discontinuities between infant capabilities and childhood language and conceptual skills. Also, it is important to note that motorically impaired "intelligent" infants are invariably underrated when tested with traditional sensorimotor examinations.

A third major finding from this study relates to prediction from infancy to childhood. The authors comment on the usefulness of psychometric testing in infancy as predictors of later achievement. However, their data show that prediction was *poor* between 6-month Cattell and 5-year Stanford Binet (0.26), moderate between 12 months and 5 years (0.51), and high only at 18 months and beyond (0.81). Thus, prediction is reasonably good only in *late* infancy. Moreover, some of the correlations might have been inflated by scores at the extreme low range, which is a point made previously by McCall et al. (1972). The *low* levels of prediction found for infants in this study are remarkably similar to data reported by Carr (1975) for Down's syndrome infants. We emphasize this low predictability because many have assumed that infancy-to-childhood prediction for "at-risk" groups is invariably high.

In summary, we mentioned the numerous problems faced by the child with spina bifida, described the variability of outcome that is found during infancy and childhood, and showed that prediction from early life to the pre-school period is low until the child is almost 2 years of age.

Although research has been directed toward exploring the impact of a spina bifida child on his family, there has been little research on the interactive aspects of caregiver and child relationships. We also know little of the means by which these infants and young children learn and cope; many important developmental issues remain to be explored.

Low Birth Weight

One of the most difficult problems in defining "risk" and discussing outcome relates to imprecise terminology. In no diagnostic entity is this confusion more apparent than in the group labeled "low birth weight." This term, characterizing infants weighing less than

2500 g, came into popular usage for two reasons: First, at one time there was a great deal of frustration encountered in accurate measurement of gestational age. Secondly, mortality and morbidity rates are highest for infants of the very lowest birth weights (Susser et al., 1972). Yet consider the infants who may be subsumed under the label "low birth weight": those who are born small due to congenital anomaly such as Down's syndrome, infants born early whose weight is appropriate for their gestational age, and those infants who are clearly underweight. Often, advantages gained by use of "low birth weight" to designate infants has been lost by admixture of very heterogeneous subgroups within study samples. Determining the actual significance of the findings for each subgroup is left to the diligent reader.

In the interests of clarification we have categorized "low birth weight" into two major diagnostic groupings: One consists of those infants who are born clearly below the expected weight for their gestational age. Within this group are two subsets: infants born at term (gestational age of 40 weeks) and those born pre-term (gestational age of 37 weeks or less). These infants are labeled "small for dates." Excluding children with congenital problems, many "small for dates" infants will have been subject to intrauterine growth retardation, meaning they were often inadequately nourished in utero. A second major classification consists of those infants born before their expected term date (37 weeks gestation or less), but whose weight is *appropriate* for their gestational age. Some may be quite immature, being born very early, while others are born several weeks later, but all have appropriate birth weight. These infants comprise a pre-term grouping. While we recognize that this subdivision may appear artificial at times, its advantages outweigh its limitations in the discussions of etiology, implications, and infant behavior.

Pre-Term Birth; Weight Appropriate for Gestational Age

The exact causes of pre-term birth are, in many cases, unclear, although numerous factors have been implicated. Included among them are maternal health and nutritional status prior to pregnancy; maternal age, height, and weight; weight gain; smoking; use of drugs during pregnancy; uterine problems; and lack of prenatal care (Bergner and Susser, 1970; Miller et al., 1976; Naylor and Myrianthopoulos, 1967). It is evident that many of these conditions can be linked, directly or indirectly, to adverse social and economic conditions; thus it is not surprising to find higher rates of pre-term birth among women who are disadvantaged.

For many years the prognosis for a substantial number of infants born pre-term has been pessimistic, for as many as 40% later showed intellectual and neurological sequelae (Drillien, 1975). With such grim statistics it was not surprising that developmental impairment was viewed as an inevitable result of prematurity. This was clearly not the case; pre-terms actually were, and are, a heterogeneous group. Some infants, though born several weeks early, are healthy and remain so; others seem stressed at birth, and experience additional stresses in the perinatal period; while still others are born so early that their systems are unable to cope with extrauterine life. The importance of recognizing within-group differences for developmental implications has been emphasized by Parmelee and Haber (1973). Infants who seemed vulnerable to later problems often were the most immature and the most physiologically distressed. It is also likely that contemporary perinatal care has had the greatest impact on infants with these kinds of problems.

For young pre-term infants, extraordinary advances in newborn intensive care have been coupled with marked improvements in provision of nutrient intake, improved body-temperature control, and better monitoring of problems that occur with rapid onset (Davies and Stewart, 1975; Drillien, 1975). Monitoring of many aspects of physiologic functioning, once considered exceptional, is now part of routine care; problems can be anticipated and, in many cases, prevented. Along with these therapeutic interventions have come dramatic changes in feeding practices. In today's intensive care nursery the pre-term is fed with a diet carefully tailored to his bodily needs, and he is kept sufficiently warm so that body heat is not lost. In contrast, Davies (1975) and Drillien (1975) note that during the 1940s and 1950s pre-terms were often relatively starved, being fed on very light, highly diluted formulas. In addition, they were probably cold-stressed by being cared for in low ambient temperatures. Therefore, whatever nutrients might have been available were probably diverted from growth to maintenance of body temperature. There are reasonable explanations for the practices of a generation ago. Adequate means of tube-feeding immature infants were not well developed. Using bottle feeding, pre-terms tended to aspirate liquids; then, developing pneumonia, they died soon after. However, light diets led to dehydration, markedly inadequate nutrient intake, and physiological distress, which contributed to high mortality and morbidity rates.

We want to emphasize that while changing patterns of care have led to a reduction in mortality and morbidity, the young and sick pre-term still constitute a vulnerable group of infants, as do infants born in areas where modern technology is a luxury rather than commonly available. Nonetheless, there are significant improvements. Mortality is being reduced even for the most immature and lightest-weight infants, those weighing under 1000 g (Hunt et al., 1974).

Our discussion of outcome thus far has been phrased in general terms. We turn now to specifics, and start by contrasting findings from earlier studies with more contemporary data. It is important to note, however, that the number of recent studies is relatively small. Therefore, some of the inferences we make may need to be modified as more data are collected.

The first contrast we make concerns rates of relative impairment. In the past, the rate of moderate to severe intellectual impairment and neurological sequelae ranged from 10 to 40%, and was highest for infants of the very lowest birth weights. In contemporary, industrialized nations the rate appears to be between 5 and 15%; the higher figure also represents children born with very lowest birthweights (Davies and Stewart, 1974; Drillien, 1975; Hagberg, 1975; Rawlings, et al, 1971; Stewart & Reynolds, 1974). We have computed the percentage of children scoring below 85 on developmental or intelligence test measures in two recent studies of children born less than 1500 g, who were appropriate weight for gestational age, and found 15% of the samples in this category (Drillien, 1972; Dweck et al., 1973).

Secondly, past research indicated that the presence of hazardous perinatal events was associated with developmental problems in the early years of life; however, analyses made when sample groups were older indicated that perinatal influences assumed considerably less importance while environmental factors assumed substantially more (Drage, et al., 1969; Drillien, 1964; Harper and Weiner, 1965; McDonald, 1964; Sameroff and Chandler, 1975; Wiener, et al., 1968). In general, these trends seem to be mirrored in recent research. Goldstein, et al. (1976), using regression analyses, found perinatal events associated with developmental outcome at 1 year of age. Of seven factors—obstetric history, delivery and related variables, complications, prematurity, maternal discomfort during pregnancy and/or delivery, socioeconomic status, and ethnicity—the largest contributors to 1-year *uncorrected* Cattell scores were prematurity, delivery and related variables, complications, and ethnicity. When Cattell scores were corrected for amount of pre-term birth, then the only independent contributor to developmental quotient was delivery and related variables. Leaving aside the merits of age-correction, which we strongly endorse, we note the powerful and consistent influence of perinatal factors irrespective of correction.

However, a longer time perspective shows a somewhat different picture. For this, we must turn to other data. In a follow-up analysis of pre-term children examined when they were between 4 and 12 years of age, Francis-Williams and Davies (1974) found no significant relationship between intelligence-test data and presence of neonatal stresses. However, when these authors divided their sample by social class groupings they found higher mean intelligence scores for the children in the higher social classes. Since the interrelationship of socioeconomic status and perinatal influences on outcome was not examined, these data can not be considered as a definitive replication of earlier findings. Nonetheless, the absence of perinatal influences on childhood outcome is undeniable.

A third point that emerged from past studies was that school and educational problems were relatively common, particularly among males. In a recent resume of several studies, Davies and Stewart (1975) found that while mean intelligence test scores of males in various samples were well within the normal range, they were consistently lower than those of females. Moreover, while both males and females showed evidence of school problems, the percentage of males with difficulties was generally greater than that of females. Learning difficulties, interactions with teachers, and language problems were among the areas causing concern.

To summarize, recent data show that the proportion of children who show serious sequelae as a function of pre-term birth is markedly reduced. Still apparent are less severe problems and school difficulties. That some of these may have basis in environmental factors, is in part, attested to by the relationship of outcome findings and social class status.

While outcome studies indicate continuing problem areas, we can clearly specify neither the causal mechanisms, the early precursors, nor the onset periods. We previously alluded to gaps in the literature on developmental risk; it is very apparent in analyses of development of pre-term children. On the one hand there is rich documentation of the abilities and problems of the school-aged child; on the other, there is an extraordinary body of information on the young pre-term, most particularly on the infant during the first days and weeks of life. In comparison there is relatively little on infants at other ages, and essentially nothing on the toddler and pre-schooler. In light of this it is hardly surprising that our attempts to link the occurrence of a risk event, infant development, and childhood ability often are unsuccessful (Parmelee and Haber, 1973; Sameroff and Chandler, 1975). An attempt to partially fill in the picture has been made in the Infant Studies Project. This study had as one of its major goals a more accurate assessment of infants at developmental risk, with pre-term infants being used as a prototypic group. We have used multiple parameters to define infant characteristics and family-social factors that may predict and explain development at age 2 years (Parmelee et al., 1976). Data analyses of predictive trends, using parameters in various combinations, are in preliminary stages, although some early and short-term predictive analyses using portions of the sample have been reported (Beckwith et al., 1976; Kopp and Parmelee, 1976; Littman and Parmelee, 1977; Parmelee, 1976). A more definitive and comprehensive monograph is in preparation.

Turning now to other sources of data on pre-term infants—that is, research on characteristics of very young pre-terms—it is apparent that two kinds of research goals have underlined many studies. The first has been to determine the nature of abilities of infants born before their expected dates of delivery. The second has been to make comparisons of groups of pre-term infants and full-term infants to determine similarities and differences in functioning. Embodied in both types of studies is the issue of the effect of pre-term birth—that is, extrauterine experience rather than intrauterine experience—on developmental abilities. Since pre-terms were known to have later intellectual problems, a common assumption was that a detrimental effect would be found early in life.

Much has been written about the early life of the pre-term infant. Some have postulated that the infant, born early and placed in an isolette or intensive care unit, not only is deprived of the opportunity to complete his fetal maturation in the protected environment of the womb, but is also denied experiences such as the warmth and gentle swaying of uterine life. Moreover, life in an isolette deprives the infant of human interactions and the opportunity to receive patterned and contingent stimuli. These conditions have been seen as partial contributors to later problems. In contrast, a few have suggested that early extrauterine life provides pre-term infants with additional experiences, particularly of a visual nature, and this condition could affect behavioral development in some way. A more recent concept is that discussions of "deprivation" or "additional" experiences have to be considered in the context of the infant's maturational level at any given point in time—that is, a maturational readiness concept. The construct implies that restrictions in experiences or, conversely, extra experiences, have far less impact on an immature organism than on one more developed. As will be evident from the ensuing discussion, there is, as yet, no definitive body of knowledge supporting one or another theories. There are, however, findings that offer hints.

Among the most interesting studies of pre-terms are those that relate to their visual functioning. Saint-Anne Dargassics (1966) observed that while pre-term infants prior to their term dates could be responsive to visual and auditory stimuli, they were not very "capable" organisms. Responses fluctuated and were poorly integrated, particularly in the earliest days of life. This is in contrast to full-terms, who are responsive and show organized patterns of behavior almost from birth. Determining just how capable the pre-term is relative to vision presents a challenge, for it is not unitl 36 weeks' gestational or conceptual age that clearly defined states of sleep and wakefulness are evident (Parmelee, 1974).[3] Nonetheless, Hack et al. (1977) evaluated the quality of attention in pre-term is relative to vision presents a challenge, for it is not until 36 weeks' gestational infants for several weeks, they found evidence of fixation for a few infants by 31 weeks, but not before. Whereas early fixation was characterized by dull staring and poor coordination of both eyes, attention observed at 35 to 36 weeks showed active scanning and alert expressions. Not only do these data confirm Saint-Anne Dargassies' statements, but they demonstrate that qualitative changes in attention coincide with better organization of sleep states.

Moreover, these patterns of organization are reflected in other sensory systems. Schulman (1968, 1969) reported heart rate responses to auditory stimuli shifted from acceleratory to deceleratory at 36 weeks' conceptional age in a low-risk sample. While these

---

[3]Considerable confusion still exists regarding terminology used to describe the age of pre-term infants. Gestational age covers the period from point of onset of mother's last menstrual period to the point of birth; thus an infant born after 30 weeks in utero has a gestational age of 30 weeks. Conceptional age refers to the total time period covered by both intrauterine and extrauterine life. An infant of 30 weeks' gestational age, who had 3 weeks of extrauterine life, would have a conceptional age of 33 weeks. "Expected date of delivery" is one of the terms used to denote the anticipated period of brith.

findings were not replicated by Berkson et al. (1974), it would be surprising if auditory responsiveness did not show some organizational change during this time. The tactual system, as measured by reflexive organization, also shows changes within this period. Rooting and sucking responses to stimuli are weak and show long latencies until infants reach a conceptional age, or are born at a gestational age, of 32 to 34 weeks (Amiel-Tison, 1968). Many other reflexes absent in the most immature pre-term infants begin to be predictably elicited between 32 and 36 weeks of age, irrespective of infant gestational age (see Robinson, 1966).

While these data suggest that a qualitative change in abilities probably occurs at about 36 weeks' conceptional age (which may indicate the infant becomes more receptive to selected experiences), the data do not provide us with information about the positive or negative effects of pre-term birth on general functioning. For this perspective we turn to studies of group differences. It is important to note that some of the studies included in this summary probably had samples comprised of normal infants as well as infants with CNS dysfunction. Thus, it may be difficult to sort out the effects of pre-term birth, in and of itself, and the effects of pre-term birth in conjunction with other stresses on the infant. In addition, some of the samples may have included a small group of infants whose birth weight was low for gestational age.

First, it will be instructive to ask if additional extrauterine experiences foster growth of abilities. For example, given that empirical data show that pre-term infants have the ability to be attentive at about 35 weeks' conceptional age, will visual abilities reflect the fact that they received visual "practice"? Clinical observations tend to be affirmative; both Gesell and Amatruda (1945) and Saint-Anne Dargassies (1966) suggested that pre-term infants observed at their expected date of delivery seemed more visually responsive than did full-terms infants. However, Gesell noted that this difference was short-lived, as in a matter of days or a few weeks there appeared to be no difference between the groups. A supporting, though slightly different, perspective is obtained from laboratory data. Kopp et al. (1975a) tested a pre-term sample at 40 weeks' conceptional age for length of first and total fixation to stimuli. They found the pre-term sample had lengthier first fixations for only the first trial of a three-trial series when the data were contrasted with those obtained with a previously tested full-term sample. Using the same paradigm in a replication study, Sigman et al. (1977) found pre-term infants tested at their term dates showed greater first-fixation time in the first trial and greater total fixation in the second trial of a three-trial series. Nonetheless, both studies show that pre-term infants can show greater length of fixation to stimuli, but the significant group differences are found only on some trials. The results are too evanescent to consider that additional extrauterine experiences made a profound impact on the development of pre-term infants, at least to their expected date of delivery. Why should this be so? The pre-term infants may have been too immature to benefit from added experiences. Parmelee and Sigman (1976) have argued that while pre-term infants may have the ability to fixate early in life, they may be unable to utilize the ability in an adequate fashion. This concept receives empirical support from the Hack et al. (1977) study previously discussed.

This finding does not preclude a possibility that extrauterine life has other effects. Indeed, it does seem to have differential impact on some developing systems, which is reflected in inconsistent response patterns. Pre-term infants tested at their term dates show instances of both mature and immature development when contrasted with full terms. This is apparent in arousal, sleep states, neuromuscular functioning, electroencephalographic patterns, visually evoked responses, and sound detection (Bench and Parker, 1971; Chappell et al., 1973; Dreyfus-Brisac, 1966, 1970; Engel, 1965; Howard et al., 1976; Michaelis et al., 1973; Parmelee et al., 1968; Saint-Anne Dargassies, 1966; Stern et al., 1969). Even the tactual system, a system ontogenetically "old" and functional early in fetal life, seems affected by pre-term birth. Rose et al. (1976) found significantly less responsiveness on the part of pre-term infants tested at their term dates on both heart rate measures and behavioral indices. The authors wondered if their results could partly be explained by pre-term infants' inability to maintain vigorous responses, or possibly by a higher threshold to tactual stimuli.

In summary, research on the very young pre-term shows that additional experiences do not seem to greatly enhance their early abilities. It is apparent, though, that extrauterine life, in the form of pre-term birth, does have some influence. Many studies show that the level of organization of behavior of pre-term infants is not identical to that of full-term infants. For the pre-term there is both immaturity and maturity evidenced in his development. We hasten to point out that this unevenness is characteristic of samples observed 10 or more years ago as well as more recently. What are the developmental implications of these findings? Can they be linked to later functioning? Are similar type signs observed in older infants?

On the basis of current data we can respond only to the last question. Examination of studies of older pre-terms lead to no definitive conclusions, but some studies show term and pre-term differences in functioning. But the number and type of differences are far fewer than those obtained in the newborn period. With reference to vision, studies of pattern vision have been made by Fantz and Fagan (1975), who examined the effects of variations in pattern size and number on visual attention with developmentally normal pre-term twins between 5 and 25 weeks of age. Analyses were directed toward exploring age-related attentional shifts, and examining whether postmenstrual or postnatal age best reflected visual abilities. In regard to the former, both pre-term and full-term infants showed size preferences decreasing with age, whereas number preferences increased. There were only a few group differences at some ages. Fantz et al. (1975) suggest this may indicate risk for impairment. This, however, remains only a supposition awaiting empirical validation.

In other analyses, Fantz and Fagan (1975) found postmenstrual age curves coincided well with curves for full-term data, suggesting that it is age from time of *expected birth,* rather than age from birth, that provides a more accurate assessment of pre-term capability.[4] Overall, the Fantz and Fagan data suggest neither acceleration nor retardation occurred as a function of pre-term birth.

Their findings are consistent with O'Connor's (1977) data. Using auditory stimuli and heart rate responses, she found no term and pre-term differences on either initial responses or habituation trials in 3- and 4-month-old infants. However, O'Connor's sample had considerable attrition due to crying and other reasons. The infants who were eliminated from the sample might have influenced the nature of the results.

In contrast to the Fantz and Fagan study, which found very few group differences across

[4]Corrections are made by two methods: In one system, age is calculated from time of *expected date of birth,* the term date, not from time of actual birth. For example, estimating an infant's birth to occur June 1, the actual birth occurs April 1; however, June 1 is the date used to calculate subsequent age. Alternatively, age correction can be made by calculating the entire number of weeks of extrauterine life (from the time of birth to the time of current measurement) then subtracting the number of weeks of pre-term birth. Thus an infant with a total amount of extrauterine life equal to 38 weeks, born 6 weeks early, is considered 32 weeks, or approximately 8 months, of age.

several age periods, Sigman and Parmelee (1974) reported a major group contrast in their study of 4-month-old pre-term (corrected-age) and full-term infants on visual preferences. Sample characteristics in relation to normality and deviance was undefined. The infants were measured on their responses to complex versus simple stimuli, and novel versus familiar stimuli were contrasted. No group differences were found with pattern complexity, whereas full-term infants showed significantly greater preference for novelty than did pre-term infants, implicating a memory process. Do pre-term infants have difficulty remembering stimuli? This is difficult to answer on the basis of a single study. Nonetheless, one explanatory factor is found in a later Sigman (1976) study in which 8-month-old (corrected-age) term and pre-term infants were contrasted by comparing their object preferences. The research paradigm utilized a familiarization procedure and subsequent paired comparisons of familiar objects with novel objects. Sigman observed that pre-term infants explored the familiar stimuli longer than did the full-term sample, but this was significant for only the first 2 of 10 trials. Separating the pre-term sample into *high-* and *low-*risk groups on the basis of performance on other measures, she found that high-risk infants explored novel objects significantly less than did low-risk infants—again, a finding that possibly implicates a memory process. Thus, these data attribute *some* term and pre-term differences to risk factors. Nonetheless, the magnitude of group differences is relatively small.

However, the fact that memory processes may be affected in high-risk pre-term infants is of interest, for memory also was found to be affected in Down's syndrome infants (Fantz et al., 1975). Too many procedural differences mark the two groups of studies; therefore, direct comparisons cannot be made. Nonetheless, a question that needs to be addressed at some time is whether there are similarities or differences in the nature of impairment for different diagnostic groups of high-risk infants.

Are risk factors the only contributors to differences in abilities found between full-term and pre-term infants? Apparently not, but whether differences are found depends, in part, on the samples selected, on the task that is given, and the techniques used to measure performance. Thus, when using a developmentally normal pre-term sample and a relatively gross measure of abilities, no differences were found between pre-term and full-term groups (Kopp et al., 1975). The infants were tested at 9 months (corrected age) on a sensorimotor series designed to examine the level of development of object permanence and awareness of means-ends relationships. When the sensorimotor measure was given to a sample of pre-term infants that included developmentally deviant infants, then group differences were apparent (Kopp, 1976a).

In contrast to the sensorimotor data, Kopp (1976b) found subtle differences were evident between developmentally normal pre-term and full-term infants when micro-analyses were made of spontaneous object interactions of 8-month-olds (corrected age). While no significant differences were found in type or frequencies of behavior, group differences were apparent in the length of time that one or another behavior was utilized. For example, pre-term infants, both male and female, spent significantly more time just holding objects and looking at them than did the full-term infants. It appeared that the full-terms were more actively engaged in direct object interactions than were the pre-terms. Moreover, full-terms, in a behavior characteristic of 8-month-olds, took the objects to their mouths to explore. While the pre-term infants also did this, they did so for a significantly shorter period. The pre-term males showed the least amount of this type of investigation. Do these differential patterns of object interaction have any meaning? It is difficult to say, as this study was made of infants at only one age period. Yet, preliminary analyses suggest some predictive utility when this measure was used as an assessment tool (Parmelee, 1977), but more definitive analyses are needed to elucidate underlying mechanisms.

Given this checkered pattern of results, what firm conclusions can be reached? We know that pre-term infants demonstrate considerable behavioral similarity to full-term infants, and this is observed across several age periods during the 1st year of life. On the other hand, group differences are found, although the proportion found in the newborn period appears greater than at later ages. Moreover, some differences were inconsistent and too dependent on task and sample characteristics for us to conclude that they had developmental significance. The differences might have been isolated phenomena totally unrelated to later developmental problems. Yet, the data are not easily dismissed, and nagging questions remain. Do high-risk pre-term infants have difficulty with recognition memory? Do low-risk pre-term infants have subtle interactional patterns that differ from those of full terms? If so, might these have any developmental significance?

It is apparent that far more research is necessary on pre-term samples. We suggest that future studies include precise definition of sample characteristics as well as measurement of responses at multiple age periods. Additionally, it seems warranted to suggest that some emphasis be placed on studies of information processing and patterns of exploration.

Intrauterine Growth Retardation: Pre-term or Full-Term Birth

In this section our focus will be on infants whose birth weights are not only low but they are low relative to gestational age; these infants may be born full-term or pre-term. Until relatively recently, there was a tendency to group all low-birth-weight infants together; it is now realized that a differential diagnosis has important implications for perinatal medical care and, possibly, for long-term outcome.

In 1961, Warkany et al. (1961) introduced the term "intrauterine growth retardation" to describe infants who are small for their period of gestation. These infants, often called "small-for-dates" or "small-for-gestational-age," are, among themselves, a varied grouping. Some may be small due to inadequate nutrition during prenatal life, others are undersized due to genetic or chromosomal anomalies, and a few are small for unexplained reasons. Infants in this latter group may not show any signs of pathology. In the ensuing analysis of intrauterine growth retardation we shall exclude, as much as possible, discussion of infants who show signs of intrauterine growth retardation due to genetic and chromosomal problems, since these conditions often impose an additional set of developmental constraints.

It is now possible to identify small-for-dates infants using fairly reliable criteria. Among them are birth weights 2 S.D. below the mean for a given gestational age (Ounsted and Ounsted, 1973), below the 3rd percentile (Ounsted and Ounsted, 1973), below the 10th percentile (Lubchenco, 1970; Lubchenco et al., 1967), or an infant with a low ponderal index (Miller and Hassanein, 1971). The ponderal index along with other clinical signs are sometimes useful in determining if growth was retarded throughout intrauterine life or if it occurred in the last weeks of the fetal period.

Although etiologic factors underlying fetal growth retardation vary considerably, the actual mechanisms that are involved relate to impairment of fetal oxygen and nutrient transport, and/or exchange of metabolic waste products (Vorherr, 1975). What influences these mechanisms? Implicated are maternal conditions such as cyanotic heart disease, toxemia, renal disease, smoking, use of drugs, viral infections (DeMyer, 1975; Gruenwald, 1975; Ounsted and Ounsted, 1973; Vorherr, 1975). Others involve physical or structural features of the uterus that restrict transport functions; still others are due to placental conditions relating to size, structural features, cysts, infections, edema, or thrombosis. Abnormal placental attachments also may lead to poor fetal nourishment. While these conditions can lead to major reduction in fetal size, there are other maternal factors that, to a lesser extent, affect fetal development. These include maternal ethnicity, size, general health, nutrition, weight gain during pregnancy, geographic locale of residence, and social class (Ounsted and Ounsted, 1973). Some of these influences are nonpathological in nature; nonetheless, it is highly probable that many maternal factors are so complexly interrelated such that an unfortunate combination of them could lead to fetal deprivation. While we have listed numerous factors related to the maternal system, it should be remembered that direct fetal-related conditions can affect nutrient transport; these can include fetal abnormalities, multiple fetuses, fetal infections, and so forth (Gruenwald, 1975; Ounsted and Ounsted, 1973).

With all of the influences listed above it is evident that the placenta itself is just one, albeit an important one, of many causes of intrauterine growth retardation. While many would readily implicate placental malfunction to causes of fetal growth retardation, Ounsted and Ounsted (1973) and Lind (1976) note that the placenta is an extremely complicated organ; because of this its direct relationship to malnutrition in utero is not always clear. What is clear, though, is that placentae age. Thus, when a fetus *moves beyond* its term date, the placenta becomes less able to provide nutrients. At one time it was thought that post-term birth—previously labeled postmaturity, dysmaturity, "placental dysfunction syndrome" (Clifford, 1954)—was the major cause of intrauterine growth retardation. It is now felt that post-term birth contributes only a small portion of growth-retarded fetuses.

By whatever means the fetus becomes malnurished in utero, delivery into extrauterine life can mean potential biological hazards. Where wastage is extreme, such that blood supply is presumed to be very inadequate, there may be signs of anoxia; asphyxia, infections, hypoglycemia, high bilirubin levels, and pulmonary hemorrhage are among other frequent complications. The ability of the infant to survive and recover from one or more of these serious events becomes an important concern.

Even without these complicating factors, questions relative to outcome have been raised. It has been presumed that malnourishment in utero must have an impact on the developing brain. However, postmortum studies made by Gruenwald (1963) suggest that brain size is less affected by intrauterine growth retardation than are organs such as lungs and liver. It is possible, however, that more subtle indices of brain insult may be found. This line of reasoning has been taken by Dobbing (1970, 1974), 1976), who has inferred that two important periods of cell growth occur for humans, one at about 15 to 20 weeks' gestational age, the other starting about 25 weeks' gestational age and continuing until 18 months' postnatal life. Malnutrition in utero could have some impact on cell growth during these periods, although Dobbing notes, as have others, that much brain development occurs in extrauterine life. Dobbing (1974) recently suggested that minor variations in cell numbers may not be critical for higher mental functioning, but rather dendritic branching and synaptic connections may play important roles. The effects of malnutrition in utero upon these neural mechanisms remain to be determined.

Turning now to follow-up studies of infants born during the mid-1960s and later, there is no unequivocal pattern of results suggesting that infants of low birth weight due to intrauterine growth retardation are considerably more disadvantaged for long-term intellectual outcome than infants of low birth weight due solely to prematurity.[5] At present, however, real differences may be masked by too few studies and inadequate delineation of small-for-dates subgroups within samples. Some striking group differences in ability were reported in earlier studies, but some of these may be attributed to inclusion of infants with known genetic and chromosomal anomalies in sample groups (Drillien, 1970). There are, however, some expected group differences among children who experienced intrauterine growth retardation and those born healthy, full size, and full term.

Findings relative to infants born *at term* who were classified as small-for-dates indicate children at follow-up are functioning with abilities in the average range—that is, with developmental or intelligence quotients in the 90s and 100s (Babson and Kangas, 1969; Fitzhardinge and Steven, 1972b; Parmelee and Schulte, 1970; Rubin et al., 1973). Nonetheless, these means may be up to 10 points lower than those of comparison full-term samples. Fortunately, only a few children are severely retarded. Yet for children who are now school-aged, there are many who evidence educational and behavioral problems. Often, more males than females experience these difficulties. In most, but not all studies, intellectual outcomes are related to socioeconomic conditions: children who had higher scores came from more supportive environments. This finding is so well documented that it does not require additional amplification.

In a comprehensive study, Fitzhardinge and Steven (1972a, 1972b) found a pattern of results not unlike those reported for low-birth-weight pre-term infants. Ninety-six children with severe intrauterine growth retardation, selected on clearly defined criteria, were followed for 5 years. The children were from lower-, middle-, and upper-class families, although a slightly higher proportion came from the lower class than from the other two social classes. Intelligence quotients of the males averaged 95, and for the females, 101; however, the mean scores of the males averaged 11 points less than those of a small comparison group of siblings, whereas no differences were found between females and their siblings. Severe neurological defects were uncommon. Moreover, there was *no* relationship between degree of intrauterine retardation and intellectual and neurological functioning. On the other hand, difficulties were noted for the school-aged subsample, with educational problems observed for 50% of the males and 36% of the females. Minor electroencephalographic abnormalities were found in a larger percentage of children than is usually anticipated. The authors wondered if the combined school and EEG findings reflected maturational problems or mild brain damage. Using samples, less precisely defined than in this study, Rubin et al. (1973) reported data on a full-term low-birth-

[5]Subsequent to writing this chapter, a study was reported on outcome comparisons made at 5 and 7 years of age, of children who had been born small-for-dates or pre-term (Neligan et al., 1976). The children, born in Newcastle during 1960–1962, were given an intensive series of evaluations. Other information pertaining to background, health histories, and birth factors was available from a variety of records and interviews. The entire Newcastle sample had been used to select (1) a small-for-dates group using criteria of birth weight below the 10th percentile and gestational age greater than 255 days (36 weeks), and (2) a short-gestation group using criteria of gestation less than 255 days and weight between the 10th and 90th percentiles. Of the total number of children who met these criteria, approximately 40% were available for follow-up. Briefly, the findings showed (1) the mean intelligence test scores of both groups were well within the normal range (excluding scores of 4 children with severe impairments), (2) both groups demonstrated poorer performance on most measures than a comparison group, (3) on most individual test measures there were *no significant differences between scores of the small-for-dates and short-gestation children,* (4) when the scores for each test were dichotomized and added together, then significant group differences were found which favored the short-gestation children, and (5) outcome was related to a complex combination of environmental, clinical, and biologic factors.

weight group; their data also show adequate intellectual performance but marked evidence of school problems.

What inferences can be made about the development of pre-term small-for-dates infants? It has been suggested that because they experience intrauterine growth retardation *and* immaturity their outcome might be poorer than that of other pre-term, or full-term growth-retarded infants. Since data are not plentiful it is difficult to respond definitively; however, a recent prospective study of London-born *pre-term* appropriate-for-dates and small-for-dates infants points to some group differences (Francis-Williams and Davies, 1974). Thirty-three children, classified in the newborn period as small-for-dates on clearly based criteria, had at follow-up a mean intelligence test score of 92 (tl55–125); in contrast, 72 children classified as having birth weights appropriate for gestational age, had at follow-up a mean intelligence score of 99 (55–>125). However, confounding factors were embedded in these scores. For example, less than 10% of the low-weight group were from the highest social classes whereas almost a third of the appropriate-weight group were. Furthermore, included in the small-for-dates sample were children of questionable genetic conditions; three of these children were among the lowest scoring in the small-for-dates group. Acknowledging these factors, it can be inferred that small-for-dates children were doing relatively well. Still, within the entire sample there was a comparatively high rate of educational problems, including a high percentage of reading problems, immaturity of Bender items, and performance IQ significantly below verbal IQ. These findings resulted from total group analyses, so it is not possible to determine the contribution made only by the small-for-dates children. Yet again, though the findings are generally positive, there is evidence of learning problems.

Turning now to the data base on small-for-dates infants we find it is extremely limited. Most studies have been made in the neonatal period; the findings show an interesting pattern. Among the neonatal characteristics that differentiate the small-for-dates full-term infant from that of his full-size contemporary are reflexive behaviors and general responsiveness (see review by Caesar and Akiyama, 1970). In one study, for example, Michaelis et al. (1970) found differences in standing and stepping responses, the Moro and asymmetric Tonic Neck Reflexes between small-for-dates and full-size full-term infants. Moreover, small-for-dates had poor head control and extraneous arm movements. Recently, Als et al. (1976) extended these findings with a similar groups of infants. Their sample, chosen on the basis of ponderal index scores, was examined with the Brazelton scales.

Their data provide a useful clinical picture of undersized infants. They found, as have others, that organization of arousal and physiologic measures were similar for small as well as full-sized infants. However, the small infants were markedly different with respect to motor and interactive behaviors. Poor tone, low activity levels, poor hand-to-mouth coordination, poor responsiveness, unfocused and unmodulated interactions, "gives the appearance of being stressed when handled" are some of the terms used by Als et al. to describe their subjects. The authors suggested the uneven quality of these behaviors might impede parent-infant interactions.

Interestingly, when the authors evaluated the infants toward the end of the 1st year of life they found them to be developing normally. However they were described by their parents as being active, intense, and unpredictable. These descriptions could be an example of "self-fulfilling prophecy" (Rosenthal and Jacobson, 1968)—parents expect their infants to be different because of neonatal qualities; therefore, they interact with them differently, and, in turn, the infants are different or are perceived to be different. That these interactive patterns could continue into childhood is possible. Small-for-dates infants often remain small and grow into children who have smaller stature, lower weight, and smaller head circumferences than children who were appropriate-for-dates (Babson, 1970; Bjerre, 1975; Davies and Davis, 1970; Fitzhardinge and Steven, 1972). In a classic study, Jones and Bayley (1950) showed that delayed maturity and small size in school-aged males evoked differential reactions from parents, peers, and teachers. Thus child size can not be ignored as a variable possibly influencing outcome.

In summary, it is clear that the infant born with intrauterine growth retardation may have severe medical problems in the neonatal period. Reflexive and behavioral differences may occur in early life, possibly leading to disrupted patterns of parent-infant interaction. The overall outcome for intellectual functioning is relatively positive, even for pre-terms who were small-for-dates. Yet, inevitable questions arise. Would the intelligence of this group of children have been higher if they had not been malnourished in utero? What is the cause of the behavioral and school problems shown by so many children? Studies of small-for-dates during infancy could elucidate some of these questions. For example, serial measurements of attention, memory, discrimination, auditory and visual, might pinpoint problem areas and validate or refute indications of brain insult. Moreover, studies of interactional patterns might focus on family and child characteristics and behaviors that could lead to maladaptive interactions.

Summary of Low Birth Weight

In discussing low-birth-weight infants we stressed the need to differentiate pre-terms, whose weight was appropriate for gestational age, from pre-term or full-term infants, who were markedly underweight for their gestational age. Infant and outcome data focused on these two major groupings.

Outcome data on recently born pre-terms show reductions in mortality and morbidity. However, the lowest-birth-weight infants are still doing less well than those of higher birth weight; social class continues to play an important role; educational problems are prevalent. The findings regarding small-for-dates samples are similar. Most children show levels of intelligence within the normal range, but educational difficulties are apparent.

With reference to infancy data, pre-term infants, examined at their expected term date, show many similarities to full-terms. They demonstrate little evidence of acceleration in development as a consequence of extrauterine experiences. In subtle ways, they do show unevenness or immaturity of developing systems when they are compared with full-terms. This pattern is also evident with older pre-term infants.

Discussion of infants suffering intrauterine growth retardation in infancy focused on outcome findings and neonatal data. Since this group was differentiated only relatively recently, there are very few studies.

In general, the small-for dates infant shows a general level of maturity that matches that of this age-mate. There is evidence of some behavioral and neurological disorganization, which may have implications for caregiver-infant interaction patterns.

SYNTHESIS, PERSPECTIVES, STRATEGIES

A substantial amount of literature has been mentioned in this chapter; using this as only one source of reference, it is apparent that for the last few years we have been grappling with the meaning and implications of prenatal and perinatal stress. The fact that we review research and search for unifying concepts suggests we have come to appreciate that hazards and stresses that once appeared specific, definitive, and direct in their influence on development, are not—their effects are complex and abstruse. Encompassed within any diagnostic category is a myriad of individual differences, many times equal in diversity to the range of variation observed in nonstressed infants and children. Use of a diagnostic label or the term "developmental risk" often is misleading, for it glosses over diversity. It is evident that although our understanding has increased—and here we reiterate the point made in an earlier section of this chapter—we do not have a conceptual model of risk that defines precisely the meaning of pre- and perinatal stress for individuals within groups as well as for groups. There is, instead, some research that permits broad generalizations.

With reference to outcome and follow-up data, the following summary points can be made:

1. A range of outcomes results as a consequence of adverse prenatal and perinatal conditions; those events linked to early prenatal life have more serious effects for a greater number of individuals than those that occur in later prenatal or perinatal life.

2. Heterogeneity of outcome is common, and was observed in all conditions that were discussed in this chapter; the specific reasons for individual variation frequently were unexplored or unexplained.

3. Supportive rearing conditions are associated with higher intellectual scores among children with Down's syndrome, pre-term birth, and intrauterine growth retardation.

4. Infant developmental status, particularly in the 1st year of life, did not show high levels of prediction to early childhood intellectual status.

5. Severe physical impairment, as found in spina bifida, was not always associated with intellectual impairment.

Turning now to the other group of studies examined in this chapter, we explored infant data, which most often involved studies of group differences. We can summarize the findings as follows:

1. Groups of infants classified by diagnosis often showed some behavioral differences when contrasted with infants not exposed to prenatal and perinatal stress. Most often the findings of group differences were "explained" on the basis of category membership—for example, Down's syndrome or pre-term birth.

2. Individual differences were found but it was the rare study where a researcher made an attempt to explore their underlying mechanisms.

3. There was evidence of uneven development for groups of pre-term and small-for-dates infants.

4. Pre-term and small-for-dates infants may show some differences in patterns of object interaction and interpersonal interactions.

5. Early information processing may be impaired in infants with Down's syndrome and, in some instances, with some infants of pre-term birth.

Despite an increasingly voluminous literature, we could not find a single group of behaviors or class of functioning that has been systematically explored across several age periods for any prenatal or perinatal diagnosis. There are, indeed, a number of excellent studies, but they are fragmented and isolated. While there is a substantial and impressive body of knowledge on neonates, the findings have not been linked empirically to later abilities or limitations. We are forced to conclude that as valuable as this research has been, it too has limitations if we try to use the findings to ascertain the implications of risk status. Why do we find ourselves with so much data and so little power and specificity?

While numerous factors may account for this state of affairs, there are two that merit emphasis. First, there has been heavy reliance on describing behaviors, on cataloging one or another type of behavior. Far less effort has been expended on trying to measure the processes or mechanisms underlying competence or impairment. A catalog indicates current status, but it has limited usefulness when we try to use it to link performance to future abilities. Second, much of the research has been atheoretical. It has not been tied to a developmental theory or developmental principles—by this we mean research formally guided by a *specific* developmental theory. Not only does this lead to unsystematic research efforts but equally important, there may be no sound developmental context in which behaviors under study can be embedded. Thus, findings often end up as isolated bits of information, which only sometimes can be tied to a developmental pattern or sequence.

In thinking about the literature on developmental risk, and indeed of atypical infants in general, it seems that the trends reflected within it, in part, mirror the patterns of research that have characterized the study of normal infants. Our first studies of normal infants tended to be descriptive and atheoretical in basis, notwithstanding the influence of Gesell, Watson, and Freud on some aspects of investigation. Generally, early studies involved cataloging behaviors at specified ages, defining sequences of change, and measuring continuities or discontinuities in development. This period of accumulation of normative and descriptive data was of undeniable importance. Then there was a change in focus.

In the last 20 years, research on normal infants has been characterized by increased use of developmental theories or developmental principles as guides to formulate research questions. Moreover, there has been a shift from descriptions of infant behavior for catalogs, to descriptions that can be used to infer psychological and social processes. There has been an enormous expenditure of energy directed toward trying to understand the *meaning* of infant responses. Much of this is represented by research endeavors reported in this volume, as well as in earlier articles (see Appleton et al., 1975; Kessen et al., 1970). Perception, problem-solving, contingent learning, recognition memory, object permanence, intentionality, vocalization, and socialization, to name just a few, have been investigated. Methodologies have varied considerably, from descriptions of motor acts to measurement of visual and auditory preferences, heart rate, sucking, inhibition of activity, and so forth.

Along with these research trends came research directed at exploring the constituents of the environment that interacted with infant characteristics to promote or facilitate development. Global variables such as social class were used less frequently as investigators focused on dimensions of home qualities, patterns of interaction, forms of communication, and other variables of interest (Beckwith, 1971; Clarke-Stewart, 1973; Lewis and Rosenblum, 1974; White and Watts, 1973; Yarrow et al., 1975).

While important gaps in our knowledge still exist, there is a substantial amount of information on the perceptual-cognitive-affective-social capabilities of infants, and the mechanisms that contribute to them. And, much of our current research on normal infants reflects a blending of earlier and more recent research trends.

In research on infants at risk, however, with few exceptions we are still in the first stage, the descriptive period—the use of theory is minimal and the search for underlying mechanisms is almost nonexistent. Why are we so late in making the transitions? Perhaps, it is because research on developmental risk "had" to go through a descriptive period, and in due time other trends will become more common. But, perhaps it is that we find it difficult to view early stress as being anything but immutable—therefore, processes and theoretical principles are considered irrelevant. Sameroff and Chandler (1975) have thoroughly addressed this bias, and have shown the pitfalls contained within such an outlook. Surely, there is an imperative need to redirect research on developmental risk. In the next section, we consider possible avenues of focus.

Expanding our Focus of Study

In an earlier section we indicated that our present conceptual perspectives of developmental risk are inadequate. We cannot, with these perspectives, answer significant questions raised in that section. We require additional approaches and other comprehensive studies of infants.

Currently, fundamental gaps exist in our knowledge. We are essentially ignorant of an "at-risk" infant's ability to handle information, and we have been inattentive to the *resources* infants mobilize to meet changing situations and tasks. If we can explore these two aspects of behavior, we will move closer to having a well-rounded picture of the infant and, in time, to developing an improved model at risk. Indeed, these two topics, if investigated in sufficient depth, hold promise of "answering" the developmental questions raised earlier. In the balance of this section, we indicate topics for investigation in information processing, and give suggestions for utilizing the concept of *resources*.

It is patently clear that information processing is complex and subsumes multiple domains. Nonetheless, during infancy some abilities can be specified that develop early in life and those that occur later. In the young infant, information processing encompassses ability to focus on stimuli, to control attention, and to store, retrieve, and exchange simple kinds of knowledge. With older infants, it also includes ability to interpret events and signals, to classify, to learn means-ends relationships, and to evolve strategies. Every one of these areas is of sufficient importance to have warranted investigation with normal infants; inevitably, though, some topics have been explored more than others. Yet the only studies of information processing thus far undertaken with groups of risk infants have been made by Fantz and his associates, Sroufe and his associates, and in our own laboratories. While granting the importance of this data base, we also emphasize the limited number of risk groups that have been sampled and the narrow repertoire that so far has been studied. Surely, the point we make is obvious. In the normal infant we study information processing, for it speaks to the mechanisms underlying cognitive growth. Are we not interested in the same topics for "at-risk" samples?

What kind of a data base on information processing are we seeking? On the one hand, we need research that addresses itself to overall group differences and attempts to answer the following: What developmental risk conditions are associated with limitations in forms of information processing? Which areas seem most vulnerable? Is vulnerability more apparent with complex skills associated with older age periods of infancy than with abilities found at younger ages? What is the interaction of risk condition and environmental influence on basic information-processing abilities and those associated with more complex functioning? In addition to the above, we can analyze an individual infant's information-processing ability, independent of diagnostic group. Asking how an "at-risk'' infant's performance compares with that of normal infants will help explain ongoing infant competence or deviance. Lastly, we need to explore possible ramifications of disparities that may be observed between an infant's measured ability to handle information and a discrepant developmental test score.

Turning now to the concept of *resources,* we note that it too is complex and embodies multiple domains, the measurement of which is difficult. Prior to discussing potential uses of the concept, it will be helpful to define the term. On the one hand, *resources* embodies the *range and diversity* of behavior; on the other, it refers to *organization and adaptability* of behavior. An increase in *range* of behavior—sometimes defined by refinement, hierarchization, or differentiation—is one of the most fundamental and pervasive characteristics of ongoing development in the first 2 years of life (Bruner, 1970, 1974; Flavell, 1972; Gesell and Amatruda, 1945; Gibson, 1969; Kagan, 1972; Kuo, 1967; Lewin, 1935; Piaget, 1952, 1954, 1971; Werner, 1948). While we are cognizant of this and frequently measure across-age *increases* in *range* of behavior, we have only minimally explored the significance of a *narrow or broad range* of behavior at any given level of infancy.

Reference to *diversity and range* of infant behavior is not an original idea. It is implicit in Piaget's (1952, 1954) writings on early development with his focus on the role of experiences in the development of multiple schemes. Moreover, Corman and Escalona (1969) describe something akin to it in their speculations about behaviors available to infants reared in supportive versus depriving situations. Their supposition was that a greater number of behaviors would be available to infants in the former condition than in the latter. Empirical support was found by Collard (1971), who observed fewer exploratory schemas demonstrated by institution-reared infants contrasted to home-reared samples.

We suggest that we utilize the construct of *resources* as an additional measurement of infants presumed to be at developmental risk. Utilizing the construct, our focus could be on the richness and diversity of infant behavior, and not necessarily on the age of attainment of a certain level of development. An example may be helpful. Consider, for instance, three infants: Infant *A,* presumed to be normal, at 14 months chronological age attains a level of cognitive skills equivalent to 14 months. Observations made in specified settings indicates that infant *A* demonstrates a wide *range* of cognitive behaviors—for example, utilizes *x* number of means-ends relationships in play, and employs *y* number of strategies in early problem-solving. Infant *B,* presumed to be at developmental risk because of extremely low birth weight due to intrauterine growth retardation, at chronological age 16 months attains a level of 14th -month cognitive skill. However, when observed in play and problem-solving situations, the *range* of behavior of infant *B* is found to be equivalent to that of infant *A,* irrespective of the fact that it took a longer period of time for the child to reach the same cognitive level. Finally, there is infant *C,* also at developmental risk because of low birth weight due to intrauterine growth retardation, who attains a 14th-month cognitive level at 15 months chronological age. However, observations show the *range* of behavior demonstrated for play is $x-1$, and for problem solving is $y-1$.

How can these observations be utilized? We can explore the implications of *range* of behavior for the next step in development, postulating that the infant with a broader *range* will show somewhat more potential. Moreover, within our risk samples, we can examine the effects of varied caregiving situations on expansion and constriction of *range*. Can, for example, the limited repertoire of infant *C* be attributed to environmental factors? Finally, we can ask whether a restricted *range* in one behavioral domain invariably is associated with restriction in another. Again, on the basis of developmental theory we would expect some independence (Werner, 1948); however, we might explore which restriction has greater implications for development.

It seems to us that a definition of infant resources has the potential of providing a rich description of capability, which can be used in multiple ways to explore the effect of risk conditions. A specific research example is provided in the previously cited study of Cicchetti and Sroufe (1976) on cognitive-affective development of Down's syndrome infants. One aspect of their study involved ascertaining age of successful performance and measuring diversity of acts accomplished. While their Down's syndrome sample ultimately attained an overall level of cognitive-affective skill commensurate with that of the normal sample, they never demonstrated a similar *range* of behavior. We view as promising the extension of this paradigm to other groups of developmentally "at-risk" infants where the childhood level of intellectual attainment is not as limited as it is with a Down's syndrome sample.

The recurring theme expressed in preceding paragraphs suggests that infants with *greater ranges* of behavior should be more advantaged than infants with *restricted ranges*. Yet, we are cognizant of the fact that this component of *resources* cannot be isolated from that of *organization*. Behavior must be integrated so that it is not manifested as fragments that are unadaptable to changing needs and situations (Lewin, 1935; Piaget, 1952).

Measurement of *organization* of behavior is far more difficult than measurement of *range;* the concept is abstract (Kagan and Kogan, 1970). Clinically, a similar construct has been used to describe infants but, to our knowledge, it has not been formally measured. For example, in the context of observing infants' play with novel objects, one might be described as showing systematic explorations, another characterized by random moves from object to object. Theoretically, both infants could demonstrate the same *range* of behavior. It will be a formidable challenge to move from clinical description to actual measurement; yet, in time, as this is accomplished we envision numerous applications to studies of developmental risk.

In summary, we have indicated that our basic knowledge of infants "at risk" is incomplete. We have suggested alternative approaches. Within the context of specific abilities, we pointed to a need to explore information processes. Within the more general context of development, we suggested exploring *resources* infants mobilize in their ongoing interactions.

Finally, concomitant with a change in research focus, we believe that changes in research strategies are required. We suggest that research endeavors can be better organized to optimize knowledge, and in times of restricted budgets becomes a prudent course. One approach that is particularly appealing would involve cooperative research endeavors involving several developmental laboratories linked together by interest, expertise, and external funding. A formal liaison, supported with sufficient funding, could permit time to generate ideas about optimal approaches, allow testing of ideas, use of sizable samples, and evaluation of methodologies. Thus, instead of fragmented and isolated studies, meritorious as they might be, there would be organized, in-depth studies of different risk groups, utilizing sophisticated methodologies and evaluation techniques. We are aware this approach has been used on an informal basis; we now suggest this be formal and organized, and sanctioned by funding.

We end this chapter as we began. Much has been accomplished toward gaining a general understanding of the hazards of prenatal and perinatal factors, too little is understood regarding individual implications of a diagnosis. We need to generate a refined, conceptual model of developmental risk that allows correct identification of an infant's problems so that the most appropriate care, services, and interventions may be provided.

BIBLIOGRAPHY

Abramowicz, H. K., and Richardson, S. A. Epidemiology of severe mental retardation in children: Community studies. *American Journal of Mental Deficiency,* 1975, **80,** 18–39.

Alden, E. R., Mandelkorn, T., Woodrum, D. E., Wennberg, R. P., Parks, C. R., and Hodson, A. Morbidity and mortality of infants weighing less than 1,000 grams in an intensive care nursery. *Pediatrics,* 1972, **50,** 40–49.

Als, H., Tronick, E., Adamson, L., Brazelton, B. The behavior of the full-term yet underweight newborn infant. *Developmental Medicine and Child Neurology,* 1976, **18,** 590–602.

Amiel-Tison, C. Neurological evaluation of the maturity of newborn infants. *Archives of Diseases in Childhood,* 1968, **43,** 89–93.

Appleton, T., Clifton, R., and Goldberg, S. The development of behavioral competence in infancy. In F. D. Horowitz, E. M. Hetherington, S. Scarr-Salapatek, and G. M. Siegel (eds.), *Review of Child Development Research,* Vol. 4. Chicago: University of Chicago Press, 1975.

Babson, S. G. Growth of low-birth-weight infants. *Journal of Pediatrics,* 1970, **77,** 11–18.

Babson, S. J. & Kangas, J. Pre-school intelligence of undersized term infants. *American Journal, Diseases in Childhood,* 1969, **117,** 553–557.

Barnard, K. E. A program of stimulation for infants born prematurely. Paper presented at the biennial meeting of the Society for Research in Child Development, Philadelphia, 1973.

Baumeister, A. A. The effects of dietary control on intelligence in phenylketonuria. *American Journal of Mental Deficiency,* 1967, **71,** 840–847.

Bayley, N. Consistency and variability in the growth of intelligence from birth to eighteen years. *Journal of Genetic Psychology,* 1949, **75,** 165 196.

Bayley, N., Rhodes, L., Gooch, B., and Marcus, M. Environmental factors in the development of institutionalized children. In J. Hellmuth (ed.), *Exceptional Infant: Studies in Abnormalities,* Vol. 3. New York: Brunner/Mazel, 1971.

Beckwith, C. Relationships between attributes of mothers and their infants' I.Q. scores. *Child Development,* 1971, **42,** 1083–1097.

Beckwith, L., Cohen, S. E., Kopp, C. B., Parmelee, A. J., and Marcy, T. Caregiver-infant interaction and early cognitive development in preterm infants. *Child Development,* 1976, **47,** 579–587.

Bench, J., and Parker, A. Hyper-responsivity to sounds in the short-gestation baby. *Developmental Medicine and Child Neurology,* 1971, **13,** 15–19.

Bergner, S., and Susser, M. W. Low birthweight and prenatal nutrition: An interpretative review. *Pediatrics,* 1970, **46,** 946–966.

Berkson, G., Wasserman, G., Behrman, R. Heart rate responses to an auditory stimulus in premature infants. *Psychophysiology,* 1974, **11,** 244–246.

Berman, J. L., and Ford, R. Intelligence quotients and intelligence loss in patients with phenylketonuria and some variant states. *Journal of Pediatrics,* 1970, **77,** 764–770.

Berman, P. W., Waisman, H. A., and Graham, F. K. Intelligence in treated phenylketonuric children—a developmental study. *Child Development,* 1966, **37,** 731–747.

Bidder, R. T., Bryant, G., and Gray, O. P. Benefits of Down's syndrome children through training their mothers. *Archives of Diseases in Childhood,* 1975, **50,** 383–386.

Birch, H. G., and Gussow, J. D. *Disadvantaged Children*. New York: Harcourt, Brace & World, 1970.

Birch, H. G., Richardson, S. A., Baird, D., Horobin, G., and Illsley, R. *Mental Subnormality in the Community: A Clinical and Epidemiologic Study*. Baltimore: Williams & Wilkins, 1970.

Bjerre, I. Physical growth of 5-year-old children with a low birthweight. *Acta Paediatrica Scandinavia* (Stockholm), 1975, **64**, 33–43.

Brocklehurst, G. Spina bifida for the clinician. Clinics in Developmental Medicine, No. 57. *Spastics International Medical Publication*. London: Heinemann, 1976.

Broman, S. H., Nichols, P. L., and Kennedy, W. A. *Preschool I.Q.: Prenatal and Early Developmental Correlates*. New York: Wiley, 1975.

Bruner, J. S. The growth and structure of skill. In K. J. Connolly (ed.), *Mechanisms of Motor Skill Development* New York: Academic, 1970.

Bruner, J. S. The organization of early skilled action. In M. P. M. Richards (ed.), *The Integration of a Child into a Social World*. London: Cambridge, 1974.

Caesar, P. and Akiyama, Y. The estimation of the postmenstrual age: a comprehensive review. *Developmental Medicine & Child Neurology*, 1970, **12**, 697–729.

Carr, J. *Young Children with Down's Syndrome: Their Developmental Upbringing and Effect on their Families*. London: Butterworth, 1975.

Carrier, C., Doray, B., Stern, L., and Usher, R. Effects of neonatal intensive care on mortality rates in the Province of Quebec. *Pediatric Research*, 1972, **6**, 408 (abstract).

Carter, C. O. Incidence and aetiology. In A. P. Norman (ed), *Congenital Abnormalities in Infancy*. Oxford: Blackwell, 1971.

Carter, C. O. Clues to the aetiology of neural tube malformations: Studies in hydrocephalus and spina bifida. *Developmental Medicine and Child Neurology*, Suppl 32, 1974, **16**, 3–15.

Cedarbaum, S. Personal communication, 1976.

Chappell, P. F., Boismier, J. D., and Meier, G. The infant's entering repertoire. Paper presented at the biennial meeting of the Society for Research in Child Development, Philadelphia, 1973.

Chase, H. C. Perinatal mortality: Overview and current trends. *Clinics in Perinatology*, 1974, **1**, 3–17.

Chess, S. The influence of defect on development in children with congenital rubella. *Merrill-Palmer Quarterly of Behavior and Development*, 1974, **20**, 255–274.

Cicchetti D., and Mans, L. Down's Syndrome and normal infants' responses to impending collision. Paper presented at the meetings of the American Psychological Association, Washington, D.C., 1976.

Cicchetti, D., and Sroufe, L. A. The emotional development of the infant with Down's syndrome. *Child Development*, 1976, **47**, 920–929.

Clarke-Stewart, A. Interactions between mothers and their young children: Characteristics and consequences. *Monographs of the Society for Research in Child Development*, 1973, **38**, (6–7, Serial No. 153).

Clifford, S. H. Postmaturity with placental dysfunction. *Journal of Pediatrics*, 1954, **44**, 1–13.

Collard, R. Exploratory and play behavior of infants reared in an institution and in lower and middle-class homes. *Child Development*, 1971, **42**, 1003–1015.

Connolly, B. and Russell, F. Interdisciplinary early intervention program. *Physical Therapy*, 1976, **56**, 155–158.

Corah, N. L., Anthony, E. J., Painter, P., Stern, J. A., and Thurston, D. L. Effects of perinatal anoxia after seven years. *Psychological Monographs*, 1965, **79**, (3) (whole No. 596.)

Corman, H. H., and Escalona, S. K. Stages of sensorimotor development: A replication study. *Merrill-Palmer Quarterly of Behavior and Development*, 1969, **15**, 351–362.

Cornwell, A. C. Development of language, abstraction and numerical concept formation in Down's syndrome children, *American Journal of Mental Deficiency,* 1974, **79,** 179–190.

Czochanska, J., and Losiowski, Z. Objawy neurologiczne stwierdzane u dzieci z nieleczona i pozno leczona fenyloketonuria. *Neurologia i Neurochirurgia Polska* (Warszawa), 1972, T. VI (XXII), NR2, 225–228.

Davies, P. Perinatal nutrition of infants of very low birth weight and their later progress. *Nutrition, Growth & Development–Modern Problems in Pediatrics,* 1975, **14,** 119–133.

Davies, P., and Davis, J. P. Very low birth weight and subsequent head growth. *Lancet,* 1970, **2,** 1216–1219.

Davies, P., and Stewart, A. L. Low birth-weight infants: Neurological sequelae and later intelligence. *British Medical Bulletin,* 1975, **31,** 85–91.

Davies, P. and Tizard, J. P.. M. Very low birth weight and subsequent neurological defect. *Developmental Medicine & Child Neurology,* 1975, **17,** 3–17.

Decarie, T. G. A study of the mental and emotional development of the thalidomide child. In B. M. Foss (ed.), *Determinants of Infant Behavior IV.* London: Methuen, 1969.

Decarie, T. G., and O'Neill, M. Quelques aspects du dévelopment cognitif d'enfants souffrant de malformation dues à la thalidomide. *Bulletin de Psychologie,* 1974, **25,** 5–9.

DeMyer, W. Congenital anomalies of the central nervous system. In D. B. Tower (ed.), *The Nervous System. The Clinical Neurosciences.* New York: Raven, 1975.

Dicks-Mireaux, M. J. Mental development of infants with Down's syndrome. *American Journal of Mental Deficiency,* 1972, **77,** 26–32.

Diller, L., Gordon, W. A., Swinyard, C. A., and Kastner, S. *Psychological and Educational Studies with Spina Bifida Children.* Washington, D.C.: U.S. Department of Health, Education & Welfare, U.S. Office of Education, 1969.

Dingman, H., and Tarjan, G. Mental retardation and the normal distribution curve. *American Journal of Mental Deficiency,* 1960, **64,** 991–994.

Dobbing, J. Undernutrition and the developing brain. The relevance of animal models to the human problem. *American Journal of Diseases of Children,* 1970, **120,** 411–415.

Dobbing, J. Prenatal nutrition and neurological development. In J. Cravioto, L. Hambraeus, and B. Vahlquist (eds.), *Early Malnutrition and Mental Development.* Symposia of the Swedish Nutrition Foundation (No. XII). Stockholm: Almquist & Wiksell, 1974.

Dobbing, J. Vulnerable periods of brain growth and somatic growth. In D. F. Roberts and A. M. Thomson (eds.), *The Biology of Human Fetal growth.* New York: Halsted, 1976.

Dodson, J. C., Kushida, E., Williamson, M. and Friedman, E. G. Intellectual performance of 36 phenylketonuria patients and their nonaffected siblings. *Pediatrics,* 1976, **58,** 53–58.

Dorner, S. The relationships of physical handicap to stress in families with an adolescent with spina bifida. *Developmental & Child Neurology,* 1975, **17,** 765–776.

Douglas, J. W. B. "Premature" children at primary schools. *British Medical Journal,* 1960, **1,** 1008–1013.

Drage, J. S., Berendes, H. W., and Fisher, P. D. The Apgar score and four-year psychological examination performance. In *Perinatal Factors affecting Human Development,* Pan American Health organization Scientific Publication No. 185, 1969.

Dreyfus-Brisac, C. The bioelectric development of the central nervous system during early life. In F. Falkner (ed.), *Human Development.* Philadelphia: Saunders, 1966.

Dreyfus-Brisac, C. Sleep ontogenesis in human prematures after 32 weeks of conceptional age. *Developmental Psychobiology,* 1970, **3,** 91–121.

Drillien, C. M. *The Growth and Development of the Prematurely Born Infant.* Edinburgh: Livingstone, 1964.

Drillien, C. M. The small-for-dates infant: Etiology and prognosis. *Pediatric Clinics of North America*, 1970, **17**, 9–23.

Drillien, C. M. Aetiology and outcome in low-birth-weight infants. *Developmental Medicine and Child Neurology*, 1972, **14**, 563–574.

Drillien, C. M. Prevention of handicap in infants of very low birth weight. In D. A. A. Primrose (ed.), *Proceedings of the Third Congress of the International Association for the Scientific Study of Mental Deficiency*. Warsaw: Polish Medical, 1975.

Driscoll, S. G. Prevention of prematurity and perinatal morbidity. In A. Milunsky (ed.), *The Prevention of Genetic Disease and Mental Retardation*. Philadelphia: Saunders, 1975.

Drotar, D., Baskiewicz, A., Irvin, N., Kennell, J. and Klaus, M. The adaptation of parents to the birth of an infant with congenital malformation: A hypothetical model. *Pediatrics*, 1975, **56**, 710–717.

Dweck, H. S., Saxon, S. A., Benton, J. W., and Cassady, G. Early development of the tiny premature infant. *American Journal of Diseases of Childhood*, 1973, **126**, 28–34.

Engel, R. Maturation changes and abnormalities in the newborn electroencephalogram. *Developmental Medicine & Child Neurology*, 1965, **7**, 498–506.

Fantz, R. L., and Fagan, J. F. Visual attention to size and number of pattern details by term and preterm infants during the first six months. *Child Development*, 1975, **46**, 224–228.

Fantz, R. L., Fagan, J. F., and Miranda, S. B. Early visual selectivity. In L. Cohen and P. Salapatek (eds.), *Infant Perception: From Sensation to Cognition*, Vol. I, *Basic Visual Processes*. New York: Academic 1975.

Fishman, M., and Palkes, H. The validity of psychometric testing in children with congenital malformations of the central nervous system. *Developmental Medicine and Child Neurology*, 1974, **16**, 180–185.

Fitzhardinge, P. M., and Steven, E. M. The small-for-date infant. I. Later growth patterns. *Pediatrics*, 1972a, **49**, 671–681.

Fitzhardinge, P. M., and Steven, E. M. The small-for-date infant. II. Neurological and intellectual sequelae. *Pediatrics*, 1972b, **50**, 50–57.

Flavell, J. An analysis of cognitive-developmental sequences. *Genetic Psychology Monographs*, 1972, **86**, 279–350.

Ford, E. H. R. *Human Chromosomes*. New York: Academic, 1973.

Fraiberg, S. The development of human attachments in infants blind from birth. *Merrill-Palmer Quarterly of Behavior and Development*, 1975, **21**, 315–334.

Francis-Williams, J., and Davies, P. A. Very low birth weight and later intelligence. *Developmental Medicine and Child Neurology*, 1974, **16**, 709–728.

Fraser, F. C. Some genetic aspects of teratology. In J. Wilson and J. Warkany (eds.). *Teratology: Principles and Techniques*. Chicago: University of Chicago, 1965.

Freeston, B. M. An enquiry into the effect of a spina bifida child upon family life. *Developmental Medicine and Child Neurology*, 1971, **13**, 456–461.

Gesell, A. L., and Amatruda, C. S. *The Embryology of Behavior; The Beginnings of the Human Mind*. New York: Harper, 1945.

Gibson, E. *Principles of Perceptual Learning and Development*. New York: Appleton-Century-Crofts, 1969.

Gold, E. M. Obstetric aspects of perinatology. *Clinics in Perinatology*, 1974, **1**, 19–24.

Goldstein, K. M., Caputo, D. V., and Taub, H. B. The effects of prenatal and perinatal complications on development at one year of age. *Child Development*, 1976, **47**, 613–621.

Graham, F. K., Pennoyer, M. M., Caldwell, B. M., Greenman, M., and Hartman, A. F. Relationship between clinical status and behavior test performance in a newborn group with histories suggesting anoxia. *Journal of Pediatrics*, 1957, **50**, 177–189.

Graham, F. K., Ernhart, C. B., Thurston, D., and Craft, M. Development three years after perinatal anoxia and other potentially damaging newborn experiences. *Psychological Monographs,* 1962, **76** (3, whole No. 522).

Gruenwald, P. Chronic fetal distress and placental insufficiency. *Biologia Neonatorum,* 1963, **5,** 215–265.

Gruenwald, P. *The Placenta.* Baltimore: University Park, 1975.

Hack, M., Mostow, A., and Miranda, S. Development of attention in pre-term infants. *Pediatrics,* 1976, **58,** 669–674.

Hagberg, B. Pre-, peri- and postnatal prevention of major neuropediatric handicaps. *Neuropaediatrie,* 1975, **6,** 331–338.

Hagberg, B. Olaw, I., and Hagberg, G. Decreasing incidence of low-birth-weight diplegia—an achievement of modern neonatal care? *Acta Paediatrie Scandinavia,* 1973, **62,** 199–200.

Harper, P. A., and Wiener, G. Sequelae of low birth weight. *Annual Review of Medicine,* 1965, **16,** 405–420.

Hayden, A. H., and Haring, N. G. The acceleration and maintenance of developmental gains in Down's syndrome school-aged children. paper presented at Fourth International Congress of the International Association for the Scientific Study of Mental Deficiency, 1976.

Hickey, M. F. Genes and mermaids: changing theories of the causation of congenital abnormalities. *The Medical Journal of Australia,* 1953, **1,** 649–667.

Hirschhorn, K. Chromosomal abnormalities I: Autosomal defects. In V. A. McKusick and R. Claiborne (eds.), *Medical Genetics.* New York: H. P. Publishing, 1973.

Howard, J., Parmelee, A. H., Kopp, C. B., and Littman, B. A neurological comparison of pre-term and full-term infants at term gestational age. *Journal of Pediatrics,* 1976, **88,** 995–1002.

Hsia, D. Y., and Holtzman, N. A. A critical evaluation of P.K.U. screening. In V. A. McKusick and R. Claiborne (eds.), *Medical Genetics.* New York: H. P. Publishing, 1973.

Hsia, D. Y., O'Flynn, M. E., Berman, J. L. Atypical phenylketonuria with borderline or normal intelligence. *American Journal Diseases of Childhood,* 1968, **116,** 143–157.

Hunt, G. M. Implications of the treatment of myelomeningocele for the child and his family. *Lancet,* 1973, **2,** 1308–10.

Hunt, G. H., and Holmes, A. E. Studies in hydrocephalus and spina bifida. *Developmental Medicine and Child Neurology,* 1975, **17,** 65–70.

Hunt, J. V. Environmental risk in fetal and neonatal life and measured infant intelligence. In M. Lewis (ed.) *Origins of Intelligence.* New York: Plenum, 1976.

Hunt, J. V., Harvin, D., Kennedy, D., and Tooley, W. H. Mental development of children with birth weights <1500 G. *Clinical Research,* 1974, **22,** 240 (abstract).

Jacobs, P. A. Human population cytogenetics. In J. deGrouchy, F. J. G. Ebling, and I. W. Henderson (eds.), *Human Cytogenetics.* Amsterdam: Excerpta Medica, 1972.

Jones, M. C., and Bayley, N. Physical maturing among boys as related to behavior. *Journal of Educational Psychology,* 1950, **41,** 129–148.

Jordan, T. E. Research on the handicapped child and the family. *Merrill-Palmer Quarterly of Behavior and Development,* 1962, **8,** 243–260.

Kagan, J. Do infants think? *Scientific American,* 1972, **226,** 74–82.

Kagan, J. and Kogan, N. Individual variation in cognitive processes. In P. H. Mussen (ed.), *Carmichael's Manual of Child Psychology.* New York: Wiley, 1970.

Kashgarian, M., and Rendtorff, R. C. Incidence of Down's syndrome in American Negroes. *Journal of Pediatrics,* 1969, **74,** 468–471.

Kelman, H. R. The effect of a brain-damaged child on the family. In H. G. Birch (ed.), *Brain Damage in Children: The Biological and Social Aspects.* Baltimore: Williams & Wilkins, 1964.

Kessen, W., Haith, M. M., and Salapatek, P. H. Infancy. In P. H. Mussen (ed.), *Carmichael's Manual of Child Psychology,* 3rd ed. New York: Wiley, 1970.

Knobloch, H., Rider, R., Harper, P., and Pasamanick, B. Neuropsychiatric sequelae of prematurity: A longitudinal study. *Journal of the American Medical Association,* 1956, **161,** 581–585.

Knox, W. E. Phenylketonuria. In J. B. Stanbury, J. B. Wyngaarden, and D. S. Fredrickson (eds.), *The Metabolic Basis of Inherited Disease.* New York: McGraw-Hill, 1972.

Koch, R., and de la Cruz, F. F. *Down's Syndrome (Mongolism): Research, Prevention and Management.* New York: Brunner/Mazel, 1975.

Koch, R., Acosta, P., Fishler, K., Schaeffler, G., and Wohlers, A. Clinical observations on phenylketonuria. *American Journal of Diseases of Childhood,* 1967, **113,** 6–15.

Koch, R., Fishler, K., Schild, S., and Ragsdale, N. Clinical aspects of phenylketonuria. *Mental Retardation,* 1964, **2,** 47–54.

Koch, R., Share, J., Webb, A., and Graliker, B. The predictability of Gesell developmental scale in mongolism. *Journal of Pediatrics,* 1963, **62,** 93–97.

Kolin, I. S., Scherzer, A. S., New, B., and Garfield, M. Studies of the school-age child with meningomyelocele: Social and emotional adaptation. *Journal of Pediatrics,* 1971, **78,** 1013–1019.

Kopp, C. B. Sensorimotor development: Studies of full term and pre-term infants. Unpublished manuscript, 1976a.

Kopp, C. B. Action-scheme of 8-month-old infants. *Developmental Psychology,* 1976b, **12,** 361–362.

Kopp, C. B., O'Connor, M., Sigman, M., Parmelee, A. H., and Marcy, T. Early cognitive development of pre-term and full term infants: Component structure of sensorimotor and developmental examinations. Paper presented at the biennial meeting of the Society for Research in Child Development, Denver, 1975.

Kopp, C. B., and Parmelee, A. H. Behavioral antecedents of cognitive abilities. *Clinical Research,* 1976, **24,** 175A (abstract).

Kopp, C. B., Sigman, M. Parmelee, A. H., and Jeffrey, W. E. Neurological organization and visual fixation in infants at 40 weeks' conceptual age. *Developmental Psychobiology,* 1975, **8,** 165–170.

Kuo, Z. Y. *The Dynamics of Behavior Development. An Epigenetic View.* New York: Random House, 1967.

Kushlick, A., and Blunden, R. The epidemiology of mental subnormality. In A. M. Clarke and A. D. B. Clarke (eds.), *Mental Deficiency: The Changing Outlook,* 3rd ed. New York: Free Press, 1974.

Laurence, K. M. The natural history of spina bifida cystica. Detailed analysis of 407 cases. *Archives of Diseases in Childhood,* 1964, **39,** 41–57.

Laurence, K. M. The survival of untreated spina bifida cystica. *Developmental Medicine and Child Neurology,* Suppl 11, 1966, **8,** 10–20.

Laurence, K. M., and Tew, B. J. Follow-up of 65 survivors from the 425 cases of spina bifida born in South Wales between 1956 and 1962. *Developmental Medicine and Child Neurology,* Suppl. 13, 1967, **9,** 1–3.

Laurence, K. M., and Weeks, R. Abnormalities of the central nervous system. In A. P. Norman (ed.), *Congenital Abnormalities in Infancy.* Oxford: Blackwell, 1971.

Leiderman, P. H., Leifer, A. A., Seashore, M. J., Barnett, C. R., and Grobstein, R. Mother-infant interaction: Effects of early deprivation, prior experience, and sex of infant. Early Development. *Research Publication, Association for Research in Nervous and Mental Disease,* 1973, **51,** 154–175.

Lemire, R. J., Loeser, J. D., Leech, R. W. and Alvord, E. C., Jr. *Stages of Embryonic Development: Growth of Fetal Structures and Organs.* New York: Harper & Row, 1975.

Lenneberg, E. H., Nichols, I. A., and Rosenberger, E. F. Primitive stages of language development in mongolism. *Disorders of Communication,* 1962, **VVL**-1, 119–137.

Lewin, K. *A Dynamic Theory of Personality.* New York: McGraw-Hill, 1935.

Lewis, M., and Rosenblum, L. A. *The Effect of the Infant on its Caregiver.* New York: Wiley, 1974.

Liedholm, M., Wessner, G., and Karlberg, P. Mental function in children with myelomeningocele: A preliminary report. *Developmental Medicine and Child Neurology,* Suppl. 32, 1974, **16,** 157 (abstract).

Lind, T. Techniques for assessing fetal development. In D. F. Roberts and A. M. Thomson (eds.), *The Biology of Human Fetal Growth.* New York: Halsted, 1976.

Littman, B., and Parmelee, A. H. Perinatal complications and developmental outcome in a group of pre-term infants, *Clinical Research,* 1977, **25,** 191A (abstract).

Lonsdale, M. B., and Foust, M. Normal mental development in treated phenylketonuria—report of 10 cases. *American Journal, Diseases in Childhood,* 1970, **119,** 440–446.

Lorber, J. Results of treatment of myelomeningocele. An analysis of 524 unselected cases with special reference to possible selection for treatment. *Developmental Medicine and Child Neurology,* 1971, **13,** 279–303.

Lubchenco, L. Assessment of gestational age and development at birth. *Pediatric Clinics of North America,* 1970, **17,** 125–145.

Lubchenco, L., Housman, C., and Backström, L. Factors affecting fetal growth. In J. Jonxis, H. Visser, and J. Trolstra (eds.), *Nutricia Symposium: Aspects of Praematurity and Dysmaturity.* Groningen, May 10–12, 1967.

Mawdsley, T., Rickham, P. O., and Roberts, J. R. Long-term results of early operation of open myelomeningoceles and encephaloceles. *British Medical Journal,* 1967, **1,** 663–666.

McCall, R. B., Hogarty, P. S., and Hurlburt, N. Transitions in infant sensorimotor development: The prediction of childhood I.Q. *American Psychologist,* 1972, **27,** 728–748.

McDonald, A. D. Intelligence in children of very low birth weight. *British Journal of Preventive and Social Medicine,* 1964, **18,** 59–74.

McKusick, V. A. *Human Genetics,* 2nd ed. Englewood Cliffs, N.J.: Prentice-Hall, 1969.

Mercer, J. *Labeling the Mentally Retarded.* Berkeley: University of California, 1973.

Michaelis, R., Parmelee, A. H., Stern, E., and Haber, A. Activity states in premature and term infants. *Developmental Psychobiology,* 1973, **6,** 209–215.

Michaelis, R., Schulte, F. J., and Nolte, R. Motor behavior of small for gestational age newborn infants. *Journal of Pediatrics,* 1970, **76,** 208–213.

Milhorat, T. H. *Hydrocephalus and the Cerebrospinal fluid.* Baltimore: Williams & Wilkins, 1972.

Miller, H. C., and Hassanein, K. Diagnosis of impaired fetal growth in newborn infants. *Pediatrics,* 1971, **48,** 511–522.

Miller, H. C., Hassanein, K., Chin, T. D. Y., and Hensleigh, P. Socieconomic factors in relation to fetal growth in white infants. *Journal of Pediatrics,* 1976, **89,** 638–643.

Miranda, S. B. Response to novel visual stimuli by Down's syndrome and normal infants. Proceedings, American Psychological Association, 1970a.

Miranda, S. B. Visual abilities and pattern preferences of premature infants and full-term neonates. *Journal of Experimental Child Psychology,* 1970b, **10,** 189–205.

Miranda, S. B. Visual attention in defective and high-risk infants. *Merrill-Palmer Quarterly of Development and Behavior,* 1976, **22,** 201–228.

Miranda, S. B., and Fantz, R. L. Visual preferences of Down's syndrome and normal infants. *Child Development,* 1973, **44,** 555–561.

Miranda, S. B., and Fantz, R. L. Recognition memory in Down's syndrome and normal infants. *Child Development,* 1974, **45,** 651–660.

Monsen, R. Adjustment in spina bifida. Unpublished manuscript, 1976.

Moore, K. L. *The Developing Human*. Philadelphia: Saunders, 1973.

National Academy of Sciences, Washington, D.C. Genetic screening programs, principles and research, 1975.

Naylor, A. F., and Myrianthopoulos, N. C. The relation of ethnic and selected socio-economic factors to human birth weight. *Annals of Human Genetics,* 1967, **31,** 71–83.

Neligan, G. A., Kolvin, I., Scott, D. M., AND Garside, R. F. Born too soon or born too small. *Clinics in Developmental Medicine,* No. 61. London: Heinemann, 1976.

Nora, J. J., and Fraser, F. C. *Medical Genetics: Principles and Practice*. Philadelphia: Lea & Febiger, 1974.

O'Connor, M. J. A comparison of pre-term and full-term infants on parameters of habituation at four months and performance on Bayley Scales of Infant Development at 18 months. Unpublished doctoral dissertation, University of California, Los Angeles, 1977.

Ounsted, M., and Ounsted, C. On fetal growth rate. *Clinics in Developmental Medicine,* No. 46. London: Heinemann, 1973.

Paine, R. S. The variability in manifestations of untreated patients with phenylketonuria. *Pediatrics,* 1957, **20,** 290–302.

Parmelee, A. H. Ontogeny of sleep patterns and associated periodicities in infants. In F. Falkner and N. Kretchmer (eds.), *Pre and Postnatal Development of the Human Brain*. Basel: Karger, 1974.

Parmelee, A. H. Diagnostic and intervention studies of high risk infants. Unpublished progress report, 1976.

Parmelee, A. H. Diagnostic and intervention studies of high risk infants. Unpublished progress report, 1977.

Parmelee, A. H., Akiyama, Y., Stern, E., and Harris, M. A periodic cerebral rhythm in newborn infants. *Experimental Neurology,* 1969, **25,** 475–584.

Parmelee, A. H., and Haber, A. Who is the risk infant? *Clinical Obstetrics & Gynecology,* 1973, **16,** 376–387.

Parmelee, A. H., Kopp, C. B., and Sigman, M. Selection of developmental assessment techniques for infants at risk. *Merrill-Palmer Quarterly of Development and Behavior,* 1976, **22,** 177–199.

Parmelee, A. H., Minkowski, A., Saint-Anne Dargassies, S., Dreyfus-Brisac, C., Lezine, I., Berges, J., Chervin, G., and Stern, E. Neurological evaluation of the premature infant. *Biology Neonate,* 1970, **15,** 65–78.

Parmelee, A. H., Schulte, F., Akiyama, Y., Wenner, W., Schultz, F., and Stern, E. Maturation of EEG activity during sleep in premature infants. *Electroencephalography and Clinical Neurophysiology,* 1968, **24,** 319–329.

Parmelee, A. H., and Schulte, F. Developmental testing of pre-term and small-for-dates infants. *Pediatrics,* 1970, **45,** 21–28.

Parmelee, A. H., and Sigman, M. Development of visual behavior and neurological organiation in pre-term and full-term infants. In A. Pick (ed.), *Minnesota Symposia on Child Psychology,* Vol. 10. Minneapolis: University of Minnesota, 1976.

Penrose, L. S., and Smith, G. G. *Down's Anomaly*. London: Churchill, 1976.

Phillippe, F., and Lézine, I. A propos du devenir de l'ancien prématuré. *Revue de Neuropsychiatrie Infantile,* 1974, **22,** 263–280.

Piaget, J. *The Origins of Intelligence in Children*. New York: International Universities, 1952.

Piaget, J. *The Construction of Reality in the Child*. New York: Basic, 1954.

Piaget, J. *Biology and Knowledge: An Essay on the Relation Between Organic Regulation and Cognitive Processes*. Edinburgh: Edinburgh, 1971.

Prechtl, H. F. R. Prognostic value of neurological signs in the newborn infant. *Proceedings of the Royal Society of Medicine,* 1965, **58,** 3–4.

Rawlings, G., Reynolds, E. O. R., Stewart, A., and Strong, L. B. Changing prognosis for infants of very low birth weight. *Lancet,* 1971, **1,** 516–519.

Reisman, L. E. Chromosome abnormalities and intrauterine growth retardation. *Pediatric Clinics of North America,* 1970, **17,** 101–110.

Roberts, D. F., and Thomson, A. M. *The Biology of Human Fetal Growth.* New York: Halsted, 1976.

Robinson, R. J. Assessment of gestational age by neurological examination. *Archives, Diseases in Childhood,* 1966, **41,** 437–447.

Rose, S., Schmidt, K., and Bridger, W. Cardiac and behavioral responsivity to tactile stimulation in premature and full-term infants. *Developmental Psychology,* 1976, **12,** 311–320.

Rosencrans, C. J. A longitudinal study of exceptional cognitive development in a partial transloca-tion Down's syndrome child. *American Journal of Mental Deficiency,* 1971, **76,** 291–294.

Rosenthal, R., and Jacobson, L. *Pygmalion in the Classroom.* New York: Holt, Rinehart & Winston, 1968.

Roskies, E. *Abnormality and Normality.* Ithaca: Cornell, 1972.

Rubin, A., Rosenblatt, C., and Balow, B. Psychological and educational sequelae of prematurity. *Pediatrics,* 1973, **52,** 352–363.

Rynders, J., and Horrobin, J. M. Project E.D.G.E.: The University of Minnesota's communication stimulation program for Down's syndrome infants. In B. L. Friedlander, G. M. Sterritt, and G. E. Kirk (eds.), *Exceptional Infant,* Vol. 3. *Assessment and Intervention.* New York: Brunner/Mazel, 1975.

Saint-Anne Dargassies, S. Neurological maturation of the premature infant of 28 to 41 weeks gestational age. In F. Falkner (ed.), *Human Development.* Philadelphia: Saunders, 1966.

Sameroff, A. J., and Chandler, M. J. Reproductive risk and the continuum of caretaking casualty. In F. D. Horowitz, M. Hetherington, S. Scarr-Salapatek, and G. Siegel (eds.), *Review of Child Development Research,* Vol. 4. Chicago: University of Chicago, 1975.

Schulman, C. Auditory stimulus on heart rate in high risk and low risk premature infants. Paper presented at the Eastern Psychological Association meeting, Washington, D.C., 1968.

Schulman, C. A. Effects of auditory stimulation on heart rate in premature infants as a function of level of arousal, probability of CNS damage and conceptual age. *Developmental Psychobiology,* 1969, **2,** 172–183.

Share, J., Koch, R., Webb, A., and Graliker, B. The longitudinal development of infants and young children with Down's syndrome (mongolism). *American Journal of Mental Deficiency,* 1964, **64,** 685–692.

Sibinga, M. S., and Friedman, C. J. Diet therapy and other sources of influence on the outcome of children with phenylketonuria. *Developmental Medicine & Child Neurology,* 1972, **14,** 445–456.

Siegel, T. S., Balow, B., Fisch, R. O., and Anderson, J. E. School behavior profiles of phenyl-ketonuria children. *American Journal of Mental Deficiency,* 1968, **72,** 937–944.

Sigman, M. Early cognitive development of pre-term and full-term infants: Exploratory behavior in 8-month-old infants. *Child Development,* 1976, **47,** 606–612.

Sigman, M., Kopp, C. B., Littman, B., and Parmelee, A. H. Infant visual attentiveness as a function of birth condition. *Developmental Psychology,* 1977, **13,** 431–437.

Sigman, M., and Parmelee, A. H. Visual preferences of 4-month-old premature and full-term infants. *Child Development,* 1974, **45,** 959–965.

Smith, D. W. and Wilson, A. A. *The Child with Down's Syndrome (Mongolism).* Philadelphia: Saunders, 1973.

Smith, I., and Wolff, O. H. Natural history of phenylketonuria and influences of early treatment. *Lancet,* 1974, **2,** 540–544.

Sroufe, L. A. Emotional development in infancy. In J. Osofsky (ed.), *Handbook of Infancy.* New York: Wiley, 1977.

Sroufe, L. A., and Waters, E. The ontogenesis of smiling and laughter: a perspective on the organization of development in infancy. *Psychological Review,* 1976, **83,** 173–189.

Stedman, D. J., and Eichorn, D. H. A comparison of the grown and development of infants and young children with Down's syndrome (mongolism). *American Journal of Mental Deficiency,* 1964, **69,** 391–401.

Steinhausen, H.-C. Psychological evaluation of treatment in phenylketonuria: Intellectual, motor and social development. *Neuropaediatrie,* 1974, **5,** 146–156.

Stern, E., Parmelee, A. H., Akiyama, Y., Schultz, M., and Wenner, W. Sleep-cycle characteristics in infants. *Pediatrics,* 1969, **43,** 65–70.

Stewart, A. L., and Reynolds, E. O. R. Improved prognosis for infants of very low birth weight. *Pediatrics,* 1974, **54,** 724–735.

Stubbe, H. *History of Genetics.* Cambridge: M.I.T., 1965. Translated from revised 2nd ed., 1972.

Susser, M., Marolla, F. A., and Fleiss, J. Birth weight, fetal age and perinatal mortality. *American Journal of Epidemiology,* 1972, **96,** 197–204.

Sutherland, B. S., Umbarger, B., and Berry, H. K. The treatment of phenylketonuria. *American Journal of Diseases of Childhood,* 1966, **111,** 503–523.

Tarjan, G. Some thoughts on sociocultural retardation. In H. C. Haywood (ed.), *Socio-cultural Aspects of Mental Retardation.* New York: Appleton-Century-Crofts, 1970.

Tew, B. J., and Laurence, K. M. The ability and attainment of spina bifida patients born in South Wales between 1956 and 1962. *Developmental Medicine and Child Neurology,* Suppl. 27, 1972, **14,** 124–131.

Tew, B., and Laurence, K. M. The validity of psychometric studies on children with spina bifida. *Developmental Medicine and Child Neurology,* 1974, **16,** 186–188.

Tew, B., Payne, H., and Laurence, K. M. Must a family with a handicapped child be a handicapped family? *Developmental Medicine and Child Neurology,* Suppl. 32, 1974, **16,** 95–98.

Thompson, J. S., and Thompson, M. W. *Genetics in Medicine.* Philadelphia: Saunders, 1973.

Tizard, J. Ecological studies of malnutrition: Problems and methods. In J. Cravioto, L. Hambraeus, and B. Vahlquist (eds.), *Early Malnutrition and Mental Development.* Symposia of the Swedish Nutrition Foundation (No. XII). Stockholm: Almquist & Wiksell, 1974.

Vorherr, H. Placental insufficiency in relation to post-term pregnancy and fetal postmaturity. *American Journal of Obstetrics and Gynecology,* 1975, **123,** 67–103.

Walker, J. H., Thomas, M., and Russell, I. T. Spina bifida and the parents. *Developmental Medicine and Child Neurology,* 1971, **13,** 462–476.

Warkany, J., Monroe, B. B., and Sutherland, B. S. Intrauterine growth retardation. *American Journal of Diseases of Childhood,* 1961, **102,** 249–279.

Werner, H. *Comparative Psychology of Mental Development,* Rev. ed. Chicago: Follett, 1948.

Wiener, G., Rider, R. V., Oppel, W. C., and Harper, P. A. Correlates of low birth weight: Psychological status of 6–7 years of age. *Pediatrics,* 1965, **35,** 434–444.

Wiener, G., Rider, R. V., Oppel, W. C., and Harper, P. A. Correlates of low birth weight: Psychological status at 8–10 years of age. *Pediatric Research,* 1968, **2,** 110–118.

White, B., and Watts, J. C. *Experience and Environment. Major Influences on the Development of the Young Child.* New York: Prentice-Hall, 1973.

Williams, C. D., and Jelliffe, D. B. *Mother and Child Health.* London: Oxford, 1972.

Wilson, J. G. *Environment and Birth Defects.* New York: Academic, 1973.

Wood, A. C., Friedman, C. J., and Steisel, I. M. Psychological factors in phenylketonuria. *American Journal of Orthopsychiatry,* 1967, **37,** 671–679.

Yarrow, L., Rubenstein, J., and Pedersen, F. *Infant and Environment. Early Cognitive and Motivational Development.* New York: Halsted, 1973.

Zeaman, D., and House, B. J. Approach and avoidance in the discrimination learning of retardates. *Child Development,* 1962, **33,** 355–372.

CHAPTER 3

Obstetrical Medication and Infant Behavior[1]

Yvonne Brackbill

Obstetrical medication is a controversial issue today. The substance of the controversy is the safety of the labor and delivery drugs for the child.

Controversy is not new to this medical practice. Medication was the object of dispute upon its very introduction into obstetrics, but the issue then was morality rather than safety. According to the Christian-Judaic belief, Eve was not only to be punished as a scofflaw but her punishment, pain during childbirth, was to be visited as well on all of her descendants. There was no serious threat to the enforcement of this divine ordination for the first 18½ centuries AD, perhaps because Christian women of the Western world did not have ready access to the naturally occurring psychoactive substances—principally opium, hemp, and mandrake—that were frequently used by primitive peoples for the relief of pain.

On January 19, 1847, however, all this changed. James Young Simpson, a Scottish obstetrician, used ether on a woman to deliver her child. The news of his success in painless birth spread like wildfire. Within 5 months etherized deliveries had also been performed in England, Ireland, France, Germany, and the United States. By the end of 1847, chloroform had also been used successfully as an obstetrical anesthetic.

News of painless childbirth was quickly followed by strong objections from both the clergy and medical profession. Clerics saw it as an act of heresy: God had ordained women to suffer during childbirth in eternal punishment for their ancestral sin: "In sorrow thou shall bring forth children" (*Genesis* III:16). Pain killers that reduced this suffering clearly flaunted divine will, as did the men who administered them. Simpson (1849), a contentious man by all accounts, was not to be outdone in biblical interpretation; he quickly drafted a long treatise entitled "Answer to the religious objections advanced against the employment of anaesthetic agents in midwifery and surgery." Simpson argued first that it was incorrect to translate the Hebrew word "בְּעֶצֶב" as "sorrow." Its correct translation was *work* or *labor,* according to Simpson, and anesthetic did not deprive women of labor. On the contrary, claimed the rebellious Scot, anesthesia *was* divine will. In proof of this one need only contemplate the "deep sleep" (i.e., anesthesia) which God caused to fall on Adam when "He removed one of his ribs and closed up the flesh instead thereof" (*Genesis* II:21). (He added that if God *had* ordained pain, pain would be felt by *all* women; but, as every one knew, the women of black tribes did not feel pain during labor and delivery.)

Simpson's arguments held the clergy at bay. They were not persuaded, but neither did

[1]The author is grateful to the many colleagues who contributed to this chapter by providing information and unpublished data and reviewing the final draft.

they spearhead legislation prohibiting use of ether or chloroform in childbirth. The event that wiped out all further moral objections was not rhetoric but demonstration by a morally unassailable figure, the secular head of the Church of England. In 1853 (and again in 1857), Queen Victoria allowed herself to be chloroformed during the birth of a royal prince.[2]

Quite apart from ministerial outrage, the medical profession also objected to the abolition of parturient pain. Physicians were not so readily persuaded by biblical argument or monarchial example. One month after the Queen's painless delivery, *Lancet* editorially admonished the Queen's physician: "In no case could it be justifiable to administer chloroform in a perfectly ordinary labour" (Haggard, 1929). In the United States, medical opposition was led by Charles Meigs, Professor of Midwifery at Jefferson Medical College and a man no less attracted to controversy than Simpson. Meigs (1849) argued that "The propriety of resorting to the use of chloroform and ether as means of obviating the pain and hazards of labor, is a question to be settled by an estimate of the safeness as well as necessity of it." On other occasions Meigs was less of an empiricist. Since pain is physiological, said he, there must be some necessary and useful connection between it and successful parturition. Elsewhere, Meigs argued against tampering with ". . . those natural and physiological forces that the Divinity has ordained us to enjoy or to suffer."

From abroad, Meigs' objections were answered by Simpson in articulate and impassioned letters that are masterpieces of veiled insult. At home, Meigs' chief adversary was Walter Channing, another prominent American obstetrician. Channing polled Boston physicians on their experiences with painless childbirth and published the results of his survey in book form. His *Treatise on Etherization in Childbirth* (1848) was an overwhelming endorsement of obstetrical anesthesia—a not surprising outcome since the author had, by his own admission, omitted all negative responses to his questionnaire.

Throughout this long period of hot debate, very little attention was being paid the infant. Queen Victoria's physician did observe that infants born to chloroformed mothers did not "kick and scream in the violent way and grasp the bedclothes with the force, during the first minute after birth, that is often observed under other circumstances" (Snow, 1853).[3]

Except for some casual observations, however, the century that followed was not one in which the infant figured prominently. One reason is that the infant is not, from the obstetrician's point of view, his chief responsibility. In judging the safety of new drugs, the obstetrician assumed (and still does?) that no matter how poor the infant's initial state, no matter how long the period before respiration began, no matter how blue his color initially, no matter how unresponsive, if the infant ultimately appeared normal then he had suffered only transient difficulties.

Only in the last decade have others begun to question this assumption as well as to question whether these measures are appropriate indices of neurobehavioral function in real-life situations. The questioners have been, for the most part, developmental psychologists. They have been joined by a few physicians from a variety of specialties, principally obstetrical anesthesiologists, pediatricians, and psychiatrists.

This chapter reviews the empirical evidence these investigators have uncovered concerning the extent and duration of the effects of medication on infant behavior. [Previous

---

[2]For some time chloroform was referred to as anesthesia à la reine.

[3]For a more detailed history of inhalation anesthesia in obstetrics see Caton (1970) and Haggard (1929). For a short history of regional block anesthesia, see Bonica (1953).

reviews relevant to this topic include those of Aleksandrowicz (1974a), Alper et al., (1975), Bowes (1970), Brazelton (1970), Dubowitz (1975), Richards (1970), and Scanlon (1974).] As background for this presentation, I first summarize current anatomical and physiological thinking concerning the infant's structural and functional immaturity at time of birth, criteria for drug evaluation from clinicians' and pharmacologists' points of view, a description of the pre-anesthetic and anesthetic medications most frequently used in childbirth, and a report on incidence of drug use in obstetrics.

STRUCTURAL AND FUNCTIONAL IMMATURITY AT BIRTH

The human baby is among the many mammals whose morphological and functional development is not complete at time of birth. The significance of this incomplete development is twofold. First, postnatal development, outside the insulative environment of the womb, means increased vulnerability to exogenous influences during this sensitive period. Second, those systems or organs most susceptible to drugs [central nervous system (CNS)] or most needed for drug clearance (liver, kidney) are those least well developed at time of birth.

At birth, the CNS is the least-well-developed system morphologically as well as functionally. Dobbing estimates (Dobbing and Sands, 1973) that the "brain growth spurt," the period of most rapid CNS development, continues for at least 18 postnatal months (Fig. 3-1) (see also Himwich, 1970). Thereafter, the CNS continues to develop, though more slowly, until early adulthood (Timiras et al., 1968). Underdevelopment at birth means, at the macro-level, that sensory structure and function are still developing, particularly in the phylogenetically younger modalities such as vision (Fitzgerald and Brackbill, 1976; Gottlieb, 1971). At the micro-level there are still major developments to take place in neuronal multiplication, dendritic arborization, synaptic connections, myelination, development of neurotransmitter mechanisms and nucleic acids, and formation of blood-brain barriers. Neuroanatomic evidence has established that trauma to developing CNS structures can effect permanent morphological and functional changes. For example, when normally developing synaptic connections are injured, collateral sprouting follows. The new connections are different from those that would have been formed if trauma had not intervened; the system, in other words, is permanently altered. (Guth and Clemente, 1975).

Liver and kidney are two other organs whose function is markedly underdeveloped at birth and which also undergo some postnatal structural change (Kleinman, 1970; Smith and Nelson, 1976; Stave, 1970; Vernier and Smith, 1968; Walsh and Lind, 1970). Blood flow to neonatal kidney is restricted. Glomeruli and tubules, which continue to grow in size until adolescence, are structurally immature. Glomerular filtration rate is low and tubular function is poor. Glomerular heterogeneity limits renal acidification and regulation of acid-base balance (Kleinman, 1970; Vernier and Smith, 1968; Walsh and Lind, 1970).

In contrast to the systems just reviewed, heart and lungs are functionally mature at time of birth (Herrington, 1970; Walsh and Lind, 1970). These organs, however, do not play a special role in drug clearance.

In summary, the newborn human being is an organism poorly positioned for dealing with toxic agents. Drugs enter the CNS readily because of incomplete blood-brain barriers; they lodge in brain structures that are still developing and therefore at high risk to damage; they cannot readily be transformed to nontoxic compounds since the necessary

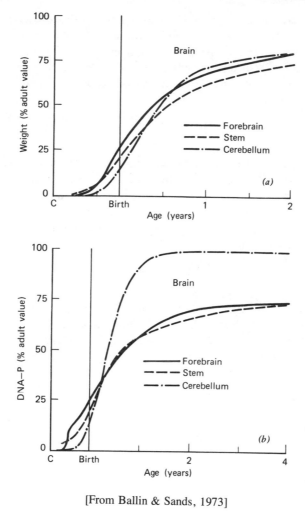

[From Ballin & Sands, 1973]

Figure 3-1. Growth of the brain (C-cells).

liver functions are immature; and they cannot readily be excreted because of inefficient kidney function.

CRITERIA FOR DRUG EVALUATION

From the obstetrician's point of view, the chemical criteria for evaluating obstetrical medications are therapeutic efficacy (principally, analgesic potency), effects on labor, side-effects on mother, and effects on fetus and newborn (Bonica, 1953). The criteria for evaluating drug effects on the fetus and newborn are mortality, clinical status at birth (especially Apgar score), presence or absence of risk indices—for example, respiratory distress or need for resuscitation at birth—and biochemical measures of newborn status, principally maternal and fetal blood levels of drug, pH, PCO_2, and buffer base measurements.

From the pharmacologist's point of view, criteria for drug evaluation follow four basic parameters: absorption, distribution, biotransformation, and excretion. Unfortunately, these parameters are affected by hormonal status and maturity, so that relatively little is known with certainty about pharmacodynamics in the pregnant woman and fetus. [For reviews of fetal, perinatal, and neonatal pharmacology, see Boréus (1973), Mirkin (1975), Morselli (1976), and Yaffe (1976)].

Absorption

Absorption rate refers to the time between drug administration and onset of action. It depends upon several factors: drug solubility, drug concentration, circulation to the site of absorption, area of absorbing surface, and, perhaps most importantly, route of administration. In general, absorption rate is fastest for intravenous (IV) administration, slower for intramuscular (IM) administration, and slowest for oral administration. To illustrate, some barbiturates peak in 2 to 4 min following IV injection, in 30 min following IM injection, and 1.5 h following oral administration.

Distribution

Distribution refers to the binding of drugs at different sites and to its localization in tissue. As Fingl and Woodbury (1970, 1975) point out, as a drug is absorbed it enters the body's fluid compartments: plasma, interstitial fluid, transcellular fluids, and cellular fluids. Drugs differ in their ability to pass cell membranes and, consequently, differ in the extensiveness of their distribution throughout the body. "In addition, some drugs may accumulate in various areas as a result of binding, dissolving in fat, or active transport. The accumulation may be at the locus of action of the drug, or, more often, in some other location. In the latter situation, the site of accumulation may serve as a storage depot for the drug (Fingl and Woodbury, 1970, p. 9).

Most if not all drugs used in obstetrical medication cross the placenta readily. (Those characterized by high lipid solubility and low ionization cross most readily.) Once across the placenta, they enter fetal circulation and tissues where their distribution is different from that for the mother (principally because of the immaturity of the blood-brain barriers, allowing ready access to the CNS). In the fetus, drugs accumulate to a disproportionate extent in the highly perfused (blood-filled) organs—such as brain, liver, and kidney—for which they have a particular affinity. For example, within 2 min of lidocaine administration to pregnant guinea pigs, lidocaine concentration is three times as great in the fetal liver as in the maternal liver and remains high thereafter (Finster et al., 1972).

Biotransformation

After entering the circulation or tissues, a drug is changed through a biochemical reaction, of which there are two general types. Nonsynthetic reactions (oxidation, reduction, and hydrolysis) generally result in inactivation of the drug. Occasionally, however, they result in increased activation by transformation of the parent drug into active metabolites. Synthetic reactions (conjugation) almost always lead to inactivation of the parent drug. They result from coupling of the drug or its metabolite with an endogenous substrate. Biotransformations occur principally in the liver and depend considerably on drug-metabolizing enzymes in hepatic microsomes (a function relatively undeveloped in the newborn).

Excretion

The kidney is the principal organ for excretion of drugs, either in unchanged form or as metabolites. (Drugs are also excreted through breast milk; inhalant anesthetics through the lungs and milk as well.) The mechanisms by which this is accomplished are passive glomerular filtration, active tubular secretion and reabsorption, and passive tubular diffusion. Renal excretion depends on the composition of the drugs and their metabolites. It is also highly dependent on the organisms' plasma protein binding capacity and acid-base balance—neither of which is favorably disposed toward maximally efficient renal function in the newborn.

MEDICATIONS FREQUENTLY USED IN OBSTETRICS

Table 3-1 lists by function, generic name, and brand name the medications most frequently used in obstetrics. By broadest classification, these are pre-anesthetic and anesthetic medications. A brief account of these follow. For more detailed information on any drug class or its use in obstetrics, the reader is referred to Bonica's *Principles and Practice of Obstetric Analgesia and Anesthesia* (1967, 1969) and to Goodman and Gilman's *The Pharmacological Basis of Therapeutics* (1975).

Pre-Anesthetic Medication

Physicians and nurses dispense a variety of drugs to laboring women. The most common classes are oxytoxics to initiate or augment labor, analgesics to relieve pain, and sedative-hypnotics and tranquilizers to relieve anxiety. I will describe each of these as well as some less frequently used drug classes—for example, narcotic antagonists.

Uterine Muscle Stimulants

Oxytocin stimulates contractile activity as well as electrical activity in uterine smooth muscle. The extent of stimulation is positively correlated with stage of pregnancy so that the later the stage of pregnancy the smaller the dose of oxytocin required to initiate uterine motility. Muscle activity increases as an exponential function of the amount of oxytocin so that administration must be carefully monitored. Too large a dose interferes with placental circulation and increases the possibility of unwanted side effects such as fetal distress or even uterine rupture.

Oxytocics serve multiple functions in obstetrics. They are used to induce labor, to augment labor in cases of prolonged uterine inertia, and to increase uterine tone following delivery. For prepartum functions, oxytocin is the drug of choice since oxytocin produces contractions intermixed with periods of relaxation. Ergot derivatives, on the other hand, produce sustained contractions and are therefore used only after delivery. (Strictly speaking, the ergot alkaloids should not be listed under Pre-anesthetic Medications in Table 3-1.)

The new alternative to oxytocics for labor induction is prostaglandin E_2.[4] For more information on the roles of prostaglandins in obstetrics, the reader is referred to Karim (1972) and Nakano and Koss (1973).

[4]The Upjohn Co. estimates that its prostaglandin E_2 will be released in 1977 for clinical use as a 10-mg vaginal insert.

Table 3-1.   Medication Agents Used in Obstetrics

Premedication Agents

Uterine Muscle Stimulants	Sedative-Hypnotics
oxytoxics	barbiturate
ergot alkaloids	pentobarbital (Nembutol)
ergonovine (Ergotrate)	secobarbital (Seconal [b])
methylergonovine (Methergine)	amobarbital (Amytal [a])
oxytocin (Pitocin, Syntocinon)	nonbarbiturate
prostaglandin E_2(see text)	diazepam (Valium)
Narcotic Analgesics	scopolamine (hyoscine)
alphaprodine (Nisentil)	Tranquilizers
meperidine (Demerol)	chlorpromazine (Thorazine)
morphine	hydroxyzine (Atarax, Vistaril)
Narcotic Antagonists	promazine (Sparine)
levallorphan (Lorfan)	promethazine (Phenergan)
nalorphine (Nalline)	propriomazine (Largon)
naloxone (Narcan)	triflupromazine (Vesprin)

General Anesthetic and Related Agents

Inhalant Anesthetics [c]	methohexital (Brevital)
cyclopropane	nonbarbiturate
enflurane (Ethrane)	ketamine (Ketalar, Ketaject)
halothane (Fluothane)	Neuromuscular Blocking Agents
methoxyflurane (Penthrane)	d-tubocurarine (Curare)
nitrous Oxide	gallamine (Flaxedil)
trichloroethylene (Trilene)	succinylcholine (Anectin, Quelicin, Sucostrin)
Intravenous Anesthetics	Antimuscarinic Agents
barbiturate	atropine
thiopental (Pentothal)	scopolamine (hyoscine)

Local Anesthetic and Related Agents

Procaine Analogs and Related Compounds	Vasopressors/Vasoconstrictors (Antihypotensives)
bupivacaine (Marcaine)	ephedrine
chloroprocaine (Nesacaine)	epinephrine (Adrenalin)
etidocaine (Duranest)	mephentermine (Wyamine)
lidocaine (Xylocaine)	metaraminol (Aramine)
mepivicaine (Carbocaine)	methoxamine (Vasoxyl)
prilocaine (Citanest)	norepinephrine, levarterenol (Levophed)
tetracaine (Pontocaine)	phenylephrine (Neo-Synephrine)

[a] British generic name is pethidine.

[b] Seconal and Amytal are often combined as Tuinal.

[c] To the list of inhalants might be added chloroform, ether, and fluroxene, which are no longer used but are in the research literature.

Narcotic Analgesics

Physicians generally consider narcotics to be the most effective drug for pain. Among the narcotic analgesics, meperidine is the most frequently administered obstetrical pain killer in the world. In Great Britain, meperidine was used in 56% of deliveries in 1958 and 68% in 1970 (Richards, 1976). In the United States it was administered to 61% of the subjects in the Collaborative Perinatal Study, 1958–1965 (Broman, 1977). In addition to its analgesic effect meperidine sedates and, in some patients, induces euphoria. Like other narcotic analgesics, its uptake and distribution rates depend on the route of administration. Meperidine is usually administered by injection since it is relatively ineffective when administered orally. The onset of analgesia is within 10 to 20 min of subcutaneous or IM administration and lasts 2 to 4 h. Biotransformation of meperidine is relatively slow and takes place primarily in the liver. Excretion proceeds primarily via the kidney.

Chief among meperidine's side effects is respiratory depression. As indirect consequences, there may be changes in maternal cardiovascular function and fetal oxygenation. Meperidine readily crosses the placenta and causes varying degrees of respiratory and CNS depression in the fetus. Meperidine's principal metabolite, normeperidine, also gains access to the fetus via the placenta. There is evidence indicating that even though normeperidine is less potent pharmacologically than its parent compound, it is more toxic—particularly with respect to respiratory depression (Brackbill et al., 1974a; Brown et al., 1976; Morrison et al., 1973).

Narcotic Antagonists

Narcotic antagonists are sometimes given to counteract narcotic-induced respiratory depression. Meperidine, morphine, and other opiates have been shown to exert their effects by binding to specific opiate receptors in the brain. Opiate antagonists, such as naloxone, are quite specific drugs that block access to opiate receptors and thus reverse the effects of opiates. There is an increasing interest in the prospect of administering naloxone directly to infants born with respiratory depression (see, for example, Williams et al., in press). When naloxone administration is helpful to the infant, it indicates that the respiratory depression is opiate-produced. [For relevant reviews of narcotic antagonists, see Marx (1977) and Snyder (1977).]

Sedative-Hypnotics and Tranquilizers

Drugs whose primary function is to reduce anxiety and excitement are frequently given mothers during childbirth. These agents reduce the amount of anesthesia needed, although preoperative interviews with the anesthesiologist have been shown to serve that purpose with much the same effectiveness (Egbert et al., 1963).

Barbiturates such as pentobarbital and secobarbital are used as sedative-hypnotics less frequently now than formerly.

Among the nonbarbiturate sedative-hypnotics, scopolamine is an agent that was very popular in the past but is less frequently used today. Scopolamine (the henbane of history) is a belladonna alkaloid with multiple effects. It generally, though not always, produces drowsiness, euphoria, and amnesia. (There is some evidence that diazepam [Valium] also produces varying degrees of amnesia.) Scopolamine suppresses parasympathetic action and may therefore be used in place of atropine to reduce excessive oropharyngeal secretions when general anesthesia is administered.

Among tranquilizers, phenothiazine derivatives are probably the most popular for obstetrical purposes. They account for all tranquilizers listed in Table 3-1 except hydroxyzine. In a recent study of obstetrical medication given to clinic patients at the University of Florida's Shands Hospital, 42% received promethazine (Phenergan). Phenothiazine reduces anxiety and responsiveness to external stimuli. (The so-called neuroleptic syndrome following its administration consists of psychomotor slowing, emotional quieting, and affective indifference.) Phenothiazines also sedate when given for the first time.

Physiologically, the most notable effects of chlorpromazine are hypotension and tachycardia.

Phenothiazines are readily absorbed after oral and parenteral administration and are rapidly distributed throughout all body tissues. A very large number of metabolites are formed through biotransformation in the liver. Many of these metabolites, along with some amount of unchanged drug, remain in the body for very long periods of time (6 to 8 months after drug discontinuance of high doses in mental patients). Some of the metabolites are excreted in urine, others in feces.

Anesthesia

The generic term "anesthesia", coined by Oliver Wendell Holmes, means lack of sensation. *General anesthesia* indicates loss of sensation throughout the entire body. Routes of administration of general anesthesia—intravenous or inhaled—also indicate its systemic nature. *Regional anesthesia* means a loss of sensation in some restricted area of the body. This areal restriction is accomplished by injecting the anesthetic agent in such a way—for example, around a nerve—that its bodily distribution is limited. General and regional anesthesia also differ with respect to types of agents used for their induction. We will now turn our attention to these very important parameters.

General Anesthesia

When is general anesthesia used in preference to regional anesthesia? One indication for its use is fetal distress and a consequent need for speeding up delivery. Another indication is the patient's refusal to tolerate delivery while conscious. As Bonica (1967, p. 879) puts it, general anesthesia is indicated for anyone who is not "emotionally suited" to remain awake during delivery. Another indicator is the need for intrauterine manipulation—for example, the need to adjust manually the position of a second twin after delivery of the first. Agents used for general anesthesia are listed in Table 3-1. The uptake, distribution, biotransformation, and elimination of inhalant and intravenously administered agents present complicated pictures; for a discussion of these parameters, the reader is referred to Bonica (1967, Vol. 1) and Goodman and Gilman (1975). For our purposes, suffice it to say that all general anesthetic agents cross the placenta rapidly, producing varying degrees of CNS depression in the fetus.

General anesthesia used traditionally to be divided into four stages: analgesia, delirium, surgical anesthesia, and respiratory paralysis. The boundaries between stages relate to degradative changes involving respiration, muscle tone, and reflex activity. It is logical to assume that the degradative changes should be important for obstetrics. For example, maternal respiratory depression interferes with fetal oxygenation, and loss of muscular control may necessitate forceps extraction. Nevertheless, the importance for obstetrics of this particular four-stage classification scheme has not been demonstrated. Thus, for a subsample of 669 women enrolled in the Collaborative Perinatal Study who received inhalant anesthesia for vaginal delivery, there was no strong or consistent relationship between anesthetic stage reached and infant outcome, as measured by the pediatric-neurological exams given at 4 and 12 months, and by the Bayley scales, given at age 8 months.

INHALANT ANESTHETICS

Of the gaseous inhalant agents, only nitrous oxide is currently used with any marked frequency. Cyclopropane and ethylene are highly explosive compounds, though cyclopropane is still used in some hospitals.

The volatile agents, which are liquid at room temperature, include ether and the halogenated hydrocarbons. Ether is not currently fashionable because it is explosive, irritating, and slow-acting. Trichloroethylene in periodic self-administrations has been widely used in Great Britain but not in the United States. Methoxyflurane is now used instead for self-administration. It is often used in low concentrations for vaginal delivery and is occasionally used to supplement nitrous oxide for cesarean section. High concentrations of halothane are also used occasionally when it is necessary to relax the uterus—for example, for intrauterine manipulation.

INTRAVENOUS ANESTHETICS

From anesthetists' point of view, the short-acting barbiturates are desirable as anesthetic agents because they induce anesthesia rapidly, allow relatively prompt recovery of consciousness, and reduce the probability of vomiting. Thiopental, which is the most popular of the short-acting barbiturates and the prototype of its class, used to be used alone. However, thiopental is an inefficient analgesic; increasing the amount of this drug to produce analgesia markedly increases the probability of fetal/neonatal depression. For this reason it is currently used as an induction agent, after which others are given by inhalation. A common technique is called "balanced anesthesia": nitrous oxide for analgesia, thiopental for unconsciousness, and succinylcholine for muscle relaxation, intubation, and immobility.

Among the nonbarbiturate anesthesias, ketamine is of the "dissociative anesthetic" class, so called because the patient feels dissociated from his environment and often his own body. Ketamine produces analgesia but also, in some cases, such unwanted effects as unpleasant dreams and muscle rigidity.

NEUROMUSCULAR BLOCKING AGENTS

A neuromuscular blocking agent is used in conjunction with general anesthesia to relax skeletal muscle and thus facilitate tracheal intubation and surgery. Succinylcholine, contrary to earlier beliefs, does cross the placenta (Finster and Marx, 1976).

ANTIMUSCARINIC AGENTS

Small doses of atropine may be given to reduce excessive salivary, bronchial, and sweat secretions associated with the administration of some anesthetics. Scopolamine has much the same antiparasympathetic effect. Contrary to earlier beliefs, scopolamine does cross the placenta, as does atropine.

CESAREAN SECTION

"Cesarean section" refers to delivery of the child surgically, by abdominal incision, rather than through the normal vaginal route. In the past, the use of cesarean section was synonymous with the use of general anesthesia. Today, some cesarean sections are being carried out under regional anesthesia. The majority, however, are still done under general anesthesia.

Cesarean section rates, once on the decline, are increasing again. To illustrate, Jones (1976) reports trends[5] based on 72,184 births during a 35-year period, at Charlotte Memorial Hospital, Charlotte, North Carolina. From 1940 to 1952, the cesarean section rate was 4.5% of all births; from 1953 to 1962, 3.7% [3.9% for 19,432 Collaborative Perinatal Study subjects (Benson et al., 1965)]; from 1963 to 1969, 6%; from 1970 to 1974, 8.2%; and for the first 6 months of 1975, 10.3%. Jones also polled 50 representative medical school departmental chairmen throughout the United States. His results indicate that 10 years ago the average cesarean section rate ranged from 3 to 8%. Today, the rate is between 9 and 12%; the upper range limit is 23%. Most respondents predicted a further increase. The rise in cesarean section rates is not restricted to the United States (Richards, 1976).

Why has the cesarean section "changed from an operation of necessity to an operation of choice?" (Jones, 1976, p. 529). Clinicians see as the basic reason a shift in priorities from mother to fetus. As one respondent remarked of the increase in cesarean sections, "It is due to an increasing desire to spare the fetus any trouble whatever" (Steer, quoted in Jones, 1976, p. 527). Indications for cesarean section have also changed over the years. Repeat cesarean sections are no longer viewed as automatic. For primary (i.e., nonrepeat) cesarean sections, the most frequent indicators are cephalopelvic disproportion (including failed use of forceps and dysfunctional labor), breech presentation, and fetal distress. Many claim that the use of fetal monitoring equipment of late has contributed significantly to the frequency of use of the diagnosis, "fetal distress" (Colen, 1976).

Local Anesthetic Agents

Local anesthetic agents are analogs—or at least distant relatives—of procaine (Novocain), first synthesized in 1905. Those more commonly used in obstetrics are listed in Table 3-1. They block pain by preventing nerve-impulse generation and conduction. Following their administration, local anesthetic agents are readily absorbed and diffuse across the placenta within minutes of their administration. They are metabolized either in the liver (aminde compounds) or liver and plasma (ester compounds), and are excreted mainly in urine. [See Covino (1972) on physiologic disposition of local anesthetic agents.] Because they indirectly produce hypotension (through relaxation of the smooth muscle of the arterioles and consequent vasodilation), their administration is sometimes accompanied by epinephrine, whose counteractive vasoconstrictive effect helps restrict the distribution of the anesthetic and its rate of absorption. Specific anesthetic agents differ in terms of their anesthetic potency, actions on cell membranes, and duration of action—from less than 1h (procaine) to more than 3h (bupivacaine).

SITE OF ANESTHETIC BLOCKING

Figure 3-2 shows the most common sites for administration of local anesthetic agents for obstetrical use. These sites differ in terms of the amount and/or concentration of an agent

---

[5]Caution must be exercised in extrapolating from obstetrics statistics based on non-national samples, since we know that rates for different obstetrical procedures differ by hospital and geographic region. Unfortunately, there is no national repository for obstetrics statistics.

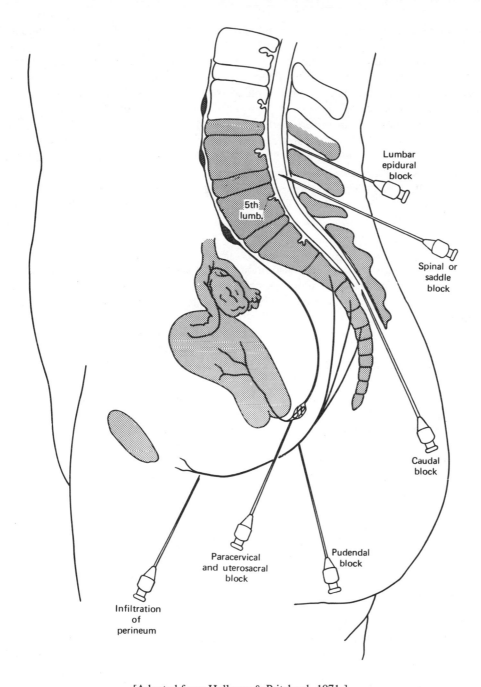

Lumbar
epidural
block

5th.
lumb.

Spinal or
saddle
block

Caudal
block

Pudendal
block

Paracervical
and uterosacral
block

Infiltration
of
perineum

[Adapted from Hellman & Pritchard, 1971.]

Figure 3-2. Routes of local anesthetic administration frequently used in blocking obstetric pain.

required for effective anesthesia. Local infiltration requires less anesthetic agent (and less skill) than does a regional block. Subarachnoid (''spinal'') anesthetics require less anesthetic than regional nerve blocks because distribution of the agent is anatomically restricted and because it is deposited directly into fluid bathing the nerve.

Anesthetic sites also differ in terms of the area anesthetized and therefore the stage of labor when they are useful. In stage 1 labor (until the cervix is completely dilated) pain emanates from the uterus and from cervical dilation. In stage 2 (until delivery), to uterine pain is now added pain from the perineal areas served by the pudendal nerve. Injection of anesthetic around the pudendal nerve blocks perineal pain but not uterine pain, whereas the reverse is true for paracervical block.

Local infiltration, which anesthetizes only a relatively small area around the genitals and anus, is not useful for labor but is commonly used for episiotomy and/or its repair.

VASOPRESSORS/VASOCONSTRICTORS

These agents are used to retard the absorption of local anesthetic agents and to counteract the hypotension produced by some anesthetic techniques and agents. They are sympathomimetic amines that raise blood pressure by altering vascular tone and/or cardiac output.

INCIDENCE OF DRUG USE IN OBSTETRICS

Before reviewing empirical studies of drug effects, it is helpful to know something about the incidence of drug use among mothers before, during, and after their deliveries.

Unlike many other developed countries, the United States maintains no registry on drugs released by the FDA for clinical use. Hence, there are no national data: no one knows the full extent of drug use nor the number and types of adverse reactions in patients for whom the drug is prescribed. The epidemiological bits and pieces that follow are the only statistics known to the reviewer. They come from studies that vary in age, sample size, and method of collection. The studies also vary somewhat in the definition of ''drug,'' depending on whether the investigators have included such compounds as vitamins, iron by mouth, and preoperative scrubs. For a review of previous studies and definitional problems, see Hill et al. (1977) and Bowes (1970).

Prenatal Drug Use

Among 50,000 Collaborative Perinatal Study subjects who enrolled in that investigation between 1958 and 1965, reported mean prenatal drug intake was 3.8 (Heinonen et al., 1977). White mothers took more drugs (M = 4.2) than Black mothers (M = 3.5), and blacks took more than Puerto Ricans (M = 2.7).

More recent studies show higher drug intake. Stewart et al. (1977) followed the prenatal, perinatal, and postnatal drug histories of 168 clinic patients at the University of Florida's teaching hospital. The mean number of different drugs consumed during pregnancy was 11.0. During 1969 to 1975, Hill et al. (1977) interviewed 241 pregnant women of urban, middle-to-upper socioeconomic class status. These women admitted taking, on the average, 6.4 different prescribed drugs and 3.2 different over-the-counter (OTC) drugs, for a grand total mean of 9.6 different drugs consumed prenatally; 25% of the subjects took at least one drug chronically. Regarding the OTC products, Hill et al. comment, "Patients do not equate drugs purchased without prescription as being pharmacological agents even though they are consumed as a treatment for a physical complaint" (1977 p. 383). As one mother said, "If I had known that aspirin was a drug, I would not have taken it" (Hill, 1973, p. 654).

Perinatal Drug Use

In 1973, obstetrician-gynecologists in private practice prescribed, for their hospitalized patients, 3.7 million doses of narcotic analgesics, 1.3 million doses of barbiturate sedatives, 1.1 million doses of nonnarcotic analgesics, and 1.1 million doses of tranquilizers. Most, but not all, of these hospitalizations were for delivery (private market survey, Doering, 1976). In 1974, my poll of 18 teaching hospitals with faculty membership in the Society for Obstetric Anesthesia and Perinatology revealed that only 5% of deliveries in those institutions were accomplished without anesthesia. By the time the Perinatal Collaborative First Study subject registration had ended in 1965, investigators had tallied 336 different premedication agents and 37 different anesthetics used in some 39,000 deliveries (Broman, 1977).

Hill et al. (1977) report for 241 middle- to upper-class women delivering between 1969 and 1975 a mean of 6.0 drugs administered (range, 0–14). Stewart et al. (1977) report, for 168 clinic patients delivering between 1974 and 1976, a mean of 7.0 different drug administrations during vaginal deliveries and 15.2 during cesarean section deliveries.

Postpartum Drug Usage in Lactating Mothers

Hill et al. (1977) report a mean intake of 7.7 different drugs by lactating mothers. These investigators comment on infant irritability and poor sleep patterns on days when mothers' coffee intake is high (see their Fig. 4: caffeine levels in breast milk). Stewart et al. (1977) report a postpartum mean intake of 2.5 different drugs. Although this mean is lower than that reported by Hill et al., the period of postpartum hospitalization for the population studied is also correspondingly lower.

Some indication of the large number of drugs excreted in breast milk can be found in reviews by Catz and Giacoia (1972), Knowles (1965), Martin (1971), and Vorherr (1974). (See Table 3-2 for a combined summary of empirical evidence.) These reviews cover available information regarding the nonbehavioral effects on the infant following the inadvertent consumption of drugs through breast milk. There is no corresponding coverage of behavioral effects.

Drug Intake on the Uptake

There is a general conviction among clinicians that the obstetrical use of drugs has decreased over the last few years. This conviction is not borne out by available statistics. The following examples serve to illustrate:

- In the Collaborative Perinatal Study, data collection spanned the years 1958 through 1965. During this period the mean prenatal drug intake of white clinic patients increased from 2.6 to 5.0.
- In 1973, Hill reported a combined prenatal-perinatal drug intake mean of 10.3 for

Table 3-2. Some Drugs Excreted in Breast Milk[a]

Alcohol	Corticosteroids
Amphetamines	e.g., cortisone, prednisone
Analgesics (nonnarcotic)	Cough suppressants
e.g., acetaminophen (Tylenol), aspirin	Diuretics
Anesthetics (inhalant)	Environmental chemicals
Antibiotics	e.g., DDT
e.g., penicillin, tetracycline	Ergot alkaloids
Anticancer	Expectorants
e.g., cyclophosphamide, methotrexate	Laxatives
Anticholinergics	Minerals, salts, metals
e.g., atropine, scopolamine	Muscle relaxants
Anticoagulants	e.g., curare, succinylcholine
e.g., warfarin	Narcotics
Anticonvulsants	e.g., codeine, meperidine
e.g., diphenylhydantoin (phenytoin),	Nasal decongestants
primidone	e.g., ephedrine, pseudoephedrine
Antidepressants	Nicotine
e.g., Elavil, Tofranil	Oral antidiabetics
Antihistamines	e.g., Orinase
Antiinfectives	Oral contraceptives
e.g., Flagyl	e.g., estrogens, progestogens
Antimalarials	Reserpine
e.g., pyrimethamine, quinine	Sedatives/hypnotics
Asthma preparations	e.g., bromides, chloral hydrate, diazepam
e.g., aminophylline	Thyroid and antithyroid drugs
Barbiturates	e.g., iodides, propylthiouracil
Caffeine	Tranquilizers
Cardiac antiarrhymthia drugs	Vitamins
e.g., quinidine	

[a]Each generic category covers an assortment of drugs, not all of which have been tested. Examples are given of those that have been studied.

middle-to-upper socio-economic class women living in Houston. Four years later, Hill et al. (1977) reported a mean drug intake of 15.6 for the same population.

- Richards (1977) reports that meperidine was used in 56% of deliveries in Great Britain in 1958 and 68% of deliveries in 1970.
- Benson et al. (1965) reported that some form of anesthesia was used in 85.4% of 1833 Collaborative Perinatal Study full-term deliveries. I found, in my unpublished 1974 poll of 18 U.S. teaching hospitals, that 95% of deliveries were carried out under some form of anesthesia.

It may be true that *some* drugs—for example, barbiturates and scopolamine—are less frequently administered nowadays. However, all available statistics indicate that for other types of drugs—for example, oxytocin—and for drugs as a class, drug administration for obstetrical purposes is on the increase.

Empirical Studies of Obstetrical Medication and Infant Behavior

At time of writing, more than 30 studies have been carried out on behavioral effects of obstetrical medication. ("Behavior" is defined broadly enough to include EEG and sleep states.) Those in which obstetrical medication is a principal focus of study are outlined in

Table 3-3 and also described narratively—first in terms of study parameters and then in terms of behavioral outcome. Those investigations in which obstetrical medication is of minor concern are not outlined in Table 3-3, but are referred to in appropriate sections of the text.

Study Parameters

Study Design and Procedure

One of the early studies of obstetrical medication effects was designed as an experimental investigation. The experimenter had control over drug administration and exercised it. "The groups were constituted by random sampling of uncomplicated obstetrical patients, and the mothers were not given the opportunity to elect or refuse the medication" (Kron et al., 1966, p. 1013). However, cumulative evidence from these early studies has made it increasingly clear that it is ethically impossible to continue using experimental designs in this area of investigation. The experimenter is left with two design alternatives: to enroll mothers before delivery and settle for a mixed bag of drugs and delivery modes, or to select along more narrowly defined lines after delivery. In either case, the resulting design is correlational. This has not been an insuperable obstacle to gathering and interpreting data. Any consequent loss of control within a single experiment has been more than compensated by cross-validation across studies.

In procedural respects, almost all studies shown in Table 3-3 were experimental. [Two exceptions are the clinical studies of Hughes et al. (1948, 1950.)]

Drugs

As Table 3-3 indicates, anesthetic agents and pre-anesthetic medication agents have shared the investigational limelight about equally. Among the premedication agents, analgesics, sedative-hypnotics, and tranquilizers have all been represented. Narcotic inhibitors and uterine muscle stimulants, on the other hand, have been relatively neglected as objects of research. (This may accurately reflect infrequent usage in the case of antagonists, but not in the case of oxytocins.) Among anesthetics, studies of specific agents have been few in number but tend to be the choice of physicians interested in behavioral outcome—for example, the Scanlon et al. (1974, 1976) studies comparing neurobehavioral test responses following bupivicaine, lidocaine, or mepivicaine; and the Hodgkinson et al. (1976c) study comparing ketamine and thiopental as general anesthetic agents.

Most obstetrical medication studies get low marks on specification of important drug parameters, including total dose, route of administration, and dosage time (time from administration or first administration or beginning of continuous administration to delivery). Total dose is often specified for premedication agents but not for anesthetics, where it is just as important. On the other hand, route of administration is clear enough for anesthetics but needs specification (IV, IM, oral, rectal) for premedication agents since effectiveness is a joint function of dosage and route; absorption is generally highest for IV and lowest for oral route. Dosage time is an extremely important variable, as we shall see in discussing outcome; it is a prime parameter in biotransformation and the conversion of parent compounds to metabolites which may themselves affect behavior. Speaking as an experimenter rather than reviewer, I think it is safe to infer that failure to specify important drug data is much less often the fault of the investigator than it is of the attending

Table 3-3. Empirical Studies of Obstetrical Medication and Infant Behavior

Study Variables	Aleksandrowicz & Aleksandrowicz (1974)	Bakeman et al. (1975)	Borgstedt & Rosen (1968)
Drugs	Mixed	Mixed; obstetricians rated potency	Mixed premed., 33 medicated, 8 unmedicated; anesthetic?
Infants (I)			
No.	44 (10 nonwhite)	45	13 white, 28 Black
test age(s)	Days 1–5, 7, 10, 28	3 days	42–78 h.
Experimenter:			
blind?	Blind	?	Blind
Mothers (M)			
parity	?	Primips & multips	?
risk	?	Low	?
Measures	Brazelton scale	M-I interaction	EEG Neurological exam Apgar
Results			
drug?	Drug-related differences? See Federman & Yang (1976); Aleksandrowicz & Aleksandrowicz (1976)	Potency predicted passivity, lack responsiveness. 1/16 analyses sig.	Exam & EEG affected, Apgar not
Other			
parity?	?	1/16 analyses parity effect; 2/16 labor	?
labor?	?	effect	?
Sex diffs.?	?	3/16 analyses sig.	?

Study Variables	Broman & Brackbill, (in progress)	Brower (1974)	Brown et al. (1975)	Conway & Brackbill (1970)
Drugs	Mixed	Meperidine	Analgesic mixed, ceiling 150 mg; anesthetic?	Mixed; obstetricians ranked for potency
Infants (I)				
No.	3528 white single births from Collab. Perinatal Project, NINCDS	45	45, 21<3000 g	23 20 17 ↓ ↓ ↓
test age(s)	Birth, 4, 8, & 12 mos.	48 h	55–80	2 days, 5 days, 1 month
Experimenter:				1 tester naive
blind?	Analysis retrospective	Computer analyzed	?	

Brackbill et al. (1974a)	Brackbill et al. (1974b)	Brackbill (1976)	Brazelton (1961)
Meperidine, 0–150 mg, IM	Mixed; obstetricians ranked for potency	Anesthesia: (1) none vs. local vs. regional or general; (2) regional vs. genl. (see Broman & Brackbill for more information on sample 2)	Mixed. High vs. low premed.
25	19 (supplementary sample)	(1) 18; (2) 3528	41
32 h	36 + 60 h	(1) 1, 4, & 8 months (2) 4 & 12 months	Days 1–6
Blind	Blind	Blind	M's own observations, feeding
11 primip; 14 multip	Primips & multips	(1) second pregnancy (2) primips & multips	Multips
Low	Low	(1) low; (2) low	?
Habituation, motor response to auditory stimulus; Brazelton scale (revised); Apgar	Habituation, motor response to auditory stimulus	Heart rate: A) habituation, HR to auditory stim.; B) abnormal HR	Responsiveness to feeding; onset, weight gain
Affected habituation and Brazelton	Affected habituation	(1) Potency-related trends in HR responding 8 months; (2) Potency→abnormal HR, 12 months	Both measures affected
Sig r, length labor[1]/ Brazelton; dosage time/habituation; no parity effect	No effect No effect	(1) Not applicable (2) Unknown (1) No effect (2) Unknown	?
?	?	(1) None; (2) unknown	?

Dubignon et al. (1969)	Emde et al. (1975)	Friedman et al. (1978)	Hodgkinson et al. (1976a)
Mixed. Premed. and anesthetic	Mixed premed.; anesthesia?	Mixed premed. & anesthetic	Anesthesia (31 spinal, 57 general)
144 lo risk 66 hi risk	10 drugged, 10 undrugged	50 ↓ 60 ↓	88
Birth–4 days	birth–10 h	4 mos., 5 mos.	Days 1 & 2
Data mechanically recorded	?	Retrospective study	Blind

93

Table 3-3. (*continued*)

Study Variables	Broman & Brackbill, (in progress)	Brower (1974)	Brown et al. (1975)	Conway & Brackbill (1970)
Mothers (M)				
parity	M=1.5	10 primips, 35 multips	22 primips	18 primips, 5 multips
risk	Low	Low	Low-risk Black	Low
Measures	Pediatric-neuro exams, birth, 4 & 12 mo.; Bayley scales, 8 mo.	EEG before & after auditory, visual, olfactory, & tactile stimulation	(1) M-I interaction (2) Graham-Rosenblith items	Graham Scale; habituation, motor response to auditory stimulus; Bayley Scales; Apgar
Results				
drug?	Approx. 40% items show sig. anesthetic effect across age	Post-stimulation changes, mostly occipital	2/14 items sig, 5/14 trend	All but Apgar affected
Other				
Parity?	Currently being analyzed	?	Yes, drugs, labor, parity jointly→8% common variance	Lower Graham scores for longer labors and firstborns (trends)
Labor?	Currently being analyzed	?		
Sex diffs.?	Currently being analyzed	?	Nonrelating to drugs	?

Study Variables	Hodgkinson et al. (1976b)	Hodgkinson et al. (1976c)	Horowitz et al. (1977) (Israeli sample)
Drugs	Anesthesia: 35 epidural v 35 general; Meperidine	(1) Anesthesia: ketamine (N=84) vs. thiopental (N=42) vs. extradural (N=101); (2) meperidine +/−; (3) oxytocin augmentation	Light analgesics (N=31) vs. no drug (N=33)
Infants (I)			
No.	70	227	65
test age(s)	Days 1 & 2	Days 1, 2	Days 1, 2, 3, 4, 1 mo., 3 mo.
Experimenter:			
blind?	Blind	Naive	2 blind, 2 naive
Mothers (M)			
parity	Primips	?	Primips & multips
risk	Low	Low	Low
Measures	Scanlon test	Scanlon test	Brazelton (5 tests) Bayley (1 test)
Results:			
drug?	Epidural→better performance than genl., both days Meperidine↓scores	(1) Extradural> ketamine>thiopental; (2) meperidine effect. (3) no effect oxytocin	2/15 items sig.

Dubignon et al. (1969)	Emde et al. (1975)	Friedman et al. (1978)	Hodgkinson et al. (1976a)
29 primips	?	56% primips	?
Some hi risk	?	Low	Low
8 nutritive & non-nutritive sucking measures	State	Habituation, visual stimuli	Scanlon test
Anesthetic related to nutritive suck.	↑quiet sleep, sleep cycles; ↓wakefulness	Analgesia, oxytocin longer responding, 4 mo.	Spinal→better performance than genl., all items, day 1 & half items, day 2
Affected nutritive sucking	?	No effect	No effect
Affected nutritive & nonnutritive sucking	?	?	No effect
None	?	None	None

Horowitz et al. (1977) (Uruguayan sample)	Hughes et al. (1948)	Hughes et al. (1950)	Kraemer et al. (1972)
51-no med., 23 mixed, unknown quantities	Secobarbital; dose? anesthetic?	Meperidine (N=16), 100 mg; (N=5), 200 mg; (N=9), 300 mg; vinbarbital (N=20) 5–8 grain, (N=9)>8 gr.; morphine (N=19) 10 mg, (N=17) 15 mg	Mixed. Pre-med. & anesthetic Two samples: (1) & (2)
80	20 neonates; 51 EEGs	95	(1) 124; (2) 32
3 days	Days 1, 2, 3	Days 1, 2, 3	(1) ?; (2) 57 h
?	?	?	(1) Data mechanically recorded; (2) ?
?	?	?	(1) ?; (2) 14 primips
Low	Low	?	(1) ?; (2) low
Brazelton	EEG	EEG	(1) Feeding intervals; (2) various observed behaviors
6/17 items sig.	Depressed activity, often at variance with clinical picture of alertness	Depressed activity, often delayed, & esp. occipit. after mep.; occasional hi volt. 1 death after vinbarb.	(1) Yes; (2) no

Table 3-3. *(continued)*

Study Variables	Hodgkinson et al. (1976b)	Hodgkinson et al. (1976c)	Horowitz et al. (1977) (Israeli sample)	
Other				
parity?	Not applicable	No effects labor, parity, low	No effect	?
labor?	No effect	forceps	Med. record info not available	med. record info not available
Sex diffs.?	None	None	No	?

Study Variables	Kron et al. (1966)	Moreau & Brich (1974)	Parke et al. (1972)	
Drugs	Sedative (secobarb. 200 mg, IV), N=10 vs. no drug, N=10	General anesthesia v no general anesthesia	Mixed; obstetrician rated potency 1-10	
Infants (I)				
No.	20	60 females	19	
test age(s)	24–36 h, 48–60h, 72–84 h	41 h	6–48 h	
Experimenter:				
Blind?	Dependent variable mechanically recorded	?	?	
Mothers (M)				
parity	?	Mixed parity (parity lower for genl. anesthesia mothers)	Primips	
risk	?	Low	Low	
Measures	Sucking rate and pressure; amount consumed	Habituation, HR & eye movement, to auditory & tactile stimuli	M-I interaction F-I interaction	
Results				
drug?	Yes, all 3 measures on all 3 test ages	Sig. decrement, eye/ aud. & HR/tactile, but not HR/and	M-I: 3/13 sig, 1 trend; F-1: 0/13 sig, 3 trend	
Other				
parity?	?	Lower for general anesthesia	No effect	
labor?	?	Not related to medication	?	
Sex diffs.?	?	Not applicable	1/13 items	

Study Variables	Tronick et al. (1976)	VanderMaelen et al. (1975)	Wiener et al. (1976)	Yang et al. (1976)
Drugs	Mixed, light analgesia & local or regional anesthesia	Mixed premed & anesthesia; 6-pt. scale potency	Following Meperidine 100–300 mg to mother, Saline, 40 μg IV or 200 μg IM naloxone to infants	Mixed premedication & anesthesia; no. drug administrations + 3 dosage time measures

Horowitz et al. (1970) (Uruguayan sample)	Hughes et al. (1948)	Hughes et al. (1950)	Kraemer et al. (1972)
?	?	(1) effects labor & parity; (2) no effect parity	
?	?	Labor affected 5 measures	
?	?	?	

Richards & Bernal (1972)	(1) Scanlon et al. (1976) (2) Scanlon et al. (1974)	Standley et al. (1974)[a]	Stechler (1964)
Premed., chiefly Pethilorfan (meperidine + antihypotensive) (N=23) 50–100 mg, IM	Anesthesia: (1) Non-epidural vs. epidural with (2) lidocaine or mepivacaine or (3) bupivacaine	Mixed analgesia & anesthesia; time-weighted dosage rating	Mixed premed., analyzed by (1) dosage time, (2) potency + dosage time
33	61	60	19
Birth–10 days	Birth–8 h	48–72 h	2–4 days
"Semi-blind"	Blind	?	Blind
Primips & multips	?	Primips	?
Low	?	Low	?
(1) M-I interaction, feeding; (2) nonnutritive sucking; (3) Prechtl-Beintema exam	Scanlon test	Brazelton, grouped into 3 clusters: alertness, irritability, motor maturity	Total looking time, 3 visual stimuli
(1) Sig. diffs.; (2) nonsig. trends; (3) 4 items sig.	For most items, bupivacaine>non-epidural>lidocaine/mepivacaine	Sig. r, drugs & irritability, motor maturity	Looking time sig. shorter for high potency, short dosage time
No effect	No effect	?	?
?	No effect	No effect	No effect
None	None	?	None

Table 3-3. *(continued)*

Study Variables	Tronick et al. (1976)	VanderMaeian et al. (1975)	Wiener et al. (1976)	Yang et al. (1976)
Infants (I)				
No.	54	24	54	85
test age(s)	Days 1, 2, 3, 4, 5, 7, 10	54 h	0.5, 4, 8, 12, 24, & 48 h	58
Experimenter:				
blind?	Blind	No	Yes	Retrospective study
Mothers (M)				
parity	Primips & multips	?	?	Primips
risk	Low	?	?	Low
Measures	Scanlon & Brazelton scales	Habituation, motor response to auditory stimulus	Scanlon test	(1) M: Schaefer-Manhe Preg. Ques.; (2) I: sleep, sucking, resp. to avers. stim. crying, motor resp., autonomic variability. $\Sigma = 15$ measures
Results				
drug?	Some items, each day	Habituation rate sig. related to drug potency, state & stimulus intensity	5/15 items sig. improvement after 200 but not 40 μg naloxone	4/15 measures affected by drug variables
Other				
parity?	?	No effect	?	Not applicable
labor?	?	No effect	?	Sig. *r,* labor & drug measures
Sex diffs?	?	None	?	None

[a]See also Hodgkinson et al. (1975) and Standley

physicians and nurses who fail to record such details on the patients' medical records.

As noted earlier, studies of obstetrical medication effects are by necessity correlational in design—meaning that the independent variable is not under the experimenter's control. A major consequence of this, if one selects subjects before delivery, is a conglomerate of drug types, times, and doses. A typical strategy for coping with this apples/oranges addition problem has been to use the obstetrician as a measuring instrument in gauging potency levels. If the number of subjects is not too large, it is possible for obstetricians to rank order patients with a fair degree of interjudge reliability (e.g., Conway and Brackbill, 1970). With more than 25 or 30 subjects it is necessary to use some sort of scaling procedure (e.g., Standley et al., 1975; Stechler, 1964). A second strategy has been to use factor analysis to arrive at groups (e.g., Aleksandrowicz and Aleksandrowicz, 1974b). A third strategy has been to use dichotomous groups, such as no premedication versus some premedication [e.g., Horowitz et al., 1977 (Israeli sample)]. None of these strategies is as satisfactory as restricting selection for each group to a single drug, a single route of administration, and so on.

Subjects

TERM, RISK, AND DELIVERY MODE

In studying obstetrical medication effects, investigators have generally had the foresight to use healthy, full-term babies and thus to avoid confounding drug effects with the effects of disease or correlates of prematurity. One might also expect that most of the subjects represented in Table 3-3 had been delivered vaginally, though this is rarely made clear.

RACE

Few nonwhites are represented in this research, which may well be subject to race differences. If Black babies are motorically more mature at birth and if a prime target of drug effects is motor coordination, then data from Black samples could be expected to show fewer drug effects.

SEX

Almost without exception, the babies studied have been of both sexes. From those studies that have analyzed sex differences, it does not appear that drugs affect boys and girls differently.

AGE

Most studies shown in Table 3-3 have used neonatal subjects. Only two studies (Richards and Bernal, 1972; Tronick et al., 1976) have tested babies as old as 10 days. Three more [Aleksandrowicz and Aleksandrowicz, 1974b; Conway and Brackbill, 1970; Horowitz et al., 1970 (Israeli sample),] have used subjects as old as 1 to 3 months of age. Only three studies (Brackbill, 1976; Broman and Brackbill, in progress; Friedman et al., 1978) have used subjects between 4 and 12 months of age. The underrepresentation of older subjects is unfortunate, since most of us expect drug effects to dissipate with age—an expectation so far unsupported by the few studies available.

Experimenter

The issue of obstetrical medication effects, like that of heredity vs. environment, has generated controversy and strong feelings. For this reason it is advisable for the investigator to collect data by mechanical means (not often feasible in obstetrical medication studies) or to use ''blind'' or ''naive'' experimenters in collecting and analyzing the data. A blind experimenter is one who is aware of the purpose of the experiment but is not aware of the subjects' status with respect to the independent variable. A naive experimenter is not even aware of the experimental purpose. Many of the studies summarized in Table 3-3 have used blind or naive experimenters.

Mothers

Like their babies, mothers who served as subjects in obstetrical medication studies have generally been healthy and low risk, with normal, uncomplicated pregnancies and deliveries. Both primiparas (women giving birth for the first time) and multiparas (women who have previously given birth) have been represented in obstetrical medication effect studies, although parity has not always been specified. The importance of parity as a variable stems from the fact that primiparas usually have longer labors, which may in itself affect infant outcome.

Measures

Given the infant's limited repertoire of behavior and the limited age range within which they have been studied, there is a remarkable diversity in the measures used as dependent variables in drug studies. Nonsocial behaviors are best represented. These include perception, attention, muscular strength, motor coordination, and vegetative functioning. About half the measures in this broad category are psychophysiologic: habituation to auditory, visual, and tactile stimuli; EEG; state; sucking; heart rate responses; motor movements. The other half are items from neurological-behavioral-pediatric scales: Brazelton's neonatal assessment scale, Scanlon's neurobehavioral test, the Bayley motor and mental scales, the Prechtl-Beintema neurological examination, the Graham-Rosenblith scale, and the Collaborative Perinatal pediatric-neurological examination.

Social behavior is represented by only four studies in Table 3-3 (Bakeman, et al., 1975; Brown, et al., 1975; Parke et al., 1972; and Richards and Bernal, 1972). (This tally excludes the "social" items on the Bayley mental scale.) In these studies, the principals are typically mother and infant, though one study (Parke et al., 1972) also measured father-infant interaction. Infants have been of neonatal age, and the situational focus has generally been on interaction during feeding.

Behavioral Outcome

In this section we examine the empirical results of obstetrical medication studies, first in terms of drug effects and then in terms of the type of dependent measure employed, and in terms of outcome as affected by subjects' age.

Drug Effects

OVERALL EFFECTS OF DRUGS

Of the studies outlined in Table 3-3, by far the largest number, 20, show substantial behavioral effects following perinatal drug administration. "Substantial" is arbitrarily defined as significant for half or more of the dependent variables at one or more of the test ages. Nine studies [Aleksandrowicz and Aleksandrowicz, 1974b; Bakeman et al., 1975; Brackbill, 1976; Friedman et al., 1978; Horowitz et al., 1977 (Uruguayan sample); Kraemer et al., 1972; Richards and Bernal, 1972; Tronick, 1976; Yang, 1976] show results that are significant but less substantial, and two [Horowitz et al., 1970 (Israeli sample); Parke, et al., 1972] show nonsignificant results, defined as significant for fewer than one-fourth of the dependent variables or items. (If one were to take the author's own assessment of outcome, this tally would be less conservative: 26 strongly positive studies, 3 less positive, and 2 negative.) The direction of these behavioral changes is uniformly toward degradation of performance or interference with normal function.

Aside from strength of results, what about strength of drugs used in these studies? Obviously, significant results *within* studies must relate to differences in total dosage of any one drug and/or to differences in potency or strength of the drugs compared.[6] But do dosage and potency also account, at least in part, for the difference in significant outcomes *between* studies? Apparently. Of the 11 studies showing negative or weakly positive results, none sampled high-potency drugs or drugs given in high total doses.[7] On the other hand, high-dosage/high-potency administrations are well represented among the studies showing strongly positive outcome. For example, almost all the studies of general anesthetic effect fall in the outcome category.

OUTCOME BY DRUG CLASS

Some investigators have not been able to specify their independent variable more narrowly than "premedication agents" or even "drugs." Others have been able to specify their variables generically as a class of drugs: analgesics, tranquilizers, and the like. It is informative to look at results by this next level of generality.

Types of Pre-Anesthetic Medication. Three investigators have singled out sedative-hypnotics (all barbiturates) for study. These investigators found that barbiturates affected sucking (Kron et al., 1966), EEG (Hughes et al., 1948), and Brazelton test scores (Aleksandrowicz and Aleksandrowicz, 1974b). Sostek et al. (1976) confirm the effect of barbiturates on Rosenblith test scores.

Eight studies have focused on the effects of analgesics, for the most part meperidine. Effects have been found on Brazelton and Scanlon test scores (Brackbill et al., 1974a; Hodgkinson et al., 1976a, 1976b, 1976c), on EEG (Brower, 1974; Hughes et al., 1950; Satran and Rosen, 1966) and on mother-infant interaction (Richards and Bernal, 1972).

Oxytocins have been the object of only two behavioral studies—without demonstrable effects in one using Scanlon test scores (Hodgkinson et al., 1976c) and with mixed effects in the other, using visual fixation and habituation measures (Friedman et al., 1978). [See Liston and Campbell (1974) on the nonbehavioral effects of oxytocin.]

Tranquilizers are difficult to assess as a class since their use is almost always ancillary and hence tends to be confounded with the administration of other drugs. Brower's (1974) EEG study is one exception. In this, meperidine administration was compared to meperidine plus diazepam and to meperidine plus promethazine. No difference was found among the three groups, though there was a significant difference between these three groups and a comparison group receiving no meperidine.

It may be important to note that with one or two possible exceptions, the strongest demonstrations of premedication effects have been found during the neonatal period.

Seven studies, four of them longitudinal, indicate that the use of general anesthetics leads to poorer infant performance scores than does the use of regional/conduction anesthetics (Hodgkinson et al., 1976b, 1976c; Broman and Brackbill, in progress; Brackbill, 1976; Moreau and Birch, 1974; Conway and Brackbill, 1970; and Aleksandrowicz and Aleksandrowicz, 1974b). In addition, one study (Scanlon et al., 1974) indicates that conduction anesthetic is more degrading than local infiltration or no anesthe-

---

[6]"Potency" is defined here in lay terms as strength or intensity of effect; its pharmacological definition, in terms of dose-response curve parameters, can be found in Goodman and Gilman (1975, p. 25).

[7]An exception is the report by Kraemer et al. (1972). High-potency drugs were apparently included here but grouped for comparison purposes in such a way that drug effects may have been cancelled out. The authors compared effects of local infiltration (low potency) *plus* general anesthetic (high potency) *to* conduction anesthetic (medium potency).

tic at all. There are no studies showing results in the opposite direction (general anesthetic better than conduction; conduction better than none or local).

SPECIFIC DRUGS

There are many studies in the obstetrical literature comparing the effects on labor and delivery of specific pre-anesthetic and anesthetic agents. With rare exception, however, these studies fall short of examining behavioral outcome for the neonatal subjects involved. The exceptions are reviewed here.

Among premedication agents, meperidine, which because of its widespread popularity is almost synonymous with "analgesia," has been the focus of seven studies as noted earlier. All have found strong effects on neonates following its administration.

Among general anesthetic agents, Hodgkinson et al (1976c) found higher scores on Scanlon scale items following ketamine than after thiopental. Among local agents used for conduction anesthesia, Scanlon et al. (1974, 1976) found higher Scanlon scale scores following bupivacaine than after lidocaine or mepivacaine.

Naloxone, a narcotic antagonist with no agonist properties, shows promise as a means of reversing meperidine-produced respiratory depression in neonates. Wiener et al. (1976) found significant and sustained improvement in some Scanlon scale items among babies affected by meperidine and subsequently treated with naloxone. Improvement on nonbehavioral measures—Apgar, respiration rate, alveolar carbon dioxide concentration, and alveolar ventilation—has also been found by Evans et al. (1975).

DOSAGE TIME

The interval between drug administration and delivery was a focus of study in four investigations. In two of the four studies, dosage time was significantly related to outcome (Brackbill, 1974a; Stechler, 1964); in the other two, dosage time was nearly significant (Conway and Brackbill, 1970; Yang et al., 1976). The results for these four studies are mixed: In two (both involving meperidine), longer dosage times were associated with poorer outcome (Brackbill et al., 1974a; Conway and Brackbill, 1970). In the remaining two studies, directional outcome is either mixed (Yang et al., 1976) or else shorter dosage times are associated with poorer outcomes (Stechler, 1964).

VARIABLES OTHER THAN DRUGS?

Some variables, principally parity and length of labor, tend to be correlated with drug administration and with each other. One may well question whether they are also related to behavioral outcome.

Parity.   Primiparous women have longer labors and are administered more drugs than multiparous women. Parity is not clearly related to infant's behavioral outcome, however. Of the 14 studies in Table 3-3 that did examine this relationship, by far the majority (10) found nonsignificant results. Results were significant, though not especially strong, for three others (Brown et al., 1975; Dubignon et al., 1969; Kraemer et al., 1972) and were suggestive for a fourth (Conway and Brackbill, 1970).

Labor.   As just noted, labor is related to both parity and drug dosage. Is it also related to infant outcome? The answer to this question is not clear. Of the 14 studies analyzing labor outcome relationships, eight found nonsignificant results, two a trend toward significance, and four significant results. For the last six studies, the direction of results was consistent: longer labor was associated with poorer infant performance, where quality of performance could be determined.

Outcome as Affected by Dependent Measure

MEASURES OF SOCIAL INTERACTION

Four studies have asked whether obstetrical medication affects social interaction between mother and infant or father and infant. None found strong evidence of drug effects (though the authors of the four articles would probably disagree with this conclusion). Evidence was positive but weak in two cases (Bakeman et al., 1975; Richards and Bernal, 1972) and lacking in the other two cases (Brown et al., 1975; Parke et al., 1972).

PSYCHOPHYSIOLOGIC MEASURES

Muscular Strength and Motor Coordination. In their analysis of 3500 8-month Bayley scale scores, Broman and Brackbill (in progress) found that 67% of the motor scale items were significantly related to prior medication, whereas only 37% of the mental scale items were so related. Most of the significant items tapped gross motor activities of a strenuous nature, principally attempts to sit, stand, and walk, rather than fine motor abilities.

Conway and Brackbill (1970) also found Bayley motor and mental scales to be differentially sensitive to potency of delivery medication. In their study, when subjects were 4 weeks of age, the correlation between quality of infant performance and Bayley motor scale scores was -0.62 $(P<.01)$ whereas the correlation between performance and mental scale scores was -0.40 (NS).

Conway and Brackbill also found, when their subjects were tested at age 2 days and again at age 5 days, that the muscle tension subscale of the Graham test was far more sensitive to obstetrical medication than the vision and maturation subscales.

Standley et al. (1974) studied the effects of analgesia and anesthesia on three clusters of Brazelton neonatal scale items: alertness, irritability, and motor maturity. Motor maturity showed by far the strongest relationship to both analgesia and anesthesia. According to Standley (1977), this cluster has the heaviest factor loadings on three items: motor maturity, tremulousness, and startle.

Finally, it should be noted that those habituation/response decrement studies (reviewed below) showing consistently strong obstetrical medication effects all made use of a motor response.

Decrement or Habituation of the Orienting Response. Several investigators have used the habituation paradigm as a test for obstetrical medication effects. For this purpose, a stimulus is presented repeatedly and note taken of the speed with which the infant decreases rate of responding or stops responding altogether. Brackbill et al. (1974a, 1974b), Conway and Brackbill (1970), Moreau and Birch (1974), and VanderMaelen et al. (1975) have used motor responding to auditory stimuli; Brackbill (1976) and Moreau and Birch (1974), heart rate responding to auditory stimulation; Moreau and Birch (1974), motor responding to a tactile stimulus; and Friedman et al. (1978), motor responding to a visual stimulus.

According to classical Pavlovian theory, the modality of the stimulus and the nature of the response should not affect rate of decrement of the unconditioned orienting reflex. According to empirical results, however, these do seem to matter. For neonatal subjects, all five studies using a motor response to an auditory stimulus have demonstrated a strong negative relationship between rate of decrement and prior medication (meaning that medication prolongs responding). On the other hand, the two studies using heart rate response to auditory stimuli have failed to find such a relationship for neonates. (Age differences provide a further complication here; see "autonomic responding" below.) Moderate relationships between decrement and obstetrical medication have also been found for heart rate responding to a tactile stimulus (Moreau and Birch, 1974) and motor responding to a visual stimulus (Friedman et al., 1978).

Are there differences by modality? Friedman et al. (1978) found response decrement to visual stimuli less closely related to obstetrical medication than had other investigators using response decrement to auditory stimuli (Brackbill et al., 1974a, 1974b; Conway and Brackbill, 1970; Moreau and Birch, 1974; VanderMaelen et al., 1975). Friedman et al. (1978) suggest that pharmacologic agents may affect information processing (or other responses) to different extents in the different modalities. On the other hand, Sigman reports (1977) for 130 4-month-olds that the distribution of visual fixation time between novel and familiar stimuli differed significantly as a function of amount of prior anesthetic medication.

Sucking, Feeding.   With one exception (Yang et al., 1976), all studies of sucking and feeding show strongly significant relationships to perinatal medication history. Furthermore, the direction of results is consistent across these studies. Specifically, obstetrical medication has been found to decrease amount of food consumed and weight gained (Brazelton, 1961; Dubignon et al., 1969; Kron et al., 1966); sucking rate and pressure Dubignon et al., 1969; Kron et al., 1966; Richards and Bernal, 1972 [(trend only)]; number and vigor of sucks (Hodgkinson et al., 1976b, 1976c); responsiveness to feeding (Brazelton, 1961); and to alter feeding intervals (Kraemer et al., 1972). The subjects in these studies were all neonates.

Autonomic Responding.   Autonomic responses, chiefly heart rate, have been used in several medication studies spanning the 1st year of life. With one exception [Moreau and Birch, 1974 (tactile-stimulus group)] significant correlations between obstetrical medication and alterations in autonomic responding appear to be age-linked. Specifically, they have not been demonstrated in newborns [Moreau and Birch, 1974 (auditory-stimulus sample); Yang et al., 1976], in 1-month-olds (Brackbill, 1976), or in 4-month-olds (Brackbill, 1976; Broman and Brackbill, in progress). (Again, the only exception is the Moreau and Birch finding of heart rate decrement to tactile stimuli in neonates.) At older ages, however, the relationship between autonomic responding and obstetrical medication becomes apparent. Brackbill's 8-month data (1976) on heart rate decrement to auditory stimulation suggest differences in form of response as a function of obstetrical medication—specifically, a shift from orienting to defensive reflex in infants born under high-potency anesthesia conditions. For 12-month-old subjects, Broman and Brackbill (in progress) found that abnormal heart rate was significantly associated with the administration of high-potency anesthetics among Collaborative Perinatal Study subjects, although this outcome had failed to reach significance for the same subjects at age 4 months. In addition it should be noted that the 12-month data also showed significant relationships between potency of anesthetic used during delivery and subsequent increases in blood pressure, respiration rate, and sweating.

EEG.   There have been four major studies and two brief reports (Rosen et al., 1974;

Satran and Rosen 1966) of obstetrical medication effects on EEG. These studies, which have all been restricted to newborns, have all shown changes in EEG following obstetrical medication. Borgstedt and Rosen (1968) found "alterations" as a function of obstetrical medication. [Their Fig. 1 implies the major alteration was low voltage, fast activity, in confirmation of an earlier finding by Satran and Rosen (1966)] Hughes et al. (1948, 1950) observed a depressed activity, often occipital and often at variance with a clinical picture of alertness. Brower (1974) found changes (also often occipital) more often following auditory, visual, olfactory, and tactile stimulation than during prestimulation, baseline periods.

Sleep; State.   Several studies, all carried out on neonates, have shown sleep and state changes following drug administration. Emde et al. (1975) found dosage positively correlated with increases in quiet sleep and decreases in wakefulness. Yang et al. (1976) found dosage time to be positively correlated with increases in quiet sleep and decreases in active sleep. An effect of medication on state lability (frequency of change from one state to another) has been found by Brackbill et al. (1974a). Horowitz (1970) for the Kansas and Israeli samples but not for the Uruguayan sample, and by Standley et al. (1974).

STANDARDIZED NEUROLOGICAL-BEHAVIORAL-PEDIATRIC SCALES

The literature on obstetrical medication effects includes use of four scales suitable for neonates—the Brazelton, Graham-Rosenblith, Prechtl-Beintema, and Scanlon scales— and two suitable for the post-neonatal period, the Bayley scales and the Collaborative Perinatal Project Pediatric-Neurological examinations. These scales were all constructed, if not for purposes of general assessment, then at least for purposes other than evaluation in behavioral toxicology. It should not be surprising then that results using these scales for the assessment of pharmacological effects on behavior are (1) sometimes contradictory and (2) never easy to interpret in terms of functional common denominators underlying the plethora of diverse items. To illustrate the point about disparity in results, consider that the Scanlon scale contains 15 items, 12 of which are the same as Brazelton items.[8] Despite this considerable item overlap, the Scanlon scale frequently appears to be sensitive to drug effects when the Brazelton scale does not. Thus, if one counts across all items and all studies using the Scanlon scale, the resulting tally is 207 items $\times$ drug comparisons, 104 of which are statistically significant (50%). The same tally for all Brazelton items across all studies yields 1335 comparisons, only 40 of which show statistically significant sensitivity to drugs (3%). How can this be if one scale is but a capsule version of the other? (There is a likely explanation for this disparity, and it will be discussed below.)

Muller et al. (1971) went beyond the infancy period to ask whether obstetrical medication (and other perinatal factors) might be related to a variety of developmental indices at age 9. Of the 12 indices, Lorge-Thorndike IQ showed a significant negative relationship to potency of anesthesia used during delivery.

Outcome as Affected by Subjects' Age

Table 3-4 indicates how obstetrical medication studies are distributed by subjects' age and overall level of significance. Although the majority of studies have been carried out on neonates, significant outcomes are by no means restricted to that age level. Two studies

---

[8]Orienting to sound stimulus, response decrement to sound stimulus, response decrement to light stimulus, decrement in response to pin prick, pull to sit, general body tone, alertness, rooting, sucking, motor reflex, arm recoil, placing.

Table 3-4. Outcome in Obstetrical Medication Studies: Effects of Age and Strength of Results

	Neonate	1–3 Months	4 Months	8 Months	12 Months
Significant and substantial	Borgstedt & Rosen (1968) Brackbill et al. (1974a, 1974b) Brazelton (1961) Brower (1974) Conway & Brackbill (1970) Dubignon et al. (1969) Emde et al. (1975) Hodgkinson et al (1976a, 1976b, 1976c) Hughes et al. (1948, 1950) Kron et al. (1966) Moreau & Birch (1974) Scanlon et al. (1974, 1976) Standley et al. (1974) Stechler (1964) VanderMaelen (1975)	Conway & Brackbill (1970)	Broman & Brackbill (in progress)	Broman & Brackbill (in progress)	Broman & Brackbill (in progress)
Less substantial	Aleksandrowicz & Aleksandrowicz (1974) Bakeman et al. (1975) Friedman et al. (1977) Horowitz et al. (Uruguayan sample, in press) Kraemer et al. (1972) Richards & Bernal (1972) Tronick et al. (1976) Wiener et al. (1976) Yang et al. (1976)	Aleksandrowicz & Aleksandrowicz (1974)	Friedman et al. (1977)	Brackbill (1976)	
Nonsignificant	Brown et al. (1975) Horowitz et al. (Israeli sample, in press) Parke et al. (1972)	Brackbill (1976) Horowitz et al. (Israeli sample, in press)	Brackbill (1976)		

that have followed subjects longest are Brackbill (1976), in which infants were tested longitudinally at 1, 4, and 8 months, and Broman and Brackbill (in progress) in which infants were examined at 4, 8, and 12 months. In each case obstetric medication effects were as strong or stronger at the oldest testing date as at the youngest. Additionally, there are two retrospective studies in which obstetrical drugs have been included among a variety of independent variables. In one study, Muller et al. (1971) found 9-year Lorge-Thorndike IQ scores to be related to use of obstetrical medication in a sample of 536 subjects. In the other, Goldstein et al. (1976) found type of anesthesia to be related to Cattell DQ score at age 1 year in a sample of 322 infants. It is important to note that in all four studies the long-term effects relate to prior use of anesthetic agents rather than to analgesics.

Other Studies

This review is limited to the effects of perinatally administered drugs on the behavior of human infants. There are related areas of research that fall beyond these limits but that are so important they must be mentioned even though they cannot be reviewed thoroughly. These research areas include epidemiological studies of the cumulative effects of exposure to low levels of inhalant anesthetics among operating-room personnel, experimental studies of behavioral effects of low-level inhalant anesthetics, experimental studies of structural and functional changes in animals exposed as fetuses or infants to anesthetics, and studies of the effects on human infants of chronic maternal addiction to narcotics. Each will be described briefly in turn.

Epidemiologic Studies of Operating-Room Personnel: Cumulative Effects of Exposure to Low Levels of Inhalant Anesthetics

In 1967, Vaisman published a study showing increases in several morbidity/mortality statistics (including excessive spontaneous abortion rates) among Soviet anesthesiologists. Vaisman attributed these unfavorable outcomes to unfavorable working conditions, including the low levels of gaseous agents that continually pollute the air in "unscavenged" operating rooms. Quite independently, and about the same time, anesthesiologists in other countries were becoming concerned about the same problems. Soon there were similar epidemiological studies underway in Europe, in the United Kingdom, and in the United States concerning occupational risks for physician anesthetists, for nurse anesthetists, for dentists who frequently administer general anesthesia, and for the unexposed wives of the male members within this category of "operating-room personnel."

The overall results of the studies examining mortality statistics may be summarized as follows: Among exposed male operating-room personnel, deaths from suicide (Bruce et al., 1968, 1974a), from diseases of the liver (Cohen et al., 1974), and from some cancers (Bruce et al., 1968) are significantly higher than for other, comparable groups. Among exposed female personnel, mortality rates are significantly higher for diseases of liver and kidney and for some forms of cancer (Cohen et al., 1974).

On statistics relating to morbidity and reproductive problems, exposed operating-room personnel show an increased frequency of liver disease (Cohen et al., 1975). Exposed females also show increased rates of involuntary infertility (Knill-Jones et al., 1972), increased rates of spontaneous abortion (Askrog and Harvald, 1970; Cohen et al., 1971, 1974; Knill-Jones et al., 1972, 1975; Rosenberg and Kirves, 1973; Vaisman, 1967), and increased rates of congenital abnormalities in their offspring [Corbett et al., 1974; Knill-Jones et al., 1972 (trend only)]. Exposed personnel also have a higher proportion of female than male children than do comparable groups (Askrog and Harvald, 1970).

As a final statistic of note, three studies have found that reproductive risk increases for *nonexposed* wives of male operating-room personnel. Cohen et al. (1975) found higher rates of spontaneous abortion among the nonexposed wives of exposed males. Cohen et al. (1974) and Knill-Jones et al. (1975) found higher rates of congenital abnormalities among the children of exposed fathers.

Experimental Studies of Behavioral Effects of Low-Level Inhalant Anesthetics

Considerable work has been undertaken to discern the effects on human and animal behavior of inhalant anesthetics, including nitrous oxide, ether, halothane, enflurane, cyclopropane, methoxyflurane, and other agents. The amount of agent administered is usually small in order to simulate the levels to which the physicians and nurses are actually exposed in unscavenged operating rooms. The human subjects in these studies have for the most part been healthy volunteers (e.g., Bruce et al., 1974b, 1975, 1976); occasionally they are patients (e.g., Adam, 1973). Animals have also served as subjects. (The animal literature is reviewed by Porter, 1972.) The dependent variables have included a wide variety of learning tasks and cognitive/perceptual/motor performance tasks. In those studies using human subjects, the experimenters have frequently chosen measures that are functionally similar to the operating-room tasks required of an anesthesiologist.

In general, results show that behavioral impairment under or following low-level anesthetic administration depends on dose, on duration of inhalant administration, and on timing of test administration relative to inhalant administration. Degree of impairment also depends upon the type of behavior measured. Among learning tasks, those most vulnerable to anesthetic effects are avoidance learning tasks, particularly passive avoidance (Porter, 1972). Among performance tasks, those most vulnerable to anesthetic effects fall in the broad category of information processing—for example, signal detection—as well as short-term auditory and visual memory. Timed motor performance also suffers. In general, as Steinberg (1954) points out, the more complex a task the greater the probability it will reflect impairment. Impairment is typically found to be greater for immature than mature animals (Porter, 1972).

Experimental Studies of Structural and Functional Changes in Animals Exposed as Fetuses or Infants to Anesthetics

In recent years, experimentalists have looked to animal models in studying physiological and behavioral effects of exposure to low-level inhalant anesthetics. Subjects in these studies have been rats, for the most part; mice, guinea pigs, and chicks have also been tested. Following prenatal exposure of these animals to inhalant anesthetics, investigators have found evidence of increased fetal death (Corbett et al., 1973), liver degeneration (Chang et al., 1975c), pathologic changes in CNS development (Chang et al., 1976; Quimby et al., 1974), teratogenic anomalies (Smith et al., 1965), and learning deficits (Quimby et al., 1974). Among immature animals exposed postnatally to inhalant anesthetics, there is evidence of liver damage (Stevens et al., 1975) and changes in blood and marrow (Aldrete and Virtue, 1968). Animals exposed as adults show similar patterns of pathologic changes in CNS (Chang et al., 1974b), liver (Chang et al., 1974a, 1975b; Kosek et al., 1972), and kidney (Chang et al., 1975a).

Studies of Children of Narcotic-Addicted Mothers

The 1960s ushered in a new problem for clinicians: the passively addicted newborn. Throughout that decade and the first part of the 1970s, the number of pregnant women addicted to heroin or to methadone increased steadily, despite a drop in the national birth rate. In one urban hospital in 1972, one of every 27 births was to a drug-addicted mother (Zelson, 1975).

Most, but not all, passively addicted infants show withdrawal symptoms involving CNS, gastrointestinal, and respiratory functions. The specific symptoms include irritability, motor disturbances (restlessness, tremors, tremulousness, hypertonicity), crying and inconsolability, sleep-pattern disturbances or inability to sleep, poor feeding and regurgitation, and, in severe cases, convulsions. Clinical characteristics in these cases have been described by Ramer and Lodge (1975) and clinical care by Neumann and Cohen (1975) and Zelson (1975). For general reviews, the reader is referred to Kron et al. (1977) as well as to the symposium proceedings published in the journal *Addictive Diseases,* 1975, vol. 2.

Of late a few behavioral studies have appeared that highlight functional aberrations in passively addicted children (e.g., Kron et al., 1975a, 1975b, (1977); McCreary et al., 1976; Strauss et al., 1975). There are some notable similarities in the test behaviors of children exposed to narcotics chronically and prenatally and those exposed acutely and perinatally. For example, on the Brazelton scale, chronically and acutely exposed neonates show the same pattern of differences from control-group scores, with the largest significant difference appearing on items measuring irritability, a smaller though still significant difference on motor maturity items, and no significant difference on items measuring alertness [cf. Standley et al. (1974) to Kron et al. (1975a].

Functional aberrations tend to persist in passively addicted children. In a follow-up study of 4-year-olds exposed prenatally to heroin, McCreary et al. (1976) found marked deficits in some cognitive skills (particularly attention and concentration), decreased rates of physical growth, and increased frequencies of behavior problems when these children were compared with three control groups matched for postnatal drug-culture exposure, prenatal and postnatal risk indices, and socioeconomic status.

DISCUSSION

Review of Major Findings

The empirical results just presented may be summarized as follows:

- Drugs given to mothers during labor and delivery have subsequent effects on infant behavior. Almost all of the studies reviewed found statistically significant effects of obstetrical medication. Furthermore, the direction of the effect is consistent across studies in showing behavioral degradation or disruption. No study has demonstrated functional enhancement following obstetrical medication.

- Obstetrical medication effects are dose-related. This conclusion relates both to within-study analyses and to between-study comparisons. Those investigations showing the most substantial results are also those in which mothers received high-potency drugs or high total doses of drugs.

- The behavioral effects of obstetrical medication are not transient. The ages of infants studied have ranged from 1 day to 1 year. There is no real evidence of decrease in overall effect within this age range. (By the same token, there is a strong possibility that effects found at later ages relate more to the prior use of anesthetic than to the prior use of pre-anesthetic medication.)

• Obstetrical medication effects are more pronounced in some functional areas than others. Overall, the strongest effects can be seen in selected areas of cognitive function and gross motor abilities. Some questions of outcome in relation to measurement parameters will be taken up in greater detail below.

• Insufficient data and contradictory results prevent drawing conclusions about differential effects of obstetrical medication by race, ethnic background, or socioeconomic status. Contradictory findings also preclude definite conclusions on the role of length of labor in determining infant behavioral outcome. There is no evidence to suggest that there are differential effects of obstetrical medication by sex of offspring or maternal parity.

Outcome in Relation to Design and Measurement Parameters

Present Stress measures Prior Stress

Results of the empirical studies reviewed in this chapter show a wide variety of behavioral effects attributable to obstetrical medication. However, it is also clear that within this array of significant results, some of the measures and some of the test conditions are more sensitive than others to drug effects. Nonsocial measures are more drug-sensitive than social variables. Measures reflecting ability to inhibit responding are more drug-sensitive than measures of ability to respond. Measures of gross motor ability, as reflected in muscular strength and motor coordination, are more vulnerable to obstetrical medication than are measures of fine motor ability. Responses innervated by the somatic nervous system more often show drug effects—at least initially—than do autonomic responses. Measures reflecting information processing appear to be more susceptible to drugs than measures reflecting stimulus intake.

In addition to drug-sensitivity differences among measures, the results also suggest drug-sensitivity differences among test conditions. Specifically, the probability that obstetrical medication effects will be found appears to be a function of the extent to which the tests, test items, or test conditions are stressful—that is, the extent to which they demand from the infant intensive efforts, strenuous exertion, high-energy output, continued coping with environmentally imposed stimuli, or sustained attention. As this reviewer has said elsewhere (1975, pp. 27–28),

> The greater the environmental demands on the infant and the more complex the action required of him to cope with these demands, the greater the difference in quality of performance among infants in terms of their perinatal medication history. It is the neonate's ability to cope effectively that is the most important predictor of later functioning and it is coping ability that most sensitively reflects the effects of perinatal medication.

In conjunction with differential sensitivity of test items themselves, it also appears that some test-scoring procedures are more sensitive than others to prior drug administration. Specifically, scoring procedures that record the infant's average, most variable, or even worst performance are apparently more revealing of perinatal history than are scoring procedures that record only the infant's best performance (as in the Brazelton scale, for example; see Brazelton, 1973, p. 9). This is the most likely explanation for the remarkable fact, presented earlier, that the same test items are significantly related to obstetrical medication when administered and scored by one experimenter but are nonsignificantly related when administered and scored by another experimenter.[9]

Modality Differences?

From studies of embryological and behavioral development we know that sensory modalities mature at different times during fetal and infant development (Gottlieb, 1971). For example, the auditory modality is ontogenetically (as well as phylogenetically) older than the visual modality. Within these sensory systems there are separate sensory functions that also mature at different times. For example, in the human being, visual acuity matures by 1 to 3 months (Banks, 1977), while binocularity does not peak until age 2 to 3 years (Banks et al., 1975). If maturation and plasticity are inversely related, it is possible that a single traumatic event—for example, a pharmacological insult—could affect a particular sensory function in one system but not in another if it occurs just prior to the onset of the sensitive period for that function. This possibility was raised earlier with respect to possible differences in drug effects on habituation in the auditory and visual systems. Although there is insufficient evidence to decide this point for human development, it is worthwhile noting supporting evidence from animal studies. Hubel and Wiesel (1970), for example, have demonstrated in the kitten that sensitivity to lack of visual input begins suddenly, near the 4th week of life. Prior to that time, monocular eyelid closure produces little or no effect, whereas starting at that time and during the ensuing sensitive period, closure for even brief periods produces permanent ocular dominance.

Labor and Parity

LENGTH OF LABOR AND ANALGESIC DOSAGE

Several of the studies reviewed found a statistically significant association between length of labor and analgesic dosage. Many investigators have interpreted this outcome directionally, concluding that the longer the labor, the greater the pain and the greater the need for a pain-relieving drug. For example, Brown et al. (1975, p. 681) state, "Mothers who had longer labors typically received more analgesic drugs." An interpretation in this direction may be empathically appealing but may not be empirically correct. Data from experimental studies of both human beings (e.g., Petrie et al., 1976) and animals (e.g., Nuite, 1976) indicate that administration of analgesics and tranquilizers decreases uterine activity (Petrie et al., 1976) and prolongs labor (Nuite, 1976). This is not to deny that prolongation of labor may contribute to increased drug consumption, but to point out that the initiating event in the cycle seems to be drug administration rather than longer labor.

Direction of interpretation aside, it is apparent that length of labor and drug dosage tend to be confounded, and their separate effects on infant outcome difficult to disentangle. It would be possible to separate these variables experimentally by studying cases of elective cesarean section (performed prior to the onset of labor) that differ in terms of anesthetic medication and/or pre-anesthetic medication.

[9]Scanlon (1977) suggests an alternative explanation: Since the Scanlon test is generally administered 24 h earlier than the Brazelton test, the Scanlon test can be expected to show higher correlations with obstetric medication parameters.

Parity and Infant Outcome

Four of the studies reviewed found a significant or near-significant correlation between parity and infant outcome (Brown et al., 1975; Conway and Brackbill, 1970; Dubignon et al., 1969; Kraemer et al., 1972). In each case, there was a direct relationship between parity and quality of infant performance—that is, laterborns performed better than firstborns. As we know from other literature, being first-born does not in and of itself predispose to impaired performance. On the contrary, there is a large body of literature documenting an inverse relationship between family size and quality of performance on achievement and ability tests (e.g., Zajonc, 1976). The Collaborative Perinatal Study data, as a case in point, consistently show a negative relationship between maternal parity and child's mental test score at 8 months, 4 years, and 7 years (Broman, 1977). Since the four studies that found a correlation between parity and infant outcome also found a correlation between length of labor and outcome, it would better serve logic and parsimony to regard the parity/outcome correlation as an artifact of the established correlations between parity/labor and parity/dosage.

Dosage Time

Clearly, the significance of dosage time for behavioral outcome depends on the toxicity of the parent drug and its metabolites. Drugs differ considerably in the number and pharmacological parameters of their metabolites. For example, it is the opinion of Morrison et al. (1973), based on their animal research, that normeperidine, the principal metabolite of meperidine, is more toxic than the parent compound. This would mean that at the time of cord clamp, infants left with relatively greater amounts of normeperidine are at a greater disadvantage than those left with relatively greater amounts of meperidine.

Nonbehavioral Measures

This review is restricted to behavioral effects of obstetrical medication. Nevertheless, some mention must be made of nonbehavioral measures that are often used in medically oriented studies of obstetrical drugs. The most popular of these measures are mortality, Apgar score, respiratory depression, skin discoloration, blood gas values, and drug levels in fetal, maternal, and cord blood. My reason for mentioning nonbehavioral measures is to draw the reader's attention to their disproportionately small contribution to the bottom-line question: the biological significance of early, acute pharmacologic stress for later functioning. More than 30 drug/behavior studies have been reviewed in this chapter. Most showed strong and behaviorally consistent drug effects even after the drug had presumably been cleared. On the whole, nonbehavioral measures show no such strength or consistency. At best, drug effects as reflected in these measures are transient and spotty. At the same time, there is no reason to suppose that nonbehavioral measures *should* predict later functioning, since our criteria of adequate functioning are dominated by behavioral components and behavioral priorities.

Ethical Considerations

Knowing what we now know about obstetrical medication effects on infants makes it ethically impossible at this point to use a research design in which women are assigned randomly to experimental and control groups differing in drug dosage or potency. Except for serendipitous experiments in nature or the like, we must confine ourselves to correlational designs and the use of multivariate analysis to unravel statistically what would otherwise be manipulated experimentally. This is not such a gloomy prospect as long as studies are cross-validated (preferably by different investigators) and as long as human research is supplemented by experimental studies using animal models in which structural and functional development at time of birth is roughly equivalent to that of the human being. There has been considerable cross-validation of studies and replication of findings at the human level, but very little research using animal models. Hopefully, more animal work will be forthcoming in the future.

Long-Term Effects: Possible Explanations and Consequences

If future research establishes that perinatal medication effects are permanent, two questions will become even more important than they are now: Where and how are these effects mediated anatomically and physiologically? What are the long-term functional consequences for the child's adaptation to his environment? Although there are at present no directly relevant studies that provide definitive answers to these questions, there are studies that may be of indirect relevance. One such set of studies are those conducted by Levine (e.g., Levine and Mullins, 1968) and by Denenberg (e.g., Denenberg and Zarrow, 1971) on long-term effects of early stress. These studies show, according to the investigators, that animals stressed (or "manipulated," in their terms) during infancy react as adults more adaptively to stressful situations than do control animals. The early manipulations include such diverse operations as hormonal modifications, handling, electric shock, or simply removing infants from maternal cages for a brief daily period. Dependent variables, which appear to reflect these earlier manipulations, measured in experimental and control groups of adult animals, include open-field activity and defecation, consumatory behavior, various tests of timidity, avoidance learning, discrimination learning, exploratory behavior, aggression, maternal behavior, body weight, sexual precocity, resistance to leukemia virus, abscorbic acid depletion, and ability to survive terminal stress.

The general finding from which these investigators concluded that early stress leads to greater adaptive potential is that as adults, experimental animals are significantly less responsive than controls to mild stimuli but significantly more responsive than controls to noxious, stressful, or potentially dangerous stimuli. Both Levine and Denenberg see developmental hormonal changes as the important mechanism underlying developmental behavioral differences. Levine hypothesizes that infancy represents a critical period for the setting of the adrenal "hormonostat" and that the number of settings (i.e., the sensitivity) of the hormonostat is a direct function of the number and breadth of infantile experiences. [Ader (1975) and Ader and Grota (1973) have criticized this conclusion and questioned the validity of its empirical base.]

A different conclusion about the later consequences of early stress may be drawn from many clinically oriented studies of human behavior development (e.g., Mednick et al., 1970). This conclusion, generally stated, is that early stress causes functional deficit and that this deficit, whether compensated or not, subtracts from the total adaptive reserves of the organism. One must consider here two sets of conditions: the number of environmentally imposed demands on the organism for adaptation and the extent of the organism's biological capabilities for coping effectively with these demands. In the laboratory, when one experimentally reduces the second factor, one may also adjust the constraints of the first. In real life, however, environmental demands are not so easily adjusted to balance functional capacities of the organism, so that loss of one function, even though compensated, may decrease the capacity of the organism as a whole to behave as the environment demands.

From their study of adolescents at risk for mental illness, Mednick et al. (1970, 1971) conclude that children who are genetically predisposed to mental illness *and* who have been subject to perinatal stress are less able to adapt to the stress of adolescence than children who are at risk in only one of these two respects. In other words, the greater the number or severity of early risks, the greater the probability that compensation will be ineffective in maintaining adaptive behavior in the face of later stress.

Mednick et al. suggest that the mechanism by which perinatal stress may produce permanent effects is through anoxia-produced damage to the hippocampus, which is not yet fully developed at time of birth. These authors print out that damage to the hippocampus has been shown to result in a failure of inhibition of ACTH released by the pituitary gland. This inhibitory influence is normally operative under stress. A damaged hippocampus under stress, however, does not provide an adequate inhibitory control of the pituitary gland, which leads to an oversecretion of ACTH. The oversecretion of ACTH underlies many behavioral aberrancies during stress, particularly a state of hyperarousal, according to Mednick et al. (1970, 1971). Whether the immediate cause of the effects reviewed in this chapter is hypoxia, the drugs themselves, their metabolites, or some combination of these is not yet clear.

Other data of possible relevance come from Ucko's (1965) study of children who had earlier experienced perinatal "asphyxiation." Ucko found no behavioral differences between these children and a normal group in routine, everyday situations. Under stress, however, the children who had suffered perinatal anoxia showed significantly more behavioral disturbances than did the normal children.

The investigations linking early stress, compensation, and breakdown under later stress, such as those of Mednick et al. and Ucko, may be similar dynamically to the present author's inference that the stress represented by obstetrical medication shows up to the extent that subsequently administered test items and conditions are themselves stressful.

Implications for Social Research and Public Policy

The Decision to Administer Drugs

For many illnesses today, treatment with drugs is the only treatment considered to be effective. In such cases both physician and patient consider drug therapy essential rather than optional. Hence, there is no real decision-making involved under these circumstances.

Neither pregnancy nor delivery is an illness. Administering drugs prenatally and perinatally is more often optional than essential, and there is plenty of room for decision-making. What are the relative contributions of the obstetrician and his patient to this decision-making process?

It is commonly assumed that the initiative for administering obstetrical pain-relieving drugs comes from the patient: the mother experiences pain, communicates this to the physician or nurse, and is in turn given an analgesic or anesthetic. This assumption is strengthened by the protocol, enacted by many obstetricians and childbirth-education teachers, of describing to the pregnant woman the veritable cornucopia of drugs available to her so that, it is implied, she may select what she needs at the appropriate time.

Nevertheless, there is no evidence to support the assumption that the mother plays a key role in the decision to use drugs. On the contrary, there is plenty of evidence, though largely circumstantial, that the patient has little if any say in the matter.

One source of empirical evidence comes from a study (Brown et al., 1972) relating maternal personality characteristics, measured prenatally and perinatally, to drugs administered perinatally. Brown et al. found no correlation between perinatal drug administration and perinatal pain or anxiety. Significant correlations were found, however, between perinatal drug administration and prenatal variables (anxiety, ego strength, and general adaptation to pregnancy). The authors conclude that labor and delivery medication does not match patient needs or demands and that the obstetrician's decision to administer obstetrical medication perinatally is based not on perinatal events but on the information he gathered about the woman during her pregnancy. A similar interpretation can be made for results found by Zuckerman et al. (1963).

In addition to this empirical evidence, there are several lines of circumstantial evidence suggesting that the mother's role in decision-making about drugs is subordinate to the physician's or nurse's role. One such line of evidence comes from the fact that there is a zero-order correlation between the number of drugs taken perinatally and the number taken during pregnancy,[10] when the intake of drugs (largely over-the counter drugs) is clearly under the woman's control.

Another line of evidence suggesting disproportionate roles in decision-making comes from the consistencies and differences among physicians' and hospitals' drug-administration practices that do not accord with the distribution of individual differences in pain sensitivity and pain relief. For example, there are wide and consistent differences in medication "habits" among obstetricians. Physicians' use of obstetrical agents is not random. It is highly selective, with little variability. Just as there are some physicians who habitually use epidural anesthetics, there are others who are known for their habitual use of general anesthetics. Similarly, there are wide and stable differences among hospitals, as the Collaborative Perinatal Study has documented (Broman, 1977). In this case as well the variability within hospitals sometimes approaches zero. For example, the author has visited obstetrical units in the United Kingdom and Africa where, without exception, every entering patient receives 100 mg of Demerol.

Still another argument against significant maternal contributions to decision-making is the widespread use by obstetricians of "standing orders" for medication. A standing order is a written directive allowing nurses and pharmacists to dispense medication in the physician's absence. It is, by definition, an order based on a general condition or illness rather than on individual needs. Therefore, the more a patient is treated according to the directives of the standing order, the less voice that patient has in decision-making about her own medication. A typical standing order for medication to be administered to all private patients of one Florida obstetrician reads as follows:

Routine Ante Partum Orders
Nembutal 200 mg. by mouth, as necessary
(Primigravida)
Demerol 75–100 mg.   Intramuscular, 1st dose
Largon 20 mg.
Scopolamine 0.4 mg.
Demerol 50 mg.
Largon 20 mg.   Intramuscular, every 2
Scopolamine 0.3 mg.   hours as necessary

[10]The source here is my calculation from adverse drug reaction data collected by Doering and others (1977).

> Deladumone OB 1 ampule intramuscular at 6 cm. dilatation,
>   as necessary
> 1000 cc Ringers lactate, intravenous (100 cc/hr.).
> All patients to have regional anesthesia.

How widespread is the use of standing orders? The existence of standing orders is not publicized. No national statistics document their distribution. In order to provide some idea of the incidence of this custom, the author interviewed Directors of Pharmacy Service for 10 hospitals geographically representative of the state of Florida. These hospitals all serve obstetrical patients. None is a teaching hospital. (Teaching hospitals frequently substitute a house staff person for standing orders.) In all 10 cases, the Pharmacy Directors reported that obstetrical standing orders are in widespread use. The estimated percentage of obstetrical staff using standing orders ranges in these 10 hospitals from 50% to 100%; the median is 85%; the mode, 100%.

To this point, the discussion on decision-making has focused on the use of drugs to relieve pain and anxiety. In the administration of drugs for other purposes, the decision-making initiative is more readily identifiable as the obstetrician's. An example is the use of oxytocin as a drug of convenience in initiating labor, as illustrated in the following editorial excerpt from the *British Journal of Anaesthesia:*

When labour is induced in the morning, in perhaps 60% of all patients, and certainly in the great majority of primigravidae, the number of deliveries occurring between midnight and 9 a.m. is much reduced. Consequently, anesthesia and the services of the anaesthetist will be required less often during the hours normally devoted to sleep.[11]

Feminist literature has denounced autocracy in the obstetrical unit (Arms, 1975; Haire, 1973; Rich, 1976; Shaw, 1974; Stewart, 1976). As yet, however, there are few empirical data on the cognitive, intrapersonal, interpersonal, and situational dynamics of decision-making in elective drug administration and consumption. Here is a clear and compelling need for the research skills and contributions of social psychology.

FDA Drug Testing: Safe and Effective for Whom?

Congress has charged the FDA with the responsibility for approving drugs as safe and effective before they are released for clinical use. In turn, drug manufacturers are charged with the responsibility for providing positive evidence of such safety and effectiveness to the FDA. Drug manufacturers have proved, to the FDA's satisfaction, the safety and effectiveness for the *mother* of drugs commonly used in obstetrical medication. However, as we have seen, empirical results obtained with adults do not automatically generalize to fetus or neonate: the neonate's pharmacologic response is often qualitatively different, and neonatal physiology is grossly immature in many important respects. Since generalization is not permissible, the neonate himself must be the object of study. However, evidence for safety and effectiveness of obstetrical medication drugs for infants has never been submitted by drug manufacturers nor required by the FDA prior to clearance of the drugs for clinical use. From the data presented in this review, it is clear that it would be difficult to find evidence that obstetrical drugs are safe and effective for infants.

THE FDA AND THE NULL HYPOTHESIS

Congressional requirements of safety and effectiveness assume the paradigm of illness or dysfunction that can be alleviated or removed altogether by a drug. This paradigm shows

[11]*British Journal of Anaesthesia,* 1974, *46,* p. 391.

up statistically as a significant difference between the drug under study and no drug at all or one already in use. However, the healthy fetus is not ill, and drugs cannot improve his status. Under such circumstances, the requirement of positive proof tends to drift toward a requirement of null "proof," so that emphasis shifts to finding no statistically significant differences between experimental and control groups as "evidence" that the drug under study does not dis-improve the infant's status. As I noted earlier, there are many gross measures of viability that have little or no relationship to later clinical status or behavioral function and that have a predictably rapid return to normal levels—for example, respiratory depression, blood gas parameters, measurable drug levels in fetal blood. If one chooses—as the FDA has chosen—to accept as necessary, sufficient, and valid indicators of drug safety and effectiveness such gross and irrevelant indicators as these rather than the more refined and biologically significant neurobehavioral indicators, one may easily conclude that obstetrical drugs are safe and effective for infants.

SUMMARY

This chapter reviews empirical evidence concerning effects of obstetrical medication on infant behavior. It also presents, in summary form, material on related topics: the early history of obstetrical anesthesia, criteria for drug evaluation, a description of the pre-anesthetic and anesthetic medications most frequently used in childbirth, estimates of the incidence of drug use in obstetrics, and results from epidemiological and experimental studies of cumulative effects on animals and human beings repeatedly exposed to low levels of inhalant anesthetics. Behavioral effects of obstetrical medication are discussed in terms of their relation to design and measurement parameters, possible explanations and long-term consequences, and implications for social research and public policy.

BIBLIOGRAPHY

Adam, N. Effects of general anesthetics on memory functions in man. *Journal of Comparative and Physiological Psychology,* 1973, **83,** 294–305.

Ader, R. Early experience and hormones: Emotional behavior and adrenocortical function. In B. E. Eleftheriou and R. L. Sprott (eds.), *Hormonal Correlates of Behavior.* I. New York: Plenum, 1975.

Ader, R., and Grota, L. J. Adrenocortical mediation of the effects of early life experiences. In E. Zimmermann, W. H. Gispen, B. H. Marks, and D. De Wied (eds.) *Progress in Brain Research,* Vol. 39. *Drug Effects on Neuroendocrine Regulation.* Amsterdam: Elsevier, 1973, pp. 395–405.

Aldrete, J. A., and Virtue, R. W. Effects of prolonged inhalation of anesthetic and other gases on blood and marrow of rats. In B. R. Fink (ed.), *Toxicity of Anesthetics* (Part 2). Baltimore: Williams & Wilkins, 1968.

Aleksandrowicz, M. K. The effect of pain relieving drugs administered during labor and delivery on the behavior of the newborn: A review. *Merrill-Palmer Quarterly,* 1974a, **20,** 123–141.

Aleksandrowicz, M. K., and Aleksandrowicz, D. R. Obstetrical pain relieving drugs as predictors of infant behavior variability. *Child Development,* 1974b, **45,** 935–945.

Aleksandrowicz, M. K., and Aleksandrowicz, D. R. "Obstetrical pain-relieving drugs as predictors of infant behavior variability": A reply to Federman and Yang's critique. *Child Development,* 1976, **47,** 297–298.

Alper, M. H., Brown, W. U., Ostheimer, G. W., and Scanlon, J. W. Effects of maternal analgesia and anaesthesia on the newborn. *Clinics in Obstetrics and Gynaecology,* 1975, **2**, 661–671.

Arms, S. *Immaculate Deception.* Boston: Houghton Mifflin, 1975.

Askrog, V., and Harvald, B. Teratogen effekt af inhalations-anestetika. *Saertyk fra Nordisk Medicin,* 1970, **83**, 490.

Bakeman, R., Brown, J., Snyder, P., and Ptacek, S. Effects of maternal medication on mother-infant interaction: Methodological considerations. Paper presented at meeting of Society for Research in Child Development, Denver, Colorado, 1975.

Banks, M. S. Personal communication, 1977.

Banks, M. S., Aslin, R. N., and Letson, R. D. Sensitive period for the development of human binocular vision. *Science,* 1975, **190**, 675–677.

Benson, R. C., Shubeck, F., Clark, W. M., Berendes, H., Weiss, W., and Deutschberger, J. Fetal compromise during elective cesarean section. A report from the Collaborative Project. *American Journal of Obstetrics and Gynecology,* 1965, **91**, 645–651.

Berkowitz, B. A., Ngai, S. H., and Finck, A. D. Nitrous oxide "analgesia": Resemblance to opiate action. *Science,* 1976, **194**, 967–968.

Bonica, J. J. *The Management of Pain.* Philadelphia: Lea & Febiger, 1953.

Bonica, J. J. *Principles and Practice of Obstetric Analgesia and Anesthesia,* Vols. 1 & 2. Philadelphia: Davis, 1967, 1969.

Boréus, L. O. *Fetal Pharmacology.* New York: Raven, 1973.

Borgstedt, A. D., and Rosen, M. G. Medication during labor correlated with behavior and EEG of the newborn. *American Journal of Diseases of Children,* 1968, **115**, 21–24.

Bowes, W. A., Jr. Obstetrical medication and infant outcome: A review of the literature. In W. A. Bowes, Jr., Y. Brackbill, E. Conway, and A. Steinschneider. The effects of obstetrical medication on fetus and infant. *Monographs of the Society for Research in Child Development,* 1970, **35** (Serial No. 137), pp. 3–23.

Brackbill, Y. Psychophysiological measures of pharmacological toxicity in infants: Perinatal and postnatal effects. In P. L. Morselli, S. Garattini, and F. Sereni (eds.), *Basic and Therapeutic Aspects of Perinatal Pharmacology.* New York: Raven, 1975, pp. 21–28.

Brackbill, Y. Long term effects of obstetrical anesthesia on infant autonomic function. *Developmental Psychobiology,* 1976, **9**(4), 353–358.

Brackbill, Y. In press.

Brackbill, Y., Kane, J., Manniello, R. L., and Åbramson, D. Obstetrical meperidine usage and assessment of neonatal status. *Anesthesiology,* 1974a, **40**, 116–120.

Brackbill, Y., Kane, J., Manniello, R. L., and Abramson, D. Obstetrical meperidine usage and outcome. *American Journal of Obstetrics and Gynecology,* 1974b, **118**, 377–384.

Brazelton, T. B. Psychophysiologic reaction in the neonate. II. The effects of maternal medication on the neonate and his behavior. *Journal of Pediatrics,* 1961, **58**, 513–518.

Brazelton, T. B. Effect of prenatal drugs on the behavior of the neonate. *American Journal of Psychiatry,* 1970, **126**, 1261–1266.

Brazelton, T. B. Neonatal Behavioral Assessment Scale. *Clinics in Developmental Medicine,* No. 50. London: Heineman, 1973.

Brazelton, T. B., and Robey, J. S. Observations of neonatal behavior: The effect of perinatal variables, in particular that of maternal medication. *Journal of the American Academy of Child Psychiatry,* 1965, **4**, 613–637.

Broman, S. Personal communication, 1977.

Broman, S., and Brackbill, Y. Analysis of obstetrical data from the NINCDS Collaborative Perinatal Study, in progress.

Brower, K. R. Effects of intranatal drugs on the newborn EEG. Unpublished M.A. thesis, University of Hawaii, 1974.

Brown, J. V., Bakeman, R., Snyder, P. A., Fredrickson, W. T., Morgan, S. T., and Hepler, R. Interactions of black inner-city mothers with their newborn infants. *Child Development,* 1975, **46,** 677–686.

Brown, S., Nuite, J. A., and Blackburn, G. The effects of meperidine as a maternal obstetrical analgesic on the postpartum status and subsequent development of the neonate. Paper presented at the American Psychological Association Meeting, Washington, D.C., 1976.

Brown, W. A., Manning, T., and Grodin, J. The relationship of antenatal and perinatal psychologic variables to the use of drugs in labor. *Psychosomatic Medicine,* 1972, **34,** 119–127.

Bruce, D. L., and Bach, M. J. Psychological studies of human performance as affected by traces of enflurane and nitrous oxide. *Anesthesiology,* 1975, **42,** 194–196.

Bruce, D. L., and Bach, M. J. Effects of trace anaesthetic gases on behavioral performance of volunteers. *British Journal of Anaesthesia,* 1976, **48,** 871–876.

Bruce, D. L., Bach, M. J., and Arbit, J. Trace anesthetic effects on perceptual, cognitive, and motor skills. *Anesthesiology,* 1974b, **40,** 453–458.

Bruce, D. L., Eide, K. A., Smith, N. J., Seltzer, F., and Dykes, M. H. M. A prospective survey of anesthesiologist mortality, 1967–1971. *Anesthesiology,* 1974a, **41,** 71–74.

Bruce, D. L., Eide, K. A., Linde, H. W., and Eckenhoff, J. E. Causes of death among anesthesiologists: A 20-year survey. *Anesthesiology,* 1968, **29,** 565–569.

Caton, D. Obstetric anesthesia: The first ten years. *Anesthesiology,* 1970, **33,** 102–109.

Catz, C. S., and Giacoia, G. P. Drugs and breast milk. *Pediatric Clinics of North America,* 1972, **19,** 151–166.

Chang, L. W., Dudley, A. W., Jr., and Katz, J. Ultrastructural evidence of hepatic injuries by chronic exposure to low levels of halothane. *American Journal of Pathology,* 1974a, **74,** 103a–104a.

Chang, L. W., Dudley, A. W., Jr., Lee, Y. K., and Katz, J. Ultrastructural changes in the nervous system after chronic exposure to halothane. *Experimental Neurology,* 1974b, **45,** 209–219.

Chang, L. W., Dudley, A. W. Jr., Lee, Y. K., and Katz, J. Ultrastructural changes in the kidney following chronic exposure to low levels of halothane. *American Journal of Pathology,* 1975a, **78,** 225–242.

Chang, L. W., Dudley, A. W., Jr., Lee, Y. K., and Katz, J. Ultrastructural studies of the hepatocytes after chronic exposure to low levels of halothane. *Experimental and Molecular Pathology,* 1975b, **23,** 35–42.

Chang, L. W., Lee, Y. K., Dudley, A. W., Jr., and Katz, J. Ultrastructural evidence of the hepatotoxic effect of halothane in rats following in-utero exposure. *Canadian Anaesthetists' Society Journal,* 1975c, **22,** 330–338.

Chang, L. W., Dudley, A. W., Jr., and Katz, J. Pathological changes in the nervous system following in utero exposure to halothane. *Environmental Research,* 1976, **11,** 40–51.

Channing, W. *A Treatise on Etherization in Childbirth.* Boston: Ticknor, 1848.

Cohen, E. N., Bellville, J. W., and Brown, B. W., Jr. Anesthesia, pregnancy, and miscarriage: A study of operating room nurses and anesthetists. *Anesthesiology,* 1971, **35,** 343–347.

Cohen, E. N., Brown, B. W., Jr., Bruce, D. L., Cascorbi, H. F., Corbett, T. H., Jones, T. W., and Whitcher, C. E. Occupational disease among operating room personnel: A national study. *Anesthesiology,* 1974, **41,** 321–340.

Cohen, E. N., Brown, B. W., Jr., Bruce, D. L., Cascorbi, H. F., Corbett, T. H., Jones, T. W., and Whitcher, C. E. A survey of anesthetic health hazards among dentists. *Journal American Dental Association,* 1975, **90,** 1291–1296.

Colen, B. D. Big increase in cesarean births noted. *Washington Post,* Mar. 5, 1976, p. B1.

Conway, E., and Brackbill, Y. Delivery medication and infant outcome: An empirical study. In W. A. Bowes, Jr., Y. Brackbill, E. Conway, and A. Steinschneider. The effects of obstetrical medication on fetus and infant. *Monographs of the Society for Research in Child Development,* 1970, **35** (Serial No. 137), pp. 24–34.

Corbett, T. H., Cornell, R. G., Endres, J. L., and Lieding, K. Birth defects among children of nurse-anesthetists. *Anesthesiology,* 1974, **41,** 341–344.

Corbett, T. H., Cornell, R. G., Endres, J. L., and Millard, R. I. Effects of low concentrations of nitrous oxide on rat pregnancy. *Anesthesiology,* 1973, **39,** 299–301.

Covino, B. G. Physiological disposition of local anesthetic agents. Paper presented at the third annual anesthesiology symposium, Naval Hospital, Portsmouth, Va., Sept. 7–8, 1972. (See also, Local anesthesia, *New England Journal Medicine,* 1972, **286,** 975–983, 1035–1042.)

Crawford, J. S., and Rudofsky, S. Some alterations in the pattern of drug metabolism associated with pregnancy, oral contraceptives, and the newly-born. *British Journal of Anaesthesia,* 1966, **38,** 446–454.

Denenberg, V. H., and Zarrow, M. X. Effects of handling in infancy upon adult behavior and adrenocortical activity: Suggestions for a neuroendocrine mechanism. *Early Childhood.* New York: Academic, 1971.

Dobbing, J., and Sands, J. Quantitative growth and development of human brain. *Archives of Disease in Childhood,* 1973, **48,** 757–767.

Doering, P. L. Personal communication, 1976.

Doering, P. L. Drug monitoring in the Obstetrical Services. In R. B. Stewart, L. E. Cluff, and J. R. Philp, (eds.), *Drug monitoring: A Requirement for Responsible Drug use.* Baltimore: Williams & Wilkins, 1977, 219–238.

Dubignon, J., Campbell, D., Curtis, M., and Partington, M. The relation between laboratory measures of sucking, food intake, and perinatal factors during the newborn period. *Child Development,* 1969, **40,** 1107–1120.

Dubowitz, V. Neurological fragility in the newborn: Influence of medication in labour. *British Journal of Anaesthesia,* 1975, **47,** 1005–1010.

Editorial. A painless revolution. *British Journal of Anaesthesia.* 1974, **46,** 391.

Egbert, L. D., Battit, G. E., Turndorf, H., and Beecher, H. K. The value of the preoperative visit by an anesthetist. *Journal of the American Medical Association,* 1963, **185,** 553–555.

Emde, R. N., Swedberg, J., and Suzuki, B. Human wakefulness and biological rhythms after birth. *Archives of General Psychiatry,* 1975, **32,** 780–783.

Evans, J. M., Hogg, M. I. J., and Rosen, M. The effect of naloxone on the depression of the early respiratory activity of neonates produced by maternal pethidine analgesia. In A.Arias, R. Llaurado, M. A. Nalda, and J. N. Lunn (eds.), *Recent Progress in Anaesthesiology and Resuscitation.* Amsterdam: Excerpta Medica, 1975, pp. 72–73.

Federman, E. J., and Yang, R. K. A critique of "Obstetrical pain-relieving drugs as predictors of infant behavior variability." *Child Development,* 1976, **47,** 294–296.

Fingl, E., and Woodbury, D. M. General principles. In L. S. Goodman, and A. Gilman (eds.), *The Pharmacological Basis of Therapeutics,* 4th ed. New York: Macmillan, 1970, pp. 1–35.

Fingl, E., and Woodbury, D.M. General principles. In L. S. Goodman, and A. Gilman (eds.), *The Pharmacological Basis of Therapeutics,* 5th ed. New York: Macmillan, 1975, pp. 1–46.

Finster, M., and Marx, G. F. Neonatal distribution of succinylcholine. *Anesthesiology,* 1976, **44,** 89.

Finster, M., Morishima, H. O., Boyes, R. N., and Covino, B. G. The placental transfer of lidocaine and its uptake by fetal tissues. *Anesthesiology,* 1972, **362,** 159–163.

Fitzgerald, H. E., and Brackbill, Y. Classical conditioning in infancy: Development and constraints. *Psychological Bulletin,* 1976, **83,** 353–376.

Friedman, S. L., Brackbill, Y., Caron, A. J., and Caron, R. F. Obstetric medication and visual processing in 4- and 5-month-old infants. *Merrill-Palmer Quarterly,* 1978, **24,** 111–128. (See also Friedman et al., Errata. *Merrill-Palmer Quarterly,* 1978, 24, in press.)

Goldstein, K. M., Caputo, D. V., and Taub, H. B. The effects of prenatal and perinatal complications on development at one year of age. *Child Development,* 1976, **47,** 613–621.

Goodman, L. S., and Gilman, A. (eds.), *The Pharmacological Basis of Therapeutics,* 5th ed. New York: Macmillan, 1975.

Gottlieb, G. Ontogenesis of sensory function in birds and mammals. In E. Tobach, L. R. Aronson, and E. Shaw (eds.), *The Biopsychology of Development.* New York: Academic, 1971.

Guth, L., and Clemente, C. D. (eds.). Growth and regeneration in the central nervous system. *Experimental Neurology,* 1975, **48,** No. 3, pt. 2, p. 251.

Haggard, H. W. *Devils, Drugs, and Doctors.* New York: Harper, 1929, p. 117.

Haire, D. B. The cultural warping of childbirth. *Environmental Child Health,* 1973, **19,** 171–191.

Heinonen, O. P., Slone, D., and Shapiro, S. *Birth Defects and Drugs in Pregnancy.* Littleton, Mass.: Publishing Sciences Group, 1977.

Hellman, L. M., and Pritchard, J. A. *Williams Obstetrics,* 14th ed. New York: Meredith, 1971.

Herrington, R. T. Pulmonary function. In U. Stave (ed.), *Physiology of the Perinatal Period,* 2 vols. New York: Appleton-Century-Crofts, 1970.

Hill, R. M. Drugs ingested by pregnant women. *Clinical Pharmacology and Therapeutics,* 1973, **14,** 654–659.

Hill, R. M., Craig, J. P., Chaney, M. D., Tennyson, L. M., and McCulley, L. B. Utilization of over-the-counter drugs during pregnancy. *Clinical Obstetrics and Gynecology,* 1977, **20,** 381–394.

Himwich, W. A. Physiology of the neonatal central nervous system. In U. Stave (ed.), *Physiology of the Perinatal Period.* New York: Appleton-Century-Crofts, 1970, pp. 717–750.

Hodgkinson, R., Kim, S. S., and Bhatt, M. Double blind comparison of neonatal neurobehavioral tests following cesarean delivery under ketamine, thiopental and spinal anesthesia. Paper presented at Society for Obstetrical Anesthesia and Perinatology, Orlando, Fla., April, 1976a.

Hodgkinson, R., Marx, G. F., and Kaiser, I. H. Local-regional anesthesia during childbirth and newborn behavior. *Science,* 1975, **189,** 571–572.

Hodgkinson, R., Marx, G. F., Kim, S. S., and Miclat, N. I. Neonatal neurobehavioral tests following vaginal delivery under ketamine, thiopental, and extradural anesthesia. Paper read at 50th Congress, International Anesthesia Research Society, Phoenix, Ariz., March, 1976c.

Hodgkinson, R., Wang, C. N., and Marx, G. F. Evaluation of the effects of general anaesthesia and pethidine on neurobehavioural tests during the first 2 days of life. *Anaesthesia,* 1976b, **31,** 143–144.

Horowitz, F. D., Ashton, J. Culp, R., Gaddis, E., Levin, S., and Reichmann, B. The effects of obstetrical medication on the behavior of Israeli newborn infants and some comparisons with Uruguayan and American infants. *Child Development,* 1977, **48,** 1607–1623.

Hubel, D. H., and Wiesel, T. N. The period of susceptibility to the physiological effects of unilateral eye closure in kittens. *Journal of Physiology,* 1970, **206,** 419–436.

Hughes, J. G., Ehemann, B., and Brown, V. A. Electroencephalography of the newborn: III. Brain potentials of babies born of mothers given "seconal sodium." *American Journal of Diseases of Children,* 1948, **76,** 626–633.

Hughes, J. G., Hill, F. S., Green, C. R., and Davis, B. C. Electroencephalography of the newborn: V. Brain potentials of babies born of mothers given meperidine hydrochloride (Demerol hydrochloride), vinbarbital sodium (Delvinal sodium) or morphine. *American Journal of Diseases of Children,* 1950, **79,** 996–1007.

Jones, O. H. Cesarean section in present-day obstetrics. *American Journal of Obstetrics and Gynecology,* 1976, **126,** 521–530.

Karim, S. M. M. (ed.). *The Prostaglandins. Progress in Research.* New York: Wiley, 1972.

Kleinman, L. J. Physiology of the perinatal kidney. In U. Stave (ed.), *Physiology of the Perinatal Period,* 2 vols. New York: Appleton-Century-Crofts, 1970, pp. 679–699.

Knill-Jones, R. P., Moir, D. B., Rodriguez, L. V., and Spence, A. A. Anaesthetic practice and pregnancy: Controlled survey of women anesthetists in the United Kingdom. *Lancet,* 1972, **1,** 1326–1328.

Knill-Jones, R. P., Newman, B. J., and Spence, A. A. Anaesthetic practice and pregnancy. *Lancet,* 1975, **2,** 807–809.

Knowles, J. A. Excretion of drugs in milk—a review. *Pediatric Pharmacology and Therapeutics,* 1965, **66,** 1068–1082.

Kosek, J. C., Mazze, R. I., and Cousins, M. J. The morphology and pathogenesis of nephrotoxicity following methoxyflurane (penthrane) anesthesia: An experimental model in rats. *Laboratory Investigation,* 1972, **27,** 575–580.

Kraemer, H., Korner, A., and Thoman, E. Methodological considerations in evaluating the influence of drugs used during labor and delivery on the behavior of the newborn. *Developmental Psychology,* 1972, **6,** 128–134.

Kron, R. E., Kaplan, S. L., Finnegan, L. P., Litt, M., and Phoenix, M. D. The assessment of behavioral change in infants undergoing narcotic withdrawal: Comparative data from clinical and objective methods. *Addictive Diseases,* 1975a, **2,** 257–275.

Kron, R. E., Kaplan, S. L., Phoenix, M. D., and Finnegan, L. P. Behavior of infants born to narcotic-dependent mothers: Effects of prenatal and postnatal drugs. In J. L. Rementaria (ed.), *Drug Abuse in Pregnancy and Neonatal Effects.* New York: Mosby, 1977, 129–144.

Kron, R. E., Litt, M., and Finnegan, L. P. Narcotic addiction in the newborn: Differences in behavior generated by methadone and heroin. *International Journal of Clinical Pharmacology & Biopharmacy,* 1975b, **12,** 63–69.

Kron, R. E., Stein, M., and Goddard, K. E. Newborn sucking behavior affected by obstetric sedation. *Pediatrics,* 1966, **37,** 1012–1016.

Levine, S., and Mullins, R. F., Jr. Hormones in infancy. In G. Newton, and S. Levine (eds.) *Early Experience and Behavior.* Springfield, Ill.: Thomas, 1968.

Liston, W. A., and Campbell, A. J. Dangers of oxytocin-induced labour to fetuses. *British Medical Journal,* 1974, **3,** 606–607.

Martin, E. W. *Hazards of Medication.* Philadelphia: Lippincott, 1971.

Marx, J. L. Analgesia: How the body inhibits pain perception. *Science,* 1977, **195,** 471–473.

McCreary, R. D., Kean, J. E., Wilson, G. S., and Baxter, J. C. An evaluation of pre-school children born to heroin addicted mothers. Paper presented at meeting of American Psychological Association, Washington, D. C., September 1976.

Mednick, S. A. Breakdown in individuals at high risk for schizophrenia: Possible predispositional perinatal factors. *Mental Hygiene,* 1970, **54,** 50–63.

Mednick, S. A., Mura, E., Schulsinger, F., and Mednick, B. Perinatal conditions and infant development in children with schizophrenic parents. *Social Biology,* 1971, **18,** S103–S113.

Meigs, C. D. *Obstetrics: The Science and the Art.* Philadelphia: Lea and Blanchard, 1849, pp. 317–319.

Mirkin, B. L. Perinatal Pharmacology: Placental transfer, fetal localization, and neonatal disposition of drugs. *Anesthesiology,* 1975, **43,** 156–170.

Moreau, T., and Birch, H. G. Relationship between obstetrical general anesthesia and rate of neonatal habituation to repeated stimulation. *Developmental Medicine and Child Neurology,* 1974, **16,** 612–619.

Morrison, J. C., Wiser, W. L., Rosser, S. I., Gayden, J. O., Bucovaz, E. T., Whybrew, W. D., and Fish, S. A. Metabolites of meperidine related to fetal depression. *American Journal of Obstetrics and Gynecology,* 1973, **115,** 1132–1137.

Morselli, P. L. Clinical pharmacokinetics in neonates. *Clinical Pharmacokinetics,* 1976, **1,** 81–98.

Moya, F., & Thorndike, V. Passage of drugs across the placenta. *American Journal of Obstetrics & Gynecology,* 1962, 84, 1778–1798.

Muller, P. F., Campbell, H. E., Graham, W. E., Brittain, H., Fitzgerald, J. A., Hogan, M. A., Muller, V. H., and Rittenhouse, A. H. Perinatal factors and their relationship to mental retardation and other parameters of development. *American Journal of Obstetrics & Gynecology,* 1971, **109,** 1205–1210.

Nakano, J., and Koss, M. C. Pathophysiologic roles of prostaglandins and the action of aspirin-like drug. *Southern Medical Journal,* 1973, **66,** 709–723.

Neumann, L. L., and Cohen, S. N. The neonatal narcotic withdrawal syndrome: A therapeutic challenge. *Clinics in Perinatology,* 1975, **2,** 99–109.

Nuite, J. A. Effects of narcotic agonists on the central nervous system of rats. Paper presented at the meeting of the American Psychological Association, Washington, D. C., September, 1976.

Parke, R. D., O'Leary, S. E., and West, S. Mother-father-newborn interaction: Effects of maternal medication, labor, and sex of infant. Proceedings of the 80th Annual Convention of the American Psychological Association, 1972, pp. 85–86.

Petrie, R. H., Wu, R., Miller, F. C., Sacks, D. A. Sugarman, R., Paul, R. H., and Hon, E. H. The effect of drugs on uterine activity. *Obstetrics & Gynecology,* 1976, **48,** 431–435.

Porter, A. L. An analytical review of the effects of non-hydrogen-bonding anesthetics on memory processing. *Behavioral Biology,* 1972, **7,** 291–309.

Quimby, K. L., Aschkenase, L. J., Bowman, R. D., Katz, J., and Chang, L. W. Enduring learning deficits and cerebral synaptic malformations from exposure to 10 ppm halothane. *Science,* 1974, **185,** 625–627.

Ramer, C. M., and Lodge, A. Neonatal addiction: A two-year study. Part I. Clinical and developmental characteristics of infants of mothers on methadone maintenance. *Addictive Diseases,* 1975, **2,** 227–234.

Rich, A. *Of Woman Born.* New York: Norton, 1976.

Richards, M. P. M. Innovation in medical practice: Obstetricians and the induction of labour in Britain. *Social Science & Medicine* 1975, **9,** 595–602.

Richards, M. P. M. Personal communication, 1977.

Richards, M. P. M. The induction and acceleration of labour: Some benefits and complications. Unpublished manuscript, University of Cambridge, 1976.

Richards, M. P. M. Obstetric analgesics and the development of children. *Midwife Health Visitor, and Community Nurse,* 1976, **12,** 37–40.

Richards, M. P. M., and Bernal, J. F. An observational study of mother-infant interaction. In N. B. Jones (ed.), *Ethological Studies of Child Behaviour.* Cambridge, England: Cambridge University, 1972, pp. 175–197.

Rosen, M. G., Scibetta, J. J., and Devroude, P. J. The use of fetal EEG in the study of obstetrical anesthesia. *Clinical Anesthesia,* 1974, **10,** 103–112.

Rosenberg, P., and Kirves, A. Miscarriages among operating theatre staff. *Acta Anaesthesiologica Scandinavica,* 1973, Suppl. 53, 37–42.

Satran, R., and Rosen, M. Effect of meperidine administered during labor on the neonatal EEG. *Electroencephalography and Clinical Neurophysiology,* 1966, **21,** 404–405.

Scanlon, J. W. Obstetric anesthesia as a neonatal risk factor in normal labor and delivery. *Clinics in Perinatology,* 1974, **1,** 465–482.

Scanlon, J. W. Personal communication, 1971.

Scanlon, J. W. Effects of local anesthetics administered to parturient women on the neurological and behavioral performance of newborn children. *Bulletin of the New York Academy of Medicine,* 1976, **52,** 231–240.

Scanlon, J. W., Brown, W. U., Jr., Weiss, J. B., and Alper, M. H. Neurobehavioral responses of newborn infants after maternal epidural anesthesia. *Anesthesiology,* 1974, **40,** 121–128.

Scanlon, J. W., Ostheimer, G. W., Lurie, A. O., Brown, W. U., Jr., Weiss, J. B., and Alper, M. H., Neurobehavioral responses and drug concentrations in newborns after maternal epidural anesthesia with bupivacaine. *Anesthesiology,* 1976, **45,** 400–405.

Shaw, N. S. *Forced Labor: Maternity Care in the United States.* New York: Pergamon, 1974.

Sigman, H. Task persistence in the two-year-old. Paper presented at the Biennial Meeting of the Society for Research in Child Development, New Orleans, 1977.

Sigman, H. Personal communication, 1977.

Simpson, J. Y. *Anaesthesia, or the Employment of Chloroform and Ether in Surgery, Midwifery, etc.* Philadelphia: Lindsay & Blakiston, 1849, pp. 110–131.

Smith, B. E., Gaub, M. L., and Moya, F. Investigations into the teratogenic effects of anesthetic agents—fluorinated agents. *Anesthesiology,* 1965, **26,** 260–261.

Smith, C. A., and Nelson, N. M. *The Physiology of the Newborn Infant.* Springfield, Ill.: Thomas, 1976.

Snow, J. On the administration of chloroform during parturition. *Association Medical Journal,* London, 1853, p. 500.

Snyder, S. H. Opiate receptors and internal opiates. *Scientific American,* 1977, **236,** 44–56.

Sostek, A. M., Brackbill, Y., Broman, S. L., and Rosenblith, J. Effects of barbiturates on newborn behavior. Part of symposium on maternal medication—short and long term effects on the offspring, presented at the annual meeting of the American Psychological Association, Washington, D.C., 1976.

Standley, K. Personal communication, 1977.

Standley, K., Klein, R. P., and Soule, A. B., III. Local-regional anesthesia during childbirth and newborn behavior. *Science,* 1975, **189,** 572.

Standley, K., Soule, A. B., III, Copans, S. A., and Duchowny, M. S. Local-regional anesthesia during childbirth: Effect on newborn behaviors. *Science,* 1974, **186,** 634–635.

Stave, U. Enzyme development in the liver. In U. Stave (ed.), *Physiology of the Perinatal Period,* 2 vols. New York: Appleton-Century-Crofts, 1970, pp. 559–594.

Stechler, G. Newborn attention as affected by medication during labor. *Science,* 1964, **144,** 315–317.

Steinberg, H. Selective effects of an anaesthetic drug on cognitive behaviour. *Quarterly Journal of Experimental Psychology,* 1954, **6,** 170–180.

Stern, L., and Peyrot, R. The functioning of the blood brain barrier at several stages of development in several species of animal (in French). *Comptes Rendu Hebdomadaies des Sánces et Memoires, Société de Biologie,* 1927, **96,** 1124–1126.

Stevens, W. C., Eger, E. I., White, A., Halsey, M. J., Munger, W., Gibbons, R. D., Dolan, W., and Shargel, R. Comparative toxicities of halothane, isoflurane, and diethyl ether at subanesthetic concentrations in laboratory animals. *Anesthesiology,* 1975, **42,** 408–419.

Stewart, R.B., Cluff, L. E., and Philp, R. Drug Monitoring: A Requirement for Responsible Drug Use. Baltimore: Williams & Wilkins, 1977.

Stewart, D., and Stewart, L. *Safe Alternatives in Childbirth.* Chapel Hill, N.C.: NAPSAC, 1976.

Strauss, M. E., Lessen-Firestone, J. K., Starr, R. H., Jr., and Ostrea, E. M., Jr. Behavior of narcotics-addicted newborns. *Child Development,* 1975, **46,** 887–893.

Timiras, P. S., Vernadakis, A., and Sherwood, N. M. Development and plasticity of the nervous system. In N. S. Assali (ed.), *Biology of Gestation,* Vol. 2. New York: Academic, 1968, pp. 261–320.

Tronick, E., Wise, S., Als, H., Adamson, L., Scanlon, J., and Brazelton, T. B. Regional obstetric anesthesia and newborn behavior: Effect over the first ten days of life. *Pediatrics,* 1976, **58,** 94–100.

Ucko, L. E. A comparative study of asphyxiated and non-asphyxiated boys from birth to five years. *Developmental Medicine and Child Neurology,* 1965, **7,** 643–657.

Vaisman, A. I. Working conditions in surgery and their effect on the health of anesthesiologists. *Eksperimental'naia Khirurgiia i Anesteziologiia,* 1967, **3,** 44–49.

VanderMaelen, A. L., Strauss, M. E., and Starr, R. H., Jr. Influence of obstetric medication on auditory habituation in the newborn. *Developmental Psychology,* 1975, **11,** 711–714.

Vernier, R. L., and Smith, F. G., Jr. Fetal and neonatal kidney. In N. S. Assali (ed.), *Biology of Gestation,* Vol. 2. New York: Academic, 1968, pp. 225–260.

Vorherr, H. Drug excretion in breast milk. *Postgraduate Medicine,* 1974, **56,** 97–104.

Walsh, S. Z., and Lind, J. The dynamics of the fetal heart and circulation and its alteration at birth. In U. Stave (ed.), *Physiology of the Perinatal Period,* 2 vols. New York: Appleton-Century-Crofts, 1970, pp. 141–208.

Wiener, P. C., Hogg, M. I., and Rosen, M. Neurobehavioral changes in neonates following maternal pethidine and bupivacaine administration and the effect of naloxone hydrochloride. Paper read at the British Obstetrical Anaesthetists Association Meeting, University of Manchester, England, September, 1976.

Williams, V., Bonta, B. W., Gagliardi, J. V., and Warshaw, J. B. Naloxone reversal of mild neurobehavioral depression in normal newborns after routine obstetrical analgesia. *Pediatric Research,* in press.

Yaffe, S. J. Developmental factors influencing interactions of drugs. *Annals of New York Academy of Science,* 1976, **281,** 90–97.

Yang, R. K., Zweig, A. R., Douthitt, T. C., and Federman, E. J. Successive relationships between maternal attitudes during pregnancy, analgesic medication during labor and delivery, and newborn behavior. *Developmental Psychology,* 1976, **12,** 6–14.

Zajonc, R. B. Family configuration and intelligence. *Science,* 1976, **192,** 227–236.

Zelson, C. Acute management of neonatal addiction. *Addictive Diseases,* 1975, **2,** 159–168.

Zuckerman, M, Nurnberger, J. I., Gardiner, S. H., Vandiveer, J. M., Barrett, B. H., and den Breeijen, A. Psychological correlates of somatic complaints in pregnancy and difficulty in childbirth. *Journal of Consulting Psychology,* 1963, **27,** 324–329.

CHAPTER 4

The Behavioral Assessment of the Neonate: An Overview

Patricia A. Self
Frances Degen Horowitz

The neonatal period—or the newborn period—begins at the moment of birth and ends when the infant has achieved 28 days of life. It is a period during which a number of physiological adjustments necessary for extrauterine existence occur; it is also a period during which the behavioral repertoire of the infant is first fully displayed and begins to function in relation to external stimulation. We have progressed, over the last several hundred years, from the largely visual inspection of the neonate in search of gross structural abnormalities, to many well-developed tools for the structural, functional, and behavioral evaluation of the newborn infant. These assessments begin in the delivery room, continue in the nursery, and can follow the infant home. While the physiological complexity and completeness of the neonate have long been appreciated—both scientifically and poetically—only recently have we come to understand that the behavioral repertoire and abilities of the newborn are more extensive and well formed than we had suspected. We have gone from thinking of the newborn infant as a behavioral "tabula rasa" specimen to the point where developmental theories must be reevaluated and revised in order to take into account the role of the initial behavioral capabilities of the neonate. Whereas, the research with newborn infants in the 1920s and 1930s focused upon the newborn as a proving ground for the nature-nurture controversy, present-day behavioral research with neonates is geared more to illuminating the abilities of the newborn infant and to investigating the possible role of both antecedent and consequent events in subsequent behavioral development (Appleton et al., 1975; Stone et al., 1973).

Current research with newborn infants involves a variety of strategies. Some of them rest largely upon experimental analyses of the behavioral repertoire and the infant's abilities, while others are aimed at descriptive efforts for both categorical and diagnostic purposes. The descriptive assessment of newborn behavior has often been part of the larger endeavor involving the developmental evaluation of infant intelligence. In their review of the history of infant intelligence testing, Brooks and Weinraub (1976) identified three waves of developments in infant assessment. Investigators who were part of the first two waves were particularly interested in the predictive validity of the assessment of infant behavior with respect to whether or not tests of infant behavior could predict later child and adult intelligence. There were persistent attempts to demonstrate continuity from early infant performance to later performance well into the 1960s, in spite of the numerous reports that showed little, if any, consistency between early and later assessments. Due, in part, to the accumulating evidence, researchers now seem to have turned their interest elsewhere and have seriously questioned even the conceptual bases employed in the discussion of infant intelligence, infant intelligence testing, and prediction of later functioning from early behavior (Horowitz and Dunn, 1976; Lewis, 1976). Recent research utilizing infant assessment techniques has focused more and more on diagnostic differentiation, theoretical conceptualization, and validation, as well as measurement of specific realms of behavior.

Several of the more well-known and widely used infant assessment techniques have been designed to provide for the evaluation of the infant's behavior over the full span of the period of infancy (e.g., Gesell Developmental Schedules and the Bayley Scales of Infant Development). However, less well known is the fact that, in addition to these full-span assessment procedures, we also have a number of assessment techniques that are specifically designed to evaluate the newborn infant. The purpose of this chapter is to review nine tests available for the measurement of neonatal behavior. Some of these are part of tests designed to cover ages beyond the newborn period while others are more restricted in their scope. Each of the newborn assessments will be discussed in terms of the specific behaviors sampled by the test, the reliability and validity of the assessment technique, and the research information available on the test. The nine tests are discussed in three different sections in accordance with their intended use: Screening Tests, Neurological Examinations, and Behavioral Assessment Techniques. Since all of the assessment procedures primarily use behavioral events as the source of data, these classifications are somewhat arbitrary. However, they do represent, to some degree, the different purposes for which the tests were designed. The screening tests were devised to quickly enable the physician, clinician, or paraprofessional to make an evaluation of whether a neonate needs special care, attention, or help. Neurological examinations evaluate the infant's sensory or reflex capabilities, or maturity. The behavioral assessments comprise the largest group of tests to be reviewed. These typically involve a fairly wide range of procedures, and thus provide for a more extensive assessment of the infant's behavioral repertoire.

After reviewing the content of each of the tests, a discussion of the general findings from research with each test is provided. The implications of these examinations for the study of neonates is included, as is a brief summary. Following the conclusion of this chapter the reader will find an appendix that presents, in tabular form, all of the behavioral items that have been included in neonatal assessment procedures. We hope this will provide the student of neonatal behavior with a convenient overview of the behaviors available for assessment in the nine tests reviewed as well as a cross-index for comparative purposes. Table 4-1 will enable a researcher selecting a neonatal assessment procedure to compare the available evaluation tools with respect to the behaviors they assess and to choose the test or tests that most fully encompass the repertoire of behavior thought important to the purposes of the research under consideration.

SCREENING TESTS

Screening techniques are usually designed to provide a quick and simple method of differentiating normal infants from possibly exceptional ones. Such techniques may provide a relatively easy method for indicating infants who may need special care (Apgar, 1953); they may also be used to identify the areas in which a particular infant needs special help or practice (Frankenburg and Dodds, 1967), and they can be used to quickly indicate

TABLE 4-1. Observations and Responses Included in Neonatal Assessments

Motor Behavior, Physiologic Characteristics, Reflexes, and Neurologic Signs

Item	Apgar	DDST	Parmelee	Prechtl-Beintema	Gesell	Dubowitz	Bayley	Griffiths	Graham-Rosenblith	Brazelton
1. Abdominal reflex				x						
2. Acoustic reflex (activity—see movement)				x						
3. Anal reflex				x						
4. Ankle clonus				x		x				x
5. Babinski				x						x
6. Biceps				x						
7. Blinking reflex				x						
8. Breast size						x				
9. Chvostek's reflex				x						
10. Ciliary reflex				x						
11. Corneal reflex				x	x					x
12. Crawling				x	x		x	x	x	x
13. Cremaster				x						
14. Crossed extension				x						
15. Cry			x		x					
16. Defensive								x	x	x
17. Doll's eye				x						
18. Ear—form, firmness						x				
19. Edema						x				
20. Facial weakness			x							
21. Galants reflex			x							
22. Genitals						x				
23. Glabella reflex				x						x
24. Hand (palmar) grasp			x	x	x			x		x
25. Hand to mouth								x		x
26. Strength of pull									x?	x
27. Head, lag; pull to sit;			x		x	x			x	x
raising to prone			x		x	x	x		x	x
28. Heart rate	x									
29. Heel to ear						x				
30. Incurvation										x
31. Irritability									x	x
32. Jaw jerk				x						
33. Knee jerk				x						
34. Lanugo (on back)						x				
35. Limbs—arms, legs;										
passive movements										x
spontaneous position									x	
traction				x						
recoil				x		x				x
standing (legs)			x							x
thrusting							x			
withdrawal (legs)				x						x
36. Lip reflex				x						
37. Moro reflex & startles				x	x			x		x
38. Motor maturity coordination				x			x		x	x

Table 4-1. Observations and Responses Included in Neonatal Assessments

Motor Behavior, Physiologic Characteristics, Reflexes, and Neurologic Signs

	Apgar	DDST	Parmelee	Prechtl-Beintema	Gesell	Dubowitz	Bayley	Griffiths	Graham-Rosenblith	Brazelton
39. Movement, activity			x		x		x		x	x
40. Muscle tone	x								x	x
41. Nasopalpebral				x						
42. Nipple formation						x				
43. Nystagmus				x						x
44. Optical reflex				x						
45. Placing reflex										x
46. Plantar: creases,						x				
grasp				x						x
47. Popliteal angle						x				
48. Posture						x				
49. Pupillary reflex				x						
50. Reflex irritability	x								x	
51. Respiratory rate	x			x						
52. Rooting			x	x						x
53. Scarf sign						x				
54. Skin color	x				x	x	x			x
opacity						x				
texture						x				
55. Square window						x				
56. Sucking			x	x						x
57. Tactile-adaptive score									x	
58. Temperature				x						
59. Tonic deviation of head & eyes										x
60. Tonic neck reflex				x	x					x
61. Traction test				x						
62. Tremulousness			x	x					x	x
63. Ventral suspension						x				
64. Walk, automatic										x

Responsiveness to Social and Nonsocial Stimuli and General Behavioral Observations

	Apgar	DDST	Parmelee	Prechtl-Beintema	Gesell	Dubowitz	Bayley	Griffiths	Graham-Rosenblith	Brazelton
65. Alertness, attention							x			x
66. Auditory behavior										
to inanimate stimuli		x			x		x			x
to voice					x		x			x
to repeated stimuli (see habituation)										
67. Consolability										x
68. Cooperativeness							x			
69. Emotional tone							x			
70. Endurance							x			
71. Energy or vigor							x			
72. Excitement, peak										x
73. Fearfulness							x			
74. Feeding needs					x					
75. Goal directedness							x			
76. Habituation										
auditory										x
visual										x
to pinprick										x

Table 4-1.   Observations and Responses Included in Neonatal Assessments

Responsiveness to Social and Nonsocial Stimuli and General Behavioral Observations

	Apgar	DDST	Parmelee	Prechtl-Beintema	Gesell	Dubowitz	Bayley	Griffiths	Graham-Rosenblith	Brazelton
77. Rapidity of build-up										x
78. Reactivity							x			
79. Responsiveness to										
bath								x		
cuddling										x
examiner							x			x
mother							x			
objects							x			x
picked up										x
80. Self-quieting										x
81. Smiling			x		x			x		x
82. State										
initial, predominant				x						x
lability										x
83. Tension							x			
84. Visual behavior										
to nonsocial stimuli			x		x	x	x			x
to social stimuli			x		x					x
coordination of							x			x
85. Vocalizations (noncrying)			x		x			x	x	

problems of development within an individual infant. There are two screening techniques commonly employed with young infants: the Apgar Scoring System (Apgar, 1953) and the Denver Developmental Screening Test (Frankenburg and Dodds, 1967). Only the Apgar Scoring System will be discussed in this review since the Denver Developmental Screening Test is primarily directed toward an older population, and samples only a very limited number of neonatal behaviors.

Apgar Scoring System

The Apgar screening technique was devised by Virginia Apgar (1953). This scoring system is now routinely used in most hospitals in the United States as well as in many other countries. It involves rating the newborn at 60 sec after birth. The same rating can be made at 3, 5, and 10 min after birth. While the timing of the repeated scoring varies, the most popular times, in addition to 1 min after birth, are 5 and 10 min after birth. Each of five signs is given a score of 0, 1, or 2, depending upon the condition of the infant. A score of 2 is given if the infant is in the best possible condition for a particular sign; a 0 is given if the sign is not present, and a 1 is given for all conditions between 0 and 2. Thus, the optimal score an infant can obtain is 10.

Test Items

The five signs upon which the infant is scored are heart rate, respiratory effort, reflex irritability, muscle tone, and color. If the infant has a heart rate of 100 to 140 beats/min, he or she receives a score of 2. If the heart rate is 100 or below, the infant receives a 1; a 0 is recorded when there is no detectable heart rate. In assessing respiratory effort, regular breathing and lusty crying results in a score of 2 for this sign; a 0 is given if the infant is apneic; for all other types of breathing, such as shallow breathing, the infant receives a score of 1. Reflex irritability is the third sign and refers to a response to some form of stimulation. The original testing method was suctioning the throat and nose with a rubber catheter. This stimulation elicits facial grimaces, sneezing, or coughing. In a revision of this, Apgar et al. (1958) used stimulation of the soles of the feet. In this procedure, a cry is given a rating of 2, a grimace or movement a value of 1, and no reaction is given a 0. The fourth sign is muscle tone. An infant whose spontaneously flexed arms and legs resist extension is given 2 points, while a completely flaccid infant receives a 0 score. The fifth sign, and the most controversial one, is that of color. An infant gets a score of 2 only when he or she is entirely pink at 1 min of age. Few children receive this 2 rating at 1 min of age, although they do often receive it at 3 or 5 min of age (Apgar, 1953). This item cannot be easily evaluated for dark-skinned infants.

Standardization

Apgar et al. (1958) found that in a group of 15,348 infants, 6% received scores of 0 to 2, 24% had scores of 3 to 7, while 70% of the infants received scores of 8 to 10 at 60 sec after birth.

Data from Apgar et al. (1958) and Apgar and James(1962) with 27,715 infants indicated that Apgar scores were inversely proportional to neonatal death rates—that is, the infants with the lowest Apgar scores had the highest mortality. These data showed the Apgar scores to be a useful tool in predicting the survival rate in groups of infants, although the Apgar score might not accurately predict neonatal death for an individual infant. Apgar scores were also related to the type of delivery experienced by the infant. Breech deliveries gave the lowest average scores, followed by the caesarian, then the vaginal. Apgar scores were also correlated with the type of anesthesia the mother was given. Infants born by caesarian section whose mothers were given general anesthesia had an average score of 5, while infants whose mothers had spinal anesthesia had an average score of 8.

Reliability

The question of observer reliability was discussed in Apgar et al. (1958). They found that when two or more people assigned scores independently, the widest variation in the total score was a disagreement of one point. These variations in scoring occurred most frequently in the mildly depressed infants—that is, infants with scores of 5, 6, or 7. Variations of scoring with infants of very high or very low scores were rare. Fewer variations occurred when the observers decided scores quickly.

Since the Apgar Scoring System was designed to evaluate the condition of the newborn at 1, 3, 5, or 10 min of age, test-retest reliability can only be done across ages. Test-retest reliability is not formally reported: usually the score, if it is not optimal at 1 min, increases over time. "Only occasionally does a good score, such as 8, 9, 10, drop after one minute" (Apgar et al., 1958, p. 1988).

Other Information

Numerous studies are now available correlating Apgar scores with a variety of other behavioral measures, including fetal heart rate, responsiveness to stimuli, neurological examinations, intelligence tests, and neonatal mortality. Maternal medication has also been examined.

Schifrin and Dame (1972) found that the normal fetal heart rate was almost completely accurate in predicting a high Apgar score in their sample of 307 neonates. However, abnormal fetal heart rate was a somewhat conservative predictor of low Apgar scores; two infants were not detected through their continuous monitoring of fetal heart rate in the last 30 min of labor.

Behavioral measures that Apgar scores have been correlated with include visual attending, head turning, and induced crying. Lewis et al. (1967) correlated Apgar scores of 18 newborns with visual-attending behavior at 3 months, and again at 9 to 13 months of age. They found that the infants who were rated 7 to 9 on the Apgar Scoring System at birth were significantly less attentive than infants who were given an Apgar score of 10 at birth. Turkewitz et al. (1968) presented somesthetic stimuli to the face, and measured the direction and latency of the head turn to repeated stimuli. Infants with Apgar scores of 9 or 10 were more responsive to stimulation from the right, and made more ipsilateral responses to the right than to the left. Infants with Apgar scores from 1 to 6 were as likely to respond preponderantly in either direction; also they made proportionately more contralateral responses. Fisichelli, et al. (1969) looked at three groups of neonates. One group of infants was characterized by high Apgar scores (8–10), another by low Apgar scores (4–6), and a third group was composed of a variety of Apgar scores similar to the normal population. Crying was induced by rubber-band stimulation. Infants with low Apgar scores seemed to fatigue earlier: at 4 compared to 6 for the infants with high Apgar scores. Otherwise there were no differences between the three groups of infants over the 3 days of the study.

Studies that have correlated the Apgar scores of infants to later neurological tests have reported conflicting results. Rosenblith (1964) presented data from 242 newborns in which the relationship of the infants' Apgar scores to neurological status at 4 months was curvilinear. Infants with very high Apgar scores or fairly low Apgar scores were not neurologically suspect at 4 months of age. Drage et al. (1966) found that the 5-min Apgar score, especially when it was combined with low birthweight of the infant, was a useful predictor of neurologic abnormality at 1 year of age.

Data reported concerning correlations of Apgar scores with later intelligence tests are also conflicting. Serunian and Broman (1975) examined 350 infants with the Bayley Mental and Motor Scale at 8 months of age. They found that the mean mental and motor scores were significantly lower for infants with Apgar scores of 0 to 3 than for infants with scores ranging from 7 to 10. The mean mental scores, but not motor scores, were significantly lower for infants with scores of 0 to 3, than for those infants with scores ranging from 4 to 6. Serunian and Broman also found that infants who died in the first 2 days of life had significantly lower Apgar scores than infants who died in the period from 1 to 8 months of age. Edwards (1968) tested 85 females and 62 males with the Stanford-

Binet and other measures at the age of 4. These scores were compared with the infants' Apgar scores at birth, both at 1 min after birth, 5 min after birth, and with a combined score of the two. Edwards found the Apgar scores to be significantly correlated to IQ at 4 years of age. Her data indicated that as Apgar scores became lower, IQ scores became lower. Only infants with Apgar scores of 7 or more at 1 min, and 8 or more at 5 min achieved superior scores on the measures taken at the age of 4.

In contrast to Serunian and Broman (1975) and Edwards (1968), Shipe et al. (1968) did not find a significant correlation between Apgar scores and later intelligence tests. These investigators evaluated 33 preschool children with low Apgar scores (5 or below) and 33 matched controls at the age of 36 months with the Stanford-Binet. They found no significant differences between the two groups and concluded that low Apgar scores at birth were not related to later performance on psychometric tests or personality ratings. Similarly, in a report that was based upon over 1200 newborn infants who participated in the Collaborative Perinatal Project, no correlation was found between the 1 min Apgar score and IQ at 4 years of age when race, sex, and socioeconomic status were controlled for statistically (Broman et al., 1975).

Two other studies have reported data on the usefulness of the Apgar score as an index of neonatal mortality. Drage et al. (1964) examined 1-min and 5-min Apgar scores as related to race, birthweight, and mortality. Caucasian infants were found to have relatively higher 1-min scores than Negroes, although this was not so at 5 min. There was a strong association between Apgar scores and birthweight; the lower the birthweight, the lower the Apgar score. They also found a trend toward lower scores with birthweights over 4001 g. Drage et al. (1964) found a strong correlation between low scores and neonatal mortality, particularly the 5-min Apgar score.

Richards et al. (1968) studied infants with low Apgar scores (0 4) and control infants matched for sex, parity, and social class, who had Apgar scores of 9 and 10 at 1 min of age. Of the 49 infants, they found high infant mortality (16%) in the neonatal period among the infants with low scores (compared with no deaths in the control cases). Follow-up on 26 of the remaining low-score cases and their matched controls a year later indicated very little difference between the two groups on a developmental test (adapted from Gesell). Thus, the authors concluded that those low-score infants who survive the neonatal period "appeared to have attained a normal developmental level at one year."

With regard to maternal medication, Yang et al. (1976) examined 85 primiparous mother-infant pairs, although restricting their sample to infants with Apgars from 7 to 10 at 5 min. Of these infants, they found that infants whose mothers were given drugs earlier in labor obtained higher Apgar scores. Also, there was a negative relation between total number of drugs and Apgar scores—that is, the more drugs the mother is given, the lower is the infant's 5-min Apgar score.

NEUROLOGICAL EXAMINATIONS

Complete neurological examinations consist of a much more extensive examination of the newborn infant than do screening tests. The infant's reflexes and responsiveness to stimulation are examined as well as muscle tone, physical condition, and general state. From the evaluation of the infant's behavior, state, and responsiveness, a diagnosis is typically made about the maturity and functioning of the infant's central nervous system (CNS) and sensory functioning. The examinations included in the section, although all dependent upon neurological functioning, serve three different purposes. The first examination, that of Dubowitz et al. (1970), is used to assess maturity: to differentiate small-for-date infants from pre-term, full-term, and post-mature infants. The second examination reviewed is the neurological examination that is most often used when a complete assessment of neurological normality is of interest. This is the neurologic examination of Prechtl and Beintema (1964). The third examination is a much more abbreviated form of neurological examination by Parmelee (1972). This examination takes only about 10 min as compared to the 40 to 60 min required for the Prechtl and Beintema examination.

Assessment of Gestational Age by Dubowitz et al.

One of the more recent and increasingly used neonatal assessments is that described by Dubowitz et al. (1970). Their scoring system, based on neurological and physical characteristics of the neonate, is designed to differentiate small-for-date, pre-term, and full-term infants through accurate estimation of the infant's gestational age. It includes 10 neurological signs from the work of Prechtl and Beintema (1964) and Robinson (1966), as well as "external criteria" from the work of Farr et al. (1966).

Test Items

The neurological criteria include

1. Supine-related posture, scored 0–4
2. Square window (hand flexion), scored 0–4
3. Ankle dorsiflexion, scored 0–4
4. Arm recoil, scored 0–2
5. Leg recoil, scored 0–2
6. Popliteal angle, scored 0–5
7. Heel to ear, scored 0–4
8. Scarf sign, scored 0–3
9. Head lag, scored 0–3
10. Ventral suspension, scored 0–4

The total possible score for the neurological criteria is 35 points.

The external criteria are based upon external characteristics of the neonate. As with the neurologic signs, they are scored variously; the total possible score on external criteria is also 35. The external criteria include

1. Amount of edema, scored 0–2
2. Skin texture, scored 0–4
3. Skin color, scored 0–3
4. Skin opacity of the trunk, scored 0–4
5. Amount of lanugo over back, scored 0–4
6. Plantar creases, scored 0–4
7. Nipple formation, scored 0–3
8. Breast size, scored 0–3

9.   Ear form, scored 0–3

10.   Ear firmness, scored 0–3

11.   Genitals, scored 0–2

In both sets of criteria, 0 was designated as the score to be given to the immature infant. Levels or steps above 0 were divided by the ease of defining a particular sign. The total score received by an infant is then converted into a gestational-age estimate. A total score of 70 results in a gestational age estimate of more than 43 weeks; a score of 50 gives a gestational age estimate of 39 weeks; a score of 20 yields a gestational age estimate of 30 weeks; and so on.

Standardization

The standardization sample included 167 infants (Dubowitz et al., 1970). This sample included only mothers who were certain of the date of their last menstrual period, had a regular cycle, no bleeding during pregnancy, and who had not been on contraceptives during the 12 months prior to conception. Assessments were made within the first 5 days post-delivery. Multiple assessments were done on 70 infants, although only the data from the first assessment was correlated to gestational age. External characteristics correlated with gestational age at the level of 0.91, while the neurological signs correlated 0.89. The correlation coefficient of the total score against gestation was 0.93. From their sample, Dubowitz et al. concluded that the best regression line for their data was a linear one, with the regression formula for the total score (x) against gestation (y) is $y = 0.2642x + 24.595$.

Reliability

Dubowitz et al. (1970) report observer reliability in their original article. Among four pediatricians scoring independently, no significant differences were obtained. In a further comparison with three naive nurses, two were found to score similarly to Dubowitz, with another scoring consistently 5 points higher.

Multiple assessments of some infants were also reported by Dubowitz et al. The investigators report that the state of the infant did not influence the score, and that the score was as reliable in the first 24 h as during the next 4 days.

Other Information

Other investigators who have substantiated the usefulness of the Dubowitz et al. scoring system include Hancock (1973) and Jaroszewicz and Boyd (1973). Hancock reported the use of the scoring system in 522 infants, of whom 434 were normal and of certain gestation by dates. The scoring system gave a gestational-age estimate that differed by 1 week or less in 400 infants. Hancock found it took less than 5 min to administer, and could easily be done during the routine neonatal examination. Usefulness of the scale with grossly abnormal infants was markedly limited, and Hancock also pointed out that misleading low scores might be obtained from resuscitated infants or those infants born by extended breech delivery.

Jaroszewicz and Boyd (1973) reported utilization of the scale with 100 nonwhite infants in South Africa. With their population, they found they had to alter the regression line for best fit, although the two regression lines differed by less than 0.2 weeks in the age range from 30 to 42 weeks.

In describing the Dubowitz et al. evaluation, Sweet (1973) reported that an abbreviated version of the scoring system was being developed by Dr. J. Ballard of Cincinnati.

Due to the increasing interest in the accurate estimation of the gestational age of the pre-term and small-for-date infants, it is expected that both clinicians and researchers alike will use this technique based on neurological and physical signs.

The Neurological Examination of Prechtl and Beintema

The Neurological Examination of the Full-Term Newborn Infant by Prechtl and Beintema (1964) was an attempt to make a diagnosis of abnormalities of the nervous system as soon as possible after birth. Abnormal signs present at birth due to birth injuries or other complications often disappear after a few days or weeks, only to recur much later as abnormal functions (Prechtl and Beintema, 1964). Prechtl and Beintema were interested in studying abnormalities present at birth to see what prognostic significance certain signs might have for later development.

As Prechtl and Beintema realized, it would be impractical to propose that the full neurological examination be given to every infant; thus, they have also devised a fairly short screening exam that can be given to each infant. Any infant evaluated as suspect on the screening examination, or considered ''high-risk'' at birth, is then recommended for the complete neurological examination.

Test Items

The complete neurological examination starts with the collection of essential data about the infant, such as when last fed, the method of feeding, drugs administered to the infant or mother, the infant's temperature, frequency of defecation and vomiting, and whether any special medical investigations have been run on the infant.

The infant is then observed in his or her crib, and state is assessed. Prechtl and Beintema have defined six states: state I, eyes closed, regular respiration, no movements except spontaneous startles; state II, eyes closed, irregular respiration, no gross movements, but small movements may occur; state III, eyes open, no gross movements; state IV, eyes open, gross movements, no crying; state V, eyes open or closed, crying; and state VI, other state—describe.

The infant's resting posture is noted after the blanket is removed. However, local practices of the nursing staff must be taken into consideration. Spontaneous motor activity of the arms and legs (separately) are now observed, as well as any athetoid (some parts flexed, other parts extended, as in the fingers) postures or movements and tremors of the infant. The skin color, respiration rate and its regularity, and any other movements are also noted.

The infant is then placed in supine position on the examining table. Any abnormalities of the skull and face are noted, as well as the presence of one of five facial expressions (bland, alert, fussing, crying, and frowning). Chvostek's sign, the lip reflex, and the glabella reflex are now evaluated.

The infant is then undressed and his posture, spontaneous motor activity, respiration, and condition of the skin are assessed. Reflexes tested for are the abdominal reflex, cremasteric reflex, and the anal reflex. The eyes are observed next to see if they are central, if there is strabismus, if they deviate in either direction, point downward, or have sustained nystagmus. The shape and size of the pupils are observed, as well as the reaction of the pupils to light. The reflexes observed are the optical blink reflex, acoustic blink reflex, corneal reflex, and the doll's eye reflex. At this time it is also convenient to check the infant's posture in supine suspension and his tonic neck reflex.

The infant is next checked for resistance against passive movements; for active power, the range of movements of the joints is recorded for the neck, trunk, shoulders, elbows, wrists, hips, knees, and ankles. The recoil of the forearm at the elbow and muscular consistency (softness, etc.) of the infant is also tested.

In the supine position, reflexes and responses that are tested are the biceps reflex, the knee jerk, ankle clonus, palmar grasp, plantar grasp, Babinski reflex, magnet response, crossed-extensor reflex, withdrawal reflex, rooting reflex, sucking reflex, jaw-jerk reflex, traction test, head control at a sitting posture, and the Moro response.

While the infant is in the prone position, the vertebral column is palpated. Then spontaneous movements of the head are noted. If crawling movements occur, hands are placed on the soles of the infant's feet and the degree of coordination in the crawl is observed.

The placing response, stepping movements, and the rotation test are observed with the infant in the upright position. Now the infant is again put in the supine position. Spontaneous motor activity is reassessed, and crying is elicited if it has not occurred. It is also noted here if the thumb has been held buried in the hand throughout most of the examination.

Finally, a summary and appraisal is made of the infant. These include an appraisal of his posture, motility, motor system, response threshold, tendon reflexes, Moro response, state, crying, pathological movements, hemisyndrome, and reaction type (normal, hyperexcitable, apathetic, and comatose). Then a diagnosis, with recommendations for further testing if necessary, is made.

Standardization

The Prechtl and Beintema assessment was originally conducted on 1500 children with a history of obstetrical complications. Since many of these infants have been repeatedly observed, Prechtl and Beintema have been able to footnote each response or reflex with not only the procedure eliciting it but also the possible significance it may have as well as its developmental course. They also gave the optimal state and position for eliciting the response.

Reliability

Prechtl (1963) reported the observer reliability on the neurological examination among three observers to be between 0.80 and 0.96. The high reliability, Prechtl maintained, was "a result of a long and intensive training programme, as well as strict definitions of the scales."

Prechtl and Beintema (1964) also stated that by standardizing the technique of the examination that the subjective elements of scoring can be largely eliminated, thus insuring a higher consistency by the same observer, or higher test-retest reliability. They reported no statistical data.

In 1968, Beintema reported testing 49 babies several times with their neurological examination, starting at 1 day of age. Thirty-one of these infants were tested eight times from 1 day of age through 9 days of age. Beintema discussed how the reflexes and responses changed from day 1 to day 9 and summarized his overall findings. The responses of the infants do change and Beintema concludes, partly due to the difficulty in altering the state of the infant, that neurological exams during the first 3 days are less valid than those given later in the neonatal period.

Other Information

In this same study Beintema divided his infants into those with obstetrical complications, low-risk infants, and fetal-distress infants. He compared these infants in terms of their prenatal history, ease of delivery, Apgar scores, and neurological examinations over the first 9 days of life. He found that age and state or state cycles significantly influenced the results of the neurological examination. For infants 4 days of age or older, the first examination was characteristic of other neurological examinations. He also found that some pre- and perinatal data of the infants was correlated with the developmental course postnatally, as well as some of the data from the neurological examination.

Prechtl (1965) reported upon the prognostic value of neurological examinations with a group of 285 high-risk infants followed up at 2 to 4 years and 8 years of age. The correlation between neonatal findings and follow-up examination was significant at the 0.00001 level. The neonatal, 2-to-4-year and 8-year findings were in complete agreement in about one-half of the cases; in another quarter, the second and third examinations gave the same results, and in the other quarter of the examinations the results were inconsistent.

Prechtl (1967) reported on a sample of 1378 infants divided into groups of low-risk, middle-risk, and high-risk infants. He found that there was a high positive correlation between nonoptimal obstetric conditions and that neurological items were shown to be different in the low-, middle-, and high-risk groups.

One of the most important contributions of this technique has been Prechtl and Beintema's definitions of state: they have been widely used in psychological and pediatric research. Beintema's (1968) report on periodicity of state and state cycles is relevant to the work of many infant researchers. Another infant assessment technique which has used several of the neurological items of Prechtl and Beintema is the assessment of gestational age technique of Dubowitz et al. (1970) discussed earlier.

Neurological Examination of Parmelee

The neurological examination described by Parmelee (1974) is designed to assess "active and myotatic reflex muscle tone, primary reflex behavior patterns, states of arousal, and spontaneous behaviors" in infants from 38 to 42 weeks of gestational age. However, it is a much less extensive examination than that of Prechtl and Beintema (1964), since it requires only 10 minutes to administer.

Test Items

The examination is divided into two sections. Section I contains all of the state observations and test items. Section II includes observations on crying, activity, and so on. Its test items include:

1. Head control: posterior neck muscles; anterior neck muscles

2. Arm recoil: each arm scored separately

3. Traction response of the arms: each arm scored separately

4. Leg recoil: each leg scored separately

5. Traction response of the legs: each leg scored separately

6. Head raising in the prone position

7. Arm release in the prone position

8. Galant reflex: each side of the midline scored separately

9. Sucking

10. Rooting reflex: each side scored separately

11. Startle

12. Leg withdrawal: each leg scored separately; only the best score is used

13. Moro reflex

State is assessed initially, after undressing, after the traction response of the legs, Galant reflex, sucking, and after the Moro reflex.

Section II includes observations of abnormal eye movements, tremor, crying, movement, and facial weakness.

Scoring for the various observations in Section I is done by assigning scores from 1 to 4, with 1 as normal. In Section II, a score of one also denotes normality. Summary scoring for each infant is accomplished through totaling the number of normal scores and subtracting for abnormal scores. A "corrected raw score" for the infant is obtained.

Standardization

Although the neurological examination described by Parmelee has been in use for the last few years, the latest version of the manual does not include standardization data. Parmelee comments that the "total score should remain within the normal range in normal babies"; however, what a normal raw score should be is not specified.

Reliability

Parmelee (1974) reported that test-retest reliability between morning and afternoon examinations by the same examiners has been established; however, the statistical analysis is not included. As noted above, Parmelee comments that the score should stay within the normal range for a normal baby across examinations or examiners.

Sigman et al. (1973) reported interobserver reliability with an earlier version of the scale to be good, $r = 0.92$.

Other Information

Investigators using the neurological examination of Parmelee have examined its relation to prematurity and visual fixation, as well as arousal level. Sigman et al. (1973) found that full-term neonatal scores on the neurological examination were significantly related to the length of first fixation of stimuli and the total length of fixation to the first stimulus. Frequency of state changes was also correlated with visual alertness. Kopp et al. (1975) reported data from a group of infants born prematurely who were tested when they reached 40 weeks' gestational age, using the procedure employed by Sigman et al. (1973). In contrast to the full-term neonates, the premature group did not evidence any significant correlations between their neurological examination scores and the visual fixation measures. In comparing the two groups of infants, the authors argued that some of the premature infants behaved similarly to the full-term neonates, whereas others were markedly different. Another study, reported by Sigman et al. (1975) replicated the lack of relationship between neurological score and visual fixation for another group of pre-term infants.

Parmelee reported that Howard et al. (1970) found that premature infants tested at 40 weeks' conceptional age on the neurological examination were generally at a higher level of arousal than the full-term infant and could not be soothed as easily by the sucking technique. These data are in contrast to data from longer neurological examinations, as reported by Michaelis et al. (1973), in which premature infants cried less throughout an examination lasting approximately 40 to 60 min. Parmelee suggests that premature infants are not able to sustain a high level of responsiveness in the longer examination, although they are more easily aroused and less able to inhibit arousal than full-term infants on the shorter neurological examination.

BEHAVIORAL ASSESSMENT TECHNIQUES

The behavioral assessment techniques tend to be much more varied in intent and design than either the neurological examinations or the screening tests. A particular behavioral assessment technique may differentiate between normal and abnormal infants, may attempt to predict the abilities of characteristic performance of infants, or may attempt to provide a measure of the individual differences of infants. While some of the behavioral assessment techniques may label some behaviors immature or mature for a certain age, in general they do not attempt to correlate the behaviors with nervous system functioning, in contrast to the neurological examination.

The behavioral assessment techniques included in this section are as follows:

1. Gesell Developmental Schedules
2. Bayley Scales of Infant Development
3. Griffiths' Mental Development Scale
4. Graham Behavior Test for Neonates and the Graham/Rosenblith Test
5. Brazelton Neonatal Behavioral Scale.

The Gesell Developmental Schedules and the Bayley Scales of Infant Development are probably the most widely used in the United States, while the Griffiths Scale is widely used in Great Britain. These three assessment techniques extend significantly beyond the neonatal period. In fact, the neonatal period is at the low end of the broad age range of these tests. In contrast, the Graham test and the Brazelton Scales were devised primarily for neonates and for different purposes than the other techniques.

Gesell Developmental Schedules

The Gesell Developmental Schedules have been widely used by both psychologists and pediatricians since the late 1920s when Arnold Gesell published his first studies. The information included here is taken from *Gesell and Amatruda's Developmental Diagnosis,* Second Edition, and the Third Edition of *Developmental Diagnosis* edited by Knobloch and Pasamanick. Behavior and development are examined at the key ages of 4, 16, 28, and 40 weeks and 12, 18, 24, and 36 months, with some comments about 48 and 60 months added by Knobloch and Pasamanick. In the latest version of the scales (Knobloch and Pasamanick, 1974), behavior is divided into five areas: gross motor, fine motor, adaptive, language, and personal-social. For the infant who is 4 weeks or less, there are nine gross motor items, two fine motor items, four adaptive, three language, and three personal-social items.

Test Items

In the gross motor area, the behaviors considered typical of 4 weeks of age are:

1. In supine, side position head predominates.
2. In supine, the asymmetrical tonic-neck-reflex postures predominate.
3. In supine, the child can roll partway to the side.
4. In prone, when pulled to sit, there is complete or marked head lag.
5. In sitting, the head predominantly sags forward on his/her chest.
6. When held prone above a surface, the head droops.
7. If placed in prone position, the infant rotates his/her head so it rests on his/her cheek.
8. In prone, the infant will raise his/her head slightly to turn it, so the infant can rest on his/her cheek.
9. Crawling movements occur in the prone position.

In the fine motor area, the behaviors to observe include:

1. The hands are fisted in the supine position.
2. The hands will clench the rattle on contact.

The behaviors considered typical in the adaptive area are:

1. The ring or rattle is regarded only momentarily in the line of vision.
2. The dangled ring will be followed to midline.
3. The infant drops the clenched rattle immediately.
4. The infant attends to the bell by diminished activity.

In the language area, the behaviors typical of 4 weeks are:

1. Vague and indirect regard of the examiner during the assessment
2. An impassive face throughout most of the examination period
3. The occurrence of small, throaty vocalizations

The behaviors typical in the personal-social area at 4 weeks are:

1.   The infant diminishing activity as he/she regards an adult face
2.   Staring indefinitely at surroundings
3.   The infant requiring two night feedings

The infant is examined for each of these behaviors in the course of the test. A minus is given if the behavior does not occur (or in older ages, if a less mature behavior occurs), a plus if the behavior occurs, and a double plus if a more mature pattern occurs. At the end of the examination the examiner assesses the infant's behavior in each of the four areas, as well as the overall behavior. This is not merely done by adding the pluses and minuses but by the examiner estimating the infant's degree of acceleration or retardedness in relation to the norms by age.

The examiner assigns a representative age to each of the four areas as well as an overall age. These ages can then be used to figure a developmental quotient, which is maturity age divided by chronological age. Gesell had continually stressed that this was not equivalent to an IQ or any estimate of intelligence in the general sense of the term.

To some extent Gesell used 50% of the infants passing an item at a certain age as criterion for including an item. He also listed the ages at which either a more mature or a less mature pattern of behavior was characteristic.

Standardization

The Gesell Developmental Schedules have apparently been standardized extensively, although exact figures are hard to ascertain. One standardization group consisted of 107 healthy children of middle socioeconomic status tested at 15 months and followed up at 18 months, 2, 3, 4, 5, and 6 years of age (Gesell, 1940). Another group (possibly comprising part of the above group) included another 107 children (middle socioeconomic status), of whom 2 to 48 of them were tested at each of 15 age levels, with a total of 524 examinations (Gesell et al., 1934). Still another group of 90 infants, both normal and abnormal, were seen a total of 429 times, from the time the infants were of the ages of under 3 months to over 48 months (Gesell, 1928). Standardization data from the latest edition of the schedules have not been reported.

Reliability

Gesell recognized the problem of examiner reliability as noted by his discussions of having an observer take notes throughout the examination, as well as having the examiner score the exam. Also, he only used trained experimenters for his examinations. The problem of examiner-observer reliability, however, was never investigated statistically.

Knobloch and Pasamanick (1974) reported reliability of DQ assignment to be 0.98 among 18 pediatric residents across 100 clinical examinations. They also commented upon the impossibility of calculating split-half reliability from the schedules, since equal numbers of items are not available.

Test-retest reliability of the Gesell schedules is apparently high. Gesell (1928) reported that in 90 infants seen 492 times, the first test indicated the overall scores 80% of the time; in subnormals it was 96%. Knobloch and Pasamanick (1974) reported test-retest reliability for 65 infants seen by different pediatricians within 2 to 3 days to be 0.82. No separate reliability of the test has been reported for the 4-week (neonatal) items.

Other Information

Only a small amount of the research with the Gesell scale has been concerned with the infant at 4 weeks of age. We are, therefore, including in this section information concerning the general utility of the scale. It should be noted, however, that the specific utility of the scale at four weeks of age (the lower limit of the scale but the upper limit of this review) has not been specifically studied.

Knobloch and Pasamanick (1959) studied 300 children. They found that the Gesell schedule at 40 weeks was correlated to maturity levels at 3 years at the 0.50 level for the entire group; a correlation of 0.75 was found for infants called abnormal at 40 weeks. Hallowell (1941) tested 250 infants from 12 months to 47 months and found correlations between the DQ of Gesell and the IQ of Binet to be 0.668 at 12 to 23 months, 0.798 at 24 to 35 months, and 0.837 at 36 to 47 months. Donofrio (1965) examined 90 infants with the Gesell Developmental Schedules at the ages of 12 weeks to 23 months, again with the Stanford-Binet at the ages of 2 to 11. The infants were rated average, above average, or below average on each scale and these ratings were compared. The contingency coefficient obtained was 0.54 (significant at less than 0.01). Both Donofrio and Hallowell reported the Gesell scale seemed particularly sensitive to subnormal behavior. Stechler (1964) administered the Gesell Developmental Schedules to 125 infants repeatedly from 6 weeks to 25 months, and the Stanford-Binet was given to the same infants at the ages of 35 to 59 months. Stechler found significant product moment ($p < 0.05$) correlations between DQ and IQ only at 20 to 25 months for all infants, although for normal infants (some infants were apneic) the correlations were significant at 46 to 51 weeks as well as 20 to 25 months.

The Gesell Developmental Schedules have also been compared to the Wechsler Intelligence Scale for Children (WISC) at various ages. McRae (1955) gave the Gesell schedules to 40 infants at 0 to 11 months, 41 at 12 to 23 months, and 21 at 24 to 35 months. The correlation coefficients to later retests were 0.56 for 0 to 11 months, 0.55 for 12 to 23 months, and 0.82 for 24 to 35 months, all significant at the 1% level. Escalona and Moriarity (1961) tested 58 normal children from the ages of 3 to 33 weeks with the Gesell schedules and retested them between 6 years, 2 months and 9 years, 3 months with the WISC. They found tests of infants 20 weeks or younger did not predict later intelligence. For infants 20 to 32 weeks of age, the Gesell DQ was positively related to later intelligence, although the relationship exceeded chance at the 10% level. A ranking of clinical appraisal of infant assessment significantly predicted difference in later intelligence range of the infants.

Knobloch and Pasamanick (1974) make a strong case for the validity of infant tests, citing their own correlations between infant and later examinations to be about 0.50, using only normal infants. Their populations included "black infants reexamined at 7 years of age, a group of noninstitutionalized infants recommended for adoption and seen at 5 years, 300 infants reevaluated at 3 years of age, and 200 followed up in the early school period at about 7 years of age." When abnormal infants are added to the above sample, the correlations rise to 0.70; if weighted for socioeconomic states of the parents and seizures of the infants, the correlations increase to 0.85, including abnormals.

The Gesell Developmental Schedules were not devised for use as a single, isolated test.

They were designed to be used repeatedly over a number of years, although it was expected that the DQ of an individual should not vary much. A series of articles by Fish and her co-workers (Fish, 1957, 1959, 1960; Fish et al., 1965, 1966) reported the longitudinal use of the Gesell Developmental Schedules in a study of 16 infants from a population that had a high incidence of social and psychiatric pathology. She and her co-workers have investigated the possibility of identifying infants vulnerable to schizophrenia by analyzing their profile of early development. At 1 month of age, 3 infants were judged to be vulnerable to schizophrenia, as judged by their abnormally uneven development. At 9 or 10 years, these 3 infants were judged by a naive psychologist as grossly pathologic compared to the other children. The pattern of development as measured by Gesell was abnormal not only at 1 month but from 1 to 18 months.

Possibly the most important contribution to come from the latest version of the Gesell scales is the Developmental Screening Inventory (DSI) (Knobloch and Pasamanick, 1974), a screening test based on the Gesell scales. It was first published in 1966, and consists of selected items from the developmental schedules for the ages of 4 to 56 weeks, 15, 18, 21, 24, 30, and 36 months. According to the data presented by Knobloch and Pasamanick (1974), careful use of the DSI should lead to the detection of all infants with significant abnormalities and discrimination between neuromotor and intellectual handicaps. It also identifies almost all with minor neuromotor impairment. The data presented indicated that it may, however, produce false-positives, mandating the need for repeated testing.

In summary, the Gesell Developmental Schedules have been widely used in infant research, and a number of reports suggest their utility for providing normative guidelines particularly for older infants. The DSI shows great promise for more adequate screening of young children. Both the original schedules and the DSI need larger standardization samples and more definitive validation studies. Their specific utility for neonates remains to be further demonstrated.

Bayley Scales of Infant Development

The Bayley Scales of Infant Development (Bayley, 1969) are essentially a revision of the California First Year Mental Scale (Bayley, 1933), the California Preschool Mental Scale (Jaffa, 1934), and the California Infant Scale of Motor Development (Bayley, 1936). Originally, the tests were designed to measure the intellectual development of a child. However, it was found that there was very little correlation between the infant's score on mental scales and his later IQ, or even his later scores on mental scales. Thus, the Bayley scales now only claim to assess the child's developmental status at a given age.

The current revision is composed of three separate scales, each of which is designed to assess a separate component of the child's total developmental status at a certain age.

The Mental Scale is designed to assess sensory-perceptual acuities, discriminations, and the ability to respond to these; the early acquisition of "object constancy" and memory, learning, and problem-solving ability; vocalizations and the beginnings of verbal communication; and early evidence of the ability to form generalizations and classifications, which is the basis of abstract thinking.

The Motor Scale is designed to provide a measure of the degree of control of the body, coordination of the large muscles and finer manipulatory skills of the hands and fingers. As the Motor Scale is specifically directed toward behaviors reflecting motor coordination and skills, it is not concerned with functions that are commonly thought of as "mental" or "intelligent" in nature.

The Infant Behavior Record is completed after the Mental and Motor Scales have been administered. The IBR helps the clinician assess the nature of the child's social and objective orientations toward his environment as expressed in attitudes, interests, emotions, energy, activity, and tendencies to approach or withdraw from stimulation. (Bayley, 1969, pp. 3, 4)

The age range for the current Bayley scales is 1 month through 2.5 years. The items on the scales are arranged in the order of which 50% of the children passed a given item, with the approximate age range noted for each item.

Test Items

The items on the Mental Scale, which were passed by 50% of the children up to 1 month of age, include 14 items:

1. Responding to the sound of a bell
2. Quieting when picked up
3. Responding to the sound of a rattle
4. Responding to a sharp sound like a light switch
5. Momentary regard of a red ring
6. Regarding a person momentarily
7. Prolonged regard of a red ring
8. Horizontal eye coordination to the red ring
9. Horizontal eye coordination to a light
10. Visual following of a moving person
11. Responding to a voice
12. Vertical eye coordination to the light
13. Vocalizing once or twice
14. Vertical eye coordination to the red ring

Items on the Motor Scale before 1 month of age include:

1. Lifts head when held at shoulder
2. Postural adjustment when held at shoulder
3. Lateral head movements in prone
4. Crawling movements in prone
5. Grasps red ring
6. Arm thrusts in play
7. Leg thrusts in play
8. Holding the head
   erect briefly while in a sitting position

The IBR provides a place for noting behaviors that characterize a given infant. The behaviors observed include:

1. Responsiveness to persons in general
2. Responsiveness to the examiner
3. Responsiveness to his mother

4. Responsiveness to objects
5. Cooperativeness
6. Fearfulness
7. Tension
8. Emotional tone
9. Goal directedness
10. Attention span
11. Endurance
12. Activity
13. Reactivity
14. Energy
15. Coordination
16. Whether the child plays imaginatively
17. Whether the child has a specific attachment to a toy
18. The sensory areas of interest (lights, sounds, body motions, etc.)

Three additional items on the IBR permit the examiner to record (1) whether the examiner felt the test was a good estimate of the child's characteristics, (2) whether there was any unusual behavior displayed, and (3) whether the child is judged, overall, normal, or exceptional.

After the child has been tested on the Mental Scale, his or her basal level (the last item passed) is noted. The raw score for the scaling is the total number of items the child passed, including all items below the basal level. The raw score is changed to the Mental Development Index (MDI) by consulting the norms for the child's given age as derived by Bayley (1969). The Motor Scale is converted similarly except that a different table of normative scores is given. Bayley does not interpret these scores as IQ scores. For clinicians using the scale, she suggests finding the child's raw score in the table of norms in the rows corresponding to an MDI or PDI of 100. then noting the age group column in which the given raw score is nearest that obtained by the child. This she calls an "age equivalent" or "mental age equivalent."

Standardization

The current Bayley Scales of Infant Development have been standardized on 1262 children from 2 to 30 months of age. In the standardization sample there were no significant differences correlated with sex, birth order, geographic location, or the patients' education. There was a consistent tendency (significant) for Negro children to obtain slightly superior scores on the Motor Scale from 3 through 14 months, although this was the only difference found by separating the racial-ethnic groups.

The 1-month-old infants were not included in this standardization sample. In an earlier standardization of the Mental and Motor Scales (Bayley, 1965) involving 87 infants there was a sample of 1-month-old infants. For these 1-month-old infants no score differences were noted as a function of sex, firstborn or laterborn, education of father or mother, or geographic location.

Reliability

Observer reliability was not reported for the latest standardization sample. Werner and Bayley (1966) did study the reliability of the immediate predecessors of the Mental and Motor Scales with 90 8-month-old infants. They found the mean percentage of observer agreement on the Mental Scale to be 89.4% and on the Motor Scale to be 93.4%. These were trained testers and observers, with a minimum of 6 months of testing experience. Agreement was higher on the Mental Scale items, which dealt with object-oriented behavior, and lower on items requiring social interaction. On the Motor Scale, high agreement was found on items dealing with independent control of head, trunk, and extremities, while items needing assistance of an adult gave lower observer realibility.

In this same study, Werner and Bayley (1966) also investigated test-retest reliability by having 28 children return in 1 week for a retest by the same examiners. For the Mental Scale agreement for test-retest was 76.4%. The test-retest agreement for the Motor Scale was 75.3%.

Other Information

Since some version of the Bayley scales has been available since the 1930s and since the Berkeley Growth Studies started in the late 1920s, a considerable amount of research has been done using some form of the Bayley scales. Most of the research has been concerned with infants older than 1 month. As with the Gesell schedules, however, we will report some of the research that has been done with the Bayley scales in order to provide a general perspective on their utility. The research to be reviewed includes longitudinal information regarding the scales, including comparisons with the Stanford-Binet, Wechsler, and other scales; comparisons with Piagetian task scores; research involving determinants of the BSID scores, such as heredity, socioeconomic status, environmental factors; and correlations with mother-infant interaction measures.

Bayley (1968) summarized many of the results up to 1968 in her report on "Behavioral Correlates of Mental Growth: Birth to Thirty-Six Years." In this and earlier reports by Bayley (1933, 1935, 1940, 1949) and Bayley and Jones (1937), the child's or adult's mental growth was correlated with environmental variables, such as socioeconomic status (SES) or parents' education, and examined for its consistency over a number of years, or the relation of mental growth to attitudes, characteristic reaction tendencies, or expressed emotions.

A number of these relationships have been clarified through more recent research. Ireton et al. (1970) and Willerman et al. (1970) looked at SES and infant scores and correlated them with IQ. Ireton et al. found that high SES was a better predictor of high 4-year IQ than was high mental score, but that a low mental score was a better predictor of low 4-year IQ than low SES. Willerman et al. found similar results, although their results pointed to an interesting interaction between SES and infant scores. They found that retarded infants were 7 times more likely to obtain IQ less than 80 at age 4 if they came from the lower social class than if they came from a higher class. Further information on this interaction is provided in a study by Ramey, et al. (1973). These investigators followed 24 infants enrolled in a day care center until they were 36 months of age and found that their behavior as measured by the Bayley Mental Scale and Stanford-Binet was significantly correlated by 9 to 12 months of age and correlations remained high. Ramey et al. concluded that "when children are reared in a relatively homogeneous environment, their behavior becomes more predictable.'' Instead of differences in ability, the tests may simply be measuring differences in environments.

Several studies have pointed, however, to the importance of hereditary or physiological influences to the infants' scores on the Bayley scales. Nichols and Broman (1974) and Wilson (1974) have examined twins to clarify this relationship. Nichols and Broman found that the intraclass correlations between monozygotic twins were 0.84 as compared with 0.55 for dizygotic twins and 0.22 with siblings. While pointing to environmental similarity as contributing to the greater concordance between dizygotic twins than among siblings, Nichols and Broman conclude that there is a substantial genetic influence in the concordance of the scores. Likewise, Wilson (1974) found greater concordance among monozygotic twins; he also pointed out that twins have a somewhat unique pattern of development, as they are initially depressed in developmental status until the age of 5 or 6 years. Hunt (1975) followed a sample of premature infants through the 1st year of life with the Bayley scales and found prediction enhanced through the adjustment of scores for prematurity. Motor scores predicted development for her sample at 2 years of age, while mental scores "permitted the identification of the children at greatest risk for developmental problems at age 2.''

Recently performance on the Bayley scales has also been correlated with measures of cognitive performance. Gottfried and Brody (1975) compared the performance of 11-month infants on the Bayley Mental Scales and on Piagetian tasks; they found a high positive correlation between the two scales. Similarly, King and Seegmiller (1973) found intercorrelations among the Bayley scales and cognitive measures at 14, 18, and 22 months of age. By contrast, however, Scott and Lewis (1974) found the relationship between the Bayley scales and measures of object permanence to be complex, inconsistent, and weak for 22 infants tested at 3, 6, 9, 12, 18, and 24 months. Matheny (1975) took probably the most fruitful approach by selecting 20 items that appeared on both the Bayley scales and the cognitive tasks and administering these to 205 sets of twins. Similar to the data reported above, he found more concordance of scores for monozygotic twins than dizygotic, supporting notions about the importance of the biological origins of sensorimotor capabilities of infants. One other study has also been concerned with cognitive measures of behavior; Matheny et al. (1974) reported on correlations between the Infant Behavior Record and the Mental Scale for 110 infants tested at 6, 12, 18, and 24 months. Composite scores were calculated for two behaviorial clusters: primary cognition and extraversion. Primary cognition included the behaviors of object orientation, goal-directedness, attention span, reactivity, language, and gross and fine motor coordination; extraversion included social orientation to the examiner, cooperation, and emotional tone. The extraversion component was correlated with concurrent mental test scores, but had no predictive validity. The Primary Cognition Component was highly correlated with concurrent test scores and also was predictive of later mental test scores.

Other interesting relationships have been found using the earlier versions of the Bayley Scales of Infant Development. Hofstaetter (1954) analyzed Bayley's data by factor analysis and found three factors accounted for a large proportion of the variance of intelligence test scores. "Sensorimotor alertness" accounted for a child's achievement on intelligence tests up to an age of 20 months. From 20 to 40 months variation was accounted for by a factor labeled "persistence." After 48 months of age, factor III, labeled "manipulation of symbols," accounted for the variance of intelligence test scores.

Cameron et al. (1967) did a cluster analysis of Bayley's California First Year Mental Scale. They found one item cluster composed largely of vocalizations that correlated significantly with 39 girls' later intelligence test scores. These correlations increased with age, and were more significant with verbal than performance scores.

Finally, measures of infant development are beginning to be correlated with observations of mother-infant interaction. Lee-Painter and Lewis (1974) reported negative correlations between the amount of maternal behavior and the infant's Bayley score at 3 months of age. Similarly, Rubenstein and Pedersen (1973) in their comparisons of mothers and surrogate caretakers found no difference in the infant's Bayley scores at 5 months in spite of evidence that mothers were consistently more stimulating than surrogate caretakers. The relationship of social stimulation to infant test behavior remains to be delineated.

The Bayley Scales of Infant Development are probably the best standardized and have had the most extensive use as a research instrument of any of the behavioral assessment techniques. This extensive use has shown that the infant scales are not especially good predictors of adult IQ, but that they are helpful in ascertaining the developmental status of a particular child at a particular age. However, their specific utility for assessing infant status at one month of age is not clear at this time.

Griffiths' Mental Development Scale

The Griffiths' Mental Development Scale (Griffiths, 1954) has an age range from 1 to 24 months, although the items for 1 month of age can be given to infants shortly after birth. The scale is divided into five sections: locomotor, personal-social, hearing and speech, eye and hand, and performance. Under each section there are two to three items for each month of age. The scale was developed from systematic observation by the author, as well as from other tests (notably Gesell). The test was designed to enable an examiner to distinguish between normal and handicapped children and to explore the abilities of each.

Test Items

The following items can be given to children shortly after birth or at one month of age:
Locomotor

1. Lifts chin when prone
2. Pushes with feet against examiner's hands
3. Holds head erect for a few seconds

Personal-social

1. Regards person momentarily
2. Quiets when picked up
3. Enjoys bath

Hearing and speech

1. Startled by sounds
2. Quieted by voice
3. Vocalizations other than crying

Eye and hand

1. Follows a moving light with the eyes
2. Looks at ring or toy momentarily
3. Looks steadily at bell-ring held still

Performance

1. Grasps examiner's finger
2. Reacts to paper—generalized physical movements
3. Hand goes to mouth

The infant is scored on each item by pass or fail. The mental age for the 1st year is the number of items passed divided by three. The general quotient is the mental age times 100 divided by the chronological age. For infants 8 months of age or younger a correction factor is used. This correction factor involves adding 8 weeks to both the mental age and chronological age before figuring the general quotient.

Standardization

The Griffiths' Mental Development Scale was standardized on a sample of 604 infants, a minimum of 20 at each month of life for the first 2 years. Of these 604, 47 tests involved retests of infants assessed at least 6 months earlier. Fourteen infant tests were excluded as they were felt to be defective or near defective. Of the 571 first tests, when the correction for infants under 8 months of age was used, the distribution of scores very closely matched a random distribution of intelligence scores.

Reliability

As yet, no observer reliability checks have been reported for the Griffiths' scale. The tests in the standardization sample were all administered by one person in order to eliminate initial errors due to different examiners. No further mass testing has been reported using different examiners.

Sixty children were retested with the Griffiths' Mental Development Scale. The retest scores were very close to the original scores, with no retest more than 12 points different from the original. The age range (7 to 70 weeks) between test-retest was large enough so that there was no overlapping of items upon which the infant was tested. One infant was tested seven times during his 1st year; his scores over the seven times varied only 4 points from 125 to 129.

Other Information

The prognostic value of the Griffiths' scale at one month is unknown. Hindley (1960) has reported on the predictive value of the Griffiths' scale from 3 to 18 months, with intercorrelations between scores at different ages reported from 0.46 to 0.58. Hindley (1965) also reported correlations between the Griffiths at either 6 months or 18 months and the Stanford-Binet at 3 or 5 years to range from 0.32 to 0.78, all of which were highly significant. However, whether the 1-month test predicts later capabilities or intelligence has not been reported.

Graham Behavior Test for Neonates and the Graham-Rosenblith Tests

The Graham Behavior Test for Neonates (Graham et al., 1956) was originally designed to differentiate normal newborns from those that might be brain injured. Thus, its age range is in the neonatal period, 1 to 14 days, although many of the items are applicable for ages up to perhaps a month. The test consists of five scales: pain threshold, maturational level, visual response, and ratings of irritability and muscle tension.

Rosenblith (1974a, 1975) has revised the Graham tests; the resultant examination has become known as the Graham-Rosenblith. Since these scales are the ones that are more commonly used currently, these are the scales that will be reviewed here. In the latest version of the scales, the pain-threshold scale has been eliminated; the maturational scales are composed of two subparts; two sensory scales have been used instead of the one by Graham; the ratings of irritability and muscle tonus or tension are still included.

Test Items

The Total Maturation Score is derived from two scales: motor and tactile-adaptive. The motor score includes:

a. Head reaction in prone position
b. Coordinated crawling motions in the prone position
c. Strength of pull as measured on a 4- or 5-pound spring balance

In the report by Rosenblith (1974a), the vigor of response to cotton and cellophane as presented in the tactile-adaptive scale was included in this scale score. The tactile-adaptive score examines responses to:

a. Cotton over the nose
b. Cellophane over the nose and mouth
c. The persistence of responses over the 20-sec period that the cotton and cellophane are applied

Each of the two subscales has a 9-point maximum, which gives a maximum General Maturation Score of 18 points.

The sensory scales consist of two subscales: visual responsiveness and auditory responsiveness. The visual scale has been taken from the original Graham scales and not changed. It consists of 11 items. The items are numbered such that the description that fits the infant's behavior indicates the infant's score:

0 = Infant does not fixate or follow an object; infant has wandering uncoordinating eyes, immobilization or pinpoint pupils.

1 = Infant does not fixate or pursue an object, but has none of the abnormalities above.

2 = Fixation is brief or obtained with difficulty.

3 = Fixation is clearly present and easily elicited.

4 = Horizontal pursuit is questionably present.

5 = Horizontal pursuit through an arc of 30° is obtained with difficulty.

6 = Horizontal pursuit through an arc of 30° is easily obtained.

7 = Vertical pursuit is present.

8 = Horizontal pursuit through 90° is present.

9 = Vertical pursuit through more than 30° is present.

10 = Horizontal pursuit through an arc of more than 90° with corresponding head movement is present.

At least five trials are given unless the infant receives at least a score of 6 in fewer trials.

The auditory responsiveness scale consists of the presentation of the sounds of a rattle and a bicycle bell, each sounded four times with a 10-sec interval between presentations and a 20-sec interval between auditory stimulus. Each stimulus is sounded first at a low intensity (about 70 db for the rattle and 76 db for the bell), and if a reaction is absent the stimuli are represented at higher and higher intensities with the highest levels being 86 db for the rattle and 88 db for the bell. The responses and the scoring of these responses are as follows (from Rosenblith, 1970):

0 = No response to either rattle or bell

1 = Reflex responses (startle or blink) to the bell

2 = Reflex responses to the rattle

3 = "Listening" responses (frowning, quieting, turning head to sound) to rattle or bell

4 = "Listening" responses to at least three of eight stimulus presentations

5 = "Listening" responses to at least six of eight stimulus presentations

If the maximum score is not obtained on the first test (i.e., at the lowest intensity level) then the test is repeated; a third test is presented if the maximum score is not obtained on the second trial.

The ratings of muscle tonus were derived from 9-point ratings of six behaviors:

1. The nature (flexed or extended) of the lower limb positions

2. The response of all four limbs to limb displacement

3. The change in muscle tone in response to the pull to a sitting position

4. The amount of spontaneous activity

5. The frequency of trembling, where it occurs, how severe it is, and what causes it

6. Response of the lower limbs to having pressure applied to the feet

Double ratings can be given in order to take into account the diverse degrees of tonicity in different parts of the body, such as the normal differences in neonates in upper and lower limbs.

The irritability ratings were derived from subjective ratings made by the examiner over the course of the entire examination. These ratings are based on the amount of irritable behavior shown by the infant together with the ease of soothing the infant. A separate judgment is then made of the appropriateness of the irritable behavior. These are then combined to compose one of the five possible irritability ratings: normal, three degrees of irritability, and no cry.

Standardization

The original Graham scales were standardized by Graham et al. (1956), who gave the scales to 176 infants without prenatal, perinatal, or postnatal complications, and to 81 infants suffering from anoxia, mechanical birth injury, or diseases or infections associated with brain damage. Socioeconomic factors and sex did not influence the scores, although age did in three scales and in two scales race did influence the scores. The test was concluded to have significantly differentiated between normal and traumatized newborns.

Further standardization samples have not been reported except the extensive sampling reported by Rosenblith (1974a, 1975) in regard to performance on other standardized infant tests, which is discussed below.

Reliability

Interscorer reliability is reported by Rosenblith (1975) from previously unpublished data of Rosenblith and Anderson-Huntington (1975). For 32 infants, the reliability of the maturation scale was 0.91; for the irritability rating it was 0.875; for muscle tonus, 0.625; and for the vision score it was 0.52. Bench and Parker (1970) report reliabilities to be 0.77 for maturation; 0.71 for muscle tonus; and 0.73 for the vision score. In the study by Brown et al. (1975), interobserver reliability was established prior to the start of the study, with the range of observer agreement found to be 0.83 to 1.00, with a mean of 0.91 across the scales of motor strength, tactile-adaptive, visual responsiveness, and auditory responsiveness.

Test-retest reliability data were reported by Rosenblith (1961) on an earlier version of the scale. She found test-retest reliability across 24 h to be 0.73 for the maturation scale, 0.63 for vision, 0.62 for muscle tonus, and 0.62 for irritability.

Other Information

Rosenblith (1974a) reported an extensive comparison of data from over 1500 infants who were part of the Collaborative Perinatal Project. The infants were examined as neonates with the Graham-Rosenblith scales, and at 8 months of age with the Bayley scales. She found that by dividing her total sample into four separate samples, that the relations between neonatal measures and 8 months measures largely replicated. There were similarities in the patterns of relations between neonatal measures and later measures. Neonatal motor scores correlated with all 8-month criteria, although male and female criteria differed slightly. Neonatal measures were less related to 8-month outcomes for Blacks than for whites. When the samples were broken by gestational age, those infants whose gestational age was less than 37 weeks had the greatest number of significant relationships, but those with gestational ages of 37 to 41 weeks also had a great number of significant relationships.

Rosenblith (1970, 1975) has reported additional data on these same infants. At 4 months of age, infants who had low neonatal scores tended to be identified as having more problems during a 4-month pediatric examination. This was true on all the neonatal scales with the exception on the irritability scale. Infants who behaved irritably had more suspect or nonnormal findings at 4 months. Rosenblith also noted that infants who did not show visual following during the neonatal period had a greater tendency to fail visuo-motor items at 8 months of age, as well as being more frequently suspect or abnormal on gross motor development and other measures, despite higher than average IQs and absence of neurological problems. Findings from a 3-year speech and hearing examination indicated that there was little evidence that children who failed to respond to auditory stimuli as neonates showed hearing deficits in later assessments, although a few hard-of-hearing infants were detected during the neonatal period.

Rosenblith and Anderson-Huntington (1972) reported on a 4-year follow-up of 400 of the infants with several different tests, including Binet IQ and concept-formation measures. The total maturation scale was not related to 4-year criteria, but the motor score was related to fine motor behavior, IQ, and to the overall impression of the child. Irritability during the neonatal period was related to irritability and attention span at 4 years of age. Muscle tonus was also related to all of the 4-year criteria.

Rosenblith (1974b) also reported that neonatal scores on the tactile-adaptive scores across ethnic subgroups in Hawaii correctly predicted differences in the incidence of sudden infant death syndrome (SIDS).

Brown et al. (1975) used the Graham-Rosenblith scales in conjunction with observations of mother-infant behavior during feeding. Mean scores on each of the subscales were as follows: motor strength, 6.23; tactile-adaptive, 6.69; visual responsiveness, 5.11; and 7.89 for auditory responsiveness. Examination behaviors did not predict behavior during feeding except that infants who were more visually responsive had their eyes open longer during feeding.

Brazelton Neonatal Behavioral Assessment Scale

The Brazelton Neonatal Behavioral Assessment Scale (Brazelton, 1973) was designed in "an attempt to score the infant's available responses to his environment, and so, indirectly, his effect on the environment." It was devised for use with the normal newborn, and it samples a broad range of neonatal behaviors. The scale is divided into 20 elicited (neurological) items and 27 behavioral items.

Test Items

The elicited responses include these reflexes and elicited movements:

1. Plantar grasp
2. Hand grasp
3. Ankle clonus
4. Babinski
5. Standing
6. Automatic walking
7. Placing
8. Incurvation
9. Crawling
10. Glabella reflex
11. Tonic deviation of head and eyes
12. Nystagmus
13. Tonic neck reflex
14. Moro
15. Rooting (Intensity)
16. Sucking (intensity)
17–20. Passive movements: right arm, left arm, right leg, left leg

The behavioral scale consists of state measures, general measures of behavior, and specific behavioral indices. The first state measure is the initial state of the infant, while the other state measure is that of predominant state throughout the examination. State is defined in six stages, from deep sleep to crying.

The specific behaviors observed or elicited on the Brazelton Scale include:

1. Response decrement to light
2. Response decrement to rattle
3. Response decrement to bell
4. Response decrement to pinprick
5. Inanimate visual orientation response—focusing and following an object
6. Inanimate auditory orientation response—reaction to an auditory stimulus
7. Animate visual orientation—reaction to persons
8. Animate auditory orientation—reaction to a voice
9. Animate visual and auditory orientation—reaction to a person's face and voice
10. Pull-to-sit
11. Defensive movements

The general behaviors to be observed throughout the course of the examination and scored as summary items are:

1. Degree of alertness
2. General tonus
3. Motor maturity
4. Cuddliness
5. Consolability with intervention
6. Peak of excitement
7. Rapidity of buildup
8. Irritability
9. Activity
10. Tremulousness
11. Amount of startles
12. Lability of skin color
13. Lability of states
14. Self-quieting activity
15. Hand-to-mouth facility
16. Number of smiles

Most of the scoring of the infant's behavior is done after the administration of all the test items with the exception of a few items where the tester marks the score sheet immediately after the administration of the item. The neurological items—elicited movements—are rated on a 3-point scale for low, medium, or high intensity of response; asymmetry and absence can be noted as well. The behavioral items are each rated on a 9-point scale, with the midpoint of the scale denoting the expected behavior of a normal 3-day-old infant. The examiner also notes items that describe the conditions under which the test was done and that describe the overall impression of the infant, as well as writing an optional descriptive paragraph. The cover sheet of the scoring sheet provides for recording background data of the parents, birthweight, type of feeding, exact age, and other identifying facts about the infant.

While there is a recommended order for administering the items after the first few items, the order is partially determined by the behavior of the infant. There is no limit on the number of times an item might be tried, though the state of the infant during which a particular item is to be administered is specified. The tester attempts to elicit the best performance from the infant. The Brazelton scale does not yield an overall score for an infant. The results of the test are the scores for each of the items, although some investigators have used clusters of items from factor analyses (Scarr and Williams. 1971).

Standardization

No formal standardization sample has been used in the development of the Brazelton scale. Unlike the Bayley scales, the Brazelton scale has not been used for any large sample assessment from which norms were derived. Researchers using the scale have provided their own normative data with the population that they were using. There have been several versions of the Brazelton scale prior to the one described in the 1973 publication of the manual (Brazelton, 1973). Some of the published research with the scale utilized earlier versions.

Reliability

Horowitz and Brazelton (1973) reported that the published studies indicated that reliabilities of independent testers trained at the same time range from 0.85 to 1.00. Brazelton and Tryphonopoulou (1972) reported that testers can be trained to a 0.90 criterion of reliability and the level of reliability remains at 0.90 or above for a prolonged period.

Test-retest reliability was reported by Horowitz et al. (1971) on the next to last version of the scale in which neonates tested at three days of age were retested at four weeks. Mean test-retest agreement within 2 points on the 9-point scale was 0.796 for males and 0.850 for females. Horowitz et al. (1973) reported on repeated testing (days 1–5, 7, 10, and 28) of a sample of American and Uruguayan infants using the final version. These investigators concluded that repeated testing revealed a good level of item intercorrelation, as well as possible diagnostic use for the individual infant.

Other Information

Horowitz and Brazelton (1973) reviewed the utilization of the Brazelton Neonatal Behavioral Assessment Scale in research. Among the earliest uses of the scale was the demonstration of cross-cultural differences in neonates. American Caucasians score reliably different than American Orientals (Freedman and Freedman, 1969), Mexican infants (Brazelton et al., 1969), African infants (Tronick et al., 1972), and Greek infants (Brazelton and Tryphonoulou, 1973). All of these studies employed earlier versions of the scale. Using the final version, Uruguayan and Israeli infants were compared (Horowitz et al., 1972). Recently it has also been used to detect socio-economic influence upon neonatal behavior (Justice et al., 1976).

The Brazelton scale has also been used to document maternal medication effects upon the neonate. Aleksandrowicz and Aleksandrowicz (1974) concluded that there were medication effects apparent in the infants' behaviors, as measured by the Brazelton scales until at least 28 days of age. Standley et al. (1974) found that infants whose mothers received anesthesia were more irritable than those whose mothers had not received any anesthesia. Horowitz et al. (1972) in a complex design looked at drug effects and ethnicity differences in the 1st month of life as measured by the Brazelton scale and at 3 months of age using the Bayley scales. These investigators reported few significant differences between infants born to medicated versus non-medicated mothers. Horowitz et al. concluded that light levels of obstetrical medication did not appear to have significant effects upon neonatal behavior in Israeli or Uruguayan infants.

The Brazelton Neonatal Behavioral Assessment Scale has also been used to document the effects of maternal narcotic addiction and maternal methadone addiction in infants. Babies of narcotic-addicted mothers were found to be less alert, more irritable, and less cuddly (Strauss et al., 1975). In babies born to heroin-addicted mothers taking methadone, the utilization of the Brazelton scale indicated that valium and thorazine could be avoided in many cases simply through soothing efforts by the nursing staff (Soule et al., 1974).

Scarr-Salapatek and Williams (1973) assessed premature infants at 1 week and at 4 to 6 weeks using an early version of the Brazelton scale and at 1 year of age using the Cattell Infant Intelligence Scale. By 4 to 6 weeks of age, infants given the stimulation program were superior on Brazelton scores; by 1 year of age the stimulated group had a significantly higher developmental status.

Recently studies have correlated Brazelton scores with mother-infant interaction during neonatal feeding sessions. Both Osofsky and Danzger (1974) and Self et al. (1976) have found that certain neonatal behaviors, notably alertness, are consistent across both settings, and that the alert, responsive neonate tends to have an attentive, sensitive mother.

Other research studies of the Brazelton scale have correlated scores with later visual responsiveness (Horowitz, et al. 1971; McCluskey and Horowitz, 1975) and with auditory conditioning in neonates (Franz et al., 1976). The complex interactions of the Brazelton scores with other tasks have not yet been clearly delineated, however.

Several investigators have described recurring clusters through factor analysis in their research. These clusters are generally four in number, and may be described as composed of interactive processes, motoric processes, organizational control, and stress measures (Adamson and Brazelton, 1975; Aleksandrowicz, 1973). Lester et al. (1976) identified two major factors—attention-orientation and temperamental arousal. Dempsey (1976) has tested the utility of an additional scoring system in which not only the best but also the characteristic behavior is scored for all the orientation items and for consolability. This has been further developed by Sullivan (Sullivan and Horowitz, 1978; Horowitz, Sullivan, and Linn, in press) to include scoring modal behaviors on the orientation items and the addition of five new scale items. The new items include orientation—inanimate, visual and auditory— quality of infant alert responsivity, examiner persistence, general irritability, and reinforcement value of the infant behavior. Sullivan reported that the addition of the modal scoring procedure and the new items did not appear to distort the scoring on the remaining items with a sample of 64 infants.

The Brazelton Neonatal Behavioral Assessment Scale, in spite of its recent development, is becoming widely used, particularly in research centers, throughout the United States and in several other countries. It appears to be a promising technique for differentiating the characteristics of normal newborns, as well as delineating the course of their early adaptation to their environment, but it remains to be demonstrated what relationship it has to later tested functioning of the child.

Summary and Conclusions

In this chapter we have reviewed nine different assessment procedures that can be used with neonates. The Apgar test and the three neurological examinations reviewed were designed specifically for the newborn infant. Of the five behavioral tests reviewed, three—Gesell, Griffiths, and Bayley—were designed to include infant assessments at 4 weeks of age, and thus they tap into the "neonatal" period. These tests were not intended for use in the first few days of life. In contrast, two of the behavioral tests—Graham/Rosenblith and Brazelton—were specifically designed for use in the first few days of life and for the duration of the neonatal period—up to 1 month. In Table 4-1, which is appended to this chapter, an item-by-item description is provided for the reader that will enable selection of test procedures and comparison between tests.

Neonatal assessment is done for a variety of reasons. When motivated by clinical needs such assessments are largely used to guide practitioners in assessing the immediate status of an infant and in making some decision concerning treatment or special care for the infant. In such instances shortened forms of longer tests and quick screening devices are often preferred. When more extended assessments are utilized they are usually done in the context of a research program in which specific questions are being asked and the measured status of the neonate is a source of data. Sometimes such research is designed to validate an assessment instrument itself. But, with the current range of neonatal assessment procedures available to researchers there is increasingly less need to develop still additional instruments, and the majority of current research efforts using neonatal assessment techniques are designed to answer substantive questions.

Because the newborn infant has had minimal exposure outside of the uterus, neonatal assessment can be used to evaluate prenatal, delivery, and birth events for their effect upon the initial behavior of the infant. Neonatal assessment can also be used to evaluate the effects of the earliest environmental events upon infant behavior. In addition, because of the increasing appreciation of the effect of the infant on the caregiver, the delineation of the role of individual differences among infants becomes an attractive research strategy for the investigation of infant-environment interaction (Lewis and Rosenblum, 1974; Horowitz and Dunn, 1976).

While the neurological assessments encompass both the normal and the different newborn, the behavioral assessments so far available to us have been largely designed for the normal, full-term newborn infant. With the growing interest in the pre-term, small-for-date, and seriously high-risk infant populations there has been a concomitant need to adapt the existing assessment procedures (see Chapter 6). This has proved to be more complex than it was first thought, but in the next few years the behavioral assessment of infants in these special populations is likely to become a focus of intense research efforts.

Almost nobody views the earliest assessment of the infant as being related to any later measurement of IQ; in this consensus is reflected the progress in infant assessment. As the review of the nine tests has demonstrated, the neonate is "available" for evaluation as a complex organism, and in describing and studying the complexity of the repertoire of the newborn it is possible to begin to provide the data base that may account for some of the earliest functional relationships affecting development. One of the more promising thrusts in our efforts to understand how development happens may come from the combination of assessment procedures and experimental analyses of functional phenomena during the neonatal period. In this way we may be able to relate descriptive data to process data and thereby arrive at more refined statements accounting for infant behavior and development.

BIBLIOGRAPHY

Adamson, L., and Brazelton, T. B. Cluster analysis of the Brazelton Neonatal Behavioral Assessment Scale. Personal communication from T. B. Brazelton, 1975.

Aleksandrowicz, M. K. *Neonatal behavioral patterns and their relation to obstetrical medication.* Ph.D. dissertation, University of Kansas, 1973.

Aleksandrowicz, M. K., and Aleksandrowicz, D. R. Obstetrical pain-relieving drugs as predictors of infant behavior variability. *Child Development,* 1974, **45,** 935–945.

Apgar, V. A proposal for a new method of evaluation of the newborn infant. *Current Researches in Anesthesia and Analgesia,* 1953, **32,** 260–267.

Apgar, V., Holaday, D. A., James, L. S., Weisbrot, I. M., and Berrien, C. Evaluation of the newborn infant—second report. *Journal of the American Medical Association,* 1958, **168,** 1985–1988.

Apgar, V., and James, L. S. Further observations on the newborn scoring system. *American Journal of the Diseases of Children,* 1962, **104,** 419–428.

Appleton, T., Clifton, R., and Goldberg, S. The development of behavioral competence in infancy. In F. D. Horowitz (ed.), *Review of Child Development Research,* Vol. 4. Chicago: University of Chicago, 1975, 101–182.

Bayley, N. *The California First-Year Mental Scale.* Berkeley: University of California, 1933.

Bayley, N. The Development of motor abilities during the first three years. *Monographs for the Society for Research in Child Development,* 1935, **1** (Serial No. 1).

Bayley, N. *The California Infant Scale of Motor Development.* Berkeley: University of California, 1936.

Bayley, N. Mental growth in young chlidren. In G. M. Whipple (ed.), *Intelligence: For the Study of Education.* Bloomington, Ill.: Public School Publishing, 1940.

Bayley, N. Consistency and variability in the growth of intelligence from birth to eighteen years. *Journal of Genetic Psychology,* 1949, **75,** 165–196.

Bayley, N. Comparisons of mental and motor test scores for ages 1-15 months by sex, birth order, race, geographical location, and education of parents. *Child Development,* 1965, **36,** 369–411.

Bayley, N. Behavioral correlates of mental growth: Birth to thirty-six years. *American Psychologist,* 1968, **23,** 1–17.

Bayley, N. *Manual for the Bayley Scales of Infant Development.* New York: Psychological Corporation, 1969.

Bayley, N., and Jones, H. E. Environmental correlates of mental and motor development: A cumulative study from infancy to six years. *Child Development,* 1937, **8,** 329–341.

Beintema, D. J. *A neurological study of newborn infants,* No. 28. *Clinics in Developmental Medicine,* London: Spastics International Medical (Heinemann), 1968.

Bench, J., and Parker, A. On the reliability of the Graham/Rosenblith behavior test for neonates. *Journal of Child Psychology and Psychiatry,* 1970, **11,** 121–131.

Brazelton, T. B. *Neonatal Behavioral Assessment Scale.* National Spastics Society Monograph. Philadelphia: Lippincott, 1973.

Brazelton, T. B., Robey, J. S., and Collier, G. A. Infant development in the Zinacanteco Indians of Southern Mexico. *Pediatrics,* 1969, **44,** 274–293.

Brazelton, T. B., and Tryphonopoulou, Y. A. A comparative study of the Greek and U.S. neonates. Unpublished manuscript. Referred to in T. B. Brazelton, *Neonatal Behavioral Assessment Scale.* National Spastics Society Monograph. Philadelphia. Lippincott, 1973.

Broman, S., Nichols, P., and Kennedy, W. A. *Preschool I.Q.: Prenatal and Early Developmental Correlates.* Hillsdale, N.J.: Laurence Erlbaum, 1975.

Brooks, J., and Weinraub, M. A history of infant intelligence testing. In M. Lewis (ed.), *Origins of Intelligence*. New York: Plenum, 1976.

Brown, J. V., Bakeman, R., Snyder, P. A., Fredrickson, W. T., Morgan, S. T., and Hepler, R. Interactions of Black inner-city mothers with their newborn infants. *Child Development*, 1975, **46,** 677–686.

Cameron, J., Livson, N., and Bayley, N. Infant vocalizations and their relationship to mature intelligence. *Science*, 1967, **157,** 331–333.

Dempsey, Jean. M.A. thesis, Kansas University, 1976.

Donofrio, A. F. Clinical value of infant testing. *Perceptual and Motor Skills*, 1965, **21,** 571–574.

Drage, J. S., Kennedy, C., Berendes, H., Schwarz, B. K., and Weiss, W. The Apgar score as an index of infant morbidity. *Developmental Medicine and Child Neurology*, 1966, **8,** 141–148.

Drage, J. S., Kennedy, C., and Schwarz, B. K. The Apgar Score as an index of neonatal mortality. *Obstetrics and Gynecology*, 1964, **24,** 222–230.

Dubowitz, L. M. S., Dubowitz, V., & Goldberg, C. Clinical assessment of gestational age in the newborn infant. *Journal of Pediatrics*, 1970, **77,** 1.

Edwards, N. The relationship between physical condition immediately after birth and mental and motor performance at age four. *Genetic Psychology Monographs*, 1968, **78,** 27–289.

Escalona, S. K., and Moriarity, A. Prediction of school-age intelligence from infant test. *Child Development*, 1961, **32,** 597–605.

Farr, V., Mitchell, R. G., Neligan, G. A., and Parkin, J. M. The definition of some external characteristics used in the assessment of gestational age inthe newborn infant. *Developmental Medicine and Child Neurology*, 1966, **8,** 507.

Fish, B. The detection of schizophrenia in infancy. *Journal of Nervous and Mental Disease*, 1957, **125,** 1–24.

Fish, B. Longitudinal observations of biological deviations in a schizophrenic infant. *American Journal of Psychiatry*, 1959, **116,** 25–31.

Fish, B. Involvement of the central nervous system in infants with schizophrenia. *Archives of Neurology*, 1960, **2,** 115–119.

Fish, B., Shapiro, T., Halpern, F., and Wile, R. The prediction of schizophrenia in infancy: III. Ten-year follow-up report of neurological and psychological development. *American Journal of Psychiatry*, 1965, **121,** 768–775.

Fish, B., Wile, R., Shapiro, T., and Halpern, F. The prediction of schizophrenia in infancy: II. Ten-year follow-up report of predictions made at one month of age. In P. Hoch and J. Zubin (eds.), *Psychopathology of Schizophrenia*. New York: Grune & Stratton, 1966.

Fisichelli, V. R., Karelitz, S., and Haber, A. The course of induced crying activity in the neonate. *Journal of Psychology*, 1969, **73,** 183–191.

Frankenburg, W. K., and Dodds, J. B. The Denver Developmental Screening Test. *Journal of Pediatrics*, 1967, **71,** 181–191.

Franz, W. K., Self, P. A., and Franz, G. N. Individual difference and auditory conditioning in neonates. Paper presented at the Southeastern Conference on Human Development, Nashville, Tennessee, 1976.

Freedman, D. G., and Freedman, N. Behavioral differences between Chinese-American and European-American newborns. *Nature*, 1969, **24,** 1227.

Gesell, A. *Infancy and Human Growth*. New York: Macmillan, 1928.

Gesell, A., Halverson, H. M., Ilg, F. L., Thompson, H., Castner, B. M., Ames. L. B., and Amatruda, C. S. *The First Five Years of Life*. New York: Harper, 1940.

Gesell, A., Thompson, H., and Amatruda, C. S. *Infant Behavior: Its genesis and Growth*. New York: McGraw-Hill, 1934.

Gottfried, A. W., and Brody, D. Interrelationships between and correlates of psychometric and Piagetian scales of sensorimotor intelligence. *Developmental Psychology*, 1975, **11**, 379–387.

Graham, F. K., Matarazzo, R. G., and Caldwell, B. M. Behavioral differences between normal and traumatized newborns: II. Standardization, reliability, and validity. *Psychological Monographs*, 1956, **70**, (21, Whole No. 428).

Griffiths, R. *The Abilities of Babies*. New York: McGraw-Hill, 1954.

Hallowell, D. K. Validity of mental tests for young children. *Journal of Genetic Psychology*, 1941, **58**, 265–288.

Hancock, B. W. Clinical assessment of gestational age in the neonate. *Archives of Diseases in Childhood*, 1973, **48**, 152–154.

Hindley, C. B. The Griffiths scale of infant development: Scores and predictions from 3 to 18 months. *Journal of Child Psychology and Psychiatry*, 1960, **1**, 99–112.

Hindley, C. B. Stability and change in abilities up to five years: Group trends. *Journal of Child Psychology and Psychiatry*, 1965, **6**, 85–99.

Hofstaetter, P. R. The changing composition of "intelligence:" A study in T-Technique. *Journal of Genetic Psychology*, 1954, **85**, 159–164.

Horowitz, F. D., Aleksandrowicz, M., Ashton, L. J., Tims, S., McCluskey, K., Culp, R., and Gallas, H. American and Uruguayan infants: Reliabilities, maternal drug histories and population difference using the Brazelton Scale. Paper presented at the biennial meeting of the Society for Research in Child Development, 1973.

Horowitz, F. D., Ashton, J., Culp, R., Gaddis, E., Levin, S., and Reichmann, B. The effects of obstetrical medication on the behavior of Israeli newborn infants and some comparisons with other populations. *Child Development* (in press).

Horowitz, F. D., and Brazelton, T. B. Research with the Brazelton Neonatal Scale. In T. B. Brazelton (ed.), *Neonatal Behavioral Assessment Scale*. National Spastics Society Monograph. Philadelphia: Lippincott, 1973.

Horowitz, F. D., and Dunn, M. Infant intelligence testing. Paper presented at 1976 NICHD conference.

Horowitz, F. D., Self, P. A., Paden, L. Y., Culp, R., Boyd, E., and Mann, M. E. Newborn and four-week retests on normative population using the Brazelton newborn assessment procedure. Paper presented at the biennial meeting of the Society for Research in Child Development, 1971.

Horowitz, F. D., Sullivan, J. W., & Linn, P. L. Stability and instability of newborn behavior: The quest for elusive threads. In A. Sameroff (ed.), Organization and Stability of Newborn Behavior: A Commentary on the Brazelton Neonatal Behavioral Assessment Scale. Monographs of the Society for Research in Child Development, in press.

Howard, J., Parmelee, A. H., Kopp, C. B., and Littman, B. A neurological comparison of premature and full-term infants at term conceptual age. *Journal of Pediatrics*, in press.

Hunt, J. V. Mental and motor development of preterm infants during the first year. Paper presented at the biennial meeting of the Society for Research in Child Development, 1975.

Ireton, H., Thwing E., and Grave, H. Infant mental development and neurological status, family, socioeconomic status, and intelligence at age four. *Child Development*, 1970, **41**, 937–945.

Jaffa, A. S. *The California Preschool Mental Scale*. berkeley: University of California, 1934.

Jaroszewicz, A. M., and Boyd, I. H. Clinical assessment of gestational age in the newborn. *South African Medical Journal*, 1973, **47**, 2123–2124.

Justice, L. K., Self, P. A., and Gutrecht, N. M. Socioeconomic status and scores on the Brazelton Neonatal Behavioral Assessment Scale. Paper presented at the Southeastern Conference on Human Development, 1976, Nashville, Tennessee.

King, W. L., and Seegmiller, B. Performance of 14-to-22-month-old black male infants on two tests of cognitive development: The Bayley scales and the psychological developmental scale. *Developmental Psychology,* 1973, **8,** 317–326.

Knobloch, H., and Pasamanick, B. Syndrome of minimal cerebral damage in infancy. *Journal of the American Medical Association,* 1959, **170,** 1384–1387.

Knobloch, H., and Pasamanick, B. The Developmental Screening Inventory. In H. Knobloch and B. Pasamanick, (eds.), *Gesell and Amatruda's Developmental Diagnosis,* 3rd ed. New York: Harper & Row, 1974.

Kopp, C. B., Sigman, M., Parmelee, A. H., and Jeffrey, W. E. Neurological organization and visual fixation in infants at 40 weeks conceptional age. *Developmental Psychobiology,* 1975, **8,** 165–170.

Lee-Painter, S., and Lewis, M. Mother-infant interaction and cognitive development. Paper presented at the Eastern Psychological Association meeting, 1974.

Lester, B. M., Emory, E. K., Hoffman, S. L., and Eitzman, D. V. A multivariate study of the effects of high-risk factors on performance on the Brazelton Neonatal Assessment Scale. *Child Development,* 1976, **47,** 515–517.

Lewis, M. *Origins of Intelligence.* New York: Plenum, 1976.

Lewis, M., Bartels, B., Campbell, H., and Goldberg, S. Individual differences in attention. *American Journal of the Diseases of Children,* 1967, **113,** 461–465.

Lewis, M., and Rosenblum, L. (eds.) *The Effect of the Infant on its Caregiver.* New York: Wiley Interscience, 1974.

McCluskey, K. A., and Horowitz, F. D. A comparison of neonatal assessment score with laboratory performance in auditory and visual discrimination tasks between the ages of one and four months. Paper presented at the biennial meeting of the Society for Research in Child Development, 1975.

McRae, J. M. Retests of children given mental tests as infants. *Journal of Genetic Psychology,* 1955, **87,** 111–119.

Matheny, A. P. Twins: Concordance for Piagetian equivalent items derived from the Bayley Mental Test. *Developmental Psychology,* 1975, **11,** 224–227.

Matheny, A. P., Dolan, A. B., and Wilson, R. S. Bayley's Infant Behavior Records: Relations between behaviors and mental test scores. *Developmental Psychology,* 1974, **10,** 696–702.

Michaelis, R., Parmelee, A. H., Stern, E., and Haber, A. Activity states in premature and term infants. *Developmental Psychobiology,* 1973, **6,** 209–215.

Nichols, P. L., and Broman, S. H. Familial resemblance in infant mental development. *Developmental Psychology,* 1974, **10,** 442–446.

Osofsky, J. D., and Danzger, B. Relationships between neonatal characteristics and mother-infant interaction. *Developmental Psychology,* 1974, **10,** 124–130.

Parmelee, A. H., Jr. Newborn neurological examination. Unpublished manuscript, August 1974.

Parmelee, A. H. Neurophysiological and behavioral organization of premature infants in the first months of life. *Biological Psychiatry,* 1975, **10,** 501–512.

Prechtl, H. F. R. The mother-child interaction in babies with minimal brain damage (A follow-up study). In B. M. Foss (ed.), *Determinants of Infant Behavior II.* New York: Wiley, 1963.

Prechtl, H. F. R. Prognostic value of neurological signs in the newborn infant. *Proceedings of the Royal Society of Medicine,* 1965, **58,** 3–4.

Prechtl, H. F. R. Neurological sequelae of prenatal and perinatal complications. *British Medical Journal,* 1967, **4,** 763–767.

Prechtl, H. F. R., and Beintema, D. *The Neurological Examination of the Full-Term Newborn Infant.* Little Club Clinics in Developmental Medicine, No. 12. London: Spastics Society, 1964.

Ramey, C. T., Campbell, F. A., and Nicholson, J. E. The predictive power of the Bayley Scales of

Infant Development and the Stanford-Binet Intelligence test in a relatively constant environment. *Child Development,* 1973, **44,** 790–795.

Richards, F. M., Richards, I. D. G., and Roberts, C. J. The influence of low Apgar rating on infant mortality and development. In R. MacKeith and M. Bax (eds.), *Studies in Infancy.* Clinics in Developmental Medicine, No. 27, London: Spastics Society (Heinemann), 1968.

Robinson, R. J. Assessment of gestational age by neurological examination. *Archives of Diseases in Childhood,* 1966, **41,** 437.

Rosenblith, J. F. Prognostic value of neonatal behavioral tests. In B. Z. Friedlander, G. M. Sterritt, and G. E. Kirk (eds.), *Exceptional Infant,* Vol. 3: *Assessment and Intervention.* New York: Bruner-Mazel, 1975.

Rosenblith, J. F. Relations between neonatal behaviors and those at eight months. *Developmental Psychology,* 1974a, **10,** (6), 779–792.

Rosenblith, J. F. Relations between newborn and four-year behaviors. Paper presented at the meetings of the Eastern Psychological Association, 1974b.

Rosenblith, J. Are newborn auditory responses prognostic of deafness? *Transactions of American Academy of Ophthalmology and Otolaryngology,* 1970 (Nov.-Dec.) 1215–1228.

Rosenblith, J. F. The modified Graham behavior test for neonates: Test-retest relability, normative data and hypotheses for future work. *Biologia Neonatorium,* 1961, **3,** 174–192.

Rosenblith, J. F. Prognostic value of behavioral assessment of neonates. *Biologia Neonatorium,* 1964, **6,** 76–103.

Rosenblith, J. F., and Anderson-Huntington, R. B. Relations between newborn and 4 year behavior. *Abstract Guide of XXth International Congress of Psychology,* Tokyo, Japan, 1972.

Rosenblith, J. F., and Anderson-Huntington, R. B. Relations between newborn and four year behavior. Eastern Psychological Association, manuscript in preparation, 1974. Cited in J. F. Rosenblith, Prognostic value of neonatal behavioral tests. In B. Z. Friedlander, G. M. Sterritt, and G. E. Kirk, (eds.), *Exceptional Infant,* Vol. 3: *Assessment and Intervention.* New York: Bruner-Mazel, 1975.

Rubenstein, J. L., and Pedersen, F. A. A comparison of maternal and surrogate care-taking behavior of five-month-old infants. Paper for biennial meeting of the Society for Research in Child Development, 1973.

Scarr, S., and Williams, M. The assessment of neonatal and later status in low birth weight infants. Paper presented at meeting of the Society for Research in Child Development, April 1971.

Scarr-Salapatek, S., and Williams, M. The effects of early stimulation of low birth weight infants. *Child Development,* 1973, **44,** 94–101.

Schrifin, B. S., and Dame, L. Fetal heart rate patterns: Prediction of Apgar Score. *Journal of American Medical Association,* 1972, 1322–1325.

Scott, E., and Lewis, M. A longitudinal study of attention and cognition in the first two years of life. Paper presented at the annual meeting of the Eastern Psychological Association, 1974.

Self, P. A., Belcastro, C. M., DeMeis, D. K., Jones, J., Justice, L. K., and Gutrecht, N. M. Individual differences in neonates and mother-infant interaction during feeding. Paper presented at the Southeastern Conference on Human Development, Nashville, Tennessee, April 1976.

Serunian, S. A., and Broman, S. H. Relationship of Apgar Scores and Bayley Mental and Motor Scores. *Child Development,* 1975, **46,** 696–700.

Shipe, D., Vandenberg, S., and Williams, R. D. B. Neonatal Apgar ratings as related to intelligence and behavior in preschool children. *Child Development,* 1968, **39,** 861–866.

Sigman, M., Kopp, C. B., Littman, B., and Parmelee, A. H. Infant visual attentiveness in relation to birth condition. Paper presented at the biennial meeting of the Society for Research in Child Development, 1975.

Sigman, M., Kopp, C. B., Parmelee, A. H., and Jeffrey, W. E. Visual attention and neurological organization in neonates. *Child Development,* 1973, **44,** 461–466.

Soule, B., Standley, K., Copans, S., and Davis, M. Clinical uses of the Brazelton Neonatal Scale. *Pediatrics,* 1974, **54,** 583–586.

Standley, K., Soule, A. B., Copans, S. A., and Duchowny, M. S. Local-regional anesthesia during childbirth: Effect on newborn behaviors. *Science,* 1974, **186,** 634–635.

Stechler, G. A longitudinal follow-up of neonatal apnea. *Child Development,* 1964, **35,** 333–348.

Stone, L. J., Smith, H., and Murphy, L. *The Competent Infant.* New York: Basic Books, 1973.

Strauss, M. E., Lessen-Firestone, J. K., Starr, R. H., and Ostrea, E. M. Behavior of narcotics-addicted newborns. *Child Development,* 1975, **46,** 887–893.

Sullivan, J. W. and Horowitz, F. D. Kansas supplements to the Neonatal Behavioral Assessment Scale: A first look. Paper presented at the International Conference on Infant Studies, Providence, 1978.

Sweet, A. Y. Classification of the low birth-weight infants. In M. Klaus and A. Fanaroff (eds.), *Care of the High-risk Neonate.* Philadelphia: Saunders, 1973, 36–57.

Tronick, E., Koslowski, B., Brazelton, T. B. Neonatal behavior among urban Zambians and Americans. Referred to in T. B. Brazelton, *Neonatal Behavioral Assessment Scale.* National Spastics Society Monograph. Philadelphia: Lippincott, 1973.

Turkewitz, G., Moreau, T., and Birch, H. G. Relation between birth condition and neurobehavioral organization in the neonate. *Pediatric Research,* 1968, **2,** 243–249.

Werner, E. E., and Bayley, N. The reliability of Bayley's revised scale of mental and motor development during the first year of life. *Child Development,* 1966, **37,** 39–50.

Willerman, L., Broman, S. H., and Fielder, M. Infant development, preschool I.Q., and social class. *Child Development,* 1970, **41,** 69–77.

Wilson, R. S. Twins: Mental development in the preschool years. *Developmental Psychology,* 1974, **10,** 580–588.

Yang, R. K., Zweig, A. R., Douthitt, T. C., and Federman, E. J. Successive relationship between maternal attitudes during pregnancy, analgesic medication during labor and delivery, and newborn behavior. *Developmental Psychology,* 1976, **12,** 6–15.

CHAPTER 5

Early Infant Assessment: An Overview

Raymond K. Yang[1]

The process of being born is a momentous occasion for it marks the developing human's entry into the peopled environment. It also finalizes what, for several preceding hours, has been a period of acute, intense physical stress and strain. Cranial compression is severe. There is a near instantaneous shift in cardiopulmonary function. Rapid superficial cooling occurs with exposure to air. Probably at no other time is so much happening in so short a span.

Recovery from the physical stress and strain, completion of cardiopulmonary adjustments, and perhaps an initial adjustment to the surrounding clamor, occurs during what is commonly thought of as the *newborn* or *neonatal* period. During this period the tumultuous changes wrought by passage from intra- to extrauterine life are receding. Type and duration of delivery, maternal medication during labor, and other perinatal factors influence neonatal behavior. The effects may be transient or more lasting. In either case, neonatal assessments reflect them as well as endogenous congenital characteristics.

The *infant* is the newborn who has gotten down to the business of growing. Transient perinatal effects have presumably disappeared; what remains are endogenous and congenital. What has entered are social influences in the form of caregiver behavior and the home environment. This is the context of infant assessment.

Assessment techniques for infants are as unique as the organism itself. To wit: the infant, although not uncommunicative, is linguistically incompetent. Therefore, control of the testing situation by instructions is not possible; the guile of the examiner and the inherent interest of the test items are critical to successful testing. While the infant cannot be relied upon to be cooperative, he can effectively control the behavior of others (especially adults) with the most compelling communications: cries and smiles. In addition to being guileful, therefore, the examiner must be wary of overresponding to a particularly skillful infant. These considerations, prior to any theoretical perspective, make infant assessment a distinctive part of the testing field. At no other time is development so rapid and the available forms of measurement so restricted.

There has been an enormous increase in the number of infant studies in the past two decades: there is increased accessibility of infants (Kessen et al., 1970) and an increased emphasis on behavioral origins. The chapters in this handbook exemplify the many issues and theoretical concepts whose beginnings are being sought.

By comparison, the field of infant assessment had its beginnings in an earlier time. Arnold Gesell was the prime mover of the infant assessment field. Nancy Bayley and Psyche Cattell were initial participants in its development. These three, more than any

[1]This chapter was prepared while the author was a Senior Staff Fellow in the Laboratory of Developmental Psychology, National Institute of Mental Health. The chapter is not copyrighted and is in the public domain.

others, were responsible for substantive development of the field. This chapter will review the work of these individuals, more from an historical than substantive perspective. Other chapters in this handbook deal with specific assessment techniques and their supporting literature.

PIONEERING EFFORTS OF ARNOLD GESELL

Gesell's commitment to infancy was singular:

It is the most consequential period of development for the simple but decisive reason that it comes first . . . . The infant learns to see, to hear, handle, walk, comprehend, and talk. He acquires an unaccountable number of habits fundamental to the complex art of living. Never again will his mind, his character, his spirit advance as rapidly as in this formative preschool period of growth. [Gesell, 1925, pp. 10–11]

Although infant assessment, as a field, was nonexistent before Gesell, his intentions did not appear to be directed at establishing an open-ended research area. Rather he focused on pragmatic goals—"infant welfare" and "infant hygiene"—and the diagnostic scales he developed were intended to distinguish among infants for whom welfare and hygiene would become important. Certainly Gesell felt that the need to develop diagnostic capability in this area had been signaled by the (then) recent establishment of the Federal Children's Bureau, departments of child hygiene, and various congressional acts promulgating mother and infant hygiene. Nevertheless, Gesell felt that pragmatic concerns should not be the sole determinant of the diagnostic approach. Indeed, he chided Binet and others for their use of chronological age to categorize abilities. While age norms were important in studying growth, Gesell argued that the *process* of growth was the vital concern of developmental psychology (Gesell, 1929).

Gesell modeled his approach after the work of Wilhelm His (1831–1904), the founder of human embryology. Gesell commented,

Just as the embryologist gets his basic conceptions of morphogenesis by building up indefatigably, step by step, detailed sectional view of growing organisms or of a growing organ, so may genetic psychology build up a continuing series of sections corresponding to the stages and moments of development. Even the cinema-film is a series of static pictures. When reproduced in close succession, this series restores the original motion . . . . Mental development is dynamic and elusive but it is essentially no more elusive than physical development and, just as the science of embryology is clarifying the phenomena of physical growth through countless sectional studies, so may genetic psychology attain an insight into the obscure developmental mechanics of the growth of behavior. [Gesell, 1925, p. 26]

Although Gesell provided perceptive descriptions of neonatal behavior, he chose not to begin his normative efforts at that early age. Rather, his initial starting point was at 3 months and included five other assessment points before 2 years: 6, 9, 12, 18, and 24 months of age. (Gesell also developed assessment procedures for children up to 6 years of age, but these are not covered in this chapter.) The purpose of these scales was broad and more clinical than not; the inclusion of specific items was based more on normative and descriptive utility than on any particular conception of intelligence. Nevertheless, Gesell contended that the scales were useful in interpreting "capacity and personality."

The initial total scale, published in 1925, consisted of 144 items divided into four general fields. *Motor behavior* included postural control, locomotion, prehension, drawing, and hand control. Items in this field were designed to assess coordination and motor capacity. *Language behavior* was assessed by means of vocabulary, word comprehension, conversation, and reproduction. *Adaptive behavior* was comprised of eye-hand coordination, imitation, object recovery, comprehension, discriminative performance, apperception and completion, and number conception. Items in this field were designed to assess responsivity to environmental change. *Personal and social behavior* included reactions to persons, personal habits, initiative and independence, play responses, and acquired information. These items were presumed to assess personality traits and were based on information obtained in maternal interviews. While Gesell cautiously noted that these four fields were ". . . simply a codification . . . not to be applied in an artificial manner," he added that, ". . . the classification followed psychological lines as far as was possible" (Gesell, 1925, p. 60).

Each of the infant schedules contained an average of 32 items, with some items appearing on more than one schedule. The composition of the scales varied. While motor items comprised 45% of the 4-month schedule, language items comprised only 3% of that schedule. By the 24th month, however, motor items were reduced to only 11% of the schedule, while language items comprised 21% of the schedule—that is, while motor items were quartered, language items had been increased by sevenfold. The percentage of adaptive behavior items remained relatively unchanged throughout the six schedules, ranging from 25 to 34% of the total number of items. The personal-social items increased from 28% of the 4-month schedule to 43% of the 24-month schedule. This meant that there was an increase in the number of items assessed by interview as the infant grew, possibly introducing increasing amounts of social desirability into the assessment.

Although Gesell's intention was to select a ". . . representative, unselective sample of the prepublic school population . . .," the composition of his longitudinal sample was difficult to ascertain. The population of infants was initially drawn from county records. While subject attrition rates were not given for the infant sample, attrition rates of 72 and 61% were noted for the 2- and 3-year-old children. The sample was generally balanced between males and females, and was composed of infants from "American homes." While infants from homes of professional classes were not excluded, the largest source of infants appeared to be from "baby welfare stations" attended by mothers from middle class homes. Markedly retarded children were excluded from the sample, as were markedly superior children.

Many of the specific items Gesell developed were adopted unchanged by later researchers. Although some have noted the need to revise the norms of certain items, no one has questioned the appropriateness of the items for use with infants. Table 5-1 presents a sampling of some of Gesell's initial items and their average age of appearance (50th percentile).

There have been no basic changes in the scale since 1925. The classification of items into motor, adaptive, language, and personal-social categories is still used. For 15 years, the major efforts of Gesell and his co-workers were directed at making finer gradations in the schedules and in restandardization. In 1938, Gesell presented normative distinctions for 4, 6, 8, 12, 16, 20, 24, 28, 32, 36, 40, 44, 48, 52, and 56 weeks; 15, 18, and 21 months; and 2-year-old infants (Gesell and Thompson, 1938; Gesell, 1940). These distinctions were achieved not by changing specific items on the schedules but by distinguishing finer gradations of response. For example, the response to the sound of the bell, once only head-turning, was changed to distinguish degrees of postural orientation as well as cessation of body movement.

The normative samples on which these schedules were based were inadequate. One

Table 5-1.　Representative Items from the 50th Percentile for each Month from Gesell's Initial Scale (1925)

4 Months	**6 Months**
Turns head toward sound of bell	Exploratory manipulation of spoon
Complete thumb apposition	Looks for fallen object
Defensive hand motions to paper placed lightly on face	Reacts to mirror image
	12 Months
9 Months	Builds tower of three cubes
Lifts inverted cup and secures cube placed under it	Spontaneously scribbles when given paper and pencil
Releases cube in cup	Walks unsupported
Holding two cubes, accepts a third (without dropping any)	
	24 Months
	Imitatively builds a three-block bridge
18 Months	Uses color names
Builds tower of four cubes	Gives full name and sex
Points to two or more parts of body	
Asks for things by words	

hundred and seven infants comprised the normative longitudinal sample, with about 35 infants seen at each age to 56 weeks. The infants were full-term and normal. The parents averaged 29 years of age and were primarily middle-class and of northern European ancestry. The 15- and 21-month schedules were based on another normative sample (20 to 30 infants) that Gesell described as "clinical cases . . . less homogeneous than normative cases . . . but relatively normal children" (Gesell, 1940, p. 321). The composition of the 18- and 24-month normative samples is not clear.

It should be noted that Gesell did defend his selection of subjects: "Our problem was *not* the construction of a scale for the evaluation of a child's behavior in terms of *all* infants of his age. We desired instead to investigate the patterning of growth" but, he added enigmatically, "to plot the course of development of a statistically average individual" (Gesell and Thompson, 1938).

Several attempts to examine the predictive validity of the Gesell schedules have been conducted since 1925. The results have not been encouraging. Wittenborn et al. (1956) examined the predictive validity of the schedules in groups of infants examined in Gesell's Yale Clinic. Wittenborn's sample was drawn from the population of the clinic and consisted largely of an adoptive sample, some tested before, and others after placement (total $N = 226$). In addition to the Gesell schedules, a number of assessments were made to cover areas possibly missed by the schedules, but still important in describing children. Most of the infants were assessed with the Gesell schedules before 40 weeks of age and in no cases were tested after 14 months of age. Some infants were tested twice if the tester was not confident of the infant's performance on the first test. Between 5 and 9 years of age the Stanford-Binet was given, and a number of selective assessments were made (scholastic achievement, physical development, and personal-social development). The correlations between the Gesell General Maturity Quotient and Stanford-Binet scores were uniformly low, ranging from -0.14 to 0.55. Excluding infants placed with families after testing and for whom Wittenborn had demonstrated related selective placement, the average correlation between the Gesell and Stanford-Binet was 0.09. Although some additional correlations were obtained between other assessments made at both ages (that is, adaptive subscale of the Gesell and hand dynamometer grip strength, $r = 0.45$), their importance was minimized by the authors. Regarding the relationships between the Gesell schedules and the Stanford-Binet, Wittenborn concluded that the correlations they obtained "were not only unreliable, but . . . too small to be of any practical interest." The other correlations "were so infrequent as to possibly have occurred by chance" (Wittenborn et al., 1956, p. 87).

Another assessment of the predictive validity of the Gesell schedules was conducted by Knobloch and Passamanick (1960). They compared the scores of slightly under 1000 full-term and premature infants on the Gesell schedules for 40 weeks of age and the Stanford-Binet for 3 years of age. In sharp contrast to Wittenborn et al., Knobloch and Pasamanick reported a correlation of 0.48 between the 40-week Gesell schedule and the 3-year Standford-Binet. This was not much different from the correlation between the 40-week and 3-year Gesell schedules ($r = 0.51$).[2] However, Knobloch and Pasamanick were predicting over a much shorter time span in this study.

Apart from the time factor, another possible explanation of the large difference between the correlations of Wittenborn et al. and those of Knobloch and Pasamanick may have involved the rater reliability of the initial assessment. The procedure used by Wittenborn included reassessment with the Gesell if the examiner was not confident about an initial assessment during infancy. Rater agreement data was not presented, but one might suspect that if the reassessment had been a part of the procedure it may have been low. Knobloch and Pasamanick reported rater-agreement correlations of over 0.98 between the training examiner and three trainees.

In a later study, Knobloch and Pasamanick (1966) reported some of the highest correlations obtained with the Gesell scales. In a heterogeneous sample of normal and clinical infants seen before 1 year of age and tested 7 years later with the Stanford-Binet, the authors obtained a correlation of 0.70 ($N = 123$) between the Gesell and the Stanford-Binet. However, it appears likely that size of the correlation was augmented by the heterogeneity of the sample.

Drillien (1961) also used a sample of heterogeneous infants in a longitudinal study of the effects of prematurity. As had Knobloch and Pasamanick (1966), Drillien obtained high correlations between Gesell schedules administered during infancy and tests administered several years later. Based on samples of more than 200 at each age, Drillien obtained correlations of 0.54, 0.57, and 0.66 between the Gesell schedules administered at 6, 12, and 24 months and the Terman-Miles administered at 5 years.

Aware of the variability in magnitude of predictive coefficients obtained by various investigators, Ames (1967) defended the use of infancy scales as a form of assessment. She correctly noted that Gesell had not intended his scale to be an intelligence test. Therefore, attempts to minimize its utility by demonstrating low correlations with later intelligence tests were misdirected. Furthermore, the use of homogeneous samples of infants, excluding neurologically damaged infants for whom the Gesell scales were also intended, artificially depressed test-retest correlations. In support of her contentions, Ames tested 33 infants between 24 weeks and 1 year of age, retesting them at 10 years with the Wechsler Intelligence Scale for Children (WISC). Twenty-one of those infants retested at 10 years had scores on both tests within 10 points of one another. Sixteen of the 21 had scores differing by 5 points or less. She concluded that "infant and preschool tests yield scores which are highly predictive of . . . 10-year-old performance on the WISC" (Ames, 1967, p. 235).

In objecting to the use of later intelligence tests as a measure of validity, it is not clear why Ames used the WISC rather than a broader form of assessment at 10 years (as had

[2]The 3-year Gesell schedule and Stanford-Binet were correlated, $r = 0.87$ in their data.

Wittenborn). In addition, the majority of the Ames sample were children of Yale faculty members, not necessarily a heterogeneous group. And although the presentation of percentages of infants maintaining scores within a given range at retesting is informative, the relation to other studies using the correlation coefficient as the index of predictive power is unclear. Nonetheless, our computation of correlation coefficients from Ames' Table 2 yielded two significant correlations (of 8) between the infant scale and the WISC: at 24 weeks, $r = 0.58$ ($p < 0.05$, $N = 11$), and at 28 weeks, $r = 0.82$ ($p < 0.02$, $N = 7$). These were the earliest testings in infancy. Why the later, more reliable infant testings did not yield significant correlations is unclear.

Three factor analyses have been performed on selected Gesell scales. Richards and Nelson (1938) contended that the 6-month Gesell scale could be broken into three factors: an "alertness" factor (items assessing attentiveness more than motor performance), a "motor ability" factor (items dealing with reaching, grasping, and manipulation), and a "testability" or "halo" factor common to all items except those assessed by the mother's report. The testability factor presumably reflected both the tester's rapport with the infant as well as the infant's predispositional set to testing on that particular day. However, in a later analysis of 6-, 12-, and 18-month Gesell schedules, Richards and Nelson (1939) reported that the testability factor did not emerge, and they could only replicate the alertness and motor factors. Furthermore, the alertness factor was described as containing items dealing with "distance reception" and " playfulness." The motor factor was present in all items "because of the obvious fact that all behavior at this early level is . . . motor" (Richards and Nelson, 1938, p. 317).

More recently, Stott and Ball (1965) performed varimax and biquartimin analyses on 6- and 12-month Gesell scales, with clearest results on the 6-month scale. It yielded eight factors dealing with manual closure and generalized manipulation, memory, directed reaching and purposeful manipulation, locomotion, reflexes, manual production of sound, visually instigated action, and body control. Factors from the 12-month scale were less clear, involving responses to general social communication, responses to verbal communication, gross psychomotor control, memory of demonstrations, and deductive reasoning. Stott and Ball attributed the contrast between the number and types of factors in these analyses and those of Richards and Nelson, in part, to recent developments in computer technology.

The results of these studies are not impressive, particularly if the Gesell scales are presumed to be compatible with the Stanford-Binet in assessing intelligence, a presumption Gesell never intended. He distinguished between psychometric intelligence and developmental status, which referred to a complete description of the child; his adaptive, linguistic, and personal-social behaviors. Gesell's interest was in assessing developmental status from a comparative perspective, feeling as he did that a moderately positive relationship between his scales and intelligence would have been theoretically appropriate.

Although Gesell did not have many students, his major publications were written with associates (Gesell and Thompson, 1938; Gesell and Amatruda, 1945, 1947). Two of his students, Hilda Knobloch and Benjamin Pasamanick, have recently published an extensively updated version of the Gesell scales (Knobloch ad Pasamanick, 1974). It is the most thorough single reference and source of documentation for the scales and is an essential resource for anyone using them.

Over the years, Knobloch and Pasamanick were able to test large numbers of children of varying backgrounds and abilities. Their data provide more adequate norms for the scales than the original data collected by Gesell. As a result, Knobloch and Pasamanick changed some of the norms for the 36- through 56-week schedules. Ten items, mostly involving adaptive behavior, were moved to adjacent later points in the scale. Thirty-two items, mostly involving personal-social and language items were moved to earlier points in the scale. Perhaps more important, Knobloch and Pasamanick divided Gesell's original motor behavior category into gross- and fine-motor behavior categories. The fine-motor category includes hand and finger movements occurring in grasping and manipulating objects.

Almost 50 years separate the first major publication of Gesell's scales and Knobloch and Pasamanick's compendium. Essentially minor changes in the scales have improved them. But, basically, the scales and the perspective maintained by Gesell remain (Knobloch and Pasamanick, 1974, pp. 140–141): the scales are not measures of intelligence, but of total development. Qualitative clinical impressions, therefore, supersede test scores (when they conflict) in assessing developmental scales. Furthermore, attempts to assess the intellectual status or derive intelligence quotients from the scales are eschewed as dangerous distortions of early development.

EFFORTS OF CATTELL AND BAYLEY

The Cattell Infant Intelligence Scale

Unlike Gesell, Psyche Cattell was less concerned with an enveloping, clinical assessment than with producing a standardized assessment of mental ability. Cattell found the Gesell scales, as well as several others available during the 1930s, wanting in objectivity, standardization, appeal to young infants, and amenability to numerical ratings rather than descriptions. Cattell was particularly dissatisfied with the proliferation of motor performance items in the scale as they were "probably only indirectly related to mental development" (Cattell, 1940, pp. 15–21).

Cattell directed her efforts toward developing an assessment free of these alleged shortcomings. The degree to which she was successful is best reflected in her own words (1940, p. 23):

The Gesell tests were used as a point from which to build. The items of the Gesell tests were first arranged in an age scale similar to that of the Stanford-Binet tests. In order to make the scale as much an intelligence scale as possible, over 100 items, the responses to which were thought to be unduly influenced by home training or to depend mainly on large muscular control, were eliminated. Other items collected from various sources were added to fill the gaps. All the directions for giving and scoring items have been written in as detailed and in as objective a manner as possible. A large majority of the items taken from the Gesell tests were modified, more or less, in order to make the giving or scoring more objective or to increase or decrease the difficulty for the purpose of attaining an equal number of items at each of the age levels covered. A total of 1,346 examinations were used in connection with the standardization, but, unfortunately, those items which were added later were not given to as many children as were those used from the beginning.

The scale was designed to be compatible with the Stanford-Binet. An inspection of the specific items in the scale indicates that, by and large, they are similar to those in the Gesell scales.

Cattell's normative sample consisted of 274 infants participating in a longitudinal study conducted at the Harvard School of Public Health. The infants were seen at 3, 6, 9, 12, 18, 24, 30, and 36 months of age. They were from normal deliveries and from families of northern European ancestry in which the father was apparently gainfully employed. Occupational descriptions indicated that the families were largely of middle-class status. A $50 fee covering prenatal, delivery, and postnatal care probably excluded lower-class families from participating. Subject attrition was 25% over a 7-year period.

The scale consists of five items for each age level, with one or two alternates. Each item is scored as pass or fail, and is proportionately weighted in determining an infant's level of performance. The split-half reliability of the 3-month scale was poor ($r = 0.56$, Spearman-Brown corrected); scales for later ages reached acceptable levels of reliability (Spearman-Brown correlations ranging from 0.86 to 0.90). Notwithstanding, correlations with the Stanford-Binet at 3 years of age were poor: $r = 0.10$ from 3 months, $r = 0.34$ from 6 months, $r = 0.18$ from 9 months, $r = 0.56$ from 12 months, $r = 0.67$ from 18 months, and $r = 0.71$ from 24 months (N range, 42 to 57). Given that her scale was intended to be a downward extension of the Stanford-Binet, Cattell did not appear to be appropriately circumspect in her general instructions regarding its use; her recommendations emphasized predictive power without respect to age. However, she did suggest that close attention be paid to clinical and other subjective impressions of the infant not specifically related to the test or testing situation. These, she admitted, could be of value in revealing areas of dysfunction which had distorted performance on a particular scale or item (Cattell, 1940, pp. 85–92).

A factor analysis of the 3- and 6-month Cattell scales performed by Stott and Ball (1965) yielded four factors at each age. At 3 months, three of the factors had visual components: visual attention, hand and arm responses to visual stimuli, and visual anticipation. The fourth factor involved activity with the fingers. At 6 months the factors remained somewhat the same: direct reaching, manipulative evaluation, persistent goal-directed behavior, and exploratory manipulation.

Escalona (1950) examined the potential effects of "non-test" considerations on the Cattell scales. Using a six-category classification of development (retarded to superior) based on either the Cattell or Gesell scales, Escalona examined the relationship of test reliability to subjective judgments of maximal performance. The subjective judgments were based on the judges' "impression as to whether the subject had performed in as mature a manner as was possible for this particular infant" (Escalona, 1950, p. 122). In a sample of 72 adoptive children, Escalona found that 38 infants had not been tested at their optimal level. Retesting the 38 placed 80% of them in a developmental category different from their original placement. In contrast, slightly less than one-third of the 34 infants initially tested under optimal circumstances were placed in another category at retesting. Unfortunately, Escalona did not describe the time interval between test and retest beyond saying that it ranged from one-half to several years.

In a similar study Gallagher (1953) retested 4- to 24-month-old adopted infants on the basis of whether or not they were judged as having done their best on initial testing with the Cattell scales. The infants were divided into two groups; one from deprived families and exhibiting poor performance at initial testing; the other, a control group of normals. Gallagher found that while one-third of the normal infants changed categories upon retesting, 42% of the deprived infants changed categories upon retesting. Gallagher also reported test-retest stabilities for both groups: for the deprived group a correlation of 0.77 at an interval of 7.9 months; for the nondeprived group a correlation of 0.83 at an interval of 7.2 months. Interestingly, while the deprived group significantly increased its average performance by 9 points at retesting, the normal group did not change. Clearly, consideration of such factors is important in obtaining accurate assessments of infants. To routinely administer test items to an infant while ignoring condition and qualitative aspects of the infant's performance, runs the risk of obtaining distorted results.

Cavanaugh, et al. (1957) compared premature, term, and postmature infants on the Cattell scales and the Stanford-Binet. Assessment with the Cattell occurred at 6, 12, 18, and 24 months. Assessment with the Stanford-Binet occurred at 36, 48, and 60 months of age. The higher correlations between tests at different ages occurred in a subsample of term infants ($N = 34$) for whom longitudinal data from 6 to 48 months was complete and from whom it was thought that generally valid test scores had been obtained. The correlations generally increased in magnitude as the infant matured and the test-retest interval decreased (i.e., the 6- and 12-month correlation saw 0.32; the 6-month and 60-month correlation was 0.21; the 48- and 60-month correlation was 0.69). These trends also characterized the correlations from the whole sample (premature, term, postmature). Changes in mean scores between the ages generally tended to be significant; differences existed between the means of the Cattell scores and those of the Stanford-Binet scores. The authors questioned whether functions tapped by the Stanford-Binet and Cattell scales were similar, suggesting that the Cattell could not be empirically defended as a downward extension of the Stanford-Binet.

Escalona and Moriarity (1961) compared the Cattell and Gesell scales with the WISC, assessing infants from 1 to 8 months with both scales and retesting them between 7 and 8½ years of age with the WISC. The correlations between the Cattell and WISC scores, and the Gesell and WISC scores were 0.05 and 0.08, respectively. Dividing the WISC scores into four categories, ranging from low-average to superior, yielded a slightly, but still umimpressive, relationship between the infant assessments and later testing. The addition of clinical appraisal data collected during the infancy assessments provided some predictive ability and appeared more useful than the scales themselves in predicting the gross categorical distinctions based on the WISC. Escalona and Moriarity concluded that "for children in this age range, a clinical appraisal based on total test performance on two test instruments is a more accurate predictor of later intelligence range than are scores obtained from either the Cattell or Gesell tests alone" (Escalona and Moriarity, 1961, pp. 604–605).

The California Infant Scales

Bayley's reasons for developing her own scale appeared to be related to her dissatisfaction with currently available scales and the manner in which they had been standardized. She was particularly critical of the use of small institutionalized samples in developing normative scales (Bayley, 1933, pp. 5–10). Although Bayley also relied heavily on Gesell's work in developing her own scale, she has continued, more than anyone else, to improve her scales over the more than 40 years since she developed them. Her efforts have been directed primarily toward strengthening the scales by revising them on larger normative samples.

Bayley's scales are divided into mental and motor areas. Among the mental test items are "tests of adaptability or learning and tests of sensory acuity and fine motor (manual) coordinations" (1933, p. 24). Motor items deal with "gross body coordinations" (p. 24). Although most of the specific test items were drawn from the Gesell scales, Bayley omitted those that did not elicit differentiating behavior at successive ages or were not observed in sufficiently large numbers.

The California First Year Mental Scale (1933) was Bayley's first formal test. It contained 115 items which were judged on a pass-fail basis. Items were not considered passed until consecutive successes had occurred to the same item on two adjacent testings. The scale started at 1 month and continued at monthly intervals until 15 months of age. Thereafter, 3-month intervals separated the tests. Thus, before an item was considered as having been successfully passed at 1 month, it must also have been passed at 2 months. Rather than meaning that a test score could not be computed until an infant had been tested twice, this meant that a score was tentative and modifiable dependent on an ensuing test. An infant's score was cumulative from month to month, and consisted of all the previous items passed on preceding tests.

Bayley's original normative sample consisted of 61 normal infants born to upper-middle-class families in the Berkeley, California area. The infants were tested longitudinally over the duration of data collection. Subject attrition reduced the sample to 53 by the second year. Split-half reliabilities (Spearman-Brown corrected) computed on this initial sample were superior to those obtained by other infant scales, averaging $r = 0.63$ for the first 3 months, $r = 0.92$ for the 4th through the 8th month, and $r = 0.82$ thereafter (until 2 years of age). Concomitantly, test-retest reliabilities between successive tests averaged $r = 0.63$ for the first three months and $r = 0.80$ thereafter.

Bayley's motor scale (1935) was initially published 2 years after her mental scale. It was similar to the earlier scale, as it was drawn largely from the Gesell. The normative sample for it was the same as for the mental scale. Testing intervals were also identical to those used in the development of the mental scale. The scale contained 76 items and was scored in a cumulative fashion identical to the scoring procedure for the mental scale. Split-half reliabilities for the motor scale was not as high as for the mental scales during the early months; an average correlation of $r = 0.58$ for the first 3 months, 0.74 for the 4th through 8th month. Following 8 months, the average correlation was as high as that of the mental scale. The test-retest correlations among consecutive tests ranging from 1 month through 15 months yielded correlations comparable to those obtained for the mental scale; they were low for the early months but reached acceptable levels by the 5th month ($r = 0.75$). Unlike the mental scales, however, the test-retest correlations were very poor from 15 to 24 months. Here, where tests occurred at 3-month rather than 1-month intervals, correlations averaged $r = 0.33$. Correlations between the initial mental and motor scales for months 1 through 24 were variable, averaging $r = 0.47$.

These initial mental and motor scales have undergone both major and minor revisions in the 40 years that Bayley has worked with them. Samples from the Collaborative Study of the National Institute of Neurological Diseases and Blindness have provided additional bases for modifications. Bayley's test manual (1969) contains a brief history of the development of the scales, standardization and reliability information, and complete instructions for administering and scoring tests. Performance on the mental scale is expressed in the form of a "mental development index"; performance on the motor scale is expressed on a "psychomotor development index." The mental scale contains 163 items and is normed at half-month intervals from 2 to 5 months, and at 1-month intervals from 6 to 30 months. The motor scale, containing 81 items, is normed at identical-age intervals. The Infant Behavior Record is described in the manual, and contains a set of ratings that provides quantitative and qualitative information regarding the infant's social, emotional, and stylistic behavior during administration of the mental and motor scales; it could possibly contribute considerably to an accurate assessment in light of the importance of the "non-test" factors discussed earlier (Escalona, 1950; Gallagher, 1953).

Bayley's sample, comprised of 1262 term and normal infants, was stratified by sex, color ("white," "nonwhite"), rural-urban residence, and education of head of household. The only difference Bayley found between these stratifications was for color: nonwhite infants scored significantly higher than white infants on the motor scale between the 3rd and 14th month. The corrected split-half reliabilities for the 1969 mental and motor scales were impressive, averaging 0.86. But these corrected split-half reliabilities did not include the half-month intervals from 2 to 5 months and the 1-month intervals from 6 to 30 months shown in the normative tables in the manual. Rather, 1-month intervals were used between 2 and 6 months, 2-month intervals between 12 and 30 months.

The only observer-agreement (simultaneous observation) data available are for a preliminary version of the scale (Werner and Bayley, 1966). Summarizing their analyses based on a sample of 90, Bayley reported 89% agreement for 59 items on the 8-month mental scale, and 93% agreement for 20 items on the motor scale (Bayley, 1969). A subsample of this group ($N = 28$) tested at a 1-week interval with 8-month scale yielded test-retest observer agreement percentages of 76% for the mental scale and 75% for the motor scale (Bayley, 1969). The correlation between the mental and motor scale ranged from $r = 0.24$ to $r = 0.78$; the higher correlations occurred at the younger ages.

Correlations between the Bayley mental scale and the Stanford-Binet have ranged from minimal to moderate. Based on her 1933 sample, Bayley reported no relation (r range: $-0.13 - 0.02$) between the initial mental scale administered before 2 years of age and the Stanford-Binet from 5 to 13 years of age (Bayley, 1949). She reported a correlation of $r = 0.53$ between the 24-month mental scale and Stanford-Binet on another sample of infants ($N = 120$).

Several attempts at a priori classifications of her 1933 and 1935 scales provided Bayley with only one categorization of the mental scale that she thought was successful—that was separating sensorimotor from predominantly adaptive behaviors (Bayley, 1933). She was unable to make more specific categorizations such as visual behavior, eye-hand coordination, reaction to sound, and so on. The Initial Motor Scale (1935) was divided into "anti-gravity" and "gross body motion" categories. Antigravity behaviors were typified by head raising and maintaining erect posture while sitting or standing. Gross body motions were represented by body turning, arm and leg thrusting, and lateral head movements.

Stott and Ball (1965) examined the factor groupings of a subset of Bayley's items at the 6- and 12-month levels. At 6 months responses to external stimuli fell into affective evaluative, exploratory, cognitive, and motoric factors. At 12 months the factors were more reflective of self-initiating behaviors: understanding of relationships, linguistic communication, cognitively adaptive behavior, and memory.

Ramey, et al. (1973) have reported high-magnitude correlations of the Bayley mental and motor scores with Stanford-Binet scores, stating that in situations where natural environmental variation was reduced, predictive power of the scales should be high, ostensibly reflecting the genetic composition of intelligence. Their sample consisted of 24 infants attending a day-care project over a 3-year period. The average age of the infants entering the project was 3 months. Socioeconomic status varied from poverty levels to upper middle-class. Correlating performance on the motor scale at 6 to 8, 9 to 12, 13 to 16 months with Stanford-Binet scores at 36 months yielded rs of decreasing magnitude (0.77, 0.56, and 0.43, respectively). Correlating performance on the mental scale at the same ages yielded rs of increasing magnitude (0.49, 0.71, and 0.90, respectively). Ramey el al.

(1973) attributed the magnitude of these correlations to the homogeneity of environmental conditions created by the day care. However, it is equally likely that the magnitude of the correlations was caused, at least in part, by chance fluctuations due to the small sample on which these correlations were based ($N = 11$). As noted earlier, Bayley has reported a correlation of 0.53 ($N = 120$) between her early scores and later Stanford-Binet scores.

Hofstaetter (1954) conducted a factor analysis of the Bayley scale. He examined Bayley's published correlation matrices for performance on selected standardized tests between 2 months and 18 years and described three orthogonal factors, each of which was impressively associated with a particular age. His first factor was similar to one described by Bayley and dealt with "sensorimotor alertness" at approximately 12 months of age. The second factor dealt with "persistence . . . , a tendency to act in accordance with an established set rather than upon interfering stimulation" (Hofstaetter, 1954, pp. 161–162). This factor peaked at about 3 years of age. The third factor became asymptotic at slightly over 7 years. This factor appeared to deal with the manipulation of "symbols" and resembled Spearman's "g." This rather dramatic analysis was severely criticized 13 years later by Cronbach (1967). Cronbach maintained that the matrices Hofstaetter used conformed to a simplex pattern—that is, one in which initially high correlations between adjacent measurements progressively decreased as the measurements became separated in time. Cronbach argued that Hofstaetter's factors were inherent in the simplex structure of the matrices, and supported his argument by replicating Hofstaetter's analysis and demonstrating that a principal-components analysis and varimax rotation did not yield similar factors. Cronbach concluded that "students of child development should drop the Hofstaetter analysis from further consideration. It was an interesting exploration, nothing more" (Cronbach, 1967, p. 289).

A PERSPECTIVE: GESELL, CATTELL, BAYLEY

The efforts of Gesell, Cattell, and Bayley span a period of nearly 70 years. During that time American psychology has moved from its early beginnings to an impressive diversity of approaches. Interestingly, it has been both a shortcoming and a strength that the cumulative efforts of Gesell, Cattell, and Bayley have reflected only a limited part of that diversity. The press to move from behavioristic descriptions of molecular phenomena toward more abstract psychological processes was least felt by those studying infancy. Thus, while able to focus their efforts on behavior change and the intricacies of its assessment, they were also somewhat unappreciative of cognitively based approaches relating early sensorimotor skills to conceptual development. Nevertheless, each of their unique efforts was coordinated by their substantive focus on developmental measurements in infancy and their commitments to eliminating the shortcomings of earlier scales.

Although all three investigators focused on the assessment of developmental changes in infancy, each had somewhat different views regarding what their scales actually measured. Gesell eschewed the concept of intelligence, choosing instead to deal with developmental status. This was a holistic descriptor representing the totality of an infant's effective functioning and was composed of motor, adaptive, personal-social, and language behaviors. And although Gesell was very much aware of the necessary interplay of genetic and environmental influences, he saw development to be primarily a result of a maturational unfolding process generally unaffected by external influences. In contrast, Cattell's specific intent was to measure "intelligence." Her scales were to be a downward extension of the Stanford-Binet. The exclusion from her scale of Gesell items that she felt were unduly reflective of home influence or large muscle control, however, suggested that she was also sympathetic to a view of intelligence that was relatively unencumbered by environmental influence. Bayley was not as averse to restricting the role of developmental tests to the measurement of intelligence as was Gesell. She noted very early, however, that intelligence was an emergent function, taking different forms at different periods of development. Thus, from her view one would not have expected correlations to appear between what were disparate forms of intelligence at different ages.

Underlying all three approaches was the presumption that the motive force of development was provided by genetic factors. Ignoring the press of environmental over constitutional interpretations of phenotypic variation, these approaches have been cast (at least tacitly) as supporting a genetic conception of intelligence.

The factor-analytic studies of these scales produced some interesting findings. Most often cited is Hofstaetter's (1954) contention that three orthogonal factors described performance at three ages, those factors and ages having a surprising correspondence with Piaget's cognitive-developmental approach to intellectual functioning. Hofstaetter's first factor, "sensorimotor alertness," peaks at 1 year and corresponds to Piaget's "sensorimotor period." Hofstaetter's second factor, "persistence," peaks at 3 years and is somewhat compatible wth Piaget's "preoperational period," a stage during which the child is beginning to establish rules of logical relationships. Hofstaetter's third factor, "planning," becomes asymptotic at about 8 years. This factor is compatible with Piaget's period of "concrete operations," a stage during which the logical relationships between numbers and objects in time and space are being established. The present writer has not encountered any studies attempting to replicate Hofstaetter's work with adjustments to accommodate Cronbach's (1967) telling criticism of the methodology used. Nevertheless, some communality has appeared in other kinds of factor analyses of the various scales (Stott and Ball, 1965). The early scales (6 months) yield sensorimotor factors (exploration of the proximal environment and demonstration of minimal temporal integration in the form of short memory and goal-directed behavior). Factors for later ages (12 months) entail primitive social awareness and communication. It therefore is likely that the Gesell, Cattell, and Bayley scales are tapping similar facets of infant behavior. This communality appears suggestive of the type of factor that Hofstaetter described for the earliest period, Cronbach's critique notwithstanding.

THE INFLUENCE OF PIAGET: TWO ORDINAL SCALES

The onset of Piaget's great influence on American developmental psychology was dependent not so much on the original publication of his work, but rather on its translation into English. Thus, it was not until the 1950s that Piaget began to gain any sizeable readership among American psychologists (Baldwin, 1967). Attempts to develop infant-assessment procedures had long been underway; and to the extent that Piaget had introduced a new theoretical approach to developmental psychology, traditional infant-assessment procedures were devoid of that approach. From a Piagetian perspective, the assumptions implicit in the traditional tests were major and largely in error (Uzgiris and Hunt, 1975): developmental progress was summative and nonhierarchical; progress was not dependent upon magnitude of achievement at one particular level, but only on the occurrence of a behavior (as assessed by a test item) within an array of other contemporaneous behaviors.

Piaget's approach was not so much psychologically oriented as it was epistemologically oriented. His concern was not with the developmental psychology of the child but with the process of the child's coming to view the basic elements of existence. As Gesell was the prime mover in characterizing the maturational unfolding of the child, Piaget was the prime mover in describing the child as the prototypical epistemic philosopher. They were both different from one another in one other important aspect: the pragmatic Gesell took development to be primarily an accretion of increasingly complex behavioral units, relatively unaffected by environmental contingencies, whereas Piaget undertook to describe development as a series of hierarchical, qualitatively different stages, containing horizontal and vertical movement, and inextricably bound to environmental exchange. The initial stages were seen as primarily reflexive; the later stages represented the progressive integration of developing internal processes and physical coordination, neither of which could develop independently. In one respect Piaget and Gesell were similar: they both undertook to describe the totality of the child's functioning, not a circumscribed area of behavior.

Two assessment procedures based on Piaget's theory have been developed recently (Corman and Escalona, 1969; Uzgiris and Hunt, 1975). The Einstein scales of sensorimotor intelligence (Escalona and Corman, 1969) are designed for infants between one month and two years of age. The procedure consists of three scales containing a total of 54 items. The prehension scale covers the development of adaptive reflexes (primary circular responses) and early systematic behavior (secondary circular responses) in the lowest age range. This scale includes spontaneous exploratory behavior, as well as items (such as object-grasping) that are identical to those developed by Gesell. The object permanence scale focuses on the growing awareness that objects in the environment exist permanently and independently of behavior. Items on this scale index the infant's ability to follow the trajectory of objects to the limits of the visual field, as well as the ability to continue behaviors initiated prior to visual obstruction. The space scale involves the infant's ability to function effectively in three-dimensional space. Included here are items assessing goal-directed behavior in the face of physical obstruction, and items eliciting object manipulation indicative of a three-dimensional perspective.

Corman and Escalona (1969) examined properties of the scales in an unselected sample of approximately 300 infants, ranging in age from slightly under 1 month to slightly over 2 years. Performance on the prehension, object permanence, and spatial relationships scales showed correlations with age ranging from 0.83 to 0.85 (rho). An appropriate indication of the adequacy of the scales was gained by determining the age at which a child entered a particular stage of performance. The scales defined four Piagetian stages and two substages. According to Piagetian theory, all of the stages should be passed in sequential order. The average age at entering into each stage was found to be sequential, beginning at 2.8 months for the first substage of Piagetian stage two and ending with entry into stage six at 10.1 months. Although some individual infants entered adjacent stages simultaneously, no infant was found to skip a stage or enter a later stage before an earlier stage. This supported the contention that the stages were invariant in sequence. Corman and Escalona correctly noted that their scales, rather than assessing "intelligence," generally defined as "the relative ability for successful problem-solving," measured the "methods and means employed in problem-solving." The scales should therefore be moderately, but not highly, correlated with standardized intelligence tests.

The assessment procedure developed by Uzgiris and Hunt (1975) is similar to the Einstein scales in coverage, but is divided into six rather than three scales. The first scale, visual pursuit and permanence of objects, is concerned with the infant's increasing awareness of the existence of objects outside of the immediate perceptual field. Visual pursuit as well as behaviors indicating search for a hidden object are presumed to index this ability. This scale is comparable to the Einstein object permanence scale. The second scale, development of means for obtaining desired environmental events, covers actions initiated by the infant to achieve a particular outcome. Included are sustained hand-watching and the use of implements to obtain objects out of reach. This scale subsumes the Einstein prehension scale. The third scale, development of imitation, is divided into two subscales: the vocal subscale begins with differentiation of distress and pleasure by crying and cooing, and ends with the repetition of words. Included are vocal behaviors apparently imitative, but also adaptive; these might be construed as externally elicited circular reactions. The gestural subscale is concerned with imitative responses requiring body action. The fourth scale is the development of operational causality. Anticipatory behavior is the earliest behavior relevant to this scale; systematic behaviors (circular reactions included) directed toward establishing antecedent-consequent relationships are also included, whether or not the attribution of causality is internal or external. The fifth scale, construction of object relations in space, involves the infant's increasing capacity to appreciate three-dimensional space. Assessed here is the infant's ability to track and/or locate objects for which visual cues have been somehow interrupted. This scale is comparable to the Einstein space scale. The sixth scale is the development of schemes for relating to objects. It is generally directed at assessing the changing role of toys in the infant's environment and is not generally related to any particular stage. Progressive use of toys as extensions of the infant, as objects of curiosity and as functional units, are noted with this scale.

The scales were tested and revised on three samples, the first two of which totaled 65. The infants were drawn exclusively from metropolitan middle-class families. The final sample consisted of 84 infants, also from middle-class families. Observer agreement and 48-h test-retest stability indices were high, ranging between 92 and 97%, and 70 and 85% stability by individual items in each scale. All of the scales were highly correlated with age (no correlation less than $r = 0.88$). Concomitantly, the intercorrelations of the scales were high, none falling below $r = 0.80$. However, with the effects of age partialled out, the intercorrelations decreased dramatically, only two of them yielded rs above 0.50. Mean ages for the achievement of each scale stage were presented, but Uzgiris and Hunt (1975) noted that their samples had not been selected with the intention of providing representative normative data for each age.

Comparisons of performance on the Uzgiris-Hunt scales and the Bayley scales were made by King and Seegmiller (1973) on a group of unselected Harlem infants. The infants were assessed with both scales at 14, 18, and 22 months of age. Although King and Seegmiller were able to find mean differences in their sample supporting the ordinality of the Uzgiris-Hunt scales, they could not produce evidence of useful prediction to the Bayley. At 14 months of age, only three of the six Piagetian scales yielded significant correlations with the mental and motor Bayley scales. At 18 months only two scales yielded significant correlations with the Bayley mental scale. At 22 months, three scales were correlated with the Bayley mental scale. The authors also noted that performance variation dropped sharply between 14 and 22 months; in some cases these standard deviations were so low as to preclude valid correlational computations. King and Seegmiller suggested that the response categories should be expanded to allow for greater variation in response and that procedures be more rigorously standardized. King and Seegmiller also suggested that the poor predictive power of the Uzgiris-Hunt scales was attributable to "uneven cognitive growth" (King and Seegmiller, 1973, p. 325). It should be noted that the poor predictive power of the scales, as indexed by between-age correlations, does not detract from their validity, as indexed by the sequential entrance of stages. The latter may be a more appropriate criterion by Piagetian as well as statistical standards. In this respect, uneven cognitive growth might even be predicted.

Wachs (1975) provided more impressive evidence for the predictive power of the Uzgiris-Hunt assessment. In a small longitudinal sample tested at 3-month intervals between 12 and 24 months, Wachs obtained correlations between all the scales and performance on the Stanford-Binet at 31 months. At 12 months only the visual pursuit and permanence of objects scale was significantly correlated to Stanford-Binet scores. By 24 months, all of the scales except means for obtaining desired environmental events were significantly correlated with Stanford-Binet performance.

CONCLUSION

Five major efforts to develop early assessment procedures have been reviewed in this chapter. The efforts of Gesell, Cattell, and Bayley were grouped together because of their substantive similarity and their common emphasis on nonenvironmental influences. The scales developed by Corman and Escalona, and Uzgiris and Hunt are based on Piagetian theory. While many items in these scales are similar to those originated by Gesell, their scoring and interpretation are quite different. Qualitative rather than quantitative changes are the units of measure; progress is ordinal rather than ratio-based.

Generally, all of the scales meet psychometrically acceptable standards. Adequate internal consistency, concurrent interrater agreement, and at least short-term test-retest stability have been shown. These facts alone reflect a considerable accomplishment, considering the unique problems encountered in working with infants. Nevertheless there is a tendency toward poor psychometric performance with the scales for younger infants. The major shortcomings of the scales relate to their normative samples. Unfortunately, only the Bayley scales have been based on large and varied samples. Bayley's samples, unlike the others, included nonwhite and rural-born infants from geographically diverse areas of the United States.

In spite of the acceptable psychometric properties of the scales, they have proved to be systematically poor predictors of later performance; the earlier in infancy the initial test, and the greater the time between initial and final testing, the poorer the predictive relationship. Thus, the loss of predictive power occurs precisely in the range for which there had been the most hope for strong relations: long-range prediction from a point early in life. The evidence for the lack of early predictive power is most convincing for the Gesell, Cattell, and Bayley scales; but of course, these are the scales that have been most extensively used and studied. The others are too recent to have accumulated an extensive literature.

The scales of Gesell, Cattell, and Bayley comprise the traditional scales. These traditional scales had been described earlier as supporting—directly, in Gesell's case, and tacitly, in Bayley's case—a maturationally and genotypically controlled conception of development. While Bayley's conception of development did not preclude an *ex post facto* determination that intelligence is composed of emergent factors rather than of one general, fixed factor, it was clearly in line with a general factor orientation. Not until Bayley had collected her data was she drawn to a conception of intelligence as emergent and functionally unique at different periods (Bayley, 1933). By comparison, the Piaget-based scales

(Uzgiris and Hunt, Corman and Escalona) were constructed from the viewpoint that qualitative changes in intelligence characterize growth.

Reflecting the increasing appreciation of Piagetian theory, and a cognitive-developmental approach, McCall et al. (1972) reanalyzed selected data from the Fels Longitudinal Study. They related early performance on the Gesell scales to later performance on the Stanford-Binet, WISC, or Wechsler-Bellevue. The Gesell scales had been administered at 6, 12, 18, and 24 months. The Stanford-Binet, WISC, or Wechsler Bellevue had been administered between 3½ and 13 years of age. The total sample was composed of approximately 150 children. Rather than correlating total scores, as had studies in the past, McCall et al. performed principal-components analyses at each infant testing age, relating those components to later performance.

Reduction of the Gesell data to principal components yielded a major component that was correlated between all ages (6, 12, 18, and 24 months). While this might have been described as a general factor in intelligence ("g"), McCall and others suggested the contrary. This factor accounted for no more than 19% of the total test variance and, up to 12 months of age, showed no relationship to any of the later tests.

Although most principal components appeared similar for males and females within each age, the pattern of cross-age correlations between the components differed. Females tended to display cross-age continuity in the form of correlations between homologous components. Males, on the other hand, tended to exhibit cross-age continuity between nonhomologous components. Thus, by applying methods of analysis appropriate to a concept of intelligence as an emergent phenomenon, showing functionally different properties at different ages, this study was able to distinguish two pathways of cognitive development in the sexes.

Correlations between the major infancy component and later performance on the Stanford-Binet, WISC, or Wechsler-Bellevue reached statistical significance at 12 months of age for females and 18 months of age for males. The correlations for the females, ranging between 0.41 and 0.69, were impressive, particularly those with the Stanford-Binet. No major increase in predictive power occurred between 12 and 24 months of age, nor did any major loss of predictive power occur in predicting performance at 3½ or 10 years. This surprising retention of predictive power was not exhibited for males, for whom the results conformed to results from earlier studies: predictive power increased later in infancy, and decreased as the testing interval lengthened.

Since there were several components in the infancy tests, and only one of these showed substantial continuity, and for only one sex, McCall et al. (1972, p. 746) concluded:

A simple conception of a constant and pervasive g factor is probably not tenable as a model for "mental" development, especially for the infancy period . . . The term "mental" as applied to infant behavior or tests should be abandoned in favor of some conceptually more neutral label, perhaps Piaget's "sensorimotor," "perceptual motor," or even more specific classes of behaviors (for example exploration of perceptual contingencies, imitation, language). The network of transitions between scales at one age and another is likely more specific and complex than once thought, and not accurately subsumed under one general concept.

The reexamination of the Gesell scales from a cognitive developmental perspective is significant in that it is part of a larger and major redirection of the critical foci of early development toward inferences about internal processes. Observable behaviors are only of significance in relation to their assumed relevance to the internal processes. This redirection is suggestive of a paradigmatic shift (Kuhn, 1962). In such a shift, preexisting data are not necessarily cast aside, but may be treated differently in terms of new formulations.

Emmerich's (1968) classification of developmental approaches into "classical," "differential," and "ipsative" orientations help to clarify this shift. The efforts of McCall et al., as well as the scales developed by Uzgiris and Hunt, and Escalona and Corman, represent "classical" orientations to development (Emmerich, 1968). This approach, which includes psychoanalytic theory, postulates a developmental progression through qualitatively different stages. Appropriate measurement is accorded through nominal classifications. Gesell's infant scales, in contrast, exemplify a "differential" orientation. Emmerich describes this orientation as the traditional area in which the study of dimensions of individual differences are pursued. This rubric subsumes testing, measurement, and other psychometric concerns. Each of the orientations—classical and differential—have traditionally maintained distinctive emphases in basic assumptions, methodology, and interpretation. The formulation of classical theory in differential terms, for the purposes of discussing test validation, runs at cross purposes to the classical orientation. Whatever the case, a differential perspective requires a reformulation of the means of specifying individual progress through Piaget's hierarchical stages that would provide a basis for diagnosis and differential prediction. Whether this can be achieved remains to be seen.

Granting that a paradigmatic shift may be occurring, it remains interesting that the raw data for infant assessment have not changed. There is a general communality in items used in the infant scales. That the pool of items used in infant assessment procedures has not varied may be indicative of two overriding concerns. In order to achieve and maintain psychometric stability, a conservatism on the part of most scale developers may have been introduced that was constructive only in the short run. While they may have improved test stability and increased the probability of accurate statistical prediction, much may have been lost in terms of broad, valid assessment.

One other possible explanation for the communality of items in various infant scales relates to the presumption that the infant, by comparison with the adult, is a relatively simple organism. In this view, the infant's behavioral repertoire is inherently more limited and, therefore, more easily assessed. It is possible that the behavioral repertoire of the infant has, in part, been limited by the assessment situation as much as by any inherent restrictions. Indeed, there may have been overconfidence that infant behavior is easy to assess when in fact it is not. These limitations might be based on the need for direct, unencumbered observation of behavior. Sophisticated electronic equipment, long periods of testing, and extensive training are not conducive to expeditious assessment. Whatever difficulties are inherent in assessing infant behavior, such as rapid transition between different levels of physiological arousal, may have been further exacerbated by the need for efficiency in the assessment situation.

The press that led to the development of standardized infant assessment techniques is still strong: the desire for accurate, early diagnosis paired with appropriate and effective intervention. The relatively recent development of neonatal assessments reflects the continued commitment of a number of researchers (see other chapters in this book) toward these ends. In the author's opinion, neonatal assessments are essentially a "downward" extension of infant tests and, as such, they contain many of the problems that are inherent in infant tests. In addition, they must parse the transient effects of labor and delivery from their more enduring effects (if any), as well as reflect the neonate's endogenous characteristics. These researchers may confront a more complex problem in separating the transient and enduring effects from the same behavioral corpus. Nevertheless, the neonatal assessment scales show promise. The scales developed by Brazelton (1973), for example, have considerable breadth, and assess behaviors relevant to human interaction.

It is admirable that researchers, in coping with the variable nature of the neonate, have maintained the same rigorous psychometric criteria for test evaluation as has been used for other ages (Horowitz and Brazelton, 1973; Horowitz, Self, Paden, Culp, Laub, Boyd, and Mann, 1971).

BIBLIOGRAPHY

Ames, L. B. Predictive value of infant behavior examinations. In J. Hellmuth (ed.), *Exceptional Infant*, Vol. 1. New York: Brunner/Mazel, 1967, pp. 207–241.

Bayley, N. Mental growth during the first three years. *Genetic Psychology Monographs,* 1933, **14,** 1–92.

Bayley, N. The development of motor abilities during the first three years. *Monographs of the Society for Research in Child Development,* 1935, **1,** (Serial No. 1).

Bayley, N. Consistency and variability in the growth of intelligence from birth to eighteen years. *Journal of Genetic Psychology,* 1949, **75,** 165–196.

Bayley, N. *Bayley Scales of Infant Development.* New York: Psychological Corporation, 1969.

Baldwin, A. L. *Theories of Child Development.* New York: Wiley, 1967.

Brazelton, T. B. *Neonatal Behavioral Assessment Scale* (Clinics in Developmental Medicine, No. 50). Spastics International Medical Publication. Philadelphia: Lippincott, 1973.

Cattell, P. *The Measurement of Intelligence of Infants and Young Children.* New York: Psychological Corporation, 1940.

Cavanaugh, M. C., Cohen, I., Dunphy, D., Ringwall, E. A., and Goldberg, I. D. Prediction from the Cattell Infant Intelligence Scale. *Journal of Consulting Psychology,* 1957, **21,** 33–37.

Corman, H. H., and Escalona, S. K. Stages of sensorimotor development: A replication study. *Merrill-Palmer Quarterly,* 1969, **15,** 351–361.

Cronbach, L. J. Year-to-year correlations of mental tests: A review of the Hofstaetter analysis. *Child Development,* 1967, **38,** 283–290.

Drillien, C. M. A longitudinal study of the growth and development of prematurely and maturely born children. Part VII: Mental development two-five years. *Archives of Disease in Childhood,* 1961, **36,** 233–240.

Emmerich, W. Personality development and concepts of structure. *Child Development,* 1968, **39,** 671–690.

Escalona, S. The use of infant tests for predictive purposes. *Bulletin of the Menninger Clinic,* 1950, **14,** 117–128.

Escalona, S., and Corman, H. H. Albert Einstein Scales of Sensorimotor Development. Unpublished manuscript, Albert Einstein College of Medicine, 1969.

Escalona, S., and Moriarty, A. Prediction of schoolage intelligence from infant tests. *Child Development,* 1961, 32, 597–605.

Gallagher, J. J. Clinical judgment and the Cattell Infant Intelligence Scale. *Journal of Consulting Psychology,* 1953, **17,** 303–305.

Gesell, A. *The Mental Growth of the Preschool Child.* New York: Macmillan, 1925.

Gesell, A. *Infancy and Human Growth.* New York: Macmillan, 1929.

Gesell, A. *The First Five Years of Life.* New York: Harper, 1940.

Gesell, A., and Amatruda, C. S. *The Embryology of Behavior.* New York: Harper, 1945.

Gesell, A., and Amatruda, C. S. *Developmental Diagnosis,* 2nd ed. New York: Hoeber, 1947.

Gesell, A., and Thompson, H. *The Psychology of Early Growth.* New York: MacMillan, 1938.

Hofstaetter, P. R. The changing composition of 'intelligence:' A study in t-technique. *The Journal of Genetic Psychology*, 1954, **85**, 159–164.

Horowitz, F. D., and Brazelton, T. B. Research with the Brazelton scale. In T. B. Brazelton (ed.), *Neonatal Behavioral Assessment Scale* (Clinics in Developmental Medicine, No. 50). Spastics International Medical Publication. Philadelphia: Lippincott, 1973.

Horowitz, F. D., Self, P. A., Paden, L. Y., Culp, R., Laub, K., Boyd, E., and Mann, M. F. Newborn and four-week retest on a normative population using the Brazelton Newborn Assessment Procedure. Society for Research in Child Development meetings in Minneapolis, 1971.

Kessen, W., Haith, M. M., and Salapatek, P. H. Human infancy: A bibliography and guide. In P. H. Mussen (ed.), *Carmichael's Manual of Child Psychology*, Vol. 1, 3rd ed. New York: Wiley, 1970, pp. 287–445.

King, W. L., and Seegmiller, B. Performance of fourteen- to twenty-two-month-old black, firstborn male infants on two tests of cognitive development: The Bayley scales and the infant psychological development scale. *Developmental Psychology*, 1973, **8**, 317–326.

Knobloch, H., and Pasamanick, B. An evaluation of the consistency and predictive value of the 40-week Gesell Developmental Schedule. *Psychiatric Research Reports*, 1960, **13**, 10–31.

Knobloch, H., and Pasamanick, B. Predicting from assessment of Neuromotor and Intellectual Status in infancy. Paper presented at the American Psychopathological Association Meeting, 1966. In H. Thomas, Psychological assessment instruments for use with human infants. *Merrill-Palmer Quarterly*, 1970, **16**, 179–223.

Knobloch, H., and Pasamanick, B. *Gesell and Amatruda's Developmental Diagnosis: The Evaluation and Management of Normal and Abnormal Neuropsychologic Development in Infancy and Early Childhood*, 3rd ed. New York: Harper & Row, 1974.

Kuhn, T. S. *The Structure of Scientific Revolutions*. Chicago: University of Chicago, 1962.

McCall, R. B., Hogarty, P. S., and Hurlburt, N. Transitions in infant sensorimotor development and the prediction of childhood IQ. *American Psychologist*, 1972, **27**, 728–748.

Ramey, C. T., Campbell, F. A., and Nicholson, J. E. The predictive power of the Bayley scales of infant development and the Stanford-Binet intelligence test in a relatively constant environment. *Child Development*, 1973, **44**, 790–795.

Richards, T. W., and Nelson, V. L. Studies in mental development: II. Analysis of abilities tested at the age of six months by the Gesell Schedules. *Journal of Genetic Psychology*, 1938, **52**, 327–331.

Richards, T. W., and Nelson, V. L. Abilities of infants during the first eighteen months. *Journal of Genetic Psychology*, 1939, **55**, 299–318.

Stott, L. H., and Ball, R. S. Infant and preschool mental tests: Review and evaluation. *Monographs of the Society for Research in Child Development*, 1965, **30** (3, Serial No. 101).

Uzgiris, I. C., and Hunt, J. McV. *Toward Ordinal Scales of Psychological Development in Infancy*. Champaign, Ill.: University of Illinois, 1975.

Wachs, T. D. Relation of infants' performance on Piaget scales between twelve and twenty-four months and their Stanford-Binet performance at thirty-one months. *Child Development*, 1975, **46**, 929–935.

Werner, E. E., and Bayley, N. The reliability of Bayley's revised scale of mental and motor development during the first year of life. *Child Development*, 1966, **37**, 39–50.

Wittenborn, J. R., Astrachan, M. A., Degooyer, M. W., Grant, W. W., Janoff, I. Z., Kugel, R. B., Myers, B. J., Riess, A., and Russell, E. C. A study of adoptive childen: II. The predictive validity of the Yale developmental examination of infant behavior. *Psychological Monographs*, 1956, **70** (2, whole No. 409).

CHAPTER 6

Specific Neonatal Measures: The Brazelton Neonatal Behavioral Assessment Scale[1]

Heidelise Als, Edward Tronick, Barry M. Lester, and T. Berry Brazelton

The examinations in use for evaluation of newborns, the Apgar (1960) examination and the neurological (Prechtl and Beintema, 1964; Parmelee, 1973) and pediatric examinations in present routine usage are successful in identifying gross abnormalities of central nervous system (CNS) and psychophysiological function. They have not, however, been as effective in detecting milder dysfunction of the CNS during the neonatal period, nor do they capture the range of temperamental variations in normal infants which predict to differential effects on the caretaking they will elicit from their environments.

The limitation in the detection of subtle differences in function by present evaluation techniques can probably be attributed to the conceptualization that underlies these examinations of the neonate's capabilities as subcortical as well as to their goals for detection of gross CNS abnormality. Pediatric and neurological examinations of the newborn focus on the detection of pathology and rely on the neonate's response to reflex and "negative" stimulation. They give little attention to the neonate's capacity to orient to and organize responses to positive or social stimuli. For example, in a neurological examination, an assessment of visual function might consist of eliciting pupillary constriction and eyelid blinks to a bright light, of assessing extraocular movements, nystagmoid movements on rotation, and the vestibular or doll's eye reflexes, along with an examination of the fundus. The newborn is capable of more sophisticated visual responses. He can habituate these blinks and the accompanying startle responses to the same bright light and can demonstrate in the process that he has the capacity to "defend" himself from assaultive, repetitive stimulation. He shows a set of visual and motor responses to a moving object, which include alerting of his face and body, widening of the pupils and eyelids, opening of the mouth, softening and raising of the cheeks, raising of the eyebrows, inhibition of generalized body movements, and coordinated tracking movements of the eyes with accompanying head turning to follow it (Brazelton and Robey, 1965). He can attend to an attractive visual stimulus for long periods (Als, 1975a), and he can make preferential "decisions" about stimuli which can be quantified by measurement of the duration of attention (Carpenter, 1974) and by a description of facial expression (Brazelton et al., 1975). In fact, he demonstrates a wide range of behaviors which can be documented in the neonatal period. The maturity of the motor system is assessed on a standard exam by eliciting important reflex responses, including biceps, triceps, jerks of the extremities, the placing and stepping responses, the Moro reflex, and the tonic neck response. Muscle tone

[1]This work was supported by grant 3122 of the Grant Foundation, New York.

may be further assessed by using manipulations of the body and stretch responses which measure passive and active resistance to movement. The quality of movement is then characterized by inequalities of tone, hyper- or hypomotility, and the presence or absence of limitation of movement, or of tremulousness or imbalances in flexor and extensor responses. Not enough attention is likely to be given to the infant's capacity to organize his motor behavior in more complicated, "purposeful" performances. Such a performance might include, for instance, the bringing of his hand to his mouth, with head turning to meet the fist, as well as insertion for sucking. The fact that this movement can be organized as an infant becomes upset to keep himself under control becomes a further opportunity for assessing his capacity for self-organization.

Prechtl's neurological evaluation (Prechtl and Beintema, 1964) has captured the important relationship between "state" behavior and reflex performances. The Graham Scale (Rosenblith, 1961) first conceptualized the gradations of responses to tactile, auditory, visual, and kinesthetic stimuli, which might add an important predictive set of measures to the existing neurological exams of the 1950s (see Chapter 7). This conceptualization of observable, measurable behavior as a reflection of CNS integrity became a major breakthrough which pointed to the possibilities for assessing measures of quality and quantity of responsiveness. In the Graham-Rosenblith Scale (Rosenblith, 1961) are measures of attention in response to "positive" or attractive stimuli. The capacity to habituate in the neonatal period as described by Bridger (1961) in the 1950s led to the next step—that he might indeed make choices and/or be equipped with a perceptual system for a certain preferred range of sensory stimuli. Indeed, his behavior to such attractive stimuli was seen as more complex and requiring more control over the physiologic demands of the immediate postdelivery period, and this pointed to a programming in the neonate for attention to and selection for positive social stimulation. The concept of strong individual differences in neonates had been raised by Fries (1944) and reinforced by Thomas and Chess' studies (Thomas et al., 1963) on older infants. The possibility of constructing an assessment that might document such individual differences in style and tempo at birth led to the idea that such an assessment might also predict how such neonatal differences might influence the newborn and infant's caregivers as they attempted to understand and interact with him or her. Out of this came the behaviors included in the Brazelton Neonatal Behavioral Assessment Scale (BNBAS) (Brazelton, 1973).

DESCRIPTION OF THE BNBAS

Concepts Underlying the Exam

The BNBAS is based on the conceptualization of the infant as complexly organized, adapted to defending himself from negative stimuli, and to controlling interfering motor and autonomic responses in order to attend to important external stimuli.

The BNBAS is based on the concept that he is adapted to the environment in order to interact with it and elicit from it the stimulation necessary for his species' specific motor, emotional, and cognitive development. It combines a series of elicited behaviors of newborns in different stiuations—that is, when they have been left sleeping, when they are disturbed by negative stimuli, and when they are presented with attractive stimuli as well as in interaction with a human caretaker, The procedure of the examination encompasses an attempt to recapitulate experiences that will be typical of future interactive situations. It attempts to capture the dimensions of the newborn's capacity to organize himself in the face of the physiological demands for recovery from labor, delivery, and exposure to the new extrauterine environment. The normal newborn is manipulated in such a way that over the course of the half-hour exam he exhibits motor, cognitive, social, and temperamental responses as well as observable psychophysiological reactions. These are observed and measured by the examiner in a way that might represent the responses of a caring mother and father. Thus the scoring of the measures becomes a way of assessing the capacity for interaction which might be expected by his environment. The response of an examiner to the particular infant then becomes a measure of prediction to the environment's response to this infant.

A second concept hinges on the fact that the examiner tries to provide optimal conditions for performance and to elicit the newborn's *best* performance. This has been adopted as a way of overcoming the problems of sampling behavior at less than optimal times, since the neonate is so powerfully influenced by temporal events that are often beyond the control of the examiner. As a result, the examiner makes efforts to influence the infant to an optimal state for the desired response, and to vary his maneuvers until he can produce the best response available to the infant. Thus a poor response may be due to the fact that the newborn cannot produce a better one, or it may be that the examiner's maneuvers were not effective enough. So the examiner must always be sensitive to the infant's particular state of consciousness, and he must learn the necessary maneuvers to adapt his procedures to the baby. This places extra demands on training examiners to reliability and on efforts to maintain it. The possibility that his typical performance is superceded by these maneuvers becomes a probability and can be seen as a weakness in evaluating typical behavior by the BNBAS.

An important difference between the Brazelton exam and many other assessments lies in the fact that the procedure has a less than fixed order of item administration. The goal of the exam is that the newborn be brought up from a light sleep state to alert states, then into more active states, to crying, and down to alert inactive states again. The intrusiveness of the stimuli and of the maneuvers is graded in order not to overwhelm the infant too early on in the exam, and the infant's behavior is followed in the order of administration of items, in order to produce his best performance at a time appropriate to his state behavior.

This leads to a fourth consideration—namely, the use and importance of states of consciousness. The exam is based on the concept that responses to negative and positive stimuli have a kind of predictability among neonates as long as the state of the newborn becomes the matrix for this expectancy, for he will have an expectable range of responses to these stimuli within each state. "State" becomes an important variable. To be able to observe the newborn as he reacts in *all* states of consciousness is very important. Furthermore, the pattern of states the infant moves through—the speed, lability, and gradation of change from one state to another—is an important characteristic. This pattern is thought to reflect his capacity to modulate his states of consciousness in order to be available for social and cognitive stimulation. Since the newborn's periods of alertness are likely to be brief, especially in the first few days of life, the assessment of orientation and responsiveness to animate and inanimate, to visual and auditory stimuli has high priority in this assessment of the infant.

A fifth point is that the BNBAS does not allow the examiner to label the baby with a simple behavioral quotient or a numerical index. More recently we have attempted to combine subscales of the BNBAS into four clusters of behavior in an effort to construct a profile of functions that might hope to capture the infant's individuality. This is an attempt to prevent oversimplified labels, and to emphasize processes in the baby rather than simple scoring of responses to stimuli.

It is implicit in the conceptualization of this scale that individual score points will not tell us whether an infant is normal or not. It is the pattern of behavior clusters that becomes decisive in making a judgment of "at risk" or normal (Tronick and Brazelton, 1975). It is in the integration and organization of more complicated responses, especially those in response to social stimulation, in which the physiological and neurological difficulties of a subtle nature may be detected and on which these decisions may be based.

Content of the BNBAS

The exam assesses the neonate's neurological intactness by 20 reflex items such as rooting, sucking, the Moro, and so on. Table 6-1 lists the reflex items. Each reflex is scored on a 4-point scale, from 0 to 3. Most healthy full-terms (approximately 80%) will receive a score of 2 on these items, with the exception of the tonic neck reflex, ankle clonus, and visual nystagmus. In these three items 0, 1, and 2 are all normal scores. The reflex items will identify gross neurological abnormalities by deviant scores. At the point where three scores are deviant, the authors suggest a detailed neurological evaluation should accompany the BNBAS. Elicitation of the reflex behavior serves as a technique for eliciting other behavioral responses as well, such as the newborn's state control and his capacity to shut out the disturbing stimuli necessary to produce reflex responses.

Table 6-1.   Reflex Behaviors

	X	O	L	M	H	A
Plantar grasp		0	1	2	3	
Hand grasp		0	1	2	3	
Ankle clonus		0	1	2	3	
Babinski		0	1	2	3	
Standing		0	1	2	3	
Automatic walking		0	1	2	3	
Placing		0	1	2	3	
Incurvation		0	1	2	3	
Crawling		0	1	2	3	
Glabella		0	1	2	3	
Tonic deviation of head and eyes		0	1	2	3	
Nystagmus		0	1	2	3	
Tonic neck reflex		0	1	2	3	
Moro		0	1	2	3	
Rooting (intensity)		0	1	2	3	
Sucking (intensity)		0	1	2	3	
Passive movement						
arms R		0	1	2	3	
L		0	1	2	3	
legs R		0	1	2	3	
L		0	1	2	3	

X = Response omitted
O = Response not elicited
A = Asymmetry of response
L = Low
M = Medium
H = High

Two global behavioral dimensions summarize the neonate's overall organization: *attractiveness* and *need for stimulation*. Each is rated on a 4-point scale. Attractiveness is a measure of the newborn's overall social attractiveness. This score allows the examiner to reflect on how much he had to contribute to the interaction and how much the infant responded to him. A score of 0 identifies that the infant was very stressed, could not tolerate handling, became cyanotic, or gagged repeatedly, during even the soothing maneuvers. A score of 1 identifies the baby who shows brief periods of organization and stability and may have been available for social stimulation for very brief periods. A score of 2 identifies the infant who shows good organization and stability for moderate periods during the several maneuvers and was available for social stimulation. A score of 3 identifies the baby who shows repeated periods of sustained responsiveness coupled with the ability to maintain physiological and state stability as he remained available to social stimulation.

Need for stimulation is a measure of the newborn's use of and need for stimulation in order to organize his responses. Many newborns become more organized and stable as they are handled; other newborns cannot tolerate handling and clearly give cues that they are better off if left alone. Some newborns can deal with stimulation but do not necessarily need it to become well organized. A score of 0 describes the newborn who cannot tolerate any kind of handling or stimulation. He disintegrates consistently and appears more stressed than when left alone. A score of 1 describes the newborn who can only poorly tolerate stimulation but gives the impression of preferring to be left alone by turning pale or mildly cyanotic or by tremors of his extremities, by gagging, respiratory irregularities, and motoric imbalance. A score of 2 describes the newborn who looks fairly well organized without stimulation, but with stimulation the organization improves. A score of 3 describes the newborn who definitely improves in organization and stability with stimulation. He looks best when he is played with and handled by the examiner.

The item *interfering variables* measures the amount of interference from the environment that prevents a quiet, undisturbed examination. A score of 0 means that there was essentially no interference from the environment. A score of 1 means there was a minimum of interference from the environment—for example, there was noise from the street or hallway, other infants cried, personnel were walking to and fro, and/or there was an additional observer such as the mother or a nurse. A score of 2 means there was moderate interference from the environment as noise, bright lights, and/or two other observers. A score of 3 means there was considerable interference from the environment as noise, light, and two or more additional observers to whom the examiner was attending.

The item *activities used to quiet self* records the various maneuvers a baby may use to quiet himself or to maintain a quiet or organized state. A *yes-no* answer is coded for each maneuver. More than one maneuver can be scored. The maneuvers listed are hand-to-mouth activity, sucking with nothing in mouth or mouthing, locking onto visual or auditory stimuli, postural changes, or state change or maintenance for no observable reason.

The major part of the examination assesses the newborn's interactive behavior repertoire on 26 behavioral items, each scored on a 9-point scale. Table 6-2 shows the 26 behavioral items. These 26 items can be grouped together into four behavioral dimensions of newborn organization:

1. *Interactive capacities:* These assess the newborn's capacity to attend to and process simple and complex environmental events.
2. *Motoric capacities:* These assess the infant's ability to maintain adequate tone,

Table 6-2.   Behavioral Items

1. Response decrement to light (2,3)	14. Cuddliness (4,5)
2. Response decrement to rattle (2,3)	15. Defensive movements (4)
3. Response decrement to bell (2,3)	16. Consolability (6 to 5,4,3,2)
4. Response decrement to pinprick (1,2,3)	17. Peak of excitement (6)
5. Orientation inanimate visual (4 only)	18. Rapidity of buildup (from 1,2 to 6)
6. Orientation inanimate auditory (4,5)	19. Irritability (3,4,5)
7. Orientation animate visual (4 only)	20. Activity (alert states)
8. Orientation animate auditory (4,5)	21. Tremulousness (all states)
9. Orientation animate visual and auditory (4 only)	22. Startle (3,4,5,6)
10. Alertness (4 only)	23. Lability of skin color (from 1 to 6)
11. General tonus (4,5)	24. Lability of states (all states)
12. Motor maturity (4,5)	25. Self-quieting activity (6,5 to 4,3,2,1)
13. Pull-to-sit (3,5)	26. Hand-mouth facility (all states)

Numbers in parenthesis refer to optimal state for assessment.

to control motor behavior, and to perform integrated motor activities—for instance, his ability to bring his hands to his mouth, insert his thumb or finger, and maintain it there long enough to establish a good suck.

3. *Organizational capacities in respect to state control:* This detects how well the infant maintains a calm, alert state despite increased stimulation; how much exhaustion enters into the picture of state modulation; how much the baby is at the mercy of the environment; and how vulnerable he is to continued stimulation.

4. *Organizational capacities—physiologic responses to stress:* This assesses how much at the mercy of the physiological demands of his immaturity and the recovery from labor and delivery the infant is at this time—how well the infant is able to inhibit startles, tremors, and interfering movement as he becomes aroused or as he attends to social and inanimate stimuli.

The most important dimension is the newborn's capacity to integrate this behavior over the first days of life. The curve of recovery of overall organization becomes the most important measure of prediction (Tronick and Brazelton, 1975). In order to be able to assess this recovery, at least two examinations are needed on an infant. These should be done on day 2 or 3 when the immediate stresses of delivery and some of the medication effects have begun to wear off, and again on day 9 or 10 when the baby has been at home and has adjusted to his home environment. The day immediately following discharge from the hospital should be avoided as an examination day, since the change from hospital to home environment tends to make for more instability in behavior.

ORDER OF TESTING

To ensure optimal assessment outcome, the authors of the scale suggest that the infant should be tested midway between feedings and before he is disturbed. When he is in light or deep sleep (state 1, 2) the initial stimuli are presented. After the initial presentation of items for response decrement, the remaining items are presented at times that will elicit the infant's best performance. Ideally, the examiner should be in a flexible working interaction with the infant, in which he can estimate the effect of all the stimuli on the infant. This is important if he is to understand the infant in the ''process'' of assimilating stimuli, of adjusting his state in order to handle them, and of responding actively to his new environment.

The examiner begins by assessing the initial state of the infant for 2 min. The state of the infant is then recorded on the scoring sheet.

The initial presentation of a flashlight to the eyes, a rattle to the ears, and a bell to the ears is done while the infant is in a state of 1, 2, or 3. After these stimuli are presented, the infant is uncovered, and his relevant reactions are observed and recorded. While the infant is still quiet, a light pinprick is applied to his foot four times. Ankle clonus, foot grasp, and the Babinski response are then determined before undressing the infant. As the infant is being undressed, he is observed for relevant reactions such as state changes, lability of skin color, and speed of buildup. His general tone is also assessed while being undressed. Passive movements of the infant are rated while he is awake but not disturbed. It is recommended that he be tested for auditory responses to the rattle and bell while in the awake state to determine responses to inanimate, visual, and auditory stimuli. While he is still in the awake state, the infant is then pulled to sit. The next assessment items include the infant's standing, walking, and placing reflexes. After elicitation of these, incurvation, body tone across the examiner's hand, and prone responses of the infant are then assessed. Next the infant is picked up, held, and spun around slowly for vestibular responses and nystagmus. The infant should then be held while assessing his responses to the orientation animate behavioral items. He should systematically be tested for his responses to animate stimulus, visual stimulus, auditory stimulus, and then visual and auditory stimuli in combination.

The most disturbing maneuvers are used last with the infant. The infant is assessed as he reacts to a cloth on the face; in addition, the infant's reactions to the elicitation of the tonic neck reflex and the Moro reflex are noted. The infant's reactions to aversive stimuli offer an excellent time to observe his graded attempts to quiet himself.

Whenever the infant becomes upset, the examiner should wait 15 sec. before intervening with comforting measures. This allows the infant an opportunity to quiet himself. If no self-quieting behavior occurs, the examiner should comfort the infant, using graded measures to quiet him, such as the examiner placing his face in front of the infant; using both his face and voice, placing his hand on the infant's abdomen; restraining one of the infant's arms; restraining both arms; holding the infant; holding and rocking the infant; and holding, rocking, and talking to the infant. These are graded estimates of the infant's need for external consoling.

The infant's responses such as hand-to-mouth movements, tremulousness, amount of startle, vigor, and amount of activity are observed throughout the entire examination. In addition, the number of discrete state changes that occur are documented.

CONDITIONS FOR ASSESSMENT

It is recommended that the infant be observed and assessed in a quiet, somewhat darkened room. If these conditions cannot be met, the disturbing aspects of a noisy, brightly lighted room or of interruptions should be documented as part of the stimuli to which the infant might be reacting.

The entire examination usually takes about 20 to 30 min. Except for the first four items, which can be scored immediately by the examiner, most of the items are scored at the conclusion of the testing. Scoring may take from 10 to 15 min. Some of the 26 items are scored during a specific interaction with the infant, such as his head turning to a voice, but others are scored according to total continuous observations which are made throughout the entire assessment examination. For example, state changes, color changes, periods of alertness, and peaks of excitement are observed throughout the examination and are scored at the conclusion of the examination.

EXAMINER TRAINING

All persons who are using the scale should be trained in the proper administration of test items, order of examination procedures, optimal conditions of testing, and method of scoring. Examiners using the scale should also be familiar with special considerations that are included during an assessment of an infant. Before an examiner can be assured of independent reliable ratings, it is essential that practice with testing of at least 10 infants be completed. By practicing with 10 infants, an examiner can be trained to achieve higher interscorer reliability, at one of the two established training centers.[2]

An interrater reliability of greater than 90% for the overall assessment is necessary before the scale should be used for research. On the reflex items, reliability scoring is based on no difference in the 3-point scores. A 1-point deviation is allowed on the 9-point behavioral items. A difference of 2 points is considered a nonreliable difference in the item.

STATISTICAL ANALYSIS OF THE BRAZELTON SCALE

A recurrent problem faced by researchers with the BNBAS has been the selection of methods for data reduction and the application of appropriate statistical tests. These problems arise due to the underlying conceptualization of the scale. Since the scale was developed as a clinical tool for describing optimal performance, a large set of descriptors is used to characterize the behavioral repertoire of the neonate. Each nominal category is designed to describe the complexity and richness of a particular qualitative dimension of behavior. As such, the scale does not lend itself to the generation of more traditional overall or summary scores—as, for example, the Bayley scales do.

Many of the scale items are metrically or distributionally inimical to common statistical manipulations. For example, the items are not a set of equal-interval scales that go from poor to excellent. For some items, such as motor tone, a midrange score is considered optimal, with different behavioral implications at either extreme. Nor are the items independent. Their order of administration, scoring, and interpretation are meaningful only in the context of the infant's changing behavior and state. Alertness, for example, is an overall rating based, in part, on performance on individual orientation items but also includes the quality of alertness during other parts of the exam, whether or not the infant uses stimulation to come to and maintain an alert state, and has to be balanced against episodes of irritability and crying.

[2]Reliability training can be obtained by writing directly to the principal investigator, Brazelton, or to Dr. Frances D. Horowitz, Department of Human Development and Family Life, University of Kansas, Lawrence, Kansas 66044. In addition, four training films are available for use with the published manual. These can be obtained by writing to the Educational Development Corporation, 8 Mifflin Place, Cambridge, Massachusetts 02138.

Because of the lack of uniformity in the statistical properties of the subscales, many different kinds of analyses have been attempted. They can be grouped into (1) item-by-item comparisons, (2) overall summary scale and subscales, (3) factor analysis, and (4) typologic and profile analysis. Obviously, the method of data reduction and analysis one chooses depends, to some extent, on the particular research question at issue. Thus, the statistical advantages or disadvantages of a given approach must be weighted against the discriminability of the scale in a particular setting.

Item-by-Item Comparisons

The most popular approach to the analysis of the Brazelton scale has been the comparison of each of the 26 items. These studies typically compare mean performance between two or more groups on each item and explain their effects by *post hoc* interpretations of items on which significant differences are found. For example, Freedman and Freedman (1969) suggest that those items that differentiate Chinese-American from European-American neonates reflect temperamental differences between the groups. In other cross-cultural studies, single-item mean differences are used to compare Zambian and American (Brazelton et al., 1976a) and Latin American and Black American babies (Coll et al., 1976). Others have considered the number of items on which performance has changed due to intervention (Solkoff and Matuszak, 1975; Scarr and Williams, 1973) and correlations between individual items and behavior during mother-infant interaction (Osofsky and Danzger, 1974).

This approach is supported by findings such as those of Soule et al. (1974) and of Kaplan and Kron (1974), where differences between narcotic-addicted and control babies were found on 12 of the same 14 items. Using a slightly different sample, Strauss et al. (1975) reported similar findings.

There are, however, certain difficulties inherent in this approach. First, the investigator does not state in advance which items are expected to differ, which would then allow for comparisons of just those items. Instead, all comparisons are made, and whatever differences are found are explained. Another problem is that the number of comparisons that this approach often entails raises serious questions as to the probability that some differences may be due to chance. This is a particular problem in large factorial designs where age and sex effects may also be tested along with group effects on each item (Horowitz et al., 1976). A third problem with this method is that although many items are inherently dependent and related, they are often treated as independent when significant effects are found. No study has reported the correlations between items that are found to show group differences. Thus, many so-called significant effects are probably accounting for behavior. A final issue is that the magnitude of reported differences is often within the margin of error used to establish reliability in training in the scale. Since a 1-point difference is treated as an agreement in scoring the scale, it may be reasonable to only consider mean differences between groups that are greater than 1 scale point. Smaller differences may be statistically reliable but conceptually meaningless, as suggested by Horowitz et al. (1976).

Summary Scale and Subscales

A second approach to the reduction and analysis of the scale has been to reduce the items to summary scores for subscales. This has the advantage of organizing planned comparisons around conceptually meaningful dimensions and reducing the number of overall comparisons. The main disadvantage of this method is that many of the items do not lend themselves to combination with other items because many items are not linear and have mid-range optimal performances. In item-by-item comparisons this problem can be avoided by using statistics such as chi square for such items (c.f. Strauss et al., 1975).

Brackbill (1974) computed summary scores for the total scale and for the neurologic items. These were then divided into elicited and emitted subscales. They also reported item-by-item comparisons for items comprising the elicited and emitted scores. Standley et al. (1974) combined the scale items into clusters of alertness, irritability, and motor maturity to study the effects of obstetric medication. Brazelton et al. (1976b), in a study of malnourished Guatemalan infants, compared means among four clusters, two of which represented optimal caretaker eliciting behaviors and the others reflecting motor and interactive disorganization. Eight subscales were used by Als and Lewis (1975) to derive five temperament types. In an intervention study, Powell (1974) constructed a responsivity score and a head control score by combining selected items, and reported that the correlation between these two scores was 0.69. Kaplan and Kron (1975) calculated an overall score by adding the scores of items that predicted positive responses and subtracting items that predicted negative responses. These scores were correlated with a sucking measure and birthweight in a study of narcotic-addicted babies.

Factor Analysis

Several authors have attempted to determine the degree to which the items on the scale are part of a common underlying structure by locating and defining dimensional space among the items through factor analysis. When orthogonal rotations are used (e.g., varimax rotation) the factors extracted are independent and the scale would be reduced to a few independent factors.

Factor-analytic studies of the scale have shown some consistent findings that highlight both the strengths and inadequacies of this approach. Scarr and Williams (1973) compared the factor structure of the scale in the same group of 30 low-birthweight infants at 7 days and 4 weeks. They found that the first two factors, which accounted for 20 and 12% of the variance, respectively, were virtually the same at 7 days and 4 weeks. The first factor had loadings of at least 0.78 for all of the items and represented the variance common to all of the scales. The second factor was composed of nine items reflecting reactivity to stimulation. Since this study used an early version of the scale and tested a very low-birthweight group (half of whom were in an intervention study), it is difficult to compare these findings with those of others.

An additional problem with this and other factor-analytic studies is that the sample size does not meet established criteria for a factor analysis of 26 items (c.f., Cattell 1966). For example, Aleksandrowicz and Aleksandrowicz (1974) produced 64 factors from Brazelton scale performance of 44 infants on 8 testing days. These were reduced to 34 factors by eliminating half of the testing days. They then selected one item from each of the 34 factors as a "marker" variable to represent the factor to study the effects of obstetric medication. However, as Federman and Yang (1976) have argued, it is not clear what these marker variables mean or how they represent the factor.

A heterogeneous sample of 52 neonates was used in an initial study by Lester et al. (1976). These infants were then included in a factor-analytic study of 140 infants in an attempt to examine the stability of the factor structure (Emory et al., 1976). In the first study, two main factors were extracted: an attention-orientation factor that accounted for

20% of the variance and included eight items, and a temperament-arousal factor that accounted for 18% of the variance and included seven items. Lower scores on the attention factor were associated with low-birthweight infants and infants of younger mothers, while low scores on the temperament dimension were related to low Apgar scores. In the second study a group of high-birthweight infants was included, and three main factors were extracted. Factor 1 accounted for 31% of the variance and included six items, five of which defined the first factor in the initial study. The arousal-temperament factor from the first study seemed to split into separate dimensions in the larger sample. Factor 2 in the second study accounted for 20% of the variance along the arousal dimension and included five items, four of which were part of the seven items called arousal-temperament in the first study. The remaining three items combined with two additional items to form a third factor called temperament, which accounted for 13% of the variance. This study also found differences in factor scores among the three birthweight groups.

A similar factor structure to the scale was reported by Bakow et al. (1973). They found two main factors that accounted for 25% of the variance and five additional factors that accounted for another 30%. Consistent with other studies, they found an alertness factor which included all of the orientation items and an irritability factor which included items such as activity level, peak of excitement, tonus, rapidity of buildup, and irritability. Comparing the factors with temperamental typologies at 4 months, one of the major and three of the minor factors were related to several of the temperamental types studied by Thomas et al. (1963).

These factor-analytic studies seem to suggest that orthogonal dimensions of alerting-orienting and arousal level are reflected in the structure of the Brazelton scale. Not surprisingly, previously mentioned studies which selected a priori subscales organized the items along similar dimensions (c.f. Standley et al., 1974; Strauss et al., 1975). However, factor-analytic studies also suggest that there may not be a simple structure in the scale that can explain the variability in individual differences assessed by the scale. For example, Bakow et al. (1973) found that no single factor accounted for a major portion of the variance in the 26 items, and that five items did not load on any of the factors. They suggested that the scale measures a large number of independent dimensions of behavior, which argues against the use of factor analysis. Scarr and Williams (1973) found only 2 of 10 factors on day 7 that accounted for more than 10% of the variance and three factors that accounted for more than 10% of the variance out of 10 factors at 4 weeks. Many of the minor factors at both ages were composed of one to three items. In the studies by Lester (Lester et al., 1976; Emory et al., 1976) the number of factors accounting for more than 10% of the variance were two of nine in the first study and three of eight in the second study. Indeed, these findings may be expected since many of the distributional and metric parameters of the scale discussed earlier are at variance with some of the assumptions of factor analysis.

Typologic and Profile Analysis

The last approach to the analysis of the BNBAS is a system of typological and profile analysis recommended by the authors and presented in Figure 6-1. This is an a priori clustering of the items in the scale along four specified dimensions (Adamson et al., 1975). This approach is not dependent on either the parametric or ordinal qualities of the scales but rather uses the conceptual information inherent in scale items prior to their numerical transformation. Unlike parametric clustering programs and factor analysis, it is

Fig. 6-1. Criteria for a priori clustering.

Dimension I. Interactive Processes

(1) ——Orientation: 4 of 5 $\begin{cases} \text{7 or above on visual reactions} \\ \text{6 or above on auditory reactions} \end{cases}$

none below 4 if done

——Alertness: 6 and above

——One of $\begin{cases} \text{cuddliness 6 or above} \\ \text{consolability NA* or 6 and above} \end{cases}$

*NA: Not answerable

(3)

——Two of $\begin{cases} \text{orientation: 3 of 5 NA or 5 and below} \\ \text{alertness: 1–4 or NA} \\ \text{one of } \begin{array}{l} \text{cuddliness 1–4} \\ \text{consolability 1–4} \end{array} \end{cases}$

Dimension II. Motoric Processes

(1) ——No more than 1 deviant reflex (excluding 0 or 1 on clonus, nystagmus, and TNR and counting both arms and both legs as one item on passive movements)

——Motor tone: 5 or 6

——Three of $\begin{cases} \text{7 or above on pull-to-sit} \\ \text{5 or above on motor maturity} \\ \text{7 or above on defensive reaction} \\ \text{5 or above on hand-to-mouth activity} \end{cases}$

——Activity: 4–6

(3)

——Two of $\begin{cases} \text{Motor tone: 1–3 or 7–9} \\ \text{Three of } \begin{cases} \text{maturity 1–3} \\ \text{pull-to-sit 1–4} \\ \text{defensive reaction 1–4} \\ \text{activity 1–3 or 8 and 9} \\ \text{hand-to-mouth 1–3} \end{cases} \\ \text{More than 3 deviant reflexes (excluding as above)} \end{cases}$

Dimension III. Organization Processes: State Control (continued)

(1) ——State 4 is scored as one predominant state

——Habituation: $\begin{cases} \text{if all done, all are 5 and above} \\ \text{if 2 done, both are 5 and above} \\ \text{if only 1 done, does not apply} \end{cases}$

——Peak of excitement: 5–7, or 4 if predominant state is 4 and not 1,2, or 3

——Three of $\begin{cases} \text{lability of states 3 or less} \\ \text{rapidity of buildup 4 or less} \\ \text{irritability 4 or less} \\ \text{self-quieting 6 or more or NA} \end{cases}$

(3) *Type I—Very Labile*

——Three of $\begin{cases} \text{rapidity of buildup 7–9} \\ \text{irritability 7–9} \\ \text{self-quieting 1–4} \\ \text{state lability 6 or above} \\ \text{peak of excitement 8 or 9} \\ \text{habituation all 4 or below if done} \\ \text{pin prick 1 or 2} \end{cases}$

196

Fig. 6-1. *(continued)*

Type II—Flat, Depressed

——Peak of excitement: 1–4

——One of $\left\{\begin{array}{l}\text{rapidity of buildup 1–3}\\ \text{irritability 3 or less}\\ \text{state lability 1 or 2}\end{array}\right.$

——Predominant states are *not* 4 or 6

Dimension IV. Organization Processes: Response to Stress

(3) If two of $\left\{\begin{array}{l}\text{tremulousness 6 or above}\\ \text{skin color 1,7,8, or 9}\\ \text{startles 6 and above}\end{array}\right.$

Figure 6-1.   Criteria for a priori clustering.

not necessary to assume that all the scales are consistent in directionality or in the spacing between scale points. In addition, items can be given relative weights rather than equal weights, to more appropriately index their significance. The a priori cluster analysis uses all the information in the assessment as contrasted to factor analysis, which ends up with some items having so small a weight that they are not usable, or analysis of variance which cannot evaluate certain items. Most importantly, an a priori cluster analysis is able to compare not only groups of infants but is able to follow and compare particular infants with each other and with themselves over time.

The heart of this method then is to cluster all the items of the BNBAS along four major dimensions of the scale listed above to summarize an individual infant's performance and to then be able to compare individual infants and groups of infants on their cluster scores for each dimension. There are four major conceptual dimensions, as mentioned earlier: (I) interactive processes, (II) motoric processes, (III) organizational processes as related to state control, and (IV) organizational processes as related to physiologic responses to stress.

These dimensions are divided into typologies which indicate the quality of the infant's performance along the dimension being scored. Dimensions I, II, and III are divided into three typologies: (1) exceptionally good performance, (2) adequate performance; and (3) deficient performance. Dimension IV is divided into two categories: (1) adequate performance and (2) deficient performance. Within each typology there are some criteria that *must* be met. Other criteria are not necessary for the particular typology score and thus are established as "either/or." For example, a necessary score for typology 1 on dimension I, interactive processes, is a score of 6 or above on alertness. If the infant does not achieve that score he cannot receive a typology score of 1. An optional, either/or score on dimension I for typology 1 is the choice of a 6 or above score on cuddliness *or* a consolability score of NA or 6-or-above. If the infant has either the cuddliness score *or* the consolability score he can receive a 1 on dimension I.

While only three typologies are defined for the first three dimensions, additional information can be retained by recording and noting the item scores actually received by a particular infant on each typology. On dimension II (motoric processes), by noting which items produced the score of 3, the score can be qualified as to whether the infant was *hyper-* or *hypo*tonic in his motor organization. Score 3 for dimension II can be further divided into labile or flat and depressed by noting the scores that produced the typology of 3.

This approach allows each infant's performance to be categorized on the BNBAS. All of the information available in the exam is used to make up the clusters. The approach allows a weighting of the different items in the assessment based on clinical experience. The approach produces a conceptually meaningful descriptor of each infant, not a summary score such as might be typified by an IQ or DQ score.

Statistical analysis of the data is then straightforward. Depending on the size of the sample and the goals of the research, either parametric or nonparametric statistics may be used. At the simplest level, if two groups are being compared, four X^2 tests could be applied to the frequencies of each typology score in each of the four dimensions. This would require a relatively small number of Ss, and a significant result would indicate distinctive differences between the groups.

This approach has been effectively used to compare a group of small-for-gestational-age (SGA) and appropriate-for-gestational-age (AGA) infants (Als et al., 1976). Ten infants in each group were examined with the BNBAS on days 1, 3, 5, and 10. The scores for each infant were given typologies along each of the four dimensions for each examination day. To illustrate this method, Table 6-3 presents the data from that study. The use of the typologies effectively discriminated between the two groups of infants. Moreover, the results indicated that the SGA infants were significantly deficient on dimension I, interac-

Table 6-3.   Comparison of Underweight (UW) and Full-weight (FW) Infants on the Four Dimensions of the Brazelton Examination

Number of Newborns Receiving a Score of 3—Judged to be Worrisome—by Days Separately and Total of 4 Examinations

Dimension	Age in Days	UW ($N=10$)	FW ($N=10$)	Level of Significance[a]	
Interactive	1	4	2	—	
process	3	7	1	<0.01[a]	
	5	2	1	—	
	10	5	0	<0.05[a]	
	Σ	18	4	<0.01	$\chi^2=14.11$
Motoric	1	3	1	—	
processes	3	3	0	—	
	5	1	0	—	
	10	4	0	<0.05[a]	
	Σ	11	1	<0.01	$\chi^2=11.86$
State	1	4	3	—	
organization	3	1	0	—	
	5	0	1	—	
	10	0	1	—	
	Σ	5	5	—	
Physiological	1	1	1	—	
organization	3	3	1	—	
	5	1	1	—	
	10	4	1	—	
	Σ	9	4	<0.10	$\chi^2=3.31$

Source: Als, Tronick, Adamson, and Brazelton (1976).
[a]Fisher's Exact Probability Test, one-tailed.

tive processes. Furthermore, the table indicates how the AGA infants improved in their performance over the 10 days, while the SGA infants failed to show the expected pattern of recovery. We feel that these results are indicators of the validity of the use of such clusters, since they also fit the clinical impression gained from these infants.

An additional approach would be to combine the typology scores for each dimension into a single profile. For example, the modal profile score of the SGA infants was 3323. The distribution of profile scores among different groups could be compared (see Fig. 6-2). This might be especially useful in cross-cultural comparisons. On the other hand, it would provide a useful description of an individual infant. Either at the cross-cultural level or at the individual level one could follow, for example, how these profile characteristics changed with development.

The utility of these profiles is also suggested by other studies. For example, in a study of the effects of phototherapy on neonatal behavior, Telzrow et al. (1976) found differences between experimental and control groups on the dimensions of interactive processes and organizational processes with respect to state control. Moreover, these effects were exacerbated by the use of phototherapy. In another study, Lester and Zeskind (1977) reported that low-birthweight and SGA infants with high-pitched cries showed poor performance along the dimensions of interactive processes and organizational processes related to state control. Also, the overall profile scored by summing the ratings on the four typological dimensions was higher (more deficient) in infants with high-pitched cries as compared to infants with low-pitched cries. Finally, Sepkoski et al. (1976) divided 153 neonates with ranging degrees of at-riskness into superior, average, or deficient performance on each of the four typologies and on the overall profile. Discriminant function analysis was then used to predict group membership in these categories on the basis of six risk variables. While there was a considerable variation in the "hit" and "false-alarm" rates from dimension to dimension, the number of infants correctly classified ranged from 58% for physiologic organization to 80% for motoric processes.

In summary, a typological analysis of the BNBAS allows for the appropriate use of

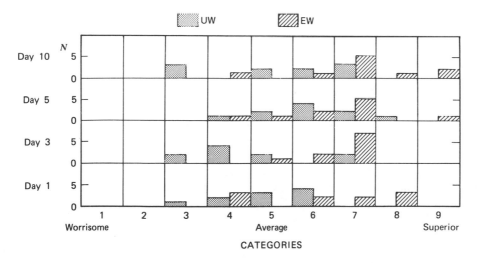

Figure 6-2.   Distribution of numbers of underweight and full-weight infants into nine profile categories on Brazelton examinations on days 1, 3, 5, and 10 separately.

inferential statistics. It allows for the comparison of groups of infants at one point in time and over time. It can be used to describe a single infant and his change over time. Most importantly, it seems to fit more closely than other approaches the underlying conceptualization of the scale—which is to provide a description and assessment of the behavioral competencies of newborn infants.

Normative Data—Standardization of the Scale

Newborn behavior is influenced by many factors, such as the health of the mother, maternal medication administered during labor and delivery (Brazelton and Robey, 1965), and events during labor and delivery—such as the length of labor, presentation of the baby, fetal heart rate patterns, mode of delivery—and many others. Newborns in different cultures have been found to behave differently (Brazelton et al., 1976; Brazelton et al., 1969). The question therefore is whether it is meaningful to collect normative data on a sample which can then be considered to be representative of the "population at large." It would have to include infants from different ethnic and social class backgrounds as well as with many different health histories. The mean performance on each subscale of such a standardization sample would be difficult to interpret.

We decided to identify homogeneous subgroups of a standardization sample and to aim for normative profile scores for these well-defined subgroups. For instance, it seems more meaningful to ask what is the behavior of the healthy full-term, white, black, Puerto Rican, or Indian newborn, than to ask what is the "typical" U.S. neonate's behavior. Similarly, it is more meaningful to ask what is the behavior of the full-term yet small-for-dates newborn, the behavior of a newborn who has suffered hyperbilirubinemia, than to ask what is the behavior of a random sample from a particular hospital. With this in mind, we have collected data from a homogeneous group of 54 healthy full-term white newborns delivered at the Boston Hospital for Women, Lying-In Division. These newborns were selected for pediatric and neurologic normalcy after delivery. Their mothers had uncomplicated obstetric histories and deliveries as defined by strict selection criteria given in Table 6-4. The medication received by the mothers during labor and delivery was classified into (1) no medication, (2) a local or a spinal, (3) analgesic (alpha-prodine and/or promazine) of less than 60 mg total, and (4) an epidural with lidocaine or mepivicaine within 4 h of delivery. No significant lasting effects of these medications were found in this particular sample (Tronick et al., 1976).

Repeated behavioral assessments with the BNBAS were made on each infant on days, 1, 2, 3, 4, 5, 7, and 10. The examinations on days 1 to 4 were performed in the hospital and often with the mother present; the examination on days 5 to 10 were performed in the home with either one or both parents present. Four examiners were involved in the study. No examiner performed more than two examinations in succession, and no examiner performed more than a total of five out of the seven examinations. At least one of the seven examinations was performed by two examiners. Overall, interexaminer reliability on each exam was better than 89%.

The data provide a picture of the behavioral change of a group of highly selected, healthy newborns, carefully controlled for optimal intrauterine and perinatal experiences.

Table 6-5 shows the means and standard deviations for the 26 behavioral items of the Brazelton scale for this group of babies. For easier presentation, the items are grouped

Table 6-4. Selection Criteria for Study of Healthy Full-Term Newborns

Infant Excluded if Mother Had
  Toxemia
  Threatened abortion
  Diabetes mellitus
  Chronic diseases
    renal
    hyper-or hypothyroidism
    neurologic disorders
  Age: under 18 years, or over 35 years

Labor
  Prolonged 1st stage greater than 24 h
  Prolonged 2nd stage greater than 6 h
  Ruptured membranes greater than 24 h
  Hemorrhage/shock
  Precipitous labor less than 3 h
  Any abnormal delivery
    breech, cesarean section
    shoulder, brow, face presentation
    high, mid-forceps

Infant Rejected at Delivery or by End of 1st 24 h if
  Gestation greater than 41 weeks or less than 38 weeks
  Birthweight under 2.7 kg or over 4.1 kg
  Ponderal index less than 2.3
  Fetal heart rate depression during labor
  Nuchal cord
  Congenital abnormality
  Apgars of less than 7 at 1 min and 5 min
  Cephalohematoma or other bruising
  Development of illness during study, e.g.
    sepsis
    seizures
    bleeding, hyperbilirubinemia

Actual Mean Value and Range on Variable Criteria
  Mother's mean age: 27.2 years
  Gravity: range 1–4, mean 1.8
  Parity: range 0–3, mean 0.7
  Mean length 1st stage labor: 7.8 h
  Mean gestation: 39.8 weeks
  Mean weight: 3.4 kg
  Mean 1-min Apgar: 8.5
  Mean 5-min Apgar: 9.2
  Sex: 50% male, 50% female

according to the a priori clusters. Only days 1, 3, 5, and 10 are presented because of space limitations. The exclusion of days 2, 4, and 7 does not change the overall picture.

The most striking finding is the definite improvement in the behavioral performance of these neonates over the first 10 days of life. To assess this, an analysis of variance was performed. There were significant changes across days in items of all four major dimensions (see Table 6-5):

Dimension I: Attention and social responsiveness. Five of the eight items making up this dimension—orientation to face, orientation to voice, orientation to face and

Table 6-5.   Mean Scores and Standard Deviations on Brazelton Neonatal Items for Days 1, 3, 5, and 10[a]

	Day 1		Day 3		Day 5		Day 10	
ITEM	M	SD	M	SD	M	SD	M	SD
Items Indicating the Infant's Capacity for Attention and Social Responsiveness								
Orientation to object	5.6	1.4	5.4	1.5	5.6	1.5	6.0	1.5
Orientation to inanimate sound	5.5	1.1	5.8	0.8	5.8	1.1	6.1	1.1
Orientation to face[b]	6.3	1.2	6.5	1.1	6.3	1.1	7.0	0.9
Orientation to voice[c]	5.5	1.3	5.8	1.9	5.9	1.3	6.2	1.0
Orientation to face and voice[b]	6.6	1.1	6.9	0.9	6.7	1.1	7.3	1.0
Alertness[c]	4.9	2.3	5.5	1.9	5.9	2.1	6.1	1.8
Cuddliness[b]	5.6	1.0	5.8	1.2	5.9	1.0	6.5	1.3
Consolability	6.4	1.7	6.2	1.4	5.7	1.5	6.0	1.9
Items Indicating the Infant's Motor and Tone Capacity								
Muscle tone[b]	5.3	0.9	5.4	1.0	5.5	0.9	5.8	0.9
Activity level[b]	3.9	0.8	4.6	0.9	4.7	1.1	4.8	1.2
Motor maturity[b]	4.2	0.6	4.7	0.9	4.8	0.9	5.2	1.0
Hand-to-mouth facility[b]	4.9	2.2	6.0	1.8	5.6	2.0	5.8	2.1
Defensive movement[b]	4.9	2.4	6.9	1.3	6.9	1.1	6.8	1.2
Pull-to-sit	5.6	1.2	5.8	1.3	5.7	1.5	6.0	1.4
Items Indicating Infant's Capacity for Controlling His State of Consciousness Response Decrement to:								
1. Repeated light stimuli[c]	6.3	1.6	7.1	1.5	7.0	1.5	6.5	1.3
2. Repeated rattle stimuli	6.7	2.1	6.8	1.8	6.6	1.9	6.2	2.1
3. Repeated bell stimuli[c]	6.9	2.1	7.1	1.8	7.6	1.5	6.7	2.1
4. Repeated pinpricks	4.4	1.5	4.2	1.2	3.9	1.3	4.5	1.6
Rapidity of buildup to crying state	3.5	2.2	3.6	1.8	3.8	2.2	3.6	2.1
Peak of excitement	5.4	1.3	5.8	1.3	5.9	1.5	5.7	1.4
Irritability	4.1	1.5	4.0	1.5	4.5	2.0	4.2	1.8
Self-quieting	5.2	1.6	5.1	1.5	4.9	1.5	5.5	2.0
Lability of states	2.7	1.2	2.8	1.1	2.7	1.2	2.6	1.3
Items Indicating Physiological Responses to Stress								
Startles[b]	4.5	1.8	4.3	1.6	3.8	1.5	3.3	1.5
Tremor[b]	5.0	1.7	4.4	1.8	3.9	1.9	3.7	2.1
Color changes	4.4	1.4	4.1	1.2	4.1	1.5	3.7	1.6

[a]Examination data for days 2,4 and 7 are not reported because of space limitations. Their exclusion does not change the results.
[b]$p < 0.01$: significant day effects.
[c]$p < 0.05$: significant day effects.

voice, alertness, and cuddliness—showed significant improvement in an almost day-by-day fashion.

Dimension II: Motor and tonic capacity. Five of the six items used to assess motor and tone capacity—muscle tone, activity level, motor maturity, hand-to-mouth, and defensive movement—showed significant improvement over the first 10 days of life.

Dimension III: State control. Two items—response decrement during sleep to a repeated light stimulus and to a repeated bell—evidenced a U-shaped curve, with the most proficient performance coming on day 3.

Dimension IV: Physiological stability in response to stress. There was a significant
decrease in the number of both startles and tremors over the first 10 days of life.

These data provide us with a picture of the behavioral recovery of a group of neonates in
which the effects of medication were minimized through the control of a multiplicity of
stress variables. Their recovery is characterized by a definite improvement over the first 10
days of life in major areas of their behavioral functioning. During this initial recovery
period, these infants became more alert and capable of orienting to external—particularly
animate—stimuli. Their motor maturity, muscle tone, and integrated motor performances
also improved. On behavioral items reflecting their physiological adjustment, there was a
clear improvement with a decrease in their number of startles and their amount of tremulousness. Items reflecting state control appeared to remain relatively stable over the first 10
days, which probably reflects their well-organized condition at birth. In other more
stressed populations, we have seen a recovery in this area as well (Tronick and Brazelton,
1975).

In addition to the group data, and the mean and standard deviations per item, we can
also look at the change of a priori profile scores over days for this group of newborns.
Fifty-four score profiles are possible, defining a different type of examination and infant.
Grouping the profiles from worrisome to superior, nine major categories can be derived,
based on the sum of the four typology scores. Category 1 is the profile yielding the highest
sum, 12, derived from the dimensional subscores 333,3, and describing a neonate who is
worrisome in all four dimensions. Category 2 encompasses profiles, the sum of which is
11, such as profiles 233,3 or 323,3 or 332,3, which describe a baby who is worrisome in
three dimensions and average in one, etc. Category 5, the average, encompasses profiles
yielding the sum of 8, such as 223,1, 322,1, or 113,3. Category 9 encompasses the
profiles yielding the sum of 4, that is the baby "superior" in all four dimensions.

Figure 6-3 shows the distribution of profiles for this healthy population on days 1, 3, 5,
and 10. On day 1 this distribution is normal and the mean is at category 5.7. The
distribution increasingly shifts toward the superior category. On day 3 the mean is 6.0, on
day 5 it is 6.7, and on day 10 it is 7.1. A comparison of the number of infants who are
average (category 5) or worse with the number of infants above average shows that there is
a significant increase of above-average babies with increasing age ($p < 0.01$). Table 6-6
shows this distribution. This supports the hypothesis that the healthy, term newborn has
become significantly more mature and organized by day 10.

RELIABILITY OF THE SCALE

The issue of test-retest reliability of the Brazelton scale deserves consideration. A measurement tool that fluctuates in the accuracy with which it assesses a trait is not useful.
Therefore, one commonly determines how comparable the readings with the tool under
consideration are over time. This is appropriate if the trait measured is assumed to be
stable. For instance, if one wants to know whether a measuring tape measures the height
of an infant accurately, one measures the infant on day 1 and again on day 2 and compares
the two measurements. If one is assured that height changes negligibly over 24 h, one can
attribute the difference in the two measurements to the inaccuracy of the measurement
instrument. Newborn behavior, as shown above, changes significantly over the first 10
days of life. It is therefore meaningless to expect good test-retest reliability in the tradi-

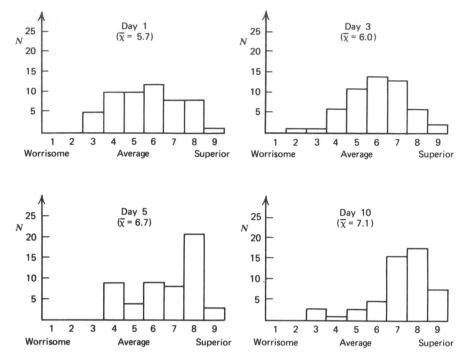

Figure 6-3.   Distribution of profile categories of healthy term newborns over the first 10 days of life (N = 54).

tional sense. So far, the number of expectable tracks of change from different starting points has not been established. Only overall group changes are available.

Interrater reliability on the BNBAS is very good—that is, persons can be trained in the administration and scoring of the scale to produce comparable results at any given time. This requires, first of all, an understanding of the conceptual framework of the scale. Once the conceptual framework is internalized and handling of the infant to produce optimal behaviors has been practiced, high accuracy in behavioral observation can be achieved and retained over extended periods, as long as the scale is being used continuously. The authors have been able to consistently train people to interrater reliability of above 90% after the appropriate theoretical and practical preparation. It is encouraging to find that even after a year of continued use of the assessment, their reliability remains above 90%.

Another significant finding over the past years of training others in the use of the scale is the importance of identification of those items of the scale in which a tester does slip.

Table 6-6.   Comparison of Number of Infants of Average and Below Average (≤ 5) with those of Above-Average profiles (>5) Across the First 10 Days of Life

	≤ 5	>5
Day 1	25	29
Day 3	19	35
Day 5	13	41
Day 10	7	47

Chi-square test: $p < 0.01$

These are consistently the behaviors in which his testing population differs from the healthy term population the scale was developed for. Therefore, when a control group is not available during field work, annual reestablishment of reliability is necessary, and is useful in identifying those areas of newborn function that differentiate the tested groups (Keefer and Dixon, 1976; Als, 1975b).

If a control group is available, it is advisable to test a "normal control" as every fifth subject. This ensures that the examiner does not slip in his scoring toward a mean for his population, thereby losing the subtlest differences in his group of infants.

PREDICTIVE VALIDITY OF THE BNBAS

An important question for any assessment tool becomes what can one predict from its use—that is, how well does it predict to later functioning.

Two studies have reported relations between Brazelton scale performance and 4-to-6-month-old behavior. Bakow et al. (1973) found that the factors of alertness, motor-maturity, tremulousness, habituation, and self-quieting were correlated with infant temperament at 4 months. Powell (1974) found that at 4 months, summary scales of head control and responsivity were correlated with the Bayley behavior record (0.47 and 0.67, respectively), and at 6 months the responsivity dimension was correlated with the Bayley motor score (0.67) and the behavior record (0.64).

A 1-year follow-up was reported in the Scarr and Williams (1971) study. With the effects of birthweight partialled out, nine Brazelton scales from day 7 correlated above 0.30 with Cattell IQ scores. Moreover, seven of these were measures that loaded highly on their second or reactivity factor. They argued that these measures of behavioral responsiveness and organization of response are most likely to predict developmental status at 1 year.

The only long-term follow-up study to date with the Brazelton exam (Tronick and Brazelton, 1975) compares the predictive value of the Brazelton exam with that of the standard neurological exam as developed by the nationwide Collaborative Study sponsored by the National Institute for Nervous Disease and Stroke (NINDS). A group of 53 newborns, who had been called neurologically suspect at the age of 3 days by two staff pediatricians, were reevaluated by pediatric neurologists from the Children's Hospital Medical Center in Boston. At this time they were labeled either neurologically suspect—if they demonstrated two minor neurological abnormalities such as clonus, or facial paresis, or similar ones—or neurologically abnormal if there were more than two minor or one major abnormality such as abnormal Moro, seizures, and high-pitched cry. The infants were followed at 4 months, 8 months, and 12 months, and then again at 2, 4, 6, and 7 years at the follow-up clinic at Children's Hospital. At the last examination at age 7 years, the child's outcome was scored as either normal or abnormal. These particular 53 newborns were also assessed with at least two Brazelton behavioral exams, done by different examiners between days 2 and 6, so that there were two exams on each baby separated by at least a day in the newborn period. A prediction was made at the time by summarizing the two neonatal exams and basing the prediction on the behaviors, but also on the "curve of recovery" implied in the separate exams. The predictive value of the respective newborn exams has been measured against the 7-year outcome.

In comparing the predictive capacity of the two exams, the following appears, as Table 6-7 shows. Both exams were comparable in their capacity for detecting abnormal chil-

Table 6-7. Comparison of Predictive Accuracy of Brazelton Assessment and Neurological Examination: Neonatal Classification vs Outcome Classification ($N=53$)

OUTCOME CLASSIFICATION

		Normal	Abnormal
NEONATAL CLASSIFICATION	Normal	$N=29$ (76%)	$N=3$ (20%)
	Suspect/ abnormal	$N=9$ (24%) False alarms	$N=12$ (80%) Hits

Brazelton Assessment

OUTCOME CLASSIFICATION

		Normal	Abnormal
NEONATAL CLASSIFICATION	Normal	$N=8$ (20%)	$N=2$ (13%)
	Suspect/ abnormal	$N=30$ (80%) False alarms	$N=13$ (87%) Hits

Neurological Examination

Source: Reproduced from Tronick and Brazelton, 1975, p. 148.

dren. The neurological exam correctly diagnosed 13 of the 15 newborns who later turned out to be abnormal. The Brazelton examination correctly diagnosed 12 of the 15 newborns. All the abnormal infants were included in the "suspect" category by each group of examiners, but there are striking differences in the discriminative capabilities of the two exams in mislabeling normal infants—that is, in their false-alarm rates. The neurological examination classified 43 newborns as suspect/abnormal, and only 13 of them turned out to be abnormal. Thirty newborns were misdiagnosed as being abnormal who later turned out to be normal. This would be a false-alarm rate of 80%. Thus, the neurological examination achieved its hit rate of 87% for detecting abnormal newborns by misclassifying a large percentage of normal newborns. In striking contrast, the Brazelton exam diagnosed 21 newborns as abnormals, and 12 of these were in fact abnormal at outcome. Only nine were misdiagnosed as suspect/abnormal; they were later found to be normal. That would be a false-alarm rate of 24%. Thus, the Brazelton exam achieved its hit rate of 80% for detecting abnormal children without including nearly as many normal newborns in the abnormal category.

What accounts for the differences between the two exams? The neurological examination classified a newborn as suspect or abnormal for the most part on grounds of abnormalities of more isolated reflex functioning, rather than CNS integration and adaptability. The Brazelton examination found these abnormalities, too, but weighed them against the infant's ability to perform those integrated acts that point to higher-level CNS functioning. Thus, despite certain abnormalities, newborns categorized as suspect/abnormal neurologically could be classified as normal by the Brazelton examination and turned out to be normal at age 7 years. This occurred when, in spite of CNS signs, the newborns evidenced a number of these capacities: (1) to alert and attend to auditory, visual, and other external events; (2) to organize and control their state of consciousness by self-quieting and to prevent themselves from becoming too upset in the exam; (3) by exhibiting smooth, fluid movements in alert states; (4) by their ability to improve in all these functions over the first few days. The infants categorized as abnormal by the Brazelton exam as well as by the neurological exams had restricted, abnormally jerky movements and/or abnormal reflexes. In addition, these infants failed to evidence successful periods of alertness during the Brazelton exam and were unable to shut down their responses to disturbing events.

There were 3 infants who were classified as abnormal on both examinations who turned out to be normal later on. In each case, both exams emphasized problems in muscle tone (hypo- or hypertonicity), jitteriness, constant flexion, and poor range of movement. Because of the high doses of prenatal medication, these signs were transient rather than fixed neurological deficits, but they were not diagnosed as transient by day 6.

In summary, it can be postulated that the BNBAS elicits higher order of functioning of the CNS and may be likely to make fewer predictions of at riskness from the error of false alarm. The assessment of alertness, state organization, quality of movement, reaction to stress, and improvement over time should add substantially to accuracy in predicting to abnormality.

USES OF THE BNBAS

The Brazelton scale has been used for a variety of purposes in different settings, including the study of high-risk infants, the effects of maternal obstetrical medication, cross-cultural comparisons of infant behavior, the relation between neonatal behavior and infant-caregiver interaction to assess the effects of intervention programs, and as an intervention tool in teaching parents about the behavior of their baby.

The largest number of studies using the scale have been concerned with the assessment of infants who range in at-riskness due to prenatal, perinatal, and/or postnatal factors. Using an early version of the scale, Scarr and Williams (1971) tested 30 neonates ranging in birthweight from 1300 to 1800 g with a mean gestational age of 32.6 weeks; they were tested at 7 days and 4 to 6 weeks of life. Although the low-birthweight infants were not compared with controls, their scores in the neonatal period were low, averaging 3 or 4 for most items. On re-test at 1 month, intercorrelations of the scales were low, whereas the factor structure was similar for the two observations. Correlations between birthweight and behavior showed nine correlations above 0.30 at 1 week, while at 1 month the number of correlations at this level did not exceed chance. Finally, both 1-week and 4-week scale scores correlated with Cattell IQ at 1 year, both with simple correlations and with birthweight partialled out. Neonatal observations were more predictive than 4-week observations, and centered around behaviors that had to do with responsivity and the organization of responses (factor 2).

In a study of 154 rural Ladino babies from Guatemala, Brazelton et al. (1976b) tested nutritionally stressed infants during the 1st month of life. Mean differences in two of four a priori cluster scores that reflected social interaction and neuromotor adequacy discriminated between groups that varied in gestational age, birthweight, age of testing, and the number of hypoxic episodes. Poor performance was also associated with long birth intervals between pregnancies of the mother, short maternal stature, and low maternal socioeconomic status (SES). This study points to a number of nongenetic variables that can affect intrauterine conditions unfavorably, and it would be useful to compare the relative contribution of these variables in predicting neonatal behavior.

This procedure was attempted in a study in which multiple regression was used to determine the relative contribution of six high-risk variables on factor scores of the Brazelton scale (Lester et al., 1976). Low attention scores were associated with low-birthweight babies and infants of younger mothers. Low Apgar babies scored lower on a temperament-arousal dimension. The 52 babies from this study were also included in a study of 140 infants of low, average, and high birthweight (Emory et al., 1976). Factor scores representing three dimensions—attention, arousal, and temperament—were compared among the three birthweight groups, with gestational age as a covariate. Both low- and high-birthweight infants scored lower on attentional behavior than infants of average birthweight. Low-birthweight males and high-birthweight females scored lower on arousal and temperament than other sex-by-birthweight groups. In another study of high-risk infants (Sepkoski et al., 1976), 153 babies from Puerto Rico were compared using typological and profile analysis of the Brazelton scale. Independent variables of birthweight, gestational age, ponderal index (ratio of weight to length), total nonoptimal obstetric conditions, age of the mother, and the age and sex of the baby were used in a discriminant function analysis to find the best linear combination capable of predicting deficient versus average or superior performance for each of the four typologies and in the overall profile. Various combinations of these variables significantly predicted group membership in all dimensions, with the percentage of infants correctly classified ranging from 58 to 80%.

The ponderal index was also used by Als et al. (1976) to compare AGA with SGA full-term infants at 1, 3, 5, and 10 days of life with the Brazelton scale. These normal, healthy but slightly malnourished infants differed from controls along behavioral dimensions that are important for the caretaker of the baby such as attractiveness, need for stimulation, interactive processes, and motor processes. The two groups also differed on reflexive behavior. Moreover, follow-up of the underweight infants showed difficulties in temperamental organization and some indication of psychosomatic reaction to stress.

Other studies have also used the Brazelton scale to look at special high-risk groups. Three studies have been concerned with infants born to narcotic-addicted mothers. In the first, Soule et al. (1974) compared infants of 19 heroin-addicted mothers taking methadone with 41 controls who, unfortunately, differed on economic, racial, and medical factors. Mean differences were found for 14 of the 26 items of the scale and reflected the methadone baby's state of narcotic withdrawal. The methadone babies were neurologically irritable as shown by more crying, state changes, tremors, hypertonicity, and less motor maturity. An interesting sidelight to this study was that information from the exam was useful in the management of these infants by using interventions from the consolability maneuvers to avoid the administration of drugs to alleviate the withdrawal. In a similar report, Kaplan and Kron (1975) found mean differences between narcotic-addicted and control infants on 12 of the items that Soule et al. (1974) found to discriminate between the two groups. Kaplan and Kron (1975) also generated summary scores from the scale and found these scores to be related to measures of sucking and to the birthweight of the baby. The latter finding led to the conclusion that lower-birthweight babies were more affected by the withdrawal than full-birthweight babies.

The last study of narcotic-addicted infants attempted to control for risk-producing factors other than maternal addiction and to control for the effects of drug therapy, since either of these sets of variables may have affected neonatal behavior in previous studies. The Brazelton scale was administered to 22 infants of heroin-addicted mothers and 22 controls on days 1 and 2 of life. All infants were full-term, full-birthweight, and their mothers were similar in terms of age, SES, Apgar, prenatal history, and length of labor. In addition to finding classic behavioral signs of withdrawal such as irritability, tremulousness, state lability, motor immaturity, and resistance to cuddling, these infants also differed along dimensions of orientation responsiveness such as habituation, alertness, and auditory and visual orientation. It was felt that the behavior patterns of addicted neonates are likely to tax the ability of the caregiver to adapt to the infant.

Another group of infants who may be at risk are infants whose mothers have received substantial doses of obstetric medication. The Brazelton scale has become a popular assessment tool in the study of the effects of maternal obstetric medication. Using a modified version of the scale, Brackbill et al. (1974) compared the analgesic effects of meperedine in full-term healthy infants whose mothers also received epidural anesthesia. Differences between meperedine and nonmeperedine groups were found on the Brazelton scale in terms of a total score, a summary neurologic score, and for four of five elicited responses and for two of five emitted responses. Group differences were also found for rate of habituation of the orienting reflex, although the relations between this measure and Brazelton scale performance is not reported. In contrast, when Standley et al. (1974) compared the effects of analgesia with that of anesthesia using the scale, they found mean differences in the a priori subscales of irritability and motor maturity due to anesthesia with analgesia controlled but no effects when analgesia was studied with the effects of anesthesia controlled. In a report somewhat muddled by confusing and perhaps inappropriate treatment of the data, Aleksandrowiscz and Aleksandrowiscz (1974) administered the Brazelton scale eight times during the 1st month of life and related 34 items chosen to represent as many factors from a factor analysis to seven drug groups. They suggested that

". . . a moderately substantial [about one-fifth to one-third] amount of variance for six of the seven Brazelton items which appeared as marker variables on at least three of the four testing days was predictable by a subset of the seven drug group scores on one of the 4 or 3 testing days (1974, p. 941)."

Two recent studies have called attention to the possible synergistic effects of medication and other stress factors. In one study (Tronick et al., 1976) strict selection criteria were used to compare the effects of eight drug groups on the behavior of full-term, healthy infants whose mothers had problem-free pregnancies, labors, and deliveries. The Brazelton exam was administered on days 1, 2, 3, 4, 5, 7, and 10. Mean differences among the drug groups were sporadic and did not persist. Local anesthesia and analgesic premedication produced few changes in behavior, and while epidural anesthesia did result in an initial diminution in the motor organization of the infant, this effect was transient. Similarly, Horowitz et al. (1976) reported the results of a series of studies comparing Israeli, Uruguayan, and American samples. Infants in the Israeli samples were tested on days 1 to 4 and on day 30 with the Brazelton scale and at 3 months with the Bayley scales. The results were dramatic in the few significant effects obtained, especially in view of the large number of statistical tests performed and for the low magnitude of the effects found. The *largest* difference was 1.7 scale points; moreover, the results from the Uruguayan sample were similar to those of the Israeli sample. These studies may suggest that low levels of obstetrical medication in very healthy infant-mother pairs have little or no direct effect on neonatal behavior.

Finally, two other studies of specific risk groups of infants can be mentioned. One study looked at the effects of phototherapy in infants suffering from hyperbilirubinimia (Telzrow et al., 1976) by comparing a jaundiced group receiving phototherapy with a jaundiced group not in therapy and a nonjaundiced group. Using a priori typologies of the Brazelton scale, they found that the effects of phototherapy may interact with the effects of jaundice to cause disorganization in state modulation that persists beyond the normal recovery from jaundice. After 10 days of discontinuation of phototherapy these infants still showed diminished alertness, social responsivity, and consolability.

The other study also used the Brazelton scale typologies and profile analysis (Lester and Zeskind, 1977) to compare pitch analysis of infant cry with Brazelton scale performance, since high-pitched cries may be related to the risk status of the infant. Deficient performance in social interactive processes and organizational processes related to state control were associated with high-pitched cries. The overall profile analysis also showed poor performance correlated with higher-pitched cries. These studies and the earlier reported study by Als et al. (1976) of full-term underweight infants suggest some of the more subtle ways in which babies declared pediatrically healthy and normal may exhibit patterns of behavior that may make caretaking more difficult.

While the majority of studies using the Brazelton scale have been concerned with some dimension of at-riskness in the infant, the scale has also been used for other purposes. We now turn to a discussion of three other uses of the scale: cross-cultural comparisons, the relation between infant behavior and infant-caregiver interaction, and in intervention settings.

Cross-cultural studies represent the earliest uses of the scale, and studies by Brazelton et al. (1969) and Freedman and Freedman (1969) employed an early version of the scale. In an investigation of the Zinacanteco Indians of southern Mexico, five neonates were examined during the 1st week of life and compared with three Caucasian infants (Brazelton et al., 1969). The Zinacanteco babies seemed to demonstrate a higher order control of state and motor behavior than the Caucasian infants, which fostered prolonged and repeated responses to auditory, visual, and kinesthetic stimuli during the 1st week. Observations of mother-infant interaction suggested that the mothers reinforced the quiet alertness of the baby providing dyadic interaction well suited to the society and a demonstration of the infants' role in shaping the environment's response to him.

Freedman and Freedman (1969) compared 24 Chinese-American with 24 European-American neonates and controlled for initial state, 5-min Apgar score, length of labor, obstetrical medication, and the age and parity of the mother. While total Brazelton scores were different between the two groups, item-by-item comparisons showed that these differences were due to behaviors reflecting temperamental dimensions. Specifically, Chinese-American neonates were less perturbable to experimenter ministrations, habituated more quickly, were better at self-quieting, and soothed easier when consoled. These differences were interpreted along genetic lines.

In a study of urban Zambian and American infants, the Brazelton scale was administered to 10 babies from each culture on days 1, 5, and 10 (Brazelton et al., 1976a). Although all infants were full-term and normal, the Zambian babies showed pediatric evidence of intrauterine depletion and placental insufficiency. The samples were compared on each item of the scale for each day of the examination. On day 1 the Zambians scored lower than the Americans on items that reflected reactivity, whereas by day 10, although the Zambians still scored low on reactivity measures, they scored higher than Americans on items indicating social attentiveness. The recovery of the Zambian infants was attributed to a combination of inherited (genetic and nongenetic) factors and cultural expectations of the caregiver.

In another study, 34 Puerto Rican infants were compared with Black and white American babies, by grouping items according to the typologies of the Brazelton scale (Coll et al., 1976). Differences were found along all four behavioral dimensions. Puerto Rican infants performed better on social responsiveness and were more capable of controlling their physiologic response to stress. They came rapidly into alert states, were highly responsive to stimulation, and showed much physical activity. They also showed more jerky movements but were successful at self-quieting.

These cross-cultural studies provide a framework for understanding the role of neonatal behavior in shaping cultural expectations. A few studies have used the scale to systematically look at the contribution of the infant to interaction with his mother in Western cultures.

Bakow et al. (1973) performed a factor analysis of the scale and used the factors to predict infant-response clusters and maternal-response clusters during a home observation at 4 months. They found that items of one of the two main factors, alertness, was related to activity in the mother and responsivity in the infant during the home-observation session. Similar findings were reported by Osofsky and Danzger (1974) with respect to neonatal style and mother-infant interaction during a feeding situation with 2- to 4-day-old infants. Scale performance was related to infant feeding behavior, which was in turn correlated with the behavior of the mother. This study showed that infant style and responsivity was consistent during the Brazelton assessment and the feeding session—for example, newborns who were alert and responsive according to the scale behaved similarly when fed. Also, patterns of maternal stimulation and style of responding were consistent with the demand and responsivity characteristics of the baby.

Als and Lewis (1975) used the scale at six ages during the first 3 months of life and also observed infant-mother interaction during feeding at these same age points. They used eight subscales to derive five temperament types and were interested in the developing organization of the baby during the first few months. They found that by 2 to 3 months mother and infant had combined efforts to achieve a well-modulated state in the baby and that the infant's temperament affected the way the mother handled the baby. For example, the mothers learned to stimulate lethargic babies and contain overreactive infants.

The last group of studies to be discussed used the Brazelton scale to assess the effects of intervention or as teaching resources for intervention. The study by Scarr and Williams (1973) was a follow-up to their earlier reported study of low-birthweight infants (Scarr and Williams, 1971). For the intervention study they divided the 30 low-birthweight infants into experimental and control groups and provided the experimental subjects with extra handling and stimulation in the nursery and later at home. Although statistical data were not provided, the authors reported that at 1 week Brazelton scale performance was better in the control than in the experimental babies, whereas following 4 weeks of intervention the reverse was true. At 1 year of age the experimental babies had a higher IQ than the controls. Relations between Brazelton scale performance and 1-year IQ were not reported. Powell (1974) attempted to replicate and extend the Scarr and Williams (1973) study and also used the early version of the scale. Scale items were combined into a responsivity score and a head-control score. Significant correlations between these scores and 4- and 6-month Bayley scale performance ranged from 0.47 to 0.67 and were stronger at 6 than at 4 months. Finally, Solkoff and Matuszak (1975) provided 7½ min of extra handling during each 16-h nursing shift for 10 days to babies of 31 weeks' gestational age. Changes of at least two points were found on 11 Brazelton scale items for the experimental babies, with the controls changing on only two items.

While these studies may suggest that the Brazelton scale can be used to assess the effectiveness of intervention procedures with very small infants, it should be cautioned that the scale was designed to tap the behavioral repertoire of healthy full-term newborns. As a result the scale may not be sensitive to some of the issues that are more relevant as the premature infant reaches full gestation.

In terms of direct intervention, the scale is used in a program directed by Katherine Barnard as a resource and guideline for teaching parents about their newborn's state changes, temperament, and individual behavior patterns (Erickson, 1976). This individualized approach facilitates parental learning about how to effectively interact with and make adjustments to their infants and to consider alternative strategies for meeting their own and the infants' needs. In this context, the scale may provide a forum for parents and child care professionals to take a more active role in exploring together the strengths of the infant to promote optimal parent-infant interactions.

One additional note has to do with the issue of neonatal sex differences. While no studies have been designed to specifically investigate sex differences using the Brazelton scale, several studies have included analyses for sex differences in their reports. While a few sex differences have been found (Horowitz, 1973; 1976; Emory et al., 1976; Lester et al., 1976), the number of nonsignificant findings seems more striking than the scattered significant effects.

In summary, the Brazelton Neonatal Behavioral Assessment Scale attempts to capture the complexity of behavioral responses to social stimuli as the neonate moves from sleep to crying and to alert states of consciousness. The 20 reflex items rule neurological integrity in or out. The 26 behavioral items attempt to assess his capacity to respond to his environment. As such they become a reflection of his capacity to organize his autonomic and central nervous systems in order to respond to stimuli (both animate and inanimate), and the exam predicts to the environment's response to him as an individual. Characteristic of this exam is that it scores his "best" performance, which is captured after a series of trials, often without a fixed order, and assesses his capacity to organize his responses within clear states of consciousness. The 46 items can be clustered into four sets of variables—interactive, motor, state, and physiologic processes—in order to simplify data analysis. Standardization, validation, and test-retest reliability have begun to be demonstrated by Horowitz et al. (1973, 1976). Reliability among observers can be maintained for at least a year. This allows for comparability of the many studies with neonates that are in progress. So far the scale has been used (1) to predict to temperament in later infancy, to CNS integrity, (2) to assess infants at risk for prematurity, SGA intrauterine undernutrition, maternal addiction, (3) in cross-cultural studies to assess genetic differences and in utero influences, (4) to assess the influence of such perinatal variables as maternal medication and anesthesia, phototherapy and hyperbilirubinemia, (5) to predict to maternal-infant interaction, (6) to assess the effect of intervention programs on high risk prematures.

In conclusion, the BNBAS is a broad-based newborn behavioral and neurological examination. One of its disadvantages is that training for research purposes requires reliability with the personnel at a limited number of training centers. Furthermore, performance must be committed to memory during the assessment unless two examiners are present, and the scale does not lend itself easily to test-retest or split-half reliability analyses or an overall score. The assessment should be limited at this time to full-term infants, although a modification suitable for prematures may be developed. Finally, like all infant tests, predictive validity to later infant or childhood behavior has not been fully demonstrated. On the other hand, the BNBAS seems to offer a total picture of the neonate as he responds to his new environment. It concentrates on interactive behaviors which contribute to home adaptation as well as sensory, state control, and neurological functioning. The Brazelton scale can be taught with relative ease to most individuals, once they have gained experience with newborns.

BIBLIOGRAPHY

Adamson, L., Als, H., Tronick, E., and Brazelton, T. B. A priori profiles for the Brazelton Neonatal Assessment. Mimeo. Child Development Unit, Children's Hospital, Boston, 1975.

Aleksandrowicz, M., and Aleksandrowicz, D. Pain-relieving drugs as predictors of infant behavior variability. *Child Development,* 1974, **45,** 935.

Als, H. The human newborn and his mother: An ethological study of their interaction. Ph.D. dissertation, University of Pennsylvania, 1975a.

Als, H. Reliability testing with J. Chisholm, after working with the Navajos. Child Development Unit, CHMC, Boston, 1975b.

Als, H., and Lewis, M. The contribution of the infant to the interaction with his mother. Paper presented at the biennial meeting of the Society for Research in Child Development, Denver, 1975.

Als, H., Tronick, E., Adamson, L., and Brazelton, T. B. The behavior of the full-term yet underweight newborn infant. *Developmental Medicine and Child Neurology,* 1976, **18,** 590.

Apgar, V. A. A proposal for a new method of evaluation of the newborn infant. *Current Researches in Anesthesia and Analgesia,* 1960, **32,** 260.

Bakow, H., Sameroff, A., Kelly, P., and Zax, M. Relation between newborn and mother-child interactions at four months. Paper presented at the biennial meeting of the Society for Research in Child Development, Philadelphia, 1973.

Brackbill, Y., Kane, J., Manniello, R. L., and Abramson, M. D. Obstetric meperidine usage and assessment of neonatal status. *Anesthesiology*, 1974, **40**, 116.

Brazelton, T. B. *Neonatal Behavioral Assessment Scale*. Clinics in Developmental Medicine, No. 50. Philadelphia: Lippincott, 1973.

Brazelton, T. B., and Robey, J. S. Observations of neonatal behavior. *Journal of the American Academy of Child Psychiatry*, 1965, **4**, 613.

Brazelton, T. B., Koslowski, B., and Tronick, E. Study of the neonatal behavior in Zambian and American neonates. *Journal of the American Academy of Child Psychiatry*, 1976a, **15**, 97.

Brazelton, T. B., Robey, J. S., and Collier, G. A. Infant development in the Zinacanteco Indians of southern Mexico. *Pediatrics*, 1969, **44**, 274.

Brazelton, T. B., Tronick, E., Adamson, L., Als, H., and Wise, S. Early mother-infant reciprocity. In *Parent-Infant Interaction*. Ciba Foundation Symposium 33. Amsterdam: North-Holland, 1975, p. 137.

Brazelton, T. B., Tronick, E., Lechtig, A., and Lasky, R. The behavior of nutritionally deprived Guatemalan infants. *Developmental Medicine and Child Neurology*, 1977, **19**, 364.

Bridger, W. H. Sensory habituation and discrimination in the human neonate. *American Journal of Psychiatry*, 1961, **117**, 991.

Carpenter, G. C. Visual regard of moving and stationary faces in early infancy. *Merrill-Palmer Quarterly*, 1974, **20**, 181.

Cattell, R. B. The meaning and strategic use of factor analysis. In R. B. Cattell (ed.), *Handbook of Multivariate Experimental Psychology*. Chicago: Rand-McNally, 1966.

Coll, C., Sepkoski, C., and Lester, B. Differences in Brazelton scale performance between Peurto Rican and North American White and Black newborns. Symposium on Research with Latin American Infants. Presented at the XVI Inter-American Congress of Psychology, Miami, 1976, E. Pollitt, Chairman.

Erickson, M. L. *Assessment and Management of Developmental Changes in Children*. St. Louis: Mosby, 1976.

Emory, E. K., Lester, B., and Eitzman, D. V. *Brazelton scale performance of infants of varying birthweight*. Presented at the fourth biennial neeting of the Southeastern Conference on Human Development, Nashville, April 1976.

Federman, E. J., and Yang, R. A critique of obstetrical pain relieving drugs as predictors of infant behavior variability. *Child Development*, 1976, **47**, 294.

Freedman, D. G., and Freedman, N. Behavioral differences between Chinese-American and European-American newborns. *Nature*, 1969, **224**, 122.

Fries, M. Psychosomatic relationships between mother and infant. *Psychosomatic Medicine*, 1944, **6**, 159.

Horowitz, F. D., and Brazelton, T. B. Research with the Brazelton Neonatal Scale. In Brazelton, T. B. (ed.). *Neonatal Behavioral Assessment Scale*. Philadelphia: Lippincott, 1973, p. 48.

Horowitz, F. D., Ashton, S., Culp, R., Yaddis, E., Levin, S., and Reichman, B. The effects of obstetrical medication on the behavior of Israeli newborn infants and some comparisons with other populations. Mimeo, University of Kansas, 1976.

Kaplan, S., and Kron, B. Correlations between scores on the Brazelton Neonatal Assessment Scale, measures of newborn sucking and birthweight in infants born to narcotic addicted mothers. Proceedings of the Gatlinburg Conference on Research and Theory of Aberrant Infant Development. Gatlinburg, Tennessee, 1974.

Keefer, C., and Dixon, S. Work in Kenya with the Kisii tribes. Child Development Unit, CHMC, Boston, 1976. Work in progress.

Lester, B., and Zeskind, P. Brazelton Scale and physical size correlates of neonatal cry features. *Infant Behavior and Development*, 1978, **4**, in press.

Lester, B., Emory, E. K., Hoffman, S., and Eitzman, D. V. A multi-variate study of the effects of high-risk factors on performance on the Brazelton Neonatal Assessment Scale. *Child Development,* 1976, **47,** 515.

Osofsky, J. D., and Danzger, B. Relationships between neonatal characteristics and mother-infant interaction. *Developmental Psychology,* 1974, **10,** 124.

Parmelee, A. H. *Newborn neurological examination* (infant-study project). Mimeo, U.C.L.A., 1973.

Powell, L. F. The effect of extra stimulation and maternal involvement on the development of low birth weight infants and on maternal behaviors. *Child Development,* 1974, **45,** 106.

Prechtl, H., and Beintema, D. *The Neurological Examination of the Newborn Infant.* Clinics in Developmental Medicine, No. 121. Spastics Society; London: Heinemann, 1964.

Rosenblith, J. F. The modified Graham behavior test for neonates. Test-retest reliability, normative data and hypotheses for future work. *Biologia Neonatorum,* 1961, **3,** 174.

Scarr, S., and Williams, M. L. The assessment of neonatal and later status in low birthweight infants. Paper presented at Meetings of the Society of Research in Child Development, Minneapolis, 1971.

Scarr, S., and Williams, M. L. The effects of early stimulation on low birthweight infants. *Child Development,* 1973, **44,** 94.

Sepkoski, C., Coll, C., and Lester, B. The effects of high risk factors on neonatal behavior as measured by the Brazelton scale. Symposium on Research with Latin American Infants. Presented at the XVI Inter-American Congress of Psychology, Miami, December 1976, E. Pollitt, Chairman.

Solkoff, M., and Matuszak, D. Tactile stimulation and behavioral development among low birthweight infants. *Child Psychiatry and Human Development,* 1975, **6,** 33.

Soule, A. B., Standley, K., Copans, S., and Davis, M. Clinical uses of the Brazelton Neonatal Scale. *Pediatrics,* 1974, **54,** 583.

Standley, K., Soule, A. B., Copans, S. A., and Duchowny, M. S. Local-regional anesthesia during childbirth: Effects on newborn behaviors. *Science,* 1974, **186,** 634.

Strauss, M., Lesser-Firestone, J., Starr, R., and Ostrea, E. Behavior of narcotics addicted newborns. *Child Development,* 1975, **46,** 887.

Telzrow, R., Snyder, D., Tronick, E., Als, H., and Brazelton, T. B. The effects of phototherapy on neonatal behavior. Presented at the Meeting of the American Pediatric Society, St. Louis, 1976.

Thomas, A., Chess, S., Birch, H. G., Hertzig, M. E., and Korn, S. *Behavioral Individuality in Early Childhood.* New York: New York University, 1963.

Tronick, E., and Brazelton, T. B. Clinical Uses of the Brazelton Neonatal Behavioral Assessment. In B. Z. Friedlander and L. Rosenblum (eds.), *Exceptional Infant,* Vol. III. New York: Brunner/Mazel, 1975, p. 137.

Tronick, E., Wise, S., Als, H., Adamson, L., Scanlon, J., and Brazelton, T. B. Regional obstetric anesthesia and newborn behavior: Effect over the first ten days of life. *Journal of Pediatrics,* 1976, **58,** 94.

CHAPTER 7

The Graham/Rosenblith Behavioral Examination for Newborns: Prognostic Value and Procedural Issues[1]

Judy F. Rosenblith

GENERAL HISTORICAL INTRODUCTION

Behavioral assessment of young infants has long been used for purposes of specifying normality of the infant or for identifying abnormal behaviors. Gesell (1953) and Gesell and Amatruda (1956) have, perhaps, made the most use of such assessments in their work. After initial enthusiasm about infant tests, their use declined. This was probably due to several factors including studies done in the 1940s and 50s indicating that infant IQ tests were not good predictors of later IQ [e.g., Bayley (1955)], Gesell's lack of statistical rigor, and his failure to control for possible examiner bias as a source of the continuity he obtained in test results.

There was a strong revival of interest in research with infants, which started in the 1950s but which especially characterized the 1960s. It included renewed interest in the diagnostic and/or prognostic usefulness of early systematized tests of behavior. The Apgar test (Apgar, 1953, Apgar and James, 1962; Drage et al., 1964, 1966) was found useful in assessing the status of newborns; this may well have contributed to the upsurge of interest in newborn testing. In addition, the Collaborative Perinatal Research Project (CPRP), which started in the late 1950s, described by Berendes (1963), meant that infants in many centers were being looked at in new ways.

People such as Knobloch and Pasamanick (1962), who were students of Gesell, had continued to use his techniques of developmental examination. Other people such as Griffiths (1954) in England developed new examination schedules which, like the Gesell and Bayley Scales of Infant Development extended down to about 1 month. Inasmuch as Griffiths demanded that people train with her if they wanted to use her scales, the scales have not been as widely used as they might have been. Perhaps because of the renewed interest in assessment of infants, Knobloch and Pasamanick (1974) have recently revised the book *Developmental Diagnosis* by Gesell and Amatruda. They include their shortened version (Developmental Screening Inventory) along with very complete instructions for its use by the practitioner, and encourage people to use it as long as proper credit is given.

[1]The author wishes to thank Dr. Glidden L. Brooks and his successor as director of Brown University's participation in the Collaborative Perinatal Research Project, Dr. Lewis P. Lipsitt, and the directors of the Women and Infants Hospital of Rhode Island. Work on portions of the data reported here was supported by the Grant Foundation. In addition I would like to thank Dr. Judith Sims-Knight and Rebecca Anderson-Huntington for reading earlier drafts of this manuscript.

In a similar vein, Honzik (1960) and Honzik et al. (1965) have shown that Bayley scores do differentiate both diagnosed and suspect infants from normals. She and her co-workers found differences on both the mental and motor scales of the 8-month Bayley tests for infants classified by two pediatricians as normal, possibly suspect, and suspect of neurological handicaps on the basis of hospital records. A definitely suspect group, which had been medically diagnosed as having neurological problems, was also differentiated from a normal group on the Bayley scales.

Newborn Testing

A pioneer in the new wave of behavioral testing applied to newborn infants was Frances Graham and her co-workers (1956)—the St. Louis group. They adapted items from earlier scales, organized them into a battery, and showed that this battery discriminated among newborns with varying degrees of anoxia, those with other problems, and normal newborns. In short, they demonstrated that the test had concurrent validity. Graham herself was involved only in the effort to establish the predictive validity of the test at 3 years. A variety of assessments were used at that follow-up period, many of them developed and standardized especially for the purpose. The analyses of relations between neonatal performance and the later outcomes were made only within the original diagnostic classifications. Graham et al. (1962) reported that there were few relations between neonatal scores and ratings and developmental criteria measured at 3 years of age. To use their own words,

In conclusion, the present study could not be said to have demonstrated the predictive value of the Newborn Behavior tests. Correlations differed depending on whether infants were premature or full term at the time of testing, and on whether they were complicated, anoxic, or normal Ss. Correlations also varied depending on the function probably measured by the newborn test. Replication is necessary before confidence can be placed in the significant correlations that did occur. They may be chance by-products of an extensive analysis [p. 39].

However, prior to the appearance of their follow-up studies, others had begun to build on the work of the St. Louis group in the effort to further develop neonatal testing. Even when the negative conclusions of the St. Louis group appeared, they were counterbalanced by the work of people such as the pediatricians Drillien et al. (1966) and Illingworth and Birth (1959), who showed that later marked subnormality could indeed be predicted by early behavioral tests.

HISTORY AND DESCRIPTION OF THE GRAHAM/ROSENBLITH SCALES

In 1957 to 1958 both Rosenblith and Brazelton were beginning work for which they studied Graham's scales. Each of these workers took quite different directions in developing their scales. [For a description of the Brazelton Neonatal Assessment Scale see Brazelton (1973) and Chapter 6.] The Rosenblith version is a modification of Graham's scales based on a 2-year study of them and is called the Graham/Rosenblith (G/R) Behavioral Examination of the Neonate (Rosenblith, 1959, 1961a, 1961b). It provides for a modest degree of quantification (more than Graham's in some instances) of systematically tested behaviors from the limited behavior repertoire of the newborn. Like Graham's, it focuses on behaviors more complicated than the simple reflexes, which are already well known in the pediatric neurological literature. [For example, see Peiper (1941, 1963), André-Thomas et al. (1960), and the valuable survey of the European neurological studies of the newborn published by Parmelee (1962).] The G/R restricts test procedures to those that can be administered in a 20-to-30 min period of time, those that can be reliably administered by para-professional personnel, and those that use no elaborate or costly instruments. The latter restriction meant that the threshold for electrotactual stimulation used by Graham was eliminated. Graham et al. (1956) had divided their test battery into those aspects that assessed developmental level (general maturation and vision scores) and those that assessed current functioning (ratings of irritability and muscle tension and the measure of pain threshold).

Some of the changes made in the Graham tests may well have been important in studying the relations between neonatal scores and later outcomes. I was not certain that the vision score reflected developmental level, but thought of it in terms of its assessing current sensory functioning. I also assumed that responses to auditory stimuli should be considered as assessing current sensory functioning. Hence, responses to sound were removed from the general maturation score and used as a separate sensory assessment, the auditory score. In addition, one item (pushing against feet) was removed from the remainder of the general maturation items and used as an additional component when making the muscle tonus rating. This was done because preliminary study showed that this item did not change with age in the same pattern as did the others. The items that remained on the maturation scale were divided into two subscales: one was composed of items that seemed to represent muscle strength and coordination and was named the motor scale (MS). All items in it except item 3 below had their scoring refined. The MS includes (1) head reaction in the prone position now scored 0 through 3 (not 2), (2) coordinated crawling movements in the prone position now scored 0 through 2 (not 1), (3) vigor of response to cotton and cellophane, scored 0 to 1 as before (see below), and (4) strength of pull, scored 0 through 3 (not 1). All three of the items whose scoring was revised had been found to be reliably scorable over the wider range. The maximum score on the MS thus is higher than for the equivalent Graham items. The other subscale was composed of items that seemed to assess a different kind of responsiveness. The responses looked at were adaptive in the sense of being functional for getting rid of the stimuli that triggered them. I called this the tactile-adaptive scale (TAS), since at least one of the stimuli had a strong tactile component (a small piece of cotton held over the nostrils). If I were to rename it, I would call it the defensive response scale. It includes (1) responses to cotton held over the nares, (2) responses to cellophane placed over the nares and mouth (with the holding fingers far enough back from the mouth to avoid triggering rooting responses), both scored 0 through 4 (as in Graham), and (3) persistence or the proportion of trials in which responses persist over most of the 20-sec stimulation period (scored 0 to 1). The vigor of response to these stimuli seemed related to muscle strength; hence, as noted above, it is included in the MS.

These two subscales are summed to provide a general maturation score (GMS) somewhat like that of Graham and her co-workers. All three of these scores have been used in all data analyses examining the prognostic value of the G/R scales.

Relatively small changes were made in the rating scales used by Graham's group. The muscle tonus rating was converted to a category scale. They had used the distance and direction from a central normal point on the rating scale, and they had included infants who did not cry during the entire examination as normal in their rating of irritability. Such infants were placed in a separate category in the G/R, since it was not clear to me that this should always be considered a normal behavior (or lack of behavior). The rating of "irritability" is supposed to allow for or discount for fussing that is due to normal causes (hunger, sleepiness, gas, etc.). However, Rosenblith and Lipsitt (1959) have shown that different examiners do not discount in the same ways. I found that it was easier to teach reliable "discounting" if one first had the examiner rate the actual amount of fussing or crying, together with the ease of calming the infant. Then the examiner can consider the infant's behaviors, that lead one to interpret the fussing as due to sleepiness, hunger, gastric discomfort, and so on, and come up with a rating of "irritability" in the physiological sense of that word—that is, irritable behavior that has no apparent cause or is presumed to be centrally determined. These revisions became the G/R test. The G/R scales have been shown to be reliable by the English researchers Bench and Parker (1970), as well as by Rosenblith (1973). The G/R scales have also been used to detect changes in behavior resulting from experimental manipulations in the early weeks of life (Katz, 1970; Neal, 1968; Novak, 1978).

PROGNOSTIC SIGNIFICANCE OF THE G/R SCALES

The goal of developing the G/R scales was to determine whether they might be useful in identifying groups of infants "at risk." The infants studied for this purpose were part of the Brown University component of the National Collaborative Perinatal Research Project (CPRP). My definition of "useful" included the requirement that it should identify infants "at risk" who were not considered medically suspect. Thus there is a marked difference from the approach of the St. Louis group who used the Graham tests to distinguish medically different groups in the neonatal period before examining its prognostic value. My goal was to identify infants "at risk" with respect to a number of different later criteria and at a number of different ages. It was not assumed that individual prediction could result from neonatal testing.

There were several important assumptions that permeated my thinking in structuring this project:

1. If there were to be relations between newborn behaviors and later criteria of developmental status they would most likely be a function of damage to or malfunctioning of the central nervous system.[2]

2. The more complicated the newborn behavior tested, the more likely it was to provide evidence of damage or deficit.

3. Motor behaviors, emotional behaviors, and intellectual behaviors are all potentially useful indices of malfunctions resulting from CNS damage or malfunction.

4. Later deficits may appear at some ages, disappear at others, and perhaps reappear at still later ages. Thus it is desirable to have follow-up assessments at several different ages.

5. Deficits or malfunctions are most likely to appear when the individual is undergoing challenge.

The last three assumptions made the CPRP both a good and a not so good vehicle for the research. It was good because the CPRP used multiple ages of assessment and multiple

[2]It is clear that constitutional differences in autonomic functioning could also provide a continuity between newborn assessment and later outcome. However, I assumed that was less likely to be the case.

criteria of function. It was not good because only the 7-year assessment is clearly at a period of marked change or stress. An unrelated good feature of using the results of the CPRP follow-up examinations for our criteria is the fact that their examiners never knew what our neonatal findings were. With these orienting remarks we shall turn to the procedures used and the answers we have found to date.

The G/R scales were administered to 1553 newborns who were part of the Providence branch of the nationwide CPRP. This was slightly less than half of the total Providence study group. The sampling was random except for not taking infants who were too ill to be tested during the period that the condition persisted. During some periods of intake, if all available babies could not be tested, preference was given to babies from the special care nursery. All infants were tested by the same neonatal examiner (Rebecca Anderson-Huntington). As noted earlier, the advantage of studying infants who were part of the CPRP was that extensive follow-up information was to be obtained on them. Medical and/or psychological assessments were obtained at 4, 8, and 12 months of age, and at 3, 4, and 7 years of age. To date, data relating neonatal scores and ratings to criteria chosen from these follow-up periods have been analyzed for all these ages except 7 years, for at least part of our total sample. Extensive presentations of these findings can be found in Rosenblith's (1964; 1966; 1974) publications, and summaries in Rosenblith's (1973; 1975) papers.

Before turning to the actual results, let me explain the general organization of Tables 7-1 through 7-6. In all of these tables the probability values are based on chi-square analyses to avoid the possibly incorrect assumption of a linear relationship between scores or ratings and outcomes. The optimal newborn score would seem to be something that should be determined in the research rather than assumed to follow the a priori scoring schemes of neonatal examiners. In all of the analyses outcomes are dichotomized into normal or not (the latter includes both the cases classified as abnormal and those classified as suspect on the CPRP measures). When maturation scores are the predictor variable they are trichotomized into high, medium, and low in such a way as to compare extreme quartiles with the middle half. When ratings are the predictor variable they are dichotomized into normal versus other, and sometimes specific non-normal categories are contrasted with normals. Details are given later. The p values shown in these tables are always those for the total population. In addition, the initial of any race or sex subgrouping for which the relation between predictor and outcome is significant at the 0.05 level or better is shown.

PROGNOSTIC VALUE OF MATURATION AND OTHER SCORES

The three scores originally used—motor (MS), tactile-adaptive (TAS), and general maturation (GMS)—have maxima of 9, 9, and 18, respectively. On the basis of post hoc analyses of the newborn behaviors of infants who later died suddenly and unexpectedly, an additional score was derived. It was based on the poorest (rather than the best) of the three responses to cotton over the nose and cellophane over the nose and mouth. This score too has a theoretical maximum of 9 points. It is called the low tactile adaptive score (LTAS).

In addition to the three scores established prior to data collection (MS, TAS, and GMS) and to the score established as part of the analysis of cases of sudden infant death syndrome (SIDS)—the LTAS—we have established a score based on a risk index. The seven ingredients for the risk index were derived from the results of our 8-month analyses and from the earlier serendipitous findings:

Item	Non-optimal characteristic	Weighting in index score
1. MS	Low score (0–3)	+3
2. LTAS	Low score (0–4)	+1
3. Irritability rating	Irritable (2, 3, or 4)	+1
4. Pull to sitting	Poor tonus (1, 2)	+2
5. Comprehensive tension rating	Poor tonus (1, 2, or 3)	+4
	Dividend Tonus (flaccid upper extremities, tense lower extremities)	
6. Light sensitivity	Unusual degree of light Sensitivity	+5
7. Questionable light sensitivity	? Light sensitivity	+4
	Highest possible total = 20	

A score of zero (0) means that the infant had none of the above non-optimal findings. The scores on this risk index were grouped into four levels of risk for the data analyses: 1 for those with scores of 0 or 1; 2 for those with scores of from 2 through 4; 3 for those with scores of 5 or 6; and 4 for those with scores of 7 or above.[3]

Although our previous summary papers have included analyses based on portions of our total population, only analyses based on our entire population will be included here. Given the current status of our data analyses, this means that only relations to the 8-month and 4-year batteries can be discussed.

Eight-Month Findings

As we can see in Table 7-1, the MS is related to all seven of the 8-month developmental criteria, including that of physical development. The latter had not been expected since variables assumed to be related to neurological status were not assumed to be predictive of physical development. The fact that they were may indicate that developmental status is a highly global phenomenon in infancy. The GMS is related to nearly as many criteria as its component MS, but the TAS is related to only four of the seven criteria.

When we examine the significant relations found within a given race or sex, we find that there are about the same number of significant relations for males (seven) as for females (five), but more for the Whites (nine) than for the Blacks (four). With respect to the latter, it is possible that the actual size of relationships could be similar, and the relations not be significant for Blacks because of the relative numbers (about one-third as many Blacks as Whites). However, this does not appear to account for the data pattern. Perhaps there are fewer relations among Blacks than Whites because of the tendency of Black infants to outperform Whites (Geber and Dean, 1957; Honzik, 1976). Honzik (1976) found that suspect Black boys and girls were more than 0.5 standard score unit above the norm on the MS. For controls the figures were 0.75 of a standard score unit for boys and 1.4 for girls. Blacks also were above Whites on the mental scale, but the results were not as clear-cut. It

[3]Basically my preference would be for an index that would simply count the number of times on which an infant had suspect standing. However, we do not have this coded for computer analysis at the present time.

Table 7-1. Relations Between Neonatal Scores and Later Outcomes: 8-Month Criteria

	Physical Devel.	Activity Level	Gross Motor Devel.	Fine Motor Devel.	Social-Emot. Devel.	Intellectual Devel.	IBR
Maturation Scores							
MS	M 0.01W	MF 0.01 B	M 0.02W	M 0.001WB	F 0.01W	MF 0.001WB	MF 0.01W
TAS		0.005	M 0.01W		0.05W		0.05W
GMS	MF W	MF 0.001W	M 0.005W	0.02	F 0.02W	M 0.005 B	M 0.01W
Other Scores							
LTAS		B	F W				

might also be tempting to speculate that environmental variables are so important among Blacks that they wipe out any initial biological differences as reflected in neonatal scores. However, as we will see later, this does not seem to be a tenable hypothesis.

To turn back to the sex differences, while the total number of significant relations on the component scores is about the same, the pattern shows an interesting difference. The neonatal MS is related to physical, gross motor, and fine motor development for boys and not girls. The only relation for girls is to social-emotional development, which is not related to the MS for boys. The TAS is related to gross motor development for boys and to no other criterion in either sex alone. The only relation to a motor criterion that is significant for girls is that of the LTAS to gross motor development.

Our more detailed analyses include the examination of relations between neonatal scores and outcomes according to subgroupings of the total population other than sex or race. These groupings included replication samples, gestational ages, birthweights, nursery placement (which is a crude indicator of medical status), ages at which examinations were done, and degrees of certainty of the examiner as to the representativeness of the results obtained. Many of these analyses yield very interesting results. Some of these analyses were reported for the 8-month data (Rosenblith, 1974). It is not possible to present the detailed information for gestational age here. However, it should be noted that there is *no one* gestational-age grouping that is important in accounting for the population difference. Rather, all the gestational-age groupings contribute to the significant effect for the total population.

There is one grouping of the population that will be considered here. This decision was dictated by our concern that the prognosis of risk should be possible for infants who were not medically considered at risk. A contrary concern stems from the fact that we have previously shown (Rosenblith and Anderson, 1968a) that taking account of nursery placement may markedly enhance risk prediction. Thus there are two partially opposed reasons for making analyses separately for groups in different medical categories. Three groupings based on nursery placement were used in our analyses: normal nursery, special care nursery because of prematurity, and special care nursery for other reasons. At 8 months one finds seven significant relations between newborn scores and outcomes in the normal nursery group ($N = 870$). For the prematures ($N = 165$) there are three scores (all scores except GMS) related to one of the criteria, mental development. Among the special care nursery infants who were not premature ($N = 178$), only the relation of the LTAS to fine motor development is significant. It thus appears that our measures not only differentiate "at-risk" infants within the group of infants considered at least roughly normal but do it better than within prematures or within a group of infants with other medical problems.

Four-Year Findings

When we turn to the criteria from the 4-year assessment, quite a different picture emerges as to which neonatal score is most prognostic (Table 7-2). For the total population, the TAS is related to 6 of the 10 criteria, including IQ classification. The other three scores are related to only one or two criteria each. The LTAS, which had not been related to outcomes at 8 months for the population as a whole, is related to two of the 4-year criteria (the behavior profile and concept formation).

Relations within the race and sex subgroups differ markedly from what was true at 8 months. There are more significant relations for females (four) than for males (two), and for Blacks (six) than for Whites (three). The nature of the relations within sexes also have a somewhat different pattern. The TAS is related to fine motor development for girls but not for boys. Among the cluster of emotional criteria it is related to irritability for girls and to the behavior profile for boys. In the intellectual cluster it is related to concept formation only for boys.

Although there were fewer significant relations of neonatal scores to outcome at 4 years than there had been at 8 months, there were a considerable number. Most of them involve the TAS, which has been less prognostic than the other scores at 8 months. Both the MS and the TAS are related to IQ classification at 4 years for the population, but they are related only for Blacks among the subgroups shown in Table 7-1. Thus the conclusion that was tempting in relation to the 8-month findings—that there were fewer relations among Blacks because the environment played a greater role in their outcomes—is untenable. By 4 years, after all, the environment should have played an even greater role in outcomes, and there should thus be fewer relations for Blacks.

Table 7-2 also shows the relation of the risk index to 4-year outcomes (based on 4-by-2 chi-squares).[4] While scores based on the risk index are not related to as many 4-year criteria as the TAS by itself is, they are, however, related to 4 of the 10 criteria. Like the TAS they are related to both gross and fine motor development. They are also related to the one criterion from among the emotional criteria that the TAS is not related to—attention span. Scores on the risk index are the only ones related to the overall impression at 4 years (for the population, girls, and Whites).

In general, when relations for the risk index are examined separately by sex and race, there are more relations to outcomes for females than males. This was the case for the scores taken as a whole. However, the risk index is related to six outcomes for Whites and only one for Blacks, in contrast with the situation for other scores where there were slightly more relations for Blacks than for Whites (five vs. three).

The important points with respect to our original idea of identifying infants "at risk" who would not otherwise be identified will be considered next. (Again these findings are not detailed in the tables.) The TAS is related to six of the criteria for infants of normal gestational age (39–41 weeks) and to only two criteria for infants born at less than 37

---

[4]A problem with our data tape has prevented our going back and analyzing the relations for this score at 8 months.

weeks gestational age. It is related to three of the criteria for infants in the normal-birthweight grouping (3–3.5 kg) and to two criteria for babies below 2.5 kg at birth. There are only five relations between neonatal scores and outcomes for the population subgroups based on medical groupings (nursery care). All of them involve the TAS and four of them are for the normal nursery infants ($N = 784$). For them the TAS is related to gross and fine motor development and to the behavioral profile and irritability; it is also related to irritability at 4 years for prematures ($N = 146$). Thus it appears that the long-range relations also are found chiefly among infants considered at least grossly normal.

As was true for the basic scores, the significant relations of the risk index to outcomes stem from those whose birthweights and gestational ages were in the normal range.

In addition, the only significant relations of scores on this index to the 4-year outcomes are found in the normal nursery population. The risk index score is related to 6 of the 10 criteria in this group. For each of these criteria there are at least twice as many suspect and abnormal 4-year-olds from those with scores above 7 as from those with scores of 0 or 1. Also for the few (5 out of 79) prematures who did have scores over 7 on the risk index, the prognosis is indeed poor.

To sum up the most important findings on neonatal scores in relation to later development we have found the following:

1. As would be expected, there are more significant relations of neonatal scores to 8-month outcomes than to 4-year outcomes.

2. There are, however, a substantial number of relations between neonatal scores and 4-year outcomes.

3. The neonatal scores are relatively undifferentiated in their predictive power at 8 months. If any score is better it is the MS.

4. There is a marked difference in the predictive power of neonatal scores when 4-year criteria are used. The MS essentially predicts nothing and the TAS is most highly predictive. In addition, scores on a "risk index" are predictive at 4 years.

5. When race and sex groups are examined separately there are complicated differences in patterns of relations between newborn and criterial behaviors, which are further complicated by the fact that they differ for the two criterial ages.

6. In general, the predictive value of all scores to both ages, including that for the "risk index" to age 4, is greatest for infants that were essentially normal in the newborn period (i.e., normal in terms of birthweight and/or gestational age or in being in the regular care nurseries).

It is obviously very important to see what happens when we can examine the data for the 7-year follow-up. That test battery will enable us to choose still more differentiated criteria to examine in relation to our neonatal scores. Will all relations have disappeared by then due to the still longer time period in which experiences can have moderated initial conditions? Or, might it be that, since 7-year-olds have just gotten a real start in school and now face demands for new levels of coping, there will be greater numbers of relations? What will the sex and race patterns be if there are relations? Will there be more relations for boys and Blacks, both of whom are widely believed to have more problems in coping with school? These are some of the questions to be answered at a later time.

RATINGS IN RELATION TO OUTCOMES

Irritable Behavior and Irritability

We have already given considerable description of these ratings. Infants were observed not to cry and fuss, and given a label for that both under "irritable behavior" and "irritability"; to cry or fuss to a degree and quiet with an ease that was considered normal (coded normal in both ratings); or to cry and fuss a major portion of the examination period (or beyond what was considered normal) and quiet with more than usual difficulty. Three degrees of such fussiness were coded under "irritable behavior." In the rating of "irritability" three degrees of irritability were possible after "discounting" for presumably normal causes of fussiness. For the purpose of the overall analysis, all three degrees of abnormal amounts of irritable behavior or of irritability are lumped into one abnormal category. Thus there are three levels for the predictor variables: no cry; normal (fussiness or irritability); and abnormal (fussiness or irritability). The significance levels in the tables are based on 3-by-2 chi-squares with three levels of neonatal behaviors and two levels of outcome, normal or not (i.e., normal vs. suspect or abnormal).

As can be seen in Table 7-2, neither of these ratings is related to outcomes either at 8 months or at 4 years in the population. There are only a few significant relations within our basic sex and race groups. There are as many of these for irritable behavior per se as for the presumably more meaningful irritability rating.

However, among the population subgroups not shown in the table, the irritability rating is related to social-emotional development at 8 months for infants of normal gestational age (37–39 weeks) but not for more premature infants. For low-birthweight babies (under 2.5 kg) both irritable behavior and irritability are related to IQ classification. Within nursery care classifications, both irritable behavior and irritability are related to mental development at 8 months for prematures, but not for babies with other problems or for normal nursery babies. Thus we might conclude that irritable behavior or irritability only has prognostic meaning at 8 months within special subgroups of the population defined by birthweight and/or gestational age.

When we turn to the 4-year outcomes we see that irritable behavior is related to IQ classification both for babies in special care for reasons other than prematurity and for those in the normal care nursery. Also for high-birthweight babies (over 4.5 kg), irritable behavior is related to concept formation. Irritability is related to IQ classification both for babies in special care for reasons other than prematurity and for those in the normal care nursery. Irritability is related to fine motor development for the prematures and to the behavior profile for babies from the normal care nursery.

The relations to 8-month outcomes might easily be dismissed as chance findings. However, the pattern of findings at 4 years has a certain consistency that appears to make it interesting. The rating based on actual irritable behavior appears to have more relation to outcome for medically suspect groups than for normals—that is, for high- or low-birthweight babies or prematures. Furthermore, the criterion measures to which it is related tend to be fine motor development or intellectual outcome in the non-normal babies and criteria in the emotional cluster for the groupings not based on medical normalcy, especially for girls.

Table 7-2. Relations Between Neonatal Scores and Later Outcomes: 4-Year Criteria

	Motor			Emotional				Intellectual		Overall
	Activity level	Gross motor devel.	Fine motor devel.	Irrita-bility	Emot. reactions	Behavior profile	Attention span	Concept formation	IQ	
Maturation Scores										
MS									0.025 B	
TAS		0.025W	F 0.005W	F 0.005 B	0.05	M 0.025 B		F	0.05 B	
GMS			0.05 B							
Other Scores										
LTAS			B	F		0.05		M 0.025W		
Risk index score	W	F 0.01 W	MF 0.01 BW			W	F 0.025W			F 0.01W

Muscle Tonus

The rating of muscle tension or tonus is based on six submeasures (Table 7-3):

1. The nature (flexed or extended) of spontaneous lower limb position
2. The response of all four limbs to displacement
3. The response of the lower limbs to having pressure applied to the feet
4. The change in tone of the neck and shoulder muscles in response to being pulled to a sitting position
5. The amount of spontaneous activity
6. The frequency of trembling, where it occurs, how severe it is, and what stimuli evoke it

Flaccidity or rigidity is judged by the amount of resistance to limb displacement. If the limbs remain floppy and return to place without a change in tone, they are considered floppy (hypotonic). On the other extreme, if they resist displacement and move or snap rapidly back to position they are considered rigid (hypertonic). Flaccidity would be represented by head lag on pull-to-sitting, while rigidity would be seen in an infant who came up to a sitting position in a stiff posture without head lag. Frequent trembling is typical of hypertonic babies, particularly of a moderate to severe degree. It is seldom seen in flaccid infants. Overactivity is typical of the hypertonic baby, while the floppy infant often remains almost motionless. Spontaneous leg position is extended and stiff in the hypertense baby, and when pressure is applied to the feet it is difficult to push them back. The converse is true of the floppy child.

A baby judged to have normal muscle tone would be typified by the following findings: (1) on limb displacement there is some resistance and slow return to position—more in the arms than in the legs; (2) often there is mild spontaneous trembling in the arms; (3) spontaneous leg position is either flexed with occasional extension or extended but not rigid; (4) on pull-to-sitting there may be some head lag but the muscles in the neck and shoulders improve in tone and give assistance; (5) there is some activity throughout the examination period.

Degrees of departure from normalcy are indicated by marking the representative space on a nine-category line scale, where five (or normal) occupies twice the space of any other designation. Double ratings may be given in order to take account of diverse degrees of tonicity in different parts of the body. Originally this possibility was provided in order to allow for differences between the two sides of the body such as might be found in hemiplegia. In practice we found (Rosenblith and Anderson, 1968a) that it was used to take account of differences between upper and lower extremities. No rating (or a rating of not rateable) is given when it is impossible to choose two categories that together seem to be adequately descriptive of the infant's muscle tonus picture during the examination.

Our early work showed that the 8-month outcomes for those in category 6 (slight degree of hypertonicity) were not distinguishable from those for normals. Our later analyses therefore have included 5 and 6 as normal and only tonus ratings of 7 to 9 are considered hypertonic. The tables showing tonus in relation to outcomes have four different lines labeled, respectively, 6 Category, *A, B,* and *C*. I was interested in several gross comparisons, not just specific comparisons of two categories; hence there are four different chi-squares computed involving muscle tonus. The first, or 6-Category comparison, examines outcome in relation to ratings of normal, hypertonic, hypotonic, not rateable, divided ratings, and a special form of divided rating where the lower extremities are markedly more hypertonic than upper extremities. As you will recognize, this latter pattern is the opposite of that normally found in newborns. This had been identified in our earlier work (Rosenblith and Anderson, 1968b) as having especially bad prognostic implications. The *A* comparison looks at outcomes for those rated normal compared to those rated hyper- and/or hypotonic. This comparison is the most basic in terms of all the literature on hypertonicity (MacKeith, 1968; Peiper, 1963; Berenberg and Ong, 1964) and on the floppy-baby syndrome (Genichel and Nelson, 1968; Shinoda, 1968). The *B* comparison examines outcomes for those rated normal and those not rateable or with divided ratings. The *C* comparison allows us to check our earlier identification of divided tonus with hypotonicity in upper and hypertonicity in lower extremities as more dangerous, prognostically speaking, than other forms of divided tonus ratings (e.g., hypertonic upper and hypotonic or normal lower extremities, etc.). This comparison involves normally rated infants compared with infants given divided ratings other than the special one, and those with the special divided rating. In the discussion that follows the numbers of significant findings will be examined across all four analyses.

Table 7-3 shows that tonus ratings are related to 8-month outcomes in a number of subgroups in our sample, although not for the total population. There are seven relations for Whites and none for Blacks. There are six relations for females and only two for males. Thus it appears that the meanings of given muscle tonus ratings depend upon the race and sex of the infant rated. This is especially noteworthy when one considers that there are absolutely no significant relations for the total population. It is also apparent that the relations of muscle tonus to 8-month outcomes primarily cluster under the criteria of gross motor development and mental development.

There is considerable similarity in the pattern of findings at 4 years to that at 8 months. However, at 4 years there are many significant findings for the total population (see Table 7-4). Tonus categories are related to five of the 4-year outcome criteria when all six tonus description categories are examined and when divided ratings of different kinds are compared with normals (*C*). The tonus comparison that involves normals compared to hypo- and hypertonic infants (*A*) is related to only two criteria (fine motor development and IQ) for the population. These are the criteria for which relations would be most expected on the basis of previous neurological studies and work such as that of Honzik et al. (1965). Also, the comparison of normals with those having divided ratings and those

Table 7-3.   Relations Between Neonatal Ratings and Later Outcomes: 8-Month Criteria

	Physical Devel.	Activity Level	Gross Motor Devel.	Fine Motor Devel.	Social-Emot. Devel.	Mental Devel.	IBR
Neonatal Rating							
Irritable behavior	B			F			
Irritability	F B						
Muscle tonus							
6-category			W			F W	
A		F,M W	F W	F		F	
B			W				
C			M W			F W	

Table 7-4. Relations Between Neonatal Ratings and Later Outcomes: 4-Year Criteria

Neonatal Rating	Motor			Emotional				Intellectual		Overall
	Activity level	Gross motor devel.	Fine motor devel.	Irrita-bility	Emot. reactions	Behavior profile	Attention span	Concept formation	IQ	Impression
Irritable behavior							W			
Irritability										
Muscle tonus					B					
6-category		F 0.005 W	M 0.001 WB			F W	F 0.05	M	0.05	F 0.025W
A		F W	0.025						F 0.01W	W
B		M 0.05	M 0.05					M		M W 0.05
C	W	F 0.001 W	M 0.001 WB			F	F 0.01	M 0.05		0.05

who could not be rated (*B*) yields significant relations to only three criteria (gross and fine motor development and the overall impression) for the population.

At 4 years there are nine significant relations for Whites and only two for Blacks. However, the sex distribution of significant relations is more even (nine for females and eight for males). The heaviest concentration of significant findings is for the cluster of criteria involving gross and fine motor development. In addition, there are some relations to intellectual development and some to items in the emotional cluster—namely, to attention span and the behavior profile. It is interesting to note that there were relations at 8 months primarily to gross motor development. However, at 4 years, both gross and fine motor development are related to neonatal tonus in several of the comparisons, but in the *A* comparison only fine motor development is related. Also, the tonus comparison that yielded the largest number of significant relations to 8-month outcomes involved the hypo- and hypertonic groups (*A*). At 4 years, however, it is the six-category breakdown or that involving the special divided tonus rating that is more frequently related to outcomes.

Table 7-5 shows the relations between tonus and outcomes according to the nursery placement and classification of the infant. Unlike the findings related to irritable behavior and irritability, the tonus ratings predict more outcomes at 8 months for normals (eight) than for prematures (two) or for babies with other problems (four). It is especially in the infants from normal nurseries that tonus is related either to motor development or to mental development. In prematures, tonus is related to later motor performance, but not to mental development; and in babies with other problems it is related to social-emotional development or the overall impression and not to motor or mental criteria.

At 4 years the neonatal tonus ratings are related to outcomes primarily for those from the normal care nursery. There are 14 significant relations between tonus categories and outcomes for these normal nursery infants. In contrast there are none for premature infants, and only one for infants with other problems in the neonatal period. Seven of the 14 relations are to criteria in the sphere of motor development, two to attention span, and two to IQ. The overall impression, of course, contains somewhat redundant information, and it accounts for three of the significant relations.

It is clear from these data that muscle tonus in the newborn period in babies not seen to need special care is related to later motor development at both 8 months and 4 years of age. It is also related to intellectual development at 8 months and 4 years and to attention span at 4 years. One might argue that this rather impressive set of relations contributes little that is new to the armamentarium of the would-be risk predictor, since pediatric neurologists have long been concerned with muscle tonus. However the specific pattern of muscle tonus identified earlier by us and included in the *C* comparisons has not been previously identified as a risk factor. It is the one that accounts for the largest number of significant relations. In addition the fact that the relations are primarily found among infants medically considered basically normal is new.

In conclusion, the two ratings are very different both in their prognostic usefulness and in the groups within which they are useful:

1. For the population neither irritable behavior nor irritability are related to outcomes—either at 8 months or 4 years.

2. Muscle tonus patterns are significantly related to 4-year outcomes for the population although they were not related to 8-month outcomes.

3. More types of 4-year outcomes are related to neonatal muscle tonus (for race and sex subgroups or the population) than was true for 8-month outcomes.

Table 7-5. Relations Between Neonatal Tonus Rating and Outcomes in Different Medical Subgroups: 8-Month Criteria

Neonatal Tonus Rating	Activity Level	Gross Motor Devel.	Fine Motor Devel.	Social-Emot. Devel.	Mental Devel.	IBR
6-Category	0.05 N	0.025 N			0.005 N	0.05 O
A	0.005 N 0.01 P	0.005 N	0.05 N		0.001 N	0.005 O
B				0.025 O		
C		0.05 P		0.025 O	0.025 N	

4-Year Criteria

| | Motor | | | Emotional | | | | Intellectual | | Overall |
Neonatal Tonus Rating	Activity level	Gross motor devel.	Fine motor devel.	Irritability	Emot. reactions	Behavior profile	Attention span	Concept formation	IQ	Impression
6-Category		0.025 N	.001 N				0.005 N		0.025 N	0.01 N
A		0.025 N	.05 N						0.005 N	
B										0.025 N
C	0.01 N .05 O	0.025 N	.001 N				0.005 N			0.05 N

N: infants in normal nursery; P: prematures; O: babies in special care nursery for reasons other than prematurity.

4.   There are a number of significant relations between irritable behavior and/or irritability and outcomes when these are looked for within the medical subgroupings of birthweight, gestational age, prematurity, or other problems. Only 3 of the 10 significant relations were for infants in the normal classifications.

5.   Muscle tonus is related to the 4-year outcomes primarily for grossly normal infants.

From these findings we can conclude that the prognostic usefulness of neonatal tonus assessments increases as the child becomes older. This is even more interesting in view of the fact that when neonatal medical status is taken into account, it is babies who were not premature and did not have other problems that led to their being in special care nurseries whose neonatal tonus is related to 4-year outcomes. This is the same pattern that was found for the neonatal scores. The reverse is true when irritable behavior or irritability is the predictor variable.

PROGNOSTIC VALUE OF SENSORY SCORES

One aspect of the G/R was carried over with little modification from Graham and her colleagues—namely, the vision score. It assesses visual-following responses (both vertical and horizontal) on a 10-point scale where 0 means not only no fixation or following but also at least one abnormal feature. One aspect of scoring was changed on the basis of my preliminary work. Graham had credited the infant with the number of points appearing next to a given ''best'' response, assuming that the responses represent an ordinal scale. Since she intermixed vertical and horizontal following in her ordering, this assumption is questionable. Indeed our preliminary work indicated that the items did not order well enough to justify the assumption, so we credited the baby with each performance actually achieved. We also further standardized the stimulus and the situation used to elicit following. The St. Louis group had used for the visual stimulus either of the objects employed to test hearing—that is, a red rattle or the bicycle bell. We used only the latter, which had the advantage of reflecting in the baby's pupil so that fixation and following were quite easy to determine. The bell was always kept silent when testing following responses, but could be sounded to aid in obtaining fixation. A further change in procedure was that the testing of visual responses was only done with the infant on the test bed in the prone position. We felt that with the infant tested in the arms of the examiner, a procedure allowed by Graham et al. (1956) and Brazelton (1973), there is too much opportunity for the tester to provide the baby with body cues. Babies not alert enough or with eyes too swollen from silver nitrate to be tested are not scored, but coded as not testable. Their responses of blinking and sometimes following to a small pen light are then determined and recorded.

I have earlier reported (Rosenblith, 1971) the relations between various levels of visual following and selected outcomes from the 8-month and 4-year assessments. The outcomes were selected to include the most general criteria (mental and motor ages at 8 months IQ plus gross and fine motor development at 4 years) in addition to specific items that seemed to demand a good ''visual-motor base.'' At 8 months these items were ''looking for the contents of a box'' and ''imitative scribbling.'' At 4 years they were copying a square and the Graham Ernhart Block Sorts (used to assess concept formation). A group of criteria presumed to reflect neurological damage (level of activity, duration of attention span, and goal orientation) were examined in order to determine the degree to which any possible findings would reflect specifically visual or visual/motor functioning, as opposed to representing general neurological damage. Based on the first 630 cases in our sample (the number available at the time I attended an international conference (Paris, 1971) on the function of gaze, several interesting findings, some statistically significant and some only tendencies, emerged. These findings suggested such specific visual-motor relations that they were exciting, but seemed to be too good to be true. Indeed a replication analysis based on the last 761 cases in our sample does not replicate the exciting aspects.

Auditory Scores

As indicated earlier, we removed the scoring of auditory responses to a rattle and bicycle bell from Graham's general maturation score and considered them separately as a sensory score. Based on both theoretical grounds and a single clinical experience, we had some hope that this assessment would detect infants "at risk" for serious hearing loss.

Both stimuli were sounded four times, with the rattle always preceding the bicycle bell. An intertrial interval of about 10 sec was used with each stimulus except for a 20-sec interval between the last trial on the rattle and the first on the bell. These intervals were chosen because they apparently avoided the rapid adaptation of response typically shown by newborns. The first trial with each stimulus was at a low intensity (approximately 70 db for the rattle and 76 db for the bell). This level is optimal for eliciting orienting responses—quieting of gross motor activity, increased eye and/or head movement (possibly but not necessarily in the direction of the sound). Louder soundings are more liable to produce reflexive blinks and/or startles. If no responses were seen, the next stimulation was more intense (circa 78 db for the rattle, 85 db for the bell), and if there was still no response seen, an even greater intensity was used (circa 86 db for the rattle, 88 db for the bell). On any one trial (which included eight stimulations) there was a confounding of intensity and location since each stimulus was sounded in each of four locations—to the left, the right, and above, and below the midline of the supine infant. In all cases the object sounded was not in the infant's line of sight.

Graham et al.'s (1956) scoring that had a 5-point maximum was used as was her procedure of seeking a high-level score. That is, the test was repeated later in the examination if the infant did not obtain the maximum score of 5 on the first series of presentations (or first trial), and a third trial was given if there was still not a maximum response or score. Other items were interspersed between trials to avoid adaptation. The scoring scheme contains three tacit assumptions which, to varying degrees, can be questioned: (1) that an orienting response, called a "listening" response in the examination (with the quotes indicating behavior "as if" listening) represents a higher or better level of functioning than more purely reflexive blinks and startles; (2) that the greater the number of listening responses, the better the functioning (or score); and (3) that a reflex response to the rattle is a higher level of response than one to the bell. I am still inclined to accept the first two of these ideas. However, my acceptance of the second is somewhat limited by the findings of Clifton et al. (Clifton and Nelson, 1976; Clifton, in press) that responses to auditory stimuli are so state-dependent.[5] While we attempted to optimize state for testing,

[5]These authors have a very sophisticated series of studies on orienting versus defensive responses of newborns (to a 72-db stimulus). The relation of heart-rate acceleration to state and to non-nutritive sucking are analyzed. When heart-rate deceleration is the index of an orienting response, it is important to be sure no sucking movements are taking place. Heart-rate decelerations are only found reliably in infants who remain awake for at least 10 min after the stimulation.

not all babies were tested in an alert state and not all of those who were alert remained so for another 10 min, a factor that Clifton and her colleagues have shown to be important. On the other hand, the best response, which is the only one we can analyze for the whole sample, is the one for which these conditions are most likely to have occurred. Although we could say that the third assumption was justified by our finding (on an analysis done long after testing procedures were in use) that the intensity of the bell is indeed greater than that of the rattle, I doubt its validity.

In this connection I would like to note the work of another project with which I was associated. This project was directed by Dr. John Farley. It was jointly sponsored by the Department of Pediatrics, Women and Infants Hospital (Providence, R. I.), and the Department of Speech and Hearing of the Rhode Island Hospital under Dr. Barry Reagan. Mrs. Anderson-Huntington of my laboratory and the Board of Lady Visitors' volunteers screened all newborns for adequate hearing responses (Rosenblith, 1970). This project used a more standardized sound source—the Rudmose Warblet. It emits a tone that warbles between 2800 and 3200 Hz. It can be sounded to produce an intensity of 80, 90, or 100 db. Of the first 6184 newborns tested, 17 failed on repeated testing to show behavioral responses to this stimulus and were then tested for heart rate and respiratory changes to pure-tone stimuli in the laboratories of Dr. Lewis Lipsitt. Four were not cleared as "hearing" by these techniques. They were examined at between 12 and 14 months of age by Dr. B. Regan to determine the adequacy of their hearing. From these tests it did not appear that the neonatal auditory screening procedures were effective in providing early detection of deafness.[6] However, children whose behavioral responses to the Warblet had been difficult to evoke appeared to be "unusual" in their later responses to sound, particularly to show less fear. This was true regardless of whether they were cleared for adequate responses to sound using the electrophysiological techniques or whether they later appeared to have hearing losses.[7]

These findings might lead one to conclude that the auditory responses should have been included with the GMS, which presumably assesses the integrity of the CNS. However, the number of trials required to elicit behavioral response would be the appropriate measure indicated rather than the level of response obtained. Thus it is particularly unfortunate that we do not have current access to data for those that received three trials. It may well be, however, that auditory assessments that attempt to distinguish between reflex (primarily defensive responses) and orienting responses are doomed to failure when it is not possible to exert exacting controls on state.

I would now suggest giving three trials or sets of presentations to all infants regardless of their level of responsiveness on the first trial. The failure to have done so greatly complicates the analysis and interpretation of the data. There is some indication (Rosenblith, 1970) that infants who needed three trials, given our procedures, differ from those who obtained maximum scores in fewer trials. I would probably also abandon the arbitrary 0 to 5 scores in favor of recording the actual numbers of responses of each type (with or without weighting them differently for orienting responses compared to reflex blinks and startles), and I would establish cutting points post hoc on the basis of an initial sample studied in relation to later outcomes. These could then be checked on later

[6]Only one of the four was clearly deaf (and had two deaf siblings), and one was not evaluated. Among the 13 who were cleared, at least two appeared to have some hearing problems later.

[7]Recently it has been shown (Galambos and Hecox, 1978) that the auditory brainstem response can be used to diagnose hearing loss in babies "with relative ease, at reasonable expense, and with surprising accuracy." This can be done in the first day or two of life and they advocate use of this procedure will all infants at discharge from intensive care and with infants who are at risk for other reasons.

samples. While I cannot reanalyze my data to do this over the three trials (due to the varying number of trials administered), I may be able to make such an analysis for the first trial at some point.

I would not have a great desire to purify the stimuli since complex sounds have long been shown to be more effective in eliciting responses than are pure tones (Eisenberg, 1970, 1971).

The usefulness of sensory scores, as they have been analyzed to date, can be summarized as follows:

1. Visual following responses in the newborn period do not seem to be predictive of later visual or visual-motor behaviors at 8 months or 4 years.

2. The techniques used to assess and score auditory responses in the G/R do not produce results that make them appear to be useful tools for early screening to detect serious hearing impairment. However, some children with profound hearing loss have been identified by their lack of response to the G/R stimuli and some by the examiner's judgment that a hearing deficit was likely despite apparent responses to the stimuli.

3. The results of the hospital-wide auditory screening project suggest that newborns who fail to respond appropriately to sound may have other—possibly neurological—problems even though they are not deaf.

SERENDIPITOUS FINDINGS

A series of unplanned or serendipitous findings has also emerged from the work with the G/R scales including the accompanying notations made by the examiner.

Unusual hypersensitivity to room light marks a small group of infants with gross developmental problems over the first years of life (Anderson and Rosenblith, 1964; Rosenblith et al., 1970). This group of infants also led to the identification of spontaneous nystagmus during the examination as related to poorer visual performance and more abnormal neurological findings at 4 months (Rosenblith and Anderson, 1968b). Infants with spontaneous nystagmus also had higher proportions of suspect and/or abnormal cases for physical development, fine motor coordination, and overall behavior ratings at 8 months. We have not yet had an opportunity to extend these analyses to the entire population or to the examination of 4-year criteria.

Attention has already been called to our findings with respect to marked discrepancy in muscle tonus for the upper and lower halves of the body, with the latter more hypertonic (Rosenblith and Anderson, 1968a). This pattern too was identified because of its occurrence in the light-sensitive infants.

We have already noted that scores from the G/R examination discriminated infants who died suddenly and unexpectedly from various control groups (Anderson and Rosenblith, 1971). In addition, notations of various other so-called "soft signs" of neurologic damage noted in the course of the G/R have been shown to distinguish the infants who died from a control group made up of a random sample of every 15th case examined (Anderson-Huntington and Rosenblith, 1976). The signs include abnormalities of muscle tonus, skin color, cry, and vision, as well as anoxic conditions, jaundice, and poor LTAS scores.

If one were to choose a cutting point of four such signs, 83.4% of the deaths would be identified and only 17.5% of a random sample would have that many of the signs or be false-positives.

EXAMINATION OF ORIGINAL ASSUMPTIONS

It would be helpful to evaluate what has been learned to date about the initial assumptions of the study. The first assumption was that behavioral differences in the newborn period that would relate to later functioning would probably reflect CNS function. Since this assumption has been an important part of the work of many investigators, it will not be further justified here. However, I would call attention to the fact that a number of the significant findings at 4 years were to criteria that are considered neurological "soft signs" at that age or have been associated with the hyperactive child or MBD. Hopefully the 7-year findings will shed further light on this association.

The second assumption was that more complicated neonatal behaviors were more likely to be predictive than more simple reflexive behaviors. This may still be only an assumption. However, the degree to which we have found some predictive validity for our measures, which were picked for their complexity, serves as at least a weak support for it. Further, we might conceive that the TAS reflects a more complex pattern of behaviors than the MS. Since the former has more predictive value at 4 years than the latter, this too provides some support for the assumption.

The third assumption was about the multiple or varied nature of criteria that might be related to CNS deficit. Again, most workers in this field have assumed that motor, emotional, and intellectual behaviors can all index CNS malfunction. Certainly Graham and the St. Louis group tried to choose criteria from all of these areas. They added social behavior as seen by both parents and teachers at their 7-year follow-up. Each of these types of criteria are predicted in some groups and/or at some ages by one or more of our neonatal measures.

The fourth assumption was that deficits may appear, disappear, and reappear. This idea receives considerable discussion in the work of the St. Louis group (Graham et al., 1962; Corah et al., 1965). Attention is called in Corah et al. (1965) to earlier statements of Teuber and Rudel (1962) relevant to the idea that deficits may be manifested in different ways at different ages and that some may decrease and others increase. Certainly it is true that some deficits cannot be manifested until development reaches a certain point. Verbal deficits cannot be assessed at 3 months. Certainly the patterns we have found in the types of deficit related to newborn measures at different ages and in the follow-up age when a given newborn score is related to behavior support this basic idea. They also add to the picture of complexity which these authors have painted.

The fifth assumption—about the importance of doing follow-up examinations at times when the child is facing challenges or new adaptations—is not one which clearly dictated previous work in this field. However, in their efforts to understand some of the unexpected aspects of their data, Corah et al. (1965) have explored this question in their thinking. They discuss the fact that they find less damage to vocabulary than to conceptual ability— the opposite of what might have been expected from theory based on adult findings. They say that it may not be the degree of learning that has taken place at the time an injury occurs that determines the degree of intactness for that performance but the degree of learning (or overlearning) that has occurred at the time the behavior is measured: ". . . Conceptual ability should continue to show relatively more impairment than many other functions, if the measure of conceptual ability does not call upon concepts that are already overlearned" [p. 49]. As indicated earlier, we will only have a way of considering this assumption in the light of our own data when we have been able to analyze the 7-year follow-up data.

PROCEDURAL ISSUES

In the course of analyzing the data relevant to the prognostic usefulness of the G/R assessments, a number of general issues arise which are important to the general field of neonatal testing. I shall take them up here.

The breaking down of the GMS score used by Graham and the St. Louis group into smaller components appears to have been exceedingly useful. At least one of these subscores always has more relations to outcomes than does their total. While the GMS was related to six of the seven 8-month criteria, the MS is related to all seven, and the TAS to only four. At 4 years the GMS is related to only one of the 10 criteria, but the TAS is related to six and the MS to only one. It should also be noted that the two subscales often predict different outcome variables, especially at 4 years when outcome measures are themselves more differentiated. The usefulness of our two subscales clearly varies according to the age at which relations to outcomes are assessed. The fact that we find relations to outcomes at 4 years, whereas Graham et al. (1962) failed to find any sizeable number of such relations at 3 years, could well reflect the usefulness of this finer breakdown of behavior. These facts based on the G/R could be seen as supporting Horowitz's (1975) contention that summing component scores on the Brazelton is not a good idea.

What is the "best" score on a neonatal scale (or item)? Number values are assigned to responses to specific stimulus situations in all the neonatal tests. These numbers are ordered according to what the examiners conceive of as best responses or top-level performance. In fact, of course, the true definition of what is *best* should rest on outcomes. "What are the scores of infants with the best outcomes?" is the question one would ask. One should not prejudge that infants with high scores should necessarily have the best outcomes. Perhaps the top level of response represents overresponsiveness. It is this concern that led me to adopt a relational model (chi-square) for analyses of the data rather than a linear relation model (Pearson-Product-Moment correlations).

Indeed we have found that while those with low scores usually have the poorest prognosis, the best prognosis, for some criteria at least, is for those with medium scores and *not* those with high scores. This is especially true for the 4-year criteria. Again, this change from the linear relation model of Graham et al. may be relevant to our finding more significant relations to 4-year outcomes than they found to 3-year outcomes.

As can be seen in Table 7-6 there is a tendency for the MS to show ordered relations to the 8-month criteria, but only a few could be said to be truly linear. Nevertheless, the highest proportion of cases that are suspect or abnormal on a criterion are always from the low-scoring group, and there are only two criteria for which the medium level score is either best or in a tie for best. Of the four criteria that are significantly related to the TAS, only one is really linearly related and the smallest proportion of suspect and abnormal cases on mental development and the infant behavior rating come from the group that had medium scores as newborns.

When we look at the data in relation to the 4-year criteria (see Table 7-7), there are, of course, no significant relations for the MS. For the TAS there are six significant relations to outcome. For the four criteria from the emotional cluster, the smallest proportion of suspect and abnormal cases come from those whose neonatal TAS was in the middle range. The highest proportion comes from those who were in the bottom quartile for three of the criteria. The highest proportion of non-normal cases on gross and fine motor development is also found for those with a low TAS. However, for one criterion (IQ) those with medium scores have the best prognosis, and both extreme quartiles are equally

Table 7-6.   Proportion of Cases from Each Neonatal Score Category Who Are Not Normal on the 8-Month Criteria

Neonatal Scores	8-Month Criteria						
	Phys devl.	Activity	Gross motor	Fine motor	Soc.-emot.	Mental devel.	IBR
MS							
Low	46	25	23	21	18	15	39
Medium	38	15	22	16	11	7	35
High	33	18	13	10	11	6	25
TAS							
Low	40	24	27	20	17	12	39
Medium	39	16	18	15	12	7	31
High	40	16	17	14	9	9	34
GMS							
Low	44	25	24	20	17	13	39
Medium	39	15	21	16	11	8	35
High	35	17	14	11	10	6	26
LTAS							
Low	40	24	29	20	15	13	41
Medium	39	19	22	17	14	9	34
High	40	16	16	14	11	7	31

disadvantaged. The one significant relation of GMS to outcome (to fine motor development) is linear despite the nonlinear TAS component. There is no significant relation between LTAS and outcome.

In the case of the scores based on the risk index, the highest proportion of suspect or abnormal cases is always found in the group with the largest number of such findings. For all criteria that are significantly related to this score, the lowest proportion of non-normal findings occurs for those with only one or no risk sign. However, there is certainly no linear ordering, as can be seen in Table 7-7. We might also note that this index, which was based on the seriousness of neonatal indicators judging from 8-month outcomes, is hardly impressive in predicting 4-year outcomes though it is better than any of the single scores.

Is it better to judge an infant by his best performance, his average or modal performance, or by his poorest performance? Graham et al. had scored their test in terms of average performance, where there was more than one trial. I felt that given the variability of infant behavior, one should credit infants with their best performance. The Brazelton test has also been scored in terms of the infant's best performance. What have we learned in the course of our data analyses relevant to this question? Before we attempt to answer this question it is important to reemphasize a procedural aspect of the testing. In both the Graham and the G/R tests the items in the motor scale were not administered more than once if the infant obtained the maximum score on the first trial. The items in the TAS were always administered three times and the responses for each administration were scored. This was done because a score was given not only for the response itself but for the vigor and persistence of responses across the six stimulus presentations (two stimuli, three trials each) that were made. As previously noted, we have studied the neonatal records of infants who later died of SIDS (Anderson and Rosenblith, 1971). In this context we learned that a score based on the poorest of the three responses to each stimulus differentiated these infants from various control groups even better than did the score based on best responses. This new score was called the low tactile-adaptive score, or LTAS.

Table 7-7. Proportion of Cases from Each Neonatal Score Category that Are Not Normal on the 4-Year Criteria: 4-Year Criteria

	Motor			Emotional				Intellectual		Overall
	Activity	Gross motor	Fine motor	Irrita-bility	Emot. reactions	Behavior profile	Attention span	Concept formation	IQ	Impression
Neonatal Scores										
MS										
Low	24	16	29	20	28	28	27	9	15	20
Medium	23	14	23	19	24	24	22	8	11	24
High	18	14	23	21	27	28	25	7	11	24
TAS										
Low	22	20[a]	32[b]	25[b]	29[a]	32[a]	28	10	15[a]	30
Medium	22	13	21	16	23	23	22	8	10	22
High	21	12	25	22	30	27	25	6	15	26
GMS										
Low	23[a]	16	29[a]	20	29	28	27	10	14	28
Medium	24	15	24	19	24	25	22	8	12	24
High	18	12	20	18	26	26	24	7	11	24
LTAS										
Low	21	18	29	21	30	31	25	8	12	26
Medium	24	15	25	21	27	28	24	11	14	28
High	21	13	22	17	22	22	23	6	11	22
Risk Index Score										
7–20	33	27	56	27	31	40	40	15	17	44
5–6	24	16	29	17	28	23	24	7	12	25
2–4	24	18	27	22	27	28	26	9	14	29
0–1	20[b]	12[b]	21[b]	18	24	24	22[a]	7	11	21[b]

[a] $p \leq 0.05$.
[b] $p \leq 0.01$.

Further, we have shown ethnic differences in these scores that parallel the ethnic differences in SIDS rates for the same locale (Rosenblith, 1970).

These findings emphasize that, at least for some outcomes, the poorest response may be most prognostic. This is clearly not true for all outcomes since our analyses of the relations of the LTAS score to the various 4-year criterion measures have shown it to be less prognostic than the TAS based on best performance. There is an exception for the infants examined on day 5. The role of the age of the baby at the time of examination will be dealt with in the next section.

It might also be interesting to examine the risk index score on this basis. It is related to four of the 4-year criteria: gross and fine motor development, attention span, and the overall impression. As previously noted, in all of these categories the smallest proportion of suspect and/or abnormal children come from those with the lowest risk score and the largest proportion (usually twice that for the low scores) from those with the highest scores. However, there is no systematic ordering in the two intermediate risk score categories (see Table 7-7).

If we were to start a new data collection we would utilize a procedure in which three trials were given on all items, and the four possible scores all examined for their relation to outcomes. The four possibilities are (1) score based on best performance, (2) score based on next best performance, (3) score based on poorest performance, and (4) score based on the total of all three performances. Strauss (1975) has also made the point that he was considering the use of modal scores on the basis of his work. He expects greater discrepancies between best and modal scores for drug-addicted than for normal infants. He also calls attention to the fact that it is necessary to empirically determine which is more useful and that this may depend on the specific criterion that is to be predicted. Horowitz (1976) is planning a study to investigate this issue systematically.

What is the optimal neonatal age for doing newborn behavioral assessments?

A number of people have assumed that the answer is "the later the better." They (and all of us who do our work during the hospital stay of the infants) are constrained in our actual work by the hospital practices with respect to the age at which normal newborns are sent home. This has been seen as a serious constraint. Our own research started out with the idea of doing two assessments on as many infants as possible, with 48 h intervening between the two. We hoped to find differences between these scores to be of some prognostic usefulness. In preliminary work based on 242 infants (Rosenblith, 1964), we established that, in and of themselves, the differences between the two scores did not have prognostic value. However, we also have found that for the first of our four samples first examinations were more predictive of 8-month outcomes than were second examinations (Rosenblith, 1966). At this point we were aware of the difficulty of separating age of examination from repeat-versus-initial examination, and modified our procedures to do more first examinations on day 3 or day 4, thus allowing us to better separate these factors. The data presented in the present paper are all based on the first examination of the infant; hence only the age of the infant at first examination is assessed in relation to the prognostic usefulness of the score or rating.

The relations between neonatal measures and outcomes at 8 months in relation to the day of life on which the neonatal assessment was made reveal some interesting facts (see Table 7-8). There are three significant relations between motor scores and outcomes if the scores were obtained on day 1 or 2 but only one if they were obtained on day 3 or 4. For the TAS there are two relations for scores in day 1 or 2, but none for those from day 3 or 4. The LTAS and GMS scores do not show any age patterns. Although we have shown more

Table 7-8. Significant Relations Between Neonatal Measures and 8-Month Criteria According to the Day that Infants Were Examined

	Physical	Activity	Gross Motor	Fine Motor	Social-Emot.	Intellect	Overall
Neonatal Score							
MS	D1 D2	D6		D5 D6	D5	D1	D4 D5
TAS		D2	D1				D5
GMS	D2 D4	D3 D6		D6			
LTAS		D4	D1 D3 D5			D5	D1
Ratings							
Irrit. behav.	D2						
irritability	D2 D6				D2 D5		D4
Muscle Tonus—							
6-category			D3			D3 D5	
A		D3 D4	D3		D3	D3 D5	
B	D1					D3	
C			D1 D5			D5 D6	

relations within normal samples than in medically suspect samples, infants who were first examined on day 5 or 6 show the greatest number of significant relations between the motor score and the outcomes (five of the nine significant findings for this score). These would all be infants who were considered too ill to be examined earlier. Day 5 and 6 scores also have one or two significant relations to outcomes for each of the other scores (TAS, GMS, and LTAS).

If we turn from the scores to the ratings we see that the pattern for irritable behavior and irritability ratings is again different from that for the muscle tonus ratings. At 8 months (see Table 7-8) half of the significant ratings (three) for the irritable grouping were for day 2 and the other half for days 4, 5, and 6 (one each). On the other hand, among the muscle tonus ratings that were significantly related to outcomes there were two from day 1, seven from day 3, two from day 4, and four from days 5 or 6.

If we look at the patterns for the 4-year criteria, the early age of examination appears to have an even stronger advantage (see Table 7-9).

When relations to 4-year criteria are examined we find that the only one of the original three scores with significant relations to a number of the criterion measures is the TAS. When it was assessed in the 2nd day of life, it is related to all four criteria in the cluster of criteria that have been labeled emotional (degree of irritability, emotional reactivity, behavior profile, and attention span). It is related to fine motor development if done on day 1, but there is only one significant relation for day 3 or day 4 scores (IQ classification, day 3).

Also the LTAS that had distinguished SIDS victims from others had usually been obtained on day 1 or day 2. When the LTAS is obtained on day 2 it is related to three of the 4-year criteria, but scores from day 1, 3, or 4 are related to none. On the other hand, the LTAS obtained on day 5 is significantly related to six of the criteria—to gross and fine motor development, to degree of irritability, to both concept formation and IQ classification, and to overall impression.

The other score that was established later, the risk score, is related to four criteria (gross and fine motor development, emotional reactivity, and the overall impression) if based on day-1 or day-2 examinations. It is related to only two criteria if based on examinations done on day 3 or day 4. However, if it is based on day-5 assessments, it is significantly

Table 7-9. Significant Relations Between Neonatal Measures and 4-Year Criteria According to the Day that Infants Were Examined

| | Motor | | | Emotional | | | | Intellectual | | Overall |
	Activity level	Gross motor devel.	Fine motor devel.	Irrita-bility	Emot. reactions	Behavior profile	Attention span	Concept formation	IQ classif.	Impression
Neonatal Score										
MS			D3			D5	D1	D5		D5
TAS			D1	D2 D5	D2 D5	D2	D2 D5		D3	
GMS			D3		D2					
LTAS		D5	D5	D5	D2 D3	D2		D2 D5	D5	D5
Risk index score	D4	D1	D1 D5		D2			D5 D6+	D3 D5	D1 D5
Ratings										
Irrit. behav.—3-level				D1 D2 D4	D4	D1	D1 D3			D1 D2
Irritability—3-level			D2	D2					D2	
Muscle tonus—6-level		D4 D5	D1					D5		D5
A		D5	D1 D5	D5				D5	D3 D5	D5
B		D3 D4 D5	D1	D5	D5	D5				D5
C			D1 D4	D5		D5				D5

242

and impressively related to four criteria—fine motor development, and the overall impression, as for day 2, and also to concept formation and IQ classification. For three of these criteria it accounts for more than 25% of the variance.

When one looks at the relation of ratings to the 4-year criteria (Table 7-9), it appears that irritable behavior or irritability is of most value if assessed in day 1 or 2. These days account for 9 of 12 significant relations found for these ratings. On the other hand, muscle tonus ratings from later days are more often related to outcome except for the criterion of fine motor development. The bulk of the remaining significant relations (16 out of 21) are for tonus ratings obtained on day 5. Day 3 and 4 ratings account for the remainder.

If one looks at the various criteria in relation to all the neonatal measures it appears that fine motor development is more apt to be predicted by measures made on day 1, items in the emotional cluster by measures made on day 2, and IQ by measures made on day 3. This ignores the day-5 data, which we will address later. This pattern further complicates an answer to the basic questions posed in research of this type.

What implications do these findings on age of examination have for neonatal testing strategies? I would argue that they strongly suggest that examinations done on day 1 or 2 would be best in hospitals that routinely send babies home on day 3 or 4. Where does this leave us with respect to the day-5 results being so meaningful and important? It is difficult to say since day-5 infants were always infants with some problem. It would appear to be valuable to look in detail at the records of the day-5 group to see if they could shed further light on the nature of this group or on any possible mediator for the strong relations found. It would also appear to be worthwhile to find hospitals that routinely keep infants for 6 to 7 days. Indeed, Tronick and Brazelton (1975) have claimed that the latest examination of babies routinely kept in the hospital for 6 days are most valuable in correctly identifying babies with long-term damage from among a group of suspect infants. However, they have not presented the data on which this statement rests, so we cannot interpret it in relation to our own findings. It would be valuable to study the relation of neonatal assessments made on days 5 through 7 to later outcome for a group that was largely normal. I do not believe that the at home examination of infants would answer the question adequately, although it would give us different information. The new accommodations the infant is making when first at home could be hypothesized to have two exactly opposite effects on the prognostic usefulness of the measures. We could hypothesize either that it would give us a very unstable, hence useless, measure of performance or we could hypothesize that it would give us a measure of great value. Why the latter? It could be that the relative effectiveness of day-1 and day-2 assessments is a result of the fact that the infant is making a major adjustment at the time and that therefore any weakness in its response system will be particularly evident. These hypotheses demand testing.

The issue of the role of state when examining newborns is one other procedural issue of importance that cannot be dealt with very fully in the confines of this chapter. What is the optimal strategy for working with state as a variable when one's goal is the prediction of future outcome? Some workers have stressed the importance of exacting control over state. Our original strategy was to vary the order of presentation of the components of the G/R assessment and to soothe or rouse infants in such a way that we hopefully optimized the state of the infant for the given test situation. We ruled out the administration of any item when the infant was crying. Present knowledge based on our own work and that of others hardly provides definitive answers to this basic question.

We have not yet analyzed the data on the MS in relation to the one state measure we recorded (whether the infant's eyes were open, closed, or both during the trial). We have shown that state thus measured does not appear to play a major role in TAS scores. However, when the infant is not manipulated to optimize state, and responses are scored in relation to state at the time of presentation, state does affect the scores (Rosenblith and Anderson-Huntington, 1975).

The work of Clifton already cited makes it appear that state is an exceedingly important determinant of responses to auditory stimuli. Indeed, some time ago Gogan (1970) showed that in adults, habituation of both startle and orienting reactions to sound depended on the variability of EEG rhythm at the time of stimulation. This might also be considered a state variable. Bell (1963) was one of the persons who early argued for strict controls on state. More recently, he and Haaf (1971) stated that their data place limits on the importance attached to state in predicting responses in young infants. They have also shown that the responses they were studying (nonnutritive sucking and responses to nipple removal) have relations to response characteristics over the next few months. Lamper and Eisdorfer (1971) have shown that state may be important when responses to mild, but not to compelling, stimuli are assessed.

The question of optimal strategy with respect to state as a variable really had two questions buried within it. Both have been addressed in some of our remarks thus far. One question is whether or not state affects a given class of responses. The other is whether the prognostic or predictive value of given response measures is greatest if you control severely for state, control loosely as the G/R procedures did, or possibly, control not at all.

The work of Strauss (1975) in studying narcotics-addicted neonates is relevant to this issue. In comparing the addicted neonates with normals he notes that for the orientation and alertness items on the Brazelton the chief differences between his groups is in whether or not scorable behavior is elicited, not in the scores of infants who have scorable behavior. One is reminded of some of the work assessing effects of severe nutritional deprivation on learning in various animal species. It is often harder to get the surviving animals to become engaged in the learning situation; but, once they are, differences from normals are minimal. It would appear that an important datum to keep track of is the difficulty of eliciting appropriate behavior as well as the scores on the behaviors. Strauss is making the point that state differences between infants or the organization of states in infants tells us something important about the infants' current functioning. Prechtl et al. (1973) have previously shown the important relation between neonatal states and jaundice. Various persons have shown that neonatal jaundice is related to later functioning (Hardy and Peeples, 1971; Lucey et al., 1964; Johnson and Boggs, 1974). This suggests the possibility that neonatal states may themselves be related to developmental outcomes. However, I know of no direct study of this matter.

Whether or not our own strategy of loose control is optimal we cannot say. In any event it has not prevented our finding relations between neonatal measures and later outcomes.

OVERALL CONCLUSIONS AND DISCUSSION

To recapitulate the major findings: The scores based on the G/R are indeed related to the outcomes as assessed using the Bayley (CPRP) 8-month assessments. This is in some sense not a very new finding since a number of aspects of newborn history and status have been shown to be related to the 8-month Bayley information. In addition to Honzik's (1960) findings that infants classified on the basis of their newborn medical records differed on the Bayley scales, Serunian and Broman (1975) have shown that the newborn Apgars are related to the Bayley 8-month scores. Correlations with mental scores are higher than with motor scores. Also correlations are higher within their ethnic subsamples than within their total sample. This tends to substantiate our conclusion that it is important to examine relations within ethnic groups. However, their finding of similar correlations for Whites, Blacks, and nonwhite Portuguese does not seem to parallel our findings.

The ratings made on the G/R have little or no relationship to 8-month Bayley criteria for our total population. However, gross motor development at 8 months is related to neonatal muscle tonus ratings for Whites.

What is very new, especially in view of the Graham-St. Louis group's negative findings regarding relations of newborn behavior or newborn anoxia to development at 3 years, is a sizeable number of relations between the G/R newborn measures and 4-year outcomes. The TAS is related to five of the 4-year criteria. There are at least two scores that relate to four of the nine basic criteria for the population. Although neonatal muscle tonus ratings were not related to 8-month criteria, they are related to 4-year criteria. When these ratings are analyzed according to all six basic categories they are related to five of the 4-year criteria (counting the overall impression). It is not possible to state which of the methodological differences beween the St. Louis work and mine accounts for this difference or whether they all act together. Dividing maturation scales into smaller, more homogeneous groupings appears very important. Analyzing data for both the whole population and within subsamples appears also to be important. The fact that children were tested at 4 rather than 3 years plays an indeterminant role in the differences between our findings.

Another reason for optimism regarding the usefulness of neonatal assessments lies in the fact that most of the relations to outcomes were found in portions of the population that were considered essentially normal in the newborn period. Hence it may be possible to predict for a group that would not be medically identified as suspect.

All of the newborn ratings are more related to 4-year than to 8-month outcomes. In the case of the irritable behavior and irritability ratings the relations only hold if they were made in the first 2 days of life or were examined within medically suspect groups. Muscle tonus ratings, on the other hand, are related to 4-year outcomes for the population, especially in the essentially normal groups. Also, they are related to more criteria if based on a G/R done after day 2. The criteria to which they are related are those that involve motor development.

The relation of sensory scores to general developmental criteria is not examined here. However, evidence is cited that they both fail to relate to the appropriate later sensory or perceptual criteria.

Several aspects of the observations made in the course of doing the G/R have been shown to be related to later developmental outcomes.

Even though these are relatively positive findings about the potential usefulness of neonatal G/R test results in identifying populations at risk, many cautions are appropriate. First of all, except for rather rare signs that have been identified in this work, the level of risk is not impressively large, and, except for muscle tonus assessed in day 5, the proportion of variance in outcome measures accounted for by the neonatal measures is not large.

Predictability of outcomes depends on the sex and race of the child and the day of life the newborn measures are made. Also, different findings have been noted depending on which predictor variables and which criterion measures have been utilized. These factors limit the feasibility of neonatal predictions.

Despite the above cautions, I would reverse the argument and say that the number, level, and patterning of significant relations means we must proceed. If we are to understand the basic relations between the biological substrate and later outcomes, we need to further investigate the variables identified here as affecting the pattern or strength of relations between newborn behaviors and later outcomes. However, these studies must take account of the factors we have identified as important to the relationships found. At a number of points in the chapter, especially in the section dealing with procedural issues, we have made recommendations as to how we would proceed in the light of our present knowledge.

The fact that we found some prognostic value for the G/R is contrary to the findings based on the original Graham tests. It is, however, difficult to compare the findings for the G/R with those for the Brazelton. The only work I know of examining its prognostic value is that reported by Tronick and Brazelton (1975). Their study compared the predictive value of the Brazelton with that of a neurological examination. However, their approach was extremely different. First, they only studied infants diagnosed as suspect or abnormal. Second, component scores were not studied—rather, an overall clinical diagnosis based on the Brazelton. Using the CPRP 7-year assessment as the criterion measure, they established that their diagnoses had almost the same hit rate as newborn neurological examinations, but fewer false-positives. Another factor making comparison difficult is that in the event of disagreements between the two assessments they had on each infant, they relied most heavily on the last examination, which would usually have been on day 5 or 6, an age at which only babies with problems would have been available to us.

Finally, I would like to agree with the point made by Gottfried (1976) in discussing research strategies for relating anoxia to later development: ". . . Control or matched group procedures in nonexperimental research . . . delete rather than provide valuable information . . . . A more fruitful approach would be to study the association of anoxia and subsequent behavior in its natural interplay with other covariances rather than in an artificially isolated context" [p. 9]. This point is equally applicable to the study of the association between newborn behavioral measures and subsequent development or functioning.

BIBLIOGRAPHY

Anderson, R. B., and Rosenblith, J. F. Light sensitivity in the neonate: A preliminary report. *Biology of the Neonate,* 1964, **7,** 83–94.

Anderson, R. B., and Rosenblith, J. F. Sudden unexpected death syndrome: Early indicators. *Biology of the Neonate,* 1971, **18,** 395–406.

Anderson-Huntington, R. B., and Rosenblith, J. F. Central nervous system damage as a possible component of unexpected deaths in infancy. *Developmental Medicine and Child Neurology,* 1976, **18,** 480–492.

Andre-Thomas, Chesni, Y., and Saint-Anne Dargassies, S. *The Neurological Examination of the Infant,* London: Heinemann, 1960.

Apgar, V. Proposal for a new method of evaluation of the newborn infant. *Anesthesia and Analgesia,* 1953, **32,** 260–267.

Apgar, V., and James, L. S. Further observations on the newborn scoring system. *American Journal of Diseases of Children,* 1962, **104,** 419–428.

Bayley, N. On the growth of intelligence. *American Psychologist,* 1955, **10,** 805–818.

Bell, R. Q. Some factors to be controlled in studies of the behavior of newborns. *Biology of the Neonate,* 1963, **5,** 200–214.

Bell, R. Q., and Haaf, R. A. Irrelevance of newborn waking states to some motor and appetitive responses. *Child Development,* 1971, **42,** 69–77.

Bench, J., and Parker, A. On the reliability of the Graham/Rosenblith behavior test for neonates. *Journal of Child Psychology and Psychiatry,* 1970, **11,** 121–131.

Berenberg, W., and Ong, B. H. Cerebral spastic paraplegia and prematurity. *Pediatrics,* 1964, **33,** 496.

Berendes, H. The Collaborative Perinatal Research Project, 5 Years of Progress. Collaborative Project Report, 1963.

Brazelton, T. B. *Neonatal Behavioral Assessment Scale.* Philadelphia: Lippincott, 1973.

Clifton, R. K. The relation of infant cardiac responding to behavioral state and motor activity. In W. A. Collins (Ed.) *Minnesota Symposium on Child Psychology* V.II, Minneapolis: University of Minnesota, In press.

Clifton, R. K., and Nelson, M. N. Developmental study of habituation in infants: The importance of paradigm, response system, and state. In T. J. Tighe and R. N. Leaton (eds.), *Habituation: Neurological, Comparative and Developmental Approaches.* New Jersey: Erlbaum, 1976.

Corah, N. L., Anthony, E. J., Painter, P., Stern, J. A., and Thurston, D. L. Effects of perinatal anoxia after seven years. *Psychological Monographs,* 1965, **79,** (Whole No. 596).

Drage, J. S., Kennedy, C., Berendes, H., Schwarz, B. K., and Weiss, W. The Apgar Score as an index of infant morbidity. *Developmental Medicine and Child Neurology,* 1966, **8,** 141–148.

Drage, J. S., Schwarz, B. K., and Kennedy, C. The Apgar Score as an index of neonatal mortality. *Obstetrics and Gynecology,* 1964, **24,** 222–230.

Drillien, C. M., Jameson, S., and Wilkinson, M. E. Studies in mental handicap: I. Prevalence and distribution by clinical type and severity of defect. *Archives of Diseases of Childhood,* 1966, **41,** 528–538.

Eisenberg, R. The organization of auditory behavior. *Journal of Speech and Hearing Research,* 1970, **13,** 453–471.

Eisenberg, R. Pediatric audiology: Shadow or substance. *Journal of Auditory Research,* 1971, **11,** 148–153.

Galambos, R. and Hecox, K. E. Clinical applications of the auditory brainstem response. *Otolaryngologic Clinics of North America,* 1978, in press.

Geber, M., and Dean, R. F. A. The state of development of newborn African children. *Lancet,* 1957, **1,** 1216–1219.

Genichel, F. M., and Nelson, K. B. Abstract of paper delivered at the annual meeting of the American Academy for Cerebral Palsy, San Francisco, 1967. Reported by Martin Bax in *Developmental Medicine and Child Neurology,* 1968, **10,** 248.

Gesell, A. Developmental procedures. In A. Weider, (ed.), *Contributions Toward Medical Psychology,* Vol. 2. New York: Ronald, 1953, 485–494.

Gesell, A., and Amatruda, C. S. *Developmental Diagnosis; Normal and Abnormal Child Development, Clinical Methods and Pediatric Applications.* New York: Hoeber, 1956.

Gogan, P. The startle and orienting reactions. A study of their characteristics and habituation. *Brain Research,* 1970, **18,** 117–135.

Gottfried, A. W. Research strategies and issues in determining the association of perinatal anoxia and human behavior development. Paper in symposium on Perinatal Asphyxia and Hypoxia in the Etiology of Behavioral Dysfunctions. Eastern Psychological Association, New York, April 1976.

Graham, F. K., Ernhart, C., Thurston, D., and Craft, M. Development three years after perinatal anoxia and other potentially damaging newborn experiences. *Psychological Monographs,* 1962, **76,** No. 3.

Graham, F. K., Matarazzo, R. G., and Caldwell, B. M. Behavioral differences between normal and traumatized newborns: I. Test procedures. II. Standardization reliability and validity. *Psychological Monographs,* 1956, **70,** No. 427, 428.

Griffiths, R. *The Abilities of Babies: A Study in Mental Measurement.* New York: McGraw-Hill, 1954.

Hardy, J. B., and Peeples, M. O. Serum-bilirubin levels in newborn infants. Distributions and association with neurological abnormalities during the first year of life. *Johns Hopkins Medical Journal,* 1971, **128,** 265–272.

Honzik, M. P. The patterning of mental test performance in infants suspected of suffering brain injury. Paper presented at meetings of the American Psychological Association, 1960.

Honzik, M. P., Hutchings, J. J., and Burnip, S. R. Birth record assessments and test performance at 8 months. *American Journal of Diseases of Children,* 1965, **109,** 416–426.

Honzik, M. P. Personal communication, 1976.

Horowitz, F. D. Discussant on symposium, "Current research using the Brazelton Neonatal Behavioral Assessment Scale." American Psychological Association, Chicago, September 1975.

Horowitz, F. D. Personal communication, 1976.

Horowitz, F. D. Discussant on symposium, "Current research using the Brazelton Neonatal Behavioral Assessment Scale." American Psychological Association, Chicago, September 1975.

Illingworth, R. S., and Birth, L. B. The diagnosis of mental retardation in infancy. *Archives of Diseases of Childhood,* 1959, **34,** 269.

Johnson, L., and Boggs, T. R. Bilirubin-dependent brain damage: Incidence and indicators for treatment. In G. B. Odel, R. Schaeffer, and A. T. Simopoulos (eds.), *Phototherapy in the Newborn: An Overview.* Washington, D.C.: National Academy of Sciences, 1974.

Katz, V. The relationship between auditory stimulation and the developmental behavior of the premature infant. Unpublished manuscript in partial fulfillment of the requirements for the D. Ed., 1970.

Knobloch, H., and Pasamanick, B. (eds.). *Gesell and Amatruda's Developmental Diagnosis: The Evaluation and Management of Normal and Abnormal Neuropsychologic Development in Infancy and Early Childhood,* 3rd ed. New York: Harper & Row, 1974.

Knobloch, H., and Pasamanick, B. The developmental behavioral approach to the neurologic examination in infancy. *Child Development,* 1962, **33,** 181–198.

Lamper, C., and Eisdorfer, C. Prestimulus activity level and responsivity in the neonate. *Child Development,* 1971, **42,** 465–473.

Lucey, J. F., Hibbard, E., Behrman, R. E., Esquivel deGallardo, F. O., and Windle, W. F. Kernicterus in asphyxiated newborn rhesus monkeys. *Experimental Neurology,* 1964, **9,** 43–58.

MacKeith, R. Maximal clarity on neurodecelopmental disorders. *Developmental Medicine and Child Neurology,* 1968, **10,** 143.

Neal, M. S. Vestibular stimulation and developmental behavior of the small premature infant. Ph.D. dissertation, 1968.

Novak, K. K. A behavioral evaluation of phototherapy in the treatment of jaundiced infants. Unpublished Ph.D. thesis, Univ. of Cincinnati, 1978.

Parmelee, A. H. European neurological studies of the newborn. *Child Development,* 1962, **33,** 169–180.

Peiper, A. The neurological foundations of psychological development. *Monatsschrift für Kinderheilkande,* 1941, **87,** 179–203.

Peiper, A. *Cerebral Function in Infancy and Childhood* J. Wortis (ed.). New York: Consultants Bureau, 1963.

Prechtl, H. F. R., Theorell, K., and Blair, A. W. Behavioral state cycles in abnormal infants. *Developmental Medicine and Child Neurology,* 1973, **15,** 606–615.

Rosenblith, J. F. Neonatal assessment. *Psychological Reports,* 1959, **5,** 971.

Rosenblith, J. F. Manual for behavioral examination of the neonate as modified by Rosenblith from Graham. Unpublished manuscript, Brown University Institute for Health Sciences, 1961a.

Rosenblith, J. F. The Modified Graham Behavior Test for Neonates: Test-retest reliability, normative data and hypotheses for future work. *Biology of the Neonate,* 1961b, **3,** 174–192.

Rosenblith, J. F. Prognostic value of behavioral assessments of neonates. *Biology of the Neonate,* 1964, **6,** 76–103.

Rosenblith, J. F. Prognostic value of neonatal assessment. *Child Development,* 1966, **37,** 623–631.

Rosenblith, J. F. Are newborn auditory responses prognostic of deafness? *Transactions of the American Academy of Ophthalmology and Otolaryngology,* 1970, **74,** 1215–1228.

Rosenblith, J. F. Visual fixation and following in the neonatal period in relation to selected behaviors and development at eight months and four years. In A. Dubois-Poulson, G. C. Lairy, and A. Remond, (eds.), *La Fonction deRegard, Colloque INSERM.* Paris: Louis-Jean, 1971.

Rosenblith, J. F. Prognostic value of neonatal behavioral tests. *Early Child Development and Care,* 1973, **3,** 31–50.

Rosenblith, J. F. Relations between neonatal behaviors and those at eight months. *Developmental Psychology,* 1974, **10,** 779–792.

Rosenblith, J. F. Prognostic value of neonatal behaviors. In B. Z. Friedlander, G. M. Sterritt, and G. E. Kirk (eds.), *Exceptional Infant,* Vol. 3. New York: Brunner/Mazel, 1975, 157–172.

Rosenblith, J. F. Newborn characteristics of infants who became SIDS victims. Paper presented at Feb., 1974 NIH Conference on Sudden Infant Death. Journal Supplement Abstract Service, Catalog of Selected Documents in Psychology, Aug., 1978.

Rosenblith, J. F., and Anderson, R. B. Prognostic significance of discrepancies in muscle tension between upper and lower limbs. *Developmental Medicine and Child Neurology,* 1968a, **10,** 322–330.

Rosenblith, J. F., and Anderson, R. B. Nystagmus in the newborn as related to later development. *Pediatrics Digest,* 1968b, **10,** 27–32.

Rosenblith, J. F., and Anderson-Huntington, R. B. Defensive reactions to stimulation of the nasal and oral region in newborns: Relations to state. In J. Bosma and J. Showacre (eds.), Development of Upper respiratory Anatomy and Function: Implications for Sudden Infant Death Syndrome. DHEW Publ. VIH 76–941, Maryland, 1975.

Rosenblith, J. F., Anderson, R. B., and Denhoff, E. Hypersensitivity to light, muscle tonus discrepancies: A follow-up report. *Biology of the Neonate,* 1970, **15,** 217–228.

Rosenblith, J. F., and Lipsitt, L. P. Interscorer agreement for the Graham Behavior Test for Neonates. *Journal of Pediatrics,* 1959, **54,** 200–205.

Serunian, S. A., and Broman, S. H. Relationship of Apgar Scores and Bayley Mental and Motor Scores. *Child Development,* 1975, **46,** 696–700.

Shinoda, M. Hypotonia, *Developmental Medicine and Child Neurology,* 1968, **10,** 143.

Strauss, M. E. Behavior of narcotics addicted neonates. Paper presented at American Psychological Association, September 1975.

Teuber, H. L., and Rudel, R. G. Behavior after cerebral lesions in children and adults. *Developmental Medicine and Child Neurology,* 1962, **4,** 3–20.

Tronick, E., and Brazelton, T. B. Clinical uses of the Brazelton Neonatal Behavioral Assessment. In B. Z. Friedlander, G. M. Sterritt, and G. E. Kirk (eds.), *Exceptional Infant,* Vol. 3. New York: Brunner/Mazel, 1975, 137–156.

PART TWO

Developmental Perspectives in Infancy

CHAPTER 8

Physical Development: Current Foci of Research

Dorothy H. Eichorn

"Growth is the only evidence of life." John Henry, Cardinal Newman, *Apologia pro Vita Sua,* 1864.

Body size, proportions, and composition and rapid changes therein are items that loom large in the personal economy of the infant. During the course of a day an older child or adult may fluctuate 2 kg or more in weight. For the full-term infant this would amount to at least two-thirds of his total weight of 3.0 to 3.5 kg. An infant born prematurely at the end of the second trimester of gestation weighs only about 1000 g, a third or less of the average full-term weight.

Furthermore, the infant has a larger surface area per unit weight than does the adult. For example, at 15 days weight is about 4.8% of the adult's, but the surface area amounts to 15%, increasing relative to the adult the potential for heat loss, the calories expended to maintain basal metabolism, and the risk of severe dehydration and acidosis. In addition, the infant must fuel a rapid growth rate—for example, 4.5 kg (a 130–150% increment) during the first 6 months. Lacking teeth, the 2-week-old infant can meet the total caloric expense only by consuming an amount of milk which, on a relative body weight basis, would be 10 to 20 quarts for an adult (Smith, 1951). Then the infant must excrete much of the prodigious amount of water in which the calories and specific nutrients, such as amino acids, are carried. Small wonder that feeding and toileting circumstances may also loom large in the physical and psychological well-being of infants.

And as yet we have only scratched the surface. Many of the salient behavioral characteristics of infants reflect their tissue composition. To illustrate, at birth water accounts for about 75% of body weight, fat for 11%, and protein for 11%. By contrast, the adult female is about 52% water, 31% fat, and 16% muscle, while the adult male distributions are, respectively, 62%, 14%, and 33%. The infant's muscles are not only small, watery, and possessed of fewer nuclei (muscles are multinucleated), but also his skeleton is primarily cartilaginous and much lower in mineral content. Thus he lacks both the strength and the leverage to support himself or objects and to direct his limbs and fingers precisely. The nervous system, while still immature, is comparatively much further advanced. As behavioral scientists have finally learned after decades of painstaking and frustrating work, the young infant's receptor systems work amazingly well; the difficulties in demonstrating this fact have been posed by the limitations of the effector systems.

Given the background of these introductory comments, the reader will not be surprised to find that the topics to be reviewed in the succeeding discussion represent not only major foci of current research on physical growth during infancy but also the interplay between physical, physiologic, and behavioral development. Yet these topics were selected because they were the most frequent among nominations by a small group of prominent investigators in physical growth when I asked each separately to suggest the most important advances and issues in the field.

GROWTH STANDARDS

Descriptive research of the sort involved in producing developmental norms may seem to some students and researchers unexciting, but as rapid physical development is a hallmark of infancy, so measures of it are bench marks for the clinician and the researcher. Small size for age or slower than average progress alerts the clinician to go beyond the rather gross norms used as screening devices to more specific norms or tests and to inquire about such influential factors as diet, feeding practices, or parent-child affectional relationships.

In research, whether the primary orientation is behavioral or biologic, measures of physical development have long served as both predictor and outcome variables. To cite but one set of examples, we have on the one hand a host of studies relating birthweight to subsequent physical or psychological health and on the other a large literature in which birthweight is the criterion for evaluating the effect of various antenatal conditions, such as maternal anxiety or diet. Reference standards are a longstanding and continuing concern for any research in which some aspect of physical growth or maturation is either the dependent variable or the criterion for selecting or categorizing participants.

Size or maturity for age standards are also used in reverse for developmental research in a variety of disciplines under circumstances in which no respondent can accurately state the child's age. In some cultural groups in which anthropological, psychological, sociological, or medical research is done the investigators must estimate the child's age from his size and physique. As we shall see in a subsequent section of this chapter, the age of embryos, fetuses, and prematurely delivered infants must also be estimated by this technique.

Historical Overview

In 1835, Quetelet, a Belgian astronomer and statistician, published the first carefully collected and analyzed set of normative data on the heights of children of each sex from birth through 18 years. He reported not only the range (minimum and maximum) heights at each age but also the annual increments—for this pioneering study was also a longitudinal one. The only precedent was the Count de Montbeillard's longitudinal record of his son's annual measurements of height from birth to 18 years (Scammon, 1927). During the 1870s, Bowditch (1877, 1891) began cross-sectional measurements on boys and girls attending school in Boston, producing in 1877 the first norms and in 1891 the first charts of average heights and weights for children of school age in the United States. The first norms for heights of British children were published by the Anthropological Committee of the British Association for the Advancement of Science (1880). In 1902, Hastings reported cross-sectional norms of heights and weights for 8000 boys and 7000 girls aged 5 to 20 years, primarily school children, whom he had measured in Omaha in 1899.

Not until the early 1920s, however, did norms and growth charts appear for a United States sample of infants and preschool children. Woodbury's (1923) sample of 172,000 boys and girls aged 1 through 6 years residing throughout the United States made the standards for this age range more nearly a representative sample of the nation than those available for older children. Further, Woodbury included not only means but also several percentile values.

An innovation introduced by the Baldwin-Wood (1925) charts was average weights for a series of heights rather than mean heights and weights by age. This feature proved so popular that these charts have been in frequent use even to the present despite their obsolescence by the secular trend (see below).

In the early 1930s tables and charts began to proliferate. Among the most widely used standards for height and weight, again, even to date, were the Gray-Ayres norms (Gray, 1931), the Bayer-Gray (1935) charts of stature relative to height and hip width, and the percentile charts of Stuart and Meredith (1946). All of the norms produced were based on samples from only one or a few cities or states, and most on samples of restricted socioeconomic range. As the standards movement gained momentum, tables and charts for many other dimensions, such as head circumference (Kasius et al., 1957; McCammon, 1970), were published, but again most were derived from small local samples.

Finally, almost a century after Bowditch's initial efforts at developing growth standards in the United States and two centuries after de Montbeillard charted his son's growth, a series of publications began to appear containing tables and charts based on a representative probability sampling of children in the United States (see, e.g., National Center for Health Statistics, 1970, 1973, 1976). Such an unusual and long-awaited set of data merits attention, so we turn next to a more detailed description of these new norms and charts.

NCHS Growth Norms and Charts

The physical growth data reported from the Health Examination Survey (HES) and the Health and Nutrition Examination Survey (HANES) of the National Center for Health Statistics (NCHS) were collected, not with the aim of conducting research on physical growth per se, but rather as part of major programs authorized by Congress under the National Health Survey Act of 1956. The HES program was intended as a continuing Public Health Service function to assess the health status of the population of the United States. The aims of the HANES program are to evaluate the nutritional status of this population and to monitor changes occurring over time. "Such a system should permit the use of health data as an objective test of programs to improve nutritional status and should provide an improved basis for allocation of scarce program resources" (Abraham et al., 1975, p. 1).

Three "cycles," each limited to a specific segment of the population and to specified aspects of health, constituted the HES. Cycle I assessed adults aged 18 to 79 years in 1959 to 1962; cycle II, done in 1963 to 1965, covered ages 6 to 11 years; and cycle III, conducted in 1966 to 1970, included ages 12 to 17 years. A sophisticated, multistage, stratified probability sampling design determined the 40 locations selected throughout the continental United States. Only noninstitutionalized persons were surveyed, and, with the exception of some children from cycle II who happened by chance also to be included in cycle III, the samples were cross-sectional. Health was broadly defined, so the assessments included not only medical and dental examinations, x-rays, tests of sensory and physiologic functions, strengths tests, and a battery of 30 anthropometric measurements, but also tests of intelligence and academic achievement, reports of social behavior and emotional problems, socioeconomic indicators, and ethnic derivation.

Clearly, these data provide a rich source of reference standards as well as of potential research data for scientists in many disciplines, although many behavioral and social scientists are as yet unaware of their availability. But by now the reader will have detected a serious omission—neither infancy, the period of most rapid development, nor the preschool years, a period of expanding socialization with attendant health risks, were included in the data collection. Yet these are the age spans in which detection of developmental disturbances could be expected to have the most potential in terms of the remediation of conditions with long-term sequelae.

HANES remedied this critical omission for the preschool years, but secured information only for the latter part of infancy. Conducted in 1971 to 1972, this cross-sectional survey included persons aged 1 to 74 years. However, in both HES and HANES each age interval includes a full year (e.g., 1.0–1.99 years), and age was as that at the last birthday. Thus the youngest ages for which norms are available are actually 1.5 and 2.5 years—the mid-points of the age intervals labeled 1 and 2 years.

The sampling design for HANES was very similar to that for HES (although the response rate was not as high), and fairly comparable data were obtained. Because the orientation of this program was nutritional, data collection included biochemical tests and reports of dietary intakes, but not behavioral assessments.

Construction of growth charts from the data of the HES and HANES programs to replace the outdated and less representative ones described in the historical overview above was urged by several expert and concerned groups. In 1971, the American Academy of Pediatrics and the Bureau of Community Health Services, U. S. Public Health Service, sponsored a study group on "The Assessment and Recording of Measurements of Growth of Children" (Owen, 1973). This panel concluded that the older standards, such as the Stuart-Meredith (1946) norms, were no longer suitable, and recommended the development of new growth charts derived from contemporary, representative samples, such as the HES. In 1974, the Committee on Nutrition Advisory to the Center for Disease Control, National Academy of Sciences–National Research Council, reached similar conclusions and recommendations, suggesting also the use of data from the Preschool Nutrition Survey (Owen et al., 1974; see below) and the Fels longitudinal study. The following year their proposals were supported by the participants in a workshop on "Physical Growth of Ethnic Groups Comprising the U. S. Population" (Roche and McKigney, 1976), sponsored by the National Institute of Child Health and Development.

Finally, in 1976 the 14 NCHS growth charts (seven for each sex) were published, the product of a task force of experts in biostatistics, physical growth, pediatrics, and public health from within and outside the federal service. Two of the charts for each sex (height for age and weight for age) cover the age span 2 through 18 years; one (weight for height), the range from 2 years until puberty; and four (length for age, weight for age, weight for length, and head circumference for age) are for the period from birth through 36 months.

But we have already noted that national samples provide no norms under 1.5 years. What is the source of the charts for infant growth? Ironically, it is a longitudinal study of nonrandom samples of predominantly middle-class, white infants from successive cohorts born in the region around Yellow Springs, Ohio, between 1929 and 1974. Six to 20 pregnant women were enrolled in each of these years with the intent of following their offspring through early adulthood. Although the total sample is large (over 800), especially for a longitudinal study, its representativeness is further restricted by the fact that a considerable proportion of its members are close relatives (over 260 parent-offspring pairs, upwards of 400 siblings, and smaller numbers of cousins).

Why, then, did an expert committee from the National Academy of Sciences recommend using these data and a task force of other authorities implement the recommendation? Larger samples exist, including at least one that consists of both Black and white infants born between 1959 and 1967, as do other carefully collected longitudinal data, although none is free from sampling bias (see Roche and Falkner, 1975, for a review of growth charts from such samples). On balance, however, the Fels data combine a rather large sample (part of which was born in the time period during which the HES data were collected), methodology and instrumentation similar to that in HES, and technical accuracy. In addition, measures of both length and standing height were available at all ages after the children could stand. Therefore, the data could be overlapped with the HES and HANES data. HES data were standing heights, whereas at the younger ages HANES data contained both kinds of measures. Until about age 4 or 5 years recumbent length is about 2 cm greater than standing height; thereafter the difference is about 1 cm. The ability to adjust for this important transition in type of height measurement plus the ready availability of the data in computer-compatible form were undoubtedly decisive factors in the choice of the Fels data.

Figures 8-1 to 8-4, a selection from the NCHS charts, which permits comparison of

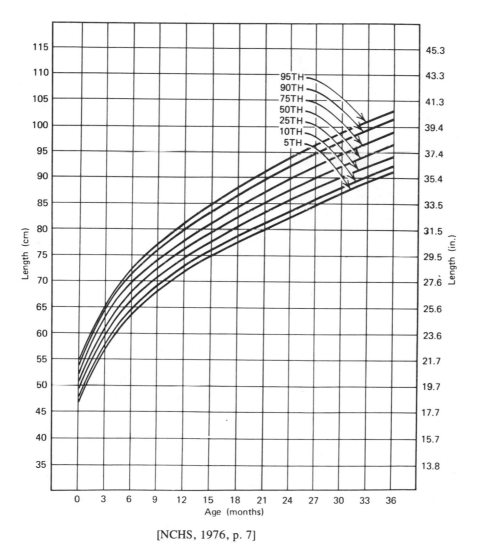

[NCHS, 1976, p. 7]

Figure 8-1. National Center for Health Statistics growth chart for length by age, birth to 36 months, for girls. Data from Fels longitudinal study.

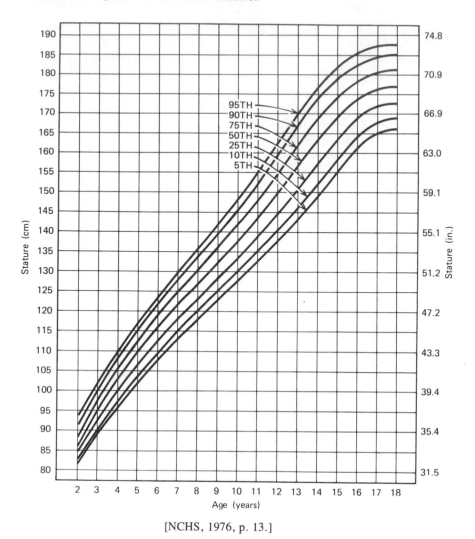

[NCHS, 1976, p. 13.]

Figure 8-2. National Center for Health Statistics growth chart for standing height by age, 2 to 18 years, for boys. Data from national probability sample.

heights and weights at the overlap ages, reveal an interesting fact with important implications. Note that the 50th percentiles for height and weight are very similar in the two samples despite the fact that most of the infants in the Fels study were measured long before 1971 to 1974, the years of the HANES data collection on infants. Given the widely documented trend toward larger size in succeeding generations (Heyneman, 1974), this similarity certainly could not be assumed a priori. Two complementary factors are probably involved.

First, a comparison of the HANES data on children aged 6 to 17 years with those on HES children of the same ages but born about 10 years earlier yielded no significant differences, at least for children at the 25th percentile and above. Very slight increases were observed at the 5th and 10th percentiles. As nearly as the investigators could estimate from earlier data available, "the secular trend to increasing body size of children

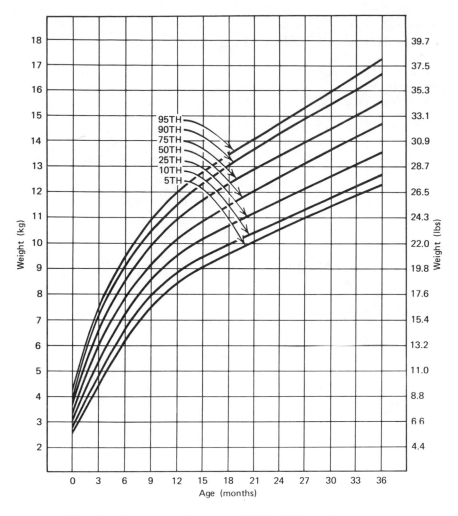

[Data from Fels longitudinal study (NCHS, 1976, p. 9).]

Figure 8-3.   National Center for Health Statistics growth chart for weight by age, birth to 36 months, for boys.

[and adults] from the prenatal period onward had ceased to be of sufficient magnitude by 1955 or 1956 to affect these rather sensitive data across most socioeconomic levels of the American population'' (NCHS, 1976, p. 19). Thus, for about 18 of the 45 years in which the Fels data were being collected, no bias from a secular trend would be expected.

Second, infants from families of lower socioeconomic status are, on the average, smaller than those from the middle and upper classes. The small proportion of lower-class infants in the Fels study compared to a representative sample would bias the mean size of the group upward, probably compensating at least in part for the secular trend operative during the period of the study before 1955.

The comparability of the Fels and HANES samples contains a double irony. In the past, developmental data from longitudinal studies such as those at Berkeley, Denver, and Fels, all of which yield quite similar values, were criticized because they were not representa-

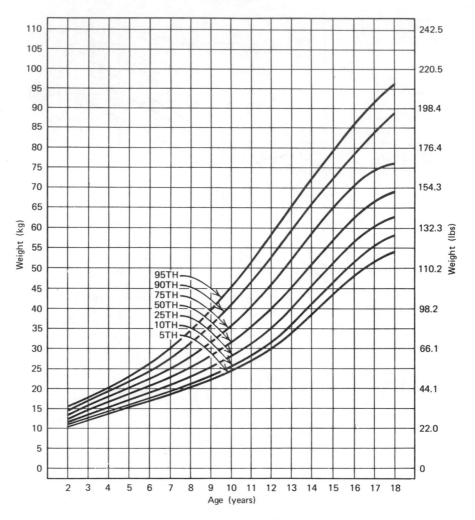

[Data from national probability sample (NCHS, 1976, p. 15).]

Figure 8-4.　National Center for Health Statistics growth chart for weight by age, 2 to 18 years, for boys.

tive of the general population, but rather biased upward by the lack of sufficient numbers of children from lower socioeconomic levels. More recently these same data have been deemed to have been made obsolescent by the secular trend. Now we find that these biased samples of yesteryear provide appropriate norms for contemporary groups and, indeed, for future groups if the secular trend does not resume or reverse. An additional twist to the whole affair is that height, the measure for which the secular trend was first and best documented, should be the one in which the diminution and cessation of this trend was first demonstrated.

Typically the data from the well-known longitudinal studies do have slightly less variance than those from larger, more representative cross-sectional samples, and this is the case with the Fels data for weight during infancy. The authors of the report on the NCHS growth charts attribute this difference to less heterogeneity—that is, the inclusion of fewer extremely fat children (NCHS, 1976, p. 18). However, the high proportion of close relatives among the Fels population would also tend to restrict variability. Good metric reasons also exist for expecting less variance among the longitudinal samples. In contrast to the wide age range included for a given age in large cross-sectional surveys such as HES and HANES, the traditional longitudinal studies allowed only a small age tolerance but measured at frequent intervals. To illustrate, in the Berkeley Growth Study measurements were made within 3 days of the monthly birthdate during the 1st year of life, and in the Fels study the limits were 1 day at 3 months, 2 days at 6 months, 3 days at 9 months, and 4 days at 12 months. Personnel making the measures were also much more consistent across children and age in these longitudinal studies, and the greatest source of error variance in anthropometric measures is the different "personal constants" of the anthropometrists. Any techniques that reduce error variance will, of course, yield a truer picture of reality.

In sum, the greatest limitation of the Fels infant data seems to be consanguinity. Geographic, class, and ethnic bias seem to introduce no serious contradictions to the use of these data as a temporary national referent, although one would feel more comfortable with more adequate tests of these assumptions, particularly for the first 12 to 18 months, for which no national data are available. No systematic significant differences between Black and white children in height and weight were found in the HES or HANES, although in these surveys and in the Preschool Nutrition Survey, Black children were slightly taller and heavier at most ages. The NICHD workshop on "Physical Growth of Ethnic Groups in the U. S. Population" concluded that use of a single U. S. standard for weight and height would be "unlikely to cause serious errors." Some socioeconomic and regional differences were found in these large surveys but, as noted earlier, the Fels sample from one region of Ohio yields norms very similar to those for the composite national sample at overlapping ages.

Criteria for Developing and Selecting Growth Standards

A dictum common to all scientific disciplines is that normative standards should be derived from carefully done, precisely defined assessments on a representative sample of the population to which they are to be applied. Yet two important considerations dictate qualification of this dictum: (1) the interpretation of the term *representative* and (2) the desirability of equating *average* with *optimal* or at least *healthy*.

In a nation with diverse ethnic, cultural, or geographic subgroups, norms can be based on a representative sample of the entire population or separate norms can be established on a representative sample of each subgroup. If real genetic differences exist in growth potential (that is, absolute size that can be achieved under comparable conditions) or in growth pattern (that is, rate of growth at different ages), then separate standards are required to avoid incorrect inferences about groups or individuals. For example, children from a genetically tall population evaluated against norms obtained on a heterogeneous population containing a sizeable number of genetically smaller persons might be judged to be of normal size when in fact their development was being retarded by malnutrition or some other factor. Conversely, a child from a genetically small family might be diagnosed as retarded and subjected to special treatment to the stress of the child and family, or at least needless expense, when in fact he or she was growing normally.

On the other hand, if subgroup differences are entirely or in considerable measure environmental (in the broadest sense), such as varying levels of income or dietary habits, the wisdom of using separate norms is debatable. Suppose a child comes from a regional or cultural group in which the diet is low in iron. Judged by regional or subcultural norms, that child's values for various measures of red blood cells, such as hematocrit, may be average or even high. Such a child might also be of average or larger size and accomplishments among the particular subgroup. Were no norms available for a population containing more advantaged individuals, the fact that this child and others of his subgroup are not developing up to their potential would not be discovered. Such a risk is particularly great when the significance of a measure has not been determined. Imagine, for example, that we could easily and routinely measure body levels of thyroid hormone but knew only that it affected basal metabolism and nothing about its effect on growth.

The environmental example serves also to illustrate the issue of normal in the sense of average versus normal in the sense of healthy. Certainly the child who is growing along the 75th percentile curve for his subgroup is growing "normally" for that group, but if that level is the equivalent of the 10th percentile in a well-fed population the pattern does not reflect "good health." The contrast does tell you that this child probably has the genetic potential for greater growth and is not suffering from an idiosyncratic growth disorder.

The logical extension of this argument is that even in populations that are not obviously deprived the standard should be those living under optimal conditions or displaying optimal development. But how do we determine what is optimal? Regimens for pre-term and small-for-age infants, as well as for normal infants and children, have often been judged to be good if they result in larger and more rapidly growing individuals. But are large or rapidly growing infants healthier, and will they be so 40 or 50 years from now? Only very comprehensive, very long-term longitudinal data permit real answers to such questions, but evidence is growing that the answer may be no (see section below on obesity). Small may even be better if it means that the individual is better adapted to maintain the quality of growth under stress, such as famine. Under most conditions the quality of structure and function is the important issue, not sheer size.

If "optimal" cannot be readily determined, are norms from socioeconomically advantaged groups a reasonable approximation? The data cited above on longitudinal samples studied in past decades suggest that they may be. However, economic privilege can be a disadvantage. Witness the increasing number of reports of the higher prevalence of deteriorative diseases among affluent adults as compared with those who must perform hard physical labor and subsist on less rich diets. Witness also the practices thought to be beneficial that were instituted first and most widely among those who could afford private care by professionals aware of new developments. Among such practices now known to have deleterious effects when excessive are administration of certain hormones or drugs to prevent miscarriage or alleviate "morning sickness," severe restriction of weight gain during pregnancy, administration of oxygen to pre-term infants, and dietary supplements of vitamins A and D. Another suspect is too early feeding of solids, particularly meats—a practice that may increase the likelihood of allergies.

Given our present state of knowledge, the best compromise in most situations is several sets of standards. Obviously, national norms or norms derived from almost any subgroup are sufficient when little diversity exists among subgroups in a particular measure. When subgroups are heterogeneous, national norms are still desirable, for they aid the communication process among researchers and clinicians by making it possible to define each special group or case in terms of where it stands with respect to this referent. This tactic, in the form of "marker variables," has been strongly advocated by the Interagency Panel, made up of representatives of many different federal agencies in the United States funding research with infants, children, and youth (Heyneman, 1974; Hertz and Harrell, 1974). More specific norms for subgroups can then be developed or used as a second step. They are useful in differential diagnosis, as illustrated in the "environmental" differences example given earlier.

Even more helpful, particularly for cases falling in the extreme percentiles of composite or subgroups norms, are what might be called "family-specific" or "child-specific" norms. Within regional, ethnic, or cultural subgroups, individual differences abound, so every group is heterogeneous in this sense. One source of the variation is genetic. Indeed, genetic differences probably are more frequently useful in accounting for variation within subgroups than between them. For this reason development and use of reference standards that adjust for parental levels has received increasing attention during the past decade (Garn, 1966; Tanner, 1970; Tanner and Thompson, 1970; Tanner et al., 1970). Examples of the increased precision provided by such standards and its utility in differential diagnosis are given by Tanner et al. (1970). Two boys described by them fell exactly at the 3rd percentile on "parent unknown" standards. One had parents both of whom also had heights at this level, so his standing rose from this "danger alert" zone to the 20th percentile—that is, within the normal range—on the standards allowing for mid-parent height (average of the two parents). The mid-parent height of the parents of the second boy was exactly average, so he moved even farther down into the abnormal zone. Another child appeared to be only moderately small on "parent-unknown" standards and had been considered to be simply a normal small child. But his parents were very tall, and plotting his height on the parent-adjusted standards led to medical follow-up, which showed that during periods when his blood sugar levels were low his secretion of growth hormone ceased. After hormonal therapy was introduced his growth rate doubled. At the other extreme was a son of parents of average height who, during his preschool years, was also within average limits. His percentile ranking then began to rise so that on parent-adjusted charts he was consistently beyond the 97th percentile. Hand-wrist x-rays showed him to be an early maturer who, after his adolescent growth spurt was completed at 16 (a precocious age), fell back to the 75th percentile.

This type of standard becomes child-specific as well as family-specific when such factors as parity order within the family are also considered. Adjustment for parity order is most important during the neonatal period and early infancy, when the fairly small absolute differences in size associated with parity order become of relatively greater importance. Because matters of size are so critical in this period, the topic of growth charts for the fetus and neonate are dealt with below in the section on anomalies of prenatal growth. Actually, more parent-adjusted norms are available for neonatal and late fetal size than for infancy and childhood. Development of parent-adjusted norms has been slowed by the fact that only the period of steady even growth from about 2 or 3 years through 9 or 10 years can be dealt with as a unit. Separate calculations are required for segments of the growth span preceding and succeeding this period. Although one might think that adjustments would be improved by special allowances for large differences in parental size, statistical tests made by Tanner et al. (1970) bearing on this possibiliy yielded negative results. They also tested the possibility of a nonadditive function of maternal and paternal heights by including the interaction of the two in their calculations. Although no significant improvement in the multiple regression was found, the number of cases in their samples was not sufficiently large to demonstrate a small degree of nonadditivity if it existed.

An obvious solution to the issue of general versus specific norms is to derive both from the same data—that is, to use a large random sample of the total population and then do analyses for subgroups as well as the composite. In fact, this is what is being done with the HES data, with subgroup norms being published subsequent to, or concomitantly with, those for the total population (see, for example, Malina et al., 1974; Roche et al., 1975). The major disadvantage of this procedure is that it requires a very large total sample if the number of subgroups for which norms are to be established is sizeable and particularly when cross-tabulation is done (e.g., sex by age by race by socioeconomic status). However, this approach yields a more satisfactory final result and is probably less expensive than series of separate studies to establish subgroup norms. Some exception to this statement occurs in the case of parent-adjusted norms. The parent-child correlations for dimensions such as height and weight are very similar from birth through adolescence in a wide variety of groups—for example, Berkeley, California (Bayley, 1954), Yellow Springs, Ohio (Garn, 1966), and London, Brussels, Stockholm, and Zurich (Tanner et al., 1970), increasing from about 0.2 to 0.3 at birth to 0.4 to 0.5 by the middle to end of the 1st year and remaining at about the 0.5 level thereafter. Thus it is not necessary to collect data for, and compute, parent-child correlations for each population and subgroup for which growth standards are constructed. Only when the rearing circumstances affecting growth are different for parents and child *and* either the parents or the child also differ in this respect from their contemporaries would the expected levels of the correlations at different ages be lower. To date, insufficient data are available to estimate the correlations under these circumstances. However, one should assume that if the parents were reared under growth-retarding circumstances, parent-adjusted norms will overadjust the placement of offspring reared under more advantageous conditions—that is, the children's expected size will be underestimated. Of course, if the comparative rearing circumstances are reversed, the direction of the error of estimate will also be reversed.

Finally, development and use of norms from groups likely to represent the best current approximation of "optimal" or "healthy" development is highly desirable, provided those who use such norms observe the caveats discussed above. At least the idealists among us believe that our aim should be to promote the best possible development of all children, not simply improve the condition of the most handicapped. The particular conditions that promote the full development of potential may often differ among individuals or groups (for example, some individuals and, particularly, members of certain ethnic groups, are allergic to milk), but the level or pattern of development that can be achieved is what the "ideal" norms exemplify.

NUTRITION AND PHYSICAL DEVELOPMENT

The study of physical growth encompasses research on bodily size, form, and composition from the molar to the molecular levels and on variables affecting these characteristics. In all these aspects the interaction of nutrition and growth is ubiquitous. The same measures of external and internal size, form, and composition used to assess the level and rate of physical development are also the most frequently used indicators of nutritional status. Among these are height, weight, skeletal maturity and mineralization, amount of muscle and of subcutaneous fat, and the types and levels of lipids, carbohydrates, proteins, minerals, and vitamins in blood and tissues. As the term *physical anthropology* has been applied to the study of external size and shape, so the term *chemical anthropology* has been coined for the study of internal form and composition (Macy and Kelly, 1957), and we can speak of chemical maturity (Owen and Brožek, 1966).

At the same time, nutrition merges structure (physique) with function (physiology), for the nutritionist's metabolic balance studies assess not only intake of nutrients but also their uptake (absorption, digestion, and assimilation or incorporation) and excretion. Again, measures serve multiple purposes. For example, hemoglobin levels tell us something about physical development, nutritional status, and physiologic function. In combination, metabolic balance studies and assessments of physical growth and health determine recommended dietary intakes and dosages of medication, both of which must be adjusted to the size of the organism, its growth rate, and its ability to absorb and utilize nutrients and excrete the waste products.

Among the factors affecting physical development both pre- and postnatally, nutrition "probably represents the most important single influence" (Barness and Pitkin, 1975). Malnutrition may be primary (deficiency or excess of one or more nutrients) or secondary to congenital defects, infections, or other illnesses that alter the capacity to handle nutrients at all stages from mastication to excretion and put additional demands on the organism for energy, maintenance, and repair. Through these latter mechanisms, congenital anomalies, genetically determined errors of metabolism, and chronic and acute illnesses retard or distort growth. Because of the special circumstances involved in antenatal and perinatal nutrition, these topics, like growth standards for these periods, are considered in the third section of this chapter.

Nutritional Status of Infants and Preschoolers in the United States

Only within the last decade have major financial and professional resources been committed to assessing the nutritional status of the child and adult population of the United States, despite at least 40 years of such investment, much of it from the United States, in other areas around the world. For example, between about 1950 and 1970, surveys and intervention studies were conducted in a number of developing nations under the aegis of such groups as the Interdepartmental Committee on Nutrition for National Defense (1963), the Pan-American Health Organization (Behar, 1968), and the National Institute of Child Health and Development (Read et al., 1975). These were concentrated in countries in which children constitute the largest proportion of the population. Although neonates were found to be somewhat smaller than those in highly industrialized nations and subject to higher rates of mortality and morbidity, the growth rates of the survivors were generally quite good during the first 6 to 12 postnatal months. Thereafter growth rates and average size relative to developed countries declined quite precipitously, and mortality rates among children aged 1 through 5 years ran to 50% or higher. Thus, the infant after weaning and the preschool child seemed especially affected by primary and secondary malnutrition. Following documentation of growth and health disturbances related to nutrition, attention turned to behavioral and social development, particularly performance on intelligence tests and in school (Behar, 1968; Kallen, 1973).

Probably because syndromes associated with severe primary nutritional deficits had rarely been reported since the decade of the Great Depression, the Congress of the United States had to be convinced that the prevalence of nutritional deficiencies was sufficiently great in this affluent nation to warrant special attention. The social unrest of the early 1960s was a major factor in precipitating congressional hearings during 1967 on the nutritional state of the nation. Following these hearings the Congress did direct the establishment of surveys to determine the prevalence, type, and location of malnutrition and associated health conditions. Two of these surveys, HES and HANES, have already been described. Two others in which infants and preschool children received particular attention were the Ten-State Nutrition Survey (USDHEW, 1972) and the Preschool Nutrition Survey (Owen et al., 1974), both conducted in 1968 to 1970.

Originally intended to be, and titled, the National Nutrition Survey, the Ten-State Nutrition Survey (TSNS) was in fact limited by exigencies of money, time, and politics to a probability sample of the population in the lowest quartile of income as indicated by the 1960 census. That is, it was a survey of the segment of the population most likely to be suffering from malnutrition. The 10 states selected (California, Kentucky, Louisiana, Massachusetts, Michigan, New York, South Carolina, Texas, Washington, and West Virginia) were judged to represent major geographic regions and to include (1) diverse economic, ethnic, and cultural subgroups, (2) highly vulnerable groups such as migrant workers, (3) some regions where maternal and infant mortality rates were above the national average, and (4) some states in which food supplements and other welfare assistance were considered to be below the national average. The procedures were based on those used in nutrition surveys conducted in 33 countries by the Interdepartmental Committee on Nutrition for National Defense (1963). Demographic data were secured on more than 86,000 members of 24,000 families, and nutritional status was assessed for almost 41,000 persons, of whom almost 8000 were 0 to 5 years old. Among the items comprising the demographic data were education of parents, family income and composition (e.g., number in family, sex of head of household), locale of residence (urban or rural), and ethnic derivation. Social factors—such as housing conditions (crowding), participation in school lunch or other food-distribution or welfare programs, alcoholism, unwanted pregnancies, and parental separation during pregnancy—were assessed in some or all families. The nutritional, health, and physical evaluations included medical examinations and histories, dental examinations, anthropometric measures and wrist X-rays, biochemical analyses on all or part of the sample (e.g., hemoglobin, serum proteins, vitamins A and C, serum iron), and, on selected groups, household food intakes and food-pattern frequencies, and individual dietary intakes. In all instances in which only subsamples were used, concentration was on pregnant and lactating females, children ages 0 to 3 and 10 to 16 years, and persons over 60 years old.

Judged as the proportion of children below the 15th percentile on the Stuart-Meredith growth standards for height and weight (see section on growth standards), retardation was found in all ethnic groups and in all states, but the prevalence varied with sex, ethnic origin, and income level. For example, the growth curve of median height for Mexican-American children living in Texas was at approximately the 16th percentile, and in some subgroups children from families with an income of less than $5000 for a family of four were 1 year retarded in height compared to those from comparable-sized families with incomes above this level. Illustrative findings for the entire sample of Black and white children at age 2 years are given in Table 8-1. Retardation in skeletal and dental maturity and other growth indices (e.g., subcutaneous fat), showed similar patterns.

Iron deficiency anemia is the most common nutritional disease found in most surveys of United States populations, and by several indices the prevalence was also quite high among older infants and preschool children in the TSNS. The percentages of children in this age range having unacceptably low levels, as evaluated by the usual guidelines (Interdepartmental Committee, 1963), ranged from 8 to 40% in several sex, state, and ethnic subgroups, and averaged 34% for Blacks, 13.1% for whites, and 9.5% for

Table 8-1. Percentage of 2-Year-Olds in the Ten-State Nutrition Survey Below the 15th Percentile for Height and Weight on Stuart-Meredith Standards

	Black		White	
	Boys	Girls	Boys	Girls
Height	46	37	42	46
Weight	34	27	26	31

Source: Adapted from Schaefer (1975), pp. 12–13.

Hispano-Americans. Exacerbating the anemias were the rather unexpectedly low levels of folate in red blood cells. Of children aged birth to 5 years, 21% of Blacks, 18% of whites, and 16% of Hispano-Americans had deficient levels. Over 90% of the children aged 1 to 3 years had dietary intakes of iron below the recommended levels, with 26 to 48% having intakes only about one-third of such levels. Although the prevalence of anemias was lower in higher income groups, anemias were found at all income levels, and their relative prevalence was greater among the more advantaged than were vitamin deficiencies. Both human and cow's milk contain little iron, so deficiencies are particularly likely in the absence of supplementation when milk constitutes a large proportion of the diet.

Despite the facts that both human and cow's milk are good sources of vitamin A and that dietary intakes were far less deficient, the TSNS found the prevalence of unacceptable serum values of this vitamin to be high among infants and preschoolers—for example, over 26% in South Carolina and 40% in Texas. This fact is particularly worrisome because serum levels remain at acceptable levels for some period after tissue stores have begun to be depleted. Associated physical signs of severe and prolonged deficiency—lesions of the eye, follicular hyperkeratosis (excessive growth of the follicles in the corneous layer of the skin) on the arms, and rickets—fortunately were far less frequent (e.g., about 4% of preschool children had some symptoms of rickets). A happy outcome of the preliminary findings on vitamin A levels in the TSNS was an edict from the Department of Agriculture in late 1968 that all skim milk provided through their food-distribution programs must be fortified with vitamins A and D. Prior to that time it had not been, although fortification for skim milk shipped to other countries had begun in 1965.

Although the prevalence of "unacceptable" levels of vitamin C was in general lower than for vitamin A, in some subgroups—for example, Black infants and young children "high risk" levels were more common for vitamin C than A. Inadequate intake of riboflavin (one of the B vitamins) is probably the most common dietary deficiency worldwide because much of the riboflavin is lost during the processing of grains for bread and cereals; and other sources, such as meat, are expensive. Among the TSNS sample a fairly high proportion of children were found to have excretory levels of riboflavin sufficiently low as to indicate deficiency, but frank physical symptoms of advanced deprivation were rare (e.g., the prevalence of cheilosis—fissuring and scaling of the lips and angles of the month—ranged from 0.6–4.1%).

As might be expected, the overall prevalence of poor health and nutrition and retarded growth was greatest among minorities and the poor—Black and Mexican-Americans, whites from Appalachia, and migrant workers of all ethnic groups—and these factors interacted. For example, riboflavin deficiency was only a minor problem in the higher income Black families but a moderate one in low-income Black families. Among low-income families, riboflavin, protein, and vitamin A deficiencies were more common among those of Latin-American descent, but this differed with cultural dietary habits.

Thus, whereas children of Puerto Rican families had a low incidence of vitamin A deficiency, this vitamin was particularly lacking in the diets of Mexican-American children. As already noted, both white and Black families whose incomes relative to family size were below the poverty level showed higher frequencies of iron deficiency than families of the same ethnic background with incomes above this level. In general, nutritional deficiencies and poor health status were less common in cities where medical care was readily available than in rural areas where it was not. Studies of special subgroups showed psychosocial factors—such as number of siblings born within 2 years, parental separation during pregnancy, and unwanted pregnancies—to increase the risk of malnutrition (Chase, 1975).

In contrast to the TSNS, which covered most of the age span but concentrated on the economically disadvantaged, the Preschool Nutrition Survey (PNS) was intended to describe the nutritional status of a socioeconomic cross-section of children aged 1 to 6 years. Further, the PNS used a national sample, drawn from the 74 Primary Sample Units of the Survey Research Center at the University of Michigan (Kish and Hess, 1965). Response rates were somewhat better for Blacks than whites, and among the latter some significant regional differences in response rates were found, perhaps because of greater frequency of illness in regions sampled during the winter. Nevertheless, on the basis of race, sex, and age, "the sample was reasonably representative of the preschool population of the United States (Owen et al., 1974)."

Like the TSNS, the PNS included not only dietary interviewing but medical and dental examinations, biochemical determinations, and demographic and other information on the family; but, again, not all measures were obtained on all children. Within selected families all children in the designated age range were included. Most of the data analyses were done by sex, age, ethnic group, and socioeconomic status, with the latter usually defined by the Warner Index Status Characteristics (Warner et al., 1949), a summed composite rating ranging from I (lowest) to V (highest) and based on four variables — source of income, occupation, dwelling type, and area. Actually, no children from category V were sampled.

Only the anthropometric data are reported for the sexes separately because other significant sex differences—for example, intakes of nutrients—were a function of body size and, thus, were not significant when calculated per unit weight. Height, weight, and head circumference increased systematically with socioeconomic level. For example, in terms of standard score for age and sex, head circumference increased from -0.28 in Warner level I to $+0.15$ in level IV. Almost identical trends were found for height, whereas the weight differences were of smaller magnitude — a difference of 0.24 SD units between classes I and IV. Skeletal maturity for age, as judged by the mean number of ossification centers present, also progressed from class I through III, with no further increase in class IV. On the other hand, "fatness" (measured by skinfold thickness), decreased from $+0.09$ to -0.09 from class I to IV. Recall, also, that the increase of height with class was greater than that for weight. Had a ratio of weight for height been calculated, the socioeconomically advantaged children would probably also have been found to be leaner by this criterion.

These associations between socioeconomic status and body size were calculated only from the data for white children because Blacks were disproportionately represented in the lower socioeconomic levels. Despite this fact, Black children were taller and heavier, but less "fat" (as judged by skinfold thickness) than whites at most ages. For girls these ethnic differences were greater for weight, whereas for boys the differences were larger for height. Had the heights of the Black children been evaluated by the Stuart-Meredith or similar norms, their growth relative to their potential would have been underestimated. The apparent contradiction between the socioeconomic and ethnic differences probably arises from the more advanced maturation rate of the Black children, who had a larger number of ossification centers at most ages than did whites. The finding of an ethnic difference in size, with Blacks lower in birthweight but larger at most ages thereafter (at least through early adolescence), is supported and extended by the data from both the TSNS and HANES. Socioeconomic handicap masks some of this difference, for it is larger when comparisons are made within comparable levels.

Although the PNS found some ethnic regional differences in dietary intakes and levels of nutrients in blood and urine, these were usually a function of, or closely associated with, socioeconomic level. The importance of the latter factor is demonstrated by analyses of variance showing highly significant ($p < 0.001$) differences among socioeconomic groups on almost all of the dietary intake and biochemical variables. Differences significant at this level were found for intakes of calories, protein, carbohydrate, fat, calcium, and the vitamins A, C, thiamin, and riboflavin. Only iron intakes failed to differentiate among classes, with quite comparably high proportions of each class containing children with low daily intakes (55% in Warner class I, 49% in II, 52% in III, and 50% in IV). However, despite the failure of intakes to differ significantly, all four blood measures related to iron (hemoglobin, hematocrit, iron, and transferrin saturation) did differ significantly ($p < 0.001$) among classes, and increased systematically from rank I through IV. Transferrin saturation, which reflects iron stores in the body, increased with age during the early years but stabilized after about 47 months. The lower level of iron-related variables among Blacks was most apparent from 12 to 23 months and less marked thereafter. Each of the dietary surveys—HANES, TSNS, and PNS—shows iron deficiences as the most common dietary lack among infants and to be frequent in all social classes. In both PNS and TSNS, evidence was found for a specific link between iron levels in the body and physical size—for example, within age and sex groups hemoglobin levels were positively correlated with height and skinfold thickness. Thus Black children are achieving greater height despite the handicap of lower iron stores and hemoglobin levels.

Other biochemical variables showing highly significant socioeconomic differences were vitamins A and C, triglycerides (one measure of fat in the blood), and blood and urinary measures of protein metabolism. Interestingly, biochemical measures of total protein in the blood tended to *decrease* with *increasing* socioeconomic level and to be higher among Black than white children of all ages, whereas levels of albumin in the urine were higher among children in classes III and IV. Only blood levels of cholesterol (another fat measure) and cholinesterase (reflecting protein and vitamin A levels) showed no overall significant class differences, although cholesterol levels in infants (12 to 23 months) did rise with socioeconomic status, an observation we shall return to later in discussing obesity. Also, cholesterol levels did not change with age, while triglyceride values decreased with age, increased with social class, and were higher among whites.

For most intake measures the socioeconomic differences arose primarily from the contrast between class I and all other classes. For example, classes II, III, and IV had about equally low proportions (0-2%) of children with low intakes of protein, thiamin, vitamin A, and riboflavin. Even the proportion of children in class I with unacceptable levels of these nutrients was small — 3% for protein, 5% for Vitamin A, 8% for riboflavin. and 9% for thiamin. As reflected in the percentage of children with unacceptably low intakes, classes III and IV were similar for vitamin C (2%) and calories (15%), whereas class II was intermediate (7% and 19%, respectively) and class I most affected (16% and 34%, respectively).

Some of the class differences in dietary and biochemical variables stem from differential use of vitamin and mineral supplements in the form of pills or fortified foods. In general the proportion of children taking such supplements decreased with age but increased with socioeconomic class within any age group. For example, among infants aged 12 to 23 months, the percentages taking supplements were 36% in class I, 51% in class II, 70% in class III, and 84% in class IV. At 24 to 35 months the comparable proportions were 31%, 46%, 65%, and 69%. Usually the supplement was a multivitamin preparation; only one-third of the supplemented children received iron, and less than 0.4% took calcium. That dietary iron intakes did not differ significantly among classes probably reflects the relatively small class differential in iron supplements. Milk contains little iron but high levels of calcium and riboflavin, and the classes did differ in calcium and riboflavin intake. Milk intakes were lower among Black than white children, and the proportion of Blacks in classes I and II was relatively higher.

The effect of vitamin supplements was seen clearly in the bimodal distributions of intake curves for vitamins. In classes III and IV most children had intakes of vitamins that were twice as high as the Recommended Daily Allowances of the National Academy of Science. The investigators comment (Owen et al., 1974) on the number of preschool children with perfectly adequate diets who were also regularly receiving vitamin supplements. Because the water-soluble vitamins (all vitamins except A, D, E, and K) are not stored in the body but must be renewed each day, these oversupplemented children were excreting sizable quantities of such vitamins.

An earlier study (Agriculture Research Service, 1969) of the diets of adults and children in the United States had shown that as per capita income of a family decreased, both the proportion of the income spent on food and the nutritional *quality* of the diet increased, despite a decrement in the total *quantity* of intake. In the PNS the nutritional quality of the children's diets was assessed by relating the amount of each nutrient to the total caloric intake. This measure is particularly relevant for children because the recommended total caloric intake is determined by the need for energy for growth a well as maintenance.

On this relative basis few differences were found among socioeconomic categories in the nutritional quality of the diet, although the absolute quantity often differed, as suggested by the data cited above on the percentages of children in different social classes with low intakes of nutrients. Among the exceptions were the relatively higher intakes of thiamin, riboflavin, and vitamin C among children in Warner classes III and IV, the former two largely because of more frequent vitamin supplementation and higher milk consumption and the last because of greater usage of citrus fruits, which are expensive. Poor families did not, however, use soft drinks instead of more nutritionally adequate fruit juices or beverages containing vitamin supplements. Use of dairy foods, a relatively cheap source of high-quality protein as well as of riboflavin and calcium, decreased with age, particularly in class I and among Blacks (who also had low calcium intakes relative to total calories).

On the other hand, not only did the intake of protein and iron per 1000 calories vary little with social class, but also the *absolute* amounts of poultry and meat consumed were similar. Indeed, on the relative basis, Black children actually averaged higher iron intakes than whites. The large intakes of animal protein in all classes caused the investigators to "question whether protein hasn't been oversold (Owen et al., 1974)," especially to those who cannot easily afford so large a portion of their income for so expensive a source. Aside from dairy products and fruit, which constituted an increasing source of both calories and specific nutrients with increasing socioeconomic level, the other dietary components actually declined in nutritional quality with social class. These included vegetables and the quality of cereal grains. The latter provide the major source of calories and iron in young children's diets. With increasing socioeconomic level the proportion of total calories derived from pie, cake, cookies, and sweet rolls increased while, with one exception, the proportion from breads, cereals, and pastas declined. The exception was that children in class I did not eat as many of the breakfast cereals, usually the ready-to-eat type, that are heavily fortified with iron. Significant consumption from "fast-food" restaurants was rare in the sample as a whole (about 3%) and essentially none of the children involved was under 4 years old.

In summary, poor families, contrary to popular belief, typically purchased wholesome food for their children. Aside from vitamin supplements, wherein, then, did the size, intake, and biochemical differences among social groups arise? A strength of the PNS was the amount of information collected that bears on feeding "styles." Social class differences in food procurement and preparation were relatively minor. In most families the mother performed these functions, although the proportion of families in which these tasks were shared with others was slightly higher in classes I and II. More mothers in classes III and IV enjoyed food preparation and tried new methods, and many more used cookbooks and public sources of information on nutrition and cooking. However, none of these factors seemed a major influence on the children's intakes. In addition to the absolute amount of food purchased, the more important variables seemed to be the kinds of food selected and parental permissiveness with respect to eating. We have already noted the high expenditure on meat protein relative to dairy products and fruit. Within the meat group, families in class I also tended to buy more pork products, such as lunch meats and hotdogs, which are more expensive per unit protein than are most other meats and poultry.

In most respects permissiveness about eating decreased with increasing social class. Catering to food preferences for infants aged 12 to 23 months did not vary systematically with class, but thereafter it did, with class IV mothers being particularly unbending as the child became older. Allowing children to eat whenever they pleased was much less common among class III and IV parents regardless of the child's age. For example, only 9% permitted this pattern for infants aged 12 to 23 months, whereas the proportions were 39% for class I and 21% for class II. Use of food as extrinsic motivation increased with the child's age in all classes but was systematically associated with social class at all ages. In the 12 to 23 months age group, for example, 54% of class I parents and 46% of class II used food as a reward, in contrast to 27% in class III and 23% in class IV. The comparable proportions who punished by withholding food were 21%, 20%, 10%, and 4%.

Other possible sources of class differences in nutrition as reflected in the child's bodily size and stores of nutrients are pre- and perinatal circumstances and postnatal health. In the PNS sample, extremes of maternal age, parity, and size were associated with social class, as illustrated in Table 8-2. On the average, mothers who are small or young (especially those who are still growing themselves) will have less adequate nutritional stores. Further, teenage mothers are less likely to have adequate diets during gestation, exacerbating any other deficiencies related to social class. Mothers depleted by frequent childbearing also may provide inadequate nutrients for the fetus. The medical histories of

Table 8-2.   Percentage Distribution by Prenatal Variables: Warner Rank for Socioeconomic Level in Preschool Nutrition Survey

	I	II	III	IV
Maternal Age at 1st Pregnancy				
less than 17	42	15	5	0
26 and above	4	7	13	23
Number of Pregnancies				
1 to 3	39	54	68	65
6 or more	30	15	10	9
Maternal Height				
less than 155 cm	17	13	9	4
Maternal Education				
9 or less years	33	12	2	0
13 or more years	3	15	45	70
Vitamin/Mineral Supplements				
During Pregnancy	75	90	92	96
infant breast-fed 1st week	21	23	29	39
infant breast-fed 2nd week	9	12	15	20
Housing Characteristics				
dwelling has indoor toilet	80	99	100	100
rooms per person	0.8	1.2	1.3	1.5

Source: Adapted from Owen et al. (1974), pp. 607, 613, 615, 617, 619.

the mothers also showed those in the lower socioeconomic classes to have had more problems during pregnancy. For example, 14% of class I mothers, but only 5% in class IV, had hypertension.

Table 8-3 presents some of the medical history items for children that showed class variations. As might be expected, the proportion of low birthweights, as defined by the World Health Organization (under 2.5 kg), is greatest in class I, and the proportion of high birthweights (3.75 kg and above) is lower than in the higher Warner categories. Note, however, that the class difference is in the marginal category (2.25–2.49 kg), whereas very low weights, which probably are associated with congenital disorders rather than suboptimal nutrition, are about equal in all classes.

The incomes per capita of the four Warner classifications in the PNS were I, $750; II, $1500; III, $2125; and IV, $2827. None of the class III and IV families were receiving assistance from federal food programs (stamps or commodities), but 28% of class I families and 2% of class II families were. That the various differences in children's size, intakes, and biochemical values were not simply a function of family income and income substitutes was shown by several special analyses. For example, where Warner socioeconomic status and income were inconsistent (usually in the lowest and highest groups), dietary intakes and biochemical values were more closely associated with the Warner ratings than with income. Further, although all indices were associated statistically, the Warner ratings correlated more highly with all the other variables examined than did income. These findings indicate that measures to improve the quality of growth of children must involve not only sufficient funds for food and medical care but also improvement in the "styles" of care. Much also remains to be done to improve methods of assessing the nutritional adequacy of diets. Current standards for children are particularly inadequate for they consist almost entirely of extrapolations from

Table 8-3.   Child Health Variables: Percentage Distribution by Warner Rank for Socioeconomic Level in Preschool Nutrition Survey

	I	II	III	IV
Birthweight (kg)				
2.24 or less	6	5	<5	<6
2.25–2.49	10	6	4	3
3.75 and above	27	34	37	35
Immunizations				
DPT	83	93	98	99
measles	56	73	86	93
polio	77	89	95	99
Illnesses—12–23 months (and 48–71 months)				
rubeola	4 (19)	3 (10)	4 (9)	0 (4)
mumps	5 (13)	2 (18)	1 (23)	0 (18)
rubella	14 (26)	13 (23)	10 (17)	8 (14)
Hospitalized, 12–23 months	12	10	7	5
Less than 12 h of sleep in 24 h, 12–23 months	40	45	33	22
Examined by M.D. within past 6 months	61	81	86	83

adult values, and even those are imperfect because they are based on only short-term balance studies.

Early Nutrition and Obesity

Thus far we have spoken mainly in terms of deficiencies, but dietary excesses are also a form of malnutrition. Among affluent countries obesity "is far more prevalent than is any other disease, except perhaps diagnosed and undiagnosed atherosclerosis (Yudkin, 1974)." Mounting evidence links obesity with a variety of disorders (Epstein, 1965; Kannel et al., 1969), most of them serious and often fatal. Obesity is not limited to the developed countries, the economically advantaged within them, nor to adolescents and adults (Adadevoh, 1974; Richards and de Casseres, 1974; Winick, 1975). One of the most frustrating aspects of attempts to control obesity in many persons is its intractibility— weight is lost with great effort only to be regained with ease. Recent research on adipose tissue suggests an hypothesis about the source of such intractibility and links some forms of obesity to events during gestation and infancy.

Development of a needle-aspiration technique for obtaining samples of subcutaneous fat opened a new approach to the study of human adipose cells, their pattern of growth and metabolism (Hirsch and Gallian, 1968). Given samples of adipocytes (fat cells), preferably from several sites, the distribution of cell sizes can be assessed by determining the lipid content of the tissue and counting the number of cells per unit of tissue. Knowing cell size, one can then estimate the total number of fat cells in the body. Total body fat is assessed by one of a variety of techniques—for example, skin fold measurements at a variety of sites or underwater weighing. The needle-aspiration technique is safe and easy to perform without hospitalization, and the methods of assessing cell size and body fat are reliable. However, controversy exists about the most valid way to measure total body fat, and the number and size of adipocytes may vary in different locations. Further, adipocytes can be identified only if they contain some lipid, so those with very small amounts are missed in cell counts.

Despite these limitations, the biopsy technique is generally regarded as a "breakthrough" leading to a new concept about obesity—that is, that persons with the more intractible "early-onset" obesity have a much larger number of fat cells than either the non-obese or those with "late-onset" obesity, and that this differential is not removed by weight loss. These observations in turn suggest that feeding during early life may be an important etiologic factor in some forms of obesity.

Evidence for the hypothesis comes from research with both humans and rats. Among human adults the obese were found to have about 100% more fat cells than the non-obese, whereas the average fat content per cell was only 20% greater (Hirsch and Knittle, 1970; Bjorntorp and Sjostrom, 1971; Salans et al., 1973). Experimentally induced obesity in adult rats or humans increased the average fat content but not cell number (Hirsch and Han, 1969; Sims et al., 1968). Conversely, after weight reduction the cell number remained the same; only average lipid content of the cells decreased (Hirsch and Han, 1969; Sims et al., 1968; Knittle and Hirsch, 1968; Knittle, 1972). When newborn rats were undernourished until weaning (3 or 4 weeks of age), the number of adipocytes remained below normal throughout life even if ad libitum feeding was instituted immediately after weaning (Knittle and Hirsch, 1968; Knittle, 1972). Histologic studies showed that regardless of early feeding practices the formation of new fat cells in the rat ceased between 2 and 4 weeks (Greenwood and Hirsch, 1974). The latter finding is consistent with well-established principles of developmental anatomy: (1) tissue grows by both hyperplasia (increase of cell number) and hypertrophy (increase in cell size), (2) hyperplasia is the more fundamental determinant of growth, (3) the most critical period in the development of tissue is the period of most rapid cell division, and (4) tissues and organs vary in the duration and timing of periods during which growth is by hyperplasia only, by hyperplasia and hypertrophy, or only by hypertrophy. Among humans, fetal fat does not appear until quite late in gestation (30 weeks) and then increases quite rapidly. During the 1st year of life the water content of adipose tissue decreases from about 48 to 37% while the fat increases from 40 to 53% (Fomon, 1966). The increase in volume of the adipose tissue is particularly great between the 2nd and 6th months—more than twice that of muscle— whereas from 6 to 12 months muscle increases slightly more than does adipose tissue (Fomon, 1966).

Several investigators have reported that persons whose histories indicate onset of obesity after puberty show primarily higher fat content of cells when compared to normals, whereas those with onsets during infancy or childhood show not only hypertrophy of adipocytes but also hyperplasia (Salans et al., 1973; Knittle, 1971; Brook, 1974; Brook et al., 1972). If the obese person is already adult, early onset is almost always determined from retrospective reports, which may not be reliable. Therefore, studies that include children are of particular interest. Brook and his colleagues (1972) examined 52 obese children in whom age at onset could be determined objectively, and categorized them into two groups—29 who had excessive weight gains during the 1st year and 23 who did not. The former had significantly more fat cells than controls and were also taller and advanced in skeletal maturation, while the latter did not differ from controls in any of these respects. Both groups did show hypertrophy in comparison with controls.

Among Knittle's (1975) sample of obese children, most had reached adult levels of average cell size, whereas no normal control children had. The obese children of all ages also had a larger number of adipocytes than did controls. Indeed, all teenagers and some younger children had attained or exceeded the normal adult number, but no control reached adult numbers before 12 years. Both his cross-sectional and short-term longitudinal data indicated that normal children had little or no increase in the number of adipocytes or of total body fat between 2 and 8 or 10 years. Then a pubescent period of increases in both cell number and size occurred. By contrast, obese children had both more and larger fat cells by 2 years, followed by rapid hyperplasia without hypertrophy until 12 to 16 years. In some children the rapid increase seemed to begin between 5 and 7.

Previous studies by Knittle (1971) and Brook (1972) agreed in finding very little age trend during childhood in cell size, but Brook's data suggested steadily increasing cell number in contrast to Knittle's (1975) recent report, cited above, of hyperplasia primarily during infancy and adolescence. Others (e.g., Heald, 1975) have suggested a third hyperplastic period from about 5 or 6 to 7 or 8, although this could reflect early pubescence among obese children who were also advanced in skeletal maturation—the group that Brook found to show both hyperplasia and excessive weight gain during the 1st year.

As with adults, both Brook and Knittle found that weight loss in children and adolescents reduced cell size but not number. However, Knittle's data suggested that under 6 years it was possible to reduce the rate of new adipose cell development if the adipocyte number did not already exceed average adult values.

Against the concatenation of evidence for the role of premature hyperplasia in the etiology of some forms of obesity must be set the fact that no longitudinal data are yet available to show that obese infants become obese adults. The widely cited reports that fat babies or children become fat adults are based either on retrospective data, as already noted, or on overweight (Eid, 1970; Taitz, 1971). Although overweight and obesity are positively correlated, the magnitude of the association changes with age and differs at some ages with sex. Among males, for example, it increases from about 0.1 at age 1 to 3 years to about 0.7 in preadolescence and adolescence (Garn et al., 1975). One may have excessive adipose tissue without being overweight, and one may be overweight because of a heavy skeleton or large muscle mass, as in the case of some athletes.

Garn et al. (1975) have also challenged the notion that obese infants necessarily become obese adults with the finding that obesity is more common during infancy and childhood among the economically advantaged of both sexes but more common in adulthood among *poor* women and *advantaged* men. (Recall here that cholesterol levels were positively related to SES among infants in the PNS.) However, Garn's data are cross-sectional, and Weil (1975) has advanced several arguments as to why they may be misleading.

Recently one large-scale longitudinal follow-up on underfeeding during gestation and infancy has been reported (Ravelli et al., 1976), although the adult measure is overweight rather than obesity. Almost 95,000 persons were measured at about 19 years who had been exposed to the acute conditions of the Dutch famine between October 1944 and May 1945. Because food was carefully rationed, intakes could be determined with considerable accuracy. Further, because the famine resulted from an embargo imposed on only certain parts of the Netherlands by the Nazis, it was highly localized. Thus, almost 213,000 persons born outside this area during the same period were available as controls. Additional controls from the study area were those conceived after the famine.

Analyses of the data in terms of the phases of gestation or infancy concurrent with acute famine (e.g., first trimester only, last trimester and early infancy, early infancy only) yielded results that are in part difficult to interpret. Two groups differed significantly from controls. The lowest incidence of obesity was found among those who were in the last trimester of gestation and the first 3 to 5 postnatal months during the famine. This finding is consistent with data on body composition showing that fetal fat increases rapidly from 30 to 40 weeks and that about 67% of the weight gain during the first 4 postnatal months is adipose tissue (Fomon, 1966); thereafter, lean and adipose tissue increase proportionately. The puzzling finding is that the highest incidence of obesity was found among those who were in the first two trimesters of pregnancy during the famine, whereas those exposed to famine only in the first trimester or during the second and third trimesters did not differ significantly from controls. The investigators suggest that among the more obese group the famine coincided with a critical period for differentiation of the appetite control centers in the hypothalamus. However, the results certainly do not indicate that one or the other of the first two trimesters is critical. Another confusing result, not sufficiently discussed by the investigators, is the high incidence of obesity among groups conceived and delivered in the postfamine period.

The complex of findings recalls an earlier study by Smith (1947) of birthweights in two cities within the famine area. He found lower birthweights among neonates whose last trimester occurred during the famine but not among those whose last two trimesters were during this period. Further, those born immediately after the famine had higher birth-weights than Dutch infants born before World War II.

Clearly, the relationship of early nutrition to later obesity is not a simple one. Even proponents of the early-feeding hypothesis believe that not all obese infants become obese adults and, conversely, that not all obese adults were obese infants (Brook, 1974). Among the complicating factors are the variety of forms of obesity (some of which are known to be genetic), the alterations in metabolism following either weight gain or loss, and the fact that the effect of nutrients is not simply on the amount or fat content of adipose tissue but also on other aspects of body composition, such as electrolyte balance, water distribution (intra- and extracellular), and cell mass. Further, illness, activity, type of feeding, and personality characteristics are also associated with at least weight gain, although the direction of the influence is not always clear. For example, overweight infants have been reported to have a higher incidence of illness (Hooper and Alexander, 1971), particularly respiratory ailments (Tracey et al., 1971). Mayer (1975) found no correlation between food intake and weight gain in babies aged 0 to 15 months. Indeed, the thin infants often had the highest intakes but were active, tense, and cried a great deal, whereas the fatter infants had only moderate intakes but were placid. Among school-age girls Mayer found no difference in the proportions of fat, protein, and carbohydrate consumed by the obese, although their caloric intakes were actually 300 to 400 *less* than the non-obese. However, the amount of time during which they were actually active (documented by movies) was only one-third that of the non-obese. Others (*Nutrition Reviews,* 1973) have reported that breast-fed infants are more active and cry more than bottle-fed, and less frequently become overweight. Introduction of cereals during 1st or 2nd postnatal months also seems to be associated with rapid weight gain (Eid, 1970; Taitz, 1971).

As yet, however, the data do not justify radical changes in infant feeding practices, although they suggest the urgency of detailed and long-term studies. One wonders, for example, whether the hyperalimentation often used as a remedial measure with infants of low birthweight will prove on balance to do more harm than good. On the other hand, marked restriction of maternal intakes during pregnancy, a common medical practice during the 1940s and 1950s, is now considered inadvisable. Also, severe restriction of fats per se either during gestation (particularly the last trimester) or during the early postnatal years may be contraindicated by the fact that these are periods of rapid myelination of the nervous system, and fat is a major component of myelin.

FETAL AND NEONATAL DEVELOPMENT

During the past decade a quiet revolution has been spreading through newborn nurseries. Physicians and nurses specializing in neonatology have been salvaging infants, particularly those with very low birthweights and marked prematurity, who previously would have constituted a sizeable proportion of the perinatal mortality rate (Usher, 1970; Lubchenco, 1972). In addition to the treatment provided in intensive care units, major factors in the higher survival rate are better identification of fetuses and neonates at risk and discrimination among them as to etiology and the likelihood of particular disorders. As the survival rate of extremely small or premature infants improved, concern about later physical and behavioral sequelae led to an increasing volume of multidisciplinary longitudinal assessments of survivors. To date this research has yielded encouraging results, that is, a secular trend toward decreasing prevalence of serious sequelae as techniques of neonatal care have improved (Hunt, 1975; Davies and Stewart, 1975). However, long-term follow-ups of infants benefitting from recent innovation in perinatal diagnosis and management are not yet available. Hence many developmental psychologists will be participating in such research, and they should be aware of the methods and problems involved in assessing physical development in the fetus and neonate.

Contributing to the better identification and differentiation of infants at risk has been the distinction between prematurity per se and low birthweight. In 1948, the World Health Organization proposed defining as premature all infants with birthweights of 2.5 kg or less. Although many obstetricians and pediatricians were aware that not all small neonates were premature, the distinction was rarely made in clinical or research reports, rendering the older follow-up literature obsolete on these grounds as well as because of changes in prenatal and perinatal medical care. Not until 1961 was the WHO recommendation changed so that infants of 2.5 kg or less were classified as "low birthweight" and the premature infant defined as one having a gestational age of 37 weeks or less. Full-term infants are those born between the onset of the 38th week of gestation and the end of the 41st. Infants with longer gestations are called post-term or postmature. As of the early 1970s, 9.2% of births in the United States were classified as premature and 6.6% as low birthweight (NCHS, 1975). The latter figure represents well over a quarter of a million babies who still had a mortality rate 17 times greater than that of other infants. Clearly, the risks associated with prematurity and low birthweight still represent a sizeable public health problem. Postmature infants, often the offspring of diabetic mothers, are also at greater risk than normals.

In the current literature, infants are designated as small-for-date (SFD) or small-for-gestational-age (SGA), large for date (LFD) or gestational age (LGA), and average for date (AFD) or gestational age (AGA). Some set the cutoff points for small and large at the 10th and 90th percentiles of the reference standards being used, respectively, whereas others use the 5th and 95th or 3rd and 97th (Tanner, 1970). Two-way classifications are becoming typical, with infants grouped, for example, as SGA, premature and AGA, full-term and SGA, post-term and SGA, or LGA. As might be expected, the prognosis in general is poorest for the SGA premature infant who has not only the handicaps associated with small size but also is ill-equipped physiologically to live outside its natural habitat—for example, to breathe for itself, resist infections, and cope with temperature variation.

An obvious problem in constructing growth standards for gestational age is determining the latter. Exact conceptional or fertilization age is never known in the human, although instances of close approximations are becoming more frequent. Gestational age is most commonly calculated from the onset of the mother's last menstrual period, with conception being estimated as 10 to 14 days later. Given a carefully taken history, authorities now consider this method quite accurate in 75 to 85% of pregnancies (Lubchenco, 1970; Korones, 1972). Sources of error are irregular menses, amenorrhea accompanying nursing, post-conceptional bleeding, and ingestion of antiovulary medications (if fertilization occurs soon after termination of birth control pills, the time between the last menstruation and the next ovulation cannot be estimated).

Other methods used during the pregnancy include various obstetric signs such as maternal perception of fetal movement (about 16 weeks), detection of fetal heart beat (18 to 22 weeks, average of 20), and the height of the uterine fundus above the pubic symphysis (e.g., about 25 cm at 26 weeks). Because of normal individual variations in mother (e.g., amount of subcutaneous fat) and fetus as well as variations with abnormal conditions, none of these methods is exact. When complications that may dictate delivery by caesarian section are present, amniocentesis (sampling of amniotic fluid via a needle inserted through the abdominal wall) may be done, and gestation age estimated from the creatinine level in the fluid. The physician tries to time the delivery to maximize the maturity of the fetus while simultaneously minimizing the risk to fetus and mother of maintaining the pregnancy. Occasionally estimates of fetal age are done by X-ray late in gestation—ossification centers normally appear at the proximal end of the tibia and the distal end of the femur by 36 to 38 weeks.

Once the fetus is delivered, age may be estimated from appearance, behavior, EEG and other electrophysiologic measures, biochemistry (e.g., creatinine, immunoglobins, amount of fetal hemoglobin, and anthropometric measurements). Physical signs include posture, contours, amount of subcutaneous fat, and condition of the skin (Korones, 1972). A widely used neurologic scale for assessing maturity is that of Dubowitz et al. (1970), which yields an estimate of age accurate to about 2 weeks (about the same range as for menstrual age estimates). Estimation of gestational age from fetal growth charts for length or weight (the more common) is, of course, a double-bind situation if one is trying to determine whether or not the infant is small, average, or large for age. However, the ratio of head circumference to chest circumference is a proportion that changes with age and avoids the ''chicken and egg'' problem.

After gestational age has been determined in some fashion, the fetus or neonate can be measured and judged against one of the available reference standards. Until the development of sonography (Garrett and Robinson, 1971; Robinson, 1973), measurement of the intact fetus was limited to gross approximations with calipers or tape applied to the maternal abdomen. Sonography or echography is a noninvasive technique that permits measurement in utero not only of length and widths (biparietal diameter is the most widely used measure) but also of specific organs, such as the heart and liver. For the ultrasound technique to be useful diagnostically, estimates of size must begin before the 30th week of gestation. This is because growth retardation resulting from maternal malnutrition or placental defects (which can result in malnutrition as well as in oxygen deprivation and other insults) occurs primarily during the last 10 weeks of gestation. Unless serial measures are begun earlier, a slowing in growth rate is difficult to detect. Crown-rump length can be measured by 6 weeks and biparietal diameter by 13. As yet reference standards of the type available for postnatal growth are not available, but sonography opens the possibility of constructing norms from fetuses who prove at birth and subsequently to be normal.

By contrast, none of the reference standards and charts for intrauterine or postnatal growth based on delivered premature infants (Tanner, 1970; Babson and Lubchenco, 1975) can fill this ideal. Even if infants with obvious defects are eliminated from the standardization sample—for example, those dead at birth or with malformations—one cannot be sure that undetected abnormalities affecting growth are not present. Nor can one be sure that even healthy premature infants grow at the same rate postnatally as they would have in utero. Despite such limitations, the better standards have proved very useful in distinguishing premature infants who are of normal size for age from those suffering from intrauterine growth retardation and differentiating among postmature infants on the basis of size for age. Standards that permit adjustment for maternal size (Tanner and Thompson, 1970) provide additional precision.

As techniques for feeding and otherwise managing small and premature infants continue to improve, norms will probably have to be revised. Not long ago such infants were fed little if anything for at least several days because of their immature digestive systems. With current feeding regimens the early course of growth of these infants is much better, particularly for the SGA (Sabel et al., 1976). Obsolescence of current standards for such a reason is an outcome devoutly to be wished.

BIBLIOGRAPHY

Abraham, S., Lowenstein, F.W., and O'Connell, D.W. Preliminary Findings of First Health and Nutrition Examination Survey, United States (1971–1972), Anthropometric and Clinical Findings. *Department of Health, Education and Welfare Publication No. (HRA)* April, 1975, 75–1229.

Adadevoh, B.K. Obesity in the African. In W.L. Burland, P.D. Samuel and J. Judkin, (eds.) *Obesity Symposium,* Edinburgh-London-New York: Churchill Livingstone, 1974.

Babson, S.G. and Lubchenco, L.O. Fetal growth. In W.K. Frankenburg and B.W. Camp (eds.) *Pediatric Screening Tests,* Springfield, Illinois: C. C. Thomas, 1975.

Baldwin, B.T. Weight-height-age standards in metric units for American-born children. *American Journal of Physical Anthropology,* 1925, **8**, 1–10.

Barness, L. W. Nutrition for the low birth weight infant. *Clinical Perinatology,* 1975, **2**, 345–352.

Bayer, L.M. and Gray, J. Plotting of graphic record of growth for children aged one to nineteen years. *American Journal of Diseases for Children,* 1935, **50**, 1408–1417.

Bayley, N. Some increasing parent-child similarities during the growth of children. *Journal of Educational Psychology,* 1954, **45**, 1–21.

Behar, M. Prevalence of malnutrition among preschool children. In N.S. Scrimshaw and J.E. Gordon (eds.) *Malnutrition, Learning and Behavior.* Cambridge, Mass.: M.I.T. Press, 1968.

Bjorntorp, P. and Sjostrom, L. Number and size of adipose tissue fat cells in relation to metabolism in human obesity. *Metabolism,* 1971, **20**, 703–713.

Bowditch, H.P. *Massachusetts State Board of Health Annual Report,* 1877, **8**, 275–324.

Bowditch, H.P. *Massachusetts State Board of Health Annual Report,* 1891, **22**, 479–522.

British Association for the Advancement of Science: *Report of the Anthropometric Committee,* 1879, London, 1880.

Brook, C.G. Obesity in Childhood, *M.D. Thesis,* University of Cambridge, 1972.

Brook, C.G. Critical periods in childhood obesity. In W.L. Burland, P.D. Samuel and J. Yudkin, (eds.) *Obesity Symposium,* Edinburgh-London-New York: Churchill Livingstone, 1974.

Brook, C.G., Lloyd, J.K. and Wolff, O.H. Relation between age of onset of obesity and size and number of adipose cells. *British Medical Journal,* 1972, **2**, 25–27.

Chase, H.P. The epidemiology of malnutrition in the United States. In C.A. Canosa, (ed.), *Nutrition, Growth and Development, Modern Problems in Paediatrics,* 1975, **14**, 1.

Committee on Nutrition Advisory to CDC, FNB, NAS-NRC, *Nutrition Review,* 1974, **32**, 284.

Davies, P.A. and Stewart, A.L. Low-birth-weight infants: Neurological sequelae and later intelligence. *British Medical Bulletin,* 1975, **31**, 85–91.

Dubowitz, M.S., Dubowitz, V. and Goldberg, C.J. Clinical assessment of gestational age in the newborn infant. *Journal of Pediatrics,* 1978, **77**, 1–10.

Eid, E.E. Follow-up study of physical growth of children who had excessive weight gain in first six months of life. *British Medical Journal,* 1970, **2**, 74–76.

Epstein, F.H. The epidemiology of coronary heart disease: A review. *Journal of Chronic Diseases*, 1965, **18**, 735.

Food Intake and Nutritive Value of Diets of Men, Women and Children in the United States, Spring, 1965, ARS-18, U.S. Government Printing Office, Washington, D.C.

Fomon, S.J. Body composition of the infant. In F. Falkner (ed.), *Human Development*, Philadelphia-London-New York: Russell Sage Foundation, 1966, 239–246.

Garn, S.M. Body size and its implications. In L.W. Hoffman and M.L. Hoffman, (eds.) *Review of Child Development Research*, Vol. 2, New York: Russell Sage Foundation, 1966, 529–561.

Garn, S.M., Clark, D.C., and Guire, K.E. Growth, body composition and development of obese and lean children. In M. Winick (ed.), *Childhood Obesity*, New York-London, Sydney-Toronto: Wiley, 1975, 23–46.

Garrett, W. J. and Robinson, D.E. Assessment of fetal size and growth rate in ultrasonic echoscopy. *Obstetrics and Gynecology*, 1971, **38**, 535–534.

Gray, H. Growth in private school children; with averages and variabilities based on 3110 measurings on boys and 1473 on girls, from the ages of one to nineteen years. *Behavior Research Fund Monographs*, 282, University of Chicago Press, 1931.

Greenwood, M.R.C. and Hirsch, J.J. Postnatal development of adipocyte cellularity in the normal rat. *Journal of Lipid Research*, 1974, **15**, 474–483.

Hastings, W.W. *A Manual for Physical Measurements for Use in Normal Schools, Public and Preparatory Schools, Boys' Clubs, and Young Men's Christian Associations, with Anthropometric Tables for Each Height of Each Age from 50 to 20 Years, and Vitality Coefficients*. Springfield, Mass., 1902.

Heald, F.P. Juvenile obesity. In M. Winick (ed.), *Childhood Obesity*, New York-London-Sydney-Toronto: Wiley, 1975, 81–90.

Hertz, T.W. and Harrell, A.V. *Toward Interagency Coordination, Fourth Annual Report*, The George Washington University, Washington, D.C., 1974.

Heyneman, S.P. *Toward Interagency Coordination, Second Annual Report*, Social Research Group, The George Washington University, Washington, D.C., 1974.

Hirsch, J. and Gallian, E.J. Methods for the determination of adipose cell size in man and animals. *Journal of Lipid Research*, 1968, **9**, 110–119.

Hirsch, J. and Han, P.W. Cellularity of rat adipose tissue: Effects of growth, starvation and obesity. *Journal of Lipid Research*, 1969, **10**, 77–82.

Hirsch, J. and Knittle, J.L. Cellularity of obese and nonobese human adipose tissue. *Federal Proceedings*, 1970, **29**, 1516–1521.

Hooper, P.D. and Alexander, E.L. Infant morbidity and obesity. A survey of 151 infants from general practice. *Practitioner*, 1971, **207**, 221–227.

Hunt, J.V. Environmental risk in fetal and neonatal life and measured infant intelligence. In M. Lewis (ed.), *Infant Development*, New York: Plenum, 1975, 223.

Interdepartmental Committee on Nutrition for National Defense, *Manual for Nutrition Surveys*, 2nd ed., Washington, D.C., U.S. Government Printing Office, 1963.

Kallen, D.J., (ed.) *Nutrition, Development and Social Behavior*, Department of Health, Education and Welfare Publication No. (NIH) 73–242, 1973, Washington, D.C., U.S. Government Printing Office.

Kannel, W.B., Pearson, G. and McNamara, P.M. Obesity as a force of morbidity and mortality. In F.P. Heald (ed.), *Adolescent Nutritional Growth*, New York: Appleton-Century-Crofts, 1969.

Kasius, R.V., Randall, A., Tompkins, W.J. and Wiehl, D.B. Maternal and newborn studies at Philadelphia Lying-In Hospital: Newborn studies, V. Size and growth of babies during the first year of life. *Milbank Memorial Fund Quarterly*, 1957, **35**, 323–372.

Kish, L. and Hess, I. *The Survey Research Center's National Sample of Dwellings*, Institute for Social Research, University of Michigan, Ann Arbor, 1965, ISR No. 2315.

Knittle, J.L. Childhood obesity. *Bulletin of the New York Academy of Medicine*, 1971, **47**, 579–589.

Knittle, J.L. Maternal diet as a factor in adipose tissue cellularity and metabolism in the young rat. *Journal of Nutrition*, 1972, **102**, 427–434.

Knittle, J.L. Basic concepts in the control of childhood obesity. In M. Winick (ed.), *Childhood Obesity*, New York-London-Sydney-Toronto: Wiley, 1975, 135–140.

Knittle, J.L. and Hirsch, J. Effects of early nutrition on the development of rat epididymal fat pods: Cellularity and metabolism. *Journal of Clinical Investigations*, 1968, **47**, 2091–2098.

Korones, S.B. *High Risk Newborn Infants*, St. Louis, Missouri: C.V. Mosby, 1972.

Lubchenco, L.O. Assessment of gestational age and development at birth. In B.F. Andrews (ed.) *The Small-for-Date Infant, The Pediatric Clinics of North America*, 1970, **80**, 509.

Macy, I.G. and Kelly, H.J. *Chemical Anthropology*, Chicago: University of Chicago Press, 1957.

Malina, R.M., Hammill, P.V.V., Leneshow, S. *Vital and Health Statistics*, 1974, Series 11, No. 143, Department of Health, Education and Welfare Publication No. (HRA) 75-1625, U.S. Government Printing Office, Washington, D.C.

Mayer, J. Obesity during childhood. In M. Winick (ed.), *Childhood Obesity*, New York-London-Sydney-Toronto: Wiley, 1975, 73–80.

McCammon, R.W. *Human Growth and Development*. Springfield, Ill.: C. C. Thomas, 1970.

National Center for Health Statistics, *Vital and Health Statistics, 1970, Series 11, No. 104, Health Services and Mental Health Administration, Washington, D.C., U.S. Government Printing Office*.

National Center for Health Statistics, *Vital and Health Statistics, 1973, Series 11, No. 124, Health Services and Mental Health Administration, Washington, D. C., U.S. Government Printing Office*.

National Center for Health Statistics, *Monthly Vital Statistics Report*, 1976, Vol. 25, No. 3, Supplement (HRA).

Owen, G. M. The assessment and recordings of measurements of rowth of children: Report of a small conference. *Pediatrics*, 1973, **51**, 461–466.

Owen, G. M. and Brozek, J. Influence of age, sex and utrition on body composition during childhood and adolescence. In F. Falkner (ed.), *Human Development*, Philadelphia: W.B. Saunders, 1966.

Owen, G.M., Kram, K.M., Garry, P.J., Lower, J.E., and Lubin, A.H. *A Study of Nutritional Status of Preschool Children in the United States*, 1974, **53**, Part II, Supplement, 597–646.

Quelet, L.A. *Sur l'Homme et le Développement de Ses Facultes, ou Essai de Physique Sociale*, Brussels, 1935.

Ravelli, G.P., Stein, Z.A., and Sussen, M.V. Obesity in young men after feminine exposure in utero and early infancy. *New England Journal of Medicine*, 1962, **295**, 349–353.

Read, M.S., Habicht, J.P., Lechtig, A., and Klein, R.E. Maternal nutrition, birth weight and child development. In C.A. Canosa (ed.), *Nutrition, Growth and Development*, Basel: S. Karger, 1975.

Richards, R. and de Casseres, M. The problem of obesity in developing countries: Its prevalence and morbidity. In W.L. Burland, P.D. Samuel and J. Yudkin (eds.), *Obesity Symposium*, Edinburgh-London-New York: Churchill Livingstone, 1974.

Robinson, H.D. Sona measurements of fetal crown-rump length as means of assessing maturity in first trimester of pregnancy. *British Journal of Medicine*, 1973, **4**, 28–31.

Roche, A.F. and Falkner, F. Physical growth charts. In W.K. Frankenburg and B.W. Camp, (eds.), *Pediatric Screening Tests*, Springfield, Ill.: C.C. Thomas, 1975, 63–73.

Roche, A.F. Physical growth of ethnic groups comprising the U.S. population. *American Journal of Diseases of Children*, 1976, **130**, 62–64.

Roche, A.F., Roberts, J. and Hamill, P.V.V., *Vital and Health Statistics*, 1975, Series 11, No.

149, Department of Health, Education and Welfare Publication No. (HRA) 76–1631, U.S. Government Printing Office, Washington, D.C.

Sabel, K.G., Olegard, R. and Victorin, L. Remaining sequelae with modern perinatal care. *Pediatrics*, 1976, **57**, 652–658.

Salans, L.B., Cushman, S.W. and Weismann, R.E. Studies of human adipose tissue. Adipose cell size and number in nonobese and obese patients. *Journal of Clinical Investigation*, 1973, **47**, 2485.

Scammon, R.E. First seriatim study of human growth. *American Journal of Physical Anthropology*, 1927, **10**, 329.

Schaefer, A.E. Epidemiology of pre- and postnatal malnutrition-USA. In C.A. Canosa (ed.), *Nutrition, Growth and Development, Modern Problems in Paediatrics*, 1975, **14**, 9.

Sims, E.A.H., Goldman, R.F., Gluck, C.M., Horton, E.S., Kelleher, P.C. and Rowe, D.W. Experimental obesity in men. *Transitional Association of American Physicians*, 1968, **81**, 153–170.

Shula, A., Forsyth, H.A., Anderson, D.M., Marwahs, M. Overfeeding in the first year of life. *Nutrition Reviews*, **31**, 1973, 116.

Smith, C.A. Effects of maternal undernutrition upon the newborn infant in Holland (1944–1945), *Journal of Pediatrics*, 1947, **30**, 229–243.

Smith, C.A. *The Physiology of the Newborn Infant*, 2nd edition, Springfield, Ill.: C.C. Thomas, 1951.

Stuart, H.C. and Meredith, H.V. Use of body measurements in school health program. *American Journal of Public Health*, 1946, **36**, 1365–1386.

Summary Report Final Natality Statistics, 1973. *Monthly Vital Statistics Report, National Center for Health Statistics* (HRA), 1975, **23**, No. 11 Supplement, 75.

Taitz, L.S. Infantile overnutrition among artificially fed infants in the Sheffield region. *British American Journal*, 1971, **1**, 315–316.

Tanner, J.M. Standards for birth weight or intra-uterine growth. *Pediatrics*, 1970, **46**, 1–6.

Tanner, J.M., Goldstein, J. and Whitehouse, R.H. Standards of children's height at ages 2–0 years allowing for heights of parents. *Archives of Diseases of Childhood*, 1970, **45**, 755–762.

Tanner, J.M. and Thomson, A.M. Standards for birthweight as gestation periods from 32–42 weeks, allowing for maternal height and weight. *Archives of Diseases of Childhood*, 1970, **45**, 566–569.

Tracey, V.V., De, N.C., and Harper, J.R. Obesity and respiratory infection in infants and young children. *British Medical Journal*, 1971, **1**, 16–18.

U.S. Department of Health, Education and Welfare, *Ten-State Nutrition Survey*, 1968–1970, DHEW Publication No (HMS) 72-8134, 1972, Volumes I–V.

Usher, R.H. The role of the neonatologist. In B.F. Andrews (ed.), *The Small-for-Date Infant, The Pediatric Clinics of North America*, 1970, **17**, 199.

Warner, W.L., Meeker, M. and Eells, K. *Social Class in America: A Manual of Procedure for the Measurement of Social Status*, Chicago: Science Research Associates, 1949.

Weil, W.B., Jr. Infantile obesity. In M. Winick (ed.), *Childhood Obesity*, New York-London-Sydney-Toronto: Wiley, 1975, 61–72.

Winick, M. (ed.) *Childhood Obesity*, New York: Wiley, 1975.

Woodbury, R.M. Statures and weights of children under 6 years of age. *Children's Bureau Publication*, 1921, **87**.

Woodbury, R.M. Tables of infancy and early childhood. *Mother and Child*, Supplement to July Issue, 1923.

Yudkin, J. Introduction in W.L. Burland, P.D. Samuel and J. Yudkin (eds.), *Obesity Symposium*, Edinburgh-London-New York: Churchill Livingstone, 1974.

CHAPTER 9

Psychophysiological Development in Infancy: State, Sensory Function, and Attention[1]

W. Keith Berg and Kathleen M. Berg

One of the first decisions to be made by the investigator or practitioner wishing to study or examine the infant is the choice of behaviors to be observed. For most readers of this text it will appear almost trite to note that the choices available are relatively few due to the "limited behavioral repertoire" of the infant, especially the very young infant. Yet it is important to note that this statement is true largely for the overt, easily observed behaviors representative of well-coordinated striate muscle activity. The more covert behavior of the infant, often denoted as "physiological" activity, is relatively well developed even at birth. The heart has been beating since the 4th week post conception and both sympathetic and parasympathetic systems exert at least some control at birth or before (Eichorn, 1970). The presence of clear sinus arrhythmia indicates a definite cardiac-respiratory coordination by well-known brainstem structures. Skin potential (though not skin resistance) responses are readily recorded in the newborn, and electroencephalographic activity is observable early in gestation. This is not meant to suggest that these systems are fully mature at birth, but that they are examples of the relative wealth of information available from "physiological" activity.

For many investigators, the dichotomy of response measures into those that are "physiological" and those that are "behavioral" is not simply descriptive but represents a fundamental and functional distinction. Further, however useful they might be in the study of infants, those responses labeled "physiological" are sometimes perceived as more indirect indicants of sensation, learning, cognition, and other such psychological constructs than are "behavioral" responses. We would argue, however, that while the dichotomy provides a useful descriptive distinction, there are no grounds for a clear functional distinction nor for a hierarchical one in which one type of response is considered to be a priori more valid or direct; we suggest both are types of behaviors differing only in the extent to which they are overt or covert.

While discarding the fundamental behavior-physiology dichotomy avoids a logical problem, it leaves us with the practical one of what to cover in a chapter on psychophysiological development, or for that matter why a separate chapter is required at all. A separate chapter serves to emphasize and outline the information that covert behaviors are able to add to that available from overt ones. However, we shall often be including research employing relatively overt behavior where it bears upon issues and problems that have been illuminated by the use of physiological responses. In large part

[1]Preparation of this manuscript was supported in part by NIH contract NO 1-NS-5-2313.

the physiological responses discussed will be heart rate and electroencephalographic activity, including evoked brain potentials. Electrodermal (skin potential and resistance), electromyographic, and respiratory activity are only briefly mentioned since there is little work available in infants.

The chapter is organized around three central topics: sleeping and waking states, the maturation and assessment of sensory capacities, and the development of more cognitive processes such as orienting, attention, and habituation. These are areas where the recording of physiological activity has had a particularly important impact. Limitations of space regrettably require restriction of the coverage of these topics and the omission of a number of other topics of relevance. Throughout the chapter we have attempted to emphasize the developmental changes taking place during infancy and, wherever possible, to relate them to physiological and neurological maturation.

STATE, SLEEP, AND BIOLOGICAL RHYTHMS

A great deal has been written about state in the developmental literature; much of it, as Ashton (1973a) has pointed out, is difficult to interpret due to a general lack of agreement concerning the number and the naming of states observed in young infants, as well as the criteria to be used in defining such states. This lack of agreement can be partly attributed to the instability of behavioral organization during early infancy. Spontaneous behaviors do tend to occur in clusters during this period, but these poorly organized clusters are quite different from the distinctive patterns of autonomic and central activity which occur in an orderly sequence as "states" in adults.

Although the complexities of waking states in adult subjects are still a matter of controversy, it is generally agreed that adult sleep may be classified into five stages: rapid eye movement (REM) sleep and four stages of non-REM or NREM sleep. During a typical night, the REM state and one or more stages of NREM sleep alternate periodically. After sleep onset, there is a progression from stage 1 to stage 4 of NREM sleep, and an associated decrease in levels of central, autonomic, and motor activity. Electroencephalographic tracings recorded from the scalp show a gradual slowing of wave frequencies; heart rate and respiration become slow and regular; and there is general muscular relaxation (Williams et al., 1973). A notable exception is spontaneous electrodermal activity which shows a dramatic increase during stages 3 and 4, frequently referred to as electrodermal "storms" (Johnson and Lubin, 1966). These patterns are reversed in REM sleep; the EEG changes to a low-amplitude–mixed-frequency pattern characteristic of increased activation; heart rate and respiration become irregular, and spontaneous electrodermal activity decreases to waking levels. Most characteristic of the REM state are bursts of rapid eye movements and phasic movements of the face and extremities, which are superimposed on a background of profound inhibition of tonic muscle activity (Williams et al., 1973).

These well-organized patterns of activity are not fully developed in the human infant until well into the 1st year of life. In the newborn, at least three distinct states can be identified: wakefulness and two stages of sleep, which are the precursors of REM and NREM sleep in the adult. A variety of terminologies for these sleep states are currently in use, but the terms "active" and "quiet" sleep recommended by Anders et al. (1971) will be used here.

Organization of States

Observations reported by Dreyfus-Brisac (1967, 1968) in previable prematures 24 to 27 weeks' conceptional age[2] indicate that at this stage of development, infants exhibit only a single state which cannot be classified as sleep or wakefulness. Body movements, generally localized to the extremities, are almost continuous with little periodic fluctuation. Eye movements are absent or very infrequent, heart rate is fixed and unvarying, and respiration is predominantly irregular and unrelated to body activity. Scalp recordings from these infants show short bursts of activity alternating with periods of quiescence which may last as long as 2 to 3 min.

With further maturation, eye movements gradually become more frequent, and by 28 to 30 weeks' conceptional age, they may occur quite regularly at a rate of 1 to 4 per min (Dreyfus-Brisac, 1967). Spontaneous skin potential responses can first be recorded from the palms and soles of the feet during this period, but they occur infrequently and are unrelated to other phasic events (Curzi-Dascalova et al., 1973).

The first signs of behavioral state organization occur at approximately 32 weeks' conceptional age with the emergence of two distinguishable EEG patterns. One of these, an intermittent pattern of slow-wave clusters interspersed with periods of relative inactivity, later develops into the *tracé alternant* pattern characteristic of quiet sleep in the full-term neonate. The second is a continuous pattern of mixed frequencies with predominant slow waves, the precursor of EEG patterns later associated with wakefulness and active sleep (Parmelee et al., 1967a; Dreyfus-Brisac and Monod, 1975). A tendency toward organization of other behavioral elements also appears at this time. Eye movements, body movements, and spontaneous skin potential responses continue to occur in association with both EEG patterns, but are most frequent during the continuous pattern (Parmelee et al., 1967a; Curzi-Dascalova et al., 1973, 1974).

Between 32 and 40 weeks (term), interrelationships between different elements become more clearly defined and the various patterns of activity gradually become organized into the two groupings, termed active and quiet sleep. Each of the components appears to mature independently, and associations may be established with certain elements at one point in development, only to be reestablished with other elements later. According to Dreyfus-Brisac (1970), active sleep may be seen in its typical form by 35 weeks', and quiet sleep by 37 weeks' conceptional age.

Although the infant at term exhibits three distinguishable patterns, which are recognizable as the precursors of wakefulness, REM, and NREM states in the adult, the interrelationships among elements of the patterns are not yet stable enough to classify all periods of observation into these categories. The typical approach to this problem is to select several criteria for each state and require that some pre-set portion of these be met before a particular period of observation can be classified as one state or another. Periods not satisfying these criteria are then classified as transitional or undefined (e.g., Anders et al., 1971). In a variant of this approach, Prechtl (1974) has proposed that each state be described as a vector in which the presence of a particular behavioral characteristic is assigned a positive value and its absence a negative value. "Transitional" states are not undefined in this system since vectors can be described for them.

As might be expected, the particular criteria selected and the number of criteria that

[2]Conceptional age refers to the time since onset of the mother's last menstrual period. The term gestational age refers to the time between onset of the mother's last menstrual period and the infant's birth.

must be met for classification may have a marked influence on the results, especially in young premature infants when state organization is just emerging. Parmelee and associates (1967b) have illustrated this influence in a comparison of two methods of defining sleep states in pre-term infants. In the first method, they classified each 20-sec period of sleep as either active sleep or quiet sleep if it included any four of six defining characteristics for each state. Analyzing the records in this way, they found that amounts of active sleep were greatest in the youngest prematures and gradually decreased in older infants. The opposite trend was obtained for quiet sleep, which was infrequent in young prematures and increased with further maturation (Fig. 9-1). When these records were reanalyzed with the requirement that all three of three criteria be met for classification, the results for quiet sleep were unchanged but active sleep showed a very different developmental course; it was infrequent in very young prematures, increased to a peak at 34 weeks' gestational age, and then steadily declined in older infants.

Definition of states is considerably less difficult in full-term infants than in prematures, but state components still show varying degrees of immaturity at term. REMs, along with other physiological parameters characteristic of active sleep, can be observed during "nonsleep" states when the eyes are open or during crying (Edme and Metcalf, 1970). Penile erections, which are a concomitant of REM sleep in adults, may occur during any state in the newborn, although they tend to be more frequent during active sleep (Korner, 1968; Wolff, 1966). And other criteria, such as body movements and respiratory and EEG patterns, show varying degrees of overlap between the different states (Parmelee et al., 1968a, 1967a). These unstable patterns disappear during the first few months of life with the development of adult sleep stages.

Maturation of Specific Elements

EEG PATTERNS

Although the EEG of prematures is routinely described as "less complex" than that of older infants, there is still considerable diversity in the EEG patterns observed in young pre-term infants. Parmelee and associates (1968b) were able to identify at least nine different EEG patterns in sleeping infants ranging from 30 to 40 weeks' conceptional age, and Dreyfus-Brisac and her colleagues have typically distinguished at least four different patterns: those most characteristic of the two stages of sleep and two that appear to be transitional (e.g., Dreyfus-Brisac, 1970). Such transitional patterns are seen at all ages, but change in character as the EEG matures (Parmelee et al., 1967a).

After term, developmental changes in the EEG pattern of active sleep are for the most part limited to changes in wave amplitudes and frequencies (e.g., Parmelee et al., 1967a). More striking developmental changes are seen in quiet sleep patterns. The intermittent pattern, which Dreyfus-Brisac has termed *tracé alternant,* is most typical of quiet sleep in the full-term newborn. This pattern develops as the low-level activity during "flat" periods of the discontinuous EEG seen in young prematures gradually increases in amplitude. The result consists of bursts or clusters of high-amplitude slow waves interspersed with periods of more attenuated activity (Parmelee et al., 1969). Parmelee et al. have noted that the burst-to-burst time appears to remain a constant 9 to 10 sec in both newborn infants and prematures as young as 29 weeks' conceptional age. However, with increasing maturation the duration of the bursts gradually increases, reducing the duration of the flat periods until the pattern becomes one of continuous slow waves at approxi-

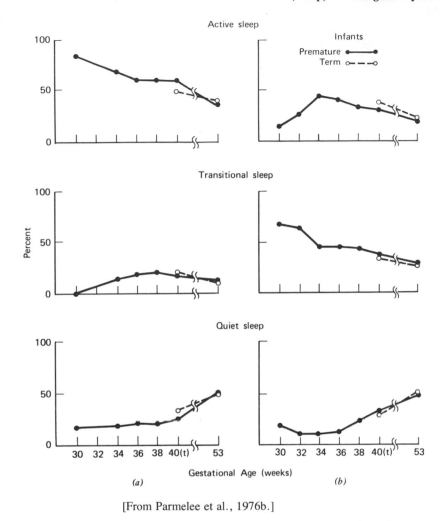

[From Parmelee et al., 1976b.]

Figure 9-1.   Percentage of each sleep state at each gestational age for two methods of state classification. For the data in panel   (a), at least four of the following six characteristics were required to be present in a 20-sec epoch. For active sleep: (1) rapid eye movements, (2) irregular respiration, (3) irregular heart rate, (4) frequent small movements, (5) absence of chin EMG, (6) continuous low-amplitude EEG. For quiet sleep: (1) no eye movements, (2) regular respiration, (3) regular heart rate, (4) no body movements, (5) some chin EMG activity, (6) tracé alternant EEG pattern. Panel (b) illustrates sleep-state percentages when all three of the following three charracteristics were required for each state. For active sleep: (1) rapid eye movements, (2) irregular respiration, (3) either presence or absence of body movements. For quiet sleep: (1) absence of eye movements, (2) regular or periodic respiration, (3) no body movements.

mately 3 to 4 weeks after term. Further, burst durations are significantly longer for prematures at term than for full-term newborns, suggesting that extrauterine experience may accelerate EEG maturation. Parmelee et al. have suggested that this rhythmic burst activity may be attributable to a subcortical pacemaker, possibly in the thalamus, which remains stable during early development.

A second significant change in the EEG of quiet sleep occurs sometime during the 2nd month of life with the appearance of sleep spindles, a waveform characteristic of NREM stage 2 in the adult. Spindles are brief bursts of rhythmic activity in the range of 12 to 15 Hz; they are typically fusiform in shape and may range from 400 msec to 3 to 5 sec in duration. In the young infant they are seen superimposed on the dominant slow-wave activity of quiet sleep. Although similar rapid rhythms are frequently seen superimposed on slow waves in pre-term infants, these patterns are typically present over posterior areas of the scalp and do not appear to be precursors of spindles, which are most prominent at the vertex and central regions (Parmelee et al., 1967a).

When spindle bursts first appear, they are very brief and variable in frequency. After first appearance their development takes place within a period of approximately 2 weeks, during which they rapidly become more regular, longer in duration, and higher in amplitude (Metcalf, 1970a). Like burst duration in the *tracé alternant,* their development appears to be accelerated in prematures compared to full-term infants of the same conceptional age (Metcalf, 1969).

Spindles are first seen only during the first third of a period of quiet sleep, but then increase in duration and frequency of occurrence with further maturation. By approximately 3 to 6 months of age they may occur with equal power throughout a quiet sleep phase (Schulte and Bell, 1973). Thereafter, duration and incidence of spindles decline until they are again restricted to the beginning of a quiet sleep period (Lenard, 1970b). At this point, the stages of adult NREM sleep are clearly differentiated; spindles characteristic of stage 2 are present early in the sleep period while the large slow waves of stages 3 and 4 dominate later portions.

Tanguay and associates (1975) have reported that the percentage of time that sleep spindles are present in the EEG reaches a minimum at approximately 2 years of age, but then increases again in 4- to 5-year-olds. A similar disappearance and later reappearance of spindle activity has been reported in the kitten (Jouvet-Mounier et al., 1970). Spindles have also been reported to disappear during maturation of the sleep EEG in infant chimpanzees (Balzamo et al., 1972), but apparently do not reappear later in development since they are minimal in the adult chimpanzee (Bert et al., 1970).

Results of animal studies have indicated that cortical spindle activity is mediated primarily by lateral nuclei of the thalamus. These structures are also the thalamic relay nuclei of the somatosensory system, and transmission of somatosensory impulses through them has been observed to be inhibited during spindle generation. However, Lenard and Ohlsen (1972) have found no consistent differences in somatosensory evoked responses recorded from the scalp during presence or absence of spindle activity in 5- to 9-month-old human infants. To account for these findings, they have suggested that during infancy, spindle activity may either originate in the cortex itself, or may originate from several different thalamic generators rather than from a single generator in the somatosensory relay nuclei.

The spontaneous K-complex, a second waveform characteristic of stage 2 sleep in the adult, first appears in infants at approximately 5 to 6 months of age (Metcalf et al., 1971). This vertex-dominant pattern generally consists of an initial sharp surface-negative wave followed by a large slow positive wave, and is thought to be homologous to sensory evoked responses to external or interoceptive stimulation. In the adult, their occurrence appears, in part, to be related to events of the cardiac cycle, suggesting that some percentage of these apparently spontaneous waveforms may be evoked by receptors of the cardiovascular system (Fruhstorfer et al., 1971). Monod and Garma (1971) have reported that K-complexes may be observed in response to external stimuli in premature infants at approximately 32 to 34 weeks' post conception, but then become obscured with further development of EEG patterns.

At 5 to 6 months after birth, K-complexes are poorly formed and may be seen over large areas of the scalp, although they are larger and better differentiated at the vertex. Vertex-dominance gradually increases over the first 18 to 24 months of life. Metcalf et al. (1971), rating development of K-complexes with respect to four different criteria, report that after their first appearance, these waveforms show rapid changes in maturation until about 2 years of age, when development reaches a plateau. A second more gradual period of developmental change is seen beginning at approximately 5 years of age, which appears to coincide with the period of increasing spindle activity observed by Tanguay et al. (1975).

Until approximately 5 to 8 months after birth there is no specific EEG pattern associated with drowsiness. Instead, this state is characterized by a gradual increase in amplitude and slowing of activity (Dreyfus-Brisac and Curzi-Dascalova, 1975). By 8 months a specific pattern of high-amplitude regular 4-to-5-Hz theta activity is present in most infants during drowsiness (Schulte and Bell, 1973). This pattern, which is occasionally referred to as "hypnagogic hypersynchrony," is characteristic of the drowsy state until at least 2 to 3 years of age.

Throughout early development, EEG patterns for wakefulness and active sleep remain quite similar. The two states cannot be differentiated until approximately 36 weeks' conceptional age, when patterns associated with active sleep become slightly more rhythmic and regular (Parmelee et al., 1967a). Evidence reviewed by Dreyfus-Brisac and Curzi-Dascalova (1975) indicates that by 3 months after birth the precursor of alpha can be distinguished in the occipital regions during the waking state. This pattern consists of an irregular frequency of 3-to-4-Hz rather than the 8-to-12-Hz alpha seen in adults but, like the adult alpha rhythm, can be blocked by opening of the eyes. This rhythm increases in regularity and frequency to reach 6 to 8 Hz by 12 months of age.

RAPID EYE MOVEMENTS

REMs, which are infrequent in young pre-term infants during sleep, rapidly increase to a high level by term (Petre-Quadens et al., 1971). In the newborn, they are superimposed on slow rolling movements of the eyes, which precede the appearance of the first REMs by 2 to 4 min, and continue for several minutes after the REMs have disappeared (Prechtl and Lenard, 1967). This is not the case in adult subjects, although similar slow eye movements have been described in adults during sleep onset (Snyder and Scott, 1972).

It is generally agreed that REMs in the young infant do not reflect a simple random process, since nonsequential histograms of the intervals between eye movements show a higher incidence of short intervals than would be expected by chance (Prechtl and Lenard, 1967; Dittrichova et al., 1972). Although REMs in the neonate occur more frequently during some periods than others, they do not appear to show the "burst" pattern which is typical of adults. Interval histograms reported by Prechtl and Lenard (1967) for newborns and by Aserinsky (1971) for adults show similar maxima at inter-REM intervals of approximately 300 msec, but a second mode corresponding to the longer intervals between bursts is evident only in the adult histogram. Evidence reviewed by Lenard (1970a) indicates that the burst pattern is present by 3 to 4 months of age, although Petre-Quadens et al. (1971) have reported observing a burst pattern in neonates for REMs that occur late in a sleep period. In infants, as in adults, periods of dense REM activity are associated with increases in the rate and irregularity of respiration and heart rate (Prechtl and Lenard, 1967; Dittrichova et al., 1972; Spreng et al., 1968). Neither Prechtl and Lenard (1967) nor Petre-Quadens et al. (1971) found any differences between vertical and horizontal eye movements during early infancy.

With further maturation, the incidence of REMs occurring at intervals of less than 1 sec continues to increase until at least 5 to 6 months after term (Dittrichova et al., 1972), but results reported by Petre-Quadens et al. (1971) suggest that they may subsequently decline in older infants and young children. The duration of eye movement bursts reportedly increases between infancy and early childhood (Ornitz et al., 1971).

Ornitz and associates (Ornitz et al., 1967, 1969) have reported that auditory evoked responses recorded from the scalp are suppressed during bursts of eye movements in adults and children older than 19 months of age, but not in 6- to 12-month-old infants. They describe a function of evoked-response inhibition during REM bursts that develops toward the end of the 1st year of life and increases with further maturation. Differential effects of external stimuli on REMs have also been described for infants and older children. Ornitz et al., (1973) have reported that mild auditory and vestibular stimulation during sleep increases the amount of REM activity in children 3 to 10 years of age, while other evidence suggests that vestibular stimulation reduces REM activity in newborn infants. On the basis of evidence from animal studies indicating that eye movements, along with other phasic activity of REM sleep, are mediated by the vestibular nuclei in the brainstem, Ornitz and associates have suggested that these developmental differences may reflect a maturational increase in the role of the vestibular nuclei in the control of REM activity.

ELECTRODERMAL ACTIVITY

On their first appearance in young pre-term infants, spontaneous skin potential responses are not consistently related to a particular EEG pattern or to the occurrence of other measurable activity. However, by 31 to 36 weeks' conceptional age, they occur significantly more frequently in active than in quiet sleep, and are usually associated with the presence of REMs (Curzi-Dascalova et al., 1973). This is the reverse of the pattern seen in adult subjects, who show greater spontaneous electrodermal activity during NREM than REM states (Johnson and Lubin, 1966; Koumans et al., 1968).

Curzi-Dascalova and Dreyfus-Brisac (1976) have reported an abrupt increase in electrodermal responses in active sleep during the 1st month of life. Frequency of spontaneous skin potential responses during active sleep appears to stabilize at a level higher than that seen in adults during REM, and remains at that level for at least 6 months, the oldest group tested. The authors suggest that this high frequency of spontaneous activity may be attributable to the immaturity of descending inhibitory influences in young infants during active sleep. The frequency of spontaneous electrodermal responses in quiet sleep also increases during this period, but appears to be related to the appearance of EEG sleep spindles rather than to chronological age. With the development of spindle activity sometime during the 2nd month of life, response frequency in quiet sleep increases rapidly to exceed frequencies seen during active sleep, and approaches levels typical for NREM electrodermal "storms" in adults (Curzi-Dascalova and Dreyfus-Brisac, 1976).

In contrast to phasic skin potential responses, skin potential level apparently does not differentiate between sleep states. However, it is lower during sleep than during wakefulness in both newborn infants (Bell, 1970) and adults (Koumans et al., 1968).

RESPIRATION

According to Dreyfus-Brisac (1968), the respiration of very young pre-term infants shows a continuous semiregular pattern which does not change with variations in the amount of body activity. This is gradually replaced by less stable patterns in slightly older prematures, and by 30 weeks postconception the most common type of respiration is an irregular pattern characterized by unequal breath-to-breath intervals (Parmelee et al., 1972). Periodic respiration, a pattern in which respiratory episodes alternate with apneic episodes, is present approximately 25 % of the time in premature infants between 30 and 36 weeks' conceptional age, but gradually becomes less frequent with further maturation of respiratory control centers. Regular respiration, which is very rare in young pre-term infants, increases rapidly after 36 weeks' conceptional age to become one of the most reliable state criteria by term. Data reported by Parmelee et al. (1967a) indicate that while regular respiration is present during only 25% of quiet sleep at 36 weeks, it is present during 78% of quiet sleep and only 10% of active sleep by 40 weeks' conceptional age. Periodic respiration, which also occurs most frequently during quiet sleep after term, is seen only rarely after 7 weeks' postnatal age (Metcalf, 1970b).

The occurrence of apneic periods during sleep has recently become a topic of considerable interest due to evidence linking sleep apneas with instances of sudden infant death (e.g. Guilleminault et al., 1975), but no clear pattern of results has yet emerged. Schulte and associates (Gabriel et al., 1976; Schulte et al., 1977) have reported that periods of apnea lasting longer than 10 sec occur predominantly during active sleep in pre-term infants, and have attributed them to inhibitory influences known to act on spinal motoneurons, including respiratory motoneurons, during REM sleep. In contrast, Guilleminault et al. (1975) found that apneic episodes in prematures were more frequent during quiet and indeterminant sleep, while Parmelee et al. (1972) found apnea associated with no-eye-movement periods at 32 weeks postconception and with eye-movement periods at term. It is likely that these inconsistencies are at least partly attributable to the ambiguities of defining sleep states in young prematures.

HEART RATE

The course of maturation for heart rate activity is initially similar to that described for respiration. Heart rates are fixed and unvarying in previable prematures 24 to 27 weeks' conceptional age, and become more irregular as central control mechanisms develop (Dreyfus-Brisac, 1968). Prior to 30 weeks' conceptional age there are no differences in heart rate activity associated with different states. Watanabe et al. (1973a) have reported that the mature pattern begins to emerge after 30 weeks, with a marked increase in heart rate range during active sleep, accompanied by only slight increases in variability during quiet sleep and wakefulness. After term, heart rate variability decreases in both sleep states, but at different rates; variability during quiet sleep decreases to a stable level within the first month of life, while variability during active sleep decreases rapidly between 2 and 4 months and more slowly between 4 and 6 months of age. Variability during the waking state increases rapidly to a peak at 3 months and then subsequently declines. Heart rate levels are consistently higher during wakefulness than during sleep, but do not differ for quiet and active sleep states. (Harper et al., 1976).

The spectra for fluctuations in cardiac rate have also been found to differ for quiet and active sleep states in the young infant. DeHaan et al. (1977) have reported that the spectrum obtained during active sleep shows most power concentrated between 1 and 10 cycles/min with pronounced peaks at 1, 4, and 8 cycles/min. In contrast, quiet sleep has a broad, low spectrum over this range. DeHaan et al. note that oscillations in heart rate are in the same range as those reported for respiration, and speculate that the rate variations for both may have a common, possibly supramedullary, origin.

ELECTROMYOGRAM

In the adult, antigravity muscles in the vicinity of the chin show tonic levels of activity during NREM sleep, and a profound suppression of activity during REM. This pattern of EMG activity appears to be one of the most immature of state-specific patterns during early infancy. Petre-Quadens (1967) has reported that at 28 to 30 weeks' conceptional age, the chin EMG is characterized by a constant low-amplitude activity which shows no state-dependent variations. By approximately 33 weeks this is replaced by the adult EMG pattern, but suppression of EMG activity during active sleep occurs only rarely. The degree of EMG suppression during active sleep increases as the infant approaches term but, according to Petre-Quadens (1967), chin EMG activity does not consistently discriminate between states until approximately 7 months' postnatal age.

Organization of State Cycles

Information obtained from daily records kept by parents indicates that the young infant sleeps 16 to 17 h/day, with periods of sleep and wakefulness evenly distributed between day and night until approximately 4 weeks of age (Parmelee et al., 1964). Clear evidence of a diurnal cycle emerges by about 5 to 6 weeks of age as sleep becomes more concentrated during the night hours and wakefulness begins to increase during the day. The length of both sleep and waking periods increases, and although there is little variation in the total amount of sleep time during the first months of life, the length of periods of sustained sleep may double within the first 16 weeks (Parmelee et al., 1964). A diurnal pattern of sleep and wakefulness is clearly established by 12 to 16 weeks of age, with daytime sleep consolidated into well-defined naps (Parmelee and Stern, 1972). Day-night differences apparently develop independently for various physiological functions. Some, such as skin resistance level and body temperature, show evidence of diurnal cycles within the first weeks of life, while others, such as aspects of kidney function, do not show a mature diurnal pattern until approximately 2 years of age (Hellbrugge et al., 1964).

Development of the diurnal sleep-wakefulness cycle is also accompanied by developmental changes in organization within the sleep cycle. During the neonatal period, infants typically begin a sleep episode in active sleep and spend approximately equal amounts of time in each of the two stages of sleep, epochs of active and quiet sleep alternating with a period of approximately 50 to 60 min (Stern et al., 1969; Roffwarg et al., 1966; Monod and Pajot, 1965). By comparison, the adult pattern typically begins with an episode of NREM, which alternates with the REM stage at intervals of 90 to 110 min, a period nearly twice that seen in young infants (Globus, 1970; Sterman and Hoppenbrouwers, 1971). During the first weeks of life there is a rapid decrease in the amount of active sleep, accompanied by an increase in quiet sleep (Dittrichova, 1966; Stern et al., 1969; Emde and Walker, 1976). While at term, active and quiet sleep are of equal duration in a sleep cycle, by 3 months of age the duration of quiet sleep is approximately double that of active sleep. However, the duration of the state cycle remains unchanged during this period. In two studies examining both short and all-night sleep episodes, Parmelee and associates found that state-cycle duration, as measured either from one period of active sleep to the next or from one period of quiet sleep to the next, was consistently in the range of 40 to 60 min from 36 weeks' post conception to 8 months past term (Stern et al., 1969, 1973). Evidence compiled by Sterman (1972) suggests that the period of the state cycle does not reach adult values until late childhood or perhaps early adolescence.

The changeover from active sleep onset to the mature pattern of quiet or NREM sleep onset apparently occurs sometime during the first 6 months, but is very susceptible to disruption by aspects of the laboratory situation (Bernstein et al., 1973). In a longitudinal study of infant sleep patterns employing behavioral observations made in the home, Kligman et al. (1975) found a great deal of variability in this developmental changeover, with ages for quiet sleep onset ranging from 8 to 22 weeks. Until recently, it was thought that the neurochemical events occurring during NREM stages performed a "priming" function for the subsequent appearance of the REM state, and the occurrence of NREM at sleep onset was explained in terms of the specific neurochemical processes underlying the different stages of sleep (e.g., Jouvet, 1969). As a result, the changeover from active to quiet sleep onset in young infants was believed to represent a major reorganization of biochemical function during development. More recently, several studies have demonstrated that REM sleep onset may occur in adults when the 24-h sleep-wakefulness cycle is disrupted (e.g., Carskadon and Dement, 1975). These findings suggest that the developmental changeover to quiet sleep onset may be associated with maturation of the diurnal cycle rather than reorganization of the sleep cycle.

Within recent years there has been a trend toward viewing the ontogeny of state cycles not as the maturation of a single sleep-wakefulness cycle, but in terms of the developing interactions between two independent biological rhythms. This view, originally proposed by Kleitman (1963), and more recently by Sterman (Sterman, 1972; Sterman and Hoppenbrouwers, 1971) emphasizes the "basic rest-activity cycle" (BRAC), a biological rhythm proposed to be more fundamental than the sleep-wakefulness cycle. As applied to adults, the BRAC is manifest in the periodic recurrence of REM periods during sleep and in cycles of increased alertness or efficiency during wakefulness. There appears to be considerable evidence to support Kleitman's view, including reports of recurrent periods of REMs during a 24-h recording session (Othmer et al., 1969), periodic changes in amplitude and latency of cortical evoked potentials (Tanguay et al., 1973), and periodicities in performance on perceptual tasks (Globus et al., 1970; Lavie et al., 1974).

Other evidence suggests that the BRAC and sleep-wakefulness cycles develop independently during ontogeny. In a study of fetal activity recorded in utero from electrodes placed on the mothers' abdomens, Sterman and Hoppenbrouwers (1971) found that activity showed an irregular alternation of peaks and troughs with one significant periodicity of 80 to 110 min corresponding with maternal REM periods, and a second of 30 to 50 min attributed to the fetus. These rhythms were detectable by 21 weeks' gestation, well before sleep and wakefulness can be distinguished in pre-term infants. Further, the 24-h periodicity of the sleep-wakefulness cycle is well established within the first 6 months of life, while the BRAC does not become stabilized at adult values for several years (Sterman, 1972).

Both Kleitman (1963) and Sterman (1972) have argued that the cyclic alternations of active and quiet sleep seen in the newborn are those of the basic rest-activity cycle, and that states of sleep and wakefulness as we know them in the adult await the maturation of forebrain mechanisms sometime during the first 3 months of life. Kleitman (1963) distinguished two levels in the development of the waking state during infancy: wakefulness of necessity, mediated by subcortical mechanisms, and wakefulness of choice, requiring cortical function. He believed the newborn to be capable of only the first type, which occurs primarily as a result of discomfort or pain, and is terminated when the discomfort is removed. However, subsequent studies have indicated that "wakefulness of necessity" is not an adequate description of wakefulness in the newborn infant. The concept was originally questioned by Wolff (1966), who observed that periods of wakefulness were significantly longer immediately after a meal when discomfort due to hunger should be minimal. Gaensbauer and Emde (1973) have since demonstrated that the distribution of waking periods in the newborn infant is dependent upon the schedule of feeding. In a comparison of infants fed on demand and on a 4-h schedule, they found no differences in the total amount of time spent in various states, but demand-fed infants showed the largest amounts of wakefulness just prior to feeding, while schedule-fed infants showed large amounts of wakefulness after feeding as well as before. To insure that the periods of wakefulness seen in these infants were endogenous, Emde et al. (1975) also observed a group of neonates during a 10-h period immediately after birth when they were neither fed nor disturbed. All infants showed prolonged periods of wakefulness immediately after birth and subsequent periods of wakefulness interspersed between sleep periods despite the absence of external stimulation.

These results suggest that an intrinsic sleep-wakefulness cycle as well as the BRAC is present in the neonate, although these states bear little resemblance to waking and NREM states in the adult. It is generally agreed that in the mature organism, brain mechanisms responsible for the more primitive REM or basic rest-activity cycle are localized in the lower brainstem, while control of NREM sleep is mediated by both brainstem and forebrain mechanisms (e.g., McGinty, 1971). In the newborn, both the sleep-wakefulness cycle and the BRAC may be regulated at the brainstem level. The appearance of high-amplitude slow waves and spindles in the EEG of quiet sleep, waking "alpha" rhythms, and alteration of the waking state in ways that suggest increasing awareness of the environment during the first months of life presumably reflect a shift in the control of the sleep-wakefulness cycle to higher levels of the brain as thalamocortical systems in the forebrain mature.

Environmental Alteration of State Cycles

The characteristics of infant state cycles have stimulated considerable speculation on the function of various sleep states during development. The large amount of active sleep during infancy and its gradual decrease with age led Roffwarg et al. (1966) to propose that these periods of intense central activation may serve to facilitate neural development in the immature organism. In a similar vein, Berger (1969) proposed that the eye movements of active sleep may establish neuromuscular pathways necessary for binocularly coordinated eye movements during wakefulness. Others have suggested that the increased amounts of sleep seen in young infants may be attributable to the higher metabolic rate of immature organisms, or perhaps to the incomplete development of neural mechanisms mediating wakefulness (McGinty, 1971).

Anders and Roffwarg (1973) recently investigated the role of active sleep in the newborn by the technique of sleep deprivation. Results of similar studies in adults have shown that after selective deprivation of REM periods there is a marked "rebound" or elevation of REM time on recovery nights, suggesting a biological need for REM sleep (Dement,

1969). Anders and Roffwarg (1973) reasoned that if REM or active sleep serves a vital function during early development, the REM-rebound effect should be particularly strong in the newborn. Initially, they attempted to selectively disturb either active or quiet sleep in two groups of infants, but found it was impossible to selectively eliminate a single sleep stage. After awakening, infants, unlike adults, either returned to the same sleep stage or remained awake. In a second experiment, subjects were first observed during a baseline control period, then kept awake during a 4-h interfeeding period and observed again during an uninterrupted recovery period. Contrary to expectations, the results showed no evidence of a REM rebound after sleep deprivation. Instead, there was a significant reduction in the proportion of active sleep during the first 30-min epoch of the recovery period.

Other investigators have described a similar alteration of the state cycle after extended periods of wakefulness. Theorell et al. (1973) compared the distribution of various states in newborn infants on the 1st and 5th days after birth and found that infants spent considerably more time in waking states on the 1st day of life. The proportion of quiet sleep remained constant from the 1st to the 5th day but the amount of active sleep nearly doubled, suggesting that the increased wakefulness on day 1 was maintained at the expense of active sleep. Similarly, Monod and Pajot (1965) reported that the relative proportions of sleep in each cycle remained constant during the neonatal period unless more than 60 % of the cycle was spent in the waking state. In this case, the proportion of active sleep was reduced while quiet sleep was unchanged. Ashton (1971a) has also noted that the first epoch of active sleep following a feeding and its associated period of wakefulness is significantly reduced compared to subsequent active sleep periods. In contrast, epochs of quiet sleep remained essentially unchanged throughout periods of observation in excess of 2 h.

Results of two recent studies by Boismier and associates (Boismier, 1977; Boismier et al., 1974) show a similar effect but have been given a different interpretation. In a study of newborn infants, Boismier (1977) manipulated the amount of alert inactivity during an observation period by presenting stimuli that elicited varying amounts of visual fixation. Infants who did not attend to the stimuli were permitted to sleep. His results indicated that the amount of active sleep was significantly reduced for those stimulus conditions that elicited the longest periods of visual fixation. Since observations were terminated at the end of the first period of active sleep, effects of visual stimulation on quiet sleep and subsequent active sleep epochs could not be determined. Boismier, following Berger's (1969) eye-movement-coordination interpretation of REM sleep, has suggested that the amount of active sleep is regulated by the proportion of time spent in attentive observation of the environment. If so, it is an effect specific to young infants since studies manipulating the amount of visual observation in adult subjects have been unable to demonstrate any significant changes in the amount of REM (e.g., Horne and Walmsley, 1976; Allen et al., 1972).

A slightly different alteration of the sleep cycle in young infants has been reported for conditions that may be considered stressful. In two experiments, Emde and associates (1971) found a significant increase in the proportion of quiet sleep during a 10-h period following routine circumcision without anesthesia, while neither active sleep nor wakefulness were significantly affected. This increase in quiet sleep was reflected both in decreased latency to the first quiet sleep episode and in increased length of quiet sleep episodes. Emde et al. (1971) speculated that this may represent an adaptive "inhibiting" response to stressful stimulation in the newborn infant. Theorell et al. (1973) have also reported an increase in the proportion of quiet sleep, which they attribute to stress factors. In a comparison of infants whose umbilicals were clamped early (within 10 sec) and late (longer than 3 min), Theorell et al. found a higher percentage of quiet sleep in late-clamped infants on both the 1st and 5th days of life. They attribute this difference to the physiological stress of increased blood volume which may occur as a result of the pumping action of uterine contractions when cord clamping is delayed.

Although results of at least two studies suggest that factors that might be interpreted as stressful increase the proportion of quiet sleep in infants, clearly painful stimuli apparently do not. Anders and Chalemian (1974) also observed infant states following circumcision, but their procedures were acute and more traumatic than the circumcision procedures of Emde et al. (1971), which involved application of a chronic ligature. In contrast to Emde et al., who reported increased quiet sleep following circumcision, Anders and Chalemian found only a significant increase in wakefulness and crying during a 1-h observation period immediately following the procedure.

In summary, those studies that have demonstrated a significant elevation of quiet sleep over baseline or control levels in newborn infants have investigated factors that might be considered chronic stressors and that appear to be effective over extended periods of time. Emde et al. (1971) reported that the effects of their circumcision procedure gradually declined over the observation period, but were still evident after 10 h and Theorell et al. reported increased quiet sleep in late cord-clamped infants after 5 days. Both groups noted a slight but nonsignificant reduction in wakefulness in their subjects. Although the data are incomplete, the pattern of available evidence suggests that those factors that increase wakefulness temporarily but do not involve the presence of chronic stress or pain produce a reduction in active sleep which is probably evident only during the first state cycle of the recovery period. This type of trade-off involving wakefulness and the period of active sleep that follows, but not subsequent states or cycles, would be expected if the alternation between active and quiet sleep in the newborn were determined by the rhythm of the basic rest-activity cycle.

Studies of sleep organization in older infants have demonstrated an alteration of sleep patterns under laboratory conditions which appears similar to the "first night effect" widely reported in adult subjects (Agnew et al., 1966). In a study of 2- and 8-week-old infants, Sostek and Anders (1975) employed a videotape recorder to monitor sleep-waking behavior over a 24-h period, which included 12 h of polygraph recording. They found that both transportation to the laboratory and application of recording electrodes resulted in increased fussiness and crying in both age groups when compared to the final recovery period, but effects on sleep organization were only noted in the 8-week-olds. These infants reportedly showed a significantly reduced proportion of active sleep during the 12 h of polygraph recording, but since observations were expressed as percentages of total sleep time or total awake time, corresponding variations in wakefulness for specific state cycles could not be determined. These subjects also failed to show evidence of diurnal variations in the periods immediately following transportation to the laboratory and application of electrodes, although diurnal variation was present, at least in 8-week-olds, during subsequent periods (Sostek et al., 1976).

Bernstein et al. (1973) have reported a comparison of sleep patterns under home and laboratory conditions in 4-month-old infants. Like Sostek and Anders (1975), they found that the percentage of active sleep was reduced in a simulated laboratory environment compared to home naps. They also noted that both at home and in their simulated laboratory, long episodes of quiet sleep at sleep onset were infrequent, occurring only in infants who had been crying for extended periods before the nap. However, in two separate longitudinal studies in which sleep states were recorded polygraphically (Kligman et al., 1975), 10 of 12 and 9 of 14 infants showed consistent quiet sleep onset beginning at 7 to 9 weeks of age. In a recent study of EEG power spectra during quiet sleep, Sterman and associates (1977) observed an increase in slow-wave activity during the first sleep epoch of the night in 2- to 4-month-old infants which was not present in younger or older infants. They have suggested that since the period between 2 and 4 months of age represents a transitional period between the more primitive organization of states seen in the newborn and the establishment of mature patterns of sleep and wakefulness, it may be a period in which state patterns are uniquely vulnerable to effects of mild stress or to disruptive effects of laboratory recording procedures on the infant's normal routine.

Arousal Thresholds and Behavioral Responsivity

In adult subjects, thresholds for arousal from different stages of sleep have been found to vary with a number of factors, including time of night, meaningfulness of stimuli, the response index employed, and the particular method used for threshold determination (Snyder and Scott, 1972). As a result, numerous inconsistencies exist in the literature. For neutral stimuli such as tones, clicks, or flashes, thresholds are typically found to be lowest immediately after sleep onset (descending stage 1) and to increase with increasing stages of NREM. Thresholds during REM sleep may be either lower or no different than thresholds during NREM, depending on the response measure. In general, those studies using EEG criteria of awakening have reported no differences between sleep stages, while those requiring a voluntary motor or verbal response from the subject have found higher thresholds during NREM, especially stages 3 and 4 (Keefe et al., 1971; Langford et al., 1974; Rechtschaffen et al., 1966). Measures of autonomic activity also show no consistent pattern during sleep. Both the threshold and the magnitude of autonomic responses vary depending upon the sleep stage and the particular response system. While thresholds for cardiovascular responses during sleep are well below arousal threshold, skin potential, skin resistance, and motor responses are seen only on awakening (Keefe et al., 1971).

Few studies of arousal thresholds have been reported in the infant, but those that do exist suggest that infant thresholds, like those of the adult, may be determined by a complex of factors. Petre-Quadens (1966) classified infant sleep into four categories rather than two and labeled them according to "depth of sleep" as determined by threshold of response to auditory and tactile stimulation. She reported that infants, like adults, were most sensitive immediately after sleep onset; thresholds were lowest during epochs of active sleep which followed periods of waking. The highest thresholds were obtained during epochs of active sleep which followed periods of quiet sleep, with quiet sleep showing intermediate threshold levels.

Several studies employing only tactile stimuli have failed to find differences in behavioral response thresholds for the two sleep stages. Schmidt and Birns (1971), using a cold thermal stimulus applied to the abdomen of 2- to 5-day-old infants, did not report thresholds for the first post-feeding period of active sleep, but did find that thresholds for behavioral arousal were lower during the first period of quiet sleep than during the second. Thresholds were slightly higher for later epochs of active sleep than for quiet sleep, but this difference was not significant. Similarly, Yang and Douthitt (1974) found no differences in thresholds for behavioral response to an airpuff delivered to the abdomen of newborns during active and quiet sleep. In addition, there were no differences in the magnitude of heart rate responses elicited by stimuli of threshold intensity in the two sleep stages. Stimuli below behavioral response threshold were also ineffective in evoking heart rate responses, suggesting that in the newborn, heart rate and behavioral response thresholds for tactile stimulation may be similar. More recently, Rose et al. (1978) compared responsivity in active and quiet sleep for a graded series of tactile stimuli. In agreement with previous studies, they found no significant differences between states in the first cycle after feeding for either heart rate or behavioral responsivity. During the second state cycle the stimuli elicited no behavioral responses in either state, but a significant heart rate acceleration was present in response to the strongest stimulus during quiet sleep.

Although the results of studies employing tactile stimulation are quite consistent in showing little or no difference in responsivity between active and quiet sleep, differences between sleep states have been reported for stimuli in other modalities. Murray and Campbell (1970) employed amyl acetate as an olfactory stimulus and determined the minimum concentration effective in eliciting a behavioral or respiratory change. Their results showed that thresholds were significantly higher during quiet sleep than active sleep. However, sleep stage was a between-subjects variable in their experimental design, and each subject was tested the first time he reached the desired state after a feeding. Since infants begin a sleep period in active sleep and proceed to quiet sleep, the separate effects of sleep stage and time from sleep onset cannot be distinguished in this experiment.

Several studies have reported state-related differences in responsivity to auditory stimulation. Goldie and VanVelzer (1965) determined thresholds for behavioral response to auditory stimuli and found that they were lower during active sleep than quiet sleep. Hutt et al. (1968b) recorded EMG responses during active and quiet sleep for both sine and square wave stimuli of several different frequencies and found higher probabilities of response during active sleep for all stimuli except a 70-Hz square wave tone which did not elicit differential responding in the two states. However, a reanalysis of their data using signal detection theory (Weir, 1976) failed to support this conclusion, suggesting that the findings may be due to differences in spontaneous response levels in the two stages of sleep.

In an extensive study of responses to click stimuli in premature infants from 30 to 39 weeks' conceptional age, Monod and Garma (1971) found significant differences for both motor and EEG reactivity in the two stages of sleep. Motor responsivity was greater in active sleep while indices of EEG reactivity were greater during quiet sleep. These differences first appeared at approximately 34 weeks' conceptional age when the number of click-elicited behavioral responses began to gradually decline during quiet sleep while frequency of responses during active sleep remained unchanged. Click-elicited K-complexes decreased with age during both active and quiet sleep, presumably obscured by developing background EEG patterns, but were always more frequent during quiet sleep. This pattern of results is very similar to those reported in adult subjects and suggests that differences in behavioral arousal thresholds in the newborn as well as in the adult do not reflect differences in sensory thresholds, but rather state-specific influences on effector systems.

Wolff (1966) reached essentially the same conclusions after observing differences in the types of behavioral responses most frequently elicited during active and quiet sleep. He noted that for a given type of response, elicited frequency closely paralleled its spontaneous frequency in the various states, startles being more frequent during quiet sleep while facial twitches and smiling responses were more frequent during active sleep. Estimates of responsivity therefore appear to be dependent upon the extent to which a given stimulus is adequate for evoking the predominant responses in each state. Auditory stimuli, at least at low to moderate intensities, seem to be less effective in evoking behavioral responses during quiet sleep than active sleep. However, the work of Ashton (1971b, 1973b) suggests that this may not be the case for higher intensity stimuli. Ashton (1973b) recorded behavioral and heart rate responses to 75-dB square wave tones for two state cycles following a feeding. In agreement with previous results, he found that the percentage of motor responses was largest during the initial epoch of active sleep and that responsivity during the second period of active sleep was still greater than either the first or second periods of quiet sleep. While only 10% of responses recorded during active sleep were startles, approximately 70% of those recorded during quiet sleep met the criteria for startle responses. When the tones were a more intense 85 dB (Ashton, 1971b), there were no significant state-related differences in responsivity.

MATURATION OF SENSORY SYSTEMS

One of the major generalizations derived from neuroanatomical studies of brain maturation is that during the course of development, peripheral structures tend to exhibit greater maturity than more central structures of the brain. The course of maturation of sensory systems in the human infant illustrates this principle quite well. Evidence recently reviewed by Hecox (1975) indicates that the structural features of the inner ear are well developed by term. Differentiation of receptor cells appears to be for the most part complete, with the possible exception of a small area in the basal (high-frequency) region of the cochlea and a portion of the outermost row of hair cells. The auditory nerve and lower brainstem pathways of the auditory system are reported to be well myelinated, inferior colliculus and medial geniculate are less so, and auditory cortex is quite immature. Similar conclusions obtain for the visual system in the newborn. Although there is some disagreement concerning the maturity of receptors in the retina, myelination of the optic nerve and brainstem structures of the visual system is well advanced compared to myelination of cortical projection fibers.

Within the cortex, development is most advanced in primary sensory areas, with the single exception of motor cortex, which exhibits greater maturity at all stages of development. Of the major sensory areas, primary somatosensory cortex is most mature, followed by primary visual and auditory projection areas. There appears to be no further increase in the number of neural cells after birth, but histological changes such as increasing fiber diameters, axon lengths, and dendritic branching continue well into childhood (Conel, 1952).

Electrophysiological data, where they are available, are in good agreement with the pattern of neurological maturation, showing greater maturity of response at lower levels of the nervous system. The neonatal electroretinogram (ERG), recorded from the retina in response to light, appears very similar to that of the adult. Several studies have reported comparable waveforms and only slight differences in latencies of components of ERGs recorded from adult and infant subjects, the major difference being reduced amplitude of response in newborns (Barnet et al., 1965; Fogarty and Reuben, 1969; Lodge et al., 1969). When light intensity is sufficiently high, ERGs recorded from both full-term newborns and premature infants accurately follow stimulus rates as high as 72 flashes/sec, the critical flicker fusion frequency of the adult ERG (Horsten and Winkelman, 1962,

1964). In contrast, responses recorded from visual cortex show extreme "fatigability" in infants as compared to adult subjects. Ellingson (1967) has reported that in some infants, especially prematures, intervals between stimuli must be as long as 4 to 5 sec before a response to each flash can be observed.

A methodology permitting examination of auditory responses in human infants at lower levels of the nervous system has been developed only within the past few years. These responses are recorded from the scalp at the vertex as a sequence of six waves occurring within the first 10 msec following stimulation (Jewett et al., 1970). Like the cortical evoked potential, they are obtained by averaging the time-locked EEG activity for a large number of stimulus presentations. Recent studies in the cat (Buchwald and Huang, 1975) and in human patients with brainstem lesions (Starr and Hamilton, 1976) have confirmed that this series of waves reflects activity generated at successive points in the auditory pathway ranging from the eighth nerve to inferior colliculus.

In newborns and young infants, the most prominent components of this brainstem-evoked response (BSER) are waves I and V, believed to represent activity in the auditory nerve and inferior colliculus, respectively (Salamy and McKean, 1976; Salamy et al., 1975). Salamy and associates have argued that the latency of wave I represents an index of peripheral transmission, and that the time between waves I and V can be interpreted as an index of central transmission through the brainstem. In tracing developmental changes in the response, they have reported differential rates of maturation for these two measures. While peripheral transmission decreases to adult levels by 6 weeks of age, central transmission through the brainstem appears to show three distinct maturational stages and does not reach adult values until approximately 1 year of age.

Rapid changes in the waveform of the BSER also occur during the period of early infancy. To some extent, these changes appear to be dependent on the parameters of stimulation. Salamy and McKean (1976), presenting click stimuli at the rate of 15 per sec, have reported differentiation of waves II and III by 6 weeks of age, but did not obtain the adult six-wave pattern until 3 months. When stimuli were presented at the slower rate of 5 per sec, a more mature response could be recorded in 6-week-old infants (Salamy et al., 1975). By comparison, adult subjects run under similar conditions showed no loss in response resolution at rates as high as 30 clicks/sec. As Salamy et al. (1975) have noted, this difference suggests that mechanisms involved in recovery processes in brainstem structures are still quite immature at 6 weeks of age.

Cortical Evoked Responses

In the adult, the evoked response to sensory stimuli recorded from the scalp consists of a complex sequence of waves of alternating positive and negative polarities. Since all but extremely large potentials are obscured by spontaneous EEG activity, the response to a single stimulus presentation can rarely be observed. It is therefore necessary to extract the waveform or "signal" from the background "noise" by averaging a number of responses together. With sufficient averaging, activity time-locked to the stimulus summates to a characteristic waveform while the random background EEG approaches zero. This technique has been used extensively for visual, auditory, and somatosensory responses, but evoked responses to olfactory and gustatory stimuli have not been recorded because of the difficulty in time-locking stimulus presentations.

Two categories of cortical evoked response components have traditionally been distinguished in the adult literature. Waves with peak latencies longer than approximately 100 msec are typically referred to as ''late components.'' These waves are generally similar for all three major stimulus modalities and can be recorded from wide areas of the scalp with a maximum amplitude near the vertex. The second category includes waves with latencies shorter than 100 msec. For visual and somatosensory evoked responses, these short-latency or ''early components'' are largest over their corresponding cortical projection areas in the occipital and contralateral parietal regions. The primary projection area for auditory stimuli, buried within the sylvian fissure in the temporal lobe, has proved to be inaccessible to scalp recording, and no early components have been recorded from the temporal region. However, with more extensive averaging, they may be recorded from the vertex (Mendel and Goldstein, 1969; Picton et al., 1974). It is generally conceded that early components of the evoked response represent activity generated in primary sensory cortex, but the origin of late components remains a matter of controversy (Arezzo et al., 1975; Lieb and Karmel, 1974; Goff et al., 1977; Picton et al., 1974).

When Ellingson (1967) reviewed the existing literature on maturation of sensory evoked responses several years ago, only responses to visual stimulation had been investigated to any extent. There were few available studies of auditory evoked responses, and no reports of responses to somatosensory stimulation in human infants. In summarizing this literature, Ellingson concluded that during infancy, the visual evoked response was of simpler waveform, longer latency, more fatigable, and topographically less widespread than in the adult. Since then, evoked responses in all three major modalities have been studied extensively during the period of early infancy, and it appears that Ellingson's conclusions may be generalized to auditory and somesthetic modalities as well.

Waveform

The early ontogenesis of cortical evoked responses in human infants is much the same as that described for other mammalian species. The first response that can be recorded from the scalp is a long-latency surface-negative wave. With further maturation, a shorter latency surface-positive or biphasic wave appears and the two components merge to form a more complex waveform. (e.g. Rose and Ellingson, 1970). In human infants, the long-latency surface-negative wave can be recorded in response to stimuli in all three major modalities sometime before 25 weeks' post-conception (Hrbek et al., 1973; Weitzman and Graziani, 1968). For visual and somatosensory stimuli, this component is largest and most distinct over the corresponding projection areas, but is present in adjacent regions as well.

In keeping with the more rapid neuroanatomical maturation of primary somatosensory cortex, the somatosensory evoked response (SER) appears to develop more rapidly than responses in other modalities. By 29 weeks' conceptional age, an initial negative-positive complex can be identified in responses recorded from primary somatosensory cortex contralateral to the stimulated area, and the large negative wave begins to gradually decrease in amplitude and duration (Fig. 9-2). These short-latency components are somatotopically represented, showing topographic distributions which vary with the site of stimulation (Vaughan, 1975). Longer latency components, which are initially largest over the contralateral hemisphere, increase in amplitude at the vertex and ipsilateral sites to become as large as contralateral responses by approximately 37 weeks' gestation. However, even at term, the short-latency components are rarely present over the ipsilateral projection area (Hrbek et al., 1968, 1969). Evidence from studies in adult patients suggests that the early components of the SER may be conducted from the contralateral to

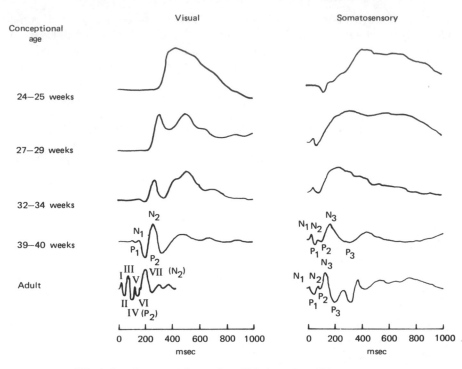

[The infant data are redrawn from Hrbek et al., 1973.]

Figure 9-2. Cortical responses evoked by visual and somatosensory stimuli in pre-term infants, full-term newborns, and adults. Derivations are bipolar; Oz–Pz for the visual response, C–F contralateral to the stimulated limb for the somatosensory response. Surface negativity is plotted upwards.

the ipsilateral projection area via an interhemispheric pathway (Halliday, 1975). The inconstancy of these short-latency components in the ipsilateral projection area of the newborn may therefore reflect the greater immaturity of horizontal as compared to vertical fiber tracts at this stage of development (Conel, 1952). In any case, it appears to be consistent with results of studies of spontaneous EEG activity, which have also indicated that interhemispheric linkages are poor in the newborn infant (Joseph et al., 1976).

During early infancy, the short-latency negative wave $(N_1)^2$, which is very prominent in the newborn, gradually decreases in size, and additional components appear. The waveform typical of the adult response is present by approximately 2 to 4 months' postnatal age, although maturation of the longer latency waves continues into early childhood (Laget et al., 1976). The prominent initial negative component of the newborn SER is also characteristic of the response in other immature mammals. However, in other species this early negative wave rapidly decreases and disappears, while in humans it persists in the adult with reduced amplitude and duration. Desmedt et al. (1976) have traced this progressive decrease in the duration of the initial negative component and note that it occurs very slowly; its time course could be fit by a negative power function, with the most rapid changes occurring within the 1st year of life, but adult values were not yet attained by 8 years of age.

Maturation of the visual evoked response (VER) follows a similar sequence of developmental changes, but its development proceeds more slowly and gradually than that of the response to somatosensory stimulation (Hrbek et al., 1973). The long-latency negative wave first seen over posterior regions of the scalp in very young pre-term infants gradually differentiates into two distinct negative components over a period of several weeks (Fig. 9-2). Sometime between 32 and 35 weeks' conceptional age, a positive wave localized to the occipital area develops to form the initial component of the response (Hrbek et al., 1973; Watanabe et al., 1972, 1973b; Umezaki and Morrell, 1970). This positive wave (P_2) gradually increases in amplitude, and is the most consistent component of the VER during the neonatal period (Ellingson, 1970). By term, shorter latency components may be present in some subjects, but there is considerable variability in the waveform of the VER throughout early infancy (Ellingson, 1970; Ferriss et al., 1967). With increasing maturation, later components of the response become more widely distributed and can be recorded from more anterior areas of the scalp, including the vertex (Umezaki and Morrell, 1970; Ellingson, 1967). Latencies of components decrease, additional components develop, and by approximately 2 months of age, the VER waveform is similar to that seen in the adult (Ferriss et al., 1967).

In the kitten, the early-developing surface-positive and long-latency negative waves have been attributed to what have been described as two independent visual systems: a direct classical visual pathway involving the lateral geniculate and primary visual cortex, and a second indirect pathway involving the superior colliculus and perhaps also the reticular formation, which projects to more widespread regions of the cortex (Rose and Ellingson, 1970; Rose, 1971). Rose and Lindsley (1965) were able to selectively eliminate the short-latency response by lesions of the lateral geniculate nucleus, and the long-latency negative wave by lesions of the superior colliculus. Considerable evidence suggests that the second visual system associated with the long-latency negativity is involved in the mediation of visually guided and attentional aspects of behavior in other mammalian species (Rose and Ellingson, 1970; Schneider, 1969), and Bronson (1974) has recently suggested that it may mediate a large portion, if not all, visual behaviors exhibited by human infants during the 1st month of life. Similar anatomical and functional distinctions can probably be made for mechanisms underlying early and late components of responses in other stimulus modalities as well. Velasco and associates (Velasco et al., 1975; Velasco and Velasco, 1975) have recently reported that lesions that selectively reduce or eliminate late components of the somatosensory-evoked response in human patients also produce a curious form of neglect or "inattention" to the contralateral limbs.

One of the unique characteristics of the VER during infancy is its extreme variability. This variability is seen in measures of latency and amplitude as well as in waveform, and appears to be unrelated to phase of the sleep-wakefulness cycle or to processes such as fatigue, sensitization, or habituation (Ellingson, 1970). Although evoked responses are in general less stable in young infants than in older subjects, variability appears to be considerably greater for the VER than for responses in other stimulus modalities. Ellingson et al. (1973, 1974) have computed test-retest reliabilities for latency and amplitude of the major components of both visual and auditory evoked responses during the newborn period. They reported that while 92% of these correlations were significant for the auditory modality, only 40% were significant for the visual response. Although the VER in adult subjects is reliable across days, homogeneous in the occipital area, and shows consistent variations associated with the sleep-wakefulness cycle, this was not the case for VERs recorded from either newborns or 3-month-old infants. Further, the 3-month-olds were not different from the neonates for any of these measures, suggesting that there is no significant decrease in VER variability during the first months of life (Ellingson et al., 1973). No data are available on variability of the VER in older infants, but the results of Dustman and Beck (1969) suggest that considerable stability of the visual response is attained by at least 3 years of age.

Auditory evoked responses (AER), unlike those of other major sensory modalities, do not exhibit a focus over auditory projection areas within the temporal lobe. In young prematures 25 to 28 weeks' conceptional age, the long-latency negative wave, which is the major component of the response, is largest over posterior and lateral regions of the scalp (Weitzman and Graziani, 1968). In some cases, this component may be followed by a slow positive wave with a latency ranging from 700 to 900 msec (Fig. 9-3). By 35 to 37 weeks, responses recorded from the vertex become clearly larger and more complex than those recorded from other regions, and the late positive wave (P_2) becomes progressively more prominent than the earlier negative wave (N_1) at this site. The pattern typical of the full-term newborn is for the most part attained by 37 to 38 weeks' post-conception, with the appearance of a small initial positive wave (P_1) and a longer latency negative wave (N_2) (Weitzman and Graziani, 1968).

During the first few postnatal weeks, the large surface negative wave seen in young prematures continues to decrease in amplitude, and later components become progressively larger. The adult waveform is achieved sometime between 3 to 6 months of age when a late positive wave (P_3) appears and rapidly increases in prominence to become a major component of the response (Ohlrich and Barnet, 1972; Barnet et al., 1975). Barnet and associates have suggested that the development of this late positive wave may reflect the development of higher cortical function since it is sensitive to probabilities of events and complex perceptual decision processes in adult subjects (e.g., Picton and Hillyard, 1974), and is reportedly absent or ill-defined in 6- and 12-month-old infants with Down's syndrome (Barnet et al., 1971).

Since responses evoked by auditory stimulation are largest and most distinct at the vertex rather than over auditory cortex, their origin has been a topic for considerable speculation. Due to the similarity of vertex responses evoked by stimuli in different sensory modalities, the vertex potential has frequently been interpreted as a diffuse, nonspecific response mediated by pathways that are interrelated, if not partially common, for all types of stimuli. In the adult literature, both nonspecific (e.g., Fruhstorfer, 1971; Davis et al., 1972) and specific (e.g., Lehtonen, 1973; Arezzo et al., 1975) characteristics of the response have been described. In newborn infants, Hrbek et al. (1969) have reported evidence for some degree of specificity in vertex responses evoked by visual stimulation. They found that while vertex potentials evoked by auditory and somatosensory stimuli were nearly identical in waveform and showed similar variations with states of sleep and wakefulness, visual vertex responses were clearly different for both these characteristics.

Activity specific to the auditory pathway, including primary auditory cortex, apparently can be observed in shorter latency components recorded from the vertex with more extensive averaging (Mendel and Goldstein, 1969; Picton et al., 1974). These early components are reportedly less stable in the newborn than the longer latency vertex waves. Engel (1971) was able to detect a short-latency response in only 8 of 24 neonates tested, and in the majority of these cases it could not be reproduced. In contrast, the larger late components of the vertex response could be reliably obtained from all infants.

AEPs: PREMATURE TO 3 YRS.

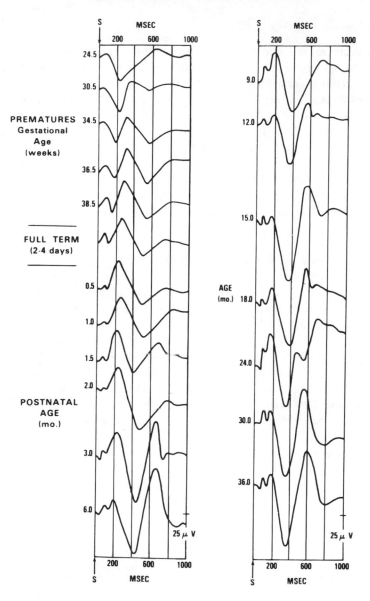

[From Barnet et al., 1975]

Figure 9-3. Schematic representation of the auditory-evoked response (AEP) recorded from the vertex, demonstrating the maturation of the response from the premature period through 3 years of age. Note that positivity at the vertex is represented by an upward deflection.

Latency

An orderly decrease in the latency of cortical evoked responses with age has been well documented for all three major stimulus modalities. In premature infants, this decrease in latency is essentially linear for prominent components of the response after 30 weeks' gestation (Hrbek et al., 1973; Weitzman and Graziani, 1968). Exceptionally long latencies have been reported in infants younger than 30 weeks, but these are observed only during the first few days after birth and have been attributed to factors such as difficulty in adapting to the extrauterine environment rather than to developmental level (Hrbek et al., 1973). During the first few weeks of life, significant negative correlations have been obtained between evoked-response latency and post-conceptional age, but not post-natal age, suggesting that extrauterine experience does not noticeably alter the course of response maturation (Umezaki and Morrell, 1970; Hrbek et al., 1973).

In describing developmental changes in the latency of P_2, the major component of the VER in young infants, Ellingson (1967) has reported a double-limbed function (Fig. 9-4) consisting of a period of rapid decrease between 1 and 2 months of age, followed by more gradual reductions in latency until adult values are reached at approximately 18 to 24 months of age (Ellingson et al., 1973). Comparable data for both auditory and somatosensory evoked responses indicate that, for these modalities as well, the decrease in latency is negatively accelerated, with the most rapid changes occurring early in infancy. Barnet et al. (1975) have reported that AER latencies decrease as a negative exponential function of age over the period from birth to 3 years (Fig. 9-5), and Desmedt et al. (1976) have described a similar function for early components of the SER from birth to 8 years of age after increases in conduction time associated with increasing body length are accounted for. However, in both cases the period of early infancy has not been examined in sufficient detail to determine if the double-limbed function described by

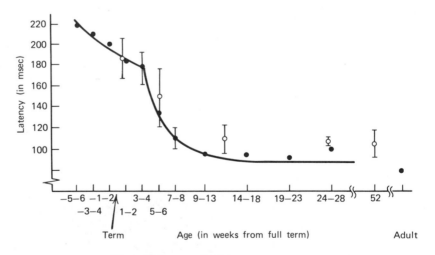

[From Ellingson, 1967.]

Figure 9-4.   Latency of the major positive component of the visual-evoked response as a function of age in weeks from full term. The solid and open dots represent data from two different experiments. The vertical lines passing through the open dots signify ± 1 SD for a group of 21 subjects.

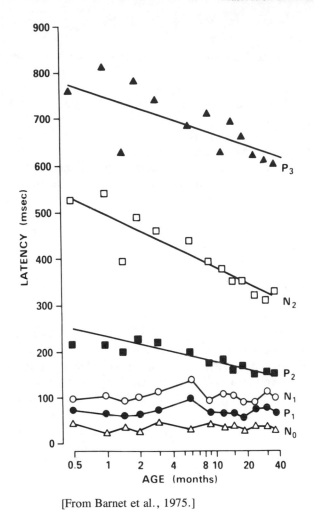

[From Barnet et al., 1975.]

Figure 9-5. Mean latencies of components N_0, P_1, P_2, *and* P_3 *of the AER with respect to logarithm$_{10}$ age. Regression lines are drawn from those components that varied significantly with age.*

Ellingson (1967) for visual responses is also characteristic of evoked-response maturation in other modalities.

Barnet et al. (1975) have also reported differences in the rates at which various components of the auditory response mature. They found no significant decrease in the latencies of earlier components from birth to 3 years of age, while the later components P_2, N_2, and P_3 showed significant decreases which also differed significantly in rate. As the authors have noted, this suggests that the neural substrates underlying the various components are to some extent independent. Systematic comparisons of rates of decrease among various response components have not been reported for other modalities, but slight differences in slope are evident in figures illustrating age changes in the latencies of various waves of the visual response (e.g., Watanabe et al., 1972; Umezaki and Morrell, 1970). Here again, the largest and most rapid changes are seen in longer latency components of the response.

Amplitude

Amplitudes of cortical evoked responses are typically larger in prematures than in full-term newborns, and larger in young than in older pre-term infants (Umezaki and Morrell, 1970; Hrbek et al., 1973). After approximately 30 weeks' conceptional age there is a gradual reduction in response amplitude, presumably due to the development of more complex patterns of cortical activity which generate fields of opposing polarity (Vaughan, 1975). Amplitude then increases again after term (Ferriss et al., 1967; Barnet et al., 1975). For auditory responses, Barnet et al. (1975) have reported that this increase is considerably larger for longer latency components, and continues until at least 3 years of age, the oldest group tested. Dustman and Beck (1969) have described a similar increase in amplitude of the VER, which is also most notable for longer latency portions of the response. They report that VER amplitude first increases until 6 years of age and then subsequently declines. The net result is that amplitude of the adult response is approximately the same as that seen in the newborn.

State-Dependent Variations

In contrast to visual responses, which show no consistent variations associated with sleep and waking states in young infants (Ellingson et al., 1973), auditory and somatosensory potentials do exhibit reliable state-dependent changes. In the newborn, these are generally equivalent to state-dependent changes observed in the adult for later components of the response; amplitudes are higher and latencies are longer during quiet sleep than during active sleep and wakefulness (e.g., Hrbek et al., 1969; Weitzman et al., 1965; Ellingson et al., 1974; Akiyama et al., 1969; Desmedt and Manil, 1970). Early components, which are relatively unaffected by state changes in adult subjects, have been found in the newborn to be either weaker and more variable, or reduced in duration during active sleep for auditory responses (Ellingson et al., 1974) and for somatosensory responses evoked by electrical stimulation of the fingers (Desmedt and Manil, 1970; Desmedt and Debecker, 1972). An interesting exception is the report by Hrbek et al. (1968, 1969) that early components of the newborn SER evoked by tapping a muscle or tendon are enhanced rather than reduced during active sleep. An explanation for this difference has yet to be proposed, but it is probably related to differences in the pattern of afferent input resulting from the two kinds of stimulation (Larsson and Prevec, 1970).

Other exceptions have been reported in premature infants for both auditory (Akiyama et al., 1969) and visual (Watanabe et al., 1973b) evoked responses. In both instances, long-latency waves were found to be significantly larger during active sleep than quiet sleep, a reversal of the pattern characteristic of the full-term newborn. Akiyama et al. (1969) have attributed this reversal to differences in the background EEG associated with the two states since the continuous slow waves of active sleep are larger, and the "flat" periods of the tracé alternant pattern of quiet sleep are longer in prematures than in full-term infants (e.g., Parmelee et al., 1967a). Similar correlations between amplitude of evoked responses and amplitude of background activity have been described in older subjects, and appear to be due to the presence of "unaveraged" EEG in the response. Tanguay and Ornitz (1972) have reported that these correlations could be reduced to nonsignificant levels by increasing the number of responses contributing to each averaged waveform.

With more extensive averaging, state-dependent response variations in pre-term infants are not determined by the amplitude of background EEG, and appear to be the same as those seen in older infants and adults. Graziani and associates (1974) have recently examined amplitude and latency of the AER in prematures for six categories of EEG patterns and found that high amplitudes and longer latencies were associated with intermittent EEG patterns, which are the precursors of quiet sleep, while low amplitudes and short latencies occurred most frequently during the high-amplitude continuous patterns characteristic of active sleep. These relationships increased with conceptional age and were significant primarily for infants older than 34 weeks' post-conception.

ASSESSMENT OF SENSORY FUNCTION

Probably the greatest source of information about sensory and perceptual capabilities in infants has been from recordings of physiological responding. A complete review of this evidence is beyond the scope of this chapter but representative research concerning sensory functioning in the auditory and visual modalities will be outlined in this section.

Auditory Capacity

In general, the same kinds of questions have been asked about the infant's auditory capacity as the adult's: To what aspects of the stimulus are infants sensitive? Possibly the most fundamental aspect of stimulation is the smallest stimulus intensity that will elicit a response—that is, the threshold of responsivity. However, it has become increasingly obvious that for infants as well as adults, variations in stimulus frequency and bandwidth (the range of frequencies within a given complex stimulus) interact with intensity in important ways to determine responsivity.

Intensity Thresholds

The majority of work with infants attempting to determine the lowest intensity that would elicit a response has employed neonates. Such threshold determinations should not be seen as necessarily assessing the lowest intensity that may be perceived, nor can this be assumed for the more traditional behaviorally determined "thresholds" in older subjects. All measures of sensitivity must be qualified both in terms of the type of response recorded and the manner in which the response is measured. The important question is the extent to which any measure of responsivity relates to the functioning of the sensory system, a question largely unanswered for infants. However, since behaviorally determined thresholds in adults are related to auditory system functioning, most studies of infant physiological response thresholds relate their data to known adult behavioral thresholds.

A great deal of information has been obtained from recordings of evoked brain potentials. Barnet and Goodwin (1965) presented 2- to 4-day-old sleeping neonates with a series of clicks at intensities ranging from 35 to 65 dB above adult behavioral thresholds. An identifiable response was reported in all subjects at 45 dB and in about 75% at 35 dB. Engel and Young (1969) found even lower thresholds when sleeping neonates were tested with brief tone pips ranging from 500 to 8000 Hz in octave steps. The lowest intensity eliciting an identifiable response averaged 5 to 18 dB above adult behavioral thresholds. Taguchi et al. (1969) also used tone bursts but did not report thresholds as low as Engel and Young. They found that thresholds were a function of both age and sleep state of the neonate, but infants 4 to 12 days old tested during quiet sleep had the lowest thresholds, about 30 dB above adult behavioral levels. The threshold values of 35 to 40 dB, which Taguchi et al. report for 2- to 4-day-olds, agree quite well with Barnet and Goodwin's (1965) click data for the infants of this age.

An especially striking finding in the results of Taguchi et al. was a marked drop in threshold over the first few days of life, which closely paralleled the apparent changes in middle-ear efficiency during this period. It has been repeatedly suggested that newborns may have a hearing loss as high as 30 to 40 dB as a result of mesenchymal tissue retained in the middle ear. Taguchi et al. tested for such a conductive hearing loss by comparing threshold differences in responses evoked by stimuli presented in the normal manner (air conduction) and those obtained when the same stimuli were presented by bone conduction, a procedure that allows stimuli to bypass the middle ear. When the data are averaged over the three frequencies used, thresholds for stimuli presented by air conduction show a drop of about 16 dB over the early days of life (Fig. 9-6). However, when the difference in thresholds between air and bone conduction, representing the portion attributable to the middle ear, are subtracted from the air-conduction thresholds, the resulting threshold curve shows little change with age. These data strongly argue that early elevations of threshold are largely peripheral rather than neural in origin and that such conductive losses rapidly diminish.

A few studies have examined evoked-potential thresholds in older infants. Onishi and Davis (1969) longitudinally tested two infants from 4 to 12 months of age using 1000 Hz tones. Like Taguchi et al. (1969), they found thresholds to be much lower in quiet than in active sleep, about 10 to 15 dB and 45 dB above adult behavioral thresholds, respectively. This difference could simply be the result of the differing background EEG levels in the two states. Hecox (1975) obtained brainstem-evoked responses (BSER) to clicks in neonates and older infants up to 3 years of age. Neonates had recognizable responses beginning at about 27 dB, compared to 20 dB for the older children and 10 dB for adults. Teas (1977) has confirmed the 20 dB figure for infants when click stimuli filtered to restricted frequency ranges are used to elicit the BSER.[3]

Thresholds for heart rate responses are generally higher than those reported for evoked responses and vary over a far greater range across studies. Schulman (1973) reported very high thresholds when a relatively strict response criterion was employed. Less than a third of her sample of neonates responded at 70 or 80 dB for pure tones, and the median threshold for one-third octave band-pass noise was 84 dB. However, using a less stringent criterion, Bartoshuk (1964) found intensities of 48 to 58 dB (re 0.0002 μbar) elicited responses that significantly differed from a control period. Using heart rate as well as motor and respiratory changes, Steinschneider and colleagues (Steinschneider, 1968; Steinschneider et al., 1966) also reported thresholds of about 55 dB. Thresholds in older infants are generally reported to be lower. Schulman and Wade (1970) obtained identifiable decelerations (criteria unspecified) to 34 dB (re 0.0002 μbar) one-third octave noise stimuli in awake infants 3 to 9 months of age. The few 6- and 8-week-old infants in their

---

[3]Various conventions for the labeling of components have been employed in the evoked-response literature, and comparisons across studies are frequently difficult due to the absence of an established nomenclature. The "Committee on Methods at the International Symposium on Cerebral Evoked Potentials in Man," Brussels, 1974, recently recommended a system in which each component is specified by its polarity and latency. However, this system seems ill-suited to developmental comparisons since latencies of components change rapidly with age. For the present discussion, evoked-response components are numbered sequentially according to their polarity, a convention commonly used in studies of evoked-response development. The labels are assigned according to the components present in the response of the full-term newborn.

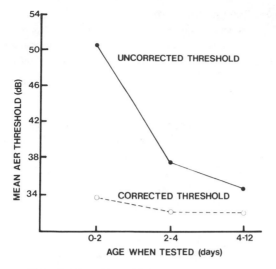

[Adapted from Taguchi et al., 1969.]

Figure 9-6. Comparison of changes in average-evoked response (AER) thresholds to auditory stimuli during the early days of life when corrected for the conductive (middle ear) loss estimated from the difference in air-conduction and bone-conduction thresholds (air-bone gap).

sample had more variable and higher thresholds than the older infants, but since the sample was at-risk for hearing damage, it is uncertain if this was truly an age effect. Berg et al. (1977) reported significant cardiac responses in sleeping 2- to 4-month-old infants to 30 and 40 dB tones, even though somewhat higher intensities did not reliably elicit responses.[4] Enhanced responding to near-threshold values has been reported in adults as well (e.g., Jackson, 1974; Rousey and Reitz, 1967).

Recently a new procedure has been developed that shows promise for assessing thresholds. The procedure is based on the reflex inhibition of startle-blink responses (Graham, 1975; Hoffman and Searle, 1968) by a brief tone presented at a specific interval preceding the blink-eliciting stimulus. Reiter and Ison (1977) have recently shown in adults that blinks induced with air puffs may be inhibited even with stimuli at the behavioral threshold level, and both Strock et al. (1978) and Hoffman and Marsh (1977) have demonstrated blink inhibition in young infants. Ongoing research with 3-to 4-month-old infants in our own laboratory[4] indicates significant inhibition of air-puff-induced blinks by 25-msec, 1000 Hz tones of 40, 60, and 80 dB (re 0.0002 μbar). Inhibition of blink amplitude averaged about 12 to 15% for each tone intensity, and at 40 dB better than 90% of the sample showed the phenomenon.[5]

Frequency and Bandwidth

There is abundant evidence from adults that both the behavioral threshold and the judged loudness of auditory signals are influenced by stimulus frequency and bandwidth

---

[4]This research was carried out under NIH contract NO 1-NS-5-2313.
[5]We are indebted to Frances K. Graham and Howard S. Hoffman and to their colleagues for generously sharing their experience with apparatus and procedures used to test startle inhibition in infants. Louis Silverstein, Marsha Clarkson, and Lori Golden have contributed significantly to this research effort.

(Licklider, 1951). In general, stimuli with frequencies at the extremes are judged less loud and have higher thresholds than middle-range frequencies. Narrow-band signals are judged less loud than wideband ones equal in total physical energy. Research using physiological responses in infants suggests a somewhat different picture. Although wider bandwidths appear to elicit stronger responses as in adults, a number of studies suggest low-frequency signals are *more* effective than middle- or high-frequency signals in eliciting responses.

The strongest evidence for an enhanced responsivity to low-frequency stimuli comes from studies by Hutt et al. (1968b). Pure tones of 125 and 250 Hz produced substantially larger electromyographic responses in neonates than tones of 70, 500, 1000, or 2000 Hz. Other reports have suggested that a similar phenomenon holds true for evoked potentials (Lenard et al., 1969) and heart rate accelerative responses (Hutt et al., 1969), but these latter conclusions are dependent on results for square-wave rather than sine-wave stimuli which, as Bench (1973) has pointed out, confound bandwidth and frequency. However, Taguchi et al. (1969) employed pure tones to elicit cortical evoked potentials and found that compared to stimuli of 1000 and 2000 Hz, 500 Hz tones had lower thresholds and elicited larger responses at all intensities tested. Other reports also indicate lower frequency stimuli are more effective in soothing crying infants (Bench, 1969; Birns et al., 1965).

Several studies of heart rate responses have failed to confirm enhanced responding at low frequencies, but even these results indicate comparatively greater responding at lower frequencies than might be expected from adult behavioral evidence. Clarkson and Berg (1977) reported no differences in neonatal heart rate responses to 125 and 1000 Hz pure-tone and square-wave signals; and Crowell et al. (1971) found no differences for warbled tones centered at 500, 1000, 2000, 4000, and 8000 Hz. Schulman (1973) reported slightly higher thresholds for narrow-band noise centered at 500 Hz than at 3600 Hz, but this difference was only about 5 dB.

Some investigators (e.g., Eisenberg, 1976) have suggested that the effectiveness of low-frequency signals may be due to a special "tuning" of the infant auditory system to the "carrier frequencies" of speech. However, two reports indicate that the apparent increased responding to low-frequency stimuli in infants compared to adults may really be a result of reduced responding to the higher frequencies. Engel and Young (1969) report that evoked-potential thresholds for neonates are within 3 dB of adult behavioral thresholds at 250 Hz but are elevated by 10 to 15 dB for frequencies over 1000 Hz. Similarly, Hecox (1975) reports that masking noises limited to frequencies above 1000 Hz have little effect on the BSER in neonates but clearly reduce the response in adults. This suggests that high frequencies contribute little to the BSER in neonates. The contribution of higher frequency elements can apparently be detected within a few weeks after birth, but is still reduced compared to adult levels. Unfortunately, there are no other studies comparing responses to low and high frequencies beyond the newborn period.

Studies examining effects of stimulus bandwidth on infant response are clearly in agreement with adult evidence; pure tones are generally less effective than various multiple-frequency stimuli in eliciting responses. Several early reports asserted that pure tones were wholly without effect for neonates (e.g., Eisenberg, 1970; Turkewitz et al., 1972b), but the results described above clearly refute this extreme view. Nevertheless, a number of studies examining cardiac responses in neonates have reported that single pure tones are less effective than (1) square-wave and synthetic speech stimuli (Clarkson and Berg, 1978), (2) two- or three-tone chords (Turkewitz et al., 1972a), and (3) narrow-band noise (Schulman, 1973). Hutt et al. (1968b) have shown that square waves elicit larger electromyographic responses than pure tones regardless of stimulus frequency, but other work by this group suggests additional factors must be operating. Lenard et al. (1969) confirmed the greater effectiveness of square-wave over pure-tone stimuli for evoked potentials, but found that square-wave stimuli were also more effective than the wider band white noise stimuli. Further, there was no difference between responses elicited by a 125 Hz square-wave and a speech stimulus despite marked differences in the bandwidth of the stimuli. Resolution of these inconsistencies awaits research in which bandwidth is varied over a wide range while other variables are held constant.

Vision

Since the development of visual perception during infancy has been reviewed in detail by Cohen, DeLoache, and Strauss in this volume (Chapter 11), the present discussion will be limited to the brief description of a few recent experiments in which cortical evoked responses have been applied to the study of visual function in young infants.

Spectral Sensitivity

Studies of the visual evoked response in adult subjects have indicated that it is primarily a photopic response, strongly dominated by the activity of cone receptors in or very near the fovea. This is generally attributed to the shorter latency of the cone response and the subsequent refractoriness of retinal ganglion cells to the longer latency activity generated by the rods (Ciganek, 1975). In a comparison of evoked responses to orange and white light in newborn infants, Lodge et al. (1969) found that the amplitude of the P_2 component of the VER was larger in response to orange light, even when the two stimuli were equated for brightness on the basis of the ERG response recorded from the retina. This suggests that the VER in the newborn is also of predominantly photopic origin.

A recent study by Dobson (1976) appears to be the first to use the VER to assess the spectral sensitivity of young infants over a wide range of chromatic stimuli. Since latency of the major positive component varies inversely with stimulus intensity, it is possible to estimate spectral sensitivity from the VER by determining the intensity necessary to produce comparable response latencies for different wavelengths of light. Dobson (1976) found that spectral sensitivity functions estimated in this manner for 2-month-old infants were very similar to the adult function for wavelengths above 550 nm. However, infants were more sensitive than adults to shorter wavelengths in the blue end of the spectrum. Dobson has suggested that this elevation of sensitivity may be due to a lower density of pigment in the macula of the infant retina.

Visual Acuity

Numerous studies in the adult literature have demonstrated that two components of the VER with latencies of approximately 100 and 200 msec are especially sensitive to patterned stimulation. When stimuli are checkerboard patterns, the amplitudes of these components show an inverted U relation with check size, which has generally been attributed to the properties of receptive fields of single neurons in the visual system (Harter and White, 1968, 1970; Karmel and Maisel, 1975). The peak of this function can be shifted toward larger checks by degrading the pattern with refractive lenses, suggesting that the check size that elicits maximum response varies with the visual acuity of the subject.

In an initial study of the response to patterned stimuli in young infants, Harter and Suitt (1970) traced changes in the VER to checkerboard patterns in one infant over a period of several months. They found that after approximately 1 month of age, the largest responses were evoked by progressively smaller check sizes, presumably reflecting an increase in visual acuity. An inverted U function was evident by 2 to 3 months of age, with a peak corresponding to that seen in adult subjects with visual acuities on the order of 20/250.

More recently, Sokol and Dobson (1976) have used the same technique to examine visual acuity in infants 2 to 6 months of age. They reported a decrease in the check size eliciting maximum response with increasing age, and an inverted U function nearly identical to that obtained for adults with Snellen acuities of 20/20 by 6 months of age. Similar results have been reported by Marg et al. (1976) for bar gratings of different spatial frequencies. Rather than matching functions for infants and adults, they determined threshold visual acuity by identifying the highest spatial frequency that evoked a response clearly different from the response to a gray field. Their results showed a very rapid improvement in acuity during the first 2 months of life, and the attainment of adult levels by 4 to 5 months. Both of these estimates suggest visual acuities that are considerably better than estimates derived from most behavioral studies in young infants. However, Cohen, DeLoache, and Strauss (Chapter 11) have reviewed several recent studies using behavioral measures that have reported acuity estimates more in line with VER results.

The VER and Visual Fixation

In a series of several experiments, Karmel and associates (Karmel, 1969; Karmel et al., 1974; Karmel and Maisel, 1975) have demonstrated that visual-fixation preferences for checkerboard stimuli are highly correlated with the amplitude of the major positive component of the VER in infants older than 6 weeks of age, and with the amplitude of a longer latency negative wave in younger infants (Hoffman, cited in Karmel and Maisel, 1975). On the basis of Rose and Lindsley's (1965) finding that early positive and long-latency negative waves of the VER are associated with two independent visual systems in the kitten, Karmel and Maisel (1975) have suggested that this correlation of visual fixation with two different components of the VER during development may reflect control of visual attention by the more primitive indirect visual system prior to 6 weeks of age and the subsequent emergence of the primary geniculostriate system in older infants.

More recently, Harter et al. (1977) have reported that even though amplitude of the major P_2 component is not correlated with visual fixation in infants less than 6 weeks of age, it does show an inverted U relation with check size over a limited range of relatively high spatial frequencies. Harter et al. have suggested that P_2 amplitude in infants less than 6 weeks old may reflect primarily the contribution of subcortical mechanisms. Considered together, the results of Harter et al. for small check sizes, and those of Karmel's group for a range of larger ones, suggest that some time after 6 weeks of age the relation between P_2 amplitude and check size may be bimodal, with peaks occurring for both small and large stimuli. However, P_2 amplitude appears to be correlated with visual fixation only over the range of larger check sizes. Presumably, this bimodality would disappear as the second mode shifted toward progressively smaller check sizes with increasing maturation.

ORIENTING AND ATTENTION
Development of Cardiac Orienting

In 1966, Lipton et al. reported, as part of a series of studies detailing infants' autonomic functioning, that there were pronounced changes in the form of the heart rate response to a brief airstream stimulus during the early months of life: monophasic acceleration at birth shifted to a predominantly deceleratory response by 2½ months of age. In that same year, Graham and Clifton (1966) reviewed a wide variety of evidence and hypothesized that heart rate deceleration was associated with orienting and attentive behavior, while acceleration above prestimulus levels represented a defensive response. Based on this, Graham and colleagues in this and in later publications (Graham and Jackson, 1970) argued that the change from neonatal heart rate acceleration to the predominantly decelerative response of the older infant may reflect development of the orienting response. Because Sokolov (1963) has hypothesized that orienting is part of a basic perceptual system geared toward taking in and processing information in contrast to the protective and information-limiting systems engaged during defensive responding, the suggestion of development of orienting had important implications for the emergence of cognitive and learning capabilities (Sameroff, 1971). Further, the suggestion implied that the developmental changes in the form of the cardiac response reflected maturation of brain systems responsible for relatively high-level behavior. In contrast to this position, Lipton et al. (1966, p. 14) argued against such an interpretation of developmental changes in cardiac response form and attributed them to ANS development, probably increasing control of the vagus nerve and maturation of baroreceptor reflexes.

Unfortunately, separation of peripheral and central influences on responding is very difficult in the human infant. In animals, and in some cases adult humans, influence of peripheral or central mechanisms may be directly assessed by surgical or pharmacological intervention. However, indirect procedures may be employed even with human infants to evaluate the likelihood that development of central orienting mechanisms is occurring. One procedure is to show that the neonate's cardiovascular system is capable of deceleratory response like that of more mature infants and adults, at least under some conditions. This would indicate that peripheral control is sufficiently developed to produce the response. More convincing would be evidence that circumstances that increase the likelihood of deceleration in neonates are predictable from the constructs underlying the concept of orienting more so than from the conditions that would favor autonomic stability.

Evidence of Deceleratory Responses in Neonates

After Graham and Jackson (1970) concluded that sustained deceleratory responses in neonates had not been unequivocally demonstrated, a concerted effort was made on the part of a number of investigators to elicit such a response. Review of this work indicates a number of false starts and dubious claims preceding the eventual success. An early problem, and one that still persists, was the failure to recognize the distinction between what appear to be two types of cardiac deceleration: a brief initial deceleration, typically preceding an acceleration above baseline, and a longer sustained deceleration. An example of the brief response may be seen in a study of neonates by Lipsitt and Jacklin (1971). They reported that immediately after presentation of the odorant asafoetida there were more instances of heart beats below the prestimulus range than above it, but subsequent to the third ordinal beat, acceleratory cases far outnumbered deceleratory ones. This presumably translates to a mean response of a brief deceleration followed by an acceleration above baseline. Porges et al. (1974) have also reported the biphasic deceleration-acceleration in response to onset of a visual stimulus, and both groups suggest the brief deceleration may be indicative of orienting in the neonate.

The general form of the brief or short-latency deceleration is illustrated in the left panel of Fig. 9-7. A curve showing the median heart rate response in three studies of neonates may be compared with responses in sleeping 6- and 12-week-olds (Rewey, 1973) and adults (Berg, et al., 1975). In two of the studies with neonates, click stimuli were presented repeatedly regardless of state over a period of several hours (Schachter et al., 1971; Williams et al. 1967).[6] In the third study, results are from the onset of 30-sec increase in room illumination in awake subjects with higher than the median prestimulus variability (Porges et al., 1974). In all cases the brief initial deceleration is followed by an acceleration above baseline. It is evident that there is little variation in response shape or latency across ages and stimulus durations.

The right panel of Figure 9-7 illustrates the sustained, monophasic deceleratory response with its longer latency to peak. Again the median response for a number of studies of neonates (see figure caption) are compared with responses to 75 dB auditory stimuli in awake 6- and 12-week-olds (Rewey, 1973) and to a 50 dB tone in awake adults (Berg, 1970). Though the latency to the peak of this longer deceleration is somewhat more variable across ages than for the brief response, none of these decelerations are followed by accelerations above baseline. Few examples of response intermediate between these forms were locatable, suggesting these are representative of a true dichotomy. Further, these two distinct forms of heart rate response are associated with different stimulus conditions. The brief decelerations are typical in sleeping subjects, at least in older infants and adults, and they do not appear to habituate (Schachter et al. 1971; Williams et al., 1967), though the later acceleratory component may. In contrast, the sustained, monophasic decelerations are rarely found in sleeping infants and habituate rapidly (Adkinson and Berg, 1976). They do not seem to be exclusive to any stimulus duration or quality since data contributing to the neonate long-latency curve are responses to auditory, visual, and vestibular stimulation with durations ranging from 7 to 20 sec, and to stimulus offset as well as onset.

It is only the sustained decelerations that appear to clearly qualify as cardiac components of orienting based on criteria outlined by Graham and Clifton (1966). Graham and Jackson (1970) suggested that the brief deceleration may represent an immature or subcortical orienting response. However, this view may require modification in light of recent evidence of sustained deceleratory responses in an anencephalic infant (Graham et al., 1978). One alternative is suggested by Graham and Slaby's (1973) report that in adult subjects, differences in the rise time of auditory stimuli affect only the initial portion of the heart rate response. They proposed that the initial portion of the response curve may be principally sensitive to stimulus-onset characteristics whereas the longer latency components are responsive to steady-state aspects of the stimulus. Figure 9-7 shows that even for neonates the short- and long-latency curves do not clearly differ until after second 2, the same point Graham and Slaby use for distinguishing such responses in adults. The implication is that the two types of responses may reflect differences in subjects' reactions to steady-state qualities of the stimulus rather than onset characteristics. If so, the data

[6]The data from these studies as represented in Figure 9-7 were obtained by averaging data points from the published individual response curves.

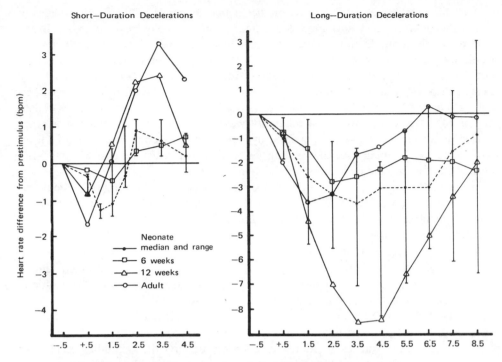

Short—Duration Decelerations   Long—Duration Decelerations

[Short-duration newborn curve based on data from Porges et al. (1974), onset response of high-variability subjects; Schachter et al. (1971), means of individual subjects. Long-duration newborn curve based on older newborns on Trial Block 1, offset response of older newborns on Trial Block 3; Clarkson (1977) response to pulsed speech; Clifton and Nelson, (1976) subjects awake longer than 10 min; Pomerleau-Malcuit and Clifton (1971) responses to auditory and vestibular stimuli; Sameroff et al. (1973), response to checkerboards; and Porges et al. (1974), offset responses of both high- and low-variability subjects. Older infant and adult data are adapted from single response curves (see text for references).]

Figure 9-7. Illustrative short-latency (left panel) and long-latency (right panel) deceleratory responses in infants and adults. The median and range (vertical lines) of data from several studies are shown for newborns.

suggest developmental changes are occurring in the way that infants process information during the steady-state portion of the stimulus, and not its onset.

Another aspect of some studies of neonatal cardiac responses that caused interpretive difficulties was a type of sampling error. Since heart rates of neonates, especially awake neonates, are highly variable, there is always a possibility of recording a deceleration by chance, especially under circumstances where the number of conditions being tested is large, the number of subjects per condition is small, and no *a priori* basis for response selection is made. A report by Kearsley (1973) is representative of this problem. In a study of heart rate, eyelid, and head-movement responses, Kearsley presented awake neonates with a wide variety of acoustic stimuli: pure-tone versus narrow-band noise at three intensities (70, 80, and 90 dB), four frequencies (250, 500, 1000, and 2000 Hz), and four onset times (0, 500, 1000, and 2000 msec). Based on characteristics of orienting and defense-startle responses, it could be predicted that longer rise time, lower intensity stimuli should be conducive to a reduced incidence of eyelid closures and greater likelihood of deceleration. Eyelid-closure data generally confirmed this, especially for the rise-time variable. However, no consistent effects of any stimulus dimensions were reported for heart rate. Therefore, four conditions from the total set of 96 were selected only because response to that condition appeared to be monophasic acceleration or deceleration; no rationale based on stimulus parameters was offered, curves were averages of data for only 4 subjects, and statistical reliability was not assessed. Although the selected decelerations were reportedly accompanied by increased eye-opening and decreased head movements possibly indicative of orienting, there remains the distinct possibility that the selected curves represent only chance fluctuations.

To a much lesser degree, a study by Pomerleau-Malcuit and Clifton (1973) could be subject to the same difficulty. They presented vestibular (rocking), tactile, and 65 dB auditory stimuli to awake and sleeping neonates either before or after feeding. Significant deceleration was reported in 2 of the 12 conditions: for vestibular and for auditory stimuli in awake infants tested before feeding. More confidence may be placed in these results than those of Kearsley (1973) not only because of the smaller number of conditions sampled and the evidence of statistical reliability but because they occurred in conditions where orienting might be most anticipated—in maximally alert infants.

Although the results of some of the studies reporting decelerations in neonates may be questioned, there are now a number of unequivocal instances of sustained deceleratory responses in awake neonates to stimuli in a variety of modalities. Studies employing visual stimuli were among the first to provide clear-cut evidence. Sameroff et al. (1973) elicited a large (8 beats/min), sustained deceleration to onset of a 12-by-12 checkerboard, and Porges et al. (1974) reported a more modest sustained deceleration to offset of room illumination, though only on later trials and in subjects with high prestimulus heart rate variability. Porges et al. (1973) also found sustained deceleration at stimulus offset and not at onset of an auditory stimulus, but Adkinson and Berg (1976) obtained sustained deceleration to both onset and offset of a field of color. Further, onset responses rapidly habituated with stimulus repetition and dishabituated when a new color was introduced, characteristics expected of an orienting response. Long-latency responses to onset of auditory stimuli have only recently been unequivocally reported in the neonate. In our laboratory, Clarkson (1977) predicted and obtained sustained deceleration to onset of various intermittent sounds, as did Clifton and co-workers (described in Clifton and Nelson, 1976). When these results for auditory and visual stimuli are added to those of Pomerleau-Malcuit and Clifton (1973) for vestibular stimuli, it is clear that the sustained deceleratory response is not exclusive to any single stimulus modality. It should not be concluded from these data, however, that deceleration is readily obtained in the neonate. Unlike the 3- to 4-month-olds who show large decelerations under a wide variety of conditions, the neonate seems to produce the response with great reluctance. It is not entirely clear exactly what conditions are necessary to elicit the elusive long-latency deceleration in the newborn, but several important parameters have been identified and are described in the following section.

Variables Influencing Decelerative Responses

A number of variables, which may be expected to influence orienting, also appear to affect heart rate decelerations of neonates as well as older infants and adults.

State

It can be argued that the awake subject is in a state more conducive to information processing and therefore to orienting than is the sleeping subject. Data on heart rate responses indicates they are profoundly influenced by sleep-wake states at all ages. During all stages of sleep the cardiac response of the adult always has a prominant accelerative component regardless of stimulus intensity, though decelerative components may occur as well (Berg et al., 1975). In contrast, with appropriately moderate stimulus intensities and rise times, the awake adult has a monophasic decelerative response.

Marked state-dependent differences in the form of the cardiac response have also been shown to occur in infants 4 months of age (Berg et al., 1971), 6 and 12 weeks of age (Rewey, 1973), 2 to 8 weeks of age (Lewis et al., 1967) and in neonates (Jackson et al., 1971). Like adults, the sleeping infants in all age groups had responses that included a prominent acceleratory component. During the awake, quiet state sustained monophasic decelerations were seen in infants older than 12 weeks of age, while for younger subjects, reactions were not always clearly decelerative but they lacked the significant acceleration seen during sleep. In view of this it is not surprising that all successful attempts to elicit sustained deceleratory responses in neonates have, with one exception (Pomerleau-Malcuit et al., 1975) resulted from tests of only alert infants. Thus, in the neonate as well as in the more mature subject, a relaxed, alert state can be considered a necessary, though not sufficient condition for eliciting long-latency decelerations.

Although state seems to influence cardiac responses at all ages, recent evidence suggests that responses of neonates may be more sensitive to this variable than those of older subjects. Clifton and colleagues (e.g., Clifton and Nelson, 1976) have found that responses of neonates who are judged to be alert at the time of testing differ depending upon the length of the alert period. Neonates tested at the beginning of an alert period of at least 10 min responded with a deceleration to the initial presentation of an intermittent auditory stimulus while those tested during periods of alertness of less than 5 min had no clear response to the stimulus. Clifton (1977) notes that the same phenomenon can be observed in a study of habituation of cardiac responses in 1- to 4-week-old infants by Campos and Brackbill (1973), and Leavitt et al. (1976) have reported a similar effect for 6-week-olds. Clarkson and Berg (1978) found that transitory alert periods in neonates attenuated but did not eliminate deceleratory responses, an effect also found in 4-month-olds (Berg et al., 1971). In any case, it is clear that deceleratory cardiac responses of neonates and very young infants are sensitive to even subtle state variations.

Visual and Auditory Stimulus Parameters

A wide variety of stimulus parameters may influence physiological responses, some of which have been discussed in earlier sections. In the visual domain, a number of variables that have been shown to have a potent effect on visual orientation also appear to exert an effect on cardiac deceleration. As discussed earlier, both visual fixation and amplitude of visual-evoked responses show an inverted U-shaped relationship with check size, or according to Karmel (1974), contour density. J. K. Keen (1974) reported more extended fixation and larger and longer decelerations for longer contour stimuli (24-by-24 checkerboards) than for shorter ones (4-by-4 checkerboards). The effect was especially marked on the initial trial block. McCall and Kagan (1967) employed random polygons and found that both visual fixation and the number of infant subjects decelerating were inverted

U-shaped functions of perimeter length, the equivalent of Karmel's contour length. McCall and Melson (1970) also found the incidence of deceleration and visual fixation to covary with changes in contour length.

Evidence of another variable with a potent effect on visual orienting is in the clear visual preference for curved over straight lines for infants 2 months of age and older (Fantz et al., 1975). While there have been no direct tests of this with cardiac responses, one preliminary study in McCall and Kagan (1967) found significantly less fixation and heart rate deceleration in 4-month-olds to straight-lined polygons than to faces, regardless of whether the faces were schematic or photographed, regular or distorted. Since the response to the face types apparently did not significantly differ, the effect may be the result of differences in the amount of curvature of the stimuli rather than their social significance, as was suggested by the authors. Finally, in a number of studies, Lewis and co-workers have found both heart rate and visual fixation to directly covary with the "complexity" of a pattern of blinking lights (Kagan and Lewis, 1965; Lewis et al., 1966) and number of items (Lewis et al., 1971). Overall, the results seem to suggest that cardiac and visual-fixation components of orienting are influenced similarly by a number of parameters of visual stimuli. However, there have been few attempts to examine visual orienting and cardiac responding in infants less than 3 months of age.

Compared with visual stimuli, influence of parameters of auditory stimuli on cardiac decelerations have been studied over a wider age range. For two of these parameters, intensity and rise time, clear predictions can be made as to their effect on orienting. Abrupt onsets should be more likely to elicit startles, a response presumably incompatible with orienting. Intensity increases, discussed earlier for responding in general, should elicit greater orienting up to the point where the threshold for defense responses are approached. Hatton et al. (1970) examined both parameters in adults and found abrupt onsets when coupled with higher intensities (90 dB) changed a monophasic deceleratory response into an acceleratory-deceleratory one. Using similar stimuli with 4-month-olds, Berg et al. (1971) found abrupt onsets attenuated decelerations to 75 dB stimuli in awake infants and increased acceleratory components to both 50 and 75 dB tones in sleeping infants. Berg (1975) found that accelerations in response to 90 dB stimuli were consistently elicited in 10-month-old infants and elicited under some conditions in 4-month-olds (Fig. 9-8). The 75 dB stimuli consistently elicited monophasic deceleration in both age groups. Only Kearsley (1973) has examined effect of intensity and rise time in awake neonates. Though there was no evidence of differential effects on decelerative cardiac responses for either of these variables, it was not clear, as noted earlier, that any reliable cardiac response was elicited in this study.

Another variable that may be related to orienting is whether the eliciting stimulus is turned on and left on for its duration or whether it is interrupted periodically. The latter pulsed stimulus with its multiple alterations in intensity might be expected to elicit greater or more extended orienting. There is ample evidence that this factor influences the cardiac component of orienting. With 4-month-olds, Clifton and Meyers (1969) reported pulsed stimuli elicited longer latency and significantly larger decelerations when compared to responses to uninterrupted signals, an effect replicated by Berg (1972). The influence of stimulus continuity appears even stronger in younger infants. Rewey (1973) compared effects of pulsed and continuous tones in 6- and 12-week-olds. Awake older infants responded with deceleration regardless of stimulus type, but significant deceleration in awake 6-week-olds was reported only for pulsed tones. Similarly, Berg (1974) and Leavitt et al. (1976) were successful in eliciting substantial decelerations in 6-week-olds

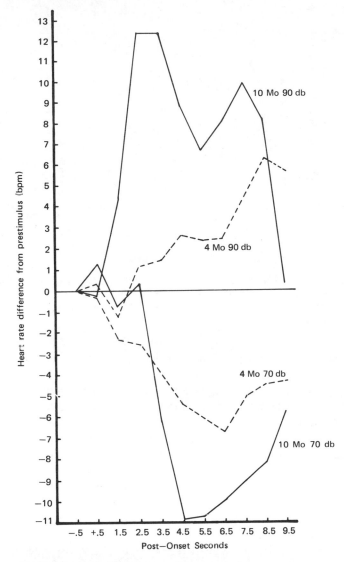

Figure 9-8.   Cardiac rate responses to 2-sec-long bursts of white noise at 70 and 90 dB (re 0.0002μbar) of infants 4 and 10 months of age.

with tones and synthetic speech stimuli that were pulsed, but Brown et al. (1977), employing a continuous warbling or chirping sound, were able to elicit significant decelerations in 9- but not in 6-week-olds. Noting this evidence, Clarkson (1977) assessed the influence of temporal pattern as well as two other parameters in eliciting deceleration in neonates. Overall, pulsed auditory stimuli elicited significant deceleration while continuous ones generally did not (Fig. 9-9). Increased spectral complexity appeared to increase magnitude of decelerations for pulsed stimuli and magnitude of accelerations for continuous stimuli. Contrary to the work of the Hutts (Hutt et al., 1968b, 1969) stimulus frequency had no influence on the response.

Taken together, the data indicate a potent and surprisingly consistent effect of pulsing

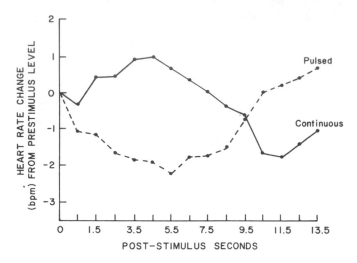

[From Clarkson, 1977, with permission.]

Figure 9-9.   Cardiac rate responses of newborns to 75 dB auditory stimuli either pulsed (0.5 sec on, 0.5 sec off) or continuous for a 10-sec period. Curves are averages of responses to pure-tone, square wave, and synthetically produced vowels.

auditory stimuli. With few exceptions, deceleration in response to auditory stimuli in infants 6 weeks of age and less have been reported only when stimuli were intermittent. The possibility arises that, ". . . the processing of temporal transitions may play as important a role in determining infant attention to auditory stimuli as the processing of spatial transitions does in the visual domain" (Leavitt et al., 1976, p. 522). Hirsh and Sherrick (1961) suggested that the ability to resolve temporal information and spatial information are of primary importance in the auditory and in the visual domains, respectively. If such a parallel between temporal and spatial processing exists, we might anticipate orienting or attention would be an inverted U-shaped function of pulse rate, similar to that for spatial frequency (Karmel, 1974). However, no studies have compared pulse rates over a wide range, though Clifton and Meyers (1969) and Berg (1974) reported no differences in effectiveness of rates of 1 and 2 per second and 0.5 and 1 per second, respectively. Some comparisons across studies are suggestive, however. The pulse rates that have proved effective in enhancing heart rate decelerations have all been in the range of about 0.5 to 2 per second. The stimulus used in the Brown et al. study (1977) may have been ineffective with 6-week-olds not because it did not alternate silent and sound intervals but because the 4-per-second warbling rate exceeded some optimal frequency. Obviously, definitive answers to this await the necessary parametric studies of pulsation rate.

Perinatal Events and Risk Factors

The events associated with birth, including physical stress, adaptation to an independent existence and recovery from maternal medication, and the various factors that can put an infant at risk for brain damage would not be expected to provide optimal conditions for the perceiving and processing of sensory stimulation. This consideration has led a number of investigators to examine whether perinatal events and risk factors might have a temporary or extended effect on orienting responses.

Evidence of a temporary influence of perinatal events has led to what might be called the "birthday" effect. Adkinson and Berg (1976) reported sustained decelerations to visual stimuli only in infants older than the median sample age of 35 h. Similarly, Friedman (1972) reported that the visual-fixation responses of 2-day-old neonates habituated but those of babies tested on the day of birth did not. Indirect confirmation of these findings comes from Porges' laboratory. In several studies Porges and colleagues have reported decelerations in neonates who have higher than the median prestimulus heart rate variance. However, in two of the three reports (Arnold and Porges, 1972; Porges et al., 1973), prestimulus heart rate variability was greater on the 2nd day of life. This led Adkinson and Berg (1976) to suggest that it was not the heart rate variance but the time since birth that was critical. In any case, both Adkinson and Berg (1976) and Porges (1974) attributed the birthday effect to recovery from undetermined events associated with the birth process rather than to any extraordinary neural maturation occurring in this brief period, as proposed by Friedman (1972). Since evidence indicates that birthday effects occur in both the autonomically ennervated cardiac system and the somatically ennervated oculomotor system, it is likely that the birthday influence is centrally rather than peripherally mediated. These results also have practical importance. With many hospitals shortening the length of nursery care, sometimes to 24 h., the influence of perinatal factors will make it increasingly difficult to adequately test for orienting in neonates.

The effect of various risk factors on heart rate deceleration has also been examined. Schulman (1968, 1969) tested 1- to 7-week-old low-birthweight infants who were otherwise relatively free from negative indications (low risk) and those who had a number of additional problems (high risk). An 80 dB "buzzer" presented for 10 trials elicited deceleration only in the awake low-risk infants. In the second study four low-risk pre-term infants were repeatedly tested and found to first exhibit decelerations when they were 33 to 36 weeks' conceptional age, 7 to 10 weeks' postnatal age. This report was surprising because of the difficulty in eliciting deceleration in even full-term infants at this postnatal age, especially with a stimulus of this intensity and quality, and because responses were averaged over 10 trials. Subsequently, Berkson et al. (1974) attempted to closely replicate Schulman's procedures, including use of the same buzzer, and failed to find even a brief deceleration in high- or low-risk subjects up to 5 postnatal weeks of age.

Lester (1975) tested a different risk variable in older infants. Severely malnourished 1-year-old Guatamalan infants were found not to decelerate in response to a tone series nor did they respond to change in tone frequency. The better-nourished infants responded with a deceleration on initial trials, which habituated with stimulus repetition and dishabituated to change in tone frequency.

Concomitant Somatic and Sucking Activity

As Obrist (1976) has reminded us, the primary function of the cardiovascular system is not to reflect attentional influences per se but to meet the varying metabolic demands of the body. Therefore, it should be expected that changes in somatic activity would be one of the important factors influencing heart rate and other cardiovascular variables. Obrist and colleagues (e.g., Obrist, 1976) have provided ample evidence of this cardiac-somatic relationship in adults and older children. If one proposes that it is the development of autonomic control of the heart that produces the age-related change in heart rate response form, then it is reasonable to presume that this increased control by the ANS should be reflected in development of the cardiac-somatic relationship.

The most detailed evidence on cardiac-somatic relationships in infants stems from studies of heart rate and sucking movements. In a series of recent studies in neonates, Lipsitt, Crook, and colleagues reported increased heart rate levels during both nutritive and nonnutritive sucking bursts, but found that during nutritive sucking the heart rate increase was accentuated by greater amounts and sweetness of fluids (Crook, 1976, Crook and Lipsitt, 1976; Lipsitt, et al., 1976). Nelson et al. (1978) showed that heart rate changes were precisely time-locked to the neonate's sucking bursts. When an auditory stimulus which had proved effective in eliciting deceleration in nonsucking infants was presented at predetermined points in the sucking bursts, no influence of the stimulus could be detected—that is, heart rate changes that occurred appeared to be the same as those that would have resulted during a sucking burst alone. Although direct comparison of heart rates during sucking plus auditory stimulation and during sucking alone were not made in this report, a point Brown et al. (1977) suggest might be critical, Gregg et al. (1976) did make such a comparison. They found that during active tracking of a visual stimulus, neonates who were sucking on a pacifier had accelerative heart rates while nonsucking infants did not. However, Clarkson and Berg (1977) reported that availability of a pacifier attenuated but did not eliminate a decelerative response in neonates. Cardiac-somatic relationships have not been studied extensively for activity other than sucking. Pomerleau-Malcuit et al. (1975) examined the effects of head movements on cardiac activity in neonates and found that deceleratory responses were obtained only when movements did not occur.

Whatever potency sucking and other somatic activity has for disrupting deceleratory heart rate responses in newborns apparently has largely dissipated by 9 weeks of age. Recording both sucking and heart rate activity, Brown et al. (1977) reported significant deceleration in 9-week-olds even for a subgroup of subjects who sucked throughout the test session. Nevertheless, heart rate was still coupled to sucking rates, and correlations were about the same for the 6- and 9-week-olds tested in this study as for the neonates tested in Nelson et al. (1978). Also, judging from published curves, the range over which heart rate fluctuates during sucking bursts and pauses remains at about $\pm$ 5 beats/min during the first 9 weeks. (Brown et al., 1977, Fig. 2; Nelson et al., 1978, Figs. 2 and 3). Apparently, the basic cardiac-sucking relationship remains constant; what changes is the extent to which the relationship can be overridden by the influence of external stimuli.

Summary. The evidence discussed above supports the view that the increase in decelerative responses over the early months of life results from development of central mechanisms of orienting. The recent work with neonates clearly indicates that sustained deceleratory responses can be elicited at birth, suggesting that the autonomic system is sufficiently functional to produce such a response. The more convincing arguments, however, are based on the conditions required to elicit such a response in the newborn. With respect to state, sustained decelerations are generally found only during waking, the state that would be optimal for orienting. Presumably, the optimal conditions for autonomic control would be during sleep when metabolic demands are minimal. Stimulus variables which in the older infant produce the largest decelerations and the longest visual orienting are the most effective in eliciting deceleration in the neonate. Peripheral autonomic control over heart rate should not be affected by such stimulus variations. It is also notable that the birthday effect is evident in somatic as well autonomically controlled responses associated with orientation. Possibly the stongest evidence comes from contrasting somatic and stimulus influences on heart rate. There is no evidence of an increased somatic-cardiac relationship with age which might indicate autonomic development. Rather, it appears that the relationship present at birth is increasingly susceptible to the influenceee of sensory stimulation, which is consistent with the interpretation that changes in cardiac responses result from modification of CNS mechanisms.

It would be premature to rule out any influence of autonomic changes on the development of cardiac deceleratory responses. Far more sophisticated research on autonomic functioning would be required to determine this. The evidence does, however, seem to indicate marked development in a central mechanism that fits the functions and definitions of an orienting response system.

Habituation and Dishabituation

The occurrence of habituation and dishabituation can both indicate fundamental cognitive processes and provide evidence of basic sensory capacity. Habituation has been demonstrated throughout the range of phylogeny (Ratner, 1970), at every level of the nervous system (Thompson and Spencer, 1966) and across all age levels in humans. In its many formats and guises the habituation paradigm is probably the procedure most often employed in the experimental study of human infant behavior. However, due to limitations of space, discussion will be restricted to questions concerning the importance of cortical structures and arousal states, both matters of special relevance to development during infancy. The influence of stimulus type as well as other questions will not be considered in detail, but may be found in recent works devoted to the topic of habituation (Clifton and Nelson, 1976; Jeffrey and Cohen, 1971).

The simple definition of habituation as a decrement in responding with repeated stimulus presentation is convenient but not wholly adequate. Using this definition, other phenomena such as adaptation occurring at the receptor site and fatigue of response effectors can masquerade as habituation. The required addition to the simple definition to make it descriptive of the phenomenon as it is normally conceived is that the observed response decrement be mediated by the CNS and be specific to the stimulus being tested. The requirement of CNS mediation eliminates processes such as receptor adaptation which can also be stimulus-specific. The stimulus-specificity requirement means that if, for example, a decrement resulting from a change in state attenuated responding to all stimuli, it would not qualify as habituation (Hutt et al., 1969). Thompson and Spencer (1966) have described habituation characteristics, some of which can be used as tests for receptor adaptation and effector fatigue, but it appears that the only true test of stimulus specificity of the decrement is presentation of a different stimulus.

The latter procedure, often referred to as dishabituation, has two forms. In the classic procedure, after presenting n trials of a given stimulus, another stimulus, typically *more* intense, is presented followed by trial $n + 1$ of the original stimulus. Dishabituation is inferred if the response on trial $n + 1$ exceeds that on trial n to a significant degree; the response to the interposed stimulus is ignored. Thompson and Spencer (1966) have argued that this type of dishabituation results from sensitization following the interposed stimulus.[7] If so it would not be an adequate test of stimulus specificity. The second procedure, far more common in research with infants, is to follow the n habituation trials with one or more trials of another stimulus, typically of the *same* intensity. Dishabituation

---

[7]Recent results on vasomotor responses in rabbits suggest such dishabituation can occur in the absence of sensitization (Whitlow, 1975).

is inferred from a significantly increased response to the new stimulus compared to that on trial *n*. Though interpretation of such results are complicated by possible generalization of habituation to the dishabituation stimulus (Graham, 1973), they provide the best test of stimulus specificity of habituation. With proper choice of stimuli, the procedure provides a powerful method for testing stimulus discrimination as well (e.g., Berg, 1972).

Cortical Involvement

Much of the interest in habituation can be attributed to the suggestion by Sokolov (1963) and others that there is cortical involvement in this process. If true, tests of habituation might provide a way to track and assess the myelination and dendritic arborization of cortex, which continues for some time after birth in the normal infant (Conel, 1952; Dobbing and Sands, 1973) and possibly indicate cortical dysfunction in the infant at-risk. Despite the continued popularity of this view and Sokolov's hypothesis, there has been for some time considerable evidence that the cortex is not a necessary structure to obtain habituation in many response systems. For example, there are demonstrations of habituation in many species that have no cortex (Ratner, 1970) and in those whose normally present cortex has been surgically removed (Sharpless and Jasper, 1956). More recently, Thompson and colleagues (Groves and Thompson, 1970; Thompson and Spencer, 1966) have provided convincing evidence that responses to both natural and artificial stimuli in isolated spinal cord neurons of the acute spinal cat habituate in a manner similar to behavioral responses in the intact organism. Groves and Thompson (1970) propose that for spinal neurons, habituation occurs right at the synapse and that the same may be true for responses mediated at higher levels of the nervous system.

The discrepancy between this suggestion that habituation may have its locus potentially anywhere in the nervous system and Sokolov's (1963) contention that it occurs specifically in cortex might be artifactual. Sokolov was only concerned with habituation of the orienting response. Sokolov's (1963) model of habituation proposes that on each stimulus presentation, characteristics of the stimulus are extracted and stored in the cortex. With continued stimulus presentation this information accumulates into an increasingly accurate representation of the stimulus, known as a neuronal model. As each stimulus is presented, it is compared with the existing model in the cortex. To the extent that there is a match between them, the orienting response is inhibited, and over trials habituation occurs as a result. When a mismatch occurs, such as when a novel stimulus is presented, the orienting response is allowed to occur uninhibited. The orienting response itself was viewed as developing in the reticular formation as well as the cortex, though Graham and Jackson (1970) have suggested that the hippocampus may play the role Sokolov attributed to the reticular formation.

Despite the intuitive appeal of having such a stimulus comparator system resident in cortex, there is little direct evidence to support the cortical involvement, though the model-comparator system itself seems to fit the experimental data. Sokolov (1963) cites some Russian studies indicating disruption of orienting-response habituation with cortical damage, and dishabituation, which occurs with change in semantic aspects of a verbal stimulus, presumably requires cortical input. Although Western literature supporting the notion is sparse, a study of an anencephalic infant by Brackbill (1971) is often cited as evidence of cortical involvement in habituation.

The subject of Brackbill's research was a 3-month-old infant with an intact cerebellum and brainstem but no telencephalon (status of midbrain and diencephalon are not mentioned). The arousal state of the infant could not be determined except to distinguish REM and NREM periods. Habituation was tested in three sessions by examining motor reactions to 80 dB stimuli presented at 20-, 30-, or 40-sec. intervals. An habituation criterion of five consecutive no-response trials was not reached in any of the 180 to 200 trial sessions even though similarly tested 2- to 28-day normal infants reached such a criterion in an average of 22 or 23 trials. The conclusion drawn was that while the cortex may not be important in eliciation of the orienting response, it is essential to its inhibition. Since there was no certain evidence that orienting rather than startle or defense responses were elicited and the infant lacked many brain structures other than a cortex, this conclusion should be viewed cautiously. Nevertheless, the data do indicate that habituation of a motor response *can* be retarded by loss of forebrain structures.

The caution in accepting the dominant role of the cortex in orienting and habituation was further underscored by recent tests of another anencephalic infant (Graham, et al., 1978). Autopsy of this infant following its death at 51 days indicated that the brain was no more complete and perhaps less so than that of the infant tested by Brackbill. Brain weight was 11% of the expected value, and only brainstem and cerebellum were grossly normal, though they too were underdeveloped. As with Brackbill's subject, state was difficult to assess but was predominantly REM. A total of 330 auditory stimuli were presented over a number of sessions when the infant was 3 to 6 weeks of age. Stimuli varied in intensity, frequency, and quality in different tests, but virtually all elicited sustained heart rate decelerations comparable to those in older, normal infants. With stimulus repetition the deceleratory responses habituated to zero in several tests and were reelicited with a change in stimulus. The form of the cardiac response and the occurrence of habituation and dishabituation must be considered precocious since such findings with this variety of stimuli would not be expected of a normal infant of this age, much less one so severely handicapped.

The interpretation made by Graham and colleagues is that in the normal infant the activity of lower brain structures may be suppressed by immature higher structures. The anencephalic infant appears precocious because the interfering immature structures have not ever developed. It is difficult to compare results of the Graham et al. and the Brackbill studies since different responses were recorded and the extent of brain damage may not be comparable. Yet, the Graham et al. results are incompatible with Brackbill's conclusion. With respect to the cardiac component of orienting, these findings indicate that, in the absence of forebrain structures, the brainstem is sufficient for habituation of what appears to be the orienting response.

This evidence should not lead one to conclude that the remainder of the brain plays no role in orienting or in habituation. The nervous system operates as a whole and this portion of it certainly could serve to modulate and integrate such basic processes. Therefore, because of the maturation taking place in the nervous system, especially in higher-level structures, it is still reasonable to anticipate the possibility of some changes in habituation with age. In the many studies exploring this possibility, there has been a surprising lack of agreement, some of which may be due to ignoring the effects of state.

Influence of State on Habituation

Waking State

In the awake infant there is little agreement about when developmental changes in habituation occur or even if they do occur, despite the use in many cases of fairly comparable stimuli and responses. Lewis et al. (1969) reported evidence of very late development of habituation for both heart rate and visual-fixation responses to 30-sec periods of blinking lights or curved shapes. In 3-month-olds, the youngest subjects tested, heart rate deceleration and visual fixation showed little or no habituation in a four-trial experiment, nor did visual fixation in several other experiments with four to nine trials. Heart rate responses appeared to habituate in 6-month-olds, but no significant age or trial effects were found due to erratic responding. The more stable visual-fixation responses showed increasing habituation rates over the 3- to 18-month age range tested. These results are contradicted by many other reports indicating rapid habituation of both visual-fixation and heart rate responses in infants as young as 3 months.

Wetherford and Cohen (1973) also report an age effect but place onset of habituation much younger. They recorded visual fixation to two-dimensional figures in infants, 6, 8, 10, and 12 weeks of age. Only the two older groups had a significant response decrement, which in the oldest subjects appeared to occur within four to six trials. Neither of these reports appear entirely consistent with several studies of habituation in neonates. Friedman and colleagues, (e.g., Friedman, 1972; Friedman et al., 1974) have reported habituation within eight 60-sec presentations of checkerboard stimuli. Also, Adkinson and Berg (1976) have reported habituation of cardiac responses in neonates over 36 h. old. A sustained deceleratory response to a 20-sec exposure of a colored field habituated completely within six presentations separated by 20- to 40-sec intervals and dishabituated when the color was changed.

Results for auditory stimuli are no more consistent than those for visual stimuli. Lewis (1971) tested infants 3, 6, and 12 months of age using eight repetitions of 30-sec auditory stimuli. Though the deceleratory responses decreased over trials for all age groups, the decrement was significant only for the 12-month-olds. Clifton and Meyers (1969) reported habituation of cardiac deceleration only after the initial six trials, but Berg (1972, 1974) found significant habituation within six trials in both 6- and 16-week-old infants. Clifton and Nelson (1976) briefly mention obtaining rapid habituation of a sustained deceleration to auditory stimuli in neonates.

Results for habituation of responses to offset of relatively long-duration stimuli present an even more discrepant picture. Lewis (1971) reported that a deceleratory response to offset of an auditory stimulus habituated for 3-month-olds and not for 6- or 12-month-olds. Clifton and Meyers (1969) also reported habituating offset deceleration in 4-month-olds. In contrast, several studies have reported *increased* magnitude of offset deceleration with repeated stimulation. Berg (1972, 1974) reports it for both 6- and 16-week-olds, and Adkinson and Berg (1976) and Porges et al. (1974) for neonates.

Careful attention to the stimulus and temporal aspects of the studies could explain some but not all of these apparent discrepancies. Without further data, it can only be concluded that awake infants of any age are capable of habituation of an orienting response. Whether the habituation will occur or not apparently depends upon stimulus characteristics or other parameters not yet fully elucidated.

Sleep

Evidence for developmental changes in habituation in the sleeping subject are rather different than for the awake subject. Whereas data indicating habituation in the awake neonate has come about only recently, there has been from nearly the onset studies suggesting habituation in the sleeping neonate. In part this may be a result of the fact that nearly all early habituation studies with neonates were carried out when they were asleep due to the brevity of the quiet awake states (Berg et al., 1973). The evidence of reliable habituation in sleeping neonates is all the more surprising in view of the difficulty of obtaining it in the adult.

For years it had been understood that habituation in adults did not take place during sleep in any of a variety of response measures, even after hundreds of stimulations. Even when responses were habituated just before sleep onset, they would reappear when sleep began (Johnson and Lubin, 1967). However, a number of recent reports have indicated that when the results of adult studies are analyzed trial by trial, heart rate, vasomotor, and skin-potential responses all seem to decline within about 10 trials, but unlike habituation in the awake state, they asymptote at a level well above zero (Firth, 1973; Johnson et al., 1975, McDonald and Carpenter, 1975). The early failures were in part attributable to the technique of averaging over many trials, which obscured all but the residual, asymptotic responding. Thus, it would appear that both the neonate and the adult have a period of rapid habituation during sleep, but only the adult maintains reduced responding over an extended number of trials.

Despite the large number of reports examining habituation in the sleeping neonate (e.g. Bartoshuk 1962; Bridger, 1961; Engen et al., 1963; Keen, 1964; Leventhall and Lipsitt, 1964), few have made the distinction between active and quiet sleep stages. In the adult work cited above, habituation occurred in NREM sleep, usually stage 2; only McDonald and Carpenter (1975) have reported habituation in REM. The Hutts, in particular (Hutt et al. 1968a, 1969), have pointed out the dangers of ignoring state changes when studying habituation. Their reports indicated that depending upon the state at the beginning of the session and the session length, either habituation or dishabituation could be mimicked by spontaneous state changes. Since they found no evidence of habituation within a state, they concluded that convincing evidence of habituation independent of state changes had not been demonstrated for the neonate.

It is still the case that evidence for habituation within sleep states is sparse, but some work has been done since the Hutts' report. In two earlier reports (Engen et al., 1963; Engen and Lipsitt, 1965), sleep state was not explicitly noted, but the procedure of presenting stimuli only in the presence of even respiration and absence of motor activity provided some assurance that testing took place in quiet sleep. In both studies odorants were presented to neonates for 10 trials of 10 sec. each, followed by a change in odorant. In the 1965 study receptor adaptation was cleverly excluded as an explanation by presenting an odor mixture on the initial trials and one of the components of the mixture on the change trial. Results for both studies showed that respiratory changes and ratings of combined motor and autonomic responses decreased linearly over the 10 trials and recovered following the change in stimulus. Ashton (1973b) more carefully examined state, but other procedures made the evidence of response decrement difficult to interpret. In two experiments, one with 75 dB and one with 85 dB tones, neonates received six or fewer stimulations at 2-min intervals in the first active and again in the first quiet sleep period following feeding, and whenever possible the second sleep-cycle states as well. General motor activity was found to habituate in nearly all conditions but heart rate accelerative responses habituated only in the first active sleep period in both studies and in the first quiet sleep period for 85 dB tones. It is difficult to rule out the possibility that the lack of consistent habituation in quiet sleep (which in neonates always follows active sleep) and in the second sleep cycle may be due to the prior habituation, which reliably occurred in the first active sleep period. Further, without a test of dishabituation, the stimulus specificity of the decrement cannot be assured. Changes in responsivity to stimulus repetition might be especially likely in the initial period following sleep onset. Schaefer (1975) examined both habituation and dishabituation of neonates' EEG desynchronization responses in quiet sleep. Both tone and white noise were tested, and recordings were made at both anterior and posterior head regions. Habituation was significant only for white-noise stimuli and for the posterior recording site; dishabituation occurred with a change to tone after 15 trials.

There are almost no studies of habituation in the older sleeping infant, and the few that exist do not clearly distinguish between sleep states. Lewis, et al. (1969) reported significant habituation of cardiac responses to 30 repetitions of tactile stimuli in 2- to 6-week-old sleeping infants. Subjects were believed to be in quiet sleep, but this was not confirmed with specific observations. These stimuli did not produce habituation in awake infants, but procedures allowed long interruptions and the restarting of sessions when awake infants became upset, which would not be conducive to habituation. Campos and Brackbill (1973) presented 80 dB bursts of white noise at 40-sec intervals to 1- to 6-week-old infants, some of whom remained asleep throughout testing. Habituation to a criterion occurred, but reportedly only about half of this group reached the criterion before state changed, apparently from active to quiet sleep.

It is evident that there is a definite need for assessment of habituation during sleep in the older infant as well as in the neonate, using procedures that (1) distinguish between quiet and active sleep, (2) present stimuli in each state independently, and (3) assess the stimulus specificity of response decrements with dishabituation trials. In general the available data are too few and too unstable to draw anything but the most tenuous conclusions regarding developmental changes in habituation during sleep. However, it may serve to summarize the results by noting that, taken as a whole, the data indicate that habituation appears to be readily elicited in active or REM sleep in neonates, at least in the first sleep cycle, but not in adults. Habituation in quiet or NREM sleep appears to occur at all ages.

BIBLIOGRAPHY

Adkinson, C. D., and Berg, W. K. Cardiac deceleration in newborns: Habituation, dishabituation, and offset responses. *Journal of Experimental Child Psychology,* 1976, **21,** 46–60.

Agnew, H. W., Webb, W. B., and Williams, R. L. The first night effect: An EEG study of sleep. *Psychophysiology,* 1966, **2,** 263–266.

Akiyama, Y., Schulte, F. J., Schultz, M. A., and Parmelee, A. H. Acoustically evoked responses in premature and full term infants. *Electroencephalography and Clinical Neurophysiology,* 1969, **26,** 371–380.

Allen, S. R., Oswald, I., Lewis., S., and Tagney, J. The effects of distorted visual input on sleep. *Psychophysiology,* 1972, **9,** 498–504.

Anders, T., and Chalemian, R. The effects of circumcision on sleep-wake states in human neonates. *Psychosomatic Medicine,* 1974, **36,** 174–179.

Anders, T., Emde, R., and Parmelee, A. A manual of standardized terminology, techniques and criteria for scoring of states of sleep and wakefulness in newborn infants, UCLA Brain Information Service, Los Angeles, 1971.

Anders, T. F., and Roffwarg, H. P. The effects of selective interruption and deprivation of sleep in the human newborn. *Developmental Psychobiology,* 1973, **6,** 77–89.

Arezzo, J., Pickoff, A., and Vaughan, H. G. The sources and intracerebral distribution of auditory evoked potentials in the alert rhesus monkey. *Brain Research,* 1975, **90,** 57–73.

Arnold, W. R., and Porges, S. W. Heart rate components of orientation in newborns as a function of age and experience. Paper presented at the meeting of the Eastern Psychological Association, Boston, 1972.

Aserinsky, E. Rapid eye movement density and pattern in the sleep of normal young adults. *Psychophysiology,* 1971, **8,** 361–375.

Ashton, R. Behavioral sleep cycles in the human newborn. *Child Development,* 1971a, **42,** 2098–2100.

Ashton, R. The effects of the environment upon state cycles in the human newborn. *Journal of Experimental Child Psychology,* 1971b, **12,** 1–9.

Ashton, R. The state variable in neonatal research. *Merrill-Palmer Quarterly,* 1973a, **19,** 3–20.

Ashton, R. The influence of state and prandial condition upon the reactivity of the newborn to auditory stimulation. *Journal of Experimental Child Psychology,* 1973b, **15,** 315–327.

Balzamo, E., Bradley, R. J., and Rhodes, J. M. Sleep ontogeny in the chimpanzee: From two months to forty-one months. *Electroencephalography and Clinical Neurophysiology,* 1972, **33,** 47–60.

Barnet, A. B., and Goodwin, R. S. Averaged evoked electroencephalographic responses to clicks in the human newborn. *Electroencephalography and Clinical Neurophysiology,* 1965, **18,** 441–450.

Barnet, A. B., Lodge, A., and Armington, J. C. Electroretinogram in newborn human infants. *Science,* 1965, **148,** 651–654.

Barnet, A. B., Ohlrich, E. S., and Shanks, B. L. EEG evoked responses to repetitive auditory stimulation in normal and Down's syndrome infants. *Developmental Medicine and Child Neurology,* 1971, **13,** 321–329.

Barnet, A. B., Ohlrich, E. S., Weiss, I. P., and Shanks, B. Auditory evoked potentials during sleep in normal children from ten days to three years of age. *Electroencephalography and Clinical Neurophysiology,* 1975, **39,** 29–41.

Bartoshuk, A. K. Human neonatal cardiac responses to sound: A power function. *Psychonomic Science,* 1964, **1,** 151–152.

Bartoshuk, A. K. Human neonatal cardiac acceleration to sound: Habituation and dishabituation. *Perceptual and Motor Skills,* 1962, **15,** 15–27.

Bell, R. Q. Sleep cycles and skin potential in newborns studied with a simplified observation and recording system. *Psychophysiology,* 1970, **6,** 778–786.

Bench, J. "Square wave stimuli" and neonatal auditory behavior: Some comments on Ashton (1971), Hutt et al. (1968), and Lenard et al. (1969). *Journal of Experimental Child Psychology,* 1973, **16,** 521–527.

Bench, J. Some effects of audio-frequency stimulation on the crying baby. *Journal of Auditory Research,* 1969, **9,** 122–128.

Berg, K. M. Heart rate and vasomotor responses as a function of stimulus duration and intensity. Unpublished M. A. thesis. University of Wisconsin, Madison, 1970.

Berg, K. M., Berg, W. K., and Graham, F. K. Infant heart rate response as a function of stimulus and state. *Psychophysiology,* 1971, **8,** 30–44.

Berg, W. K. Cardiac components of defense response in infants. *Psychophysiology,* 1975, **12,** 224.

Berg, W. K. Cardiac orienting responses of 6- and 16-week-old infants. *Journal of Experimental Child Psychology,* 1974, **17,** 303–312.

Berg, W. K. Habituation and dishabituation of cardiac responses in four-month-old, awake infants. *Journal of Experimental Child Psychology,* 1972, **14,** 92–107.

Berg, W. K., Adkinson, C. D., and Strock, B. D. Duration and frequency of periods of alertness in neonates. *Developmental Psychology,* 1973, **9,** 434.

Berg, W. K., Jackson, J. C., and Graham, F. K. Tone intensity and rise-decay time effects on cardiac responses during sleep. *Psychophysiology*, 1975, **12**, 254–261.

Berg, W. K., Silverstein, L. D., Verzijl-Tweed, N., and Clarkson, M. Enhanced cardiac decelerations to near-threshold stimuli in infants. *Psychophysiology*, 1977, **14**, 98 (abstract).

Berger, R. J. Oculomotor control: A possible function of REM sleep. *Psychological Review*, 1969, **76**, 144–164.

Berkson, G., Wasserman, G., and Behrman, R. Heart rate response to an auditory stimulus in premature infants. *Psychophysiology*, 1974, **11**, 244–246.

Bernstein, P., Emde, R., and Campos, J. REM sleep in four-month infants under home and laboratory conditions. *Psychosomatic Medicine*, 1973, **35**, 322–329.

Bert, J., Kripke, D. F., and Rhodes, J. Electroencephalogram of the mature chimpanzee: twenty-four-hour recordings. *Electroencephalography and Clinical Neurophysiology*, 1970, **28**, 368–373.

Birns, B., Blank, M., Bridger, W. H., and Escalona, S. K. Behavioral inhibition in neonates produced by auditory stimuli. *Child Development*, 1965, **36**, 639–645.

Boismier, J. D. Visual stimulation and wake-sleep behavior in human neonates . *Developmental Psychobiology*, 1977, **10**, 219–227.

Boismier, J. D., Chappell, P. F., and Meier, G. W. Wakefulness and REM sleep in human neonates . *Developmental Psychobiology*, 1974, **7**, 304.

Brackbill, Y. The role of the cortex in orienting: Orienting reflex in an anencephalic human infant. *Developmental Psychology*, 1971, **5**, 195–201.

Bridger, W. H. Sensory habituation and discrimination in the human neonate. *American Journal of Psychiatry*, 1961, **117**, 991–996.

Bronson, G. The postnatal growth of visual capacity. *Child Development*, 1974, **45**, 873–890.

Brown, J. W., Leavitt, L. A., and Graham, F. K. Response to auditory stimuli in 6- and 9-week-old human infants. *Developmental Psychobiology*, 1977, **10**, 255–266.

Buchwald, J. S., and Huang, C. Far field acoustic response: origins in the cat. *Science*, 1975, **189**, 382–384.

Campos, J. J., and Brackbill, Y. Infant state: Relationship to heart rate, behavioral response and response decrement. *Developmental Psychobiology*, 1973, **6**, 9–20.

Carskadon, M. A., and Dement, W. C. Sleep studies on a 90-minute day. *Electroencephalography and Clinical Neurophysiology*, 1975, **39**, 145–155.

Ciganek, L. Visual evoked responses. In A. Remond (ed.), *Handbook of Electroencephalography and Clinical Neurophysiology*, Vol. 8A. Amsterdam; Elsevier, 1975.

Clarkson, M. Effects of frequency, complexity, and temporal pattern of auditory stimuli on cardiac orienting in neonates. Unpublished M.A. thesis, University of Florida, 1977.

Clarkson, M., and Berg, W. K. Cardiac deceleration in neonates is influenced by temporal pattern and spectral complexity of auditory stimuli. *Psychophysiology*, 1978, **5**, 284 (abstract).

Clifton, R. K. The relation of infant cardiac responding to behavioral state and motor activity. In W. A. Collins (ed.), *Minnesota Symposia on Child Psychology*, Vol. 11. Chicago: Crowell, 1977.

Clifton, R. K., and Meyers, W. J. The heart-rate response of four-month-old infants to auditory stimuli. *Journal of Experimental Child Psychology*, 1969, **7**, 122–135.

Clifton, R. K., and Nelson, M. N. Developmental study of habituation in infants: The importance of paradigm, response system and state. In T. J. Tighe and R. N. Leaton (eds.), *Habituation: Perspectives from Child Development, Animal Behavior, and Neurophysiology*. Hillsdale, N.J.: Erlbaum, 1976.

Conel, J. L. Histologic development of the cerebral cortex. In *Biology of Mental Health and Disease*, The twenty-seventh annual conference of the Milbank Memorial Fund. New York: Hoeber, 1952.

Crook, C. K. Neonatal sucking: Effects of quantity of response-contingent fluid upon sucking rhythm and heart rate. *Journal of Experimental Child Psychology,* 1976, **21,** 539–548.

Crook, C. K., and Lipsitt, L. P. Neonatal nutritive sucking: Effects of taste stimulation upon sucking rhythm and heart rate. *Child Development,* 1976, **47,** 518–522.

Crowell, D. H., Jones, R. H., Nakagawa, J. K., and Kapuniai, L. E. Heart rate responses of human newborns to modulated pure tones. *Proceedings of the Royal Society of Medicine,* 1971, **64,** 8–10.

Curzi-Dascalova, L., and Dreyfus-Brisac, C. Distribution of skin potential responses according to states of sleep during the first months of life in human babies. *Electroencephalography and Clinical Neurophysiology,* 1976, **41,** 399–407.

Curzi-Dascalova, L., Pajot, N., and Dreyfus-Brisac, C. Spontaneous skin potential responses during sleep: Comparative studies in newborns and babies between 2 and 5 months of age. *Neuropadiatrie,* 1974, **5,** 250–257.

Curzi-Dascalova, L., Pajot, N., and Dreyfus-Brisac, C. Spontaneous skin potential responses in sleeping infants between 24 and 41 weeks of conceptional age. *Psychophysiology,* 1973, **10,** 478–487.

Davis, H., Osterhammel, R. A., Weir, C. C., and Gjerdigen, D. B. Slow vertex potentials: Interactions among auditory, tactile, electric and visual stimuli. *Electroencephalography and Clinical Neurophysiology,* 1972, **33,** 537–545.

DeHaan, R., Patrick, J., Chess, G. F., and Jaco, N. T. Definition of sleep state in the newborn infant by heart rate analysis. *American Journal of Obstetrics and Gynecology,* 1977, **127,** 753–758.

Dement, W. C. The biological role of REM sleep (circa 1968). In A. Kales (ed.), *Sleep: Physiology and Pathology.* Philadelphia: Lippincott, 1969.

Desmedt, J. E., Brunko, E., and Debecker, J. Maturation of the somatosensory evoked potentials in normal infants and children with special reference to the early N_1 component. *Electroencephalography and Clinical Neurophysiology,* 1976, **40,** 43–58.

Desmedt, J. E., and Debecker, J. The somatosensory cerebral evoked potentials of the sleeping human newborn. In C. D. Clemente, D. P. Purpura, and F. E. Mayer (eds.), *Sleep and the Maturing Nervous System.* New York: Academic, 1972.

Desmedt, J. E., and Manil, J. Somato-sensory evoked potentials of the normal human neonate in REM sleep, in slow wave sleep and in waking. *Electroencephalography and Clinical Neurophysiology,* 1970, **29,** 113–126.

Dittrichova, J. Development of sleep in infancy. *Journal of Applied Physiology,* 1966, **21,** 1243–1246.

Dittrichova, J., Paul, K., and Pavlikova, E. Rapid eye movements in paradoxical sleep in infants. *Neuropadiatrie,* 1972, **3,** 238–257.

Dobbing, J., and Sands, J. Quantitative growth and development of the human brain. *Archives of Disease in Childhood,* 1973, **48,** 757–767.

Dobson, V. Spectral sensitivity of the 2-month infant as measured by the visually evoked cortical potential. *Vision Research,* 1976, **16,** 367–374.

Dreyfus-Brisac, C. Sleep ontogenesis in early human prematures from 24 to 27 weeks of conceptional age. *Developmental Psychobiology,* 1968, **1,** 162–169.

Dreyfus-Brisac, C. Ontogenesis of sleep in human prematures after 32 weeks of conceptional age. *Developmental Psychobiology,* 1970, **3,** 91–121.

Dreyfus-Brisac, C. Ontogénése du sommeil chez le prematuré humain: étude polygraphique. In A. Minkowski (ed.), *Regional Development of the Brain in Early Life.* Oxford: Blackwell, 1967.

Dreyfus-Brisac, C., and Curzi-Dascalova, L. The EEG during the first year of life. *Handbook of Electroencephalography and Clinical Neurophysiology,* Vol. 6B. Amsterdam: Elsevier, 1975.

Dreyfus-Brisac, C., and Monod, N. The electroencephalogram of full-term newborns and premature infants. *Handbook of Electroencephalography and Clinical Neurophysiology,* Vol. 6B. Amsterdam: Elsevier, 1975.

Dustman, R. E., and Beck, E. C. Effects of maturation and aging on the wave form of VERs. *Electroencephalography and Clinical Neurophysiology,* 1969, **26,** 2–11.

Eichorn, D. Physiological development. In P. H. Mussen (ed.), *Carmichael's Manual of Child Psychology.* New York: Wiley, 1970.

Eisenberg, R. B. *Auditory Competence in Early Life.* Baltimore: University Park, 1976.

Eisenberg, R. B. The organization of auditory behavior. *Journal of Speech and Hearing Research,* 1970, **13,** 454–471.

Ellingson, R. J. The study of brain electrical activity in infants. In L. P. Lipsitt and C. C. Spiker (eds.), *Advances in Child Development and Behavior,* Vol. 111. New York: Academic, 1967.

Ellingson, R. J. Variability of visual evoked responses in the human newborn. *Electroencephalography and Clinical Neurophysiology,* 1970, **29,** 10–19.

Ellingson, R. J., Danahy, T., Nelson, B., and Lathrop, G. Variability of auditory evoked potentials in human newborns. *Electroencephalography and Clinical Neurophysiology,* 1974, **36,** 155–162.

Ellingson, R. J., Lathrop, G. H., Danahy, T., and Nelson, B. Variability of visual evoked potentials in human infants and adults. *Electroencephalography and Clinical Neurophysiology,* 1973, **34,** 113–124.

Emde, R., Harmon, R., Metcalf, D., Koenig, K., and Wagonfeld, S. Stress and neonatal sleep. *Psychosomatic Medicine,* 1971, **33,** 491–497.

Emde, R. N., and Metcalf, D. R. An electroencephalographic study of behavioral rapid eye movement states in the human newborn. *Journal of Nervous and Mental Disease,* 1970, **150,** 376–386.

Emde, R., Swedberg, J., and Suzuki, B. Human wakefulness and biological rhythms after birth. *Archives of General Psychiatry,* 1975, **32,** 780–789.

Emde, R. N., and Walker, S. Longitudinal study of infant sleep: Results of 14 subjects studied at monthly intervals. *Psychophysiology,* 1976, **13,** 456–461.

Engel, R. Early waves of the electroencephalic auditory response in neonates. *Neuropadiatrie,* 1971, **3,** 147–154.

Engel, R., and Young, N. B. Calibrated pure tone audiograms in normal neonates based on evoked electroencephalographic responses. *Neuropadiatrie,* 1969, **1,** 149–160.

Engen, T., and Lipsitt, L. P. Decrement and recovery of responses to olfactory stimuli. *Journal of Comparative and Physiological Psychology,* 1965, **59,** 312–316.

Engen, T., Lipsitt, L. P., and Kaye, H. Olfactory responses and adaptation in the human neonate. *Journal of Comparative and Physiological Psychology,* 1963, **56,** 73–77.

Fantz, R. L., Fagan, J. F., and Miranda, S. B. Early visual selectivity. In L. B. Cohen and P. Salapatek (eds.), *Infant Perception: From Sensation to Cognition,* Vol. 1. *Basic Visual Processes.* New York: Academic, 1975.

Ferriss, G. S., Davis, G. D., Dorsen, M., and Hackett, E. R. Changes in latency and form of the photically induced average evoked response in human infants. *Electroencephalography and Clinical Neurophysiology,* 1967, **22,** 305–312.

Firth, H. Habituation during sleep. *Psychophysiology,* 1973, **10,** 43–51.

Fogarty, T. P., and Reuben, R. N. Light-evoked cortical and retinal responses in premature infants. *Archives of Ophthalmology,* 1969, **81,** 454–459.

Friedman, Steven. Habituation and recovery of visual response in the alert human newborn. *Journal of Experimental Child Psychology,* 1972, **13,** 339–349.

Friedman, S., Bruno, L. A., and Vietze, P. Newborn habituation to visual stimuli: A sex difference in novelty detection. *Journal of Experimental Child Psychology,* 1974, **18,** 242–251.

Fruhstorfer, H. Habituation and dishabituation of the human vertex response. *Electroencephalography and Clinical Neurophysiology,* 1971, **30,** 306–312.

Fruhstorfer, H., Partanen, J., and Lumio, J. Vertex sharp waves and heart action during onset of sleep. *Electroencephalography and Clinical Neurophysiology,* 1971, **31,** 614–617.

Gabriel, M., Albani, M., and Schulte, F. J. Apneic spells and sleep states in pre-term infants. *Pediatrics,* 1976, **57,** 142–147.

Gaensbauer, T., and Emde, R. N. Wakefulness and feeding in human newborns. *Archives of General Psychiatry,* 1973, **28,** 894–897.

Globus, C. G. Quantification of the REM sleep cycle as a rhythm. *Psychophysiology,* 1970, **7,** 248–253.

Globus, G., Phoebus, E., and Moore, C. REM "sleep" manifestations during waking. *Psychophysiology,* 1970, **7,** 308.

Goff, G. D., Matsumiya, Y., Allison, T., and Goff, W. R. The scalp topography of human somatosensory and auditory evoked potentials. *Electroencephalography and Clinical Neurophysiology,* 1977, **42,** 57–76.

Goldie, L., and Van Velzer, C. Innate sleep rhythms. *Brain,* 1965, **88,** 1043–1056.

Graham, F. K. The more or less startling effects of weak prestimulation. *Psychophysiology,* 1975, **12,** 238–248.

Graham, F. K. Habituation and dishabituation of responses innervated by the autonomic nervous system. In H. V. S. Peeke and M. J. Herz (eds.), *Habituation: Behavioral Studies and Physiological Substrates.* New York: Academic, 1973.

Graham, F. K., and Jackson, J. C. Arousal systems and infant heart rate responses. In L. P. Lipsitt and H. W. Reese (eds.), *Advances in Child Development and Behavior,* Vol. V. New York: Academic, 1970.

Graham, F. K., and Clifton, R. K. Heart-rate change as a component of the orienting response. *Psychological Bulletin,* 1966, **65,** 305–320.

Graham, F. K., Leavitt, L. A., Strock, B. D., and Brown, J. W. Precocious cardiac orienting in a human, anencephalic infant. *Science,* 1978, **199,** 322–324.

Graham, F. K., and Slaby, D. A. Differential heart rate changes to equally intense white noise and tone. *Psychophysiology,* 1973, **10,** 347–362.

Graziani, L. J., Katz, L., Cracco, R., Cracco, J. B., and Weitzman, E. D. The maturation and interrelationship of EEG patterns and auditory evoked responses in premature infants. *Electroencephalography and Clinical Neurophysiology,* 1974, **36,** 367–375.

Gregg, C., Clifton, R. K., and Haith, M. M. A possible explanation for the frequent failure to find cardiac orienting in the newborn infant. *Developmental Psychology,* 1976, **12,** 75–76.

Groves, P. M., and Thompson, R. F. Habituation: A dual-process theory. *Psychological Review,* 1970, **77,** 419–450.

Guilleminault, C., Peraita, R., Souquet, M., and Dement, W. Apneas during sleep in infants: Possible relationship with sudden infant death syndrome. *Science,* 1975, **190,** 677–679.

Halliday, A. M. Somatosensory evoked responses. In A. Remond (ed.), *Handbook of Electroencephalography and Clinical Neurophysiology,* Vol. 8A. Amsterdam: Elsevier, 1975.

Harper, R. M., Hoppenbrouwers, T., Sterman, M. B., McGinty, D. J., and Hodgman, J. Polygraphic studies of normal infants during the first six months of life: I. Heart rate and variability as a function of state. *Pediatric Research,* 1976, **10,** 945–951.

Harter, M. R., Deaton, F. K., and Odom, J. V. Maturation of evoked potentials and visual preference in 6–45-day-old infants: Effects of check size, visual acuity and refractive error. *Electroencephalography and Clinical Neurophysiology,* 1977, **42,** 595–607.

Harter, M. R., and Suitt, C. D. Visually-evoked cortical responses and pattern vision in the infant:

A longitudinal study. *Psychonomic Science,* 1970, **18,** 235–237.

Harter, M. R., and White, C. T. Effects of contour sharpness and check size on visually evoked cortical potentials. *Vision Research,* 1968, **8,** 701–711.

Harter, M. R., and White, C. T. Evoked cortical responses to checkerboard patterns: Effects of check-size as a function of visual acuity. *Electroencephalography and Clinical Neurophysiology,* 1970, **28,** 48–54.

Hatton, H. M., Berg, W. K., and Graham, F. K. Effects of acoustic rise time on heart rate response. *Psychonomic Science,* 1970, **19,** 101–103.

Hecox, K. Electrophysiological correlates of human auditory development. In L. B. Cohen and P. Salapatek (eds.), *Infant perception: From Sensation to Cognition.* 11. *Perception of Space, Speech, and Sound.* New York: Academic, 1975.

Hellbrugge, T., Lange, J. E., Rutenfranz, J., and Stehr, K. Circadian periodicity of physiological functions in different stages of infancy and childhood. *Annals of the New York Academy of Sciences,* 1964, **117,** 361–373.

Hirsh, I. J., and Sherrick, C. E. Perceived order in different sense modalities. *Journal of Experimental Psychology,* 1961, **62,** 423–432.

Hoffman, H. S., and Marsh, R. Personal communication, 1977.

Hoffman, H. S., and Searle, J. L. Acoustic and temporal factors in the evocation of startle. *Journal of the Acoustical Society of America,* 1968, **43,** 269–282.

Horne, J. A., and Walmsley, B. Daytime visual load and the effects upon human sleep. *Psychophysiology,* 1976, **13,** 115–120.

Horsten, G. P. M., and Winkelman, J. E. Electrical activity of the retina in relation to the histological differentiation in infants born prematurely and at full term. *Vision Research,* 1962, **2,** 269–276.

Horsten, G. P. M., and Winkelman, J. E. Electro-retinographic critical fusion frequency of the retina in relation to the histological development in man and animals. *Documenta Opthalmologica,* 1964, **18,** 515–521.

Hrbek, A., Hrbkova, M., and Lenard, H. G. Somato-sensory, auditory and visual evoked responses in newborn infants during sleep and wakefulness. *Electroencephalography and Clinical Neurophysiology,* 1969, **26,** 597–603.

Hrbek, A., Hrbkova, M., and Lenard, H. G. Somato-sensory evoked responses in newborn infants. *Electroencephalography and Clinical Neurophysiology,* 1968, **25,** 443–448.

Hrbek, A., Karlberg, P., and Olsson, T. Development of visual and somatosensory evoked responses in pre-term newborn infants. *Electroencephalography and Clinical Neurophysiology,* 1973, **34,** 225–232.

Hutt, C., Bernuth, H. V., Lenard, H. G., Hutt, S. S., and Prechtl, H. F. Habituation in relation to state in the human neonate. *Nature,* 1968a, **220,** 618–620.

Hutt, S. J., Hutt, C., Lenard, H. G., Bernuth, H. V., and Muntjewerff, W. J. Auditory responsivity in the human neonate. *Nature,* 1968b, **218,** 888–890.

Hutt, S. J., Lenard, H. G., and Prechtl, H. F. R. Psychophysiological studies in newborn infants. In L. P. Lipsitt and H. W. Reese (eds.), *Advances in Child Development and Behavior.* New York: Academic, 1969.

Jackson, J. C. Amplitude and habituation of the orienting reflex as a function of stimulus intensity. *Psychophysiology,* 1974, **11,** 647–659.

Jackson, J. C., Kantowitz, S. R., and Graham, F. K. Can newborns show cardiac orienting? *Child Development,* 1971, **42,** 107–121.

Jeffrey, W. E., and Cohen, L. B. Habituation in the human infant. In H. Reese (ed.), *Advances in Child Development and Behavior,* Vol. 6. New York: Academic, 1971.

Jewett, D. L., Romano, M. N., and Williston, J. S. Human auditory evoked potentials: Possible brain stem components detected on the scalp. *Science,* 1970, **167,** 1517–1518.

Johnson, L. C., and Lubin, A. The orienting reflex during waking and sleeping. *Electroencephalography and Clinical Neurophysiology,* 1967, **22,** 11–21.

Johnson, L. C., and Lubin, A. Spontaneous electrodermal activity during sleeping and waking. *Psychophysiology,* 1966, **3,** 8–17.

Johnson, L. C., Townsend, R. E., and Wilson, M. R. Habituation during sleeping and waking. *Psychophysiology,* 1975, **12,** 574–584.

Joseph, J. P., Lesevre, N., and Dreyfus-Brisac, C. Spatio-temporal organization of EEG in premature infants and full term newborns. *Electroencephalography and Clinical Neurophysiology,* 1976, **40,** 153–168.

Jouvet, M. Biogenic amines and the states of sleep. *Science,* 1969, **163,** 32–41.

Jouvet-Mounier, D., Astic, L., and Lacote, D. Ontogenesis of the states of sleep in rat, cat and guinea pig during the first postnatal month. *Developmental Psychobiology,* 1970, **2,** 216–239.

Kagan, J., and Lewis, M. Studies of attention in the human infant. *Merrill-Palmer Quarterly,* 1965, **11,** 95–127.

Karmel, B. Z. Contour effects and pattern preferences in infants: A reply to Greenberg and O'Donnell. *Child Development,* 1974, **45,** 196–199.

Karmel, B. Z. The effect of age, complexity and amount of contour on pattern preferences in human infants. *Journal of Experimental Child Psychology,* 1969, **7,** 339–354.

Karmel, B. Z., Hoffman, R. F., and Fegy, M. J. Processing of contour information by human infants evidenced by pattern-dependent evoked potentials. *Child Development,* 1974, **45,** 39–48.

Karmel, B. Z., and Maisel, E. B. A neuronal activity model for infant visual attention. In L. B. Cohen and P. Salapatek (eds.), *Infant Perception: From Sensation to Cognition.* 1. *Basic Visual Processes.* New York: Academic, 1975.

Kearsley, R. B. The newborn's response to auditory stimulation: A demonstration of orienting and defensive behavior. *Child Development,* 1973, **44,** 582–590.

Keefe, F. B., Johnson, L. C., and Hunter, E. J. EEG and autonomic response patterns during waking and sleep stages. *Psychophysiology,* 1971, **8,** 198–212.

Keen, J. K. Fixation and cardiac responses of four-month infants to repeated visual stimuli of varying complexities. Unpublished M.A. thesis, University of Iowa, 1974.

Keen, R. Effects of auditory stimuli on sucking behavior in the human neonate. *Journal of Experimental Child Psychology,* 1964, **1,** 348–354.

Kleitman, N. *Sleep and Wakefulness.* Chicago: University of Chicago, 1963.

Kligman, D., Smyrl, R., and Emde, R. A. A "nonintrusive" longitudinal study of infant sleep. *Psychosomatic Medicine,* 1975, **37,** 448–453.

Korner, A. F. REM organization in neonates. *Archives of General Psychiatry,* 1968, **19,** 330–340.

Koumans, A. J. R., Tursky, B., and Soloman, P. Electrodermal levels and fluctuations during normal sleep. *Psychophysiology,* 1968, **5,** 300–306.

Laget, P., Raimbault, J., D'Allest, A. M., Flores-Guevara, R., Mariani, J., and Thieriot-Prevost, G. La maturation des potentiels evoques somestheseques (PES) chez l'homme. *Electroencephalography and Clinical Neurophysiology,* 1976, **40,** 499–515.

Langford, G. W., Meddis, R., and Pearson, J. D. Awakening latency from sleep for meaningful and non-meaningful stimuli. *Psychophysiology,* 1974, **11,** 1–5.

Larsson, L. E., and Prevec, T. S. Somato-sensory response to mechanical stimulation as recorded in the human EEG. *Electroencephalography and Clinical Neurophysiology,* 1970, **28,** 162–172.

Lavie, P., Lord, J. W., and Frank, R. A. Basic rest-activity cycle in the perception of the spiral after-effect; a sensitive detector of a basic biological rhythm. *Behavioral Biology*, 1974, **11**, 373–379.

Leavitt, L. A., Brown, J. W., Morse, P. A., and Graham, F. K. Cardiac orienting and auditory discrimination in 6-week-old infants. *Developmental Psychology*, 1976, **12**, 514–523.

Lehtonen, J. B. Functional differentiation between late components of visual evoked potentials recorded at occiput and vertex: Effect of stimulus interval and contour. *Electroencephalography and Clinical Neurophysiology*, 1973, **35**, 75–82.

Lenard, H. G. Sleep studies in infancy: Facts, concepts and significance. *Acta Paediatrica Scandinavica*, 1970a, **59**, 572–581.

Lenard, H. G. The development of sleep spindles in the EEG during the first two years of life. *Neuropadiatrie*, 1970b, **1**, 264–276.

Lenard, H. G., Bernuth, H. V., and Hutt, S. J. Acoustic evoked responses in newborn infants: The influence of pitch and complexity of the stimulus. *Electroencephalography and Clinical Neurophysiology*, 1969, **27**, 121–127.

Lenard, H. G., and Ohlsen, I. Cortical responsivity during spindle sleep in young children. *Neuropadiatrie*, 1972, **3**, 258–267.

Lester, B. M. Cardiac habituation of the orienting response to an auditory signal in infants of varying nutritional status. *Developmental Psychology*, 1975, **11**, 432–442.

Leventhal, A. S., and Lipsitt, L. P. Adaptation, pitch discrimination and sound localization in the neonate. *Child Development*, 1964, **35**, 759–767.

Lewis, M. A developmental study of the cardiac response to stimulus onset and offset during the first year of life. *Psychophysiology*, 1971, **8**, 689–698.

Lewis, M., Bartels, B., and Goldberg, S. State as a determinant of infant's heart rate response to stimulation. *Science*, 1967, **155**, 486–488.

Lewis, M., Dodd, C., and Harwitz, M. Cardiac responsivity to tactile stimulation in waking and sleeping infants. *Perceptual and Motor Skills*, 1969, **29**, 259–269.

Lewis, M., Goldberg, S., and Campbell, H. A developmental study of information processing within the first three years of life: Response decrement to a redundant signal. *Monographs of the Society for Research in Child Development*, 1969, **34**, (9, Ser. 133).

Lewis, M., Kagan, J., Campbell, H., and Kalafat, J. The cardiac response as a correlate of attention in infants. *Child Development*, 1966, **37**, 63–71.

Lewis, M., Wilson, C. D., and Baumel, M. Attention distribution in the 24-month-old child: Variations in complexity and incongruity of the human form. *Child Development*, 1971, **42**, 429–438.

Licklider, J. C. R. Basic correlates of the auditory stimulus. In S. S. Stevens (ed.), *Handbook of Experimental Psychology*, New York: Wiley, 1951, 985–1039.

Lieb, J. P., and Karmel, B. Z. The processing of edge information in visual areas of the cortex as evidenced by evoked potentials. *Brain Research*, 1974, **76**, 503–519.

Lipsitt, L. P., and Jacklin, C. N. Cardiac deceleration and its stability in human newborns. *Developmental Psychology*, 1971, **5**, 535.

Lipsitt, L. P., Reilly, B. M., Butcher, M. J., and Greenwood, M. M. The stability and interrelationships of newborn sucking and heart rate. *Developmental Psychobiology*, 1976, **9**, 305–310.

Lipton, E. L., Steinschneider, A., and Richmond, J. B. Autonomic function in the neonate: VII. Maturational changes in cardiac control. *Child Development*, 1966, **37**, 1–16.

Lodge, A., Armington, J. C., Barnet, A. B., Shanks, B. L., and Newcomb, C. N. Newborn infants' electroretinograms and evoked electroencephalographic responses to orange and white light. *Child Development*, 1969, **40**, 267–293.

Marg, E., Freeman, D. N., Peltzman, P., and Goldstein, P. J. Visual acuity development in human infants: Evoked potential measurements. *Investigative Ophthalmology,* 1976, **15,** 150–153.

McCall, R. B., and Kagan, J. Attention in the infant: Effects of complexity, contour, perimeter, and familiarity. *Child Development,* 1967, **38,** 939–952.

McCall, R. B., and Melson, W. H. Complexity, contour and area as determinants of attention in infants. *Developmental Psychology,* 1970, **3,** 343–349.

McDonald, D. G., and Carpenter, F. A. Habituation of the orienting response in sleep. *Psychophysiology,* 1975, **12,** 618–623.

McGinty, J. Encephalization and the neural control of sleep. In M. B. Sterman, D. J. McGinty, and A. M. Adinolfi (eds.), *Brain Development and Behavior.* New York: Academic, 1971.

Mendel, M., and Goldstein, R. Stability of the early components of the averaged electroencephalic response. *Journal of Speech and Hearing Research,* 1969, **12,** 351–361.

Metcalf, D. The effects of extrauterine experience on the ontogenesis of EEG sleep spindles. *Psychosomatic Medicine,* 1969, **31,** 393–399.

Metcalf, D. R. EEG sleep spindle ontogenesis. *Neuropadiatrie,* 1970a, **1,** 428–433.

Metcalf, D. The ontogenesis of sleep-awake states from birth to 3 months. *Electroencephalography and Clinical Neurophysiology,* 1970b, **28,** 421.

Metcalf, D. R., Mondale, J., and Butler, F. K. Ontogenesis of spontaneous K-complexes. *Psychophysiology,* 1971, **8,** 340–347.

Monod, N., and Garma, L. Auditory responsivity in the human premature. *Biologia Neonatorum,* 1971, **17,** 292–316.

Monod, N., and Pajot, N. Le sommeil du nouveau-né et du prématuré I. Analyse des études polygraphiques (mouvements oculaires, respiration et E.E.G.) chez le nouveau-né à terme. *Biologia Neonatorum,* 1965, **8,** 281–307.

Murray, B., and Campbell, D. Differences between olfactory thresholds in two sleep states in the newborn infant. *Psychonomic Science,* 1970, **18,** 313–314.

Nelson, M. N., Clifton, R. K., Dowd, J. M., and Field, T. M. Cardiac responding to auditory stimuli in newborn infants: Why pacifiers should not be used when heart rate is the major dependent variable. *Infant Behavior and Development,* in press.

Obrist, P. A. The cardiovascular-behavioral interaction—As it appears today. *Psychophysiology,* 1976, **13,** 95–107.

Ohlrich, E. S., and Barnet, A. B. Auditory evoked responses during the first year of life. *Electroencephalography and Clinical Neurophysiology,* 1972, **32,** 161–169.

Onishi, S., and Davis, H. Auditory evoked responses in the sleeping infant. *Electroencephalography and Clinical Neurophysiology,* 1969, **26,** 114.

Ornitz, E. M., Forsythe, A. B., and de la Peña, A. The effect of vestibular and auditory stimulation on the rapid eye movements of REM sleep in normal children. *Electroencephalography and Clinical Neurophysiology,* 1973, **34,** 379–390.

Ornitz, E. M., Ritvo, E. R., Carr, E. M., Panman, L. M., and Walter, R. D. The variability of the averaged evoked response during sleep and dreaming in children and adults. *Electroencephalography and Clinical Neurophysiology,* 1967, **22,** 514–524.

Ornitz, E. M., Ritvo, E. R., Lee, Y. H., Panman, L. M., Walter, R. D., and Mason, A. The auditory evoked response in babies during REM sleep. *Electroencephalography and Clinical Neurophysiology,* 1969, **27,** 195–198.

Ornitz, E. M., Wechter, V., Hartman, D., Tanguay, P., Lee, J. M., Ritvo, E., and Walter, R. The EEG and rapid eye movements during REM sleep in babies. *Electroencephalography and Clinical Neurophysiology,* 1971, **30,** 350–353.

Othmer, E., Hayden, M. P., and Segelbaum, R. Encephalic cycles during sleep and wakefulness in humans: A 24-hour pattern. *Science,* 1969, **164,** 447–449.

Parmelee, A. H., Akiyama, Y., Schultz, M. A., Wenner, W. H., Schulte, F. J., and Stern, E. The electroencephalogram in active and quiet sleep in infants. In P. Kellaway and I. Petersen (eds.), *Clinical Electroencephalography of Children*. New York: Grune & Stratton, 1968a.

Parmelee, A. H., Akiyama, Y., Stern, E., and Harris, M. A. A periodic cerebral rhythm in newborn infants. *Experimental Neurology*, 1969, **25**, 575–584.

Parmelee, A. H., Schulte, F. J., Akiyama, Y., Wenner, W. H., Schultz, M. A., and Stern, E. Maturation of EEG activity during sleep in premature infants. *Electroencephalography and Clinical Neurophysiology*, 1968b, **24**, 319–329.

Parmelee, A., and Stern, E. Development of states in infants. In C. B. Clemente, D. P. Purpura, and F. E. Mayer (eds.), *Sleep and the Maturing Nervous System*. New York: Academic, 1972.

Parmelee, A. H., Stern, E., and Harris, M. A. Maturation of respiration in prematures and young infants. *Neuropadiatrie*, 1972, **3**, 294–304.

Parmelee, A. H., Wenner, W. H., Akiyama, Y., Stern, E., and Flescher, J. Electroencephalography and brain maturation. In A. Minkowski (ed.), *Symposium on Regional Development of the Brain in Early Life*. Philadelphia: Davis, 1967a.

Parmelee, A., Wenner, W., Akiyama, Y., Schultz, M., and Stern, E. Sleep states in premature infants. *Developmental Medicine and Child Neurology*, 1967b, **9**, 70–77.

Parmelee, A. H., Wenner, W. H., and Schulz, H. R. Infant sleep patterns from birth to 16 weeks of age. *Journal of Pediatrics*, 1964, **65**, 576–582.

Petre-Quadens, O. On the different phases of the sleep of the newborn with special reference to the activated phase, or phase d. *Journal of Neurological Sciences*, 1966, **3**, 151–161.

Petre-Quadens, O. Ontogenesis of paradoxical sleep in the human newborn. *Journal of Neurological Sciences*, 1967, **4**, 154–157.

Petre-Quadens, O., de Lee, C., and Remy, M. Eye movement density during sleep and brain maturation, *Brain Research*, 1971, **26**, 49–56.

Picton, T. W., and Hillyard, S. A. Human auditory evoked potentials. II: Effects of attention. *Electroencephalography and Clinical Neurophysiology*, 1974, **36**, 191–199.

Picton, T. W., Hillyard, S. A., Krausz, H. I., and Galambos, R. Human auditory evoked potentials. I: Evaluation of components. *Electroencephalography and Clinical Neurophysiology*, 1974, **36**, 179–190.

Pomerleau-Malcuit, A., and Clifton, R. K. Neonatal heart-rate response to tactile, auditory, and vestibular stimulation in different states. *Child Development*, 1973, **44**, 485–496.

Pomerleau-Malcuit, A., Malcuit, G., and Clifton, R. K. An attempt to elicit cardiac orienting and defense responses in the newborn to two types of facial stimulation. *Psychophysiology*, 1975, **12**, 527–535.

Porges, S. W. Heart rate indices of newborn attentional responsivity. *Merrill-Palmer Quarterly*, 1974, **20**, 231–254.

Porges, S. W., Arnold, W. R., and Forbes, E. J. Heart rate variability: An index of attentional responsivity in human newborns. *Developmental Psychology*, 1973, **8**, 85–92.

Porges, S. W., Stamps, L. E., and Walter, G. F. Heart rate variability and newborn heart rate responses to illumination changes. *Developmental Psychology*, 1974, **10**, 507–513.

Prechtl, H. F. R. The behavioral states of the newborn infant (a review). *Brain Research*, 1974, **76**, 185–212.

Prechtl, H. D., and Lenard, H. G. A study of eye movements in sleeping newborn infants. *Brain Research*, 1967, **5**, 477–493.

Ratner, S. C. Habituation: Research and theory. In J. Reynierse (ed.), *Current Issues in Animal Learning*. Lincoln: University of Nebraska, 1970.

Rechtschaffen, A., Hauri, P., and Zeitlin, M. Auditory awakening thresholds in REM and NREM sleep stages. *Perceptual and Motor Skills*, 1966, **22**, 927–942.

Reiter, L., and Ison, J. Inhibition of the human eyeblink reflex: An evaluation of the sensitivity of the Wendt-Yerkes method for threshold detection. *Journal of Experimental Psychology: Human Perception and Performance,* 1977, **3,** 325–336.

Rewey, H. H. Developmental change in infant heart rate response during sleeping and waking states. *Developmental Psychology,* 1973, **8,** 35–41.

Roffwarg, H., Muzio, J., and Dement, W. Ontogenetic development of the human sleep-dream cycle. *Science,* 1966, **152,** 604–619.

Rose, G. H. Relationship of electrophysiological and behavioral indices of visual development in mammals. In M. B. Sterman, D. J. McGinty, and A. M. Adinolfi)eds.), *Brain Development and Behavior.* New York: Academic, 1971.

Rose, G. H., and Ellingson, R. J. Ontogenesis of evoked potentials. In W. A. Himwich (ed.), *Developmental Neurobiology.* Springfield, Ill.: Thomas, 1970.

Rose, G. H., and Lindsley, D. B. Visually evoked electrocortical responses in kittens. Development of specific and nonspecific systems. *Science,* 1965, **148,** 1244–1246.

Rose, S. A., Schmidt, K., and Bridger, W. H. Changes in tactile responsivity during sleep in the human newborn infant. *Developmental Psychology,* 1978, **14,** 163–172.

Rousey, C. L., and Reitz, W. E. Respiratory changes at auditory and visual thresholds. *Psychophysiology,* 1967, **3,** 258–261.

Salamy, A., and McKean, C. M. Postnatal development of human brainstem potentials during the first year of life. *Electroencephalography and Clinical Neurophysiology,* 1976, **40,** 418–426.

Salamy, A., McKean, C. M., and Buda, F. Maturational changes in auditory transmission as reflected in human brainstem potentials. *Brain Research,* 1975, **96,** 361–366.

Sameroff, A. J. Can conditioned responses be established in the newborn infant? *Developmental Psychology,* 1971, **5,** 1–12.

Sameroff, A. J., Cashmore, T. F., and Dykes, A. C. Heart rate deceleration during visual fixation in human newborns. *Developmental Psychology,* 1973, **8,** 117–119.

Schachter, J., Williams, T. A., Khachaturian, Z., Tobin, M., Kruger, R., and Kerr, J. Heart rate responses to auditory clicks in neonates. *Psychophysiology,* 1971, **8,** 163–179.

Schaefer, A. B. Newborn responses to nonsignal auditory stimuli: I. Electroencephalographic desynchronization. *Psychophysiology,* 1975, **12,** 359–366.

Schmidt, K., and Birns, B. The behavioral arousal threshold in infant sleep as a function of time and sleep state. *Child Development,* 1971, **42,** 269–277.

Schneider, G. E. Two visual systems, *Science,* 1969, **163,** 895–902.

Schulman, C. A. Heart rate audiometry. Part I. An evaluation of heart rate response to auditory stimuli in newborn hearing screening. *Neuropadiatrie,* 1973, **4,** 362–374.

Schulman, C. A. Effects of auditory stimulation on heart rate in premature infants as a function of level of arousal, probability of CNS damage, and conceptional age. *Developmental Psychobiology,* 1969, **2,** 172–183.

Schulman, C. A. Differentiation in the neonatal period between infants at high risk and infants at low risk for subsequent severe mental retardation. Paper presented at the meeting of the Eastern Psychological Association, Washington, D.C., 1968.

Schulman, C. A., and Wade, G. The use of heart rate in the audiological evaluation of nonverbal children. Part II. Clinical trials on an infant population. *Neuropadiatrie,* 1970, **2,** 197–205.

Schulte, F. J., and Bell, E. F. Bioelectric brain development. An atlas of EEG power spectra in infants and young children. *Neuropadiatrie,* 1973, **4,** 30–45.

Schulte, F. J., Busse, C., and Eichhorn, W. Rapid eye movement sleep, motoneuron inhibition, and apneic spells in preterm infants. *Pediatric Research,* 1977, **11,** 709–713.

Sharpless, S. K., and Jasper, H. Habituation of the arousal reaction. *Brain,* 1956, **79,** 655–680.

Snyder, F., and Scott, J. The psychophysiology of sleep. In N. S. Greenfield and R. A. Sternbach (eds.), *Handbook of Psychophysiology*. New York: Holt, Rinehart and Winston, 1972.

Sokol, S., and Dobson, V. Pattern reversal visually evoked potentials in infants. *Investigative Ophthalmology*, 1976, **15,** 58–62.

Sokolov, E. N. *Perception and the Conditioned Reflex*. New York: Macmillan, 1963.

Sostek, A. M., and Anders, T. F. Effects of varying laboratory conditions on behavioral state organization in two- and eight-week-old infants. *Child Development*, 1975, **46,** 871–878.

Sostek, A. M., Anders, T. F., and Sostek, A. J. Diurnal rhythms in 2- and 8-week-old infants: Sleep-waking state organization as a function of age and stress. *Psychosomatic Medicine*, 1976, **38,** 250–256.

Spreng, L. F., Johnson, L. C., and Lubin, A. Autonomic correlates of eye movement bursts during stage REM sleep. *Psychophysiology*, 1968, **4,** 311–323.

Starr, A., and Hamilton, A. E. Correlation between confirmed sites of neurological lesions and abnormalities of far-field auditory brainstem responses. *Electroencephalography and Clinical Neurophysiology*, 1976, **41,** 595–608.

Steinschneider, A. Sound intensity and respiratory responses in the neonate. *Psychosomatic Medicine*, 1968, **30,** 534–541.

Steinschneider, A., Lipton, E. L., and Richmond, J. B. Auditory sensitivity in the infant: Effect of intensity on cardiac and motor responsivity. *Child Development*, 1966, **37,** 233–252.

Sterman, M. B. The basic rest-activity cycle and sleep. In C. B. Clemente, D. P. Purpura, and F. E. Mayer (eds.), *Sleep and the Maturing Nervous System*. New York: Academic, 1972.

Sterman, M. B., Harper, R. M., Havens, B., Hoppenbrouwers, T., McGinty, D. J. and Hodgman, J. E. Quantitative analysis of infant EEG development during quiet sleep. *Electroencephalography and Clinical Neurophysiology*, 1977, **43,** 371–385.

Sterman, M. B., and Hoppenbrouwers, T. The development of sleep-waking and rest-activity patterns from fetus to adult in man. In M. B. Sterman, D. J. McGinty, and A. M. Adinolfi (eds.), *Brain Development and Behavior*. New York: Academic, 1971.

Stern, E., Parmelee, A. H., Akiyama, Y. Schultz, M. A., and Wenner, W. H. Sleep cycle characteristics in infants. *Pediatrics*, 1969, **43,** 65–70.

Stern, E., Parmelee, A., and Harris, M. Sleep state periodicity in prematures and young infants. *Developmental Psychobiology*, 1973, **6,** 357–365.

Strock, B. D., Graham, F. K., and Zeigler, B. L. Startle and startle inhibition in early development. *Psychophysiology*, 1978, **15,** 285.

Taguchi, K., Picton, T. W., Orpin, J. A., and Goodman, W. S. Evoked response audiometry in newborn infants. *Acta oto-laryngologica Supplementum*, 1969, **252,** 5–17.

Tanguay, P., and Ornitz, E. Two measurements of evoked response amplitude and their relationship to background EEG. *Psychophysiology*, 1972, **9,** 477–483.

Tanguay, P. E., Ornitz, E. M., Forsythe, A. B., Lee, J., and Hartman, D. Basic rest-activity cycle rhythms in the human auditory evoked response. *Electroencephalography and Clinical Neurophysiology*, 1973, **34,** 593–603.

Tanguay, P. E., Ornitz, E. M., Kaplan, A., and Bozzo, E. S. Evolution of sleep spindles in childhood. *Electroencephalography and Clinical Neurophysiology*, 1975, **38,** 175–181.

Teas, D. C. Personal communication, 1977.

Theorell, K., Prechtl, H. F. R., Blair, A. W., and Lind, J. Behavioral state cycles of normal newborn infants: A comparison of the effects of early and late cord clamping. *Developmental Medicine and Child Neurology*, 1973, **15,** 597–605.

Thompson, R. F., and Spencer, W. A. Habituation: A model phenomenon for the study of neuronal substrates of behavior. *Psychological Review*, 1966, **73,** 16–43.

Turkewitz, G., Birch, H. G., and Cooper, K. K. Patterns of response to different auditory stimuli in the human newborn. *Developmental Medicine and Child Neurology,* 1972a, **14,** 487–491.

Turkewitz, G., Birch, H. G., and Cooper, K. Responsiveness to simple and complex auditory stimuli in the human newborn. *Developmental Psychobiology,* 1972b, **5,** 7–19.

Umezaki, H., and Morrell, F. Developmental study of photic evoked responses in premature infants. *Electroencephalography and Clinical Neurophysiology,* 1970, **28,** 55–63.

Vaughan, H. G. Electrophysiologic analysis of regional cortical maturation. *Biological Psychiatry,* 1975, **10,** 513–526.

Velasco, M., and Velasco, F. Differential effect of task relevance on early and late components of cortical and subcortical somatic evoked potentials in man. *Electroencephalography and Clinical Neurophysiology,* 1975, **39,** 353–364.

Velasco, M., Velasco, F., Maldonado, H., and Machado, J. Differential effect of thalamic and subthalamic lesions on early & late components of the somatic evoked potentials in man. *Electroencephalography and Clinical Neurophysiology,* 1975, **39,** 163–171.

Watanabe, K., Iwase, K., and Hara, K. Heart rate variability during sleep and wakefulness in low birthweight infants. *Biologia Neonatorum,* 1973a, **22,** 87–98.

Watanabe, K., Iwase, K., and Hara, K. Visual evoked responses during sleep and wakefulness in pre-term infants. *Electroencephalography and Clinical Neurophysiology,* 1973b, **34,** 571–577.

Wantanabe, K., Iwase, K., and Hara, K. Maturation of visual evoked responses in low-birthweight infants. *Developmental Medicine and Child Neurology,* 1972, **14,** 425–435.

Weir, C. Auditory frequency sensitivity in the neonate: A signal detection analysis. *Journal of Experimental Child Psychology,* 1976, **21,** 219–225.

Weitzman, E. D., Fishbein, W., and Graziani, L. Auditory evoked responses obtained from the scalp electroencephalogram of the full-term human neonate during sleep. *Pediatrics,* 1965, **35,** 458–462.

Weitzman, E. D., and Graziani, L. J. Maturation and topography of the auditory evoked response of the prematurely born infant. *Developmental Psychobiology,* 1968, **1,** 79–89.

Wetherford, M. J., and Cohen, L. B. Developmental changes in infant visual preferences for novelty and familiarity. *Child Development,* 1973, **44,** 416–424.

Whitlow, J. W. Short-term memory in habituation and dishabituation. *Journal of Experimental Psychology: Animal Behavior Processes,* 1975, **104,** 189–206.

Williams, H. L., Holloway, F. A., and Griffiths, W. J. Physiological psychology: Sleep. *Annual Review of Psychology,* 1973, **24,** 279–316.

Williams, T. A., Schachter, J., and Tobin, M. Spontaneous variation in heart rate: Relationship to the average evoked heart rate response to auditory stimuli in the neonate. *Psychophysiology,* 1967, **4,** 104–111.

Wolff, P. H. The causes, controls and organization of behavior in the neonate. *Psychological Issues,* 1966, **5,** 1–105.

Yang, R. K., and Douthitt, T. C. Newborn responses to threshold tactile stimulation. *Child Development,* 1974, **45,** 237–242.

CHAPTER 10

Learning in Infancy: A Developmental Perspective

Arnold J. Sameroff

Patrick J. Cavanagh

Although learning has been defined in a variety of ways through the ages, its current connotation is synonymous with conditioning. The vast majority of studies in infant learning have utilized conditioning paradigms for both the investigation and interpretation of early behavior. This chapter will review these studies. In the course of the review we shall argue that the major contribution of conditioning research to the understanding of infant behavior has been through the production of empirical anomalies rather than theoretical explanations.

The anomalies result from a view inherent in the conditioning approach that the organism is subject to the whims of environmental contingencies independent of any contribution of its own. What shall be seen is that the infant's response to the environment is regulated by a variety of internal functions. These processes intrinsic to the child appear to play as significant a role in controlling inputs and establishing contingent relations to outputs as the experimental manipulations of the researcher.

The infant places constraints on the character of the associations that can be made. These constraints can be divided into three categories which will be elaborated at length in the following chapter. They are the consequences of (1) the phylogenetic experience of the species, (2) the ontogenetic experience of the particular individual, and (3) the state of arousal during conditioning. The phylogenetic constraints have come into recent prominence (Hinde, 1973; Seligman and Hager, 1972). Seligman (1970) has postulated a dimension of preparedness which he primarily relates to evolutionary considerations. However, preparedness for learning has other constituents as well. The developmental experience of the individual child appears to play a major role in determining the range of associations an infant can make. This ontogenetic perspective begins with prenatal experience (Schneirla, 1966; Gottlieb, 1976) and extends into the postnatal period (Piaget, 1960; Sameroff, 1972). In addition, the state of the child plays a significant role in moderating responsivity to experimental manipulations (Hutt et al., 1969).

The consequences of taking these constraints into account requires a change in theoretical perspective. The behaviorist tradition, embodied in the conditioning approach, views the child as the passive recipient of the world's teachings. The contrasting position is that children are actively engaged in the construction of their world using structures adapted through the evolution of the species and the experience of the individual. These theoretical implications are captured in the contrast between mechanistic and organismic models of development (Reese and Overton, 1970). The organismic model embeds the individual in a biological context in which the principles of adaptation are seen to play a superordinate role to the laws of conditioning.

The view that shall be expounded in this chapter is that the traditional definitions of learning are inadequate for understanding psychological change, that psychological functioning is a continuation of biological functioning, and that the same general principles that apply to biological functioning apply to psychological functioning as well. To achieve this end we will need to define what we mean by psychological functioning, define what we mean by biological functioning, and then to identify the general principles that apply to both as well as the specific principles that differentiate between them.

Infancy is a period of functional transition between two modes of functioning which have been traditionally isolated as scientific disciplines: the biological and the psychological. Most psychologists view biological functioning as a necessary substrate for psychological functioning, but view the relationship as one of parallelism rather than of continuity. The parallelism view is easy to maintain when the object of study is an adult organism, for in the adult both physiological and psychological functioning have reached high levels of organization which can be independently studied. Physiological psychology is the specific sub-discipline devoted to identifying the biological mechanisms that are related to psychological functioning. Such psychological functions as memory, perception, intelligence, language, and personality can be assessed and then related to a variety of electrophysiological and biochemical processes in the brain. However, during infancy parallelism is less obvious because the psychological and biological functioning of the child are closely intertwined. A question to be addressed is whether it is more meaningful to think of psychological behavior during infancy as being confounded with biological behavior or whether it is more meaningful to think of psychological behavior as developing out of biological behavior.

Traditional theories of learning have attempted to interpret the development of behavior as the concatenation of a few simple stimulus-response relationships. It has become clear that these S-R relationships permit only a limited perspective on what infants do. By changing our view of the infant from an organism passively controlled by the contingencies provided by the environment to one of an organism actively engaged in controlling inputs by assimilating the environment to existing behavioral schemata, we can initiate a rapprochement between the psychological and biological principles of development.

PLAN OF PRESENTATION

If one were to make an age distribution of the samples used in studies during infancy, there would be a bimodal distribution with one peak during the first few days of life and the second between 3 and 6 months of age. The peak during the newborn period is a consequence of the relative ease with which research can be done with infants who are already in the hospital as well as a desire to seek information on innate capacities at the earliest possible time. The peak following 3 months of age is a practical consequence of the mother's willingness to bring the infant into the laboratory after negotiating the initial settling-in process at home and her increased security about the fragility of the child. From the investigator's perspective, 3 months is the point at which a number of responses such as smiling and vocalization become available for utilization in conditioning tasks. Our presentation will be subdivided in accord with these two peaks, an initial presentation of the newborn data followed by a consideration of the research done later in infancy.

In our review of newborn learning we shall begin with the traditional approach. Since the majority of studies of infant learning have used a classical or instrumental conditioning paradigm, we shall present the data under these two rubrics. We will then see how closely the data in these studies fit the expected pattern in order to identify anomalies. We shall then propose alternative models for understanding early learning; these incorporate not only the traditional paradigms but the anomalies as well. In the last major section we shall deal with studies of learning in older infants. Again we shall begin with the traditional conditioning perspective, but we shall also raise the question of the nature of the infant's contribution to the learning process.

NEWBORN LEARNING

Let us begin by defining our terms so that we will have a set of clear categories into which we can sort the data we will be reviewing. Kimble (1961), in his standard text on the issue, cites a general agreement that "learning refers to a more or less permanent change in behavior which occurs as a result of practice." By not being more specific, Kimble can stretch this definition to include most traditional contemporary theories of learning whether they be based on S-R conceptions, which emphasize the establishment of new associations between stimuli and responses, and S-S (Bolles, 1972) conceptions, in which the learner sees new relationships among the stimuli in his environment.

Conditioning is generally viewed as a less general conception than learning and includes the two subvarieties called classical and instrumental conditioning. Grant (1964) saw learning as primarily the establishment and strengthening of S-R connections or associations. Classical and instrumental conditioning are seen as being simpler than most other forms of learning in that fewer S-R connections are involved. Current research on learning has found it increasingly difficult to separate these two forms of learning. However, since most research in the infant period has been done within one or the other framework, we will use the distinction between classical and instrumental conditioning to aid the presentation of the review of the literature.

Studying Classical Conditioning

Kimble (1961) states that the basic distinction between the two forms of learning is in terms of the consequences of the conditioned response. In classical conditioning the subject has no control over the sequence of events. By contrast, in instrumental conditioning the subject's response or failure to respond determines whether rewards or punishments will occur.

An unconditioned response (UCR) is reliably elicited by an unconditioned stimulus (UCS). By pairing a previously neutral stimulus, the conditioned stimulus (CS), with the UCS, a new association is established in which the CS can now serve to elicit a conditioned response (CR) similar to the UCR.

The criterion for learning to occur in the classical conditioning situation is that at the end of the training period the CS will elicit a CR more frequently than before the training period. Typically, when an investigator wants to test for the occurrence of a CR in infant conditioning, the UCS is omitted either on selected test trials during the training period or during an extinction period following the training period.

A good example of the classical conditioning paradigm can be found in a study by Wickens and Wickens (1940) in which they tried to condition foot withdrawal. The response could be easily elicitied by a mild electrotactual shock. By pairing a buzzer CS with a shock UCS for 36 trials over a period of 3 days they hoped that the buzzer would come to elicit a foot withdrawal CR. Indeed, during extinction the CS reliably elicited a CR. However, to differentiate conditioning phenomenon from possible artifacts, a variety of control groups are necessary.

It is difficult to find a truly neutral CS since any stimulus has at least a small probability of eliciting any particular UCR. To control for this possibility, experiments usually include a control condition in which only the CS is presented for the same number of trials as in the paired CS-UCS conditon. In addition, it has been found that after a series of trials of UCR elicitation by a UCS, the response becomes sensitized so that any stimulus might elicit it. To control for this possibility, a condition is included in which only the UCS is presented for the same number of trials as in the paired CS-UCS condition. When the effect of the CS was examined during the extinction period in these two control groups, the Wickens' found that no response was elicited in the CS-only group, but foot withdrawal was elicited in the UCS-only group. They concluded that the effect they had found was not classical conditioning, since there was no specific association established between the buzzer and the foot withdrawal, but rather "pseudo-conditioning," since any stimulus might elicit the response after sensitization had occurred.

Controlling for State of Arousal

In newborns the total stimulus picture assumes great importance because of the evanescent quality of the infant's behavioral state. State has come to be seen as an important determinant of behavior patterns in the human newborn (Prechtl, 1969; Wolff, 1966). Complex change in behavior is found in habituation studies, and the simple elicitation of reflexes have been found to be profoundly influenced by changes in the infant's state of sleep or wakefulness (Hutt et al., 1969).

Recent research has demonstrated a need for additional procedures to control for the state of the infant. For example, increases in responding during a training period might be the result of changes in level of arousal, rather than a result of learning. The subject may simply be becoming more active, and the general increase in behavior is accompanied by an increase in the specific response being trained. Therefore, it is important to control for the total amount of stimulation in the conditioning situation. During paired CS-UCS presentations there is more stimulation than in either the CS-only or UCS-only control conditions. Thus, a control condition is required that presents the same total amount of stimulation. Initially, investigators utilized an unpaired CS-UCS condition in which the CS and UCS were presented for the same number of times as in the paired situation, but the CS never preceded the UCS. This procedure was criticized because if the CS is never paired with the UCS, nor followed by the UCR, it might become a signal "not to respond," thereby spuriously increasing any difference in response rate between the paired experimental group and the unpaired control groups. To circumvent this problem, Rescorla (1967) suggested the use of a control group in which the CS and UCS were presented at random intervals for the same number of trials as in the paired CS-UCS condition. This random control group would avoid the problems of negative conditioning in the unpaired control group but still would not completely solve the problem of equating for total stimulation in the conditioning procedure.

In order that the amount of stimulation be the same in the unpaired or random control group as in the paired experimental group, one has to assume that the infant can summate the total amount of stimulation during the conditioning period. However, if the infant has a high threshold to stimulation then the unpaired presentation of either the CS or UCS alone might not get above this threshold while the combined CS-UCS stimulation in the paired presentation would. An example of these problems can be found in the study of Babkin response conditioning in the newborn.

The Babkin reflex is a reaction to the simultaneous pressing of the palms of the hands of the infant (Babkin, 1960). It consists of opening the mouth or gaping, turning the head toward the midline, and raising or flexion of the head. It can also be accompanied by closing of the eyes and flexion of the forearm.

Kaye (1965) used an arm-raise as a CS in an attempt to classically condition the Babkin reflex. He raised the infant's arms from the extended to the flexed position and then pressed the palms to elicit the gaping response. When the conditioned group was compared with a US control group that received only palm presses, the conditioned group showed more responses to the arm-raise during an extinction period when no palm presses were administered. Encouraged by these findings, Connolly and Stratton (1969) replicated Kaye's study. In addition they went a step further and reported successful conditioning of the Babkin reflex to an auditory CS in addition to the arm-raise.

A concern that certain experimental issues were not fully dealt with in these studies led Sostek et al. (1972) to investigate the phenomenon further. The unresolved issues related to the nature of appropriate control groups, the neutrality of the arm-raise CS, and the effect of the infant's behavioral state on the response. Kaye did not systematically control for responding to the CS alone, nor did he control for pairing the stimuli by the use of a noncontingent CS-UCS control group. While Connolly and Stratton did use a CS control, they also omitted a noncontingent CS-UCS control group. A random CS-UCS control seemed important in order to control for the total amount of stimulation provided in the paired CS-UCS group.

Neither of the previous Babkin conditioning studies recorded state throughout the experimental session, although Connolly and Stratton took it into consideration for their auditory CS study. State changes in the neonate may play a large part in the acquisition of conditioned responses. Lenard et al., (1968) found that the Babkin reflex can be elicited only during irregular sleep or wakefulness. Papousek (1969) has noted the reciprocal relationship between state and stimulation during the course of conditioning.

Sostek et al. (1972) repeated the Babkin conditioning study with the arm-raise CS using modifications designed to answer some of the unresolved issues. They included a random CS-UCS control group in addition to the traditional CS- and UCS-only controls. Both CS and UCS baseline measures were also taken to test for initial response to the arm movement as well as the palm press. In addition, systematic observations of state were made before each trial to investigate the effect of state changes on the infant's responsivity and conditionability.

The results did not replicate either the Kaye (1965) or Connolly and Stratton (1969) findings. In no subject was the rate of responses to the CS during extinction higher than the rate to the CS during the baseline period. Figure 10-1 shows the Babkin reflex responses to the stimuli given by the various groups. The decline in responding was the

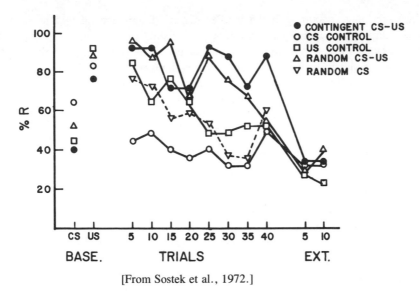

[From Sostek et al., 1972.]

Figure 10-1. Percentage responses for the contingent CS-US group and control groups. The responses to the CS in the random CS-US condition are indicated by a dashed line. Each point is an average of five trials for 5 Ss.

opposite of the result expected for learning, and could be better explained as habituation or fatigue to the UCS.

In the contingent CS–UCS group, the CS–only control, and the UCS-only control, the infant could only respond once per trial, but in the random CS-UCS group the subjects could respond twice, once to the UCS and once to the unpaired CS. Figure 10-1 shows responses to the CS in the random condition in a separate curve from the responses to the UCS.

The decrease in responding during the training trials seen in Figure 10-1 was associated with a decline in level of arousal from the first to last trial blocks. The behavioral state of the infants did play a role in their responsiveness. As a further indication of the relation between arousal and responsiveness, the rate of response decrement was different for each of the treatments. Although somewhat obscured in Figure 10-1, the response rates were directly related to the amount of stimulation inherent in each condition, the paired condition having the highest rate and the CS-only condition having the lowest.

Classical Conditioning of Newborns

Several reviews of conditioning in young infants have been published in the last decade. Since the rate of research in this area is relatively slow, there is little new empirical data to be added to these reviews (Fitzgerald and Porges, 1971; Fitzgerald and Brackbill, 1976; Lipsitt, 1963; Sameroff, 1971, 1972). Except for a section devoted to some recent attempts at classical conditioning of a heart rate response (Clifton, 1974, Stamps and Porges, 1975), most of the following will focus on issues raised by research in this area rather than an exhaustive review.

Most reviews conclude that classical conditioning has been demonstrated in the newborn infant. In contrast, Sameroff (1971, 1972), while accepting the findings that changes in performance have occurred in the studies reviewed, has argued that these changes cannot be interpreted in what is usually understood as the classical conditioning paradigm. Sameroff attempted to integrate the anomalous results of newborn conditioning studies in a framework derived from Piaget's theory of development (Piaget, 1960). The present review will make a more articulated attempt to place all forms of infant learning into a developmental framework with both ontogenetic and phylogenetic components. But first let us review the anomalies.

Conditioned Headturning

Attempts to condition headturning in infants have led to some of the most successful research on infants' learning abilities, but have also led to confusion in judging the significance of these findings. The headturning paradigm was first described by Papousek (1959). The UCS was a tactile stimulus to the side of the mouth, which elicits a headturning response about 25% of the time. The UCR was headturning, commonly called the rooting reflex. Typically, an auditory stimulus has been used as a CS and paired with the tactile UCS. If the procedure ended at that point, it would be an example of a classical conditioning paradigm. However, when the infant turned his head to the UCS, he received a milk reinforcer. The addition of the reinforcer brings this procedure close to an instrumental conditioning paradigm and converts the significance of the auditory stimulus from a conditional stimulus to a discriminative stimulus. To confuse the picuture further, if the infant learned to turn his head to the auditory stimulus, the tactile stimulus was not administered at all. Despite all these variations on standard themes, the essential bit of data is that the procedure seems to work (Papousek, 1961, 1967).

Papousek was primarily interested in studying the course of conditioning rather than the speed. His procedure called for the administration of 10 trials a day until the infant reached a criterion of five successive "correct" responses within a session. A correct response was defined as a head turn in the appropriate direction to the auditory stimulus. In newborns the criterion was reached in an average of 177 trials over 3 weeks of conditioning (Papousek, 1967).

Siqueland and Lipsitt (1966) adapted the Papousek procedure and did three studies to determine whether conditioning would occur in a single session during the newborn period. Initially, headturning occurred about one-fourth of the time to a perioral tactile stimulus. In their first study a buzzer presentation was followed by the tactile stimulus and a dextrose reinforcer. In the experimental group the dextrose reinforcer immediately followed a head turn to the tactile stimulus, while for a control group the dextrose was given 8 to 10 sec after the tactile stimulus, irrespective of response. In the control group the headturning rate remained at about 25%, while in the experimental group the rate increased after 30 trials to about 80%. Papousek (1967) similarly reported that only 3 of 14 infants responded to the tactile stimulus in the first trial, while 3 to 22 trials were necessary before the remaining subjects would respond. Siqueland and Lipsitt found no evidence that the buzzer had any effect on the responding. The infants did not turn their heads to the presentation of the auditory signal but waited until after the tactile stimulus had been delivered.

In their second experiment they used two auditory stimuli which signaled a tactile stimulus to either the right or left side of the mouth. The positive auditory stimulus was paired with a tactile stimulus eliciting headturning to one side, while on alternate trials the negative auditory stimulus was paired with tactile stimulation eliciting headturning to the other side. After training by reinforcing the response to the positive stimulus with dextrose solution, these investigators were able to show an increase of headturning to the stroke on the positive side and a decrease of headturning to the stroke on the negative side. Again, however, there was no evidence that the auditory stimuli played any role in the learning since the infants responded only after the differential stroking of the cheek to one side or the other.

In the third experiment some evidence for differentiation of the auditory stimuli was demonstrated. They again used the buzzer and tone as positive and negative stimuli, presented alternately as in the previous experiment; but this time both were paired with a tactile stimulus eliciting headturning to only one side. When the positive stimulus sounded, the tactile stimulus was applied, and if a head-turn occurred the infant was reinforced with dextrose solution. When the negative stimulus sounded, the infant was stroked on the same side, but a head-turn did not result in reinforcement. In this situation the infant increased his responding to the tactile stimulus following the positive auditory stimulus, while the stroke associated with the negative stimulus did not increase in effectiveness to eliciting head-turns.

The Siqueland and Lipsitt (1966) studies are interesting in that the last one showed the beginning ability of the infant to use auditory stimulation discriminately, although in none of their studies was the infant able to make the response to the auditory stimulus alone. The auditory stimulus supplemented the tactile stimulus but could not replace it. Papousek (1969) attempted to use two auditory cues as discriminative stimuli as in the second Siqueland and Lipsitt study, but the auditory stimuli were both positive, signaling tactile stimuli to opposite sides. He found this procedure extremely difficult for newborns. At the rate of 10 training trials a day, it took the subjects an average of 814 trials to reach a criterion of five successive correct responses to the auditory stimuli. By that time they were 4 months old.

In follow-up studies on the Siqueland and Lipsitt (1966) work (Clifton et al., 1972a, 1972b) several confounding factors were found in the original studies. As in the Babkin conditioning studies, a primary nuisance variable was the behavioral state of the newborn. Clifton et al. (1972a) used the headturning technique in an attempt to assess effects of medication during delivery on the infant's conditionability during the newborn period. They were surprised that they could not replicate the increase in responding to the tactile stimulus found by Siqueland and Lipsitt (1966). The experimental groups in their study never reached a response rate much over 50%, and even this rate tended to taper off toward the end of the 30-trial session. Clifton et al. attributed the differences between their results and those of Siqueland and Lipsitt to a number of differences in experimental procedure. Instead of using spontaneously awake subjects as Siqueland and Lipsitt had done, Clifton et al. used a wake-up procedure and included initially drowsy infants in their study. They found that the infants that had been awakened tended to fall back asleep, depressing the average response rate of the group in the later part of the session. In addition, although Siqueland and Lipsitt used a perceptible head turn (5–10°) as their criterion, Clifton et al. used a more stringent 15° as their criterion. The stricter criterion might not have permitted an adequate shaping of the response since it might be beyond the capability of newborn infants.

To resolve the discrepancies between the two studies, Clifton et al. (1972b) ran a third study with only spontaneously awake infants in two different criterion conditions, a 5° and a 15° head-turn. Although the subjects in this last study were selected for being awake, many of them fell asleep or drifted in and out of drowsiness during the experiment. The results showed a clear relationship between state of wakefulness and the probability of obtaining a positive response to the tactile stimulus. The difference in response criterion did not make a significant difference in the training.

The investigators concluded that their results provided reliable evidence of conditioned headturning in newborn infants. However, it should be noted that their data (Fig. 10-2) indicate that the differences in response rate between the experimental and control groups in their study appeared during the first block of training trials and remained relatively constant across the rest of the conditioning blocks. As in the Sostek et al. (1972) study discussed earlier, the high level of response to the CS in the experimental group seemed to be already present in the first few trials. Sameroff (1968) found similar results in his attempt to condition components of sucking. He attributed this type of phenomenon to already prepared response systems rather than conditioning. What the Clifton et al. study seemed to demonstrate was that this prepared headturning response to the tactile stimulus is very sensitive to state variables. Prechtl (1958) made the point that only if the infant is awake and alert can the headturning response be reliably elicited.

Reinforcement does seem to affect headturning, but the effect seems to be related more to maintaining the built-in reflexive behavior rather than to establishing it. The next section, on conditioned sucking studies, provides further elaboration of this point.

Classically Conditioned Sucking Behavior

Marquis (1931) observed 10 infants in conditioning sessions during the first 10 days of life. During each session a 5-sec buzzer was followed by the insertion of the milk bottle into the baby's mouth. This procedure was followed throughout the feeding. Marquis felt

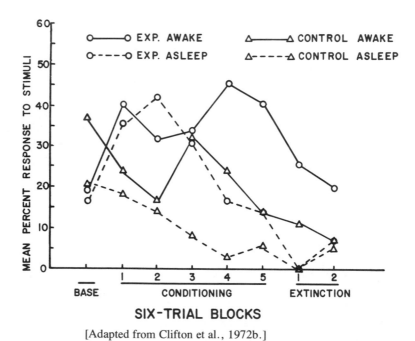

[Adapted from Clifton et al., 1972b.]

Figure 10-2. Comparison of the mean percentage response for four sub-groups over baseline, conditioning, and extinction phases.

that conditioning had occurred in that many of the infants were responding to the buzzer with sucking and mouth-opening responses within 5 days. Wenger (1936) criticized the study because Marquis did not report any statistical analyses, used a subjective-response scoring procedure, and omitted appropriate control groups. Using only two infants, he was unable to replicate Marquis's findings.

Since there were no CS-only or USC-only control groups, Marquis' results could be another example of the pseudoconditioning or sensitization effect described above in the Wickens and Wickens (1940) study.

More recently, Lipsitt and Kaye (1964) attempted to study classically conditioned sucking behavior in newborns. The infants were seen for only one session within the first 4 days of life. For the experimental group, a tone CS was followed after 1 sec by insertion of a nipple into the infant's mouth. After every four paired presentations, the USC was omitted to test for the development of the conditioned response to the tone. A control group, in which the tone and nipple were presented, but unpaired for each trial, was used as a comparison. Lipsitt and Kaye's results are confusing because during the training period, when the CS and US were paired, the experimental group did not respond more frequently than the control group during CS-only test trials. The control group gave as many sucking responses to the tone as the experimental group (see Fig. 10-3). Only during extinction did the groups begin to show a difference in responsivity to the CS. A fuller report of this study might be helpful in understanding these findings since it is possible that temporal conditioning could have occurred. Something seems to have happened to the

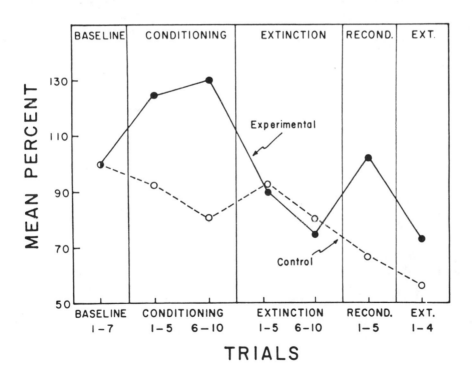

[From Lipsitt & Kaye, 1964.]

Figure 10-3. Percentage and number of sucking responses to the CS in the experimental and control groups.

infant's performance related to the administration of the tone, even though it was not a clear-cut conditioning phenomenon.

Again, as in the Marquis (1931) success followed by the Wenger (1936) failure to replicate, Lipsitt and Kaye's (1964) complex findings were followed by more complex findings in a study by Clifton (1971, 1974). Clifton attempted to classically condition sucking to a tone CS. She found no evidence of conditioned sucking responses during training nor during extinction. However, the study also was an attempt to condition heart rate responses. The results of this aspect of the study will be reviewed in the next section.

A summary of the attempts to classically condition the sucking response would not give strong support to the success of these attempts. Of the two studies that yielded conditioning-like results, the Marquis (1931) study seems the more clear-cut. That she continued training for many sessions over 10 days would have given her subjects training equivalent to Papousek's (1967) infants who learned to turn their heads. The Lipsitt and Kaye (1964) and Clifton (1971) studies require more complex interpretations.

Studies in which sucking on a nipple was the UCR and anticipatory sucking without a nipple was the CR have questionable aspects related to the prepotency of the sucking response in the hungry infant. Jensen (1932) has reported onset of sucking to squeezing the infant's toe or pulling his hair. More recent evidence calls into question the neutrality of an auditory CS in sucking studies since an unconditioned sucking response to onset of auditory stimulation has been found (Keen, 1964; Semb and Lipsitt, 1968). The prepotency of this response and the inability of the investigator to decide conclusively what elicited the response when it occurs makes sucking a response requiring complex controls in studies of classical conditioning. Sucking movements can be elicited by the infant touching his lips with his tongue or even by touching the two lips together. Since feeding is one of the more necessary animal functions, it is considered to be the most highly organized behavior of the young infant (Kessen, 1967).

Seligman (1970) has described a number of prepared responses that are easily conditionable because of their biological significance to the organism. In a later section it will be argued that from a developmental perspective the sucking response system may already be adapted to assimilate certain classes of environmental stimuli.

Classical Conditioning of Heart Rate

Advances in the technology of recording newborn responses have made possible the study of autonomic conditioning in the newborn. Several recent studies have been devoted to demonstrating classical conditioning of heart rate change.

Clifton attempted to study the conditioning of sucking and heart rate. While she was unsuccessful with the sucking response (Clifton, 1971), she reported better results with heart rate (Clifton, 1974). Inserting a nipple in the baby's mouth produces heart rate acceleration. A comparison was made between a group of infants who had a tone CS paired with a nipple-insertion UCS, and a control group in which the CS and UCS were presented at random intervals during the conditioning period. No conditioned response to the tone developed in the course of the training period. During the first extinction trial a large heart rate deceleration occurred to the absence of the UCS for the paired CS-UCS group but not for the random control group. Clifton interpreted these results as an orienting reaction to the absence of an expected event, a reasonable "cognitive" explanation of the data. However, she goes on to argue as follows:

Data from the present work would not meet the criterion of a CR elicited by a previously neutral

CS. However, if one accepts the formation of an expectancy as conditioning, the present study . . . affirms that the newborn can be classically conditioned . . . . [p. 19]

Certainly, the formation of an expectancy can be interpreted as learning, but why should the classical conditioning paradigm be twisted to incorporate these anomalous data? Would it not be better to utilize a paradigm in which the definitions need not be interpreted in a convoluted form?

Stamps and Porges (1975), in another attempt at heart rate conditioning, were even more articulate in their reinterpretation of the classical conditioning paradigm. These investigators trained a group of newborn infants in a trace conditioning procedure using a tone CS and a blinking light UCS. In trace conditioning there is a delay between the offset of the CS and the onset of the USC such that any association formed is not between the UCS and CS but between the UCS and a trace of the CS. Although conditioning is usually much harder to achieve in a trace situation than in the standard situation in which the CS and UCS are overlapped in time, these investigators felt justified in this procedure in order to examine anticipatory responses to the UCS independent of responses to the CS. Two of the three differences between the infants in the control and experimental groups were only reliable for subsets of the 10 babies in each group. The single main effect found was that the experimental group showed more heart rate deceleration when the UCS was omitted. This finding is quite comparable to Clifton's (1974) results described above. How do Stamps and Porges explain their findings?

The deceleration in the absence of the UCS could be described as a ''searching'' response for the missing stimulus . . . The conditioned responses are based on the CS-UCS contingency, or what might be called a stimulus-stimulus (S-S) association . . . from some theoretical points of view, S-S relationships may be accepted as evidence of classical conditioning. [pp. 428–429]

Thus, the data presented appears to support an argument for classical conditioning of the neonate. The only aspects of conditioning which have not been demonstrated conclusively in the study are the *acquisition* and *extinction* of the conditioned responses. [p. 431, italics added]

If acquisition and extinction of the CR have not been demonstrated, why call the phenomenon classical conditioning? Stamps and Porges cover another bet by arguing for an S-S cognitive learning theory explanation of classical conditioning. We will argue in a later section that, indeed, a cognitive learning theory is necessary to describe the results of the two heart rate conditioning studies. But, we will argue further that classical conditioning phenomena require an even broader conception of learning than the S-S paradigm.

Instrumental Conditioning

Instrumental conditioning is generally defined as a situation in which a particular response is reinforced. To avoid the controversy over the nature of reinforcement, a more general definition of instrumental conditioning states that, contingent upon the subject's response, other stimuli are made available, and the subject's interaction with these stimuli changes the rate of emission of the original response (Grant, 1964).

Although the forms of instrumental conditioning include both appetitive and aversive conditions, there are few if any examples of avoidance or escape conditioning with newborns. Studies of instrumental conditioning in the newborn have centered on two response systems: headturning and sucking. Indeed, as we have already pointed out in the previous discussion of classical conditioning, these two responses are important constituents of the infant's primary pattern of survival, the feeding system. In the next two sections we shall review the research with these responses.

Instrumental Conditioning of Sucking

The attempts to classically condition sucking behavior to novel conditional stimuli have led to complicated results. Studies of sucking, in which reinforcement contingencies have been manipulated, have led to more traditional outcomes and placed sucking in the category of operant behaviors that are modifiable in the newborn period.

Lipsitt and Kaye (1965) had noted that different oral stimuli varied in effectiveness in eliciting sucking behavior. Specifically, a nipple was a better elicitor of sucking than a rubber tube. Lipsitt et al. (1966) speculated that reinforcement of the weak sucking response to the tube should enhance its value as an elicitor of sucking. In an experimental group the tube was inserted into each infant's mouth during 15-sec trials, in the last 5 sec of which dextrose was delivered through the tube. A control group received the tube insertion for the same period of time but no nutrient was delivered. Instead, an amount of dextrose equal to that received by the experimental group was inserted into the infant's mouth during the intertrial interval.

It can be seen in Figure 10–4 that giving the dextrose increased the effectiveness of the tube as an elicitor of sucking. However, it can also be noted that the increased sucking occurred almost *immediately* in the first blocks of trials. During extinction the effects of the reinforcement procedure were immediately washed out. The same results were obtained during a reconditioning and second extinction period. Given the great difficulty found in attempts to classically condition responses in newborns, what can be said about conditioning that occurs so rapidly? It is not clear whether anything was indeed learned. The Lipsitt et al. data seem to show that the newborn infant has a capacity for moderating his sucking behavior on a moment-to-moment basis but without an extended change in performance, which usually characterizes learning. The next series of studies reported

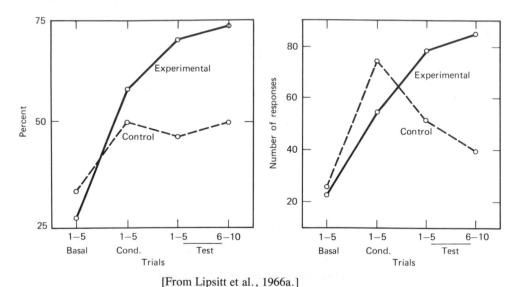

[From Lipsitt et al., 1966a.]

Figure 10-4. *Changes in sucking rate for experimental and control groups represented as the mean ratio of number of sucks per trial in each of the periods divided by the number of sucks per trial during the baseline period. A trial consisted of the first 10 sec of the tube presentation prior to reinforcement for the experimental group. The data are averaged over trials as indicated on the abscissa.*

below (Sameroff, 1965, 1968) attempted to separate some of the variables involved in the infant's sucking behavior and to determine which components lent themselves to the most rapid modification—that is, were most sensitive to reinforcement contingencies—and which components were least sensitive—that is, required prolonged training periods before they were modified.

Two responses have been described for getting milk out of a nipple: "expression," the squeezing of the nipple between tongue and palate (Ardran et al., 1958), and "suction," the generation of negative pressure in the mouth (Colley and Creamer, 1958). These two components seemed to offer the opportunity to attempt differential conditioning within the organized sucking response.

An apparatus was devised to provide nutrient either when the baby performed the positive-pressure (expression) component of sucking or when he performed the negative-pressure (suction) component (Sameroff, 1965).

The nutrient delivery apparatus could be set to operate in one of three modes: (1) a direct-suction condition permitted nutrient to be delivered as a direct consequence of negative pressure applied to the nipple, (2) a suction threshold condition in which a liquid pump delivered nutrient whenever the negative pressure exceeded a threshold, and (3) a similar expression threshold condition in which the threshold was for the positive-pressure component.

A series of studies were completed that included a variety of contingencies to evaluate the infant's ability to modify his behavior (Sameroff, 1968, 1972). In each study the infant was seen at two feeding sessions, 4 h apart. In each session, the 1st min of sucking was nonnutritive—that is, no milk was delivered through the nutrient delivery tube. During the next 5-min period, the infant was given milk under the appropriate response condition: direct-suction or expression threshold in the first study, high- and low-expression threshold in the second study. This cycle of 1 min of nonnutritive sucking followed by 5 min of nutritive sucking was repeated until the infant completed his feeding.

Sameroff (1968) attempted to differentiate between those parameters of the sucking response that could be conditioned—that is, were gradually modified by the effects of differential reinforcement—and those parameters of the sucking response that were preadapted by some form of developmental preparedness—that is, were immediately modified as soon as the newborn could determine the contingency required.

Certain expectations could be stated for the directions in which the components of the sucking response would be changed. In the direct-suction condition one would expect the infants to use a greater negative pressure amplitude than in the expression-threshold condition. Similarly, in the expression-threshold condition one would expect the infants to use a greater positive pressure than in the direct-suction condition.

The question of whether the expected changes in response components would be the result of learning or the adaptation of already existing response abilities could be examined through several comparisons. Evidence for learning would be (1) greater differences between the direct-suction and expression-threshold conditions in the second feeding session than in the first, (2) greater differences between the direct-suction and expression-threshold conditions in the nonnutritive sucking period following the training period than in the one preceding the training period, (3) greater differential effect of restarting nutrient delivery during the second feeding cycle than during the first, or (4) increasing differences between the direct-suction and expression-threshold conditions during the feeding period.

Evidence for adaptation would be (1) equality of differences between the second feeding session and first, (2) no differences between the direct-suction and expression-threshold groups during the nonnutritive periods, following the first 6-min cycle, (3) no increase in differences during the second feeding cycle as compared with differences in the first feeding cycle, and (4) immediate occurrence of differences between the direct-suction and expression-threshold conditions—that is, during the 1st min of feeding—and no alteration by subsequent feeding experience.

Most of the data did not lend themselves to a learning interpretation—that is, (1) the differences between the two conditions were not greater in the second feeding session than the first, (2) the differences between the two conditions were not greater during the second nonnutritive minute than the first, and (3) there was no greater differential effect of restarting nutrient delivery in the second feeding cycle than during the first.

However, there were some differences between the direct-suction and expression-threshold conditions which increased during the feeding period. For the expression-threshold group a trend developed across the 5-min feeding period in the ratio between the positive- and negative-pressure components. Figure 10-5 shows the change in the ratio of number of negative-pressure responses to the number of positive-pressure responses as a percentage during the first 6 min of each session.

In a second study, infants were fed in an expression-threshold condition for two feedings. During one feeding, a high positive-pressure threshold was required to obtain nutrient; during the other feeding, a low threshold was required. Half the infants had the low-expression-threshold condition at the first feeding and half had it at the second feeding. The infants exhibited greater positive-pressure amplitude in the high-expression-threshold condition than in the low-expression-threshold condition. Although there was no initial difference between the positive-pressure amplitude in the high-expression-threshold

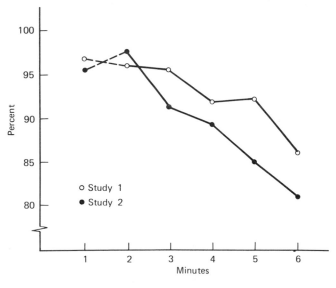

[From Sameroff, 1968.]

Figure 10-5.   The ratio of the negative-pressure component to the positive-pressure component during the first nonnutritive sucking minute (NNI) and the 5 min feeding period (F1-F5) in the Expression Threshold condition for study 1 and study 2.

and low-expression-threshold conditions, the amplitude of the infants in the low-expression-threshold condition decreased during the feeding period, and the amplitude of the infants in the high-expression-threshold condition was maintained at the initial level. As in the expression-threshold condition of the first study, an analysis of the ratio between the negative-pressure and positive-pressure components of the sucking response showed that the ratio declined during the feeding period (see Fig. 10-5).

Newborn human infants could change their sucking behavior as a function of the consequences of their activity. Most of the effects found in the two studies seem to be the result of previously organized abilities of newborns to adapt their sucking response. However, some changes in performance may have been the result of new learning, or new accommodations of the sucking response.

Instrumental Conditioning of Headturning

The complexities of utilizing the headturning paradigm in attempts to classically condition newborns (Siqueland and Lipsitt, 1966) led Siqueland (1968) to simplify the procedure into a free operant task. A band was placed around the head of newborn infants such that the number of degrees of head-turns could be continuously assessed. A head-turn of more than $10°$ in any direction was reinforced by giving the infant a nonnutritive nipple to suck on for 5 sec. After 25 reinforcements, a group of eight infants that had been reinforced for every head-turn had increased its rate of response from 5 to 18 responses/min. In a second group of eight infants that had been started on continuous reinforcement but shifted to a 3:1 schedule (every third response reinforced) for the last 15 reinforcements, the headturning rate increased to over 25 responses/min. As expected from the operant literature the intermittent-reinforcement group showed slower extinction rates than the continuous-reinforcement group. Siqueland included a third group of subjects who were given reinforcement only when they had held their heads still for 20 sec. The last group showed a nonsignificant decrease in the number of head-turns during the training period. The success in getting the last group to reduce their headturning rate argued against the possibility that the results obtained in the first two groups could be a simple excitation effect of the nipple administration.

Bakow (1975) attempted to explore the relationships between individual differences in newborn temperament and performance in the conditioning situation used by Siqueland. Using a sample of 40 newborns, each of whom was tested on two separate occasions, Bakow could not produce an increase in operant headturning. The difference in outcomes between the two studies may have been related to two procedural differences. Bakow used a 5-min baseline period prior to conditioning where Siqueland had used only a 3-min baseline. It is possible that the extra 2 min might have been too tiring for some of the subjects. Siqueland's infants had been swaddled, inhibiting all movement except for the head. Bakow did not swaddle his infants in order to make an observation of each infant's activity during the conditioning procedure. Bakow reasoned that his inability to find a conditioning effect was because the child's unrestrained motor activity perpetuated an agitated state of arousal that prevented successful performance.

Krafchuk et al. (1976) performed two further studies to assess the effect of eliminating the differences in procedure between the Siqueland and Bakow studies of operant headturning. In the first study, two groups of swaddled infants were trained, one group after a 4-min baseline period and the second group after a 2-min baseline period. The 2-min baseline group significantly increased their headturning rate between the baseline and extinction periods. In addition, when the time required to complete 25 responses was divided into four equal periods, the number of responses increased linearly across the four quarters of the training period. The 4-min baseline group showed neither of these effects. Thus, it would appear that the length of baseline and the swaddled condition of the infant were important parameters in conditioning operant headturning.

Since neither Siqueland nor Bakow included noncontingent control groups in their studies, Krafchuk et al. did a second experiment in which 21 swaddled newborns were conditioned after a 2-min baseline period and then matched to 21 yoked controls who received nipple reinforcements at the same points in time that the contingent group had. The group that received contingent reinforcement showed a greater increase in headturning than the noncontingent controls, confirming Siqueland's original results. Figure 10-6 shows the number of headturning responses for each group.

A methodological complication can be seen during the training period where the rate of headturning in the yoked controls was much higher than in the contingent-reinforcement group. The reason is that head-turns occur during bursts of activity. In the contingent group, as soon as the first head-turn occurred, the nipple reinforcement was given, which quieted the infant, preventing the continuation of the headturning activity. In the control group the nipple administration was independent of head-turns, so that each burst of activity generated a greater absolute number of turns. In such instances the criteria for learning must be carefully chosen. If one used the difference between baseline and end of training as a learning criteria, the control group would have shown much more "acquisition" than the experimental group.

During the Krafchuk et al. studies the state and behavior of the infant were monitored during the experimental period. In addition each infant was tested with the Neonatal Assessment Scales (Brazelton, 1973) to assess individual differences. These individual differences were then related to the conditioning data. One of the rationales for studying conditioning in infants is that it taps higher mental functions than the standard neurologic or sensory-motor tasks. If one were testing complex intellectual functions, one would expect that alertness should be positively related to conditionability. Surprisingly, in-

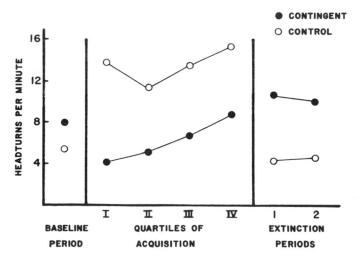

Figure 10.6.   Average number of headturning responses/minute in 2-min blocks during baseline and extinction periods and during quartiles of the total acquisition period.

creases in response rates were not related to alertness, but rather to higher activity level and muscle tonus. These correlations were high for both the contingent group and also the noncontingent control group. In other words, in both groups infants who showed increased headturning had higher activity and tonus levels. The difference between the groups occurred because 80% of the infants in the contingent group showed increases in headturning, while only 48% of the infants in the noncontingent group did.

The infant's state of arousal had been assessed 2 sec prior to each headturning response. Figure 10-7 shows the distribution of head-turns across four states: drowsiness, quiet awake, active awake, and active crying. It can be seen that the vast majority of head-turns were made while the infants were in an active awake state. This curve is almost identical to that reported by Papousek and Bernstein (1969) for headturning in which discrete trials were used. An alternate expectation would be that the infant should be in a quiet alert state awaiting the impulse to respond. Instead, the data from these four studies show that the infant must be in an active state if conditioned responses are to occur.

Papousek (1967) feels that a major problem in this area of research has been the lack of familiarity of researchers with their experimental subjects. This lack of knowledge has been especially true in the manner in which the problem of state has been ignored in most early studies. Papousek found that the conditioning process could best be studied if infants were kept on a controlled feeding and sleeping schedule to assure maximum wakefulness during the conditioning procedures.

The Krafchuk et al. study raised important questions about the manner in which contingent reinforcement affects responsivity. The simple explanation is that the response is reinforced. Another explanation is that contingent reinforcements act to arouse infants.

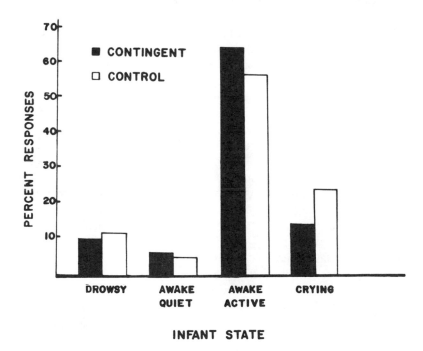

Figure 10-7. Percent of headturning responses occurring in each state during acquisition period for contingent and noncontingent yoked control groups.

Aroused infants then make more headturning responses. The effect of contingencies on newborn behavior offers many possibilities for further investigation.

Conclusions About Newborn Learning

The implications derived from the preceding selective review of the literature on classical and operant conditioning of newborn infants can be summarized in four points, two methodological and two theoretical.

The first methodological point is that working with newborn infants is at best difficult and at worst frustrating. Whenever a study has reported some interesting result, a second study has been unable to replicate that result. A constraint on the generalization of most findings has been that complex statistical analyses have been used to obtain significant results from the data obtained from small numbers of subjects. In many cases, fewer than 10 subjects per group have been used, and then subdivided even further. From a historical perspective, the data from newborn learning studies have rarely stood the test of time. Those that have survived may have done so because no one has had the ambition or energy to repeat them. It is clear that replications of successful studies with larger numbers of subjects continues to be necessary.

The second methodological point is that the unsuccessful replications have pointed up the inadequate assessment of state in the initial studies. In the early studies, infants who were spontaneously awake were mixed with those who needed to be awakened, or kept awake during the procedure. In later studies concurrent evaluations of state have shown a close correlation between the arousal level of the infant and the number of responses irrespective of reinforcement condition. In high-stimulation situations—paired or un-paired CS-UCS groups—high levels of responding were found, whereas in low-stimulation situations—CS-only or USC-only groups—lower levels of responding were found. It is necessary, then, to closely evaluate the state of the infant during the course of each study, especially at those points where stimuli were presented or responses required.

The first theoretical point relates to the results using the classical conditioning paradigm with newborns. The most successful studies have not found the establishment of S-R connections, but rather the establishment of S-S connections. Both the Clifton (1974) and Stamps and Porges (1975) studies found expectancy relationships developing between the CS and UCS. It should be appropriate to focus on the S-S nature of this relationship in its own right, and reject attempts to convert these results into an anomalous version of S-R classical conditioning, which may only serve to cloud our already minimal understanding of newborn learning. Awaiting a clear demonstration of classical conditioning in the newborn may no longer be worthwhile because there already exist more fruitful paradigms for understanding newborn and infant behavior. This conclusion brings us to the next point.

The second theoretical point relates primarily to the results obtained using the instru-mental paradigm, but also interacts with some of the classical conditioning studies. Successful results have generally been reported for those response systems that are con-nected with the biological survival of the newborn—that is, sucking and headturning. Investigators have used these responses since they are among the few organized capacities of the newborn, but they may also represent those responses that have been developmen-tally prepared for interaction with environmental stimulation and contingencies. If indeed these response systems are already prepared for adaptation to specific stimuli, then the demonstration of these adaptations would not be the result of learning but rather the result of developmental processes more fundamental than learning. The empirical differentiation between learned associations and prepared adaptations in the newborn can only be made on the basis of the speed of association. In those situations in which the association was immediate, preparedness would be implicated. In those situations where the associations increased in frequency or strength over time, learning would be implicated. However, as we have already noted, these latter situations have been clouded by the infant state problem. Those studies that have shown behavioral changes over time may have only reflected state changes during which the infant became sufficiently aroused to demonstrate the prepared adaptation rather than learning a new association.

If such be the case, the preparedness issue becomes central to our understanding of newborn behavior. What do we mean by "preparedness"? The next section will try to explore this concept and its implications for our understanding of infant learning. Subsequently we will apply this analysis to the data from studies of learning in older infants where more subtle examples of preparedness can be identified.

CONSTRAINTS ON LEARNING

Biology and Psychology

Psychology is typically defined in introductory texts as the study of behavior. Surprisingly, biology is also defined as the study of behavior. What differentiates psychological behavior from biological? One answer focuses on the size of the behavioral unit. Psychological behavior is thought to involve larger units—for example, the whole organism moving through space. On the other hand, biological behavior involves smaller units such as the action of enzymes on ingested nutrients. A second answer focuses on the medium of exchange between the organism and its environment. Biological behavior involves responses to material stimulation and results in *material exchange* with the environment as when a one-celled organism incorporates chemicals from the environment into its body. Psychological behavior involves responses to patterned stimulation and results in *informational exchange,* as when a child learns to respond in a situation where the color or shape of a stimulus is the cue. A third answer focuses on the plasticity of the behavioral system. Biological behavior is seen as innate, instinctual, motivated by physiochemical causes, and relatively unmodifiable. Psychological behavior is seen as a function of experience, and relatively changeable.

Each of these three differences can be dimensionalized rather than dichotomized. Size of the behavioral unit is clearly a dimension and not a dichotomy. Material versus informational exchange is less clearly a quantitative dimension, but once the complex patterning of the genetic code is taken into account, it can be seen that on even the most primitive biological levels information is a major determinant of behavior. The remaining difference relates to the plasticity of behavior, and what we shall discuss in this section will be directed at demonstrating that this dimension as well does not lend itself to simple dichotomization.

Preparedness

Learning has been traditionally viewed as a functional capacity, which either exists or does not exist. This ability, if found, is considered to be a structural capacity of the organism in question. Seligman (1970) has expanded on these assumptions in his definition of a "general process learning theory." Citing Pavlov, Estes, and Skinner, Seligman makes the point that in their view the particular nature of the stimuli and responses to be associated in the learning process are irrelevant to the learning ability itself. He argues that classical and instrumental models of learning make an "assumption of equivalence of associability" [p. 407] in which any stimulus, response, or reinforcement can be associated with approximately equal facility.

In contrast to this position, Seligman posits a dimension of "preparedness." In addition to an organism's differential ability to perceive stimuli in one modality or another, and to make responses of one kind or another, organisms may have the differential ability to make one kind of association or another. In this view certain combinations of stimuli, responses, or reinforcers are biologically prepared such that their association is almost immediate without the apparent necessity of a learning process to occur, while other combinations of stimuli, responses, and reinforcers are unprepared so that a learning process must occur for associations to form. Still other combinations are counterprepared so that no amount of conditioning will produce an association.

Seligman cites the work of Garcia and his associates (Garcia and Koelling, 1966; Garcia et al., 1966) as a clear example of the preparedness notion. Rats immediately will learn to associate taste CSs with stomach illness UCSs, an example of prepared associations, or after a more extended training learn to associate exteroceptive CSs with a shock UCS, an example of unprepared associations, but will not learn to associate taste with shock or exteroceptive stimuli with stomach illness, an example of counterprepared associations. Similarly, pigeons almost instantly learn to peck a key to obtain food, a prepared association, but cannot learn to key peck to avoid a shock (Hoffman and Fleshler, 1959), a counterprepared association.

The force of Seligman's argument is that one cannot view the behavior of a particular organism as a function of an arbitrarily defined general capacity such as learning, but rather one must determine the particular stimuli, responses, or reinforcers that that organism can associate and then as a secondary question attempt to determine how those elements come to be related.

Breland and Breland (1966), working within an operant framework, reported on a number of anomalies where conditioned behavior broke down under the constraints of what they labeled "instinctive drift." Pigs were readily conditioned on a ratio schedule to carry large wooden coins and deposit them in a piggy bank after which they were reinforced with food. But after the initial conditioning the behavior would deteriorate. The pigs would eagerly get the coins, but would then drop them, root them, and play with them instead of depositing them in the bank. The deterioration in conditioned behavior violated the law of least effort since it required additional work in the playing, and also delayed the reinforcement unnecessarily. An additional contradiction to traditional views was that increasing the drive intensified the deterioration of the learned response.

Breland and Breland argued that the behaviors to which the animals drifted were the natural food-getting responses of the particular species involved. The arbitrary associations that were learned in the conditioning situation broke down when the food reinforcement began to "elicit" species' typical food-getting behaviors. The Brelands concluded that "the behavior of any species cannot be adequately understood, predicted, or controlled without knowledge of its instinctive patterns, evolutionary history, and ecological niche" [p. 684].

When we reflect on our previous review of newborn learning, Seligman's theory of preparedness gives us a context for understanding the success or lack of success of the various studies. Successful studies have utilized species' typical patterns of response related to food-getting behavior. The typical feeding situation of the human newborn is a touch on the cheek from the nipple as the baby is cradled by the mother preparatory to sucking. The infant turns his head in the direction of the tactile stimulus, and opens his mouth—the rooting reflex. The open mouth engages the nipple and then begins to suck—another reflex. In this situation, it is reasonable to believe that the infant is prepared to make modifications in behavior related to the form of the nipple, as found by Lipsitt et al. (1966a), or in the kind of pressure necessary to get milk, as found by Sameroff (1968).

From the failure of studies to demonstrate the newborn's ability to associate exteroceptive cues such as tones with the feeding situation it would be reasonable to assume that these associations are unprepared or counterprepared. They are not totally unprepared because after a period of a few weeks these associations become possible. Papousek (1967), for example, was able to demonstrate conditioned headturning to an auditory stimulus for a milk reinforcer after an average of 3 weeks of age. We must conclude that these associations are initially not prepared but that a change occurs within the first few weeks that alters the associability of exteroceptive stimuli to motor responses. What this change may entail requires an analysis of a classic issue in the history of psychology—that of maturation versus experience.

Models of Development

Why are different species prepared or not prepared to make a variety of associations? Seligman (1970) and the Brelands (1966) follow the lead of the ethologists in suggesting that there are species-specific innate behaviors. This argument, however, does not allow us to understand the *development* of behavior in any single organism or species. We are again stuck in the same bind as when we initially considered learning as a capacity that an organism had or did not have. Now the terms are different but the model is the same. The question is converted to whether an organism is prepared to make certain associations or not. The question is still not a developmental one.

To ask the appropriate question we must step back for a moment from our empirical concerns and explore the theoretical context in which our research is organized. Under the impact of Piaget, psychologists over the last decade have been exploring the epistemological foundations not only of children's thought but also of their own science. The reason is that Piagetian-type theories could not be integrated into the existing behaviorist-type theories without radical distortions which made both types of theories lose their coherency. Reese and Overton (1970; Overton and Reese, 1972) have been the most articulate in contrasting the different methodologies and conclusions to be drawn from these two perspectives. They contrasted a mechanistic model with an organismic one, which paralleled the dichotomy between behaviorist theory and Piagetian theory.

In general, a model is used to represent a body of empirical data because it is simpler and better organized than the data, thus aiding in understanding and explaining the subject matter. However, in addition to being an aid, a model causes one to see the data with a specific focus. It establishes the basic categories for interpreting the data, including certain theoretical constructs, while excluding others. At the same time a model acts to define the problems that should be investigated. Some areas of interest are legitimate to a particular model while others are irrelevant. Reese and Overton (1970) emphasized the point that it is very important for the scientist to be explicit about his underlying model, at least to himself, since it influences both the selection and interpretation of research problems.

Organismic and Mechanistic Models

A crucial aspect of a model as defined by Reese and Overton is that it is based on a metaphor and the properties of that metaphor become the properties of the model. The contrasting properties of the mechanistic and organismic as related to infant development were reviewed by Sameroff (1972). For present purposes we will need to deal with only three of these properties: (1) the nature of the unit of behavior to be investigated, (2) the source of motivation for behavior, and (3) the source of structural change.

The basic metaphor of the mechanistic model is the machine. In this view any part of the universe under investigation is represented as being composed of machinelike parts whose interrelationships form reality. To understand the machine one must understand the parts. Once the parts are understood, the machine is understood. The basic metaphor of the organismic model is the living cell. In the cell, parts cannot be taken out of context because their role is defined by that context, by the cell's total functioning.

This distinction is made clearer when we consider the second contrast between models, the source of motivation. The machine is intrinsically passive, and only responds when an external power source is applied, while the cell is intrinsically active. The cell requires external nutrients in order to continue functioning, but makes its own selections based on its current level of functioning.

The third contrast relates to the source of the current level of functioning, which brings us to the development issue. Machines do not develop; they only change by some external agent adding, subtracting, or altering the parts. Cells do develop by constantly restructuring themselves. External input plays a necessary role but only as nutrition for the cell's activity. The new structures that will be formed are determined not by the nature of the input but by the nature of the cell.

To concretize these model issues as applied to infant behavior, one can place the experimental findings reviewed earlier in a model context. From a mechanistic orientation, each organism has a number of inputs, outputs, and functions. The inputs are the stimuli that can be sensed; the outputs are the responses that can be made; and the functions are the ways in which connections can be made between inputs and outputs. In classic S-R theory the function is associative learning. Individual and species differences determine which stimuli, which responses, and which functions are or are not in the repertory of the organism in question.

The "preparedness" critique did not alter the model, only the built-in functions. Whereas before it was thought that any stimulus could be associated with any response, now it is thought that there is a prior screening device that sorts out stimulus and response combinations into the prepared, unprepared, and counterprepared categories. Associative learning becomes a second-order function instead of a first-order function.

From an organismic orientation the view is quite different. There are no specified entities such as stimuli, responses, or learning, which are independent of the current structure of the organism. Depending on the point in development at which an assessment is made, the organism will be sensitive to different inputs, be capable of different outputs, and have different capacities for relating both to the internal structure. The biological metaphor of the living cell is quite rich when explored analogously. Depending on the state of the genetic structure, the same environmental biochemicals will be incorporated into different structures or not incorporated at all. In turn, the environmental biochemicals change the state of the genetic structure by turning on or off various combinations of genes. These transactions between the organism—that is, the genome—and its effective environment—the rest of the cell—are prototypical of all succeeding developmental processes.

Piaget (1960) has made an almost literal translation of this organismic model in his theory of cognitive development. The developmental process is defined as identical with adaptation, the organism's self-regulatory activity, which functions to maintain an equilibration between the organism and its environment. Adaptation is subdivided into the transactional properties of assimilation and accommodation. Assimilation is the process by which the organism can incorporate inputs from the environment without a modification in structure. Accommodation is the process by which the input from the environment causes the organism to modify its structure. Piaget has elaborated this theory to cover the range of cognitive development from infancy to adolescence. For the present purposes we are limiting our focus to the young infant's sensory-motor functioning.

When dealing with the specific question of learning, Piaget (1964) argues that learning is subordinated to development, and not the opposite. Further, he states that the fundamental relation involved in all development and learning is not association.

In the stimulus-response schema, the relation between the response and stimulus is understood to be one of association. In contrast to this I think that the fundamental relation is one of assimilation. Assimilation is not the same as association, I shall define assimilation as the integration of any sort of reality into a structure, and it is this assimilation which seems to be fundamental in learning. . . . [p. 19]

Learning according to Piaget is the assimilation of reality—in our case the stimulus—into a structure. If this is the case we must address ourselves to defining the nature of the structure. In addition, we must investigate the source of the structure, and how it changes. Discerning the source of structure requires us to reexamine the dichotomy between maturation and experience. From a mechanistic approach, structure is either given through the biological maturation of organs or imposed through psychological experience. From an organismic viewpoint the maturation-experience dichotomy is a false one since both are necessary for the development of any and every structure. This point will become clear in the following discussion of the embryological foundations of behavior.

Adaptation, Maturation, and Experience

The essence of an organismic orientation to development is that each successive state of the organism is the result of a continuous interplay with its environment. Traditional ethologists (Lorenz, 1965; Tinbergen, 1951) spent a major part of their efforts identifying species-specific patterns of behavior that were independent of experience. This nativist orientation postulated that innate behavior patterns unfolded that were basic to behavior, and that the effects of learning were then added to these hereditary unfoldings. Schneirla (1966) has argued that this approach overlooks the major functions that intervene as variables between genes and behavior. Schneirla went on to argue that improved empirical techniques would not resolve the problem unless accompanied by a redefinition of terms together with a clarification of assumptions. Such a reformulation would not exclude genetic factors but it would exclude the traditional concept of "maturation" as the unfolding of gene-determined patterns because no emerging system is independent of external factors.

After his extensive investigations of the embryogenesis of behavior, Kuo (1967) defined development as a set of gradual and complex changes arising from a series of progressive biochemical, physiological, and physical events, with the pattern of each stage resulting from a reorganization of previous patterns in earlier stages. This position is in contrast to the conventional view that genetic and environmental factors are separate entities that engage in distinct functional relationships.

Gottlieb (1976), in a recent review, contrasts the older view of a unidirectional structure-function relationship in which genes produce structural maturations that produce functions with a newer view of a bidirectional structure-function relationship. In the newer version, gene actions enter into a reciprocal relationship with structural maturations, which themselves are in a reciprocal relationship with functions even before complete maturity is achieved. Gottlieb notes that in the past it was unusual to include neural activity, sensory stimulation, and feedback from motor movement among the determinants of neuroembryological development. Yet recent research has demonstrated maintaining, facilitating, and even inductive roles for these factors in the development of both species-typical behaviors and the nervous system.

The traditional bifurcation in which biological variables were thought to produce invariant material structures, while psychological variables were thought to produce plastic informational associations, has broken down from both sides. Biologists such as Schneirla (1966), Kuo (1967), and Gottlieb (1976) were sensitive to the role that function and experience play in physiological development, while psychologists such as Piaget (1960) and Seligman (1970) were sensitive to the constraints placed on behavioral plasticity by the anatomical and physiological structures of the particular organism. This breaking down of conceptual barriers between biology and psychology has opened the way for a search for communalities in the role of structure and function in both areas. The picture that is beginning to emerge is that there is a continuity of process from biological to psychological functioning. The continuity resides in the organism's active engagement in an adaptive transaction with its environment. The organism's activity produces functional and experiential consequences that act to modify existing structures.

Traditional reviews of learning have tended to ignore the structural basis for the successful association of stimulus and response. In this review we cannot do much better in delineating this structural basis. This would require not only much more space than is available but also much more theory and data than are available. For these reasons we must limit ourselves to presenting the problem and drawing together as much evidence as possible to demonstrate the inadequacy of any theory that does not incorporate species-typical and individual organismic and environmental constraints.

In the preceding review of newborn learning we tried to show that whenever modifications of behavior occurred, they have been artifacts of inappropriate control of infant arousal or they have been based on biologically relevant systems related to the adaptive functioning of the human infant in a human social context.

In the following review of learning in older infants we shall continue this theme. We shall argue, on the one hand, that behavioral plasticity has been overstated for a variety of socially relevant response systems and, on the other hand, that whatever successful modifications have been produced have been rooted in a process of cognitive development more basic and pervasive than conditioning.

LEARNING IN LATER INFANCY

The preceding discussion has argued that different experimental approaches, methodological paradigms, and theoretical models are necessary to understand the learning process.

However, since most past research was done under other constraints, we must return initially to traditional categories to facilitate the literature review. We will begin again with studies of classical conditioning, and then move to instrumental conditioning studies. During the review of instrumental learning research a number of points will arise that cannot be explained within the conditioning paradigm. The most important of these issues is the distinction between learning effects and elicitation effects. Elicitation effects must be treated as artifacts from a conditioning perspective, but are central to understanding behavior from an organismic perspective.

Classical Conditioning

Fitzgerald and Brackbill (1976), in a review of classical conditioning studies during infancy, examined each parameter of the conditioning paradigm in detail. These parameters included the modality of CS and UCS, the autonomic versus somatic character of the response, interstimulus intervals, orienting reactions, and age. Kasatkin (1972) had proposed that a constraint on conditioning was that stimulus and response modalities matured at different rates. He suggested that the earliest conditioning would be possible using CSs in phylogenetically older modalities—that is, vestibular, cutaneous, gustatory, and olfactory—and phylogenetically older response systems—that is, autonomic. Conditioning using phylogenetically younger modalities—auditory and visual—and younger response systems—somatic—would be possible later in development.

Fitzgerald and Brackbill, in reviewing the few studies of infant classical conditioning, could find no evidence to support Kasatkin's hypothesis. Instead, they proposed that certain CS-CR combinations were more conditionable than others. With data derived from a series of studies done by these authors and their collaborators (Brackbill et al., 1967, 1968; Fitzgerald et al., 1967; Fitzgerald and Brackbill, 1968; Abrahamson et al., 1970), they argued that a temporal CS is readily linked by classical conditioning procedures to an autonomic response—the pupillary reflex—but not to motor responses—eyeblink and sucking—while tactile, auditory, and visual CSs were more readily conditioned to somatic responses than to autonomic responses. These data support the notion that stimulus-response specificity plays a major role in regulating early learning. If viewed with the caveat that there have been no replications of these studies, these studies are in accord with the preparedness notions of Seligman (1970). A direction for further exploration would be the biologically adaptive significance of these proposed specificities.

Fitzgerald and Brackbill (1976), after reviewing conditioning studies that tested infants at different ages, could find no evidence that older infants were more easily conditioned. However, in none of these studies was the same procedure used with infants of different ages. Papousek (1967) did use the same procedure at all ages when he investigated conditioned headturning in newborns, 3-month-old infants, and 5-month-old infants. He found that there was an inverse relationship between age of infant and trials to criteria; 177, 42, and 28 respectively. This increasing efficiency of learning with age need not be associated with changes in the association mechanism. In fact, when trials to extinction were examined in the same three groups, there were no differences; 27, 25, and 27, respectively. The extinction data are evidence that the neurological mechanisms are not radically different in the three groups. A better explanation for the differential conditionability with age would be in the differential development of the infant's cognitive organization. The older infants would have had more experience with the conditional stimuli in their natural environment prior to the conditioning procedure.

Action-Consequence Relationships

In discussing the learning literature, we need some terminological mechanism that will allow us to change our focus from the "teaching" activity of the environment connoted by the word conditioning to the "learning" activity of the child connoted by the word adaptation. As an interim solution we have adopted the phrase *action-consequence learning* to substitute for the traditional operant or instrumental learning. The use of a different label will, at a minimum, signal that we are taking a different perspective on learning during infancy.

Although we have reported the gap in research between the newborn period and the 3rd month of life as the consequence of empirical expediency, it is highly likely that a major transformation is occurring in the infant's capacities during this period. Emde and Robinson (1976) have marshalled an impressive array of cognitive affective, neurological, and physiological data to indicate that there is a marked developmental discontinuity between newborn functioning, which they define as the first 2 months, and functioning afterwards. Behaviorally, the change is most evident in the child's social-affective development. The infant moves from a quiescence-distress state organization to the dramatically different social smiling and prominent eye-to-eye contact which emerges after 2 months. Emde and Robinson go on to argue that there is a shift from endogenous to exogenous control. The infant has a major reduction in nonhunger fussiness, which permits the use of wakefulness to explore the environment.

Piaget, as well, speaks of a marked change during this period from the use of primary circular reactions to the use of secondary circular reactions. While the primary circular reaction is restricted to a single activity, the secondary circular reaction coordinates action in one modality with that in another.

It is perhaps necessary to justify the use of our new label, action-consequence learning. The first 3 months of life are taken up primarily with the task of intramural coordination of the reflex modalities. However, after 3 months infants develop a relatively more active mode of interaction with the environment, and rapidly become more and more effective at controlling the world around them. The term action-consequence learning is intended to designate this new and increasingly active form of coordinated activity without the implication that the infant necessarily understands cause-effect relationships.

This term is preferable over the term operant learning. The responses involved are not free operants. It will be argued that response elicitation plays an important role in such learning, and that response elicitation can be seen as an indicator of the presence of an expectancy that instructs the infant about the further possibility of action-consequence interaction with the environment. It will be argued further that such expectancies constitute facilitating or limiting conditions for learning, and that they become increasingly flexible with age.

The theme of this chapter up to this point has been to show that there is less plasticity in newborn behavior than a "general-process" (Seligman, 1970) learning theory would lead one to expect, and where plasticity occurs it is largely the result of evolutionary preparedness as opposed to learning. In the case of older infants there is greater plasticity in their behavior. However, it will be argued that a combination of evolutionary preparedness and experience (developmental preparedness) equips the infant with a set of response-elicitation tendencies that encourage or inhibit learning.

The Role of Response-Elicitation

It is generally accepted that there are certain classes of stimuli—for example, social stimuli, and novel visual stimuli—whose contingent application can increase the rate of responses such as vocalizing, smiling, and panel pressing. However, as pointed out by Lipsitt (1963), a simple demonstration that response rate during contingent acquisition is greater than in baseline or extinction does not permit one to conclude that the change in response rate is due to learning. A stimulus can effectively control a response not only by facilitating learning but also by a reflexive or other elicitation of the response—or, in the case of newborn infants, by altering the state of the infant. To discriminate a learning effect from an elicitation effect it is necessary to use an appropriate noncontingent control group to show that the increased response rate occurs only in the presence of the contingency and not in the general presence of the stimulus, contingent or noncontingent. If response rate increases in the noncontingent group, it can be argued that an elicitation effect is present.

The case of learning to manipulate an object to gain access to interesting stimuli provides a good example. After hand-eye coordination has been achieved, the hands become an increasingly important modality for interaction with the environment. It is therefore reasonable to expect that, especially after the first half-year of life, the hands will be brought to bear upon interesting stimulation whenever possible, and some of these stimuli will produce interesting (reinforcing) variations as a consequence of manipulation. Thus, in the infant's ordinary interactions with the environment many stimuli will elicit manipulative responses; as a consequence of manipulation these same stimuli will reinforce the responses they elicit.

This circular relationship between responses and their consequences has been previously described by Piaget (1952b) under the label of the secondary circular reaction. An observation of this pattern was made on an infant who was lying on her back in a bassinet looking at some cloth dolls suspended from the hood of the bassinet. When the baby moved her legs, the bassinet shook and the dolls on the hood moved. Piaget observed that the baby saw these movements and smiled with pleasure while continuing to kick her legs. Later, when the infant was still, he shook the dolls on the bassinet and observed that the infant began kicking again. The point of this observation and of the concept of circular reaction is that an action and its consequence are organized in a reciprocal fashion; the action produces the interesting result because of the organization of the environment; the interesting result produces the action because of the organization of the infant. If this relationship holds, then the secondary circular reaction describes a behavior pattern in which a stimulus both reinforces and elicits the same response.

An experiment by Cavanagh and Davidson (1977) attempted to replicate the observation of the circular reaction and to determine whether an elicitation effect might be seen in a case of manipulative responding for auditory-visual reinforcement. Six-month-old infants had to press on a clear plexiglass panel located directly in front of them in order to see a multicolored light display located immediately behind the panel and hear a bell located on the ceiling directly above their heads. The infants were divided into three groups: (1) a group that received auditory-visual stimulation contingent upon panel pressing, (2) a yoked noncontingent group in which each subject was matched with a subject in the first group for amount and distribution of stimuli, and (3) a contingent group in which the locus of the visual reinforcement was spatially separated from the manipulandum. In order to assess the presence or absence of a circular reaction (i.e., responding to the stimuli), the stimuli were presented noncontingently every 20 sec during the baseline and extinction phases of the experiment.

The results supported both the observation of the circular reaction and the idea that response elicitation can play a role in such learning (Fig. 10-8). The analysis of the changes in response rate from baseline to acquisition and from acquisition to extinction showed significant changes in all groups—that is, each group showed increased responding in the presence of the stimulus during acquisition in comparison with either the baseline or the extinction phase. However, there were no differences between the groups in the degree of change from one phase of the procedure to the other. The yoked noncontingent group produced a response curve for the entire session similar to that of the two contingent groups. Clearly, response elicitation played a role in maintaining the increased response level in the noncontingent group and in the contingent group in which the response manipulandum and the reinforcement were spatially contiguous.

The analysis of the infants' response pattern following the periodic noncontingent stimuli during the baseline and extinction phases supported the observation of the circular reaction. The infants in the contingent group with the manipulandum and spatially contiguous reinforcement showed more responding following stimulus onset in extinction than they did during the baseline phase, and this difference was greater in this group than it was in the other two (Fig. 10-9). Thus, as a consequence of contingent interaction with the

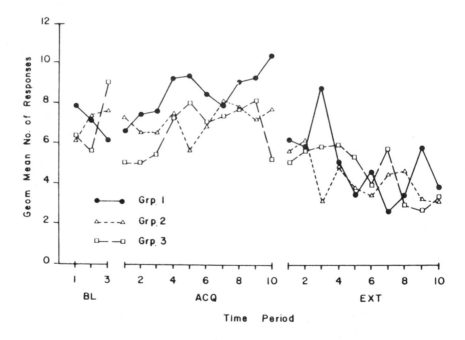

[From Cavanagh & Davidson, 1977.]

Figure 10-8. Number of responses during successive 20-sec periods during baseline, acquisition, and extinction for infants in a contingent condition (group 1), a yoked noncontingent condition (group 2), and a spatially separated contingent condition (group 3).

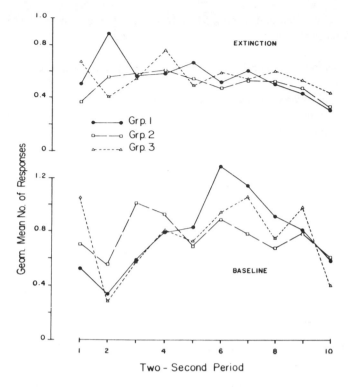

[From Cavanagh & Davidson, 1977.]

Figure 10-9. Number of responses during successive 2-sec periods following stimulus onset in baseline and extinction for infants in a contingent condition (group 1), a yoked noncontingent condition (group 2), and a spatially separated contingent condition (group 3).

reinforcing stimulus in spatial contiguity to the response, these infants developed an increased tendency to respond following the reinforcement.

It now becomes possible to give an account of learning in this group of infants in terms of two processes: unconditioned elicitation and conditioned elicitation. Because of the growth of hand-eye coordination, the 6-month-old infant enters an experiment with the prehensile system already adapted to interaction with the environment. By this point in his life, the infant has found that many interesting events can be produced through the use of the hands. Thus, when faced with an interesting stimulus within reach, the young infant responds by reaching out to contact the stimulus. The stimulus, therefore, elicits the response without concurrent contingent interaction, as shown in the increased response rate produced by the noncontingent group in this experiment. This result is an example of an unconditioned elicitation effect. However, when contingent interaction was available in addition to the elicitation effect, learning was enhanced, as seen in the fact that the contingent group showed a greater change in elicited responding from baseline to extinction than did the noncontingent group. This greater change reflects conditioned elicitation. The infant entered the learning situation with the expectancy that a particular response system would be effective. This expectancy made it possible for the related response to be elicited in an unconditioned manner. As a result of this elicitation the infant encountered a portion of the environment that responded to him in a reliable fashion. The contingency established a conditioned cycle of mutually sustained activity between the organism and the reinforcing stimulus.

Now that we have seen a special case of the effect of unconditioned and conditioned elicitation effects, the question arises to what extent unconditioned and conditioned elicitation are present in other studies of action-consequence learning. In a review of operant training of social behaviors in infancy, Millar (1976a) concluded that researchers may have been "precipitous" in their optimism about the infant's social conditionability. Millar goes on to state that the data are equivocal primarily because of inadequate controls. Elicitation effects were evident in almost all studies, and their presence must be taken into account in any claim for conditioning effects. We will now review these studies of social conditioning with an eye to this issue.

We do not use the term social conditioning to imply that the infant has an understanding of the difference between social and nonsocial stimuli and responses. Our use is limited to the fact that the stimuli and responses that fall in this category generally occur in a social context as well as the fact that they seem to have a meaning for maintaining and communicating social interactions.

SOCIAL BEHAVIOR

Vocalization

The case of responses that have a social component provides a good starting point because the problem is intuitively clearer in this domain, and infant vocalization in particular has generated an interesting literature. Perhaps the first study of conditioned vocalization was that by Rheingold et al. (1959) done with 3-month-old infants. Following a baseline period, infant vocalization was reinforced by adult social stimulation, continuously at first, then on a partial schedule in the latter part of acquisition period. Rheingold et al. were able to show that vocalization increased significantly during the acquisition phase. It was interesting that although there was no control group in this study, the authors did discuss the possibility that the reinforcing stimulus might have elicited the response although the infant did not seem to respond following presentation of the social stimulation. The issue was taken up explicitly in a study by Weisberg (1963) in which he compared, among other things, the effect of contingent and noncontingent social stimulation. Weisberg found an increase in vocalization rate during contingent social stimulation but not during noncontingent stimulation. He therefore concluded that the results of his and the Rheingold et al. study could be attributed to learning effects. The issue appeared to have been settled at that point, and a number of studies of various aspects of conditioned vocalization were carried out without using noncontingent control groups until the appearance of a study by Bloom and Esposito (1975).

Bloom and Esposito argued that the Weisberg study needed reexamination because the results of the noncontingent group were in opposition to the casual observation of most adults that infant vocalization can be elicited by adult social stimulation. In addition, the results of Weisberg's contingent group may have been dominated by a single very active infant, with the implication that learning may not have occurred.

In their first experiment, done with 3-month-olds, Bloom and Esposito used a yoked noncontingent control group. The yoked procedure was argued to be an appropriately rigorous control because it provided the same amount and distribution of stimuli as in the contingent reinforcement group. The procedure included baseline, acquisition, extinction, and reconditioning for some of the subjects. The results were that application of the social stimulation significantly increased response rate for both the acquisition and reconditioning phases of the procedure, but there were no differences between the response rates of the contingent and noncontingent groups (Fig. 10-10). Adult social stimulation caused a significant increase in the rate of vocalization regardless of the contingency.

In a second experiment, Bloom and Esposito compared a condition in which the experimenter continuously tried to elicit vocalizing by means of social stimulation with a condition in which the experimenter stopped applying social stimulation for a period of 5 sec whenever the infant vocalized. Although the continuous-elicitation condition provided twice as much social stimulation as the time-out condition, there was no significant difference between the two in response rate (Figure 10-11). In a later study (Bloom, 1975), it was again shown that both response-independent and response-dependent social stimulation could increase vocalization but with the additional restraint that eye-to-eye contact with the experimenter was necessary.

Inasmuch as other studies of conditioned vocalization did not have appropriate controls, it is reasonable to conclude that increases in the rate of infant vocalization in a situation where adult stimulation is present are due at least in part to unconditioned elicitation.

Smiling

The literature on conditioned smiling, although smaller than the literature on vocalization, raises some parallel questions. In a study with 4-month-olds, Brackbill (1958) demonstrated a partial-reinforcement effect. She used a complex visual, auditory, and tactile reinforcing stimulus of 30-sec duration, and administered a lengthy series of trials over a period of time ranging from 8 to 16 days. During this period the infants were kept on a schedule of social deprivation. "In effect, this meant elimination of all social and body

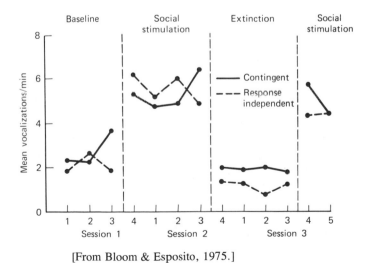

[From Bloom & Esposito, 1975.]

Figure 10-10. Changes in vocalization rate as a function of experimental treatment.

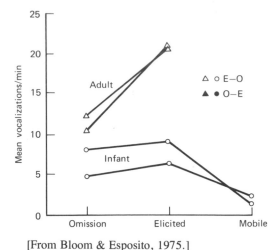

[From Bloom & Esposito, 1975.]

Figure 10-11.   Changes in adult and infant vocalization as a function of experimental treatment.

contacts that were not absolutely necessary for S's well being" [Brackbill, 1958, p. 117]. One group of infants received continuous reinforcement throughout the procedure, while another group received continuous reinforcement during the early phases of conditioning followed by a progressively thinner schedule of partial reinforcement during the latter phases. Brackbill reported that during extinction the partial-reinforcement group showed significantly more responses than the continuous-reinforcement group. It is difficult to contrast the acquisition and baseline performance of these infants because the data are presented in cumulative form with the groups combined. However, examination of the response curve suggests that continuous reinforcement did not produce an increase in the operant rate of responding in either group. It seems that a substantial increase over operant level, if it exists, would be found only in the latter trials of the partial-reinforcement procedure.

The idea that infant smiling can be manipulated by operant techniques gained further support from studies by Etzel and Gewirtz (1967) and Wahler (1967). In the Etzel and Gewirtz study crying was extinguished and smiling was increased during the appropriate part of the experimental procedure in two institutionalized infants. The Waller study showed more effective control of infant smiling when the infant's mother was the experimenter than when a stranger was the experimenter.

However, an interesting pair of experiments with 3-month-olds by Zelazo (1971) raised some important questions about these studies. In his first experiment Zelazo contrasted the effect of a male and female experimenter as vehicles for social reinforcement, and found differential effects dependent upon the sex of the experimenter. In the second study, using only the female experimenter, he contrasted the effects of a contingent experimental group with both contingent and noncontingent control groups. For our purposes, two aspects of the results are important: (1) in both experiments the frequency of smiling decreased steadily across the experimental session, and (2) in the second experiment, there were no differences between the groups with the exception of a higher response rate in the contingent group during the first part of each of the three sessions of the experiment. Zelazo pointed out that this initial difference could have been inadvertently caused by the subject-selection procedure.

At first glance the results of this study appear to be vastly discrepant from the studies cited above. However, upon closer examination this is not necessarily the case. In none of these studies does smiling behave like a typical operant. If the data in the Brackbill (1958) study were presented simply in terms of number of responses across blocks of trials for the entire experiment for each group separately, it is quite likely that there would be no marked increase in response rate due to reinforcement in the continuous-reinforcement group, and an increase only during the latter part of acquisition in the partial-reinforcement group. However, the most salient aspect of the curves for both groups would be the fact that response rate fell well below the operant level by the end of the session. Furthermore, there was no noncontingent control group in this study, and responses were not recorded during the 30-sec reinforcement procedure. In the Wahler (1967) study, which contrasted the mother and stranger as reinforcers, the response curve for the stranger (basically the same condition as in the Zelazo study) showed no increase in response rate as a result of reinforcement. Again the dominant property of the response curve was a decline to well below the baseline level by the end of the experiment. The response curve for the mother as reinforcer did show a substantial increase during acquisition. However, it is precisely in the case of a mother reinforcing her own infant for smiling that one would need a noncontingent control for unconditioned elicitation. The latter was not present in the Wahler study. The Etzel and Gewirtz study perhaps presents the strongest evidence for conditioned smiling because it seemed that it was necessary to overcome a learned crying response in the presence of adults. But the pattern of responding was again unusual. Although reinforcement produced an increase over the baseline phase, extinction did not produce a subsequent decline. In the 20-week-old infant, the highest peak of responding for any day of the session occurred during extinction, and the rate of responding in acquisition appeared to be no greater than during extinction. In the 6-week-old infant the rate of smiling during extinction was clearly much higher than it was during reinforcement. As in the other studies, Etzel and Gewirtz had no noncontingent controls.

As Zelazo (1972) pointed out, smiling appears as a response that is not very amenable to laboratory study in general and operant analysis in particular. It has a low frequency of occurrence relative to other responses in the infant's repertoire, especially in strange places and in the presence of strange persons. A major portion of the work on smiling has studied it as an elicited rather than a conditioned response (e.g., Schultz and Zigler, 1970; Wolfe, 1963; Zelazo and Komer, 1971). Furthermore, as pointed out by Sroufe and Waters (1976), smiling may be an affective discharge related to the perception of a contingency, social or otherwise. Even the learning work suggests an unconditioned elicitation component as seen in the failure of Zelazo (1971) to find a response difference between the contingent and noncontingent group, and in the experimenter effects found in both the Zelazo (1971) and Wahler (1967) studies. Such findings indicate that the infant may be differentially prepared to smile under varying conditions.

Learning to Look

Looking behavior is a component of both social and nonsocial responding. Several studies have attempted to demonstrate that visual fixation and headturning in order to look can be operantly as well as tropistically controlled. Although not controversial, these studies will be examined here in order to emphasize how difficult it is to demonstrate a purely operant effect.

Watson (1968) raised the question whether operant control by the preferred stimulus might account for differences found in studies of infant visual fixation where preference was assessed in terms of duration of visual fixation. He presented an inverted and an upright schematic face to 5-month-old infants in trials of 30-sec duration and examined the duration of fixation during 5-sec intervals. The results were no differences in fixation during the 5 sec of the first presentation, but greater looking to the upright stimulus during the remainder of the first presentation. During the second presentation the positions of the stimuli were reversed and the infants showed greater looking to the inverted face during the first 10 sec of the presentation, but reversed their looking by the end of the presentation. Watson interpreted the looking behavior in the first 10 sec of the second presentation as operant learning of the position of the upright stimulus. Presumably this is operant learning because there was no preference apparent during the first 5 sec of the first presentation. However an elicited preference did emerge during the remainder of this presentation, which persisted into the second presentation.

Levison and Levison (1967) attempted to condition headturning in 3-month-olds using a visual reinforcement presented at the midline. Such a procedure would presumably avoid an elicitation effect because the infant was required to turn his head away from the stimulus. However, in order to facilitate the procedure, a small blinking light on the appropriate side of the viewing panel was used to elicit the first three responses in each session. Although these responses were not counted in the data analysis, the response under investigation was nonetheless an elicited response.

The same comment can be made about a set of studies by Caron (1967) and Caron et al. (1971). In both these studies a patterned visual stimulus was presented at the midline as a reinforcement for a 20° turn of the head to the left. At the beginning of the acquisition phase (Caron, 1967) the response was elicited by means of stimuli such as beads or a rattle, which were held at the midline and moved to the left side. When the infant's tracking behavior produced a 20° head-turn, reinforcement was delivered. For most of the infants in the study, this procedure was carried out for the first two or three responses. These responses were not counted in the data analysis, but again the response was elicited. The Caron et al. study simply states that the response was shaped, but it is reasonable to assume that the same procedure was used. Furthermore, because of the procedural requirements for this study, 68% of the infants who entered the project could not complete their participation. This raises questions about the representative nature of both the sample and the task.

This discussion is not an attempt to minimize the role of contingent consequences in the development of looking behavior. The objective is simply to point out that, especially in the case of looking behavior, elicitation can play an important role in action-consequence interactions.

Learning Manipulative Response

Manipulative responses like reaching and touching have been studied in both social and nonsocial contexts. The early studies of manipulative responses did not engage the question of elicitation effects directly. Rheingold et al (1962) demonstrated an apparatus that could be used to condition manipulative responses in infants and older children. The response was a touch to a spherical object within the infant's reach; the reinforcement was an auditory-visual stimulus directly in front of the infant at a distance of 30 in. Because the report emphasized the description of the apparatus, few data were presented and fewer conclusions could be made. However, it is interesting that of the two individual cumulative records presented, one showed a response pattern that differentiated between contingent reinforcement and noncontingent reinforcement, and the other showed a response pattern that did not make the differentiation (Fig. 10-12). In the case of the second infant, it seemed that the response apparatus and/or the noncontingent stimuli elicited a response rate similar to the acquisition rate of the infant who discriminated between contingent and noncontingent reinforcement.

Another of the early studies of manipulative responding is that by Lipsitt et al. (1966b) with 12-month-olds. The response consisted of pressing on a clear panel within the infant's reach. The reinforcement was a visual display presented directly behind the response panel. This study used conjugate reinforcement: a procedure in which the reinforcing stimulus is continuously present but varies in intensity as a direct function of response rate. Since a noncontingent control group was not used in this study, no definitive conclusion can be drawn. However, it is interesting that in both of the experiments the data did not exhibit a completely consistent set of effects.

The adequate design of learning experiments require a baseline recording period of sufficient duration (Hulsebus, 1973). When the baseline period is too short it can produce an artificially low response rate because it does not permit habituation of the initial orienting reaction to the apparatus. When this artificially low response rate is compared to

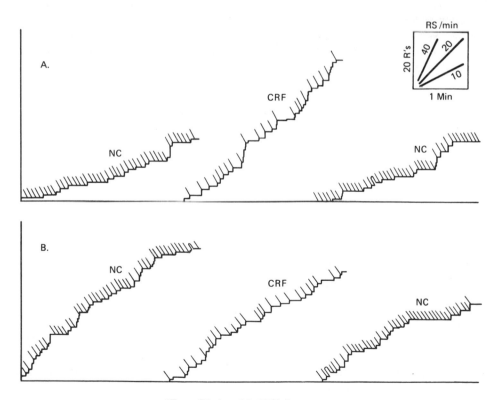

[From Rheingold, 1962.]

Figure 10-12. Cumulative response curves for two infants, showing (A) performance sensitive to changes in experimental conditions, and (B) performance not sensitive.

performance in the latter part of acquisition, it yields differences that can be erroneously attributed to conditioning effects. In Lipsitt et al.'s first experiment the duration of the baseline phase was 15 sec and the comparison between the baseline and acquisition response rates was significant. However, the comparison between acquisition and extinction response rates was not significant. In their second experiment the comparison of response rate during the first minute of conditioning with that of the last minute of conditioning was not significant. Thus, although the data were not conclusive, there is a possibility that the pattern of responding was not completely under the control of the contingency in either experiment.

Another study that used conjugate reinforcement was that by Rovee and Rovee (1969). This was not a study of manipulative responding, but it is of interest here because it used a noncontingent control group and because, like the Cavanagh and Davidson (1977) study cited earlier, it is derived from Piaget's (1952) observation of the circular reaction. The infants were tested in their own homes while in the supine position in their cribs. A mobile was attached to the crib and connected to the infant's left foot by means of a silk cord. The infant could move the mobile by kicking his or her leg. As leg-kicking increased, the amount of stimulation increased. Two noncontingent groups were used in which the experimenter continuously moved the mobile independently of the infant's kicking: in one group, a silk cord was attached to the infant's foot; in the other group no cord was attached. The results showed appropriate increases and decreases in response rate during acquisition and extinction in the experimental group. The control groups, on the other hand, showed no change in response rate across the phases of the experiment, and unconditioned elicitation does not seem to have been present. It should be said that for a number of reasons the stimulus conditions were probably not identical for the groups. The leg movements in the contingent group were accompanied by proprioceptive stimulation from the pull on the mobile. In neither of the two control groups was this proprioceptive stimulation available, although a silk cord was attached to the infant's foot in one of these groups. The continuously moving stimuli presented by the experimenter to the control groups may have produced habituation of interest more rapidly than the variably moving stimuli produced by the infants in the experimental group. Furthermore, although the report is not clear, the experimenter may have been positioned within the visual field of the control infants, but outside the visual field of the experimental infants.

Millar and Schaffer performed an interesting set of studies (Millar, 1972, 1974; Millar and Schaffer, 1972, 1973) on the spatio-temporal parameters of operant conditioning with manipulative responses and audio-visual reinforcements. All of these studies used noncontingent control groups, and none of them report an elicitation effect. In the majority of cases, noncontingent stimulation suppressed responding.

The first of these (Millar, 1972) was a study of the effect of delayed reinforcement. The infants, who were 4 and 8 months of age, sat before a white plexiglass panel behind which were colored lights and a pair of miniature loudspeakers. The reinforcing stimulus consisted of sound and light originating approximately 16 in. in front of the infant. The reinforced response was an arm movement. Nylon cords were pinned to the cuffs of the infant's clothing and attached to silent pull-switches located on either side of the stimulus panel. The cords were somewhat slack so that extensive arm movements were required to produce a reinforcement. It can be seen from this description of the stimulus apparatus and manipulandum that a response in a direction away from the stimulus source was required to produce a reinforcement. It is unlikely that such responses could be elicited in an unconditioned manner; therefore, it is not surprising to find no evidence of unconditioned elicitation in this study.

However, conditioned elicitation in this study is another matter. Millar's thorough control procedures provided four different instances in which it was possible to compare the effect of random noncontingent stimulation following a period of contingent stimulation with the effects of random noncontingent stimulation following a period of no stimulation. As argued earlier, the relationship between a response and a reinforcement may be reciprocal and, if so, the reinforcement will develop an increasing capacity to elicit the learned response as a result of contingent interaction with the stimulus. If this is true, noncontingent stimulation following contingent should elicit responses and show a higher response rate than noncontingent stimulation following no stimulation. An examination of Millar's data shows that all four of the comparisons mentioned above support this reasoning, and in at least two of the cases the difference appears to be significant. In one instance, response rate did not decline from contingent to noncontingent stimulation. In one other instance it is possible to compare the effects of delayed reinforcement (1, 2, and 3 sec) following a period of immediate reinforcement with the effects of delayed reinforcement following a period of no stimulation. Again, the same logic applies; response rate in the former condition should be higher because of conditioned elicitation. Again, the data are supportive. When a period of delayed reinforcement followed a period of immediate reinforcement it produced a greater response rate than it did when administered following a period of no stimulation. In the case of the 3-sec delay, the response rate after immediate reinforcement was almost double the rate that occurred after no stimulation. Although the combination of ceiling and suppression effects might have worked in favor of a higher response rate following contingent stimulation, the data did not rule out the possibility of conditioned elicitation, and their consistency provided mild support for this hypothesis.

In the other Millar and Schaffer studies (Millar, 1974; Millar and Schaffer, 1972, 1973) it is not possible to construct an argument for the presence of conditioned or unconditioned elicitation. In the case of unconditioned elicitation, the necessary comparison groups were not available. In the case of conditioned elicitation it is appropriate to point out that the stimulus and response parameters of the Millar studies were considerably different from those of other studies. Compared with the other studies of manipulative learning reviewed here, the stimuli in the Millar studies were weaker, and the responses were more specific. Furthermore, the maximum response rates in the other studies were twice as high as the maximum response rates in the Millar studies. Thus, it is possible that potential elicitation effects were erased by the stringent stimulus-and-response conditions of Millar's procedures.

It can be argued that removing the possibility of eliciting effects is precisely the purpose of stringent control procedures in an operant learning experiment. The underlying learning process is assumed to be one in which the frequency of freely emitted responses is increased as a function of contingent reward. To study this process it is necessary to remove from the experiment all conditions that might elicit the response more or less independently of reinforcement conditions.

The question now arises whether such a research strategy sets up an arbitrary organism-environment relationship (Seligman, 1970). Response systems such as vocalizing, smiling, and prehension have a very high degree of adaptive significance. In the case of the human infant from 3 to 6 months of age, both the history of the species and the history of the organism (developmental preparedness) have prepared vocalizing, smiling, and prehension to be highly interactive mechanisms capable of engaging the environment under a variety of conditions both contingent and noncontingent (Bowlby, 1969). Therefore, the effort to design contingency relations that are free of eliciting effects, in spite of the fact that such effects are probably quite common in the natural environment, is an imposition of arbitrariness in the infant domain that is exactly the same as the arbitrariness described by Seligman within the animal domain. If elicitation is seen not as an experimental artifact but as an integral part of infant behavior, it is appropriate to examine its role.

FACILITATING EFFECTS OF RESPONSE ELICITATION

Despite the fact that recent animal literature has tended to emphasize constraints on learning (e.g., Hinde, 1973; Shettleworth, 1972), it is important to emphasize that the infant's level of preparation provides facilitating conditions as well. The environment is not random and infinite in its natural possibilities. In many ways it is highly structured, with salient properties that strongly impose themselves on the infant. In other ways it is weakly structured, but the preparedness of the infant compensates to make learning possible. Hunt (1961) has suggested that the effect of evolutionary and ontogenetic processes is to construct a match between environmental properties and the response systems of the infant, which will enhance adaptive mutual accommodation by making some kinds of interactions highly probable and very easy to maintain. An illustration of the facilitating and constraining effects of infant expectancy can be seen by examining the effects of reinforcement modality and spatial displacement on infant learning.

Reinforcement Mode

The effects of reinforcement modality can be explored by examining three studies (Millar, 1976b; Ramey and Watson, 1972; and Weisberg, 1963). Weisberg (1963) attempted to condition vocalization in 3-month-olds using social and nonsocial reinforcement. The study used a variety of stimulus conditions including (1) contingent and noncontingent social stimulation, (2) contingent and noncontingent nonsocial stimulation, (3) an unresponsive adult, and (4) no stimulation. The social stimulus was vocal and tactile; the nonsocial stimulus was auditory. The results showed that an increased response rate was found only under contingent social stimulation, and that nonsocial stimulation, both contingent and noncontingent, produced a lower vocalization rate than all other conditions with the possible exception of the no-stimulation condition.

Similar results were reported by Ramey and Watson (1972). They attempted to condition vocalization in 10- and 16-week-old infants using two nonsocial reinforcers: a visual stimulus and a compound auditory-visual stimulus. The use of noncontingent controls was not reported. The results showed increased response rate during acquisition only for 16-week-old males under visual reinforcement. In all other groups (age, sex, and stimulus conditions) the stimuli were not effective in controlling response rate. Thus, in both the Weisberg (1963) and Ramey and Watson (1972) studies, nonsocial reinforcement was relatively ineffective for controlling the rate of a social response.

A recent study by Millar (1976b) turned the paradigm around and attempted to condition a nonsocial response using a social reinforcer with 6- and 9-month-old infants. The response was a touch to a small canister attached to a table directly in front of the infant. The reinforcing stimulus was a "peek-a-boo" from the infant's mother who was seated directly in front of the infant on the far side of the manipulandum. The experimental design used contingent and noncontingent stimulation in both age groups. The results showed learning in the 9-month-old contingent group. The 6-month-olds showed a steadily declining response rate across the phases of the procedure under contingent and noncontingent stimulation. Once again, it is the case that mixing social and nonsocial modalities proved relatively ineffective for controlling the infant's behavior.

The failures to achieve response control in these three studies are significant because, as Millar (1976a) points out, there is ample evidence that social responses and manipulative responses can be conditioned when the appropriate reinforcers are used. Millar goes on to speculate that in the case of social responses combined with social feedback, the effectiveness of this paradigm for controlling vocal behavior may be related to its "natural" quality, inasmuch as the reinforcement involves "the reciprocal performance by the reinforcing agent of the operant under consideration" [Millar, 1976a, p. 13]. If the term natural is intended to refer to those instances where the reinforcement more or less imitates the response, then its use seems too restrictive because manipulative responses are readily controlled by reinforcing stimuli that do not imitate the response. However, if the term natural is intended to refer to the situation where laboratory conditions replicate organism-environment interactions that frequently and naturally occur outside the laboratory, then its use seems entirely appropriate. The social mode of interaction (social response and social feedback) and the manipulative mode of interaction (manipulative response and perceptual feedback) are highly practiced in the natural environment of infants 3 to 6 months of age. It is therefore reasonable to speculate that the infant has internalized these modes as schemas of interaction with the environment. In the case of younger infants, these schemas constitute facilitating conditions for learning when response and reinforcement are in the same mode, but they constitute constraining conditions for learning when the response and the reinforcement are in different modes.

Spatial Displacement of the Reinforcement

Similar speculation is supported by the results of studies by Millar and Schaffer (1972, 1973) and Millar (1974) on the role of attention in learning manipulative responses under conditions of displaced reinforcement. In the first of these studies Millar and Schaffer (1972) used the canister manipulandum described earlier. The reinforcement consisted of light display and a tone whose locus varied in three conditions. In the 0° condition the display originated from the response canister; in the second condition, it originated in another canister placed 5° to the side of the manipulandum; and in the third condition the reinforcement was positioned 60° to the side. The reinforcement in all three conditions was administered contingently or noncontingently to groups of 6-, 9-, and 12-month-old infants. The results showed that 6-month-old infants learned in the 0° and 5° conditions but not in the 60° condition; 9- and 12-month-olds, on the other hand, learned in all three conditions. It is interesting to note that response rates during acquisition for 6- and 9-month-old infants were very similar for both the 0° and 5° conditions. Only the 12-month-olds seem to have differentiated between the 0° and 5° conditions. And for this group the response rate in the 5° condition is similar to the 60° condition. Millar and Schaffer (1972) speculated that the failure of the 6-month-olds to learn in the 60° condition occurred because the experimental arrangement was such that the reinforcement drew attention away from the manipulandum and the infants therefore could not coordinate the simultaneous motor and perceptual activities involved.

Accordingly, a further study (Millar and Schaffer, 1973) was done using the 60° condition with 6- and 9-month-olds, and the infant's visual attentional responses to the manipulandum and the reinforcement were recorded. Again, the 6-month-olds failed to show learning while the 9-month-olds were successful. Analysis of the infants' visual behavior showed that under contingent stimulation the younger infants looked at the display stimulus as much as the older ones, but the frequency of simultaneous looking at the reinforcement while responding was much greater for the older infants. For the younger infants, looking at the reinforcement seemed to have inhibited responding to the manipulandum. In a later study (Millar, 1974) it was shown that the presence of a cue that marked the locus of the reinforcement supported learning in 6-month-olds. In the absence of the cue, learning was not evident at this age. Again, the varying conditions of reinforcement did not disrupt the behavior of 9-month-olds. In this study, the same manipulandum was used; audio-visual reinforcement came from a small screen located in front of the infant on the opposite side of the manipulandum.

These studies emphasize the spatial aspects of infant learning, and clearly point out the role of attentional coordination in spanning the spatial gaps between actions and their consequences. The studies of action-consequence learning reviewed above included a dimension of spatial relatedness between the locus of the response and the locus of the consequent stimuli. At one end of the spatial dimension, the response and its consequences are continuous and simultaneously comprehendible by the infant. At the other end they become angularly dissociated into two separate vectors of action, where the infant cannot attend to the locus of response and the locus of contingent changes at the same time.

At the extreme of spatial contiguity the reinforcing stimulus is provided by the manipulandum and occurs in the same location as the response (Cavanagh and Davidson, 1977; Lipsitt et al., 1966b; Millar and Schaffer, 1972). Perception of the stimulus does not require the infant to remove his attention from the locus of the response.

Toward the middle of the dimension are examples of linear noncontiguity. In these cases the reinforcing stimulus originates from a source distant from the manipulandum, but the two are within the same span of action. Attending to the stimulus requires that the infant's attention be removed from the manipulandum or response activity, but not very far. This category includes most cases of social conditioning, some cases of manipulative learning (Millar, 1972, 1974, 1976b; Millar and Schaffer, 1972; Rhinegold et al., 1962), as well as some other cases of motor learning (Rovee and Rovee, 1969).

At the other end of the dimension is displaced noncontiguity. In this case the manipulandum and the reinforcement are in different vectors of action for the infant. In this situation the infant cannot simultaneously attend to the locus of the response and the locus of reinforcement. Studies using displaced feedback (Cavanagh and Davidson, 1976; Millar and Schaffer, 1972, 1973) fall into this category.

In the case of complete contiguity the infant's expectancy of manipulative interaction with an interesting object within reach is clearly a facilitating condition for learning. Unconditioned elicitation leads the infant to explore the manipulandum. This manipulation produces a stimulus from the manipulandum, which leads to further unconditioned elicitation; and in a matter of seconds a circular reaction is established as the infant constructs an interactive relationship with the reinforcing stimulus, developing a conditioned elicitation. The infant's expectancy also facilitates attentional coordination because the elicitation properties of the task are such that they direct the infant's attentional activities to a single spatial location.

In the case of linear noncontiguity, learning should be somewhat more difficult because the unconditioned elicitation directs the infant's attention to two spatial locations—one for the manipulandum, another for the reinforcement. However, successful stimulus control has been demonstrated under these conditions quite readily. The results of these studies suggest that attentional coordination of action-consequence relationships within the same span of action is quite easy for the young infant. The only suggestion that coordination is more difficult under these conditions comes from the results of Millar's (1974) study of the role of spatial holding cues. In this study, 6-month-olds were not able to learn to control a distal audio-visual stimulus in the noncued condition.

In the case of displaced noncontiguity, learning becomes more difficult. The elicitation properties of the situation draw the infant's attention to two different locations separated by a relatively large spatial gap. The results of studies in the previous two categories suggest that the infant expects to find action-consequence coordinations within contiguity or linear noncontiguity. Such an expectation conflicts with the learning required in a displaced arrangement and the expectation becomes a constraint on new learning.

It is reasonable to propose that an infant moves through a temporal sequence of phases of attentional coordination relative to displaced action-consequence coordinations. Initially, there is a phase of uncoordinated attention in which attention to the consequence inhibits performance of the action. Then there is a phase of attending to the relationship that is under construction, and one would expect to see alternation from attention to the action and the manipulandum to attention to the consequent stimuli. In a third phase, the response activity would have been learned and would no longer require focused attention. The infant can attend to the consequences without having to attend to the action.

Support for the existence of these phases comes from the Millar and Schaffer (1973) study cited above and from a study by Koslowski and Bruner (1972). In the Millar and Schaffer study, 6-month-old infants under displaced reinforcement showed the same amount of looking to the contingent stimulus as the 9-month-olds, but they showed less responding and failed to learn the relationship. Looking at the consequence appeared to inhibit the action as in the first phase described above. The 9-month-olds, on the other hand, learned the relationship and showed a greater frequency of looking at the stimulus while responding as in the third phase described above.

In the Koslowski and Bruner (1972) study, infants between 12 and 24 months of age worked on a problem in which a toy attached to the end of a lever could be reached by rotating the near end of the level which was within the child's reach. The apparatus was such that at the beginning of the procedure the child, manipulandum, and the toy were in a linear arrangement. However, the solution required the child to move the toy into a different vector relative to his frontal position. The results were that a series of strategies were used by the infants. The youngest infants began with a strategy that produced direct attention to and preoccupation with the goal and no attention to the manipulandum. They moved through a set of strategies that included alternating attention to the goal and the manipulandum and finally a phase of attention to the goal while operating the manipulandum.

It is clear that there is a need to explore manipulative learning in relation to the classes of looking behavior required across ages and phases of an experiment within different ranges of displacement. As infants get older, their ability to transpose spatial gaps by means of coordinated attention becomes greater and their strategies for manipulating the environment become more flexible as the expectation for complete contiguity or linear noncontiguity is reduced.

THE 7-TO-9-MONTH SHIFT

We have divided our review into a section on the newborn period and a section on later infancy on the pragmatic basis that studies have clustered in the newborn period and at 3 months. We added to that a theoretical rationale that there may be a major shift in behavioral organization during the first 3 months of age. We must now add a second major shift in behavioral organization, which appears to occur between 7 and 9 months of age. Emde et al. (1976) have reviewed evidence for major changes in behavior that occur in emotional, cognitive, and psychophysiological domains during this age period. Between these ages the infant achieves the ability to find a hidden object (Piaget, 1954) as well as to become upset by strangeness. These shifts imply an increased facility of the infant to utilize memorial processes in order to coordinate past with present information. The studies reviewed above offer experimental evidence for some aspects of this shift in behavioral organization.

CONCLUSIONS

We began our presentation by stating that we were not going to make a traditional presentation of the learning literature. We claimed that the main contributions made by a traditional approach to explaining infant learning have been through the prediction of inconsistencies rather than consistencies. Whether or not we have succeeded in our goal, we will have to leave to the judgment of the critical reader. To aid in that reappraisal, let us reiterate the major conceptual issues we have raised.

The central point is that the conditioning paradigm, whether classical or operant, attempts to understand behavior by imposing a structure on the activities of the child which neglects both the biological and psychological uniqueness of the human infant. The biological uniquenesses derive from a phylogenetic and ontogenetic development history, which has prepared infants for activities appropriate to their environmental niche. Studies that have taken advantage of these prepared activities have found connections between responses and their consequences, while those studies that have attempted to establish arbitrary relationships between behavior and its consequences have been unable to do so. The psychological uniquenesses derive from the experiential history of children as they activate and coordinate their initial response capacities.

In the newborn period, those studies that have claimed to have succeeded to establish new contingencies between organism and environment have been quite limited. Controls have proven necessary for the infant's state of arousal as well as the eliciting properties of the conditional and reinforcing stimuli. In later infancy, both conditioned and uncon- ditioned elicitation effects have further contributed to doubts about successes claimed for the conditioning of behavior.

Have we offered a meaningful alternative to the conditioning approach? We argued that a stronger integration was necessary between principles of biological and psychological functioning. The biological principle most cogent to our view is that each organism operates in an adaptive relation with its specific environment. This adaptive relation is developmentally structured in the functioning of young infants. We have followed Piaget in arguing that learning is better defined as assimilation, not association. Assimilation implies that there is a prior structure to which experience can be assimilated. The newborn's structures are the biologically given perceptual and response capacities. The "preparedness" argument has focused on these givens, which constrain the organism's range of assimilation. To the preparedness notion, we must add a development perspective. The problem for biologists is to explain the development of the newborn's initial set of sensitivities and action capacities. The analogous succeeding problem for psychologists is to explain how this initial set becomes differentiated and integrated as a function of the infant's activity in his or her environment.

The developmental problem may be even more complicated. It may be that the transitions in behavioral organization that occur at 2 to 3 months and at 7 to 9 months are based on further developments in biological organization. Conversely, it may be that the transitions in biological organization that occur during the fetal period may have a basis in behavioral organization. What all of the above implies is that one must understand psychological structures and functions in the context of biological structures and functions and, further, that both psychological and biological organization may be unique for a given organism in a given niche.

Given the above context, we can again attempt an understanding of infant learning. The first question is, can infants learn? If the answer is in the affirmative, the next question is, what can the infant learn? Our review of the literature would lead us to the conclusion that infants can learn. What they can learn, however, is a more complex issue. There are clear constraints in this learning. One of these constraints is that infants will not learn to arbitrarily associate any stimulus with any response. An opposing constraint is that some studies that have purported to show learning have merely manipulated the infant into a state where already organized behavior can be demonstrated. The foundation for this conclusion was in the discussion of elicitation effects throughout infancy.

However, we have argued that elicitation effects should not be viewed as artifacts, but rather as evidence of the contemporary status of the infant's behavioral organization. New learning can only build on already existing organization.

While the account of infant learning given here may be novel, placing the study of infant learning within its evolutionary and developmental context can be a fruitful enterprise. On the one hand, an area of research that restricted itself to attempted replications of the phenomena of animal learning now finds itself with a host of indigenous problems. These problems include the relative contributions of unconditioned and conditioned elicitation, the role of attention in action-consequence learning, and the parameters of the infant's ability at various ages to span the temporal and spatial gaps of organism-environmental interactions in social and manipulative modes of behavior.

The awareness of phylogenetic and ontogenetic constraints necessitates a new relationship between laboratory and naturalistic methodologies. There has been antipathy between these two approaches—the former claiming supremacy because of its rigorous control and the precision of the causal explanations that it yields, the latter claiming supremacy because of the richness of its behavioral descriptions. This competitiveness should be replaced by cooperation. While the richness of naturalistic methodology can provide insights for improving experimental designs, it is the rigor of laboratory methodology that can provide clear illustrations of processes that are too submerged in variability to be visible in the natural environment.

We end this review with the hope that we have stimulated the reader into an awareness of the vast array of parameters that intersect in the study of infant learning. A further hope is that we may have contributed something to the integration of these parameters.

BIBLIOGRAPHY

Abrahamson, D., Brackbill, Y., Carpenter, R., and Fitzgerald, H. E. Interaction of stimulus and response in infant conditioning. In H. E. Fitzgerald and Y. Brackbill (eds.), *Design and Method in Infant Research*. Chicago: University of Chicago, 1970.

Ardran, G. M., Kemp, F. H., and Lind, J. A cineradiographic study of bottle feeding. *British Journal of Radiology,* 1958, **31,** 11–22.

Babkin, P. S. The establishment of reflex activity in early postnatal life. In *The Central Nervous System and Behavior*. (Translated from the Russian by the U.S. Department of Health, Education and Welfare, Public Health Service.) Washington, D.C.: U.S. Government Printing Office, 1960, 24–32.

Bakow, H. A. Conditioning and individual differences in human newborns. Unpublished Ph.D dissertation, University of Rochester, 1975.

Bloom, K. Social elicitation of infant vocal behavior. *Journal of Experimental Child Psychology,* 1975, **20,** 51–58.

Bloom, K., and Esposito, A. Social conditioning and its proper control procedures. *Journal of Experimental Child Psychology,* 1975, **19,** 209–222.

Bolles, R. C. Reinforcement, expectancy and learning. *Psychological Review,* 1972, **79,** 394–407.

Bowlby, J. *Attachment and Loss,* Vol. 1. *Attachment*. New York: Basic Books, 1969.

Brackbill, Y. Extinction of the smiling response in infants as a function of reinforcement schedule. *Child Development,* 1958, **29,** 115–124.

Brackbill, Y., Fitzgerald, H. E., and Lintz, L. M. A developmental study of classical conditioning. *Monographs of the Society for Research in Child Development,* 1967, **32** (8, ser. 16).

Brackbill, Y., Lintz, L. M., and Fitzgerald, H. E. Differences in the autonomic and somatic conditioning of infants. *Psychosomatic Medicine,* 1968, **30,** 193–201.

Brazelton, T. B. *Neonatal Behavioral Assessment Scale*. London: Heinemann, 1973.

Breland, L., and Breland, M. *Animal Behavior*. New York: Macmillan, 1966.

Caron, R. F. Visual reinforcement of head-turning in young infants. *Journal of Experimental Child Psychology,* 1967, **5,** 489–511.

Caron, R. F., Caron, A. J., and Caldwell, R. C. Satiation of visual reinforcement in young infants. *Developmental Psychology,* 1971, **5,** 279–290.

Cavanagh, P., and Davidson, M. L. The secondary circular reaction and response elicitation in the operant learning of six-month-old infants. *Developmental Psychology,* 1977, **13,** 371–376.

Clifton, R. Heart rate conditioning in the newborn infant. Paper presented at the meeting of the Society of Psychophysiological Research, St. Louis, November 1971.

Clifton, R. Heart rate conditioning in the newborn infant. *Journal of Experimental Child Psychology,* 1974, **13,** 43–57.

Clifton, R. K., Meyers, W. J. and Solomons, G. Methodological problems in conditioning the head turning response of newborn infants. *Journal of Experimental Child Psychology,* 1972a, **13,** 29–42.

Clifton, R., Siqueland, E. R., and Lipsitt, L. P. Conditioned head turning in human newborns as a function of conditioned response requirements and states of wakefulness. *Journal of Experimental Child Psychology,* 1972b, **13,** 43–57.

Colley, J. R. T., and Creamer, B. Sucking and swallowing in infants. *British Medical Journal,* 1958, **ii,** 422–423.

Connolly, K., and Stratton, P. An exploration of some parameters affecting classical conditioning in the neonate. *Child Development,* 1969, **40,** 431–441.

Emde, R. N., Gaensbauer, T. G., and Harmon, R. J. Emotional expression in infancy: A biobehavioral study. *Psychological Issues Monograph Series,* Vol. 10, No. 37. New York: International Universities Press, 1976.

Emde, R. N., and Robinson, J. The first two months: Research in developmental psychobiology and the changing view of the newborn. In J. Noshpitz and J. Call (eds.), *Basic Handbook of Child Psychiatry,* New York: Basic Books, 1976.

Etzel, B. C., and Gewirtz, J. L. Experimental modification of caretaker-maintained high-rate operant crying in a 6- and a 20-week-old infant (Infans Tyrannotearus): Extinction of crying with reinforcement of eye contact and smiling. *Journal of Experimental Child Psychology,* 1967, **5,** 305–317.

Fitzgerald, H. E., and Brackbill, Y. Interstimulus interval in classical pupillary conditioning. *Psychological Reports,* 1968, **23,** 369–370.

Fitzgerald, H. E., and Brackbill, Y. Classical conditioning in infancy: Development and constraints. *Psychological Bulletin,* 1976, **83,** (3), 353–376.

Fitzgerald, H. E., Lintz, L. M., Brackbill, Y., and Adams, G. Time perception and conditioning of an autonomic response in young infants. *Perceptual and Motor Skills,* 1967, **24,** 479–486.

Fitzgerald, H. E., and Porges, S. W. A decade of infant conditioning and learning research. *Merrill-Palmer Quarterly,* 1971, **17,** 79–117.

Garcia, J., Ervin, F., and Koelling, R. Learning with prolonged delay of reinforcement. *Psychonomic Science,* 1966, **5,** 121–122.

Garcia, J., and Koelling, R. Relation of cue to consequence in avoidance learning. *Psychonomic Science,* 1966, **4,** 123–124.

Gottlieb, G. Concepts of prenatal development: Behavioral embryology. *Psychological Review,* 1976, **83,** 215–234.

Grant, D. A. Classical and operant conditioning. In A. W. Melton (ed.), *Categories of Human Learning.* New York: Academic, 1964.

Haugan, G. M., and McIntire, R. W. Comparisons of vocal imitation, tactile stimulation, and food reinforcers for infant vocalizations. *Developmental Psychology,* 1972, **6,** 201–209.

Hinde, R. A. Constraints on learning—an introduction to the problem. In R. A. Hinde and J. Stevenson-Hinde (eds.), *Constraints on Learning.* New York: Academic, 1973.

Hoffman, H. S., and Fleshler, M. Aversive control with the pigeon. *Journal of the Experimental Analysis of Behavior,* 1959, **2,** 213–218.

Hulsebus, R. C. Operant conditioning of infant behavior: A review. In H. W. Reese (ed.), *Advances in Child Development and Behavior,* Vol. 8. New York: Academic, 1973, 111–158.

Hunt, J. McV. *Intelligence and Experience.* New York: Ronald, 1961.

Hutt, S. J., Lenard, H. G., and Prechtl, H. F. R. Psychophysiological studies in newborn infants. In H. W. Reese and L. P. Lipsitt (eds.), *Advances in Child Development and Behavior,* Vol. 4. New York: Academic, 1969, 127–172.

Jensen, K. Differential reactions to taste and temperature stimuli in newborn infants. *Genetic Psychology Monographs,* 1932, **12,** 363–479.

Kasatkin, N. I. First conditioned responses and the beginning of the learning process in the human infant. In G. Newton and A. H. Riesen (eds.), *Advances in Psychobiology,* Vol. 1. New York: Wiley, 1972.

Kaye, H. The conditioned Babkin reflex in human newborns. *Psychonomic Science,* 1965, **2,** 287–288.

Keen, R. Effects of auditory stimulation on sucking behavior in the human neonate. *Journal of Experimental Child Psychology,* 1964, **1,** 348–354.

Kessen, W. Sucking and looking: Two organized patterns of behavior in the human newborn. In H.

W. Stevenson, E, H. Hess, and H. L. Rheingold (eds.), *Early Behavior: Comparative and Developmental Approaches*. New York: Wiley, 1967, 147–179.

Kimble, K. A. *Hilgard and Marquis' Conditioning and Learning*, 2nd ed. New York: Appleton-Century-Crofts, 1961.

Koslowski, B., and Bruner, J. Learning to use a lever. *Child Development*, 1972, **43**, 790–799.

Krafchuk, E. E., Sameroff, A. J., and Bakow, H. Newborn temperament and operant head turning. Paper presented at Southeast Regional Meeting of the Society for Research in Child Development, Nashville, April 1976.

Kuo, Z.-Y. *The Dynamics of Behavior Development*. New York: Random House, 1967.

Lenard, H. G., von Bernuth, H., and Prechtl, H. F. R. Reflexes and their relationships to behavioral state in the newborn. *Acta Paediatrica Scandinavica*, 1968, **55**, 177–185.

Levison, C. A., and Levison, P. K. Operant conditioning of head turning for visual reinforcement in three month old infants. *Psychonomic Science*, 1967, **8**, 529–530.

Lipsitt, L. P. Learning in the first year of life. In L. P. Lipsitt and C. C. Spiker (eds.), *Advances in Child Development and Behavior*, Vol. 1. New York: Academic, 1963.

Lipsitt, L. P., and Kaye, H. Conditioned sucking in the human newborn. *Psychonomic Science*, 1964, **1**, 29–30.

Lipsitt, L. P., and Kaye, H. Change in neonatal response to optimizing and non-optimizing sucking stimulation. *Psychonomic Science*, 1965, **2**, 221–222.

Lipsitt, L. P., Kaye, H., and Bosack, T. N. Enhancement of neonatal sucking through reinforcement. *Journal of Experimental Child Psychology*, 1966a, **4**, 163–168.

Lipsitt, L. P., Pederson, L. J., and Delucia, C. A. Conjugate reinforcement of operant responding in infants. *Psychonomic Science*, 1966b, **4**, 67–68.

Lorenz, K. Z. *Evolution and Modification of behavior*. Chicago: University of Chicago, 1965.

Marquis, D. P. Can conditioned responses be established in the newborn infant? *Journal of Genetic Psychology*, 1931, **39**, 479–492.

Millar, W. S. A study of operant conditioning under delayed reinforcement in early infancy. *Monographs of the Society for Research in Child Development*, 1972, **37** (2), 1–44.

Millar, W. S. The role of visual-holding cues and the simultanizing strategy in infant operant learning. *British Journal of Psychology*, 1974, **65**, 505–518.

Millar, W. S. Operant acquisition of social behavior in infancy: Basic problems and constraints. In H. Reese (ed.), *Advances in Child Development and Behavior*, Vol. 11. New York: Academic, 1976a.

Millar, W. S. Social reinforcement of a manipulative response in six- and nine-month-old infants. *Journal of Child Psychology and Psychiatry*, 1976b, **17**, 205–212.

Millar, W. S., and Schaffer, H. R. The influence of spatially displaced feedback on infant operant conditioning. *Journal of Experimental Child Psychology*, 1972, **14**, 442–452.

Millar, W. S., and Schaffer, H. R. Visual manipulative response strategies in infant operant conditioning with spatially displaced feedback *British Journal of Psychology*, 1973, **64**, 545–552.

Overton, W. F., and Reese, H. W. Models of development: Methodological implications. In J. R. Nesselroade and H. W. Reese (eds.), *Life-Span Developmental Psychology: Methodological Issues*. New York: Academic, 1972, 65–86.

Papousek, H. A method of studying conditioned food reflexes in young children up to the age of 6 months. *Pavlov Journal of Higher Nervous Activities*, 1959, **9**, 136–140.

Papousek, H. Conditioned head rotation reflexes in infants in the first months of life. *Acta Pediatrica*, 1961, **50**, 565–576.

Papousek, H. Experimental studies of appetitional behavior in human newborns and infants. In H.

W. Stevenson, E. H. Hess, and H. L. Rheingold (eds.), *Early Behavior*. New York: Wiley, 1967.

Papousek, H., and Bernstein, P. The functions of conditioning stimulation in human neonates and infants. In A. Ambrose (ed.), *Stimulation in Early Infancy*. New York: Academic, 1969.

Piaget, J. *The Language and Thought of the Child*. London: Routledge and Kegan Paul, 1952a.

Piaget, J. *The Origins of Intelligence in Children*. New York: Norton, 1952b.

Piaget, J. *The Construction of Reality in the Child*. New York: Basic Books, 1954.

Piaget, J. *Psychology of Intelligence*. New York: Littlefield, Adams, 1960.

Piaget, J. Development and learning. In C. S. Lavatelli and F. Stendler (eds.), *Readings in Child Behavior and Development*. New York: Harcourt Brace Janovich, 1964.

Prechtl, H. F. R. The directed head turning response and allied movements of the human baby. *Behavior,* 1958, **13,** 212–242.

Prechtl, H. F. R. Brain and behavioural mechanisms in the human newborn infant. In R. J. Robinson (ed.), *Brain and Early Behavior*. New York: Academic, 1969, 115–138.

Ramey, C. T., and Watson, J. S. Nonsocial reinforcement of infants' vocalizations. *Developmental Psychology,* 1972, **6,** 538.

Reese, H. W., and Overton, W. F. Models of development and theories of development. In L. R. Goulet and P. B. Baltes (eds.), *Life-Span Developmental Psychology: Research and Theory*. New York: Academic, 1970, 116–154.

Rescorla, R. A. Pavlovian conditioning and its proper control procedures. *Psychological Review,* 1967, **74,** 71–80.

Rheingold, H. L., Gewirtz, J. L., and Ross, H. W. Social conditioning of vocalization in the infant. *Journal of Comparative and Physiological Psychology,* 1959, **52,** 68–73.

Rheingold, H. L., Stanley, W. C., and Colley, J. A. Method for studying exploratory behavior in infants. *Science,* 1962, **136,** 1054–1055.

Rovee, C. K., and Rovee, D. T. Conjugate reinforcement of infant exploratory behavior. *Journal of Experimental Child Psychology,* 1969, **8,** 33–39.

Sameroff, A. J. An apparatus for recording sucking and controlling feeding in the first days of life. *Psychonomic Science,* 1965, **2,** 355–356.

Sameroff, A. J. The components of sucking in the human newborn. *Journal of Experimental Child Psychology,* 1968, **6,** 607–623.

Sameroff, A. J. Can conditioned responses be established in the newborn infant? *Developmental Psychology,* 1971, **5,** 1–12.

Sameroff, A. J. Learning and adaptation in infancy: A comparison of models. In H. W. Reese (ed.), *Advances in Child Development and Behavior,* Vol. 7. New York: Academic, 1972, 169–214.

Schneirla, T. C. Behavioral development and comparative psychology. *Quarterly Review of Biology,* 1966, **41** (3).

Seligman, M. E. P. On the generality of the laws of learning. *Psychological Review,* 1970, **77,** 406–418.

Seligman, M. E. P., and Hager, J. L. *Biological Boundaries of Learning*. New York: Meredith, 1972.

Semb, G., and Lipsitt, L. P. The effects of acoustic stimulation on cessation and initiation of non-nutritive sucking in neonates. *Journal of Experimental Child Psychology,* 1968, **6,** 585–597.

Shettleworth, S. J. Constraints on learning. In D. S. Lehrman, R. A. Hinde, and E. Shaw (eds.), *Advances in the Study of Behavior,* Vol. 4. New York: Academic, 1972, 1–68.

Shultz, T. R., and Zigler, E. Emotional concomitants of visual mastery in infants: The effects of stimulus movement on smiling and vocalizing. *Journal of Experimental Child Psychology,* 1970, **10,** 390–402.

Siqueland, E. R. Reinforcement patterns and extinction in human newborns. *Journal of Experimental Child Psychology,* 1968, **6,** 431–442.

Siqueland, E., and Lipsitt, L. P. Conditioned head-turning behavior in newborns. *Journal of Experimental Child Psychology,* 1966, **3,** 356–376.

Skinner, B. F. Two types of conditioned reflex: A reply to Konorski and Miller. *Journal of General Psychology,* 1937, **16,** 272–279.

Sostek, A. M., Sameroff, A. J., and Sostek, A. Failure of newborns to demonstrate classically conditioned Babkin responses. *Child Development,* 1972, **43,** 509–519.

Sroufe, L. A., and Waters, E. The ontogenesis of smiling and laughter: A perspective on the organization of development in infancy. *Psychological Review,* 1976, **83,** 173–189.

Stamps, L. E., and Porges, S. W. Heart rate conditioning in newborn infants: Relationships among conditionability, heart rate variability, and sex. *Developmental Psychology,* 1975, **11** (4), 424–431.

Tinbergen, N. *The Study of Instinct.* Oxford: Clarendon, 1951.

Wahler, R. C. Infant social attachments: A reinforcement theory interpretation and investigation. *Child Development,* 1967, **38,** 1079–1088.

Watson, J. S. Operant fixation in visual preference behavior of infants. *Psychonomic Science,* 1968, **12,** 241–242.

Weisberg, P. Social and non-social conditioning of infant vocalizations. *Child Development,* 1963, **34,** 377–388.

Wenger, M. A. An investigation of conditioned responses in human infants. *University of Iowa Studies in Child Welfare,* 1936, **12,** 1–90.

Wickens, D. D., and Wickens, C. A study of conditioning in the neonate. *Journal of Experimental Psychology,* 1940, **26,** 94–102.

Wolff, P. Observations on the early development of smiling. In B. M. Foss (ed.), *Determinants of Infant Behavior II.* New York: Wiley, 1963.

Wolff, P. H. The causes, controls, and organization of behavior in the neonate. *Psychological Issues,* 1966, **5** (1, monog. 17).

Zelazo, P. R. Smiling to social stimuli: Eliciting and conditioning effects. *Developmental Psychology,* 1971, **4,** 32–42.

Zelazo, P. R. Smiling and vocalizing: A cognitive emphasis. *Merrill-Palmer Quarterly,* 1972, **18,** 349–366.

Zelazo, P. R., and Komer, M. J. Infant smiling to nonsocial stimuli and the recognition hypothesis. *Child Development,* 1971, **42,** 1327–1339.

CHAPTER 11

Infant Visual Perception[1]

Leslie B. Cohen
Judy S. DeLoache
Mark S. Strauss

We were originally asked to contribute a chapter on infant perception to this volume. Ten or 20 years ago that task might have been possible. But the growth of research in the past 10 years has been so incredibly rapid that today it would be impossible to condense this vast literature into a single chapter and still do justice to the field. Recently, two entire volumes (Cohen and Salapatek, 1975a, b) have been devoted to infant perception, and they could not cover all of the relevant literature.

Instead of attempting to summarize an entire body of research, we have elected to restrict our discussion to infant visual perception. We have chosen this strategy for several reasons. First, most research on infant perception has been on infant vision. We believe that the evolution of research on infant visual perception can serve as a valuable guide for the more recently emerging literature on infant perception in other sensory modalities. Second, the methodological techniques used to investigate infant visual perception are the most varied, virtually all are sophisticated and efficient, and all have tended to yield similar results. We are firmly convinced that one can have the most confidence about results in an area when experiments using different methodologies arrive at the same conclusions. The area of infant visual perception has been characterized by this type of convergence. We do not mean to imply that there are no longer any disagreements or controversies. Controversies abound, but most of these disagreements seem resolvable. Besides, controversies keep an area interesting and exciting.

Even within infant visual perception, we cannot hope to cover the entire literature. While we do mention some of the older pioneering work, we have emphasized more recent research. We have also tried to go beyond a simple summary of results. Whenever possible, experiments are placed within the theoretical or methodological context that generated them. In this way we hope to provide the reader with the flavor of the area as well as the facts.

METHODOLOGICAL ADVANCES

This section will discuss the major techniques that have been developed for studying infant visual development. The first part will review the behavioral and physiological

[1]Preparation of this chapter was supported in part by National Institute of Child Health and Human Development Grants, HD 03858, HD 05951, and HD 00244. Our grateful appreciation is extended to Jane Maynard for her thoughtful suggestions and for the many hours she put in editing and reediting earlier versions of this manuscript.

measures which have commonly been used to measure the infant's responses to visual stimulation. The second part will then describe three major procedures—visual preferences, habituation, and conditioning—used in infant perceptual research. In addition, more recently developed methodologies which have combined the above three procedures will be discussed.

Response Selection: Behavioral and Physiological Measures

In 1913, Valentine dangled colored yarn balls in front of his 4-month-old son to see if the child would prefer one ball over the other. If he did, Valentine would be able to infer that his son had sufficient color vision to discriminate between the two colors. Since Valentine's time we have developed increasingly sophisticated physiological and behavioral measures of infant responses, but the basic logic remains the same: if we can get an infant to behave differently to two stimuli, we can infer that he can discriminate between them.

In visual perception research the most frequently used behavioral measure is fixation time—the length of time a subject spends looking at a stimulus. Fixation time is often assessed using the corneal reflection technique introducted by Fantz (1958): an infant is scored as fixating a stimulus when its image can be seen superimposed on his or her pupil. Some investigators record cumulative looking (total fixation time), while others argue that the first fixation alone is a more reliable and sensitive measure (McCall, 1971). The principal problem with using fixation time to infer interest or preference is that sometimes "blank staring" occurs: infants appear to be locked in visually to a stimulus without processing it. This problem occurs more with younger infants.

Various refinements of fixation time measures have been introduced. Cohen (1972) suggested recording separately both fixation time and latency of fixation to differentiate between attention-getting and attention-holding processes. The amount of looking back and forth between two patterns has been used to study visual comparison processes in infants (Ruff, 1975). The most sophisticated visual measures are recordings made with infrared cameras of infant scanning patterns, which permit investigators to determine exactly which features of a visual display an infant is fixating foveally (Salapatek, 1968; Salapatek and Kessen, 1966, 1973). A potential difficulty with this procedure is that due to certain characteristics of the young infant's eye, the measurements may be slightly off, leading to incorrect inferences as to just what point is fixated (Slator and Findley, 1972). However, the degree of error is probably not enough to be of practical significance (Salapatek et al., 1972).

Although fixation time measures have the greatest face validity for inferring that visual information is being processed, a variety of other behavioral measures also have been employed, sometimes singly and sometimes in conjunction with other measures. Suppression of ongoing physical activity (Haith, et al., 1969) and of sucking (Haith, 1966) reflect attention to a visual stimulus. Differential smiling to stimuli has been used, especially in the study of face perception (e.g., Watson, 1966), and surprise reactions have been assessed to determine if an event violates some expectancy of the infant (Charlesworth, 1969).

The above behavioral measures nave, for the most part, been developed specifically for studying infant visual perception. There are a number of other dependent measures, however, which originated in research on adult visual perception and were adapted for studying the infant. These measures are primarily electrophysiological and are recorded from the naturally occurring electrical activity that originates from all neurosensory functions.

Several of these electrophysiological measures directly record responses from the eye. The electroretinogram (ERG), for example, is a measure of the electrical potentials produced by the retina when it is exposed to light. The ERG has been particularly useful in assessing the degree to which the infant's central versus peripheral retinal regions are functional. This differential assessment can be made because the wave that results from an ERG recording has two main components—the a-wave that originates from the activity of the cones and the b-wave that originates from the activity of the rods.

Another direct measure of the eye is the electrooculogram (EOG). This measure is a recording of the electric potential that exists between the cornea and the retina and is used to plot the infant's eye movements. As the infant's eye moves, the electrically positive cornea moves closer to and farther from recording electrodes placed around the orbital rim. This movement causes small electrical changes which can be used to keep track of the infant's eye position.

The EOG is a more sensitive measure of the infant's eye movements than the previously discussed corneal reflection technique and has been most useful in accurately recording the optokinetic nystagmus (OKN) response. The OKN response is a partially reflexive eye movement which occurs when a repetitive pattern, such as black and white stripes, is continuously moved in front of the subject. The OKN response consists of a short fixation, a small following movement, and then a return to the original eye position. It occurs repeatedly as the subject attempts to track the moving stimulus. As will be noted later in the chapter, the OKN response has primarily been used to measure the infant's visual acuity. A more detailed discussion of the above physiological measures can be found in Maurer (1975).

In addition to the visual measures described above, other electrophysiological responses have been used as dependent measures in experimental assessments of the infant's perceptual abilities. The infant's heart rate, for example, has been used to measure such diverse behaviors as the degree of attention to visual displays, reactions to discrepant visual stimuli, reactions to a repetitively presented visual stimulus, and defensive reactions to certain threatening visual stimuli (Campos, 1976).

Finally, one of the more recently developed electrophysiological measures is the visually evoked potential (VEP), a measure of brain wave activity recorded in direct response to a visually presented stimulus. The VEP is a measure that must be mathematically derived with a computer from the infant's ongoing brain activity and represents a measure of the brain's actual processing of the visual stimulus. Until recently, the VEP has primarily been used to assess the maturity of the infant's response to visual patterns (Karmel and Maisel, 1975) and colors (White et al., 1977).

Techniques for Assessing Discriminative Capacity

As we noted earlier, almost any question about the infant's perceptual capabilities can be translated into a question concerning which stimuli the infant can discriminate. Operationally, the question reduces to whether or not infants respond differently under varied stimulus conditions. If they do, the ability to discriminate can be assumed; but if they do not, one cannot necessarily assume a failure to discriminate.

In the simplest case of perceptual discrimination experiments, a single stimulus is introduced and infants' behavior in the presence of the stimulus is compared to their behavior in its absence (Haith, 1976; Lewis and Maurer, 1977). If infants' responses change in the presence of the stimulus, one can assume that they perceive something about that stimulus. Many experiments investigating infant discrimination have used the same basic logic, but a slightly more complicated design. Two stimuli are simultaneously presented to the infants, and one of the stimuli contains a visual feature not present in the other. Presumably, if the infants can discriminate the feature, they will respond differently than if they cannot. Salapatek et al.'s (1976) study of visual acuity provides an example of this technique. Infants were presented with vertical striped patterns that varied in spatial frequency paired with homogeneous gray patterns. The minimum frequency needed to produce sustained attention to the striped target was used as an estimate of acuity. In a sense, the experiment could be described as an attempt to find the point at which infants could perceive a pattern rather than no pattern. Other researchers have used this simple technique effectively to demonstrate early perception of color (Oster, 1975), contour (Kessen, Salapatek, & Haith, 1972), and pattern (Fantz, 1961).

While this procedure is useful in determining if the infant can perceive anything at all, it usually is of little help in answering more specific questions. For example, suppose an infant looks longer at a black-and-white schematic drawing of a face than at a plain white or a plain gray surface (Fantz, 1961). One can assume the infant is perceiving something when he or she looks at the face; but is the infant responding to a high-contrast area, a patterned surface, or a picture of a face? To answer such questions, the visual preference test (Berlyne, 1958; Fantz, 1958) was developed to provide researchers with more specific information about an infant's discriminatory abilities. The test is based upon the infant's existing tendency to attend more to some stimuli than others. Two patterns, A and B, are presented simultaneously on each trial, and the responses to each, usually fixation times, are recorded. Left-right positions of the stimuli are counterbalanced across trials. If the infants looks reliably longer at pattern A than at B, a preference for A is assumed, as is the ability to discriminate between A and B. This visual preference test has proven to be a valuable tool for assessing infant discrimination of curved versus straight lines, complex versus simple patterns, one pattern arrangement versus another, faces versus nonfaces, and a host of other perceptual variables.

The chief limitation of the technique is that frequently infants can discriminate between two visual stimuli, but do not show an initial preference for one over the other. In order to overcome this difficulty, two modifications of the preference test have been devised to experimentally induce artificial preferences. In the first, the infant is habituated or familiarized to one stimulus, thereby decreasing his or her response to it relative to a novel stimulus. In the other, a conditioning paradigm is used to increase the infant's response to one of the stimuli by making it either a discriminative stimulus or a secondary reinforcer.

In the habituation technique one stimulus is repeatedly shown either for a fixed number of trials or until the infant's response (e.g., visual fixation, heart rate, or sucking rate) drops to some criterion level. A discrimination test is then given, and the infant's response to the familiar and one or more novel stimuli is compared. If the infant's response increases upon presentation of only the novel stimuli, it indicates that he or she can discriminate them from the familiar one. Again, as in the preference test, if the infant does not respond longer to the novel stimuli, one cannot necessarily assume an inability to discriminate. Habituation and related paired-comparison techniques have been used to demonstrate perception and discrimination of colors, forms, faces, objects, concepts, and even meaningful temporal events. It has become the method of choice for many studies of infant perception, particularly those at the interface between perception and cognition, where the investigator is interested in determining both how the infant encodes visual information and how well he or she remembers that information.

Operant conditioning techniques have also been employed to study infant perception. In several studies, Bower (1966a, b) has conditioned infants to turn their heads in response to one visual stimulus. Degree of generalization of the conditioned head-turn to other related stimuli was used as an indication of discrimination. Both conditioning and habituation paradigms employ approximately the same logic: modify the infant's tendency to respond to one stimulus, transform the original stimulus in some way, and then see to what extent the response generalizes to the new stimulus. Clear-cut conditioning is usually more difficult to establish than habituation, frequently requiring several sessions over several days, which may be one reason for the increased popularity of the habituation technique over the conditioning procedure.

One innovative approach, the conjugate reinforcement paradigm (Siqueland and DeLucia, 1969), makes use of both conditioning and habituation. Visual stimuli are presented contingent upon the infant's high rate of nonnutritive sucking or some other response. The procedure typically produces first an increase in sucking rate and then a decrease. Once the decrease reaches a preset criterion, the original stimulus is changed for some subjects and kept the same for others. Recovery of sucking to the novel stimulus, but not the familiar, indicates discrimination.

In this section, we have not included all procedures used to test infant discrimination. Most procedures, however, can be viewed as variants of one or more of those given above. The classic visual cliff studies on infant depth perception have much in common with the visual preference technique since they also exploit the infant's tendency to respond differentially to two stimuli. Two stimuli are presented simultaneously (i.e., the deep side and shallow side of the cliff), and differential responding is recorded. The visual scanning studies by Salapatek and Kessen (1966, 1973) may be viewed as asking whether an infant prefers looking at a high-contrast edge or a uniform white or black surround. Even studies that record infants' surprise to a disappearing object may be viewed as habituation-type studies in disguise. Infants are first familiarized with one particular toy or object, and then their reaction is noted when the object vanishes or is transformed into a novel object.

Subsequent sections of this chapter will examine more closely results from numerous experiments that have used these techniques. However, it is safe to conclude at this point that their development over the past two decades has provided a major impetus to the burgeoning volume of research on infant visual perception.

SENSORY PROCESSES

This section will discuss research examining the maturity of the young infant's visual system and the infant's ability to detect and discriminate visual stimuli. A brief overview of the physiological changes that occur in the visual system during the first months of life will be followed by a more extensive review of the behavioral studies that have attempted to determine the infant's basic visual abilities.

Physiological Development of the Visual System

Our present knowledge of the physiological maturity of the newborn's visual system and its rate of development during infancy is limited. Detailed anatomical and histological studies of the infant's visual system are relatively scarce, and those that exist are of questionable accuracy. One major source of inaccuracy in these studies results from changes in the eye and neurological tissues that occur after death, and the inevitable damage inflicted when preparing and staining anatomical specimens (Maurer, 1975).

A second major problem complicates interpretation of the anatomical and histological research. In many of these studies, the cause of the infant's death is either not reported or unknown. The possibility exists, therefore, that the infant may have been developmentally retarded, and the results of the study may yield an inaccurate picture of the normal newborn or older infant (Haith, 1978).

To circumvent some of the above problems, lately a greater emphasis has been put on inferring knowledge about the ontogeny of the infant's visual system from studies conducted with other developing infant animals, particularly kittens and rhesus monkeys. By comparing measures such as nerve-conduction velocity, evoked potentials, and ERGs, it is possible to assess the relative maturity and growth rates of different developing animals (Parmelee and Sigman, 1976). The anatomical and histological results from various species are then compared, and extrapolations are made to the relative maturity of the human infant's visual system. However, many researchers still question the validity of this type of inference. It is within the context of these problems that the following brief review of infant physiological development is offered.

The Retina

The retina of the adult eye is composed of two primary types of receptors, the rods and cones, which are located in the second, third, and fourth neural layers. The cones, a more recent evolutionary development, number about 6 million and are sensitive to color. The approximately 120 million rods, on the other hand, are sensitive to all light waves within the visible spectrum and serve as our primary source of night vision.

Rather than being uniformly distributed about the retina, the cones are primarily concentrated in a single area behind the lens, especially within an area called the fovea, which contains only cones and no rods. The concentration of cones relative to rods decreases away from the fovea, so that the peripheral regions of the retina contain only rods.

Within the fovea, the cones are connected on an almost one-to-one basis with other higher-order neurons, thus allowing for a maximum degree of visual resolution in this area. The fovea is also unique since in this region the other retinal neural elements such as the bipolar, amacrine, and ganglion cells are displaced, causing a depression in the retina. This depression allows the foveal cones to be directly stimulated by entering light waves. Visual acuity, therefore, is most sensitive in this foveal area of the retina and decreases gradually toward the peripheral regions.

Researchers disagree on the maturity of the retina at birth and its development during early infancy. The main source of the dispute concerns the state of the fovea at birth. Traditional sources of visual embryology (Duke-Elder and Cook, 1963; Mann, 1964; Peiper, 1963) maintained that at birth the various neural layers have not been displaced from in front of the fovea and prevent direct stimulation of its high-resolution receptors. They also believed that the foveal cones of the newborn were shorter and stubbier than those of adults. It was generally believed that it was not until around the 4th month that the infant's fovea was basically equivalent to the adult's. As a result, the infant's central visual abilities were considered quite limited. Early ERG research supported this view, finding that only the scoptic b-wave, which is mediated by the rods, was present at birth; the photopic a-wave, which is mediated by the cones, was not fully present until much later (Zetterstrom, 1951, 1955).

More recently, a number of researchers have come to question this pessimistic view of the young infant's central visual abilities. Haith (1978) claims that both Duke-Elder and Cook (1963) and Mann (1964) based their conclusions on work with newborns who died for unknown reasons, and who may have been developmentally retarded. Haith cites a very comprehensive study of retinal development in rhesus monkeys by Ordy et al. (1965), which showed that the monkey (a species usually believed to be visually less mature at birth than humans) has a fairly well-developed fovea at birth, with clear evidence of an advanced, although not complete, foveal depression.

Haith (1978) also discusses the more recent ERG work of Horsten and Winkelman (1962, 1964), which has shown that if the infant is dark-adapted and bright flashes are used, both the a- and b-waves can be seen in the newborn's ERG. It should be noted, however, that the mere presence of the a-wave gives no indication of how well the infant's foveal vision is functioning; it only indicates that it functions to some degree. As Maurer (1975) has noted, a normal ERG can be elicited from subjects with subnormal visual acuity, color-defective vision, and even macular degeneration and central scotomas. Conversely, people with normal vision sometimes do not show normal ERG patterns.

In summary, the degree of anatomical development of the retina at birth is still an open question. The view an individual researcher takes depends largely on his or her belief in the validity of the traditional human anatomical studies versus the comparative studies.

Visual Pathways

Simplifying greatly, from the retina there are two main pathways the visual signal can take. The primary pathway travels from the retina through the optic nerve and chiasm to the lateral geniculate nucleus (LGN) of the thalamus. From the LGN, there are projections to the occipital cortex (areas 17, 18, and 19) which, in turn, connect with the temporal regions of the cortex.

The second visual pathway projects from the retina to the superior colliculus within the midbrain; and from there to the higher cortical areas, both directly and through the thalamus by way of the pulvinar. There are also known, but not well understood, pathways from the optic tract to the reticular formation, which project to a widely distributed area of the cortex.

Again, little is known of the ontogeny of these various pathways. The infant's optic nerve at birth is both thinner and shorter than the adult's and not completely myelinated. Estimates of the completion of myelinization range from 3 weeks (Last, 1968) to 4 months postnatal age (Duke-Elder and Cook, 1963). In general, there is evidence that the primary visual pathways mature postnatally in a manner consistent with the order in which information is processed—that is, the retina matures first, then the LGN, striate cortex, and so on—and that the secondary visual pathways develop faster and prior to the primary visual pathways (Bronson, 1974).

The Striate Cortex

The most extensive anatomical studies of human infant cortical development have been reported by Conel (1939, 1941, 1947, 1951, 1955, 1959). According to these studies, the infant's visual cortex is quite underdeveloped at birth. This is especially true of areas 18 and 19, which throughout the first few months of life are less developed than area 17.

Although all the adult cortical neurons are present at birth and there is no evidence of mitosis occurring after the 8th gestational month (Rabinowicz, 1964), a number of cortical changes do occur after birth. Many fibers are unmyelinated at birth, with continuing myelinization occurring throughout the first 10 years of life (Yakovlev and Le Cours, 1967). Additionally, the cortical neurons undergo prodigious changes in the size of their cell bodies, length of their axons and dendritic branches, and the extent of their differentiation and arborization (Conel, 1939, 1941, 1947).

Despite these changes, which occur during infancy, the visual cortex is, to some degree, functional at birth. Evidence for this position derives primarily from studies of the newborn's visually evoked potential (VEP) which, although quite immature, shows evidence of cortically originated components (Karmel and Maisel, 1975).

Unfortunately, the extent to which anatomical changes within the visual system during infancy are related to emerging visual and cognitive behaviors is almost totally unknown, and physiological knowledge is of little help in the assessment of the infant's basic visual competence. Consequently, several behavioral techniques have been developed for this purpose and will be discussed in the next section.

Behavioral Studies

Central Vision and Acuity

Early infant researchers, knowledgeable of histological studies that showed the newborn's retina to be highly underdeveloped, were not very interested in trying to assess the young infant's visual-acuity threshold. As research in the late 1950s and early 1960s made it evident that even newborn infants show distinct and stable visual preferences and, hence, are far from blind, there was a growing concern with establishing behaviorally determined acuity thresholds.

The first attempts to evaluate the young infant's central acuity employed the optokinetic nystagmus (OKN) response to determine what minimal width moving stripes would elicit an OKN response. Studies by Dayton et al. (1964), Fantz et al. (1962), Gorman et al. (1957, 1959), and Kiff and Lepard (1966) found that newborn infants respond to lines of approximately 20.0 to 41.4 min of arc (20/400 to 20/820 Snellen equivalent). The best acuity was demonstrated in the Dayton et al. study where 9 of the 39 infants responded to lines of only 7.5 min of arc (20/150).

The accuracy of the OKN response as a measure of central acuity became questioned, however, in the study by Kiff and Lepard, when it was found that the response did not vary when infants' acuity was changed through the use of corrective lenses or cycloplegic drugs. Amigo (1972) has also suggested that the OKN response may be an inaccurate measure of foveal acuity, since the striped patterns employed in all of the above studies extend beyond the macula so nonfoveal receptors may be mediating the response. Finally, Maurer (1975), in her review of the OKN literature, concluded that since ablation studies have shown that the OKN response may not require the optic tract, lateral geniculate nucleus, and possibly the occipital lobes, there is little reason to expect it to be an accurate measure of central acuity.

A second behavioral technique used to assess the young infant's acuity threshold makes use of the visual-preference method. This technique involves determining the minimal width of striped pattern that will elicit a visual preference when the striped pattern is paired with a homogeneous gray pattern of the same overall brightness. Studies by Fantz et al. (1962), Harter and Suitt (1970), Teller et al. (1974), and Leehy et al. (1975) using this technique have all found the acuity threshold of infants under 2 months of age to be somewhere between 15 and 40 min of arc (20/300 to 20/800). These estimates agree well with those produced in the OKN studies.

A study recently reported by Lewis and Maurer (1977), however, has suggested that the newborn's central vision may be considerably better than the above estimates indicate. In their study, the infants were first shown a column of red lights located in the center of their visual field. The column of lights was then turned off, and the infants were presented with a 10-sec trial of either a single centrally located line, a single line displaced either 10, 20, or 30 degrees from center, or a blank field. The lines varied in width between 4 min to 4 degrees, 24 min. The infants looked longer at the center of the field when it contained a line as narrow as 8 min than when the field was blank. The amount of looking between a blank field and one that contained a 4-min line was essentially the same.

The authors suggest that the reason they found neonates capable of detecting such a fine stimulus was due to their use of a single line as opposed to black-and-white gratings. They cite research showing that ". . . adults can detect a single line which is much finer than the narrowest stripe they can resolve in a grating" [Lewis and Maurer, 1977, p. 10]

Visual acuity improves rapidly during the 1st year and appears to be within the range of normal adult vision by 6 months to 1 year. Fantz et al. (1962), using the visual-preference technique, found that infants could resolve 10-min-of-arc stripes at 5 months of age and 5-min stripes at 6 months of age. These results were supported by Teller (1973), who found one of her subjects to be close to the adult norm of 1 min of arc by 6 months of age.

Teller also tested whether infants displayed orientational anisotropy, the tendency to show better visual acuity for horizontal and vertical edges than for oblique ones, which is found with adults. The usual explanation for this effect, based on a number of studies with kittens raised from birth in environments of lines in one exclusive orientation (Blakemore and Cooper, 1970; Hirsch and Spinelli, 1970; Pettigrew and Freeman, 1973), is that our environment is dominated by horizontal and vertical edges that, at an early age, shape the sensitivity of the visual system. Teller found no indication of orientational anisotropy in her subjects.

Leehy et al. (1975), however, applied a more sensitive method by showing infant's pairings of identically striped targets in different orientations, under the assumption that the infants would spend more time viewing the visually clearer of the two targets. With this technique, they found a preference for vertical and horizontal edges over oblique edges as early as 6 weeks of age and thus called into question conclusions from animal studies implicating early visual experience as the sole cause of orientational anisotropy.

Almost all of the acuity studies have presented the visual stimulus at a distance of approximately 19 cm from the infant, based on the common belief that infants cannot accommodate to farther or closer distances because they have this fixed focal distance. This belief emerged from two studies that used dynamic retinoscopy (Haynes et al., 1965; White and Zolot, cited in White, 1971), a technique that can objectively measure the extent to which the lens is focusing as a subject fixates targets at varying distances.

A more recent study by Salapatek et al. (1976) questioned the logic of this common belief among infant researchers. They used the visual-preference paradigm to determine the acuity threshold of 24- to 63-day-old infants viewing targets at distances of 30, 60, and 150 cm. In line with the previously cited visual-preference studies, the results of this study indicated that 1- to 2-month-old infants showed acuity thresholds of about 20 to 30 min of arc with, interestingly, no improvement within this age range. More significantly, it was found that acuity thresholds were the same at all four distances tested.

The authors point out that retinoscopic studies have found the refractive power of the infant's lens to be considerably different (5 diopters) between waking and sleeping states, evidence that the lens itself is not rigid and the cause of the lack of accommodation. They believe the reason that young infants do not show visual accommodation is that they are only sensitive to low spatial frequencies. As adult research has shown, it is the high-spatial-frequency information of a stimulus that provides the primary cues for accommodation, since low spatial frequencies look similar over a large range of refractive error. Because infants are insensitive to high spatial frequencies, they are consequently insensitive to the visual cues for accommodation.

In summary, although current research has established rough estimates of the newborn's central visual acuity and its improvement over the 1st year, individual studies have yielded a large disparity in their estimates of the infant's visual competence. For example, Lewis and Maurer (1977) found newborns able to detect a line of only 8 min of arc, whereas the best estimate found by Miranda (1970) was 66 min of arc. This diversity is probably largely due to differences in the methods used to test the infants. It is not known how comparable the various behavioral paradigms are to one another. For example, it is not known to what extent the different methods measure central versus peripheral visual processes. In addition, the response requirements associated with different paradigms are not comparable. Some procedures merely require the detection of lines to elicit a response, whereas others require some greater degree of resolution or recognition before a response is made. Unfortunately, the contribution of both these factors may lead to different acuity estimates. Much more research will be needed to resolve the difficulties arising from such methodological differences.

Peripheral Vision and Acuity

Much less research has investigated the infant's peripheral visual capabilities. Most of the existing studies have been attempts to determine, first, whether the newborn is able to detect the presence of a stimulus presented at varying distances in the periphery and, second, if with development there is an expansion in the size of the effective visual field.

All of the detection studies to be discussed have used the same basic paradigm. First, a stimulus is presented centrally until it is fixated by the infant. A second stimulus is then presented in the periphery at a particular distance from the center of the visual field. Of primary interest is whether or not the second stimulus will elicit an appropriately directed eye movement.

The possibility that the newborn's visual field is very narrow at birth and expands with development during the first few months was suggested by Tronick's (1972) results. Using colored rectangular solids as central and peripheral stimuli, he found that 2-week-old infants had a rather narrow visual field of 15° to either side of center. The effective visual field expanded with age, however, so that it had more than doubled by 10 weeks of age. Unfortunately, this study was faulty since the central stimulus was always present, even after the peripheral stimulus had been introduced and, hence, may have caused the infants to ignore the peripheral stimulus even though they had detected it.

This possibility was tested in two more recent experiments (Harris and MacFarlane, 1974; MacFarlane et al., 1976). Both experiments used a light that subtended a visual angle of 3° as their stimulus, and compared results in conditions where the central stimulus light either remained on (competing condition) or was turned off (noncompeting condition) upon presentation of the peripheral stimulus. Combining the results of the two studies, it was found that the newborn infants in the noncompeting condition could detect a stimulus that was horizontally displaced by as much as 25° to 30°. The size of the visual field expanded with age so that by 6 to 7 weeks of age the infants could detect a stimulus as far as 45° from center. The results were very different in the competing conditon. The effective visual field of both age groups was smaller in this condition than in the noncompeting condition. In addition, the influence of the competing stimulus was greater for the older infants—that is, peripheral responding decreased over age in the presence of a competing central stimulus.

Aslin and Salapatek (1975) performed a similar type of study with 1- and 2-month-old infants. The study used electrooculography to record the infant's eye movements so the authors could actually describe the form of the localizing saccades in addition to their directional appropriateness. The stimuli used were 4° angular targets. Aslin and Salapatek (1975) found that infants of both ages could detect a peripheral stimulus introduced as far as 30° from center along the horizontal axis. Expanding the results of the previously discussed studies, they found equally successful detection along the diagonal axes, but only 10° detection along the vertical axis. In form, the first saccades made to the peripheral targets were very short in comparison to an adult's eye movements, and were followed by additional saccades of an approximately equal distance until the target was reached.

In the previously mentioned study on central acuity, Lewis and Maurer (1977) also tested the newborn's ability to detect a line presented at either 10°, 20°, or 30° from center. This study was unique in that the authors varied the size of the peripheral stimulus between 4 min of arc and 3 degrees, 18 min. The results indicated that newborns could detect a line of 33 min at both 10° and 20° from center, and a 1-degree, 6-min line at a horizontal displacement of 30°.

The studies of peripheral vision discussed so far were concerned with the infant's ability merely to *detect* the presence of a peripheral stimulus. Research has also tested the ability of older infants to *discriminate* stimuli presented in the periphery and then to respond differentially as a result of the discrimination.

Several studies done by Cohen and his associates (Cohen, 1972; Cohen et al., 1975; DeLoache et al., 1977) have established that by 4 months of age infants are able to discriminate among different checkerboard patterns (e.g., 2×2, 8×8, 16×16) when they are presented in the periphery. These studies recorded the infant's latency of turning from a central fixation control point to a pattern presented on either the left or right. Infants were able to peripherally discriminate the different checkerboard patterns; how readily they oriented to the patterns was dependent on factors such as their size, complexity, or novelty.

Maurer and Lewis (1977) have recently reported evidence of 3-month-old infants' ability to discriminate between two stimuli presented in the visual periphery. In this study infants' attention was first attracted to the center of the visual field by a strip of red lights. The lights were then turned off and two patterns introduced, one on each side of the lights, each displaced from the center of the field by either 10°, 20°, or 30°. The authors had purposely chosen pairs of stimuli for which they expected a preference for one member of the pair over the other. These preferences were then determined within a pilot study by recording which member of each pair received longer visual attention.

This information allowed the authors to study whether the infants could discriminate the patterns in the periphery well enough to allow them to make their first fixation to the preferred stimulus of the pair. The results showed that, for pairs of stimuli where the two patterns differed from each other on a number of dimensions, such as size, color, and amount of contour, the infants made appropriate first fixations to patterns displaced as much as 30° from the center. When the two stimuli were more similar to each other—for example, differing only with respect to the curvature of three internal elements—the infants could discriminate them at 10° and possibly at 20°.

As a result of the research discussed in this section, we now know that although the infant's visual system is quite underdeveloped at birth, the newborn can detect visual stimuli presented both centrally and peripherally. We also know that many physiological changes occur within the visual system during the first 6 months of life. The consequences of these physiological changes can be observed in the behavioral studies which document the infant's increasing central and peripheral visual abilities.

A number of questions, however, remain. For example, it is still not known to what extent the newborn's fovea is functional. As we noted, physiological research is ambivalent on this issue. The behavioral studies also do not answer this question of foveal functioning, since the best estimate of central acuity found in the newborn (20/150) can be found in an adult using peripheral retinal receptors at least 15° from the fovea (Alpern, 1962).

Another issue that needs further clarification is the relationship between central and peripheral vision. The mature visual processor uses peripherally detected information to help guide his or her eye movements and to determine what aspects of the visual environment should be centrally fixated in order to abstract greater detail. This process has been most clearly demonstrated in visual search tasks which have shown that both children and adults use peripherally detected cues such as color, size, and shape to guide their eye movements (Day, 1975; Luria and Strauss, 1975; Williams, 1966). Although infant research has shown that by 6 months of age both the infant's central and peripheral systems are quite mature, little is known about the interaction of these systems. The studies on peripheral discrimination have shown that by 3 to 4 months of age the infant is capable of some integration of central and peripheral information. The development of this ability and its relation to the guidance of eye movements is still unknown. These questions represent just two of the many important questions that remain to be answered before our understanding of the infant's basic visual processes can be complete.

VISUAL INFORMATION PROCESSING

Now that we have reviewed the studies concerned with determining the infant's basic visual sensory abilities, we can turn to the existing research on the infant's higher-order visual perceptual abilities. The topics chosen for discussion in this section do not represent the totality of research on infant perception but, rather, those areas that have received the most attention from infant researchers during the past two decades.

Color Perception

As early as the turn of the century, researchers were concerned with testing the ability of infants to discriminate colors. Preyer (1888) tested his own son with forms that varied only in color and concluded that the child was not able to discriminate them until 21 months of age. Marsden (1930a, b) showed his son two different colored stimuli and slowly moved them apart to see if there would be a preference for tracking one of the two colored cards. He found a differential response to color starting at about 4 months of age, in contrast to Holden and Bosse (1900), who first found color discrimination in their subjects at around 6 months of age.

However, these studies as well as a number of other early studies on infant color perception (see Kessen et al., 1970) ignored a problem that, in fact, has only been successfully dealt with recently: controlling for the perceived brightness of different colored stimuli. This problem exists because people are differentially sensitive to brightness at differing wavelengths. In general, more light energy is needed to achieve a brightness match for colors at either end of the visible spectrum than for colors in the middle region. Because of this pheonomenon, an infant being shown two colors in a discrimination task may be responding to a difference in *brightness* rather than a difference in *hue*. Indeed, Hershenson (1964) has shown that infants do readily perceive and respond to stimuli differing only in brightness. Let us now examine those studies that have attempted to control for brightness in tests of infant color vision.

Brightness versus Hue

Several studies have attempted to control for brightness cues by equating the relative brightness of their different-hue stimuli according to adult standards (Chase, 1937; Fagan, 1974; Spears, 1966; Staples, 1931). For example, in a study by Chase (1937), infants were shown a stimulus consisting of a small colored circular field moving within a second larger field of a different color. The dependent measure was visual tracking of the smaller moving field. Prior to testing the infants, the two fields were subjectively equated for brightness by an adult with normal color vision. Infants' responses in this first condition were compared to those in a second condition in which the two fields were of the same hue but differed in perceived brightness.

More recently, Fagan (1974) showed 4- to 6-month-old infants two colored checkerboard patterns made of Munsell chips that were equated for brightness according to the adult photopic C.I.E. sensitivity curve. Preference for the checkerboard as opposed to a solid field provided a measure of hue discrimination. Fagan's results indicated that infants were capable of discriminating hue differences by 4 to 6 months.

As a number of researchers (Kessen et al., 1970; Munn, 1965; Oster, 1975; Schaller, 1975; Wooten, 1975) have noted, equating brightness to adult standards is not an adequate control in tests of infant color vision. First, in order to use adult standards, one must assume that infants and adults have the same spectral-sensitivity curves. Although one study indicates that this may be the case (Trinker and Trinker, 1967), this study used a rather unsophisticated dependent measure, a tonic neck reflex, and was only able to yield a very rough estimate of the infant's spectral sensitivity curve. Recent studies, using more advanced measures (Dobson, 1975; Munsinger and Banks, 1974; Teller and Peeples, 1974), have indicated that adults' and infants' curves are indeed different. This difference is not surprising since changes in the absorption of light by preretinal material and changes in the pigmentation of the retina will both result in changes in spectral sensitivity, and there is sufficient evidence that both of these changes do occur with development (Cooper and Robson, 1969; Ruddock, 1972).

Fortunately, there appears to be an answer to the problem posed by brightness cues in infant color perception studies. The solution is to purposely vary brightness cues so that infants' responses can be made only on the basis of differing hues. Recently, there have been three studies of infant color perception that have used this technique to bypass the problem of equating the brightness of differing hues (Bornstein, 1976; Oster, 1975; Schaller, 1975). Interestingly, each of these experiments has applied a different infant testing paradigm. Pattern preferences, conditioning, and habituation were each used in different studies.

Oster (1975) used the standard visual-preference paradigm to test infant color perception. The stimuli she presented to her 9- to 10-week-old infants were similar to those used by von Frisch (1950) to test color vision in bees. Each pattern had nine ¾-in. squares of widely different brightness values arranged in a 3 × 3 matrix on a medium gray background. There were three different sets of stimuli. The first set consisted of stimuli with nine achromatic squares varying only in brightness. In the second set of stimuli, the center square of the 3 × 3 matrix was a highly saturated chromatic color (red, green, yellow, or blue), and the surrounding eight squares were achromatic. The final set of stimuli was identical to the first set, except that its central square differed in brightness from that of the first set. The infants were presented with 12, 20-sec trials where comparisons between all three sets of stimuli were made.

The use of these stimuli eliminated the effect of brightness in three ways. First, any differences in brightness between the central squares were camouflaged by the large brightness differences within each of the patterns themselves. Second, any preference for either darker or lighter central squares could be cancelled out by a counterbalancing of colors and neutral values. Finally, comparisons of stimuli from the first and third sets allowed a measure of the infants' responses when only the relative brightness of the central square differed. As a result of this study, Oster was able to conclude that infants by the age of 10 weeks do indeed perceive colors ranging over a fairly large portion of the visible spectrum.

Schaller (1975) also purposely varied brightness to prevent it from being used as a cue by infants in a color-discrimination task. He did so, however, within a discrimination conditioning paradigm, training 11- to 12-week-old infants to look longer at the "red" (or "green") member of "red-green" pairs by reinforcing them with social, visual, and auditory stimulation. Each of the two stimuli in the pair varied from trial to trial over a relative brightness range from 200 to 1. Schaller found that six of the seven infants tested demonstrated longer fixation times for the reinforced stimulus, a discrimination that could not be based on brightness cues.

Finally, Bornstein (1976) used similar logic in a habituation experiment. In this study he tested whether infants had normal adultlike trichromatic as opposed to dichromatic vision, specifically protonopic or deuteranopic vision, the two most common types of adult color vision defects. He did this by making use of what is known as the dichromatic neutral zone. This is a region in the visible spectrum between 490 and 500 nm where an adult with normal color vision sees a saturated blue-green color, but where the dichromat sees white or gray.

Bornstein habituated 3-month-old infants to a series of 12 stimuli that varied randomly between 490 and 500 nm in hue and ranged in luminance 0.8 log units from a mean of 0.50 cd/m². The infants were then shown two test stimuli of white light selected from the same brightness range, and two more stimuli from the 490- to 500-nm range.

It was predicted that infants with dichromatic vision would see the first 12 stimuli as achromatic and hence not dishabituate during the two test trials with the white light. On the other hand, infants with normal trichromatic vision would habituate in the 12 initial trials to a blue-green hue, dishabituate in the two test trials to white light, and then decrease their looking on the last two trials when the original habituation hue was again shown. Bornstein found this latter result, indicating that his subjects had trichromatic vision.

The above three experiments have only tested a limited number of hues, and although they appear to indicate a similarity between color vision functioning in adults and infants as young as 10 weeks of age, they do not presume to show that the infant's perception of color is identical to the adult's. They have, however, established basic methods needed to further explore this question. The next section will discuss research that has extended the habituation technique to explore the question of whether infants, in addition to discriminating among different hues, also perceive the hues as belonging to distinct color categories.

Categorical Perception

Studies concerned with how adults name colors have found that most wavelengths can be adequately named with one or two of the primary color terms. Research has shown that color-naming functions generally take the form of plateaus, where a single color name is primarily used for wavelengths in a given region of the spectrum. These regions are separated by boundary areas where subjects differ in their application of color terms to wavelengths—for example, some subjects will consider a given hue in the blue-green boundary as primarily blue, whereas others will perceive it as primarily green (Boynton and Gordon, 1965). This research indicates that although the underlying physical dimension of wavelength is continuous, adults perceive broad categories in the spectrum within which wavelengths are quite similar in hue and are easily distinguished from hues in adjacent categories.

Evidence from both comparative studies and human cross-cultural research demonstrates that the categorical perception of color is not learned, but rather is due to the physiological structure of the visual system (Bornstein et al., 1976). Given this finding, it is logical to expect that infants also perceive colors in a categorical fashion.

This possibility was examined in two recent experiments. In the first, Bornstein et al. (1976) tested whether 4-month-old infants categorically perceived the colors of blue, green, yellow, and red. The infants were first habituated to a single wavelength of light for 15, 15-sec trials. Then, they received test trials with a set of three wavelengths. Two of the test wavelengths were physically equidistant from the habituation stimulus; however, one test stimulus was in the same hue category as the habituation stimulus, while the second was in an adjacent hue category. It was expected that if the infants perceived colors categorically, they would dishabituate to a test wavelength from the color category adjacent to the habituation color category, but show no dishabituation to a wavelength from the same color category as the habituation stimulus. Different groups of subjects were used to test each of the different color categories.

The results supported the view that 4-month-old infants do, indeed, perceive colors categorically. That is, recovery from habituation occurred when the habituation and test wavelengths were from different categories, but not when they were both from the same color category. The one exception to these results was provided by a group of subjects who were habituated to a red hue and tested with a yellow hue. This group showed less looking at the novel yellow color than the familiar red. The authors believe that this result was probably due to a particularly strong preference for the color red.

The above findings were partially replicated in a second experiment with 3-month-old infants (Bornstein, 1976). This experiment used the same paradigm as the earlier study, but the infants were tested only with wavelengths from the yellow-green categories. Specifically, the infants were first habituated in 15 trials to a 570-nm light that looks yellow in color to an adult. The infants then received test trials with a 580-nm light that also appears yellow to adults, and with a 560-nm light that looks green to adults. The infants showed reliable evidence of dishabituation to the 560-nm light, but did not dishabituate to the 580-nm light.

These two studies, in conjunction with the previously discussed hue-discrimination experiments, suggest that by at least 3 to 4 months of age infants are perceiving color in a relatively mature manner. Unfortunately, the possibility exists that the research techniques used in these studies may not be applicable to the study of color vision in younger infants or newborns. The applicability of these techniques to newborn research is an important issue, since research on early color vision may help to clarify the previously discussed question of infant foveal functioning. Bornstein's paradigm requires habituation, which many believe is not easily obtained in infants under 8 to 10 weeks of age (see Cohen and Gelber, 1975). Oster's paradigm may be applicable to research with younger infants but, again, may encounter problems since it requires the infant to scan extensively a stimulus, a behavior that previous research (Salapatek, 1975) has shown is difficult to elicit in young infants. While very young infants can be conditioned, it is a long and arduous process and, therefore, use of this technique poses difficulty for Schaller's paradigm as well. The above experiments, however, have successfully demonstrated the solution to the previously very problematic issue of brightness control, and constitute an important first step in infant color vision research.

Form Perception

Devising a concise yet comprehensive definition of form is a difficult, if not impossible, task. As Zuzne (1970, p. 1) notes, definitions of form ". . . range from the shape of a solid object to the values of coordinates in objectless space; from a synonym for the manner in which some event takes place to the philosophical notion of form as opposed to substance." While the diversity of definitions used by researchers of infant form perception certainly has not been as great, it is true that there has been no universally agreed-upon definition. Fantz (1961) includes shape, pattern, size, and solidity. Hershenson (1967) is more restrictive, requiring the form to be perceived as a whole. Salapatek (1975) distinguishes between a contour, a figure or shape, and a form, the latter term being reserved for a three-dimensional figure. And Bond (1972) admits to the possibility that no operational measure of form may be entirely satisfactory. Nevertheless, researchers working within the general rubric of infant form perception have usually presented one of four types of visual stimuli: high-contrast edges and angles; simple closed figures such as triangles, circles, or squares; compound patterns including two or more simple figures; or three-dimensional objects. In the present section we shall restrict the discussion to studies that have presented two-dimensional line drawings or photographs and have assessed either infant scanning patterns or discrimination abilities. Both the section in this chapter on perceptual constancies and Chapter 12 in this volume will examine infants' reactions to real objects.

High-Contrast Edges and Angles

A variety of experiments investigating infant form perception have used the corneal reflection apparatus to trace infant eye movements. The results of studies using this technique have provided abundant evidence that newborns can perceive high-contrast edges and angles. Kessen et al. (1972) reported that newborns would fixate a vertical but not a horizontal high-contrast edge. A subsequent study by Haith (1976) found that under appropriate conditions newborns would fixate a horizontal line as well as a vertical one. Others (see Salapatek, 1975) have also examined infant eye movements to geometric figures such as triangles, circles, and squares and have found that 1-month-old infants tend to concentrate their fixations about a single edge or angle. On the other hand, infants 2 months or older tend to scan the figures much more extensively.

Similar results were also obtained when newborns were shown a compound figure such as a line drawing of a face (Bergmann et al., 1971; Maurer and Salapatek, 1976). Newborns again responded much as they did with a single figure, scanning only a small portion of the outermost contour. When 2-month-old infants were shown a compound, however, they rapidly moved their eyes from the outer contour to one or more internal features. Results of studies with both simple and compound figures, therefore, support the notion that more extensive scanning of figures occurs with development.

Results consistent with this developmental change in scanning patterns were reported by Milewski (1976). He presented a compound visual pattern, a circle with a square, to 1- and 4-month-old infants contingent upon their high-amplitude nonnutritive sucking. Once the sucking had habituated, either the inner or outer figure was changed to a triangle. Sucking increased to either change in the 4-month old, but only to a change of the outer figure in the 1-month-old infants. Additional tests showed that the lack of discrimination of a change in the inner figure by 1-month-old infants was not caused by the smaller size of the figure, but by the fact that it was embedded within another figure.

Still a third technique has produced much the same conclusion. Using a paired comparison procedure, Fantz and Miranda (1975) examined newborn visual preferences for patterns with curved versus straight lines. On each trial, infants were shown two patterns (e.g., a bull's-eye versus stripes), and fixation times were recorded. When the patterns themselves formed the outer contour of the stimuli, newborns looked longer at the curved lines. However, when the same forms were embedded within large white squares, no consistent preferences were found. Presumably, the newborn fixations stopped at the outer contour of the square, and they did not attend to the internal forms. A previous study by Fantz and Nevis (1967) showed that older infants, 2 to 4 months in age, did prefer curved over straight lines, whether or not they were embedded in the square. Ruff and Birch (1974) have also shown that by 3 months of age infants discriminate features such as concentricity, curvilinearity, and number or directions of the elements in the pattern when they are embedded within a square.

Components versus Compounds

While the evidence presented so far indicates that infants beyond 2 months of age perceive both the internal and external parts of a compound figure, it does not answer the question of whether the parts are perceived as independent components or as a unified whole. For example, if an infant is shown a cross inside a circle, does he perceive a cross *within* a circle or just a cross *and* a circle? Cornell and Strauss (1973) examined this question in 4-month-old infants using a habituation-novelty paradigm. During an eight-trial habituation phase, infants were given four successive alternations of the cross and the circle. They were then tested either with a compound made of familiar components (i.e., the cross within the circle) or with a completely novel compound (i.e., a square within a triangle). Only the males' fixation times recovered in the test, and then only to the square-triangle. These results are consistent with the view that the males were responding on the basis of separate components rather than on the basis of the compound. If they had perceived the cross-circle as a novel compound, they should have recovered to that stimulus as well as to the square-triangle.

In a series of experiments, Miller and her associates (Miller, 1972; Miller et al., 1976) performed essentially the opposite manipulation. They habituated 4-month-old infants to a compound consisting of a circle surrounding an X and two dots. Both prior to and following habituation, fixation times to each independent component were assessed. If during habituation, infants were attending to the separate components, one might expect habituation to the components to occur at different rates, depending upon which was initially preferred. The results were consistent with this interpretation. Fixation times in the posthabituation test dropped most to the component that had initially been looked at longest.

The stimuli used by Miller were taken from an earlier report by Bower (1966), in which 8-, 12-, 16-, and 20-week-old infants were conditioned to make a left head turn when shown the compound—that is, the circle with an X and two dots. A generalization test was then given with the compound and each of the components separately. Bower reasoned that if the compound were perceived as a "whole," the number of generalized responses to it should be greater than the sum of the responses to the components. If it were not perceived as a "whole," the number of responses to the compound should equal the sum of the responses to the components. For the youngest two ages the whole did equal the sum of its parts, while for the 20-week-old subjects, the whole was greater than the sum of its parts. Thus, the evidence seems to indicate that while infants 2 to 4 months of age do perceive internal as well as external figures, they do not yet integrate them into a more complex whole or compound. Bower's research also suggests that this ability to integrate internal with external parts may begin to appear at about 5 months of age.

One can ask the same compound-component question about multidimensional stimuli. When infants attend to a colored form such as a red circle, do they perceive the red circle as a single unit or as something red and something circular? Although less evidence is available in this instance than for compound forms, the conclusion appears to be the same.

Several studies using one variation or another of the habituation-novelty paradigm have found that within the first 6 months of life infants can discriminate one colored form from another (Cohen et al., 1971; Milewski and Siqueland, 1975; Miranda and Fantz, 1974; Pancratz and Cohen, 1970; Welch, 1974; Wetherford and Cohen, 1973), and three of them (Cohen et al., 1971; Milewski and Siqueland, 1975; Miranda and Fantz, 1974) have shown that infants can discriminate a change in color or form alone. For example, Cohen et al. (1971) habituated 4-month-old infants to a red circle and then tested for dishabituation with the same red circle, a green circle, a red triangle, and a green triangle. A change in either color, form, or both produced increased looking. Furthermore, the effect was additive, with greater dishabituation when both dimensions were changed than when only one was changed.

While these experiments indicate that young infants can perceive both color and form, they do not bear directly on the question of whether the infants perceive these dimensions as compounds or separate components. In a more direct test of the compound-component issue, Cohen (reported in Cohen and Gelber, 1975) habituated 4-month-old infants to alternating trials of a red circle and a green triangle. The infants were then tested either with the same stimuli (i.e., a red circle and green triangle), the same components arranged in novel compounds (i.e., a red triangle and a green circle), or totally novel compounds (i.e., a blue square and a yellow dumbbell). Dishabituation occurred only in the last group, indicating that the infants were perceiving the components. Rearranging the components into novel compounds had little or no effect.

Recently Fagan (1977) reported a compound-component study with 22-week-old infants. All of his subjects were first familiarized to a red diamond pattern. They were then divided into four groups for the novelty test. Group 1 was shown a green diamond versus a green square. If that group looked longer at the green square, it would indicate form discrimination. Group 2 was given a red diamond versus a red square. Greater looking to the red square would also indicate form discrimination. However, in this case since one of the stimuli was exactly the same compound as that seen during the familiarization period, longer looking to the red square could also be based upon responding to a novel versus a familiar compound. If infants' preferences for novelty were greater in group 2 than in group 1, perception of the compound as well as form could be assumed. Groups 3 and 4 were similar to groups 1 and 2 except that they were used to test for discrimination of color and compound plus color. The results indicated that by 5 months of age infants could indeed perceive compounds as well as components. Thus, as in the compound-form studies, the evidence suggests a developmental transition at about 5 months of age, with infants younger than 5 months perceiving colored forms in terms of their components and those over 5 months perceiving the compound as well.

Pattern Arrangement

In the present section, we have considered infant perception or discrimination of simple lines, forms, or compounds composed of one form or color embedded within another form. It is also possible to construct complex stimuli out of two or more simple forms arranged side by side in some type of larger pattern. For example, Fagan's (1977) stimuli were actually produced by arranging 24 small diamonds or squares into larger diamond or square patterns. Much of the research on pattern arrangement, particularly that on infants' preference for complex versus simple patterns, will be covered in the next section. In this section, we shall ask three related questions about infants' perception of patterns: First, if two or more forms are placed next to one another, can infants perceive more than one? Second, if the pattern arrangement is altered in some way, either by rotating the individual forms or rearranging them, will the infant notice a change? And third, does the infant perceive the pattern arrangement as a unified whole or as a collection of independent parts?

The answer to the first question appears to be a qualified yes. Recall that Milewski (1976) found that 1-month-old infants did not dishabituate when only the internal form of a compound-form stimulus was changed. In another experiment in this series he placed the internal and external forms side by side and found that changing either form produced dishabituation. Apparently, when one form was not contained within the other, the infants could attend to both, even at 1 month of age. On the other hand, negative evidence was obtained by Salapatek and Maurer (Salapatek, 1975) with 8- and 11-week-old infants and more complex stimuli. They recorded infant eye movements to a series of 7×5 matrices composed of forms. All but one of the forms in each matrix were squares. The discrepant form could be either a triangle, circle, diamond, angle, or horizontal lines. Under these conditions no directed attention was obtained to the discrepant form.

Several experiments have reported that infants over 2½ or 3 months of age can discriminate one pattern from another when both patterns consist of different arrangements of the same simple form (Cornell, 1975; Fagan, 1977; Fantz and Nevis, 1967; Ruff, 1976·

Vurpillot et al., 1977). One might assume that these studies also provide evidence for infant perception of multiple forms, since in order to respond differently to the arrangements of the forms the infants attend to more than one form at a time. Unfortunately, for most of these experiments, that assumption need not hold, for in constructing the patterns the forms were not only arranged differently, but were rotated at different angles as well. Thus, the infants could have based their discriminations on different rotations of a single form rather than on different overall pattern arrangments.

One experiment (Vurpillot et al., 1977) is of particular interest since it examined infant discrimination of pattern arrangements without rotating the forms, and at the same time asked whether the infants perceived the pattern as a unified whole or as a collection of parts. Two- and 4-month-old infants were first habituated to a large cross pattern made up of nine smaller crosses. They were then tested with a square pattern made from the same nine crosses versus a cross pattern made fron nine small squares. When the size of the pattern elements was large, infants at both ages dishabituated only to a change in the shape of the elements and not to a change in the overall shape of the pattern. However, when the size of the elements was small, both 2- and 4-month-old infants dishabituated to a change in the shape of the pattern, but not to a change in elements. These results with small elements suggest perception of the pattern as a unified whole.

The possibility that poor visual acuity may have prevented the infants from discriminating a cross pattern made up of squares from the square pattern made up of crosses was partially ruled out by a pretest. Vurpillot et al. found that 2-month-old infants could discriminate between a single small square and a single small cross. The acuity explanation is not totally eliminated since, as we have reported in a previous section of this chapter, the acuity threshold to an isolated element is quite a bit lower than the acuity threshold for the same element when it is part of a larger configuration. However, this version of the poorer acuity explanation was also negated by Vurpillot et al. with 4-month-old infants. They could discriminate two similar irregular patterns, one made up of small crosses and the other composed of small squares. Unfortunately, the 2-month-old infants were not tested with the irregular patterns, so poorer acuity may still have accounted for their behavior.

Thus, the evidence is reasonably convincing that at some point within the first 6 months of life infants can perceive multiple forms and can respond to, and prefer, a change in pattern arrangement. Also, by 4 months of age, and possibly even by 2 months of age, certain configurations of elements that are arranged into simple, symmetric, regular forms can be perceptually organized into unique wholes.

The Invariance of Form

No discussion of infant form perception would be complete without considering whether infants can perceive a form as invariant despite certain nondistorting transformations. In fact, some investigators in this area (Hershenson, 1967; Schwartz 1975) have argued that infant perception of form, as opposed to infant sensation of form, should be reserved for those instances in which the infant responds on the basis of the unity, integrity, and plasticity of the sensory information rather than just to the physical shape in one spatial orientation. In essence, their point is that true form or shape perception implies form or shape constancy.

Very little is known about shape constancy in infants, and it is not even clear that shape constancy is a unitary phenomenon. For example, perceiving a form as the same when it is rotated in the frontoparallel plane may involve quite different perceptual mechanisms from perceiving it as the same when it is rotated in depth. In the former case, the projective shape remains intact. In the latter, the projective shape changes, but additional cues such as changes in size and depth are also available. We shall restrict our discussion in the present section to those cases where a form is rotated in the frontoparallel plane. In the section on perceptual constancies we shall consider the evidence for infant shape (rotation in depth), size, and object constancies.

The first experiment testing the age at which infants could perceive the identity among different rotations of the same form in the frontoparallel plane was done by McGurk (1972). In this experiment, McGurk habituated 3-, 6-, 9-, and 12-month-old infants to a simple stick figure form in four 20-sec trials. In the first experimental condition, the orientation of the same form was changed in each of the four habituation trials. In a second experimental condition, the orientation of the form remained constant. Comparison of the results of both selective test trials and rate of habituation of the two groups indicated that by 6 months of age, infants recognized the identity of the habituation form despite changes in its orientation.

The most extensive investigation of infant perception of the invariance of form over rotations in the frontoparallel plane has recently been conducted by Schwartz (1975). Infants between 2 and 4 months of age were habituated to a single angle or form and then tested for dishabituation to variations of the habituation stimulus. In the first three experiments, infants were habituated to connected line segments. Dishabituation occurred when the angles formed by the lines were changed, but not when the original line segments were merely rotated. In another experiment infants were habituated to a square. They dishabituated to some degree when the square was rotated 45° to form a diamond, but dishabituated more when the angles of the square were altered to produce a rhomboid. Finally, in two other experiments, infants were habituated to a rectangle. Dishabituation occurred only when the rectangle was changed to a square and not when the rectangle was rotated.

Overall, the evidence was remarkably consistent. If the shape of the angle or form was altered, infants responded; if the angle or form was merely rotated, they did not. The only exception occurred when a square was rotated to produce a diamond. In this case, infants did dishabituate to some extent. But a diamond is an unusual figure; even an adult perceives a diamond as a unique form and not simply as a rotated square.

The evidence suggests that young infants' perception of simple angles and forms is quite sophisticated. By 2 to 4 months of age infants are no longer simply responding to vertical and horizontal lines, or to high-contrast edges and angles. They respond to the relationship among the parts of the form and to the form as a unique whole. It may be that at this age infants cannot integrate multiple forms into higher-order units, such as patterns or objects, but at least circumstantial evidence exists from the face-perception, constancy, and object-permanence literatures that by 7 or 8 months of age they are capable of such integration.

Complexity

Infant researchers have generally assumed (McCall, 1971) that, infant attention provides an ". . . avenue to the study of cognitive development . . ." [p. 107]. Since attention involves selective orientation to a stimulus or set of stimuli, the identification of those stimulus characteristics that determine attention may reveal something about the underlying cognitive development of the infant. This sort of assumption has motivated much of the research into the stimulus determinants of infant attention, including a fairly large body of work on stimulus complexity. The effect of a dimension generally referred to as "complexity" has been clearly established, the basic finding being that as infants get older they prefer increasingly complex stimuli. Less clear, however, is the meaning of complexity or the basis for its effect. Operational definitions of complexity abound: number of squares in a checkerboard pattern (Brennan et al., 1966; Greenberg, 1971; Thomas, 1965), number of elements in other patterns (Greenberg and O'Donnell, 1972), number of positions taken by a flashing light (Cohen, 1969; Haith et al., 1969), number of turns in a random shape (Hershenson et al., 1965), degree of redundancy or asymmetry in a pattern (Fantz and Fagan, 1975; Karmel, 1969a,b), and amount of contour (Karmel, 1969a,b).

The largest amount of data and the most reliable results have been obtained with checkerboard patterns. The classic study in this area was done by Brennan et al. (1966). They showed three different black and white checkerboards (2×2, 8×8, 24×24) to infants of 3, 8, and 14 weeks. Their fixation-time results revealed a positive relation between age and checkerboard complexity. While the younger infants preferred a checkerboard pattern comprising only a few, large squares, and older infants looked longer at a the pattern of intermediate complexity.

This general complexity preference has been replicated frequently for infant fixation times (Cohen, 1972; Greenberg, 1971; Greenberg and O'Donnell, 1972). Additionally, Cohen et al. (1975) and DeLoache et al. (1977) have shown that complexity preferences are also reflected in the speed with which infants turn toward a visual stimulus. Four-month-old infants turn more rapidly to look at many-element checkerboards than to simpler patterns.

There is little argument with respect to the data on checkerboard preferences, but the interpretation of those data is very much in doubt. Two main questions occur in this respect: (1) what is the physical stimulus dimension responsible for infants' checkerboard preferences; and (2) what is the underlying mechanism mediating them?

Amount of Information

Greenberg (1971) offers a perceptual-cognitive interpretation of the complexity preference. He assumes that the most important dimension underlying complexity preferences is the amount of information contained in a stimulus; more complex patterns contain more units and hence more information to be processed. Thus, for any infant at any given time there is an optimal level of complexity such that stimuli above and below the optimal level will be less preferred than those that match it. As infants develop, the amount of stimulus information they are capable of processing increases. Consequently, the optimal level for complexity also increases over age, with infants preferring increasingly complex stimuli. Greenberg (1971) showed that the optimal level could be accelerated by providing specific relevant experience. In support of the optimal level position, Greenberg et al. (1972) found a positive correlation between degree of complexity preference and rate of visual habituation (often thought to reflect rate of information processing) (Miller et al., 1976).

Contour Density

Although the optimal level concept is intuitively appealing, there are alternative explanations for complexity preferences. Karmel's (1969) interpretation differs from Greenberg's

(1971) with respect to both the stimulus dimension and the underlying mechanism. According to Karmel, the relevant physical dimension for infants from 6 weeks on is contour density, a measure of the black-white transitions in stimuli of a given overall size. Stimuli referred to as "complex" checkerboards have more black-white transitions and hence higher contour density than simpler patterns. An inverted U-shaped function relates contour density to looking time, and the maximum of the curve progressively shifts upward to higher-density values with age.

Karmel and Maisel (1975) believe that the mechanism underlying contour density preferences over age is not cognitive development [as Greenberg (1971) claims], but rather neurological maturation of the visual system. When one looks at a visual pattern, certain receptive fields of the visual system respond to contours or edges of the stimulus. Visual attention is a function of the amount of neuronal activity resulting from the interaction of contour stimulation and receptive field characteristics. Over development, neural receptive field sizes become smaller and better defined. Thus, with respect to checkerboard patterns, progressively smaller checks become capable of producing maximum neuronal activity as the infant gets older.

Karmel's noncognitive explanation in terms of changes in the size of neural receptive fields is supported by his observation that visual choice in behavior of rats and chicks, as well as human infants, is an inverted U-shaped function of contour density (Karmel, 1969b). Additionally, Karmel et al. (1974) measured visually evoked potentials (VEPs) to tachistoscopically flashed checkerboards of varying contour density. They found that the relation between VEPs and contour density was very similar to that between fixation time and contour density—that is, peak amplitude responses were an inverted U-shaped function of contour density, and with increasing age were elicited by stimuli of increasingly high contour density. A similar result reported for adults (Harter and White, 1968, 1970) was attributed to size-dependent properties of visual receptive field neurons, and Karmel et al. (1975) argued that the same explanation was appropriate for the infant data.

Size and Number of Elements

Fantz et al. (1975) agreed with Karmel that the neurological maturation of the infant visual system is the most important mechanism underlying checkerboard preferences, but they disagreed as to the relevant stimulus dimension affecting infant responses. These investigators pointed out that in complexity research, two stimulus dimensions have almost always been confounded—size and number of elements. If two checkerboard patterns are of the same overall size, the individual squares in the pattern with more checks are necessarily smaller than those in a simpler pattern. Fantz and Fagan (1975) and Miranda and Fantz (1971) independently manipulated size and number of squares in black-and-white patterns.

With number and size of internal elements now unconfounded, both variables influenced visual attention in newborn to 6-month-old infants. Generally, given patterns with the same number of elements, the infants looked longer at one with larger elements; given patterns made up of elements of the same size, the infants preferred the pattern with a greater number of elements. However, a developmental shift occurred in the prepotency of the two variables. Size had a strong effect on the fixation time of the youngest infants, but had a smaller effect with increasing age. Fantz and Fagan (1975) argued that description of the data in terms of the interaction of the two variables with age is more adequate than a unidimensional description in terms of contour density. Thus, Fantz and Fagan

(1975) concluded that the typical preference function for checkerboard patterns is based on two stimulus dimensions—size and number—whose relative importance changes over development.

Poorer visual acuity may be in large part responsible for the younger infants' preferences for larger elements, but the number preferences must be accounted for by some other mechanism. Fantz and Fagan (1975) discounted a cognitive explanation of the preference and pointed out that the number preferences of younger subjects are directly counter to the optimal level position. They suggested instead that it has to do with neurological maturation, although they do not specify the precise mechanism.

Face Perception

An extensive literature exists on infants' perception of faces, because the topic is of interest to investigators from a wide range of perspectives. Here we will restrict ourselves to a consideration of face perception as it relates to the general development of visual perception in infants. The main question that will concern us is whether the development of face perception can be described with the same general principles as other aspects of form perception, or whether, as some suggest, there is something different or unique about an infant's response to a human face. Since Gibson (1969) and Bond (1972) reviewed the area a few years ago, we will concentrate on more recent evidence not available to them. Much of our discussion will follow Gibson's organization of the area.

Preference for Faces: The Innateness Hypothesis

The first question, then, concerns the existence of an innate preference for human faces. According to Bowlby (1958) and other ethologically oriented investigators (Freedman, 1974; Goren, 1975), there is an innate, evolved tendency for human newborns to attend to human faces. This hypothesis is not supported by the several studies that have compared newborns' visual fixations of faces versus other stimuli. Reported preferences for looking at faces over other simple stimuli (Fantz, 1963; Stechler, 1964) can be attributed to a variety of other variables, especially complexity. When very young infants have been shown faces versus other fairly complex stimuli, no face preference has emerged (Hershenson, 1964; Thomas, 1965). Furthermore, neither the orientation nor arrangement of facial features influences the attention of newborns or infants younger than 2 months (Fantz, 1965, 1967; Haaf, 1974; Hershenson, 1964; Watson, 1966).

Just one study contradicts the above statement and reports differential responding by newborns to face stimuli differing only in arrangement of internal features. Goren (1975) found that a regular schematic face elicited greater visual following than scrambled or blank faces when the stimulus was slowly moved in an arc around the infant. She also reported that a real face was followed more than a mannequin or photograph. Goren concluded that "The infant enters the world predisposed to respond to a face, any face" [p. 6].

Since Goren's results are discrepant from any others with newborns, we feel they must be viewed with caution. The study needs to be replicated with better controls for observer bias and a different set of stimuli; there may be some idiosyncratic features of her set of stimuli which have little or nothing to do with "faceness," but which determine the amount of following of patterns moved into the periphery.

Development of Attention to Facial Features

The second question concerns infants' attention to facial features. Do infants respond to faces as a whole or to individual features, and how does the basis of their response change with development? With the exception of Goren's study, there is no evidence that the variables that influence young infants' responses to faces are different from the variables that influence their attention to other stimuli.

Recent experiments analyzing infants' patterns of eye movements as they scan faces (Bergman et al., 1971; Donnee, 1973; Maurer and Salapatek, 1976) have found that young infants scan faces in a manner similar to the way they scan two-dimensional shapes (Salapatek, 1968, 1975; Salapatek and Kessen, 1966, 1973). Maurer and Salapatek (1976) reported that 1-month-olds fixated away from a real face most of the time and scanned only a limited portion of the perimeter (hairline and chin) of the face. They very rarely fixated inside the face. In contrast, 2-month-olds spent most of their time looking at the internal features of the face and were especially likely to fixate the eyes. Whether the eyes attracted the 2-month-old's gaze because they had acquired some special meaning or simply because they were the internal feature with the most contrast, these results corroborated Gibson's (1969) view that the eyes were the first facial feature to be differentiated. Her conclusion was based mainly on Ahrens' (1954) finding that the eyes were the first isolated part of the face sufficient to elicit smiling and Wolff's (1963) report that 3½-week-olds fixate the eyes in a real face.

Caron et al. (1973) investigated the relative salience of a number of different facial features for 4- to 5-month-old infants. For 4-month-olds, the eyes were a more salient feature than the nose-mouth area, but by 5 months the nose and mouth were also perceptually salient. Caron et al. (1973) also found that at 4 months the outer head contour was more salient than the inner face configuration and that the degree of "faceness" did not determine responding. Thus, a number of studies show that until 4 months, infants respond to faces on the basis of isolated features, usually the eyes and other high-contrast areas.

According to Gibson (1969), an important transition in the development of face perception occurs at approximately 4 months. Infants begin noticing invariant relationships between facial features and respond to the configuration of features rather than to individual features. At this age infants show spontaneous preferences, as indicated by longer fixations or greater smiling for regular faces over faces with their features scrambled (Haaf and Bell, 1967; Kagan, 1967; Kagan et al., 1969; Thomas, 1973), and faces in an upright orientation elicit most smiling (Watson, 1966). More realistic versions of faces seem to be preferred over less realistic ones (Ahrens, 1954; Kagan, 1967; Kagan et al., 1966; Lewis, 1969; Lewis et al., 1966; Polak et al., 1964a,b; Thomas, 1973; Wilcox, 1969), although the basis for the observed preferences is not completely clear. Additionally, realistic faces are often preferred over a wide range of other nonface stimuli (Fantz and Nevis, 1967; Kagan and Lewis, 1965). Thus, a large number of studies have been interpreted as showing that by approximately 4 months, infants become capable of responding to the facial configuration as a whole and not just to isolated features, and that their response to facelike stimuli depends on how closely the stimulus resembles a human face.

The conclusion that a preference for viewing faces gradually emerges has not gone unchallenged. Several of the individual experiments cited above can be faulted for not including relevant controls (e.g., for not controlling symmetry of the scrambled faces or for not comparing realistic versions of faces to realistic versions of other objects), and often not all response measures assessed were in agreement. A more telling criticism is Thomas' (1973) objection to the common procedure of averaging response measures rather than assessing individual infant's preference functions. He claims that when individual preference orderings are examined, a preference for facelike stimuli is found in infants as young as 5 weeks. A recent study by Thomas and Jones-Molfese (1977) supports this position. Preference orderings for four stimuli—a blank oval, a scrambled schematic face, a regular schematic face, and a black-and-white photograph of a face— were obtained from infants from 2 to 9 months of age. The best description of a dimension underlying the obtained preference data was in terms of faceness: at all ages the more facelike stimuli were preferred.

One can reconcile the discrepancy between Thomas' (1973; Thomas and Jones-Molfese, 1977) findings and the earlier literature by accepting his criticisms of the methodological and conceptual difficulties involved in inferring preference from group data analyzed by procedures assuming preferences to be a linear function. However, it is still difficult to reconcile his finding of a face preference in 5-week-old infants with the scanning studies showing that infants of this age tend to scan only a part of the perimeter of faces (Maurer and Salapatek, 1976). These results also seem contrary to the general finding that configural information only becomes important in determining attention at around 5 months (Fantz et al., 1975).

By 5 months, infants seem to have differentiated faces as a distinct class of stimuli possessing a particular configuration of features. Although infants can now discriminate between two fairly dissimilar face photographs in a memory task (Cohen et al., 1977; Fagan, 1972), they do not discriminate between two upside-down faces (Fagan, 1972). Only if they have learned that faces represent a class of mono-oriented stimuli with certain distinctive features should their discriminatory ability be affected by the orientation of the stimuli.

From 5 months on, infants become increasingly capable of abstracting invariant features or relations among features. Cornell (1974) reported data suggesting that 24-week-old subjects discriminated between photos of men versus women, and Cohen (1977) and Fagan (1976) have shown that at 6 or 7 months infants can discriminate between two faces of the same sex. Furthermore, different poses of the same person can be discriminated from one another. This discrimination could only be based on abstract configural information. Infants were also able to recognize a new picture of a person they had previously seen in a different pose (Cohen, 1972; Fagan, 1976). Thus, they must have abstracted unique aspects of individual faces which remained invariant from one pose to another. Dirks and Gibson (1977) have also shown abstraction of facial information in a study in which 5-month-olds showed generalization from a real face to a color photograph of the same person, and Strauss et al. (1977) reported generalization by 5-month-olds from a color photograph of a woman's face to a black-and-white photograph and a line drawing of the same woman.

Discrimination of facial expressions requires that the infant abstract information that remains invariant over different faces. Although Browne (1975) found that 3-month-old infants in a habituation study discriminated between two expressions (happy and surprised), their discrimination could easily have been made on the basis of differences in a single feature (i.e., the eyes). Kreutzer and Charlesworth (1973) presented infants between 4 and 10 months with an adult who portrayed a variety of facial expressions accompanied by appropriate vocalizations. Before 6 months no evidence was found for discrimination among the expressions. Using a visual preference technique, Wilcox and

Clayton (1968) found no evidence of discrimination of facial expressions by 5-month-olds. Recently, however, LeBarbera et al. (1976) reported that their 4- and 6-month-old subjects looked significantly longer at black-and-white photographs of faces depicting an expression of joy than at faces with neutral or angry expressions. The reason for the disparity in ages at which infants show evidence of discrimination of facial expressions is not clear. However, it is safe to conclude that by 6 months infants respond differentially to different facial expressions, and may do so as early as 4 months.

In summary, infant perception of faces seems to follow the same general course as other aspects of form or pattern perception. There is little evidence of an innate preference for human faces, and infants younger than 2 months seem to respond to only one or a few isolated high-contrast facial features. By 4 months or perhaps earlier, infants respond to the whole configuration of features, so arrangement of features is crucial in determining their attention. From 5 months on they become increasingly adept at abstracting invariant features from faces. They notice the structure that distinguishes one face from another and that remains constant over a variety of poses. They are also able to recognize the aspects of facial expressions that remain invariant over individuals.

Perceptual Constancies

The term perceptual constancy refers to the perceived stability of an object or event in the face of marked changes in the sensory stimulation that it provides the perceiver. For example, when we walk about a room, we perceive a chair as the same, or invariant, even though its projective shape, size, and location on the retina are continually changing. The existence of constancies in adult perception has been well documented, but little is known about their existence in infant perception. A recent review by Day and McKenzie (1977) has summarized and evaluated most of the existing evidence for constancies in infant perception. Therefore, we shall not attempt to duplicate the Day and McKenzie chapter; instead we shall briefly mention the most convincing evidence that they present and add new evidence which has recently emerged.

In their review of the constancy literature, Day and McKenzie distinguish three main classes of constancies: object, egocentric, and identity-existence constancies. Object constancy refers to the perceived stability of certain physical characteristics of an object, such as its size, shape, color, or brightness. The stability of these characteristics persists despite changes in the location of the object, the orientation of the object, or the ambient light level of the room. In this first class of constancies, only size and shape constancy have been systematically investigated in infants. Egocentric constancy, the second class of constancies, refers to the perceived stability of the location of an object despite movements by the perceiver. Thus, egocentric constancy includes all situations in which a stationary object is perceived as stationary even when the projection of that object on the retina moves. The infant-perception literature also includes a few studies of egocentric constancy. The last class of constancies, identity-existence constancy, refers to belief in the continued existence of an object despite its partial or total disapearance. As we know, objects in the foreground occlude objects in the background; and every time we cover an object, turn off the lights, or blink our eyes, the projective image of an object disappears. However, despite the object's disappearance from our visual field, our knowledge of its continued existence remains, and this knowledge constitutes identity-existence constancy. Of the three classes of constancies, identity-existence constancy has been investigated the most extensively in infants within the context of Piagetian theory under the label of "object permanence." Since the object-permanence literature has been discussed elsewhere in this volume (see Chapter 12 by Gratch), we shall not discuss it here.

Shape Constancy

One of Day and McKenzie's (1977) major conclusions was that good evidence existed for the occurrence of shape constancy by 2 months of age. Recent studies suggest that this conclusion was premature. Day and McKenzie based their conclusion on two sets of experiments, the principal one reported by Bower (1966c), who conditioned a headturning response in 2-month-old infants to a rectangular piece of wood rotated 45° from the frontoparallel plane. Following the establishment of the conditioned response, infants participated in a generalization test with the rectangle they had seen previously, the same rectangle now facing front, a trapezoid facing front that had the same projective shape as the conditioned stimulus, and a trapezoid rotated 45°. The infants made approximately the same number of generalized responses to both rectangles and made fewer responses to both trapezoids. Since the infants had generalized to the same objective rather than to the same projective shape, Bower concluded from this and two other related studies that "young infants possess the capacity for shape constancy, the capacity to detect invariants of shape under rotational transformation in the third dimension," [Bower, 1966b].

A recent study by Caron et al. (1977), however, casts some doubt on the validity of Bower's conclusion. In an attempt to replicate and extend Bower's original study, Caron et al. habituated 12-week-old infants to one of six stimuli and then tested all infants with the same vertically oriented square. The first group was habituated to the vertical square, the second group to the square tilted back 30° and the third group to the square tilted 60°. Thus, groups 2 and 3 habituated to the same objective stimulus they would receive in the test but to different projective views of this stimulus. Group 4 was habituated to a trapezoid tilted back 60°. This stimulus had the same projective shape as the test square, but a different objective shape. Dishabituation in groups 2 and 3 would provide evidence that the infants responded on the basis of projective shape. Dishabituation in group 4, but not in groups 2 or 3 *could* provide evidence of response to the objective shape—that is, of shape constancy. Dishabituation in group 4, however, could also be produced by a response to an area difference rather than to a difference in objective shape. The response to the area difference might occur because the trapezoid with the same projective shape as the vertical square necessarily had a greater area than the square. To facilitate interpretation of the response of infants in group 4, two more groups were included. Group 5 was habituated to a small trapezoid of the same area as the test square, and group 6 was habituated to a larger square.

The results did not support either the projective-shape or objective-shape interpretations. Infants in every group dishabituated but those in group 1, the group that received exactly the same stimulus in habituation and the test. The authors concluded that while infants were not perceiving projective shape they were also not demonstrating shape constancy.

The second bit of supportive evidence for infant shape constancy comes from a study by Day and McKenzie (1973). These researchers habituated 6- to 16-week-old infants to either a cube in a constant orientation, to the same cube in varying orientations, or to photographs of the cube in varying orientations. They found that the infants habituated both to the cube in a constant orientation and to the cube in different orientations, but did not habituate to the photographs. The authors concluded that these results demonstrated shape constancy, reasoning that infants should habituate more rapidly to the same stimulus than to changing stimuli. In the variable-orientation condition, infants habituated as rapidly as in the constant-orientation condition. Hence, Day and McKenzie concluded that this similarity in rate of habituation indicated that in the variable condition the depth cues were sufficient for the infants to perceive the cube as the same regardless of orientation. Unfortunately, their conclusion, which was equivalent to saying that the infants had shape constancy, was unwarranted, since all Day and McKenzie really demonstrated was that infants habituated more rapidly to three-dimensional stimuli than to photographs. Even the conclusion that the rates of habituation were comparable may be questioned, since a floor effect may have prevented differences between the constant- and variable-orientation conditions from occurring.

A more powerful technique for demonstrating shape constancy may involve a combination of both Caron et al.'s (1977) use of dishabituation and Day and McKenzie's (1973) multiple-habituation procedure. One must first demonstrate that infants can discriminate among different orientations of the same object. Second, one must show that when infants are habituated to different orientations of the same object, they dishabituate to an object with a different shape but not to the same object in a novel orientation. Successful demonstration of both would provide potent evidence that orientation had become irrelevant and that infants had shape constancy. A few experiments have now used similar procedures with pictures of faces (Fagan, 1976; Cohen, 1977) and with real objects (Ruff, 1977b). In one experiment, for example, (Cohen, 1977) 18-, 24-, and 30-week-old infants were habituated either to a single three-quarter profile of a face or to multiple three-quarter profiles. They were then tested with front views of the same face and a different face. Thirty-week-old infants in the single-photograph condition dishabituated to both test stimuli, but infants in the multiple-photograph condition dishabituated only to different faces. Dishabituation to the familiar face in the single condition indicated that the infants could discriminate between a three-quarter and frontal orientation of the same face. The lack of dishabituation in the multiple condition indicated that presentation of multiple examples of profiles enabled the infants to disregard the orientation and respond to the face per se. The younger infants, in contrast, could not disregard orientation; they dishabituated to the same face in both conditions. These results demonstrate shape constancy, or at least face constancy, but at a much older age than proposed by McKenzie and Day. The results also indicate that most depth cues are not necessary for the recognition of a face as the same regardless of orientation. Similar results, indicating the existence of shape constancy at 9 but not at 6 months, have been obtained by Ruff (1977b), with three-dimensional objects.

In conclusion, Day and McKenzie's statement that shape constancy exists by 2 months of age should be modified. No clear-cut experimental evidence supports the existence of shape constancy in infants under 7 months of age. Perhaps if simpler stimuli than those used by Cohen or Ruff were presented and if the multiple-habituation technique were employed, evidence for shape constancy at an earlier age would emerge. At present, however, the existence of shape constancy in the first 6 months of life remains an open question.

Size Constancy

Much less is known about visual size constancy than shape constancy in infants. Once again, the key experiment supporting the existence of size constancy was reported by

Bower (1964). After conditioning 6- to 12-week-old infants to turn their head to a 12-in cube at a distance of 3 ft, he examined generalization to the same stimulus, to a 12-in. cube at 9 ft, to a 36-in. cube at 3 ft, and to a 36-in. cube at 9 ft. The greatest generalization occurred to the conditioned stimulus (i.e., the 12-in. cube at 3 ft) and the least to the 36-in. cube at 9 ft. Since the infants responded least to the cube that had the same projective size as the conditioned stimulus, Bower concluded that some degree of size constancy was present in infants. Since infants also responded more to any cube at 3 ft than to any cube at 9 ft, however, the existence of size constancy alone could not explain his results. In general, the infants also appeared to respond more to near objects than to far ones.

Several attempts have recently been made to replicate Bower's results. In some attempts (McKenzie and Day, 1972) a habituation paradigm was used, while in others (summarized by McKenzie and Day, 1977) conditioning paradigms were employed. Infants in these experiments ranged from 6 weeks to 4 months of age. Although most studies replicated the tendency of infants to respond more to near than to far objects, none found evidence of size constancy.

Thus, examination of the evidence yields the same conclusion in the case of size constancy as shape constancy. To date, there has been no unequivocal demonstration of size constancy in the first 6 months of life, perhaps because distance is a more potent variable for young infants than size. If a multiple-habituation paradigm were used and infants habituated to the same cube at a number of different distances, distance per se might become irrelevant and evidence for size constancy might emerge. Unfortunately, such an experiment has not yet been conducted.

Egocentric Constancy

As we mentioned earlier, egocentric constancy refers to the perceived stability of the location of an object despite alterations in the location of the observer. The few studies that have begun to appear on egocentric constancy in infants have been based upon a rather unusual phenomenon in the object-permanence literature known as the stage-IV error. If a 9- or 10-month-old infant is shown an object hidden under one of two cloths, without hesitation he or she will remove the cover and obtain the object. If the object is hidden several times under one cloth, however, and is then hidden under a new cloth in a different location, the infant will look for the object at the old location rather than at the new one. Two possible explanations have been offered for the infant's error. According to these explanations, the infant has learned either to associate the object with a particular location in space or to associate the object with a particular response.

Bremner and Briant (1977) conducted a study to distinguish between these competing explanations of the stage-IV error. Nine-month-old infants were placed in a chair facing a table. In the first phase of the experiment a toy was hidden five times under one of the two cloths on the table, while in the second phase the object was hidden under either the old or new cloth. Prior to the second phase, the previously correct location of the object relative to the infant was changed in one of two ways. Infants in the first group had the table rotated 180°, while infants in the second group were moved to the opposite side of the table. The only conditions in which the infants consistently obtained the toy were those in which their previous response was correct. The previous location of the object appeared to be an irrelevant factor.

In another experiment investigating egocentric constancy (Acredelo, 1977) 6-, 11-, and

16-month-old infants were placed in the center of a room with one window on the left and one on the right. The infants were conditioned to turn their head to one window whenever they heard a buzzer. They were then rotated 180°, the buzzer was sounded, and the experimenter recorded whether the infants turned to the previously correct window or made the previously correct response. Although there was some evidence of a developmental change from 6 to 11 months, only the 16-month-old infants consistently turned to the correct window.

Both the experiments by Bremner and Briant and by Acredelo, therefore, indicated that locating an object in space independently of one's own location or response is a very difficult task. One reason for this difficulty may be that, as Piaget assumes, infants define objects in terms of their actions on the objects in the first 2 years of life. The difficulty may also result from the particular task used thus far, since they depend heavily on left-right discriminations. Such discriminations are notoriously difficult even for pre-school children (Mandler and Day, 1975).

To summarize, the evidence for perceptual constancies under 6 months of age is equivocal at best. At 8 to 10 months of age there is a hint of shape constancy, a lack of support for egocentric constancy, and no information on the existence of size constancy. These early studies on constancies, although not conclusive, have been valuable both in focusing attention on perceptual constancies as a research area and in demonstrating viable techniques for future experimentation. This area remains wide open to investigation, and we expect much more definitive evidence on the existence of perceptual constancies in infants to be available in the near future.

CURRENT ISSUES RELATED TO INFANT PERCEPTION

To complete our discussion on infant visual perception, we will now consider how infants' perceptual abilities are related to other organismic variables. As has been obvious throughout this chapter, visual attention is determined not simply by the physical characteristics of a stimulus but by the relation of that stimulus to various internal processes. In this section we will briefly discuss some of the important issues with respect to the relation between visual attention and motivational and memory systems, as well as the infant's developing maturational status.

Perception and Physiology

At present, our understanding of the effects of neural maturation on emerging, observable perceptual behavior is very poor. To a large extent, this lack of understanding can be attributed to the relative paucity of research on the physiological development of the infant's visual and sensory systems. It further results from the complexity of the physiological-behavioral interactions themselves; simple correspondences between emerging behaviors and observed physiological changes are very rare. Infant researchers are faced with an especially difficult task in searching for such relationships, for unlike the neuroscientist, they cannot directly effect such changes through manipulations of the infant's physiological system or physical environment. At best, infant researchers hope to find emerging behaviors that are indirectly compatible with existing notions of the development of the infant's visual system.

In spite of these handicaps, interesting comparisons between existing physiological and behavioral research have emerged—comparisons that, at present, are most useful for their ability to guide research in the two separate disciplines. The behavioral-acuity and form-perception studies, for example, have been aided by the anatomical studies, which have established both the basic limits of the infant's visual abilities and rough time estimates for predicting their improvement. Additionally, knowledge that the central and peripheral retinal regions are not equally mature at birth has emphasized the need for research that clearly distinguishes behaviors mediated by the development of central versus peripheral processes.

The current work on cortical receptive fields provides another example of the complimentary relationship between existing physiological and behavioral work. Research by sensory physiologists such as Hubel and Weisel (1959, 1963, 1968) has clearly established the existence of cortical cells that are differentially sensitive to stimulation by particular shapes, features, line orientations, and colors. This work on receptive fields corresponds with the early infant form-perception literature, which has shown that even newborns detect and differentially attend to particular contours in the visual environment. The exact relationship between the infant's attentive behaviors and the organization and development of underlying cortical units is not known, but interactions between behavioral and physiological research will continue to guide future attempts to specify the nature of this relationship. Studies examining the features to which infants differentially respond and changes in this response with development will help to shape the search for specific types of cortical units. Conversely, research on the extent to which cortical units are innate and on changes in these units with development will improve our understanding of the infant's changing visual behaviors. Indeed, Karmel and Maisel (1975) have discussed how knowledge of changes in the receptive field size can be used to explain developmental changes in the infant's selective attention to black-and-white checkerboard patterns.

Bronson (1974) has also aptly demonstrated how existing behavioral and physiological knowledge can be integrated to help explain infant perceptual development. Although a detailed explanation of his theory is beyond the scope of this chapter, Bronson basically attempted to show how a large amount of the visual behavioral research could be explained by existing physiological data. According to Bronson's theory, the visual system is actually made up of two phylogenetically differentiated subsystems which mature at different rates during infancy and are responsible for controlling different types of visual behaviors.

Although there is much disagreement concerning the accuracy and validity of Bronson's theory (see discussions by Haith & Campos, 1977; and Salapatek, 1975), the type of integration between physiological and behavioral data which Bronson attempts to provide is prominently missing from the infant perceptual development literature. At this point in time, any theory that attempts to integrate these two research areas must be speculative and, hence, poses an easy target for attack and criticism; however, it is our belief that such theorizing is needed and will be extremely useful as a guide for future research in infant perceptual development.

Perception and Motivation

Motivational variables clearly influence infants' attention to different stimuli, and must always be considered in our investigation of their perceptual abilities. The dominant point of view in this area is derived from discrepancy theory (Dember and Earl, 1957; Hunt,

1965; McClelland and Clark, 1953). Several investigators have theorized that a major determinant of attention is the extent to which a stimulus matches some internal model or schema (Kagan, 1967; McCall, 1971; McCall and McGhee, 1977) or the extent to which it matches an internal optimal level (Greenberg, 1971; Thomas, 1973). (The latter approach has been discussed previously in the section on complexity.)

The discrepancy hypothesis asserts that an infant will display maximum attention to stimuli that offer an optimal amount of discrepancy—that is, stimuli sufficiently familiar that they can be assimilated but sufficiently novel that they provide some new information, "stimuli that are a blend of new but processable information" [McCall and McGhee, 1977]. A stimulus that is extremely similar to a familiar stimulus (i.e., one stored in memory) presents no new information and hence is not interesting. However, a stimulus that is extremely different from the familiar standard may present *too much* new information and require too much processing effort to be attractive to the infant. Attention is thus predicted to be an inverted U-shaped function of stimulus discrepancy, with stimuli that are too familar or too discrepant recruiting little attention. For a recent detailed explanation of the discrepancy hypothesis, see McCall and McGhee's (1977) excellent summary.

Two main strategies have been adopted in attempts to demonstrate the validity of the discrepancy hypothesis in infant visual attention. One strategy followed in this research has been to focus on a naturally developing schema or internal model—for example, the face—and assess infants' attention to various levels of discrepancy from that schema (Kagan, 1967; Kagan et al., 1966). While the face-perception data are by no means completely consistent, they do conform fairly well to the discrepancy position. Initially, presumably before the infant has had sufficient experience to have developed a schema for human faces, there is no preference for either regular or scrambled face stimuli. However, at around 4 months, when a schema for faces is inferred to be developing, infants come to prefer regular faces, which presumably provide a moderate degree of discrepancy from the developing schema. Once the face schema becomes firmly established, regular faces become too familiar and scrambled faces present an optimum amount of discrepancy. This schema-discrepancy position has been strongly criticized by Thomas (1973) on both conceptual and methodological grounds, one of his main objections being that averaged group data distort the preference functions of individual subjects.

A second strategy for investigating the discrepancy hypothesis has been to attempt to induce the creation of an internal model or schema for some stimulus. Generally infants are familiarized to a stimulus and then tested for attention to variations of the original, some involving slight modifications, others extreme changes in the stimulus. McCall and McGhee (1977), major proponents of the discrepancy hypothesis, restrict the hypothesis to experimental evidence derived from this approach. They expect maximal attention to the moderate discrepancy, with the slight and extreme changes receiving less attention. The McCall et al. (1973) study exemplifies this approach. In this experiment, infants were familiarized to a single arrow in a vertical or horizontal position. Then the arrow was rotated varying numbers of degrees from its initial position, presenting the infant with different levels of discrepancy from the original stimulus.

The results of such investigations have been mixed. Sometimes an inverted U-shaped function is found, but often it is found for one sex but not the other, for one experimental group but not another, for one dependent variable but not another. At times data are reported that can be interpreted ad hoc to be consistent with the predicted inverted-U shape, such as a linear increasing function or a decreasing function; but such data offer very weak support and lend themselves to other interpretations. According to Thomas

(1971), these mixed results are not surprising since unambiguous tests of discrepancy theory are quite difficult and require specification of a number of parameters that are typically not known. "In the absence of parameter specification, almost any data may be mapped into or found at variance with the models by making different assumptions about parametric values [Thomas, 1971, p. 253]." McCall and McGhee (1977) argue that when a number of infant studies investigating the discrepancy hypothesis are considered together, a pattern of results emerges supporting the position. However, by far the most common finding in infant-attention research is a linear function—that is, attention increases as degree of discrepancy increases.

The discrepancy hypothesis has intuitive appeal: we have all been bored by stimuli that are too simple for our cognitive level, overwhelmed by information too complex for us to comprehend, and attracted to material that adds a new dimension or insight into what we already know. One reason that such a confusion of results has occurred in studies of infant visual attention may have to do with the type of stimuli used. Other than the face studies, most experiments have presented relatively simple, meaningless stimuli like those commonly used in studies of infant attention. The stimuli are arbitrary and so are the changes made in them—simple rearrangements or distortions of elements, or other physical modifications. It seems unlikely that purely physical nonmeaningful changes could be sufficient to present an infant with too much discrepant information to be comfortably processed. For a stimulus to be so discrepant that it results in reduced attention or avoidance, it probably must violate more than a simple perceptual schema—it must involve a change in meaning that requires extensive cognitive restructuring. An example of infant behavior that does seem to be a negative reaction to extreme discrepancy comes from studies of infants' responses to their own mothers' face. They often refuse to look at or become emotionally upset when presented with an immobile, unsmiling mother (Carpenter et al., 1968; Maurer and Salapatek, 1976) or multiple versions of their mother (see Bower, 1974). Perhaps, a fruitful course for investigators of the discrepancy hypothesis would be to apply it to recent topics in infant behavior that clearly involve cognitive processes—for example, concept formation and event perception.

Perception and Memory

Many of the studies discussed in this chapter have taken advantage of the infant's tendency to attend more to novel than familiar stimuli. The specific procedures have varied. In some procedures, one stimulus is repeatedly presented until the infant's looking or sucking habituates. In others, the infant is given one long exposure to the stimulus. But in all these procedures, following the initial familiarization period, the infant is tested with the now-familiar stimulus versus novel ones. In this chapter we have emphasized how these procedures may be used effectively to study infant perceptual discrimination. However, they also provide information about infant recognition memory. Assuming that the novel and familiar stimuli were equally preferred at the onset of the experiment, the only basis for the infant's differential response to the test stimuli is the difference in stimulus familiarity. Responding on the basis of familiarity also implies memory for some aspect of the familiar stimulus and requires that the infant encode or store information received during the familiarization period for use in the test. Thus, the same procedures that tell us what the infant can discriminate also tell us what the infant can remember.

A body of literature produced in recent years has investigated the infant memory process itself, examining not only what infants can remember, but also the earliest age at which they can remember, how long they can remember and the susceptibility of their memory to interference. Recent summaries are available (Cohen and Gelber, 1975; Cohen, 1976) and, in general, the evidence indicates that infants as young as 2 months (perhaps even newborns) can habituate to a repeated visual stimulus and dishabituate to a novel one. At 4 or 5 months of age infants can retain previously encoded visual information for minutes, hours, days, and even weeks. Infant memory is also remarkably immune to interference. Inserting novel stimulation in the delay interval between initial familiarization and later testing usually has little or no effect.

Several models of infant habituation and memory have been developed (Cohen and Gelber, 1975; Fagan, 1977; McCall and McGhee, 1977; Olson, 1976). They all start with the premise that the infant compares the test stimulus to information that has been stored from previous visual stimulation. They differ, however, on a number of important issues. These issues include the nature of the habituation process (is it gradual or all-or-none?), the infant's preference for novel test stimuli (do infants prefer the most novel stimulus or one of intermediate novelty?) and the necessity of proposing long- and short-term memory mechanisms.

Most infant researchers agree that it is important to distinguish between behaviors that merely reflect visual discrimination of test stimuli and those that reflect high-order perceptual processing. Although there are a number of ways of distinguishing between discrimination and perception, one of the more important distinctions is the extent to which memory processes are involved. As Schwartz (1975) has stated, perception as opposed to discrimination requires ". . . the integration of sensory information" [p. 1] and ". . . a suitably developed storage and retrieval mechanism with which to make comparisons" [p. 2]. Thus, the ability to discriminate among stimuli may be a necessary condition for perception, but it need not be a sufficient condition.

In this chapter we have discussed the similarities between the visual-preference and the habituation paradigms for determining infant visual discriminations. Although the procedures are generally comparable, the results obtained from habituation studies will be influenced much more by the infant's memory ability than those obtained from visual-perference studies. For this reason, habituation may be a more suitable procedure for investigating perceptual processes, and visual preference better suited for investigating basic discriminatory abilities. Even when habituation-type paradigms are used, slight differences in procedure can occasionally yield quite different results. If, following a preliminary familiarization period, the test stimuli are presented simultaneously, infants may be less likely to respond differentially to novel versus familiar stimuli than if the test stimuli are presented successively (McGurk, 1975). If the test stimuli are withheld for a time following familiarization, greater responding to novelty may occur to fewer stimulus dimensions than if the test stimuli are presented immediately after familiarization (Strauss and Cohen, 1977). Clearly, it is not enough to assert that infant perception involves both discrimination and memory. Much more needs to be known about the interactions between specific discrimination abilities and specific memory processes before our understanding of infant visual perception can be complete.

CONCLUDING COMMENTS

In this chapter we have attempted to include most of the current research on infant visual perception. As we noted at the outset of the chapter, the field has expanded rapidly, although much more information is needed before a complete understanding of infant vision is possible. Nevertheless, a coherent picture of the origins of visual perception is beginning to emerge. Newborn infants are neither blind nor a "tabula rasa" waiting for visual experiences to completely mold their understanding of the visual world. Even though at birth the visual system is still quite immature, newborns are capable of turning toward a stimulus in the periphery and of seeing high-contrast, low-frequency edges and angles. Newborns also tend to look more at curved than at straight lines and at simple than at complex patterns. This latter result may be partially due to their poor visual acuity.

By 2 to 4 months of age, infant perception is much more sophisticated. Simple figures are perceived as organized wholes whether they are constructed from connected line segments or discrete elements arranged in a simple pattern. Infants begin to respond to the relationship among the elements rather than to the elements as independent units. Colors tend to be perceived categorically rather than along a gradually changing continuum. Complex patterns, such as checkerboards or pictures of the human face, are looked at more than simple ones, and infants are able to traverse an external boundary in order to perceive an internal figure or feature. They still have some difficulty integrating component features such as a square within a circle or a color and a form, but even this integration appears possible by 4 or 5 months of age. It is also at this age infants are able to integrate the features of a face and recognize the identity of an individual face despite changes of pose and facial expressions.

Perceptual constancies do not make their appearance until somewhat later, about 7 to 13 months of age. Very little research has examined the development of constancies, and new procedures such as the use of multiple stimuli during habituation could show the existence of perceptual constancies within the first 6 months of life.

At the beginning of this chapter we indicated that the experiments we were planning to discuss would be placed within the theoretical contexts that generated them. Yet, one obvious omission from this chapter has been a discussion of global theories of perceptual development. [The reader is referred to Salapatek (1975) for a brief survey of these theoretical positions.] We omitted these theories in the present chapter for two reasons. First, many of the experiments were not specifically designed to test the theories. Either the investigators simply wanted to learn what infants were capable of perceiving at a particular age, or they had more circumscribed theories in mind, such as a test of primary versus secondary visual systems, or the validation of an optimal level of motivation theory. Second, taken as a whole, the evidence does not unequivocally support any one global theory. The Hebbian view of the development of higher neural organization from primitive cell assemblies gains support from the eye-movement research on newborn infants and from the newborn's tendency to fixate external contours. It is not supported by the evidence that newborn fixations do not necessarily concentrate at the angles of a figure or by research that shows slightly older infants capable of considerable perceptual organization. The Gestalt position that "good" figures are innately perceived is supported by evidence that at 2 to 4 months of age, infants perceive simple figures as unified wholes whether the figures are constructed from connected line segments or separated elements. Gestalt theory would have some difficulty, however, explaining the newborn research on eye movements, or the evidence that 2- to 4-month-old infants respond to components rather than compounds. The Gibsonian position stresses perception of invariant features in the environment. This position would be supported by the research on perceptual constancies and the invariance of form and face. However, it is difficult to extract from the Gibsonian view the precise ages when different perceptual abilities should appear. Salapatek (1975) interprets the theory as predicting neonatal organization of simple shapes and immediate perceptual constancy with three-dimensional objects. Neither prediction is supported by the evidence.

Finally, Piaget's theory agrees with the late development of perceptual constancies, but his theory stresses a much more active role of motor behavior in perception than would seem to be indicated by the evidence for early perceptual organization of colors and forms.

Despite the absence of a viable, global theory, the area of infant visual perception has made continual progress. Most new experiments tend to confirm and extend the results of earlier ones rather than contradict them. We know that neither a strict nativist nor a strict empiricist position is correct. The infant's perceptual abilities gradually develop throughout the 1st year of life. Much is already known about the nature of that development, and we are optimistic that much more will be learned in the near future as researchers continue to explore the visual world of the infant.

BIBLIOGRAPHY

Acredelo, L. P. The development of spatial orientation in infancy. *Child Development,* 1977.

Ahrens, R. Beitrage zur Entwicklung des Physiognomie-und Mimikerkennes. *Zeitschrift fur Experimentelle und Angewandte Psychologie,* 1954, 412–454, 599–633.

Alpern, M. Muscular mechanism. In H. Davson (ed.) *The Eye,* Vol. 3. New York: Academic, 1962.

Amigo, G. Visuo-sensory development of the child. *American Journal of Optometry and Archives of American Academy of Optometry,* 1972, **49** (12), 991–1001.

Aslin, R. N., and Salapatek, P. Saccadic localization of peripheral targets by the very young human infant. *Perception and Psychophysics,* 1975, **17,** 292–302.

Bergman, T., Haith, M. M., and Mann, L. Development of eye contact and facial scanning in infants. Paper presented at the meeting of the Society for Research in Child Development, Minneapolis, 1971.

Berlyne, D. E. The influence of the albedo and complexity of stimuli on visual fixation in the human infant. *British Journal of Psychology,* 1958, **49,** 315–318.

Blakemore, C., and Cooper, G. F. Development of the brain depends on the visual environment. *Nature,* 1970, **228,** 447–478.

Bond, E. K. Perception of form by the human infant. *Psychological Bulletin,* 1972, **77,** 225–245.

Bornstein, M. H. Infants are trichromats. *Journal of Experimental Child Psychology,* 1976, **21,** 425–445.

Bornstein, M. H., Kessen, W., and Weiskopf, S. The categories of hue in infancy. *Science,* 1976, **191,** 201–202.

Bower, T. G. R. Discrimination of depth in premotor infants. *Psychonomic Science,* 1964, **1,** 368.

Bower, T. G. R. Heterogeneous summation in human infants. *Animal Behaviour,* 1966a, **14,** 395–398.

Bower, T. G. R. The visual world of infants. *Scientific American,* 1966b, **215,** 80–72.

Bower, T. G. R. Slant perception and shape constancy in infants. *Science,* 1966c, **151,** 832–834.

Bower, T. G. R. The development of object permanence: Some studies of existence constancy. *Perception and Psychophysics,* 1967, **2,** 411–418.

Bower, T. G. R. *Development in Infancy,* San Francisco: Freeman, Company, 1974.

Bowlby, J. The nature of the child's tie to his mother. *International Journal of Psychoanalysis,* 1958, **39,** 350–373.

Boynton, R. M., and Gordon, J. Bezold-Brucke hue shift measured by color-naming technique. *Journal of the Optical Society of America,* 1965, **49,** 654–666.

Bremner, J. G., and Briant, P. E. Place versus response as the basis of spatial errors made by young infants. *Journal of Experimental Child Psychology,* 1977, **23,** 162–171.

Brennan, W. M., Ames, E. W., and Moore, R. W. Age differences in infants' attention to patterns of different complexities. *Science,* 1966, **151,** 354–356.

Bronson, G. W. The postnatal growth of visual capacity. *Child Development,* 1974, **45,** 873–890.

Browne, G. Y. Discrimination of normative facial expressions by 12-week-old infants. Paper presented at the meeting of the Society for Research in Child Development, Denver, 1975.

Campos, J. Heart rate: A sensitive tool for the study of emotional development. In L. Lipsitt (ed.), *Psychobiology: The Significance of Infancy.* Washington, D.C.: Erlbaum, 1976.

Caron, A. J., Caron, R. F., Caldwell, R. C., and Weiss, S. Infant perception of the structural properties of the face. *Developmental Psychology,* 1973, **9** (3), 385–399.

Caron, A. J., Caron, R. F., and Carleson, V. R. Do infants see objects or retinal images? Shape constancy revisited. Paper presented at the meeting of the Society for Research in Child Development, New Orleans, March 1977.

Carpenter, G. C., Tecce, J. J., Stechler, G., and Friedman, S. Differential visual behavior to human and humanoid faces in early infancy. *Merrill-Palmer Quarterly,* 1968, **14,** 25–46.

Charlesworth, W. R. The role of surprise in cognitive development. In D. Elkind and J. H. Flavell (eds.), *Studies in Cognitive Development: Essays in Honor of Jean Piaget.* New York: Oxford University, 1969, 257–314.

Chase, W. P. Color vision in infants. *Journal of Experimental Psychology,* 1937, **20,** 203–222.

Cohen, L. B. Observing responses, visual preferences, and habituation to visual stimuli in infants. *Journal of Experimental Child Psychology,* 1969, **7,** 419–433.

Cohen, L. B. Attention-getting and attention-holding processes of infant visual preferences. *Child Development,* 1972, **43,** 869–879.

Cohen, L. B. Habituation of infant visual attention. In T. J. Tighe and R. N. Leaton (eds.), *Habituation: Perspectives from Child Development, Animal Behavior, and Neurophysiology.* Hillsdale, N.J.: Erlbaum, 1976.

Cohen, L. B. Concept acquisition in the human infant. Paper presented at the meeting of the Society for Research in Child Development, New Orleans 1977.

Cohen, L. B., DeLoache, J. S., and Pearl, R. An examination of interference effects in infants' memory for faces. *Child Development,* 1977, **48,** 88–96.

Cohen, L. B., DeLoache, J. S., and Rissman, M. W. The effect of stimulus complexity on infant visual attention and habituation. *Child Development,* 1975, **46,** 611–617.

Cohen, L. B., and Gelber, E. R. Infant visual memory. In L. Cohen and P. Salapatek (eds.), *Infant Perception: From Sensation to Cognition: Basic Visual Processes,* Vol. 1. New York: Academic, 1975, 347–403.

Cohen, L. B., Gelber, E. R., and Lazar, M. A. Infant habituation and generalization to differing degrees of stimulus novelty. *Journal of Experimental Child Psychology,* 1971, **11,** 379–389.

Cohen, L. B., and Salapatek, P. (eds.). *Infant Perception: From Sensation to Cognition: Basic Visual Processes,* Vol. 1. New York: Academic, 1975a.

Cohen, L. B., and Salapatek, P. (eds.). *Infant Perception: From Sensation to Cognition: Perception of Space, Speech, and Sound,* Vol. 2. New York: Academic, 1975b.

Conel, J. L. *The Postnatal Development of the Human Cerebral Cortex,* Vol. 1. *The Cortex of the New Born.* Cambridge, Mass.: Harvard University, 1939.

Conel, J. L. *The Postnatal Development of the Human,* Vol. 2. *The Cortex of the One-Month-Old Infant.* Cambridge, Mass.: Harvard University, 1941.

Conel, J. L. *The Postnatal Development of the Human Cerebral Cortex,* Vol. 3. *The Cortex of the Three-Month Infant.* Cambridge, Mass.: Harvard University, 1947.

Conel, J. L. *The Postnatal Development of the Human Cerebral Cortex,* Vol. 4. *The Cortex of the Six-Month Infant.* Cambridge, Mass.: Harvard University Press, 1951.

Conel, J. L. *The Postnatal Development of the Human Cerebral Cortex,* Vol. 5. *The Cortex of the Fifteen-Month Infant.* Cambridge, Mass.: Harvard University, 1955.

Conel, J. L. *The Postnatal Development of the Human Cerebral Cortex,* Vol. 6. *The Cortex of the Twenty-Four-Month Infant.* Cambridge, Mass.: Harvard University, 1959.

Cooper, G. F., and Robson, J. G. The yellow colour of the lens of man and other primates. *Journal of Physiology* (London), 1969, **203,** 411–417.

Cornell, E. H. Infants' discrimination of faces following redundant presentations. *Journal of Experimental Child Psychology,* 1974, **18,** 98–106.

Cornell, E. H. Infants' visual attention to pattern arrangement and orientation. *Child Development,* 1975, **46,** 229–232.

Cornell, E. H., and Strauss, M. S. Infants' responsiveness to compounds of habituated visual stimuli. *Developmental Psychology,* 1973, **9** (1), 73–78.

Day, M. C. Developmental trends in visual scanning. In H. W. Reese (ed.), *Advances in Child Development and Behavior,* Vol. 10. New York: Academic, 1975.

Day, R. H., and McKenzie, B. E. Perceptual shape constancy in early infancy. *Perception,* 1973, **2,** 315–320.

Day, R. H., and McKenzie, B. E. Constancies in the perceptual world of the infant. In W. Epstein (ed.), *Stability and Constancy in Visual Perception. Mechanisms and Processes.* New York: Wiley, 1977.

Dayton, G., Jones, M., Aiu, P., Rawson, R., Steele, B., and Rose, M. Developmental study of coordinated eye movements in the human infant: I. Visual acuity in the newborn human: A study based on induced optokinetic nystagmus recorded by electro-oculography. *Archives of Opthalmology,* 1964, **71,** 865–870.

DeLoache, J. S., Rissman, M. D., and Cohen, L. B. An investigation of the attention-getting process in infants. *Infant Behavior and Development,* 1978, **1,** 11–25.

Dember, W., and Earl, R. Analysis of exploratory, manipulatory, and curiosity behavior. *Psychological Review,* 1957, **64,** 91–96.

Dirks, J., and Gibson, E. Infants' perception of similiarity between live people and their photographs. *Child Development,* 1977, **48,** 124–130.

Dobson, M. V. Spectral sensitivity of the two-month infant as measured by the visually evoked cortical potential. Unpublished Ph.D. thesis, Brown University, 1975.

Donnee, L. H. Infants' developmental scanning patterns to face and nonface stimuli under various auditory conditions. Paper presented at the meeting of the Society for Research in Child Development, Philadelphia, 1973.

Duke-Elder, S., and Cook, C. *Systems of Ophthalmology,* Vol. III. St. Louis: Mosby, 1963.

Fagan, J. F. Infants' recognition memory for faces. *Journal of Experimental Child Psychology,* 1972, **14,** 453–456.

Fagan, J. F. Infant color perception. *Science,* 1974, **183,** 973–975.

Fagan, J. F. Infants' recognition of invariant features of faces. *Child Development,* 1976, **47,** 627–638.

Fagan, J. F. An attention model of infant recognition. *Child Development,* 1977, **48,** 345–359.

Fantz, R. L. Pattern vision in young infants. *Psychological Record,* 1958, **8,** 43–49.

Fantz, R. L. The origin of form perception. *Scientific American,* 1961, **204,** 66–72.

Fantz, R. L. Pattern vision in newborn infants. *Science,* 1963, **140,** 296–297.

Fantz, R. L. Visual perception from birth as shown by pattern selectivity. In H. E. Whipple (ed.), *New Issues in Infant Development, Annals of the New York Academy of Science,* 1965, **118,** 793–814.

Fantz, R. L. Visual perception and experience in early infancy: A look at the hidden side of behavior development. In H. W. Stevenson, E. H. Hess, and H. L. Rheingold (eds.), *Early Behavior: Comparative and Developmental Approaches.* New York: Wiley, 1967, 181–224.

Fantz, R. L., and Fagan, J. F. Visual attention to size and number of pattern details by term and preterm infants during the first six months. *Child Development,* 1975, **16,** 3–18.

Fantz, R., Fagan, J., and Miranda, S. Early visual selectivity. In L. Cohen and P. Salapatek (eds.), *Infant Perception: From Sensation to Cognition: Basic Visual Processes,* Vol. 1. New York: Academic, 1975, 249–341.

Fantz, R. L., and Miranda, S. B. Newborn infant attention to form of contour. *Child Development,* 1975, **46,** 224–228.

Fantz, R. L., and Nevis, S. Pattern preferences and perceptual-cognitive development in early infancy. *Merrill-Palmer Quarterly,* 1967, **13,** 77–108.

Fantz, R. L., Ordy, J. M., and Udelf, M. S. Maturation of pattern vision in infants during the first six months. *Journal of Comparative and Physiological Psychology,* 1962, **55,** 907–917.

Freedman, D. G. *Human Infancy: An evolutionary perspective.* Hillsdale, N.J.: Erlbaum, 1974.

von Frisch, K. *Bees: Their Vision, Chemical Senses, and Language.* Ithaca, N.Y.: Cornell University, 1950.

Gibson, E. J. *Principles of Perceptual Learning and Development.* New York: Appleton-Century-Crofts, 1969.

Goren, C. Form perception, innate form preferences and visually-mediated head turning in human newborns. Paper presented at the meeting of the Society for Research in Child Development, Denver, 1975.

Gorman, J., Cogan, D., and Gellis, S. An apparatus for grading the visual acuity of infants on the basis of opticokinetic nystagmus. *Pediatrics,* 1957, **19,** 1088–1092.

Gorman, J., Cogan, D., and Gellis, S. A device for testing visual acuity in infants. *Sight Saving Review,* 1959, **29,** 80–84.

Greenberg, D. J. Accelerating visual complexity levels in the human infant. *Child Development,* 1971, **42,** 905–918.

Greenberg, D. J., and O'Donnell, W. J. Infancy and the optimal level of stimulation. *Child Development,* 1972, **43,** 639–645.

Greenberg, D. J., O'Donnell, W., and Crawford, D. Complexity levels, habituation, and individual differences in early infancy. *Child Development,* 1973, **44** (3), 569.

Haaf, R. A. Complexity and facial resemblance as determinants of response to face-like stimuli by 5 and 10 week old infants. *Journal of Experimental Child Psychology,* 1974, **18,** 480–487.

Haaf, R. A., and Bell, R. Q. The facial dimension in visual discrimination by human infants. *Child Development,* 1967, **38,** 893–899.

Haith, M. M. The response of the human newborn to visual movement. *Journal of Experimental Child Psychology,* 1966, **3,** 235–243.

Haith, M. M. Organization of visual behavior at birth. Paper presented in a symposium on Perception in Infancy at the XXIst International Congress of Psychology Meetings, Paris, July 1976.

Haith, M. M. Visual competence in early infancy. In R. H. Held, H. Leibowitz, and H. L. Teuber (eds.), *Handbook of Sensory Physiology (VIII).* Berlin: Springer-Verlag, in press.

Haith, M. M., and Campos, J. J. Human infancy. *Annual Review of Psychology, Vol. 28,* Palo Alto, Calif.: Annuals Reviews, 1977.

Haith, M. M., Kessen, W., and Collins, D. Response of the human infant to level of complexity of intermittent visual movement. *Journal of Experimental Child Psychology,* 1969, **7,** 52–69.

Harris, P., and MacFarlane, A. The growth of the effective visual field from birth to seven weeks. *Journal of Experimental Child Psychology,* 1974, **18,** 340–348.

Harter, M. R., and Suitt, C. D. Visually-evoked cortical responses and pattern vision in the infant: A longitudinal study. *Psychonomic Science,* 1970, **18,** 235–237.

Harter, M. R., and White, C. T. Effects of contour sharpness and check-size on visually evoked cortical potentials. *Vision Research,* 1968, **8,** 701–711.

Harter, M. R., and White, C. T. Evoked cortical response to checkerboard patterns; Effect of check-size as a function of visual acuity. *Electroencephalography and Clinical Neurophysiology,* 1970, **28,** 48–54.

Haynes, H., White, B. L., and Held, R. Visual accommodation in human infants. *Science,* 1965, **148,** 528–530.

Hershenson, M. Visual discrimination in the human newborn. *Journal of Comparative and Physiological Psychology,* 1964, **58,** 270–276.

Hershenson, M. Development of the perception of form. *Psychological Bulletin,* 1967, **66,** 326–336.

Hershenson, M., Munsinger, H., and Kessen W. Preference for shapes of intermediate variability in the newborn human. *Science,* 1965, **147,** 630–631.

Hirsch, H. V. B., and Spinelli, D. N. Visual experience modifies distribution of horizontally and vertically oriented receptive fields in cats. *Science,* 1970, **168,** 869–871.

Holden, W. A., and Bosse, K. K. The order of development of color perception and color preference in the child. *Archives of Ophthalmology,* 1900, **29,** 261–277.

Horsten, G. P., and Winkelman, J. E. Electrical activity of the retina in relation to histological differentiation in infants born prematurely and at full term. *Vision Research,* 1962, **2,** 269–276.

Horsten, G., and Winkelman, J. Electro-retinographic critical fusion frequency of the retina in relation to the histological development in man and animals. *Documenta Ophthalmologica,* 1964, **18,** 515–521.

Hubel, D. H., and Weisel, T. N. Receptive fields of single neurones in the cat's striate cortex. *Journal of Physiology* (London), 1959, **148,** 574–591.

Hubel, D. H., and Weisel, T. N. Receptive fields of cells in striate cortex of very young visually inexperienced kittens. *Journal of Neurophysiology,* 1963, **26,** 994–1002.

Hubel, D. H., and Weisel, T. N. Receptive fields and functional architecture of monkey striate cortex. *Journal of Physiology* (London), 1968, **195,** 215–243.

Hunt, J. McV. Intrinsic motivation and its role in psychological development. *Nebraska Symposium on Motivation,* 1965, **14,** 189–282.

Kagan, J. The growth of the "face" schema: Theoretical significance and methodological issues. In J. Hellmuth (ed.), *The Exceptional Infant,* Vol. 1. *The Normal Infant.* New York: Brunner/ Mazel, 1967.

Kagan, J., Henker, B. A., Hen-Tov, A., and Lewis, M. Infants' differential reactions to familiar and distorted faces. *Child Development,* 1966, **37,** 519–532.

Kagan, J., and Lewis, M. Studies of attention in the human infant. *Merrill-Palmer Quarterly,* 1965, **11,** 95–127.

Karmel, B. Z. Complexity, amount of contour, and visually dependent preference behavior in hooded rats, domestic chicks, and human infants. *Journal of Comparative and Physiological Psychology,* 1969a, **69,** 649–657.

Karmel, B. Z. The effect of age, complexity, and amount of contour on pattern preferences in human infants. *Journal of Experimental Child Psychology,* 1969b, **7,** 339–354.

Karmel, B. Z., Hoffman, R. F., and Fegy, M. J. Processing of contour information by human infants evidenced by pattern-dependent potentials. *Child Development,* 1974, **45,** 39–48.

Karmel, B. Z., and Maisel, E. B. A neuronal activity model for infant visual attention. In L. B. Cohen and P. Salapatek (eds.), *Infant Perception: From Sensation to Cognition: Basic Visual Processes,* Vol. 1, New York: Academic, 1975.

Kessen, W., Haith, M., and Salapatek, P. H. Human infancy: A bibliography and guide. In P. H. Mussen (ed.), *Carmichael's Manual of Child Psychology,* Vol. I. New York: Wiley, 1970, 287–445.

Kessen, W., Salapatek, P., and Haith, M. The visual response of the human newborn to linear contour. *Journal of Experimental Child Psychology,* 1972, **13,** 9–20.

Kiff, R. D., and Lepard, C. Visual response of premature infants. *Archives of Ophthalmology,* 1966, **75,** 631–633.

Kreutzer, M. A., and Charlesworth, W. R. Infants' reactions to different expressions of emotions. Paper presented at the meeting of the Society for Research in Child Development, Philadelphia, March 1973.

LaBarbera, J. D., Izard, C. E., Vietze, P., and Parisi, S. A. Four- and six-month-old infants' visual responses to joy, anger, and neutral expressions. *Child Development,* 1976, **47**(2), 535–538.

Last, P. *Eugene Wolff's Anatomy of the Eye and Orbit.* London: Lewis, 1968.

Leehey, S. C., Moskowitz-Cook, A., Brill, S., and Held, R. Orientational anistropy in infant vision. *Science,* 1975, **190**(4217), 900–902.

Lewis, M. Infants' responses to facial stimuli during the first year of life. *Developmental Psychology,* 1969, **2,** 75–86.

Lewis, M., Kagan, J., Campbell, H., and Kalafat, G. The cardiac response as a correlate of attention in infants. *Child Development,* 1966, **37,** 63–71.

Lewis, T. L., and Maurer, D. Newborns' central vision: Whole or hole? Paper presented at the meeting of the Society for Research in Child Development, New Orleans, March 1977.

Luria, S. M., and Strauss, M. S. Eye movements during search for coded and uncoded targets. *Perception and Psychophysics,* 1975, **17,** 303–308.

MacFarlane, A., Harris, P., and Barnes, I. Central and peripheral vision in early infancy. *Journal of Experimental Child Psychology,* 1976, **21**(3), 532–538.

Mandler, J. M., and Day, J. Memory for orientation of forms as a function of their meaningfulness and complexity. *Journal of Experimental Child Psychology,* 1975, **20,** 430–443.

Mann, I. *The Development of the Human Eye.* London: British Medical Association, 1964.

Marsden, R. W. A study of the early color sense. *Psychological Review,* 1903a, **10,** 37–47.

Marsden, R. W. The early color sense—further experiments. *Psychological Review,* 1903b, **10,** 297–300.

Maurer, D. Infant visual perception: Methods of study. In L. B. Cohen and P. Salapatek (eds.), *Infant Perception: From Sensation to Cognition: Basic Visual Processes,* Vol. 1. New York: Academic, 1975, 1–76.

Maurer, D., and Lewis, T. L. What the infant sees from the corner of his eye. Paper presented at the meeting of the Society for Research in Child Development, New Orleans, March 1977.

Maurer, D., and Salapatek, P. Developmental changes in the scanning of faces by young infants. *Child Development,* 1976, **47,** 523–527.

McCall, R. B. Attention in the infant: Avenue to the study of cognitive development. In D. Walcher and D. Peters (eds.), *Early Childhood: The Development of Self-Regulatory Mechanisms.* New York: Academic, 1971, 107–137.

McCall, R. B., Hogarty, P. S., Hamilton, J. S., and Vincent, J. H. Habituation rate and the infant's response to visual discrepancies. *Child Development,* 1973, **44,** 280–287.

McCall, R. B., and McGhee, P. E. The discrepancy hypothesis of attention and affect in infants. In F. Weizmann and I. C. Uzgiris (eds.), *The Structuring of Experience.* New York: Plenum, 1977.

McClelland, D. C., and Clark, R. A. Antecedent conditions for affective arousal. In D. C. McClelland, J. W. Atkinson, R. A. Clark, and E. L. Lowell (eds.), *The Achievement Motive*. New York: Appleton-Century-Crofts, 1953.

McGurk, H. The role of object orientation in infant perception. *Journal of Experimental Child Psychology*, 1970, **9**, 363–373.

McGurk, H. Infant discrimination of orientation. *Journal of Experimental Child Psychology*, 1972, **14**, 151–164.

McKenzie, B. E., and Day, R. H. Distance as a determinant of visual fixation in early infancy. *Science*, 1972, **178**, 1108–1110.

Milewski, A. E. Infants' discrimination of internal and external pattern elements. *Journal of Experimental Child Psychology*, 1976, **22**, 229–246.

Milewski, A., and Siqueland, E. R. Discrimination of color and pattern novelty in one-month human infants. *Journal of Experimental Child Psychology*, 1975, **19**, 122–126.

Miller, D. J. Visual habituation in the human infant. *Child Development*, 1972, **43**, 481–493.

Miller, D. J., Ryan, E. B., Sinnott, J. P., and Wilson, M. A. Serial habituation in two-, three-, and four-month-old infants. *Child Development*, 1976, **47**, 341–349.

Miller, D. J., Sinnott, J. P., Short, E. J., and Hains, A. A. Individual differences in habituation rates and object concept performance. *Child Development*, 1976, **47**, 528–531.

Miranda, S. B. Visual abilities and pattern preferences of premature infants and full-term neonates. *Journal of Experimental Child Psychology*, 1970, **10**, 189.

Miranda, S. B., and Fantz, R. L. Distribution of visual attention of newborn infants among patterns varying in size and number of details. *Proceedings*, American Psychological Association, Washington, D.C., 1971.

Miranda, S. B., and Fantz, R. L. Recognition memory in Down's Syndrome and normal infants. *Child Development*, 1974, **45**, 651–660.

Munn, N. L. *The Evolution and Growth of Human Behavior*, 2nd ed. Boston: Houghton-Mifflin, 1965.

Munsinger, H., and Banks, M. S. Pupillometry as a measure of visual sensitivity among infants, young children, and adults. *Developmental Psychology*, 1974, **10**, 677–682.

Olson, G. M. An information-processing analysis of visual memory and habituation in infants. In T. J. Tighe and R. N. Leaton (eds), *Habituation: Perspectives from Child Development, Animal Behavior, and Neurophysiology*. Hillsdale, N.J.: Erlbaum, 1976.

Ordy, J. M., Samorajski, T., Collins, R. L., and Nagy, A. R. Postnatal development of vision in a subhuman primate (Macacca Mulatta). *Archives of Opthalmology*, 1965, **73**, 674–686.

Oster, H. S. Color perception in ten-week-old infants. Paper presented at the biennial meeting of the Society for Research in Child Development, Denver, 1975.

Pancratz, C. N., and Cohen, L. B. Recovery of habituation in infants. *Journal of Experimental Child Psychology*, 1970, **9**, 208–216.

Parmelee, A. H., and Sigman, M. Development of visual behavior and neurological organization in pre-term and full-term infants. In A. D. Pick (ed.), *Minnesota Symposia on Child Psychology*, Vol. 10. Minneapolis: University of Minnesota, 1976.

Peiper, A. *Cerebral Function in Infancy and Childhood*. New York: Consultants Bureau, 1963.

Pettigrew, J. D., and Freeman, R. D. Visual experience without lines: Effect on developing cortical neurons. *Science*, 1973, **182**, 599–601.

Polak, P. R., Emde, R. N., and Spitz, R. A. The smiling response to the human face. I. Methodology, quantification, and natural history. *Journal of Nervous and Mental Disorders*, 1964a, **139**, 103–109.

Polak, P. R., Emde, R. M., and Spitz. R. A. The smiling response to the human face. II. Visual discrimination and the onset of depth perception. *Journal of Nervous and Mental Disorders,* 1964b, **139,** 407–415.

Preyer, W. *The Mind of the Child. Part I. The Senses and the Will.* New York: Appleton, 1888. (Translation of W. Preyer, *Die Seek des Kindes.*)

Ruddock, K. H. Light transmission through the ocular media and macielar pigment and its significance for psychological investigation. In D. Jameson and L. M. Hurvich (eds.), *Handbook of Sensory Physiology,* Vol. VII/4. *Visual Psychophysics.* New York: Springer-Verlag, 1972, 455–469.

Rabinowicz, T. The cerebral cortex of the premature infant of the eighth month. *Progress in Brain Research,* 1964, **4,** 39–92.

Ruff, H. A. The function of shifting fixations in the visual perception of infants. *Child Development,* 1975, **46,** 857–865.

Ruff, H. A. Developmental changes in the infant's attention to pattern detail. *Perceptual and Motor Skills,* 1976, **43,** 351–358.

Ruff, H. A. The role of stimulus variability in infant perceptual learning. Paper presented at the meeting of the Society for Research in Child Development, New Orleans, March, 1977a.

Ruff, H. A. The development of form perception in human infants. Unpublished paper, 1977b.

Ruff, H. A., and Birch, H. G. Infant visual fixation: The effects of concentricity, curvilinearity, and number of directions. *Journal of Experimental Child Psychology,* 1974, **17,** 460–473.

Salapatek, P. Visual scanning of geometric figures by the human newborn. *Journal of Comparative and Physiological Psychology,* 1968, **66,** 247–258.

Salapatek, P. Pattern perception in early infancy. In L. B. Cohen and P. Salapatek (eds.), *Infant Perception: From Sensation to Cognition: Basis Visual Processes,* Vol. 1. New York: Academic, 1975.

Salapatek, P., Bechtold, A. G., and Bushnell, E. W. Infant visual acuity as a function of viewing distance. *Child Development,* 1976, **47,** 860–863.

Salapatek, P., Haith, M., Maurer, D., and Kessen, W. Error in the corneal-reflection technique: A note on Slater & Findlay. *Journal of Experimental Child Psychology,* 1972, **14,** 493.

Salapatek, P., and Kessen, W. Visual scanning of triangles by the human newborn. *Journal of Experimental Child Psychology,* 1966, **3,** 155–167.

Salapatek, P., and Kessen, W. Prolonged investigation of a plane geometric triangle by the human newborn. *Journal of Experimental Child Psychology,* 1973, **15,** 22.

Schaller, M. J. Chromatic vision in human infants: Conditioned fixation to 'Hues' of varying intensity. Paper presented at the meeting of the Society for Research in Child Development, Denver, April 1975.

Schwartz, M. Visual shape perception in early infancy. Unpublished Ph.D. thesis, Monash University, 1975.

Siqueland, E., and DeLucia, C. A. Visual reinforcement of nonnutritive sucking in human infants. *Science,* 1969, **165,** 1144–1146.

Slater, A. M., and Findlay, J. M. The corneal reflection technique: A reply to Salapatek, Haith, Maurer, & Kessen. *Journal of Experimental Child Psychology,* 1972, **14,** 497.

Spears, W. C. Assessment of visual preference and discrimination in the four-month-old infant. *Journal of Comparative Physiological Psychology,* 1964, **57,** 381–386.

Staples, R. Color vision and color preference in infancy and early childhood. *Psychological Bulletin,* 1932, **28,** 297–308.

Stechler, G. Newborn attention as affected by medication during labor. *Science,* 1964, **144,** 315–317.

Strauss, M. S., and Cohen, L. B. Infant immediate and delayed memory of perceptual dimensions. Unpublished paper, 1977.

Strauss, M. S., DeLoache, J. S., and Maynard, J. Infants' recognition of pictorial representations of real objects. Paper presented at the meeting of the Society for Research in Child Development, New Orleans, March 1977.

Teller, D. Y. A visual psychophysicist turns to infants. Paper presented at the meeting of the Society for Research in Child Development, Philadelphia, March 1973.

Teller, D., Morse, R., Borton, D., and Regal, D. Visual acuity for vertical and diagonal gratings in human infants. *Vision Research,* 1974, **14,** 14–33.

Teller, D. Y., and Peeples, D. Grating acuity and color sensitivity in infants. Paper presented at the meeting of the Association for Research in Vision and Ophthamology, Sarasota, April 1974.

Thomas, H. Visual fixation responses of infants to stimuli of varying complexity. *Child Development,* 1965, **36,** 629–638.

Thomas, H. Discrepancy hypotheses: Methodological and theoretical considerations. *Psychological Review,* 1971, **78,** 249–259.

Thomas, H. Unfolding the baby's mind: The infant's selection of visual stimuli. *Psychological Review,* 1973, **80**(6), 468.

Thomas, H., and Jones-Molfese, V. Infants and I Scales: Inferring change from the ordinal stimulus selections of infants for configural stimuli. *Journal of Experimental Child Psychology,* 1977, **23**(2), 329–339.

Trincker, D., and Trincker, I. Development of brightness vision in infants. In Y. Brackbill and G. G. Thompson (eds.), *Behavior in Infancy and Early Childhood.* New York: Free Press, 1967.

Tronick, E. Stimulus control and the growth of the infant's effective visual field. *Perception and Psychophysics,* 1972, **11,** 373–375.

Valentine, C. W. The colour perception and colour preferences of an infant during its fourth and eighth months. *British Journal of Psychology,* 1913–1914, **6,** 363–386.

Verly, R. Essai sur les criteres electrophysiologiques qui permettraient de comparer entre elles les evolutions de diverses especes, en pariuclier de l'homme. In S. R. Berenberg, M. Caniaris, and N. P. Masse (eds.), *Pre- and Postnatal Development of the Human Brain,* Vol. 13. Basel: Karger, 1974.

Vurpillot, E., Ruel, J., and Castrec, A. L'organisation perceptive chez le nourrisson: Reponse au tout ou à ses éléments. *Bulletin de Psychologie,* 1977, **327,** 396–405.

Watson, J. Perception of object orientation in infants. *Merrill-Palmer Quarterly,* 1966, **12,** 73–94.

Wetherford, M. J., and Cohen, L. B. Developmental changes in infant visual preferences for novelty and familiarity. *Child Development,* 1973, **44,** 416–424.

White, B. L. *Human Infants.* Englewood Cliffs, N.J.: Prentice-Hall, 1971.

White, C. T., White, C. L., Fawcett, W., and Socks, J. Color evoked potentials in newborns. Paper presented at the meeting of the Society for Research in Child Development, New Orleans, March 1977.

Wilcox, B. M. Visual preferences of human infants for represenations of the human face. *Journal of Experimental Child Psychology,* 1969, **7,** 10–20.

Wilcox, B. M., and Clayton, F. L. Infant visual fixation on motion pictures of the human face. *Journal of Experimental Child Psychology,* 1968, **6,** 22–32.

Williams, L. G. The effect of target specification on objects fixated during visual search. *Perception and Psychophysics,* 1966, **1,** 315–318.

Wolff, P. H. Observations on the early development of smiling. In B. M. Foss (ed.), *Determinants of Infant Behavior,* Vol. II. New York: Wiley, 1963, 113–134.

Wooten, B. R. Infant hue discrimination? *Science,* 1975, **187,** 275–277.

Yakovlev, P., and LeCours, A. The myelogenetic cycles of regional maturation of the brain. In A. Minkowski (ed.), *Regional Development of the Brain in Early Life.* Oxford: Blockwell, 1967, 3–70.

Zetterstrom, B. The clinical electroretinogram. IV. The electroretinogram in children during the first year of life. *Acta Opthalmologica,* 1951, **29,** 295–304.

Zetterstrom, B. Flicker electroretinography in newborn infants. *Acta Opthalmologica,* 1955, **33,** 157–166.

Zusne, L. *Visual Perception of Form.* New York: Academic, 1970.

CHAPTER 12

The Development of Thought and Language in Infancy*

Gerald Gratch

I think that most people would agree that infants neither think nor talk, at least on a manifest level. Therefore if we are going to study how infants develop such activities then we had best have a clear idea of what we mean by them. However, agreement on what is meant by thinking and language is hard to come by, and it will be the burden of this chapter to try to make plain what is involved in one set of ideas about thinking and language which evolved at the turn of the century and which guides much of the present study of these issues. The discussion will focus primarily on thinking rather than language for reasons that I shall describe during the course of the chapter. My aim will not be to provide the reader with a review of the current literature. That would serve no function as there are a number of able reviews that bear on the issues to be discussed—for example, Appleton et al. (1975), Bloom (1975), Bruner (1974), Gratch (1975), Haith and Campos (1977), Harris (1975a), Kessen et al. (1970), and Salapatek (1975).

In recent years, John Flavell seems to have been best able to capture for wide audiences the spirit of the set of ideas about thinking and language that will be examined here. He has excited a great many students of the field with his idea of metamemory (Flavell and Wellman 1977), and, more recently, he has announced another domain of study, metacommunication (Flavell, 1976). There are two messages inherent in Flavell's discussions. One is the importance of studying the difference between doing and knowing what you are doing. The other is that the study of metamemory and metacommunication, and such possible other fields of study as "metaperception," do not constitute separate fields of study. To investigate what a person knows about how he remembers involves communication, with other, with self, and to study what a person knows about how he communicates with others involves memory and other cognitive processes.

The first point, the difference between doing something and being aware of that activity, captures the sense in which the term thinking will be used in the present chapter. As will be discussed below, there is a long tradition that holds that most conduct, of adults as well as children, goes on unthoughtfully. Such conduct may be skilled, foresightful, empathic, and so on, but it simply involves an actor in a continuous transaction with his environment. On this view, there is another level of conduct, the thoughtful, wherein the actor steps out of the stream of activity and treats aspects of it as objects of study. The

*The preparation of this chapter was supported in part by funds from the Department of Psychology and the College of Social Sciences of the University of Houston. I want to thank my Chairman, Kenneth Laughery, and Dean, David Gottlieb, for their encouragement and support. Thanks also are due Michael Agar, Andrew Meltzoff and Alan Sroufe for their thoughtful comments.

occasions may be our asking him why he acted as he did or other obstacles that block the line of activity. Whatever the reason, the person engages in a process of symbolizing aspects of what transpired; he represents it in order to view it differently. I chanced to read the following quote and offer it as an illustration and evidence of the fact that this notion of thinking is part of our popular culture. Larry Dierker, a sore-armed veteran pitcher of the Houston Astros, had pitched a no-hitter, and his manager, Bill Virdon, praised the performance that came so late in his career by saying, "You don't have to be a bright person to pitch and win but knowing how to pitch, how to use your ability to get batters out is important. . . . And that is intelligence" [*Houston Chronicle,* 1976].

Flavell's second point, the unity among fields of analysis, highlights the centrality of the actor and the continuity between the activities of the person observed and the scientific observer. Just as the scientist analyzes people's activities into components, so do people. And it is important to not reify the analyses, to not lose sight of the fact that the categories are functional ones, created by someone for some purpose. In that same regard, Flavell's analysis emphasizes the social elements in thinking about lines of activity. The scientist has in mind the audience he will share his analyses with, and the claim is that there are similarities between the process of sharing information with others and sharing information with oneself, and that both evolve from the same developmental roots.

While such an approach as Flavell's has been around for a long time, it has seldom captured the sustained interest of American psychologists. However, present infancy studies are dominated by themes inherent in such an approach. On the one hand, the study of the development of thinking is keyed to Piaget's ideas and observations. On the other hand, the study of language development has shifted from a focus on how the "instrument" is acquired to issues of meaning as captured by such terms as semantics, speech acts, and pre-linguistic communication. These themes are not well articulated at present, and their explication and articulation seems to be the main activity of inquiry, in at least the near future. In important part, the current lack of relatedness of these themes, seems to stem from the preeminence of Piaget's position, one that does not place either language or social communication at the core of the development of thinking. These themes were more closely related at the turn of the century. That time contained the roots of Piaget's ideas as well as those ideas developed at Clark University by Werner and his associates (e.g., Werner and Kaplan, 1963), which form the background of Flavell's investigations. To give you a guide to these ideas, I shall begin by focusing on one of the turn-of-the-century figures, George Herbert Mead (1934). Rightly or wrongly, Mead attempted to account for the development of the thinker and his thoughts in terms of the infant's social matrix.

THEORETICAL POSITIONS

George Herbert Mead

At present, we are witnessing a widespread return to late 19th century attempts to account for complex social organizations and higher mental processes in terms of the idea of evolution, sociobiology being one vigourous exemplar (e.g., Wilson, 1975; Campbell, 1975). Mead, like many other thinkers of the turn of the century, was captured by the idea of accounting for the existence of the mind and social life in terms of its emergence from a biological process. Further, like Durkheim (1933), he was preoccupied with understanding community and its disruption by industrialization and nationalism. He turned to social psychology as a basis for getting perspective on the nature of the group and the relation of the individual to it. His approach was to explain how individuality developed out of group life. His approach was behavioristic, but his behaviorism was not the strong form advocated by Watson. He believed that there are thoughts and feelings and group norms, and their presence or absence can be inferred on the basis of how creatures act. He believed the actor learns about his own mental processes in comparable terms. For example, he learns how to identify when he is angry because such acts are treated as such by others, and he in turn learns to attend to aspects of his angry act and its consequences and thereby knows his feeling.

Mead saw the infant as an active, unreflective creature who was embedded in a social context. The infant's caretakers and nature set the stages upon which he acts. The infant, a creature with impulses and selective sensitivities, does not know his own impulses and abilities. Rather he is only aware of things as they bear on the completion of his line of activity—that is, he knows things in a functional and context-bound manner. For Mead, this did not mean that the infant is a solipsist. Rather, he assumed that there were features of things that the infant could selectively know, "affordances." Through the course of his transactions with things, both the infant's acts and the aspects of things he is attuned to would change. In this, Mead shares a view of the perceptual process which, in recent years, J. J. Gibson (1966) has been explicating, one that holds that there are describable properties in things that correspond to each level of adaptive perception.

Mind arises out of the infant's transactions and is present when the infant achieves a means of stepping out of the flow of conduct. When selected aspects of the process become focal, when they become objects of attention as such, then they are no longer sensed only in relation to the line of activity. With the ability to attend to events as relevant to various possible lines of activity, the infant can control his conduct; the stage is no longer set by the larger context alone. Thus, putting things in perspective was Mead's metaphor for thought, and he viewed such perspective-taking in communicative terms. The infant contacted the world in the context of a social field, and Mead believed that through taking the role of the "other"—person or thing or larger setting—the child would come to construct ideas of thing, self, and society. In particular, Mead believed that, in the words of Morris, "Language, in the form of the vocal gesture, provides the mechanism for their emergence [Mead, 1934, p. xiv].

To capture the development of the active child, Mead proposed three levels of activity or "communication." The first, what Piaget has called the sensorimotor, involved a course of relatively momentary mutual regulations between the actor and those persons and things that bore on his line of activity. As indicated earlier, the meanings of things at this level are determined by how things bear on the completion of situationally specific acts.

Mead used the metaphor of "the conversation of gestures" to describe the second level of activity. He had in mind such events as a dog fight, fencers, and a mother and infant in a caretaking encounter. In the heat of such encounters, at least once they are launched, it seldom makes sense to talk of thinking and planning because the quickness of the mutual adjustments rules out thought in the sense we have been discussing. How then to account for the seeming intentionality and intelligence that often is displayed? Mead's answer was to note that acts occur on a time line, that acts unfold in phases. One may react to an early phase of the act. One need not wait for the dog to bite to know that raised hackles and bared teeth indicate that consequence. The latter are the early phases of the attack. If the other dog reacts to the early phases of the act then we may talk of a response to a gesture.

Both dogs are simply acting, and we can account for the elaborate series of moves and countermoves without invoking consciousness, planfulness, and so on.

In talking about gestures, Mead did not impute to the initial actor any intention to make a gesture. The dog is attacking, not feinting. It is the other who gives the gesture meaning by his reponse to it. When others respond to the early phases of the acts, then new acts are created. Mead saw in these new acts, the partial completions of acts and their consequences, the basis of mind, the third level of activity. When the infant can know the meaning of his act before he has carried it out in its entirety, can react to the early phases of his act as does the other, then the infant has the basis for stepping out of the stream of conduct. Gestures provide a basis for acting toward things variously, and that in turn provides the basis for developing voluntary control of the gestures. With such voluntary control, the infant has a basis for analyzing events. Control over conduct is achieved by voluntary selective attention to events.

This is what you are doing when you act in a rational fashion: you are indicating to yourself what the stimuli are that will call out a complex response, and by the order of stimuli you are determining what the whole response will be. . . . We can directly control the sensory but not the motor process; we can give our attention to a particular element in the field and by giving such attention and so holding on to the stimulus we can get control of the response.'' [Mead, 1934, p. 94]

Mead believed that there could be various indicators, "whether one points with his finger or points with the glance of the eye, or motion of the head, or the attitude of the body, or by means of a vocal gesture in one language or another is indifferent. . . .'' [1934, p. 97]. However, he attached central importance to the vocal gesture. It was through this medium that he believed mindedness emerges. He saw it as a particularly usable tool, easily separable from the flow of conduct and hence useful as an indicator of what is going on. Moreover, he saw organized language as a major vehicle through which the actor becomes aware of how significant others view him and that which he acts on, and thereby provides a basis for the child to become an individuated member of his community.

However, Mead gave a special color to language and other representational systems. This can be seen in terms of two of his influential concepts, the significant symbol and the-I-and-the-Me. Mead argued that vocal gestures become significant symbols when the speaker takes the role of the other into account. When an infant cries in an instrumental fashion, the meaning of the gesture is the response of the other—succor or not. But it is the caretaker who must contextualize the gesture, must figure out what it is the infant is crying about, and what will satisfy him. Woe betide the caretaker who expects the infant to take his situation into account. The referent of the infant's cry is not only not explicit but the cry does not take into account the attitude of the listener. When the social interaction occurs at the significant symbolic level, both the speaker and the listener attempt to deal with the issues of who is saying what about that to whom for what purpose, and the string of words only carries part of the message. Mead reserved the terms communication and language for these circumstances. In other words, Mead argued that the linguistic utterance takes on its meaning within a larger social context. With development, the actor becomes consciously aware of the relevance of ever broader contexts to his particular lines of action and communicative efforts.

Moreover, Mead held that saying something to someone is not a simple matter of putting one's ideas into words. Rather it is a constructive act. Just as the sculptor "resees'' both his medium and his intention in the course of trying to mold the material, so too does the speaker with communicative intent. One speaks to someone about something for some purpose, and therefore must tailor one's utterances to the listener and his assumed attitude. The consequences of that act determine whether one has communicated or not, and the process takes at least two parties who must work to share not only the referents of the terms but their social purpose. Thus Mead suggested that words do not "mean" in any abstract way. They mean particular things in particular contexts; they are vehicles of social action. Further, Mead believed that scientific thought was of this form—critical "conversations" with nature which could be shared with an interested audience—and ordinary thought had the same general form—namely, conversations with oneself that evolved out of conversations with others.

The-I-and-the-Me was the notion Mead used to capture the latter process, and its structural form was the concept of the self. He argued that we come to know our feelings, motives, abilities, and so on, in terms of how others react to our actions. There is a "me" when "I" can present to myself the reactions of others to me, and the self is an abstract organization of these "me's." The "me" of a transaction is clearly not solely determined by what others think. Their reactions have to be interpreted. But what is always missing from the "me" is the actor, the "I." The "I" for Mead is not just an empty term, nor is it Freud's "Id." The actor develops. The reconstructions of our activity, the "me's." lead to a different kind of actor. The impulses and selective sensitivities of the infant are not the same as those of the child, let alone the adult. The reconstructive acts of trying to say who "I" was in a particular situation or who "I" am in general never capture the "I" but they serve the function of restructuring the flow of conduct. Mead used the idea of games both to point out how a sense of oneself in an organized system gives one control of one's conduct and to suggest where the child develops a sense of larger social systems and himself as an actor therein. Mead's idea was that sustained social encounters—friendships, families, societies—have an organization involving positions and roles. Playing one's position in the light of knowledge of the other positions is what a game-player must do. To be a "solo" player is to neither be a game-player nor does it lead to effective conduct in the long run. Children and strangers have to come to learn to know things, themselves, and others within a frame of reference that includes them all, the "game." Knowing the setting of conduct gives one control over conduct in that any number of possibilities are excluded. On the other hand, to return to my earlier baseball example, to know that you are the pitcher does not determine how you will pitch; one's control over one's actions and those of others is only partial.

Mead generalized this analysis of knowing self in action—"me"—and out of particular action contexts—"self"—to words in general. Pointing to oneself, saying "I," saying "cat," and so on, all indicate something, but their meaning has a functional core. On the one hand, the meaning of the terms vary with the action context. On the other hand, they do have a meaning that can be abstracted from the various action contexts. Such meanings have to do with generalized possibilities of action by self and other with respect to objects, and come to involve physical descriptions as well as functional ones—for example, the definition of "bicycle" shifts with development from "to ride on" to indications of the features that make such a course of action possible. But again, the meanings are not "definitional" in the sense of capturing things or the "I" essentially or exhaustively. With development, our gestures, our strings of words, may point to ever finer or larger aspects of what is involved in conduct, but the meanings of these events have ever to be reconstructed. Mead saw these meanings as social. It is in coming to know how "we" give meaning to such abstractions that the social process influences thought, and Mead believed that our knowledge of "anything" was influenced by our social matrix. In the case of the infant, the influence was asymmetric and took in a limited compass. With development, the influence process becomes increasingly symmetric and refers to more encompassing events.

This rather lengthy and selective presentation of Mead's views hopefully has served to indicate a view of the nature and function of thought. I have dwelled on it even though Mead knew relatively little about infants in particular because I think it is important to know that the issues Piaget took up have a deep history and that the current developments regarding thought and language are importantly prefigured in Mead and other thinkers of his time. In other words, I think perspective on our present endeavors can help us act on them more effectively.

Jean Piaget

Piaget was influenced by the same intellectual milieu as Mead. He too set out to trace the ontogenesis of thought and group membership in the light of phylogenetic themes and saw language as playing a critical role in the process. In his early work, he played on such issues as morality, conceptions of the world, and language and thought. Like Mead, he too favored a dialectical metaphor and saw self-knowledge and object knowledge as emergents from the activities of an actor who was aware of things only in the context of action. His early explanatory concept, egocentrism, shared much in common with Mead's concepts. It was a loosely defined functional term, used to characterize an actor who did not take the other into account. The infant was egocentric because he knew objects only in relation to his own activities. The preconceptual child was egocentric because he failed to distinguish self from other in his communicative acts and self from thing in his attempts to conceptualize objects. Anyone who did not have a larger perspective on the elements involved in conduct was egocentric in that regard. Like Mead, Piaget saw imitation and play as important processes in development. The child tries to copy events around him, but he only understands them in his own terms. Play with such imperfectly understood and copied models creates the conditions for seeing new meanings and new skills which will enable the child to come to have more adequate ideas.

But Piaget departed from Mead in his search for the mind in several significant ways. He immersed himself in infancy through reading the infant biographers and researchers and adapting their notions and techniques to the study of the course of development of his own three infants. As such, his ideas about infancy are both much more specific and are lodged in the whole course of infancy. Moreover, his observations were primarily oriented to how the infant interacts with the world of things rather than persons. Further, his program of study came to be an account of the structure of action, and he sought that structure in the individual. Mead turned to the metaphor of the "game" and tried to describe how the child's action and play within a social system led him to be conscious of himself in terms of the system. Piaget, on the other hand, focused less on the organization of nature and social life and more on describing the growth of the mental structures that are responsible for the particular ways in which children order their acts and the world around them at different periods of life. Piaget's metaphor was "the construction of reality."

The Origins of Intelligence in Children

Piaget's three infancy books (1951, 1952, 1954) describe his program as it bears on infancy. The three books go over the same territory from somewhat different vantage points. In *The Origins*, Piaget gives his account of how the infant comes to control his conduct, and ceases to be embedded in the context of activity. He describes a sequence of steps from reactiveness to planfulness. Initially the infant is reactive in terms of disjoint reflex-schemes. Things serve to signal relatively direct reactions (stage 1). The exercise of the schemes and the attendant consequences lead the schemes to be elaborated and coordinated with other schemes. Such new schemes lead to a kind of pre-intentionality—namely, attempts to capitalize on accidental consequences of action (stages 2 and 3). Such directed efforts lead to the emergence of intentionality in the sense that the infant now persists toward perceptually present objects despite obstacles. Events now have an index quality. One can react to events directly but one also is aware that they portend other events. Because the infant has some sense of event sequences and has elaborated and coordinated skills, the infant has some ability to stage the conditions of his activity. He can keep his "eye" on the goal while trying various means to that end (stage 4). Such voluntary skillfulness creates the conditions that enable the infant to be able to make his first focal analyses of aspects of the course of conduct (stage 5). The infant now first thinks, but it is a sensorimotor thinking. It is focused on perceptually present events, and the exploration of the action possibilities of objects goes on in a groping fashion. Such trial-and-error analyses lead to a sense of objects and actions as such, and hence to forethought (stage 6). In this stage, the infant can think representationally. The infant can invent, mentally, means, and can set aim for objects that are not in the perceptual field. As such, he can plan—he can set the stage on which he will play in a way that is not dependent solely on the perceptual field.

The Construction of Reality in the Child

In *The Construction*, Piaget describes development from the point of view of knowing. He explains how the development of the action schemes leads the infant to develop those contextual categories of space, time, and cause which permit one to know objects "objectively." In early infancy, infants may appear to follow objects in space-time and note their relations to other objects and action, but the organization is in nature and not in the child. The child does not know objects, causes, spatial-temporal organization. His awareness is action-dominated and only appears knowledgeable in an objective sense because of the constraints imposed by the external events. The infant may recognize his bottle when he sees the nipple, but the anticipatory sucking stops when the bottle is oriented so that the nipple is not visible. He may follow the movement of an object as it goes behind a screen and look to the other side of the screen as if anticipating its emergence. But if the object fails to emerge, he may either not look further or may look back to where he first saw the object. The infant may pull on the strings attached to the crib to free the desired parrot enmeshed in them. But, he will pull on those self-same strings when he sees the desired parrot resting on the adjoining bedstand.

The infant imposes different organizations upon his experience at each stage of development. The organizations correspond to the stages of action and are underlaid by the same schemes. Very generally, the infant moves from recognizing and locating things in terms of disjointed schemes to broader subjective notions which permit him to keep track of visible objects in relation to one another in more diverse places over longer time spans. Such awareness is egocentric, is still keyed to the infant's ongoing activities, but is followed by the exploration of objects and their relation to other objects, actions, and places. In this sense, there is objective knowing. The infant is able to step outside of the stream of activity and regard aspects of objects as such. But such thoughtful knowing is limited to perceptually present objects or perceptually present indices of such objects. Such explorations lead the infant to be able to deal with events representationally. In particular, Piaget describes how the infant comes to develop a sense of persons as causes, as things who one can turn to as independent agents who can be instrumental in effecting the infant's intentions. When the infant has achieved such a level of organization, he is able to know objects as independent, substantial, and permanent entities which are controlled by his activities only under certain conditions and which have some definite relations to other objects independent of him. The objects are located in an organized mapping of possible places and trajectories which does not include a privileged position for the infant. Such a level of awareness permits the infant to think representationally about objects and courses of action; the infant is not just limited to acting on objects.

Play, Dreams, and Imitation

In *Play,* Piaget offers his answer to how the instrument of thought emerges. The necessary condition is the establishment of voluntary control of habits that have to do with things in relatively familiar contexts, and play is important in establishing voluntary control. The voluntary control of habits permits the infant to recreate, to re-present the events. That is Piaget's answer to the means by which early thinking occurs, *reenactment,* a copying of what one has done. Imitation in the narrower sense of copying observed events is part of this general process of habit development. Piaget describes a sequence in which imitation of the actions of another moves from repeating what one already is doing, "pseudo-imitation," to copying those movements that one can observe oneself do to being able to copy movements of the other that are not visible to oneself and hence involve some kind of inner mental process. The imitation is not the thought; it is its vehicle. One can only copy, reenact, aspects of the observed. The reenactment serves as a means of singling out the event, indicating it, but the meaning is in the thinker, and not in the symbol.

There are two forms of early imaging: overt sensorimotor reenactments and perceptual activity. The latter is Piaget's answer to "interiorized" imagery and is possible because the same complex schemes underlie both perceptual and sensorimotor activity. Reenactments occur in both natural and social contexts, but in Piaget's view the form of the infant's awareness of social events is no different from that of natural events. Hence he views the child as asocial and pays no special attention to how the social world influences the infant's conduct. In that same regard, he treats the role of language in no special way. They are events that must be assimilated and accommodated to in the same way as things and people. Because of the omnipresence of speech and its relation to events, the child ultimately comes to use words to represent events. But when they first are used, they are only part of the stream of activity. They play no special role with respect to planning or problem-solving—to say "cat" in its presence involves no more than to indicate the cat by pointing. Later, language does play a special role, but the meaning of the utterances is always determined by the child's, and not the adult's, point of view. However, the fact that adults use words in a relatively common social context sets the stage for the child to give common categorical meanings to words. But such a process comes late in development—when the child's thought is operational, when the child can coordinate his perspective with that of others. Before that the child's thought, and his sense of what words stand for, is first preconceptual and then intuitive.

Discussion of the Infancy Books

Thus Piaget's account of the development of thought both significantly extends and modifies Mead's account. On the one hand, Piaget concretizes the energence of thinking. His description of the development of intentionality describes how one gets a sense of a thing separate from the act and thereby can set the stage on which one acts. His description of the development of the categories of awareness sharpens up the sense in which one can distinguish between acting on things, where the order is in the sensorimotor complex, and knowing things and their orderly relations to other things and actors. His account characterizes the nature of early thought in a way that rings truer than does Mead's, with its heavy emphasis on the word as the vehicle. Piaget captures the similarity between the obviously nonverbal and thoughtful conduct of chimpanzees (Köhler, 1959) and the infant. On the other hand, Piaget clearly departs from Mead in devaluing the social as important in the development of thought and in not looking to external forms as a direct source of the internal organizations.

The three books represent a striking achievement. My account of them is selective and does not contain their force. The reader must turn to them or better paraphrases of them for direct evidence of this assertion (e.g., Flavell, 1963; Furth, 1969; Piaget, 1950). Much of the appeal of the books lies in how they reveal a mind at work, struggling to impose order on events, sensitive to alternative possibilities and resourceful in searching out new data to decide among them, sweeping in its reach. Flavell (1963) predicted that replicating Piaget's infancy observations would become a cottage industry, and that indeed has come to pass. So many of his observations are so counterintuitive that many have needed little more than that as a basis for following in his wake. But it is in his seeking for an encompassing order in the flux of infancy that Piaget has struck so many both positively and negatively. His observations involve diverse ages and settings, but they are hardly a complete catalogue. Yet he talks about *the* infant. He talks about stages of development, not in a nominal way but as statements about what kind of an organized creature the infant is in that stage. For most of us, order is hard to conjure, let alone find. Thus whether on common-sense grounds or because one has the empiricist's persuasion, Piaget's claims raise the question of, whether in Cartesian fashion (Furth, 1970; Gardner, 1972), Piaget has not imposed an order where there are only particularities.

Further, there are some striking qualities to the particular order that he has announced. Thought is fundamentally an individual matter. While Piaget is as cognizant as the next man that infants live among people and are influenced by them, he does not really believe that thought becomes social until late childhood. Again and again, Piaget and his able interpreter Furth (1969) announce that "you can lead a horse to water but . . ." While Mead and Vygotsky (1962) saw the educative process as playing a constitutive role in the development of thinking, Piaget seems bent on saying "Yes, but . . ." In keeping with this emphasis on how the child gives meaning to the events he encounters, Piaget does not try to carefully document the child's environment. As I have already suggested, this is not just an oversight on his part nor is it just a consequence of his functional approach to awareness. In large measure, it is because he is focused on how the infant organizes his particular experiences. Piaget is part of a tradition that is antiempiricist in the sense that it is held that particular experiences only lead to fragmentation and confusion unless they are ordered by a larger conception. Particular experiences take on meaning in terms of the general (assimilation), and particular experiences are the occasion for changes in the general (accommodation). If you want to understand how the mind works and develops then you have to study the general, and the general is a construction, not something that simply arises out of many impressions. Thus rightly or wrongly, Piaget uses his particular observations as opportunities to infer the nature of the underlying structure. He is looking for the general order where many of us have as our object to study the conduct of particular infants in particular situations.

A consequence of this view of the knowing child is that the underlying structures will become an object of knowing later than will the events that the structure organizes. Both in action and in thought, it is the object of activity that is focal. Second, as already noted, the development of the structures is out of the direct control of both the educator and the child. Furth (1969) has sharpened this aspect of Piaget's view by making a distinction between "interiorization" and "internalization." The latter refers to the taking on of external representations—for example, language—and using them to direct conduct. The former is the critical process and refers to the structures of knowing. It is these that give meaning to words and other gestures, and it is these that are responsible for conduct, thoughtful or otherwise. These underlying schemes, which Piaget has tried to capture in terms of various logical models, are like an underlying cybernetic machine, out of the direct control of either the educator or the self-conscious actor, though influenced by inputs from them. The "machine" develops through a process called "reflective abstraction," but it operates on itself and in its own terms. Reflection here does not mean conscious reflection, and the terms are fundamentally not such vehicles as words, gestures, and images. The ground for this idea is "imageless" thought. Piaget believes that much of the creative adult's thinking is intuitive, is not reflective in the conscious sense, and that there is a continuity between such directly unknowable thinking and the activity of the infant. Manifest symbolically guided thinking, in the form of pretense and recall and planning, does not emerge until the 2nd year of life. It forms a basis for the child to consciously join with adults to think about the bases for conduct, to get some control over the "machine" in socially conditioned terms. But fundamentally neither the adult nor the child can represent the "machine."

I have dwelled on these aspects of Piaget's general thinking at some length to provide a basis for seeing why his approach to the study of infancy and childhood emphasizes so much the individual nature of thought and why he places conscious reflection and language in a secondary position. The idea that we cannot write the blueprint for the "machine" is captured in Mead's "I" and in the greatly acclaimed analyses of the relation of the knower to the known of Polanyi (1958) and Popper (1963). But there is a troubling quality to Piaget as I have presented him. Piaget is certainly aware of the importance of thinking in the consciously reflective and socially implicated sense, his writings on attempts to model the mind being one exemplar. But whereas a Popper views knowing as a process of conjectures and refutations with respect to a focal aspect of the larger scene—one takes on issues one at a time—Piaget's (1971) attempts to capture the "whole" of thought in logical terms has led him increasingly far away from the concrete events and into speculations about the root of mature thought being in the logical organization of cells. Piaget's theorizing has come under increasing attack, in part for its holistic emphasis, in part for its abstractness, (Feldman and Toulmin, 1974–5). Critics increasingly wonder whether Piaget has lost the child in his structural models, whether he has fallen into the error of reifying his models. Nonetheless, it is this mixture of moving between the particular and the abstract that has aroused so much interest in his treatment of infancy. When presented at the level of abstraction of the present discussion, it is hard to evaluate. It is hard to know whether one can more profitably look at thought as an individual matter or a social matter, as conscious or fundamentally not conscious. In a certain sense it is all of these, and it is only when such orientations are put to work in making sense of concrete events that their merits come to the fore. Current work in infancy is in large part addressed to this process of concretizing the large themes I have raised in terms of Mead and Piaget, and I shall try to give the reader some sense of that process. I shall organize my presentation in terms of the three general issues raised in Piaget's three infancy volumes: (1) the nature of action, the problem of *The Origins* (1952), (2) the nature of awareness, the problem of *The Construction* (1954), and (3) the relation of sensorimotor knowing and doing to language, the problem of *Play* (1951). The second and third issues are the ones being pursued most vigorously, and the third also is characterized by a focus on the themes that Mead developed.

CURRENT DEVELOPMENTS

The Nature of Action

Intention and the problem of how to relate the particular to the general, within a period and across the course of infancy, seem to be the central issues in thinking about the development of skilled action. There seems to be fairly general agreement that skilled conduct should be looked at from the point of view of intentions and their development. This is a marked shift from the context within which Mead and Piaget developed their ideas. In part, it stems from a widespread turning away from S-R analyses of conduct to information-processing ones. In part it stems from confirmations of many of Piaget's observations. For example, investigators who have developed Piaget-inspired infancy scales have broadly documented Piaget's account of the account of the development of intention (e.g., Uzgiris and Hunt, 1975) and particular aspects of the general sequence have been carefully replicated—for example, the development of visually guided reaching (White, 1971). In part it has stemmed from Bruner's (1973) theoretical and empirical work on how the "automatization" of simpler skills sets the stage for their integrated use in pursuing higher-order purposes. He and his associates have nicely documented how infants come to foresee such events as the need to create a storage space if they want to grasp and hold more than two objects, the need to use one hand to hold and one hand to grasp when dealing with a box which contains an object and which has a top that slides down when the examiner releases it, and so on. This is not to say that the problems of the nature of the skilled components and their organization have been solved. Rather, I am suggesting that there is general agreement that one should approach the study of the development of skills in terms of the idea of intention and mobilization of means thereto.

Piaget has answered the questions of the relation between skills in a period of life and the relation between periods of life in schematic form within the framework of the concepts of assimilation, accommodation, and equilibration. The latter term names the fact that skills coordinate and enter into hierarchical relations, but the answer is very general. Bartlett (1958) and Werner (1956) raised the ontogenetic question in a more open form—namely, what are the similarities and differences between microgenesis and macrogenesis and how do the two processes articulate? Bower (1974a) has nicely re-opened one old form of this issue by asking what is the relation between early maturationally determined components of a later skill and the later skill? What is the relation between early swimming movements which typically disappear without practice and later swimming? What is the impact of exercising the early components on the nature of the skill? Zelazo et al. (1972) have shown that early exercising of the stepping and placing reflexes leads to the early onset of walking, just as McGraw (1946) once showed for swimming. But how does it work? Why can we develop the skill later even though the early components are not systematically exercised? Bower (1974b) also has highlighted these issues in other ways—for example, his study, with Mounod, of the development of an infantile version of the conservation of mass; his study, with Paterson, of the impact of early training in the visual tracking of moving objects upon later manual search for covered objects.

The question of how the various skills fit together within a time period, the issue of the reality of stages, has also been studied to no present resolution. For example, Schofield and Uzgiris (1969) attempted to substantiate Piaget's belief that how infants act on objects is related to whether they can search for them. They did not find the expected close relation between search and the emergence of object inspection, as opposed to treating objects as "assimilables"—for example, "bangables," "mouthables." Further, Uzgiris (1973) has not been able to find meaningful patterns of correlation between infants' performance on the various tasks that comprise the Uzgiris-Hunt infancy schedule.

The Nature of Awareness

The relation between early and late also is a major organizing issue in studies relevant to the issues Piaget raised in *The Construction* (1954). Since Piaget wrote his books, there has been a great deal of study of how very young infants perceive the world, (e.g., Kessen et al., 1970; Salapatek, 1975). These studies have thrown into question the idea that Piaget shared with William James—namely, that the neonate experiences a "buzzing, blooming confusion."

Moreover, there have been a number of studies that have claimed that very young infants know things "objectively" and are able to represent absent things. These claims are at great variance with Piaget's ideas and observations, and the evidence for such precocity on the part of infants is conflicting. In support of the claim, Bower et al. (1970) report that within the first 2 weeks of life, infants will reach toward objects in a directed manner, their fingers will be molded to correspond to the size and shape of the object, and they will be distressed when their hand contacts the place where they localize a virtual image of the reached-for object. The lack of correspondence between this report and Piaget's notions is striking. Not only does there seem to be evidence of eye-hand coordination, but it appears that the neonate perceives objects as such—solid, three-dimensional forms. Meltzoff and Moore (1977) have shown that infants as young as 12 to 21 days old can imitate non-visible movements such as tongue protrusion, mouth opening, and lip protrusion. Gardner and Gardner (1977) and Smillie and Coppotelli (1977) also provide evidence that such imitation, which Piaget thinks of as a Stage 4 achievement, is a capacity of young infants. Not only does the infant appear to be capable of selectively copying the conduct of the other very early in life, but he seems to have a means of referring the conduct of others to things he can do which he has no visible knowledge of. Ball (1973) has reported that very young infants see collisions between objects as causal, a claim that runs contrary to both associationistic and action accounts of the development of causality. Bower et al. (1971) and Gardner (1971) report that by 5 months of age infants are able to visually track moving objects in Piaget's Stage 6 sense of object permanence. Not only do they anticipate the reappearance of an object that moves behind a screen, but, if a different object emerges, they will look back to the screen to find the missing object. The fact that 5-month-old infants appear to ignore the visible object and search for the missing one seems to indicate that they are able to represent objects as enduring entities. There are many other studies that I could report, but these suffice to bring out several points. One is that, as Gibson (1966) and Michotte (1955) argued, there appears to be a great deal of information in the visual array, and very young infants seem to be able to appreciate it without much experience on either a visual or tactual level. Another is that there appear to be important coordinations between sensorimotor modalities or schemes early in life. A third is that if these claims are taken on their face, then there is a major puzzle still to be solved—namely, why is it that these very competent infants do so many of the "foolish" things that Piaget noted and why is it that they take so long to make their competencies manifest in the course of everyday conduct?

One solution is to doubt the claims of early competence. The burden of the evidence makes it plain that infants have more competence and orderly awareness than Piaget assumed when he began to observe his infants (consider how sketchy his observations were with regard to the first months of life relative to the later ones). On the other hand, one may doubt the facts in particular studies, and one may interpret the facts differently in the case of other studies. For example, Dodwell et al. (1976) report that they did not find that infants in the first weeks of life know objects as solid three-dimensional forms. The infants they studied did not reach differently for a solid object and its two-dimensional representation. Further evidence of very young infants' lack of "objectivity" is provided by Caron, Caron, and Carlson (52). They attempted to replicate Bower's claim that such infants have shape constancy and found evidence that 60 and 80 day old infants discriminate only proximal cues specifying slant rather than real shape-at-a-slant. In the case of the claim that 5-month-old infants exhibit object permanence in visual-tracking situations, Goldberg (1976) and Nelson (1971) did not find as clear evidence of anticipatory looking as did Bower et al. (1970), and Meicler (1976) found that the looking back to the screen when a different object emerged neither occurred often nor did it have the characteristics of a search for a missing object. Rather, when it occurred, it took the form of a stereotyped look at the screen entrance or a look at points along the path of the object before it went behind the screen. Moreover, she found that the responses of 9-month-olds paralleled the behavior of 9-month-olds studied by LeCompte and Gratch (1972) and Saal (1975). The latter authors hid objects under covers. In support of Piaget's views, those authors found that it was not until 18 months that infants were surprised by the object change and searched for the missing toy. At 9 months, they, like Meicler, found that the infants reacted in a mildly distressed and confused manner to the trick. They seemed to have only a vague sense of the contingent relation between the disappearing and reappearing objects as opposed to the 18-month-olds' seemingly clear idea of what had been hidden and where it ought to be. Yonas and Pick (1975), reviewing the infant spatial-perception literature, wonder whether many of the instances of purported spatial knowledge cannot be better explained in terms of responses to specific features of the perceptual array which have quite a different meaning for the infant than the adult. In other words, they counsel that we should approach the various claims of early competence with a question in mind: Is there evidence that the infant has a representation of space or only evidence that he is responding to some aspect of space?

Another solution is to make a competence-performance distinction. One assumes that the problem for the infant is a combination of developing an appropriate motor apparatus and identifying the occasions where his knowledge is appropriate, in analogy to the problem of applying mathematical models to concrete instances different from those that were the base from which the model was developed. Bower (1967) adopted this tack, but he has dropped it for much the same reason that Bruner (1974) counsels we abandon the tactic in trying to account for early language acquisition—namely, that it assumes more than it explains and tends to undercut inquiry.

Thus most investigators have adopted some mix of the following solutions. They do more empirical work, keyed to unearthing further curiosities that stem from asking Piaget-based or Piaget-like questions—that is, asking in what way do infants orient to a different world than do adults and children. Or they accept Piaget's idea that there are emergents in development, but they offer different accounts of their nature and origin. As an example of the first approach, LeCompte (1976) reports an interesting difference between how 9- and 18-month-olds react to tricks of hiding one (or two) objects and finding two (or one), when the objects are copies of one another. Nine-month-olds are more distressed when one object is hidden and they find two than they are when two are hidden and they find one. The opposite pattern is shown by the 18-month-olds. LeCompte speculates that the differential distress may have to do with the infants' stage of object conception. In the case of the 18-month-olds, they may have a clear enough idea of objects to know they just do not disappear and also that there may be replicas. To lose one of two is distressing; finding an extra may be puzzling, but it is also intriguing. The 9-month-olds not only do not play well with more than one toy at a time, they cannot think of them well. Therefore the loss of one is not distressing, whereas the finding of two poses them a confusing conceptual problem.

At present, most exemplars of the second approach are addressed to Piaget's posing of the object-permanence problem, and I shall comment on only this work. This theme of Piaget's, the infant's singling out of the object from the sensorimotor stream, has captured many investigators for such diverse reasons as the manageableness of the procedure and the concept's seeming relevance to the question of when infants really know their significant others and to the question of when can their words stand for things. In other words, many believe that an infant neither truly has an attachment to his caretaker until he can represent her in her absence, nor can he be said to properly use words until he can use them representationally. Most current attempts to account for the phenomena have focused on the intimate interplay between object and spatial knowledge that Piaget pointed out was involved in knowing about an object as abstracted from any particular context. But most of these accounts take a different tack than Piaget's. In large part, they are keyed to the fact that infants seem to do many of the same kinds of inappropriate things toward objects that are moved about in full view as they do when objects are hidden in various places. For example, not only do infants often search at the first place they found a hidden object when they see it hidden at a second place, as Piaget observed, but they often do this when the objects are either not covered or are covered with transparent objects. Harris (1975a) has marshalled this evidence well, and he, and also Butterworth (1975), have been trying to develop an explanation involving the idea that throughout the course of development one must struggle to coordinate two developing frames of reference: an egocentric spatial frame of reference—for example, front of me, to side of me—and an external frame of reference. Bower (1975) has been developing an argument that focuses on an object as a "bounded volume of space in a place or on a path of movement" [p. 45]. He tries to account for various facets of development in terms of how the infant comes to appreciate the identity among the spatial transformations in the object introduced by its being moved in space relative to objects it neighbors, goes behind, goes under, and so on.

Moore (1975) also has offered an explanation that focuses on how the infant develops a sense of the identity of the object as it undergoes spatial and featural transformations. He focuses on identity in the sense of the spatial rules that define a distinct thing—two things cannot occupy one place, one thing cannot occupy two places. Such rules permit one to tell the difference between same and similar, and Moore argues that the infant achieves them through developing a sequence of incomplete object notions. These notions are contradicted by various experiences of place, trajectory, and object feature, and the contradictions set the stage for the infant to develop the next level of object notion.

The Relation of Sensorimotor Knowing and Doing to Language

The relation of language to thought and communication is presently being studied in ways that pick up on the lines of analysis that Mead considered. This is not to say that investigators of this domain do not look to Piaget's notions of the development of sensorimotor intelligence for guidance. However, much of the work is either critical of key Piagetian assumptions or pursues issues that are not central to his line of thought. I shall discuss these developments under four heads: the acquisition of language, word meanings, language as communication, and prelinguistic communication.

The Acquisition of Language

The tradition that Mead and Piaget represent has never been focused on linguistics, and my commentary will follow their lead. On the other hand, it is important to note that in the last two decades the study of the acquisition of language as a system has been a dominant undertaking. As Bloom (1975) and Brown (1973) point out, its early form was dominated by Chomsky's ideas about generative grammar and the importance of syntax. Increasingly investigators are turning to problems of meaning and communication, whereas the earlier work contained the implication that we could understand these issues if we could understand the nature of the linguistic system and its acquistion. Brown takes a somewhat bemused attitude toward his early enthusiasm for the collection and intensive study of corpora of children's first spontaneous utterances. In effect, he seems to say that if language is an object of interest to you, then he is sure you will find much profit in the study of its development. We all use language, but we all need not reflect on that instrument to know its objects.

Much attention has been paid to the phonological aspect of language (e.g., Eimas, 1975), but I shall not discuss these developments. Instead, I shall dwell on a major issue that has emerged among investigators trying to diagnose what kind of a language system children are acquiring by the study of corpora of their early spontaneous utterances. Currently such investigations focus upon the relationship between the children's world-knowledge, their communicative intentions, and the word-strings they emit. This is a difficult task. One of the difficulties lies in maintaining a boundary between semantics and world-knowledge—between the sense in which the child has category within the linguistic system in his head and the sense in which he has the world-category in his head. When one is primarily interested in thought, as were Mead and Piaget, the problem is simpler. One draws inferences from what children say and do about what and how they know. However, those focused on determining what kind of linguistic structure the child is acquiring have the problem of matching the utterance to a linguistic category that captures more than just what he meant. Many investigators are seeking to find a relation between Piaget's account of the sensorimotor period and the linguistic structure of first words. It is a reasonable idea, but Sinclair (1973) rightly cautions that one must go beyond simply seeking correlations between the two sets of achievements.

The difficulty of the boundary problem is exemplified in the attempts to identify the linguistic status of children's early word-combinations (Bowerman, 1976). The exemplar I shall touch on is the contrast between the positions taken by Bloom (1973) and Braine (1976). Bloom believes children have and express certain semantic relations such as nomination or existence, recurrence, nonexistence, and so on, when they say things like "this," "more," and "all gone." Moreover, she sees a close relation between the emergence of such sensorimotor knowledge as object permanence and nomination and recurrence. Braine, on the other hand, attributes less linguistic knowledge to children making such utterances. He believes the semantic status of such terms in early word-combinations is far narrower than is implied when one classifies them in case grammatical terms. Moreover he argues that much of what one observes can be characterized as "groping patterns," attempts by children to express a meaning before they learned the rules that determine what position the words should take in a linguistic string.

Word Meanings

The boundary problem also is central in determining what lexical items mean. Can we infer the meaning of a term by noting the array of instances that it is used with reference to? One tradition says yes. By noting the physical features that the instances have in common, we can both note the meaning of the term for the child and chart the development of the criterion.

Clark (1973) has reexamined many of the baby biographies in this light. On the other hand, the tradition of Mead, Piaget, and Werner emphasizes the functional-expressive meaning of words, and Werner and Kaplan (1963) have given particular importance to the expressive. Nelson (1974, 1976) and Rosch (1973) have been developing this idea. In the framework of both empirical studies and conceptual analyses, they have been pointing out that the exemplars of common nouns like cat and chair bear only a "family resemblance" to one another from the point of view of physical features. In other words, any two exemplars share some features in common, but the search for the feature(s) that all proper exemplars share in common leads to null sets. They argue that one must look to experience, to function and feeling, for the core meanings. Features, as relevant to core prototypes, are useful in helping to identify new instances, but the core meaning is lodged in prototypically organized experiences which come to be elaborated with further experience. Their account of this elaboration, as instanced in such higher-order concepts as animals and furniture, leads them to be critical of Piaget. They believe these concepts develop in the same analogical way as do the lower-order concepts. The ordering of such concepts into logical classification systems is not part of some individually inspired process of "reflective abstraction." They argue that we think in an analogical way, in a "family way," all through life. We develop logical notions through the many, many concrete exchanges we have with the "educative" system. When we have logic, we have it only in part, and we use it only some of the time—namely, when we try to make a logical analysis of our sense of the relatedness of events. I have presented these views as if they are the shared idea of Nelson and Rosch. But they each develop these notions in different manners, and, in particular, Nelson (1976) is critical of that aspect of Piaget's idea of object permanence which emphasizes the achievement of the idea of a unique object. She doubts such an idea emerges in infancy, and as such would question the accounts of object permanence that have the idea of identity at their core.

The treatment of the status of abstract notions by Nelson and Rosch is very much like that of Mead's. Moreover there is a sense in which their analysis is not unlike that of Piaget's (see *Play, Dreams, and Imagination*), but they place far more emphasis on the open-ended, the one-thing-at-a-time, manner in which children develop ways of organizing their experience and the relevance of social experiences throughout the process of development.

Language as Communication

Olson (1970) has made some of the above points in a way that, like Mead, brings out their relevance to the communicative situation. His analysis takes the point of view of the child as the stranger who must somehow interact with people in a framework that includes words. His emphasis is on how children comprehend, rather than produce, speech, and he points out that one cannot think of reference simply in terms of ostentation, pointing. Speech occurs in a framework of action. We name events relative to some purpose in some context. Words do not stand for things; rather, they serve to differentiate some event from a set of alternatives relative to a listener. How explicit we are about our intentions, our view of the listener, the focal event, the context, and so on, depends on who we are talking to, when, and so on. Olson sensitively points up the cognitive problems for the child in comprehending such speech acts and the lack of sufficient emphasis in the literature on the study of comprehension. But interestingly, he does not recognize what Mead emphasized—namely that saying what you mean is as much a cognitive task as understanding what the other means. Vygotsky (1962) long ago pointed out how different a task it is to write than to speak face to face because in the former case you have to imagine your audience. The muteness of the toddler on the telephone is well known. But though the audience's presence may diminish the problem for the speaker, it does not eliminate it.

Prelinguistic Communication

This emphasis upon the intimate interplay between speaker and listener, thought and message, and so on, has become the focus of workers in what can be loosely called the speech act tradition. Bruner (1975, 1974), Harris (1975b), and Ryan (1974) have ably reviewed much of this growing body of literature and its relation to the nonverbal origins of communication. They call our attention to the possibility that during infancy there may arise means of mutual reference to common sets of objects that have common meanings. There are a number of themes in this literature, and I shall briefly describe some of those that bear on the nonverbal roots of communication. One line of inquiry has to do with the emergence of mutual reference. Lampers et al. (1975) have documented that early in the 2nd year of life infants can take the perspective of the other—for example, when infant and adult are so positioned that each sees a different facet of an object, the infant is differentially aware of what he and the other see. This achievement does not seem to fit in a simple fashion with Piaget's ideas. Many other investigators are trying to trace out the origins of such a performance by seeking connections between very early mutual gazing, following the gaze of the other, and the use of the gaze and manual and vocal pointing as referential vehicles. There is a good deal of interest in looking at such regular social contexts as feeding and games, like peek-a-boo, as occasions for understanding how infants evolve a sense of the nature of communication and communicative systems (e.g., Brazelton et al., 1974; Greenfield, 1972; Sander, 197 ; Schaffer et al., 1977; and Stern, 1974a). In other words, there is a focus on how infants develop a sense of turn-taking, of roles within a social structure, of objects that have a common meaning, and so on. These are the kinds of issues that Mead's metaphor of the game and his analysis of it in terms of different levels of communication signalled as important to study, and a number of workers have also been exploring the relation between symmetries and asymmetries in the infant-mother communication system—that is, the sense in which infant and mother share on one level and its relation to the larger perspective from which the mother acts (Sameroff, 1975; Sander, 1977; Stern, 1974a).

CONCLUSION

The previous subsection brings me full circle. I began with a presentation of G. H. Mead's ideas because I sense a general movement in the field toward an attempt to understand the development of thought and language in infancy in terms of a focus on the social links that the dependent infant and its caretakers build between them. In less than 30 years, the field has shifted from a relative lack of interest in thought and language at any age to a serious consideration of Piaget's ideas to a beginning rejection of them, in part in the name of looking for their social roots. This movement can be seen in the literature I have touched on, and it can also be seen in such sources as Riegel's (1975) call for studying development as a dialectical process, in the character of the chapters Richards (1974) brought together, in Smillie's (1977) attempt to describe the function of infancy as a period in which the respective partners come to make an affective commitment to one another, and in Lewis and Brooks' (1975) attempt to account for the origins of self-identification.

My sense of these developments is that they are both promising and yet preliminary. As I noted earlier, Mead's account is not an empirical one, and much of the promise of current work lies in its attempt to determine the facts with respect to the important questions highlighted by Mead and others. But the preliminary character of these developments can be illustrated by considering a not atypical example of the literature on prelinguistic communication, namely Stern's (1974b) oft-cited work. Stern addresses the important task of identifying early turn-taking patterns in the interactions of infants and their mothers. He believes he has identified a stochastic process with analogies to that seen in adult face-to-face situations. With 3- to 4-month-old infants, he examined the relation between the gaze-toward and the gaze-away of mother and infant, the gazes being coded every 0.6 sec. However, the reported matrices reveal that basically what is going on is that mother is looking at the infant. Only two of the possible contingencies are of consequence—mother-infant look at each other followed by the same event, or mother looks at the infant and infant looks away followed by the same event. As Stern notes, the conduct of the mother probably is determined by her acceptance of the experimenter's task demand that she get her infant to "play." It is likely that what was of interest in the situation was not where the partners were looking but how they were looking. But such data is difficult to collect, and even then the value of such information would have to be qualified by the importance of the experimenter's setting condition for the mother. These comments are not made to be critical of Stern's work (he makes essentially the same points), rather they are made to emphasize the difficulty that investigators are having in getting a handle on a particularly exciting set of questions. The problem in part lies in establishing satisfactory empirical procedure. But in part, the problem lies in having an organized set of ideas about the issues which can guide empirical activity.

I introduced Mead by way of providing a possible perspective for this line of inquiry. In this, I had several reasons. I wanted to point out that the present emphasis on the study of prelinguistic communication is an old one. More importantly, Mead's ideas are far-ranging and articulate. They provide a frame of reference within which to lodge the many diverse probes at the questions. While Mead's ideas do not translate into obvious empirical paradigms—the symbolic interaction tradition in sociology derives directly from Mead and has not been notable for its empirical success (Stone and Farberman, 1970)—they do have important links with Piaget's notions, which notions have had important empirical as well as theoretical consequences.

Earlier, in my general discussion of Piaget's infancy books, I highlighted some differences between the emphases of Mead and Piaget; Piaget underplays the social as a content to be studied and as a determiner of thought. He strongly emphasizes the importance of holistic structures, the infant as a total system. Mead sees conduct as socially influenced at every level and sees the structures as far less organized, as far more open than Piaget. In part their differences stem from their trying to answer different abstract questions: How is it possible that people become logical? How is it possible for people to exist as citizens in a democratic society? Piaget's focus upon individual rationality would seem to have been influenced by the almost religious role of science relative to human conduct. The current interest in the social nature of thought, and in part the reaction against Piaget, can be viewed as determined by a diminution of faith in science and great concern with the problem of community (White, 1976). The different emphases lead one to look for different things. But it is not obvious that one emphasis will necessarily tell us more about the nature of the development of thought than the other. In keeping with current sociobiological ideas, it may be profitable to think of infants (and their caretakers) as phylogenetically programmed to be social, thoughtful, and linguistic, but it is not at all clear what the program is nor how it is translated into ontogenetic terms. The infant exists in a community but is not a socially significant, in Mead's terms, member of that community. While it seems intuitively obvious that we must come to focus on socially common objects and share our knowledge of them, it is not obvious that the process of knowing is best captured by a social metaphor. The infant, like the artist and the scientist (Chandrasekhar, 1975), does much of his exploration and problem-solving off on his own.

In conclusion, I have tried to indicate that much of current investigation of language and thought in infancy can be looked upon as plays upon the emphases inherent in the positions of Mead and Piaget. The views of Mead and Piaget share some common limitations and virtues. Both positions are vague on the mechanism of development. Their metaphor of the child as problem-solver and "sense-maker" leaves many unanswered questions. However, the metaphor is no less magical than the assumption that the course of development is a cumulation of mutual regulations between the child and his caretakers or of reinforcements or is a result of an unspecified maturational process. Moreover, their metaphor has the virtue of focusing our attention on the phenomenon to be explained— namely, how does a child think and communicate.

Both positions are vague on how to specify the nature and number of the structures, stages. One may question the basis on which Piaget identified three or six levels, rather than 15 or 30, with regard to a particular task situation or how one combines various task performances into an indication of a general stage of development. On the other hand, the notion of levels serves to focus our attention on important questions. It is all too easy to notice a mutual regulation between an infant and a mother and conclude there is communication without simultaneously asking in what way such communication differs from the communication between two adults or children and adults. It is all too easy to note an infantile performance in a particular context that seems most intelligent and not wonder if the specificity of that performance to that context implies a different form of knowing rather than just ignorance of the other contexts. For example, it is indeed impressive that children come to talk in the 2nd year of life to significant others, but what accounts for the fact that such talk does not become self-guiding until much later (Kohlberg et al., 1968). In closing, the rightness or wrongness of the views of Mead and Piaget seem less important than the role these positions can play in highlighting and structuring the ways to look at the unintelligent and dependent infant.

BIBLIOGRAPHY

Appleton, T., Clifton, R. and Goldberg, S. The development of behavioral competence in infancy. In F.D. Horowitz (ed.), *Review of Child Development*, Vol. 4, Chicago: University of Chicago, 1975.

Ball, W.A. The Perception of Causality in the Infant. Report No. 37. *Developmental Program*, Department of Psychology, University of Michigan, 1973.

Bartlet, F.C. *Thinking: An Experimental and Social Study*, New York: Basic, 1958.

Bloom, L. *One Word at a Time: The Use of Single Word Utterances before Syntax*. The Hague: Mouton, 1973.

Bloom, L. Language development. In F.D. Horowitz (ed.), *Review of Child Development Research*, Vol. 4, Chicago: University of Chicago, 1975.

Bower, T.G.R. The development of object permanence: Some studies of existence constancy. *Perception and Psychophysics, 1967*, **12**, 411–418.

Bower, T.G.R., Broughton, J.M. and Moore, M.K. Assessment of intention in sensorimotor infants. *Nature*, 1970, **228**, 679–681.

Bower, T.G.R., Broughton, J.M. and Moore, M.K. Development of the object concept as manifested in the tracking behavior of infants between seven and twenty weeks of age. *Journal of Experimental Child Psychology*, 1971, **11**, 182–193.

Bower, T.G.R. *Development in Infancy*. San Francisco: Freeman, 1974.

Bower, T.G.R. Repetition in human development. *Merrill-Palmer Quarterly*, 1974, **20**, 303–318.

Bower, T.G.R. Infant perception of the third dimension and object development. In L.B. Cohen and P. Salapatek (eds.), *Infant Perception*, Vol. 2, New York: Academic, 1975.

Bowerman, M. Commentary. In Braine, M.D.S. Children's First Word Combinations. *Monographs of the Society for Research in Child Development,* 1976, **4**(1).

Braine, M.D.S. Children's First Word Combinations. *Monographs of the Society for Research in Child Development*, 1976, **4**(1).

Brazelton, T.B., Koslowski, B. and Main, M. The origins of reciprocity: The early mother-infant interaction. In M. Lewis and L.A. Rosenblum (eds.), *The Effect of the Infant on its Caregiver*. New York: Wiley, 1974.

Brown, R. *A First Language: The Early Stages*. Cambridge, Mass: Harvard University, 1973.

Bruner, J.S. The organization of early skilled action. *Child Development*, 1973, **44**, 1–11.

Bruner, J.S. From communication to language—a psychological perspective. Mimeographed manuscript, Oxford University, 1974.

Bruner, J.S. The ontogenesis of speech acts. *Journal of Child Language*, 1975, **2**, 1–19.

Butterworth, G. Object identity in infancy: The interaction of spatial location in determining search errors. *Child Development*, 1975, **46**, 866–870.

Campbell, D.T. On the conflicts between biological and social evolution and between psychology and moral tradition. *American Psychologist*, 1975, **30**, 1103–1126.

Caron, A.J., Caron, R.F., and Carlson, V.R. Do infants see objects or retinal images? Shape constancy revisited. *Infant Behavior and Development*, 1978, in press.

Chandrasekhar, S. Shakespeare, Newton, and Beethoven or patterns of creativity. The Norah and Edward Ryerson Lecture, Center for Policy Study, University of Chicago, 1975.

Clark, E.V. What's in a word? On the child's acquisition of semantics in his first language. In T.E. Moore (ed.), *Cognitive Development and the Acquisition of Language*, New York: Academic, 1973.

Dodwell, P.D., Muir, D., and DiFranco, D. Responses of infants to visually presented objects. *Science*, 1976, **194**, 209–211.

Durkheim, E. *The Division of Labor*. Glencoe, Ill.: Free Press, 1933.

Eimas, P.D. Speech perception in infancy. In L.B. Cohen and P. Salapatek (eds.), *Infant Perception*, Vol. 2, New York: Academic, 1975.

Feldman, C.F. and Toulmin, S. Logic and theory of mind. Proceedings of Nebraska Symposium on Motivation, 1974–75.

Flavell, J.H. *The Developmental Psychology of Jean Piaget*. New York: Van Nostrand, 1963.

Flavell, J. The development of metacommunication. Paper given at the Symposium on Language and Cognition, 21st International Congress of Psychology, Paris, July, 1976.

Flavell, J. and Wellman, H.M. Metamemory. In R.V. Kail and J.W. Hagen (eds.), *Memory in Cognitive Development*, Hillsdale, N.W.: Erlbaum, 1969.

Furth, H.G. *Piaget and Knowledge*. Englewood Cliffs, N.W.: Prentice-Hall, 1969.

Furth, H.G. On language and knowing in Piaget's developmental theory. *Human Development*, 1970, **13**, 241–257.

Gardner, J. The development of object identity in the first six months of infancy. Paper presented at the Biennial Meeting of the Society for Research in Child Development. Minneapolis, 1971.

Gardner, J. and Gardner, H. A note on selective imitation by a six-week-old infant. *Child Development*, 1970, **41**, 1209–1213.

Gibson, J.J. *The Senses Considered as Perceptual Systems*. Boston: Houghton-Mifflin, 1966.

Goldberg, S. Visual tracking and existence constancy in five-month-old infants. *Journal of Experimental Child Psychology*, 1976, **22**, 478–491.

Gratch, G. Recent studies based on piaget's view of object concept development. In L.B. Cohen and P. Salapatek (eds.), *Infant Perception,* Vol. 2, New York: Academic, 1975.

Greenfield, P.M. Playing peekaboo with a four-month-old: A study of the role of speech and nonspeech sounds in the formation of a visual schema. *The Journal of Psychology*, 1972, **82**, 287–298.

Haith, M.H. and Campos, J.J. Human infancy. In *Annual Review of Psychology*. Palo Alto, Calif.: Annual Reviews, 1977.

Harris, A.E. Social dialetics and language: Mother and child construct the discourse. *Human Development*, 1975, **18**, 80–96.

Harris, P.H. Development of search and object permanence during infancy. *Psychological Bulletin*, 1975, **82**, 332–344.

Houston Chronicle, Sec. 3, p. 4, July 11, 1976.

Kessen, W., Haith, M.H. and Salapatek, P.H. Infancy. In P.H. Mussen (ed.), *Carmichael's Manual of Child Psychology*, 3rd Edition, New York: Wiley, 1970.

Kohlberg, L., Yaeger, J. and Hjertholm, E. Private speech: Four studies and a review of theories. *Child Development*, 1968, **39**, 691–736.

Kohler, W. *The Mentality of Apes*. New York: Vintage, 1959.

Le Compte, G.K. Personal Communication, Hacettepe University, Ankara, Turkey, 1976.

LeCompte, G.K. and Gratch, G. Violation of a rule as a method of diagnosing infants' level of object concept. *Child Development*, 1972, **43**, 385–396.

Lempers, J.D., Flavell, E.R. and Flavell, J.H. The development in very young children of tacit knowledge concerning visual perception. Mimeographed Manuscript, 1975. Institute of Child Development, University of Minnesota.

Lewis, M. and Brooks, J. Infant's social perception: A constructive view. In L.B. Cohen and P. Salapatek (eds.), *Infant Perception*, Vol. 2, New York: Academic, 1975.

McGraw, M.B. Maturation of behavior. In L. Carmichael (ed.), *Manual of Child Psychology*, New York: Wiley, 1946.

Mead, G.H. *Mind, Self and Society*, Chicago: University of Chicago, 1934.

Meicler, M.C. The level of object conceptualization in human infants as manifested by tracking responses to a moving object. Unpublished Ph.D. Dissertation, University of Houston, 1976.

Meltzoff, A.N. and Moore, M.K. Imitation of facial and manual gestures by human neonates, *Science*, 1977, **198**, 75–78.

Michotte, A. Perception and cognition. *Acta Psychologica*, 1955, **11**, 69–91.

Moore, M.K. Object permanence and object identity: A stage developmental model. Paper presented at the Biennial Meeting of the Society for Research in Child Development, Denver, April, 1975.

Nelson, K. The conceptual basis for naming. Mimeographed Manuscript, 1976, Yale University, New Haven.

Nelson, K.E. Concepts, word and sentence: Interrelations in acquisition and development. *Psychological Review*, 1974, **81**, 267–285.

Olson, D.R. Language and thought: Aspects of a cognitive theory of semantics. *Psychological Review*, 1970, **77**, 257–273.

Piaget, J. *Biology and Knowledge*. Chicago: University of Chicago, 1971.

Piaget, J. *The Construction of Reality in the Child*. New York: Basic, 1954.

Piaget, J. *The Origins of Intelligence in Children*. New York: International Universities, 1952.

Piaget, J. *Play, Dreams, and Imitation*. New York: Norton, 1951.

Piaget, J. *The Psychology of Intelligence*. New York: Harcourt-Brace, 1950.

Polanyi, M. *Personal Knowledge: Toward a Post-Critical Philosophy*. London: Routledge and Kegan Paul, 1958.

Popper, K.R. *Conjectures and Refutations*. London: Routledge and Kegan Paul, 1963.

Richards, M.P.M. (ed.), *The Integration of a Child into a Social World*. London: Cambridge University, 1974.

Riegel, K.F. (ed.), *The Development of Dialectical Operations*. Basil: Karger, 1975.

Rosch, E. On the internal structure of perceptual and semantic categories. In T.E. Moore (ed.), *Cognitive Development and the Acquisition of Language*, New York: Academic, 1973.

Ryan, J. Early language development: Towards a communication analysis. In M.P.M. Richards (ed.), *The Integration of a Child into a Social World*. London: University of Cambridge, 1974.

Saal, D. A study of the development of object concept in infancy varying the degree of discrepancy between the disappearing and reappearing object. Unpublished Ph.D. Dissertation, University of Houston, 1975.

Salapatek, P. Pattern perception in early infancy. In L.B. Cohen and P. Salapatek, (eds.), *Infant Perception*, Vol. 1, New York: Academic, 1975.

Sameroff, A. Transactional models in early social relations. *Human Development*, 1975, **18**, 65–79.

Sander, L.W. Infant and caretaking environment: Investigation and conceptualization of adaptive behavior in a system of increasing complexity. In E.J. Anthony (ed.), *The Child Psychiatrist as Investigator*, New York: Plenum, 1977.

Schaffer, H.R., Collis, G.M. and Parsons, G. Vocal interchange and visual regard in verbal and pre-verbal children. In H.R. Schaffer (ed.), *Studies in Mother-Infant Interaction*. London: Academic, 1977.

Schofield, L. and Uzgiris, I.C. Examining behavior and the development of the concept of the object. Paper presented at the Biennial Meeting of the Society for Research in Child Development, Santa Monica, California, March, 1969.

Sinclair-de Zwart, H. Language acquisition and cognitive development. In T.E. Moore, (ed.), *Cognitive Development and the Acquisition of Language*. New York: Academic, 1973.

Smillie, D. Sketch for a theory of human development. Mimeographed manuscript, New College of the University of South Florida, Sarasota.

Smillie, D. and Coppotelli, H. Imitation in early infancy: A critical reappraisal. Mimeographed manuscript, New College of The University of South Florida, Sarasota, 1977.

Stern, D.N. The goal and structure of mother-infant play. *Journal of American Academy of Child Psychiatry*, 1974, **13**, 402–421.

Stern, D.N. Mother and infant at play: The dyadic interaction involving facial, vocal, and gaze behaviors. In M. Lewis and L.A. Rosenblum (eds.), *The Effect of the Infant on its Caregiver*. New York: Wiley, 1974b.

Stone, G.P. and Garberman, H.A. (eds.), *Social Psychology Through Symbolic Interaction*. Waltham, Mass: Xerox, 1970.

Uzgiris, I.C. Patterns of cognitive development in infancy. *Merrill-Palmer Quarterly*, 1973, **19**, 181–204.

Uzgiris, I.C. and Hunt, J. McV. *Assessment in Infancy*. Urbana: University of Illinois, 1975.

Vygotsky, L.S. *Thought and Language*. Cambridge: M.I.T., 1962.

Werner, H. Microgenesis and aphasia. *Journal of Abnormal and Social Psychology*, 1956, **52**, 347–353.

White, B.L. *Human Infants: Experience and Psychological Development*. Englewood Cliffs, N.J.: Prentice-Hall, 1971.

White, S.H. Social implications of IQ. In S.H. White (ed.) *Human Development in Today's World*. Boston: Educational Associates, 1976.

Wilson, E.O. *Sociobiology: The New Synthesis*. Cambridge: Belknap, 1975.

Yonas, A. and Pick, H.L., Jr. An approach to the study of infant space perception. In L.B. Cohen and P. Salapatek (eds.), *Infant Perception*, Vol. 2, New York: Academic, 1975.

Zelazo, P.R., Zelazo, N.A. and Kolb, S. "Walking" in the newborn. *Science*, 1972, **176**, 14–15.

CHAPTER 13

Socioemotional Development[1]

L. Alan Sroufe

The loving mother teaches her child to walk alone. She is far enough from him so that she cannot actually support him, but she holds out her arms to him. She imitates his movements, and if he totters, she swiftly bends as if to seize him, so that the child might believe that he is not walking alone . . . And yet, she does more. Her face beckons like a reward, an encouragement. Thus, the child walks alone with his eyes fixed on his mother's face, not *on the difficulties in his way. He supports himself by the arms that do not hold him and constantly strives towards the refuge in his mother's embrace, little suspecting* that in the very same moment that he is emphasizing his need of her, he is proving that he can do without her, *because he is walking alone. (Kierkegaard, 1846)*

The child grows not as a perceptive being, not as a cognitive being, but as a human being who experiences anxiety, joy, and anger, and who is connected to its world in an emotional way. The infant's engagement of the observable and manipulable world is not merely a cognitive engagement but an affective engagement as well. It seeks and moves away, turns toward and shrinks back, opens up and shuts out.

As does cognition, affect organizes the infant's behavior. In many ways affect *is* the meaning of a transaction with the surround for the infant (Stechler and Carpenter, 1967); affective life is the meaning and motivational system that cognition serves. As Vygotsky (1962) has pointed out, a separation between cognition and affect "makes the thought process appear as an autonomous flow of thoughts thinking themselves, segregated from the fullness of life, from the personal needs and interests, the inclinations and impulses of the thinker" [p. 8].

Viewing the task of infant research as understanding the total organization of development, it becomes clear that emotion and cognition must be studied together. The infant is an affective being whose experience is made up of sensation, action, and feeling—not thought (e.g., Piaget, 1952; Stechler and Carpenter, 1967; Tennes et al., 1972). But awareness and recognition are cognitive processes, processes without which emotion proper does not exist. Emotions, as opposed to autonomic arousal or facial expressions, are cognitive as well as affective events, being the result of a cognitive engagement and later of an appraisal process. Likewise, emotional growth and experience and affective expression contribute vitally to cognitive and social development (e.g., Sroufe and Waters, 1976a).

There is now growing acceptance in developmental psychology of this integrative, organizational view of development (e.g., Brody and Axelrod, 1970; Escalona, 1968;

[1]This paper was supported by a contract grant from the National Institute of Mental Health (278-75-0030 ER). Send reprint requests to L. Alan Sroufe, Institute of Child Development, University of Minnesota, Minneapolis, Minnesota 55455.

Emde et al., 1976). Papers and volumes are appearing on cognitive factors in affect expression (Zelazo, 1972; McCall, 1972), the effect of infant temperament and affect expression on caregiver behavior (e.g., Lewis and Rosenblum, 1974), the effects of attachment on cognitive development (e.g., Bell, 1970; Clark-Stewart, 1973), affect in cognitive assessment (Haviland, 1975b), social cognition (Flavell et al., 1968), and developmental studies of cognitive-motivational variables (Yarrow et al., 1975). Chapters in a volume such as this may be arbitrarily divided into perception, learning, and so forth, but increasingly what is being sought is an integrated picture of infant development. How do perception and learning work together, and how are they to be integrated with what can be called cognition? How do learning and cognition contribute to social development, and how does social development influence cognitive growth? In short, we are moving away from an interest in the capacities of the infant toward the goal of understanding the organization of infant development that is built upon those capacities.

Within the organizational view, the emergence of affects is related to central nervous system maturation and concurrently to central themes in social and cognitive development (Cicchetti and Sroufe, 1976; Emde, et al., 1976; Sroufe and Waters, 1976a). Emotional development is studied in relation to major behavior systems in infancy—attachment, wariness, affiliation, curiosity/exploration (e.g., Bischof, 1975; Bowlby, 1969; Bretherton and Ainsworth, 1974)—and with regard to major developmental tasks, such as physiological regulation, differentiation of self and others, and mastery of the object world (e.g., Mahler, 1975; Sander, 1969, 1974). And emotional life is related to major stages and processes within ego theory: ego formation, self-awareness, self-regulation and self-control, mastery, and autonomy (Block and Block, 1973; Brody and Axelrod, 1970; Escalona, 1968; Mahler, 1975; Loevinger, 1976; Spitz, 1959).

At the same time, the organizational point of view, with a central place for affect and motivation, sheds light on such traditional areas of study within infant social development as attachment, stranger fear, affiliation, and personality formation itself. Frequently, conceptual confusion in these problem areas has resulted from explanatory attempts divorced from consideration or understanding of the infant as a complex emotional being. When the organizational viewpoint is adopted, evidence that infants are wary of novel persons gains perspective and may be integrated with information concerning infants' affiliative tendencies, rather than sparking debate about the true nature of the infant's reaction. And questions about whether cognitive, in contrast to affective, factors underlie the formation of attachment lose their force. These factors are not in competition; in the emphasis on attachment as an affective bond it is assumed that this bond is built upon learning and is dependent upon cognitive development. At the same time, the attachment relationship likely influences exploration, problem-solving attitude, the sense of efficacy and other factors vital to cognitive development and performance.

Studying emotional development, then, is necessary for formulating a total, integrated view of the infant and for engaging central topic areas in social and personality development. Moreover, it has importance for major problems that cut across domains of developmental psychology. For example, following the demise of drive reduction as central in explanations of human behavior (White, 1959; Bowlby, 1969; Mandler, 1975), what is to be the role of motivational constructs in developmental theory? Given the strong situational influences on discrete behaviors and the lack of evidence for homotypic continuity (Kagan and Moss, 1962; Mischel, 1968), how is continuity in personal and social adaptation to be demonstrated? And how is a model of development to be formulated in which the transitions between stages or phases of development can be conceptualized?

The relevance of studies of emotional development for each of these problems will be illustrated on subsequent pages. By investing in the study of emotional development, we not only uncover certain phenomena of great interest we also may expect important advances in the field in general.

THE ORGANIZATION OF DEVELOPMENT

The organization of development refers to the nature of the developmental process, the way in which behaviors are hierarchically organized into more complex patterns within developmental systems, the way in which later modes and functions evolve from earlier prototypes, and the way in which part functions are integrated into wholes (Breger, 1974; Emde et al., 1976; Escalona, 1968; Santostefano and Baker, 1972; Spitz, 1959; Werner and Kaplan, 1964). It refers to relationships between systems—physiologic and psychological, cognitive, social and affective, and subsystems within these—and to consequences of advances and lags in one system for other systems (Brody and Axelrod, 1970; Cicchetti and Sroufe, 1976; Emde et al., 1976; Sroufe and Waters, 1976a). It refers to the consequences of earlier adaptations for later adaptation (Brody and Axelrod, 1970; Erikson, 1950; Escalona, 1968; Mahler, 1975; Sander, 1962; Spitz, 1959; Yarrow and Goodwin, 1965). And it refers to the increasingly smooth and synchronous flow of the stream of behavior and to the tendency for this flow to be increasingly under the control of psychological (anticipation, memory, intentionality) as opposed to physiological processes.

As is cognitive development, emotional development itself is organized; it reflects and is influenced by the organization of development in general. Understanding the ontogenesis and function of affect requires an understanding of developmental organization; yet, the study of emotional development reveals the principles of organization with great clarity.

The discussion of some principles of organization below is arbitrarily sectioned into those operating primarily in the first half and those operating in the second half year. This is for emphasis only; each principle operates across the course of infancy. Moreover, what is perhaps the primary principle of developmental organization, the repeated emergence of new levels of organization (converging lines of development and subsequent intersystemic reorganizations), applies to both the early and later infancy periods (Brody and Axelrod, 1970; Emde et al., 1976). This principle will be expanded in the discussion of stages of affective development.

Themes in the Organization of Early Development

The Physiological Context of Behavior

While temperament, state, and physiological regulation exert influence throughout infancy, they are prominent major themes in the early weeks and months of life when maturation is dominant in development (Emde et al., 1976). Indeed, establishing some regularity in physiological cycles is widely considered the first adaptive task of the infant (e.g., Emde et al., 1976; Sander, 1962, 1974). Important individual variation is captured by the infant's activity level, reactivity, and ability to settle itself or be settled (Brazelton, 1961, 1973; Emde et al., 1976; Escalona, 1968; Thomas et al., 1968). Wide individual differences in sleep-wake cycles, crying time, and reactivity are reported (Birns et al.,

1966; Brackbill, 1975; Clemente et al., 1972; Osofsky and Danzger, 1974; Robinson, 1970; Wolff, 1966). And cyclic or transient neurophysiological state and maturation of neurofunctioning are primary determinants of behavioral expressions later to be linked with emotions (Bell et al., 1971; Korner, 1969, 1971; Moss, 1967; Parmalee, 1972; Sroufe and Waters, 1976a).

For example, the REM sleep smile of the newborn apparently reflects fluctuation in CNS arousal, a process that declines with maturation of the cortex, dropping out entirely by about age 3 months (Emde et al., 1976; Spitz et al., 1970; Sroufe and Waters, 1976a). Even early elicited smiles are heavily dependent on state, with alert smiles ontogenetically later than smiles elicited while asleep or drowsy (Wolff, 1963). Likewise, there is wide agreement that early distress derives primarily from enteroceptive (e.g., pain, hunger) stimulation; infants in the first 3 or 4 weeks of life are quite insensitive to noxious external stimulation (e.g., Tennes et al., 1972; Wolff, 1969). This insensitivity is also reflected in the difficulty of establishing conditioning, habituation, and heart rate deceleration (the cardiac OR) during early infancy (see Emde et al., 1976, for a review).

One might say in summary that in early infancy behavior is heavily influenced by the physiological context within which the stimulation occurs. Such contextual factors include enduring characteristics of the individual (temperament) and transient state of arousal. While temperament, state, and neurological maturation remain important, interacting with experience (e.g., Escalona, 1968), they become subordinated to other principles of developmental organization. For example, after the first half-year, hunger no longer evokes excitation or even significant behavioral change (Escalona, 1968). The physiological prototypes of behavioral organization give way to psychophysiological processes (Emde et al., 1976; Sroufe and Waters, 1976a).

The Trend Toward Active Involvement in Producing Stimulation

In parallel to the increasing amount of time the infant is awake and alert is a psychological process, reflected in an increasing involvement in the surround and a trend toward more active participation in producing affectively effective stimulation. This trend toward active participation is perhaps the central developmental theme in infancy (see Sroufe and Waters, 1976a). In early infancy this tendency takes the form of arousal becoming increasingly a function of the infant's transaction with external events, rather than being in one-to-one correspondence to the quantity of stimulation. At first this is a matter of sustaining attention and following changes in stimulation; by the 3rd month it involves processing the *content* of the stimulation as well.

In the ontogenesis of smiling, for example, gentle modulated stimulation is first effective. Here, quantity and other physical parameters of the stimulation are crucial; any stimulation that sufficiently jostles the nervous system will do. Later smiles that occur when the infant is alert and attentive are larger and have a shorter latency (Wolff, 1963). This trend toward a more active role for the infant and more vigorous smiling continues as dynamic stimuli (e.g., nodding head and voice) and, by 8 to 12 weeks, static visual stimuli become effective, the latter presumably requiring the greatest cognitive effort (Sroufe and Waters, 1976a). Here, the content of the event is crucial—that is, the arousal is produced by a cognitive process. We know that *awareness* of the content of the stimulation is involved because repeated presentations of the *same* event (e.g., toy clown; Shultz and Zigler, 1970) will lead to smiling, whereas substitutions will produce continued orienting and attention without positive affect. The active involvement concept also captures Watson's (1972) observation of vigorous smiling and cooing in the 3rd month to mobiles which move contingent upon the infant's actions.

The trend toward active participation in stimulation is also apparent in negative reactions. Distress at first is produced primarily by enteroceptive stimulation, later by noxious or captivating external stimulation, still later by the cessation of pleasurable interaction, and finally by stimulation with a specific negative meaning (e.g., Bronson, 1972; Escalona, 1968; Brody and Axelrod, 1970; Tennes et al., 1972). For example, obligatory attention (Stechler and Latz, 1966), which produces distress, seems to be increasingly a function of incongruity rather than attractive visual stimulation (see Wariness-Fear, below).

As will be discussed further in considering specific affective systems, the baby's increasingly active participation in its experience continues throughout infancy, as does the tendency for the content of stimulation (and, later, specific meaning in relation to the baby's acts) to take precedence over the quantity of stimulation. Of course, just as state and temperament remain important, quantity of stimulation is never irrelevant; even older infants may laugh with joy in vigorous play or may become distressed by overstimulation.

From Global-Diffuse to Specific-Coordinated Actions

In early infancy when the infant is distressed, even by a specific external source, the reaction tends to be a diffuse total-body reaction; only later is there a directed, coordinated reaction with specificity in terms of the event. Charlotte Buhler (1930), in a classic work, has described the ontogenesis of negative reactions to a common early event—having the nose wiped. At first this tends to produce total-body involvement with flailing of the limbs. Only later do arm movements become sufficiently coordinated to bat away the hand, and a directed reaction to the nose being covered occurs even later. It is not until about 8 months that the infant will execute an anticipatory blocking movement. Such increased organization is also seen in the clear biphasic response in fear situations at about this time: behavioral and physiological orienting (evaluation), then negative reaction (Emde et al., 1976; Sroufe et al., 1974).

Similarly, positive reactions are increasingly characterized by specificity and coordination of behavior. General activity often builds to smiling and cooing in young infants, but later this is replaced by focused attention and anticipatory quieting, and later smiling can occur in the absence of motility (Escalona, 1968). Still later, the execution of specific intended acts, with anticipated consequences (e.g., pulling off a mask in peek-a-boo), are associated with positive affect. In general, anticipation and specificity in reaction are two signs of the infant's increased ability to interact meaningfully with objects and events. Such criteria are highly relevant to designating the emergence of emotions proper (e.g., pleasure, rage, and wariness, and later joy, anger, and fear), as distinct from their precursors.

Sensory, Sensorimotor, and Sensoriaffective Integration: The Roots of Control

Early in infancy repeated stimulation is responded to with little evidence of carry-over from one stimulus presentation to another (e.g., Tennes et al., 1972) or from one day to another in a habituation series (e.g., Emde et al., 1976; Sameroff and Cavanaugh, Chapter 10). Soon, however, a cumulation of effect can be observed. For example, Tennes et al. (1972) reported that in the 3rd month increased motor activity and then distress were noted with several presentations of a loud horn, whereas prior to that time there was a decrement in responsivity over trials or no consistent response. Such sensory integration is relevant to positive affect as well, since both positive and negative affect may be presumed to involve increases in tension (Sroufe et al., 1974; see Pleasure-Joy, below).

Tennes et al. (1972) also provide an example of the coordination of sensory, motor, and affective behaviors. Early in infancy, engaging visual stimulation sometimes leads to a prolonged cessation of behavior (obligatory attention), occasionally resulting in distress. But in the 2nd month such fixations are punctuated by periods of motor activity, smiling, and cooing ("positive discharge"), and brief glances away, which become the dominant reaction:

> This waxing and waning marked the onset of pleasurable responses . . . It represents a modulation of motor activity and of gazing, each preempting the other in alternation . . . The increased responsivity to stimulation results in irritability, but the concomitantly occurring increased coordination between sensorimotor systems increases the capacity to sustain more stimulation over longer periods of time without distress. As links between visual input and motor action develop, the infant becomes equipped with a means of dealing with stimulation, before a specific means of turning away or avoiding visual stimulation has developed. [p. 218]

Thus, the coordination of attention and motor activity initiates what will become positive emotion.

The affective component is so prominent in the punctuation and regulation of early behavior that Stechler and Carpenter (1967), in a paper of basic importance, propose the term "sensory-affective" to replace "sensory-motor" for the initial stage of development. Affective expression can be seen to mark, pace, or complete transactional loops in social and nonsocial interactions and to play a role in modulating arousal in continued engagements (Robson, 1967; Sroufe and Waters, 1976a; Stechler and Carpenter, 1967; Stern, 1974a, 1974b, 1975). Stern, (1974b) for example, has described how positive affective expression and gaze-aversion are coordinated to structure caregiver-infant interaction. By the 4th month the infant also has some ability to ignore stimulation (i.e., to redirect attention), even stimulation of a rather compelling, noxious nature (Tennes et al., 1972).

Later sensory-sensory and sensory-motor integrations, which Piaget (1952) described with the term "coordination of schemes," also have clear relevance for emotional development. As shall be presented below, the squeal of laughter in mock attack, wariness of novelty, fear, and focused anger—all, in one way or another—call upon coordinated sensory impressions or the failure (interruption) of an anticipated coordination. For example, the 5-month-old laughs at loud sounds made by the caregiver when face to face but cries when the sounds are made from behind, unexpectedly. Later, the 10-month-old laughs as it stuffs a cloth back into the caregiver's mouth, coordinating its action with a remembered visual experience. Or the infant may cry when, instead of the expected mother, a stranger steps from behind a screen, and it may be angry when an attempted securing action fails to produce a sought-after object. The tendency to impose order on experience is ever present. When order can be attained from novelty, incongruity (Berlyne, 1969) or uncertainty (Kagan, 1971), through mastery or repetition (Piaget, 1972), there is positive affect; when the orderly flow of cognition or behavior is inalterably interrupted (Mandler, 1975), there is negative affect.

Much more could be said about these and other early organizational principles, and they will receive some elaboration in presenting the specific affect systems. But, continuously relevant as they are, these are not the principles that characterize the second half-year, when basic human emotions (anger, joy, and fear) emerge. Here, we are concerned with the organization of meaning, with the organization of behavior of an active agent that is influenced by past experience and anticipated outcomes and that is beginning to know objects and persons as existing independent of its actions. Any impression of discontinuity between the principles outlined above and the organizational concepts to be discussed, however, is due to limits of exposition, and not to the behavior of infants. Nor should it be implied that experiential factors are not influential in early infancy when temperamental and maturational factors are so dominant (Yarrow and Goodwin, 1965). Sander (1962, 1974) for example, has argued that the task of early biological regulation is strongly influenced by the quality of care. And Stern (e.g., 1974a) among others, has shown that the character of early mother-infant interaction is a function of both infant and caregiver (Lewis and Rosenblum, 1974; Klaus et al., 1972).

Later Organization: Context, Behavioral Systems, and the Meaning of Behavior

A major obstacle in the study of emotional development has been the failure of researchers to go beyond the occurrence of behavior to its meaning and, in doing so, to put the affective reaction in its behavioral and situational context. In addition, there has been a failure to recognize the basic developmental proposition that a given behavior can have multiple meanings (serve multiple functions or multiple behavioral systems) and that multiple behaviors can serve the same function (e.g., Escalona,, 1968; Santostefano and Baker, 1972). The position taken here is that even descriptive studies of emotion entail inferences concerning the meaning of behavior, since emotions as constructs must be inferred. The problem of meaning is all the more apparent when the task at hand is comprehending the place and function of affect in the organization of behavior.

The Behavioral Context and the Meaning of Behavior

Obviously, behaviors do not occur in isolation; rather, there is a stream of behavior, and behaviors are integrated with other behaviors into reaction patterns (e.g., Escalona, 1968; Sroufe and Waters, 1976b). Increasingly with development, behavior is organized into complex patterns, with the meaning of a behavior depending on other behaviors that occur with it or precede and/or follow it. For example, contact-seeking mixed with pushing away, squirming to be put down, or general petulance has different significance than relaxed molding to the caregiver (see Attachment, below). Ten-month-old infants frequently smile at strangers in a standard stranger-approach situation, but these smiles occur predominantly when the stranger enters and is at a distance, becoming decreasingly likely as the stranger approaches, and are absent at pick-up (see Sroufe, 1977, for a review). Also, smiles to strangers may be followed or accompanied by looking away or other aversive reactions (Bretherton and Ainsworth, 1974; Waters et al., 1975). And, unlike responses when the caregiver enters, they typically are not integrated with bouncing and vocalization into what can be described as positive greeting behaviors (Vaughn, 1977). These observations point up the inadvisability of simple frequency counts of discrete behaviors and also make it clear that the presence of a single discrete behavior (e.g., a smile) is not sufficient for determining the affective tone of an episode.

The Situational Context

By the end of the second half-year the infant no longer responds to isolated stimulus events (e.g., an approaching stranger). Behavior becomes organized with respect to context. Setting (lab versus home), familiarization time, preceding events (e.g., a mother-separation episode), presence and location of the caregiver, and other aspects of the situation influence the reaction (Sroufe et al., 1974). With rather substantial alterations, context effects can be demonstrated in early infancy, as in Stechler and Carpenter's (1967) observation of distress to the sight of mother's face decontextualized (in a *gansfeldt*). But in the second half-year the effects are subtle and wide-ranging; for example, the generally positive reaction to mother approaching with a mask or negative reaction to a masked-stranger or to standard-stranger approach can be influenced by the order of the approaches or other preceding events (Emde et al., 1975; Skarin, 1976; Sroufe et al., 1974). These context effects reflect the infant's abilities to remember and anticipate experience, and to be more differentiated from the event, which increasingly leads to the infant's subjective relation to the event. For example, heart rate data indicate that sequence and setting effects are not due to changes in state; rather, they are assumed to reflect changing thresholds for threat (Sroufe et al., 1974). By the end of the 1st year, infants evaluate events in context, and their behavior must likewise be interpreted in terms of its organization within context.

As Escalona (1968) suggested, "What remains relatively stable in the behavioral organization of infants is not overt behavior, but the direction and extent of behavior change in response to different states and external conditions" [p. 200]. For example, stable individual differences in the quality of attachment simply cannot be assessed without considering situational factors (Ainsworth, 1974; Sroufe and Waters, 1977). Infants are expected to seek proximity, contact, or interaction not under all conditions, but under conditions of threat or need. An infant who requires a great deal of physical contact when external threat is minimal is probably insecurely attached. *Failure* to seek proximity when stress could be presumed (e.g., following a separation) is also significant. It is not proximity-seeking, but proximity-seeking in context that conveys information about the quality of the attachment relationship. In general, it is behavior in context that allows observers to infer emotional state in the preverbal infant, without sole reliance on the presence of adult facial expressions.

The Organization of Behavioral Systems

By the end of the 1st year, social behavior readily can be viewed as organized into major systems—attachment, affiliation, wariness, and curiosity/exploration—which interact in predictable ways (Bischof, 1975; Bowlby, 1969; Bretherton and Ainsworth, 1974). Particular behaviors can serve multiple systems; for example, looking, depending on its integration with other behaviors and the situational context, can serve any of the four systems mentioned above. Smiling too, if appeasement (van Hooff, 1972) and tension-modulation (Sroufe and Waters, 1976a) meanings are accepted, can serve the exploratory and wariness systems, as well as affiliation and attachment. Smiling certainly occurs during visual exploration and solitary play, as well as during interaction with the caregiver, and it occurs on encounters with strangers, even when followed by clear signs of wariness (e.g., Waters et el., 1975). Moreover, a given system can serve multiple motives, and multiple systems can be activated simultaneously or sequentially in the same external situation. Infants have been observed to smile and turn away (coy behavior) and to retreat to the caregiver following approach to a stranger, only to turn and visually explore the stranger once again (Bretherton and Ainsworth, 1974). Here, the attachment system is serving both exploration and comfort-seeking.

Such complexity does not preclude accurate interpretation of infant behavior, but it does require that meaning be inferred from patterns or constellations of behavior in context. Ainsworth (e.g., Ainsworth et al., 1974) has argued convincingly that individual differences in the security or quality of attachment must be conceptualized in terms of the organization of attachment behaviors, not in terms of frequencies of discrete behaviors. For example, smiling and showing a toy on reunion following separation can be functionally equivalent to proximity-seeking (see Attachment, below), and ignoring the caregiver or avoiding eye contact on reunion suggests a maladaptive (insecure) attachment relationship, regardless of the number of looks during pre-separation play (see Attachment, below).

It should be restated that the complexity resides in infant behavior, and comprehending infant emotional development requires a commensurate complexity of analysis. In particular, the human infant's motivation concerning novelty is quite complex: both strong tendencies to be wary of novel objects and persons *and* to approach, to explore, and to affiliate are well documented in the empirical literature (e.g., Bretherton and Ainsworth, 1974; Bronson, 1972; Rheingold and Eckerman, 1973; Schaffer and Emerson, 1964; Sroufe et al., 1974). The need for such complexity in a species whose adaptation is based on flexibility and opportunism has been discussed by a number of investigators (e.g., Breger, 1974; Bronson, 1972; Bowlby, 1973; Sroufe and Waters, 1976a). It makes sense that the strong curiosity/exploratory tendency is in dynamic balance with wariness (e.g., that immediate approach be inhibited in the face of novelty (Schaffer, et al., 1972), and that presence of the caregiver be crucial in this balance (see Sroufe, 1977, for further discussion).

Finally, comprehending emotional development and individual differences in adaptation requires an appreciation of the interaction of various behavioral systems. Attachment, for example, has been defined in terms of an attachment-exploration balance and in terms of its relationship to the wariness and affiliation systems (Bretherton and Ainsworth, 1974; Bischof, 1975). Securely attached infants should be able to use the caregiver as a secure base for exploration, mastery of the object world being a major task of the 1-year-old (Ainsworth, 1973; Mahler, 1975). The inability to part from the caregiver for the purpose of exploration suggests an insecure attachment, not a strong attachment (see Attachment, below). Similarly, the relationship between attachment and wariness-affiliation is one of dynamic balance, *not* a one-to-one correspondence (e.g., *not:* the more attachment the more wariness of strangers). In the caregiver's presence, the securely attached infant should warm up to and be able to engage a novel person; but when distressed, contact with an unfamiliar person may well be avoided (Ainsworth et al., 1971).

THE ONTOGENESIS OF THE EMOTIONS

The ontogenesis of the emotions poses a problem for the student of developmental organization, but at the same time it provides clues concerning the nature of that organization. From the developmental perspective, there must be a logic in the appearance of the emotions and there must be an orderly process in the unfolding of later emotions from their precursors. Coemergence of different emotions often points to common underlying development, and major developmental reorganizations will be associated with the emergence of new emotions or qualitative changes in previously existing emotional systems. Similarly, major changes in the emotional repertoire signify major developmental changes in other domains as well (e.g., Brody and Axelrod, 1970; Emde, et al., 1976; Sroufe and Waters, 1976a).

Bridges' paper on the ontogenesis of the emotions has been *the* reference since 1932 and certainly qualifies as a developmental analysis (Table 13-1). The principle of differentiation sets   rd for studying emotional development, clearly suggesting an integration with general development. The idea that specific emotions evolve out of earlier, undifferentiated distress or nondistress states (away from global to more specific reactions) retains validity and has even received further support (see Principles of Early Organization). However, Bridges did not specify the basis on which she inferred particular affect in her subjects, and her formulation requires considerable revision and elaboration.

As early as 1934, Florence Goodenough pointed out that very young infants are more capable and complex than Bridges supposed. "General excitement" does not cover the infant's repertoire (see Early Organization). Bridges was correct in thinking that, if overly excited, the young infant's reaction would be distress, and that distress is related to arousal in a continuous fashion.[2] There are no emotions in the early weeks of life. Her view can be elaborated, however, by considering the different routes to distress, within which are the roots of later emotional reactions. In general, Bridges did not really link the specific emotions with their precursors or really illustrate the process of differentiation. She did not, for example, indicate the common elements between rage and anger, or the precursors of fear, or indicate *how* one emotion evolved to another. Finally, she did not call upon general development to explain why particular emotions appeared when they did.

Table 13-1. Showing the Approximate Ages of Differentiation of the Various Emotions During the First 2 Years of Life (Bridges, 1932)

					EX.						Birth
				DI.	EX.	DE.					3 months
FE.	DG.	AN.		DI.	EX.	DE.					6 months
FE.	DG.	AN.		DI.	EX.	DE.		EL.	Affection		12 months
FE.	DG.	AN.	JE.	DI.	EX.	DE.		EL.	A.A.	A.C.	18 months
FE.	DG.	AN.	JE.	DI.	EX.	DE.	JO.	EL.	A.A.	A.C.	24 months

Key: A.A.: affection for adults; A.C.: affection for children; AN.: anger; DE.: delight; DG.: disgust; DI.: distress; EL.: elation; EX.: excitement; FE.: fear; JE.: jealousy; JO.: joy.

[2]One way of putting this is that prior to maturation of limbic structures, there is only undifferentiated brianstem arousal and not arousal associated with various emotions.

There has been an attempt to draw upon the empirical literature and current theory in developing the reformulation to be presented. With Bridges and others, it is assumed here that true emotions do not begin until a basic differentiation between the "self" and the surround has been made—that is, until the emergence of rudimentary consciousness or Ego (e.g., Spitz et al., 1970). Prior to this point, however, the infant can, for obvious survival purposes, communicate distress, and also exhibits a prototype of later positive emotions (a "turning toward"; Spitz, 1963). In the endogenous smiles of the neonate (fluctuating states of arousal) and the global distress reactions caused by pain, hunger, physical restraint, arresting stimulation, or sudden noxious stimulation, are the precursors of delight and joy, anger, fear, and surprise; yet, this early distress and quiescence is not properly called emotion, because it is simply a function of *amount* of global arousal.

The conceptualization here is more differentiated than that of Bridges. Fear, for example, is traced out of early obligatory attention and then the psychological arrest due to a mixture of familiar and unfamiliar elements (wariness). With both precursors, it is assumed that stopping the flow of behavior ultimately will lead to increased arousal and distress (see Mandler, 1975). Wariness is considered an emotional reaction because the content (quality versus quantity) of the external event is relevant; both wariness and obligatory attention are considered precursors of fear because the stilling, locked attention, and distress are due to an external event (psychological arrest). In this view, the precursors of rage are related to precursors of wariness. Here, however, the spontaneous flow of overt behavior is physically blocked, as in head restraint, or earlier, due to intense distress itself. When the rage reaction is due to blocking or termination of an established motor sequence or the termination of an interaction, it is considered an emotional response in the present scheme (see below). It is analogous to the failure of assimilation/accommodation in wariness, but here it is a failure of motor assimilation rather than cognitive assimilation.

While the developmental chart outlined in Table 13-2 is based on available empirical literature (see Affect Systems, below), it is to some extent theoretically derived. There has been a deliberate attempt to draw developmental parallels across affect systems. Thus, fear, anger, and joy are presented as emerging during the same developmental period. While this parallel is not completely established, it is a reasonable working assumption that the major developmental reorganization during the third quarter of life—with major advances in object concept, intentionality, and causality—would have implications for each of the affect systems (and that major changes in affect would be associated with such cognitive advances). In the positive affect system, for example, "delight" refers to laughter in response to vigorous stimulation (reflexive laughter) in the second quarter. The term joy is reserved until the third quarter to capture the active mastery apparent at this time (Piaget, 1952; Sander, 1962; Sroufe and Waters, 1976a). Although the tendency toward active participation continues throughout infancy, there seems to be a qualitative turning point here. A similar case will be made with the other affect systems, and with other periods of developmental reorganization.

Stages in the Development of Affect

In a sense, when affect is viewed as the "force," and cognition the "structure" of mental life (Piaget, 1952), there can be no stages of affective development. But in an integrated view of development, affect and cognition are interdependent, and the stages of development therefore apply to both domains:

Table 13-2. The Ontogenesis of Some Basic Human Emotions[a]

Month	Pleasure-Joy	Wariness-Fear	Rage-Anger	Periods of Emotional Development
0	Endogenous smile	Startle/pain	Distress due to: covering the face, physical restraint, extreme discomfort	Absolute stimulus barrier
1	Turning toward	Obligatory attention		Turning toward
2				
3	Pleasure		Rage (disappointment)	Positive affect
4				
	Delight Active laughter	Wariness		
5				
6				Active participation
7	Joy		Anger	
8				
9		Fear (stranger aversion)		Attachment
10				
11				
12	Elation	Anxiety Immediate fear	Angry mood, petulance	Practicing
18	Positive valuation of self-affection	Shame	Defiance	Emergence of self
24			Intentional hurting	
36	Pride, love		Guilt	Play and fantasy

[a]The age specified is neither the first appearance of the affect in question nor its peak occurrence; it is the age when the literature suggests that the reaction is common.

The cognitive schemes which are initially centered upon the child's own action become the means by which the child constructs an objective and "decentered" universe; similarly, and at the same sensori-motor levels, affectivity proceeds from a lack of differentiation between the self and the physical and human environment toward the construction of a group of exchanges or emotional investments which attach the differentiated self to other persons (through interpersonal feelings) or things (through interests at various levels). [p. 21]

The stages outlined below, then, are not coincidentally parallel to descriptions of cognitive development (Table 13-3), though they have been to some extent independently derived. The three major developmental reorganizations described, which are taken from Spitz (e.g., 1965), were in fact inspired by observations of emotional development, as were the eight "stages" of emotional development listed in Table 13-3. Parallels between the cognitive and affective stages will be discussed in the section on the affect-cognition interchange.

Developmental Organizers and Affect Development

Spitz has suggested three qualitative turning points in early development, each marked by a change in affectivity and each reflecting a basic transformation in psychological life— the emergence of new functions and a qualitatively different process for interacting with the environment (Spitz, 1959, 1965; Emde et al., 1976). Spitz postulated, with some evidence (e.g., Spitz et al., 1970), that such converging lines of development, and the consequent developmental reorganization, were linked to CNS maturation. Recently, Emde et al. (1976) have presented further documentation for this position, drawing on comparative literature and psychological and physiological data on human infants. Developmental changes in the EEG, sleep patterns, autonomic responses, and affective expression have been shown to converge, consonant with the first two periods of reorganization described by Spitz.

The first "organizer," marked by the reliable *social* (exogenous) *smile,* represents the infant's basic distinction between the "in here" and the "out there." There is beginning recognition of repeatability in the surround and awareness moving toward anticipation (Spitz, 1963; Spitz et al., 1970). There can be pleasure as the infant finds familiarity in the "out there" and disappointment when the contact is broken. To Spitz, these are the first true emotions because they reflect a *relation between the infant and the surround.* The very fact of the exogenous smile reveals such an awareness, because such elicited smiling occurs only to highly familiar events (e.g., the face) or following a number of presentations of a novel event. The infant "recognizes" this *particular* event (Sroufe and Waters, 1976a). This is a qualitative turn in development. Before this time infant behavior seems to fit a discharge, hydraulic, or homeostatic model; now seeking and maintaining contact with stimulation are prominent (Emde et al., 1976).

The new sensitivity to reliability in the surround moves development forward at an ever-increasing rate until the press of development forces another reorganization. In part this can be viewed as recognition memory leading to recall memory, object permanence, and other cognitive-motivational advances, as the infant can begin coordinating experiences. Experience becomes more organized as current and previous events can be related and as events are engaged with expectation. Ultimately, infants in the 1st year can act with regard to objects not visually present, affectively respond to their loss or recovery, and *experience this affective reaction in connection with the event.* This is a new level of awareness (see Brody and Axelrod, 1970). In Spitz' view (1965), this reorganization is signaled by *stranger anxiety*—the failure of the stranger's face to match the stored image of the mother. A broader view of recall memory and expectation, as associated with the differentiation of persons, object relations, and *fear* in general, seems more defensible (see also Emde et al., 1976). Stranger fear, reflecting anxiety over loss of mother, is contestable (e.g., Emde et al., 1976; Fraiberg, 1969). Still, the view of a major developmental reorganization in the third quarter seems descriptively accurate, with implications for positive affect, as well as fear and anger.

As an intentional being in a world with permanent objects, which can be acted on in planned ways [Kagan's (1969) "activation of hypotheses"], the infant moves toward a third reorganization. Many theorists have described the emergence of the autonomous self in the 2nd year with *awareness of the self as a separate being* (e.g., Erikson, 1950; Mahler, 1975; Sander, 1962). For Mahler, for example, the infant's moving out into the world ("practicing") necessarily leads to the awareness of separateness. Spitz emphasizes more the infant's discovery of will. In any case, the increased capacity for internal representation, object mastery skills, and increased mobility *converge* to support the infant's use of the caregiver as a secure base for exploration. This experience in mastering the surround on one's own in turn leads to the emergence of the autonomous self and to qualitative change in the child's cognitive transactions with the environment, perhaps influenced by CNS maturation (see Emde et al., 1975). This developmental reorganization is supported by evidence that at 18 months infants typically recognize themselves in a mirror, whereas at 12 months they do not (Amsterdam, 1972; Brooks and Lewis, 1975). It is also supported by apparent changes in the cognitive domain [e.g., Piaget's stage 6, the transition from the sensorimotor behavior to representational thought and Lenneberg's (1967) biological readiness for language] and in the affective domain. Spitz argued that this third major developmental reorganization was marked by negativism. More generally, it can be argued that *defiance, shame, affection,* and *positive valuation of the self* evolve only with the emergence of the autonomous self. For example, while infants certainly become attached in the 1st year and express joy and pleasure upon greeting, exploring, and interacting with the caregiver, true *affection* is perhaps best conceived as an emotion experienced by a well-differentiated self with regard to a clearly represented other. Nonelicited "love pats" are quite common in 18-month-olds, rare in 12-month-olds (unpublished data).

Extrapolating from Spitz' system, a fourth organizer would also be marked by a major affective change, advances in cognitive development, and further differentiation of the self-concept. Such a nodal point is suggested by the 3-year-old's capacity for fantasy play, role-taking, and beginning identification. It is only after the infancy period, when with continued differentiation of the self there is identification and internalization of standards, that we see *guilt, love,* and *pride,* which evolve from the emotions of the preceding period. The more separated being is capable of a greater connectedness and a wider range of emotions.

Eight "Stages" of Infant Affective Development[3]

Drawing on the work of a number of investigators (e.g., Bronson and Pankey, 1977; Escalona, 1968; Mahler, 1975; Sander, 1962, 1969; Sroufe and Waters, 1976a; Sroufe

---

[3]These "stages" are not proposed as a necessary, invariant sequence, but rather as normatively descriptive. Whether they are true "stages" (cf. Flavell, 1971) is an empirical question.

Table 13-3. Stages of Cognitive Development and Related Changes in the Affective and Social Domains

Cognitive Development (Piaget)	Affective Development (Sroufe)	Social Development (Sander)
0–1 Use of reflexes Minimal generalization/accommodation of inborn behaviors	**0–1 Absolute Stimulus Barrier** Built-in protection	**0–3 Initial Regulation** Sleeping, feeding, quieting, arousal Beginning preferential responsiveness to caregiver
1–4 Primary Circular Reaction First acquired adaptations (centered on body) Anticipation based on visual cues Beginning coordination of schemes	**1–3 Turning Toward** Orientation to external world Relative vulnerability to stimulation Exogenous (social) smile	
4–8 Secondary Circular Reaction Behavior directed toward external world (sensorimotor "classes" and recognition) Beginning goal orientation (procedures for making interesting sights last; deferred circular reactions)	**3–6 Positive Affect** Content-mediated affect (pleasurable assimilation, failure to assimilate, disappointment, frustration) Pleasure as an excitatory process (laughter, social responsivity) Active stimulus barrier (investment and divestment of affect)	**4–6 Reciprocal Exchange** Mother and child coordinate feeding, caretaking activities Affective, vocal, and motor play
	7–9 Active Participation Joy at being a cause (mastery initiation of social games) Failure of intended acts (experience of interruption) Differentiation of emotional reactions (initial hesitancy, positive and negative social responses, and categories)	**7–9 Initiative** Early directed activity (infant initiates social exchange, preferred activities) Experience of success or interference in achieving goals

476

8–12 Coordination of Secondary Schemes & Application to New Situations

Objectification of the world (interest in object qualities & relations; search for hidden objects)
True intentionality (means-ends differentiation, tool-using)
Imitation of novel responses
Beginning appreciation of causal relations (others seen as agents, anticipation of consequences)

9–12 Attachment

Affectively toned schemes (specific affective bond, categorical reactions)
Integration and coordination of emotional reactions (context-mediated responses, including evaluation and beginning coping functions)

10–13 Focalization

Mother's availability and responsivity tested (demands focused on mother)
Exploration from secure base
Reciprocity dependent on contextual information

12–18 Tertiary Circular Reaction

Pursuit of novelty (active experimentation to provoke new effects)
Trial-and-error problem-solving (invention of new means)
Physical causality spatialized & detached from child's actions

12–18 Practicing

Mother the secure base for exploration
Elation in mastery
Affect as part of context (moods, stored or delayed feelings)
Control of emotional expression

14–20 Self-Assertion

Broadened initiative
Success and gratification achieved apart from mother

18–24 Invention of New Means Through Mental Combination

Symbolic representation (language, deferred imitation, symbolic play)
Problem-solving without overt action (novel combinations of schemes)

18–36 Emergence of Self-Concept

Sense of self as actor (active coping, positive self-evaluation, shame)
Sense of separateness (affection, ambivalence, conflict of wills, defiance)

and Wunsch, 1972; Tennes et al., 1972; White, 1971), a further differentiation of phases of affective development can be delineated (Table 13-2). Initially, there is a period of rather absolute nonresponsivity, which Tennes et al. (1972), following Benjamin, refer to as a *passive stimulus barrier* (stage 1). During this period, infants are relatively invulnerable to external stimulation, though Bergman and Escalona (1949) have pointed to important individual variation in this regard. Next, there is a period of *turning toward* the environment (stage 2). This is a period of relative vulnerability, since the infant is open to stimulation and has only preadapted tension-modulation devices (Tennes et al., 1972). These devices include the beginning coordination of attention, motor activity, and smiling and cooing, which help bring an end to the distress of obligatory attention (see Early Organization). In "turning toward" are the roots of interest and curiosity, as well as positive affect.

The crowning achievement of stage 2, the reliable social smile, ushers in the period of positive affect (stage 3), roughly 3 to 6 months (e.g., Escalona, 1968; White, 1971). Since during this phase there is awareness and "anticipation" (Spitz, 1963), motor expectations, and secondary circular reactions (Piaget, 1952), there can be disappointment and failures of assimilation. Consequently, frustration and such negative emotions as rage and wariness can be experienced. But the social smile and generally increased responsivity elicit positive engagement from the caregiver (e.g., Emide et al., 1976; Stern, 1974; Sroufe and Waters, 1976a), and many general schemes can be exercised without disruption. Probably based on maturation, infantile fussiness disappears during this period (Emde et al., 1976), and the infant has the capacity to actively avoid noxious stimulation (Tennes et al., 1972). The infant smiles and coos at its own feet, at its toy giraffe, and especially at the caregiver. For the first time it *laughs* in response to vigorous stimulation. "Pleasure has become an excitatory phenomenon," associated with high states of excitation (Escalona, 1968, p. 159). With eyes sparkling, caregiver and infant set out upon the task of establishing reciprocal exchanges (Sander, 1962).

The social awakening continues in the fourth stage (7–9 months), when the infant participates in social games (Sroufe and Wunsch, 1972) and makes "persistent efforts to elicit social responses" (Escalona, 1968, p. 188), even from other infants (Goodenough, 1934). In the first half-year infants will look at another infant and perhaps smile. But now they will vocalize, touch, cajole, and otherwise try to elicit a response from the baby. Infants also *initiate* interactions with the caregiver (Sander, 1962), explore the caregiver's person (Mahler, 1975), and, with budding intentionality, produce consequences in the inanimate environment (Escalona, 1968; Piaget, 1952). As there is increasing meaning in the infant's transactions with the surround, emotional reactions become more differentiated in this phase, with an initial hesitancy in the face of novel objects (Schaffer et al., 1972) and sober faces for strangers (e.g., Emde et al., 1976; Schaffer, 1966). This is the *period of active participation*, engagement, and mastery. It is also the period in which the infant becomes aware of its emotions. Joy, fear, anger, and surprise are its products.

Although infants continue to manifest strong affiliative tendencies toward people, including strangers (e.g., Bretherton and Ainsworth, 1974; Rheingold and Eckerman, 1973), an exclusive preoccupation with the caregiver may follow in stage 5 (e.g., Sander, 1962). This is accompanied by a temporarily subdued affective tone (Sroufe and Wunsch, 1972) and an intensification of stranger fear (Sroufe, 1977). This is the *period of attachment*, when immediate positive greetings to the caregiver emerge, the caregiver becomes a source of security, and emotional expression becomes highly differentiated and refined.

By the end of this stage one can see gradations of feeling, ambivalence, and moods, and rather clear communication of emotion.

In what can be called a *practicing phase* (Mahler, 1975), attachment-exploration balance (Ainsworth, 1973; Ainsworth, et al., 1971) or a phase of self-assertion (Sander, 1962), the infant is again ebullient in stage 6 (roughly 12–18 months). It actively *explores* and *masters* the inanimate environment. As when the infant grinned on pushing itself to hands and toes in stage 4, it appears delighted and even cocky with the first steps now. But as Mahler (1975) has described, this rather complete confidence and sense of well-being cannot endure unchallenged. Inevitably, the infant's moving out into the world leads to an awareness of separateness from the caregiver—a necessary but temporarily deflating step in the *formation of self-concept* (stage 7). To maintain the new-found sense of autonomy in the face of anxiety over separation and the increasing awareness of its limited power is the emotional task of the 2-year-old, a task that is ultimately resolved with the development of *play and fantasy* skills and, later, identification (stage 8; Breger, 1973).

Criteria for Judging the Presence of Emotion

To establish the heuristic value of the ontogenetic frameworks just presented or of any developmental conception of affect, it is necessary to have criteria for determining the appearance and unfolding of the emotions. Assessing emotion brings one to the center of major problems of definition and conceptualization (Ekman and Friesen, 1975b; see Charlesworth and Kreutzer, 1973, for a review).

If one takes the position that the facial expressions of emotion are isomorphic with the felt experience of the individual (e.g., as proposed by Izard, 1971) most problems of assessment disappear. An observer can assume that a particular affective experience is within the capacity of the infant when the particular affective expression is first seen. This approach assumes, however, that facial expressions that communicate affective states are identical in adults and infants and that the expressions will emerge in their most stereotyped, recognizable forms—assumptions that cannot be verified from existing data (see, however, Vaughn and Sroufe, 1976, with respect to facial expressions of surprise). It is also the case that while the stereotyped expressions of the primary affects are quite recognizable to adults living in a variety of cultures (Izard, 1971; Ekman, 1972; Ekman and Friesen, 1975b) these expressions are very rare in the facial displays of adults. Therefore, the presence of the expression is good prima facie evidence that a particular emotion is being experienced, though, if reports of fear faces during birth are taken seriously (e.g., Stirnimann, 1940), such expressions can be misleading. Certainly, the absence of such an expression cannot be conclusive concerning the absence of that experience.

Currently, a number of investigators are studying infant facial movement and expressions (e.g., Haviland, 1975a; Oster, 1976; Vaughn and Sroufe, 1976). These investigations include attempts at identifying static "face" or expressions, development of a *facial action code* (c.f. Oster, 1976; Ekman and Friesen, 1976a) and assessments of concomitant autonomic and behavioral measures of particular expressions (Vaughn and Sroufe, 1976). When fully developed, this work will undoubtedly make an important contribution to the study of infant emotional development. Of special interest for the study of emotional differentiation will be the proposed facial movement codes (e.g., Oster, 1976), since it may be that early, "primitive" preemotional states may contain facial movements that show up later in the differentiated emotions. Additional research coordinating autonomic, overt behavior, and facial expression, in context (i.e., convergent measures; Sroufe and Waters, 1976), can provide information about the question of whether the infant is experiencing an affective state prior to the time he displays facial expression which communicates that affect. It may be that the facial expression lags behind the capacity for experience but further amplifies and sharpens the experience.

There are several specific drawbacks of the exclusive emphasis on facial expression that should be mentioned. Relationships among phenotypically different emotional reactions cannot be pursued. Links with other development are unidirectional (find the age of emergence of the facial expression, then seek its correlates). Finally, vast areas of what we would include in the domain of emotional development (e.g., control and modulation) are relegated to a secondary status when emotional life is so tied to the facial expression.

The problem of validating facial expressions and the assessment of emotion in general can be illustrated by recent research on infants' reactions to strangers and incongruity. Even with careful study of videotape records of 200 8- to 16-month-old babies, being approached by strangers or in the face of incongruity, we have rarely seen a classic fear face (cf., Ekman and Friesen, 1976a). Much more frequently we have seen gaze-aversion, avoidance, and distress (especially when we violate a strong expectation[4]). Since babies in the first half-year rarely show these behaviors (Sroufe, 1977; Sroufe et al., 1974; Waters et al., 1975), a developmental change in emotion (or a change in the appraisal of the event) is thus implied. But which, if any, of these infants are afraid?

If fear is operationally defined as behavioral avoidance or crying (cf., Rheingold and Eckerman, 1973), then those babies that turn away from the stranger or cry are afraid. If fear is defined in psychological terms, for example, as a recognition of threat (cf. Arnold, 1960), then those babies that cry or turn away, especially at the *sight* of the stranger and especially on a second exposure, are fearful. Certainly, this reflects some kind of immediate, categorical negative reaction, which seems different from earlier distress following prolonged contact, and could reasonably be called fear (Bronson, 1976). Also, such crying and turning away are differential to stranger-approach compared to mother-approaches (Waters et al., 1975). And the incidence of such negative reactions is influenced by setting, familiarization time, sequence of events, and other aspects of context which could be presumed to alter the infant's threshold for threat (Sroufe et al., 1974).

What of responses like gaze-aversion and frowns or "wary brow" (Waters et al., 1975)? While more common in older infants, such reactions fail to meet the facial expression, operational definition, or response to threat criteria (they are, for example, less likely on a second trial).

However, gaze aversion, as one example, has been demonstrated to have important temporal correlates with autonomic arousal (Waters et al., 1975). During stranger-approach, gaze-aversion (partial closing of lids and downward turning of eyes) tended to occur near the peaks of heart rate (HR) acceleration. Following gaze-aversion, the HR recovered, and the infant once again regarded the stranger. Thus, this indicator of emotion was actually related to physiological arousal, as is crying. Behavioral avoidance (complete turning away early in the sequence) was not associated with HR acceleration. From this point of view, then, it might be said that avoidance *prevented* the fear response, whereas gaze-aversion was part of a fear reaction (Sroufe and Waters, 1976b).

[4]In one study (Vaughn and Sroufe, 1976), after playing peek-a-boo from behind a screen, the mother comes out wearing a mask or a stranger appears and approaches the baby.

The fact that determining the experience of an emotion in a nonverbal infant is complex and frequently involves a certain amount of inference does not produce a hopeless situation. We are able to say that fear, for example, emerges in the second half-year, though not with the certainty that would come with accepting the "fear face" as the index of fear. Ultimately, ties between the emergence of fear and earlier emotional development, fear and cognitive and social development, and even the emergence of what is being called "fear" here and the reliable presence of the fear face, can be traced. This is more consistent with the objectives of the discipline of emotional development, as defined in this chapter, than is determining the age at which emotions emerge by any given definition.

Specific Affect Systems

To accurately describe the ontogenesis of the various emotions, it is necessary to consider both continuity and discontinuity. In humans, no emotion suddenly appears full-blown; yet periods of rapid reorganization of behavior bring forth transitions such that a reaction, fleeting and irregular before, or occurring in certain defined circumstances, now becomes highly reliable, even in response to events previously impotent with respect to the affect in question. In the view presented here, there is a lawful ontogenetic trail for all of the classic emotions, originating in early infancy. At the same time there are qualitative changes in emotion and affective expression which capture and reflect reorganizations in psychological development (see Emde et al., 1976). Whether one wishes to call the social smiles of the 3-month-old indications of pleasure, or the reaction of the 10-month-old to an intruding stranger, fear, these reactions are qualitatively different from earlier expressions of positive and negative affect. Yet, they have their roots in these earlier expressions and are also logically related to later affect expression, as emotional life continues to evolve.

As a consequence, the following discussion will be built around evolving systems, and will point to relations between these systems and emotional development beyond the infancy period. As the discussion of developmental organization must have implied, even this division is somewhat arbitrary, made necessary for the sake of exposition.

Pleasure-Joy

In an earlier paper, a logical link between the early endogenous smiles of the neonate (e.g., Emde and Harmon, 1972; Emde et al., 1976; Wolff, 1963) and later smiles to external stimulation was established (Sroufe and Waters, 1976a). The neonatal smiles apparently reflect a fluctuating level of moderate arousal; they occur in bursts primarily during REM sleep and do not occur for some time following a startle or when the infant is alert. Soon smiles can be elicited, after a notable delay, by gentle, modulated stimulation, most easily while the infant is asleep or drowsy, later when awake and alert. Again, it is a matter of arousal rising above some hypothetical threshold, with the smile occurring with the relaxation, as arousal again declines (Figure 13-1).[5] It is not until about the 3rd month, however, that *psychological processing of the stimulus content* (recognition) leads to the smile, which may be suggested to indicate *pleasure*. At first smiling is a completely passive process, and static visual stimuli are ineffective in any state. Now, with highly

---

[5]Emde et al. (1976), rousing neonates from sleep to a drowsy state, were able to produce smiles repeatedly with gentle stimulation.

familiar stimuli or following repeated presentation of visual stimuli, smiling is observed as the infant assimilates or visually masters the event (Kagan, 1971; Shultz and Zigler, 1970; Zelazo and Komer, 1971; Zelazo, 1972). And, unlike the earlier sleep-smile reaction to a rattle or bell, the smile of recognition wanes with repeated presentations. A review of this substantial literature can be found in Sroufe and Waters (1976a).

Drawing from these observations, Sroufe and Waters (1976a) characterized this content-mediated smile in terms of tension fluctuation, analogous to the arousal fluctuation that underlies the neonatal smile. *Tension* refers to *arousal based on the infant's engagement of the event* rather than on stimulation per se. As with the neonatal smiles, the process is again arousal–relaxation–smile. But here the hypothetical tension threshold is exceeded due to the effort involved in the infant's engagement of the event. There is a genuine transaction between infant and event (the event is in part a function of the infant's cognitive processes), and a genuine emotional reaction. The smile occurs with the tension fluctuation as the recognition process is completed. Though engaged, there is no smile on early presentations of the novel event because the assimilation is not accomplished, and thus there is no rapid fluctuation in the tension. In our model

it is proposed that cortically mediated (content-based) tension increases and recovers rapidly, producing the ''arousal jag'' (Berlyne, 1969) required for smiling and laughter, and that this occurs against the backdrop of slowly recovering global arousal produced by stimulation per se. [Sroufe and Waters, 1976a, p. 178]

There is no smile on final presentations because assimilation is no longer effortful—tension is minimal (see, also, Kagan, 1971).

Based on this analysis, early *pleasure* might be defined as the modulation of tension around some moderate level. In this view tension is not always negative; in fact, as we shall discuss further, quite high levels of tension may be positive. Although the distinction may seem arbitrary, early neonatal smiles, while reflecting a comfortable level of arousal or a pleasant state, are not considered to indicate positive affect (*pleasure*) because they do not involve even the beginnings of meaning. (Of course, the beginnings of meaning do come out of such arousal fluctuations.) Only when the smile is mediated by a cognitive (conscious) process—a connection between the infant and the surround (an awareness, see

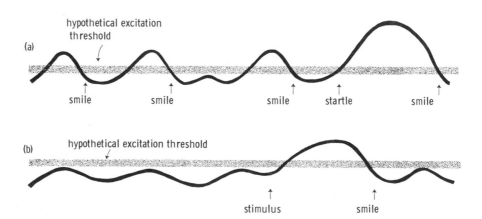

above)—is the *emotion* of pleasure inferred from the smile. Interestingly, there seem to be qualitative changes in the smile itself at this time (Wolff, 1963), which may be argued to reflect the steeper gradient of tension in cognitively mediated smiles. Further, the *pleasure* of the 2- to 3-month-old is not considered *joy*, the latter term being restricted to more active mastery and a higher level of meaning, which probably includes awareness of the affect itself.

Laughter, the most intense expression of positive affect, apparently requires a steeper gradient and more rapid fluctuation of tension than does smiling, and in the present analysis is related to *delight* or *joy*. Metaphorical as such a description is, it adequately and aptly summarizes rather substantial empirical evidence (Cicchetti and Sroufe, 1976; Rothbart, 1973; Sroufe and Waters, 1976). Interestingly, laughter is rare before the 4th month (e.g., Escalona, 1968; Sroufe and Wunsch, 1972), though vigorous smiling and cooing may be common. Infants first laugh to physically vigorous, intrusive stimulation and only in the third or fourth quarter are more subtle events (e.g., playing tug, pulling a cloth from mother's mouth, the sight of mother sucking on a bottle) reliably capable of producing laughter. Especially with incongruous events, laughter builds from neutral reactions and smiles on early presentations and fades again with further trials (Sroufe and Wunsch, 1972). More rapid processing of the event is implied (since laughter succeeds smiling trials), as is a greater amount of tension, because laughter fades again to smiling as presentations continue. That a great deal of tension is required for laughter is also suggested by the fact that many stimuli adequate for laughter are potent for fear (e.g., loud sounds, loss of balance). Items producing crying before the onset of laughter are among the first to produce laughter. And an event that previously produced laughter can produce crying if a distressing experience is interpolated (see Sroufe et al., 1974; Sroufe and Waters, 1976a). More tension is required for laughter than for smiling and, in the second half-year, such a steep tension gradient may be produced by the infant's cognitive processes (the relationship between subject and event), minimizing the role for stimulation per se.

As was the case with smiling, the expression of laughter illustrates the infant's increasingly active involvement, from processing the stimulation in its surround, and later in its temporal and situational context, to participating in the event (playing tug, uncovering mother's face), to actually creating the spectacle (e.g., laughing uproariously while stuffing the cloth back into mother's mouth). This is the progression over the 1st year. *Joy* is placed on our chart in the third quarter. Given the laughter of the 5-month-old to vigorous stimulation (''delight'') and the sophisticated games of the 12-month-old, this may again seem arbitrary, but it is in the third quarter that the infant laughs in anticipation of mother's return in peek-a-boo, laughs at a variety of social games, laughs at visual spectacles across a distance, and begins to lose interest in mere stimulation. In short, the *meaning of the event in relation to the infant* becomes dominant, in comparison to mere stimulation. Of course, meaning becomes even more dominant in the fourth quarter, with visual incongruities paralleling social games in potency for eliciting laughter (Sroufe and Wunsch, 1972).

By the end of the 1st year and throughout the 2nd, the infant increasingly expresses positive affect in anticipation of events, especially events it plans or carries out (personal observation). It thus has the capacity for the sustained feeling of joy we call *elation*. From the end of the 1st year, situations, not just discrete events, can produce joy—for example, the infant becomes joyous on entering a room full of toys. And given a rather well-established sense of self, with joy and elation in response to positive social evaluation, we have the roots of *pride*. Pride, however, is reserved for those positive feelings that derive from meeting one's own standards, a capacity that develops after the infancy period.[6]

Wariness-Fear

The wariness-fear distinction comes from Bronson's (1972) work on the development of fear. Wariness, a negative reaction to the unfamiliar or unknown, appears in the first half-year (see also Escalona, 1968). Fear, a categorical negative reaction, does not appear until about 9 months (Emde et al., 1976; Sroufe, 1977). Bronson presents some evidence that the two are separate systems, with wariness having a heavier temperamental influence (babies receive similar rankings of apprehension in various novel situations; Bronson and Pankey, 1977). Here, a finer developmental gradation of the system will be presented. Wariness-fear has its roots in early infancy, but the case can be made for placing the onset of fear at various developmental points, including the end of the 1st year of life or later.

Infants as young as 10 to 15 days have been observed to become distressed following unbroken inspection of a visual stimulus. Stechler and Latz (1966) termed this "obligatory attention" (Table 13-2). More commonly in early weeks, however, infants fixate for a time, with greatly reduced activity, then lose the target, requiring an adjustment by the experimenter (Tennes et al., 1972). By about 5 weeks, unbroken attention for periods up to 2 min is noted. If the baby looks away, its eyes again return quickly to the target, as though it were "stimulus-bound." An initial long period of inactivity is followed by increasingly vigorous activity and hard crying (Tennes et al., 1972). As described earlier (Early Organization), this negative response is replaced in a few weeks by smiling and cooing, as sensory and motor activity become more coordinated. These early negative reactions could be termed fear, since they involve an interaction between organism and an external stimulus. But the excess of arousal here seems to be due merely to the infant's being locked into the stimulus and unable to continue the flow of behavior. The *content* of the stimulus is largely irrelevant. Still, this reaction appears to be the precursor of wariness and fear.

What Bronson and others (e.g. Schaffer, 1974) call "wariness" is similar to this precursor reaction, yet in an important way different. After prolonged inspection (up to 30 sec) of a stranger's immobile, sober face, 4-month-old infants frequently show great distress. Bronson (1972) has discussed this as a reaction to the unassimilable unfamiliar. It could also be seen as a further case of obligatory attention, but here the attention arrest derives from a mixture of familiar, attractive elements and unfamiliar elements. The content of the event is important. Four-month-old infants frequently can divert their attention from noxious stimulation (Tennes et al., 1972), and they appear to try that here (Bronson, 1972). But an unfamiliar human face is a very attractive stimulus, presumably because of an established general face scheme and the possible "pre-potency" of the face in early life. The engagement cannot be broken. There is no modulation of the tension, and distress results (Meili, 1955). A better case can be made that this is a fear reaction because the content or meaning of the event, the mixture of known and unfamiliar elements, is involved. Certainly this reaction (*wariness*) is an emotional reaction, as defined in this chapter.

With Bronson, Arnold (1960), and others, however, the position here is that fear involves a negative categorization of an event, rather than the inability to assimilate an event—that is, the event is *assimilated to a negative scheme*. In the second half-year, for

[6]This is reminiscent of James' (1890) view of self-esteem as the ratio of one's expectations for himself to his actual accomplishments.

example, infants commonly show negative reactions to intruding strangers without a lengthy period of study. Despite a number of critiques of this literature (e.g., Rheingold and Eckerman, 1973), it is rather well established that many babies will show such reactions by 9 months, and almost all will do so sometime in the 1st year (e.g., Emde et al., 1976; Goldberg, 1972; Klein and Durfee, 1975; Schaffer, 1966; Scarr and Salapatek, 1970; Waters et al., 1975). Since ethical considerations mandate rather innocuous procedures and since strangers also activate infants' curiosity and affiliative systems (Bretherton and Ainsworth, 1974; Rand and Jennings, 1975; Morgan, 1973; Rheingold and Eckerman, 1973), care is required to illustrate the phenomenon. The data are clear, however, that when strangers intrude on the infant, especially picking it up without mediating their approach with a toy or game and without a prolonged familiarization period, the majority of 10- to 12-month-old infants show some degree of negative reaction (Emde et al., 1976; Meili, 1955; Rand and Jennings, 1975; Waters et al., 1975; see Sroufe, 1977, for a comprehensive review).

Is the negative reaction to strangers fear? Unlike the wary reaction described above, it is not strictly due to a failure to assimilate, though increasing the assimilability of the event and baby's response options, through toy play or a game, greatly reduces the negative reaction. Stranger fear in the second half-year is linked to cognitive growth, including changes in object concept. As Meili (1955) suggests in a classic paper, not only does a stimulus have to be assimilated as a sensory impression (as the stranger is by this time), but it must also be "worked in" meaningfully—that is, integrated into the existing world of objects. The stranger cannot be worked into the world of objects, with the same consequence as the earlier failure of sensory assimilation.

This is a viable position and is developmentally sound. The present analysis differs only in suggesting that the stranger is in a sense assimilated as an object, but assimilated to a negative scheme (perhaps "unfamiliar persons"). In distressed babies, the reaction occurs more quickly on a second trial (Bronson and Pankey, 1977; Sroufe, 1977), suggesting not faster failure of assimilation/accommodation but rather a categorical negative reaction. The *intrusive* stranger is perceived as a member of a class of aversive events.

As a categorical reaction, based on the relationship of the event to the infant, this negative reaction can qualify as *fear* (see Emde et al., 1976). And this is where fear has been located on the developmental chart (Table 13-2). Consistent with this are behavioral data on a variety of fear situations (Scarr and Salapatek, 1970) and the data showing HR acceleration and obvious aversive behavioral reactions to a looming stimulus (Hruska and Yonas, 1971; Cicchetti and Mans, 1976) or to the visual cliff (Schwartz et al., 1973) at this time, as well as to approaching strangers (Campos et al., 1975; Waters et al., 1975). Since discrimination of loom (versus zoom) and the "deep" (versus the "shallow") side of the "cliff" occur earlier, it seems that this shift is due to the changing *meaning* of the event.[7] Emde et al. (1976) have provided substantial documentation, including compara-

---

[7]Bower et al. (1970) and Ball and Tronick (1971) reported defensive reactions to a looming stimulus in the first weeks of life. Cicchetti and Waters elicited the same response from infants 3 to 5 weeks of age in our own lab (unpublished data). Recently, Cicchetti and Mans (1976) occasionally observed such reactions in Down's syndrome infants, even with head movement controlled (the head tilting back could cause the arms to go up). Unlike reactions in the second half-year, these occur only on "impact," rather than in anticipation, and must be considered reflexive rather than cognitive. This early defensive reaction apparently drops out, to appear again in the second half-year with great reliability. Since the reactions are as common in Down's syndrome infants as in normal controls, the prepotency of the looming stimulus is indicated, as opposed to an explanation based on abstraction of meaning. Faster, anticipatory responses of older normal babies on subsequent trials, on the other hand, represent a reaction that can be called fear.

tive and physiological data, for a developmental shift in the fear system at this time. Fear reactions emerge rather precipitously across species at comparable developmental points and are preceded by maturational changes in the EEG in humans, as well as by the shift to HR acceleration in response to stimulus events with negative meaning. Emde et al. (1976) refer to this as an "anticipatory" acceleration, because it happens without any physically noxious stimulation.

Nevertheless, the term fear could also be reserved for the subsequent developmental step. The negative reaction to strangers, relatively dependable only with intrusion and avoidable through a variety of familiarizing maneuvers, seems to be due in part to the lack of response options, to not knowing how to behave, or to a loss of control (Sroufe, 1977). Babies free to crawl away will not so often cry as babies who are restrained (Bronson, 1972). Fear upon *sight* of the stranger across the room is very rare (Bretherton and Ainsworth, 1974; Rheingold and Eckerman, 1973; Waters et al., 1975). And frank distress is uncommon at any point, unless intrusion is protracted (Emde et al., 1976) or the baby is further stimulated following pickup (Rand and Jennings, 1975). More typically, the negative reaction consists of a frown, cry-face, or gaze-aversion (which are accompanied by HR acceleration), or by turning from the stranger.

Rather than calling these reactions "mild fear," suggesting a fear scale, they might be considered negative or "wary" reactions, to be described and examined as to their functional significance (Waters et al., 1975). Fear could be reserved for full-blown negative reactions, immediate on perception of the threatening event. The latter reaction is what mothers and other observers describe following a trip to the doctor for shots. In our laboratory we quickly learned to abandon lab coats because of the occasional extreme reactions that occurred following such visits. These reactions were immediate and were apparent in face and body as the infant turned and clutched the mother. Some trial-2 reactions in stranger-approach studies have this same quality.

Some may prefer to restrict the term fear to these conditioned responses, occurring late in the 1st year (fear 2). The noxious event is recognized and impending. However, the emphasis on the qualitative shift in meaning over the third quarter is congruent with the developmental analysis of other affect systems.

With the acquisition of language and facility with abstraction, fear is no longer wedded to conditioning, as is demonstrated in an example from Goodenough's (1934) text. A 3-year-old, previously delighted with water, was terrified on a subsequent visit to the very familiar lake. This fear reaction followed exposure to ideation about how well the fish were "biting" on the preceding visit. Several days later he explained, "Mummy, do you know why I couldn't go in ze water one day? I was afraid ze pish would bite my peat" [p. 319]. Probably by age 2 fear is no longer necessarily tied to the previous occurrence of events (Jersild and Holmes, 1935). And with the development of self-awareness (18 months) and, later, the internalization of standards, fear may be linked to shyness, shame, and guilt.

Rage-Anger

Many observers have described "angry" cries and "mad" faces as early as the newborn period (Stirnimann, 1940; Watson, 1924), while others require some degree of intentionality before using the term anger. In accord with this latter view, *anger* is located on the developmental chart in the third quarter of the 1st year, becoming common by 12 months when the infant is capable of an "angry" mood (e.g., Ainsworth et al., 1978; Goodenough, 1934). Still, anger in the third quarter has its roots in earlier *rage*.

While there are great difficulties of definition here, and little convincing data, a precursor of rage seems to be a primitive response to prolonged distress which may originate in many ways. Spectographic studies have distinguished "mad" cries of newborns from other crying (Wolff, 1969), though comparisons have not been made with later angry crying, where the observer would have additional bases for judging the emotion. And young infants do sound and appear mad to mothers and other observers.

Shortly after the newborn period, head or limb restraint is apparently an adequate stimulus for extreme distress, a second rage-anger precursor (Stirnimann, 1940). Here, the negative reaction comes from blocking the flow of behavior, analogous to the wary reaction described above, though in this case the stoppage of behavior is physical. The "object" (in Arnold's, 1960, sense) is not recognized by the infant.

Only when the *rage* is due to "disappointment"—the failure of a *motor* expectation or interruption of specific ongoing activities—is it considered an emotional reaction in the present scheme. The reaction derives from the infant's involvement with a *particular* event—for example, the failure of a well-established action sequence to be continued. The infant's increasing role is also suggested by the increasing directedness of the reaction (Buhler, 1930; see Early Organization). Bridges (1932) referred to this behavioral reaction (kicking, pushing, "protest shouts," less tearful crying) as anger, again presenting a less differentiated account than the present analysis.

As in the analysis of fear, specific *anger* toward objects and people emerges out of rage in the second half-year, with qualitative advances in other aspects of development. The infant now perceives in a new sense the *cause* of an interruption, as when a sought-after toy cannot be reached. Situations much more diverse and subtle than physical restraint or disruption of an ongoing action pattern can now produce anger and rage, including disruption of an *intended* action. Whether at this time there is also a qualitative change in the nature of what is disappointing to the infant (becoming independent of fixed-action sequences) is an important area for research. It is the age of onset of separation protest (e.g., Schaffer and Emerson, 1964). Also, in contrast to earlier rage, the *anger* here rather directly follows the unwanted event, rather than building from distress, though the reaction still involves crying. The angry reaction is common, though not frequent, in the second half-year, because by then the infant persists in its intended acts, will not readily accept substitute objects, and has more specific plans with respect to these objects (see Affect-Cognition Interchange, below). "With the growth of meaning come more definite and stronger desires, and the more frequent the desire, the stronger the impulse, the greater will be the likelihood of interference or thwarting and the more frequent will be the occasions for anger" (Goodenough, 1934, p. 222). A number of observers have noted such angry reactions during this period (Brody and Axelrod, 1970; Escalona, 1968; Goodenough, 1931).

Although the outline above is speculative and the ontogenesis of this system awaits systematic study (Goodenough, 1931, is the exception), there is no doubt that angry reactions are well within the repertoire of the 12-month-old, including foot stomping, batting away objects, kicking the feet and, slapping, pushing, or hitting at persons. By the end of the 1st year they may be directed against the source of the interference or disappointment, may occur in the absence of crying, and may take the form of petulance or an angry mood (Ainsworth et al, 1978; Bridges, 1932; Brody and Axelrod, 1970; Goodenough, 1934; Main, 1973).

Defiance, negativism, and aggression are products of the 2nd year, which, in part, reflect maturation of the self-concept and the development of autonomy. The infant may express anger with a purpose (e.g., stopping occasionally to note its effects; Goodenough,

1934), and interpersonally it becomes more closely linked with agression and resistance. By the end of the 2nd year some infants can be observed to engage in unprovoked aggression (e.g., pinching the mother). Later, in a complex way, anger is mixed with fear and directed against the self in the reaction of guilt.

As with fear, an increasing specificity in the instigation of the reaction and an increasing directedness and focus of the response (obliterate the obstacle) is apparent in the rage-anger system. As with pleasure-joy and wariness-fear, however, the earlier manifestation of the system (the prototype) remains operative, as any observer of older children knows. In an extreme tantrum, the diffuse quality of the primitive response is again apparent.

A Summary: The Infant As An Emotional Being

By 3 months the infant exhibits the first true emotional reactions, involving an awareness of the surround, a *transaction* with the event. These are subjective experiences (cf. Arnold, 1960), in the sense that the effectiveness of the event depends in part on structures *within* the infant (a psychophysiological versus a physiological process). With the advent of cognitive schemes, the content of the *particular* event becomes important. Effortful assimilation to the cognitive scheme produces the affect of pleasure (e.g., Kagan, 1971). With failures of assimilation/accommodation and violation of "expectancies" based on ongoing action sequences, there can be frustration, unresolved cognitive tension, and rage and wariness as negative affects. This is the beginning of emotional life, the birth of the ego (Spitz et al., 1970).

But *by 9 months the infant is an emotional being*. Now the subject-object relationship is primary. In a new way the *meaning* of the event *for the infant* is responsible for the affect. Thus, by about 9 months the infant laughs *in anticipation* of mother's return in peek-a-boo, rather than in response to the completed sequence. It is angry in the face of an obstacle blocking an *intended* act (a particular relationship and a psychological invest-ment). And it can experience threat in advance of noxious stimulation (fear). This is also the age at which surprise, as opposed to startle, appears (Charlesworth, 1966; Vaughn and Sroufe, 1976). Awareness has become anticipation. While in the second quarter the infant has motor anticipation based on well-established action sequences, by 9 months there is cognitive anticipation. It can expect to secure the ball from under the couch though it has never reached there before, and it can be surprised (or even angry) at the result.

The 9-month-old infant also is an emotional being because it no longer has an omnibus class of schemes. Some schemes are positive, some are negative. There are gradations, and there is considerable fluidity in the system, but mental images (representations, cognitive schemes) are *affectively toned*. Thus, the stranger may be assimilated to a negative scheme. Similarly, it is not coincidental that at this time, following a period of exploring her person, immediate positive greetings to the caregiver emerge. These bounc-ing, smiling, arms-raised gestures are differential to attachment figures, reflecting the positive value of the special scheme to which the attachment figures are immediately assimilated. It is no longer the smile of simple recognition or the joy of anticipated interaction. It is feeling happy to see the caregiver, which is the root of affection.

Finally, the 9-month-old is an emotional being because there is now awareness of the affect itself. The perception of the feeling becomes part of the event. Arnold (1960), in her exhaustive review of theories of emotion, concluded that emotion is not the behavior, not the physiological reaction, and not the perception of either of these—rather, it is the *felt action tendency*. Certainly, by 9 months, affective expression portends behavior (Emde et al., 1976), rather than terminating an interaction with the environment. It becomes part of the continuing appraisal process. In discussing stranger fear, Bronson (personal communication) has put it as follows:

> These associated emotions, linked with salient features of the encounter circumstances, should by the present thesis be part of the developing framework within which a baby evaluates further encounters with unfamiliar adults.

Again, by now there is an awareness of affect and there are affective components to memory. Negative affect no longer requires a failure of assimilation, and a strong positive affective experience can be set off by the mere perception of a member of a class, without the need for effortful assimilation.[8]

As was the case with the specific affects, referring to the infant as an emotional being (or to the emergence of ego) at 9 months may seem arbitrary. One could also say that the infant is an emotional being after 12 months, when it is capable of moods, when it more purposefully exhibits and communicates affect, when it acts within a prevailing affective state, and *when affect provides a context for behavior;* or at 18 months, when the infant begins to be aware of self as experiencing. Certainly, the criterion of subjectivity (meaning) is better met at each of these points in development, and, increasingly, the contribution of the infant to the reaction (the relative independence from the event) is apparent. A continuous developmental process can be discerned. Still, there *is* a qualitative turning point after the third quarter of life, with profound developmental implications, as Emde et al. (1976) determined in an independent analysis. Now there is distress to specific patterned stimuli. Now affect portends action and apparently motivates learning (e.g., Buhler's anticipatory blocking). Now infants can turn from a goal for help *without losing interest* (Escalona, 1968), and now they can establish truly reciprocal relationships, in part based on positive valuation of the caregiver.

EMOTIONAL DEVELOPMENT

Emotional development encompasses more than the ontogenesis of the specific affects or even changes in the organization of their expression. It includes the ties between affect and the social and cognitive domains, the mutual influences of these systems, and their organization around major developmental tasks or "issues" (Sander, 1962). Emotional development is intimately related to attachment, which is affective in nature, which is promoted by affective interchanges between infant and caregiver, and which has consequences for emotional growth and health. As is attachment, emotional development is closely linked with the development of identity and self-awareness (e.g., Breger, 1974), individuation-separation (Mahler, 1975), and ego development (Brody and Axelrod, 1970; Loevinger, 1976). The domain of emotional development also includes developmental changes in conditions in which affect is expressed, the developing control of the infant over the expression of affect, and the continually elaborating function of affect in the organization of development.

Behavior becomes more coordinated and precise with development (e.g., Buhler, 1930; see Principles of Organization, above). Similarly, even though the number of different

---

[8]From a neurophysiological perspective one would discuss the establishment of cortical-limbic interactive loops by this age, such that recognition automatically activates limbic structures associated with affect.

situations capable of arousing a given emotion increases (Goodenough, 1934), conditions for the expression of emotional behavior become more specific (versus general arousal), more categorical (e.g., fear versus wariness), and less tied to the actual presence of an irritant. For example, by the end of the 1st year the infant's anger can be directed at a specific object or person in recognition of the source of irritation. Some babies express anger at the caregiver on her *return* from a separation, showing a recognition of the source independent of the event. By the end of the 1st year we see the beginnings of what can be called moods. The infant's behavior is not so constantly fluctuating with the vicissitudes of current events. It responds to what it remembers, expects, and has been experiencing within the given situation and outside of it. Its own feelings increasingly become a part of the stimulus field.

As the infant is becoming less influenced by the immediate situation, it is also developing the capacity to modulate and control emotional experience and expression. The young infant apparently has built-in mechanisms for modulating tension when further increases would lead to distress (e.g., Stern, 1974a; Tennes et al., 1972). But by the time the infant is 10 months old, these capacities are smoothly functioning and apparently much more under its control. For example, Waters et al. (1975) reported a precisely synchronized coordination between gaze-aversion and HR acceleration during stranger-approach. Gaze-aversions occurred when HR accelerations were near peak. With the gaze-aversion, HR again declined and the infant returned its gaze once again. This process seems to reflect an early coping mechanism, preventing a disorganizing distress reaction and allowing the infant to assimilate the event. (Babies showing this pattern were even more tolerant of the stranger on the second trial.) These are perhaps the roots of delay and other coping strategies Murphy (1962) has described in the preschool years.

Competent as these 10-month-olds are, equally dramatic changes occur in the next few months. For 10-month-olds, crying in a stressful situation appears to be an all-or-none response. But even by 12 months, infants have much more capacity to stop crying to take in new information (Vaughn and Sroufe, 1976). In our attachment studies, we commonly see 12-month-olds controlling their emotion, fighting back their tears when mother has left. This is suggested not only by pouts and cry-faces, which appear and evaporate, but by elevated HRs and subdued play (Mahler's "low keyedness"). Most revealing, such infants may burst into tears upon the mother's return, something we do not observe in younger babies. In general, infants are much more fluid in their emotional expression by the end of the 1st year.

The infant's control over emotional experience and expression and the elaboration of emotion in the organization of behavior are vastly influenced by the development of representation and language. While internal representation is influential in examples such as those described above, it plays a much more obvious part in the behavior of the 18-month-old, especially those who are verbally precocious. When, for example, the 18-month-old is told by mother, "I'll be right back; you play with the dolly," and the infant looks at the door, fighting back tears, then turns to the doll and repeats "Momma go, play dolly," and plays with occasional long looks at the door, it seems apparent that language and play are helping the child modulate or control emotional experience. Another child, having been distressed by separation and having been physically comforted, is now sitting face to face on mother's lap. She says "Momma go," and mother responds, ("Did Momma go?") "Cry." ("Did you cry?"). This illustrates both that in the 2nd year the emotional experience transcends the immediate event and that the infant has a developing means for working through the experience to a satisfactory resolution. A final example further illustrates the elaboration of the child's methods for control as well as the impact of emotion on the organization of complex behavior. This child, having been left alone, was mildly upset but not at all disorganized. He picked up the teddy bear and patted it; then, still holding the bear, he picked up mother's purse and put it over his shoulder. Then he waved "bye bye" to the mother's chair and walked out the door! In play he had reworked the experience to a satisfactory resolution, one that probably reflected an adaptive attachment relationship.

These examples are suggestive of the interrelationships among the affective, cognitive, and social domains, the functions of affect, and the relationship between security of attachment and emotionally healthy development. These are topics to which this section of the paper is devoted. An adequate developmental theory must be able to embrace these developmental changes in emotional life, as well as account for the ontogenesis of emotions from their early precursors.

The Affect-Cognition Interchange

Affect and cognition are inseparable, two aspects of the same process. As Piaget and Inhelder (1969) have said,

There is no behavior pattern, however intellectual, which does not involve affective factors as motives; but, reciprocally, there can be no affective states without the intervention of perceptions or comprehensions which constitute their cognitive structure. Behavior is therefore of a piece, even if the structures do not explain its energetics and if, vice versa, its energetics do not account for its structures. The two aspects, affective and cognitive, are at the same time inseparable and irreducible. [p. 158]

No one has or can have a noncognitive theory of emotional development—that is, a theory of emotional development with no place for cognition. When, for example, Lester (1974) proposed a "cognitive interpretation" as a contrast to an affective bond concept of attachment (cf. Ainsworth, 1973), they overlooked entirely the linking of the affective bond concept with differentiation of persons, person permanence, and other cognitive factors. Since the work of Schacter (1966) and Lazarus (1968) on cognitive set, the role of cognition in emotion is virtually beyond question. Similarly, consideration of infant development, even given the limited information available, is compelling concerning the reciprocal influence of affect on cognition. It is as descriptively accurate to say that emotional experience and expression promote cognitive growth as it is to say that cognitive factors underlie emotional development (Sroufe and Waters, 1976a).

Cognitive Influences on Affect

The influence of cognitive factors on the development and expression of affect has been apparent throughout this chapter. There has been the implicit assumption that cognitive factors underlie the unfolding of emotions: only with recognition is there pleasure and disappointment; only with some development of causality, object permanence, intentionality, and meaning are there joy, anger, and fear; only with self-awareness is there shame. Also, distinctions among affects and their precursors call upon cognitive achievements— for example, fear, as reflected in more immediate distress upon a second exposure to a stranger, has been referred to as a categorical reaction, dependent upon assimilation to a negative scheme. Finally, the effects of sequence, setting, and other aspects of context on emotion are obviously mediated by cognition.

Theoretical ties between cognition and affect are clear from a consideration of Piaget's stages of cognitive development (Table 13-3). For example, in Piaget's stage 2 (1–4 months) the first acquired adaptations are seen; behavioral searchings produce new results, and functional assimilation assures repetition of new responses. During this stage, there are *anticipatory* nursing postures and later *anticipatory* sucking on the basis of visual cues. The apex of this stage is visually guided reaching. In our scheme, this is the period of the first emotions, which require primitive recognition, coordination of schemes, awareness, and primitive anticipation. The smile is testimony to functional assimilation and to rudimentary coordination of attention and motor behavior (Tennes et al., 1972; see Organization of Behavior, above).

Piaget's stage 3 (4–8 months) marks the first step toward intentionality. There is now forward-looking adaptation rather than simply repetition of the old, but goals are established only after means are put into effect. For the first time, interruption in Mandler's (1975) sense (see Developmental Theory of Emotion, below) is possible and, consequently, by the end of this stage, there can be anger. Also, in this stage there is the joy of being an *active* agent. Rage (due to disappointment) and wariness (failure to assimilate) emerge early in stage 3.

Fear and surprise would emerge at the beginning of Piaget's fourth stage (8–12 months). Here, the infant searches for hidden objects, has true intentionality and means-ends relationships. Novelty presents a *problem for understanding* rather than the simple opportunity to exercise schemas [cf. Schaffer et al.'s (1972) hesitance or "wariness"]. By the end of this period, the world is more objectified, less tied to the infant's actions. For example, there are anticipatory reactions (crying when mother puts on her coat). In the affective domain we see the onset and formation of attachment, deferred emotional reactions (anger and crying on mother's return), the onset of moods, the strong influence of context, and affect as part of that context. In general, affect becomes less tied to specific events and becomes a determinant of behavior. By this time the infant has the capacity to appraise or *evaluate* an event.

What was called the mastery or "practicing" phase (cf. Mahler, 1975) in the affective domain corresponds closely to Piaget's stage 5 (12–18 months), characterized by the discovery of new means through experimentation, pursuit of the novel, and provoking new results. Causality becomes detached from the child's own actions, and people and objects become independent centers of causation. Clearly, these developments are closely tied to the emergence of self-awareness. Finally, in emotional development we see affection, shame, defiance, and positive self-evaluation after 18 months. These developments are based upon the emergence of symbolic representation and the functioning of schemes internally, independent of actions (Piaget's stage 6). There is a representation of the self.

The most compelling empirical evidence for the specific influence of cognitive factors upon affect expression is found in studies of positive affect. The onset and course of smiling to the face—from irregular to reliable but general, to differential in recognition of the caregiver—is an obvious case in point (e.g., Emde et al., 1976; Kagan, 1971; see Sroufe and Waters 1976a for a review). Also, there are developmental trends in the nature of events that elicit positive affect; previously adequate stimuli lose their effectiveness, while others become more potent (Kagan, 1971; Sroufe and Wunsch, 1972). Age differences in speed of response and number of trials to produce the affective reaction (e.g., Sroufe and Waters, 1976a; Zelazo, 1972) also reflect differing abilities to assimilate information, and trial-by-trial effects within experiments (see Pleasure-Joy, above) suggest scheme-formation, effortful assimilation leading to positive affect, and finally, effortless assimilation and disinterest. It is the tension generated through cognitive effort that is expressed in positive affect (Sroufe and Waters, 1976a).

There is also data suggesting that surprise reactions emerge after 8 months, as Piaget's theory would predict. Charlesworth and Kreutzer (1973) have summarized findings with regard to this ''epistemic'' emotional reaction, including Charlesworth's own data. In a recent study Vaughn and Sroufe (1976) corroborated these findings. Mothers and babies played a peek-a-boo game during which the mother ''peeked'' around the edge of a screen. After the baby was engaged in the game (i.e., smiling, looking, and/or leaning toward the screen) the mother called to the baby and stepped out wearing a mask. On other trials a stranger stepped out wearing the same mask. Television records of the babies' postures indicated that these episodes clearly disrupted the babies' ongoing stream of behavior, that the babies ''misexpected'' the events. When recognizable facial expressions of surprise were seen, they always followed the onset of the ''misexpected'' events. More often, elements of facial expressions of surprise (e.g., raised brows, lowered jaw) were seen. These elements of the surprise expression were seen in babies as young as 8 months, though only one baby in the 8-month-old group ($N = 12$) displayed the stereotyped surprise facial expression. Interestingly, *no* 8-month-old without demonstrated ''person permanence'' (i.e., those infants who seemed to forget the game and their mother when she disappeared behind the screen) even showed the *elements* of the surprise facial expression.

Not surprisingly, a number of investigators have sought the affective correlates of object concept development. For example, Cicchetti and Sroufe (1976) present a relationship between stage-4 object permanence and laughter to certain items in their sample of Down's syndrome infants. Although several investigators have failed to find a relationship between stranger fear and object permanence (see Sroufe, 1977, for a review), there is some support for the idea that person permanence rather than object permanence would be related to stranger reactions. Paradise and Curcio (1974) found the predicted relationship between wariness of strangers and person permanence, but the finding remains tentative; the more frightened infants may have been more motivated to find mother, since the person-permanence assessments always followed the stranger approach. Finally, in an intriguing study, Sylvia Bell (1970) revealed a *décalage* between person permanence and object permanence, with person permanence in advance. Only securely attached infants showed this *décalage,* along with a tendency to be less wary of strangers in the presence of mother. Also, Lamb (1974) found a negative *décalage* among ''nonattached'' institutionalized infants. These findings are provocative, but the search for specific affective correlates of cognitive development has only begun. It is clear already that relationships will be complex, partly due perhaps to the reciprocal influence of affect upon cognition.

The Influence of Affect on Cognition

The reciprocal influence of affect *upon cognition* has received little attention, except among psychoanalytically oriented researchers (e.g., Brody and Axelrod, 1970; Escalona, 1968; Spitz, 1965). A notable exception is the recent monograph by Emde et al. (1976). Such an influence has been frequently mentioned by cognitive theorists (e.g., Piaget, 1952), and a role for affect in cognition has been pointed to in an occasional empirical study, for example, Charlesworth's (1969) paper on the role of surprise in cognition. But until quite recently affect has been the ''weak sister'' of cognition in developmental studies.

This is surprising because the case can well be made that affect is the infant's primary medium of communication and meaning, and that affect-laden exchanges are a major source of cognitive growth (e.g., Escalona, 1968). In many ways, affect *is* the meaning of a social exchange or an encounter with the object world; it is through affective experience that the infant can be touched, moved along (e.g., Stechler and Carpenter, 1967; Stern, 1974a). Moreover, it seems likely that the first *awareness* of causality and intentionality would occur in affective exchanges. For example, it could be argued that the experience of anger when an action is blocked crystalizes the relationships between self, object, and obstacle. To be sure, it is not a one-way street; developments in directedness of behavior, persistence in the pursuit of goals, coordination of schemes, and other aspects of cognitive growth set up the anger experience. The infant that becomes distracted from the goal (attracted to the obstacle) is not likely to become angry. But the experience of affect further promotes cognitive growth.

In Brody and Axelrod's (1966, 1970) work, anxiety, cognitive development, and ego formation are interrelated, flowing out of a common process. They suggest that

. . . physiological arousals promote the exercise of perceptual and motoric structures, and perception of the tension states thus aroused is reacted to with affect. Cognitive and affective recognition continue, in concert, to promote normal development of ego functions . . . anxiety is one of the principal affects with which the ego is ushered into being. [Brody and Axelrod, 1966, p. 219]

Ego formation is thus dependent on cognitive *and* affective processes and, of course, the *organization* of cognition, affect and action *is* ego (Loevinger, 1976). Similarly, separation anxiety influences and is influenced by the formation of attachment; fear sharpens categories and is dependent upon them.

The premise of Piaget (1952), Janet (1937), and others that affect and cognition are inseparable is showing up in many research and conceptual efforts. Haviland (1975b), for example, in a fascinating paper, illustrates how those assessing cognition and cognitive growth in infants, including Piaget and infant testers, repeatedly rely on interest, surprise, and other expressions of affect to determine level of cognitive performance. Yarrow and his colleagues (e.g., Yarrow et al., 1975) are studying what they call cognitive-motivational variables, acknowledging with Piaget that secondary circular reactions, creating a spectacle, and so forth are not possible without the sustained affective investment of the infant. Without affect, problems would not be posed and there would be no intelligence (Piaget and Inhelder, 1969).

Others have demonstrated that affective measures are useful predictors of cognitive performance. Birns and Golden (1972), for example, found pleasure in the task to be a better predictor of later cognitive performance than early cognitive measures. Likewise, Sameroff (1975) found that IQ at 30 months was better predicted from temperament measures than developmental test scores at 4 months. Cicchetti and Sroufe (1976) found that laughter to a preselected set of items at age 9 months *predicted the Bayley scores of a group of Down's syndrome infants at 16 months with no overlap between groups* defined by a median split. The overall correlation between the laughter index and Bayley score was 0.89. Early laughter to complex events is probably such an excellent predictor because it taps the motivational, attentional, affective, *and* cognitive capacities (e.g., the competence) of the infant. *Emotion is necessarily integrative.*

Attachment

The further integration of affect and cognition with the social domain can be illustrated and summarized by examining qualitative aspects of the caregiver-infant interaction and the attachment relationship. Because it lies at the intersection of the cognitive, social, and affective domains, attachment is a key construct in the organization of infant development (Sroufe and Waters, 1977). Its centrality in the study of infant emotional development is readily apparent. Not only can affective development and expression be organized with respect to consequences for the formation and functioning of attachment, the affective bond itself has consequences for social/emotional and cognitive development as well. Moreover, the adaptation represented by the attachment relationship has important consequences for later adaptations.

The Organizational View of Attachment

Within the organizational view of attachment (Ainsworth, 1974; Bowlby, 1969; Sroufe and, Waters, 1977), attachment is an enduring affective tie between infant and caregiver. This position is in stark contrast to the currently prevailing social learning position that attachment is merely the interaction between infant and caregiver (e.g., Cairns, 1972; Rosenthal, 1973), that attachment can be operationally defined in terms of frequencies of discrete behaviors independent of meaning (Feldman and Ingham, 1975), and that stable individual differences in attachment cannot be found or are irrelevant to an understanding of attachment (e.g., Masters and Wellman, 1974). Nor is it compatible with the view that the caregiver-infant relationship is just another relationship, the concept of attachment having "little scientific value" (Weinraub et al., 1977). These views emerged with the collapse of attachment as a static trait. When it was shown that frequencies or duration of discrete behaviors, assumed to be "indices" of attachment, showed little consistency across samples, situations, or time, and yielded very low individual stability, it was concluded that the attachment construct itself was wanting (e.g., Masters and Wellman, 1974).

From the organizational perspective, however, attachment is not, nor has it ever been, viewed as a trait (Ainsworth, 1974; Bowlby, 1969; Sroufe and Waters, 1977). It refers to an organized behavioral system and to an affective bond between infant and caregiver. It has the status of an intervening variable (Ainsworth, 1974) or a developmental/organizational construct (Sroufe and Waters, 1977), to be evaluated in terms of its integrative power. From this perspective, contextual influences on the expression of attachment behaviors are expected and predicted, from the notion of the caregiver as a secure base for exploration and the notion of preferential treatment under stress, rather than disconfirming the construct (see below).

It is assumed, following Bowlby (1969), that attachments will be formed in the natural course of events. Given continued exposure (familiarization) to a caregiver, human infants will become attached, and, though based on underlying cognitive processes, this attachment will be affective. When there is the rare failure to form such an affective bond, as in infantile autism, the infant is considered profoundly maladapted (e.g., Kanner, 1943; Zaslow and Breger, 1969). Generally, then, it is not the existence but the quality of the attachment that is at issue.

Further, the uniqueness of the infant's relationship with the caregiver is not *presumed;* rather, it is deduced from the observation of the caregiver's centrality in the infant's life. Similarly, the common emphasis on the *mother*-infant relationship derives from the usually greater involvement of the mother in caregiving. The quality of the attachment relationship is a product of learning, of countless experiences. When fathers or others are similarly engaged with infants, attachments are formed with them as well (Cohen and Campos, 1974; Kotelchuck, 1973; Lamb, 1975), and, if the father's ministrations are sensitive, responsive, and cooperative, a secure relationship would result. Infants, of course, have important relationships with other people—fathers, siblings, grandparents, caregivers (Weinraub, et al., 1977), but the relationship with mother is typically primary. How and whether these other relationships derive from the primary relationship is a largely unexplored empirical question (but see Mahler, 1975, for beginning).

ATTACHMENT AS AFFECTIVE BOND

When the concern is comprehending emotional development, one cannot neatly sidestep the central problems in attachment with operational definitions (e.g., attachment *is* those behaviors that, with differential frequency, are directed to the caregiver; cf. Cohen, 1974). The nature of the developmental/organizational construct in question must be appreciated. As an organizational *construct,* attachment is not any behavior or set of behaviors, just as intelligence or competence is not any behavior (Sroufe and Waters, 1977). The term affective bond is meant as a metaphorical description of this construct, and it pointedly suggests that there is an enduring, stable quality to the attachment relationship (Ainsworth, 1973). Not discrete behaviors but the patterns of behavioral organization, the quality of the attachment, *the affective bond* is what endures (Ainsworth, 1973, 1974).

Some evidence for an enduring affective bond comes from observations of infants' behavior during prolonged separations (Bowlby, 1973; Robertson and Robertson, 1971). The protest, despair, and detachment sequence observed in the absence of the caregiver makes it clear that attachment is more than the interaction. And the fact that infants with good attachment relationships more readily form new attachments (e.g., Yarrow, 1972) suggests that there are important individual differences in, and consequences of, the quality of the bond. The sequence of ignoring, anger, and rapprochement on reunion following significant separations (Heinicke and Westheimer, 1966) also suggests an affective core to the attachment relationship.

In addition, *only within the conceptualization of attachment as an affective bond,* and of individuals as varying in the quality of the attachment, *has it been possible to demonstrate stable individual differences in attachment* (e.g., Sroufe and Waters, 1977). As noted above, attempts to measure consistency in the amount or strength of attachment using frequencies or duration of discrete behaviors (within sampling periods utilized) have been consistently unsuccessful. The *quality* of the attachment, however, determined from assessments of the attachment-exploration balance and the ability to seek and obtain comfort when distressed, can be reliably assessed and does yield stability. It seems at first paradoxical that an abstraction such as quality or security yields stability when discrete behaviors do not. But the quality of the affective bond is inferred from the *patterns* and organization of behavior, in keeping with the principles outlined earlier. It is well known psychometric theory that constellations of behavior are more stable than individual behaviors, as Block (1975), in an important paper, has illustrated with respect to stability in personality.

Patterns of adaptive and maladaptive (secure and insecure) attachment in 12-month-olds, described in detail elsewhere (Ainsworth et al., 1971, 1978), illustrate the concepts of affective bond and security of attachment. The modal adaptive pattern reveals the secure base phenomenon and preferential treatment under stress. Even in an unfamiliar setting, the securely attached infant, accompanied by the caregiver, would be expected to be attracted to available toys and objects (e.g., Bretherton and Ainsworth, 1974; Bischof,

1975). The infant may occasionally check back visually with the caregiver, may interact across a distance, and may even bring a toy to share. But the business at hand is exploration, and the mere presence of the caregiver is sufficient security. Such infants would be curious about a stranger; and while they might be temporarily hesitant, they would soon warm up and become engaged with her. When left by the caregiver with the stranger, the securely attached infant may or may not be distressed. [Except in consideration of the total pattern of behavior in context, separation protest cannot be used to define the quality of attachment, though it is important in determining the formation of the attachment bond (Schaffer and Emerson, 1964; Sroufe and Waters, 1977; Yarrow, 1972)]. Especially if distressed, it would engage in search behavior; it certainly would notice the caregiver's departure, perhaps reacting with subdued play. If still distressed, it would seek contact and comforting upon return, would *maintain contact until comforted,* then would part from mother again to return to play. When distressed, it would clearly show preferential treatment of the caregiver, possibly physically resisting the stranger's overtures.

There are variants of this adaptive pattern: (1) Some infants simply are not as competent at seeking proximity and maintaining contact when they need it; nonetheless, they get the job done. (2) Some infants rarely become distressed, cry little, and seek little physical contact. Still, their positive affective bond shows in greeting behavior, distance interaction, and the quality of play. (3) Other babies are unusually timid and wary of novel situations and novel persons. They are extremely distressed by separation, and they require a great deal of contact prior to separation and especially following separation. These babies can be described as anxious, but their behavior is adaptive (though perhaps not reflecting optimal emotional health) in that they seek and maintain the contact they apparently need, and they find comfort in the caregiver's arms.

Several patterns are more clearly maladaptive and, following Ainsworth (Ainsworth et al., 1971, 1978), suggest insecure attachment relationships: (1) Some 12-month-olds seek contact on reunion but they also show signs of resistance to contact (pushing away, batting away toys, squirming to get down), are not readily settled, and therefore do not get back to play. These *behaviors* are not unique to this subgroup. Securely attached babies exhibit the same behaviors but to the *stranger,* not to the caregiver. It is the organization of the behaviors, not the discrete behaviors per se, that reflects the quality of attachment. These ambivalent infants cry and show contact-seeking and impoverished exploration even before separation, show wariness of the stranger, and exhibit extreme distress on separation. (2) One variant of this pattern is characterized by passivity; the infant, for example, sits and cries, rather than actively seeks contact. Still, the defining feature is the inability of the infant to be truly settled when distressed.

Two other maladaptive patterns center on *avoidance* of the caregiver. (3) Even after being distressed some infants turn away from, look away from, pull away from, or ignore the returning caregiver. (4) Such avoidance may be mixed with proximity-seeking, giving the impression of ambivalence, but in either case it is maladaptive because the *infant's feelings* (we presume anger; cf. Ainsworth et al., 1978; Main, 1973) *interfere with seeking and maintaining contact.* These infants play during preseparation but do not affectively share their play (Waters, Wippman and Sroufe, 1978). They engage the stranger and, in fact, are as readily comforted by the stranger as the caregiver; they are not distressed *unless left alone.*

The validity of the observations cited above receives support from concurrent HR records (see Sroufe and Waters, 1976b). The avoidant babies are aroused during and following separation; their turning away or ignoring the caregiver does not represent indifference. Also, unlike the securely attached babies, their post-reunion play is not accompanied by the pronounced HR decelerations characteristic of involvement with objects and toys. Similarly, the ambivalent babies are extremely aroused and remain so long into the reunion, as their overt behavior would suggest.

More important validation comes from the stability of these patterns (Waters, 1977). In a study of 50 12-month-olds, all but a few babies (10%) fit one of the eight patterns described above, though, of course, many possible patterns could be imagined. Moreover, when 50 babies were reclassified at 18 months, by two independent coders completely blind to the previous classification, *all but two* fell in the same major category as at 12 months ($p < .001$). Avoidant infants were still avoidant; ambivalent infants still displayed resistance to contact or difficulty in settling; and, securely attached infants still sought contact (physical or psychological) upon reunion and used the caregiver as a secure base for exploration. There were 30 exact subcategory predictions ($p < .001$). All of this suggests the power of the theory based on the affective bond.

There are two fundamentally important points to be made from this research. First, it was not the discrete behaviors that were stable; touching and looking at the mother, for example, showed zero stability. Contact maintenance showed a striking developmental decrease. Avoidance and resistance *categories* were stable (in the 0.60s), but infants who, for example, showed one type of avoidant behavior (e.g., turning the head when picked up), may have shown a different form of avoidance at 18 months (e.g., ignoring). It was *the organization of the behaviors* that *remained stable*. Securely attached infants perhaps were not distressed at separation at 18 months; if not, they may not have sought physical contact on reunion, but they did positively greet and initiate interaction. It was reestablishing contact on reunion (physical or psychological) that was stable. Perhaps they did not cry and go to the door following separation; they may have instead said, "Momma go," to the stranger, but somehow they showed their interest in mother's comings and goings. Throughout, they showed their ability to use mother as a secure base. And this is the second point. It is the felt security or lack of security—*the quality of the affective bond*—that *is stable*. It is the *security* derived from the attachment relationship that is the thread around which attachment behaviors are organized.

ATTACHMENT AND THE ORGANIZATION OF DEVELOPMENT

It can reasonably be proposed that affective development and expression are organized around the caregiver. There is, of course, positive affect as a consequence of mastery of the inanimate world, and negative affect with failures to assimilate and with interruptions of action sequences. Still, a great deal of early pleasure and distress is centered around the caregiver's ministrations. In addition, affective developments such as the differential smile, the integration of positive greeting reactions, and early separation protest have in common their link with the caregiver and the attachment system.

Not only do smiles and other affective signals promote responsiveness by the caregiver even before the infant is attached, but affective expression, via its role in the modulation of arousal, is vital to the infant's own participation in interaction (Sroufe and Waters, 1976a; Stern, 1974a, 1975). Affective expression (smiling, gaze-aversion) also has been shown to have an important role in mother-infant play (e.g., Stern, 1974b), which no doubt has a role in the *familiarization process which becomes attachment*. Moreover, the reciprocity, sustained attention, and tension regulation (holding of the self) that derive from caregiver-infant play (Brazelton et al., 1974; Brody and Axelrod, 1970; Sander, 1969) would be related to the quality of the attachment.

There is clear evidence that sensitive caregiving is related to the patterns of attachment outlined above—to the quality or security of the attachment relationship (Ainsworth, 1973, 1974; Brody and Axelrod, 1970). While contingency and responsivity are central to many views of adequate caregiving (Clarke-Stewart, 1973; Lewis and Goldberg, 1969; Yarrow et al., 1972), mood-setting, acceptance, cooperation, and sensitivity to affective signals are also important (Ainsworth, 1974). The sensitive caregiver provides the proper affective climate, helps the infant achieve and maintain an optimal level of tension, and actually helps it to organize the behavior to which she then contingently responds (Brazelton et al., 1974; Brody and Axelrod, 1970; Stern, 1974b).

The organizational significance of attachment can also be underscored by noting its contemporary correlates. When defined in terms of attachment-exploration balance, the quality of attachment is logically related to exploration and mastery of the object world. Following the formation of attachment in the "practicing sub-phase" of the separation-individuation process (approximately 10–18 months; Mahler, 1975), the infant actively moves out to the environment. Empirically, security of attachment has been related to exploratory play in an unfamiliar situation and to the infant's engagement of unfamiliar persons (Ainsworth et al., 1971; Sroufe, 1977). A substantial literature on exploration and play is readily integrated within the concept of the caregiver as a *secure base* (Bretherton and Ainsworth, 1974; Carr et al., 1975; Feldman and Ingham, 1975; Maccoby and Feldman, 1972; see Sroufe and Waters, 1977, for a review).

For securely attached infants it also appears that the caregiver is the first permanent object (Bell, 1970; see Affect-Cognition, above). In time the touching, tugging, hair-pulling, hearing, and seeing, which are promoted by positive affective exchanges and which reach an apex at about 7 months (Mahler, 1975), become coordinated into the scheme of caregiver. One might reason that, as the securely attached infant formulates the myriad of impressions of the caregiver into schemes and finally coordinates these schemes into the person (she who is touchable, seeable, hearable, etc.), so too does it attain the concept, "I am he who is touched, spoken to, who sees, hears, etc."[9] The relationship between security of attachment and the emergence of self-concept is an important area for research, touched upon by Mahler (1975).

Finally, from the organizational view, there are predictable consequences of the quality of the attachment relationship for development and later adaptation. As predicted, quality (security) of attachment at 12 months has been shown to be related to the quality of exploratory play at age 2 years (Main, 1973). Recently, we have collected data (Matas, Arend, and Sroufe, 1978) suggesting that security of attachment is also related to later problem-solving style (spirit of engagement, persistence), joy in problem solution, compliance to maternal requests, and other aspects of a dyadic problem-solving situation at age 2. Finally, Clarke-Stewart (1973), whose measures of attachment and maternal sensitivity were rather coarse, found these measures to be related to later toddler competence defined in a multivariate manner, suggesting the robustness of these constructs.[10]

Attachment as an affective bond would also have consequences in the social domain. Data here are scanty, but theoretical predictions are clear and testable. Securely attached infants should more readily broaden their social ties. There should be transfer of trust of caregivers to trust of others and an expectation that others will be responsive to the child's requests and signals (Mahler, 1975). Effective help-seeking, cooperation, and affective contact would be specifically predicted. [In this regard, Waxler and Marian Yarrow

[9]I am indebted to Everett Waters for this provocative formulation.
[10]She assessed attachment using Ainsworth's system, for example, but without including the important reunion episodes (Sroufe and Waters, 1977).

(1975), in an important study, have shown that characteristics of the caregiver influence her effectiveness in modeling cooperation.] Securely attached infants also should be competently engaged with peers as pre-schoolers. In addition to interactive skill, the ability of these children to be involved in the object world, to seek out rewarding aspects of the environment, and to be affectively as well as verbally expressive would attract the attention and positive regard of other children (Waters, Wippman, and Sroufe, 1978).

There are now procedures for assessing peer competence and peer-group ranking (e.g., Hold, 1975), as well as the quality of attachment, so important advances may be expected in this vital area of research. Some children may be expected to be self-isolates; others may be isolated by their peer group because of their lack of competence. If it is found that securely attached infants are later characterized by competence with peers, as well as by their more general emotional involvement with the inanimate and social world, the study of attachment will take on new significance for developmental psychopathology. The linking of felt security within the infant attachment relationship to emotional involvement (initiative, Erikson, 1950; efficacy, White, 1954; competence, W. Bronson, 1974; zest, Birns and Golden, 1972) in the pre-school years is perhaps the central task in the study of emotional development.

The Function of Affect

The discussion of attachment and the affect-cognition interchange necessarily touched upon the function of affect and affective expression. Any adequate description and theory of emotional development requires a broad view of such functional considerations.

The communicative function of affect is most widely appreciated. Vocal and motoric expressions of affect signal need, communicate feeling, and elicit approach and care (Darwin, 1872; Izard, 1971; Vine, 1970, 1973). As suggested in the discussion of affect and cognition, these social functions apparently are supported by the arousal-modulating functions of affective expression:

> *Thus, the social function of the smile complements the function of positively toned tension release by providing opportunities for the infant to exercise its tendency to perpetuate novel stimulus situations.* The tension-release mechanism enables the infant to remain oriented toward novel or incongruous stimulation and maintain organized behavior. At the same time, the smile signals well-being and encourages the caregiver to continue or repeat interesting events. In addition, as a behavior each partner can exhibit, as well as elicit from the other, it has an important place in the learning of mutual effectance. [Sroufe and Waters, 1976a, p. 185]

So as the infant's smile encourages the caregiver to continue and vary the stimulation provided in face-to-face play, the expression of positive affect also may help the infant maintain tension within tolerable limits. Similarly, gaze-aversion, as an expression of negative affect, is associated with a reduction of arousal in face-to-face play (Robson, 1967; Stern, 1974a) and in engaging a mildly threatening event (Waters et al., 1975). Such mechanisms have also been suggested to be the *counterpart of the* behavior-arresting *orienting reaction* to novel events, *releasing behavior* following processing of the event (Sroufe and Waters, 1976a).

Affect may also have a role in supporting or amplifying behavior. Negative affect, especially when intense, *can* of course have a disorganizing effect on behavior. In contrast to 12-month-olds, who exhibited sustained interest and positive affect, Kramer and Rosenblum (1970) found that infants who quickly became distressed or angry were less persistent and competent in dealing with a barrier (see also Block and Block, 1973). And we believe that the angry feelings of avoidant and ambivalent infants prevent their getting the contact they need following separation (see Attachment, above). Even paroxisms of laughter make organized behavior impossible. *Still, within limits, even negative affect can support organized behavior.* As Arnold (1960) suggested in her exhaustive review of functional positions, anger, for example, may support and maintain vigorous responding. Fear may reinforce flight behavior long after the immediate cues are no longer present. Focusing, tuning, and guiding functions also seem likely. Certainly, surprising or threatening events elicit and maintain orientation and attentiveness (e.g., Charlesworth, 1969). Affective experience, including feedback from the facial muscles and the autonomic nervous system (Izard, 1971), likely becomes part of the child's continuing appraisal of the event and consequently its behavior. By the end of the third quarter affect expression "portends" behavior (Emde et al., 1976).

The possible mediating (motivational) role of emotion may be especially significant for understanding infant behavior and development. Breger (1974), in his synthesis of Piaget, neoanalytic theory and ethology, points out that affect, in taking over functions served by instinct in other animals, in part accounts for the flexibility of man's behavior. More even than our primate relatives, we respond to *feelings* aroused by environmental events. Thus, it is when separation from the caregiver arouses anxiety that the infant signals or seeks contact, not whenever a fixed physical distance is exceeded, in the manner of a duckling. The set goal of attachment for humans is best conceived as security, and with development this can be maintained or violated in a variety of ways. Human infants can be insecure even in the presence of their caregivers and can be secure even in brief separations, especially when internal representation is firmly established through language. With man, one may talk of instinctual boundaries or dismiss instincts altogether, but it is clear that behavior patterns are much more flexibly employed. Affect is the link between the instinctual behavior of animals and the flexible behavior of man.

Affect also mediates behavior in a more indirect manner, through its apparent reinforcing properties. Seeking conditions associated with positive affect (or even surprise; Charlesworth, 1969) and avoiding those associated with negative affect seems to be a rather general law of learning. Infants repeat (over and over again) actions that result in smiling and laughter, and pre-schoolers are attracted to expressions of mirth. Similarly, some infants, or most infants when stressed by a previous separation, are alert to the slightest sign of distance or separation and behave to prevent such an occurrence. The infant's negative affective experience would seem to play a large role in supporting this attentive and contact behavior. In our observation of pre-school children, it is clear that there are children who expect positive affective experiences in their social and nonsocial encounters with the surround and others who seem not to expect such experiences or even to expect negative experience. They behave accordingly.

Developmental Theory of Emotion

According to Arnold (1960), a "balanced" theory of emotion differentiates emotional experience from other experience, accounts for the arousal of emotion and bodily change, and specifies the role of emotion in goal-directed action. A "complete" theory also distinguishes one emotion from other related emotions and feelings, specifies neurophysiological mechanisms, and points to the significance of emotion in personality integration. A developmental theory would, of course, also have to account for the ontogenesis of emotion and the role of affect in the organization of development.

Ethological and learning positions have not been developmental to any important extent, and therefore have little to offer in a search for an adequate development theory of emotions. Postulating that the emotional expressions are innate (Darwin, 1872), mature when needed (Izard, 1971), or recapitulate phylogeny suggests few developmental questions or few insights into the relations of earlier and later affective states. As Meili (1955) has stated, the assumption that fear, for example, occurs when and because it is biologically useful, "certainly presents no solution to the problem, since it presupposes the question to be explained and at the utmost indicates that it is naturally given" [p. 195].

The incremental model assumed by most learning theorists simply does not fit the data on emotional development. However adequate learning positions may be to explain later conditions for affective expression, and however important learning may be in attachment and healthy or unhealthy emotional development in general (and it *is*), reinforcement principles are inadequate to account for the ontogenesis of emotion or even the expression of affect in infancy. For example, learning principles cannot account for the distress of obligatory attention, wariness in response to unfamiliar faces, or the link between these reactions and later fear. They cannot account for the rage in head restraint (there is no pain), the displeasure in interaction being terminated (there is no noxious stimulus, and this cannot be a random behavior shaped up by reinforcement), or the anger directed at an object prior to the period of deferred imitation. And they can in no obvious way account for initial instances of separation protest.

Moreover, learning positions are totally inadequate to account for positive affect. For example, while operant techniques can reduce the *decline* in smiling to a familiar stimulus (Brackbill, 1958), reinforcement is secondary to cognitive factors. With 3-month-olds, smiling will first increase to a novel visual stimulus, then decline, regardless of reinforcement condition (Zelazo, 1972; see Sroufe & Waters, 1976a, for a detailed discussion). Wahler (1967) was unable to demonstrate any operant effect at all in laughter. Also, it seems unlikely that operant techniques can account for the integration of smiling, vocalizing, and bouncing into positive greeting behaviors; rather the infant seems *happy* to see the caregiver. Finally, Bloom (e.g., Bloom 1975; Bloom and Esposito, 1975) demonstrated in a series of studies that the operant model provides an inadequate account of vocal behavior. Rather, when proper controls are instituted, it becomes clear that social facilitation, not reinforcement, accounts for vocal responsivity. Typical baseline procedures (a nonresponsive adult) suppress social responsivity, and subsequent noncontingent experimenter responsiveness is as effective as contingent responsiveness in overcoming this suppression. Reciprocity in caregiver-infant relationships is characterized by synchrony not reinforcement. ". . . (F)or early social development the operant conditioning paradigm has ecological validity only in structure and not in function" [Bloom, 1975, p. 6].[11]

To extend the case, it has also been found that contingent responding to crying has the consequence of *reduced* crying later in the 1st year and generally is associated with a secure attachment relationship (Ainsworth et al., 1974; Bell and Ainsworth, 1972). While based on correlational studies and therefore not conclusive with respect to causality, such a finding at least suggests the relatively greater power of a viewpoint stressing the quality of the relationship as apposed to unmodified reinforcement theory. What seems to be learned is the trustworthiness and dependability of the surround, rather than a set of discrete behaviors.

---

[11]Gewirtz (1965) has described the inadequacies of classical conditioning to account for positive affect.

Developmental theories of emotion typically have been psychoanalytic in their heritage (e.g., Brody and Axelrod, 1970; Escalona, 1968; Mahler, 1975; Spitz, 1963). These theories are developmental not only in their ontogenetic emphasis but because of their emphasis on integrated developmental processes—the ties of emotional growth to the social and cognitive domains. In the most elaborated positions, affect is viewed as central in major developmental reorganizations (e.g., Spitz et al., 1970) or even as causal in qualitative developmental change (Brody and Axelrod, 1966), the latter being closer to Freud's position on the emergence of the ego. All workers with a psychoanalytic leaning have stressed the integrated nature of development and the differential sensitivities of infants with development. Although the terms used are object relations, anticipation, and ego mastery, rather than intentionality, object concept, and goals, these developmental theorists assume that infants in the second half-year of life experience the world in a qualitatively different way than do younger infants. The emotions of anger when an *intended* act is blocked or fear when a threat is *recognized* are transformations of earlier rage and wariness. They develop out of these roots but not in a linear, incremental way.

Though developmental in nature, psychoanalytic theories have been encumbered by drive-reduction or energy-distribution notions, inherent in the closed hydraulic model. Even in his extensive elaborations of psychoanalytic theory, Spitz (1959), for example, continued to assume that tension increase was negative and tension relief was positive, and also that need gratification was central in emotion. Despite the importance of Freud's views on the relations between affect and behavior and Spitz' views on the organization of emotional development, theories of emotion based on tension reduction are clearly inadequate. Such a position cannot, for example, adequately account for the expression of positive affect—smiling at inanimate stimuli following sufficient exposure, laughing in social games where arousal is clearly high (see Sroufe et al., 1974), or the ecstasy in watching the seascape (see Pleasure-Joy, above). Nor does it seem congruent with the active way in which infants seek and maintain contact with stimulation, reproduce challenging incongruities, or, in general, master their experience (e.g., Emde et al., 1976; Brody and Axelrod, 1970; Sroufe and Wunsch, 1972; White, 1959).

Bowlby's (1969) monograph, while centering on attachment, provided a general refutation of tension release and distribution of a fixed quantity of energy as explanations for behavior. He was able to account for attachment behaviors in terms of goals and information without postulating drive concepts and pointed out similarities of human attachment behavior to that of other animals. In Bowlby's system, information reaching the infant that the set-goal of proximity is not being maintained will activate behaviors to reinstate proximity. Such behavior will continue until the goal is accomplished, without any postulation of an attachment *motive*. Mandler (1975), while not proposing a developmental theory, presents a more general statement of the power of control systems-information theory (cf. Miller et al., 1960) in accounting for emotions. In Mandler's scheme, interruption of plans produces arousal and, depending on the cognitive interpretation of arousal in context (cf. Schacter, 1966), the various emotions may be activated; again, no drive, energy, or motivational concepts are postulated.

Elsewhere we have presented a critique of theories of attachment without tension, motives, or feeling states (Sroufe and Waters, 1977). In brief, Bowlby's position can account for the activation of attachment behaviors but it cannot account for the changing sensitivity of infants to separation following a first separation or, in general, the changing settings of the set-goal when the external situation is the same. Moreover, the set-goal of proximity is developmentally inadequate (infants seek less proximity with age while obviously remaining attached); only an affective concept like "security" is developmentally robust and adequate to the complex manifestation of attachment behavior (see Sroufe and Waters, 1977). Mandler's position has a similar problem, having plans calling for their own fulfillment, but is most notably inadequate in accounting for positive affect. No interruption of plans is obviously involved in the infant's repeated laughter at uncovering the mother's face in peek-a-boo or in the ecstasy in viewing a sunset from a mountain top. Moreover, the *affect* associated with such experiences remains to be explained, even if the behaviors are accounted for adequately.

Bowlby, Mandler, and others stressing informational factors in emotional behavior have presented a strong challenge to motivational theories. And they have rather clearly demonstrated that *drive-reduction* concepts are not only insufficient but unnecessary in accounting for emotional development and affect expression. With the further accumulation of evidence, the declining status of drive reduction as the central concept in explaining human behavior continues (cf. White, 1959). An adequate theory of emotional development, then, must not be encumbered by drive-reduction concepts; yet it must be able to account for the range of emotional experiences and overcome the limitations of a purely informational position.

Outline for a Developmental Theory

A beginning toward an adequate developmental theory can be made by integrating powerful cognitive and control systems models with motivational concepts, feeling, and even tension. It is drive *reduction,* tension *reduction,* and the idea of a fixed amount of energy that have been shown to be inadequate in accounting for human emotion. It has not been shown that feeling does not mediate behavior (and there is evidence to the contrary), that motivation, as linked to feeling, is superfluous in explaining behavior, or that tension itself is an extraneous construct in conceptualizing emotional behavior and development (e.g., Engel, 1971).

Feelings are required in a cognitive-informational position to account for carry-over from one event to another, for changing thresholds for threat, and for sequences of reactions that unfold without further external information. Changing sensitivities *can* be conceptualized in terms of cognitive factors (certain kinds of information are given increased priority) or neurophysiological factors (a cortical-limbic loop is established and can be immediately activated by certain information). We would only add that emotional reactions (e.g., to a separation experience) play a large role in determining the changing salience of information, since the infant evaluates its *feelings* as part of the total event. Following Arnold (1960), it is a subjective evaluation, rather than a purely cognitive interpretation. Thus, after a separation experience, the infant may be more alert to certain classes of cues and may be more readily distressed by the same external information (e.g., the caregiver changing her position in the room). The baby may cry at a stimulating event that had produced laughter before the stress experience. The same information has new meaning, based in part on the affective experience with which the information has been associated. Since feelings as well as external information determine behavior, the infant can show the progression from protest to despair to detachment without changes in external information. And it may be angry on *reunion* with the mother. This anger is not explicable by the visual stimulus of the mother or by the interruption of plans (the infant may have been seeking her); rather, the reunion reactivates the pain of the loss with which the image of the mother was linked. However adaptive or biologically useful such an anger reaction might be (e.g., punishing the mother), we must still account for its occurrence in the human infant. The account will include preceding affective experience and the emotional relationship with the caregiver, in general.

A tension construct, including tension fluctuation and a *cumulative* process, is also required in elaborating a cognitive position. It is required to account for the range of emotions and their precursors, the positive emotions in particular, the vigor of the affective response, and the continuity and discontinuity in the development of emotion.

To be explained is the manner in which what was a physiological process becomes a psychophysiological process. Our account of the precursors of negative emotions suggested that, at first, quantity of arousal was related to distress. This arousal may have been due to head restraint or captivating visual stimulation, or later to a mixture of familiar and unfamiliar elements (wariness). In these cases, a cumulation of arousal is implicated, which is as sufficient as acute arousal due to pain in producing distress. In wariness, for example, there is no noxious stimulation; rather, what is required is that the event

have a certain insistence but also sufficient duration . . . Only in that case can the general tension cumulate to a sufficiently strong load . . . The tenseness of the whole system . . . remains and rises, evidently with the duration of the stimulus . . . It can often be observed how the expression of the child changes more and more towards anxiety.'' [Meili, 1955, p. 204.]

If the infant disengages the event, or if the engagement is punctuated with smiling, cooing and motor activity (positive discharge; Tennes et al., 1972), distress does not result. It is *unbroken* arousal or unbroken tension that produces distress. Later in infancy, distress also can result rather immediately, even in the absence of noxious stimulation. The tension increase is a function of the negative meaning of the event, a psychophysiological process.

Although a cumulative process seems unavoidable in accounting for many early negative reactions, those advocating a cognitive position might handle the points made above by assuming a developmental transition from physiological to psychological arousal. But cognitive arousal *is* what is meant by the term tension, and it is the distinction between the two kinds of arousal that the concept serves to make.[12] Tension is a product of the infant's engagement of the event, not of stimulation per se. Such a concept serves to underscore the continuity between the earlier cumulative process and a hypothesized rapid buildup of arousal in later emotion. It also metaphorically suggests that a subjective relationship, a transaction or tie, between the infant and event is descriptively more accurate than conceiving of arousal as *in response to* an event.

The tension construct is helpful in accounting for the range of emotions and the expression of affects. On the face of it, affect is often energetic and vigorous. From a purely cognitive point of view, there is no direct link between discrepant information and affect expression. A physiological link must be postulated. To say that arousal caused by interruption is (in an unspecified way) translated into fright or anger still leaves positive

[12]Such a distinction helps resolve the controversial issue regarding the temporal relationship between arousal and appraisal. If arousal refers to the immediate consequences of an encounter with a novel or disrupting event, as Mandler (1975) argues (i.e., the pronounced HR deceleration which occurs initially on encounters with any novel or salient event, threatening or otherwise), then interpretation follows or is coincidental with arousal. But if arousal is restricted to the subsequent acceleration in the negative situation, it follows appraisal, as suggested by Arnold (1960). Our summary of this situation is that, with a salient event, there is orienting and appraisal (tension is generated) and the outcome of the appraisal results in either positive *or* negative affect. Tachycardia precedes distress and is rapid and extensive; with laughter, the deceleration continues to the point of the laughing, then there is acceleration with the motor discharge (Sroufe et al., 1974; Sroufe and Waters, 1976b).

affect largely to be explained. Tension, as a product of engagement and transaction, can be produced when the infant is successfully engaging a cognitively challenging or psychologically captivating event, without postulating a disruption. Squeals of laughter can be accounted for as well as wariness or anger.

As a concept of cumulation seems necessary to account for wariness, a concept of tension fluctuation is required to account for positive affect. When young infants break from a captivating event, they not only avoid distress with the modulation of arousal but also frequently express positive affect. Also, with many types of events, laughter occurs at a focused termination point (e.g., poking the ribs), where the transaction precipitously ends (and the tension precipitously drops). Moreover, on early trials with a novel stimulus, 3-month-olds do not smile, though they orient and sustain attention; smiling requires assimilation/accommodation and a fluctuation of tension following an increase, analogous to REM smiles when relaxation follows arousal. Laughter, which builds from and fades again to smiling with repeated presentations of an event, would seem to require a more rapid tension fluctuation than smiling. In support of this, Down's syndrome infants, especially the most hypotonic, laugh relatively little, even when they are equated with controls on DQ and are smiling differentially to the items (Cicchetti and Sroufe, 1976). They seem unable to process the items with sufficient speed to produce the tension "jag" required for laughter (cf. Berlyne, 1969).

In this framework, tension is not a quantum material inside the organism, always increasing and demanding relief. Motivation is not conceived as escape from tension. Rather, tension is a product of engagement. A moderate level of tension is actively sought, and, in a positive context, even great amounts of tension can lead to positive affect. When the infant repeatedly attempts to stuff the cloth back into mother's mouth, squealing with laughter and showing dramatic HR acceleration, it is not only actively repeating the tension-arousing situation but tolerating a great amount of physiological arousal. Joy is not a product of tension relief but tension fluctuation. And *no set amount of tension is necessarily aversive*. Salient stimulus situations (e.g., mother with mask) have been shown to lead to the range of emotional reactions (fear, neutral, joy), depending on manipulation of age, setting, sequence of events, and familiarization time (Sroufe and Wunsch, 1972; Sroufe et al., 1974). There is little a mother can do in a playful home context that will distress her infant, however arousing.

In agreement with Mandler (1975), it is not the arousal (tension) per se but the interpretation (evaluation) that determines the nature of the affective reaction. Factors like discrepancy (Kagan, 1971; McCall and McGhee, 1976) can account for the amount of arousal and the magnitude of the affect but not for the hedonic tone (Stechler and Carpenter, 1967). Babies being vigorously jostled or stimulated with loud sounds will become very aroused and will express strong affect; depending on context (e.g., agent and setting), this may be *crying or laughter*. Similarly, an engaging novel event or discrepant visual event (e.g., mother with mask) will produce tension, but the direction of the affect is determined by contextual factors. The stimulus situations most potent for producing fear are often most potent for laughter in infancy; considerable tension is required for both (Sroufe et al., 1974).

An outline for a developmental theory of emotion, therefore, retains important cognitive components. The instigation of emotion is tied to recognition, appraisal, and other cognitive processes, and particular emotions depend on circumstances surrounding the increase in tension (e.g., threat versus blocking of an intended act or perceived attack). But an adequate account of infant emotion also encompasses a dynamic viewpoint. There is not a fixed amount of energy (arousal), sprung loose by interruption of plans; rather, tension is produced by the infant's engagement with and investment in the surround, at a level commensurate with its *valuing* of the plans in question. Thus, different amounts of arousal in similar circumstances and positive as well as negative affects are encompassed.

In summary, supplementing a cognitive position with a tension concept, as described above, makes it possible to account for the range of emotional reaction and their close relationships. Only acute or unbroken tension results in negative affect. Moderate levels of tension, modulated tension, and tension under the individual's control can be associated with interest, curiosity, pleasure, and even ecstacy (tension hovering around an ideal level). In certain contexts, even rapid increases of tension or considerable amounts of tension can lead to positive affect (roller coasters and vigorous infant play). In addition, the concept of tension, and affect expression as related to tension increases and fluctuation, is compatible with the variety of functions outlined in the preceding section. Affect can be seen as central in the stream and organization of behavior, from orienting through perception and appraisal to direct action. The organism *seeks* stimulation, subjectively evaluates its experience, which includes the event and its reaction, and modulates its level of tension via affective expression and/or direct action. It is *not* always acting *in order to modulate* tension, but its behavior has such consequences, and these consequences further influence behavior (cf. Arnold, 1960).

The integration proposed has numerous implications for developmental research. First and foremost, the question of what develops broadens. Beyond the influence of cognitive factors such as recognition, object concept, and intentionality, which we are beginning to study, there are important questions concerning the development of tension tolerance (capacitance) and the ability to control and modulate tension. For example, 5- and 6-month-old infants often laugh at events that produced crying in younger infants (e.g., loud sounds, vigorous bouncing). This *may* be because of an increased ability to assimilate the event or because the *ratio* of cognitively generated tension (anticipation and tuning to the patterning of the stimulation) to stimulation produced arousal (Sroufe and Waters, 1976a) has changed in a favorable direction. But it may be that the older infant can tolerate more arousal or tension, as well.

Other questions will concern the continually elaborating function of affect. Early in infancy affective expression punctuates and paces the flow of behavior, both because of its arousal-modulating effects and because of its influence on caregivers (Sroufe and Waters, 1976a). But increasingly with development there are guiding and amplifying functions as well. Infants respond to their affective experience, act within it, modulate, control, and cope with it, and may even behave in order to produce or avoid certain affective experiences. At present, such guiding and organizing functions are poorly understood, as is early development of capacities for coping with stress.

Finally, important roles for caregivers in fostering healthy emotional development can be seen within this viewpoint. The sensitive caregiver would promote cognitive growth, competence, and confidence by responding contingently (Ainsworth, 1974; Ainsworth et al., 1976; Clarke-Stewart, 1973). But, in addition, there may also be a role for assistance in developing tension tolerance, for example through caregiver-infant play. Or the caregiver may help the infant learn that tension can increase and still be under control and even can be associated with positive affective experience. Even contingency may be more than timing. Caregivers may be so effective in promoting development because they help create the appropriate affective climate and tune their behaviors to the infant's tension level, catching it at the peak of organized engagement, rather than simply because they respond to its behavior in a reliable, mechanical fashion. There are important questions for infant development and child mental health here.

CONCLUSION

This, then, is a sketch of the domain of emotional development. It includes the ontogenesis of the emotions, their interrelationships, and their ties to precursor reactions in early infancy. It includes development of the infant as an emotional being and the influence of emotion on developmental organization. And it includes the continually elaborating function of affect.

Within the organizational view of emotional development, it is obvious that its domain overlaps considerably with other major areas of developmental psychology—for example, differentiation of the self (e.g., Mahler, 1975) or ego (e.g., Loevinger, 1976) and what psychoanalytic theorists call object relations (Brody and Axelrod, 1970; Ainsworth, 1969). Differentiation of the self is related to emotional development in numerous ways. Only when the differentiating baby forms a specific tie to a recognized social object can there be the anxiety and grief associated with separation and loss. Only when the separation-individuation process is carried further can there be the experiences of shame, and later pride and guilt, which comes with self-awareness and a sense of responsibility for one's acts. Moreover, within the context of the attachment relationship, the infant has a source of security (and self trust) against which may be balanced the wariness and anxiety resulting from its encounters with the environment as a separate self (e.g., Breger, 1974; Mahler, 1975). These are complex and important topics, and the student of emotional development would do well to read widely in the work of neo-analytic theorists (e.g., Ainsworth et al., 1978; Brody and Axelrod, 1970; Escalona, 1968; Sandler and Joffee, 1965; Loevinger, 1976; Mahler, 1975; Murphy and Moriarty, 1976; Spitz, 1959). To date, it is the workers from this tradition that have attempted to put together a whole picture of the developing child, emphasizing its connectedness with the world.

Emotional development also encompasses the literature on adaptation and competence. Competence clearly involves more than veridical perception and cognitive facility; in early infancy it involves the regulation of physiology and behavior (e.g., Sander, 1962), the seeking of *aliment* (White, 1959), and establishing a smoothly functioning relationship with the caregiver (e.g., Brazelton et al., 1974; Stern, 1974b). Modulation of tension, motivation, and communication are all within the province of affect in infancy. Later, competence will involve "the freedom to engage in creative exploration . . . and persistence in working on problems that pose difficulties" (Yarrow et al., 1975) and the related constructs of ego strength and ego resiliency (Block and Block, 1973).

The ontogenesis of individual differences in competence and styles of adaptation (whatever the interaction between temperament and quality of care) is an important part of the domain of emotional development. The posture with which the pre-school child faces the world—the quality of affective engagement of the social and nonsocial environment (ego resiliency; Block and Block, 1973)—must have profound consequences for future development. In an important way, understanding emotional development is understanding the development of the zestful, affectively expressive child, who enjoys and is a source of enjoyment for others, who seeks out sources of gratification and pleasure using personal and environmental resources, and who generally moves toward its experience, as well as understanding the child who is retreating from affective contact with the environment, being unable to cope with the tensions inherent in such contact.

BIBLIOGRAPHY

Ainsworth, M. Infant-mother attachment and social development: Socialization as a product of reciprocal responsiveness to signals. In M. Richards (ed.), *The Integration of the Child into the Social World*. Cambridge: Cambridge University, 1974.

Ainsworth, M. The development of infant-mother attachment. In B. Caldwell and H. Ricciuti (eds.), *Review of Child Development Research*, Vol. 3. Chicago: University of Chicago, 1973.

Ainsworth, M. Object relations, dependency and attachment: A theoretical review of the mother-infant relationship. *Child Development*, 1969, **40**, 969–1025.

Ainsworth, M., Bell, S., and Stayton, D. Individual differences in strange situation behavior of one-year-olds. In H. Schaffer (ed.), *The Origins of Human Social Relations*. London: Academic, 1971.

Ainsworth, M., Blehar, M., Waters, E., and Wall, S. Strange-situation behavior of one-year-olds: Its relations to mother-infant interaction in the first year and to qualitative differences in the infant-mother attachment relationship. New York: Lawrence Erlbaum, 1978.

Amsterdam, B. Mirror self-image reactions before age two. *Developmental Psychobiology*, 1972, **5**, 297–305.

Arnold, M. *Emotion and Personality*. New York: Columbia University, 1960.

Ball, W., and Tronick, E. Infant responses to impending collision: Optical and real. *Science*, 1971, **171**, 818–820.

Bell, S. The development of the concept of object as related to infant-mother attachment. *Child Development*, 1970, **41**, 291–311.

Bell, S., and Ainsworth, M. Infant crying and maternal responsiveness. *Child Development*, 1972, **43**, 1171–1190.

Bell, R., Weller, G., and Waldrop, M. Newborn and preschooler: Organization of behavior and relations between periods. *Monographs of the Society for Research in Child Development*, 1971, **36**.

Bergman, P., and Escalona, S. Unusual sensitivities in very young children. *Psychoanalytic Study of the Child*, 1949, **3–4**, 332–352.

Berlyne, D. Laughter, humor and play. In G. Lindzey and E. Aronson (eds.), *Handbook of Social Psychology*, Vol. 3. Boston: Addison-Wesley, 1969.

Birns, B., Blank, M., and Bridger, W. The effectiveness of various soothing techniques on human neonates. *Psychosomatic Medicine*, 1966, **28**, 316–322.

Birns, B., and Golden, M. Prediction of intellectual performance at three years from infant test and personality measures. *Merrill-Palmer Quarterly*, 1972, **18**, 53–58.

Bischof, N. A systems approach towards the functional connections of fear and attachment. *Child Development*, 1975, **46**, 801–817.

Block, J. Recognizing the coherence of personality. Paper presented at the Meetings of the American Psychological Association, New Orleans, September 1975.

Block, J., and Block, J. Ego development and the provenance of thought: A longitudinal study of ego and cognitive development in young children. Progress Report for NIMH, 1973.

Bloom, K. Does the operant conditioning model have ecological validity for early social development? Paper presented at the Meetings of the International Society for the Study of Behavioural Development, Guilford, England, July, 1975.

Bloom, K., and Esposito, A. Social conditioning and its proper control procedures. *Journal of Experimental Child Psychology*, 1975, **19**, 209–222.

Bower, T., Broughton, J., and Moore, M. Infant responses to approaching objects. *Perception and Psychophysics*, 1970, **9**, 193–196.

Bowlby, J. *Attachment and Loss*. Vol. 1. *Attachment*. New York: Basic Books, 1969.

Bowlby, J. *Attachment and Loss*. Vol. 2. *Separation: Anxiety and Anger*. New York: Basic Books, 1973.

Brackbill, Y. Extinction of the smiling response in infants as a function of reinforcement schedule. *Child Development*, 1958, **29**, 115–124.

Brazelton, T. Psychophysiologic reactions in the neonate. I. The value of observation of the neonate. *Journal of Pediatrics*, 1961, **58**, 508–512.

Brazelton, T. *Neonatal Behavioral Assessment Scale*. National Spastics Society Monograph. London: Heinemann, 1973.

Brazelton, T., Koslowski, B., and Main, M. The origins of reciprocity: The early mother-infant interaction. In M. Lewis and L. Rosenblum (eds.), *The Effect of the Infant on its Caregiver*. New York: Wiley, 1974.

Breger, L. *From Instinct to Identity: The Development of Personality*. Englewood Cliffs, N.J.: Prentice-Hall, 1974.

Bretherton, I., and Ainsworth, M. Responses of one-year-olds to a stranger in a strange situation. In M. Lewis and L. Rosenblum (eds.), *The Origins of Fear*. New York: Wiley, 1974.

Bridger, W., and Birns, B. Neonates' behavioral and autonomic responses to stress during soothing. *Recent Advances in Biological Psychiatry*, 1963, **5**, 1–6.

Bridges, K. Emotional development in early infancy. *Child Development*, 1932, **3**, 324–341.

Brody, S., and Axelrod, S. Anxiety, socialization and ego formation in infancy. *International Journal of Psycho-Analysis*, 1966, **47**, 213–229.

Brody, S., and Axelrod, S. *Anxiety, and Ego Formation in Infancy*. New York: International Universities, 1970.

Bronson, G. Infants' reaction to unfamiliar persons and novel objects. *Monographs of the Society for Research in Child Development*, 1972, **37**.

Bronson, G., and Pankey, W. On the distinction between fear and wariness. *Child Development*, 1977, **48**, 1167–1183.

Bronson, W. Mother-toddler interaction: A perspective on studying the development of competence. *Merrill-Palmer Quarterly*, 1974, **20**, 275–300.

Brooks, J., and Lewis, M. Mirror-image stimulation and self-recognition in infancy. Paper presented at the Meetings of the Society for Research in Child Development, Denver, April 1975.

Buhler, C. *The First Year of Life*. New York: Day, 1930.

Cairns, R. Attachment and dependency: A psychobiological and social learning synthesis. In J. Gewirtz (ed.), *Attachment and Dependency*. New York: Winston, 1972.

Campos, J., Emde, R., and Gaensbauer, T. Cardiac and behavioral interrelationships in the reactions of infants to strangers. *Developmental Psychology*, 1975, **11**, 589–601.

Carr, S., Dabbs, J., and Carr, T. Mother-infant attachment: The importance of the mother's visual field. *Child Development*, 1975, **46**, 331–338.

Charlesworth, W. The role of surprise in cognitive development. In D. Elkind and J. Flavell (eds.), *Studies in Cognitive Development*. London: Oxford University, 1969.

Charlesworth, W., and Kreutzer, M. Facial expressions of infants and children. In P. Ekman (ed.), *Darwin and Facial Expression*. New York: Academic, 1973.

Cicchetti, D., and Mans, L. Down's syndrome and normal infants' responses to impending collision. Paper presented at the Meetings of the American Psychological Association, Washington, September 1976.

Cicchetti, D., and Sroufe, L. The relationship between affective and cognitive development in Down's syndrome infants. *Child Development*, 1976, **47**, 920–929.

Clarke-Stewart, K. Interactions between mothers and their young children: Characteristics and consequences. *Monographs of the Society for Research in Child Development*, 1973, **38**.

Clemente, C., Purpura, D., and Mayer, F. (eds.). *Maturation of Brain Mechanisms Related to Sleep Behavior*. New York: Academic, 1972.

Cohen, L. The operational definition of human attachment. *Psychological Bulletin,* 1974, **81**, 207–217.

Cohen, L., and Campos, J. Father, mother, and stranger as elicitors of attachment behaviors in infancy. *Developmental Psychology,* 1974, **10**, 146–154.

Darwin, C. *Expression of the Emotions in Man and Animals*. London: Murray, 1872.

Ekman, P., Friesen, W., and Ellsworth, P. *Emotion in the Humar Face*. New York: Pergamon, 1972.

Ekman, P., and Friesen, W. The facial atlas. Cited in P. Ekman, and W. Friesen, *Unmasking the Face*. Englewood Cliffs, N.J.: Prentice-Hall, 1975a.

Ekman, P., and Friesen, W. *Unmasking the Face*. Englewood Cliffs, N.J.: Prentice-Hall, 1975b.

Emde, R., and Koenig, K. Neonatal smiling, frowning, and rapid eye movement states. II. Sleep-cycle study. *Journal of the American Academy of Child Psychiatry,* 1969, **8**, 637–656.

Emde, R., and Harmon, R. Endogenous and exogenous smiling systems in early infancy. *Journal of the American Academy of Child Psychiatry,* 1972, **11**, 177–200.

Emde, R., Gaensbauer, T., and Harmon, R. Emotional expression in infancy: A biobehavioral study. *Psychological Issues Monograph Series,* 1976, **10**, (Monog. No. 37).

Engel, G. Attachment behavior, object relations and the dynamic-economic points of view: Critical review of Bowlby's Attachment and Loss. *International Journal of Psycho-Analysis,* 1971, **52**, 183–196.

Erikson, E. *Childhood and Society*. New York: Norton, 1950.

Escalona, S. *The Roots of Individuality*. Chicago: Aldine, 1968.

Escalona, S., and Corman, H. The impact of the mother's presence upon behavior: The first year. *Human Development,* 1971, **14**, 2–15.

Feldman, S., and Ingham, M. Attachment behavior: A validation study in two age groups. *Child Development,* 1975, **46**, 319–330.

Flavell, J. Stage-related properties of cognitive development. *Cognitive Psychology,* 1971, **2**, 421–453.

Flavell, J., Bottkin, P., Fry, C., Wright, J., and Jarvis, P. *The Development of Role-Taking and Communication in Children*. New York: Wiley, 1968.

Fraiberg, S. Libidinal object constancy and mental representation. *Psycho-Analytic Study of the Child,* 1969, **24**, 9–47.

Gewirtz, J. The course of infant smiling in four child-rearing environments in Israel. In B. Foss (ed.), *Determinants of Infant Behavior*. III. London: Methuen, 1965.

Goldberg, S. Infant care and growth in urban Zambia. *Human Development,* 1972, **15**, 77–89.

Goodenough, F. *Anger in Young Children*. Minneapolis: University of Minnesota, 1931a.

Goodenough, F. The expression of emotions in infancy. *Child Development,* 1931b, **2**, 96–101.

Goodenough, F. *Developmental Psychology: An Introduction to the Study of Human Behavior,* 2nd ed. New York: Appleton-Century, 1934.

Haviland, J. Individual differences in affect. Paper presented at the Meetings of the Society for Research in Child Development, Denver, April 1975a.

Haviland, J. Looking smart: The relationship between affect and intelligence in infancy. In M. Lewis (ed.), *Origins of Infant Intelligence*. New York: Plenum, 1975b.

Heinicke, C., and Westheimer, I. *Brief Separations*. New York: International Universities, 1966.

Hold, B. An ethological study of rank order behavior in preschool children. Unpublished Ph.D. dissertation (in German), University of Munich and Max Planck Institute für Verhaltensphysiologie, Arbeitsgruppe für Humanethologie. Percha/Starnberg, West Germany, 1975.

Hruska, K., and Yonas, A. Developmental changes in cardiac responses to the the optical stimulus of impending collision. Paper presented at the Meetings for Psychophysiological Research, St. Louis, 1971.

Izard, C. *The Face of Emotion*. New York: Appleton-Century-Crofts, 1971.

James, W. *The Principles of Psychology*. New York: Holt, 1890.

Janet, P. Psychological strength and weakness in mental diseases. *Factors Determining Human Behavior*. Cambridge: Harvard University, 1937, 64–106.

Jersild, A., and Holmes, F. *Children's Fears*. New York: Teachers College, 1935.

Kagan, J. On the meaning of behavior: Illustrations from the infant. *Child Development*, 1969, **40**, 1121–1134.

Kagan, J. *Change and Continuity in Infancy*. New York: Wiley, 1971.

Kagan, J., and Moss, H. *Birth to Maturity*. New York: Wiley, 1962.

Kanner, L. Autistic disturbances of affective contact. *The Nervous Child*, 1943, **2**, 217–240.

Klaus, M., Jerauld, R., Kreger, N., McAlpine, W., Steffa, M., and Kennell, J. Maternal attachment: The importance of the first post-partum days. *New England Journal of Medicine*, 1972, **286**, 460–463.

Klein, R., and Durfee, J. Infants' reactions to unfamiliar adults versus mothers. Revised version of paper presented at the Meetings of the Society for Research in Child Development, Denver, April 1975.

Korner, A. Neonatal startles, smiles, erections and reflex sucks as related to state, sex and individuality. *Child Development*, 1969, **40**, 1039–1053.

Korner, A. Individual differences at birth: Implications for early experience and later development. *American Journal of Orthopsychiatry*, 1971, **41**, 608–619.

Kotelchuck, M. The nature of the child's tie to his father. Paper presented at the Meetings of the Society for Research in Child Development, Philadelphia, April 1973.

Kramer, Y., and Rosenblum, L. Response to frustration in one-year-old infants. *Psychosomatic Medicine*, 1970, **32**, 243–257.

Lamb, M. Fathers: Forgotten contributors to child development. *Human Development*, 1975, **18**, 245–266.

Lazarus, R. Emotions and adaptation: Conceptual and empirical relations. In W. Arnold (ed.), *Nebraska Symposium on Motivation*. Lincoln: University of Nebraska, 1968.

Lenneberg, E. *Biological Foundations of Language*. New York: Wiley, 1967.

Lester, B., Kotelchuck, M., Spelke, E., Sellers, M., & Klein, R. Separation protest in Guatemalan infants: cross cultural and cognitive findings. *Developmental Psychology*, 1974, **10**, 79–85.

Lewis, M., and Goldberg, S. Perceptual-cognitive development in infancy: A generalized expectancy model as a function of the mother-infant interaction. *Merrill-Palmer Quarterly*, 1969, **15**, 81–100.

Lewis, M., and Rosenblum, L. (eds.). *The Effect of the Infant on its Caregiver*. New York: Wiley, 1974.

Loevinger, J. *Ego Development: Conceptions and Theories*. San Francisco: Jossey-Bass, 1976.

Maccoby, E., and Feldman, S. Mother-attachment and stranger-reactions in the third year of life. *Monographs of the Society for Research in Child Development*, 1972, **37.**

Mahler, M., and Pine F. *The Psychological Birth of the Infant*. New York: Basic Books, 1975.

Main, M. Exploration, play, and cognitive functioning as related to child-mother attachment. Unpublished Ph.D. dissertation, Johns Hopkins University, 1973.

Mandler, G. *Mind and Emotion*. New York: Wiley, 1975.

Masters, J., and Wellman, H. Human infant attachment: A procedural critique. *Psychological Bulletin*, 1974, **81**, 218–237.

Matas, L., Arend, R. and Sroufe, L. Continuity in adaptation in the second year: Quality of attachment and later competence. *Child Development,* in press.

McCall, R. Smiling and vocalization in infants as indices of perceptual-cognitive processes. *Merrill-Palmer Quarterly,* 1972, **18**, 341–347.

McCall, R., and McGhee, P. The discrepancy hypothesis of attention and affect. In F. Weizmann and I. Uzgiris (eds.), *The Structuring of Experience.* New York: Plenum, 1976.

Meili, R. Angstentstehung bei Kleinkindern. *Schweizerische Zeitschrift fur Psychologie und ihre Anwendungen,* 1955, **14**, 195–212.

Miller, G., Galanter, E., and Pribram, K. *Plans and the Structure of Behavior.* New York: Holt, Rinehart and Winston, 1960.

Mischel, W. *Personality and Assessment.* New York: Wiley, 1968.

Morgan, G. Determinants of infants' reactions to strangers. Revised version of a paper presented at the Meetings of the Society for Research in Child Development, Philadelphia, April 1973.

Moss, H. Sex, age and state as determinants of mother-infant interaction. *Merrill-Palmer Quarterly,* 1967, **13**, 19–36.

Murphy, L. *The Widening World of Childhood: Paths Toward Mastery.* New York: Basic Books, 1962.

Murphy, L. & Moriarty, A. *Vulnerability, Coping and Growth.* New Haven: Yale University, 1976.

Osofsky, J., and Danzger, B. Relationships between neonatal characteristics and mother-infant interaction. *Developmental Psychology,* 1974, **10**, 124–130.

Oster, H. Measuring facial behavior in human infants. Paper presented at the Meetings of the Animal Behavior Society, Boulder, 1976.

Paradise, E., and Curcio, F. The relationship of cognitive and affective behaviors to fear of strangers in male infants. *Developmental Psychology,* 1974, **10**, 476–483.

Parmelee, A., Jr. Development of states in infants. In C. Clemente, D. Purpura, and F. Mayer (eds.), *Maturation of Brain Mechanisms Related to Sleep Behavior.* New York: Academic, 1972,

Piaget, J. *The Origins of Intelligence in Children.* New York: Rutledge and Kegan Paul, 1952.

Piaget, J., and Inhelder, B. *The Psychology of the Child.* New York: Basic Books, 1969.

Rand, C., and Jennings, K. Reactions of infants and young children to a stranger in an unfamiliar setting. Paper presented at the Meetings of the Society for Research in Child Development, Denver, April 1975.

Rheingold, H., and Eckerman, C. Fear of the stranger: A critical examination. In H. Reese (ed.), *Advances in Child Development and Behavior,* Vol. 8. New York: Academic, 1973.

Robertson, J., and Robertson, J. Young children in brief separation: A fresh look. *Psychoanalytic Study of the Child,* 1971, **26**, 264–315.

Robinson, R. (ed.). *Brain and Early Behaviour.* New York: Academic, 1969.

Robson, K. The role of eye-to-eye contact in maternal-infant attachment. *Journal of Child Psychology and Psychiatry,* 1967, **8**, 12–25.

Rosenthal, M. Attachment and mother-infant interaction: Some research impasses and a suggested change in orientation. *Journal of Child Psychology and Psychiatry and Allied Disciplines,* 1973, **14**, 201–207.

Rothbart, M. Laughter in young children. *Psychological Bulletin,* 1973, **80**, 247–256.

Sameroff, A. This volume.

Sander, L. Issues in early mother-child interaction. *Journal of the American Academy of Child Psychiatry,* 1962, **1**, 141–166.

Sander, L. The longitudinal course of early mother-child interaction—cross-case comparison in a sample of mother-child pairs. In B. Foss (ed.), *Determinants of Infant Behavior,* IV. London: Tavistock, 1969,

Sandler, J., & Joffee, W. Notes on childhood depression. *International Journal of Psychoanalysis,* 1965, **46**, 88–96.

Santostefano, S., and Baker, H. The contribution of developmental psychology. In B. Wolman (ed.), *Manual of Child Psychopathology.* New York: McGraw-Hill, 1972.

Schacter, S. The interaction of cognitive and physiological determinants of emotional state. In C. Spielberger (ed.), *Anxiety and Behavior.* New York: Academic, 1966.

Schaffer, H. Cognitive components of the infant's response to strangeness. In M. Lewis and L. Rosenblum (eds.), *The Origins of Fear.* New York: Wiley, 1974.

Schaffer, H., and Emerson, P. Patterns of response to physical contact in early human development. *Journal of Child Psychology and Psychiatry, 1964,* **5**, 1–13.

Schaffer, H., Greenwood, A., and Parry, M. The onset of wariness. *Child Development,* 1972, **43**, 165–175.

Schwartz, A., Campos, J., and Baisel, E. The visual cliff: Cardiac and behavioral correlates on the deep and shallow sides at five and nine months of age. *Journal of Experimental Child Psychology,* 1973, **15**, 85–99.

Shultz, T., and Zigler, E. Emotional concomitants of visual mastery in infants: The effects of stimulus movement on smiling and vocalizing. *Journal of Experimental Child Psychology,* 1970, **10**, 390–402.

Skarin, K. Cognitive and contextual determinants of stranger fear in 6 and 11 month old infants. *Child Development,* 1977, **48**, 537–544.

Spitz, R. *A Genetic Field Theory of Ego Formation.* New York: International Universities, 1959.

Spitz, R. Ontogenesis: The proleptic function of emotion. In P. Knapp (ed.), *Expression of the Emotions in Man.* New York: International Universities, 1963.

Spitz, R. *The First Year of Life. A Psychoanalytic Study of Normal and Deviant Development of Object Relations.* New York: International Universities, 1965.

Spitz, R., Emde, I., and Metcalf, D. Further prototypes of ego formation. *Psychoanalytic Study of the Child,* 1970, **25**, 417–444.

Sroufe, L. Wariness of strangers and the study of infant development. *Child Development,* 1977, **48**, 731–746.

Sroufe, L., and Wunsch, J. The development of laughter in the first year of life. *Child Development,* 1972, **43**, 1326–1344.

Sroufe, L., Waters, E., and Matas, L. Contextual determinants of infant affective response. In M. Lewis and L. Rosenblum (eds.), *The Origins of Fear.* New York: Wiley, 1974.

Sroufe, L., and Waters, E. The ontogenesis of smiling and laughter: A perspective on the organization of development in infancy. *Psychological Review,* 1976a, **83**, 173–189.

Sroufe, L., and Waters, E. Heartrate as a convergent measure in clinical and developmental research. *Merrill-Palmer Quarterly,* 1976b,

Stayton, D., Ainsworth, H., and Main, M. Development of separation behavior in the first year of life: Protest, following, and greeting. *Developmental Psychology,* 1973, **9**, 213–225.

Stechler, G., and Carpenter, G. A viewpoint on early affective development. In J. Hellmuth (ed.), *The Exceptional Infant,* Vol. 1. Seattle: Special Child Publications, 1967.

Stechler, G., and Latz, E. Some observations on attention and arousal in the human infant. *Journal of the American Academy of Child Psychiatry,* 1966, **5**, 517–5 .

Stern, D. Mother and infant at play: The dyadic interaction involving facial, vocal and gaze behaviors. In M. Lewis and L. Rosenblum (eds.), *The Effects of the Infant on its Caregiver.* New York: Wiley, 1974a.

Stern, D. The goal and structure of mother-infant play. *Journal of the American Academy of Child Psychiatry,* 1974b, **13**, 402–421.

Stern, D. The infant's stimulus "world" during social interaction: A study of the structure, timing and effects of caregiver behaviors. In R. Schaffer (ed.), *Studies on Interactions in Infancy.* New York: Academic, in press.

Stirnimann, F. *Psychologie des neugebornen Kindes.* Munich: Kindler Verlag, 1940.

Tennes, K., Emde, R., Kisley, A., and Metcalf, D. The stimulus barrier in early infancy: An exploration of some formulations of John Benjamin. In R. Holt and E. Peterfreund (eds.), *Psychoanalysis and Contemporary Science.* New York: Macmillan, 1972.

Thomas, A., Chess, S., and Birch, H. *Temperament and Behavior Disorders in Children.* New York: New York University, 1968.

Tomkins, S. *Affect, Imagery, Consciousness,* Vol. 1. New York: Springer, 1962.

van Hooff, J. A comparative approach to the phylogeny of laughter and smiling. In R. Hinde (ed.), *Non-Verbal Communication.* Cambridge, England: Cambridge University, 1972,

Vaughn, B. The development of greeting behavior in infants from 6 to 12 months of age. Unpublished Ph.D. dissertation, University of Minnesota, 1977.

Vaughn, B., and Sroufe, L. Unpublished data, 1978.

Vaughn, B., and Sroufe, L. The face of surprise in infants. Paper presented at the Meetings of the Animal Behavior Society, Boulder, 1976.

Vine, I. The role of facial visual signalling in early social development. In M. von Cranach and I. Vine (eds.), *Social Communication and Movement: Studies of Men and Chimpanzees.* London, Academic, 1973,

Vygotsky, L. *Thought and Language.* Boston: MIT, 1962.

Wahler, R. Infant social attachments: A reinforcement theory interpretation and investigation. *Child Development,* 1967, **38**, 1074–1088.

Waters, E. The stability of individual differences in infant-mother attachment. *Child Development,* in press.

Waters, E., Matas, L., and Sroufe, L. Infants' reactions to an approaching stranger: Description, validation and functional significance of wariness. *Child Development,* 1975, **46**, 348–356.

Waters, E., Wippman, and Sroufe, L. Attachment, positive affect, and competence in the peer group: Two studies in construct validation. Unpublished manuscript, 1978.

Watson, J. *Behaviorism.* New York: Norton, 1924.

Watson, J. Smiling, cooing and "the game." *Merrill-Palmer Quarterly,* 1972, **4**, 323–339.

Waxler, C., and Yarrow, M. An observational study of maternal models. *Developmental Psychology,* 1975, **11**, 485–494.

Weinraub, M., Brooks, J., and Lewis, M. The social network: A reconsideration of the concept of attachment. *Human Development,* 1977, **20**, 31–47.

Werner, H., and Kaplan, B. *Symbol Formation: An Organismic-Developmental Approach to Language and the Expression of Thought.* New York: Wiley, 1964.

White, B. Fundamental early environmental influences on the development of competency. In M. Meyer (ed.), *Third Symposium on Learning: Cognitive Learning.* Bellingham: Western Washington State College, 1972.

White, R. Motivation reconsidered: The concept of competence. *Psychological Review,* 1959, **66**, 297–333.

Wolff, P. Observations on the early development of smiling. In B. Foss (ed.), *Determinants of Infant Behaviour,* II. London: Methuen, 1963.

Wolff, P. The causes, controls, and organization of behavior in the neonate. *Psychological Issues,* 1966, **5** (whole No. 17).

Wolff, P. Crying and vocalization in early infancy. In B. Foss (ed.), *Determinants of Infant Behavior,* IV. New York: Wiley, 1969.

Yarrow, L. Attachment and dependency: A developmental perspective. In J. Gewirtz (ed.), *Attachment and Dependency.* Washington, D.C.: Winston, 1972.

Yarrow, L., and Goodwin, M. Some conceptual issues in the study of mother-infant interaction. *American Journal of Orthopsychiatry,* 1965, **35**, 473–481.

Yarrow, L., Rubenstein, J., Pedersen, F., and Yavkowski, J. Dimensions of early stimulation and their differential effects on infant development. *Merrill-Palmer Quarterly,* 1972, **18**, 205–218.

Yarrow, L., Klein, R., Lomonaco, S., and Morgan, G. Cognitive and motivational development in early childhood. In B. Friedlander, G. Sterritt, and G. Kirk (eds.), *Exceptional Infant,* Vol. 3. New York: Brunner/Mazel, 1975.

Yarrow, L., Rubenstein, J., and Pedersen, F. *Infant and Environment: Early Cognitive and Motivational Development.* New York: Wiley, 1975.

Zaslow, R., and Breger, L. A theory and treatment of autism. In L. Breger (ed.), *Clinical-Cognitive Psychology: Models and Integrations.* Englewood Cliffs, N.J.: Prentice-Hall, 1969.

Zelazo, P. Smiling and vocalizing: A cognitive emphasis. *Merrill-Palmer Quarterly,* 1972, **18**, 349–365.

Zelazo, P., and Komer, M. Infant smiling to nonsocial stimuli and the recognition hypothesis. *Child Development,* 1971, **42**, 1327–1339.

PART THREE

Early Parent–Infant and Infant–Infant Relationships

CHAPTER 14

Mother-Infant Interaction: An Integrative View of a Complex System

Joy D. Osofsky
Karen Connors

From the time of conception, mothers and infants share a very complex relationship which is developing, evolving, and changing throughout the course of the prenatal period in terms of mother's feelings and emotions, and then in a very dramatic way during labor and delivery and the subsequent birth. From the moment of birth, all of the fantasies, fears, hopes, and aspirations come into play as the imagined baby becomes a reality and the dramatic interplay between mother and infant begins. In this chapter, we will attempt to elaborate the various factors that play a part in the influencing and determining the ways in which the evolving relationship will develop. The hopes, expectations, experiences, and attitudes of the mother as well as the style, characteristics, and disposition of the infant play a very significant role in the type of relationship that will develop and the process that will be involved in forming the relationship. Over the course of the first 2 years of life there will be changes that will occur in both the infant and mother that will influence their interactive patterns in very meaningful ways. One of the objectives of the present chapter is to gain an understanding of some of the factors that are contributed to the interaction process by both the infant and the mother and then to gain an understanding of the complex process of interaction in its own right. Finally, we will consider what the interactive process means in terms of the development of the child, both positively and negatively, as well as the developing relationship.

THEORY

While a variety of different theoretical views about infant development and capabilities influence the way research is carried out and interpreted, on the whole there is a paucity of firm theoretical evidence to guide work in the area of mother-infant interaction. As can be noted in other chapters throughout this volume, theory has played a differential role depending on the perspective of the investigator. It is clear, however—for instance, in Chapter 15, "Father-Infant Interaction," by Ross Parke—that the lack of a clear theoretical base has been a limiting factor in the development of frameworks for studying parent-infant relationships. The approach of most investigators has been to follow the theoretical orientation that seemed most compatible with their ideas and to develop a broader theoretical system either as they went along, or based on findings that emerged from one study and that lead into another study. When we consider the topic of the present chapter, what

519

we see evolving is a changing concern from the traditional socialization model, which viewed development in a unilateral way in terms of the effect of parents on children, to a bidirectional model, concerned with gaining a greater understanding of the interactive process. Along the way, there have been transitional periods during which some investigators have focused primarily on the infant's effect on the parent in order to change the emphasis. However, if a broader theoretical base had been present, the investigations would likely have focused earlier on trying to understand the interaction rather than attempting to separate the components and then come back to the integrative whole.

One of the most popular theoretical positions underlying interaction research at present is an eclectic one, and it can be very appropriate for this kind of research. It allows the researcher to interpret his or her data in a flexible way so that differential explanations can be put forth, depending on the kinds of data that are gathered. While in some ways this approach is less tightly or conservatively based, it can be a fruitful way to lay the foundation for firmer theoretical positions to be developed. However, a note of caution may be warranted. An eclectic approach can allow individuals to avoid taking a stand on the issues due to a lack of firm foundation in the area; this obviously is to be avoided.

The importance of the early experiences of mothers and infants can be interpreted from a number of different perspectives. From a biological viewpoint, it has been demonstrated that even minimal changes in the early environment may have profound effects on a developing organism. Within the first 18 months after birth, the human brain grows more rapidly than it ever will again. During this period, the brain is most plastic, and with proper evaluation, diagnosis, and treatment, certain problems can be prevented. After this period, the same results may not be obtained (Brackbill et al., 1974). Particularly during this time, internal maturational factors are at work and interaction with different kinds and forms of stimuli are extremely important (Yarrow et al., 1972).

From a somewhat different point of view, an interpretation from modern psychoanalytic ego psychology proposes that the biological properties present at birth foreshadow the development and characterological pattern of development (Escalona, 1962, 1968; Escalona and Corman, 1971). While early psychoanalytic writings showed that the development of object relationships was dependent upon the drives (Freud, 1953; Abraham, 1953a,b; Fenichel, 1945), Mahler (1960, 1975) has shown that the growth of object relationships in parallel with the early life history of the ego, can be set in the context of concurrent libidinal development. The cognitive-affective achievement of an awareness of separateness as a precondition of true object relationships and the role of ego functions in fostering such awareness are crucial to Mahler's work.

From a behavioristic viewpoint, Skinner (1971) sees the infant as controlling parental behavior to achieve certain consequences but without adjusting his own behavior. Since the parents act to achieve certain consequences as well, this position makes behavior a means-end, push-pull action on an individual basis rather than interaction within a dyadic unit. Early learning theory approaches emphasized the importance of the association between maternal presence and behavior, and infant gratification. Thus, the presence of the mother was considered to become a powerful secondary or learned reinforcer because of the repeated pairing of her presence with primary reinforcers such as feeding and discomfort-reduction (Sears et al., 1953).

From the Piagetian framework, Wolff (1963) described the infant's need to function at each new phase of development as an active reorganization of past experiences bringing these experiences into closer correspondence with assimilated novelty. Piaget's (1952) experimental accretion model is one that describes the way an infant's interaction with his or her mother and the environment functions in a technological society. A qualitatively adaptive role may simply be an imitative one in other societies (Brazelton, 1972). The infant and the combination of organization mechanisms of his or her caretaking environment are important to consider, rather than the study of the infant in a social vacuum (Sander, 1976; Wolff, 1976).

The ethological-evolutionary view of attachment (Blurton-Jones, 1974; Bowlby, 1951, 1969; Ainsworth, 1969) suggests that the young of most animal species are born with certain instinctive tendencies which promote the development of attachment to the primary adult caretaker and, thus, the development of the interactive relationship. These instinctive tendencies include for the newborn such behaviors as rooting, sucking, grasping, following with the eyes, and crying, all intended to gain the attention of the mother and to stimulate a maternal response. The interactive system is influenced by the infant's initial primitive responses, the maternal reactions, and the further developing interactive systems. In the section of this chapter in which we deal with infant capabilities as well as maternal characteristics, some of the specific behaviors and factors that contribute to the developing interactive relationship from this theoretical point of view will be elaborated further.

In any theory or position underlying studies of mother-infant interaction, a comprehensive view must be taken which acknowledges the child as a developing organism within a multifaceted society. Analyses that best capture the essence of the relationship must consider the child's developmental level, the area of behavior under investigation, and the parental or environmental involvement (Blank, 1964a).

Mother-infant interaction research certainly cannot be atheoretical, and the methodology chosen for any study presupposes a theoretical basis of some sort, whether it is stated or not (Overton and Reese, 1973). Not all views and approaches can be integrated and combined. Carefully specified and logically formulated concepts about early development and dyadic interaction need to be stated when embarking on research in this area. Assessment techniques which capture observable mother and infant behavior pertinent to these concepts, need to be utilized (Greenberg, 1971).

METHODOLOGY

Methodological problems in interaction studies pertain to the subjects studied, methods and measure utilized, timing of the study, and statistical analyses. Characteristically, many studies involve newborn infants and their mothers who provide a captive population for the few days they are in the hospital. There is a methodological advantage to this timing in that study of infants during this period eliminates as much environmental influence and as much learned behavior as possible. All of the data presented concerning the normative patterns of mother-infant interaction during the first few days after birth are from this sample.

One of the areas of importance, but also one of much deliberation, is the meaning of infant responses at different ages (Beckwith, 1971a). Observation of a single response over time can lead the researcher astray, since even the simplest responses undergo denotative changes (Lewis, 1967). For example, the cry of a newborn is a very active way for him or her to affect his or her environment, but a cry at 1 year of age can be a much more passive way of acting, or reacting on the environment.

For the sake of methodological tightness, studies often utilize small units of behavior.

However, the smaller or the more molecular the unit of behavior under consideration, the less assured one can be about its representativeness over time. Also, the contextual cues in the interactive process facilitate the understanding of events. One solution to the problem of determining the meaning of a response is to study responses with multiple measures on a longitudinal basis (Lewis, 1967). It is also important that when preestablished behavioral categories are used in observations that the design remain open for relevant events which are not listed under established categories (Gerwitz and Gerwitz, 1969).

It is important to realize that the results obtained in parent-infant interaction research is dependent to a great extent on the kind of model of analysis that is used. Lewis and Lee-Painter (1974) have reviewed the models that have formed the basis for mother-infant interaction research. The most common model, the element model, is asymmetrical and depicts the environment (or mother) as having a major effect on infant behavior, while the infant's effects are of a lesser magnitude. The second model, the interactionist model, fits a behavioristic framework in that behaviors are seen either as stimuli or responses. This model is symmetrical and can indicate equal maternal and infant contributions to the interaction. In the third model, a flow model, Markovian sequences indicate the conditional probability of events. One problem with the flow model is that it assumes that the last behavior in a pair of behaviors is responsible for the next behavior's occurrence. In addition, point of entry is not indicated from the model. Therefore, it is not known whether a behavior is an initiator or a response. The fourth model, which is highly recommended for use in interactional research, is a complex interactional model. The information from this type of model yields four kinds of data: (1) frequency distribution, (2) simultaneous behaviors, (3) directional interactional analyses (cause and effect), and (4) sequential analyses. This latter analysis includes chains of behavior from which one can obtain length of the behavior chain, initiators and terminators of behavior, and the nature of the chain in terms of transitional probabilities. In this type of analysis, individual differences as well as group data can be examined in the context of their occurrence.

A note of caution is warranted at this point. Analyses that evaluate behavior second by second are very impressive. However, the researcher must take care not to lose both himself or herself and the meaning of the data in the mire of statistical operations. We feel that the use of multiple measures, some molecular, some molar, would provide an appropriate data balance in order to produce meaningful results. This would appear to meet Lytton's (1971) standards: "The loss in specific richness is counterbalanced by the gain in clarity and analyzability" [p. 668].

Another set of problems concerns the issue of generalizability. Moss (1974) summarized the problem of comparing data from different sample populations with different controlled variables. He pointed out that the influence of maternal variables such as race, social class, previous experience, education, and so on, needs to be clarified in all studies and that such clarification is not always easy. He also used parental behavior toward different sexed infants as an example of one problem in interactional data and pointed out that specific behaviors may be present only under certain circumstances. Wolff (1971) noted that experience may be a more potent factor than others in influencing the way a mother interacts with her infant. Such issues need to be resolved and controlled for in the research in order to have clear, concise studies. At the same time, it is important to have studies that are sufficiently broad to allow generalizability to populations at large and not just the groups studied in the laboratory.

Naturalistic observations have provided an alternative approach for some researchers. However, naturalistic studies quite often serve as "fishing expeditions" in which the method of analysis of the data is not fully determined prior to the experimentation (McDowell, 1973). According to Yarrow et al., (1972), correlational models, which show the relationship of single variables to each other, have a number of drawbacks. They are simple and easy to do, but they ignore the realities of environment-child interaction. They do not permit predictions of high accuracy, and cannot indicate whether individual variables are responsible for infant functioning. However, they do allow one to ask the meaningful question of whether, and to what extent, a given variable makes a contribution to the interaction.

In studies where behavioral relationships are investigated it is often difficult or impossible to assign causal roles to specific behaviors. During the neonatal period, because of the limitations of infant behavior and the significant amount of time spent in a sleep state, it is especially difficult to determine causal relationships. However, performing analyses of maternal and infant behaviors that occur within a short time span facilitates interpretations about direction of effects, as well as providing some information about possible causality.

In a later section of the chapter, the issue of methodology will be reconsidered in a different way in terms of ways of understanding the interaction process of synchrony and mutual adaptation.

INFANT CHARACTERISTICS AND BEHAVIORS

Infant Capabilities

The ability of the young to influence the behavior of their caretakers has been well demonstrated in the animal research (Beach and Jaynes, 1956; Harper, 1971; Noirot, 1965), in work with human infants (Korner, 1965, 1970, 1971, 1973; Korner and Grobstein, 1967; Osofsky and Danzger, 1974; Osofsky, 1976; Moss, 1967; Stern, 1974), and children (Bell, 1968; Cantor and Gelford, 1977; Rheingold, 1969; Osofsky, 1970, 1971; Osofsky and O'Connell, 1972; Osofsky and Oldfield, 1971; Gerwitz and Boyd, 1976; Pedersen, 1975).

In studies involving humans, a number of infant characteristics have been found to affect the mother-infant relationship. These characteristics include temperament (Carey, 1970; Fries and Wolff, 1953; Rutter, 1970; Thomas et al., 1963; Thomas and Chess, 1977), sex (Korner, 1974; Moss, 1967, 1974; Moss and Robson; 1968; Parke and O'Leary, 1975; Wolff, 1966; Freedman, 1974), birth order (Brody, 1966; Parke and O'Leary, 1975; Thoman et al., 1970, 1971, 1972), state (Ashton, 1973; Bennett, 1971; Brazelton, 1961; Brown, 1964; Jones and Moss, 1971; Korner, 1973; 1974; Lewis, 1972; Moss, 1967), and responsiveness to tactile, visual, and auditory stimuli (Brazelton et al., 1974; Lusk and Lewis, 1972; Moss, 1967; Osofsky, 1976; Osofsky and Danzger, 1974; Robson and Moss, 1970; Wolff, 1971; Conners and Osofsky, 1977). Results from the increasing number of studies with neonates compel us to recognize infants as complex organisms with individualized patterns of reactivity and activity preferences from birth that coincide with, impinge upon, and affect maternal interests.

Infant characteristics such as sighs, helplessness, and crying facilitate the initiation of caretaking behaviors by parents (Moss, 1967; Richards, 1971). Responses common in adult social relationships are important for parents to see in their babies in order for parents to feel that they are relating socially to their infants. Robson and Moss (1970) and Bennett (1971) hypothesized that a combination of adult and infant characteristics are better elicitors of maternal attention than either one treated separately. This suggestion emphasizes the fact that actions, characteristics, and styles of behavior exhibited by the infant play an important role in determining the stimulation that he or she receives. The infant's physical characteristics trigger a number of normative responses in the mother. For example, upon the first chance to examine her baby, a mother will gaze into his or her eyes in an "en face" position and talk about the baby's eyes (Klaus and Kennell, 1976). The first physical contact with the infant progresses from fingertip touching of the extremities to palm contact with the trunk. In addition, mothers attempt to find some physical traits that resemble those of someone in the family, which is one way of integrating the baby into the family. When speaking to their infants, parents speak in a high-pitched voice. A high-pitched sound is the sound to which the infant is most responsive. Parents also tend to respond to any given infant behavior in the same modality. For example, they are likely to give a vocal response to a vocal behavior (Gerwitz and Gerwitz, 1969).

Physical characteristics of infants may also affect the mother in a negative way. The infant's posture and muscle tone affect the mother's movements and her way of handling him or her. They also affect how she feels—rejected, loved, and so on (Wolff, 1971). Noncuddlers may be so extreme in their physical preferences that mothers may feed them on a pillow; as a result, the babies do not have physical contact with their mothers (Lourie, 1971). Initial cuddlers have also been observed to become noncuddlers by the end of their 1st year (Ainsworth et al., 1972). The wide variety of infant responses that are interwoven with maternal responses are important in relation to the mother's feelings, her behavior toward the infant, and the infant's development.

In situations where the infant is beginning life with disadvantages, maternal stimulation can differentially influence the infant's behavior and facilitate development considerably. Goldberg (1972) studied the mother-infant relationship of Zambian mothers and their infants. These infants were inherently fragile at birth. However, the cultural practice of carrying infants on the mothers' backs provided the infants with close physical contact, and the vestibular stimulation that resulted from the mothers' movement in walking advanced the infants' development.

A number of researchers have investigated individual differences in infants that are present at birth and that influence the way the mother relates; these characteristics can affect the way a child will experience and master each developmental stage. Different labels have been assigned to varying observable differences among infants' behaviors. Terms such as reaction tendencies, styles of assimilation, temperament, and organismic characteristics emphasize aspects of the same phenomenon (Bakow et al., 1973).

Individual infant consistency has been a focus of considerable interest. Infants have been observed to vary greatly from one another in their responses to identical efforts to manipulate their state (Bridger and Birns, 1963). Individual rankings of differential responsivity ratings were also found to remain the same, regardless of the modality or nature of the stimulation (Birns, 1965). Responses of visual alertness (Korner, 1970), crying behavior, and arousal in response to visual stimulation (Korner, 1971, 1973) and availability and responsiveness to soothing techniques (Korner, 1973) are a few areas in which infants demonstrate wide and consistent variations.

Fries and Wolff (1953) were among the first to note what was termed an infant's "congenital activity type," relating it to later personality development through longitudinal followup. Individual differences in autonomic reactivity play a role both in mediating experiences and in determining social interaction (Lipton et al., 1961). Differences in levels of stimulation tolerance are examples of constitutional variations that play a role in the modification of experience. According to Wolff (1971), "Congenital differences in muscle tonus, motility, duration of alertness, vigor of sucking, frequency of smiling, and stability of sleep-wake cycles certainly contribute as much to the mother-infant relations as the mother's individuality" [p. 96]. However, the above-mentioned differences are of little relevance unless they are taken within the context of what each trait means for each individual mother.

Escalona (1963) investigated individual differences in sensory responsiveness among infants. These differences, which were apparent shortly after birth, may contain the rudiments of an individual's later characteristics and may differentially affect the development of his later personality. Korner (1969) stressed the significance of primary ego- and drive-endowment, both in relation to later development of the infant and to the effects of these endowments on parental reactions. Korner noted nine infant variables related to individual differences and studied them for their effect on parents' behavior. They include (1) frequency and length of periods of alert inactivity, an index of availability to external stimuli, (2) singular or global versus multiple responses to external stimuli, (3) influence of internal state on behavior (particularly sensory responsiveness), (4) response to multiple and competing external stimuli, (5) distinctiveness of state, (6) zone reliance (choice of discharge channel), (7) mode reliance, (8) dedifferentiation of behavior, and (9) predictability. These infant variables affected maternal behavior, and are thought to be present at birth since Korner's measures were obtained on the 3rd and 4th day of life when behaviors had stabilized following delivery, but when environmental influences were likely to be limited.

Individual differences that are beyond the range of normalcy cause problems for both parents and infants. Psychotic children demonstrate early a relative lack of eye contact, increased gaze-aversion to the human face, and disinterest in or withdrawal from interpersonal relationships (Hutt and Ounsted, 1966). Abused children often have strange, irritable, and difficult cries and behaviors, which are exasperating to their parents (Gil, 1970). Cases in which infants have shown only two states, such as sleeping and crying, have been extremely frustrating for parents (Brazelton, 1961). Parents often have inclinations to blame themselves. Although problems like those listed above are not the fault of the mother, she does have to make an adjustment in her care and behavior when confronted with an abnormal child. If maternal forces can be mobilized, the mother can facilitate the development of the infant (Brazelton et al., 1971).

Infant temperament is a characteristic than can affect the mother-infant relationship beneficially or detrimentally. Thomas, et al. (1963) conducted a longitudinal study to investigate the relationship of the behavioral style of young children to their later behavior. Categories of reactivity related to temperament were found, and these provided information concerning the way behavioral style of infants can pattern and shape (influence) parental behavior. These categories included: Activity level, rhythmicity, approach-withdrawal, adaptability, intensity of reaction, threshold of responsiveness, quality of mood, distractibility, attention span, and persistence. General consistencies of these characteristics were noted over time, and no indication was found that the temperamental characteristics were caused by parents.

Since the responsiveness of the infant to stimuli provided by the mother may affect her feelings of attachment and competency, and the frequency of her attempts to elicit responsiveness, these measures are important when considering the infant's role in the interaction process. The Brazelton Neonatal Assessment Scale (Brazelton, 1973) contains measures of neurological as well as social responses to animate and inanimate stimuli that may be potential elicitors of maternal responses. In addition, early behavioral characteristics such as self-quieting ability, irritability, consolability, and activity are included in the scale. These measures help ". . . identify those early behavioral characteristics . . . , [and] in turn, will advance our understanding of what it is that the infant brings to his environment which makes a difference in how he develops . . ." [Horowitz et al., 1971]. Temperament measures for older children have been developed and used in research and applied settings (Carey, 1970, 1972, 1973; Chess, 1966; Chess et al., 1959; Thomas and Chess, 1977; Garside et al., 1975).

The importance of infant state as a variable in research has been stressed by Ashton (1973), Brazelton (1961, 1972), Korner (1973, 1974), Levy (1958), Lewis (1972), Moss (1967), Yarrow and Goodwin (1965), and Jones and Moss (1971). State reflects the need as well as the availability of the infant for contact with the external environment and, thus, is important in the study of mother-infant interaction. In addition, state influences the infant's awareness of the environment, and, as a result, affects maternal behavior. An alert infant is usually very receptive to interaction with his or her mother. Ministrations to arouse an infant from a sleep state or to calm an infant in a crying state provide different experiences for mothers. Infant modulation of state provides an index of the control an infant can exert over his or her behavior.

Levy (1958) reported differences in maternal greeting responses which varied depending on the state of the infant. During the first week after delivery, mothers greeted quiet or awake infants one-third of the time, while crying infants were greeted one-sixth of the time. Moss (1974a) observed that the amount of time an infant was awake and crying was a potent modifier of maternal treatment since these two states elicit maternal surveillance and contact.

The variability of states related to stimulation affects the relationship between mothers and infants. Some infants are difficult to arouse while others are easy to arouse; some may be easily soothed while the responsiveness of others is minimal or delayed. Infants who respond to any type of stimulation with rapid state changes may be highly responsive to stimulation in general, and may be easily overstimulated. Feelings of competence as a caregiver may presumably be related to these variables.

According to Wolff (1971), there has been insufficient cognizance of the fact that the infant's behavior influences a mother's behavior as much as her past experience does. With very young infants, much of the modification that occurs in interaction is based on maternal behavioral variations in response to the infant's state or feeding behavior. A mother usually learns the appropriate way to deal with her infant's states, but, in rare exceptions, the repertoire of states is inadequate, and maternal ministrations, however appropriate, will be ineffective (Brazelton, 1961, 1971).

Infant Sex

Moore (1967) observed that female infants, ranging from 9 to 14 weeks of age, learned to orient more readily to auditory stimuli than did male infants, while males oriented more readily to visual stimuli. Moore hypothesized that if this difference in orientation persisted over time, females might be more sensitive to auditory stimuli in general, reinforce their own vocalizations, and elicit more responses from others. Moore's speculation for males is that with their increased responsiveness to moving visual stimuli, males might be more attracted to objects in motion, and therefore, to stimuli that demonstrate cause-and-effect relationships. A number of studies have indicated that male infants are more irritable and difficult to soothe than female infants during the neonatal period (Horowitz et al., 1971) as well as when they are older (Moss, 1967). In addition, Horowitz et al. found that during the neonatal period, male infants exhibited more variable auditory responses than did females. Thus, males may be more difficult to care for and less responsive to auditory stimulation.

On the basis of available data, and especially in studies that have attempted to determine possible predictability, the data on behavioral sex differences in infants are somewhat contradictory (Lamb, 1977). After analyzing a number of mother-infant interaction studies in the first months of life, Moss (1974) stated that the early differences related to infant sex were moderate, not sufficient enough to be categorized according to magnitude, and the presence of differences varied from sample to sample. Additional research is needed in this area, but it may be that significant sex differences do not occur consistently during the early period, or that they may be observed only under certain conditions.

Social Class Differences

The issue of social class is a complex one, which will be discussed briefly in this section and again in the section concerned with maternal characteristics. Tulkin and Kagan (1972) reported social class differences in the reactions of 10-month-old female infants to their mothers' and to strangers' voices. Middle-class infants listened to their mothers' voice, vocalized more following her voice, and looked at their mothers following her voice and at the stranger following her voice. Similar differential responses were not observed with the lower-class infants. Tulkin attributed this difference to the fact that middle-class infants may have received more contingent verbal stimulation from their mothers prior to the experiment. Lower-class infants were less attentive during the experiment, and did not distinguish readily between the mother's voice and that of the stranger.

Messer and Lewis (1972) have also reported social class differences related to infant behavior. Middle-class infants were observed to vocalize as much as seven times more frequently than did lower-class infants when the infants were in the presence of their mothers. This behavior, which is contingent on maternal presence, may be related to the observation that middle-class mothers tend to respond to infant vocalizations with vocalizations. This practice may create an expectancy set for the infants, the result of which can be observed when the mother is present.

Auditory Capabilities of the Infant

Communication between mothers and infants begins in the immediate postpartum period, but whether communication is the intended purpose of infant vocalizations may not be discernible. Intent to communicate is often inferred by parents and other persons wishing to "understand" the infant or believe that he or she is attempting to communicate. Purposeful communication on some levels does appear to develop very quickly.

Tonkova-Yampol'skaya (1969) described the first cry as a reflex biological phenomenon evoked by stimulation of the subcortical respiratory center in the medulla. The first cry also provides the mother with a sense of well-being and assurance that her infant is alive and responding as expected. Later, crying acquires a communicative function and remains the sole form of vocal communication signaling discomfort, hunger, and pain (Wolff, 1971). Wolff noted that mothers were able to differentiate three distinct cries produced by their infants and to categorize them according to hunger, pain, or anger. Discriminations were made on the basis of pitch, pattern, and intonation.

Infants listen selectively to auditory stimuli as early as 2 days of age. Condon and Sander (1974a, b) have noted that patterning of movement during speech is a panhuman phenomenon, occurring across cultures, involving interactional synchrony with the speaker's vocal patterns. This synchronous movement was observed between adult speech and infant movement whether the voice was live or on tape, spoken in Chinese or English. Such movement, however, was not obtained in response to tapping or vowel sounds alone. According to Condon and Sander (1974a), ". . . If the infant, from the beginning moves in precise shared rhythms with the organization of the speech structure of his culture, then he participates developmentally through complex sociological entertainment processes in millions of repetitions of linguistic forms long before he later uses them in speaking and communication" [p. 101]. Thus, in terms of interaction in a linguistic manner, there is no such thing as a "prelinguistic" child (Crystal, 1973; Kaplan and Kaplan, 1971).

A number of other studies have noted auditory responsivity in infants of different ages. In a study with 8- to 14-week-old infants, Culp (1973) observed increased visual attending to unchanging visual stimuli with the addition, but not subtraction, of the mother's voice. Therefore, the addition of the mother's voice was an interesting stimulus, but the subtraction of the mother's voice was not. Hammond (1970) found positive-orienting behavior in 25 of 31 2-week-old infants in response to the calling of the infant's name by the mother. Barrett-Goldfarb and Whitehurst (1973) found that infants who were vocalizing suppressed their vocalizations during records of their parents' voices. Their results indicated that the relative amount of suppression produced by vocal stimuli in the child's environment is a measure of the degree to which he or she chooses to listen to the vocalizations. This ability to suppress babbling when presented with an important sound in the environment has adaptive significance and likely influences a mother's behavior.

The development of intonation appears to be a significant factor involved in early interaction. The first articulated speech sounds appear during the 2nd month of life. These sounds appear to have no linguistic significance (Tonkova-Yampol'skaya, 1969). Apparently, adults respond appropriately to intonational nuances rather than to sound content. The manner in which mothers respond to intonation in cooing and babbling noises produced by infants is similar to the way persons speaking different languages understand each other through basic forms of intonation.

Logical relationships exist between primary intonational patterns, their development into intonational forms, and a number of events occurring in the life of an infant (Tonkova-Yampol'skaya, 1969).

Although infant communication apparently need not be "linguistic" in the sense of formal language, early vocal communicative systems are precursors of formal language, and also foster personal interaction with adults. During infancy, listening and the limited production of sounds provide opportunities to become aware of contingent relationships between vocalizations and responses. Listening, or attentiveness to auditory stimuli, provides a means through which infants can participate in vocal communication behaviorally before they can initiate meaningful speech. The frequency and type of vocalizations produced by the infant are affected by the linguistic surroundings; through the linguistic environment, parent-infant interactions attain their importance for linguistic development.

MacNamara (1972) hypothesized that infants can deduce the intended meaning in a spoken message regardless of their ability to produce it themselves. At a later time, the relationship between the meaning of the message and the words spoken is learned. Thus, an infant is capable of abstracting meaning from language before he or she can produce it.

Ainsworth (1967) commented on the importance of vocalizations for imitative behavior and the functional significance of infant vocalizations as demonstrations of attachment behavior. Six-month-old Ugandan infants were observed to vocalize more readily and more frequently when interacting with their mothers than when interacting with others. Ainsworth emphasized that even though physical contact is of great importance to the infant, many significant interactions between the infant and a meaningful caregiver involved distance receptors. Differential vocalization is one means by which infant attachment can be maintained through a middle distance. Production of sounds serves to further communication and interaction with others, and allows the infant practice to facilitate these processes. Babbling, rather than fulfilling a single function, most likely serves a multiplicity of functions (Crystal, 1973).

Visual Capabilities of the Infant

Because data related to visual capabilities of infants is included in several other chapters, only brief mention will be made of a few particularly relevant points. Infants appear to be inherently prepared for visual responsiveness even within a few hours after birth. Unless the infant's mother has been heavily sedated, the newborn usually spends about 4 h in a visually responsive state. In addition, in those first hours after birth, infants have shown visual distinction and preference for human facial configurations as opposed to nonfacial configurations (Goren et al., 1975).

Periods of infant visual attentiveness, or alertness, are extremely important, especially in the first few months of life when the visual field is greatly limited due to the infant's immobility and extended periods of sleep. The amount of infant visual responsiveness is dependent upon the amount of time spent in an alert state (Korner, 1970). Korner observed that infants who were in an alert state more frequently than other infants also alerted for longer periods of time, and were more capable of visual pursuit than the other infants.

MATERNAL CHARACTERISTICS

Attitudes and Perceptions

A number of investigators have explored maternal attitudes and perceptions about their infants. Brazelton et al. (1974) have observed that mothers endowed the smallest behavior of their neonates as a very significant communication. By the time the infants are 2 weeks of age, mothers have developed individual styles and fantasize about the infant's personality. The infant's unique style of temperament combining such elements as alertness, visual behavior, activity level, and facial movement, provides cues for this development in the mother (Bennett, 1971). For example, mothers may interpret bright, wide eyes with searching movement as intelligent or curious behavior. They often interpret visual attitude accompanied by mouthing as an approach and greeting response and as a sign of positive affect, even before the development of the social smile.

Caldwell et al. (1963) found that mothers progressively develop confidence about their care of their infants and their infants' well-being. They noted that mothers had more confidence in their skills and were more exhibitionistic with their 6-month-old babies than they had been previously. After 1 year of age, the mothers were more emotionally dependent on the infants, less intellectualizing, and more personal about their feedback for the mother-infant situation.

Broussard and Hartner (1970, 1971) found that maternal perceptions measured in the immediate postpartum period were not correlated with later infant outcome. These initial maternal perceptions appeared to be "fluid" and related more to the mothers' fantasies about their babies than to actual infant characteristics. However, when the infants were 1 month old, mothers' perceptions of whether their infants were average or high-risk were related to subsequent determinations at 4½ years of age. Two explanations for the findings appear possible. The infant's personal characteristics may be perceived accurately early in the relationship, and this is a true picture of what the infant outcome will be. Or the expectations that the mother holds for the child's behavioral outcome may become a self-fulfilling prophecy.

Effects of Maternal Attitudes and Behaviors

The mother's early interaction with her infant may facilitate or interfere with his or her adaptive development (Ritvo and Solnit, 1958). Some aspects of the maternal-infant relationship during the first days or months after birth may be indicative of subsequent parent-child relationships, and thus influence the personality of the child (Broussard and Hartner, 1970, 1971; Thoman et al., 1970). Animal studies of the effect of separation shortly after birth indicate that this is a sensitive period for bonding of mother to the young (Herscher et al., 1963; Klopfer et al., 1964; Moore, 1968; Rosenblatt, 1969). Reduction of sensory contact has been found to impair maternal behavior in animals (Harlow et al., 1963). For humans the first 24 h after birth have been labelled by some researchers as a sensitive period for the normal maternal reaction to the newborn (Salk, 1970; 1973). Studies with human mothers and infants have shown qualitative and quantitative differences in later maternal behavior dependent on the amount of contact during the postpartum period (Kennell et al., 1973, 1974; Klaus et al., 1970; 1972; Klaus and Kennell, 1976; Leifer, et al., 1972).

Stress upon the early neonatal period for mothers and the development of maternal-infant interaction is not new. McBryde (1951) advocated compulsory rooming-in for mothers and their newborns, and noted that not only were the infants' needs more easily met, but mothers also benefited psychologically from the procedure. Wolff (1971) observed that technological societies like our own tend to leave little opportunity for a mother to establish a relationship with her infant immediately after birth. Wolff suggested that efforts should be made to maximize contact between mothers and infants during their hospital stay. Significant advances have been made in maternity care since Wolff's observation.

Advances in maternal-infant care during the postpartum period have been made largely due to public demand. Insistent mothers have persuaded policy makers to allow them to be with their babies as soon after birth as possible, and for a longer period or all the time that they are in the hospital. There has been a growing trend toward shorter hospital stays for mothers and infants. A small portion of the childbearing population are choosing home deliveries as another option. However, as maternity care is becoming more family oriented, a growing number of mothers are able to have additional contact with their families and spend longer times with their infants within a hospital setting.

There are a number of indicators of maternal problems that may adversely affect infant development (Fischhoff et al., 1971; Haka-Inse, 1975). For example, disturbances in a mother's early attitude toward her infant may lead to a chronic disturbance in the mother-child relationship (Bibring, 1961). Maternal insensitivity, or a mother who cannot or will not respond to her infant's cues, can severely impede the relationship with her infant (Korner, 1974).

Benedek (1949) noted that a child incorporates the emotional state of its mother, embodies her anxiety, and has the developmental problems its mother has or used to have. By 3 months, an infant usually settles and sleeps through the night. Patterns of feeding and minor illnesses do not seem related to the timing of settling. High levels of maternal anxiety, which are reflected in inconsistent handling or insufficient nonfeeding play, can delay settling (Anders and Weinstein, 1972). After 6 months of age, parental concern and anger toward their infants who were awakening at midnight or early morning frequently worsened the existing problem.

It is possible that maternal attitudes are irrevelant to a child's developmental status. Blank (1964b) found no relationship between the manifest maternal attitudes and the way of handling the child's sensorimotor development. However, Thoman (1975) noted accurate perceptions and responses to infant's needs as facilitating infant development. Self-confidence is extremely important in a mother's care of a child (Benedek, 1949). Mothers who are tense while feeding their infants transmit this tension to their infants (Kulka, 1968).

Klaus and Kennell (1976) and Klaus, et al., (1972) have observed a number of behaviors that should be of concern in a new mother's interaction with her baby. Kempe (1976) has observed similar behaviors that indicate a lack of maternal interest or problems in dealing with the infant. The indicative maternal behaviors include not looking at the infant, expressing disappointment in the infant's sex, physical characteristics, or temperament for an extended period of time, continuing to call the baby "it" even after a name has been chosen for the baby, gaze-aversion, and other extreme inattentive behaviors. It has been emphasized that the likelihood of problems increases when a mother deviates significantly from the normative maternal behaviors in the labor or delivery room or in the initial postpartum period.

Social Class Differences

Research on differences in maternal behavior related to social class variables has indicated some general background differences (Brown et al., 1975). Lower-class mothers had less education, experience, and pre- and postnatal care than did middle-class mothers (Moss, 1974; Moss et al., 1969). Some maternal behavior appears related to the background differences and some to culturally embedded beliefs (Brazelton, 1972; Zunich, 1971). For example, lower-class mothers were found to believe they had little control over their child's development (Tulkin and Kagan, 1972; Tulkin, 1970). Lower-class mothers were more physically stimulating with their infants (Moss et al., 1969). Middle-class mothers provided more opportunities for distinct auditory stimulation and more verbal and imitative responses and responded more quickly to their infants' behavior than did lower-class mothers (Tulkin, 1970). In addition, middle-class mothers had attitudes that encouraged reciprocity and face-to-face vocal imitation, and they provided more objects for their infants to use in play than did lower-class mothers (Tulkin and Cohler, 1973).

Quantitatively equal but qualitatively different maternal responses to infant cues also differentiated lower- and middle-class mothers (Lewis and Wilson, 1972; Tulkin and Kagan, 1972). Although no differences were observed in the frequency of maternal vocalization, vocalizations to their infants took place in consistently different contexts. Middle-class mothers responded to infant vocalizations with a vocalization, and responded to crying with touching behavior. Lower-class mothers responded to infant vocalizations with touching, and to crying with vocalizations. Since vocalizations occur when the infant is in an alert, receptive state, and a vocalization response is a more distant cue than touching, the middle-class mothers appeared to respond in a manner that would enhance the development of representational thought (Sigel, 1968).

Other types of social class and cultural differences have also been reported. Gerwitz and Gerwitz (1969) noted differences in maternal behavior related to family constellation. Mothers in nuclear families talked a great deal to their infants, while mothers living in a kibbutz smiled more frequently at their infants. Both of these family constellations provided more physical variation in the environment than could be found in an institutional setting. A somewhat related finding demonstrated that the higher a mother's educational level, the higher the scores on a developmental test her infant received (Ivanans, 1975). The areas most affected in this relationship were adaptive language and social development.

MOTHER-INFANT INTERACTION: A BIDIRECTIONAL APPROACH

Reciprocal Effects

Bell (1968) has stated that according to the model of socialization traditionally used in parent-infant research, the action of the parent on the child is clearly structured, and the influence of the child as a biological organism has been neglected. "... The parent-child system is a reciprocal relation involving two or more individuals who differ greatly in maturity although not in competence, in terms of ability to affect each other" [Bell, 1974, p. 15]. For parents, the young have a compelling way of behaving, and they selectively reinforce parental behavior (Bell, 1971). The saliency of infant behavior for parents can maintain the social interaction system between the parent and the infant (Cairns, 1967). Developmental changes that the infant experiences in one period of development alter his or her behavior; the infant, therefore, has a different effect on parents in various periods of development. While evidence has been supplied concerning the importance of the early interactive relationship for infant development and the establishment of the mother-infant bond, and while maternal and infant characteristics have been considered, it is extremely important at this point to consider the mutual influence of both on the interactive process.

The quantity and timing of mother's responses to her infant's behavior and the degree of consistency of her responses play important roles in developing and reinforcing the infant's belief that his or her behavior can affect the environment (Lewis, 1972). The expectation of the infant that he or she can reep benefits with his or her behavior appears to be learned early in life. Failure to gain this expectation may reduce interest in exploration and in practicing new skills.

Richards (1971) studied the relationship between the temporal phasing of mothers' and infants' behavior in the feeding situation. Particularly during the first 8 weeks of life it was necessary for mothers to adapt their own temporal characteristics to the endogenous timing and serial ordering of infant behavior. Of interest is the fact that the infant pacemaking mechanisms of behavior systems are linked together so that a wide range of infant behavior induced maternal ministrations. Almost any change in infant activity (state, general or facial movement, hiccupping, etc.) served as an elicitor of maternal attention. The wide range of Richard's attention elicitors is in striking contrast to those noted by Bowlby (1969). According to Bowlby, inducers of maternal proximity are crying, sucking, following, clinging, and smiling during the newborn period; and for approximately the first 3 weeks of life, clinging, following, and smiling occur relatively infrequently. Richard's findings indicate that more interaction may be taking place during this period than Bowlby's findings would suggest.

Vocalization

Certain maternal variables have been found to be related to infant vocalization. Yarrow et al. (1972) observed that the amount that an infant vocalized while exploring an object was related to the mother's responsiveness to his or her vocalizations. Bell and Ainsworth (1972) brought to light an interesting relationship between maternal responsiveness and infant crying, which they related to later verbal behavior. Infants whose mothers most consistently picked them up when they cried in any one quarter of the 1st year tended to cry less in the next quarter. A low frequency of crying at the end of the 1st year was associated with a high frequency of other communicative behavior. They postulated that maternal responsiveness to infant signals fosters the development of communication by facilitating the growth of confidence in the child and by positively encouraging the later development of means-ends relationships and activities.

Maternal behaviors that foster attention were studied by Beckwith (1971b) in a longitudinal investigation of male and female infants and their mothers in the home. Beckwith observed that during the first session, when infants were approximately 8 months of age, the more a mother talked to her infant about the infant's own behavior, the less the infant vocalized. On the other hand, when the mother talked to observers, more infant vocalizations were produced. Across two of the sessions, at approximately 8 and 10 months of age, the frequency with which mothers ignored infant crying or social approach was inversely correlated with the amount of babbling that occurred in the second session.

High assertive maternal control during the first session as measured by the Parent Attitude Research Inventory was related to low infant vocalization, and vice versa. Encouraging docility and overprotectiveness during the second session were inversely related to infant vocalization. The amount of verbal and physical stimulation provided by mothers was not related to the amount of infant crying or babbling in either session. Agents that influenced infant vocalizations appeared to be more specific than the amount of verbal and physical contact. The amount of speech that reflected interest and maternal acceptance of the infant's immediate behavior were inversely related to infant babbling. Beckwith (1971b) suggested that maternal restrictiveness tends to decrease the effectiveness of the infant's instrumental acts, thus fostering less interest in attaining or imitating speech.

Eye Contact

In early mother-infant interaction, the nature of specific patterns of interaction are determined by the interplay of maternal attitudes and a few specific infant behaviors (Robson and Moss, 1970). During this period mutual gazing or eye-to-eye contact is extremely important to the mother for a number of reasons. Eye contact helps mothers feel less strange with their babies (Robson, 1967). It also gives them a sense that the baby is a real person, a social being who can enter into a social relationship with them, and arouses their positive feelings for the baby (Klaus, 1970; Robson and Moss, 1970). When eye-to-eye contact is grossly absent, such as occurs with blind infants, the effect is extremely disruptive of the usual course of development of the mother-infant relationship (Fraiberg, 1974). Eyes appear to be the most compelling of infant cues, and mothers read into them intelligence, curiosity, or other personality traits (Bennett, 1971). In addition, the eyes as distance receptors (Walters and Parke, 1965) allow visual interaction to occur more often than just when the mother is in physical contact with her baby.

In the visual relationship between mother and baby, the infant guides maternal behavior. Mothers tend to look where their babies look (Collis and Schaeffer, 1975). In general, the infant initiates and terminates the mutual gazing. If the infant initiates a gaze, the mother will usually respond and return the gaze immediately. If the mother initiates a gaze, she usually maintains it until the infant looks (Brazelton et al., 1974; Jaffe et al., 1973; Stern, 1974). The infant's intrinsic biological process of gaze-alteration allows him or her to modulate and thus maintain an optimal level of stimulation.

Since the mother is the major mediator of stimulation, her visual attentiveness can affect the visual activity patterns of her infant. Bennett (1971) emphasized the importance of the infant's alertness, which is necessary for interaction with the environment. However, in addition to the infant's capacity to remain in an alert state, infant alertness is dependent on the mother's ability to elicit such a state and the cultural norms that influence the attainment and maintainence of certain states. The amount of maternal facilitation of infant visual behavior is culture bound. For example, Dutch infants are usually left alone in their cribs and have less human contact and opportunity for visual pursuit than American infants (Rebelsky and Abeles, 1969). On the other hand, infants in the Bushman society have almost constant opportunity for eye-to-eye contact (Konner, 1974).

Eye contact has been shown to be a "setting" stimulus or catalyst for response-reinforced learning (Bloom, 1974). Maternal ministrations including proprioceptive stimulation and upright positioning have been found to evoke visual alertness in infants (Korner and Thoman, 1966). Therefore, infants whose mothers are more adept at eliciting visual activity would have more opportunities for social or inanimate visual pursuit. Osofsky (1976) and Osofsky and Danzger (1974) reported that, in the neonatal period, visually attentive mothers tended to have infants who were visually attentive. In addition, Noll (1971) reported findings related to maternal and infant visual attentiveness. Mothers were classified as being in a high-looking group or a low-looking group depending on how often they looked at their infants during an observation situation. Infants whose mothers looked at them more frequently attained a higher visual attentiveness score. In a study with 6-month-old infants and their mothers, Rubenstein (1967) found maternal attentiveness to be related to the amount of infant exploratory behavior.

Although the direction of the interaction pattern is not known, these findings are of interest in light of their implications for the infant's awareness of the environment and subsequent stimulation. All of these studies accentuate the importance of maternal visual attentiveness which may facilitate infant attentiveness to the environment in general. The amount of visual responsiveness is highly dependent on the amount of time an infant spends in an alert state. This state may be attained through the mother's attempts to elicit an alert state, a tendency for an alert state to be predominant, or a combination of both factors.

According to Walters and Parke (1965), ". . . The social significance of the imitative responses of early infancy reside largely in their capacity for fostering adult-child interaction" [p. 80]. This type of action was demonstrated in Piaget's (1951) report of interaction between his wife and daughter. "At 0:6[25], J. invented a new sound by putting her tongue between her teeth. It was something like 'pfs.' Her mother then made the same sound. J. was delighted and laughed as she repeated it in her turn. Then came a long period of mutual imitation. J. said 'pfs,' her mother imitated her, and J. watched her without moving her lips. Then, when her mother stopped, J. began again, and so it went" [p. 19]. J's imitative behavior served to prolong and intensify the visual and auditory stimulation that her mother was providing.

Infant Sex as an Interactive Factor

A number of investigators have observed differences in maternal behavior during the neonatal period related to the sex of the infant. Both primiparous breast-feeding mothers (Thoman et al., 1971) and primiparous bottle feeding mothers (Thoman et al., 1972) were found to stimulate, talk, and smile more to females than to male infants. However, this difference did not occur with multiparous mothers. Thoman (1976) observed that mothers of females could more easily calm their infants than could mothers of males after the infants had been crying for a period of time.

A number of investigators have found differences in parental vocal behaviors directed toward infants, which may be related to sex of the infant. Bell (1968) hypothesized that parent-infant interaction favors females, especially in the auditory domain. Other studies have supported this hypothesis. Female infants have been observed to receive more vocal stimulation from their fathers in the home during the first few weeks of life (Rebelsky and Hanks, 1971), and from their mothers, in the case of the first-born females, during the first few days of life (Thoman et al., 1971, 1972). Greater amounts of vocalization directed toward females has also been found in a home setting at 3 months of age (Lewis, 1972) and in a laboratory setting at 6 months of age (Goldberg and Lewis, 1969).

Lewis (1972) observed that sex of the infants affected maternal responsivity regardless of the behavior of the infant. Of infant behaviors, vocalizations were most often associated with general maternal responsiveness. However, when female infants vocalized, mothers also specifically tended to vocalize. Lewis concluded that ". . . girl infants' vocalizations are more frequently found to be associated with maternal vocalizations than are boys'. The potential consequences of this difference for subsequent language and cognitive development is considerable" [p. 110].

Moss (1967) and Lewis (1967; Ban and Lewis, 1974) offered additional explanations for the mother-infant interaction differences that were related to infant sex. They observed that at both 3 weeks and 3 months of age, male infants slept less, cried more, and were more involved in extensive and stimulating interaction with their mothers than were female infants. Females were more responsive and received more frequent imitation of their vocal interaction with their mothers. By the time the infants were 3 months old, in general, females were receiving more attention than males. Moss hypothesized that mothers had been positively reinforced by female responsiveness and negatively reinforced by the irritability of the male infants. He concluded that in this case the infants' behavior affected the quality as well as the quantity of maternal behavior, and this, in turn, altered their linguistic environment and the amount of interaction.

Infant Age as an Interactive Factor

One of the changes in maternal behavior that appears to be a function of infant age is the shift from proximal to distal behavior (Lewis and Ban, 1971). As the infant develops, he or she becomes more active, and more responsive to distal stimulation and social situations. In successive observations, Beckwith (1971b) observed that mothers initially touched and held their crying infants as a soothing maneuver, but that as development proceeded, mothers utilized more distal and less proximal stimulation with their infants. Lusk and Lewis (1972) also noted this proximal-distal shift in both maternal and infant behaviors as the infants matured. Their findings indicated that the pattern of caretaker-infant interaction was more strongly related to the age of the infant than to any other variable.

A number of factors are influential in the age-related shift from proximal to distal behaviors. The most obvious factor, of course, is the increased maturity of all aspects of the infant's physique. Heightened agility and mobility in conjunction with increased awareness of an interest in the social and nonsocial aspects of his or her environment make the infant a creature of curiosity and adventures. Striking out on his or her own, however, does not make the infant any less dependent upon or needy of his or her mother's attention and direction.

In 1967, Moss explained the qualitative change in maternal behavior related to the infant's age in this light:

Maternal behavior initially tends to be under the control of the stimulus and reinforcing conditions provided by the young infant. As the infant gets older, the mother if she has behaved contingently toward his signals, gradually acquires reinforcement value which in turn increases her efficacy in regulating infant behavior. Concurrently, the earlier control asserted by the infant becomes less functional, and diminishes . . . Thus, at first, the mother is shaped by the infant and this later facilitates her shaping the behavior of the infant. [pp. 29–30]

The infant's cognitive growth, in which increasing distance between the self and objects are realized, also contributes to the proximal to distal shift. The infant's expectancy of control may be developed and reinforced if contingent responses to infant behaviors are consistent (Ainsworth et al., 1971). The proximal to distal shift provides one lucid example of an infant age-related change that can be conceptualized as an interactive factor in the developing relationship.

SYNCHRONY IN THE MOTHER-INFANT RELATIONSHIP

Regardless of the characteristics that each mother and infant bring to the relationship, an appropriate "match" of maternal and infant characteristics is necessary to foster an adaptive relationship (Ritvo and Solnit, 1958; Brazelton, 1961; 1971; Hunt, 1961). This relationship takes time to evolve, and is much more difficult to develop if not fostered early in life. Thus, the development of "synchrony" in the early relationship is of great importance, for both mother and infant contribute to the synchronous or dysynchronous interactions that occur.

A number of terms have been used in the literature to denote the ingredients for positive interactions between mothers and their infants. Descriptive global terms for this phenomenon include synchrony, reciprocal interaction, mutual modification of behavior, mother-infant equilibrium, and being "in tune with each other." All these terms imply a positive interactive process on a more molecular level. Cyclic behavior, rhythmic behavior, and temporal phasing of behavior all describe the basis for infant behavior. This changing behavior, which escalates and diminishes, leads to necessary modification in maternal behavior. For example, a young infant can be in an alert state and be responsive to visual stimulation from his mother for only brief periods. Upon reaching threshold, he or she will then become quieter and unavailable for visual interaction for a period of time. Thresholds such as these vary from infant to infant and with the circumstances; a mother needs to be sensitive to her infant's thresholds in order to be in synchrony with his or her needs. In addition, a mother should respond to infant cues with responses that facilitate behavioral organization. Infants may be in a more organized or receptive state as a function of maternal intervention (Korner and Thoman, 1972).

The interdependency of maternal and infant cyclic or rhythmic behaviors are at the root of many positive interactions. Mutual modification of behavior is characteristic of this process, which is psychobiological in nature, since both infants and mothers enter the relationships with characteristics that are developed prior to the infant's birth (Thoman, 1976). Thoman and her colleagues have postulated prerequisites for both mothers' and infants' behaviors before they can be labelled as synchronous. The infant must be capable of signaling his or her status and needs, and responding to maternal interventions. The mother must have the ability to perceive the cues given by the infant and to respond appropriately.

Sander (1964, 1965, 1970) has pointed out that timing, intensity, and modality of mothers' and infants' behavior must become organized together in order to achieve and maintain the coordination and relative stability of interaction patterns. During the first day of life, some infant behaviors are vulnerable to what might seem to be minor variations in the environment. Thus, vulnerability can in turn affect interaction with the mother. Sander has observed that the first 10 days of life was the optimal period in which to establish initial regulatory coordinations of the cyclic functioning of neonates with their caretaking environments. For example, neonates who were rooming with their mothers achieved a "synchronous" sleep-wake cycle with their mothers. In comparison with infants who stayed in the nursery, these infants were active during the day and spent most of their evening hours asleep. The nursery infants were more "asynchronous" and unpredictable in their schedule. Kaye and Brazelton (1973) noted the importance of maternal sensitivity to the infant's needs and the effects of dysynchronous interaction during feeding. Maternal effectiveness in that situation was found to be related to behaviors during the infant's suck-pause sequence. For example, auditory stimulation too early in the pause period was most likely to prolong the pause and to delay feeding. The appropriateness of a mother's response to her infant's cessation in sucking either facilitated or impeded the feeding organization.

Timing of vocalization has been found to affect the rhythm of mother-infant interaction. Richards (1971) reported that mothers of infants older than 2 months of age spent a great deal of time attempting to elicit vocalization and smiling during interaction when their infants were alert. He reported a phase relationship which consisted of three parts: (1) an infant-attention phase in which the mother is restrained, (2) a phase in which the infant becomes excited at the same time that the pitch of the mother's voice rises in conjunction with her production of rapid vocalizations, and (3) a final phase when the infant is about to smile or vocalize and the mother reduces her movements, thus allowing the infant time to "reply." Mothers who subjected their infants to a constant barrage of stimulation, without pauses during which the infant could "reply," overwhelmed their infants. On the other hand, mothers who were able to establish synchrony in this time relationship with their infants were able to engage in this form of activity for long periods of time.

In identifying triads of behavior that occur most frequently in mother-infant interactions, Thoman (1976) noted sequences of "dovetailing" behaviors in which infant behavior served as a cue for maternal behavior, which in turn affected infant behavior. Both the Richards (1971) and Thoman (1976) studies demonstrate the importance of delay and consistency of feedback provided by both mother and infant. They have implications for the content of the developing communication within the mother-infant relationship.

Menaker (1973), among other investigators, feels that "the internalization of the communicative interaction between mother and child is the primary basis for all personality development, for all social action and interaction, and ultimately for all we know as culture."

The importance of the mother's sensitivity to infant needs and the proper timing of her stimulation or intervention applies across all modalities. Greenberg (1971) described the comprehensive impact of synchronous interactions on a variety of infant behaviors, when the infant behavior was the cue for the mother's attentions. The mothers utilized the infant's sensorimotor mechanisms to regulate behavior states. The behaviors involved include nutritive and nonnutritive sucking, holding, movement, and auditory and visual stimulation, including the smiling mechanism. After being given a certain amount of stimulation, an infant turned his or her head away for a while before further interaction could take place. Mothers soon developed a sensitivity to the infant's capacity for a need for partial or complete interaction. Infants appeared to be exhibiting rules about managing their needs which could be utilized by their mothers to regulate behavior states if they were perceptive. The rules for interaction, however, were constantly changing, the quality of a specific behavior change always had a meaning, substitution of behaviors was possible, and maternal sensitivity in this area was of crucial importance. Mothers could learn only from their infants which behaviors could be substituted for others. It would appear that the mother-infant equilibrium can be thought of as two systems which interact through specific mechanisms of stimulation and pacification, and with corresponding shifts of arousal level.

In a longitudinal study of primiparous mothers and their infants during the first 3 years after birth, Sander (1976) observed the early relationship to be one that revolves around a series of issues to be negotiated during the interaction. During the initial period of adaptation, which covers the first 2½ months, most of the activity is based upon the mother's adjusting her behavior to the cues that the infant gives her regarding state. During the period of reciprocal exchange, which occurred from 2½ to 5 months, pleasurable interactions including reciprocal sequences of interchange between mother and child predominate. Concurrent with this highly satisfying form of interaction, maternal anxiety is also lower than in the early postpartum months. From approximately 5 to 9 months, directed activities were observed revolving around the infant's effort to be successful in establishing areas of reciprocity in interaction with his or her mother. During the period of focalization, which occurs from 9 to 15 months of age, the infant behaves in a manner that implies that his mother alone can fulfill his or her needs. During the self-assertive period, which takes place between 12 and 18 months, the child and mother negotiate areas in which the child can be self-assertive and the cost at which this would be done.

The studies presented in this section provide some examples of the concept of synchrony or mutual adaptation in the mother-infant relationship. Work in this area is in the stage of infancy itself, but the prospects with this approach of gaining a more complete understanding of this complex relationship are very promising.

CONCLUSION

In the course of this chapter we have attempted to look at early infant development, tracing the interaction process between mothers and infants and trying to understand the contribution of the infant and the mother to the process. Mothers and infants interact through a complex process of mutual adaptation or synchrony rather than a simple unidirectional relationship. We have seen that it is not possible to understand the complexity of the process by simply separating out component parts and then putting them back together. Rather it is necessary to conceptualize how the infant may influence the mother and the mother affect the infant through a reciprocal process which develops and becomes more complex as the relationship becomes stronger and also more complex.

If one accepts this interactionist position, it becomes necessary to develop new theoretical, methodological and overall research strategies. A number of the chapters in this book have dealt with the different ways of thinking that are necessary for a thorough understanding of the interaction process. Some of the special considerations for this area of approach include a careful selection of the individuals to be studied, the variables to be considered, the degree to which the approach is molecular or molar, and the constitution of the samples. These considerations will determine the degree to which one will be able to understand the processes as well as generalize to broader populations. From a theoretical point of view, it is extremely important to base observations and strategies within the framework that provides the initial basis for the investigation and the opportunity for interpretations of the observations and overall data.

One may speculate about directions where this position is likely to lead. For years, parent-child relationships have been characterized in terms of parents' effects on children with the assumption that the effects were unidirectional. The change in orientation has added complexity as well as attributing a great deal more competency to the developing infant. With this position, we need to be as concerned about the specific characteristics of the infant as we are about those of the parent. We have to focus on the effects of these characteristics on the parent in the interaction process as well as those of the parent on the infant. If the expectations of the parents are met by the infant and if the parents are able to modulate their behaviors to meet the infant's needs in an appropriate fashion, it is likely that development will proceed relatively smoothly. If, however, these conditions do not occur, difficulties or abnormalities may develop in the developmental process. As researchers and observers of infant and parent behaviors, we need to recognize and define the factors that contribute to a harmonious relationship and optimal development, those that may lead to a poor relationship, and those that may not optimize development but will not be deleterious. We also need to be able to determine characteristics of parents that may be useful when infant characteristics match poorly with theirs or deviate from normal—and characteristics of infants that are protective when parental influences are suboptimal or even adverse. The task is an enormous one.

It will be extremely difficult to determine the patterns of relationships and the contingencies that may influence the interaction process and steps of development. Assets of parents and infants, as well as their deficiencies, and the influence of these characteristics will need better definition. The changing process and the steps in its evolution will require careful investigation. However, although the task will be hard to accomplish, it will be gratifying and extremely important both in providing more knowledge and in meeting the needs of parents and children.

BIBLIOGRAPHY

Abraham, K. (1921) Contributions to the theory of anal character. In *Selected Papers of Karl Abraham,* translated by D. Bryan and A. Strachey. New York: Basic Books, 1953a, 370–392.

Abraham, K. (1924): The influence of oral eroticism on character formation. In *Selected Paper of Karl Abraham,* translated by D. Bryan and A. Strachey. New York: Basic Books, 1953b, 393–406.

Ainsworth, M: D. S. *Infancy in Uganda.* Baltimore: Johns Hopkins, 1967.

Ainsworth, M. D. S. Object relations dependency and attachment: A theoretical review of the infant-mother relationship. *Child Development,* 1969, **40**, 969–1025.

Ainsworth, M. D. S. Patterns of attachment behavior shown by the infant in interaction with his mother. *Merrill Palmer Quarterly,* 1964, **10**, 51–58.

Ainsworth, M. D. S., and Bell, S. M. V. Some contemporary patterns of mother-infant interaction in the feeding situation. In J. A. Ambrose (ed.), *Stimulation in Early Infancy.* London: Academic, 1969, 133–170.

Ainsworth, M. D., Bell, S. M., Blehar, M. P., and Main, M. B. Physical contact: A study of infant responsiveness and its relation to handling. Paper presented at the Biennial Meeting of the Society for Research in Child Development, Minneapolis, 1971.

Ainsworth, M. D. S., Bell, S. M., and Stayton, D. J. Individual differences in strange-situation behavior of one-year-olds. In H. R. Schaffer (ed.), *The Origins of Human Social Relations.* London: Academic, 1972, 17–52.

Anders, J. F., and Weinstein, P. Sleep and its disorder in infants and children: A review. *Pediatrics,* 1972, **50**, 312–324.

Ashton, R. The state variable in neonatal research: A review. *Merrill Palmer Quarterly,* 1973, **19**, 3–20.

Bakow, H., Sameroff, A., Kelley, P., and Zax, M. Relation between newborn behavior and mother-child interaction at four months. Paper presented at Biennial Meeting of Research in Child Development, Phildelphia, 1973.

Ban, P. L., and Lewis, M. Mothers and fathers, girls and boys: Attachment behavior in the one-year-old. *Merrill Palmer Quarterly,* 1974, **20**, 195–204.

Barrett-Goldfarb, M., and Whitehurst, C. Infant vocalizations as a function of parental voice selection. *Developmental Psychology,* 1973, **8**, 273–276.

Beach, F. A., and Jaynes, J. Studies of maternal retrieving in rats. I. Recognition of young. *Journal of Mammalogy,* 1956, **37**, 177–180.

Beckwith, L. Relationships between attribute of mothers and their infants' I.Q. scores. *Child Development,* 1971a, **42**, 1083–1097.

Beckwith, L. Relationships between infants' vocalizations and their mothers' behavior. *Merrill Palmer Quarterly,* 1971b, **17**, 211–226.

Bell, R. Q. A reinterpretation of the direction of effects in studies of socialization. *Psychological Review,* 1968, **75**, 81–95.

Bell, R. Q. Contributions of human infants to caregiving and social interaction. In M. Lewis and L. A. Rosenblum (eds.), *The Effect of the Infant on Its Caregivers.* New York: Wiley, 1974, 1–19.

Bell, R. Q. Stimulus control of parent or caretaker behavior by offspring. *Developmental Psychology,* 1971, **4**, 63–72.

Bell, S. M., and Ainsworth, M. D. S. Infant crying and maternal responsiveness. *Child Development,* 1972, **43**, 1171–1190.

Benedek, T. The psychosomatic implications of the primary unit: Mother-child. *American Journal of Orthopsychiatry,* 1949, **19**, 642–654.

Bennett, S. Infant-caretaker interactions. *Journal of American Academy of Child Psychiatry,* 1971, **10**, 321–335.

Bibring, G. S. A study of the psychological processes in pregnancy and of the earliest mother-child relationship. *Psychoanalytic Study of the Child,* 1961, **16**, 9–72.

Birns, B. Individual differences in human neonates' response to stimulation. *Child Development,* 1965, **36**, 249–256.

Blank, M. The mother's role in infant development: A review. *Journal of the American Academy of Child Psychiatry,* 1964a, **3**, 89–105.

Blank, M. Some maternal influences on infants' rates of sensorimotor development. *Journal of the American Academy of Child Psychiatry,* 1964b, **3**, 668–687.

Bloom, K. Eye contact as a setting event for infant learning. *Journal of Experimental Child Psychology,* 1974, **17**, 250–263.

Blurton-Jones, N. G. (ed.). *Ethological Studies of Child Behavior,* Cambridge: Cambridge University, 1974

Bowlby, J. Maternal care and mental health. *Bulletin of the World Health Organization,* 1951, **3**, 534–555.

Bowlby, J. *Attachment and Loss,* New York: Basic Books, 1969, **1**.

Brackbill, Y., Kane, J., Manniello, R. L., and Aberamson, D. Obstetric premedication and infant outcome. *American Journal of Obstetrics and Gynecology,* 1974, **118**, 377–384.

Brazelton, T. B. Implications of infant development among the Mayan indians of Mexico. *Human Development,* 1972, **15**, 90–111.

Brazelton, T. B. *Neonatal Behavior Assessment Scale.* Spastics International Medical Publications, London: Heinemann, 1973.

Brazelton, T. B. Psychophysiologic reactions to the neonate. I. The value of observation of the neonate. *The Journal of Pediatrics,* 1961, **58**, 508–512.

Brazelton, T. B., Young, G. G., and Bullowa, M. Inception and resolution of early developmental pathology: A case history. *Journal of the American Academy of Child Psychiatry,* 1971, **10**, 124–135.

Brazelton, T. B., Koslowski, B., and Main, M. The origins of reciprocity: The early mother-infant interaction. In M. Lewis and L. A. Rosenblum (eds.), *The Effect of the Infant on Its Caregiver.* New York: Wiley-Interscience, 1974, 49–76.

Bridger, W., and Birns, B. Neonates' behavior in automatic responses to stress during soothing. *Recent Advances in Biological Psychiatry,* 1963, **5**, 1–6.

Brody, S. *Patterns of Mothering.* New York: International Universities, 1966.

Broussard, E. R., and Hartner, M. S. Further considerations regarding maternal perceptions of the first born. In J. Hellmuth (ed.), *Exceptional Infant,* Vol. II. New York: Brunner/Mazel, 1971.

Broussard, E. R., and Hartner, M. S. Maternal perception of the neonate as related to development. *Child Psychiatry and Human Development,* 1970, **1**, 16–25.

Brown, J. States in newborn infants. *Merrill Palmer Quarterly,* 1964, **10**, 313–327.

Brown, J., Bakeman, R., Snyder, R., Fredrickson, W., Morgan, S., and Hepler, R. Interactions of Black inner-city mothers with their newborn infants. *Child Development,* 1975, **46**, 677–686.

Cairns, R. B. The attachment behavior of mammals. *Psychological Review,* 1967, **73**, 406–426.

Caldwell, B. M. The effects of infant care. In M. L. Hoffman, and L. W. Hoffman (eds.), *Review of Child Development Research,* Vol. I. New York: Russell Sage, 1964, 9–87.

Caldwell, B. M., Hersher, L., Lipton, E. L., Richmond, J. B., Stern, G. A., Eddy, E., Drachman, R., and Rothman, A. Mother-infant interaction in monomatric and polymatric families. *American Journal of Orthopsychiatry,* 1963, **33,** 653–664.

Cantor, N. L., and Gelford, D. M. Effect of responsiveness and sex of children on adults' behavior. *Child Development,* 1977, **48,** 232–238.

Carey, W. B. A simplified method for measuring infant temperament. *Journal of Pediatrics,* 1970, **77,** 188–194.

Carey, W. B. Clinical applications of infant temperament. *Journal of Pediatrics,* 1972, **81,** 823–828.

Carey, W. B. Measurement of infant temperament in pediatric practice. In J. C. Westman (ed.), *Individual Differences in Children.* New York: Wiley-Interscience, 1973, 293–306.

Chess, S. Individuality in children: Its importance to the pediatrician. *Journal of Pediatrics,* 1966, **69,** 676–684.

Chess, S., Thomas, A., and Birch, H. Characteristics of the individual child's behavioral response to the environment. *American Journal of Orthopsychiatry,* 1959, **29,** 791–802.

Collis, G. M., and Schaffer, H. R. Synchronization of visual attention in mother-infant pairs. *Journal of Child Psychology and Psychiatry,* 1975, **16,** 315–320.

Condon, W. S., and Sander, L. W. Neonate movement is synchronized with adult speech: Interactional participation and language acquisition. *Science,* 1974a, **183,** 99–101.

Condon, W. S., and Sander, L. W. Synchrony demonstrated between movements of the neonate and adult speech. *Child Development,* 1974b, **45,** 456–462.

Connors, K., and Osofsky, J. D. Patterning of behaviors during early mother-infant interaction. Paper presented at the Biennial Meeting of the Society for Research in Child Development, New Orleans, 1977.

Crystal, D. Linguistic mythology and the first year of life. *British Journal of Disorders of Communication,* Sixth Jenson Memorial Lecture, 1973, **8,** 29–36.

Culp, R. E. Effect of mothers' voices on infant looking behavior. Paper presented at the American Psychological Association Meeting, Montreal, 1973.

Escalona, S. The study of individual differences and the problem of state. *Journal of the American Academy of Child Psychiatry,* 1962, **1,** 11–37.

Escalona, S. Patterns of infantile experience of the developmental process. *Psychoanalytic Study of the Child,* 1963, **18,** 197–244.

Escalona, S. *Roots of Individuality.* Chicago: Aldine, 1968.

Escalona, S., and Corman, H. H. The impact of mother's presence upon behavior: The first year. *Human Development,* 1971, **14,** 2–15.

Fenichel, O. *Psychoanalytic Theory of Neurosis.* New York: Norton, 1945.

Fischhoff, J., Whitten, C. F., and Petit, M. G. A psychiatric study of mothers and infants with growth failure secondary to maternal deprivation. *Journal of Pediatrics,* 1971, **79,** 209–215.

Fraiberg, S. Blind infants and their mothers: An examination of the sign system. In M. Lewis and L. A. Rosenblum (eds.), *The Effect of the Infant on its Caregiver.* New York: Wiley, 1974. 215–232.

Freedman, D. G. *Human Infancy: An Evolutionary Perspective.* New York: Wiley-Interscience, 1974.

Freud, S. (1905) Three essays on the theory of sexuality. In A. Strachey, (ed.), *Standard Edition,* Vol. 7. London: Hogarth, 1953, 135–243.

Fries, M., and Wolff, P. Some hypotheses on the role of the congenital activity type in personality in development. *Psychoanalytic Study of the Child,* 1953, **8**, 48–62.

Garside, R. F., Birch, H., Scott, D. McI., Chambers, S., Kolvin, I., Tweddle, E. G., and Barber, L. M. Dimensions of temperament in infant school children. *Journal of Child Psychology and Psychiatry,* 1975, **16**, 219–231.

Gerwitz, J. L., and Boyd, E. Mother-infant interaction and its study. In H. W. Reese (ed.), *Advances in Child Development and Behavior,* Vol. II. New York: Academic, 1976, 141–163.

Gerwitz, H. B., and Gerwitz, J. L. Caretaking settings, background events and behavioral differences in four Israeli child-rearing environments: Some preliminary trends. In B. M. Foss (ed.), *Determinants of Infant Behavior,* IV. London: Methuen, 1969, 229–295.

Gil, D. G. *Violence Against Children.* Cambridge, Mass.: Harvard University, 1970.

Goldberg, S. Infant care and growth in urban Zambia. *Human Development,* 1972, **15**, 77–89.

Goldberg, S., and Lewis, M. Play behavior in the year-old infant: Early sex differences. *Child Development,* 1969, **40**, 21–31.

Goren, C. C., Sarty, M., and Wu, P. Y. Visual following and pattern discriminations of face-like stimuli by newborn infants. *Pediatrics,* 1975, **56**, 544–549.

Greenberg, N. H. A comparison infant-mother interactional behavior in infants with atypical behavior and normal infants. In J. Hellmuth (ed.), *Exceptional Infant,* Vol. 2, *Studies in Abnormalities.* New York: Brunner/Mazel, 1971, 390–418.

Haka-Inse, K. Child development as an index of maternal mental illness. *Pediatrics,* 1975, **55**, 310–312.

Hammond, J. Hearing and response in the newborn. *Developmental Medicine and Child Neurology,* 1970, **12**, 3–5.

Harlow, H., Harlow, M., and Hansen, E. The maternal affectional system of rhesus monkeys. In H. Rheingold (ed.), *Maternal Behavior in Mammals.* New York: Wiley, 1963.

Harper, L. V. The young as a source of stimuli controlling caretaker behavior. *Developmental Psychology,* 1971, **4**, 73–88.

Hersher, L., Richmond, J., and Moore, A. Modification of the critical period for the development of maternal behavior in sheep and goats. *Behavior,* 1963, **20**, 311.

Horowitz, F. D., Self, P., Paden, L., Culp, R., Laub, K., Boyd, E., and Mann, M. E. Newborn and four-week retest on a normative population using the Brazelton Newborn Assessment Procedure. Paper presented at the Biennial Meeting of the Society for Research in Child Development, Minneapolis, 1971.

Hunt, J. McV. *Intelligence and Experience.* New York: Ronald, 1961.

Hutt, C., and Ounsted, C. The biological significance of gaze aversion with particular reference to the syndrome of infantile autism. *Behavior Science,* 1966, **11**, 346–356.

Ivanans, T. Effect of maternal education and ethnic background on infant development. *Archives of Disturbed Childhood,* 1975, **50**, 454–457.

Jaffe, J., Stern, D. N., and Percy, J. C. Conversational coupling of gaze behavior in prelinguistic human development. *Journal of Psycholinguistic Research,* 1973, **2**, 321–329.

Jones, S. J., and Moss, H. A. Age, state, and maternal behavior associated with infant vocalization. *Child Development,* 1971, **42**, 1039–1051.

Kagan, J., and Moss, H. A. *Birth to Maturity.* New York: Wiley, 1962.

Kaplan, E. L., and Kaplan, G. A. The prelinguistic child. In J. Eliot (ed.), *Human Development and Cognitive Processes.* New York: Holt, Rinehart, and Winston, 1971.

Kaye, K. and Brazelton, T. B. Personal Communication, 1973.

Kempe, H. Paper presented at the Perinatal Medicine Meeting, Snowmass, Colorado, 1976.

Kennell, J. H., Chesler, D., Wolfe, H., and Klaus, M. H. Nesting in the human mother after mother-infant separation. *Pediatric Research,* 1973, **7**, 269.

Kennell, J. H., Jerauld, R., Wolfe, H., Chesler, D., Kreger, N. C., McAlpine, W., Seffa, M., and Klaus, M. H. Maternal behavior one year after early extended post-partum contact. *Developmental Medicine and Child Neurology,* 1974, **16**, 172–179.

Klaus, M. H., Jerauld, R., Kreger, N. C., McAlpine, W., Steffa, M., and Kennell, J. H. Maternal attachment: Importance of the first post-partum days. *New England Journal of Medicine,* 1972, **286**, 460–463.

Klaus, M. H., Kennell, J. H., Plumb, N., and Zuehlke, S. Human maternal behavior at the first contact with her young. *Pediatrics,* 1970, **46**, 187–192.

Klaus, M. H., and Kennell, J. H. *Maternal-Infant Bonding.* St. Louis: Mosby, 1976.

Klopfer, P., Adams, D., and Klopfer, M. Maternal "imprinting" in goats. *Proceedings of the National Academy of Sciences,* 1964, **52**, 911.

Konner, M. Aspects of the developmental ethology of a foraging people. In N. G. Blurton-Jones (ed.), *Ethological Studies of Child Behavior.* Cambridge: Cambridge University, 1974.

Korner, A. F. Mother-infant interaction: One or two-way street. *Social Work,* 1965, **10**, 47–51.

Korner, A. F. Neonatal startles, smiles, erections, and reflex sucks as related to state, sex, and individuality. *Child Development,* 1969, **40**, 1039–1053.

Korner, A. F. Visual alertness in neonates: Individual differences and their correlations. *Perceptual and Motor Skills,* 1970, **31**, 499–509.

Korner, A. F. Individual differences at birth: Implications for early experiences and later development. *American Journal of Orthopsychiatry,* 1971, **41**, 608–619.

Korner, A. F. State as variable, as obstacle, and as mediator of stimulation in infant research. *Merrill Palmer Quarterly,* 1973, **18**, 77–94.

Korner, A. F. The effect of the infant's state, level of arousal, sex, and ontogenetic stage on the caregiver. In M. Lewis and L. A. Rosenblum (eds.), *The Effect of the Infant on its Caregiver.* New York: Wiley, 1974, 105–121.

Korner, A. F., and Grobstein, R. Individual differences in irritability and soothability as related to parity in neonates. Unpublished manuscript, 1967.

Korner, A., and Thoman, E. Visual alertness as related to soothing in neonates: Implications for maternal stimulation and early deprivation. *Child Development,* 1966, **37**, 867–876.

Korner, A., and Thoman, E. The relative efficacy of contact and vestibular-prioceptive stimulation in soothing neonates. *Child Development,* 1972, **43**, 443–453.

Kulka, A. M. Observations and data on mother-infant interaction. *Israeli Annals of Psychiatry,* 1968, **6**, 70–84.

Lamb, M. E. Father-infant and mother-infant interaction in the first year of life. *Child Development,* 1977, **48**, 167–181.

Lamb, M. E. Twelve-month-olds and their parents interactions in a laboratory playroom. *Developmental Psychology,* 1976, **12**, 237–244.

Leifer, A. D., Leiderman, P. H., Barnett, C. R., and Williams, J. A. Attachment behavior. *Child Development,* 1972, **43**, 1203–1218.

Levy, D. M. *Behavioral Analysis: Analysis of Clinical Observations of Behavior as Applied to Mother-Newborn Relationships.* Springfield, Ill.: Thomas, 1958.

Lewis, M. State as an infant-environment interaction: An analysis of mother-infant behavior as a function of sex. *Merrill Palmer Quarterly,* 1972, **18**, 95–121.

Lewis, M. The meaning of a response or why researchers in infant behavior should be oriental metaphysicians. *Merrill Palmer Quarterly,* 1967, **13**, 7–18.

Lewis, M., and Ban, P. Stability of attachment behavior: A transformational analysis. Paper presented at the Biennial Meeting of the Society for Research in Child Development, Minneapolis, 1971.

Lewis, M., and Goldberg, S. Perceptual-cognitive development in infancy: A generalized expectancy model as a function of mother-infant interaction. *Merrill Palmer Quarterly,* 1969, **15**, 81–100.

Lewis, M., and Lee-Painter, S. An interactional approach to the mother-infant dyad. In M. Lewis and L. A. Rosenblum (eds.), *The Effect of the Infant on Its Caregiver.* New York: Wiley, 1974, 21–48.

Lewis M., and Wilson, C. D. Infant development in lower class American families. *Human Development,* 1972, **15**, 112–127.

Lipton, E. L. Steinschneider, A., and Richmond, J. B. Autonomic function in the neonate: IV. Individual differences in cardiac reactivity. *Psychosomatic Medicine,* 1961, **23**, 472–484.

Lourie, R. The first three years of life: An overview of a new frontier in psychiatry. *American Journal of Psychiatry,* 1971, **11**, 33–39.

Lusk, D., and Lewis, M. Mother-infant interaction among the Wolof Senegal. *Human Development,* 1972, **15**, 58–69.

Lytton, H. Observation studies of parent-child interaction: A methodological review. *Child Development,* 1971, **43**, 651–684.

MacNamara, J. Cognitive basis of language learning in infants. *Psychological Review,* 1972, **79**, 1–13.

McBride, A. Compulsory rooming-in in the ward and private newborn service at Duke University. *Journal of the American Medical Association,* 1951, **145**, 625.

McDowell, E. H. III. Comparison of time-sampling and continuous recording techniques for observing developmental changes in caretakers and infant behaviors. *Journal of Genetic Psychology,* 1973, **23**, 99–105.

Mahler, M. Symposium on psychotic object relationships: III. Perceptual de-differrentiation and psychotic object relationships. *International Journal of Psychoanalysis,* 1960, **41**, 548–553.

Mahler, M., Pine, F., and Bergman, A. *The Psychological Birth of the Human Infant.* New York: Basic Books, 1975.

Menaker, E. The social matrix: Mother and child. *Psychoanalytic Review,* 1973, **60**, 45–58.

Messer, S. B., and Lewis, M. Social class and sex differences in the attachment and play behavior of the year-old infant. *Merrill Palmer Quarterly,* 1972, **18**, 295–306.

Moore, A. U. Effects of modified maternal care in the sheep and goat. In G. Newton and S. Lewis (eds.), *Early Experience and Behavior.* Springfield, Ill.: Thomas, 1968.

Moore, T. Language and intelligence: A longitudinal study of the first eight years. Part I. Patterns of development in boys and girls. *Human Development,* 1967, **10**, 88–106.

Moss, H. A. Sex, age, and state as determinants of mother-infant interaction. *Merrill Palmer Quarterly,* 1967, **13**, 19–36.

Moss, H. A. Early sex differences and mother-infant interaction. In R. C. Friedman, R. M. Richart, and R. L. Vande Wiele (eds.), *Sex Differences in Behavior,* New York: Wiley, 1974, 149–163.

Moss, H. A. and Robson, K. S. Maternal influences in early social visual behavior. *Child Development,* 1968, **39**, 401–408.

Moss, H. A., Robson, K. S., and Pedersen, F. Determinants of maternal stimulation of infants and consequences of treatment for later reactions to strangers. *Developmental Psychology,* 1969, **1**, 239–246.

Noirot, E. Change in responsiveness to young in the adult mouse. III. The effect of immediately preceeding performances. *Behavior,* 1965, **24**, 318–325.

Noll, R. The relationship between visual behavior of mothers and infant attentiveness. *Dissertation Abstracts International,* 1971, **32** (1A), 250.

Osofsky, J. D. The shaping of mother's behavior by children. *Journal of Marriage and the Family,* 1970, **32**, 400–405.

Osofsky, J. D. Children's influences upon parental behavior: An attempt to define the relationship with the use of laboratory tasks. *Genetic Psychology Monographs,* 1971, **83**, 147–169.

Osofsky, J. D. Neonatal characteristics and mother-infant interaction in two observational situations. *Child Development,* 1976, **47**, 1138–1147.

Osofsky, J. D., and Danzger, B. Relationships between neonatal characteristics and mother-infant characteristics. *Developmental Psychology,* 1974, **10**, 124–130.

Osofsky, J. D., and O'Connell, E. J. Parent-child interaction: Daughter's effects upon mothers' and fathers' behaviors. *Developmental Psychology,* 1972, **7**, 157–168.

Osofsky, J. D., and Oldfield, S. Children's effects on parental behavior: Mothers' and fathers' response to dependent and independent child behaviors. *Proceedings of the 79th Annual Convention of the American Psychological Association,* 1971, **8**, 143–144 (summary).

Overton, W. F., and Reese, H. W. Models of development: Methodological implications. In J. R. Nesselroade and H. W. Reese (eds.), *Lifespan Developmental Psychology.* New York: Academic, 1973, 65–86.

Parke, R. D., and O'Leary, S. Father-mother-infant interaction in the newborn period: Some feelings, some observations, and some unresolved issues. K. Riegel and J. Meacham (eds.), *The Developing Individual in a Changing World,* Vol. 2. *Social and Environmental Issues.* The Hague: Mauton, 1975.

Pedersen, F. Relationships between paternal behavior and mother-infant interaction. Paper presented at the Annual Meeting of American Psychological Association, Chicago, 1975.

Piaget, J. *Play, Dreams, and Imitation in Childhood.* London: Routeledge and Kagan Paul, 1951.

Piaget, J. (1936) *The Origins of Intelligence in Children.* New York: International University, 1952.

Rebelsky, F., and Abeles, G. Infancy in Holland and the United States. Paper presented at the Biennial Meeting of the Society for Research in Child Development, Santa Monica, 1969.

Rebelsky, F., and Hanks, C. Fathers' vocal interaction with infants in the first three months of life. *Child Development,* 1971, **42**, 63–68.

Rheingold, H. L. The social and socializing infant. In D. Goslin (ed.), *Handbook of Socialization Theory and Research.* Chicago: Rand McNally, 1969.

Richards, M. P. M. A comment on the social content of mother-infant interaction. In H. R. Schaffer (ed.), *The Origins of Human Social Relations.* New York: Academic, 1971, 187–193.

Ritvo, S., and Solnit, A. Influences of early mother-child interaction on identification processes. *Psychoanalytic Study of the Child,* 1958, **13**, 64–86.

Robson, K. S. The role of eye-to-eye contact in maternal infant attachment. *Journal of Child Psychology and Psychiatry,* 1967, **8**, 13–25.

Robson, K. S., and Moss, H. A. Patterns and determinants of maternal attachment. *Journal of Pediatrics,* 1970, **77**, 976–985.

Rosenblatt, J. S. The development of maternal responsiveness in rats. *American Journal of Orthopsychiatry,* 1969, **39**, 36–56.

Rubenstein, J. Maternal attentiveness and subsequent exploratory behavior in the infant. *Child Development,* 1967, **38**, 1089–1100.

Rutter, M. *Maternal Deprivation Reassessed.* Baltimore; Penguin Education, 1972.

Rutter, M. Psychological development—Predictions from infancy. *Journal of Child Psychology and Psychiatry,* 1970, **11**, 49–62.

Salk, L. The critical nature of the post-partum period in the human for the establishment of the mother-infant bond: A controlled study. *Diseases of the Nervous System,* 1970, **31** (suppl.), 110–116.

Salk, L. The role of the heartbeat in the relations between mother and infant. *Scientific American,* 1973, **288**, 24–29.

Sander, L. W. Adaptive relationships in early mother-child interaction. *Journal of American Academy of Child Psychiatry,* 1964, **3**, 231–264.

Sander, L. W. The longitudinal course of early mother-child interaction. In B. M. Foss (ed.), *Determinants of Infant Behavior,* III. London: Methuen, 1965, 89–227.

Sander, L. W. Regulation and organization in the early infant-caretaker system. In R. Robinson (ed.), *The Brain and Early Behavior.* London: Academic, 1970, 313–331.

Sander, L. W. Issues in early mother-child interaction. In E. N. Rexford, L. W. Sander, and T. Shapiro (eds.), *Infant Psychiatry: A New Synthesis,* New Haven: Yale University, 1976, 127–147.

Shaffer, H. R., and Emerson, P. E. The development of social attachments in early infancy. *Monographs of the Society for Research in Child Development,* 1964, **29** (3), Ser. 94.

Sears, R. R., Whiting, J. W. M., Nowlis, V., and Sears, P. S. Some child rearing antecedents of dependency and aggression in young children. *Genetic Psychology Monographs,* 1953, **47**, 135–234.

Sigel, I. The distance hypothesis: A casual hypothesis for the acquisition of representational thought. Symposium on the Effect of Early Experience, University of Miami, 1968.

Skinner, B. F. *Beyond Freedom and Dignity.* New York: Knopf, 1971.

Stern, D. N. Mother and infant at play: The dyadic interaction involving facial, vocal, and gaze behaviors. In M. Lewis and L. A. Rosenblum (eds.), *The Effect of the Infant on its Caregiver.* New York: Wiley, 1974, 187–213.

Tonkova-Yampol'skaya, R. V. Development of speech intonation in infants during the first two years of life. *Soviet Psychology,* 1969, **1**, 48–54.

Thoman, E. B. The role of the infant in early transfer of information. *Biological Psychiatry,* 1975, **10**, 161–169.

Thoman, E. B. Development of synchrony in mother-infant interaction in feeding and other situations. Proceedings of the 58th Annual Meeting of the Federation of American Societies for Experimental Biology, 1976.

Thoman, E. B., Barnett, C., and Leiderman, P. Feeding behaviors of newborn infants as a function of parity of the mother. *Child Development,* 1971, **42**, 1471–1483.

Thoman, E. B., Leiderman, P. H., and Olson, J. P. Neonate-mother interaction during breast feeding. *Developmental Psychology,* 1972, **6**, 110–118.

Thoman, E. B. Turner, A., Leiderman, P. H., and Barnett, C. Neonate-mother interaction: Effects of parity on feeding behavior. *Child Development,* 1970, **41**, 1103–1111.

Thomas, A., Chess, S., Birch, H., Hertzig, M., and Korn, S. *Behavioral Individuality in Early Childhood.* New York: New York University, 1963.

Thomas, A., and Chess, S. *Temperament and Development.* New York: Brunner/Mazel, 1977.

Tulkin, S. R. Mother-infant interaction the first year of life: An inquiry into the influences of social class. Unpublished Ph.D. dissertation, Harvard University, 1970.

Tulkin, S., and Cohler, B. Childrearing attitudes and mother-child interaction in the first year of life. *Merrill Palmer Quarterly,* 1973, **19**, 95–106.

Tulkin, S. R., and Kagan, J. Mother-child interaction: Social class differences in the first year of life. *Child Development,* 1972, **43**, 31–41.

Walters, R. H., and Parke, R. D. The role of distance receptors in the development of social responsiveness. *Advances in Child Development,* 1965, **2**, 59–96.

Wolff, P. H. Observations on the early development of smiling. In B. M. Foss (ed.), *Determinants of Infant Behavior,* II. New York: Wiley, 1963, 113–134.

Wolff, P. H. The causes, controls, and organization of behavior in the neonate. *Psychological Issues,* Monog. 17. New York: International University, 1966.

Wolff, P. H. Mother-infant interaction in the first year. *New England Journal of Medicine,* 1976, **295**, 999–1001.

Wolff, P. H. Mother-infant relations at birth. In J. G. Howels (ed.), *Modern Perspectives in International Child Psychiatry.* New York: Brunner/Mazel, 1971, 20–97.

Yarrow, L., and Goodwin, M. Some conceptual issues in the study of mother-child interaction. *American Journal of Orthopsychiatry,* 1965, **35**, 473–481.

Yarrow, L. J., Rubenstein, J. L., Pedersen, F. A., and Jankowski, J. J. Dimensions of early stimulation and their differential effects on infant development. *Merrill-Palmer Quarterly,* 1972, **18**, 205–218.

Zunich, M. Lower class mothers' behavior and attitudes toward child rearing. *Psychological Reports,* 1971, **29**, 1051–1058.

CHAPTER 15

Perspectives on Father-Infant Interaction[1]

Ross D. Parke

Until quite recently, there has been little consideration of the role of the father during infancy. This is the sharp contrast to the extensive research and interest in maternal roles and mother-infant interaction. The importance of the father's role in the development of older children has been indicated in a large body of research (Biller, 1971, 1974); however, it has generally been assumed that his influence begins to take on importance only in late infancy and early childhood. As Margaret Mead once noted "fathers are a biological necessity, but a social accident."

The purposes of the chapter are threefold. First, the cultural, historical, comparative, hormonal, and theoretical arguments that have limited father-infant research will be examined. Second, the recent empirical evidence derived from both naturalistic and experimental studies concerning the father's role in infancy will be examined. Third, an alternative view of early interaction, which reconceptualizes early adult-infant interaction in terms of caretaking functions and styles independently of biological sex, will be offered. As our review will indicate, fathers play an active but often distinctive and different role than mothers in the development of their infants.

FACTORS THAT LIMITED FATHER-INFANT RESEARCH

In this section, a variety of arguments that have been traditionally offered to justify our traditional sex role viewpoints will be examined. It will be demonstrated that there is no conclusive evidence supporting traditional views of male and female roles concerning their responsibility and impact on early infant development. This re-analysis of our traditional assumption has led to a revival of interest in empirically examining the role of the father in infancy.

Cultural and Historical Evidence

In Western industrialized society there has been a clear set of roles prescribed for males and females, with child care being assigned almost exclusively to the mother. In fact, as Josselyn (1956) has noted, it is even considered inappropriate in our culture for fathers to be nurturant toward their infants. Nor is the attitude restricted to our own culture: an

[1]Preparation of this chapter and the research reported here was supported by the following grants: NICHD Training Grant, HD-00244, Office of Child Development Grant, OHD 90-C-900, and a grant from the Grant Foundation. Thanks are extended to Douglas Sawin and Thomas Power for their helpful comments on the manuscript and to Brenda Congdon and Mary Schroeder for their preparation of the manuscript.

examination of a wide range of other cultures suggests a similar demarcation of roles, with the mother nearly always being the primary caretaker (Lynn, 1974; Stephens, 1963). In part, this was due to the assumption that the feeding context was critical for the adequate development of social responsiveness.

Father's roles have been examined historically with the same outcome. Over a wide span of history and across a large variety of economies, the father has played a minor role in the care of infants and young children (Lynn, 1974; Biller, 1971).

However, the cultural and historical evidence does not yield a homogeneous view. Rather, there is a great deal of variation in the contribution of males and females to early infant and child care across cultures; the definitions of sex roles vary with the social, ideological, and physical environmental conditions in different cultures (Friedl, 1975; Munroe and Munroe, 1975). The evidence clearly indicates that the father is not consistently assigned a secondary role in all cultures. There are exceptions in which males and females play a more equal role in the care of young children. Among the Trobianders of Melanesia, the father has considerable share in the caretaking, feeding, and transport of young children. Similarly, in a number of other cultures including the Taira of Okinawa, the Nyansongo of Kenya, and the Ilocos of the Philippines, father and mother share more equally in infant and child care. Nor are the exceptions limited to primitive cultures as evidenced by recent trends in both Sweden and the United States toward more active paternal involvement in child care.

Just as the cross-cultural evidence can be questioned, the historical view of the uninvolved father can be challenged as well. In fact, some have argued that the current diminished role of the father is a relatively recent phenomenon, beginning with the "advent of the Industrial Revolution in the mid-nineteenth century." (DeFrain, 1975). More important than the dispute concerning the purity of the historical view of fathers is the misuse of historical arguments. It is often assumed that male and female role relations are inevitably biased by prior historical arrangements. However, this position ignores the fact that secular trends which reflect shifts in technological and economic spheres can and are supporting the possibilities of new roles for males and females. As students of socialization, it is important to consistently monitor shifts in the larger social and economic structure which may, in turn, affect the definition and allocation of sex roles. In our preoccupation with the search for universal laws, too often we have ignored the fact that behavior shifts with social, economic, and possibly medical developments (Porges, 1976; Riegel, 1972). To cite a single example, consider the impact of bottlefeeding; by a single stroke, fathers were able to overcome a biological difference which limited their participation in caretaking of young infants. The shift from breastfeeding to bottlefeeding has been dramatic: in the late 1920s, 80% of firstborn infants were breastfed and by the early 1960s only 25% were still being breastfed (Hirschman and Sweet, 1974), although there is a recent swing among middle-class mothers back to breastfeeding.

Closely related to this issue is a common distinction that needs to be brought to bear on the present context—namely, the competence/performance distinction. Too often the fact of low father involvement throughout history in the caretaking of children has been extended to the conclusion that the low level of involvement was equivalent to a low level of competence. However, the fact that historical, social, and economic arrangements meant that fathers were allocated to other roles *need not necessarily imply that they are incapable of assuming a caretaking function*. Evidence in support of this distinction will be discussed in detail later in this chapter.

Comparative Evidence

In addition to cultural and historical sources, evidence from the organization and behavior of animals has been examined, in part, to determine the extent to which these sex role demarcations are prevalent among nonhuman species. Typically cited are studies of nonhuman primates either in captivity or in the wild. For example, DeVore (1963) found that male cynocephalus baboons take little interest in infants, and play a protective role for the troupe as a whole. Few instances of either play or affectionate physical contact were observed. Laboratory studies often present a similar picture. In a study from Harlow's laboratory (Chamove et al., 1967), 20- to 40-day-old infants were introduced to male-female pairs of preadolescent monkeys. The males and females played clearly different roles: females were four times as likely to express nurturant behavior to an infant compared to males, while the males were ten times as hostile as the females. In short, in animals as well as man, there is evidence indicating that fathers are less interested and involved in the care and nurturance of infants than mothers.

However, the animal literature cannot be completely relied upon to support traditional views of fatherhood. Recent animal evidence has demonstrated that males can assume a parental role vis-à-vis infants (cf. Redican, 1976, for an excellent review). Not only do some nonhuman primate species occasionally engage in nurturant caretaking of infants in the wild (Mitchell, 1969), but recent evidence suggests that male rhesus monkeys, who rarely display parental behavior in the wild, "are certainly capable of doing so when given the opportunity in the laboratory" (Mitchell et al., 1974, p. 8). As Redican (1976) notes,

In general the results . . . indicate a significant potential both for adult males to form attachments with infants and for infants to form attachments to adult males . . . If such an aggressive and inflexible creature as the rhesus monkey male is capable of such positive interactions with infants, there is reason to expect at least comparable potential in less sexually dimorphic, relatively monogamous more flexible creatures such as Homo sapiens. [p. 359]

However, there are wide species differences, and the extent of adult male parental care varies, in part, with the extent of maternal permissiveness. Paternal behavior, in short, can be elicited even in species that typically do not show this type of parental pattern.

Hormonal Evidence

Another body of evidence that has been used to limit the father's role in infancy is the literature on the effects of hormones on "caretaking behavior." According to this work, the hormones associated with pregnancy and parturition are thought to "prime" the female to engage in caretaking activities. For example, Rosenblatt and his colleagues have shown that as the duration of pregnancy increased, responsiveness of the female to young rat pups increases (Rosenblatt and Siegel, 1975); in conjunction with other studies that suggest that hormonal levels (estradiol levels) increase as labor approaches (Shaikh, 1971), this work provides support for the role of hormonal influence on caretaking behavior in rats. Recent evidence suggests that a similar rise in estradiol takes place in the 5 weeks preceding labor in the human mother (Turnball et al., 1974). Whether these hormonal shifts in humans alter responsiveness to infants remains to be determined. Other experimental animal evidence (Lott and Rosenblatt, 1969; Rosenblatt, 1969; Moltz et al., 1970) indicates that virgin females treated with female hormones show maternal behavior more rapidly than nontreated control females.

However, the relationship between hormones and caretaking is more complex. As Maccoby and Jacklin (1974) recently concluded from a review of the parenting behavior of subhuman mammals,

the hormones associated with pregnancy, childbirth, and lactation are not necessary for the appearance of parental behavior. With sufficient exposure to newborns, virgin females and males will show parental behavior—although the behavior is not so readily aroused as it is in a female that has been hormonally primed. [p. 219]

Moreover, Rosenblatt (1969) clearly showed that maternal behavior is under the control of two systems: a short-term hormonal system surrounding parturition that controls maternal behavior in the prepartum and early postpartum period, and a second system that predominates in the postpartum period that relies on the presence of the infant as a necessary elicitor to maintain maternal behavior. Therefore, the tyranny of hormonal control may be short-lived, and environmental factors may be more important in the long run in determining maternal responsiveness.

Finally, a number of writers (Lamb, 1976a; Bernal and Richards, 1973) have questioned the generalizability of the rat model to the human level.

In summary, the hormonal evidence is not sufficiently clear-cut to maintain our traditional views of low father involvement in early infancy.

Theoretical Evidence

Perhaps the factor that has most severely limited our view of the father-infant relationship has been the guiding theoretical frameworks in early social development. Most influential has been psychoanalytic theory, which emphasized the feeding situation as the critical context for the development of social responsiveness and the mother as the primary object of infant attachment. Although the influence of the original theory waned, the translation of psychoanalytic theory into the drive-reduction language of learning theory extended the life of the assumption of the centrality of both the feeding situation and the mother for early social development. According to this revised view, the mother, as a result of being paired with drive-reducing feeding activity, acquires positive secondary-reinforcement properties and consequently is valued by the infant in her own right. Since father was typically less involved in feeding activities, his role in infant development was minimized. Although the assumptions of drive-reduction theory were replaced by an ethological-evolutionary analysis, Bowlby (1969) similarly presented a theory of early social development that, like his predecessors, stressed the primary role of the mother in the development of social responsiveness. In fact, much of the research in infancy over the past decade has focused on the development of the mother-infant interaction system and specifically on the ways in which the infant's attachment to the mother develops and in turn affects other later relationships.

There have been theories aimed at articulating the father's role; however, these theories, such as Parsons (1954), Parsons and Bales (1954), and some of Freud's writings (Freud, 1933a, b) focus on the father's role in the family structure—but only in the oedipal period. Little or no attention was paid to the functions that the father played in infancy. Only in recent years have contemporary psychoanalytic thinkers recognized the importance of the father in early social development (Abelin, 1975; Machtlinger, 1976). In light of this paucity of theory that gave explicit recognition to the role that the father might play in infancy, it is not surprising that active empirical research on this topic has only recently emerged.

The stage was set for a reemergence of father by the general decline of secondary-drive theory (Hunt, 1961; White, 1959). Specifically, Harlow's (1958) classic demonstration that the feeding situation was not the critical context for early social development, combined with the emerging evidence that social and sensory stimulatory activities were important determinants of infant development (Rheingold, 1956; Brackbill, 1958), led to a revival of interest in the role of noncaretaking socializing agents—including fathers. The critical turning point, however, was Schaffer and Emerson's (1964) demonstration that the human infants showed "attachment" to individuals, such as fathers, who never participated in routine caretaking activities. They found that the amount of social stimulation and the responsiveness of the social agent to the infant's behaviors were important determinants of attachment. Fathers, of course, are just as capable of providing these important ingredients for early social development as mothers. Therefore, by the mid 1960s, theoretical shifts finally legitimized the active investigation of the father's role in early infant social and cognitive development.

CURRENT TRENDS IN FATHER-INFANT INTERACTION RESEARCH

A number of general trends in the area of early parent-infant interaction over the past decade are reflected in the current research scene and in our current state of knowledge about father-infant interaction. Traditionally, most approaches to social development have assumed a unidirectional model whereby the parent influences the child's development; the child's contribution to his own socialization was rarely recognized. Schaffer (1977) captures this view nicely in his descriptive phrase "mothering as stimulation." In a second phase, under the influence of Bell's (1968) classic paper, the historical imbalance has been corrected and the infant's contribution to his own socialization is now widely accepted (Lewis and Rosenblum, 1974). In part, this shift came about because of the experimental analyses of infant competencies of the 1960s which demonstrated the wide range of capacities (Kessen et al., 1970) as well as the readiness of the infant for social interaction (Bell, 1974). A third phase is not being increasingly recognized. In our enthusiasm to correct a historical imbalance we focused on the infant's impact on the parent instead of the more appropriate focus on the reciprocal nature of the interaction process. The current zeitgeist, however, has clearly shifted to a study of the reciprocity of interaction, in which the ways in which parents and infants mutually regulate each other are of central interest.

These shifts have been paralleled by corresponding changes in our methodological strategies (Parke, 1978a). To appreciate the subtleties of the interactive process, there is less reliance on noninteractive time-sampling and global-ratings approaches and an increasing use of microanalytic techniques that more adequately capture sequences of behavior and the moment-to-moment shifts in patterns of dyadic interaction with both mothers (Stern, 1974; Brazelton et al., 1974; 1975) and fathers (Yogman et al., 1977a). An understanding of the dynamics of interpersonal synchrony is increasingly the aim of parent-infant interaction research.

Another important characteristic of research in father-infant interaction is a developmental orientation. Increasingly, interest lies in tracking the continuities and discontinuities across time in the nature of the father-infant dyad as well as the family triad of mother, father, and infant. Implicit in this developmental orientation is a recognition that all members of the interactive network—father and mother as well as the infant—are changing over time. As recent theorists (Ahammer, 1973; Hartup and Lempers, 1973;

Schaffer, 1977) have reminded us, the study of early parent-infant interaction involves a dual set of developments—namely the processes that govern changes in adult development as well as shifts in the developing infant. Due to the fact that our theoretical models of parent-infant interaction emerged out of infancy research and due to the more rapid and dramatic developmental changes on the infant side, we have given insufficient attention to the developmental shifts that occur as adults become parents. The study of early parent-infant interaction is typically viewed as the study of infancy, but it is equally a part of life-span developmental psychology with its focus on the shifts in adult behavior across age and role changes.

Consistent with this developmental viewpoint is an increasing interest in the earliest stages of interaction, with observations often beginning during labor and delivery (Anderson and Standley, 1976) or in the early postpartum hospital period (Osofsky and Danzger, 1974; Parke et al., 1972) and then continuing in the home in order to track developmental shifts in parent-infant interaction patterns (Parke and Sawin, 1977). This is a noteworthy shift in emphasis and in contrast to earlier research guided by attachment theory (Bowlby, 1969). Under the influence of attachment theory, the first 6 months were largely ignored, since it was assumed that the infant could only form an attachment with the parent after the achievement of object permanence. Recent research has shown that the process of mutual recognition and regulation on both the infant side (Cassel and Sander, 1975) and the parent side (Klaus and Kennell, 1976) begins much earlier than prior theory suggested; the processes whereby both the *parent and the infant* become familiar with and responsive to each other is a necessary aspect of the paradigm (Parke and Sawin, 1975). And, of course, even if we had continued to accept the necessity of the achievement of object permanence as a landmark for attachment onset, it was hardly necessary for parents to wait 6 months to reach this milestone in cognitive development.

Moreover, by explicitly recognizing the parent as a thinking organism, it becomes clear that in recent studies of parent-infant interaction the impact of parental cognitions, perceptions, attitudes, and knowledge on the interactive process has not been given adequate attention. Implicit in many of our models of interaction is the assumption that the parent reacts to the behavior of the infant in a mechanical or unthinking fashion. Again this is, in large measure, a legacy of our S-R heritage, which has led us to ignore the role of subjective events in an effort to develop an objective analysis of interaction patterns. Nor has the recent trend of replacing our S-R models with biologically derived ethological approaches resulted in any correction of this denial of cognitive factors in social interaction. Another explanation may be that in our enthusiasm to give the infant his proper recognition as a contributor to the interactive process, we have oversimplified our assumptions concerning the relative capacities of parents and infants in the dyadic exchange by treating them as co-acting equals. This failure to recognize parents as information-processing organisms is particularly surprising in light of the general cognitive revival within psychology in the past 15 years.

One reason for the limited recognition of cognitive variables in current theoretical conceptualizations of parent-infant interaction is the failure to adequately distinguish between *parental reports as objective measures of parental behavior* and *parental reports as indices of parental knowledge, attitudes, stereotypes, and perceptions* (Parke, 1978a). These latter classes of variables are legitimate and important sources of data in their own right and are reports that provide information about ways in which parents perceive, organize, and understand both their infants and their roles as parents. The assumption of a cognitive mediational model of parent-infant interaction (Parke, 1978a) is that these cognitive sets serve as filters through which the objective behaviors of the infant are processed. It is not assumed that parent perceptions of infant behavior are short-hand routes to circumvent the task of directly observing the infant. Rather it is assumed these perceptions, attitudes, and values *are* different and to some degree independent sources of data. In fact, it is probably a mistake to assume that actual and perceived behaviors are necessarily similar and can be treated as parallel sources of information. Recent evidence (Borussard and Hartner, 1971) indicates that early maternal labeling of their infants at 1 month was related to the infant's later behavior at 4 years of age. Others (Barnard, 1976) have recently demonstrated the utility of both maternal and paternal expectations in understanding parent-infant interaction patterns and infant developmental shifts in the 1st year of life. As illustrated later, in studies of fathers, measures of parental sex role expectations (cf. Bem, 1974) will be of particular value.

In summary, there is an increasing recognition that a multiple set of assessment strategies are necessary for adequately understanding early father-infant (as well as mother-infant) interaction patterns, including observational assessments as well as verbal reports of parental perceptions, attitudes, and knowledge about infants and their development.

Next, we turn to the broader social context in which father-infant interaction should be conceptualized; in contrast to a traditional focus on the father-infant dyad, a systems approach in which the family triad of mother, father, and infant is the focus of analysis will be advocated.

CONCEPTUALIZATION OF THE EFFECTS OF FATHERS IN INFANCY

Fathers have an impact on their infants in a variety of ways. The most common view is a direct effect model, whereby the impact of direct face-to-face interaction between father and infant is the focus. Restricting our views to the father-infant dyad alone is too narrow. Rather, by viewing the father as one member in a family network, other ways in which father can influence the infant can be explicitly recognized. Fathers alter infant behavior in indirect as well as direct ways (Parke and O'Leary, 1976; Pedersen et al., 1975; Lewis and Weinraub, 1976; Clarke-Stewart, 1977). These direct and indirect effects can be conceptualized in a number of ways, as summarized in Figure 15-1. Let us take each aspect of the figure, in turn (see Parke et al., 1978, for a detailed discussion of this conceptual issue).

Part A indicates a direct-effects model, whereby the father (or mother) directly affects the behavior of the infant; note that the bidirectional quality of the interaction is represented by the arrow running from the infant to the father, and vice versa. Indirect effects are represented in Part B of the diagram. As indicated in B(i), father may affect the infant by altering the mother-infant interaction patterns. First, father may provide economic, emotional, and physical support for the mother, which, in turn, will alter both the amount of time that mother has available for infant interaction and the quality of the interaction patterns. Emotional support of a woman by her spouse in her role as mother and caretaker may affect the quality of the mother-infant relationship. Physical support in the form of sharing of household responsibilities or of infant caretaking tasks may affect the mother-infant relationship. By having the father relieve the mother of some of these routine responsibilities, the quality of the mother-infant interaction may improve by permitting more time for playful and other noncaretaking activities.

Figure 15-1.   Direct and indirect effects in father-infant (dyadic) and father-mother-infant (triadic) interaction.

(A) DYAD

Direct-Effect Model

F $\longleftrightarrow$ I

M $\longleftrightarrow$ I

(B) TRIAD

Direct and Indirect Models

(i) Impact of father modification of mother's behavior on infant

F $\rightarrow$ M $\rightarrow$ I

(ii) Impact of father-infant relationship on the mother-infant interaction

F — I $\rightarrow$ M — I

(iii) Impact of father modification of the infant's behavior on mother-infant interaction

F $\rightarrow$ I $\rightarrow$ M — I

(iv) Impact of the father-mother relationship on the infant

F — M $\rightarrow$ I

(v) Impact of the father-infant relationship on the father-mother relationship

F — I $\rightarrow$ F — M

The father's attitudes and behaviors directed toward the infant may, in turn, affect the mother's attitudes toward her infant [see B(ii)]. As Pedersen et al. (1975) note:

If the father feels positively towards the infant, it is likely that the mother's positive feelings and behaviors may be enhanced. But at the pathological extreme one mother may be jealous of the father's affection for the child and may be more demanding and harsh in her treatment of the infant. [p. 3]

Similarly, if the father's behavior is negative, the mother may either treat the child similarly or may compensate for the harsh treatment and behave in an indulgent fashion toward the infant. These effects can be viewed as "reactive" effects whereby the mother reacts either in a complementary or compensatory fashion to the father's attitudes toward or treatment of the infant.

Another way in which the father may indirectly influence the infant's treatment by other agents is by modifying the infant's behavior [B(iii)]. Infant behavior patterns that develop as a result of father-infant interaction may, in turn, affect the infant's treatment by other social agents. For example, irritable infant patterns may be reinforced by an impatient father which, in turn, alters the mother's feelings toward the infant. Note that the mother may have similar kinds of effects on the father-infant dyad, by modifying infant behavior patterns which, in turn, will alter the father-infant relationship.

Next, B(iv) depicts the impact of the husband-wife relationship on the infant. The nature of the husband-wife interaction patterns can have an impact at a variety of points during pregnancy, childbirth, and infancy. The extent to which the father has been supportive of his wife during pregnancy, labor, and delivery and in the immediate postpartum hospital period will probably determine the ease with which women adjust to their new mothering role. For example, Shereshefsky and Yarrow (1973) found positive relationships between the wife's successful adaptation to pregnancy and the husband's responsiveness to the wife's pregnancy. Similarly, husband support during labor and delivery lessens maternal distress (Anderson and Standley, 1976; Hennenborn and Cogan, 1975; cf. Macfarlane, 1977). Finally, one would expect on the basis of observations of family interaction in the early postpartum period (Parke and O'Leary, 1976) that "postpartum blues"—a condition suffered by two-thirds of all postparturitional women (Yalmon, 1968) might be lessened by the presence of a supportive other such as a husband or relative. Nor is the relationship unidirectional; a number of studies have demonstrated that the birth of an infant alters the husband-wife relationship (Cowan et al., 1978; Rausch et al., 1974), as represented in B(v).

Other data offer empirical support for the continuing influence of the husband-wife relationship on parent-infant interaction patterns beyond the newborn period. Pedersen (1975) assessed the impact of the husband-wife relationship on mother-infant interaction during feeding. Ratings were made of the quality of the mother-infant relationship in connection with two time-sampled home observations when the infants were 4 weeks old. Of particular interest was "feeding competence," which refers to the appropriateness of the mother in managing feeding. "Mothers rated high are able to pace the feeding well, intersperse feeding and burping without disrupting the baby and seem sensitive to the baby's needs for either stimulation of feeding or brief rest periods during the course of feedings" (Pedersen, 1975, p. 4). The husband-wife relationship was assessed through an interview; and, finally, Brazelton neonatal assessments were available. Pedersen summarized his results as follows:

> The husband-wife relationship was linked to the mother-infant unit. When the father was more supportive of the mother, that is, evaluated her maternal skills more positively, she was more effective in feeding the baby. Then again, maybe competent mothers elicit more positive evaluations from their husbands. The reverse holds for marital discord. High tension and conflict in the marriage was associated with more inept feeding on the part of the mother. [Pedersen, 1975, p. 6]

The picture is even more complex, however, as indicated by the observation that the status and well-being of the infant—as assessed by alertness and motor maturity—is also related to the marital relationship. With an alert baby, the father evaluated the mother more positively; with a motorically mature baby, there appeared to be less tension and conflict in the marriage. In Pedersen's (1975) view, "a good baby and a good marriage go together."

Further support for conceptualizing the father not simply as another influence source but as part of a family system of mother, father, and infant comes from another investigation by Pedersen and his colleagues (Pedersen et al., 1977). These investigators observed fathers and mothers both alone and together with their 5-month-old infants in their homes. The results revealed a positive relationship between the amount of positive affect expressed by mother to her baby and by father to his baby either when a father was present or the mother was observed alone. Surprisingly the expression of positive affect between spouses was unrelated to the level of positive affect that they directed toward the infant. Just as in the case of positive affect, the level of negative affect that the two parents directed toward the infant was positively related. More interesting is the finding that the level of negative affect between spouses affected the negative affect directed toward the infant; in short, husband-wife conflict was related to higher levels of parental expression of negative affect to their infant. Another measure, Perception of Baby Temperament Scales (Pedersen et al., 1976), which indexes the degree of discrepancy in the parent's separate perceptions of their infants' temperament, was related to the other's relationship with her infant. In families where husband and wife perceive infant temperament differently, mother is more likely to direct negative affect to her infant. Moreover, discrepancy in perception of their infant was related to the wife's verbal criticism of her husband, but not vice versa; discrepancy was unrelated to the husband's level of verbal criticism. In summary, father's behavior toward his infant is more closely related to the type of husband-wife interaction, while the wife's behavior is more closely linked to the degree of agreement between spouses in their views of the infant's routine temperamental characteristics. This study underlines the importance of a systems analysis of early family interaction in which the father is recognized as embedded in a family network. In addition, the investigation provides support for our earlier argument of the utility of parental reports, such as perceptions and attitudes for understanding early parent-infant interaction patterns (Parke, 1978a).

The nature of the indirect effect of father on the mother-infant relationship will vary with the social context or setting. While indirect effects of the father on the mother-infant dyad occur even when the father is not physically present (Pedersen et al., 1978b), the modifying impact of the father is seen very clearly when the family triad is together. Interacting alone with the infant and in the presence of the father alters the nature of the interactive experience for both the mother and infant. This general issue of the impact of a third person on the interaction patterns of a dyad has been described as second-order effects (Bronfenbrenner, 1974). To illustrate the second-order effect, Parke and O'Leary (1976) observed mother-newborn interaction both alone and in the presence of the father. They found that mothers smile more at their newborn infants and explore their infants more than when they are alone with their infants. Father-infant interaction is affected in a similar fashion: fathers smile and explore more in the presence of their wives than alone. In addition, the overall quantity of mother-infant interaction is decreased by the father's presence whether in the hospital with newborn infants (Parke and O'Leary, 1973, 1976) or in the home with 15- to 22-month-old infants (Clarke-Stewart, 1977).

As Pedersen et al. (1975) note, the experience for the infant in the dyadic and triadic interaction situations may be different as well. The triadic situation "provides the infant with opportunities for paired stimulus comparisons. He is able to compare and discriminate the mother and father to become aware of differences in voice quality, visual configuration of the face, vigor of behavior and the extent to which parents are responsive to his behavior" [p. 4]. In short, for both parents and infants, the presence of the father clearly modifies the nature of the mother-infant interaction experience and illustrates another "indirect" effect of fathers on both infants and mothers.

It should be noted that these indirect effects of father are not restricted to mother-infant relationships; father may indirectly influence his infant through his interaction patterns with other members of a family network, such as other children, visitors, or relatives, such as grandparents. Nor should this social systems view of family functioning be restricted to fathers. As Feiring and Taylor (1977) recently demonstrated, high maternal-infant involvement was positively related to the mother's perceptions of support from a secondary parent—an individual who was not necessarily the father. Clearly, evaluation of the importance of the father in contrast to other social figures in providing support for the mother is necessary in order to determine the uniqueness of the father in the family network.

QUANTITY AND QUALITY OF FATHER-INFANT INTERACTION

A useful distinction concerns the *quantity* of time that fathers spend with their infants in different activities such as caretaking, feeding, or playing and the *qualitative* nature of the interaction within these contexts. In this section, descriptions of the quantity as well as the quality of father-infant interaction will be described from the newborn period through approximately the 2nd year of life.

Quantity of Father-Infant Interaction

In spite of current shifts in cultural attitudes concerning the appropriateness and desirability of father participation in infancy, the shifts should not be exaggerated. Although more mothers are entering the workforce, current occupational arrangements still mean that the vast majority of fathers have less opportunity for interaction with their infants than mothers. Estimates of the amount of time that fathers spend with their infants varies considerably, but most reports indicate that the amount of time is surprisingly limited. Pedersen and Robson (1969), using maternal reports of father involvement, indicated that fathers were available 26 h/wk during the babies' awake periods; approximately 8 h/week were spent playing with their 9-month-old infants, with a wide range of 45 min to 26 hrs. across their sample of fathers. A similar finding was reported recently by Kotelchuck (1976), who interviewed a middle-class Boston sample and found that mothers had principal childrearing responsibilities for infants from 6 to 21 months of age. Mothers were present for more time with their infants than fathers (9.0 versus 3.2 h/day). The amount of father-infant involvement is clearly less than mother involvement with infants.[2]

However, the nature of the activities in which fathers and mothers engage differ as well. For example, Kotelchuck (1976) reported that mothers spent more time feeding than the fathers, 1.45 h versus 0.25 h, and spent more time than fathers cleaning the child (0.92 h versus 0.15 h). Of the mothers, 64% were totally and solely responsible for child care; 9.1% shared caretaking responsibility jointly with another person. Only 7.5% of the fathers shared infant-caretaking responsibilities equally with their wives, and only 25% had a regular caretaking responsibility. In short, 75% of this middle-class sample took no responsibility for the physical care of their infant on a routine basis. In fact, 43% of all fathers reported they never changed diapers at all. While mothers spent more absolute

[2]Some reports (e.g., Rebelsky and Hanks, 1971) have probably underestimated the degree of father-infant interaction in infancy. These investigators recorded father-infant verbal interaction from 2 weeks to 3 months and found that fathers verbalized to their infants 2.7 times per day for an average of 37.7 sec. However, these findings apply *only* to vocalizations and no information concerning nonvocal physical interaction is provided by this study. As Rebelsky and Hanks note, "it may be that fathers are more physical than verbal with their infants" [p. 67]. In short, low verbal involvement *does not* suggest a general pattern of low father involvement.

time in play with their children than fathers (2.3 to 1.2 h), fathers spent a greater percentage of time (37.5%) in play activities than the mothers did (25.8%).

A similar pattern was reported recently by Rendina and Dickerscheid (1976), who found that social involvement, including play, accounted for 10.4% of the father's activities while caretaking accounted for only 3.8%. These data are derived from two 5-min observation periods in the home of either 5- or 13-month-old infants; therefore the absolute amounts cannot be compared to the Kotelchuck report; unfortunately, Rendina and Dickerscheid did not report comparison data for mother-infant activities.

Nor are these differences in mother and father participation restricted to U.S. samples. Similar findings have been reported from an English study (Richards et al., 1975). As part of a longitudinal investigation of parent-infant interaction, these investigators interviewed mothers concerning fathers' participation in a wide range of caretaking and noncaretaking activities when the infant was 30 and 60 weeks old. At both ages, play was the most common activity, with over 90% of the fathers regularly playing with their infants. Regular routine participation in routine caretaking, such as feeding, was less common, with only approximately 35% regularly feeding their infants at 30 weeks and 46% participating in feeding by 60 weeks. From 30 to 60 weeks, there was an increase in the extent to which the father took the child out of the house without the mother, with almost 50% of the fathers assuming this responsibility regularly by 60 weeks. In general there was a clear hierarchy of paternal activities, with diaper-changing and bathing as the rarest categories of regular participation and playing as the most common activity.

In another study, Lamb (1977a) observed interactions among mother, father, and infant in their homes at 7 to 8 months and again at 12 to 13 months. Based on 2½ to 3 h of home observation, Lamb reported marked differences in the reasons that fathers and mothers pick up infants: fathers were more likely to hold the babies simply to play with them, while the mothers were far more likely to hold them for caretaking purposes. Moreover, Lamb (1976b) reported that middle- and upper-class fathers held their infants for caretaking purposes more often than lower-class fathers.

It is not merely the quantity of time per se that discriminates between mother and father involvement in infancy—it is the quality of activity as well. A variety of studies across a wide developmental span from the newborn period to 2 years have explored the qualitative differences in father-infant and mother-infant interaction. A complex, but consistent, pattern of similarities and differences emerges from these studies with clear role differentiation between fathers and mothers evident from the early days of life.

Father-Infant Interaction in the Newborn Period: Qualitative Effects

A number of recent studies have explored the qualitative nature of father involvement with newborn infants. Greenberg and Morris (1974) questioned two groups of fathers: (1) a group whose first contact with their newborn occurred at the birth (in the delivery room), and (2) a group whose first contact with the newborn occurred after the birth when it was shown to them by nursing personnel. Both groups of fathers showed evidence of strong paternal feelings and of involvement with their newborn, with 97% of the fathers rating their paternal feelings as average to very high. The majority were generally "very glad" immediately after the delivery and pleased about the sex of their infant (97%). While both groups of fathers judged themselves able to distinguish their own newborn from other babies by the way he looked (90%), fathers who had been present at birth thought they could do this all the time while the fathers who were not present thought they could do this only some of the time. Finally, there was some indication that fathers who were present at the delivery felt more comfortable in holding their baby. Combined with clinical interview data, Greenberg and Morris (1974) suggest that "fathers begin developing a bond to their newborn by the first three days after birth and often earlier. Furthermore, there are certain characteristics of this bond which we call 'engrossment' . . . a feeling of preoccupation, absorption and interest in their newborn'' [p. 526].

Although suggestive, these verbal reports need to be supplemented by direct behavioral observations to determine whether these self-reports of feelings and interest are reflected in behavior. In fact, there is no reason to expect that attitudes and behavior toward infants will be necessarily directly related in any simple fashion (cf. Parke, 1978a).

A series of observational studies by Parke and his associates have been conducted in order to describe—in behavioral terms—the nature of father's interaction with his new-born infant. In the first study, Parke et al. (1972) observed the behavior of fathers in the family triad of mother, father, and infant. Observation sessions lasted 10 min and oc-curred during the first 3 days following delivery. A time-sampling procedure was used in which 40 intervals of 15-sec duration were scored for the following behaviors for each parent: holds, changes position, looks, smiles, vocalizes, touches, kisses, explores, im-itates, feeds, hands over to other parent.

The results indicated that fathers were just as involved as mothers and that mothers and fathers did not differ on the majority of the measures. In fact, fathers tended to hold the infant more than mothers and rock the infant in their arms more than mothers. Fathers, in short, in a context where participation was voluntary, were just as involved as the mother in interaction with their infants.

However, there is a variety of questions that could be raised about this study. First, the context was unique since the mother and father were together, and possibly the high degree of father-infant interaction observed was due to the supporting presence of the mother.

Moreover, the sample of fathers was unique in ways that may have contributed to their high degree of interaction with their infants. Over half of the fathers had attended Lamaze childbirth classes, and with one exception all fathers were present during the delivery of the child. Both of these factors are likely to have increased the fathers' later involvement with their infants. Finally, these fathers were well educated and middle-class, and their high degree of involvement may be more common in middle-class groups; parental in-volvement may be less in lower-class samples due to a typically more rigid definition of parental roles among lower-class parents.

To overcome the limitations of the original study, a group of lower-class fathers who neither participated in childbirth classes nor were present during delivery were observed in two contexts: (1) alone with their infant and (2) in the presence of the mother (Parke and O'Leary, 1976). This study permitted a much more stringent test of father-infant involve-ment and permitted wider generalization of the previous findings. As in the earlier study, father was a very interested and active participant. In fact, in the family triad, father was more likely to hold the infant and visually attend to the infant than the mother. Nor is the mother's presence necessary for the father's active involvement; the father was an equally active interactor in both settings—alone and with his wife. Fathers in our studies (Parke et al., 1972; Parke and O'Leary, 1976; Parke and Sawin, 1975) are just as nurturant as mothers. For example, in the first study, they touched, looked, vocalized, and kissed their newborn offspring just as often as mothers did. In the second study, an even more striking picture emerged—with the father exhibiting more nurturant behavior in the triadic context than the mother and an equal amount when alone with the baby. There was only a single nurturant behavior—smiling—in which the mother surpassed the father in both studies.

Although there were few differences in the nurturance and stimulatory activities of the parents, fathers do play a less active role in caretaking activities than mothers. In the second Parke and O'Leary (1976) study in which all infants were bottle-fed, fathers fed significantly less than mothers when they were alone with the baby. Additional support for this mother-father difference comes from another study (Parke and Sawin, 1975) of father-newborn interaction, which involved a detailed examination of early parent-infant interaction in a feeding context. Comparisons of the frequencies and durations of specific caretaking activities of mothers and fathers while alone with their infants in a feeding context indicate that mothers spend more time engaged in feeding the infant and in related caretaking activities, such as wiping the baby's face, than do fathers. These findings suggest that parental role allocation begins in the earliest days of life.

These findings are consistent with the more general proposition that pregnancy and birth of a first child, in particular, are occasions for a shift toward a more traditional division of roles (Arbeit, 1975; Cowan et al., 1978; Shereshefsky and Yarrow, 1973). Cowan and her co-workers (1978) studied couples before and up to 6 months after the birth of a first child. They reported that the shift was most marked in the household tasks, next in the family decision-making roles, and least in the baby care items. Of particular interest is the fact that these patterns held regardless of whether their initial role division was traditional or equalitarian. "Despite the current rhetoric and ideology concerning equality of roles for men and women, it seems that couples tend to adopt traditionally defined roles during times of stressful transition such as around the birth of a first child" (Cowan et al., 1976, p. 20).

However, the lower level of father involvement in feeding does not imply that fathers are less competent than mothers to care for the newborn infant. Competence can be measured in a variety of ways, but one approach is to measure the parent's sensitivity to infant cues in the feeding context. Success in caretaking, to a large degree, is dependent on the parent's ability to correctly "read" or interpret the infant's behavior so that their own behavior can be regulated in order to achieve some interaction goal. To illustrate, in the feeding context, the aim of the parent is to facilitate the food intake of the infant; the infant, in turn, by a variety of behaviors, such as sucking or coughing, provides the caretaker with feedback concerning the effectiveness or ineffectiveness of their current behavior in maintaining the food intake process. In this context, one approach to the competence issue involves an examination of the degree to which the caretaker modifies his/her behavior in response to infant cues. Parke and Sawin (1975) found that father's sensitivity to an auditory distress signal in the feeding context—sneeze, spit up, cough—was just as marked as mother's responsivity to this infant cue. Using a conditional probability analysis, they demonstrated that fathers, like mothers, adjusted their behavior by momentarily ceasing their feeding activity, looking more closely to check on the infant, and vocalizing to their infant. The only difference concerns the greater cautiousness of the fathers, who are more likely than mothers to inhibit their touching in the presence of this signal. The implication of this analysis is clear: in spite of the fact that they may spend less time overall, fathers are as sensitive as mothers to infant cues and as responsive to them in the feeding context.

Moreover, the amount of milk consumed by the infants with their mothers and fathers was very similar (1.3 oz. versus 1.2 oz. respectively). In short, fathers and mothers are not only similar in their sensitivity but are equally successful in feeding the infant based on the amount of milk consumed by the infant. Invoking a competence/performance distinction, fathers may not necessarily be frequent contributors to infant feeding, but when called upon they have the competence to execute these tasks effectively.

Moreover, fathers are just as responsive as mothers to other infant cues, such as vocalizations and mouth movements. Mothers and fathers both increased their rate of positive vocalizations following an infant vocal sound; in addition, parents touched the infant and looked more closely at the infant after the infant vocalizations. However, mothers and fathers differ in the behaviors that they show in response to this type of infant elicitor: upon vocalization, fathers are more likely than mothers to increase their vocalization rate. Mothers, on the other hand, are more likely than fathers to react to infant vocalization with touching. Possibly, fathers are more cautious than mothers in their use of tactile stimulation during feeding due to their concern about disrupting infant feeding behavior. A further demonstration of the modifying impact of the infant's behavior on his caregivers—fathers as well as mothers—comes from an examination of the impact of infant mouth movements: parents of both sexes increase their vocalizing, touching, and stimulation of feeding activity in response to mouth movements. These data indicate that fathers and mothers both react to the newborn infant's cues in a contingent and functional manner even though they differ in their specific response patterns. The interaction patterns in the newborn period are reciprocal; while our focus in the Parke and Sawin (1975) study was on the role of infant cues as elicitors of parent behavior, in a later study (Parke and Sawin, 1977) it was shown that parent vocalizations can modify newborn infant behavior, such as infant vocalizations. Interaction between fathers and infants—even in the newborn period—is clearly bidirectional in quality; both parents and infants mutually regulate each other's behavior in the course of interaction.

Beyond the Newborn Period: Qualitative Effects

Many of the qualitative features that are evident in father-infant interactions in the newborn period characterize the interaction patterns in later infancy as well. In this section, the qualitative nature of father-infant interaction in older infants observed both in the laboratory and the home will be presented.

Parke and Sawin (1977) recently found that mother and father patterns of stimulation show shifts across the first 3 months. Structured observations of 10 min of feeding and 5 min of toy play were made at the newborn period, 3 weeks, and 3 months. As expected, there was more role differentiation for mothers and fathers over time in the play context than in the feeding context; this is consistent with the Brazelton et al. (1975) hypothesis that more variation in styles of parent-infant interaction would be exhibited by parents in a less structured or stereotyped context. In the Parke and Sawin study, although fathers stimulated their infants during the play session both visually (show toy) and auditorily (shake toy) more than mothers at the newborn observation, at 3 weeks and at 3 months mothers used this type of stimulation a little more than did fathers. A similar role reversal occurred for parental caretaking: in the early observation, mothers engaged in more routine caretaking (checks diapers, grooms, wipes face) while fathers did more as the infant develops. By 3 months, fathers—in a structured observation context—engaged in more of these behaviors. These indications of role reversals and convergence suggest that mutual modeling effects are operating in the family system during early infancy. It appears that as the parents share the care and stimulation of their infant they are adopting their partner's behaviors, which are reflected in shifts in each other's behavior in the direction that was more characteristic of their mate at an earlier time. Parents may learn from each other and at the same time provide a model for each other's learning. A great deal of this early learning probably occurs in the triadic context—a possibility that under-scores again the importance of considering the full family system.

As a partial evaluation of the utility of our cognitive-mediational analysis of parent-infant interaction (Parke, 1978a), Parke and Sawin (1977) administered a questionnaire to mothers and fathers at the same time points used for the observational phases of this investigation. Of particular relevance are two factors derived from this questionnaire. The first factor, the parent's perceptions concerning the infant's need for affection and stimula-tion, included such items as "it's good to cuddle babies," "diapering is a good time for play," and "it doesn't matter if you talk to babies." The second factor tapped the parent's knowledge of infant perceptual capacities; this factor included such items as "newborns can follow a moving object" and "infants can discriminate among people." On the first factor—the need for affection—fathers scored higher than mothers at the hospital period, at 3 weeks there was only a slight difference, and by 3 months mothers scored sig-nificantly higher than fathers on this factor. In general, fathers decreased while mothers increased on this factor over the 3-month period. Parental knowledge about infant compe-tence increased over time; however, fathers attributed greater perceptual competence to their infants than did mothers during the newborn period. At both 3 weeks and 3 months mothers attributed greater competence to their infants than did fathers. Of interest is the parallel between these attitudinal and knowledge patterns and the sex of parent shifts in their *behavioral* patterns of visual and auditory stimulation across time. As described earlier, fathers were more active stimulators early, while mothers played a more active role later. Consistent with a cognitive-mediational model, these shifts in attitudes and knowledge, in part, may be mediating the changing patterns of parent behavior.

Not only are there developmental changes, but the style of play during father-infant and mother-infant interaction differs—as revealed in a recent study by Yogman & his col-leagues (Yogman et al., 1977b). These investigators compared mothers, fathers, and strangers in their interactions with infants in a face-to-face play context. Each of five infants were studied for 2 min of interaction with their mothers, fathers, and a stranger from 2 weeks to 6 months in a lab arrangement whereby infant and adult face each other with instructions to play without using toys and without removing the infant from an infant seat. Using videotaped records, a variety of microbehavioral analyses of the adult-infant interaction patterns were scored. Adults differ in their play with infants as indicated by differences in vocalization and touching patterns. Mothers vocalized with soft, repetitive, imitative burst-pause talking (47%) more often than fathers (20%), who do so significantly more often than strangers (12%). Fathers, however, touched their infants with rhythmic tapping patterns (44%) more often than either mothers (28%) or strangers (29%). As Yogman et al. (1977b) comment,

> These adult behaviors were often part of an interactive "game" in the sense defined by Stern (1974): "a series of episodes of mutual attention in which the adult uses a repeating set of behaviors with only minor variations during each episode of mutual attention" . . . mothers' repetitive activities or games were more often verbal than tactile. [Yogman et al., 1977b, p. 8]

This appears to be a very promising approach to discriminating subtle differences in father versus mother styles of interaction. Moreover, these findings suggest that earlier reports of similarity between mothers' and fathers' style of interaction with young infants may have been due to insufficiently molecular measurement techniques. However, due to the small sample, replication is necessary to establish the reliability of these findings. Whether these stylistic differences are related to more molar measures of social interaction or whether similar patterns are detectable in other less structured contexts, such as home settings, clearly needs to be determined.

Stylistic differences in mothers' and fathers' play are not restricted to either young infants or structured laboratory settings. Recent observation of father- and mother-infant interaction in unstructured home contexts indicate mother-father differences in their style of play. Lamb (1977a), in an observational study of infants at 7 and 8 months and again at 12 to 13 months in their home, found that fathers engage in more physical (i.e., rough-and-tumble type) and unusual play activities than mothers. Similar findings emerged from home observations of the infants at 15, 18, 21, and 24 months of age (Lamb, 1977b). Again, fathers played more physical games, and engaged in more parallel play with their infants. Mothers, in contrast, engaged in more conventional play activities (e.g., peek-a-boo, pat-a-cake), stimulus toy play (where a toy was jiggled or operated to stimulate the child directly), and reading than fathers.

Similar differences in the style of play patterns were found by Clarke-Stewart (1977) in a study of 15- to 30-month-old infants and their parents: ''Fathers' play was relatively more likely to be physical and arousing rather than intellectual, didactic or mediated by objects—as in the case of mothers'' (Clarke-Stewart, 1977, p. 37).

In all studies reviewed, a reasonably consistent pattern emerges: fathers are tactile and physical while mothers tend to be verbal. Clearly, infants do not experience simply more stimulation from their fathers, but a qualitatively different stimulatory pattern.

Father's role as playmate shows developmental changes; in the Clarke-Stewart study, at 15 months the child's primary playmate was the mother, by 20 months mother and father shared this role, and by 30 months the father played more than the mothers. Similarly, the mother's role as caretaker was diminishing over this same period, and by 30 months there was little difference in caretaking between mothers and fathers. Of particular interest is the pattern of relationships between playful behaviors and other behavior patterns. For mothers, positive emotion and physical stimulation were highly correlated with other measures of stimulation and responsiveness. For fathers, on the other hand, expressions of negative emotion, including scolding, criticizing, and speaking sharply were related to father's physical playfulness.

In general, this pattern of findings suggests that father involvement in infancy is quantitatively less than mother involvement, but the types of roles that mother and father play clearly differ as well. The fact of less quantity of interaction, however, does not imply that fathers do not have an important impact on infant development. Just as earlier research (e.g., Hoffman and Nye, 1974; Schaeffer and Emerson, 1964) has indicated that quality rather than quantity of mother-infant interaction was the important predictor of infant cognitive and social development, it is likely that a similar assumption will hold for fathers as well.

SEX OF INFANT AS A DETERMINANT OF FATHER-INFANT INTERACTION

One of the most consistent determinants of parental expectations, perceptions, and organizers of behavior is the infant's sex. There are marked and relatively consistent differences in paternal and maternal reactions to male and female infants.

Evidence of differential parental reactions to males and females is evident even before the infant is born. Parents prefer male offspring across a wide variety of cultures (Poffenberger and Poffenberger, 1973; Arnold et al., 1975) including India, Asia, as well as the United States. In a 1975 survey of 1500 women and approximately one-fourth of their husbands in the United States, Hoffman (1977) found that there was a 2:1 preference for boys over girls. Coombs et al. (1975) reported a similar result. The respondents were given a series of choices about the sexes they would prefer if they had three children; a consistent pattern of choosing more male than female babies emerged from the Coombs et al. investigation. Of particular relevance is Hoffman's finding that the pattern of boy preference was more pronounced for men: "between 3 and 4 times as many men preferred boys than girls" (Hoffman, 1977, p. 11). Reproduction patterns are revealing as well. According to Hoffman (1977), "couples are more likely to continue to have children if they have only girls. They will have more children than they originally planned to try for a boy," [p. 11].

After the birth of the infant, parents have clear stereotypes concerning the particular types of behavior that they expect to be associated with infants of diffferent sexes. In a recent study, Rubin et al. (1974) asked mothers and fathers to rate their newborn sons or daughters in the first 24 h after birth. Although male and female infants did not differ in birth length, weight, or Apgar scores, daughters were significantly more likely than sons to be described as little, beautiful, pretty and cute, and as resembling their mother. Fathers, who had seen but not handled their infants, were more extreme in their ratings of both sons and daughters than were mothers. Sons were rated as firmer, larger featured, better coordinated, more alert, stronger, and hardier, and daughters as softer, finer featured, more awkward, more inattentive, weaker, and more delicate by their fathers than by their mothers. As the authors note,

the central implication of the study, then, is that sex-typing and sex role socialization appear to have already begun their course at the time of the infant's birth, when information about the infant is minimal. The "Gestalt" parents develop and the labels they ascribe to their newborn infant, may well affect subsequent expectations about the manner in which their infant ought to behave as well as parental behavior itself [pp. 518–519].

Nor is this sex stereotyping restricted to parents of newborn infants. In a study by Condry and Condry (1976), male and female college students rated a videotaped infant who was labeled either a "boy" or "girl." Observers rated the infant's emotional reaction to different stimuli (e.g., a Jack-in-the-Box) differently as a function of the sex label. The "boy" was rated as "angry" while the same reaction by an infant girl was labeled "fear." Although their study was not designed to reveal treatment differences, Condry and Condry (1976) note, "it seems reasonable to assume that a child who is thought to be afraid is held and cuddled more than a child who is thought to be angry" [p. 16]. Finally, the "boy" was viewed as more "active" and "potent" than the girl on semantic differential ratings.

To the extent that these types of early sex stereotypes are predictive of parental behavior, this evidence suggests that a social mediational approach, which gives explicit recognition to the role of parental expectations and attitudes as organizers of parent-infant interaction, is worthwhile (Parke, 1978a). Next, we turn to evidence of differential *treatment* of boys and girls by mothers and fathers.

As early as the newborn period, fathers treat male and female infants differently. Parke and O'Leary (1976), in the hospital-based observational study, found that fathers touched first-born newborn boys more than either later born boys or girls of either ordinal position. Fathers vocalized more to first-born boys than first-born girls, while they vocalized equally to later-born infants irrespective of their sex. A similar finding has emerged from our sequential analyses of the impact of infant vocalizations on parent behavior (Parke and Sawin, 1975). Fathers are particularly likely to react contingently to this infant cue by vocalizing—but especially in the case of the male infant. Clearly, there may be some basis to the claim that fathers really do prefer boys—especially first-born boys.

Nor are the differences in father behavior with male and female infants restricted to the newborn period. Parke and Sawin (1977) observed parent-infant interaction in a structured bottle-feeding and a toy-play situation at the newborn period in the hospital and again at 3 weeks and 3 months in the home. Although there were few consistent differences in father and mother treatment of their sons and daughters in a routine caretaking context, there were marked differences in the play context. First, fathers held their daughters close and snugly more frequently and for longer periods during play than they did their sons. Mothers, in contrast, held their sons close more than their daughters. In contrast, for visual attending and stimulation behaviors, fathers consistently favored their sons, and mothers more often favored their daughters. Fathers looked at their sons more than their daughters and more frequently visually checked on their sons, by looking more closely at their sons than at their daughters. Fathers provided more visual and tactual stimulation for their sons while mothers played a complementary role by providing more stimulation for their daughters. During the play sessions, fathers visually presented the toy and touched their sons more than they did their daughters. Mothers, on the other hand, more frequently visually stimulated their daughters with the toy than they did their sons and touched and moved their girls more than their boys. During feeding, a similar same-sex effect was evident: fathers made more frequent attempts to stimulate their sons' feeding by moving the bottle than they did for their daughters; mothers showed the opposite pattern. These findings indicate that parents stimulate their same-sex infant more than the opposite-sex infant; fathers and mothers play complementary roles with their male and female infants.

A similar pattern of father-son involvement is evident in unstructured home observational studies as well. Rebelsky and Hanks (1970), for example, noted that fathers decreased their vocalizations across the first 3 months of life to female infants more than to male infants. Similarly, Rendina and Dickerscheid (1976) reported that fathers spent more time attending to male infants than female infants, while there was a trend for fathers to play more with boys than girls. A more provocative finding concerns the differential involvement of fathers with temperamentally difficult male and female infants. Using Carey's Infant Temperament Scale, these investigators reported that fathers were involved in social activities with temperamentally difficult boys (14.6%) more than difficult girls (4%). In short, fathers apparently are willing to persist with difficult male infants more than with troublesome female infants. Unfortunately no mother-infant data is available to determine whether this a general same-sex parent-infant relationship, whereby the same-sex parent assumes responsibility for difficult infants.

Consistent with the Parke and O'Leary finding is Kotelchuck's (1976) report that fathers report that they play about ½ h/day longer with their first-born sons than with their first-born daughters. Although Lamb (1977a) found no sex-of-parent–sex-of-infant relationships in his home observations at 8 and 13 months, Lamb (1977b) did find differences in father and mother treatments of their sons and daughters in his study of 15- to 24-month-old infants in their homes. Fathers vocalized to their sons more than did mothers; in fact, fathers were twice as active in interaction with their sons than with their daughters. Both parents vocalized to their daughters equally.

Finally, Fagot (1974), in a study based on parent interviews, found that parents of 2-year-old boys believed that the father's role involved playing with and providing role models for their sons, while parents of girls did not subscribe to different roles for mothers and fathers.

Although these father-mother differences in treatment of male and female infants remain only suggestive, there are threads of evidence from both cross-cultural and comparative studies that support these general trends.

In a study of visiting patterns in Israeli kibbutzum, Gewirtz and Gewirtz (1968) found that fathers stayed for longer periods in the children's house with their 4-month-old sons than they did with their infant daughters. West and Konner's (1976) observations of male parental behavior among the Kung San (Bushmen) of Botswana, a warm-climate hunting and fathering group, reveal sex-of-infant differences. Although fathers interact more with male than female infants at both age levels studied (0–26 weeks and 27–99 weeks) the effect was significant only for the older infants.

The final evidence of greater father–male-infant interaction comes from Redican's (1975) long-term laboratory study of male-infant interaction in wild-born rhesus monkeys. In adult-male–infant pairs, sex differences in contact were more pronounced than in adult-female–infant pairs. Male adults had more extensive contact with male infants: "Mothers tended to play with female infants whereas adult males did so with male infants. In general mothers interacted more positively with female infants and adult males with male infants" (Redican, 1976, pp. 358–359).

Two aspects of these findings merit discussion. First, what are the implications of these findings on our theories of sex typing? Second, what accounts for the differential role played by fathers in the sex typing of his children?

The patterns of findings clearly indicate that the sex-typing process begins at a much earlier age than previously determined (cf. Lynn, 1974; Mischel, 1970; Maccoby and Jacklin, 1974, for reviews). As this review indicates, the process may begin as early as the newborn period. In support of previous studies with older children (Goodenough, 1957; Sears et al., 1957), these recent observational studies suggest that fathers play a more intrusive and paramount role in the sex-typing process (Johnson, 1963), fathers discriminate more than mothers in their treatment of male and female infants. In addition, boys are treated more discriminatively by their fathers than are girls, which is consistent with other studies indicating that pressures toward sex-role adoption are stronger and occur at an earlier age for sons than daughters (Lansky, 1967). Finally, father-absence studies (Hetherington and Deur, 1972; Herzog and Sudia, 1973) underline the importance of the father's behavior in determining sex-role adoption in boys—especially in the early years (Hetherington, 1966; Stoltz, 1954).

Although social learning theory (cf. Mischel, 1970) can provide a framework for explaining the processes by which the differential socialization strategies of fathers and mothers develop, recent cross-cultural surveys suggest that caution must be exercised in generalizing the specific patterns observed in United States samples to other cultures. As West and Konner (1976) note, a variety of ecological, economic, and ideological variables must be considered in order to understand the particular sex-typing pressures in different cultures. It is clear that no single pattern can survive a cross-cultural comparison. Nor is it certain that the present picture will survive the next decade—in light of the rapidly shifting sex-typing attitudes.

FATHER-INFANT INTERACTION AND INFANT SOCIAL RESPONSIVENESS

Although it has been already established that fathers are involved with their infants, do infants reciprocate their fathers' investment? Both laboratory studies and home observational studies indicate that infants react positively to *both* mothers and fathers, but the quality of the father-infant interaction history is an important determinant of the infant's social responsiveness.

Laboratory-Based Evidence

First, recent evidence indicates that infants can discriminate among mothers, fathers, and strangers at a relatively early age. In a recent study, five infants ranging in age from 2 weeks to 6 months were observed interacting at weekly intervals with either mother, father, or a stranger (Yogman et al., 1977a). Based on a microanalysis of 2 min of playful communication between the adults and the infant, reliable differences in infant behavior were observed as early as 2 months of age. Using frowning as a measure, Yogman et al. demonstrated that infants display less frowning to either mother (5.3%) or father (7.8%) than to a stranger (28.2%). After 2 months, they found that infants frown differentially to mother (2.2%) as opposed to the father (7.7%) as well as stranger (30.4%). Infant smiles, vocalization, and limb movement also discriminated between mothers and fathers versus strangers.

It is of interest not simply to determine that infants can discriminate among different social agents but to explore their preferences for different social agents.

Under the influence of earlier laboratory assessments of the infant's "attachment" to the mother (cf. Ainsworth and Bell, 1970), a series of investigations of father-infant interaction in laboratory settings appeared. By comparing father-infant versus mother-infant interaction, the relative importance of the two parents could be brought into sharper focus. In contrast to the earlier studies, where the primary question concerned father and mother activities and involvement, these studies focus on the *infants'* active involvement with their mothers and fathers. While this is an arbitrary distinction, these lab studies are designed to yield information about infant behavior in reaction to the presence or absence of father versus mother.

Theoretically, these studies can be viewed of an evaluation of the assumptions underlying the Bowlby-Ainsworth attachment theory (Bowlby, 1951; 1969; Ainsworth, 1973) that infants will be attached to mothers earlier than fathers and that they will prefer their mothers to their fathers.

The historical precursor of the current lab studies was the earlier interview study of Schaffer and Emerson (1974). They reported that the infants in their investigation protested separation from their mothers more than their fathers, but that multiple attachments (as indexed by separation protest) was present for the majority of the infants in their sample. Moreover, the sex-of-parent separation differences were observed principally in the 1st year, and by 18 months there were few sex-of-parent differences, with 75% of the infants showing separation protest to their fathers as well as their mothers.

The subsequent laboratory studies have yielded some consistent findings—namely, that both mothers and fathers are clearly preferred to strangers; however, the question of whether there is a preference for mother versus father has yielded less consistent results. Three patterns of results have emerged across various studies: (1) no preference for either parent, (2) mother preferred to father, or (3) father preferred to mother. In short, father is clearly an important and salient social figure, but his position relative to mother is less clearly established. The inconsistent picture across investigations is due, in part, to a failure to carefully distinguish among variations in the social context, the physical setting, the length of the session, and the nature of the dependent indices used in different studies.

First, the exact constellation of social agents present prior to and at the time of measurement needs to be specified; comparisons across stranger alone, parent alone, parents together with, and parents without a stranger need to be carefully made. Second, the familiarity of the measurement context is important, since the degree of stress in the situation may alter the infant's behavior (Lamb, 1976c, Sroufe et al., 1975). Third, the nature of the dependent variable—protest behavior or different types of social approach behaviors—need to be distinguished. Recently, Bretherton and Ainsworth (1974) have distinguished between "attachment" behaviors such as protest behaviors (cry, fuss), approach behaviors (approach, reach), proximity-seeking behavior, and seeking to be held—all of which are theoretically aimed at maintaining proximity to a particular person. In contrast, affiliative behaviors, such as smiling, looking, vocalizing, laughing, and preferring are not limited to one specific person but are useful for social interaction with a wide range of social agents in the child's environment. While alternative theoretical analyses of the manner in which these various social behaviors develop and the functions that they serve may differ (Bretherton and Ainsworth, 1974; Gewirtz, 1972; Cairns, 1972), for heuristic purposes this distinction is useful.

The fact that fathers and mothers are both preferred to strangers is illustrated in a series of studies by Kotelchuck and his colleagues. In the initial study, Kotelchuck (1972) introduced mother and father and their infant to a playroom situation: the infant is exposed to a series of episodes in which either parent or a stranger depart and reappear according to a predetermined schedule. The order allows an unconfounded comparison of the child's response to each of the three adults: mother, father, and stranger alone or with one other adult. No comparisons of both parents and the stranger were included in these studies. Playing, crying, proximity to an adult, touching, vocalizations, smiles, looking, and social interactions are scored. Using infants from 6 to 21 months of age, Kotelchuck (1972) found that children protest the departure of not just the mother but both parents; play was depressed and crying increased after departure of either mother or father, while play increased and crying lessened after the departure of the stranger. Children more often followed their parents to the door and were more likely to remain there following their departures than they were following the stranger's departures. Upon reunion, there was more touching and clinging directed to mothers and fathers than strangers. Similarly, starting at 12 months, children remained proximal, initiated interaction, smiled, and vocalized more to either parent than to strangers. This basic set of findings—namely, that in a laboratory playroom setting children react similarly to mothers and fathers in contrast to strangers—has been replicated in other studies by this group of investigators in the United States (Spelke et al., 1973) as well as cross-culturally in Guatemala (Lester et al., 1974).

Preference for mother versus father can be determined by examining the episodes where both parents are present in the playroom. After 12 months, the majority of children showed a maternal preference as indexed by a proximity measure; however, many showed equal or paternal preference. As Kotelchuck (1976) summarizes his findings,

approximately 55% of the 12 to 21 month old children showed maternal preferences, 20% joint preferences and 25% paternal preferences . . . The percentage of children relating to mothers and fathers and the percentage of children showing maternal or paternal preferences agree remarkably well with the findings of Schaffer & Emerson (1964) . . . [who] estimated that 80% of 18 month old infants are attached to their fathers [compared with 70% from the Kotelchuck, (1972) study] . . . The present data strongly imply that a monotropic matricentric model of early infant interpersonal preference is simplistic. [pp. 337–338]

Other investigators have reported similar findings. Feldman and Ingham (1975), for example, compared 1- and 2-year-old children's reactions to the presence or departure of the mother alone, father alone, stranger alone, or mother or father and stranger. As Kotelchuck et al. found, mother or father were both preferred to the stranger, whether attachment (proximity) or affiliative measures (look, smile) were used. Few consistent differences were found in the infants' reactions to mothers and fathers.

On the other hand, others have replicated this basic finding—namely, that parents of either sex are preferred to a stranger, particularly in a stressful and unfamiliar setting—but have found that infants "prefer" mothers more than fathers. Cohen and Campos (1974) compared 10-, 13-, and 16-month-old infants' reactions to mother, father, and stranger. In both conditions where the mother and father were both present with the stranger or where the mother *or* father were alone with a stranger, the infants maintained more proximity to their mothers and touched their mothers more than their fathers.

Lamb (1976c, d) has demonstrated that this maternal preference may be most likely to occur under stressful conditions. Twelve- and 18-month-old infants were observed under the following conditions in a laboratory context: (1) both parents present, (2) either mother present or father present, and (3) mother, father, and stranger present. While there were no differences in the infants' preference for either parent when both parents were simultaneously present or were observed individually with the infant, the infants showed a clear preference for the mothers over the fathers as indexed by greater touching and fussing (attachment indices) when the stranger was present. In support of the utility of the attachment/affiliation distinction, however, Lamb found no shift in the differential degree of affiliative behaviors directed toward mother versus father in the presence of the stranger. Only the measures classified as "attachment" indices were affected by the stress induced by the appearance of an unfamiliar person. As Lamb (1976c) notes, "These results provide strong support for Bowlby's (1969) notion that in times of stress, infants do, in fact, show preferences for their mothers" [p. 5].

Lamb's findings suggest that the preference for mother over father may be limited to a very narrow set of conditions—namely, to a triadic context in which mother, father, and stranger are present, which permits the infant a choice between two simultaneously available familiar adults. In light of our earlier discussions of the differential roles played by mother and father, with mother assuming primary caretaking responsibility, the infant's choice of mother in a time of stress is not surprising. However, in Lamb's (1976c, d) studies, order of testing, and therefore fatigue, was confounded with the appearance of the stranger; replication is clearly necessary before a definitive statement can be made concerning the conditions under which infant preferences for their mothers and fathers emerge.

In addition, this effect may be time-bound as well, since Lamb (1977b) failed to replicate his own interaction of infant-mother preference in the presence of a stranger with 24-month-old infants. Rather, at 2 years of age, infant proximity to *both* parents increased in the presence of a stranger, but no differences between preference for mother versus father were evident.

In summary, infants react with a high degree of similarity to mothers and fathers—familiar figures—in contrast to unfamiliar strangers. However, the degree of "preference" for mother and father will vary with a variety of factors, including the familiarity of the setting, the social context (the constellation of familiar and unfamiliar individuals), as well as the age and sex of the infant.

Another important determinant of children's reactions to fathers in laboratory contexts is the type of prior father-infant interaction patterns in home settings. A number of laboratory studies have found that children's preferences and extensiveness of interaction with fathers are related to the amount of father caretaking. In these investigations, positive relationships between overall proximity to the father for 12- to 21-month-old infants and paternal caretaking have been reported by Kotelchuck (1972; $r = 0.35$) and by Ross et al. (1975; $r = 0.43$). In fact, Ross et al. (1975) found that paternal proximity in the joint mother-father-present situation correlated highly ($N = 0.51$) with the number of diapers changed by the father per week.

Moreover, the infant's reaction to separation and the age span of intense separation protest in the laboratory is affected by paternal involvement in the home. Spelke et al. (1973) examined the effects of separation on infants of high-, medium-, and low-interacting fathers. In their sample of 12-month-old infants the most separation distress occurred in infants with the lowest paternal involvement, an intermediate amount of distress in infants with medium involvement, and the least distress in the infants with highest paternal involvement. Protest is inversely related to paternal involvement. In the earlier study, Kotelchuck (1972) showed that the less frequently fathers bathed and dressed their infants at home, the greater amount of time the infants cried when left alone with a stranger ($r = -0.40$). In short, children whose fathers are active caretakers are better able to handle the stress of being left alone with a stranger. Perhaps, more egalitarian families not only share caretaking more but expose the infant to a wider range of other individuals, which, in turn, might reduce the impact of a strange adult. Also,

the child's familiarity or lack of familiarity with parental departures should vary with the extent of caregiver exclusiveness. One can hypothesize that infants are exposed to more parental departures in high paternal interacting and caregiving families than in exclusive maternal caregiving families, perhaps making those infants less vulnerable to separation trauma at this early age. [Kotelchuck, 1976, p. 341]

Cross-cultural comparisons confirm these findings. Separation protest occurs earlier in Guatemala (9 months of age versus 12 months for U.S. samples of Ross et al., 1975, and Lester et al., 1974) and in Uganda (6 months; Ainsworth, 1967). In both cultures father involvement is very low.

To date, little attention has been paid to two important variables that are likely to impact significantly on the infant's selection of mother or father for interaction—namely, the type of activity and the behavior of the social agent. For example, mothers and fathers typically serve different functions for the child: the mother serves as caretaker while fathers serve more often as a playmate. Comparisons of infant choices of mother and father, therefore, are likely to vary with the type of activity available in the laboratory setting, with mother versus father being preferred in different activity settings.

Similarly, the *behavior* of the social agents in the laboratory studies has not been systematically examined; instead the adults—whether parents or strangers—have been instructed not to initiate any social interaction with the infant. Recently, investigators have found that infant reactions to strangers vary considerably with the behavior of the stranger; Ross and Goldman (1977), for example, found that infants approached an active friendly stranger more than a passive figure. It would be expected that studies in which fathers and mothers are permitted to play an active eliciting role with their infants would produce greater degrees of father preference than prior studies have yielded. In part, this is due to the fact that fathers often play an active and initiating role under naturalistic home conditions (Lamb, 1977a). In general, the usefulness of these laboratory probes will be enhanced by *systematically* approximating activities and behaviors patterns displayed in real-life environments (cf. Parke, 1978b).

Home Observational Evidence

A number of recent studies have focused on infants' reactions to their mothers and fathers under naturally occurring conditions in the home. The aim—as in the laboratory studies—is to assess the adequacy of Bowlby's assumption concerning infants' preference for their mothers.

In a longitudinal study of infants at 7 to 8 and 12 to 13 months, Lamb (1977a) observed male and female infants in their homes for 1½ to 2 h when both parents and a female stranger were present. The stranger functioned as a guest and interacted with both parents and child. While both parents were preferred to the visitor, the effect was most reliable in the infant's display of attachment behaviors (approach, proximity, reach, touch, seek to be held, fuss). The infants preferred fathers over mothers, as indicated by more frequent display of affiliative behavior (vocalize, smile, look, laugh) toward their fathers. In the home environment, the infants showed no preference for either parent in terms of their display of "attachment" behaviors (fuss, proximity, reach, etc.). As Lamb (1977a) notes, "there was certainly no evidence to support the popular presumption that infants of this age should prefer—indeed be uniquely attached to—their mothers." In a follow-up observational assessment of father-mother-infant interaction, when the infants were 15, 18, 21, and 24 months of age, Lamb (1977b) reported a similar pattern: infants directed more affiliative behaviors (smile, look, laugh, prefer) and attachment behaviors (proximity, touch, approach, fuss, but especially seek to be held, reach) toward fathers than to mothers.

In another naturalistic observational study of children at 12, 20, and 30 months of age in their homes with mother and father, Clarke-Stewart (1977) reported few differences between infant behaviors directed toward mothers and fathers—after controlling for the time each parent was available for interaction. Nor were there marked differences in the children's "attachment" to their mothers and fathers; this was indexed by the reactions of 20-month-old infants to separation and reunion of mother and father in the home environment. No measure of the child's attachment (positive or negative reactions during either brief separation or reunion) differentiated between the children's behavior with mother or father. In fact, the children's reactions to the two parents were highly similar ($N = 0.76$). For both boys and girls, reunion with father was correlated with paternal social stimulation and responsiveness and maternal responsiveness, while reunion with mother was correlated with maternal social stimulation, maternal responsiveness, and paternal play. While the relationships between parental variables and children's reactions to reunion were generally higher for boys than girls, the relationship between father's physical contact and length of interaction and the boy's reunion behavior with the father was strikingly high. In the home as in the laboratory (e.g., Kotelchuck, 1976; Lamb, 1977b), children by 18 or 20 months are attached to *both* mother and father.

Another index of social development used by Clarke-Stewart was the child's reaction to a female stranger in the home at 20 months. "A friendly but unfamiliar woman" interacted with the child in specified ways that included looking, smiling, talking, approaching, playing with a toy, and playing a physical-social game. The impact of the father on the infant's sociability to a stranger varied with sex of infant. Girls who had a highly available father, who frequently engaged them in conversation, showed a high degree of sociability to the stranger. In contrast, for boys, sociability with a stranger was more likely to be associated with a negative—and possibly even punitive—paternal attitude. Both these relationships between father's and children's reactions to strangers were embedded in a context where the behavior of boys and girls was clearly and consistently related to maternal stimulation and responsiveness. This finding is reminiscent of earlier studies that indicate the father dominance and punitiveness combined with positive affection and nurturance facilitates children's use of the father as a model (Biller, 1969; Hetherington, 1965; Hetherington and Frankie, 1967); clearly, information concerning the fathers' sociability would be helpful in interpreting Clarke-Stewart's findings.

These findings concerning the impact of variations in amount and type of father involvement on infants' responsiveness to their fathers are consistent with the results of the earlier Pedersen and Robson (1969) investigation. Although limited by their reliance on maternal interviews to assess father participation, they found a number of interesting relationships. In their 8- to 9-month-old first-born infants, father involvement in routine caretaking, emotional investment in their infant, and the stimulation level of paternal play were positively related to the male infants' attachment to their fathers as assessed by the age of onset and intensity of greeting behavior directed to the fathers. The fathers' irritability level was negatively related to male infants' attachment, while apprehension over well-being was negatively correlated for girls. Measure of availability and time spent in play were not related to infant attachment for infants of either sex. In a later study, which utilized maternal reports of father involvement, Pedersen et al. (1978b) found that 5-month-old male infants who experienced greater amounts of father interaction were more socially responsive. Social development was indexed by a cluster of Bayley Test items such as vocalizing to a social stimulus, making an anticipatory adjustment to being lifted, and enjoying frolic play. Similarly, social responsiveness of the male infants was lower in father-absent than in father-present homes.

In summary, infants are responsive to both fathers and mothers in the home environment, but father involvement is an important determinant of the level of infant responsivity.

Play: A Special Context for Fathers and Infants

As noted earlier, play is an important ingredient of the father-infant relationship. Not only do fathers and mothers differ in their play patterns, infants react differently to mother and father play. Lamb (1976b), in his study of 8- to 13-month-old infants, found that the infants' response to play with their fathers was significantly more positive than play with their mothers.

Consistent with Lamb's observations is Clarke-Stewart's (1977) finding that 20-month-old children were significantly more responsive to playful social interaction initiated by the father than to play initiated by the mother. At 2½ years of age, children were more cooperative, close, involved, excited, and interested in play with their fathers. Over two-thirds of the children chose to play with their fathers first in a choice situation and displayed a stronger preference for him as a playmate. Just as the structured/unstructured distinction is important in the "attachment" studies, a similar distinction is useful in the play sphere. Although there were clear mother-father differences in the play-probe sessions, fewer differences in infant initiations occurred in unstructured home observations (Clarke-Stewart, 1977).

Just as fathers and mothers behave differentially toward male and female infants, the infants, in turn, react differently to their mothers and fathers. In the Lamb studies (1977a, b) boys were in proximity of, approached, and fussed to their fathers more than girls; female infants, on the other hand, were in proximity of and fussed to their mothers more than the boys, while they approached their mothers about as often as did boys. Spelke et al. (1973) observed that 1-year-old infants vocalized more to the same- than to the opposite-sexed parent, while Ban and Lewis (1974) found that 1-year-old boys look more at their fathers than at their mothers. Finally, Lynn and Cross (1974) found that 2-year-old boys prefer to play with their fathers rather than their mothers; girls, on the other hand, show a shift between 2 and 4 years of age to preferring mother as a play partner.

In summary, evidence from a variety of settings (home and lab) as well as a range of cultures indicates that quality of father-infant interaction has a clear impact on the infant's developing social responsiveness. Both mothers and fathers contribute to this development but in different ways: paternal physical-playful stimulation complements mothers' verbal interaction. More attention needs to be given to delineating these complementary contributions of mothers and fathers to the development of early social competence. And the differential impact of fathers and mothers on boys and girls requires further attention; the same-sex hypotheses, however, appears to have merit, with boys, in particular, showing greater responsivity to their fathers from the 1st year of life.

In future research, the range of social assessment situations needs to be expanded. To date there has been an excessive reliance on a few structured social situations (e.g., Ainsworth's separation situation) and a few social agents (e.g., parents or strange adults). Of particular importance will be the examination of the impact of variation in father-infant (and mother-infant) interaction patterns on the development of infant-infant interaction patterns—sibs as well as other young children. The recent work by Lieberman (1977) on the relationships between mother-infant relationship and friendship patterns with peers needs to be extended to include the father-infant relationship as an antecedent of later peer relations.

FATHER-INFANT INTERACTION AND INFANT COGNITIVE DEVELOPMENT

In spite of the extensive documentation of the course of early cognitive development (Lewis, 1976; McCall, 1976) and the role of maternal influence in infant intellectual progress (Yarrow et al., 1975), there has been little attention paid to the unique role of the father in fostering the infant's cognitive development. To date, efforts have focused on the impact of the father on the intellectual achievement of pre-school children (Baumrind, 1971; Radin, 1972, 1973) or adolescents (Heilbrun, 1973; Bowerman and Elder, 1964). A majority of early studies approached the issue of the father's impact on his child's cognitive progress through the study of father absence (Biller, 1974, 1976); more recently efforts have focused directly on the father's current contribution to the child's intellectual development. This research indicates that fathers do play a significant role in early cognitive development. Paternal involvement and nurturance, in particular, are associated with cognitive competence, but boys are more generally affected than girls (Radin, 1976). Fathers may influence female intellectual development, but possibly in a less direct fashion through changes in the mother-daughter relationship—a further reminder of the importance of viewing the family as a social system. The underlying assumption of these studies is that the current interaction patterns are a result of the cumulative impact of earlier father-child interaction patterns. In combination with the findings from studies that indicate that father absence is most damaging if the child is under 5 years of age, the importance of examining the effects of father-infant interaction on cognitive development is clearly established. Next we turn to a review of this evidence in order to determine whether father involvement in infancy affects infant cognitive development or whether the father's impact is evident only in post-infancy periods.

To answer this question, Pedersen et al. (1978b) examined the impact of father absence on the intellectual development of 5- to 6-month-old lower-class Black infants. Male infants from father-absent families were lower on the Bayley Mental Development Index than male infants from intact families. Similarly these infants from father-absent homes spent less time manipulating a novel object—a measure related to later cognitive development (Yarrow et al., 1974). Using a second measure—the amount of father-infant interaction in order to provide a more differentiated examination of father involvement—these investigators found a similar pattern of relationships. Bayley mental scores and preference for novel stimuli were both correlated positively with the amount of father contact. However, neither father absence nor amount of father interaction was related to the cognitive development of the female infants. In contrast to the vast majority of earlier studies of father absence (cf. Biller, 1974), Pedersen et al. examined the possibility that father-absent households were significantly smaller than father-present households. If this is true, the father may merely be another source of stimulation to the infant. However, Pedersen et al. found no difference between father-absent and father-present infants in the number of household members (2.8 and 2.9 for the two groups). "With the number of people who are potential sources of stimulation comparable, it appears that the father has an impact that is qualitatively different from other adults" (Pedersen et al., 1978, p. 9). In addition, these investigators presented preliminary evidence that mothers' behavior in father-present and father-absent homes was similar, which suggests that it is the father's direct interactions with his male infant that is responsible for the observed "father" effects, or cognitive development.

In a study of 16- and 22-month-old infants, Clarke-Stewart (1977) found that it was the father's ability to engage the child in play in the structured interaction context, his positive attitude toward the child (derived from observer rating scales), the father's anticipation of the child's independence, and the duration of his interactions with the child in the unstructured natural observations in the home environment that best related to infant Bayley scores. In contrast, for mothers, verbal and material stimulation and the expression of positive emotion were predictive of children's cognitive development. In addition, the mother's expectations concerning the ages at which certain skills should be mastered was positively related to intellectual competence. As in earlier studies, quality, not quantity of interaction, was the important predictor of cognitive development. In light of these paternal and maternal predictors it is interesting to note that fathers' social physical play is highly related to mothers' verbal stimulation and their toy play. As Clarke-Stewart notes,

These maternal behaviors have been found in other research with slightly younger children to be central components of a pattern of so-called "optimal maternal care," while mother's social physical play has not (Clarke-Stewart, 1973). The correlations found in the present study seem to suggest, therefore, that the comparable role for a father to go along with (be married to) an "optimal mother" centrally involves social-physical play. [1977, p. 18]

Just as there were marked differences in the impact of fathers and mothers on their sons' and daughters' social development, there are similar effects in the intellectual sphere as well (Radin, 1976). While no simple picture emerges, indications of same-sex influence are evident. In the Clarke-Stewart (1977) investigation, the amount, quality, and prominence of fathers' play were more highly related to boys' development than to girls' development; but the father-son link was not found for independence-granting (expecting independence and acceptance rating), which was part of the father's relation with both boys and girls. Similarly, maternal physical contact and play were positively related to boys' cognitive development.

Fathers affect their daughters' intellectual development during the 2nd year, but in different ways than they affect their sons. Instead of physical play, verbal interaction, including talks, praise, expressions of positive emotion, and responsiveness to their daughters' social behavior, were strongly associated with girls' intellectual development. For mothers, similar kinds of variables predicted daughter cognitive competence—namely, verbal stimulation and intellectual acceleration; these relationships were stronger for girls than boys. This pattern suggests that greater attention should be addressed to the types of stimulation provided by different parents in order to understand intellectual achievement; it is physical stimulation for boys and verbal stimulation for girls that is most closely associated with cognitive development. The same-sex hypothesis may have merit simply because fathers tend to engage in more physical playful behavior than mothers while mothers may provide more verbal stimulation.

Although it is typically assumed that parent-infant relationships are bidirectional, rarely is this assumption empirically evaluated. In her study, Clarke-Stewart examined the directionality issue by a series of cross-lag correlations between the child and parent measures at two time points—15 and 30 months. Does parental behavior at 15 months predict child competence at 30 months or does the relationship proceed in the opposite direction? For mothers, verbal stimulation of girls and material stimulation of boys predicted subsequent intellectual competence. For fathers, it is the opposite direction of influence; children's superior cognitive competence at 15 months predicted that the father would be more likely to talk and play socially with girls and play with toys with boys at 30 months. "The 'chain of family influence' that affects children's intellectual competence may be from mother, to child, to father . . . the mother stimulates the child's development by talking and playing with objects and the child's competence then is reacted to by the father, inducing father-child conversation and play" (Clarke-Stewart, 1977, p. 35). However, the picture may be even more complex if the time-lagged correlations between mothers' and fathers' behavior for these variables are examined. The father's talking and playing with the child at one age was highly predictive of the mother's talking and playing with the child 10 months later. A chain in which mother influences child, who in turn affects father, who in turn modifies mother, suggests, at least, that a systems analysis in which the triadic nature of family interaction is necessary in order to represent the complexity of early parent-infant relationships.

This study is valuable not only by demonstrating that intellectual competence is affected by both fathers and mothers, but in illustrating the necessity of considering the complex fashion in which mother, father and infant each influence each other and the course of infant development.

In summary, many of the same trends that have been discovered in studies with older children are evident in these investigations of younger infants. Fathers do play an influential role in their infant's cognitive development—from a *very* early age; the task remains to detail the mechanisms through which this influence is mediated, which cognitive capacities are most affected by fathers, and at what ages these effects occur.

CULTURAL SUPPORT SYSTEMS FOR FATHERS

An important task is to provide cultural supports for fathering activities. First, there needs to be an increase in opportunities for learning fathering skills. These supports can assume a variety of forms such as the provision of both pre- and postpartum training classes for fathers to both learn and practice caretaking skills, and to learn about normal infant development (Biller and Meredith, 1974). Parenthood training, however, need not wait until pregnancy or childbirth. As many have advocated both early (PTA, 1925, cited by Schlossman, 1976) and more recently (Hawkins, 1971; Sawin and Parke, 1976), parenthood training, including information about infant development, infant care, as well as the economic realities of child-rearing should be provided in high school or even at an earlier age in light of the increasing number of teenage pregnancies. As noted elsewhere (Parke,1978c; Parke and Collmer, 1975) such training would also aid in the prevention of child abuse.

Second, there needs to be increased opportunities to practice and implement these skills. To provide the opportunity to share in the early caretaking of the infant, paternity leaves should be given wider support. These leaves could be usefully extended to the pregnancy period to permit the father to attend classes and to share in obstetrician visits with the mother. Other shifts in societal arrangements such as shorter work weeks, flexible working hours, and split jobs, whereby a male and female share the same position, are all changes that will increase the potential participation of males in fathering.

Another positive change involves modification of maternity ward visiting arrangements to permit fathers to have more extended contact with the newborn infants. To date, father-infant interaction in the newborn period is largely under institutional control, and as a result it is frequently hospital policy rather than father interest that determines the degree of father-newborn involvement. Although some countries are still highly restrictive of father-infant visitation, such as Russia, other countries such as Denmark and Sweden encourage father involvement in labor and delivery, and support frequent visitation during the immediate postpartum period (Klaus and Kennell, 1976). In the United States, there is an increasing trend toward greater father participation. For example, in New York City, 60% of the hospitals permit father-infant visitation (*New York Times,* December 5, 1975). As Klaus and Kennell (1976) have documented, opportunities for early contact in the postpartum period with the infant may alter mother-infant interaction patterns. Some preliminary evidence from Sweden (Lind, 1974) suggests that a parallel effect may hold for fathers as well. Fathers who were provided the opportunity to learn and practice basic caretaking skills during the postpartum hospital period were more involved in the care of the infant and in household tasks at 3 months in the home. More recent evidence of the impact of hospital-centered intervention for fathers comes from a recent investigation by Parke et al. (1979). Fathers viewed a film that portrayed other male caretakers engaged in play and feeding and diapering. In contrast to a control group who saw no film, the fathers exposed to this 15-min film increased the amount of feeding and diapering that they engaged in at home at three months. However, the effect held only for fathers of boys; fathers of girls were unaffected by the intervention. This same-sex effect is similar to other reports of greater father involvement with sons than daughters. In light of these demonstrations, it would appear that opportunities for fathers to take an active role with their newborn infants is an important antecedent to fuller actualization of nurturant and caretaking capacities in post-hospital contexts. These initial interactions with the newborn may serve as the basis for the subsequent formation of strong attachment bonds between father and infant. However, this remains a working hypothesis in wait of a direct and adequate empirical test.

As Zelazo et al. (1977) have recently demonstrated, efforts to modify father-infant interaction need not be restricted to young infants. These investigators selected 20 very low-interacting fathers and their 12-month-old first-born sons. These parents did little caretaking or playing and were present only occasionally when their child was awake. Twelve fathers received an intervention involving playing with their infants for ½ h/day for 4 weeks in their homes. To facilitate the play interaction, a schedule of games and toys were provided for the father. Using a social learning strategy (cf. Bandura, 1977), the experimenters both demonstrated the games, toys, and styles of interaction and coached the fathers in these activities prior to the intervention period. A control group of eight low-interacting fathers received no intervention. To assess the impact of the intervention on the infant's behavior, a parent-infant laboratory was held before and after the training period. This consisted of a 20-min free-play period, with both parents in the room reading, followed by a series of maternal and paternal departures. In comparison to the control group, infants in the experimental group increased their interaction with their fathers in the free-play session; these infant boys looked more at their fathers and initiated more interaction with them. Separation protest was not affected by the experimental intervention. This was surprising in view of earlier reports that as father involvement increased, separation upset in the presence of a stranger lessened (Kotelchuck, 1972; Spelke et al., 1973). Although it was a pioneering study, there were a number of limitations. First, the fathers were instructed not to initiate interactions in the lab sessions, and so it is unclear whether there were increases in father behaviors directed to their infants. Second, it is unfortunate that these investigators did not monitor the amount of interaction between fathers and infants in their homes as a follow-up to their intervention program. In spite of these limitations, the investigation underlines the modifiability of the infant-father relationship. Third, it serves as a corrective reminder of the fact that modification of early social interaction patterns are not necessarily limited to a particular "critical" period. As both Zelazo and his colleagues and many earlier intervention (Rheingold, 1956; Skeels, 1966) studies have demonstrated, infant responsiveness can be modified at a variety of age levels. A similar caution applies to the development of parental responsiveness to infants. Although the early contact studies (cf. Klaus and Kennell, 1976) suggest the importance of the immediate postpartum period for the facilitation of parental responsiveness to their infants, it should be recalled that adoption studies indicate that parents can learn to develop satisfactory relationships with infants and children who are adopted at older ages. The capacity of both parents and infants for continual adaptation to shifting social circumstances probably overrides the paramount importance of any single time period for the formation of social relationships (Cairns, 1977).

Considerable care must be taken in the implementation of these support systems; the important issue of parent's rights needs to be considered. The infliction of these supports, with their implicit scenario of the liberated family, who endorses egalitarian in contrast to more traditional family organization on all families is not the aim. The goal should be to provide as much support as the couple's ideology and role definition dictates is necessary for the successful fulfillment of these functions. Too often "more" is equated with "improvement"; however, in many families, increased father participation may cause conflict and disruption as a result of the threat to well-established and satisfying role definitions. Intervention, therefore, should be sensitively geared to the needs of individual families where the dynamics and ideology of the couple are given primary recognition.

SOME REMAINING ISSUES AND FUTURE TRENDS

Toward an Androgynous View of Parenting

It has been common to fail to differentiate biological sex from sex roles, and thus to treat sex of parent as a dichotomous variable. Recent research indicates that individuals differ in their rigidity of sex-role attitudes and that it may be more useful to classify both males and females along a continuum of sex roles. According to Bem's (1974) recent conceptualization of androgyny, some individuals are not rigidly masculine or feminine in their self-defined sex roles, but integrate aspects of both masculine and feminine sex roles into their sex-role concept. In a recent study with college students, Bem et al. (1976) compared androgynous individuals with others who rated themselves as masculine or feminine. When observed while interacting with a 4- to 7-month-old infant, the students who were rated androgynous and feminine displayed more nurturant behavior toward the infant as indexed by smiling, talking, kissing, and touching the baby than students rated as masculine—regardless of their biological sex. These results suggest that the biological sex of the caretaker may be less important than their sex-role definition.

Just as self-definitions of sex role are important determinants of adult-infant interaction, possibly the amount and kind of prior experience with infants is another factor that may override biological sex boundaries. Differences between fathers' and mothers' interaction patterns may be due, in part, to the differential amount of time and type of activities that male and female parents typically spend with their infants. Recent trends indicate that more fathers are serving as primary caretakers for their infants (Orthner et al., 1976; Mendes, 1976). Comparisons of fathers and mothers who act as primary caregivers with fathers who are secondary caregivers may provide some clarification of this issue. In a recent study, Field (1978) compared three types of caretakers: mothers and fathers who were primary caretakers with fathers who were secondary caretakers. Using the same face-to-face interaction situation that was described earlier (Yogman et al., 1977a), these investigators found a variety of interesting differences across the three groups of parents. First, fathers engaged in less holding of the infants' limbs, and in more game-playing and poking than mothers, which is consistent with the earlier findings of Yogman et al. (1977a). However, primary caretakers—both mothers and fathers—exhibited less laughing, and more smiling, imitative grimaces, and high-pitched vocalizations than did secondary-caretaker fathers. In short, fathers who were primary caretakers shared some of the same interactional qualities as mothers who assumed the same level of caretaking responsibility. It is unfortunate that Field did not include a comparison group of working mothers, who were comparable to the secondary caretaking fathers. Would these mothers look more like the traditional father in terms of play patterns? Although it is intriguing to speculate that experience with infants is the critical factor that results in the increased similarity between primary mothers and fathers, further information about these fathers' sex-role attitudes (i.e., Bem's androgyny index) in contrast to the sex-role attitudes of the secondary fathers is necessary to adequately interpret these data. Perhaps sex-role attitudes and interaction patterns shift as a result of exposure to infants or possibly Field's primary male caretakers already had sex-role attitudes that served to shape and direct their degree of infant involvement—even before exposure to the infant.

Monitoring Secular Trends

In any case, these studies argue for further exploration of the impact of shifting secular arrangements, such as work schedules, on male and female interaction patterns with infants. Instead of our continuing reliance on terms, such as "mothers" and "fathers," perhaps it will be useful to replace these terms by a conceptualization of a continuum of caretaking styles. Individuals would be organized along the continuum in terms of the quality and quantity of their caretaking activity, which, in turn, would vary with variables such as cultural attitudes and prior experience with infants and children. Perhaps, it is less important *who* plays *which* role in relation to the infant; rather it is only important that the infant experience a variety or range of social experiences. Clearly, little is known about the impact of these shifting family arrangements, in which traditional male and female roles are either equalized or reversed on infant social, sex-role, or cognitive development.

Nor do we know about the processes by which secular shifts affect parenting patterns. Secular change is complex and clearly does not impact on all individuals equally or on all behavior patterns to the same extent. In fact, it is a serious oversimplification to assume that general societal trends can isomorphically be applied to individual families. An important task for students of social behavior is to develop a taxonomy of influence sources which permits more precise prediction of how secular change influences current family attitudes and behaviors. Second it is important to determine which behaviors are most susceptible to secular change. For example, the structural dynamics of early interaction (cf. Stern, 1974; Brazelton et al., 1974) may be less susceptible to secular change than quantitative aspects of early caretaking that define parental roles. However, as the Field study suggests, even these aspects of early parent-infant interaction may shift as a result of increased father participation in infant care. Finally, by explicitly recognizing that the current patterns of father-infant interaction are highly susceptible to secular trends, one of our tasks is to consistently monitor changes in father-infant interaction patterns across time. Eventually we may be able to not only describe the changes but isolate the laws that govern the process of change in social interaction patterns (Parke, 1976).

A Sociobiological View of Parenting

In spite of our arguments concerning the limitations involved in organizing our conceptual discussions of parent-infant relationships around biological sex, it is premature to ignore the implications of a biosocial perspective of parenting. Almost no information at the human level is available concerning the role of hormonal or physiological factors in mediating reactions to infants or to the readiness to undertake caretaking and nurturant activities. Nor is there any information about the impact of caretaking experience on hormonal levels in males (or females). As recent advances in endocrinology indicate, relationships between differing levels of a hormone and behavior need not necessarily imply that the hormones are influencing the behavior patterns. It is possible that the behavior may alter the hormonal secretion levels (Astwood, 1972). For example, are there shifts in hormonal levels in a male as a result of his wife's pregnancy or as an outcome of being present at childbirth or as a consequence of different degrees of contact with his infant or different levels of involvement in infant caretaking? Are there relationships between sex-role attitudes, such as androgyny measures (Bem, 1974), and hormonal levels? Do shifts in one sphere result in shifts in the other domain? Complex research designs in which multiple assessments of hormones, sex-role attitudes, and social interaction patterns are simultaneously and repeatedly measured over time are necessary to adequately address these types of questions. In spite of our enthusiasm for socioenvironmental explanations of parenting, studies of this type are necessary to determine what role biological factors play in interaction with socioenvironmental variables in modulating the behavior of males and females in infant-interaction contexts.

Developmental Changes in Father-Infant Interaction: An Unsolved Problem

Much remains to be determined about the nature and course of father-infant interaction. First, more detailed assessment of the developmental changes that occur over the first 2 years is required. At present, there is only scattered evidence concerning the description of the developmental shifts in father-infant interaction—as a function of changes in the social and cognitive capacities of the infant. This will require the simultaneous assessment of infant competencies—outside the interaction context as well as measures of father-infant interaction. Similarly, how do changes in infant cognitive and social development alter paternal sex-role attitudes and paternal behavior?

Perhaps the most urgent conceptual problem that faces researchers and theoreticians in the area of early social development is how to adequately represent the changing nature of social-interaction patterns. It is no longer adequate simply either to describe differences over time or to search for simple continuities between one time point and another. Rather, an approach that recognizes that the behavioral patterns that characterize the individual at any point in time are constantly undergoing revision and reorganization is required. Similarly, the interaction patterns that characterize the mother-infant, father-infant, and mother-father dyad, as well as the nuclear family triad, are susceptible to shifts in organization across time.

This process of reorganization is most clearly seen in studies of how the couple adapts to the birth of a first infant. Although often viewed as a "crisis" (Le Masters, 1957), more recent conceptualizations suggest a more sophisticated and complex view of this event. As Cowan et al. (1978) note,

the birth of a baby is one facet of a complex process of disequilibrating shifts in identity, role behavior and communication patterns . . . Developmental theories (Freud, 1936; Piaget, 1967) suggest that disequilibrium may indeed induce stress, crisis and even dysfunction. But these theories also suggest that some disequilibrium is *necessary as a condition for developmental growth*. [p. 7; emphasis in original]

Whether or not the disequilibrium imposed on a couple will produce growth depends on a variety of factors, including the characteristics of the infant, their own role definitions, and their own willingness to adapt and change in the face of the shifting demands imposed by a new family member. Any model of adaptation is repeated across time, as characteristics of the developing infant change and as the contextual restraints shift. Just as Bower (1974) indicates that individual behavior systems reorganize themselves in a systematic fashion at different time points, it would be surprising if social behavior systems (e.g., the family) did not follow a similar pattern of repeated organization, disorganization, and change.

On the Need for Multiple Methodological Strategies

It is likely that no single methodological strategy will suffice in order to understand the development of father-infant interaction. Instead a wide range of both designs, data-collection, and analyses strategies are necessary (Parke, 1978b). To date, however, little information is available concerning the interrelationships across different levels of analyses. For example, what is the relationship between the microanalytic levels of analysis and coarser measure of interaction, such as time sampling or global ratings? Similarly, greater attention needs to be paid to the role of context in determining father-infant interaction. How do father-infant interaction patterns shift across lab and home settings and across play and caretaking contexts?

Finally, it is important to consider the social context as well as the physical setting. Just as our prior exclusive emphasis on mother-infant interaction was myopic, repeating our historical error by an equally restrictive focus on fathers and infants would be equally unfortunate. As repeatedly demonstrated in this chapter, father-infant interaction is often only fully appreciated when fathers are viewed as part of a larger social network. Although this will typically mean viewing fathers as part of a nuclear family system, there is no need to restrict ourselves to the family. Single fathers, for example, may be more directly embedded in a community-based social network, a larger social system than the traditional nuclear family.

In conclusion, fathers are clearly no longer forgotten. Nor is Margaret Mead's famous claim that "fathers are a biological necessity, but a social accident" any longer valid. Rather, fathers, as a member of the family network, play an important, active, and distinctive role in infant social, emotional, and cognitive development.

BIBLIOGRAPHY

Abelin, E. L. Some further observations and comments on the earliest role of the father. *International Journal of Psychoanalysis,* 1975, **56**, 293–302.

Ahammer, I. M. Social learning theory as a framework for the study of adult personality development. In P. Baltes and K. Schaie (eds.), *Life-Span Developmental Psychology: Personality and Socialization.* New York: Academic, 1973.

Ainsworth, M. D. *Infancy in Uganda: Infant Care and the Growth of Love.* Baltimore: Johns Hopkins, 1967.

Ainsworth, M. D., and Bell, S. M. Attachment, exploration and separation: Illustrated by the behavior of one-year-olds in a strange situation. *Child Development,* 1970, **41**, 49–67.

Ainsworth, M. D. The development of infant-mother attachment. In B. M. Caldwell and H. N. Ricciuiti (eds.), *Review of Child Development Research,* Vol. 3. Chicago: University of Chicago, 1973.

Anderson, B. J., and Standley, K. A methodology for observation of the childbirth environment. Paper presented to the American Psychological Association, Washington, D.C., September 1976.

Arbeit, S. A. A study of women during their first pregnancy. Unpublished Ph.D. dissertation, Yale University, 1975.

Arnold, R., Bulatao, R., Buripakdi, C., Ching, B. J., Fawcett, J. T., Iritani, T., Lee, S. J., and Wu, T. S. *The Value of Children: Introduction and Comparative Analysis,* Vol. 1. Honolulu: East-West Population Institute, 1975.

Astwood, E. (ed.). *Recent Progress in Hormone Research.* New York: Academic, 1972.

Ban, P., and Lewis, M. Mothers and fathers, girls and boys: Attachment behavior in the one-year-old. *Merrill-Palmer Quarterly,* 1974, **20**, 195–204.

Bandura, A. *Social Learning Theory.* Englewood, N.J.: Prentice-Hall, 1977.

Barnard, K. Unpublished report, School of Nursing, University of Washington, 1976.

Baumrind, D. Current patterns of parental authority. *Developmental Psychology Monographs,* 1971, **4**, 1–103.

Bell, R. Q. A reinterpretation of the direction of effects in studies of socialization. *Psychological Review,* 1968, **75**, 81–95.

Bell, R. Q. Contributions of human infants to caregiving and social interaction. In M. Lewis and L. A. Rosenblum (eds.), *The Effect of the Infant on Its Caregiver.* New York: Wiley, 1974.

Bem, S. L. The measurement of psychological androgyny. *Journal of Consulting and Clinical Psychology,* 1974, **42**, 155–162.

Bem, S. L., Martyna, W., and Watson, C. Sex typing and androgyny: Further explorations of the expressive domain. *Journal of Personality and Social Psychology,* 1976, **34**, 1016–1023.

Bernal, J. F., and Richards, M. P. M. What can the zoologist tell us about human development? In S. A. Barnett (ed.), *Ethology and Development*. London: Heinemann, 1973.

Biller, H. B. Father dominance and sex role development in kindergarten-age boys. *Developmental Psychology,* 1969, **1**, 87–94.

Biller, H. B. *Father, Child and Sex Role*. Lexington, Mass.: Heath, 1971.

Biller, H. B. *Paternal Deprivation,* Lexington, Mass.: Heath, 1974.

Biller, H. B. The father and personality development: Paternal deprivation and sex-role development. In M. E. Lamb (ed.), *The Role of the Father in Child Development*. New York: Wiley, 1976.

Biller, H. B., and Meredith, D. L. *Father Power*. New York: McKay, 1974.

Borussard, E. R., and Hartner, M. S. S. Further consideration regarding maternal perception of the first born. In J. Hellmuth (ed.), *Exceptional Infant: Studies in Abnormalities,* Vol. 2. New York: Brunner/Mazel, 1971.

Bower, T. G. R. Repetition in human development. *Merrill-Palmer Quarterly,* 1974, **20**, 303–318.

Bowerman, C. E., and Elder, G. H. Variations in adolescent perception of family power structure. *American Sociological Review,* 1964, **29**, 551–567.

Bowlby, J. *Maternal Care and Mental Health*. World Health Organization, 1951.

Bowlby, J. *Attachment and Loss,* Vol. 1. *Attachment*. New York: Basic Books, 1969.

Brackbill, Y. Extinction of the smiling response in infants as a function of reinforcement schedule. *Child Development,* 1958, **29**, 1–12.

Brazelton, T. B., Koslowski, B., and Main, M. The origin of reciprocity: The early mother-infant interaction. In M. Lewis and L. A. Rosenblum (eds.), *The Effect of the Infant on Its Caregiver*. New York: Wiley, 1974.

Brazelton, T. B., Tronick, E., Adamson, L., Als, H., and Wise, S. Early mother-infant reciprocity. In M. A. Hofer (ed.), *Parent-Infant Interaction*. Amsterdam: Elsevier, 1975.

Bretheron, I., and Ainsworth, M. D. Responses of one-year-olds to a stranger in a strange situation. In M. Lewis and L. A. Rosenblum (eds.), *The Origins of Fear*. New York: Wiley, 1974.

Bronfenbrenner, U. Developmental research, public policy and the ecology of childhood. *Child Development,* 1974, **45**, 1–5.

Cairns, R. B. Attachment and dependency: A synthesis. In J. L. Gewirtz (ed.), *Attachment and Dependency*. Washington, D.C.: Winston, 1972.

Cairns, R. B. Beyond social attachment: The dynamics of interactional development. In T. A. Alloway, P. Pliner, and L. Krames (eds.), *Attachment Behavior*. New York: Plenum, 1977.

Cassel, T. Z. K., and Sander, L. W. Neonatal recognition processes and attachment: The masking experiment. Paper presented at the Society for Research in Child Development, Denver, April 1975.

Chamove, A., Harlow, H. F., and Mitchell, G. D. Sex differences in the infant-directed behavior of preadolescent rhesus monkeys. *Child Development,* 1967, **38**, 329–335.

Clarke-Stewart, K. A. Interactions between mothers and their young children: Characteristics and consequences. *Monographs of the Society for Research in Child Development,* 1973, **38** (6–7, Ser. 153).

Clarke-Stewart, K. A. The father's impact on mother and child. Paper presented at the biennial meeting of the Society for Reseach in Child Development, New Orleans, March 1977.

Cohen, L. J., and Campos, J. J. Father, mother and stranger as elicitors of attachment behaviors in infancy. *Developmental Psychology,* 1974, **10**, 146–154.

Condry, J., and Condry, S. Sex differences: A study of the eye of the beholder. *Child Development,* 1976, **47**, 812–819.

Coombs, C. H., Coombs, L. C., and McClelland, G. H. Preference scales for number and sex of children. *Population Studies,* 1975, **29**, 273–298.

Cowan, C., Cowan, P. A., Coie, L., and Coie, J. D. Becoming a family: The impact of a first child's birth on the couple's relationship. In L. Newman and W. Miller (eds.), *The First Child and Family Formation*. Carolina Population Center, The University of North Carolina at Chapel Hill, 1978.

DeFrain, T. D. Androgynous parenting. Paper presented at the International Society for the Study of Behavioral Development, Guilford, Surrey, England, 1975.

DeVore, I. Mother-infant relations in free ranging baboons. In H. L. Rheingold (ed.), *Maternal Behavior in Mammals*. New York: Wiley, 1963.

Fagot, B. I. Sex differences in toddler's behavior and parental reaction. *Developmental Psychology,* 1974, **10**, 554–558.

Feiring, C., and Taylor, J. The influence of the infant and secondary parent on maternal behavior: Toward a social systems view of infant attachment. *Merrill-Palmer Quarterly,* 1977, in press.

Feldman, S. S., and Ingham, M. E. Attachment behavior: A validation study in two age groups. *Child Development,* 1975, **46**, 319–330.

Field, T. Interaction patterns of primary versus secondary caretaker fathers. *Developmental Psychology,* 1978, **14**, 183–185.

Freud, S. (1923) *New Introductory Lectures on Psychoanalysis*. New York: Norton, 1933a.

Freud, S. (1925) The passing of the oedipus-complex. In *Collected Papers,* Vol. II. London: Hogarth, 1933b.

Friedl, E. *Women and Men: An Anthropologist's View*. New York: Holt, Rinehart & Winston, 1975.

Gewirtz, J. L. On the selection and use of attachment and dependence indices. In J. L. Gewirtz (ed.), *Attachment and Dependency*. Washington, D.C.: Winston, 1972.

Gewirtz, H. B., and Gewirtz, J. L. Visiting and caretaking patterns for kibbutz infants: age and sex trends. *American Journal of Orthopsychiatry,* 1968, **38**, 427–443.

Goodenough, E. W. Interest in persons as an aspect of sex difference in the early years. *Genetic Psychology Monographs,* 1957, **55**, 287–323.

Greenberg, M., and Morris, N. Engrossment: The newborn's impact upon the father. *American Journal of Orthopsychiatry,* 1974, **44**, 520–531.

Harlow, H. F. The nature of love. *American Psychologist,* 1958, **13**, 673–685.

Hartup, W. W., and Lempers, J. Attachment: A problem for life-span psychology. In P. Baltes and K. Schaie (eds.), *Life-Span Developmental Psychology: Personality and Socialization*. New York: Academic, 1973.

Hawkins, R. P. Universal parenthood training: A proposal for preventative mental health. *Educational Technology,* 1971, **11**, 28–35.

Heilbrun, A. B., Jr. *Aversive Maternal Control*. New York: Wiley, 1973.

Henneborn, W. J., and Cogan, R. The effect of husband participation in reported pain and the probability of medication during labor and birth. *Journal of Psychosomatic Research,* 1975, **19**, 215–222.

Herzog, E., and Sudia, C. Children in fatherless families. In B. M. Cladwell and H. N. Ricciuti (eds.), *Review of Child Development Research,* Vol. 3. Chicago: University of Chicago, 1973.

Hetherington, E. M. A developmental study of the effects of sex of the dominant parent on sex role preference, identification and imitation in children. *Journal of Personality and Social Psychology,* 1965, **2**, 188–194.

Hetherington, E. M. Effects of paternal absence on sex-typed behaviors in negro and white preadolescent males. *Journal of Personality and Social Psychology,* 1966, **4**, 87–91.

Hetherington, E. M. and Deur, J. The effects of father absence on child development. In W. W. Hartup (Ed.), *The Young Child* (Vol. 2). Washington D.C.: National Association for the Education of Young Children, 1972.

Hetherington, E. M., and Frankie, G. Effects of paternal dominance warmth and conflict on imitation in children. *Journal of Personality and Social Psychology, 1967,* **6**, 119–125.

Hirschman, C., and Sweet, J. A. Social background and breastfeeding among American mothers. *Social Biology,* 1974, **21**, 39–57.

Hoffman, L. W. Changes in family roles, socialization and sex differences. *American Psychologist,* 1977, **32**, 644–58.

Hoffman, L. W. and Nye, F. I. *Working Mothers.* San Francisco: Jossey-Bass, 1974.

Hunt, J. McV. *Intelligence and Experience.* New York: Ronald, 1961.

Johnson, M. M. Sex role learning in the nuclear family. *Child Development,* 1963, **34**, 315–333.

Josselyn, I. M. Cultural forces, motherliness and fatherliness. *American Journal of Orthopsychiatry,* 1956, **26**, 264–271.

Kessen, W., Haith, M. M., and Salapatek, P. H. Infancy. In P. H. Mussen (ed.), *Manual of Child Psychology.* New York: Wiley, 1970.

Klaus, M. H., and Kennell, J. H. *Parent-Infant Bonding.* St. Louis: Mosby, 1976.

Kotelchuck, M. The nature of the child's tie to his father. Unpublished Ph.D. dissertation, Harvard University, 1972.

Kotelchuck, M. The infant's relationship to the father: Experimental evidence. In M. E. Lamb (ed.), *The Role of the Father in Child Development.* New York: Wiley, 1976, 329–344.

Lamb, M. E. The role of the father: An overview. In M. E. Lamb (ed.), *The Role of the Father in Child Development.* New York: Wiley, 1976a.

Lamb, M. E. Interactions between eight-month-old children and their fathers and mothers. In M. E. Lamb (ed.), *The Role of the Father in Child Development.* New York: Wiley, 1976b.

Lamb, M. E. Twelve-month olds and their parents: Interaction in a laboratory playroom. *Developmental Psychology,* 1976c, **12**, 237–244.

Lamb, M. E. Effects of stress and cohort on mother- and father-infant interaction. *Developmental Psychology,* 1976d, **12**, 435–443.

Lamb, M. E. Father-infant and mother-infant interaction in the first year of life. *Child Development,* 1977a, **48**, 167–181.

Lamb, M. E. The development of mother-infant and father-infant attachments in the second year of life. *Developmental Psychology,* 1977b, **13**, 639–649.

Lansky, L. M. The family structure also affects the model: Sex role attitudes in parents of preschool children. *Merrill-Palmer Quarterly,* 1967, **13**, 139–150.

Le Masters, E. E. Parenthood as crisis. *Marriage and Family Living,* 1957, **19**, 352–355.

Lester, B. M., Kotelchuck, M., Spelke, E., Sellers, J. J., and Klein, R. E. Separation protest in Guatemalan infants: Cross-cultural and cognitive findings. *Developmental Psychology,* 1974, **10**, 79–85.

Lewis, M., and Rosenblum, L. A. (eds.), *The Effect of the Infant on Its Caregiver.* New York: Wiley, 1974.

Lewis, M., and Weinraub, M. The father's role in the infant's social network. In M. E. Lamb (ed.), *The Role of the Father in Child Development.* New York: Wiley, 1976, 157–184.

Lewis, M. (ed.). *Origins of Intelligence: Infancy and Early Childhood.* New York: Plenum, 1976.

Lieberman, A. F. Preschoolers' competence with a peer: Influence of attachment and social experience. *Child Development,* 1977, **48,** 1277–1287.

Lind, R. Observations after delivery of communications between mother-infant-father. Paper presented at the International Congress of Pediatrics. Buenos Aires, October 1974.

Lott, D., and Rosenblatt, J. In Foss, B. M. (eds.), *Determinants of Infant Behavior* (IV). London: Methuen, 1969.

Lynn, D. B. *The Father: His Role in Child Development.* Monterey, Calif.: Brooks/Cole, 1974.

Lynn, D. B., and Cross, A. R. Parent preference of preschool children. *Journal of Marriage and the Family,* 1974, **36,** 555–559.

Maccoby, E. E., and Jacklin, C. N. *The Psychology of Sex Differences.* Stanford: Stanford University, 1974.

Marfarlane, A. *The Psychology of Childbirth.* Cambridge, Mass.: Harvard University, 1977.

Machtlinger, V. J. Psychoanalytic theory: Pre-oedipal and oedipal phases, with special reference to the father. In M. Lamb (ed.), *The Role of the Father in Child Development.* New York: Wiley, 1976.

McCall, R. B. Toward an epigenetic conception of mental development in the first three years of life. In M. Lewis (ed.), *Origins of Intelligence: Infancy and Early Childhood.* New York: Plenum, 1976.

Mendes, H. A. Single fathers. *Family Co-ordinator,* 1976, **25,** 439–444.

Mischel, W. Sex typing and socialization. In P. H. Mussen (ed.), *Manual of Child Psychology,* Vol. 2. New York: Wiley, 1970.

Mitchell, G. D. Paternalistic behavior in primates. *Psychological Bulletin,* 1969, **71,** 399–417.

Mitchell, G. D., Redican, W. K., and Gomber, J. Males can raise babies. *Psychology Today,* 1974, **7,** 63–67.

Moltz, H., Lubin, M., Leon, M., and Numan, M. Hormonal induction of maternal behavior in the overiectomized rat. *Physiology and Behavior,* 1970, **5,** 1373–1377.

Munroe, R. L., and Munroe, R. H. *Cross-Cultural Human Development.* Monterey, Calif.: Brooks/Cole, 1975.

Orthner, D., Brown, T., and Ferguson, D. Single-parent fatherhood: An emerging life style. *Family Co-ordinator,* 1976, **25,** 429–438.

Osofsky, J. D., and Danzger, B. Relationships between neonatal characteristics and mother-infant interaction. *Developmental Psychology,* 1974, **10,** 124–130.

Parke, R. D. Social cues, social control and ecological validity. *Merrill Palmer Quarterly,* 1976, **22,** 111–123.

Parke, R. D. Parent-infant interaction: progress, paradigms and problems. In G. P. Sackett and H. C. Haywood (eds.), *Application of Observational-Ethological Methods to the Study of Mental Retardation.* Baltimore: University Park, 1978a.

Parke, R. D. Interactional design and experimental manipulation: The field-lab interface. In R. B. Cairns (ed.), *Social Interaction: Methods, Analysis and Illustration,* Lawrence Erlbaum, 1978b, in press.

Parke, R. D. Child abuse: An overview of alternative models. *Journal of Pediatric Psychology,* 1978c, **3,** No. 1, in press.

Parke, R. D., and Collmer, C. W. Child abuse: An interdisciplinary perspective. In E. M. Hetherington (ed.), *Review of Child Development Research,* Vol. 5. Chicago: University of Chicago, 1975.

Parke, R. D., Hymel, S. Power, T. G., and Tinsley, B. Fathers and risk: A hospital based model of intervention. In D. Sawin and R. C. Hawkins (eds.), *Psychosocial Risks During Pregnancy and Early Infancy,* 1979, in press.

Parke, R. D., and O'Leary, S. E. Father-mother-infant interaction in the newborn period: Some findings, some observations and some unresolved issues. In K. Riegel and J. Meacham (eds.), *The Developing Individual in a Changing World,* Vol. II, *Social and Environmental Issues.* The Hague: Mouton, 1976.

Parke, R. D., O'Leary, S. E., and West, S. Mother-father-newborn interaction: effects of maternal medication, labor and sex of infant. *Proceedings of the American Psychological Association,* 1972, 85–86.

Parke, R. D., Power, T. G., and Gottman, J. Conceptualizing and quantifying influence patterns in the family triad. In M. E. Lamb, S. J. Suomi and G. R. Stephenson (eds.), *The Study of Social Interaction: Methodological Issues*. Madison: University of Wisconsin, 1978, in press.

Parke, R. D., and Sawin, D. B. Infant characteristics and behavior as elicitors of maternal and paternal responsibility in the newborn period. Paper presented at the biennial meeting of the Society for Research in Child Development, Denver, April 1975.

Parke, R. D., and Sawin, D. B. The father's role in infancy: A re-evaluation. *The Family Co-ordinator,* 1976, **25**, 365–371.

Parke, R. D., and Sawin, D. B. The family in early infancy: Social interactional and attitudinal analyses. Paper presented to the Society for Research in Child Development, New Orleans, March 1977.

Parsons, T. The father symbol: An appraisal in the light of psychoanalytic and sociological theory. In L. Bryson, L. Kinkelstein, R. M. MacIver, and R. McKeon (eds.), *Symbols and Values*. New York: Harper & Row, 1954.

Parsons, T., and Bales, R. F. *Family, Socialization and Interaction Process*. Glencoe, Ill.: Free Press, 1954.

Pedersen, F. A. Mother, father and infant as an interactive system. Paper presented at the Annual Convention of the American Psychological Association, Chicago, September 1975.

Pedersen, F. A., Anderson, B. J. and Cain, R. L. A methodology for assessing parental perceptions of infant temperament. Paper presented at the 4th Biennial Southeastern Conference on Human Development, 1976.

Pedersen, F. A., Anderson, B. J., and Cain, R. L. An approach to understanding linkages between the parent-infant and spouse relationships. Paper presented at the Society for Research in Child Development, New Orleans, March 1977.

Pedersen, F. A., and Robson, K. S. Father participation in infancy. *American Journal of Orthopsychiatry,* 1969, **39**, 466–472.

Pedersen, F. A., Rubinstein, J., and Yarrow, L. J. Infant development in father-absent families. *Journal of Genetic Psychology,* 1978, in press.

Pedersen, F. A., Yarrow, L. J., and Strain, B. A. Conceptualization of father influences and its implications for an observational methodology. Paper presented at I.S.S.B.D., Guildford, England, July 1975.

Poffenberger, T., and Poffenberger, S. B. The social psychology of fertility in a village in India. In J. T. Fawcett (ed.), *Psychological Perspectives on Population*. New York: Basic Books, 1973.

Porges, S. W. Cohort effects and apparent secular trends in infant research. In K. F. Riegel and J. A. Meacham (eds.), *The Developing Individual in a Changing World*, Vol. II, *Social and Environmental Issues*. Chicago: Aldine, 1976.

Radin, N. Father-child interaction and the intellectual functioning of four-year-old boys. *Developmental Psychology,* 1972, **6**, 353–361.

Radin, N. Observed paternal behaviors as antecedents of intellectual functioning in young boys. *Developmental Psychology,* 1973, **8**, 369–376.

Radin, N. The role of the father in cognitive, academic, and intellectual development. In M. E. Lamb (ed.), *The Role of the Father in Child Development*, New York: Wiley, 1976.

Raush, H. L., Barry, W. A., Hertel, R. K., and Swain, M. A. *Communication, Conflict and Marriage*. San Francisco: Jossey-Bass, 1974.

Rebelsky, F., and Hanks, C. Fathers' verbal interaction with infants in the first three months of life. *Child Development,* 1971, **42**, 63–68.

Redican, W. K. A longitudinal study of behavioral interactions between adult male and infant rhesus monkeys (Macaca mulatta). Unpublished Ph.D. dissertation, University of California, Davis, 1975.

Redican, W. K. Adult male-infant interactions in nonhuman primates. In M. Lamb (ed.), *The Role of the Father in Child Development*. New York: Wiley, 1976, 345–385.

Rendina, I., and Dickerscheid, J. D. Father involvement with first-born infants. *Family Coordinator*, 1976, **25**, 373–379.

Rheingold, H. L. The modification of social responsiveness in institutional abies. *Monographs of the Society for Reseach in Child Development*, 1956, **21**, (63).

Richards, M. P. M., Dunn, J. F., and Antonis, B. Caretaking in the first year of life: The role of fathers', and mothers' social isolation. Unpublished manuscript, University of Cambridge, 1975.

Riegel, K. F. Influence of economic and political ideologies on the development of developmental psychology. *Psychological Bulletin*, 1972, **78**, 129–141.

Rosenblatt, J. S. The development of maternal responsiveness in the rat. *American Journal of Orthopsychiatry*, 1969, **39**, 36–56.

Rosenblatt, J. S., and Siegel, H. I. Hysterectomy-induced maternal behavior during pregnancy in the rat. *Journal of Comparative and Physiological Psychology*, 1975, **89**, 685–700.

Ross, G., Kagan, J., Zelazo, P., and Kotelchuck, M. Separation protest in infants in home and laboratory. *Developmental Psychology*, 1975 **11**, 256–257.

Ross, H. S. and Goldman, B. D. Infant's sociability toward strangers. *Child Development*, 1977, **48**, 638–642.

Rubin, J. Z., Provenzano, F. J., and Luria, Z. The eye of the beholder: Parents' views on sex of newborns. *American Journal of Orthopsychiatry*, 1974, **43**, 720–731.

Sawin, D. B., and Parke, R. D. Adolescent fathers: Some implications from recent research on parental roles. *Educational Horizons*, 1976, **55**, 38–43.

Schaffer, R. *Mothering*. Cambridge, Mass.: Harvard University, 1977.

Schaffer, H. R., and Emerson, P. E. The development of social attachments in infancy. *Monographs of the Society for Research in Child Development*, 1964, **29** (3) (whole No. 94).

Schlossman, S. L. Before home start: Notes toward a history of parent education in America, 1897–1929. *Harvard Educational Review*, 1976, **46**, 436–467.

Sears, R. R., Maccoby, E. E., and Levin, H. *Patterns of Child Rearing*. Evanston, Ill.: Row, Peterson, 1957.

Shaikh, A. A. Estrone and estradiol levels in the ovarian venous blood from rats during the estrous cycle and pregnancy. *Biological Reproduction*, 1971, **5**, 297–307.

Shereshefsky, P. M., and Yarrow, L. J. *Psychological Aspects of a First Pregnancy and Early Postnatal Adaptation*. New York: Raven, 1973.

Skeels, H. Adult status of children with contrasting early life experiences. *Monographs of the Society for Research in Child Development*, 1966, **31** (3).

Spelke, E., Zelazo, P., Kagan, J., and Kotelchuck, M. Father interaction and separation protest. *Developmental Psychology*, 1973, **9**, 83–90.

Sroufe, A., Waters, E., and Matas, L. Contextual determinants of infant affective response. In M. Lewis and L. A. Rosenblum (eds.), *The Origins of Fear*. New York: Wiley, 1975.

Stephens, H. N. *The Family in Cross-Cultural Perspective*. New York: Holt, 1963.

Stern, D. N. Mother and infant at play: The dyadic interaction involving facial, vocal, and gaze behaviors. In M. Lewis and L. A. Rosenblum (eds.), *The Effect of the Infant on Its Caregiver*. New York: Wiley, 1974.

Stoltz, L. M. *Father Relations of War-Born Children*. Stanford: Stanford University, 1954.

Turnball, A. C., Patten, P. T., Flint, A. P. F., Keirse, M. J., Jeremy, J. Y., and Anderson, A. Significant fall in progesterone and rise in oestradiol levels in human peripheral plasma before onset of labor. *Lancet*, 1974, **1**, 101–103.

West, M. M., and Konner, M. J. The role of the father: An anthropological perspective. In M. Lamb (ed.), *The Role of the Father in Child Development*. New York: Wiley, 1976, 185–216.

White, R. W. Motivation reconsidered: The concept of competence. *Psychological Review,* 1959, **66**, 297–333.

Yalom, I. D. Post-partum blues syndrome. *Archives of General Psychiatry,* 1968, **28**, 16–27.

Yarrow, L. J., Klein, R. P., Lomonaco, S., and Morgan, G. A. Cognitive and motivational development in early childhood. In B. Z. Friedlander, G. M. Sterrit, and G. E. Kirk (eds.), *Exceptional Infant: Assessment and Intervention*. New York: Brunner/Mazel, 1974.

Yarrow, L. J., Rubinstein, J. L., and Pedersen, F. A. *Infant and Environment: Early Cognitive and Motivational Development*. New York: Halsted, 1975.

Yogman, M. J., Dixon, S., Tronick, E., Als, H., and Brazelton, T. B. The goals and structure of face-to-face interaction between infants and fathers. Paper presented at the biennial meeting of the Society for Research in Child Development, New Orleans, March 1977.

Zelazo, P. R., Kotelchuck, M., Barber, L., and David, J. Fathers and sons: An experimental facilitation of attachment behaviors. Paper presented at the biennial meeting of the Society for Research in Child Development, New Orleans, March 1977.

CHAPTER 16

Infant-Infant Interaction[1]

Edward Mueller

Deborah Vandell

"In 1974 the subject of peer relations is frontier research." Marian Radke Yarrow

In 1979, life on the frontier remains strenuous, though less lonely. Our boat came over in 1971, and since then many settlers have arrived. In these pages, we will tell you about their work. Also, two explorers named Lewis and Clark just returned from a trip deep into the territory. They found it to be most fertile, and even put together the first guidebook (Lewis and Rosenblum, 1975). Be sure to get a copy!

We're sure you realize that this isn't the first attempt to settle the territory. The settlers under Raleigh at Roanoke Island left some classic exploratory work (e.g., Bridges, 1933; Parten, 1932). But they disappeared, 30 years ago, leaving the territory uninhabited for years.

This time we think that the colony is much stronger. If you decide to come over on the next boat, don't forget the supplies we have been using from Geneva (Piaget, 1971) and England (Blurton Jones, 1972). We are not quite independent yet! But be sure to come. You may like it here. This is no Roanoke Island anymore!

THE GAP IN WORK ON INFANT PEER RELATIONS

The causes of the long gap in research on infant peer relations have been explored elsewhere (see Lewis and Rosenblum, 1975). The reason cited most often was the pervasiveness of psychoanalytic thinking. Freudian theory held that the mother-infant relation was primary and that all other relationships were derivative. Currently we are witnessing a period of reaction, with some workers stressing the autonomy of the growth of peer relations (see Chapters 2, 9, and 11 in Lewis and Rosenblum, 1975). The few existing studies on the relationship between parent-infant and infant-infant interaction will be reviewed here.

There are several sources of the rebirth of interest in early peer relations. With mothers placing their children increasingly in group care setting, there is a heightened cultural pressure for knowledge. Also, recently the methodology of psychology has been broadened to include more observational techniques. The stimulation has come largely from animal ethologists. For some time they have been saying that ethological methods

[1]Parts of this paper were presented at a colloquium at the University of Texas at Austin, March 1976. Its preparation was supported by National Institute of Mental Health research grant MH24824 and predoctoral fellowship MH05292. The authors are grateful to George Michel and Robert Kavanaugh for comments on an earlier draft, and to Laura Hubbs for her unpublished translation of parts of Lichtenberger (1965).

ate well suited for the study of early social relations (e.g., Blurton Jones, 1967). During the same period, sophisticated technical equipment for observational work has become available in developmental psychology laboratories. Much of the recent work would have been impossible without this equipment (see the Appendix to this chapter). Finally, there are the simple demographic facts of increased numbers of research psychologists. No interesting and potentially important aspect of infant development should remain unstudied for long.

THE CULTURAL MYOPIA OF EXISTING RESEARCH

Nearly all existing data on early peer relations comes from Western industrialized countries. Most of it comes from middle-class North American subjects, where Lewis et al. (1975) found that only about 20% of parents provide their infants with regular peer experience. Thus the often-heard phrase ''infant peer relations do not exist'' has a certain cultural validity to it. In this culture, most parents do not provide opportunities for them to develop. However, this review provides ample evidence that, in the right context, such relationships can flourish. This review will consider how a wide variety of contextual variables influences infant peer relations. However, work in one culture will never resolve issues of the universality of existing developmental patterns. As in most areas of early social development, cross-cultural work is lacking and needed.

INFANT PEER RELATIONS IN EVOLUTIONARY PERSPECTIVE

Konner (1975) suggested that during 99% of human evolution, infant peer relations were almost nonexistant. During this period modal band size is believed to have been about 30. Using natality and mortality rates, Konner determined that the probability of a 1-year-old being exposed to a child within 3 months of his own age was 0.44. The chance of having two peers was 0.11 and three was 0.03. These data ignored multiple births, presumably viewing twins as siblings rather than peers. Konner argues that infants never developed relations with peers because they were never called on to do so across millions of years of human evolution. What is the implication of saying that there has been no bioadaptive evolution favoring peer relations? If they are biologically unnatural, must their existence be impossible or maladaptive? Not at all. First note that if infant peer relations did not exist across evolutionary time, there was no biological selection *against* peer relations. Second, intelligence has largely supplanted instinct as the mechanism for programming adaptive behavior (Piaget, 1971). Cultural evolution is moving more rapidly than is biogenetic change. Indeed, much of our everyday behavior would have been bizarre and maladaptive during most of our evolution. We live in a self-synthesized environment, and we rely on our minds more than on our genes to survive here.

It is this same cultural evolution that has produced infant peer contact in cases varying from orphanages for the abandoned, to enrichment programs for the infants of parents who find their offspring bored at home. Without prejudicing their value, it is clear that cultural evolution is producing situations where infants are in contact. To prejudge infant peer relations as ''bizarrely inept'' (Konner, 1975, p. 122) based only on evolutionary and comparative arguments is a mistake. We must evaluate the direct evidence from studies of infants in contacts. As cultural change rushes on, clearly it would be maladaptive to do otherwise.

WHAT IS A PEER?

While suggesting the ultimate importance of peer relations, Yarrow (1975) provided a definition:

Peers are the life of people—not only of children. With the exception of the brief infancy and toddler years, the individual is likely to be with near-age mates for very considerable portions of his time and for very widely varying relationships. [p. 299]

Yarrow defines peers as *near agemates.* Obviously "near" differs at 30 weeks and 30 years. But as Lewis and Rosenblum (1975) noted, there seems to be, in the very idea of peers, the idea of reciprocity or sharing of capacities and common physical features.

   Are siblings peers? Despite their unquestionable importance, the study of sibling relations lags behind even that of peer relations. Surely some cross-age sibling play is reciprocal and includes shared capacities and abilities (Parten, 1933). Yet at other times siblings may be more parent than peer, sometimes directly charged with the care of a young child, and sometimes imitating their parents. It would follow from the above definitions that twins are both siblings and peers. We will review the small number of studies referring to their relationships during infancy.

ORGANIZATION OF THIS CHAPTER

The chapter is divided into two sections. Part 1 is a review of the existing empirical research. Part 2 is a review of important concepts and hypotheses in the developmental study of infant peer relations. Part 1 shows that we are no longer at the starting line. There is good agreement between existing studies in what behaviors enter into infant peer relations, and what factors influence those interactions.

   However, the study of infant peer relations has not progressed very far conceptually. The very definition of infant-infant social interaction is in dispute. Hinde (1972) notes that "when there is difficulty in obtaining agreement over a dull matter of definition, one can be sure that unresolved conceptual issues lie concealed" [p. 1]. Part 2 explores these conceptual issues and suggests hypotheses for guiding the further study of infant-infant interaction.

   One final prefatory note. This review will be limited to children under the age of 2. In general we will call children aged under 1 year *infants,* and children aged 1 to 2 *toddlers.*

PART 1: A REVIEW OF THE EMPIRICAL RESEARCH

Contrary to the claim (Appolloni and Cooke, 1975) that little research has been done on early peer interaction, there is a burgeoning literature that describes just such interactions. This literature indicates that infants and toddlers can and do direct social behaviors to their peers. It also indicates that infant peers can develop increasingly complex interaction sequences with each other. Unfortunately, however, many of the studies documenting infant-infant interaction are unpublished or are not readily available. At the same time, those studies that are published have not been integrated into a comprehensive picture of early social behavior and interaction. In view of these two problems, the following sections are designed to outline in some detail the recent unpublished literature about infant-peer interaction as well as to integrate these studies with other, more available work.

As part of this integration, the review that follows is organized into sections. In the first section the emergence of specific peer social *behaviors* over the first 2 years is outlined. Subsequent sections then report other aspects of early peer encounters: (1) the development of social *interaction* as opposed to social behaviors, (2) the conceptual and empirical importance of objects to early social encounters, (3) situational constraints on infant-infant encounters, and (4) individual differences in infant-infant relations. Part 1 concludes with a comparison of infant-infant and mother-child interactional systems.

Appearance of Early Social Behaviors

During the 1930s, a series of investigations (Bühler, 1927; Bridges, 1933; Maudry and Nekula, 1939; Mengert, 1931; Parten, 1932) were conducted on early peer encounters. Although most of these studies found not only evidence of peer contacts but also a systematic progression of peer-directed behaviors, research in this area came to a virtual standstill by the early 1940s. For the next 30 years almost no new work was reported.

After that hiatus, the 1970s have been marked by a resurgence of interest in infant-infant encounters. The bulk of these new studies have reported a remarkably similar progression of peer-directed behavior in the first 2 years to that presented years earlier.

Throughout this section the ages provided are approximate. There is, of course, variation in the precise age at which a behavior might be expected to appear. Here, the ages are given more as an ordinal index—that is, visual regard can be expected to precede peer "touches," and touching should precede smiles and laughs. Even with the different samples of children observed, and the different measures incorporated, there has been considerable agreement on the approximate age a behavior might be expected.

In the current work as well as in the early research, social skills were found to be closely tied to the child's other developing motor and vocal skills. It appears that as infants master a particular motor or vocal skill they begin to direct that behavior to a peer, *if a peer is available*. For example, looking at infants who were frequently together, Lichtenberger (1965), Vincze (1971), and Bridges (1933) each reported extended visual regard of the peer even in the first 2 months. Touching the peer was then reported at 3 to 4 months (Shirley, 1933; Lichtenberger, 1965; Vincze, 1971) for infants who were placed in close proximity.

It is, of course, unlikely that these behaviors are truly "social" in the sense of an infant anticipating and seeking the social potential of the peer. It is much more likely that the behaviors are simply exploratory, similar to what the young infant does with any interesting object or display (Berlyne, 1960). Still, these gazes and touches suggest some awareness of the peer's presence, even if that awareness is not specific to the peer's social potential. More clearly, social encounters may emerge from this increasing interest and awareness.

Around 6 months, most observers agree that additional behaviors that may be "social" appear. As Bühler (1933) has described it, infants become more actively engaged with each other from this age on. Part of this more active involvement is evident in the appearance of peer-directed smiles (Bühler, 1927; Bridges, 1933; Maudry and Nekula, 1939; Vincze, 1971). At around 6 months, infants are observed to smile in response to their peers' coos and vocalizations. By 7 to 8 months, as the infants become more mobile, they are observed to approach, follow, and reach for peers (Bridges, 1933; Durfee and Lee, 1973).

There should be some care not to exaggerate the infant's skills at this point, however. The smile may indicate pleasure at familiarity, while the approach and reach may be orienting responses to an object of interest. Still, in those instances where infants were allowed to spend a great deal of time together (Lichtenberger, 1965; Vincze, 1971), these behaviors to the peer "looked" social to the observers.

From around 9 to 12 months, more clearly "social" behaviors developed with increasing frequency. It is at this point that the "offer" and the social "take" are observed regularly between acquainted peers. (Durfee and Lee, 1973; Lichtenberger, 1965; Vincze, 1971). According to Bronson (1975), these behaviors may be most important because they maximize the likelihood of evoking feedback from the partner, be it peer or parent. With this feedback, Bronson argued that the possibility of sustained encounters was enhanced.

During the 9- to 12-month period, acquainted infants have also been observed playing games with each other. Vincze, Maudry and Nekula, Bridges, and Lichtenberger have each reported instances of run-and-chase, peek-a-boo, and ball games. To most observers, these games have a decidedly social flavor. Slightly later, at 13 to 14 months, infants have been observed to socially imitate one another (Bridges, 1933; Eckerman et al. 1975). About that same time, they begin to make noises back and forth, much like an adult conversation (Bridges, 1933; Lichtenberger, 1965).

With the acquisition of these component behaviors (vocal exchanges, offer, approach, smile, etc.) the repertoire for the infant's social encounters is fairly complete. What then occurs is an overall increase in the frequency of the behaviors. Between 12 and 24 months, Eckerman et al. reported an increase in the frequency of imitation of the peer's activity—taking, offering, and receiving toys as well as in coordinated activities with toys. Similarly, Maudry and Nekula reported an increased incidence of personal as opposed to impersonal encounters. On the negative side, struggles over toys and negative hair-pulling and biting became more common across the 2nd year (Maudry and Nekula, 1939; Missakian, 1975).

Beyond the simple increase in behaviors over time, there is every indication that the complexity of the behaviors increases over the first 2 years as well. For example, Mueller and Brenner (1977) have found systematic increases for more complex combinations of social behavior between 12 and 23 months for acquainted children. Thus, as children developed over the 2nd year, they were more capable of combining a smile with an offer to yield a coordinated social behavior. Using a different sample than Mueller and Brenner, Mueller and Rich (1976) reported similar systematic changes in the number and complexity of acquainted toddlers' (13–15 months) behavior over a 3-month period. In addition, Mueller and Rich noted that positive affect marked by smiles and laughs increased over the three month period.

Summary

From the outline above, certain conclusions about early peer-directed behavior can be drawn. These conclusions are not based on a single study but rather a whole series of studies conducted over a 50-year period. After examining these studies of acquainted infants it is fair to say that:

1. Infants at an early age can direct behaviors to each other
2. These behaviors become increasingly social through the 1st year
3. The ordinal relation of these behaviors can be predicted

Perhaps the most striking result of the studies of early social behavior is their high degree of agreement on the order of appearance of social behaviors. Because of this agreement, it may be safe to say that it is time for the research to turn to other issues in infant-infant encounters. It is to these other issues that the remainder of Part 1 will be directed.

Social Interaction

In this chapter the distinction is made between social *behavior* and social *interaction*. Before outlining the little work on social interaction, it is necessary to clarify the distinction between behavior and interaction as it is used here.

In the research on *social behavior,* the appearance or nonappearance of particular behaviors such as "smile" and "offer" is recorded. In looking at these behaviors, the unit of analysis is the individual child. Thus, Vincze, in a study referred to in the previous section, observed infants in a group care setting. There, she recorded the *behaviors* that one child directed to another.

In contrast to the individual's social behavior, analysis of *interaction sequences* considers the behavioral states of two children at once and focuses on their interrelation. Rather than examining various individuals' specific behaviors, interaction studies are more likely to include measures like "number of actor changes" and "organization of the exchanges." In examining the interaction sequences, the important aspect of interaction (namely, that more than one person has to be actively involved) is incorporated into the measures used.

In a longitudinal study across the 2nd year, Mueller and Brenner (1977) examined several measures of interaction sequences. Corresponding to increases in the number of social behaviors observed, Mueller and Brenner reported that the frequency of interaction sequences (contingencies in which one child directs a behavior to another child and the second child responds contiguously) increased in a linear fashion. They also found growth in both short-interaction sequences (child A act–child B act) and longer sequences (three units or more). While the shorter exchanges were initially more common, the longer sequences increased markedly for older children.

Results of one earlier study, Maudry and Nekula (1939), correspond to Mueller and Brenner's findings. Maudry and Nekula also reported increases in the length of interaction sequences across time, while looking at a wider range (6–25 months).

Organizational Characteristics of Interaction Sequences

In addition to quantitative measures of interaction, other examinations of interaction sequences have outlined the organizational characteristics of peer exchanges. Mueller and Lucas (1975), for example, conceptualized interactions in a day-care-like setting as progressing through three distinct stages that differed organizationally. In the first stage, the peer contacts were seen as object-centered and as not including social interaction. Thus, the infants might cluster around a given toy but they did not contingently direct behaviors to each other. If one child did direct a behavior to another child, the second child did not respond or reciprocate.

During the second stage, however, Mueller and Lucas observed that a series of contingencies were set up. These contingencies marked the appearance of true social interaction. In them, child A would direct a behavior to child B, and child B would respond contingently. These contingent responses were used to build longer and longer chains of "interacts."

With stage three, the structure of the interactions was seen as progressing a step further. Now the interactions were characterized by role reversal and role complementarity. The child, through his role reversal, was able to then demonstrate his understanding of his partner's role. Thus the child who offered an object in turn received one, and the child who received an object offered one.

Durfee and Lee (1973) have provided independent validation of the stages of interaction outlined by Mueller and Lucas. They reported one-way contacts to be more common than contingent contacts in the 1st year. After that time, they found that reciprocal contacts of the form A-B-A-B-A-B increased.

Further independent validation of the stages of interaction given by Mueller and Lucas has been provided by Ross and Goldman (1977). In 25-min toddler dyad sessions, Ross and Goldman observed that instances of turn-taking and repetition increased with age, while isolated social behaviors declined.

Finally, Garvey's (1974) structural analysis of peer interaction in preoperational children parallels Mueller and Lucas' findings for sensory-motor children. Garvey found that children's verbal play progressed from (1) imitative/repetitive responses to (2) differential responses to (3) role reversals. Her examples of each of these levels corresponded to those given by Mueller and Lucas for preverbal children.

The Role of Objects in Early Social Encounters

The development of social behaviors and interaction sequences outlined above did not occur in a vacuum. There are several indications that in the emergence of both social behaviors and interaction sequences, objects (i.e., things) play a special role.

First, on a superficial level, some social behaviors and exchanges require, by definition, the presence of objects. An offer-receive interaction, for instance, requires an object of exchange. Similarly, take-cry or take-resist interactions utilize an object as the focus of interest. The importance of objects to the development of social behavior appears to be greater than a mere definitional constraint, however.

Mueller and DeStefano (1973) have outlined in theoretical terms why objects may be so important. In their analysis, objects provide both the "carrot" and "stick" to subsequent social development. As a "stick" the presence of objects can force infants to notice a peer and his impact. For example, if a peer takes a toy with which another infant is engrossed, the infant is forced to realize the peer's impact if he is to regain the treasured toy.

At the same time, in other circumstances, objects can encourage and invite contacts. In those circumstances, contacts around the same or similar objects invite the mutual discovery of interpersonal contingencies. Through the objects, infants can discover their control over the peer. Mueller and DeStefano provide an example that illustrates how this mutual discovery of interpersonal contingencies might work.

The observation begins with two toddlers, Larry and Russell, being attracted to the same toy train. Larry is pushing the train's smoke stack and the train makes an interesting noise. Russell comes over to the toy. In the meantime, Larry begins to pull the train with Russell in pursuit. Larry then notices Russell following and changes directions several times, running back and forth across the room. Russell watches and then imitates Larry's running. Larry then imitates Russell. By this point, both children are looking at each other and making excited sounds. The purely object-centered contact allowed the toddlers to discover their mutual control over each other.

With the potential importance of objects in terms of their demand and invitation characteristics, it is noteworthy that an abundance of early social contacts do, in fact, include objects. Durfee and Lee, for instance, found that in 6- to 9-month-olds observed over 5 months, at least 60% of the contact sequences observed incorporated inanimate objects. Looking at infants from 12 to 24 months, Mueller and Brenner (1976) found an even higher proportion of contacts around objects. In their observations, 88% of the contacts involved nonsocial objects of some kind. Eckerman et al. (1975) have also noted the central role of objects. As did the others'subjects, their toddlers (12–24 months) tended to play with the same toys at the same time. In Eckerman et al.'s words, the nonsocial objects seemed to "act as vehicles" for various forms of interaction.

Development of Objects Contacts

While objects may play an important role in the early contacts, the precise role of the objects in social contacts is not stable through this period. The particular role of objects appears to vary at different periods during the first 2 years. For example, Mueller and DeStefano cited a shift during their observations from peer contacts in which the emphasis was on the object (called object-centered contacts) to contacts where the focus was on the peer, with the object in a mediating role. Maudry and Nekula (1939), years before, outlined a similar progression. In their observations, Maudry and Nekula found the focus to be first on the object and its properties. Eventually, however, they noted that the objects became merely a means for establishing social relations.

Lichtenberger (1965) has presented in more detail the development of object contacts. In extensive observations of his own twin infants, Sigrid and Horst, Lichtenberger documented changes in the children's social behavior with each other. He was particularly interested in the role of objects in the twins' exchanges.

According to Lichtenberger, the early object contacts passed through seven periods. These periods were often overlapping. The author asserted that the same infant was capable of functioning at several levels, depending on the circumstances. In the first period (3–6 months), there was *proximity* around objects, but no social contact. During that period, the twins were observed to be simultaneously active on the same object without being aware of the effects of their behavior on the other. Contacts were completely object-centered.

This stage was then followed by the *first conflict period* (5–9 months). During that period, object seizures abounded, but with a marked interest in the object, not the peer. Thus, one of the twins would take a toy from the other, all the while concentrating on the object. The peer might then try to retrieve the object, but with no visible awareness of the other twin's role in the loss of the object in the first place.

According to Lichtenberger, out of this conflict emerged more *gamelike exchanges* (6–11 months), the third period. As in the first conflict stage, the twins were taking and retrieving objects, but these exchanges were distinguished by the increasing awareness of the peer's presence and impact. These exchanges were also characterized by their playful appearance and vigorous babbling to the peer.

In contrast, the *second conflict period* (9–12 months), which followed the playful exchanges, was marked by a high degree of negative affect. In this second conflict period, the object seizures centered on the process of taking away from the peer, not just on the object as in the first conflict period. During the second conflict period, the twins showed their awareness of the other by hiding and withdrawing toys from the other.

Between 8 and 17 months, the fifth period, which involved *voluntary offers and exchanges,* emerged. Several markers were observed in this period including mutual visual regard during the exchanges and offering syllables *Da!* (*There!*) to the twin.

Finally, in the last two periods (six and seven), the twins began to use objects to meaningfully pursue common activities and to distinguish verbally and motorically the concepts of ''yours'' and ''mine.''

As is apparent from inspection of the periods outlined by Lichtenberger, early object contacts between the twins stressed the object. With the playful exchanges and then the second conflict stage, however, the social potential of the peer began to be realized. Then the objects played a different mediating role in the contacts.

Contrary Evidence about Object Contacts

While there is a general consensus about the importance of objects to early peer relations, the picture is still not without some ambiguity. Hubbs (1975), for example, has made the point that the object contacts in Lichtenberger's observations were not the precursor to other, more social encounters. Hubbs noted that Lichtenberger observed exchanges such as ''look-laugh'' between the twins long before (i.e., before 3 months) objects were facilitating their interactions. From this lag, Hubbs argued that while objects may be used by infants, they are in no way the only source of interaction, especially for infants who have ample exposure to each other.

Lewis et al. (1975) argue even more strongly that object contacts are uncommon and relatively unimportant. In their study, Lewis et al. examined unacquainted toddlers in a playgroup setting. Surprisingly, they found objects to play only an insignificant role in the toddlers' social behavior compared to proximal and distal contacts without objects. These results run directly counter to results outlined earlier in this section.

The explanation of why most researchers have found such different results from Lewis et al. remains an open question and one that needs further research. While the explanation in some cases may be differences in definitions about what constitutes toy play and object contacts, the explanation is likely to be more complex than that. For example, Bronson (1975) reported object offers and takes to be the dominant activity between toddler peers, while Lewis et al. found these activities to occur much less frequently. The reason for these very different findings remains to be explained.

Situational Constraints on Peer Behavior

A topic that one might consider as an explanation of the differential results about the role of objects is the situational constraints on peer behavior and interaction. Recent research (Dragsten and Lee, 1973; Mueller and Brenner, 1977; Vandell, 1976), in addition to some older work (Klein and Wander, 1933; Shirley, 1933) has shown that infant-infant encounters can be very much dependent on a variety of situational constraints. These constraints include (1) peer familiarity, (2) experience with infant peers, (3) size of the peer group, (4) the particular objects available, and (5) behavioral setting (home versus laboratory). All have been found to influence peer behavior and interaction. The impact of each of these environmental factors will be discussed in turn.

Familiar versus Unfamiliar Peers

Several researchers (Apolloni and Cooke, 1975; Bronson, 1972; Mueller and Rich, 1976) have hypothesized that a major variable influencing infant-infant encounters is the familiarity/unfamiliarity of the infants. At the present time, such hypotheses have been supported by circumstantial and empirical evidence.

In a classic study, Bridges (1933) conducted observations of institutionalized infants during their daily activities. Bridges noted that the greatest increase in social behavior occurred between 9 and 10 months. Prior to 9 months, the infants were observed in their separate cribs, which allowed few opportunities for the babies to interact. Only at 9 months were the infants placed together regularly. When first placed together, however, the infants tended to ignore one another. Only after a few weeks did they interact. It could be hypothesized that this increase was in part the result of increasing peer familiarity.

Empirical evidence is accumulating to support such an hypothesis. Becker (1977), for example, in an examination of dyads of 9-month-olds who did and did not know each other found that the amount of peer-directed behavior was greater among familiar peers than among unfamiliar ones. Similarly, Lewis et al. (1975) found in two separate studies different kinds of behavior between peer friends and strangers.

In the first study, Lewis et al. brought 12-month-olds together in dyads with familiar and unfamiliar peers. There, the occurrence of 20 social behaviors was recorded. Significant differences were found in the peer behavior between the infant "friends" and "strangers." More proximal contacts (like touching, lean–lie-on) were noted between friends, while distal contacts (like looking and vocalizing) were found to be about the same. In addition, "friends" initiated more interactions with each other than did the strangers. Finally, the amount of positive versus negative affect was greater for the friends. Three times the negative affect occurred with unfamiliar as opposed to familiar peers.

In the second study, Lewis et al. experimentally manipulated peer familiarity. They arranged for previously unfamiliar peers to play together several times over a week. They compared the peers' encounters before and after these play sessions along with encounters between unfamiliar peers at the end of the sessions. Lewis et al. found that, as with the peer friends in the earlier study, proximity seeking was greater for familiar peers. Gesturing to the peer also increased with familiarity.

Conceptually there is good reason to believe that peer familiarity might enhance the social behaviors and interactions observed. Bronson (1974) has suggested the important role that *control* might play in differentiating between familiar and unfamiliar peers. Arguing that consistent contingencies are important in fostering interaction in general, Bronson contended that unfamiliar peers provide each other with feedback that is too delayed and variable. Whereas familiar infants may develop social schemes that work with each other, the unfamiliar peers may have no way of knowing what response is expected, and needed to maintain an interaction. For instance, they may not know that the peer running away and vocalizing may actually be an invitation to a run-chase game. The attempt at interaction would then fall apart before it could start. Bronson has argued that peers may require considerable exposure with each other before reliable expectations can be developed.

Contrary Evidence to the Importance of Peer Familiarity

Now that the empirical and conceptual basis for the argument that familiar peers interact differently from unfamiliar ones has been provided, there is some additional evidence that should be outlined.

This evidence suggests that just because peers are not familiar with each other does not mean that they cannot interact (Eckerman et al., 1975; Ross and Goldman, 1977). In examinations of unfamiliar 12-, 18-, and 24-month-olds, Eckerman et al. found that direct involvement with peers increased reliably with age until by 2 years social play exceeded solitary play. Similarly, Ross and Goldman, observing unfamiliar peers, found over 2000 examples of intentional social overtures in 800 min of observation. In addition, they reported up to 3 min of continuous interaction between unfamiliar peers, a duration long even for familiar peers at this age (Durfee and Lee, 1973; Mueller and Brenner, 1977).

Studying Israeli infants, Fischoff (1974) also failed to find a difference in the *overall* frequency of social behaviors between familiar and unfamiliar peers. Fischoff did find, however, differences in the type of behaviors directed to peers. There were tendencies for the familiar infants to laugh, smile, and imitiate their peer, while unfamiliar infants simply looked or offered objects.

Peer Experience

Related to the familiar/unfamiliar dimension is the effect of peer experience on the infant's social behavior and interaction. While in the familiar/unfamiliar situational constraint, the effect of *acquaintance with a particular peer* on infant-infant encounters was investigated, "peer experience" refers to *prior experience interacting with peers in general*. Peer-experienced infants, for example, could be observed with either familiar or unfamiliar peers.

As was the case with familiarity, it appears that peer experience can influence aspects of the infants' and toddlers' social encounters. Mueller and Brenner (1977), for example, in a study of the impact of peer experience, compared familiar toddlers with 4½ months of peer experience to familiar toddlers with less peer experience. The more experienced toddlers (although they were slightly younger chronologically) showed a higher frequency of more complex social behaviors as measured by the appearance of several social behaviors in combination. The more peer-experienced toddlers also engaged in significantly longer interaction sequences.

Peer experience was not such an important factor on other measures Mueller and Brenner used, however. There were no differences between the groups on frequency of contacts (a time when the toddlers were mutually engaged with common objects but not necessarily interacting together) or in the frequency of less complex social behaviors (such as a single social behavior in isolation, like a single smile or offer.).

Thus it seems that while peer experience was advantageous for sustaining peer-toddler encounters, the simpler aspects of the infants' and toddlers' social skills were developing with less peer experience.

Dyad versus Group Encounters

In the 1930s, there was a feeling that the size of the infant group might also influence the infant social encounters observed. Thus, Maudry and Nekula (1939) cited a study by Klein and Wander (1933) as their reason for observing infant dyads instead of infant groups. Klein and Wander had found that infants less than 2 years of age were unable to engage in "cooperative" play with more than one other child at a time.

Subsequent observations have further suggested the increased saliency of the dyad as opposed to larger groups of infants. Durfee and Lee (1973), for instance, found that at all age levels (6–14 months) babies were more likely to contact another infant if the second infant was alone—that is, not interacting with another baby. Similarly, Bronson (1975) and Bridges (1933) observed that almost all early peer events were dyadic. In observations of 933 peer events, Bronson found only 29 triads.

Vandell (1976) has specifically compared toddlers' social behaviors and interactions in a group situation and a dyadic setting. Six toddlers who were participating in a daily play-group were videotaped numerous times over a 6-month period in both dyadic and group familiar settings. Results showed that the group size had a significant influence on the pattern and size of interactions observed. While the amount of time spent in interaction increased for dyads over the 6 months, it was stable in the group setting. Similarly, the number of coordinated social behaviors (a measure of behavioral complexity) increased for the toddlers in dyadic settings while no developmental change was registered in the group setting. In all, 11 measures showed systematic increases during dyads, while no changes were found over the 6 months in the group setting.

Quantitative differences in the amount of interaction and behavior in the two settings reflected other differences. Toddlers spent significantly more time in interaction in the dyadic setting. The number of actor changes in the longest interaction, a measure of optimal performance, was also significantly greater in the dyadic setting. As for behaviors observed, toddlers during dyads used significantly more vocalizations and coordinated behaviors than in the group setting.

The question may be raised as to why the dyadic situation is such an important factor in the infant's social behavior and interaction. An important part of the constraint may be the infant's own level of cognitive and social skills. The dyad may help the infant to focus his behavior on a social partner. In the group situation, the numerous peers may divert and distract the infant from the attention needed for a successful interaction.

The distinction between interactions when only a single partner is available and when a group is available may be relevant to two recent studies with surprising results.

Bronson (1972, 1974, 1975) in a wide-reaching examination of the development of competence, brought groups of toddlers (12–24 months) together in a playgroup setting. There, with the aid of videotapes, she observed the various toddler contacts, behaviors, interactions, and so on. In her observations, Bronson found most of the peer interactions to be very brief and to not increase over time. Over the 2nd year, Bronson reported no change in the willingness to sustain social encounters or in overall social responsiveness to the peer. Throughout her observations, Bronson found a predominance of disagreements over agreements.

Bronson's findings are interesting in light of distinctions made in this section. Her findings are contrary to most recent researchers, who have reported numerous social contacts with a predominance of positive affect over negative. The question becomes why the discrepancies between her research and other studies.

In her own discussion, Bronson (1972) cites the possibility of the impact of unfamiliar peers as an explanation, but as pointed out in an earlier section of this chapter, there is evidence that in some circumstances (Eckerman et al., 1975; Ross and Goldman, 1977) unfamiliar peers do interact increasingly over time with a minimum of negative affect. Why then do Bronson's findings differ so substantially from Eckerman et al. and Ross and Goldman who also looked at unfamiliar peers?

The one major difference in the studies was the size of the peer groups observed. Bronson typically tried to have a group of toddlers present (usually four toddlers), while Ross and Goldman and Eckerman et al. studied a dyadic situation. One is led to hypothesize, based on Vandell (1976) and the other work on group size, that this difference was critical in determining Bronson's results of low, nonchanging social contacts between infant peers.

Dragsten and Lee (1973) further illustrate the potential importance of group size to infant-infant encounters. In a study designed to compare a strange laboratory setting and a familiar setting, Dragsten and Lee confounded a number of variables now recognized as important. In their design, the social behaviors of infants during a group care session (a daycare program in which 6- to 18-month-old infants had been participating for several months) were compared to dyads of other children (one daycare, one home-reared) in an unfamiliar setting. Thus, Dragsten and Lee had two groups of children who differed on (1) peer familiarity, (2) setting familiarity, and (3) group size.

Dragsten and Lee had predicted that the daycare group, since they were in a familiar setting with familiar peers, would be involved in more social episodes. In fact, however, they found the opposite. The experimental group (unfamiliar setting, unfamiliar peer), which was observed in dyads, participated in a greater number of social episodes. Based on Vandell's findings of dyadic versus group differences, this finding is less surprising, however. The group size variable appears to have overshadowed the other situational differences.

Behavioral Setting

The discussion of group size and its impact on the infant's social behavior leads to another possible situational constraint—namely, the behavioral setting where the observations are made. Generally, studies have been conducted in (1) a child's own home, (2) a familiar setting that is not the child's home, such as a daycare center which the child regularly attends, or (3) an unfamiliar setting such as a university laboratory or a stranger's home.

One might predict that the particular behavioral setting adopted would influence the infant-infant encounters observed. It might be hypothesized that a familiar setting would offer fewer new experiences and diversions as well as being potentially less intimidating to the infants. A by-product of the familiar setting would then be an increased number of peer contacts.

The empirical results concerning the impact of physical location support this view. Becker (1977), for example, found that 9-month-olds observed over 10 sessions directed more behaviors to peers in their own home than in an unfamiliar house. Rubenstein and Howes (1976) reported extensive peer contacts (60% of the time) from toddlers observed in their own home with a friend, higher levels than have been reported in any other setting (Bronson, 1975; Mueller and Brenner, 1977; Vandell, 1976).

Fischoff (1974), looking at kibbutz infants in three settings (infant's house, parent's house, and unfamiliar house), found additional evidence of behavioral setting differences. First, infants typically directed more behaviors to their peers in the infant house where they spent most of their time than in their parent's home, which they visited each afternoon. Specifically, the infants showed significantly more mutual regard, vocalizations, and approach in the infant house than in the parents' house. While in their parents' house, the kibbutz infants were more intent on interacting with their mothers, rather than trying to interact with the peer. The infants appeared to treat the infant house as a place for peer contacts and the parents' house as a place for mother contacts.

In a second comparison, Fischoff found the infants also to be more involved in social episodes in the infant house than in the other, unfamiliar houses at the kibbutz. In the completely unfamiliar setting, the number of social behaviors observed was significantly smaller.

Objects Available

In the description of the development of social behavior earlier, emphasis was placed on the role of objects in general in the emergence of social interaction. From this general facilitating role it might be hypothesized that specific objects, their number, and their arrangement in a playroom could have specific influences. In fact, several studies have indicated how the presence or absence of particular objects influence the peer observations made.

In two classic studies, Maudry and Nekula (1939) and Bühler (1933) illustrated the differential impact of objects. In the first study, Maudry and Nekula conducted a series of experimental procedures in which infant dyads were placed in close proximity and alternately presented with 0, 1, 2, and 3 objects. Maudry and Nekula found the infants' responses varied with the number of objects presented. With no objects, no negative reactions between children were observed. When both children had materials, nearly as many positive as negative reactions were observed. With one object and two children, however, conflict and negative reactions were maximized. In the second study, Bühler also found conflict and negative reactions to be predominant when infant dyads were presented with a single toy.

DeStefano (1976) has reported on the impact of other object configurations on peer contacts. He experimentally manipulated a daycare-like setting for a group of toddlers. On some days, only large nonportable objects (such as a slide and rocking boat) were present, while on other days only small manipulable toys such as small balls, trucks, xylophone, and so on, were included. On two other types of days, either no objects or all kinds of toys were present.

Comparing these four situations, DeStefano found that the type of objects in the room significantly influenced the interactions observed. Peer social contacts were maximized in the "large-object" and "no-objects" conditions. The least number of interactions occurred in the "small-toys-only" condition. Then, the toddlers were most involved in object exploration.

Positive and negative affect were dependent on the objects present. More negative affect was expressed in the "small-toy" condition than in either the "large-objects" or "all-kinds-of-objects" condition. The "no-objects" condition also had a good deal of negative affect. Positive affect, on the other hand, was common with either "no objects" or "large objects."

Affect of Social Encounters

In the discussion of social behaviors to this point, the emotional tone of the early encounters has been dealt with only peripherally. Several studies, however, have seen affect as having an important role in the developing social encounters. Ross and Goldman (1977), for example, have hypothesized that positive affect serves as a meta-communication. They observed that smiles and laughs tend to mark certain encounters with the special quality "This is a game!"

In their research, this game marker emerged developmentally, with 72% of the games of 2-year-olds marked by positive affect, and none of the games of 1-year-olds so marked. Positive affect in 18-month-olds' games then varied with the social partner. With a 12-month-old partner, 25% of the games were marked by smiles and laughter while 33% of the games with 24-month-olds were.

In addition to positive encounters, Ross and Goldman observed instances of negative affect. They found, however, all instances of negative contact and vocalizations to be less common than the positive ones.

This superiority of positive to negative contacts is consistent with other recent research (Eckerman et al.; Mueller and Brenner, 1977; Mueller and Rich, 1976).

These studies have agreed that in dyadic free-play situations smiling and laughing were more common than fussing, crying, or whining. There was agreement that throughout the 2nd year both positive and negative affect increased, with positive behaviors continuing to outweight the negative.

Not all peer encounters favor positive affect, however. It is possible to design a situation in which negative affect is maximized, as the older research (Bühler, 1933; Maudry and Nekula, 1939) demonstrated. In those cases where two children are presented with a single toy, tears and taking objects can be guaranteed with some confidence.

Although both positive and negative affect can be either fostered or discouraged, it would be a mistake to assume that extremes of affect are the norm. In dyadic naturalistic situations, Mueller and Brenner and Eckerman et al. each observed that neutral affect was the predominant mode. In Mueller and Brenner, fully 70% of the interactions coded were marked by *no* particular affect, and in Eckerman et al. most of the observed contacts were affectively neutral. It appears that for infants and toddlers learning to interact with a peer is often "serious" business.

Individual Differences

Thus far the description of infant social encounters has stressed a normative account. These descriptions have included outlines of what might typically be expected at various ages during the first 2 years and what situational factors might be expected to influence these behaviors in general. Individual differences, or the variability between infants, has been a much less investigated topic. As it stands now, research in individual differences can be briefly summarized.

Bronson (1975), in a study whose primary focus was on the normative development of social competencies, noted that individual differences were apparent. She observed significant differences in the frequency that her same-aged toddlers initiated interaction; and those differences were correlated over the trimesters of the 2nd year. If an infant was a frequent initiator of interaction at 12 months, then s/he was likely to be a frequent initiator at 18 and 24 months as well. Bronson reported that initiations by a characteristically nonpeer-oriented toddler were unlikely even under the most favorable circumstances for interaction.

Vandell (1976) has reported other instances of variability in different toddlers' performance with peers. While one 16-month-old toddler initiated only 11% of his interactions with a peer, another toddler initiated 86%. During the same observation period at 16 months, different toddlers terminated between 29 and 73% of the interactions in which they were involved. When the organization of the behaviors observed was examined, the percentage of behaviors that were coordinated (a measure of the ability to combine a series of social behaviors into more complex patterns) varied from 11 to 48% for different toddlers.

Vandell also examined the stability across time in the rankings of the toddler boys. She found that toddlers who directed numerous behaviors to a peer at 16 months could be expected to direct many social behaviors to a peer at 22 months as well. The toddlers who unsuccessfully tried to initiate interactions at 16 months tended to be the same toddlers who were unsuccessful at interaction initiations at 22 months. Furthermore, the use of coordinated behaviors was correlated over the 6-month period; the toddler who ranked lower on the use of coordinated behaviors in period 1 continued to be ranked lower in later periods.

Lee (1973), investigating another aspect of individual differences, looked at the most- and least-preferred social partner in a playgroup. Lee defined "most-preferred" to be the infant with whom other infants most tried to interact and "least-preferred" to be that infant who other infants avoided. Looking at a playgroup of five infants, Lee found consistency in the infants' preferences. All infants in the group most preferred one infant, Jenny, while three of the four other infants least preferred another infant, Patrick. Examining what Jenny and Patrick did during social encounters, Lee tried to account for their different popularity.

In her examination, Lee found some potentially important differences. Jenny initiated only 44% of the interactions in which she participated, while Patrick initiated 59%. The choice of behaviors during interaction also varied, with Jenny typically using more distal contacts while Patrick adopted more proximal ones. Specifically, Jenny was more likely to initiate with a simple look or an approach, while Patrick was more likely to "grab." Once the interactions began, the differences in least- and most-preferred persisted. While most of Jenny's contacts were reciprocal whether she initiated the interaction or not, Patrick participated reciprocally only if he had initiated the interaction.

Attempts to account for the individual differences observed have met with ambiguous results. Bronson (1975) and Eckerman et al. (1975), for example, examined social behaviors and interaction sequences for evidence of birth-order differences and sex differences. Neither study of toddlers found any significant differences on either of these measures. Boys and girls and first-born/later-born were similar on a variety of measures including number of social behaviors and frequency and duration of interaction.

In contrast to Bronson (1975) and Eckerman et al. (1975), birth-order differences—in contradictory directions—have been reported by other researchers. Shirley (1933) reported that babies with older siblings responded more cooperatively than did those infants without older siblings. For her study, Shirley placed unfamiliar infants face to face and presented them with a series of toys. Those infants without older siblings were less responsive to their peer's social overtures than were those infants with older siblings. Shirley further observed that mothers reported that their babies with older brothers and sisters were generally more responsive (as shown by more smiles, laughs, and kicks) with older children than they were with adults.

More recently, Kelly (1976) has shown other differences in the peer-directed behavior of children with siblings and those without siblings. In observations of 40 children (30–36 months) in a playgroup setting, Kelly found significant differences in the social skills of the two groups of children. Children with older siblings were significantly more likely to initiate interactions with a peer and significantly less likely to initiate interactions with a teacher. At the same time, the children without siblings were most likely to engage in solitary play.

Lewis et al.'s (1975) results, on the other hand, run directly counter to Kelly's (1976) and Shirley's (1933). Lewis et al. (1975) observed that the variable "sibling number" was inversely related to the amount of peer-directed social behavior. In other words, the more children in an infant's family, the less social the child.

Thus, the impact of siblings on early infant sociability remains a matter for further research. This issue, as well as the overall role of individual differences and subject variables in general, stands as an obvious gap in the growing literature.

Infant-Infant Interaction and Mother-Child Interaction

While this chapter is primarily concerned with infant-infant social encounters, it is important to remember that these encounters are part of the infants' larger social experience. For most infants, most of the day is spent with adults, not peers, and for many infants that adult is the mother. With the outline of the infant-infant literature completed, the issue of the relationship between mother-child and child-child encounters can be examined. In the discussion that follows two successive issues are addressed. First, studies that compare infant encounters with both mother and peer present are outlined. With these studies, the question, "Given the choice of interacting with mother and peer when both are present, who is chosen?" is asked. After comparisons between these mother-child-peer contacts are made, a second question is pursued. It is, "What are the differences in mother-child dyads and child-child dyads, when these dyads are observed alone?" Several recent studies have dealt with this question, and those results are given in the final section of Part 1.

Mother-Infant-Peer Encounters

Most of the studies (Eckerman et al., 1975; Lewis et al., 1975; Rubenstein and Howes, 1976; Lenssen, 1975) that have examined infants' preferences for mother versus peer have reached similar conclusions even though they varied in behavioral setting, peer familiarity, and playgroup size. These studies have almost unanimously recorded an infant preference for peers when both kinds of partners were available.

Lenssen, for example, compared 10-month-olds' reactions to a 10-month-old stranger, to a 5-month-old stranger, and to their own mothers in a laboratory setting. She found a marked propensity for an infant to look at his mother when alone with her and at a peer stranger when s/he appeared. With both mother and peer present, the infant directed more "looks," "touches," and "proximity-seeking" behavior to the peer, not the mother. With the peer present, behaviors to the mother declined.

Using a situation that varied in some significant ways from Lenssen's, Rubenstein and Howes (1976) reported a similar toddler preference for peers. They observed eight toddlers in their home on two occasions, once with the mother alone and once with mother and infant friend present. During the peer visits, the toddlers were found to play with, imitate, talk to, and offer objects more often to their peer friends than to their mothers. When the mothers' and infants' behaviors were compared during the peer friends' visits and when they were alone, other significant differences were found. Both mother and child initiated verbal interactions and responded to each other's verbalizations significantly less frequently when the toddler friend was present. On one measure, however, there was no effect on the mother-child behavior by the peer's presence. The amount of tactile contact did not vary across the two situations.

Two additional studies that examined the child's behavior to mother and peer in still another situation, a group setting of unfamiliar peers, should also be discussed. These studies, while sharing some important features, illustrate a difficulty in cross-study comparisons.

During their observations of playgroups between unfamiliar toddlers, Lewis et al. (1975) found a differential preference for mother and peer, with the toddlers directing more proximal behaviors to their mothers (touching and proximity-seeking) and more distal behaviors (looking, etc.) to their peers. On other behaviors they found additional variation in which "taking an object" was much more likely to be directed to a peer as was simple "looking." Object offers, on the other hand, were equally likely to be directed to mother or peer. Overall, more social interaction was found between toddler peers than between mother-toddler pairs.

While similar to Lewis et al. in the use of playgroups of unfamiliar children, Bronson's (1974, 1975) finding of infant preferences differs. Bronson reported that, in her obsevations, peers were noticeably infrequent targets for interaction. Thus, in Bronson's study, the toddlers directed most of their behaviors toward toys, then toward their mothers, and only then toward their peers.

How may Bronson's results be reconciled with Lewis et al.'s, or can they? While the two studies are very similar in many situational variables, they differ in one significant aspect. Their definition of what constitutes a social behavior varied. Bronson did not record "visual regard alone" as a social behavior, while Lewis et al. did. Since both studies noted that "looking" was the modal peer-directed behavior, this difference in measures adopted may account for the differences reported.

Comparison of Mother-Child and Child-Child Encounters

The final issue to be addressed in Part 1 concerns the similarities and differences that one might expect from toddler-toddler and mother-toddler encounters. The outline of these similarities and differences may be seen as a first step in the attempt to understand the development and relationship of the two kinds of social encounters. Ultimately, the question to which an answer is sought is a three-pronged one: (1) does the parent-child system act as a precursor to the child-child system?, or (2) do the parent-child and child-child systems develop in a simultaneous, parallel fashion?, or (3) are the two systems basically dissimilar and nonoverlapping? Before these questions can be pursued, observations that establish the similarities and differences of the two systems over time are required. Such observations are beginning to accumulate.

Vandell (1976) compared the mother-child and child-child encounters of six male toddlers over a 6-month period. With both peers and mothers, the toddlers were observed in a dyadic, familiar setting with a familiar social partner. Comparisons of these two interactional experiences revealed significant underlying similarities and differences.

First of all, in looking at the relative contributions of the social partners to the interactions, differences in the two kinds of interaction experience became apparent. In Vandell's mother-child observations, the mothers were almost always the initiator of the interactions, and the toddlers the terminators. Furthermore, the mothers almost always responded to the toddlers' attempts to initiate an interaction, while the toddlers for their part were significantly less likely to respond to the mother.

These patterns of initiation and termination were significantly different from those seen in the toddler-toddler situation. For example, both the number and percent of unsuccessful interaction attempts were found to be greater in the toddler-toddler setting. The responsibility for initiating and terminating interactions was also distributed more evenly in the toddler setting. In the peer system there was not one partner (like the mother) who consistently maintained and sought interactions.

Examination of the content of the toddlers' behavior to mother and peer showed still other differences in the two interaction experiences. With their mothers, toddlers (16–22 months) became increasingly vocal; with their peers, the toddlers became relatively more motoric. It looked as if the toddlers adopted different modes of interaction with their different social partners (vocalizations with mother and motor behaviors with peer).

When the specific types of motor behaviors used with mother versus toddler peer were examined, still other differences in the two systems were apparent. The percentage of behaviors that were "agonistic," "look-alone responses," and "object-taking" were significantly higher toward the peer than toward the mother. This discrepancy between the toddlers' behavior to mothers and peers was particularly apparent when the three most commonly occurring behavior categories in each observation period were compared. At 16 and 19 months, there was no overlap in the toddlers' three most common kinds of behavior to the two different social partners. Only at 22 months did the toddlers begin to direct similar kinds of behavior to mother and peer.

With these differences between the parent-toddler and toddler-toddler systems in terms of relative participation and content areas, one may question how closely the systems are related. Indeed, Lewis et al. (1975) have argued that differences are so pervasive as to indicate that the two systems develop in a nonoverlapping fashion. Can that argument be made yet, however?

On other types of analyses, underlying similarities in the two kinds of experiences were evident. For example, Vandell noted similar developmental trends in the mother-toddler and toddler-toddler dyads she observed. Measures of interaction like number of actor exchanges, percent time in interaction, and mean interaction duration increased systematically with both partners. Similarly, individual measures of toddler performance showed systematic increases with both kinds of social partners. Thus, the number of toddler-coordinated behaviors increased with both partners as did the number of interactions initiated by the toddler.

Quantitatively, however, the rates of occurrence of the individual and interaction measures were greater in the mother-toddler setting. The toddlers directed many more social behaviors to the mother when only she was available than they did with the peer in the toddler-toddler situation. The toddlers also had significantly more interactions of longer duration in the mother-child setting. A measure of optimal performance, the number of actor exchanges in the longest interaction, further illustrated the quantitative differences observed. With the peer, 17 alternations was the maximum number observed, while with the mother interactions with 38 alternations were seen.

Eckerman et al. have argued from similar developmental trends and quantitative differences that toddler-toddler interaction lags behind mother-toddler interaction. As Eckerman et al. (1975) have conceptualized,

Both the correspondence in forms of behavior toward the mother and the peer and the initially greater frequency of these behaviors toward the mother suggest that young children generalize to peer relations developed through interaction with familiar adults. [p. 48]

The issue then of the relationship between mother-child and child-child interaction is far from resolved. Existing data point to contrary conclusions. Thus, this section must end with a call for additional empirical and conceptual work on the relationship between the two social systems.

PART 2: A REVIEW OF CONCEPTS AND DEVELOPMENTAL HYPOTHESES

In summarizing the existing research, we did not pause very long over concepts such as peer "social behavior" or "social interaction." Yet these terms are being used in a variety of ways, and it is important to recognize these differences and their implications. Part 1 attempted an integration of the empirical findings. Here we attempt an integration of concepts and hypotheses regarding infant peer relations.

This is a working paper. The rebirth of interest in early peer relations is so new that we have no entrenched concepts. Such flexibility could serve as a strength, as we seek a more adequate conceptualization for the study of early peer relations.

There is probably no one "best" conceptualization for studying all facets of our subject. Concepts are more or less useful for answering certain kinds of questions. Here the questions will be developmental in focus. For example, at one point we will consider whether physical objects (things) mediate the emergence of early peer social relationships. So this review will represent an interplay between hypotheses and concepts. The question will be, "What concepts could be useful in testing these hypotheses?"

We will seek not to isolate infant peer relations from broader issues of early human development. On the contrary, the concepts and hypotheses discussed will seek to integrate the study of parent-infant and peer-peer interaction. Data from early parent-infant relationships will be employed to illustrate similarities and differences with infant-infant relationships.

At the end of this review, we will summarize the major hypotheses and concepts introduced and discussed.

Alternation and Coaction: The Problem of Timing

All specifically interactive research on infancy is forced to deal with the problem of timing. The two major concepts employed in descriptions of timing are *coaction* (or synchrony) and *alternation* (or turn taking). The importance of coaction in infant social interaction has been championed by Brazelton, Stern, and others, based mostly on work on the early infancy period (e.g., Brazelton et al., 1974; Stern, 1974). The importance of alternation has been championed in work on the toddlers by Durfee and Lee (1973), Mueller and Lucas (1975), and others. The infant workers point to the way that mother and baby sustain periods of mutual gaze with each other and the way even their vocalizations coincide in time. The toddler workers, some having moved to infancy, from earlier work on verbal interaction, stress sustained turn-taking and perfect alternation sequences in toddlers' spontaneous play.

Each group defines what *it* studies as social interaction, yet *what* is studied seems different, almost opposing. Thus, one conceptual issue that will be treated here is what kinds of relatedness in behavior to define as social interaction. But before recommending our definition, we will explore the hypothesis that coaction, in the form of synchronous attention or engagement, is developmentally prior to alternation or turn-taking.

Mutual Engagement: A Developmental Pathway to Peer and Parent-Infant Relations

Despite the small number of fully interactional studies completed to date, there is considerable agreement among them regarding the developmental primacy of mutual engagement. Indeed, the work on early infancy suggests that sustained periods of mutual visual attention are the earliest contacts of any kind between an infant and its mother. Brazelton et al. (1974) described mother-infant contacts from 2 to 20 weeks. By 4 weeks, they were engaging in cyclic periods of shared attention and withdrawal. As observations continued it appeared that some mothers adjusted their rhythm to that of their infants while others did not. In the former cases infant looking at mother increased, while in the later cases it declined. In general, Brazelton et al. attribute the primary role in the production of this synchrony to the mother.

Stern (1974) conceptualizes the infant's gaze-alternation as an "intrinsic biological process" [p. 210], and Bruner (1969) argues that after 1 month, the infant's visual attention has moved from "diffuse distractability in the weeks immediately following birth to a stage of stuckness where attention has an 'obligatory character' " [p. 255]. The infant's attention is controlled by its biology and is "hooked onto" the mother's face. Stern's (1974) data on mutual visual gaze at 3 to 4 months supports the Brazelton et al. view that the mother produces the mutual engagement, through her unfailing attention to her offspring. Specifically, Stern reported that the infant initiated and terminated 94% of all mutual gazes. The infant cycled in and out of attention, but the mother was always ready and watching!

There is evidence that a state of mutual engagement is important in early peer relations as well. However, here the literature does not examine its developmental primacy. Bleier (1976) studied 480 peer-directed behaviors among 1-year-olds. He found that prior mutual looking was among the significant predictors of peer response. Thus, in 1-year-olds, mutual engagement increases the likelihood that a child will find his social behavior receiving a response from his peer. At this early age, however, Bleier's multiple-regression analysis showed that children's proximity and quality of the social behavior were of even more importance in response elicitations.

Data on verbal interaction in 2-year-olds (Mueller et al., 1977) and 3- to 5-year-olds (Mueller, 1972) showed that states of prior engagement were the *best* predictors of verbal interaction, more important even than what the speaker said!

In summary, there is evidence both from the peer and parent-infant systems pointing to the importance of mutual engagement in emerging social interaction. The parent-infant literature also suggests that states of mutual engagement are the first form of parent-infant relationship, developmentally prior to a relationship marked by sequencing of mutually elicited behaviors.

Infant Peer Relations and Infant-Parent Relations Contrasted

Lately, J. J. Gibson has spoken frequently about the affordances of the environment. They are what the environment offers or provides to actors. Thus chairs afford sitting and sidewalks afford walking. Using Gibson's concept, we will explore the hypotheses that (1) parents afford engagement at a point in development where peers do not and (2) peer-peer engagement emerges in a different context than parent-infant engagement.

Consider the data from Stern (1974) and Brazelton et al. (1974) already introduced. The parents were always available for engaging their infant's eyes. Their "mother love" made them into almost perfect engagement-affording creatures to their largely incompetent offspring. Indeed, Stern (1974) notes that, of the motor systems that will eventually mature, the visual motor system is the earliest to become functionally mature (by the 3rd month). The infant can attend actively before it can do much else.

The situation vis-à-vis infant peers is very different. Even if an *en face* position could be sustained, which is doubtful given weakness of neck musculature, the biological rhythms of attention and withdrawal would prevent all but random synchronies in their gaze. Therefore, purely on the basis of relative affordances, it is possible to conclude that normal parent-infant engagement will occur prior to normal peer-peer engagement.

The second hypothesis states that when peer relations do emerge, they do so indirectly from fortuitous contacts with physical objects. Again, the Stern and Brazelton et al. research provides valuable evidence regarding the emergence of parent-infant relations: there are no physical objects involved. The mother and infant engage each other directly using visual attention, smiling, and vocalization as the tools for building the relationship.

The situation with agemates may be very different, yet much more evidence on the first 12 months is needed. As was shown in the empirical review, the role of objects in mediating the foundation of peer relations may be universal, or it may be mediated by developing interest and skill with objects and by situation and culture. Lichtenberger's (1965) clinical observation of his infant twins does not resolve this issue. Some of the sequences he observed at 3 months appear to be object-free social interactions between the twins. Yet other of his observations, such as the stage from 3 to 6 months where contacts around objects are totally lacking in social interaction, make one wonder how far the twins' social interaction has progressed.

Vincze (1971) was the first to observe that the mediating role of things in toddlers' relationships increases with age, presumably as toddlers' skills with things also increase. Studying 12-month-old boys, Mueller and Brenner (1977) recently have demonstrated that peer interaction may begin in an object-mediated context. They studied all times when playgroup toddlers were in contact. Contact was defined to include both those periods when two children were active with the same toy (parallel play time) or with each other (social-interaction time). When over half the duration of a given contact was parallel play, the contact was called "object-focused." At 12 months, 92% of all social interaction observed was embedded in object-focused contacts. This percentage declined over time, and by 18 months, only 69% of social interactions were similarly embedded. In other words, just under one-third of all interaction now occurred during contact where peer interaction, rather than parallel play, was the predominant focus of activity. Summarizing across the entire period studied, 12 to 24 months, no more than 17% of all social interactions were free of mediating objects.

Yet the generality of these results remains in doubt. Do much younger children, say 3- to 8-month-olds, children less skilled with things, form peer social relationships directly? Is the developmental pathway through object contacts stamped "made in the United States"? One of us recently observed that urban poor children in Colombia, South America, have very few toys, but many siblings, at their disposal from birth. Would this environment not foster a different pathway to peer and sibling relations? We need not seek one universal pathway to peer relations for all children. However, the existing data suggest that at least some children first meeting their agemates around their first birthday in fact begin to interact in object-mediated contacts. This is very different from the way a parent and infant first appear to interact with each other.

Thus, we reach a paradox of early social development. Some infants who are able to engage one part of their social environment—namely, parents—before engaging either objects or peers, return to explore peers only after a long period of developing object competencies. And indeed, the return is indirect, at first contacting peers largely because of mutually shared interest in and skills with objects.

Lee (1975) and Cooney (1975) suggest that social schemes are more difficult to construct than are schemes with objects. The variability and complexity of social responsiveness is seen as more difficult to master, thus retarding social development.

Yet, this argument may overlook the large extent to which parents are disposed to interact with their offspring. Just as the child's linguistic environment is simpler than was once thought, so may be the infant's nonverbal social environment. As Brazelton and Stern have shown, the earliest skills at the infant's disposal—looking, smiling, cooing— interact with parents, not with things. Thus skills with things may well have their developmental basis in social experience, and not the reverse. Incidentally, this conclusion is in agreement with Piaget's early (1954) and contemporary (1971) statements on the matter. Yet Piaget's own research data focus on the object side of cognitive growth, making his theoretical stance easy to forget!

Perhaps once again here the issue of skill growth is best resolved by reference to relative affordances. Parents afford interactive relationships before anything else, including even the infant's own hands. Yet peers afford very little, while nonsocial objects are intermediate, being easier to control than are peers for many months.

To summarize, it may not be possible to make general statements about the relative complexity of social and nonsocial objects. "Mother love" may appear silly or mindless but it may be exactly the kind of behavior that permits the early growth of social interaction. Peers are not programmed in a similiar way and thus do not afford relationships for some time.

Peer Social Development as an Interplay between Cognitive and Social Systems

Recently many students of early social development have called for more research in a dyadic or interactional framework (e.g., Bronson, 1974; Cairns, 1972; Edwards and Whiting, 1976). Lewis and Lee-Painter (1974) state, "Psychology of all the sciences, may be the most interactive; the study of elements per se the least fruitful" [p. 21]. Yet an interacting dyad—two peers or a mother and her infant—is a social system, abeit a small one. Its analysis does not let one distinguish the social competence of either participant. One can of course say that one dyad has longer or more diverse interactions than another dyad, but this is all.

Yet, the growth of *individual* social competence, particularly the infant's, is of ultimate interest to the developmental psychologist.

Therefore methods must be found for assessing the individual's social skills and preferences at the same time, and using the same spontaneous behavior that composes the social interactions under study. Yet the only evidence about the individual's skill contributing to natural interactions are the behavioral units or elements that compose those interactions. The behavioral elements are attributable to individuals. Thus, despite Lewis and Lee-

Painter's admonition that analysis of the elements does not appear fruitful, there is no where else to turn for information about individual contributions to ongoing interactions.

In the early seventies, working independently, Bronson (1972), and Mueller and Lucas (1975) adopted novel yet similiar conceptualizations of peer social behavior. Rather than viewing social actions as indivisible units of meaning (e.g., hit, smile, laugh, push), they analyzed social behaviors as organized *coordinations* of specific actions (e.g., look and smile; vocalize and point). The focus of this approach was both developmental and Piagetian. When a child is able to coordinate looking at a peer with banging on the table, one recognizes a developmental achievement, a coordination not possible at an earlier period of infancy. It was Piaget (1952) who demonstrated that the general course of infant development could be seen as a progressive series of such coordinations.

Mueller and Rich (1976) identified two levels of coordination in toddlers' social behavior. The first was the coordination between looking at another child while doing something else—either smiling or vocalizing or performing some motor pattern. In all the studies from our laboratory, this coordination was called a socially directed behavior (SDB). The second level of coordination simply joined looking and one action to a second action, usually in a different modality. Here, for example, a child offered an object to another child, while also vocalizing, while also looking at his peer (look and vocalize and offer).

This approach proved to be useful in several ways. First it revealed the continued growth of cognitive skills relevant to peer interaction in the 2nd year—a time when most specific sensory-motor social behaviors are already established (see Mueller and Rich, 1976; Mueller and Brenner, 1977; and Part 1 of this review).

Second, and most relevant for the present discussion of cognitive and social systems, this approach provided a measure of spontaneous social skill which was conceptually and operationally independent of the interactions themselves. Thus, it became possible to ask how infants' social skills, and the interactions in which they participate, influence one another. Is a certain level of skill necessary for social interactions to occur? Do skill levels and interaction complexities develop apace? Does experience in the social system itself act as a source of skill? The results of Mueller and Brenner (1977), Mueller (in press), and Vandell (1976) support affirmative answers to all three questions. Without reviewing those results here, it may be valuable to note how participation in the social system could generate cognitive changes. We stress this direction of influence because so much modern psychology tends to see social interaction only as a product of cognitive change and not the opposite.

An example: After toddlers have interacted for some time, they begin to offer each other things. But our data reveal that, for several months, the offering and receiving is never reciprocal. That is, one child offers over and over, and the other receives over and over. They do not hand a single object back and forth. Why not? Mueller and Lucas (1975) hypothesized that offering and receiving are complementary roles in a social interaction. Toddlers appear to require considerable experience in such interactions, sometimes as "offerer" and sometimes as "receiver" before they can intercoordinate both roles in a single action. That is, the child receiving the toy must rapidly role-reverse (i.e., assume the prior role of other) and offer the toy back again. The toddler may acquire this skill from repeated participation in already established peer social interaction. We do not claim to know how social interaction participation works. The example is simply illustrative of the importance of conducting research that is conceptually sensitive to the degree of organization present *both* in the cognitive system and in the social system. Such research must recognize the possibility of mutual influence (i.e., interaction!) between the two systems. This may require complex analysis, but we agree with Hinde (1974) that understanding human behavior may make landing on the moon look easy.

Toward a Working Definition of Social Interaction

In the previous section we conceptualized social skill as a coordination of separate actions. A socially directed behavior was seen as a developmental achievement, requiring practice with the initially separate components (Piaget, 1952). In analogous fashion, early social interaction may be conceptualized as a developmental product composed of sustained mutual engagement and sequences of mutually elicited actions. Here we part company with Brazelton and Stern, whose research has been so useful; and even here, the departure concerns only definition, not substance.

Brazelton and Stern both considered states of mutual engagement as a type of social interaction. Yet for us the concept of social interaction connotes the idea that "individuals influence each other's behavior" (Hinde, 1974, p. 49). Yet in those early parent-infant engagements there is no demonstration of reciprocal elicitation sequences. The devoted parents watch their infant, whose cycling of attention is biologically rhythmic and whose attention to the parents' faces is stimulus-directed and obligatory. Rather than constituting social interaction, these periods of engagement seem to provide the necessary context where an infant and parent can first become aware of their powers to reciprocally influence each other through use of their eyes, smiles, and vocalizations. Peer interaction lags so far behind because the necessary mutual engagement is at first impossible and later occurs chiefly through indirect object-mediated channels.

Stern et al. (1975) studied mother-infant vocalizations at 3 to 4 months. Examining only vocalizations, they proposed that coaction (i.e., synchrony) and alternation "develop as distinct modes serving separate communicative functions" [p. 99]. Alternating vocalizations are thought to lead to conversational exchange while "the coaction mode transmits emotional communications expressing the nature of the ongoing interpersonal relationship, as well as contributing to the foundation of the relationship" [p. 99]. From a developmental perspective, it is the last phrase that is so important. Stern et al. note that "coactional vocalizing occurs almost invariably during mutual gaze" [p. 98]. Thus *it is in a time of preexisting engagement that the mutual vocalizing occurs*. Stern and his co-workers have provided a striking demonstration of the extent of overlap in infant-mother vocalizing. However, when the total relationship is viewed, the mutual vocalizations may be seen as punctuating the preexisting state of engagement based in visual attention. In the same regard, it should be noted that the Stern et al. coaction vocalizations may be as much elicited responses as are their alternating vocalizations. Their results suggest that each partner tends to follow the other's initiation, and that the mother tends to sustain her own vocalization for the duration of her infant's utterance.

In summary, there is a growing body of research that is compatible with the view that a first step in early social development is the achievement of engagement, usually seen in terms of sustained mutual gazing. Within these engagements develop the first mutual elicitations of discrete social behaviors. It seems preferable to limit the definition of social interaction to instances that reflect *both* engagement and elicitation, and not only the former.

The Further Development of Social Interaction: Interact Versus Interchange

Let us label as "interacts" those interactions containing but a single initiation and response. Let us call longer-chained interactions "interchanges." Mueller and Lucas (1975) introduced these terms for theoretical reasons. They proposed that interchanges were more difficult to achieve since some of their component actions were bidirectional, responding to one social behavior while also anticipating and seeking another.

Now we have some empirical results supporting this view. There is a preponderance of interacts among the interactions of 1-year-old boys (Fig. 16-1). It suggests that, at this age, children have difficulty sustaining their peer interaction beyond the initial response. Other data (Mueller and Brenner, 1977) show that prior peer experience elevates the spontaneous rate of interchanges, but does not increase the rate of interacts. Thus at age 17 months, toddlers *without* peer experience can vocalize to their peers and receive a laugh in response. But that is all. Without 4 months of peer experience they cannot turn the fun into something sustained, something that one might call a "game." Interchanges appear to involve more than the simple extension of elicited responses. They have a more complex but identifiable structure (Mueller and Lucas, 1975) and they evolve only through sustained experience with given social partners.

To summarize, we see sustained games called interchanges as the last major achievement of infant peer social development. Considering only the social system, the earlier achievements are mutual engagements followed by mutual engagement with interacts. But as we discussed earlier, cognitive change is occurring alongside the social system change. That is, the coordination of the behavioral components of social interaction is developing also. It has proved difficult to devise concepts that are bias-free regarding the potential roles of both cognition and interaction in early social development. The next section suggests a resolution.

"Contingent Upon" Versus "Elicited By": Alternate Criteria of Interactions

As treated here, social interaction is a concept that must utilize the idea of *efficient causation*. We have said that to interact is to *have an influence upon*. Since the "object" influenced is always another person, then the influence is always *external*, which is compatible with the idea of efficient cause. (Bunge, 1959).

Yet the idea of causation is seen as subjective in much science, and the zeitgeist is such that the idea of "contingency" is often substituted. Contingency usually implies only contiguity in time or in time and space, without including the causal trapping implicit in the idea of elicitation. Much peer research (including our own) followed this line of reasoning and recognized social interaction whenever two socially directed behaviors (SDB) were close in time, say within 3 sec (Vandell, 1976). This approach seemed quite satisfactory with our 1-year-olds since SDBs were well developed and contingencies between them in fact averaged under 2 sec (Mueller and Brenner, 1977). However, in still younger children, SDBs may not be so well developed, and it may be invalid to assume that interaction is the outcome of stringing SDBs together. Other observations added to the problem. Mueller and DeStefano (1973) found that not all peer interactive sequences were composed of SDBs. One example, preserved on videotape, shows one child systematically closing a surprise box while the other child depresses the lever which reopens it. Yet they never look at each other as they inadvertently control each other's behavior. Also studying toddlers, Bleier (1976) found that among all responses to sampled SDBs, only

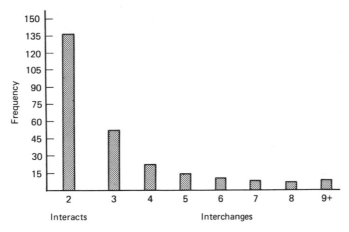

Figure 16-1.   Frequency of social interactions of differing lengths (as measured in number of component behaviors) among 1-year-olds in a playgroup.

47% were SDB responses. That is, much social behavior, while clearly influencing the peer, did not produce a socially engaged response. Yet it *did* constitute interaction in the sense of response elicitation. Thus there are a number of grounds for supposing that among peers many interactions *precede* the sustained social engagement necessary for sequences of SDBs to occur. Thus the only unbiased conceptualization for studying the emergence of peer social interaction must capture all early social behaviors as well as all interactions. Only then can one show clearly how participation in interaction makes the child social, and how the social child makes interaction.

Yet how is one to identify interactions that are *not* composed of SDBs? Here, we submit the criterion of contingency becomes hopelessly inadequate because, given two active toddlers, on the basis of chance alone there are an almost unlimited number of contingencies between their behavior. Therefore, it is necessary to identify interactions based on coder judgments of response elicitation. In our laboratory Bleier (1976) was the first to approach the problem in this way. Using a three-value code—(1) elicited, (2) possibly elicited by, and (3) not elicited—he found that coders could reach 90% simple agreement. Therefore, it may be possible to identify elicited sequences reliably.

The end result of this analysis is a recommendation. Further studies of the origins of peer social relations are advised to consider two types of basic units. The first is SDB, the basic cognitive-social unit. The second is instances of an elicitation relationship between the two infants' behavior. It is proposed as the basic unit of the interactive system, a system that has been found to exist before many of its component behaviors are socially directed.

Summary and Conclusion

A summary listing of the main hypotheses developed in the conceptual review may be useful. They are listed in order of discussion in Part 2.

1.   Mutual engagement is hypothesized to be a necessary and, in some instances, prior achievement on the developmental pathway to social interaction.

2.   Parents are hypothesized to afford engagement earlier than peers.

3.   Physical objects are hypothesized to play major contextual roles in the emergence of peer social interactions in children first meeting their peers at age 12 months or beyond. However, the generality of this pattern remains untested or in dispute. Children at younger ages, in different behavioral settings, or from different cultures may not mediate their early contacts with things. Nevertheless, whenever it occurs, object mediation is seen as an important and very different pathway to social interaction than the object-free pathway hypothesized for early infant-parent relationships.

4.   An adequate conceptualization of spontaneous early peer relations requires analysis of both individual social competence and social interaction itself.

5.   Individual social competence may be analyzed as series of coordinations of specific actions. The primary achieved coordination is the socially directed behavior.

6.   In similar fashion, it is hypothesized that social interaction is an achieved coordination between mutual engagement (mutual attention) and mutual influence (reciprocal control).

7.   Yet clinical evidence exists suggesting that toddlers achieve some object-mediated reciprocal control before they achieve mutual engagement. Conceptualizations of the origins of peer relations must incorporate the possibility that peer relations move from reciprocal control to mutual attention, and not just the opposite. It is argued that such a conceptualization will need to define interaction in terms of elicitation rather than in terms of a simple contiguity of behaviors.

Two themes in the conceptual review (items 1 and 7, above) appear to be contradictory. At first, we developed the hypothesis that mutual engagement, usually defined as sustained periods of reciprocal visual gaze, is a developmental achievement preceding reciprocal social interaction. Later, we suggested that some nonsocial interactions precede social interactions. Yet nonsocial interactions are precisely those *lacking* engagement between the participating actors. Thus at one point we argued that engagement leads to social interaction and at another point that interaction chains exist and only later become social.

It is possible that parent-infant relations follow one path while peer relations follow the other. Or possibly the parallel play of toddlers is itself a much more sophisticated kind of mutual engagement than is presently recognized. Whatever the ultimate outcome, the study of early social development has achieved a level of methodological and conceptual acuity that should permit a resolution of such issues.

APPENDIX: USEFUL EQUIPMENT AND DEFINITIONS

The rebirth of interest in early peer relations may well have had a technological basis. Bronson, Lee, and ourselves all based large peer research projects on videotape. Mueller and Brenner (1977) have shown that the rate of social behaviors in toddlers' interactions is so rapid that the interactions could never be fully analyzed without film or tape assistance.

Half-inch black-and-white videotape systems with two cameras and devices for mixing their output, thus keeping track of both members of a dyad, cost about $3000. Single-camera systems cost about half as much. Whatever system is employed, a most valuable accessory item is the *time-date generator*. It places a digital clock and date directly on the videotape record, and is invaluable in relocating sequences and timing durations.

As many concepts were introduced in the course of this review, we append a summary listing.

Concepts Related to Social Behavior

- *directed behavior*: any discrete act by an infant directed toward some object, either social or nonsocial
- *socially directed behavior (SDB)*: any directed behavior accompanied by visual attention to another person
- *coordinated SDB*: combinations of behaviors usually in different modalities accompanied by visual attention to another person

Concepts Related to Interaction

- *engagement*: a period of mutual attention between an infant and another person
- *object-focused contact*: a period of time when both an infant and another person are directing behavior to a common nonsocial object
- *interaction*: an elicitation (or a series of elicitations) between the directed behaviors of an infant and another person
- *social interaction*: same as interaction except composed exclusively of SDBs, thus indicating maintained engagement between the children
- *interact*: an interaction containing only a single elicitation
- *interchange*: an interaction containing two or more elicitations

BIBLIOGRAPHY

Apolloni, T., and Cooke, T. Peer behavior conceptualized as a variable influencing infant and toddler development. *American Journal of Orthopsychiatry,* 1975, **45**, 4–17.

Becker, J. A learning analysis of the development of peer oriented behaviors in nine-month-old infants. *Developmental Psychology,* 1977, **13**, 481–491.

Berlyne, D. *Conflict, Arousal, and Curiosity.* New York: McGraw-Hill, 1960.

Bleier, M. R. Social behaviors among one-year-olds in a playgroup. Unpublished Ph.D. dissertation, Boston University, 1976.

Blurton Jones, N. G. An ethological study of some aspects of social behavior of children in nursery school. In D. Morris (ed.), *Primate Ethology.* Chicago: Aldine, 1967.

Blurton Jones, N. (ed.). *Ethological Studies of Child Behaviour.* London: Cambridge University, 1972.

Brazelton, T. B., Koslowski, B., and Main, M. The origins of reciprocity: The early mother-infant interaction. In M. Lewis and L. A. Rosenblum (eds.), *The Effect of the Infant on its Caregiver.* New York: Wiley, 1974.

Bridges, K. M. B. A study of social development in early infancy. *Child Development,* 1933, **4**, 36–49.

Bronson, W. C. Competence and the growth of personality. In J. S. Bruner and K. J. Connolly (eds.), *The Early Growth of Competence*. New York: Academic, 1972.

Bronson, W. C. Mother-toddler interaction: A perspective on studying the development of competence. *Merrill Palmer Quarterly*, 1974, **20**, 275–301.

Bronson, W. Peer-peer interactions in the second year of life. In M. Lewis and L. A. Rosenblum (eds.), *Friendship and Peer Relations*. New York: Wiley, 1975.

Bruner, J. S. Eye, hand and mind. In D. Elkind and J. H. Flavell (eds.), *Studies in Cognitive Development: Essays in Honor of Jean Piaget*. New York: Oxford University, 1969.

Bühler, C. Die ersten sozialen Verhaltungsweisen des Kindes. In C. Buhler (ed.) *Soziologische und psychologische Studien über das erste Lebensjahr*. Jena: Gustav Fischer, 1927.

Bühler, C. The social behavior of children. In C. Murchison (ed.), *Handbook of Child Psychology*. Worcester, Mass.: Clark University, 1933.

Bunge, M. *Causality: The Place of the Causal Principle in Modern Science*. Cambridge, Mass.: Harvard University, 1959.

Cairns, R. B. Attachment and dependency: A psychological and social-learning synthesis. In J. L. Gewirtz (ed.), *Attachment and Dependency*. Washington, D.C.: Winston, 1972.

Cooney, E. W. Social-cognitive development: Applications to intervention and evaluation in the elementary grades. Paper presented at the meeting of the American Psychological Association, Chicago, September 1975.

DeStefano, C. T. Unpublished Ph.D. dissertation, Boston University, 1976. Environmental determinants of peer social activity in 18-month-old males.

Dragsten, S. S., and Lee, L. C. Infants' social behavior in a naturalistic vs. experimental setting. Paper presented at the meeting of the American Psychological Association, Montreal, August 1973.

Durfee, J. T., and Lee, L. C. Infant-infant interaction in a daycare setting. Presented at the meeting of the American Psychological Association, Montreal, August 1973.

Eckerman, C. O., Whatley, J., and Kutz, S. Growth of social play with peers during the second year of life. *Developmental Psychology*, 1975, **11**, 42–49.

Edwards, C. P., and Whiting, B. B. Dependency in dyadic context: New meaning for an old construct. Paper presented at the meeting of the Eastern Psychological Association, New York, April 1976.

Fischoff, A. A comparison between peer-oriented social behavior of kibbutz and city infants in different settings. Unpublished masters thesis, Hebrew University, 1974.

Garvey, C. Some properties of social play. *Merrill Palmer Quarterly*, 1974, **20**, 163–180.

Hinde, R. A. (ed.). *Nonverbal Communication*. London: Cambridge University, 1972.

Hinde, R. A. *Biological Bases of Human Social Behavior*. New York: McGraw-Hill, 1974.

Hubbs, L. Infant-infant interaction. Unpublished paper, Boston University, 1975.

Kelly, K. R. The effects of peer and sibling exposure on social development in young children. Unpublished paper, Boston University, 1976.

Klein, R., and Wander, E. Gruppenbildung im zweiten Lebensjahr. *Zeitschrift für Psychologie*, 1933, **128**, 257–280.

Konner, M. Relations among infants and juveniles in comparative perspective. In M. Lewis and L. A. Rosenblum (eds.), *Friendship and Peer Relations*. New York: Wiley, 1975.

Lee, L. C. Social encounters of infants: The beginnings of popularity. Paper presented at the International Society for Behavioral Development, Ann Arbor, August 1973.

Lee, L. C. Toward a cognitive theory of interpersonal development: Importance of peers. In M. Lewis and L. A. Rosenblum (eds.), *Friendship and Peer Relations*. New York: Wiley, 1975.

Lenssen, B. G. Infants' reactions to peer strangers. Paper presented at the biennial meetings of the Society for Research in Child Development, Denver, March 1975.

Lewis, M., and Lee-Painter, S. An interactional approach to the mother-infant dyad. In M. Lewis and L. A. Rosenblum (eds.), *The Effect of the Infant on its Caretaker*. New York: Wiley, 1974.

Lewis, M., and Rosenblum, L. A. (eds.). *Friendship and Peer Relations*. New York: Wiley, 1975.

Lewis, M., Young, G., Brooks, J., and Michalson, L. The beginning of friendship. In M. Lewis and L. A. Rosenblum (eds.). *Friendship and Peer Relations*. New York: Wiley, 1975.

Lichtenberger, W. *Mitmenschliches Verhalten eines Zwillingspaares in seinen ersten Lebensjahren*. Munchen: *Ernst Reinhardt*, 1965.

Maudry; M., and Nekula, M. Social relations between children of the same age during the first two years of life. *Journal of Genetic Psychology*, 1939, **54**, 193–215.

Mengert, I. G. A preliminary study of the reactions of 2-year-old children to each other when paired in a semi-controlled situation. *Journal of Genetic Psychology*, 1931, **39**, 393–398.

Missakian, E. A. Gender differences in agonistic behavior and dominance relations of communally reared children. Unpublished manuscript, 1975.

Mueller, E. The maintenance of verbal exchanges between young children. *Child Development*, 1972, **43**, 930–938.

Mueller, E. (Toddlers + toys) = (an autonomous social system). In M. Lewis and L. A. Rosenblum (eds.), *The Child and its family,* New York, Plenum, in press.

Mueller, E., and Brenner, J. The growth of social interaction in a toddler playgroup: The role of peer experience. *Child Development,* 1977, **48**, 854–861.

Mueller, E., Bleier, M., Krakow, J., Hegedus, K., and Cournoyer, P. The development of peer verbal interaction among two-year-old boys. *Child Development,* 1977, **48**, 284–287.

Mueller, E., and DeStefano, C. Sources of toddlers' peer interaction in a playgroup setting. Unpublished paper, Boston University, 1973.

Mueller, E., and Lucas, T. A developmental analysis of peer interaction among toddlers. In M. Lewis and L. A. Rosenblum (eds.), *Friendship and Peer Relations*. New York: Wiley, 1975.

Mueller, E., and Rich, A. Clustering and socially-directed behaviors in a playgroup of 1-year-old boys. *Journal of Child Psychology and Psychiatry,* 1976, **17**, 315–322.

Parten, M. Social participation among preschool children. *Journal of Abnormal and Social Psychology,* 1932, **27**, 243–269.

Parten, M. B. Social play among preschool children. *Journal of Abnormal and Social Psychology,* 1933, **28**, 136–147.

Piaget, J. *The Origins of Intelligence in Children*. New York: International Universities, 1952.

Piaget, J. *The Construction of Reality in the Child*. New York: Basic Books, 1954.

Piaget, J. *Biology and Knowledge*. Chicago: University of Chicago, 1971.

Ross, H. S., and Goldman, B. M. Establishing new social relations in infancy. In T. Alloway, L. Krames, and P. Pliner (eds.), *Advances in Communication and Affect,* Vol. 3. New York: Plenum, 1977.

Rubenstein, J., and Howes, C. The effects of peers on toddler interaction with mother and toys. *Child Development,* 1976, **47**, 597–605.

Shirley, M. *The First Two Years: A Study of Twenty-Five Babies*. Minneapolis: University of Minnesota, 1933.

Stern, D. N. Mother and infant at play: The dyadic interaction involving facial, vocal and gaze behaviors. In M. Lewis and L. A. Rosenblum (eds.), *The Effect of the Infant on its Caregiver*. New York: Wiley, 1974.

Stern, D. N., Jaffe, J., Beebe, B., and Bennett, S. L. Vocalizing in unison and in alternation: Two modes of communication within the mother-infant dyad. *Annals of the New York Academy of Science,* 1975, **263**, 89–100.

Vandell, D. L. Toddler sons' social interaction with mothers, fathers, and peers. Unpublished Ph.D. dissertation, Boston University, 1976.

Vincze, M. The social contacts of infants and young children reared together. *Early Child Development and Care,* 1971, **1**, 99–109.

Yarrow, M. R. Some perspectives on research on peer relations. In M. Lewis and L. A. Rosenblum (eds.), *Friendship and Peer Relations.* New York: Wiley, 1975.

CHAPTER 17

The Lag Sequential Analysis of Contingency and Cyclicity in Behavioral Interaction Research[1]

Gene P. Sackett

Research on the behavior of people interacting has recently proliferated. These studies employ human observers who code behavior from live, film, or videotape material. Test situations vary from laboratories to real-world settings such as schools, hospitals, and homes. Research goals also vary from simple description to testing specific hypotheses. A number of methods exist for the statistical analysis of overall, nonsequential, aspects of observational data (e.g., Gottman, 1977). However, the development of *practically useful* statistical tools for identifying contingent relationships among large numbers of behaviors poses a more difficult problem. The purpose of this chapter is to present the details of a general analysis technique for the study of these dependency relationships in multivariate observational data.

Dependency relationships can be studied in the flow of behaviors emitted by one individual or by two or more individuals measured at the same time. These dependencies can take a number of forms. Relatively simple relationships involve *pairs* of behaviors which (1) occur together at the same time (concurrent contingency), or (2) immediately precede or follow each other. Greater difficulty arises in identifying relationships among more than two behaviors. A number of behaviors can (3) occur concurrently, (4) precede or follow each other in ordered chains, or (5) follow each other at predictable future time periods. The time relationships can even involve repetitive cycles of occurrence (6) by individual behaviors (auto-contingency) or (7) between many behaviors (cross-contingency).

Much of the past work in this area has focused on simultaneously (e.g., Bakeman, 1977) or sequentially (e.g., Altmann, 1965) occurring patterns of behavior. Analysis proceeds by computer, or by hand calculations with very limited amounts of data. The analysis goal is to identify nonrandom conditional probabilities. Suppose that five behaviors *A-B-C-D-E* are studied. The data are searched for patterns of behaviors occurring at the same time or for sequential chains up to some maximal chain length. If five-step chains were of interest, a frequency count would be made of all sequential patterns of this

[1] The research reported here and preparation of this paper was supported by grant FR-00166 from the Animal Resources branch of NIH to the Regional Primate Research Center at the University of Washington and by grant HD-08633 from the Mental Retardation branch of NICHHD to the author. The model presented in this paper is an extension and refinement of the paper, "A Nonparametric Lag Sequential Analysis for Studying Dependency among Responses in Behavioral Observation Scoring Systems," which I presented at the 1974 meeting of the Western Psychological Association in San Francisco. Subsequent work on the model owes much to the thoughtful criticism and computer programming provided by my colleague Dr. Richard Holm. A Fortran computer program, with documentation, exists for performing the lag analyses described in this paper. Copies of the program can be obtained by writing to me.

623

size occurring in the flow of behavior. For example, the search might find behavior *A* followed by *B-C-D-E* in that order. A count of 1 would be made, and every time this pattern is found again another count would be added. If each of these behaviors can follow any other except itself, there are 1280 possible patterns that could occur in five-step chains. Luckily, many will not exist in real data, but a very large number will occur at least once. The situation tends to sicken when more than a few behaviors (say 10) and larger chain lengths (say 10 again) are of interest. The amount of computer output can then be physically staggering and intellectually overwhelming, and hand computation becomes practically impossible.

The model presented next is an alternative to the pattern counting method. A complete analysis will yield some of the information generated by counting actual patterns, and will suggest which among the many behaviors measured are most likely to form patterns. This will greatly reduce the effort for a subsequent pattern count. More important, the analysis allows study of conditional relationships in indefinitely long sequences, and is especially sensitive in detecting cyclic dependencies.

THE LAG CONCEPT

The basic idea in this model is an *event* or a *time* lag. The lag concept was developed for auto- and cross-correlation with quantitative variables, and the basic analytic procedure used with qualitative behaviors is as follows: (1) Choose one of the behaviors occurring in the data as a *criterion* conditional behavior. (2) Count the number of times that every behavior follows the criterion as (a) the very next behavior (lag 1), (b) the second behavior after the criterion (lag 2), (c) the third behavior after the criterion (lag 3), . . . , (d) the MAX LAG behavior after the criterion. MAX LAG is the largest sequential step of interest to the investigator. For every criterion under study, *event lags* represent the number of times that each instance of the criterion is followed by all other possible matching behaviors up to the MAX LAG event in the sequence of behavioral flow. *Time lags* are counted in the same manner as event lags, except the data are lagged in successive real-time intervals instead of sequences of events. An example should serve to remove any confusion.

Table 17-1 presents a real-time sequence of behavior changes among four events *A-B-C-D*. The left portion shows each sequential event and its duration. On the right the data are listed in successive 1-sec time unit intervals.

Event Lags

The upper portion of Table 17-2 shows results of an event lag analysis taken to lag 5. The first row (Overall) gives the frequency of occurrence *(n)* and the unconditional probability *(n/N*TOTAL) for each behavior in the data as a whole. The next five rows give the lagged matching frequencies and lagged conditional probabilities. Now, how were these numbers generated? Refer to the right half of Table 17-1, and use behavior *A* as the criterion. *A* occurs three times. *B* matches (follows) it after each of these occurrences as the next event (lag 1). So, the matching frequency for *B* at lag 1 is 3, which is seen in the lag 1 row of Table 17-2. The 3 in the "Total" column of Table 17-2 indicates that the criterion could be followed by other behaviors at lag 1 a total of three times. The lag conditional probability for any behavior matching the criterion at any lag is *n*MATCH/*N*TOTAL OF CRITERION. At lag 1 these values are 3/3 = 1.00 for behavior *B* and 0.00 for the other behaviors.

Table 17-1. Data Used to Illustrate the Event and Time Lag Concepts

Real Time Sequence			1-Sec Time Intervals					
Sequential event	Behavior	Duration (sec)	Time	Behavior	Time	Behavior	Time	Behavior
1	A	3	1	A	9	D	17	A
2	B	2	2	A	10	A	18	A
3	D	4	3	A	11	B	19	A
4	A	1	4	B	12	B	20	A
5	B	3	5	B	13	B	21	B
6	C	1	6	D	14	C	22	B
7	D	2	7	D	15	D	23	B
8	A	4	8	D	16	D	24	C
9	B	3						
10	C	1						

Table 17-2. Event and Time Lag Matching Frequencies and Probabilities for the Example Data in Table 17-1, with Behavior A as the Criterion

	Lag	Number of Matched Occurrences					Probability			
		A	B	C	D	Total	A	B	C	D
EVENT LAGS										
Overall [a]		3	3	2	2	10	0.33	0.33	0.20	0.20
	1	0	3	0	0	3	0.00	1.00	0.00	0.00
	2	0	0	2	1	3	0.00	0.00	0.67	0.33
	3	1	0	0	1	2	0.50	0.00	0.00	0.50
	4	1	1	0	0	2	0.50	0.50	0.00	0.00
	5	0	1	1	0	2	0.00	0.50	0.50	0.00
TIME LAGS										
Overall [b]		8	8	2	6	24	0.33	0.33	0.08	0.25
Level Triggered										
	1	5	3	0	0	8	0.63	0.38	0.00	0.00
	2	3	5	0	0	8	0.38	0.63	0.00	0.00
	3	1	6	0	1	8	0.13	0.75	0.00	0.13
	4	0	4	2	2	8	0.00	0.50	0.25	0.25
	5	0	2	1	4	7	0.00	0.29	0.14	0.57
Trailing Edge Triggered										
	1	0	3	0	0	3	0.00	1.00	0.00	0.00
	2	0	3	0	0	3	0.00	1.00	0.00	0.00
	3	0	2	0	1	3	0.00	0.67	0.00	0.33
	4	0	0	2	1	3	0.00	0.00	0.67	0.33
	5	0	0	0	2	2	0.00	0.00	0.00	1.00
Leading Edge Triggered										
	1	2	1	0	0	3	0.67	0.33	0.00	0.00
	2	2	1	0	0	3	0.67	0.33	0.00	0.00
	3	1	2	0	0	3	0.33	0.67	0.00	0.00
	4	0	2	1	0	3	0.00	0.67	0.33	0.00
	5	0	1	0	2	3	0.00	0.33	0.00	0.67

[a] Event lag: n = overall frequency in data; p = proportion of all behavior changes.
[b] Time lag: n = total seconds in data; p = proportion of total test duration.

At lag 2 (two steps away from each criterion occurrence) C follows A twice and D follows once, yielding probabilities of 0.67 and 0.33, respectively. At lag 3 the total number of behaviors that can possibly match the criterion is reduced by 1. This happens because at event 8 the criterion can only be followed by two more events due to the end of the data. This "falling-off-at-the-end" will reduce the total N available for lagging by 1 each time the criterion occurs at a position in the sequence equal to the current lag size from the end of the data. At lag 3, A and D each occur once yielding probabilities of 0.50. You should now try out lags 4 and 5, checking the results against the Table 17-2 data.

Time Lags

The lower portions of Table 17-2 present three types of time lag analyses. The "Overall" row gives the total duration and proportion of total test time for each behavior. Before computations can begin, however, two decisions must be made. First you must select the time unit in which the behaviors will be lagged. The most useful unit will be sufficiently short so that one, and only one, behavior can occur in the interval. For this example I chose a 1-sec unit. If more than one behavior can occur during some or all of the intervals (concurrent data), you can still make the lag counts. However, some complications arise in using the probabilities. This situation will be illustrated and discussed later.

The second decision concerns where to start lagging (the lagging trigger). Three possibilities are available. The first, called a *level* trigger, initiates lagging after every instance of the criterion in the data. To illustrate, refer to the right half of Table 17-1. Behavior A, the criterion, occurs at seconds 1, 2, 3, 10, 17, 18, 19, and 20. Each of these is a trigger (lag zero) for count initiation. The trigger at second 1 is followed by A at lag 1, A at lag 2, B at lags 3 and 4, and by D at lag 5. The trigger at second 2 is followed by A at lag 1, B at lags 2 and 3, and D at lags 4 and 5. At the second 3 trigger we find B at lags 1 and 2, and D at lags 3, 4, and 5. This procedure continues for the other five criterion triggers, yielding the matching frequencies and probabilities shown in the first "Time Lags" section of Table 17-2. These probabilities measure the chances that each behavior will follow the criterion up to 5 sec after every 1-sec occurrence of the criterion.

A second method triggers on the *trailing edge* (offset) of the criterion. The final time unit in a continuous sequence of the criterion serves as lag 0. Refer again to Table 17-1. Behavior A has offsets at seconds 3, 10, and 20. Notice that the offset at second 20 can only be followed by four lags due to "falling-off-at-the-end" of the data. Following each of these trailing edge triggers we find B at lags 1 and 2. At lag 3, B follows twice and D once. Lag 4 contains two instances of B and one of D, while lag 5 has two of D. These matching frequencies and associated conditional probabilities are shown in the second set of "Time Lag" values of Table 17-2.

The final method uses the *leading edge* (onset) of the criterion event as the lag 0 trigger. Lags are triggered from this point—but *not* from the other time unit instances of the criterion during its total duration, as was done with the level trigger. For the Table 17-1 data, behavior A has onsets at seconds 1, 10, and 17. A follows these twice and B once at lags 1 and 2. At lag 3, A follows once and B twice. At lag 4, B occurs twice and C once, while at lag 5, B occurs once and D twice. The bottom "Time Lag" section of Table 17-2 shows these matching frequencies and their probabilities.

Trigger choice may produce quite different results because each one relates the time sequence to a different question. The level trigger assesses the probability that a matching behavior will follow every time unit instance of the criterion up to MAX LAG, regardless of when the criterion began or ended. The trailing edge analysis gives the probability for following offset up to MAX LAG time units, regardless of the duration of the criterion. The leading edge yields probabilities for following criterion onset up to MAX LAG time units, and reflects the average duration of the criterion by high probabilities at the early time lags.

One important consideration in choosing a trigger concerns the possibility that some behaviors may be dependent on criterion offset, while others may be tied to onset. If the criterion has large variation in its duration from occurrence to occurrence, trailing and leading edge triggers can generate markedly different outcomes for the same matching behaviors. The level trigger will reflect both of these potential dependencies, but with reduced sensitivity and lower accuracy.

Multiple Test Sessions

Actual observational data usually consist of a number of testing sessions on the same individual or group. In this case analysis proceeds using the event or time sequences *without* lagging over the sessions. The lag counts are made separately for each session. Then the matching frequencies for each behavior at each lag are summed, with these totals being used to compute the conditional probabilities.

DISPLAYING RESULTS AND HYPOTHESIS TESTING THE EASY WAY

Lag probabilities are tested for statistical significance against a null hypothesis for the chances of matching the criterion at random. For event lags, a starting place is the null hypothesis that there are *no* dependencies among the sequential events. If this is really true, then a particular behavior will match the criterion at *any* lag in proportion to its occurrence in the data as a whole—its unconditional probability. A similar situation holds for time lags, where a reasonable null hypothesis is that a behavior will match the criterion at any future time interval simply in proportion to its occurrence at any random second in the time sequence—its proportion of total test time. In the Table 17-2 example the unconditional probability for behavior B as an event was 0.33, and as a behavior filling time it had the unconditional probability of 0.33 also. If B simply followed A by chance we would expect event matches to occur one-third of the total possible times that A could be matched. We would also expect time matches to occur one-third because behavior B occupies 0.33 of the total test seconds.

An appropriate way of testing the reliability of the difference between observed and expected lag probabilities is to apply the binomial test. With reasonably large N for the total number of criterion occurrences at a given lag (at least 30) and an expected probability that is not too close to zero (0.05–0.10 or larger) we can estimate binomial probabilities by the well-known formula:

$$z = \frac{P_{\text{OBSERVED}} - P_{\text{EXPECTED}}}{\text{SD}_{\text{EXPECTED}}}$$

where

$$\text{SD} = \left[\frac{P_{\text{EXP}} * (1 - P_{\text{EXP}})}{N_{\text{TOTAL CRITERION}}} \right]^{1/2}$$

If the z equals or exceeds ± 1.96, the difference between observed and expected probabilities has reached the 0.05 level of significance. If z is positive, the matching behavior occurs *more* than expected by chance (an excitatory or positive dependency). If z is negative, the observed probability occurs less than expected by chance (an inhibitory or negative dependency). The variability about the expected probability is estimated by $CI = P_{EXP} \pm (1.96 * SD)$, the upper and lower 95% confidence points.

Hypothesis testing can now proceed by plotting graphs of the observed probabilities and confidence bands against lag for any particular matching behavior and criterion. Figure 17-1 provides examples of some basic types of *lag profiles* that might be obtained. The upper section illustrates a chance relationship. Only 2 of the 25 lags are outside the confidence bands, and no clear rising, falling, or cyclic patterns can be seen.

In the second section the matching behavior occurs above chance for several lags, then falls into the chance level. Here we can predict when the matching behavior will be excited (above chance) following the criterion, and for how many lag steps (events or time) it will remain above chance (exhibit a positive dependency). However, we cannot predict within the 25 lags studied when the matching behavior will reoccur. In the inverse form of this function the matching behavior would be inhibited (below chance) for some lags after the criterion, then rise into and remain in the chance band.

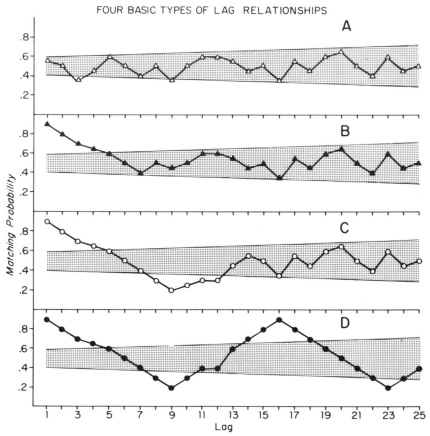

Figure 17-1. Profiles showing some of the basic types of event or time lag functions. Statistically reliable points lie above or below the confidence bands.

In the third section the matching behavior is excited for several lags, then falls into an inhibited state, followed by return to chance levels. Here we can predict the occurrence and depression of the behavior following the criterion, but we cannot predict reoccurrence of the match within 25 lags. In the inverse of this relationship the behavior would be initially inhibited, then rise above chance, then return to chance for the remaining lags.

The last section illustrates a cyclic dependency. The behavior starts above chance, becomes inhibited by lag 8, rises to another excitatory level by lag 14, and falls below chance by lag 23. If more lags had been tested this cycle might have reoccurred with a *period* of about 16 lags (the number of steps between excited and inhibited peaks), thereby identifying a repetitive cycle. If the function simply "damped" into the chance range following lag 25, we would have identified a single-cycle dependency.

Suppose that this example of cyclic dependency was the profile for a criterion behavior lagged against itself. This would show that the criterion can be predicted from its own prior occurrences. Such auto-contingencies force a strong structuring on the occurrences of behaviors that are dependent on the criterion. Take a case in which a criterion behavior is repetitively cyclic with a period of 16 lags, and behavior *B* matched above chance levels at lags 1, 2, and 3. Then *B must* also be cyclic in its relationship to this criterion, being above chance at lags 17 to 19, 33 to 35, and so on, as well as at lags 1 to 3. Thus, the existence of strong auto-contingencies can often simplify (1) the identification of dependency in the behavior flow, and (2) understanding and explaining the observed relationships among the behaviors. The ability to detect auto-contingency and cyclic dependency in long chains of behaviors is a primary virtue of the lag method. It allows an investigator to test a variety of complex hypotheses that are beyond the scope of traditional pattern counting models, and are not studied in concurrent or single step dependency analyses.

DATA TYPES FOR SEQUENTIAL ANALYSIS

Not all data are appropriate for sequential analysis. Whether a data set can be analyzed yielding outcomes that actually answer questions under study depends on methods of data sampling and behavioral code definitions. Problems of measurement and code definitions have been discussed in detail elsewhere (Sackett, 1977), while some of the material presented next borrows heavily from the thoughtful work of Bakeman (1977).

Table 17-3 illustrates a hypothetical interaction sequence in which three social behaviors—looking (L), vocalizing (V), touching (T)—code all interactions between a mother and 1-month-old infant. A nonsocial (N) category codes all behaviors that are not directed toward the partner. A second dimension codes positive (+), negative (−), and neutral (o) affect. For example, looking with smiling is coded L+, crying V−.

Real-Time Data

The first section in Table 17-3 presents a real-time sequence in 1-sec time units. Such data might have been collected with an electronic digital data-acquisition system (e.g., Sackett, et al., 1973). The sampling method initiated a score whenever *either* interactor changed on any aspect of the codes, with the current behavior of *both* individuals being scored. This sequence contains all possible information about frequencies, durations, and event and time sequences for the code categories measured and can be studied for conditional relationships both *within* and *between* either person. Thus, the mother behaviors can

Table 17-3.   Mother-Infant Interaction Data to Illustrate the Basic Data Types in Observational Scoring Systems[a]

REAL-TIME SEQUENTIAL (sec)

Time	Mother	Infant	Time	Mother	Infant	Time	Mother	Infant
1	L+	No	11	Lo	LV−	21	LV−	N−
2	LV+	No	12	L+	LV−	22	LT−	LV−
3	LVT+	No	13	LT+	LV−	23	LT−	LV−
4	LVT+	L+	14	LVT+	LV−	24	L− T+	L−
5	LV+	LV+	15	LV+	L+	25	LT+	Lo
6	No T+	LV+	16	L+	L+	26	LT+	L+
7	No	LV+	17	L+	L+ No	27	LT+	L+
8	No	No	18	L− T+	L+ No	28	LV+	L+
9	No	L− No	19	LT−	N−	29	LV+	LV+
10	No	LV−	20	LV−	N−	30	LV+	LV+

EVENT SEQUENTIAL

Event	Mother	Infant	Event	Mother	Infant	Event	Mother	Infant
1	L+	No	7	Lo	L+	13	LT−	L+
2	LV+	L+	8	L+	L+ No	14	LV+	
3	LVT+	LV+	9	LT+	N−	15	LT−	
4	LV+	No	10	LVT+	LV−	16	L− T+	
5	No T+	L− No	11	LT	L−	17	LT+	
6	No	LV−	12	L− T+	Lo	18	LV+	

INTERVAL TIME SAMPLING (5 sec)

Int	Mother	Infant	Int	Mother	Infant	Int	Mother	Infant
1	L+ LV+ LVT+ No L+		3	Lo L+ LT+ LVT+ LV+	LV− L+	5	LV− LT− L− N− LV− T+ LT+	LV− L− Lo
2	No T+	LV+ No L− LV−	4	L+ L− T+ LT− LV−	L+ No N−	6	LT+ LV+	L+ LV+

POINT TIME SAMPLING (5 sec)

Point	Mother	Infant	Point	Mother	Infant	Point	Mother	Infant
1	LV+	LV+	3	LV+	L+	5	LT+	Lo
2	No	LV−	4	LV−	N−	6	LV+	LV+

[a]Behaviors: Look (L) Vocalize (V) Touch (T) Nonsocial (N)
Affect: Positive (+) Negative (−) Neutral (o)

be lagged against each other or against the behaviors of the infant. For a complete interaction analysis the behaviors of each individual would be used as criteria and matches both within and between interactors. A less complete analysis might focus on the behaviors of one individual as criteria against which the behaviors of the other are matched.

Mutual Exclusivity

The behavior categories in Table 17-3 are not independent—more than one can occur at a time. However, independent (mutually exclusive) categories can be generated from the category combinations. For example, looking-and-vocalizing is a different, mutually exclusive, event from looking or vocalizing alone. This property of mutual exclusivity is an essential feature that coding systems must possess for complete interpretation of lag probabilities. If the individual behavioral events are not defined in a mutually exclusive fashion, unconditional and conditional probabilities will not reflect the actual occurrences of the behaviors.

To illustrate, suppose that the coding rules of an observational system required that only a single behavior be scored at any time. This might be done by a hierarchy defining the importance or priority of each behavior. For the social behaviors in Table 17-3 this might be *touch* over *vocalize* over *look*. *Touch*, being most important, would always be scored when it occurred. *Vocalize* would be scored when it occurred alone or in combination with *look, but not* when coupled with *touch*. *Look* would be scored only when it occurred alone. Thus, overall frequency or duration scores will not accurately measure the actual totals for *vocal* and *look* behavior, and lag probabilities will not yield a true picture of sequential dependencies. As suggested above, this problem is readily cured by defining the seven combinations (T,V,L,TV,TL,VL,TVL) as independent categories.

Exhaustiveness

A second aspect of coding systems concerns their completeness. In an exhaustive system some codable event must be possible at every instant of observation. Although the lag method can be applied to time data without exhaustive coding, the event method makes little sense when uncodable behavior changes can occur in the data. Exhaustiveness is usually attained by defining a "wastebasket" category consisting of the absence of any other codable behavior. In Table 17-3 the nonsocial category serves this function. If the wastebasket contains only uninteresting behaviors or only a few relatively infrequent ones, the technique is probably adequate. If it contains behaviors that are related in important sequential ways to the criterion behaviors, or if it occupies a large percentage of the total test time, the power of the lag analysis may be greatly reduced. In such cases it is probably wise to break up the wastebasket into at least some of its specific components.

Concurrency

A third aspect of some coding systems is illustrated in Table 17-3. From seconds 1 to 5 the mother behaviors are all combinations of the social categories coupled with a single affect code. However, at the 6th sec the mother performed a neutral nonsocial behavior (looking at something in the room) while simultaneously touching the infant with positive affect. Although a violation of the mutual exclusivity principle, this type of concurrency does represent co-occurrence of conceptually independent responses which seem to share incompatible attributes—namely social *and* nonsocial behavior, as well as positive *and* neutral affect. The problem can, of course, be handled by forming a compound category containing these behaviors in combination. But, this might produce the need for a very large number of compounds if many of these "incompatibilities" occurred in the data. Further, some research questions might require that incompatible behaviors be studied as separate categories. Finally, some sampling methods (see "Time Sampling" below) always yield concurrent behaviors. This produces an apparent problem for the lag method.

To identify this problem we will use mother behavior L+ as criterion from the Table 17-3 real-time data. L+ occurs at time units 1, 12, 16, and 17. Its first three lag 1 matches are LV+, LT+, and L+. At second 17 the lag 1 match is L− *and* T+. Conditional probabilities for these matches are each $\frac{1}{4} = 0.25$. Unfortunately, these probabilities sum to 1.25—a violation of the basic probability principle that a set of exhaustive probabilities must sum to 1.00. Will this invalidate the lag model? We have no real problem in terms of the descriptive probabilities for any individual behavior, because 0.25 is the actual conditional value for each match. But, will the z-score hypothesis testing model still be valid?

To answer this question empirically we will use the basic z model with its corresponding null hypothesis to estimate the number of times we expect these behaviors to follow the criterion at lag 1 by chance. Assume that the unconditional probabilities are 0.1 for LV+, LT+, L+, and L−; 0.2 for T+, and 0.4 for any other behavior in the exhaustive set of independent codes (note that the sum of these unconditional probabilities *must* equal 1.00). The expected number of matches under our null hypothesis is nEXP = NCRITERION $* P$UNC, as we expect each behavior to follow the criterion by chance in proportion to its occurrence in the data as a whole. This yields expected frequencies of LV+ = 0.4, LT+ = 0.4, L+ = 0.4, L− = 0.4, T+ = 0.8, and other behaviors = 1.6. The sum of these expected frequencies is 4, which it should be because the criterion was followed four times at lag 1. Thus, the unconditional probabilities appear to provide legitimate estimates for chance expectations even though more than one behavior was scored per interval or event. This means that the z technique can be employed with concurrent behaviors, a conclusion also reached by Bakeman (1977) in his model for studying simultaneous behavior patterns. In the lag model concurrency thus produces a situation where lag 0 (the trigger positions in the time or event series) contains meaningful information measuring the probability of behaviors occurring at the same time as the criterion.

Two points should be emphasized for concurrency data. In calculating the total N in the data as a whole (the divisor for each unconditional probability) every single or concurrent code must be counted, not just the total number of events or time units. Thus, if three behaviors occur together, a count of 3 should go into the NTOTAL. If this is not done the sum of the unconditional probabilities will exceed 1.00. Secondly, with concurrent data the sum of conditional probabilities over all matching behaviors at a given lag will always be greater than 1.00 with an exhaustive coding system. In this case it will not be possible to perform some types of analyses testing hypotheses about the joint distribution of all conditional probabilities at a particular lag. An example is the information theory measure of entropy, which studies an exhaustive set of probabilities that must sum to 1.00 (Gottman and Notarius, 1976). To conclude, it appears that lag methods can be applied with concurrent data systems, but the basic issue should probably receive more attention than has been attempted here.

Event Data

The second section of Table 17-3 shows a typical event sequence that might come from an observational study. The data were generated by simply scanning down the original 1-sec time sequence and entering a new code when any codable behavior change occurred. This type of event sequence could be used to study lags *within* the mother or infant series. However, lag dependencies *between* interactors *could not* be assessed because the mother and infant behaviors do not change at exactly the same times nor are there the same number of events in each set. Therefore, it is impossible to pair the event sequences between the partners. This is cured by focusing on the sequence of behavior changes for one individual and listing the behavior that was occurring for the other individual at each of these behavior-change points. For the Table 17-3 data with the mother as focus, the first two mother events (L+, LV+) would be coupled with infant behavior No; the third mother event (LVT+) with infant No *and* concurrently with L+; the fourth mother event (LV+) with infant LV+; and the fifth and sixth mother events (No T+, No) with infant LV+. Using this technique to extract event sequences from real-time data or using an original data-collection scheme that generates these event sequences, we would then proceed by using the *focal individual behaviors as matches* against the focal or interactor behaviors as criteria. To calculate expected values we will, of course, have to know the total number of behavior changes for each code category for both the focal individual and the interactor.

Time-Sampling Techniques

The bottom section of Table 17-3 illustrates the two principal time-sampling methods used in observational research. The first (modified frequencies) involves sampling categories in successive time intervals. The behaviors occurring in these intervals are given a score of 1 count per block regardless of the number of times they actually happened during the interval. For the Table 17-3 data, a 5-sec time-sampling interval was chosen and the real-time data were scanned for behaviors occurring in each 5-sec block. For example, in block 1 (the first 5 sec) mother behaviors L+, LV+, and LVT+ occurred at least once, so they constitute the mother entries for interval 1 of the interval sampling data. Note that concurrence will always occur with this sampling technique.

The second method involves sampling behavior only at fixed time points. All behaviors occurring at these points are scored, with behaviors occurring at other times being ignored. In Table 17-3, a 5-sec point-sampling interval was chosen and those behaviors occurring at 5, 10, 15, 20, 25, and 30 sec into the data were listed as the sequential point-sampled values. This technique may or may not have concurrent data depending on whether concurrencies actually occurred at the sample points.

Both of these sampling techniques suffer serious shortcomings for sequential analysis. Interval sampling does not preserve the order of occurrence of behaviors during the time block so all event sequence information is lost. More important, these "modified frequency" scores have no unambiguous unit of measurement. Behaviors receive a score of one interval if they occur only for a brief time among many other behaviors in the interval, and if they are the only code occurring in the interval. So, one subject may score 10 intervals for a particular behavior because it occurred 10 times for 1 sec each time in 10 different intervals. A second subject might get the same score with this behavior occurring only once, but being the only category appearing in 10 continuous time intervals. The meaning of these identical scores is quite different, with those for the first person being frequency-weighted, the other duration-weighted. This produces a situation much like the comparison of apples with oranges. If data such as these were subjected to sequential analysis, the results would be unclear at best and probably meaningless. However, if interval-sampled data approached a situation where only one code occurred per time block (the block is shorter than the average behavior duration) a time lag analysis could be meaningfully applied.

Point sampling shares all of the interval sampling problems, except scores will be duration-weighted. When sampling at instantaneous points, long-duration behaviors are more likely to be observed than behaviors having the same frequency but lasting for a shorter time. Thus, a time-point lag analysis will be relatively insensitive in detecting contingencies between long- and short-duration behaviors. However, in the special case when category durations are relatively equal, point-sampled lag probabilities might generate meaningful outcomes.

Table 17-4 summarizes the discussion in this section. Coding systems vary in terms of sampling methods—data can be collected in event sequences, real-time sequences, or by some time-sampling schemes. Systems also vary in the basis for code definition—some consist entirely of mutually exclusive codes scored one at a time during the behavioral flow, others allow more than one event to be scored at a time. Concurrent data can be studied sequentially if the simultaneous behaviors are independent and yield a true count of total occurrence. Using Bakeman's (1977) notation, this breakdown yields six basic data types. Types Ia and IIa allow the full use of lag sequential methods. Types Ib and IIb can also be lag-analyzed. They will include a lag 0 term for probabilities of behaviors occurring simultaneously with the criterion, and they may yield data in which the sum of conditional probabilities at a particular lag for a given criterion exceeds 1.00. This can cause problems in analyzing overall lag-profile distributions. Type III data will generally not produce meaningful (unambiguously interpretable) sequential probabilities except under special conditions involving very short time-sample intervals or equal overall durations of the code categories. Interval time sampling will always produce concurrent data, while point time sampling may or may not.

Table 17-4. Basic Data Types in Observational Coding Systems

	METHOD OF SAMPLING		CODE CATEGORIES	
			Mutually Exclusive	Concurrent
EVENTS	Score initiation	Event onset (behavior changes)	Ia[a]	Ib [b]
	Measurement unit	Frequency of occurrence		
REAL TIME	Score initiation	Event onset (behavior changes)	IIa[a]	IIb[b]
	Measurement unit	Frequency, duration of each occurrence		
INTERVAL TIME SAMPLING	Score initiation	First occurrence of a code during a sampling interval		
	Measurement unit	Number of intervals in which code occurred at least once		IIIb[c]
POINT TIME SAMPLING	Score initiation	Occurrence at end of elapsed time interval	IIIa[c]	
	Measurement unit	Number of interval end-point occurrences		

[a] Allows full use of lag sequential analysis for events (Ia) or time and events (IIa).

[b] Allows use of lag methods for events (Ib) or events and time (IIb), but some statistical analyses may not be possible.

[c] Will generally not yield meaningful sequential analyses except when the sampling interval is shorter than the behavior durations (IIIb) or when all behaviors have approximately equal durations (IIIa).

AN APPLICATION WITH REAL INTERACTION DATA

We will now illustrate some complexities involved in applying the lag method with interaction data from a crab-eating monkey (*M. fascicularis*) mother and her 1-month-old son. The pair lived alone in a small room and were observed for five 30-min morning sessions on five different days. Nine behaviors were scored in real time by writing down a code number and an elapsed time whenever a behavior change occurred by either the mother or infant, with the behaviors of both being scored. The behaviors that actually occurred form the nearly mutually exclusive, exhaustive, set shown in Table 17-5. Some behaviors could not be reliably scored for initiation and so were pooled with the initiator ignored. The total data base included 1000 behavior changes occurring in sequence (within sessions) out of a true total of 1109.

Event Lags

Table 17-6 presents the lag 1 event analysis of all behaviors tested against infant gross activity (IGA) as the criterion. Row 1 shows the matching frequencies for following the criterion as the next event. The criterion occurred 95 times. Dividing each matching frequency by 95 we obtain the conditional probabilities shown in row 2. The blank cells down the IGA column reveal a first complexity in the proper application of the lag method.

Because the coding scheme is mutually exclusive, a criterion behavior cannot follow itself at event lag 1—the criterion cannot be on and off at the same time! The sampling method has restricted chance, limiting the possible ways that the categories can follow each other. For this type of restriction, only the noncriterion behaviors can occur at event lag 1. Therefore, the total number of events in the whole data that can possibly be lag 1 event matches is reduced by the number of times that the criterion occurred, because these criterion events are the ones that cannot happen. Row 3 of Table 17-6 gives the overall frequency for each matching behavior, which when summed yield $1000 - 95 = 905$ as

Table 17-5.   Overall Summary Data for Five 30-min Scoring Sessions with a Single *M. fascicularis* Mother-Infant Pair

Behavior	Freq	Prob	Dur	% Dur	X̄ Dur/Freq
(PC) passive contact [a]	39	0.039	843	0.094	21.6
(HC) hold-cling [a]	133	0.133	2167	0.241	16.3
(PSJ) pat-stroke-jiggle [b]	130	0.130	960	0.107	7.4
(GR) groom [b]	101	0.101	805	0.089	8.0
(NR) nurse [b]	148	0.148	2353	0.261	15.9
(MBC) mother break contact	58	0.058	151	0.017	2.6
(SL) social looking [a]	74	0.074	125	0.014	1.7
(NSE) nonsocial exploration [a]	142	0.142	998	0.111	7.0
(MGA) mother gross activity	10	0.010	34	0.004	3.4
(IBC) infant break contact	70	0.070	218	0.024	3.1
(IGA) infant gross activity	95	0.095	346	0.038	3.6
Total	1000	1.000	9000	1.000	

[a] Initiated by mother or infant: Freq=number of occurrences; Dur=number of seconds; X̄ Dur/Freq=average duration per occurrence=Dur/Freq.

[b] Mother Initiated: Prob=Freq/total occurrences; % Dur=Dur/total test time.

Table 17-6.   Calculation of Event Lag 1 Probabilities and Summary Statistics for Mother-Infant Data with IGA as the Criterion Behavior

Measure	Behavior											Total
	PC	HC	PSJ	GR	NR	MBC	SL	NSE	MGA	IBC	IGA	
$n_{L}1$	0	19	65	0	11	0	0	0	0	0	——	95 [N_{CRIT}]
$P_{L}1$	0.000	0.200	0.684	0.000	0.116	0.000	0.000	0.000	0.000	0.000	——	1.00
N	39	133	130	101	148	58	74	142	10	70	——	905 [N_{TOT}]
P_E	0.043	0.147	0.144	0.112	0.164	0.064	0.082	0.157	0.011	0.077	——	1.00
n_E	4.1	14.0	13.7	10.6	15.6	6.1	7.8	14.9	1.0	7.3	——	95.1
P_E SD	0.021	0.036	0.036	0.032	0.038	0.025	0.028	0.037	0.011	0.027	——	
z	2.05	1.47	15.0	*3.50*	*1.26*	2.56	2.93	4.24	*1.00*	2.85	——	negative italicized
P_z	0.040	0.142	0.000	0.000	0.208	0.010	0.003	0.000	0.317	0.004	——	
+99 CI	0.097	0.239	0.236	0.194	0.261	0.128	0.154	0.252	0.039	0.146	——	
−99 CI	*0.011*	0.055	0.052	0.030	0.067	0.000	0.010	0.062	*0.017*	0.008	——	
$\chi^2 df=1$	4.10	1.79	192	10.6	1.36	6.10	7.80	14.9	(1.0)	7.30	——	246.04 $df=8$

$P_{L}1$=observed matching prob.=$n_{L}1/N_{CRIT}$
$n_{L}1$=observed matching freq.
SD=$\{[P_E*(1-P_E)]/N_{CRIT}\}^{1/2}$
χ^2 =$(n_{L}1-n_E)^2n_E$
z=$(P_{L}1-P_E)/$SD
P_E=expected matching prob.=N/N_{TOT}
n_E=expected matching freq.=P_E*N_{CRIT}
CI=confidence interval=$P_E\pm($SD$*2.56)$
N=number available for matching

the N_{TOTAL} of events that can potentially occur at lag 1. (The 95 is the number of times that the criterion was actually matched at lag 1.) Dividing each N by N_{TOTAL} yields the unconditional expected probabilities shown in row 4. Note that these are different from the relative frequencies shown in Table 17-5 for each behavior because of the adjustment to N_{TOTAL}.

Row 5 gives the number of matches expected by chance ($P_E * N_{CRIT}$), and row 6 the standard deviation of the expected probability. Row 7 gives the z values for significance testing, and Row 8 the probabilities of z taken from a standard table of the normal distribution. Negative z values equal to or less than -2.56 indicate significant inhibition at the two-tailed 0.01 level. Positive z values equal to or greater than 2.56 indicate excess of observed over expected probability reliable at the two-tailed 0.01 level. Rows 9 and 10 show the upper and lower 99% confidence points about each expected probability.

Row 10 shows chi-square ($df = 1$) values for each behavior, an alternative method for significance testing. These values are not as useful as z scores. Chi-square values are always positive, but the sign of differences between observed and expected probabilities is an important piece of information in lag analysis. However, chi-square is useful in testing the null hypothesis that there are no significant differences among any of the observed and expected probabilities. Summing the individual values yields a total chi-square with $K - 1$ degrees of freedom (K is the number of categories in the sum). A significant total chi-square allows rejection of this null hypothesis. In the example of row 11, the chi-square for MGA was not included due to its very low overall probability and expected frequency.

As usual with chi-square the legitimate application of this technique requires that no more than a few expected frequencies be below 5. This problem is discussed by Cochran (1954) and in most statistics textbooks.

The lag 1 results can be summarized as follows: (1) There were at least some significant lag 1 dependencies. (2) The mother behavior pat-stroke-jiggle (PSJ) had the highly significant conditional probability of 0.684, and was the only behavior to occur *above* chance. (3) Groom (GR), mother break contact (MBC), social looking (SL), nonsocial explore (NSE), and infant break contact (IBC) were all significantly inhibited after IGA. The other four behaviors were all within the 99% confidence points.

Table 17-7 illustrates calculation of event lags beyond lag 1, using data for lag 2 as the example. Row 1 gives the matching frequencies for each category at the *immediately preceding* lag—in this case at lag 1. Row 2 gives the observed matching frequencies at lag 2. Row 3 shows the original N for each behavior out of the total 1000 events. Row 4 gives an adjusted N for each behavior, revealing a second complication in performing lag analyses.

Because of mutual exclusivity, any instances of a particular behavior that occurred at the previous lag cannot possibly occur at the next lag. For a behavior to occur at event lag 2 some other behavior must have gone off, so the lag 2 event cannot be the same as the lag 1 event that has just gone off. Therefore, the number of times that a behavior can occur at the current lag may not be the same as its occurrence in the total data. Rather, it will be the total occurrences reduced by the number of occurrences at the preceding lag. The N_{ADJ} row presents these reduced values. Now the probabilities can be calculated. Row 5 gives the observed probability (n_L/N_{CRIT}), and row 6 the expected probabilities (N_{ADJ}/N_{TOTAL}). The remaining rows give the z values and 99% confidence points.

The lag 2 results can be summarized as follows: (1) Nursing (NR) has the highly

Table 17-7. Calculation of Event Probabilities and Summary Statistics at Lags (Lag 2) Greater than 1 for Mother-Infant Data with IGA as Criterion

Measure	PC	HC	PSJ	GR	NR	MBC	SL	NSE	MGA	IBC	IGA	Total
n_L-1	0	19	65	0	11	0	0	0	0	0	0	95 $N_{CRIT\ L-1}$
n_L	0	0	10	0	65	0	0	11	0	0	9	95 N_{CRIT}
N	39	133	130	101	148	58	74	142	10	70	95	1000 (total in data)
N_{ADJ}	39	114	65	101	137	58	74	142	10	70	95	905 N_{TOT}
P_L	0.000	0.000	0.105	0.000	0.684	0.000	0.000	0.116	0.000	0.000	0.095	1.00
P_E	0.043	0.126	0.072	0.112	0.151	0.064	0.082	0.157	0.011	0.077	0.105	1.00
P_E SD	0.021	0.034	0.027	0.032	0.037	0.025	0.028	0.037	0.011	0.027	0.031	
z	*2.07*	*3.70*	1.24	*3.46*	14.5	*2.55*	*2.91*	1.10	1.03	*2.82*	0.32	negative italicized
P_z	0.038	0.000	0.215	0.000	0.000	0.001	0.004	0.271	0.303	0.005	0.749	
+99 CI	0.096	0.213	0.140	0.195	0.245	0.128	0.154	0.253	0.038	0.147	0.186	
−99 CI	*0.011*	0.039	0.004	0.029	0.057	*0.003*	0.010	0.061	*0.016*	0.007	0.024	

n_L-1 = number of matches at preceding lag
N_{TOT} = total available for matching = ΣN_{ADJ} = overall total in data − $N_{CRIT\ L-1}$
N_{ADJ} = number available for matching = $N - n_L - 1$

significant probability of 0.684 two steps from the occurrence of IGA. (2) The other behaviors are either within the chance band or are depressed.

The event analysis was calculated out to MAX LAG = 15. Mother gross activity (MGA) was dropped because of its low (0.01) unconditional probability, and the lag profiles for the other 10 behaviors are displayed in Figure 17-2. Although a number of points lie outside the confidence band—many more than the 1 per 100 expected by chance—only several behaviors show any remarkably high dependency on IGA. PSJ at lag 1 and NR at lag 2 exhibit the greatest departure from chance. Other behaviors showing reasonably high dependency are IBC at lag 9, GR at lag 3, and NSE at lag 5. The latter may even be cyclically related to IGA. Finally, IGA itself may be somewhat autocorrelated, as both lags 6 and 12 are outside the confidence band. Note that contingencies do exist out to lag 15, and these would be missed if fewer lags had been studied.

Pattern Identification from Lag Outcomes

The three-step sequence IGA-PSJ-NR suggests an interesting psychological hypothesis. The infant may have learned to use gross motor activity as a way to get the mother to

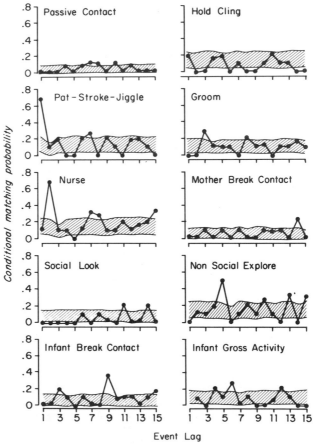

Figure 17-2.   Conditional probabilities and 99% confidence interval for event lag matches with the IGA criterion out to 15 MAX LAGS.

manipulate and cuddle him, for which he then rewards the mother by nursing. (If longitudinal sequential data were available, the ontogeny of this dependency could be very interesting.) However, the lag results, in themselves, do not actually identify the existence of this sequence as a real three-step chain in the flow of behaviors, but a little further work can do so.

Figure 17-3 presents the lag profiles with PSJ by the mother as criterion. As predicted from the IGA analysis, nursing does actually follow PSJ with a high lag 1 probability (0.662). It also appears that nursing may be cyclically related to PSJ with a period of about six to seven event lags. (In fact, a number of behaviors appear to have cyclic relationships with PSJ, suggesting that this mother behavior may play an important role in organizing the interactions.) However, the fact that PSJ follows IGA at lag 1 with a probability of 0.684 and NR follows PSJ at lag 1 with a probability of 0.662 *does not* mean that the three-step sequence actually occurs more than expected by chance. Thus, PSJ does not follow IGA $1 - 0.684 = 0.316$ of the events. These 31.6% of the IGA events may all be instances where NR occurs at lag 2, thereby resulting in a fairly frequent pattern of IGA—not PSJ-NR. However, we can calculate the chance expectation for the actual three-step chain by the product of the successive lag 1 probabilities of the events in the

CRITERION: PAT, STROKE, JIGGLE

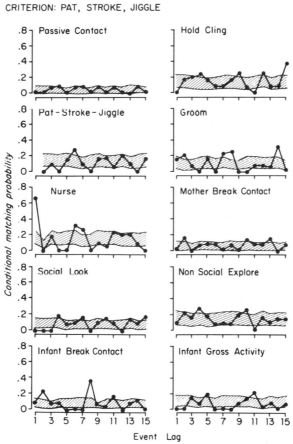

Figure 17-3. Conditional probabilities and 99% confidence interval for event lag matches, with PSJ as the criterion out to 15 MAX LAGS.

chain (the multiplicative rule for joint probabilities). This yields (IGA-PSJ) 0.684 times (PSJ-NR) 0.662 = 0.453 for the probability that the three-step chain will occur only by chance. This is equivalent to the hypothesis that these dependencies are a first-order Markov process in which all sequential steps are predictable from the first order (lag 1) transition matrix (see Gottman and Notarius, 1976, for a full exposition of the Markov method).

The analysis proceeds by searching the original event sequence for the actual frequency of occurrence of this three-step pattern. Sixty-four instances were found among the 95 three-step chains beginning with IGA in the data as a whole. This yields the observed probability of IGA-PSJ-NR equal to 0.674. We can test for significance of the difference between observed and expected probabilities by the usual z test, which yields $0.674 - 0.453 = +0.221$ divided by the square root of $[0.453 * (1 - 0.453)]/95$ for a value of 4.33. This being significant well beyond the 0.01 level allows us to conclude that the actual IGA-PSJ-NR pattern is a real one.

Because pattern identification is an important research problem in many interaction studies we will spend a bit more time on the issue. Lag outcomes will contain implications about actual patterns under two general conditions: (1) If the probability for one and only one matching behavior at successive lags is very high—1.00 in the limiting case—the behaviors forming chains will be exactly specified. For example, if IGA was followed by PSJ at lag 1 with $P = 1.00$, by NR at lag 2 with $P = 1.00$, and by IBC at lag 3 with $P = 1.00$, the four-step chain IGA-PSJ-NR-IBC would be an invariant sequence and the only four-step chain occurring that begins with IGA. (2) The occurrence of a pattern is suspected from the lag profile study, and the number of times this pattern actually occurred in the total event sequence is counted. The resulting observed pattern probability is then tested against an expected value calculated from the lag 1 probabilities of the successive behaviors in the pattern. For example, suppose that the pattern IGA-PSJ-NR-IBC actually occurred 18 times out of a total of 95 four-step chains beginning with IGA. This yields the pattern probability of $18/95 = 0.189$. If the successive lag 1 probabilities were IGA-PSJ $= 0.684$, PSJ-NR $= 0.662$, and NR-IBC $= 0.205$, the expected pattern probability would be the product, 0.093. The observed is greater than the expected, and the z value is 3.22, which is significant beyond the 0.01 level. Thus, this four-step chain does occur more than expected by chance, although it is far from invariant.

Time Lags

Computing time lags is identical to the illustration for events. The null hypothesis is that lag matches will occur in proportion to the number of matching behavior time units in the data as a whole ("% Dur" in Table 17-5). Generally, adjusted N values for calculating expected probabilities will not be necessary. In time units behaviors will always follow themselves at least one lag unit whenever the time unit is shorter than the event duration (see the Table 17-3 real-time sequence if this is unclear). Although categories may be mutually exclusive, this in itself will not usually restrict which behaviors can follow each other at successive intervals from the lagging triggers. However, an exception occurs with the *trailing edge* trigger. If categories are mutually exclusive, the criterion behavior cannot follow itself in the lag 1 time unit after its offset. If the total N of time units in the data as a whole is large, a lag 1 adjustment (Table 17-6) will yield expected probabilities almost the same as those using the unadjusted NTOTAL TIME UNITS. If the total N is not large, the number of trailing edge triggers should be subtracted from NTOTAL UNITS before calculating the lag 1 unconditional probabilities. After lag 1 the behaviors are not restricted, so adjustments at the higher lags are not required.

Figure 17-4 presents the *level*-triggered time lag profiles for infant gross activity matched against itself and against pat-stroke-jiggle and nurse. The left portion gives second-by-second matching probabilities (a 1-sec time unit was used for lagging) for 30 sec from each IGA trigger. On the right are displayed the matches at 10-sec steps out to 300 lags (5 min). IGA follows itself for 5 sec at probabilities above the 99% confidence limits, then is depressed from seconds 7 to 27. The high probabilities for the first three to four lags reflect the average duration for IGA of 3.6 sec (see Table 17-5, "$\overline{X}$ Dur/Freq"). There is a slight tendency for IGA to reoccur at 50 sec, but thereafter the chance probabilities suggest that there is no strong auto-contingency relationship.

As would be expected from the event lag analysis, PSJ follows IGA at a level well above chance for 15 sec, and may reoccur about 240 lags (4 min) later. Nursing probabilities are inhibited for 7 sec following IGA, then are well above chance for 25 sec. Nursing appears to be cyclic, reoccurring at about 80, 180, and 250 lag units from IGA occurrences.

These time lag relationships not only provide the information found in the event analyses—identification of the sequence PSJ, then NR—but also illustrate the time-locked dependencies underlying these event sequences. In essence, by applying the time analysis to a large MAX LAG size we are able to see very far into the "future" states of these behaviors.

Figures 17-5 and 17-6 show the time lag profiles for these behaviors, with PSJ and NR

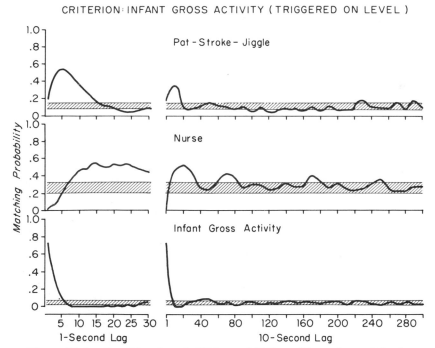

*Figure 17-4.   Conditional probabilities and 99% confidence interval for the time lag analysis matching PSJ, NR, and IGA, with the IGA as criterion. Lag was **level-**triggered out to MAX LAG 300 sec.*

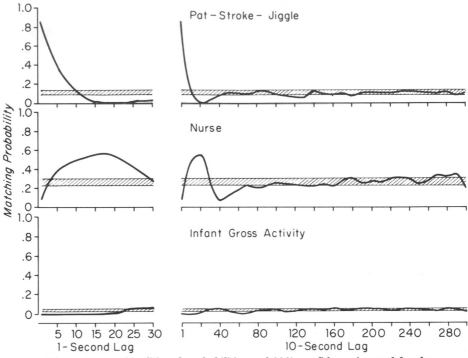

Figure 17-5.   *Conditional probabilities and 99% confidence interval for the time lag analysis matching PSJ, NR, and IGA, with PSJ as criterion. Lag was* **level-***triggered out to MAX LAG of 300 sec.*

as criteria. In Figure 17-5 we see that (1) PSJ is excited and then inhibited during the first 40 sec from its own occurrences with a recurrence of inhibition at 120 to 130 sec, (2) nursing lasts for about 25 sec, commencing 5 sec after PSJ occurrences, then is inhibited, followed by reoccurrence after about 3.5 min, and (3) IGA has a zero probability for about 20 sec after PSJ instances, and shows no strong tendency to reoccur over the total remaining lags. For nursing (Fig. 17-6) we see (1) about 15 sec of excitation followed by 25 sec of inhibition in the auto-contingency function, (2) while PSJ and IGA are initially inhibited and show little trend toward above-chance occurrences throughout the total 5 min after NR.

RESEARCH APPLICATIONS OF THE LAG MODEL

The lag model can be applied in any research situation where categorical events are measured in an ordered event or time sequence. Such situations vary from the elegant microanalyses (filmed sequences in millisecond time units) of mother-infant interactions performed by Stern (1974) to the study of behaviors between residents in group homes measured in 15-min intervals for full 24-h periods (Landesman-Dwyer, 1977). There are also several special applications for which the lag method is appropriate involving identification of rhythmicities such as diurnal cycles or shorter ultradian cycles.

CRITERION: NURSE (TRIGGERED ON LEVEL)

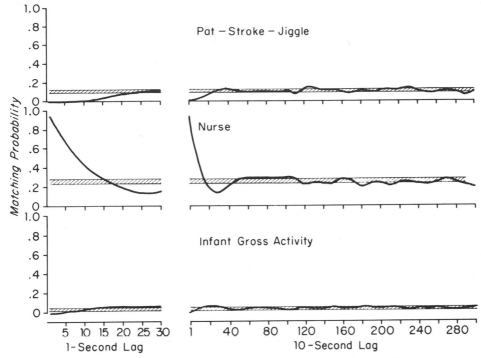

Figure 17-6.   Conditional probabilities and 99% confidence interval for the time lag analysis matching PSJ, NR, and IGA, with Nurse as criterion. Lag was level-triggered out to MAX LAG 300 sec.

Landesman-Dwyer and Sackett (1977) studied sleep-wakefulness cycles in nonambulatory retarded children living in an institution. Subjects were observed once per 10 min, 24 h/day, for 5 days. Their state was coded as either behaviorally asleep, awake-but-inactive, or awake-and-active at each observation. This produced 144 sequential observations per day for a total of 720 scores per individual. A 10-min time unit lag analysis studied auto- and cross-contingencies for these states up to the MAX LAG of 144, a full 24-h day. The resulting lag profiles were used to study the extent of diurnal cyclicity during a pretreatment period, and after 30 days of treatment by adding daily social and nonsocial stimulation for an experimental group. Using a trend analysis of variance applied to the time lag probabilities, the results showed marked positive changes in cyclicity for experimental subjects but no changes for nontreated controls. An application such as this could be very useful for studying prenatal and perinatal factors influencing cyclic state organization in newborn human infants. Michaelis et al. (1974) did use this technique to assess differences in sleep cycles of full-term and premature newborns. The lag method was also used by Maxim et al. (1976), who identified 60- to 90-min cycles in the interactive behaviors of rhesus monkey dyads.

A final, as yet untried, use of the lag method is in studying contingencies between categorical states and *quantitative* variables. An example would be the relationship between a continuously varying physiological measure and a set of observationally coded behaviors (e.g., Smith et al., 1971). Suppose that in the monkey mother-infant dyad situation we had recorded the infant's heart rate by telemetry while we coded behavior. This could produce heart rate values for every behavioral event occurring at each second in the real-time sequence. For lag analysis the heart rates would be recoded into categories. For example, we might code a rate as high or low by replacing the actual values with an "H" when the rate was above the median of all rates and an "L" when at or below the median. Finer distinctions could be made by recoding into more categories such as quartiles of the total heart rates obtained. This would yield categories of low, moderately low, moderately high, and high rates. The usual time lag analysis would then be run for auto-contingency within the heart rate categories, and cross-contingency between the rate and behavioral categories, with each code type as criteria and matching variables. Such an analysis would identify dependency of behaviors on ranges of rates and of rates on specific behaviors. Such a scheme could be used to study relationships of behavior with any quantitative measure of interest.

Analysis of Within-Subject, Between-Subject, and Group Differences

To be of wide use lag probabilities should be amenable to tests for (1) changes in values for a single individual over time or different conditions, (2) similarity (homogeneity) of values between a number of subjects, and (3) differences in values between groups of subjects. A number of methods are available for such tests. For between-group comparisons the standard arsenal of psychological inferential statistics can be applied. t or U tests will assess differences between two groups in lag probabilities of a given category at a given lag. For factorial designs standard analyses of variance can be run on probabilities for a particular behavior, and repeated measure ANOVA can be used to study all behaviors at a given lag or the lag profile for a given behavior. Between group differences on the total output of a complete lag analysis with all behaviors as criteria and matches can be made using multivariate ANOVA or multiple-regression techniques (e.g., Harris, 1975).

There are also a number of procedures, less well known in the behavioral sciences, for studying differences between sets of probabilities in a more direct fashion. These tests are especially useful in single-subject (N of 1) experiments and for studying between-subject similarities and differences. The remainder of this section will describe some of these procedures.

Lag Probabilities for a Single Behavior

Let us consider questions concerning a single behavior matching a given criterion at a specific lag—for example, the contingency between pat-stroke-jiggle and infant gross activity at lag 1 in the monkey dyad data (Fig. 17-2). Suppose that data were collected on this dyad in morning and evening sessions to see if the contingency varied with time of day. The morning lag 1 probability for PSJ matching IGA is found to be 0.684 out of 95 possible matches, while the evening value is 0.450 out of 120 possible matches. The morning versus evening difference can be tested by the 2 × 2 contingency test shown on the left in Table 17-8. The chi-square value being highly significant, we conclude that the evening dependency is weaker than that found in the morning.

Now, suppose that we test another dyad whose results are those shown in the right portion of Table 17-8. This contingency has exactly the same numbers as the first dyad, except the morning and evening values are reversed. The fact that the two chi-square values are identical shows that this statistic gives no information about the *direction* of a

Table 17-8. Lag 1 Frequencies for PSJ following IGA in the Morning versus the Evening for Two Monkey Mother-Infant Dyads. Expected Frequencies are the Product of the Row and Column Totals for Each Cell, Divided by the Overall Total. The Chi-Squares $[\Sigma(O\text{-}E)^2/E]$ have $df=1$.

		Dyad 1			Dyad 2		
		PSJ	Not PSJ	TOTAL	PSJ	Not PSJ	TOTAL
Morning	Observed	65	30	95	54	66	120
	Expected	52.6	42.4		66.4	53.6	
Evening	Observed	54	66	120	65	30	95
	Expected	66.4	53.6		52.6	42.4	
	TOTAL	119	95	215	119	95	215
	χ^2		11.85			11.85	
	$z=(\chi^2)^{1/2}$		+3.44			−3.44	

significant contingency. What test can we make that will be sensitive to the direction of contingencies?

A test for "homogeneity" of contingencies is based on the fact that $(\chi^2)^{1/2}$ with $df = 1$ is equal to z. We can sign z values by a rule like the following: z will be positive if the morning has the higher probability, but negative if the evening probability is higher. The z sum test proposed next was developed by Cochran (1954), and extended to social interaction data by Bobbitt et al. (1969). A sum of independent z values is, itself, normally distributed with a mean of zero and $\sigma = n^{1/2}$; where n is the number of z values being summed. The null hypothesis tested here is that the summed z values are a random sample from a population having a mean z of zero. If the ratio $\Sigma z/n^{1/2}$ is significant when referred to the normal distribution, we can reject the hypothesis that the average z is zero. The implications of this outcome are that (1) the mean z is different from zero (either positive or negative depending on the signs of the individual value), (2) the individual z values tend to vary in the same direction, and (3) we have no evidence *against* the hypothesis that the original contingencies were homogeneous. For the example in Table 17-8 we have a z of 3.44 and one of −3.44. The sum z test yields a value of 0.00. This statistically "proves" the obvious conclusion that these dyads are not the same in their morning-versus-afternoon probabilities.

The sum z test can be made on any number of independent signed values. Even if few, or none, of the individual z values are statistically reliable, if they are mostly in the same direction (their signs are almost all the same) the sum z test may still provide evidence for departure from a mean z of zero. For example, suppose that eight monkey dyads generated 2×2 contingencies for the morning-versus-afternoon comparison. If the z values were 3.42, 2.61, 1.67, 1.59, 1.42, 1.31, 1.29, and −3.42, the resulting sum z test would be $9.89/\sqrt{8} = 3.50$. This value allows rejection of the zero mean z hypothesis beyond the 0.01 level, and is much more powerful than the alternative binomial sign test (Siegel, 1956).

Lag Profiles and Criterion Profiles

Lag profiles are being defined here as the probability of matching a criterion by a *single* behavior across all lags up to MAX LAG. A criterion profile is defined to be the probabilities with which all behaviors studied match a given criterion at a single lag. Lag profiles are shown in all of the data plots in this chapter. A criterion profile would consist of a histogram or other type of bar graph of observed probabilities such as those shown in Tables 17-6 or 17-7. Differences for single subjects under different conditions and similarity between subjects can be studied for such profiles using chi-square tests.

Suppose that we wished to study morning-versus-evening differences in all lag 1 probabilities for the IGA criterion of a single dyad. Data for such a comparison might be those in Table 17-9. Four of the original behaviors were not included because they had zero matching frequencies on *both* the morning and evening sessions. A standard chi-square test can be applied to see if these two criterion profiles differ. The value in this case of 43.10 ($p < 0.001$), allows us to conclude that the distributions differ in at least some ways. For this test to be valid, not too many of the expected frequencies can be less than five. The standard practice of pooling categories to increase expected frequencies may not make sense with this type of data, because behaviors with no shared attributes (i.e., "apples and oranges") might have to be pooled to achieve acceptable expected values. For example, it would make little psychological sense to pool nonsocial exploration together with grooming. The cure for this problem is to collect sufficient data so that the total number of criterion occurrences is large enough to yield few expectations less than five.

The same basic test can be used to study criterion profiles for a number of subjects tested under the same conditions. Columns would contain the matching behaviors, and rows the individual subjects. A significant chi-square provides evidence that at least some of the criterion profiles differ from the overall column probabilities. This is the same as saying that there is evidence against profile homogeneity between the subjects.

Chi-square tests can also be used to study lag profiles. Columns of these contingency tables would contain the successive lags from 1 to MAX LAG. In the case of single-subject data, the rows would contain different times of measurement or measurement under different conditions. For between-subjects data the rows would contain the data for each individual when tested under the same conditions. Lag profiles can also be studied graphically. Simply plot the various lag profiles with their corresponding confidence bands, or with confidence bands generated from all of the data pooled together (the column probabilities from the chi-square contingency tables). Inspection will reveal

Table 17-9.   Criterion Profile of IGA at Lag 1 for Morning and Evening Sessions. Only Behaviors with Total Matching Frequencies over Zero are Shown. Expected Values are Calculated as in Table 17-8, Yielding Chi-Square=43.10 with df=5.

| | | \multicolumn{6}{c}{Matching Behavior} | |
		PC	HC	PSJ	GR	NR	NSE	N TOT CRIT
Morning	Observed	0	19	65	0	11	0	95
	Expected	8.84	12.81	52.58	4.42	11.49	4.86	
Evening	Observed	20	10	54	10	15	11	120
	Expected	11.16	16.19	66.42	5.58	14.51	6.14	
	TOTAL	20	29	119	10	26	11	215
Overall Prob.		0.093	0.135	0.553	0.047	0.121	0.051	

whether points collected under one condition lie within the confidence band for the other, or whether a large number of points lie outside of the confidence bands for the data as a whole.

The Information Theory Approach

The methods of information theory (e.g., Attneave, 1959) provide another technique for analyzing the lag output probabilities. Gottman and Notarius (1976) have provided a readable and elegant description of estimating information theory statistics for conditional probabilities generated from observational data. These techniques allow calculation of the amount of information (restriction on pure randomness) contained in each lag probability, the amount of information contained in total lag or criterion profiles, and the significance of differences between these measures within and between subjects and for different test groups. Exposition of these methods is beyond the scope of this chapter. However, investigators planning to use the lag method will certainly benefit from study of the Gottman and Notarius paper if they wish to fully exploit the analytic power of their lag probabilities.

A FINAL WORD

The purpose of this chapter is to present the lag technique, with as little mathematical, symbolic, and theoretical trapping as possible. The primary goal is to show that it is possible to study sequential dependencies in observational data, it is fairly simple, and for those so inclined it can be very interesting. However, two issues of some importance should be discussed. First, the method is vulnerable to capitalization on chance. Second, the hypothesis-testing techniques are too simple.

Capitalization on chance means that if a sufficiently large number of measurements are made on a phenomenon, some will almost certainly be extreme. In hypothesis testing the more tests made the more likely some will be "significant," even when the variable under study has no effect. The problem is called guarding against Type-I error—the probability of rejecting the null hypothesis when it is true.

A wise investigator will scan the criterion and lag profiles of individual subjects to be sure they make psychological (zoological, biological, physiological, sociological) sense, whether the lag probabilities are or are not statistically reliable. At the very least, it is necessary to check that (1) more than *alpha* (Type-I error rate) of the probabilities are significant, or (2) the probabilities that are significant generate a *function* that is meaningful. Such functions might be reoccurrence at specific lag periods, or bunching together at some consecutive lags in the total profile.

The null hypotheses concerning individual probabilities used in this chapter all assume that the sequential flow of behavior is random. Yet, it is a truism of behavior that almost everything is correlated with everything else, and that behaviors that occur close together in time will be more similar than those occurring far apart. These two "facts" mean that these types of simple null hypotheses will almost always be rejected. Thus, the lag analysis will always show *something* significant, as will any of the concurrent or pattern sequential methods, when a large number of behaviors are studied. What seems needed is a *model*-testing rather than a null-hypothesis-testing approach.

Models of cyclic phenomena are well understood in electrical engineering. The parametric approach to lag analysis—spectral analysis—performs the same basic type of computations, but uses product-moment correlation coefficients. Spectral analysis yields a number of mathematical parameters which describe the lag profiles, and often "explain" the characteristics of the underlying process that generated the sequential dependencies. Jenkins and Watts (1969) can be consulted for a reasonably comprehensible exposition of spectral analysis techniques. The same basic approach might be taken with this non-parametric lag analysis. Probability models can be derived for generating theoretical lag and criterion profiles. These profiles would serve as expectations, against which empirical profiles would be tested for goodness of fit. Successive experiments might search for generating models that fit the data well *and* have implications about the processes that underlie the observed behavior. A beginning has been provided by the work of Glass et al. (1975), but there is still a long way to go for models of multivariate observational data. Perhaps those of us using the lag model can persuade a friend in the Statistics Department that these are interesting and worthy problems for study at the theoretical level.

BIBLIOGRAPHY

Altmann, S. A. Sociobiology of rhesus monkeys. II: Stochastics of social communication. *Journal of Theoretical Biology,* 1965, **8**, 490–522.

Attneave, F. *Applications of Information Theory to Psychology.* New York: Holt, 1959.

Bakeman, R. Untangling streams of behavior. In G. P. Sackett (ed.), *Observing Behavior,* Vol. 2. *Data Collection and Analysis Methods.* Baltimore: University Park Press, 1977.

Bobbitt, R. A., Gourevitch, V. P., Miller, L. E., and Jensen, G. D. Dynamics of social interactive behavior: A computerized procedure for analyzing trends, patterns, and sequences. *Psychological Bulletin,* 1969, **71**, 110–121.

Cochran, W. G. Some methods for strengthening the common chi square tests. *Biometrics,* 1954, **10**, 417–451.

Glass, G. V., Willson, V. L., and Gottman, J. M. *Design and Analysis of Time-Series Experiments.* Boulder: Colorado University, 1975.

Gottman, J. M. Nonsequential data analysis techniques in observational research. In G. P. Sackett (ed.), *Observing Behavior,* Vol. 2. *Data Collection and Analysis Methods.* Baltimore: University Park Press, 1978.

Gottman, J. M., and Notarius, C. Sequential analysis of observational data using Markov chains. In T. Kratochwill (ed.), *Strategies to Evaluate Change in Single Subject Research.* New York: Academic, 1976.

Harris, R. J. *A Primer of Multivariate Statistics.* New York: Academic, 1975.

Jenkins, G. M., and Watts, D. G. *Spectral Analysis and its Applications.* San Francisco: Holden-Day, 1969.

Landesman-Dwyer, S. A behavioral and ecological study of group homes. In G. P. Sackett (ed.), *Observing Behavior,* Vol. 1. *Theory and Applications in Mental Retardation.* Baltimore: University Park Press, 1977.

Landesman-Dwyer, S., and Sackett, G. P. Behavioral changes in nonambulatory, mentally retarded individuals. *Monograph of the American Association on Mental Deficiency,* No. 3, 1978, 55–144.

Maxim, P. E., Bowden, D. M., and Sackett, G. P. Ultradian rhythms of solitary and social behavior in rhesus monkeys. *Physiology & Behavior,* 1976, **17**, 337–344.

Michaelis, R., Parmelee, A. H., Stern, E., and Haber, A. Activity states in premature and term infants. *Developmental Psychobiology,* 1973, **6**, 209–216.

Sackett, G. P. Measurement in observational research. In G. P. Sackett (ed.), *Observing Behavior,* Vol. 2. *Data Collection and Analysis Methods.* Baltimore: University Park Press, 1978.

Sackett, G. P., Stephenson, E. A., and Ruppenthal, G. C. Digital data acquisition systems for observing behavior in laboratory and field settings. *Behavior Research Methods & Instrumentation,* 1973, **5**, 344–348.

Siegel, S. *Nonparametric Statistics.* New York: McGraw-Hill, 1956.

Smith, O. A., Jr., Reese, D., Weiss, G. K., Spelman, F., Wilson, C., and Snow, E. Studies of cardiovascular physiology in controlled and unrestrained environments. *Medical Primatology,* 1971, **1**, 442–454.

Stern, D. N. Mother and infant at play: The dyadic interaction involving facial, vocal, and gaze behaviors. In M. Lewis and L. A. Rosenblum (eds.), *The Effect of the Infant on Its Caregiver.* New York: Wiley, 1974.

PART FOUR

Continuity and Change: Relationships Among Infant Behaviors Over Time

CHAPTER 18

Developmental Continuity[1]

Michael Lewis and Mark D. Starr

The childhood shows the
man as morning shows the day.

John Milton, *Paradise Regained*

A 9-year-old sits before a table on which nine pictures, one taken on each yearly anniversary of his birth, are arranged before him. What do we know of this set of pictures? First, they are all pictures of the same child. We know this both because we have taken these pictures, and because they resemble each other. Second, these pictures have an order. Although not marked, we know their order because of the increased size of the child standing there and because of the change in the facial features. These changes are invariant, the order is fixed. The final issue, the one of major concern for this discussion, is the relationship between the picture at time t and $t + 1$. Is there any relationship between the child at these two points in time or development? They are the same person; metaphysically the death of the child at t would have resulted in no picture at $t + 1$. Within this sameness what do we know of the child at $t + 1$ from our knowledge of the child at t? Does the childhood show the man?

The study of change demarcates the area of developmental inquiry. At its most basic level, the problem of development is that of finding order in change, identifying continuities in behavioral systems that are rapidly transforming and reorganizing. On the whole, we have not been particularly successful in addressing this problem. Current theories of development are predominantly descriptions of the child at different points or stages in ontogeny, and little is known about the functions relating an individual's actions and abilities at one developmental point to those at another. At first glance it appears that theorists regard the child as advancing through a series of qualitatively distinct steps, a conceptualization which, in Flavell's (1971) words, "leads logically to the paradoxical conclusion that the individual spends virtually all his childhood years 'being' rather than 'becoming' " [p. 426]. This situation has arisen in part from the failure of researchers to find continuity or stability in their studies of the child's development, and in part from the emphasis of major theories of development, especially those of Piaget and Werner, on questions of structural differences in behavior observed at different points in development (cf. Wohlwill, 1973). The study of continuity in developmental processes has been relatively neglected.

Most theorists recognize invariant sequences of change and growth over development. Much of the infant's physical and mental growth follows sequences which are fixed: the

[1]This research is supported by NICHD contract No. 1, HD 42803.

653

child moves his head before his trunk, rolls over before sitting, sits before crawling, and crawls before standing. Likewise, vowel sounds precede consonants, one-word utterances precede two-word utterances, and the mean length of utterance increases with age (see Brown, 1973). Piaget's descriptions of invariant stages of mental growth in infancy provide further examples too familiar to need discussion. Identifying and abstracting invariant sequences is, as Wohlwill (1973) notes, an important first step in the study of developmental change. Identifying sequences of growth, however, does not solve our problem, and we must further ask whether ability (either competence or performance, an unnecessary distinction for this issue) in any area—social, cognitive, perceptual, and so on—at one point in time or at one stage of development, is related to ability at another (Flavell, 1971; Piaget, 1954; Van den Daele, 1969; Wohlwill, 1973).

In recent years, "stage theories" have achieved popularity as approximate descriptions of growth and change. These theories are generally considered "structural" in that they emphasize the organization or structure of psychological items underlying behavior. In the study of developmental change, stage theories that have focused on the differences between stages or periods have typically employed cross-sectional research designs, and have specified nomothetic developmental patterns. As Wohlwill (1973) notes, the interest of theorists in this area has typically been in the formal relationships between one stage and the next, and not in the transition processes governing the development of an individual through the described stages. Nonetheless, at least four assumptions about the nature of developmental change are implicit in many stage theories:

(1) Stage-to-stage development entails qualitative rather than quantitative changes . . .; (2) the development of individual stage-specific items is characteristically abrupt rather than gradual; that is, there is a zero-order transition period between the appearance of each item and its state of functional maturity; (3) the various items which define a given stage develop concurrently, i.e., in synchrony with one another; (4) stage-specific items become organized and interrelated to form cognitive structures. [Flavell, 1971, pp. 423–433]

The use of stage theories to characterize development has fostered the assumption that behavior is discontinuous in the sense that past performance or experience, while necessary for subsequent development, is not necessarily an antecedent of that development. While stage theory does not logically preclude the possibility that specific antecedent conditions affect or predict subsequent behavior, it is usually contrasted against models that hold development is continuous. These latter models postulate development through quantitative changes in underlying functions, and have generally emphasized individual differences in behavior and the gradual acquisition of abilities. Unfortunately, no careful analysis of continuity in developmental change exists. Most studies gauge continuity in development by the stability of individual differences over time in the sample observed; for example, the Bell et al. (1971) study of the stability of the neonate's and the 3- and 4-year-old child's behavior. However, the failure of this type of study has been common: the study of IQ (Bayley, 1970; although McCall et al., 1972, report stability), the study of temperament (Bell et al., 1971), the study of attachment (Lewis and Ban, 1971; Maccoby and Feldman, 1972), and the study of cognition (Kagan, 1971) are but a few examples. These studies have not encouraged continuous models of development. This has led some to conclude that continuity exists but that infancy is a period of too rapid change in behavior to allow predictability. It has led others to accept discontinuous models of development.

Our purpose here is not to contrast continuous and discontinuous models of development. Instead, we focus specifically on problems involved in identifying continuity in developmental change. Moreover we assume that social and psychological growth is continuous. The alternative assumption that there is no continuity in early development is unattractive for a number of reasons, and before proceeding it is useful to consider some of these briefly.

First, while it is not disputed that certain abilities are best described as qualitatively distinct from earlier modes of functioning, the utility of such descriptions will always depend on the level of analysis at which one chooses to work. For example, consider the relationship between a butterfly and the caterpillar from which it grew. Few would challenge the observer who characterizes the butterfly in terms qualitatively distinct from those used to describe the caterpillar. Yet such a characterization does not imply that the process of change from caterpillar to butterfly was necessarily discontinuous. At the cellular level of analysis the change that occurred was gradual and continuous. Similarly, the choice of time frames in which observations take place will affect assessments of continuity and discontinuity. To return to our example, observing first a caterpillar and then a butterfly gives the impression of dramatic qualitative change. But when observed within the cocoon, butterfly-like characteristics are gradually accrued and we are thus more likely to describe the process of change as continuous. From a practical standpoint, while we may describe behavior in two developmental periods as qualitatively different, it is reasonable to assume that, in principle, given another level of analysis or a different time base for our observations, the functions relating the two observations will be found continuous.

A second reason for assuming continuity in developmental change derives from considerations of logic. When describing a pattern of behavior, we are inevitably plagued by the fact that we can never be sure our measurement instruments are adequate or that our constructs are the best possible. Describing a stage of development as qualitatively unique implies that the descriptors are not applicable at some earlier point in time. For example, to say that the child is able to "conserve" implies that the child was once at a developmental point when the label "conserver" was not applicable. But can we ever be sure that some other measure of conservation or some other test situation will not reveal an ability warranting the label "conserver" (or partial conserver)? To affirm the *absence* of competency or ability at a particular developmental period requires reasoning from negative results, and is therefore not logically justifiable. The failure to demonstrate competency with a given measure cannot be taken as evidence against continuous-change theories of development, nor as evidence for strict stage (i.e., discontinuous-change) theories. In addition to being of questionable logical value, it is not clear that it is even desirable to describe a child's behavior in terms of the absence of given abilities. For both theoretical and practical purposes, the child is best characterized in terms of what he *can* do. Speaking of a given behavior pattern as being without developmental antecedents gives us little in the way of useful knowledge. Supplementing these theoretical reasons for focusing on continuity in development are also pragmatic concerns. Understanding individual differences in behavior and intervening to change the course of development are both important practical issues, and have generated interest in the prediction of subsequent development from knowledge of present levels.

Together, these arguments suggest that to accept the assumption that the processes underlying development are discontinuous is neither desirable nor likely to be required by data. Instead, in our opinion, development is best studied as a continuous process. As we have argued, however, this is largely a matter of personal choice: the continuity-discontinuity debate is not an empirical issue (see Wohlwill, 1973, for a similar argument).

In the following discussion we examine a number of interrelated issues. First we consider response continuity—that is, the development and organization of response patterns. The child's behavior is, of course, the empirical anchor of our theoretical constructs, and it is important to examine the conceptual and methodological issues encountered when investigating continuity in behavioral change. Here we discuss both *continuity of development* in a theoretical sense, which includes considerations of underlying processes and their interaction, and continuity in a practical sense—that is, the *stability or consistency of an individual's behavior* over development, relative either to other individuals or to other behavior patterns within the same individual. Second, we discuss continuity and the determinants of behavior, focusing specifically on the problem of changes in the individual's perception of the world over development.

RESPONSE CONTINUITY: STABILITY AND CONSISTENCY OF BEHAVIOR

Infancy and early childhood are periods of rapid behavioral change. The individual's physical capacities increase dramatically during these periods, and a wealth of new experience quickly accumulates. To what extent are actions at one point in development related to those at another? In discussing this question, three issues will be raised; and while these are presented separately, they are, in fact, interwoven. These are (1) the problem of response reliability and measurement, (2) the problem of multiple response attributes or dimensions, and (3) the question of response meaning and organization—that is, the relation of observable behaviors to underlying psychological processes.

Reliability of Measures

Although the measurement and short-term reliability of responses used to infer theoretical constructs should not be an issue, it is unfortunately one of considerable concern. The study of development requires repeating observations and measurements of behavior. But before we can conclude that we have identified change in a developmental function, we must be confident that our initial measures of the function are, in fact, stable.

In many areas of social and psychological inquiry, responses are notoriously variable. Masters and Wellman (1974), for example, document that the behaviors used to measure mother-infant attachment are not stable from day to day. An infant upset by his mother's departure one day may take little notice of it the next. There are, of course, an indefinite number of reasons for the failure to find short-term reliability of response measures. These range from the failure on the investigator's part to control the conditions under which the behavior is observed, to the possibility that infants and young children are simply not consistent in their reactions to particular observer-defined events.

Consider, for example, the influence of the situation on the child's behavior. In assessing both short-term and long-term reliability of repeated measures, it is important to control the situational and organismic-status (state) conditions in which measurement is made. It may be the case that low reliabilities reflect the failure on the investigator's part to insure that repeated measurement takes place under the most identical conditions. Thus, if the infant is tired or sick, his behavior may be dramatically affected. When a mother leaves her infant alone in a room, for example, the infant may well be more likely to cry when sick or tired than when healthy and alert. Moreover, the external environment must be kept consistent if reliable measures are to be obtained. The mother leaving the child at home is quite a different situation than her leaving him in an unfamiliar playroom, and it would not be reasonable to expect good reliability across these different situations, although the mother's actions are similar in each case.

It is important to remember that our primary interest is not in the responses themselves but in the processes and functions underlying them. Over the course of development, the responses expressing a given process may change or be transformed. For these reasons it may be desirable to use multiple measures of a construct when doing developmental investigations. It is possible that only a subset of the responses used to represent a construct show low short-term reliability. Similarly, it is conceivable that a given process has alternative and roughly equivalent modes of expression. For example, an infant may maintain contact with his mother by either touching or looking. Considered independently, individual differences in the frequency of touching and looking may show little stability, while summed frequencies including both touching and looking may be stable.

Before addressing the larger theoretical issues of development, it is essential that careful consideration be given to studies of reliability. Unfortunately, this has rarely been undertaken; reliability has, for the most part, been an issue of the accuracy of the observer in obtaining or scoring data, rather than the ability of the subject to produce the same response. It is of considerable methodological importance to know the short-term reliability of each measure used.

If it is the case that short-term reliability continues to be difficult to demonstrate in infants, then it may be of interest to study developmental changes in reliability as an issue in itself—that is, if consistency of action is a function or outcome of development, then the short-term reliability of response measures, all other things held constant, should increase with age. For example, early in development response systems may be more labile and sensitive to environmental impact than later in development. If this is in fact the case, we would expect early measures of continuity to be less stable than later ones.

Response Attributes

In practice, a "response" is an experimenter-defined unit of behavior measured along some dimension. The response selected and measure employed in a given instance is, of course, fairly arbitrary. In the following discussion we consider briefly possible dimensions or attributes of a response. By considering that a particular response may have a variety of attributes, we may question the relation of these attributes over time. It may be the case that stability over time for a particular response is dependent on the attributes of the response measured.

Salient attributes of responses include quantity, quality, speed of acquisition, utilization, affective tone, generalizability, organizational properties, and intention. *Quantity* refers to the gross frequency and/or duration with which the behavior is expressed in a given unit of time. In the case of language, for example, this is how much a person speaks. *Quality* refers to the extent the response is effective, efficient, or elaborately differentiated. For example, we can ask whether an infant uses syntactically, correct language in a situation. *Speed of acquisition* refers to how quickly the response is acquired. *Utilization* refers to the circumstances in which the behavior is displayed. The *affective* tone refers to the degree of affect associated with use. *Generalizability* refers to the use of the target behavior in the place of other responses, while *organizational properties* refer to the relationship of the particular response to others in the individual's repertoire. *Intention* refers to the infant's control of the response and awareness of that control.

It is possible to dimensionalize a response so that one can focus upon a particular attribute of that response. This approach allows comparisons that normally would not be made. For example, a particular dimension of a response can be studied in children of different ages and sexes, or within the same group of children in different situations, and for some attributes, in animals other than man.[2] One analysis of response attributes relevant to the present discussion involves one measure of behavior at a time t and a different measure of the same behavior at $t + 1$. Suppose we are interested in language acquisition and consider the activity involved in terms of quantity, quality, and utilization. If quantity is measured at t and quality or usage at $t + 1$, it is unlikely that any consistency can be observed. Recently, Lewis and Cherry (1977) recorded the vocalizations of 50 3-month-old infants and their mothers, and the linguistic behavior of these same 50 infants and mothers when they were 2 years old. For the infants all that was available at 3 months was the quantity of vocal behavior, while at 2 years, quantity, quality [as measured by mean length of utterance (MLU)], and use (as measured by question-asking) were available. For their mothers, quantity, quality, and usage were available at both age points. Figure 18-1 represents the correlation matrix representing the various relationships. The highest correlation for the child's behavior alone across the two ages was for the quantity-quantity comparison. The same was true for the mother's behavior. There was no relationship when quantity at 3 months was compared to quality or use at 2 years. Thus continuity could be established, but only when language behavior was broken into its various dimensions as a result of the analysis of response attributes.

As in the case of response meaning, response attributes may be controlled by a number of underlying processes, and these may change over development. Returning to Flavell's (1972) classification of cognitive-development sequences for examples, "modification" and "inclusion" are both possible systems for describing developmental changes in response complexity. Response attributes may be modified in a variety of ways: skills become differentiated, generalized, and stabilized with development. Other changes in behavior occur as the response system becomes integrated with more complex and extended behavioral systems (inclusion). The point emphasized here is that responses are not static entities existing in isolation from other behavioral systems. When seeking continuity in development, care must be taken in both examining various dimensions of the response and specifying the relation between the given dimension and other components of the response system.

Response Meaning and Response Organization

Let us assume we have achieved adequate short-term reliability of our response measures at two points in development. The assumption that the responses at the two times should be related—that is, that the subjects should maintain their respective positions vis-à-vis the sample studied—underlies many studies of developmental continuity. But when given careful consideration, this assumption is not justified. The similarity of response topographies at two points in time is not of critical importance to the issue of continuity in development. Our primary interest is in the continuity of processes or functions. Since we use responses in our definitions of these central processes, our concern is with the meaning of the response—that is, its relationship to the process or construct it is used to index—rather than with the physical characteristics of the response per se.

If we assume a given construct or process is stable or continuous over development,

---

[2]For example, it would be foolish to study the feature of language called syntax in both man and apes, but the feature called communication competency might well be related for the two animals.

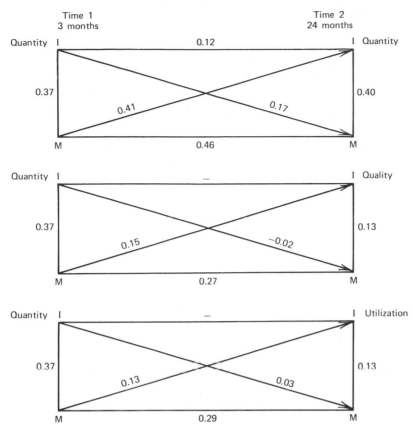

Figure 18-1. Correlation matrices for quantity (frequency of vocalization), quality (mean length of utterance) and utilization (number of yes/no questions) measures of mother and infant vocalization. Data were collected from 50 mother-infant dyads first when the infant was 3 months old (Time 1) and later when the infant was 24 months old (Time 2).

must we also assume the response we measure in the test situation is also stable? The answer to this question is clearly no. Moreover, if the responses at the two observation points are the same, we are not justified in concluding that the underlying construct has remained stable. Theoretical constructs and observable responses may appear in a variety of combinations. To use Kagan's (1971) terminology, we may observe *homotypic continuity* (also termed phenotypic or isomorphic continuity; Bell et al., 1971), where the response remains stable or constant, but the process controlling the response has changed; *heterotypic continuity* (or genotypic or metamorphic continuity), where the process has remained stable but the behavioral expression of that process has undergone change; and *complete continuity,* where both process and behavior are stable across two observation points. It is only with complete continuity that the meaning of a response is retained over development.

A hypothetical case of homotypic continuity will illustrate the implications of these process-response relationships. Suppose we observe that a 1-year-old infant cries when his mother leaves him alone in a room. Our measures tell us that this response is controlled solely by affective processes—for example, the infant cries because he is afraid. One year later, when the infant is 2 years old, we repeat our observation and find that again he cries when his mother leaves him. But now we find, with independent measures, that the infant is no longer afraid in the situation. Instead, crying is a goal-directed instrumental activity, a vocalization intended to retrieve the mother, perhaps controlled by the pleasure the infant experiences when his mother is nearby. Thus we have observed continuity, a topographically similar response to a standard situation at two points in time. But this is homotypic continuity; the process controlling the response is not the same during each observation.

Homotypic continuity can arise as an outcome of a number of developmental sequences. Consider as examples three sequences categorized by Flavell (1972)[3]: (1) Addition (also described as "cumulative" by Van den Daele, 1969): The original process (X1) is still active (e.g., the child still cries when afraid), but a second process (X2) has developed independently and is also able to control the response (e.g., the child will cry for reasons other than fear). (2) Substitution (Van den Daele's "simple"): A second developmental process, X2, completely replaces and assumes the function of the first process, X1. (3) Mediation: The first process, X1, is a bridge to the second process, X2, but X2 oeprates independently of X1. For example, without fear (X1) crying would never appear in the situation, and the infant would not learn that mother returns when he cries (X2).

Heterotypic continuity is also a common developmental phenomenon. Overt behavior is subject to a variety of influences, and it is often the case that the response through which a given underlying process finds expression changes over development. One set of factors that influence behavioral expression may be loosely described as socialization. It would appear that the effects of socialization are, in part, to alter or create responses and response meanings, and it may be that socialization acts to change response meaning as a function of level, situation, or cultural demand. Lewis and his associates (Lewis, 1967; Lewis and Ban, 1971; Lewis and Weinraub, 1974), in discussing infant behavior and the meaning of responses, have argued for a *transformational analysis* to identify changes in response meaning. The transformational approach is based on the premise that responses change their meaning over time as a function of developmental level. This change can be maturational or social; nonetheless, response meanings are expected to change in predictable ways. Infant crying in response to frustrating experiences is a good example of changing response meaning. Both with increased age and as a function of sex (possibly also as a function of cultural demands), crying becomes less socially acceptable, and as such the meaning assigned to it by the adult caregivers, and consequently their responses to it, change. As a result, in a sample of infants, crying at 12 months in response to a frustrating experience is unrelated to crying at 24 months, also in response to frustration. However, if other response measures are taken, it may turn out that crying at 12 months is related to another response to frustration at 24 months, such as actively trying to remove the frustrating obstacle.

More specific to the relationship between mother and child is the child's contact behavior. Lewis and Ban (1971), Lewis and Weinraub (1974), and Maccoby and Feldman (1972) have shown that across the first 3 years the amount of physical-proximity maintenance and seeking engaged in by the child toward its mother decreases. Moreover there is little relationship between the amount of proximity seeking shown at 1 and 2 years of age.

---

[3]Note: Flavell lists these as cognitive processes, but they may equally well be applied to motivational processes—i.e., processes controlling the expression of responses.

Lewis and Ban (1971) argued that proximity seeking may have changed its meaning as a function of socialization: at 1 year it is an appropriate response for a child to make and for parents to accept; however, by 2 years children should both want to be and are encouraged to be more independent. If proximity seeking has changed its meaning as a function of socialization, then the direct measurement of it at two age points should be unrelated, as it has been shown to be (Lewis and Ban, 1971). The question then becomes, are there other responses that we can identify which have the same or similar meaning? Lewis and Weinraub (1974), using a small sample of infants, were able to show that by looking for responses with similar meaning—that is, responses that enable the child to maintain contact—continuities can be located. In this particular case it was found that although proximity seeking—specifically touching—was not related between 1 and 2 years, touching and looking were related such that high touchers at 1 year became high lookers at 2. It was hypothesized that looking was a more adult form of contact maintenance than touching; thus the continuity in contact maintenance, although changing in form, was established.

The issue of response meaning is particularly difficult in the study of organisms undergoing rapid change. Consider that the infant can be characterized as an organism with relatively few response systems and that a major developmental outcome is the differentiation of these responses. At birth the differentiation of these domains and skills is a major task of the organism; and by the end of the 3rd year of life major differentiation has occurred. The search for consistency in response meaning becomes particularly difficult in an organism that at time t is undifferentiated but at $t + 1$ has become considerably differentiated. For example, we have observed over 50 infants at 1 and 2 years in a standard laboratory playroom setting where the mother and infant play together for 15 min and then the mother leaves the room. At 1 year, all 50 infants cried when the mother left, while at 2 years, approximately half cried. It would be impossible to predict crying at 2 years from crying at 1, since all cried at 1. Thus, the lack of variability (differentiation) at one point in time makes it extremely difficult to predict subsequent differentiated behavior. Crying at 1 year could have represented anger, fear, and instrumental responding, but because of the relatively undifferentiated state of the organism, crying subsumed all of these. At 2 years, crying appeared to have a more restricted meaning since other responses were available.

One difficulty with studying continuity in early childhood is the changing meaning of responses. The change in meaning can be the consequence of socialization and/or it can be the consequence of a relatively undifferentiated organism becoming differentiated at a very rapid rate. In either case, responses alone or in combination may be difficult to use in order to demonstrate continuity. Higher order levels of analysis allowing for transformations in response meaning may be necessary.

The preceding discussion has focused on a single response or set of responses. Now we take up the issue of the organization of these responses as they are related to underlying constructs.

The utilization of single responses in exploring continuity is filled with risks: such an approach loses sight of a more fundamental issue—that is, the fact that responses in and of themselves are of relatively little importance, since these responses are reflections of more basic constructs. Part of the difficulty lies in the attempt to simplify the task by avoiding multivariate approaches to construct analysis. To limit the study of a construct to a single, or to two or three responses, is to forget that most of our conceptualizations demand a multivariate approach. Aggression, attachment, distress, and cognition as constructs cannot be characterized by a single variable, and should not be measured in this fashion. What is required is a reassessment of what behaviors characterize a given construct at a particular point in time and the nature of their organization. Following this, the set of variables characterizing the construct at time t should be compared to the set of variables characterizing the construct at time $t + 1$.

Factor analysis as a multivariate procedure seems most useful in this regard. Sets of responses make up a factor or construct. The responses making up the items of the factors have particular loadings. These coefficients give an estimate of the relative importance of each item (or response) in the factor (or construct). At different points in time, factors may be highly correlated, but either the items making up the factors (responses making up the constructs) change or the items remain the same but their loadings change. Thus, while there may be no relationship across time when one response is measured, the factors subsuming this response may show consistency. An example of the use of the factor-analysis technique for the study of early social development is reported by Emmerich (1966). Using ratings and factor analysis, three personality factors or dimensions were identified, autonomy being one. While autonomy remained a factor over time, the meaning of this personality dimension underwent change—that is, the behaviors making up the factor changed.

Other examples in response organization are available. Infant IQ tests, for example, have been widely used as indicators of later intellectual status. However, data indicate little consistency in IQ scores during the infancy period or between infancy and later periods of development (Bayley, 1970; Lewis, 1973; Lewis and McGurk, 1972). The use of a single score based on all the different items of the test seems unwarranted in light of these findings. McCall et al. (1972) factor-analyzed the scores for each item for each age. These factors, reflecting different skills at different ages, were stable and reflected heterotypic stability and continuity.

Reconsider the construct of attachment as presented by the Lewis and Ban (1971) and Lewis and Weinraub (1974) transformational analysis. Since behaviors subsuming attachment as a construct change as a function of age (Weinraub et al., 1977), one would expect to find little relationship across like behaviors, a finding repeatedly reported. If, on the other hand, the construct is valid, one might expect to find different behaviors related across time. Lewis and Weinraub (1974) report that proximity seeking at 1 year, while irrelevant to proximity seeking at 2, is related to distal behaviors such as looking at 2 years. If we assume the attachment construct to be related to the maintenance of contact, and if both socialization and growth pressures alter responses, then contact can be maintained either by proximity or by visual regard, thus the continuity in the absence of response specificity. While factor analytic procedures were not used in this study and have not been widely used in the study of infant development in general, interest in the organizational features of constructs as they change with development, and their stability and continuity, requires the measurement of a wide variety of behaviors and the use of multivariate procedures. There is no guarantee that continuity can be observed if these techniques are used, but without an attempt to utilize these procedures our models of development are forced to rest on univariate procedures and thereby limit tests of continuity.

To summarize, the failure to demonstrate continuity in development may be due to a variety of factors. Besides the lack of reliable measures, this perhaps a function of development itself, response measures may not indicate continuity if we fail to consider the changing meaning of the response, the various attributes of a response, or the organizational features of the construct underlying the response.

CONTINUITY AND THE DETERMINANTS OF BEHAVIOR

The determinants of development, and of behavior more generally, have historically been classified as either endogenous—that is, residing in processes internal to the organism—or exogenous—residing in the environment and owing to experience with the external world. When following an individual through an invariant developmental sequence—as when observing the emergence of classification skills—or when assessing the stability of individual differences over development—as when relating vocalization in infancy to verbal ability in childhood (cf. Kagan, 1971)—it is difficult to disentangle the contributions of endogenous and exogenous processes. It is naive to suppose that one class of processes operates to the exclusion of the other. As most theorists would argue, the task is to determine the relative contribution of both endogenous and exogenous influences, and their interaction, to the emergence of a particular response pattern or developmental sequence.

Although difficult to do so in practice, we can distinguish among various sources of continuity at the level of theory. Biological maturation, for example, is a clear instance of an endogenous influence on development. Given a minimally adequate environment, we can predict that certain developmental sequences, such as walking before running, will appear simply because of the individual's biological heritage.

Other developmental patterns appear fixed by their very structure, insofar as one point in the sequence is dependent on and follows logically from an earlier point. Flavell (1972) discusses this issue in some detail, noting that in some instances earlier skills are "analytically contained" in later ones. For example, Flavell and Wohlwill (1969) cite an experiment that ". . . tested the prediction that children would acquire the ability to group two like objects together before they acquire the ability to recognize that such groupings should be exhaustive: i.e., that each and every object possessing the common attribute should be put in the same pile—none should be left apart and unclassified" [p. 87]. As the authors discuss, the ordering of this sequence is logically determined: The reverse sequence, as presently defined, is not logically possible. The movement from one level of competency to another, in this example, may be either endogenously or exogenously determined, but the relationship between the two points is, in Flavell's terms, fully given by the item structure of the more advanced level.

Instances of analytical containment are special cases. More usual is the problem of determining if the relationship between behaviors observed at two age points is due to internal (endogenous) trait factors or to external (exogenous) situational factors. In general, constructs such as aggression, attachment, and intelligence refer to characteristics or traits of the organism, and it is assumed that infants possess these characteristics. Psychology in general, and personality theory in particular, has been concerned with the broad topic of trait versus situational analysis. As a counter position to the trait theory, situational analyses have been offered (see, for example, Mischel, 1973; or for a review, Pervin, 1975).

Briefly, situational analyses suggest that observed behavior is controlled not by traits possessed by and existing within the organism, but is instead situationally determined. A strict trait or situational analysis alone would appear to be an inadequate explanation of behavior. However, since responses occur to and in situations, it would seem critical that situations be kept consistent in order to determine the stability of responses and their continuity. The measurement of a response or set of responses in one situation at t and $t + 1$ is essential to the understanding of continuity. If situational constraints are not considered, the nature of responses and their stability across time cannot be accurately assessed.

For example, proximity-seeking in a stable free-play situation at t may bear little relation to proximity-seeking during stress, such as mother leaving the child alone at $t + 1$, although proximity-seeking in a stable free-play situation at t may be stable when compared to the same situation at $t + 1$. The strong form of situational determinism requires stable situations in order to observe response stability and continuity; and while the strong form of situational determination is unacceptable, it does suggest that continuity requires a situational analysis.

Consider the attachment construct. Since the nature of the attachment relationship is reported to reside either within the organism or as a trait or attribute of the dyad, situational constraints are only useful so as to enable us to measure this phenomenon and its change over time. If, however, one allows for external influences, then the phenomenon and its change may become more apparent. For example, Brooks and Lewis (1974) among others (e.g., Clarke-Stewart, 1974) have found that such external variables as time in room, number of toys available to the child, room size, and familiarity of the setting all influence the infant's behavior toward its mother. It may be the case that continuity can be observed only when exogenous variables are replicated. This model of development would argue for a strong individual continuity only in the face of exogenous continuity. Alternatively it might be the case that continuity exists only under a subset of exogenously stable situations. An important principle of development might be that given a consistent set of external events over time, some response systems maintain their consistency, whereas others do not. This raises the general issue of continuity as a principle for all development versus continuity as a principle for only a subset of developmental processes.

If we are interested in observing continuity over time (or development) then a careful consideration of these factors is necessary. Unfortunately, little attention (or care) is given to these exogenous variables since most of our theories emphasize endogenous factors as the cause of development. Thus, even when replicating studies at a given age period, not a large amount of care is given to the proper control of these exogenous variables.

The Problem of the Stimulus

Our topic concerns the quest for orderly functions of developmental change and the problem of identifying continuity in development. Our subject is, in Emmerich's (1966) words, "the life of the individual extended through time." We have talked as if the environment and stimulus situations in which the individual behaves are fixed or constant over time, and have implied that transformation in development takes place only in the individual's response systems. In the next section we will retrace our steps and question this assumption. Changing perceptions of the world will affect how the child responds to situations that may appear to an adult to be equivalent. Moreover, the problems and events with which the child is faced change with time themselves. Below we discuss certain theoretical issues that arise when examining, developmentally, the stimulus situations in which the child is observed, as well as certain methodological tactics for compensating for changes in the child's perception of stimulus events.

Stimulus Consistency

Is the event the child responds to the same event the adult responds to? We cannot assume that the situation defined by the experimenter-observer is seen, perceived, or interpreted in the same way by the child at different points in development. This confounds the problem of identifying continuity in change enormously. In studies of response continuity, we generally require that the stimulus be equated as much as possible during repeated observations. The attempt to hold the stimulus constant has been an important factor in experimentation, since the ability to seek and find causality rests in the control of all variables save one, the independent one, and the observation of its effects on the other(s), the dependent one(s). When comparing behavior at two different ages, the stimulus situation must be held constant or controlled so that continuity and change in responses may be observed. It may be the case, however, that this is harder than imagined to operationalize.

For the purpose of the present discussion, stimulus, situations and environments can be subsumed under the same general meaning (see, for example, Stevens, 1951; Frederiksen, 1972; Lowenthal, 1972; Pervin, 1975). American psychology has, for the most part, neglected the study of the stimulus, concerning itself more with the questions of categorizing, observing, and assigning meaning to the organism's responses. J. J. Gibson (1960), in a rather interesting article, reflected on the lack of concern for the stimulus, "It seems to me that there is a weak link in the chain of reasoning by which we explain experience and behavior, namely, our concept of the stimulus" [p. 694]. Of particular concern for the issue of continuity is the issue of the stimulus, for if we are to find stability in response, it may be necessary to speak of consistency of the stimulus or situation. This is no easy task, especially in light of the philosophical issues that are raised by its consideration (Hamlyn, 1961). The study of the stimulus is full of complications, the first of which is its all-inclusive nature. Anything can be a stimulus. Added to this difficulty is the problem of who shall define the stimulus. Barker (1965) holds the view that the situation can be defined by the experimenter in objective terms or measurable characteristics—for example, room size. An alternative approach is to define the situation in terms of the subjects' perception of it (Endler and Magnusson, 1974). In either case, the task remains to specify the dimensions used for differentiating stimulus situations.

For example, the situation can be defined in terms of physical properties, which can vary along several dimensions such as temperature, area, and so on. Situations can also be defined in terms of location, such as rooms or buildings. Daily activities, such as washing and going to bed, or adaptation functions are still other methods of dividing situations. Requirements of situations—skills involved or affect elicited—are still other dimensions. Finally, people involved in the situation would be another. For this consideration, classification across specific dimensions or combinations would be possible, and in addition it would seem that certain dimensions might be more interrelated than others. Recently, Pervin (1975) has undertaken some exploration of some of these dimensions and their interrelatedness; however, the enormity of the problem remains. The taxonomy of situation involves an enormous problem at both the levels of characterization and interrelationship.

In general, but more specifically in the case of infancy and early childhood, the situation may also include other significant social objects—the mother, father, and so on. Behavior measured in dyadic interaction (a type of situation) may be quite different than the same behavior measured alone. For example, smiling behavior as a consequence of a dyadic interaction may be quite different than the smiling behavior produced when the child is alone although the measurement of this smiling took place in the same physical context (in its bed in its room). Stimuli are not as they appear. Both Salapatek (1969) and Haith (1976) have shown that the scanning ability of infants varies as a function of age, a finding reported previously for older children (Zaporozhets, 1965). Salapatek (1969) demonstrated an increase in whole-part perception with younger infants engaging in less whole perception. For example, given a triangle, young infants are more likely to fixate on an angle than to scan the whole figure. Haith (1976) has shown a similar finding for faces;

the contour of a face is scanned initially, and only after 5 weeks of age do infants fixate on the internal features. These developmental changes in what the infant fixates upon when an entire stimulus is presented have important implications for the understanding of the meaning of their responses and for our inquiry into the nature of development.

Consider that the problem under study involves the changes in infants' responses to a stimulus as a function of age; it is found that 5-day-old infants respond differently than 2-month-old infants; the 2-month-olds smile to a face while the 5-day-olds do not. Since each has been presented with the same stimulus, the age difference in smiling has to do with some aspect of a developmental function; perhaps one would offer increased cognition, affective response capacity, or memory capacity—social stimuli have come to have a meaning. Although the same physical stimulus event was presented to each aged child, from what we know of perceptual abilities it is clear that the same stimulus was not perceived by each.

In the context of the study of continuity, age changes in the perception of the stimulus have important consequences. There may be no consistency in response from age to age because the effective stimulus has changed. Continuity may not be observable, not because the stimulus event in which responses are observed has not been held constant by the experimenter, but because the stimulus has not been perceived consistently by the subject.

This model of the organism's transaction with its environment has empirical implications for the demonstration of continuity. For example, visual fixation to the same event over the first 2 years of life may be a function of the organism's reconstruction and hypothesis generation. Kagan (1971) found a U-curve function in fixation time to a series of visual events (human faces), with much looking at 4 months, relatively little at 8 to 13, and again much looking at 27 to 36 months. He argues for the concept of hypothesis generation to explain how a particular event at 2 years and beyond can elicit as much attention as when that event was less familiar. Differential hypothesis generation at different ages is the explanatory device. This would correspond to the familiar phenomenon parents observe when their infants play with a new toy, grow bored with it, and once again become interested in it 2 years later. Observation reveals that the second interest is generated by a new way of playing with the toy, quite different from the first way of interacting.

In terms of consistency, play with the same toy at two points in time is not necessarily related, since a new set of hypotheses controlling the toy play may be at work. To demonstrate consistency, it may be necessary to decipher changing hypotheses generated by the same event. The child who at 1 year cries as its mother leaves the room may cry because it does not know where or why she is leaving. When the mother leaves when the child is 2 years, the child may now know where or why she is leaving and, therefore, not cry. The ability to form hypotheses may be the underlying factor affecting consistency from year 1 to 2 in the separation situation. Continuity can only be inferred once infants' mental abilities to construct the stimulus event—understand the situation—are accounted for.

Stimulus Control

Holding the physical stimulus constant during repeated observations is one method for studying continuity in development. That the same stimulus event may not be the same for the organism, as a function of development or individual difference, presents us with both a problem and possible alternative methods for gaining stimulus control.

One alternative to holding the stimulus constant during repeated tests is to adjust or modify the stimulus for different age groups. Quite different results may be obtained when this procedure is followed. Gelman's (Bullock and Gelman, 1977; Gelman and Tucker, 1975) studies of numerical abilities in young children is one example. In this work, it was found that children as young as 3 years are sensitive to complex arithmetical relationships, such as greater-than–less-than and reversibility relations, when the number of items in the stimulus array is sufficiently small. These abilities were not apparent when the children were tested on the larger set sizes typically used with older children. Thus, when using large sets, it appears that certain arithmetical abilities are absent in young children. However, from Gelman's work we may conclude that the abilities are there, but that they are not applied to the same stimulus configurations (here set sizes) at all points in development.

Stimulus control is not easy. Orne (1973) has challenged the traditional view that the stimulus dimension can be well controlled by the experimenter, independent of the subject. Orne points out that the mind of the subject and its past experiences affect stimulus meaning, and therefore the subject's response is dependent on the subject's perception, needs, and cognitions concerning the stimulus. Presenting the same stimulus to an infant at two points in time may not be a control of the stimulus. One solution would be to present the same stimulus as determined by the organism itself. This solution calls for the organism rather than the experimenter to define the situation. The use of this type of phenomenological approach, although full of difficulties, could be one way of equating exogenous events.

Pervin (1975) has examined adults' perceptions of situations and has attempted to extract a multidimensional taxonomy. For example, consider that affective tone is used by the subject for equating two situations across time. Although situation a and b are not at all similar in terms of external dimensions, both a and b are examples of frustration-producing situations. Consistency in response might be obtained if a and b are used instead of two situations deemed more alike by the experimenter. It is important to keep in mind that a and b may be suitable only for one subject; another child may require two different situations in order to equate them for frustration. Thus, through a phenomenological approach frustrating experiences at time t and $t + 1$ are obtained even though the external situations may differ across time and the situations may differ across subjects.

An example of the latter may be in order. Lewis (1967) was interested in individual differences in infants' responses to frustration. Each infant was placed in front of a glass screen behind which a toy was presented. The infant reached forward, came in contact with the screen, and typically (1) continued reaching forward and contacting the screen, (2) reached around the screen, or (3) stopped reaching and cried. Individual differences became apparent in these 6-month-olds, but what were the causes of the individual differences observed?—differences in response to frustration, or differences in motivation to get the particular toy placed behind a screen? The bright red truck may have been of little interest to some infants, but of great interest to others. How could we be sure the response being measured reflected some attribute independent of the particular stimulus used? It would appear that there would be no solution as long as one saw the problem from the point of view of controlling the stimulus by using the same object (toy) for each child. While one could present many toys (the same) to each child, there might always be a toy that would alter the results. The solution could only be reached by concluding that the same toy was not the same for each infant. Having reached that conclusion it was possible to vary the object but to control its psychological sameness, in this case its interest and value. In this particular case, each mother was asked to bring her child's *favorite* toy to the experiment. Thus, the objects were different but were the same along the dimension of value. Parenthetically, this procedure produced a set of problems itself since mothers brought toys they thought the research scientist would consider to be better—that is, more educational. The toys received were not the infants' favorites but rather the perceived favorites of psychologists. This example points out both a method for obtaining consistency in situations across subjects and also some of the potential difficulties.

CONCLUSIONS

Consistency and continuity of development remain issues of importance for theories of development. We began with the question "Does childhood show the man?" Our answer will provide little satisfaction to those of a pragmatic bent: individual differences in behavior as detected by measurement instruments currently employed are not particularly stable over development. Some reasons for the apparent lack of stability are methodological. We have suggested that to detect stability in development, more attention should be paid to such factors as the short-term reliability of measures, replication of the stimulus situation in which observations are made, and the use of multiple measures of constructs under study. Other reasons for the failure of stability measures to indicate continuity in development are conceptual. Even with continuity in the psychological substrate, between-individual measures may not be stable. For example, when individuals do not differ on initial measures of a behavior, differing rates of change and patterns of differentiation will result in seeming instability, although within-individual development is continuous. Conversely, an individual's initial behavior in a given situation may be variable, giving way to increased stability with age. It was argued that knowledge of changes in response meaning and response organization is necessary before these issues can be fully explored. Additionally, the study of response continuity is confounded by changes in perception of the stimulus situation over development, and a careful analysis of the stimulus is required before adequate models of developmental continuity can be constructed. It may be necessary to define the stimulus in relation to the child's response competencies for continuity in the development of given behavior patterns to be revealed. Along these same lines, in some cases, especially those involving social interaction, continuity may be more apparent when a dyadic unit is considered in the place of the individual's behavior in isolation.

Our answer is both that in principle childhood does show the man and that this principle is not open to denial by fact. Rather, the continuous nature of development should be taken as a premise. The value of this premise is that it leads one to consider the child in positive terms, in terms of those competencies and abilities the child does possess at each point in development, and in terms of the transformations these competencies undergo over development.

BIBLIOGRAPHY

Barker, R. G. Explorations in ecological psychology. *American Psychologist*, 1965, **20**, 1–14.

Bayley, N. Development of mental abilities. In P. Mussen (ed.), *Carmichael's Manual of Child Psychology*, Vol. I. New York: Wiley, 1970.

Bell, R. Q., Weller, G. M., and Waldrop, M. F. Newborn and preschooler: Organization of behavior and relations between periods. *Monographs of the Society for Research in Child Development*, 1971, **36**, 1–2.

Brooks, J., and Lewis, M. The effect of time on attachment as measured in a free play situation. *Child Development*, 1974, **45**, 311–316.

Brown, R. *A First Language*. Cambridge, Mass.: Harvard University, 1973.

Bullock, M., and Gelman, R. Numerical reasoning in young children: The ordering principle. *Child Development*, 1977, **48**, 427–434.

Clarke-Stewart, K. A. Interactions between mothers and their young children: Characteristics and consequences. *Monographs of the Society for Research in Child Development*, 1974, **38** (5, Ser. 153).

Emmerich, W. Continuity and stability in early social development: II. Teacher ratings. *Child Development*, 1966, **37** (1), 17–27.

Endler, N. S., and Magnusson, D. Interactionism, trait psychology, and situationism. *Reports from the Psychological Laboratories*, University of Stockholm, No. 418, 1974.

Flavell, J. H. Stage-related properties of cognitive development. *Cognitive Psychology*, 1971, **2**, 421–453.

Flavell, J. H. An analysis of cognitive-developmental sequences. *Genetic Psychology Monographs*, 1972, **86**, 279–350.

Flavell, J. H., and Wohlwill, J. F. Formal and functional aspects of cognitive development. In D. Elkind and J. H. Flavell (eds.), *Studies in Cognitive Development: Essays in Honor of Jean Piaget*. New York: Oxford University, 1969, 69–120.

Frederiksen, N. Toward a taxonomy of situations. *American Psychologist*, 1972, **27**, 114–123.

Gelman, R., and Tucker, M. F. Further investigations of the young child's conception of number. *Child Development*, 1975, **46**, 167–175.

Gibson, J. J. The concept of the stimulus in psychology. *American Psychologist*, 1960, **15**, 694–703.

Haith, M. M. Visual competence in early infancy. In R. Held, H. Liebowitz, and H. L. Teuber (eds.), *Handbook of Sensory Physiology*, Vol. VIII. Berlin: Springer-Verlag, 1976.

Hamlyn, D. W. *Sensation and Perception*. London: Routledge & Kegan Paul, 1961.

Kagan, J. *Change and Continuity in Infancy*. New York: Wiley, 1971.

Lewis, M. The meaning of a response or why researchers in infant behavior should be oriental metaphysicians. *Merrill-Palmer Quarterly*, 1967, **13** (1), 7–18.

Lewis, M. Infant intelligence tests: Their use and misuse. *Human Development*, 1973, **16**, 108–118.

Lewis, M., and Ban, P. Stability of attachment behavior: A transformational analysis. Paper presented at the Society for Research in Child Development meetings, Symposium on Attachment: Studies in Stability and Change, Minneapolis, Minnesota, April 1971.

Lewis, M., and Cherry L. Development and change in conversation and linguistic skill. *Unpublished manuscript*, 1977.

Lewis, M., and McGurk, H. Evaluation of infant intelligence: Infant intelligence scores—true or false? *Science*, 1972, **178** (4066), 1174–1177.

Lewis, M., and Weinaub, M. Sex of parent × sex of child: Socioemotional development. In R. C. Friedman, R. M. Richart, and R. S. Vande Wiele (eds.), *Sex Differences in Behavior*. New York: Wiley, 1974.

Lowenthal, D. Research in environmental perception and behavior: Perspectives on current problems. *Environment and Behavior*, 1972, **4**, 333–342.

Maccoby, E. E., and Feldman, S. S. Mother-attachment and stanger-reactions in the third year of life. *Monographs of the Society for Research in Child Development,* 1972, **37** (1, Ser. 146).

Masters, J. C., and Wellman, H. M. The study of infant attachment: Procedural critique. *Psychological Bulletin*, 1974, **81**, 218–237.

McCall, R. B., Hogarty, P. S., and Hurlburt, N. Transitions in infant sensorimotor development and the prediction of childhood IQ. *American Psychologist*, 1972, **27**, 728–748.

Mischel, W. Toward a cognitive social learning reconceptualization of personality. *Psychological Review*, 1973, **80**, 252–283.

Orne, M. T. Communication by the total experimental situation: Why it is important, how it is evaluated, and its significance for the ecological validity of findings. In P. Pliner, L. Krames, and T. Alloway (eds.), *Communication and Affect: Language and Thought*. New York: Academic, 1973.

Pervin, L. A. Definitions, measurements, and classifications of stimuli, situations, and environments. Research Bulletin 75-23. Princeton, N.J.: Educational Testing Service, 1975.

Piaget, J. *The Construction of Reality in the Child*. New York: Basic Books, 1954.

Salapatek, P. The visual investigation of geometric patterns by the one and two month old infant. Paper presented at meetings of the American Association for the Advancement of Science, Boston, December 1969.

Stevens, S. S. (ed.). *Handbook of Experimental Psychology*. New York: Wiley, 1951.

Van den Daele, L. D. Qualitative models in developmental analysis. *Developmental Psychology*, 1969, **1** (4), 303–310.

Weinraub, M., Brooks, J., and Lewis, M. The social network: A reconsideration of the concept of attachment. *Human Development,* 1977, **20**, 31–47.

Wohlwill, J. F. *The Study of Behavioral Development*. New York: Academic, 1973.

Zaporozhets, A. V. The development of perception in the preschool child. In P. H. Mussen (ed.), European Research in Cognitive Development. *Monographs of the Society for Research in Child Development*, 1965 **30** (2, whole No. 100).

CHAPTER 19

Prediction of Emotional and Social Behavior[1]

Leila Beckwith

The origins of personality pose an intriguing mystery. While the basic assumption might be that the child is father to the man, several additional beliefs entice the student of infancy. It seems reasonable that responses practiced early would shape future behavior by altering the availability of later responses; that the younger the organism the more potent the impact of environmental events, since the primacy of early experience would augment the effect; that infancy may involve sensitive periods for the acquisition of some aspects of social/emotional development; that the younger the organism, the more its behavior might reveal individual constitutional determinants.

Extensive careful study of human infants show dramatic individual differences (Stone et al., 1973). Which of these differences have persistent meaning and which are transient? Can we trace forward the functional consequences of some individual characteristics? Do they affect the caregiver? Do they become subordinated to other principles of developmental organization, or can the derivatives be seen? Or can we trace backwards the precursors of specific strengths and vulnerabilities to identifiable predispositions in infancy? To do so would be a major contribution not only to theoretical questions but also to clinical issues by facilitating early diagnoses of adverse or desirable syndromes and by promoting more cogent interventions.

While theory provides for, and some empirical evidence corroborates, that experience and individual differences evident during infancy may have enduring consequences, the proposal is not of a rigid unfolding of autonomous behavior traits. The premise is that individual organismic characteristics shape the child's experiences by evoking, controlling, and modifying the impact of early and later events.

The infant is social from the outset. There is a growing body of evidence that the infant is genetically programmed to be particularly responsive to perceptual features of the human caregiver. The infant is inclined to behave in ways that promote contact with other humans (Ainsworth, 1973). From the earliest weeks of life the infant effectively promotes many of the interactions. The infant, through discriminative crying, looking, and smiling, facilitates and maintains interaction (Bell, 1974). The influence is not only immediate but shows long-term effects on the caregiver (Rheingold, 1969a, b). Furthermore, infants actively seek out stimulation, attend selectively, and show strong preferences among stimuli and for certain levels of stimulus change. Along with all the capacities that have been demonstrated in infants, significant individual differences have also been noted.

The major developmental tasks—for example, physiological regulation, differentiation of self and others, mastery of the inanimate world—are shaped in the social-emotional

[1]Research supported by USPHS Contract No. J-HD-3-2776, "Diagnostic and Intervention Studies of High-Risk Infants," and NICHD Grant No. HD-04612, Mental Retardation Research Center, UCLA.

surround. Interactions with the caretaking environment are essential for development. Social transactions, in themselves, and as they mediate the infant's interactions with the inanimate environment, underlie cognitive growth. Cognitive growth underlies social-emotional development (see Sroufe, Chapter 13). Social-emotional adaptation, as well as cognitive development, derives from the ongoing creative process of an infant acting on the environment.

Whereas cognitive-perceptual and social-emotional development are intertwined (e.g., Ainsworth and Bell, 1974; Birns and Golden, 1972; Yarrow and Pedersen, 1976), we shall make an arbitrary separation. For purposes of this chapter we shall further focus our examination on individual differences within infants. An emphasis on individual differences within infants is compatible with theoretical views that construe social-emotional organization as the property of the individual. On the other hand, more recent theoretical views in early infancy suggest organization to be the property of the infant-environment system (e.g., Denenberg, 1978; Sameroff and Chandler, 1975). We shall return to the latter views in the conclusion. Although they hold much promise, they have not yet guided many research studies examining stabilities and changes over time.

Since the concern of the chapter is with observed relations, not theoretical predictions, the primary emphasis will be placed on the literature that deals with empirical evidence of the continuities and discontinuities evident from infancy. Since retrospective information is subject to a host of distortions (Yarrow et al., 1968) only those studies that collected descriptive data during infancy (0–3 years for purposes of this chapter) and a subsequent period will be included here. Those longitudinal studies, recently completed or still underway, that detail change and continuity or concurrent relations within the infancy period (e.g., Ainsworth, 1973; W. C. Bronson, 1974; Kagan, 1971) will be discussed as they illuminate findings from the other studies.

The goal of explicating individual development by reference to historical antecedents in infancy encounters the difficulty that greater stability of behavior can be predicted, in general, over a shorter time span and from a more mature personality (Kessen et al., 1970). Other dilemmas also exist (Rutter, 1970). The amount of development still to occur ensures that there is very little overlap between personality characteristics at infancy and later. Further, since psychological development can be modified by subsequent experiences, it appears almost presumptuous to expect continuity from infancy to later in the face of a myriad of subsequent uncontrolled events. Finally, some of the variation in infancy behaviors may be related to the effect of differing rates of maturation rather than to any differences in the ultimate level achieved.

Although this chapter is concerned with stability of individual characteristics over time, it will not stress genetic factors, nor attempt to parcel out perinatal or postnatal environmental influences. Although there is some evidence of genetic determination of personality, the fact of genetic cause does not foreclose the question of continuity and change. Genetic determinants of IQ scores do not exclude experiential influences (Honzik, 1976) nor ensure individual stability (Bayley, 1949; Honzik et al., 1948). In that individual instability is marked (e.g., Hunt and Eichorn, 1972), it has generated issues about the adequacy of measurement and differential rates of maturation (Lewis, 1976). Although the issues were discussed in reference to intellectual development, the issues are equally relevant to emotional-social development.

The present chapter will review these issues in the light of evidence arising from longitudinal studies. The chapter will present descriptions of some of the completed efforts and some of the ongoing efforts to examine the nature of social-emotional continuity, and some of the focal research issues involved. New approaches in theory and research will also be discussed.

The plan of the chapter is as follows: (1) The meaning of continuity will be discussed. (2) The methods and methodological problems in the measurement of continuity will be detailed since they are as significant as the empirical findings. (3) The meaning of discontinuity will be presented. (4) Selected longitudinal studies will be described as to samples and procedures. We will hold off presentation of the findings until the next section in order to synthesize data, where relevant, and cross-check, where possible. (5) The overall findings from the selected studies will be reported and synthesized. (6) Conclusions, which include new directions in research and theory, will be presented.

THE MEANING OF CONTINUITY

Although the focus of this chapter is on empirical relationships, the question of continuity is more than empirical. The conceptual fictions that are held about the nature of human beings and the nature of early development guide the investigative search (Hunt, 1976). An implicit belief in preformationism or predeterminism dictates a search for behaviors that have the same appearance earlier and later without concern for intervening experiences and without concern for developmental restructuring. A number of authorities have cautioned against this tempting fiction. Phenotypic consistency which assumes an isomorphic identity in traits or behavior patterns throughout the age span has been distinguished from dynamic consistency which represents overt behaviors that are developmental transformations of earlier response patterns (Yarrow, 1964). Emmerich (1967) proposes a paradigm that differentiates the continuity or developmental transformations of a trait from the stability or instability of persons on that trait. At issue is the question of whether social/emotional traits manifest during infancy limit subsequent social/emotional development to derivatives in the expression of the traits, or whether social/emotional development consists of a series of personality reorganizations. Bell et al. (1971) describe the latter as metamorphic consistencies. They suggest, since metamorphic rather than isomorphic consistencies are more likely to occur, that longitudinal studies institute comprehensive searches between age periods, rather than depending on logical models. W. C. Bronson (1968) suggests that the early characteristic be considered as a predisposition to certain modes of interaction which influence the nature of the person's experience, and effectiveness in coping with age-tasks.

More than the continuity or change in the appearance of the behavior needs to be considered (Kagan, 1969; Lewis, 1967). Behavior may remain stable because of endogenous or exogenous factors (Kagan, 1971). Either an internal process may remain stable over time, or an environmental process may retain stability. Homotypic stability, the search for behaviors that look alike, is based on the assumption that the forces that promoted the initial manifestation are maintained over time. That assumption is not always defensible. Homotypic stability may mask changes in motivating conditions. For example, Kagan (1974) suggests at least five occasions for anxiety and distress states: (1) unassimilated discrepancy, (2) anticipation of an undesirable event, (3) unpredictability, (4) recognition of inconsistency between belief and behavior, and (5) recognition of dissonance between or among beliefs. These states probably have different origins, eliciting conditions, phenomenologies, and consequences. Therefore, it is not surprising that there is no relation between crying in infancy (probably due to unassimilated discrepancy) and anxiety in adulthood often due to dissonance and unpredictability.

Heterotypic continuity represents a continuity of expectancies, motives, goals, and sources of anxiety, that are expressed in different behaviors (Kagan, 1971). In a similar vein, W. C. Bronson (1966b), has proposed a construct of "central orientations," which sets the limits on the repertoire of responses used by an individual. Within any orientation a variety of behaviors, functionally equivalent, would be possible depending on temporal or environmental appropriateness.

Escalona (1965) further extends our understanding of the complex effects of intervening experiences on the continuity of behavior. She suggests that neither organismic nor environmental factors, nor a combination of both, operate directly on the developing personality organization. Rather, the resultant of their interaction is an intervening variable, designated as patterns of concrete experience, which, in turn, determines personality development. The possibility therefore exists of a wide variety of combinations of organismic factors and environmental events which would generate equivalent patterns of concrete experience, and thereby have grossly equivalent effects on subsequent behavior.

Although the need to understand metamorphic changes, and to do so in terms of ongoing experience, is clear, the theoretical structure to provide clarification is insubstantial.

The demands on such a theory would be stringent. It would have to include understanding of developmental sequences in affect and personality, as well as in cognitive functions. It would need to consider varieties of experience. Individual differences in temporal processes, in the rate of acquisition and consolidation of developmental stages, would have to be considered as well as structural differences. The complexities involved in unraveling such intricate interrelationships are multiple (Kessen et al., 1970).

METHODS AND METHODOLOGICAL PROBLEMS IN THE MEASUREMENT OF CONTINUITY

The phases of a longitudinal study have been characterized as follows (Thomas et al., 1963): (1) identification of initial characteristics that can be objectively and reliably studied, (2) development of data-collection techniques that will provide objective data, (3) study of continuity of initial characteristics utilizing valid and reliable and appropriate methods of data analysis, (4) development of similar measures of objectivity and reliability for study of later personality phenomena, and (5) relating of initial characteristics to later functional organization. There are problems inherent in each phase.

Measures

Since unifying conceptual systems are absent and there is a paucity of standard measures (Kessen et al., 1970), the selection of variables and the measurement thereof have been diverse. It is not only the mapping of infant behavior that has been insufficient. Variability in instrument and procedure is marked in personality studies at a later age.

Rutter (1970) has described two approaches used in studying continuity. One is "personal prediction" in which the investigator uses all the information at his/her disposal to make a personal judgment about the individual's later characteristics. That approach was used by Neilon (1948) as well as by Escalona and Heider (1959). Such an approach can use different kinds of information for each subject. The second approach specifies individual measures both early and late, and systematically compares each subject on every variable.

Many of the studies used ratings. Since ratings summarize a wholistic memory, they suppress or ignore deviations from the modal response, and tend to yield more consistent assessments than do behavioral observations (Maccoby and Masters, 1970). The judge is used as a filtering and integrating instrument (Block, 1977). Some cautions must be recognized, however. Even when interjudge reliability is established, the formulations from which the ratings are derived may be idiosyncratic in some ways and not easily reproducible. Ratings also tend to be vulnerable to "halo effects." Some studies, but not all, minimized this source of error by independently scoring one category at a time over all the subjects (Murphy and Moriarty, 1976; Thomas et al., 1963), and ensuring that the raters were independent from one time period to the next (Kagan and Moss, 1962).

Some of the studies used behavioral observations of molecular, discrete behaviors (Bell et al., 1971; Kagan, 1971). Evidence for personality consistency is erratic as derived from studies wherein selected, specific, readily identified, or enumerated behaviors are focused upon as indicators of particular personality variables (Block, 1977). Such measures are very subject to changing circumstances and transient conditions. The measures tend to be unstable. Therefore, much effort in measure evaluation must be exercised in order to ensure construct validity.

Whether ratings or behavioral observations were used, noteworthy was the dependence on careful, systematic observation. The essential tool was the insightful human observer (Stone et al., 1973).

Situational Contexts

The situations in which individual characteristics were assessed may determine the continuities found. During infancy, some investigators used naturally occurring situations in which spontaneous patterns could be assessed (e.g., Bell et al., 1971; Escalona and Leitch, 1953; Thomas et al., 1963). Other studies sampled infant behavior in a testing situation with a stranger in a strange place (Schaefer and Bayley 1963). The latter assessed behavior under heightened object and social stimulation.

Further, it is important to be aware of the nature of the situations sampled at follow-up. A nursery school (Bell et al., 1971), group trips to the zoo, and group parties (Murphy and Moriarty, 1976)—that is, interaction with unfamiliar peers—evokes different patterns of behavior than do interactions with long-term playmates, or with the mother, or with a friendly examiner. For example, W. C. Bronson (1974), in a short-term longitudinal study of the development of competence, found to her surprise that (at least on initial analysis) there was no orderly progression of quantity or quality of peer interactions during the 2nd year of life in an experimentally contrived playgroup, and further that the largest percentage of social contacts was apparently agonistic. She suggested that the feedback given by strangers may be too variable to develop predictable contingencies of behavior in contrast to that provided by the caregiver or a long-term playmate. In addition, reactions to novelty may either swamp characteristic behavior patterns or may highlight individual differences. One may wonder what kinds of continuities would have been found by Bell et al. (1971) if the relationship to the mother had been studied or behaviors during mental testing, in contrast to nursery school in which activity and assertiveness appear prominently as organizers of behavior.

Data Reduction

For most studies the number of assessments made during both the infancy and later periods has been formidable. The number may even exceed the number of subjects. On one hand, it is difficult to assess significance, since the number of continuities that may be found are probably not many relative to the number of correlations computed. On the other hand, vigorous standards are premature when applied to exploratory investigations. Statistical rigor in data analysis has to yield to the necessity of an extensive search since the later nature of early behavior is not known.

Data reduction by clustering or factor analyses serves practical and theoretical goals. Clustering measures increases the reliability of measurement. Establishing independent composites allows exact tests of statistical significance to be used which may be ambiguous for correlated measures. But composite measures that span 0 to 3 years of age (e.g., Fels Institute Study) may distort salient individual differences that might have been revealed through finer age groupings (Honzik, 1965). For example, the Berkeley Growth Study found complex relationships to later behavior which were specific to particular 3-month periods during infancy. For boys, ratings at the 10- to 12-month period not only showed as many or more significant relations with later behaviors than any other period during infancy but only at that period did ratings of rapidity and vigor relate to later unfriendliness, lack of cooperativeness, and inattentiveness at 53 to 96 months (Schaefer and Bayley, 1963), a finding that has provoked much speculation. Additionally, data reduction by factor analysis or clustering may reflect the organization of measures at one age but may mask individual measures important for later behavior. Thus, Bell et al. (1971) found that composites of newborn behavior did not show better predictive power to later behavior than individual newborn measures; if anything, they showed less.

The determination of clusters of behavior at any age period have as an aim more than statistical vigor. Investigators have strived to describe the configuration of personality characteristics considering that single behaviors only acquire meaning from the other sensitivities, skills, motives, responses, of which they are a part (Block, 1971; Thomas et al., 1963; Escalona and Heider, 1959; Murphy and Moriarty, 1976). For example, Escalona and her associates (Escalona, 1968; Escalona and Heider, 1959) suggested that significant discrepancies among areas of development (e.g., motor versus language) may in itself be a significant individual variable. Fish (1963) corroborated the significance of variability in developmental functions in infancy by linking it to a vulnerability to later childhood schizophrenia and other personality disorders in children who were born to schizophrenic mothers. Consideration of the patterning of infant characteristics was a strategy used very successfully by Thomas et al. (1968) in understanding the development of behavior problems. W. C. Bronson (1966b) suggests that a stable framework for understanding the continuity within personality development might be found not in isolated behaviors but in behaviors that are consistently good predictors of a variety of other contemporaneous behaviors.

Data Analysis

Regardless of whether single or composite behaviors are used, the correlation coefficient has been the primary index of continuity or change. It has also been used, as in factor analyses, to clarify the organization of social-emotional behaviors at different ages (e.g., Bell et al., 1971; Schaefer and Bayley, 1963). Its use derives from a search for personality attributes by which to describe all persons, and a definition of stability as a consistent ordering over time of individual differences with respect to those attributes (Emmerich, 1967). Essentially variables have been correlated over time using the entire available sample, sometimes segregated as to sex. Limitations of the correlation coefficient, therefore, will affect the meaning of the empirical relationships found.

First, the correlation, reflects group averages derived over the entire sample. As Denenberg (1978) suggests, the effects of such averaging may be misleading as to general laws. For example, the average growth curve typically may not show the pubertal growth spurt, because different children begin the growth spurt at different ages. Averaging smooths out the rapidity of the individual increases. Further, the correlation, even if significant, reflects tendencies manifested in some children but not all. There is a difference between a variable-centered and person-centered approach. Whereas correlational analyses traditionally focus on variables, a matching technique (Neilon, 1948) and "Q" analyses, in contrast to "R" analyses, can be used to identify homogeneous persons or subgroups within the larger undifferentiated sample (Block, 1971). Such person-centered approaches can highlight the significance of personality discontinuities as well as continuities, while correlational analyses of the "R" type can only attribute significance to continuities.

Second, whereas the correlation coefficient reflects the degree of correspondence between two orderings, it does not respond to the level of one set compared to another, nor does it reflect or evaluate the salience of a particular characteristic for those individuals at that developmental stage (Block, 1971). For example, Hoffman (1972) offers a reinterpretation of a perplexing finding of Kagan and Moss (1962). She suggests that the fact that maternal protectiveness during infancy correlated inversely with females, but not males, adult achievement behavior does not reflect an inherent sex difference. To the contrary, to the extent that girls as a group experience more overprotectiveness than boys, girls who receive the lesser amount are equivalent to boys who receive the greater amount.

Third, a limited range within one variable tends to attenuate the size of the correlation coefficient and to minimize the significance or stability attributed to that variable. In another population, or under more homogeneous circumstances, the correlation might achieve statistical and, thereby, theoretical significance. As Honzik (1965) indicates, the size and nature of the available sample is crucial in correlational analyses. Inclusion of siblings for some but not all children in a sample (e.g., Fels Institute, New York studies) may markedly alter the size of the correlation obtained.

Fourth, inherent in a correlation coefficient is the assumption that a trait varies in amount or intensity and does so in a linearly ordered way. Nonlinear relationships, however, may be of more interest. For example, one might speculate that very high levels and very low levels of infant irritability might lead to lessened social interaction with the caregiver. Further, qualitative classifications may show more stability and provide more information than quantitative differences in single behaviors. Attachment behaviors do not intercorrelate highly, nor are they significantly stable over time (Masters and Wellman, 1974). If, however, attachment is considered as a construct that refers to the organization of attachment behaviors, and qualitative differences in the organization of such attachment relationships are specified, then stable individual differences are revealed (Ainsworth, 1973; Sroufe, Chapter 13; Sroufe and Waters, 1977; Waters and Sroufe, 1977). For example, when infants were characterized at 12 months as securely attached or insecurely attached, as assessed from the organization of attachment behaviors shown during the "strange situation," then such characterizations were stable at 21 months, although there was little stability in frequencies of individual behaviors (Waters and Sroufe, 1977).

THE MEANING OF DISCONTINUITY

Understanding the sources of instability may be as informative as finding stabilities. Many investigators find some children of their sample to be more predictable than others (Block, 1971; Murphy, 1964; Neilon, 1948; Thomas et al., 1963). It seems likely that stable homogeneous environments, free from traumas and congenial to the child's natural style, may foster constancy (Murphy, 1964). It has been hypothesized that congruence with expected gender roles may enhance consistency, whereas behavior that conflicts with prescribed gender behavior may be expressed in alternative derivative behaviors that are socially more acceptable (Kagan and Moss, 1962).

Some traits may be more stable than others. Although there is some agreement about the nature of those traits, there is also contradictory evidence. For example, W. C. Bronson (1966, 1967) found emotional expressiveness and reactivity control to be enduring orientations of personality functioning, but only as examined post infancy. Escalona (1968) found activity level and perceptual sensitivity to be salient organizers of experience, as did Heider (1966) who found that the amount of available energy was a consistent trait. But Thomas et al. (1963) found that their measure of activity was the least stable of their variables. Similarly, Bell et al. (1971) could not even include measures of spontaneous gross movements in the study of neonates because they were not stable from one time period to the next.

On a broader level, discontinuity is as significant as continuity. There is a need to understand change, differentiation, and growth. A child is not a composite of consistent traits, but rather an individual adapting to changing pressures and opportunities (Murphy and Moriarty, 1976). Emmerich (1967) suggests further that in a complex society such as ours, it is essential that most of its members retain potential for personality change throughout the life span.

SELECTED LONGITUDINAL STUDIES: SAMPLES AND PROCEDURES

A description of the samples, measures, and procedures of the major longitudinal studies will be given in this section. In order, where possible, to integrate findings across studies, discussion of results will be presented in the next section.

Although many of the integrated accounts of the longitudinal studies were written by researchers who came after the original pioneers, the information derives from the hard work, persistence, and foresight of the original investigators. The accounts represent a culmination of many people's efforts and diligence.

It should also be pointed out that the descriptions that follow will indicate more sources of data were included for many projects than have yet been analyzed. To that extent, it becomes confusing to the reader to determine which measures contributed and which so far have been ignored in testing predictions from infancy. The problems in organizing and selecting conceptually relevant measures from the mass of information that is obtained in longitudinal studies challenges the investigator, as well as the reader. The investigator's solutions are significant and fruitful endeavors, in themselves, and are as subject to reinterpretations as are the findings about continuity.

The projects differed in data-collection procedures, methods of data analysis, and in psychological constructs. The differences make congruences all the more notable, and make the task of synthesis, reported in the next section, all the more uncertain.

The children studied in the major longitudinal investigations were screened to include only normal full-term babies without any manifest sensory or motor handicaps. They were also white, and tended to be economically advantaged, a fact that was reflected in the above-average mean IQ scores obtained. The children cannot be considered, therefore, to be randomly selected samples of all children, and propositions based on the continuity and change demonstrated by these samples might be generalized to other samples only with caution. To the extent that sample differences exist in level and range of congenital behavior patterns, and if these differences are further modified by differential patterning of experiences, then the salience and predictability of specific behaviors must be analyzed anew for each group. To that end, recent studies of lower-class and Black infants (Clarke-Stewart, 1973; Engel et al., 1975) provide a welcome addition. Atypical babies, deliberately excluded, might also reveal different patterns of salience and persistence. Further, cross-cultural studies, or reports of children growing up in alternative rearing styles, even those that now exist in our society, might show radically different sequences (Kagan and Klein, 1973).

Gesell and Ames (1937)

Five normal infants were rank-ordered on 15 behavior traits on the basis of film records taken monthly throughout the 1st year of life. Similar rank orderings were assigned at age 5 from behavior observed during psychological testing, photographing, and a party. The 15 recorded traits were notable because they previewed later studies. They were: energy output, motor demeanor, self-dependence, social responsiveness, family attachment, communicativeness, adaptivity, exploitation of environment, humor, emotional maladjustment, emotional expressiveness, reaction to success, reaction to restriction, readiness of smiling, and readiness of crying. Of the 75 ranks assigned at infancy, 48 exactly matched those at age 5. The authors concluded that certain fundamental traits of individuality exist early, persist late, and assert themselves under varying environmental conditions. Thus, the stage was set for longitudinal examination of individual personality differences.

Shirley (1933) and Neilon (1948)

Shirley (1933) studied 25 babies intensively from birth to 2 years of age using standardized developmental tests as well as behavioral observations. She then wrote personality sketches of each baby. Fifteen years after the original study, Neilon (1948) interviewed and tested 19 of the original 25 subjects, and gathered complete data on 16 subjects. The follow-up included two personality tests, independent ratings by the subject and their mothers of 23 personality traits and 6 specific abilities, interviews with each of the subjects and their mothers, and rating scales and ability scales mailed to the fathers. Personality sketches at age 17 were then written without knowledge of the matching infancy descriptions. Since the subjects' gender was obvious from the descriptions, boys and girls were analyzed separately. Ten judges were asked to match six female infant sketches to five adolescent sketches, and five judges were asked to match 13 male infant sketches with 10 sketches at adolescence. For the females, the mean number of successes for all judges involved was 3.2, which significantly exceeded chance. The largest number of successful matchings, achieved by 3 of the 10 judges, was four of the six subjects. For the males, the mean number of successes was 2.6, again exceeding chance. The most accurate matching for the males, achieved by only one judge, was 5 of the 13 infant sketches. Since the successful matchings exceeded chance, the findings are usually interpreted as a demonstration of the persistence of personality from infancy to late adolescence. However, with the recognition that the judges averaged only three correct matchings for the 15 subjects involved, the findings might equally well be interpreted as the inconstancy of personality.

There were clear-cut differences in the success with which individual subjects could be matched. Among the girls, for example, one subject was identified correctly by all 10 judges, while another subject was not matched correctly by any of the judges. The author offered three possible explanations for the individual differences. There might have been more adequate description at one or both of the ages for some subjects. Or, some subjects may maintain greater degree of similarity from infancy to adolescence. Or, the personality traits of some individuals are more salient to human judges even though the degree of continuity between early and later stages was identical for all. That there may be significant and valid differences among individuals in the stability of personality is a proposition taken up by other investigators.

The Neilon follow-up study described subjects in a global fashion using all of the information at the investigator's disposal. Since the basis for prediction was not made objective, the study allows little generalization beyond that sample and procedure (Rutter, 1970).

In contrast, the following studies mapped specific infancy measures and specific subsequent functions.

Newborn and Pre-Schooler: Organization, Behavior, and Relations Between Periods

The study by Bell et al. (1971) is unique in relating individual differences among neonates to later behavior. Although significant individual differences in a variety of response systems have been shown in neonates, their persistence and significance for later personality must still be demonstrated. The study was guided by a desire to study congenital contributors to development before differential effects of maternal handling exerted an important mediating influence.

The sample comprised 75 full-term, white, second- or later-born neonates, with no complications of pregnancy, delivery, or immediate postnatal course, and whose mothers were neither extremely disturbed nor anxious.

The neonates were studied for two 3½-h interfeeding periods that covered complete cycles of sleep and awakening. Uniform caretaking (if necessary), by the investigators of additional feeding, burping, diapering, and cleaning, was provided in order to minimize effects due to differences in maternal care. Time-sample observations were made of movements and of respirations. Measures of oral vigor and response to frustration of drive state were obtained through (1) onset-suck group, (2) average size of such group, (3) suck-rate during nonnutritive sucking, and (4) latency to a cry or movement and number of cries following interruption of nonnutritive sucking. Tactile threshold was measured during sleep. State of arousal following anthropometric measurements and bodily adjustments were noted on a 6-point scale. In addition, the amount consumed in 14 bottle feedings, for those babies who were not breastfed, provided an additional measure of oral drive. The authors noted that out of 31 neonatal measures only 12 were sufficiently stable from one session to the next, even within the neonatal period.

Thirty males and 25 females, who had been studied in the newborn period, were assessed at age 27 to 33 months during 4 weeks spent in an experimental nursery school in groups of five same-sex peers. At that period, there were over 70 stable measures derived through observations, mechanical recordings, and ratings of behavior in free-play and experimental situations.

Several procedures were used to group pre-school measures into meaningful classes of behavior. One, the pre-school measures were assigned to a priori groups guided by constructs of intensity, approach-avoidance, agonistic, affiliative, and exploratory behavior. Second, empirical data-reduction methods were then used to provide independent sets of pre-school measures. For each sex, seven internally consistent and independent classes of behavior were constructed in relation to the a priori groups. The most notable class, similar in both sexes, combined three a priori groups including general intensity, barrier behavior, and peer behavior. Children at one extreme of this class were active, assertive, and sociable, at the other extreme, inactive, submissive, and detached. The other classes of behavior for boys were as follows: verbal communication, contact with caretakers, preference for solids, breakfast liquids, response to restricted space, and barrier-behavior–goal-orientation. They were as follows for girls: gross movement and motor ability, verbal communication, contact with caretakers and peers, preference for solids, response to restricted space, and qualities of sleep and emotion.

Predictability from the neonatal period to later was disappointing. Bell et al. (1971) noted that ''newborn behavior is more like a preface to a book than a table of its contents yet to be unfolded. Further, the preface is itself merely a rough draft undergoing rapid revision'' [p. 132].

The New York Longitudinal Study

The New York Study, begun in 1956 under the directorship of Alexander Thomas (Thomas et al., 1961, 1963, 1968; as well as Rutter et al., 1963, 1964) has provided a major impetus in the identification of temperamental characteristics in infants as those characteristics contribute to normal and aberrant personality and social development. The investigators defined temperament as the behavior style of the individual child, which they identified as the ''how'' of behavior in contrast to the ''what or how well'' (abilities) and the ''why'' (motives) of behavior. Although their emphasis was on temperament as an organismic contributor to the course of psychological development, they did not assume it to be fixed but rather affected by physiological and experiential influences.

The sample comprised 85 families of middle- or upper-middle-class background, resident in New York City or its suburbs. They contributed 141 children to the study, including siblings and sets of twins. The families were not representative of the general population of the United States since 78% of the families were Jewish, and 75% of the mothers and 82% of the fathers had graduate as well as college education.

Information about the temperamental characteristics of the infant subjects was obtained through interviews with the parents which began when the children were at a mean age of 3.3 months, and continued at quarterly, semiannual, and annual intervals. The interviews were focused on descriptions of concrete objective behaviors during the preceding 3- to 6- to 12-month periods, during situations representative of daily life.

Interview data were coded on a 3-point scale for nine categories of functioning, which were determined empirically as being scorable and sufficiently variable to permit interindividual comparison. The categories were named as follows: activity level, rhythmicity, approach/withdrawal, adaptability, intensity of reaction, threshold of responsiveness, quality of mood, distractibility, attention span, and persistence. Single behavioral items in the interviews were frequently scored in two or more categories as relevant, thus providing differential numbers of items for the nine categories and differential numbers of items for each subject. Each protocol was analyzed for each category independently and no more than one interview of a given child was scored at any one time in order to diminish "halo effects."

As Rutter (1970) has indicated, there were several methodological questions. Although the ratings were based on concrete descriptions, the adjectives used by the parents in describing their infants might have influenced the ratings. That the obtained ratings might yield quite different results than would objective observations is suggested by the author's report that behavioral observations and parent interviews showed agreement at the 0.01 level of confidence (Thomas et al., 1968, p.16). Although agreement at the 0.01 level of confidence indicates some significant concordance between the two sources of data, it may also indicate much independent information. Further questions about the meaning of the ratings were raised by a recent study (Campbell, 1977) that found no systematic differences in observed infant behavior between infants who differed in ratings of irritability, irregularity, and nonadaptability. Rather, differences in ratings were reflective of differences in maternal behavior.

A further question was raised by the authors themselves about the nature of rating scales and of the instability of infant behaviors during the first 6 months of life. Three ways of rating the interview material were attempted. One, a "pre-ponderance" rating, which, similar to conventional ratings, ignored deviations from a modal point, described subjects in terms of the most frequently occurring scale point for each behavioral category. The two other procedures that were used took into account, as would behavior-frequency observational counts, the number of occurrences of behaviors at each of the scale points. The rank-order method characterized each child, for each temperamental attribute, as to the preponderance of ratings at each point of the 3-point scales. A third procedure, a percent-rank index, was used to rank-order the subjects, for each temperamental quality, as to the percentage of their own behavior that fell on the least frequent point on the scale for the entire sample. The first procedure revealed stability of ratings from the first 6 months of life to the 24-month period, which ranged from 38% for activity ratings to 88% for adaptability. Using the third procedure, the rank-order stabilities from the first 6 months of life to the 24-month period were minimal: ranging from rho = -0.15 for activity to 0.30 for intensity. With such instability, it is not surprising that antecedent-subsequent associations could not be made from the 1st year of life to year 5 (Rutter et al., 1963, 1964). They could be made from the 2nd year to year 5, however.

This study supports the previous study in detailing the poor predictability in the first 6 months of life.

Menninger Foundation Studies

An infancy project, begun in 1951 by Sibylle Escalona and Mary Leitch, has proved to be seminal in generating hypotheses of individual differences in the functioning of normal infants (Escalona, 1968; Escalona and Leitch, 1952; Escalona and Heider, 1959). The subjects of the project were 128 infants, comprising 8 boys and 8 girls studied at each 4-week age level from 4 to 32 weeks. Each infant was studied in two situations: a 4-h observation in the laboratory and a 1-h home visit observation made within 10 days of the laboratory session. Additional information was obtained by infant testing and pediatric examination, and some descriptive material about the families was also available. The sample included only white infants, free from defect, born to families who had lived in Topeka, Kansas, for at least 5 years prior to their infant's inclusion in the study, and whose economic status ranged from upper-middle-class to skilled workers. Children of the Menninger Foundation clinical staff were excluded.

Of the 128 infants included in the infancy study, 32 of the most available children from 27 families were selected as subjects for a pre-school coping project, under the directorship of Lois Barclay Murphy (e.g., Murphy and Moriarty, 1976). This project and its continuation initiated the study of normal children's efforts to cope with their own problems and to explore these efforts in relation to temperamental characteristics. The work has provided a rich source of hypotheses about normal children's adaptations to real-life events.

Ages at follow-up in the pre-school coping project and ages at the time of infant assessments varied widely. In some cases, predictions were made from a 4-week-old to a 5½-year-old, while in other cases from a 7½-month-old to a 2½-year-old. Relationships, therefore, involved comparisons of characteristics from different basal ages to different outcome ages. The authors, aware of the difficulty, have analyzed for effects associated with (1) the 7-month spread during the 1st year of life during which initial data were collected and (2) use of follow-up data involving a span of more than 3 years from toddler to school child.

The data-collection sessions for the pre-school coping project included parental interviews, pediatric examinations, psychiatric play sessions, standardized play sessions, and mental and projective testing. In addition, behaviors exhibited during the trips to and from the laboratory, and during project parties of groups of five to six children were also coded. The assessment items focused on ways in which the children confronted separation from the mother, new and strange situations, challenge, difficulty, or failure and bodily threat, damage, or pain (Escalona and Heider, 1959; Heider, 1966; Moriarty, 1961; Murphy, 1964). The procedures yielded 640 pre-school scores, including ratings from examinations and behavioral ratings.

Several strategies were used to examine the continuity from infancy to pre-school (Escalona and Heider, 1959). In one, the infancy data were reviewed, and a series of predictive statements (from 16 to 55) were made by Escalona for each of the 31 babies. Two methods were then used to judge the accuracy of the predictions. In one, Escalona and Heider independently studied the follow-up material and judged the degree to which the later behavior corroborated the predictions. Only 48% agreement could be established between the two judges; and despite the overlapping of the predictor and the evaluator, only 66% of the predictions were judged to be predominantly correct. In the second, Heider wrote personality sketches of the subjects from the coping project data. She then judged whether the infant predictions matched her descriptions. However, interjudge reliability could not be established at an acceptable level. Finally, Heider developed 134 rating scales which she used to assess each infant prediction sketch and each pre-school child description. It was these ratings scales upon which much of the understanding of the continuity of behavior is based. The number of strategies, and the difficulties involved, illustrate a basic problem of longitudinal research. Much data is generated—in fact, at times more measures than subjects. Meaningful data reduction then becomes a significant issue.

A latency study provided follow-up of the same children at ages 5 to 8. Detailed notes and narrative records were kept of the children's behavior and conversations going to and from the research center, during laboratory examinations, and during the home visits. When the children were 11 to 13 years of age, and then again during the senior year of high school, examinations and home visits were again made.

Change and Continuity in Infancy

The research by Kagan (1971) and his associates examined the stability of infant attentional-cognitive behaviors as precursors of reflectiveness-impulsivity. The sample included 91 boys and 89 girls, first-born, from white families. Most of the data characterizing the infants was obtained at the laboratory in a series of experimental situations that were administered at 4 months, 8 months, and 13 months of age. The laboratory situations included visual attention, auditory attention, free play when alone with the mother in the laboratory, and, at the older months, a separation situation. The behavioral and physiological measures concerned attentiveness, tempo of play, gross motor activity, and affective display.

The first follow-up data were gathered at 27 months and again included visual attention measures, auditory attention, a free-play situation, as well as a vocabulary test, an embedded figures test, and an experimentally presented conceptual conflict measure. The second follow-up data were gathered at 10 years of age and included the Matching Familiar Figures Test as a prototype measure of reflection-impulsivity (Kagan, 1976).

Berkeley Growth Study

The Berkeley Growth Study, University of California at Berkeley, one of the three longitudinal studies of the Institute of Human Development, was established by Nancy Bayley in 1928. Its purpose at inception was to represent the progression of normal mental, motor, and physical development of infants by frequent tests and measurements (Bayley, 1956, 1964; Bayley and Jones, 1937). Subjects were selected to be healthy full-term infants born in hospitals to white, English-speaking parents. Their families were predominantly middle-class, native born, and above the norm of educational level for that time. Of the 75 infants whose families agreed to participate, anywhere from 35 to 54 subjects were seen regularly for mental and motor tests at the institute through the first 18 years and at follow-up at 21 years, 26 years, and 36 years (Eichorn, 1973; Hunt and Eichorn, 1972). Additionally, the data included birth, prenatal, and perinatal histories, socioeconomic facts, and family histories, as well as body photographs, skeletal x-rays, health histories, and medical examinations.

For our purposes, it must be noted that the essential information, to date, about the continuity of social/emotional behavior was obtained solely through ratings based on observations made during mental and physical tests. Further, the ratings from one age period to the next were not always independent since the tester, who tended to remain constant, made many of the ratings. Even more important, the stimulus situation faced by the subjects remained the same.

The ratings that have been analyzed most thoroughly to date cover four age periods: 10 to 36 months, 3 to 8 years, 9 to 12 years, and adolescence (Schaefer and Bayley, 1963). Since the ratings were planned to include age-appropriate behaviors, they were not exact duplicates from age to age. Behaviors rated during infancy included seven point scales of activity, speed of movement, irritability and sensitivity to stimulation, emotional mood, shyness, responsiveness to persons, and amount of positive behaviors. Behaviors rated during childhood continued to include measures of cooperativeness and sociability to the examiner as well as measures of task orientation and activity control.

Behaviors rated during adolescence described a priori sectors of a circumplex model with two orthogonal poles: extraversion-introversion and love-hostility. Thus, the ratings included positive behavior to the examiner and mood, which had been measured before, and assessments of negative behavior and hostility to the examiner, which had not been measured in as much detail before, but the ratings did not provide for the assessment of continuity of task orientation.

When the subjects were aged 36 years, intensive interviews were conducted, coded, and Q-sorted by judges who did not know the subjects. While that data have been used for some purposes, they have not yet been used to test the continuity of social-emotional behavior from infancy (Eichorn, 1973; Hunt and Eichorn, 1972).

Data about caregiver-infant interaction during infancy were also obtained through observations made during mental and physical tests only. Additional data on the mother and family were obtained through interviews with the mother in the home on either one or two occasions when the subjects were between the ages of 9 and 14 years. These records were later systematized into ratings of maternal personality and child-rearing attitudes and practices (Schaefer and Bayley, 1960, 1963; Schaefer et al., 1959).

Guidance Study

The Guidance Study represents the second of the three longitudinal studies conducted at the Institute of Human Development, University of California at Berkeley. Under J. W. Macfarlane's directorship in 1928, a prospective study of normal infants was begun whose original aims were to determine (1) the frequency of behavior problems in a normal sample, (2) the factors associated with the presence or absence of such behavior problems, and (3) the effects of guidance through intensive discussions with parents about child-rearing procedures (Eichorn, 1973: Honzik and Macfarlane, 1973; Macfarlane, 1963, 1964; Macfarlane et al., 1954). In order to obtain a sample more representative of the general population than that of the Berkeley Growth Study, a randomized method of selection of every third birth in Berkeley from 1928 through 1929 was used. Despite the method of selection, the families were of higher educational and occupational status than that of the general United States population.

Of the obtained sample of 123 males and 125 females, a guidance and a control group of equal size was constituted by matching on sex, size of family, age of parents, income at birth of child, father's occupation, education, ethnic membership of parents, and neighborhood. In addition, the groups did not differ in birth conditions, developmental status, or the number of behavior problems evident at 21 months.

Although prenatal and perinatal data, and measurements of height and weight, were taken prior to 21 months, the information most relevant to our interests was collected only from 21 months on. Mental tests, and ratings of behavior during testing, were begun at 21 months, and continued semiannually, annually, and then biennially through age 18. Interviews with the parents also began when the subjects were aged 21 months and continued on a yearly basis until they were 17 years old. These interviews yielded 42 variables rated on 5-point scales. When the children of both guidance and control groups were aged 17, a retrospective interview was held with subjects and parents.

Information about the subjects' behaviors in a wider range of situations than only the laboratory was obtained from teacher interviews, sociometrics administered to classmates, and occasional planned social events with peers.

At age 30, an assessment battery of intellectual, personality and interest inventories, projective techniques, as well as interviews were used to prepare descriptive categorizations by 100-item Q-sorts.

For our purposes, note that the infancy data were derived from behavior during mental tests in the laboratory at age 21 months and from maternal interviews about behavior problems also at age 21 months.

Oakland Growth Study (Adolescent Growth Study)

The Oakland Growth Study, initiated in 1931 by Harold Jones and Herbert Stolz and continued from 1960 under the directorship of John Clausen, is the third longitudinal study from the Institute of Human Development at the University of California (Jones, 1960). The study will be referred to in a later section as it provided an example of a very interesting statistical and theoretical analysis of the continuity and discontinuity of behavior (Block, 1971). However, since the project did not include direct information about infancy, it will not be described in detail here.

Study of Human Development, Fels Research Institute

Under the directorship of Lester W. Sontag, the Study of Human Development, Fels Research Institute, was begun in 1929, and sample selection continued for the next 10 years (e.g., Sontag et al., 1958). Approximately 300 subjects were included, of whom 89 were assessed from 6 months through adulthood—that is at ages 20 to 29. Some question has been raised about the fact that the 89 children came from 63 different families, with 19 families supplying 2 to 3 children to the total sample, including one set of triplets (Honzik, 1965). (A similar question could be raised about the New York Study.) To the extent that 25% of the sample lived in rural areas, 50% in small towns, and only 25% in a large city, the sample differed from those of the Institute of Human Development, University of California at Berkeley. To the extent that the majority of the families could be placed in the middle-class by education and vocation, although fathers' occupations ranged from laborer to professional, the samples were similar.

Data collection during infancy not only included mental tests but also comprised observations of the behavior of mother and child at home. These data were collected semiannually and then annually during the 1st year of life through 12 years of age. Following the visits the parents were rated on parent-behavior scales which yielded clusters identified as acceptance, hostility, autonomy, control, protectiveness, rational or arbitrary disciplinary practices, and severity of discipline.

Behavior was assessed post-infancy in a variety of situations including attendance at a 3-week session at the Fels experimental nursery school, and 1 week in the Fels experimental day camp. Ratings of dependency, aggression, achievement, dominance, motoricity, sex-role interest, and conformity were made of behavior evident at the nursery school and day camp. The children as well as their mothers were interviewed annually from age 6 through 14. Projective techniques were administered to the subjects beginning at age 8 and continuing through age 18.

Of the 89 subjects for whom longitudinal information was available from infancy through adolescence, 71 participated in a follow-up assessment in adulthood. That follow-up consisted of a formal testing battery which included projective techniques, self-rating inventory, concept-sorting task, tachistoscopic recognition task, an intelligence test, and measures of autonomic reactivity. In addition, interviews were conducted by someone who had no knowledge of the test results nor of any of the longitudinal information (Kagan and Moss, 1962; Moss and Kagan, 1964).

Note that, in contrast to the Berkeley study, infancy data included home observations of mother-infant interaction as well as laboratory observations during mental tests; and, further, childhood data comprised behavior with peers in a nursery school and day camp setting as well as behavior during mental testing. Note also that in the analyses used to compare early to late behavior, infancy assessments were summarized over the entire 0- to 3-year period. That implicit assumption of behavioral stability during the entire infancy period may have obscured significant continuities and discontinuities (Honzik, 1965).

OVERALL FINDINGS

This section shall present an overview of the findings of predictability of emotional-social behavior from infancy. The findings do not submit to easy generalization. A coherent framework by which to organize the studies and their data is lacking. There is little agreement about emotional-social dimensions in either the infant or the adult. The ways in which we understand the infant are not necessarily congruent with our conceptions of the older child and the adult, particularly since the infant has a much narrower array of responses by which to assess any construct. Finally, there is a paucity of accepted theoretical formulations by which to integrate the transitions from infancy to later.

In an effort to comprise the diversity of infancy studies, Kessen et al. (1970) collected and sorted studies by categories which, in general, seem useful for our purposes. We have omitted some categories and added others in order to represent longitudinal research to date. The categories, admittedly, are arbitrary and not mutually exclusive. The ones we shall use are entitled as follows: the infant as oral, the infant as sensory surface, the infant as doer (intensity and magnitude of activity), the infant as emerging affective behavior, the infant as thinker, and the infant as social partner. In addition, we shall consider the predictability from infancy of vulnerability to personality disturbance. The categories shall be considered in that order.

The Infant as Oral

The meaning of oral behaviors for later personality has been investigated from several vantage points. The degree of oral satisfaction and frustration in the feeding experience occupy a prominent place in psychoanalytic and social learning theory. Attachment theory sets aside drive gratification and proposes alternative implications for oral behaviors. Individual differences in infants' skill in evoking and terminating nutritive sucking may preview differences in the quality of attachment (Ainsworth and Bell, 1969; Ainsworth, 1973) and, thereby, shape later behavior. Finally, individual differences in nonnutritive sucking and mouth movements, per se, have been investigated.

Two of the longitudinal studies under consideration have attempted to assess degree of oral satisfaction. The classic study by Heinstein (1963), using the Berkeley Guidance Study data, assessed the incidence of problem behavior from infancy to 12 years under a multivariate categorization of infancy feeding experience. Consideration was given to the "warmth" of the mother, her stability, the length of nursing, and whether done by breast or bottle. The findings were complex and helped to lay to rest gross equivalencies between oral satisfaction and breast-feeding or between oral satisfaction and long nursing. That is, there appeared to be no overall benefit for boys and girls to be breastfed or to be nursed long periods. Rather, the incidence of behavior problems was related to the matrix of maternal attitudes, maternal stability, method and length of feeding, and sex of infant.

Murphy and Moriarty (1976), in the Menninger project, used observational data to judge differences in oral demand, gratification, autonomy in satisfying oral needs, and capacity to protest or terminate unsatisfying oral situations. Characterizing the feeding experience in these ways did reveal relations to later behavior. Although the findings were established in only a very small sample ($n = 17$), they were supported in a short-term longitudinal study done independently (Ainsworth and Bell, 1969), and they are of great interest methodologically and conceptually. Infant boys who were more able to terminate, protest, and resist disliked foods, showed themselves as pre-schoolers to be judged to be more active in controlling the environment, in exercising impulse control, and to have greater clarity of self-concept. The significant outcome behaviors could be described as self-directed ways of managing one's situation in the environment. Boys who as infants experienced greater oral gratification appeared as pre-schoolers to have a greater sense of self-worth, to be less critical of people, to be less concerned with being rejected, as well as greater ability to control the environment. The results intriguingly affirm a relation between oral gratification and optimism and/or trust.

The import for pre-school behavior of neonatal rate of nonnutritive sucking (onset suck group, average size of such group, and suck rate per minute) and number of mouth movements during sleep was investigated by Bell et al. (1971). Male neonates who showed a greater rate of nonnutritive sucking, as well as more mouth movements during sleep, tended to be more distractible, more restless in a confined space, to show less play continuity, to be less goal-directed in following a game, to be more hesitant in overcoming a barrier, to do less running, to do more mouthing, to eat less breakfast solids. In sum, greater rate of nonnutritive sucking and mouth movements during sleep were linked to lesser involvement in the nursery school situation. In contrast, oral behaviors in female neonates showed different and fewer correlates with later behavior. Female neonates who showed more mouth movements during sleep were more advanced in speech development and more verbally communicative.

Thus, several studies, with different samples and procedures, suggest intriguing continuities from early oral behavior, nutritive and nonnutritive, to later personality.

The Infant as Sensory Surface

The degree of responsiveness to environmental stimuli show large individual differences that tend to be stable over at least a short period of time during infancy (Stone et al., 1973). Although it has been proposed that sensory modality preferences should also exist as a stable individual difference and should influence social and personality development, research evidence, at least for neonates, indicates that response thresholds tend to be consistent across modalities (Birns, 1965; Korner, 1971). In any case, there has been little examination in longitudinal studies of this very significant area of infancy research.

Among the few studies that do exist, Bell et al. (1971) examined the pre-school derivatives of neonatal high or low threshold to tactile stimuli. In essence, the less sensitive female neonate was later found to be more vigorous and more sustained in her efforts to tear down a barrier. She was better coordinated and more active in gross motor activity. She was also more attentive to the teacher during story time. The pattern was similar and approached significance for males.

Escalona and Heider (1959) also found pre-school derivatives of infancy sensory thresholds. A majority of their sample remained stable in level of responsiveness to perceptual stimuli from infancy to pre-school. Further, there was some evidence that sensory threshold was related to later expressive behavior, fantasy intensity, and social empathy. That is, only children with low sensory thresholds as infants (but not all such infants) were judged to be high in expressive behavior, fantasy intensity, and social empathy later. A low sensory threshold, therefore, appeared to be a necessary but not sufficient condition for later social sensitivity.

Although the data are few, they do suggest that sensory threshold in infancy may be associated with later assertive environmental activity at one extreme, and with heightened social-emotional awareness at the other.

The Infant as Doer (Intensity and Magnitude of Activity)

"Infantile activity has survived as a prominent indicator of the baby's behavior because . . . it holds promise as a revealing mark of stable differences among babies" (Kessen et al., 1970, p. 296). Three points are important: first, the internal consistency of the construct; second, short- and long-term stability; third, the consequences of various activity levels for other behaviors such as abstract thought, frustration tolerance, and expansiveness of bodily orientation in space.

Activity or activity pattern is not a simple construct agreed upon by all investigators. The distinctions in measurement and definition become important in reconciling differences found in stability and in reconciling differences found in subsequent behavior. The problems in definition become apparent when one examines the classic studies by Fries (1937, 1944). On one hand, she defined activity pattern as observable in the number, extent, and tempo of movements throughout the day and night, thus emphasizing individual differences in spontaneous activity and state organization; and on the other hand, she suggested that the assessment of activity pattern be made from duration of cry and movement as response to a startling stimulus, and duration of cry and movement as response to presentation, removal, and restoration of breast or bottle. Some investigators have used the former procedure of measuring spontaneous activity and some have used the latter procedure, and measured response to interrupted sucking. Note that measures of spontaneous gross motor activity in neonates failed to show test-retest reliability (Bell et al., 1971) and ratings of activity level in the 0- to 6-month period were the least predictive to later behavior of all the behaviors assessed in the New York longitudinal study (Thomas et al., 1963). In contrast, objective measures of neonatal response to interrupted sucking did show stability over time (Bell et al., 1971). Further, Escalona (1963, 1968), who has generated a wealth of hypotheses and findings comparing most- and least-active infants, has suggested that pace of motor development, range and qualitative aspects of motility, and availability of energy may be better predicted than activity level.

Despite differences in method, there is some evidence, though not unequivocal, that more active, rapid, intense behavior early may be linked to later decreased social interest and decreased involvement in tasks. Kagan and Moss (1962) found that "hyperkinesis" (defined as perennially restless, impulsive, aimless motor discharge) showed a high degree of stability from age 3 on (the earliest age measured), which was linked to lesser involvement in intellectual pursuits as an adult. Halverson and Waldrop (1975) similarly found "hyperactivity" to be longitudinally stable from pre-school to age 7½, with negative implications for intellectual functioning. Corroborating evidence from infancy was found by Schaefer and Bayley (1963), but only for males. Ratings of rapidity and vigor during developmental exams of males aged 10 to 12 months of age were correlated to inattentiveness, lack of cooperation, and unfriendliness during mental tests administered during the early school years.

Bell (1975) has proposed an "inversion of intensity" hypothesis. The hypothesis is based on data from his own longitudinal study in which he found that longer latency to cry and fewer cries following interruption of nonnutritive sucking in the newborn period were associated with more active involvement in games and more assertiveness in barrier situations in the pre-school period. Further, male newborns with high respiration rates during sleep were low in interest, coping, and peer interaction in nursery school.

Since the findings violated phenotypic continuity, in that frequency, and magnitude of newborn behavior were associated with less vigor and participation in nursery school, whereas lower levels of functioning in the newborn period were associated with greater involvement later, Bell (1975) sought and found substantive support in other studies. In addition, most recently, for example, a follow-up at age 3 in nursery school of infants observed at 3 months of age in their homes with their mothers, indicated substantial predictability—for males—of early high arousal (e.g., frequent vocalizing, high tonicity, much kicking and thrashing) to later lower general activity level and less frequent positive social behavior (Halverson et al., 1977).

There are several issues to be considered. One is the sturdiness of the phenomenon. Although Bell cites several studies consistent with the hypothesis, there is one study that is contradictory. Yang and Halverson (1976) repeated Bell et al.'s study, with various changes in sample and procedures, and could not replicate the findings. One may further question whether the "inversion of intensity" phenomenon is relevant to general intensity of activity or whether it is relevant specifically to sucking and breathing behaviors. It is conceivable that those behaviors, essential for infant survival, would be most salient in organizing later behavior.

Significant effects of infancy activity level on other behavioral systems has been proposed and in some ways demonstrated during the infancy period, but not subsequently.

Moss and Robson (1970) have suggested that activity levels need to be examined as they influence the infant's developmental status as well as responsiveness to external stimuli. They found that infants who had spent a greater amount of time at activity levels that were optimal for visual observation of the environment (alert inactivity) also looked longer at experimentally presented visual stimuli. Escalona (1963, 1968) has observed that activity levels underlie infantile differences in the frequency of nonnutritive oral behavior, prolonged gazing, and tactile exploration of immediate surroundings. Low activity level, Escalona proposes, is associated with a facility for restricted and modulated behavior, which in turn enhances visual responsivity. Some support for that hypothesis is adduced by the finding that developmental tests administered at age 7½ months showed inactive infants to be advanced in visual and auditory discrimination as well as fine visual-motor coordination. High activity level, in contrast, facilitated gross motor development and purposive manipulation of objects.

Schaffer and Emerson (1964) have suggested that activity type may also have consequences for social interaction between caregiver and infant. In a short longitudinal study from birth to 18 months with 37 mother-infant pairs, 19 infants were found to be cuddlers and 9 to be noncuddlers, as characterized by their mothers' responses to questions about the infants' behavior in commonly occurring contact situations. Cuddlers consistently enjoyed, accepted, and actively sought out physical contact of all sorts. Noncuddlers responded negatively to cuddling even when tired, frightened, or ill. Cuddlers were more placid, slept more, and formed special attachments to others earlier and with greater intensity. They were also more likely to get attached to transitional objects and to engage in autoerotic activities. Noncuddlers were more active, more restless, and intolerant of any physical restraint. Since Schaffer and Emerson were unable to find any consistent differences between mothers of the cuddler babies on the one hand and mothers of noncuddler babies on the other, they concluded that a difference existed in temperament, primarily expressed in the level of activity.

Schaffer (1966) also proposed that inactive infants were more likely to be adversely affected by environmental deprivation than more active infants. In support, he showed that those infants who were the most quiet and withdrawn in the hospital suffered the greatest losses in cognitive performance in the hospital as demonstrated by their showing the largest increase in test scores on their return home.

In sum, infantile activity patterning, both of basal intensity and reactive intensity, has been implicated in a variety of concurrent behavioral systems, including visual attention, object manipulation, and "cuddliness." Infantile activity intensity has been connected subsequently to peer interaction and assertive coping in nursery school, and to task orientation during the early elementary school years.

The Infant as Emerging Affective Behavior

How quick the infant is to cry, and how intensely he/she does it, or how much the infant smiles and shows calm, happy behavior, or how fearful the infant is to strange situations and persons, show some predictability to later behavior. Further, differential patterns for boys and girls found in some studies suggest that affective behaviors may have different meaning for the sexes. The following categories are not mutually exclusive.

Irritability

In general, early irritability (specifically in males) tends to be associated with later decreased social interest to peers and adults (Bell et al., 1971, as discussed in a preceding section). A finding consistent with that showed that greater irritability (in both male and female infants) during anthropometric examination during the first 3 years of life was associated with less social responsiveness to adults during the same period (Shirley, 1933). More irritability by male infants in the testing situation was similarly related to greater shyness from age 3 to 8 (G. W. Bronson, 1969, 1971).

Early irritability seems also to be associated with task orientation, but perhaps differentially for boys and girls. Kagan (1971), in a short-term longitudinal study, found that 4-month-old infants who became restless and irritable after several presentations of an interesting stimulus were most likely to be fretful at 8 and 13 months in the laboratory when their mothers left them alone. A further examination of the 21 children who, at 4 months, were so irritable that the laboratory sessions could not be continued, showed that the extremely irritable girls—but not boys—looked longer at discrepant events at 13 and 27 months of age, vocalized more following termination of auditory stimuli, showed less stereotyped play, and were more talkative at 27 months. Irritability in girls, then, if anything, may be correlated with active interest in intellectual tasks. A similar finding was stated by Karelitz et al. (1964). They reported that the more cries a female neonate made in response to sole flicks, the higher was the Stanford-Binet score at age 3. However, our examination of their data seems to indicate no difference between boys and girls.

Although the evidence presented here suggests the significance of irritability as a temperamental disposition that appears early in infancy and persists (Thomas et al., 1968), there are contrary findings. Bell and Ainsworth (1972), in a short-term longitudinal study, indicated that for normal infants the source of stability in infant crying may reside more in the mother's responsiveness to the infant than in a temperamental quality of the infant. Within the 1st year of life no correlations were found between the infants' fuss/cries in the first 3 months and in the last 3 months. Rather, infants cried less in the latter months if their mothers had been responsive during the early months to their fuss/cries, whether few or many. Even within the New York study, in which ratings of negative mood were a significant component of a cluster of behaviors labeled the "difficult baby" syndrome (Thomas et al., 1968) there was evidence of instability. For example, the ratings of mood within the 1st year of life did *not* differentiate subjects who would later show behavior problems from those who would not. That group difference only became evident in the 2nd year of life (Rutter et al., 1964).

Smiling

Antecedent-subsequent relations of smiles, and ratings of happy, calm behavior have also been considered. Kagan (1971) found that infants who at 4 months smiled more frequently at human masks, and at 27 months smiled more following successful solution of a perceptual problem, showed longer epochs of sustained play and less impulsiveness in an intellectual conflict situation at 27 months. A follow-up of these infants at age 10 continued to show them to be less impulsive and more reflective (Lapidus et al., 1977). Similarly, for males—but not for females—ratings of happy, calm, positive behavior during testing during the 3rd year of life showed a consistent pattern to task mastery behaviors of attentiveness, concentration, systematic approach, and swift comprehension from childhood through 12 years (Schaefer and Bayley, 1963). In contrast, infancy ratings for females showed exactly the opposite relationship, although inconsistently for different age periods. That is, girl infants who were judged to be happy, positive, and calm later tended to be judged to be shy, not cooperative, inattentive, and lacking in facility in a testing situation (Schaefer and Bayley, 1963).

Wariness

Despite divergence within psychology on the meaning, and the appropriate operational definition, of fear of the strange and/or the stranger, remarkable consistency was shown over several studies, each using different samples and procedures. G. W. Bronson (1968, 1971, 1972) has presented data, from both Ainsworth's short-term longitudinal study of the 1st year of life and the Berkeley Growth Study, that indicates that for males—but not for females—a relatively early onset of wariness or fear to the strange situation or strange person predicted a greater degree of shyness from infancy into the pre-school years.

In the Ainsworth study, the earlier the onset of wariness or fear of the stranger at the home observation, the greater the shyness at 1 year with a stranger in the strange laboratory situation, even when the mother was present. The relationship was, in part but not completely, mediated by variations in maternal sensitivity. Although variations in maternal sensitivity and responsiveness to infant signals in the first 3 months of life were associated with age of onset of fearfulness—that is, the more responsive the mother, the later the onset—the relationship was negligible with the intensity of fear by age 1.

In the Berkeley Growth Study, male infants who showed fear of the strange situation by or before 6 months of age, as shown by judgments that the strangeness of the situation had induced crying, were significantly more shy at the end of the 1st year and during the age period 2 to 3½ years than male infants who developed fear reactions only after 6 months. From 4 to 8½ years, the trend remained but was not statistically significant. An additional remarkable finding was noted. Retrospective analysis showed that the two males of the sample who had been hospitalized during adulthood for schizophrenia had both showed extreme fear of the strange situation during the 4- to 15-month period. No continuities were found for females.

Such findings were bolstered by the Fels Study in which male infants who showed a fearful approach to strangers and strange situations tended to be fearful in the pre-school and early school years and, in turn, to exhibit anxiety in social interactions in adulthood (Kagan and Moss, 1962).

Conflicting evidence, however, has been obtained. Findings from the Menninger study (Escalona and Heider, 1959) showed that children's responses to unfamiliar situations and shyness with strangers were significantly poorly predicted. Although the authors suggest that the lack of behavioral continuity may be accounted for by the lability of recently acquired behavior, I wonder if the explanation does not lie in the insufficiency of the infant observations for that variable. Thus, neither response to unfamiliar situations nor behavior with strangers was directly assessed. Further, since babies were studied at varying ages from 4 to 32 weeks, the construct would not be relevant to the early ages.

Anxiety

For both males and females, metamorphic continuity was evident from infancy anxiety over bodily harm (fear of cars, animals, the dark, and excessive disturbance over injury and illness) to later affiliative behavior (Kagan and Moss, 1962). For males, greater anxiety was related to increased dependency on the love object, and for females, less dependency conflict. For both males and females, greater early anxiety was related to less opposite-sex activity as an adult.

Summary of the Infant as Emerging Affective Behavior

Derivatives of individual differences among infants in affective displays of crying, smiling, anxiety, and wariness have been traced into childhood and even into adulthood. The findings are stronger for males than for females, and they differ in kind, as well as degree. In sum, the more wary the male infant at a young age and/or the more irritable, the less social interest he will later show to peers and adults. The more pleasure (i.e., smiles) a male infant shows in mastering a cognitive task, the more reflective and the more attentive he will later be in cognitive tasks. In contrast, although the evidence is more equivocal, the more irritable the female infant, the more interest she will later show in intellectual tasks, whereas the more smiles she early shows, the less interest in the task and the examiner she will later display. The strength and the nature of the relationships between infancy and later behavior may as well reside in the interaction between the infant and its environment as in the infant itself. But there is little evidence as to the processes.

The Infant as Thinker

Variously conceptualized as contingency awareness, sense of mastery, effectance behavior, competence, task orientation, and achievement motivation, the constructs reflect overlapping behaviors that define the individual's readiness to be involved in a task, to persist even in the face of difficulties, to master the challenge, and finally, to take pleasure and/or pride in the achievement (Heinicke, 1977). There are distinct limitations to our understanding of the phenomena. Do the different definitions reflect distinct behaviors, eliciting conditions, and processes? Are they correlated components or are they chained together in some sort of a developmental sequence? What evidence do longitudinal studies provide that personality dimensions involved in task orientation occur early in life and show continuity thereon?

The available data is spotty and contradictory. But, in essence, the findings suggest that the significant factors during infancy may be affect variables and lack of motor restlessness more than persistence in sensory-motor tasks.

As reported in a previous section, smiling in infancy at visual social stimuli predicted reflectiveness (longer decision time and fewer errors on an embedded figures test) at age 10 (Kagan, 1971; Lapidus, et al., 1977). Tempo of play and act changes in infancy, however, did not. In contrast, Schaefer and Bayley (1963) found that ratings of rapid, active behavior in the 1st and 2nd years of life were related to decreased attentiveness, more distractibility, and lesser task interest later.

The results from both studies are in contrast to those from the Fels Institute Study, which found no continuity between the infancy period and later task orientation. Kagan and Moss (1962) defined general achievement-mastery behavior as the child's persistence with challanging tasks, games, and problems, and involvement in activities in which a standard of excellence was applicable. Mastery behavior for the age period 0 to 3 showed no relationship to childhood, adolescent, or adult achievement strivings or performance. In considering the apparent discrepancies between the studies, one should note the different infancy periods considered. Only Kagan and Moss generalized over the entire 3-year period and thereby, perhaps, obscured the significance of specific developmental changes within that period.

While there is little evidence to date of predictability within the infant to later task behavior, there is evidence of predictability from early experience, at least within this culture. For example, Brody and Axelrad (1970) found that certain styles of mothering (high empathy, high efficiency, and moderate control) with 6-week-old infants were related to significantly higher IQ scores and verbal and arithmetic achievement test scores on follow-up at age 7. Yarrow et al. (1973) found that amount of physical contact, appropriateness of stimulation, responsiveness of the mother to the infant's attempts at communication, degree to which the mother individualized the infant, expressed positive affect, and was emotionally involved with the infant, were correlated with IQ at age 10 (for boys, but not for girls). There is additional evidence from the Berkeley Growth Study (Eichorn, 1973) and the Berkeley Guidance Study (Honzik and Macfarlane, 1973) of the impact of the family environment during infancy on later intellectual functioning. Further, the Fels Institute Study (Kagan and Moss, 1962) showed a pattern of associations between maternal practices during infancy and later child and adult achievement strivings that occurred specifically for the infancy period, lending credence to the point of view that suggests that some motivational factors are particularly sensitive to infancy experience. Their findings indicated that task-mastery strivings in adult men had been fostered by maternal protectiveness (or nurturance) during infancy followed by encouragement and acceleration of mastery behaviors during the age period 3 to 10 years. In contrast, maternal protectiveness to a female infant was likely to decrease achievement strivings, whereas maternal criticalness to a female infant was likely to increase achievement strivings as an adult.

Although the findings are provocative, many questions remain. At issue is not only the initiation of individual differences but their maintenance through adulthood, and the differential pattern shown by males and females.

The Infant as Social Partner

The human infant develops in a social environment—that is, in part shaped by the infant itself. The infant is responsive to stimuli likely to emanate from other persons, and the infant responds in ways to evoke and maintain physical closeness and social attention from other persons. Within the 1st year of life, the infant recognizes, discriminates, and prefers one or more selected individuals, and the presence of those individuals provides a secure base from which to explore. There are several theories of the origin, course, and consequences of these phenomena, which have been cogently summarized by Maccoby and Masters (1970). The theories are not equally represented in the longitudinal studies. To the extent that the theories dictate the selection and organization of relevant behaviors, they influence the predictions that can be made from early behaviors.

Kagan and Moss (1962) focused on dependency in early social affiliations. In so doing, they combined the affiliative and succorant components of dependency. These components were conceptualized as affectional dependency, instrumental dependency, passivity, and withdrawal from stress. Kagan and Moss reported that their ratings of affectional dependency during infancy (i.e., seeking of affection and instrumental aid from female adults, primarily the mother; and anxiety, crying, protest over loss of nurturance) showed no relationship with adult behavior. Thus, they concluded that the seeking of instrumental assistance may be less predictive to adult traits than a passive orientation to frustration (i.e., withdrawal from social stress or goal loss). (These behaviors, in our categorization, might have been included in "The Infant as Doer"). For boys, passivity during infancy was related to dependency on the love object as an adult, and unrelated to dependency on parents or friends. For girls, although Kagan and Moss summarized their findings (from early childhood to later) as showing a remarkable degree of continuity in passivity and dependency, isomorphic predictions from infancy could actually not be made. Rather, female infants who showed greater anxiety about loss of nurturance became adults who were more active in dealing with stress.

Attachment theory, a very significant part of infancy study today (e.g., Ainsworth, 1973; Bowlby, 1969, 1973), has not yet guided prospective studies from infancy to later. As a central thesis, this theory investigates species-specific developmental sequences rather than individual differences. Nevertheless, conceptualizing attachment as an organization of behaviors, characterizing qualitative differences in that organization (rather than quantative differences in a unidimensional trait), and positing changes in the organization dependent on situation, yield coherent and predictive descriptions within infancy.

Studies of short-term longitudinal design that have followed the course of attachment through the 1st and 2nd years of life find qualitative characterizations of "securely attached" or "insecurely attached," as shown by the organization of behaviors in the "strange situation" (Ainsworth and Wittig, 1969) to remain stable from 12 to 21 months

(Waters and Sroufe, 1977) Further, the differences in quality of attachment were significant antecedents to social behavior to a stranger as well as to object exploration. Main (1973) studied 40 infant-mother pairs in the strange situation when the infants were 12 months of age. When the infants were 20½ months of age they were tested on the mental scale of the Bayley Scales of Infant Development and were videotaped in a play situation by persons having no knowledge of the previous assessments. Infants who were judged to be securely attached at 12 months attained higher Bayley mental scores at 21 months. They also played more intensely, for longer bouts, and with more positive affect in the free-play session. They made more approaches to a stranger in the play situation, and were more cooperative with the test examiner and approached the test with a more gamelike spirit. The findings were supported by Londerville (1977), who found in a mini-longitudinal study of 36 mother-infant pairs that security of attachment at 12 months, as judged from the strange situation, predicted to more positive social behaviors with a stranger in a play session at 21 months. Moreover, the quality of attachment at 12 months was found to be affected by the mother's responsiveness and sensitivity of the infant's cues (Ainsworth, 1973) and the quality of attachment in the 1st year of life predicted to the mother's sensitivity, acceptance, and expressiveness of positive affect to her infant at 21 months of age (Tolan and Tomasini, 1977).

The findings are promising. But they do not as yet span infancy and later periods, and it is difficult to integrate them with older longitudinal studies. Since the infant as a social partner represents one of the most exciting areas of investigation within infancy research today, the paucity of integrated longitudinal data is disappointing.

Peers

There may be several distinct affectional systems, of which the mother-infant relationship is one, peer relations are another, and adult sexual relationships yet a third (Harlow, 1961).

Maccoby and Masters (1970) have indicated that during infancy and early childhood, aggressive and affiliative behaviors, specifically to peers, are correlated. Waldrop and Halverson (1975) obtained data on peer relations when a group of children were 2½ years of age and again when they were 7½ years old. The correlation between aggressive and affiliative behaviors to peers at 2½ years of age was confirmed. Further, the children who at age 2½ were friendly, involved with their peers, and able to cope with aggressive peers were likely, at age 7½, to spend many hours outside school with peers, to be socially at ease, and to be the ones who decided with whom they would play and what they would play. Significant stability between sociability in peer relations from one age period to the next was therefore demonstrated.

More far-reaching sequelae to peer relations during infancy have also been documented. Aggression to peers during infancy was linked to adult social ease, as well as less anxiety in sexual behavior by Kagan and Moss. The more a male infant was judged to show indirect aggression to peers (verbal taunts, teasing, destruction or seizure of a peer's property), the less discomfort he as an adult experienced in social situations. The more a female infant was judged to show indirect as well as direct physical aggression to peers, the less anxiety she had about sexual relations. That link between infant peer relations and adult sexual behavior has been detailed in animal studies as well (Harlow, 1961).

Bronson and Pankey (1977) are presently engaged in a short-term longitudinal research, from 12 months of age to 3½ years of age, to study the development of peer behavior during infancy. The study seeks to describe (1) the behavioral expressions, (2) the nature of the latent psychological mechanisms they reflect, and (3) the salience that such mechanisms attain for different individuals as they develop over time. The data consist of videotaped records of the activities of 40 toddlers, each of whom—accompanied by the mother—participated (among other assessments) in a series of 10 small playgroup sessions spaced throughout the 2nd year of life. Each playgroup involved three or four mother-child pairs who were generally unacquainted at the outset of each session. The study is noteworthy for its care and thoughtfulness in data reduction and data analysis. Frequency counts of a multiplicity of possible behaviors were summed into several categories to make a single profile. The pool of profiles were then reduced to a set of prototype configurations. In order to guard against unconstrained post hoc hypotheses, the data were then fitted to a series of analytic models, which were compared statistically. The study holds promise for increasing our understanding of the organization of peer behavior and its evolving nature during infancy, as well as the coherence of individual differences.

Sociability and/or Extraversion

Extraversion (expressive, outgoing behavior to other persons, adults as well as peers) is often reported to be one of the most stable dimensions found in the Berkeley Guidance Study. Yet, it must be remembered that the stability was established for the years 5 through adolescence, not from infancy. Adult derivatives were then found, as well as antecedents searched for in infancy (W. C. Bronson, 1966a, b, 1967).

What is most significant for the purposes of this chapter are the infancy antecedents of expressive outgoing behavior. Only very limited data about infancy were available, some about family relationships obtained through parental interview, and some about the number of behavior problems, also obtained through maternal interview. A greater number of maternally reported behavior problems in the first 21 months of life were related to more outgoing behavior from age 8 through adolescence, for boys and girls. In turn, extraversion during childhood and adolescence for males, but only during adolescence for females, tended to be associated with adult behaviors of gregariousness, expressiveness, and social poise.

A continuity in socially extraverted behavior from infancy to later was corroborated in the Fels Institute Study as well as in the Berkeley Growth Study. Social spontaneity, a rating of responsiveness and affective expression with peers and adults, in male infants, tended to be linked to less adult anxiety about social interaction (Kagan and Moss, 1962). Schaefer and Bayley (1963) found that ratings of responsiveness to persons—that is, socially extraverted behavior during the 10- to 12-month period for male infants—related during later childhood to socially extraverted behavior. There were no relationships to adolescent behavior.

The data also suggested an unexpected inverse relation between extraverted behavior during infancy and task attentiveness and task mastery during early childhood (Schaefer and Bayley, 1963). In turn, task facility and cooperation during infancy correlated with socially extraverted behaviors at adolescence.

Agonistic Behavior

While aggressive behaviors may reflect a dimension of social interest, particularly with peers, they may also reflect an independent dimension of anger and hostility. In general, the five infancy measures of aggression in the Fels Institute Study (aggression to mother, physical aggression to peers, indirect aggression to peers, behavioral disorganization including violent crying and tantrums, and conformity to adults) showed minimal correlates with anger and aggression as an adult. There were some slight relationships between a more conforming infant, male and female, and a less competitive adult. Also, the more a female infant was judged to show indirect as well as direct physical aggression to peers, the less anxiety she had about angry thoughts as an adult.

Summary

The studies have provided some suggestive leads for unraveling antecedent-subsequent relations of early social-affective behavior to target persons, adults, and peers. In addition, sociability, per se, appears to be a pervasive and enduring characteristic, whose origins in infancy need to be examined further.

THE PREDICTABILITY FROM INFANCY OF VULNERABILITY TO PERSONALITY DISTURBANCE

The wish to identify specific precursors, antecedent events, and experiences that make for later competence, confidence, and generosity is particularly compelling (Stone et al., 1973), as is the goal of discovering in infancy some of the sources of vulnerability that make for later emotional disturbance. Conflicting evidence has been obtained as to our success in this endeavor. Efforts have varied in the nature and assessment of relevant behaviors during infancy and later.

One method of assessing adjustment used in the Berkeley Guidance Study was to note the number, kind and severity of behavior problems (Macfarlane et al., 1954). The authors concluded that although problems frequently did show a low to moderate year-to-year consistency, change rather than persistence was of the greater significance. Further, there were epochs (kindergarten entrance, junior high school entrance, adolescence) coincident with ages at which children make major readjustments, when problem patterns tended to become disrupted.

Macfarlane (1963, 1964) has stressed the potentiality of error in predictions of psychological adjustment from early behavior and early home environment. She reported that almost 50% of the Berkeley Guidance sample became more stable and effective adults than was predicted, and 20% of the sample became less so. The discontinuities in "adjustment" were not only a reflection of the instability or nonrelevance of the infancy period, since discontinuities occurred throughout childhood and adolescence (Block, 1971; Livson and Peskin, 1967).

Two points are important. Many stress situations may facilitate problem-solving, clarify goals, and increase stability. Major developmental issues continue throughout the lifespan (e.g. parenthood) and provide occasions for change and growth (Macfarlane, 1963, 1964).

Investigators in the Menninger studies used a variety of other approaches. One was an infancy vulnerability index (Murphy and Moriarty, 1976), which was a rating based on the extent of extremes, limitations, or imbalances of sensory, motor, cognitive, affective, and vegetative behavior. The score on the infancy vulnerability index did correlate with boys' ability in early childhood to deal actively with the environment (a rating named coping I) and with both boys and girls' capacity to maintain internal integration during stress (a rating named coping II). A second approach was a classification system used by Heider (1966), which took into account high sensory reactivity plus high drive, as well as wide scatter in the Gesell Infant Test, and physique, and quality of mother-child relationship. Heider's clinical judgments of vulnerability as infants were significantly correlated with coping techniques (coping I and coping II) as pre-schoolers.

Interesting is the emphasis on low sensory thresholds or unusual sensory sensitivity as a significant element in vulnerability. The hypothesis has been supported by the investigations of G. W. Bronson (1971).

Fish (1957, 1959, 1960, 1963) hypothesized that poor integration of early neurological development might be a precursor to serious personality disorders in infants vulnerable to schizophrenia. In a series of studies of 13 infants born to schizophrenic mothers, infants were observed from birth to age 2 by repeated administrations of the Gesell Developmental Schedules. Poor integration of neurological maturation was judged to have occurred if there was wide scatter between the subtests of the Gesell, or wide scatter within a subtest, or marked irregularities in the longitudinal sequence of development over the course of time. Independent psychological evaluations were then made at age 10 to 11. At follow-up only two children were considered to be relatively healthy, and those two children as infants had shown minimally uneven development in infancy, whereas the other eight had shown severely uneven neurologic integration (Fish and Hagin, 1973). Although the findings are provocative, they must be considered tentative because they derive from such a small sample based essentially on clinical judgment.

The New York Longitudinal Study is unique in focusing directly on the contribution of infancy traits to the emergence of actual behavior problems in normal children (Thomas et al., 1968). By school age, 42 of the original sample of 136 children had developed behavioral problems serious enough for the parent and/or school to express concern. No evidence was found that the parents of the children with behavioral problems had acted differently from others of the parent group. Rather, evidence was found that identifiable infant "temperamental" qualities played a significant role in the genesis of behavior disorders. No single temperamental trait resulted in behavioral disturbance, but a cluster of traits seemed to act as a predisposition to behavioral disturbance. That is, 70% of the temperamentally difficult infants (irregularity in biological functions; a high frequency of intense negative reactions; a predominance of negative, withdrawal responses to new stimuli; and excessive slowness in adapting to changes in the environment) developed behavior problems, whereas only approximately 22% of the "easier" infants did. A clinical comparison, by the investigators, of those "difficult" infants who did and those who did not develop behavioral disturbances, and of those "easy" infants who did and those who did not develop behavioral disturbances, provided dramatic and useful information as to how styles of caregiving interacted with temperamental patterns to produce pathogenic development.

One further approach has been used by Block and Block (1977). Their study, although it begins just past the infancy stage, is reported here because it is conceptually and methodologically significant. It includes theoretically derived constructs—ego strength and ego resilience—that, by definition, are context responsive. The constructs are carefully measured by a number of procedures in laboratory situations and judges' ratings. Each measurement technique is standardized and assessed for convergent-discriminant validity. The study shows promise for extension into the infancy period.

Summary

The studies in this area have yielded scattered and tentative findings. That is, the strongest continuities were found in those studies with the fewest subjects. Nevertheless, the research suggests that consideration of a cluster of behaviors (e.g., developmental subtest scatter, unusual perceptual sensitivity when combined with high intensity, the "difficult infant" syndrome) merit further examination. Much promise was demonstrated by that study that categorized infants on clusters of behaviors and then examined outcome in terms of transactions of the infant and its environment.

CONCLUSIONS

The task in longitudinal studies is mammoth. The charge is to search for stability in a confusion of theoretical unknowns. The work includes conceptualizing, assessing and integrating individual differences, developmental changes and differential experiences. Previous reviews (Kessen et al., 1970; Sameroff, 1976) have found little evidence that behavior in the first 2 years is predictive to later overt behavior. Even by highlighting positive findings and deemphasizing the overwhelming number of negative findings, we conclude that the statistically established evidence for predictability from infancy is meager and scattered, albeit intriguing.

Theoretical problems obstruct the empirical examination of continuity from infancy in emotional-social functioning. Linear chains of causality are probably not an appropriate model (Sameroff, 1976). The infant does not maintain inborn characteristics as static traits. Kessen et al. (1970) have pointed to the need for better charting of affective-emotional development in all infants as a basis from which to understand individual differences and continuities. Not only the facts of development but the processes of development must be considered. One compelling view holds that development proceeds through a sequence of regular restructurings within and between the infant and his/her environment (Denenberg, 1978; Sameroff, 1976). Emotional-social functioning would then be the outcome of an interactive process in which the infant's characteristics are only one of the multiplicity of factors in the social context of development. Placing both the child's individuality and its environment in a common reciprocal system and assessing the transactions between the child and its environment may explain some of the continuities as well as qualitative shifts that have been found and reveal further stabilities.

There is also a question of whether the appropriate behavioral dimensions for study have yet been found (Emmerich, 1967; Stone et al., 1973). The necessary conceptualizations may have to include more than observable behaviors. To be included may be constructs that propose a difference between latent mechanisms and behavioral expression, and further posit specific modifications of behavioral expression as a function of increasing age of the child as well as demand characteristics of the situation.

The constructs will also need to include the organization of behaviors into feedback systems. These systems would imply and predict a hierarchy of possible behaviors governed by a plan and responsive to situational specificities. (Attachment and ego-resiliency are two such constructs). Finally, considering the directional effects of one behavioral system upon another would help to specify the mutual influences of developing emotional-social systems and cognition.

BIBLIOGRAHY

Ainsworth, M. D. S. The development of infant-mother attachment. In B. M. Caldwell and H. N. Ricciuti (eds.), *Review of Child Development Research*, Vol. 3. Chicago: University of Chicago, 1973.

Ainsworth, M. D. S., and Bell, S. M. Some contemporary patterns of mother-infant interaction in the feeding situation. In J. A. Ambrose (ed.), *Stimulation in Early Infancy*. London: Academic, 1969.

Ainsworth, M. D. S., and Bell, S. M. Mother-infant interaction and the development of competence. In K. J. Connolly and J. S. Bruner (eds.), *The Growth of Competence*. New York: Academic, 1974.

Ainsworth, M. D. S., and Wittig, B. Attachment exploratory behavior of one-year-olds in a strange situation. In B. M. Foss (ed.), *Determinants of Infant Behavior*, Vol. 4. London: Methuen, 1969.

Bayley, N. Consistency and variability in the growth of intelligence from birth to eighteen years. *Journal of Genetic Psychology,* 1949, **75**, 165–196.

Bayley, N. Individual patterns of development. *Child Development,* 1956, **27**, 45–74.

Bayley, N. Consistency of maternal and child behaviors in the Berkeley Growth Study. *Vita Humana,* 1964, **7**, 73–95.

Bayley, N., and Jones, H. E. Environmental correlates of mental and motor development: A cumulative study from infancy to six years. *Child Development,* 1937, **8**, 329–341.

Bell, R. Q. Contributions of human infants to caregiving and social interaction. In M. Lewis and L. A. Rosenblum (eds.), *The Effect of the Infant on Its Caregiver.* New York: Wiley, 1974.

Bell, R. Q. A congenital contribution to emotional response in early infancy and the preschool period. In R. Porter and M. O'Connor (eds.), *Parent-Infant Interaction* (CIBA Foundation Symposium 33). New York: Associated Science, 1975.

Bell, R. Q., Weller, G. M., Waldrop, M. F. Newborn and preschooler: Organization of behavior and relations between periods. *Monographs of the Society for Research in Child Development,* 1971, **36** (1–2, Ser. 142).

Bell, S. M., and Ainsworth, M. D. S. Infant crying and maternal responsiveness. *Child Development,* 1972, **43**, 1171–1190.

Birns, B. Individual differences in human neonates' responses to stimulation. *Child Development,* 1965, **36**, 249–256.

Birns, B., and Golden, M. Prediction of intellectual performance at 3 years from infant tests and personality measures. *Merrill-Palmer Quarterly,* 1972, **18**, 53–58.

Block, J. (In collaboration with N. Haan). *Lives through Time.* Berkeley: Bancroft, 1971.

Block, J. Recognizing the coherence of personality. Unpublished manuscript, 1977.

Block J., and Block, J. H. The developmental continuity of ego control and ego resiliency: Some accomplishments. In L. A. Sroufe (Chm.), The organization of early development and the problems of continuity in adaptation. Symposium presented at the meetings of the Society for Research in Child Development, New Orleans, March 1977.

Bowlby, J. *Attachment and Loss*, Vol. 1. *Attachment.* London: Hogarth, 1969.

Bowlby, J. *Attachment and Loss,* Vol. 2. *Separation.* London: Hogarth, 1973.

Brody, S., and Axelrod, S. *Anxiety and Ego Formation in Infancy.* New York: International Universities, 1970.

Bronson, G. W. The fear of novelty. *Psychological Bulletin,* 1968, **69**, 350–358.

Bronson, G. W. Fear of visual novelty: Developmental patterns in males and females. *Developmental Psychology,* 1969, **2**, 33–40.

Bronson, G. W. Fear of the unfamiliar in human infants. In H. R. Schaffer (ed.), *The Origins of Human Social Relations*. London: Academic, 1971.

Bronson, G. W. Infants' reactions to unfamiliar persons and novel objects. *Monographs of the Society for Research in Child Development*, 1972, **37** (3, Ser. 148).

Bronson, W. C. Early antecedents of emotional expressiveness and reactivity control. *Child Development*, 1966a, **37**, 793–810.

Bronson, W. C., and Pankey, W. B. The evolution of early individual differences in orientation towards peers. In L. A. Sroufe (Chm.), The organization of early development and the problem of continuity in adaptation. Symposium presented at the meetings of The Society for Research in Child Development, New Orleans, March 1977.

Bronson, W. C. Central orientations: A study of behavior organization from childhood to adolescence. *Child Development*, 1966b, **37**, 125–155.

Bronson, W. C. Adult derivatives of emotional expressiveness and reactivity-control: Developmental continuities from childhood to adulthood. *Child Development*, 1967, **38**, 801–817.

Bronson, W. C. Stable patterns of behavior: The significance of enduring orientations for personality development. In J. P. Hill (ed.), *Minnesota Symposia on Child Psychology*, Vol. 2. Minneapolis: University of Minnesota, 1968.

Bronson, W. C. The growth of competence: Issues of conceptualization and measurement. In H. R. Schaffer (ed.), *The Origins of Human Social Relations*. New York: Academic, 1971.

Bronson, W. C. Competence and the growth of personality. In K. J. Connolly and J. S. Bruner (eds.), *The Growth of Competence*. New York: Academic, 1974.

Campbell, S. B. Maternal and infant behavior in normal, high risk, and "difficult" infants. Paper presented at the meetings of the Society for Research in Child Development, New Orleans, March 1977.

Clarke-Stewart, A. Interactions between mothers and their young children: Characteristics and consequences. *Monographs of the Society for Research in Child Development*, 1973, **38** (6–7, Ser. 153).

Denenberg, V. H. Paradigms and paradoxes in the study of behavioral development. In E. B. Thoman (ed.), *The Origins of the Infant's Social Responsiveness*. Hillsdale, N.J.: Erlbaum, 1978.

Eichorn, D. H. The Berkeley longitudinal studies: Continuities and correlates of behavior. *Canadian Journal of Behavioral Sciences*, 1973, **5** (4), 297–320.

Emmerich, W. Stability and change in early personality development. In W. H. Hartup and N. L. Smothergill (eds.), *The Young Child. Reviews of Research*. Washington, D.C.: National Association for the Education of Young Children, 1967.

Engel, M., Nechin, H., and Arkin, A. M. Aspects of mothering: Correlates of the cognitive development of black male infants in the second year of life. In A. Davids (ed.), *Child Personality and Psychopathology: Current Topics*, Vol. 2. New York: Wiley, 1975.

Escalona, S. K. Patterns of infantile experience and the developmental process. *The Psychoanalytic Study of the Child*, Vol. 18. New York: International Universities, 1963.

Escalona, S. K. Some determinants of individual differences. *Transactions of N.Y. Academy of Sciences*, 1965 (Ser. 27), 802–816.

Escalona, S. K. *The Roots of Individuality: Normal Patterns of Development in Infancy*. Chicago: Aldine, 1968.

Escalona, S., and Heider, G. M. *Prediction and Outcome*. Menninger Clinic Monograph Series, No. 14, London: Imago, 1959.

Escalona, S. K., and Leitch, M. Early phases of personality development: A normative study of infant behavior. *Monographs of the Society for Research in Child Development*, 1953, **17** (1, Ser. 54).

Fish, B. The detection of schizophrenia in infancy. *Journal of Nervous and Mental Disease*, 1957, **125**, 1–24.

Fish, B. Longitudinal observations of biological deviations in a schizophrenic infant. *American Journal of Psychiatry*, 1959, **116**, 25–31.

Fish, B. Involvement of the central nervous system in infants with schizophrenia. *Archives of Neurology*, 1960, **2**, 115–121.

Fish, B. The maturation of arousal and attention in the first months of life. *The Journal of the American Academy of Child Psychiatry*, 1963, **2**, 253–270.

Fish, B., and Hagin, R. Visual-motor disorders in infants at risk for schizophrenia. *Archives of General Psychiatry*, 1973, **28**, 900–904.

Fries, M. E. Factors in character development, neuroses, psychoses, and delinquency; A study of pregnancy, lying-in period, and early childhood. *American Journal of Orthopsychiatry*, 1937, **7**, 142–181.

Fries, M. E. Psychosomatic relationships between mother and infant. *Psychosomatic Medicine*, 1944, **6**, 159–162.

Gesell, A. L., and Ames, L. B. Early evidence of individuality in the human infant. *Scientific Monthly*, 1937, **45**, 217–225.

Halverson, C. F. Jr., Moss, H. A., and Jones-Kearns, S. Longitudinal antecedents of preschool social behavior. Paper presented at the meetings of the Society for Research in Child Development, New Orleans, March 1977.

Halverson, C. F., and Waldrop, M. F. The relations between preschool activity and aspects of intellectual and social behavior at age 7½. *Developmental Psychology*, 1976, **12**, 107–112.

Harlow, H. F. The development of affectional patterns in infant monkeys. In B. M. Foss (ed.), *Determinants of Infant Behavior*. New York: Wiley, 1961.

Heider, G. Vulnerability in infants and young children: A pilot study. *Genetic Psychology Monographs*, 1966, **73**, 1–216.

Heinicke, C. The correlates and continuity of task orientation. Unpublished manuscript, 1977.

Heinstein, M. E. Behavioral correlates of breast-bottle regimes under varying parent-infant relationships. *Monographs of the Society for Research in Child Development*, 1963, **28** (4, Ser. 88).

Hoffman, L. W. Early childhood experiences and women's achievement motive. *Journal of Social Issues*, 1972, **28**, 129–155.

Honzik, M. P. Prediction of behavior from birth to maturity. Review of J. Kagan and H. Moss, Birth to maturity: A study in psychological development. *Merrill-Palmer Quarterly*, 1965, **11**, 77–88.

Honzik, M. P. Value and limitations of infant tests: an overview. In M. Lewis (ed.), *Origins of Intelligence. Infancy and Early Childhood*. New York: Plenum, 1976.

Honzik, M. P., Macfarlane, J. M., and Allen, L. The stability of mental test performance between two and eighteen years. *Journal of Experimental Education*, 1948, **17**, 309–324.

Honzik, M. P., and Macfarlane, J. W. Personality development and intellectual functioning from 21 months to 40 years. In L. F. Jarvik, C. Eisdorfer, and J. Blum (eds.), *Intellectual Changes from Childhood Functioning in Adults: Psychological and Biological Aspects*. New York: Springer, 1973.

Hunt, J. McV. Environmental programming to foster competence and prevent mental retardation in infancy. In R. N. Walsh and W. T. Greenough (eds.), *Environments as Therapy for Brain Dysfunction*. New York: Plenum, 1976.

Hunt, J. V., and Eichorn, D. H. Maternal and child behaviors: A review of data from the Berkeley growth study. *Seminars in Psychiatry*, 1972, **4** (4).

Jones, H. E. The longitudinal method in the study of personality. In I. Iscoe and H. Stevenson (eds.), *Personality Development in Children*. Austin: University of Texas, 1960.

Kagan, J. On the meaning of behavior: Illustrations from the infant. *Child Development,* 1969, **40,** 1121–1134.

Kagan, J. *Change and Continuity in Infancy.* New York: Wiley, 1971.

Kagan, J. Discrepancy, temperament, and infant distress. In M. Lewis and L. A. Rosenblum (eds.), *The Origins of Fear.* New York: Wiley, 1974.

Kagan J. Commentary. In T. Zelniker and W. E. Jeffrey. Reflective and impulsive children: Strategies of information processing underlying differences in problem solving. *Monographs of the Society for Research in Child Development,* 1976, **41** (Ser. 168).

Kagan, J., and Klein, R. E. Cross-cultural perspectives on early development. *American Psychologist,* 1973, **28,** 947–961.

Kagan, J., and Moss, H. A. *Birth to Maturity. A Study in Psychological Development.* New York: Wiley, 1962.

Karelitz, S., Fisichelli, V. R., Costa, J., Karelitz, R., and Rosenfeld, C. Relation of crying activity in early infancy to speech and intellectual development at age 3 years. *Child Development,* 1964, **35,** 769–777.

Kessen, W., Haith, M. M., and Salapatek, P. H. Human infancy: A bibliography and guide. In P. H. Mussen (ed.), *Carmichael's Manual of Child Psychology* Vol. I, 3rd Ed. New York: Wiley, 1970.

Korner, A. F. Individual differences at birth: Implications for early experience and later development. *American Journal of Orthopsychiatry,* 1971, **41,** 608–619.

Lapidus, D. R., Kagan, J., and Moore, M. S. A longitudinal study of development from infancy to age 10. Paper presented at the meetings of the Society for Research in Child Development, New Orleans, March 1977.

Lewis, M. The meaning of a response or why researchers in infant behavior should be oriental metaphysicians. *Merrill-Palmer Quarterly,* 1967, **13,** 7–18.

Lewis, M. (ed.) *Origins of Intelligence: Infancy and Early Childhood.* New York: Plenum, 1976.

Livson, N., and Peskin, H. The prediction of adult psychological health in a longitudinal study. *Journal of Abnormal Psychology,* 1967, **72,** 509–518.

Londerville, S. Socialization in toddlers. Paper presented at the meetings of the Society for Research in Child Development, New Orleans, March 1977.

Maccoby, E. E., and Masters, J. C. Attachment and dependency. In P. H. Mussen (ed.), *Carmichael's Manual of Child Psychology,* Vol. II, 3rd Ed. New York: Wiley, 1970.

Macfarlane, J. W. From infancy to adulthood. *Childhood Education,* 1963, **39,** 336–342.

Macfarlane, J. W. Perspectives on personality consistency and change from the guidance study. *Vita Humana,* 1964, **7,** 115–126.

Macfarlane, J. W., Allen, L., and Honzik, M. P. *A Developmental Study of the Behavior Problems of Normal Children between 21 Months and 14 Years.* Berkeley: University of California, 1954.

Main, M. Exploration, play, and cognitive functioning as related to child-mother attachment. Unpublished Ph.D. dissertation, Johns Hopkins University, 1973.

Masters, J., and Wellman, H. Human infant attachment: A procedural critique. *Psychological Bulletin,* 1974, **81,** 218–237.

Moriarty, A. E. Coping patterns of preschool children in response to intelligence tests demands. *Genetic Psychology Monographs,* 1961, **70,** 3–127.

Moss, H. A., and Kagan, J. Report on personality consistency and change from the Fels longitudinal study. *Vita Humana,* 1964, **7,** 127–138.

Moss, H. A., and Robson, K. A. The relation between the amount of time infants spend at various states and the development of visual behavior. *Child Development,* 1970, **41,** 509–517.

Murphy, L. B. Factors in continuity and change in the development of adaptational style in children. *Vita Humana*, 1964, **7**, 96–114.

Murphy, L. B., and Moriarty, A. E. *Vulnerability, Coping, and Growth: From Infancy to Adolescence*. New Haven: Yale University, 1976.

Neilon, P. Shirley's babies after fifteen years. *Pedagogical Seminary and Journal of Genetic Psychology*, 1948, **73**, 175–186.

Rheingold, H. L. The effect of a strange environment on the behavior of infants. In B. M. Foss (ed.), *Determinants of Infant Behavior*, Vol. 4. New York: Wiley, 1969a.

Rheingold, H. L. The social and socializing infant. In D. A. Goslin (ed.), *Handbook of Socialization Theory and Research*. Chicago: Rand McNally, 1969b.

Rutter, M. Psychological development—predictions from infancy. *Journal of Child Psychology and Psychiatry*, 1970, **11**, 49–62.

Rutter, M., Birch, H. G., Thomas, A., and Chess, S. Temperamental characteristics in infancy and the later development of behavioral disorders. *British Journal of Psychiatry*, 1964, **110**, 651–661.

Rutter, M., Korn, S., and Birch, H. G. Genetic and environmental factors in the development of primary reaction patterns. *British Journal of Social and Clinical Psychology*. 1963, **2**, 161–173.

Sameroff, A. J. Early influences on development: Fact or fancy? In S. Chess and A. Thomas (eds.), *Annual Progress in Child Psychiatry and Child Development*. New York: Brunner/Mazel, 1976.

Sameroff, A., and Chandler, M. Reproductive risk and the continum of caretaking casualty. In F. D. Horowitz, E. M. Hetherington, M. Siegel, and S. Scarr-Salapatek (eds.), *Review of Child Development Research*, Vol. 4. Chicago: University of Chicago, 1975.

Schaefer, E. S., and Bayley, N. Consistency of maternal behavior from infancy to preadolescence. *Journal of Abnormal and Social Psychology*, 1960, **61**, 1–6.

Schaefer, E. S., and Bayley, N. Maternal behavior, child behavior, and their intercorrelations from infancy through adolescence. *Monographs of the Society for Research in Child Development*, 1963, **28** (Ser. 87).

Schaefer, E. S., Bell, R. Q., and Bayley, N. Development of a maternal behavior research instrument. *Journal of Genetic Psychology*, 1959, **95**, 83–104.

Schaffer, H. R. Activity level as a constitutional determinant of infantile reaction to deprivation. *Child Development*, 1966, **37**, 595–602.

Schaffer, H. R., and Emerson, P. E. Patterns of response to physical contact in early human development. *Journal of Child Psychology and Psychiatry*, 1964, **5**, 1–13.

Shirley, M. M. *The First Two Years of Life. A Study of Twenty-Five Babies*, Vol. 3. *Personality Manifestations*. Minneapolis: University of Minnesota, 1933.

Sontag, L. W., Baker, C. T., and Nelson, V. L. Mental growth and personality development: A longitudinal study. *Monographs of the Society for Research in Child Development*, 1958, **23** (Ser. 68).

Sroufe, L. A., and Waters, E. Attachment as an organizational construct. *Child Development*, 1977, **48**, 1184–1199.

Stone, L. J., Smith, H. T., and Murphy, L. B. *The Competent Infant: Research and Commentary*. New York: Basic Books, 1973.

Thomas, A., Birch, H. G., Chess, S., and Robbins, L. C. Individuality in responses of children to similar environmental situations. *American Journal of Psychiatry*, 1961, **117**, 798–803.

Thomas, A., Chess, S., Birch, H. G., Hertzig, M. E., and Korn, S. *Behavioral Individuality in Early Childhood*. New York: New York University, 1963.

Thomas, A., Chess, S., and Birch, H. *Temperament and Behavior Disorders in Children*. New York: New York University, 1968.

Tolan, W. J., and Tomasini, L. Mothers of "secure" vs. "insecure" babies differ themselves nine months later. Paper presented at the meetings of the Society for Research in Child Development, New Orleans, March 1977.

Waldrop, M. F., and Halverson, C. F., Jr. Intensive and extensive peer behavior: Longitudinal and cross-sectional analyses. *Child Development,* 1975, **46**, 19–26.

Waters, E., and Sroufe, L. A. The stability of individual differences in attachment. In L. A. Sroufe (Chm.), The organization of early development and the problem of continuity in adaptation. Symposium presented at the meetings of the Society for Research in Child Development, New Orleans, March 1977.

Yang, R. K., and Halverson, C. F., Jr. A study of the "inversion of intensity" between newborn and preschool age behavior. *Child Development,* 1976, **47**, 350–359.

Yarrow, L. J. Personality consistency and change: an overview of some conceptual and methodological issues, *Vita Humana,* 1964, **7**, 67–72.

Yarrow, L. J., Goodwin, M. S., Manheimer, H., and Milowe, I. D. Infancy experiences and cognitive and personality development at ten years. In L. J. Stone, H. T. Smith, and L. B. Murphy (eds.), *The Competent Infant: Research and Commentary*. New York: Basic Books, 1973.

Yarrow, L. J., and Pedersen, F. A. The interplay between cognition and motivation in infancy. In M. Lewis (ed.), *Origins of Intelligence. Infancy and Early Childhood*. New York: Plenum, 1976.

Yarrow, M. R., Campbell, J. D., and Burton, R. V. *Child Rearing: An Inquiry into Research and Methods*. San Francisco: Jossey-Bass, 1968.

CHAPTER 20

The Development of Intellectual Functioning in Infancy and the Prediction of Later IQ

Robert B. McCall

Early attempts to study infant mental development grew out of the testing movement that flowered in the United States during the early 1900s (Brooks and Weinraub, 1976). Several tests of infant mental functioning were created during the late 1920s, and additional instruments have been developed periodically since then. The availability of tests of mental ability for infants as well as for children and adults coupled with the movement of the 1920s and 1930s toward studying development longitudinally were sufficient ingredients to spawn numerous attempts to predict later IQ from infant mental test scores. Implicit in such ventures was the assumption that an individual's "intelligence," however defined, was an attribute possessed from birth which remained fairly constant throughout development and which governed most functions people call mental or intellectual. But, after nearly one-half century of data collection and analysis, the results unequivocally show that scores on instruments of infant mental performance assessed during the first 18 months of life do not predict later IQ to any practical extent.

While Americans were vainly trying to predict later IQ, Piaget (1952) was busy depicting the sequence of abilities that characterizes mental development during the first few years of life. To Piaget, the prediction of later IQ—indeed, individual differences in general—is essentially irrelevant to the primary goal of describing the stages of mental development through which all infants must pass.

This chapter attempts to bring together these heretofore disparate orientations toward the study of mental development in infancy. Much of the pertinent literature was reviewed a few years ago (e.g., Bayley, 1970; McCall, et al., 1972; Rutter., 1970; Starr, 1971; Stott and Ball, 1965; Thomas, 1970) and more recently in Michael Lewis' edited volume, *Origins of Intelligence*. Therefore, this research will only be summarized here, and relatively more emphasis will be invested in stepping back from this literature, assessing its conceptual and methodological implications, and attempting elements of a synthesis which might point toward a comprehensive integrated theory of mental development during the first few years of life.

A FUNDAMENTAL DISTINCTION

The attempt to predict later IQ and the characterization of stages of mental development are two quite different, even potentially independent, pursuits. While they are both focused on continuity and change in mental performance, they pertain to two different realms.

Developmental Function versus Individual Differences

A behavior can increase or decrease in frequency or amount across age, or one behavior can replace, supplement, or grow out of another with development. This is the *developmental function* for a given behavior (Wohlwill, 1973), and it is illustrated in Figure 20–1. Suppose this is a plot of the development of verbal fluency for a hypothetical group of subjects. The heavy line—the group mean over age—is an estimate of the developmental function for verbal fluency. Developmental functions can take a variety of forms (e.g., Flavell, 1972; Van den Daele, 1969). For example, verbal fluency might follow an ogive or S-function, as in Figure 20–1, while Piaget's sensorimotor stages might be represented by a series of curves in which the abilities of each stage are added to or replace those of the previous stage. In any case, the developmental function refers to the amount or frequency of a given attribute across age for an individual or group of individuals.

But change and continuity can also pertain to *individual differences*. That is, does the relative rank-ordering of individual subjects on a given attribute relate to the relative rank ordering of those individuals on the same or another attribute assessed at a subsequent age? Typically, we approach this question by correlating scores at the two ages. In Figure 20–1 the smaller lines (both dashed and solid) around the main developmental function connect scores for individual subjects across age. The more these lines run parallel to one another, the higher the cross-age correlation.

The important point is that consistency and change in developmental function are potentially independent from consistency and change in individual diffeences. Statistically, since the correlation coefficient is independent of the means of the two distributions entering

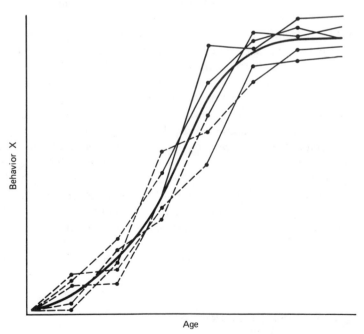

Age

[From McCall et al., 1977. Reprinted by permission.]

Figure 20-1.   Hypothetical plot of the development of behavior X for five subjects illustrating the developmental function (heavier line) and the stability/instability of individual differences (thinner lines).

its calculation, correlations of individual differences across age are potentially independent of consistency and change in developmental function. To emphasize this potential independence, I will follow Emmerich's (1964) convention of using the terms *continuity-discontinuity* to refer to the status of the developmental function, and stability-instability to characterize the relative consistency of individual differences across age.

Maintaining the Distinction

Succinctly, the quest for predictive correlations between infant tests and later IQ is an examination of the stability-instability of individual differences in assessments of mental performance, whereas Piaget's description of sensorimotor stages is a theory of the continuity-discontinuity of developmental function.

I believe progress in the field of mental development has been slowed by the failure to keep this distinction in mind. For example, the statement that 50% of a child's adult intelligence is developed by the age of 4 (Bloom, 1964) reflects the statistical fact that the correlation between IQ at 4 and at 17 years is approximately 0.71. But this claim concerning the development of "intelligence" is based solely on the stability of individual differences and completely ignores the fact that the average child's mental age (i.e., developmental function) will increase several fold during this interval.

The heredity-environment-intelligence controversy is another area in which the distinction between individual differences and developmental function has not always been upheld. Honzik's (1957) interpretation of Skodak and Skeels' (1949) data showed that the correlation of individual differences for measures of intellectual accomplishment between child and biological parent was higher than between child and adoptive rearing parent, a result that has been widely cited as favoring a genetic contribution to intelligence. However, the *average* performance of the children was closer to that of their rearing than to their biological parents, a result that is not often reported and that emphasizes the influence of the rearing environment. These two results do not conflict—the rearing environment had a greater effect on developmental function while genetic dispositions were more strongly reflected in the stability of individual differences.

The above examples illustrate rather clear cases of failing to distinguish between results pertaining to individual differences versus developmental function. But, this contrast can become more subtle. Consider, for instance, individual differences in the developmental function itself. Suppose in Figure 20–1 that the small lines are plots of the developmental functions of each of five subjects. Because these five patterns are not identical, there are individual differences in developmental functions. However, once again, the determinants of individual differences (even individual differences in developmental functions) are potentially different from those controlling the common developmental function of the group—that is, the mean curve (the heavy solid line in Fig. 20–1). This may appear to be hairsplitting, but it has serious implications for understanding mental development in infancy. For example, this distinction means that the variables controlling the sequence in which infants pass through Piaget's six sensorimotor stages may be quite different from those that produce individual differences in the rate at which infants progress from stage to stage. Perhaps the sequence (i.e., developmental function) is under considerable genetic/maturational control, while individual differences in the rate of stage progression might be governed more by nongenetic circumstances. The contrast between individual differences and developmental function is especially salient to issues of genetic influences, since all the commonly used methods to assess heritability are based upon individual differences—even individual differences in developmental functions. No methods deal directly with the heritability of a species-typical developmental function per se.

I believe it is extremely important to maintain this distinction when interpreting research results and formulating conceptions of early mental development. We must not confuse these realms nor glibly generalize results from one to the other. Therefore, the literature on the stability-instability of individual differences in mental performance will be reviewed separately from that on the continuity-discontinuity of developmental function.

STABILITY-INSTABILITY OF INDIVIDUAL DIFFERENCES IN MENTAL PERFORMANCE

Although individual differences in infant test performance are not highly stable across age, such correlations are not precisely zero. How stable are infant test scores from age to age within infancy and how poorly do they correlate with later IQ?

Cross-Age Correlations

Within Infancy

Table 20–1 presents the median correlation observed across a sample of studies of essentially normal infants which reported age-to-age correlations for traditional psychometric assessments of infant performance (i.e., Gesell, Bayley, Cattell, and Griffiths, but not Piaget-based infant tests). The decimal number in each cell indicates the median correlation, and the numbers in parentheses reflect the number of correlations and the number of different studies involved in determining that median value. When more than one correlation was available from the same study or sample, the median correlation from that study was determined first and then used to calculate the median over all studies. This was done so that each sample would carry equal weight in the determination of the summary value. However, it should be noted that some studies contributed to many cells in Table 20–1, whereas other studies are reflected in only one cell.

Observe that the correlations along the major diagonal are the highest in the table and that the *r*'s decline as one moves farther from the diagonal. If this were perfectly true, the correlation matrix would be called a "simplex." It is evident that the correlation matrix for infant test performance within the first 2 years of life approximates a simplex (the correlation between 1–3 months and 4–6 months is slightly higher because the age span is shorter than for the other values in the table). Basically, this simplex-like matrix indicates that the longer the age span, the lower the correlations.

Although these correlations are not zero, they are relatively modest in size, especially when compared with cross-age correlations for IQ during childhood. The correlations for the Stanford-Binet IQ scores from yearly assessments between 9 and 12 years of age for the Fels and Berkeley longitudinal studies are presented in Table 20–2 for comparison. While the correlation between infant tests given only a few months apart between 1 and 2 years of age is approximately 0.46, the median year-to-year correlation for childhood IQ in these two longitudinal studies is 0.90. Although cross-age correlations tend to be higher in the Fels and Berkeley studies than in other samples, the age-to-age stability of indi-

Table 20-1.   Median Correlations Across Studies Between Infant Test Scores at Various Ages During the First 2 Years of Life.[a]

4–6	0.52 (8/6)			
7–12	0.29 (14/6)	0.40 (18/10)		
13–18	0.08 (3/3)	0.39 (6/6)	0.46 (9/6)	
19–24	−0.04 (3/3)	0.32 (6/6)	0.31 (9/6)	0.47 (7/6)
	1–3	4–6	7–12	13–18

Age in Months

Data taken from Anderson (1939); Bayley (1933); Bayley (1954); Birns and Golden (1972); Cattell (1940); Cavanaugh et al. (1957); Elardo et al. (1975); Escalona and Moriarty (1961); Fillmore (1936); Goffeney et al. (1971); Hindley (1965); Honzik et al. (1948); Ireton et al. (1970); Kangas et al. (1966); Klackenberg-Larsson and and Stensson (1968); McCall et al. (1972); Moore (1967); Nelson and Richards (1939); Werner et al. (1968).
[a] Decimal entries indicate median correlation, the numbers in parentheses give the number of different r's and the number of independent studies used to calculate the median. In the case of more than one r per study, the median r for that study was entered into the calculation of the cell median.

Table 20-2.   Age-to-Age Correlations for Childhood IQ from the Fels and Berkeley Longitudinal Studies; Fels (above) and Berkeley (below), Stanford-Binet[a]

Years	9	10	11	12
9		0.90	0.82	0.81
10	0.88		0.90	0.88
11	0.90	0.92		0.90
12	0.82	0.90	0.93	

From McCall, R. B. Toward an epigenetic conception of mental development. In M. Lewis (ed.), *Origins of Intelligence*. New York: Plenum, 1976, 100. Reprinted with permission.
[a] Stanford-Binet age-to-age correlations for the Fels study above the diagonal (from Sontag ct al., 1958, p. 28) and for the Berkeley Growth Study below the diagonal (Bayley, 1949, p. 183).

vidual differences within the first 2 years of life is nevertheless markedly lower than for analogous IQ tests given during childhood.

Predictive Correlations

Given the modest inter-age correlations within the first 2 years of life, it is not surprising that predictions from infancy to later IQ tests are not high. Table 20–3 presents the median correlations between infant tests given during the first 30 months of life and IQ assessed

Table 20-3.   Median Correlations Across Studies Between Infant Test Scores and Childhood IQ

Age of Childhood Test (years)	Age of Infant Test (months)				
	1–6	7–12	13–18	19–30	
8–18	0.06 (6/4)	0.25 (3/3)	0.32 (4/3)	0.49 (34/6)	0.28
5–7	0.09 (6/4)	0.20 (5/4)	0.34 (5/4)	0.39 (13/5)	0.25
3–4	0.21 (16/11)	0.32 (14/12)	0.50 (9/7)	0.59 (15/6)	0.40
	0.12	0.26	0.39	0.49	

Data taken from Anderson (1939); Bayley (1933); Bayley (1954); Birns and Golden (1972); Cattell (1940); Cavanaugh et al. (1957); Elardo et al. (1975); Escalona and Moriarty (1961); Fillmore (1936); Goffeney et al. (1971); Hindley (1965); Honzik, et al. (1948); Ireton et al. (1970); Kangas et al. (1966); Klackenberg-Larsson and Stensson (1968); McCall et al. (1972); Moore (1967); Nelson and Richards (1939); Werner et al. (1968).
[a] Decimal entries indicate median correlation, the numbers in parentheses give the number of different r's and the number of independent studies used to calculate the median. In the case of more than one r per study, the median r for that study was entered into the calculation of the cell median. Marginal values indicate the average of the median r's presented in that row/column.

from 3 to 18 years (this is an expanded revision of Table 20–1; McCall et al., 1972). There are essentially two "main effects" in this table, which are expressed in the marginal correlations. The first and strongest effect is that the correlations increase linearly with the age at which the infant test is administered. The later in infancy the infant test is given, the higher the prediction to childhood IQ. This is summarized in the column marginals at the bottom of the table. The second and weaker trend expressed in the marginal correlations at the right of the table is the fact that prediction is better when the childhood IQ test is given at a younger age. That is, the shorter the developmental period spanned, the higher the correlation. These two trends predict the actual median correlation in each cell within 0.02 on the average and always within 0.04—that is, there is no "interaction" in the table.

Atypical Samples

The above data are from samples of essentially normal infants. However, one of the original purposes of creating the infant tests was to reveal infants who might have severe pathologies. For example, infant tests have been invoked to detect mental retardation (Hunt and Bayley, 1971; Illingworth, 1961), prematurity (Drillien, 1964), schizophrenia (Fish, 1957, 1960; Fish et al., 1965), neonatal apnea (Stechler, 1964), and fetal and neonatal risk factors (see a review by Hunt, 1976). Predictions to later test performance tend to be better for clinical groups and for samples involving children with mental deficiency than for "normal" infants (e.g., Knobloch and Pasamanick, 1960, 1963, 1967). Moreover, a low score on an infant test or a prognosis of risk made by a pediatrician at 20 months of age can predict low levels of mental test performance well into childhood (Werner et al., 1968). Therefore, the infant tests appear to have greater prognostic value for mental subnormality than for normal and superior levels of performance (Erickson, 1968; Illingworth and Birch, 1959; Knobloch et al., 1956).

Factors Affecting Stability Coefficients

Why are the correlations within infancy and from infancy to childhood so modest? Perhaps other factors obscure a higher predictability.

Reliability

One possibility is that the infant tests are not very reliable. Actually, the reliability of infant tests is quite good, especially after 3 to 4 months of age (Werner and Bayley, 1966) when internal consistency (e.g., split-half) and test-retest reliabilities (covering intervals of 1½ to 30 days) are consistently in the high 0.80s and low 0.90s. Therefore, because tests given 3 to 4 months after birth are almost as reliable as childhood IQ assessments, reliability does not appear to be responsible for the low cross-age stability of individual differences.

Sex Differences

Most stability coefficients have been reported for combined-sex samples. Perhaps prediction would be better if the sexes were analyzed separately.

There is some evidence that infant tests predict later IQ better for girls than for boys (McCall et al., 1972; Moore, 1967; Goffeney et al., 1971). The clearest demonstration of possible sex differences was reported by McCall et al. (1972) for the Fels Longitudinal Study, in which Gesell scores at 6, 12, 18, and 24 months of age were correlated with Stanford-Binet IQ at 3½, 6, and 10 years of age separately for girls and boys. The data are contained in the columns labeled "Gesell-IQ" in Table 20–4. Correlations to later IQ occur at younger ages for girls than boys.

Relative to the prediction coefficients from other studies given in Table 20–3, the r's in Table 20–4 are some of the highest correlations in the literature for normal samples, but they may not owe their superiority to the sex differences. For example, some studies have not found sex differences in prediction (e.g., Werner et al., 1968). Moreover, the Gesell test may do a better job in predicting later IQ than other infant tests. McCall et al. (1972), and Honzik (1976) have suggested that the Gesell (and Griffiths) may predict better than other tests because mothers are permitted to report behavior that occurs at home, whereas most other tests score only the behavior displayed in the test situation. The inclusion of maternal reports may make the assessments more accurate, or bright parents likely to have children with higher IQs may be more observant or more eager to report the accomplishments of their offspring.

In any case, while there may be sex differences (as well as differences between infant tests) in the level of prediction from infancy, the correlations are nevertheless not high enough to encourage practical predictions for individual subjects.

Type of Infant Test

Alternative assessment instruments based on Piaget's theory of sensorimotor development have recently been constructed (e.g., Casati and Lézine, 1968; Corman and Escalona, 1969; Uzgiris and Hunt, 1975). Although cross-age correlations and the prediction of later IQ are irrelevant to Piaget's theoretical concerns (Uzgiris, 1976), American psychologists have nevertheless pursued these activities. While there appears to be rather marked consistency in demonstrating clear scalability for the items composing these tests, there does not

Table 20-4. Bivariate and Multiple Correlations of Infant Gesell Score and Parental Education (Ed) with Childhood Stanford-Binet IQ for Different Age Combinations (Fels Data)

Age at Testing		Males			Females		
Infant (Mos)	Child (Yrs)	Gesell-IQ	Ed-IQ	Multiple R	Gesell-IQ	Ed-IQ	Multiple R
6	3½	−0.01	0.36[c]	0.36[a]	0.26[b]	0.40[c]	0.49[c]
6	6	−0.06	0.33[b]	0.33[a]	0.22[a]	0.50[c]	0.56[c]
6	10	0.07	0.47[c]	0.49[c]	0.05	0.42[c]	0.43[b]
12	3½	0.16	0.36[c]	0.39[a]	0.57[c]	0.40[c]	0.68[c]
12	6	0.22[a]	0.33[b]	0.39[a]	0.51[c]	0.50[c]	0.69[c]
12	10	0.12	0.47[c]	0.48[b]	0.37[b]	0.42[c]	0.54[c]
18	3½	0.35[c]	0.36[c]	0.53[c]	0.50[c]	0.40[c]	0.67[c]
18	6	0.28[a]	0.33[b]	0.46[b]	0.43[c]	0.50[c]	0.69[c]
18	10	0.27[a]	0.47[c]	0.57[c]	0.42[b]	0.42[c]	0.63[c]
24	3½	0.58[c]	0.36[c]	0.68[c]	0.74[c]	0.40[c]	0.80[c]
24	6	0.39[c]	0.33[b]	0.51[c]	0.65[c]	0.50[c]	0.77[c]
24	10	0.59[c]	0.47[c]	0.75[c]	0.53[c]	0.42[c]	0.63[c]

From McCall, R. B., Hogarty, P. S., and Hurlburt, N. Transitions in infant sensorimotor development and the prediction of childhood IQ. *American Psychologist,* 1972, 27, 728–748 (Table on page 734). Copyright 1972 by the American Psychological Association. Reprinted by permission.

Gesell and Ed: $r = 0.17, 0.04, 0.10, 0.01$ at 6, 12, 18, 24 months for mates; $-0.07, 0.06, -0.10, 0.15$ for females. N's between 57 and 112.

[a] $p < 0.05$
[b] $p < 0.01$
[c] $p < 0.001$, one-tail.

appear to be any greater stability of individual differences either within infancy or from infancy to later IQ with Piaget-based tests than with traditional assessment procedures (Birns and Golden, 1972; King and Seegmiller, 1973; Kopp et al., 1974; Lewis and McGurk, 1972; Uzgiris, 1973, 1976; Uzgiris and Hunt, 1975; Wachs, 1976).

Socioeconomic Class

Perhaps the prediction of later IQ could be improved by combining the infant test with socioeconomic class in a multiple regression. But such is not the case, at least not until 18 to 24 months of life. For example, parental education or socioeconomic status is typically a better single predictor for normal infants than the infant test during the first 12 to 18 months of life (Hindley and Munro, 1970; Ireton et al., 1970; McCall et al., 1972). This trend is revealed in the correlations between the infant test ("Gesell-IQ") relative to parental education ("Ed-IQ") with childhood IQ at various ages for the Fels sample displayed in Table 20–4. Moreover, multiple correlations combining infant test score and parental SES ("Multiple R" in Table 20–4) do not produce levels of prediction to later childhood IQ that exceed those associated with parental SES alone until 18 to 24 months. Finally, even when infant test score is partialed out, SES predicts later IQ almost as well as when the infant test score is not partialed out (Hindley and Munro, 1970). Therefore, prior to 18 months of life parental education or SES correlates 0.40 to 0.60 with later childhood IQ, and the level of prediction is not substantially increased by considering the infant's own performance on a mental test.

At 18 to 24 months, as seen in Table 20-4, there is some indication that the infant's mental test score and parental SES can be combined to raise the level of association with later IQ over either predictor variable taken alone (McCall et al., 1972). The advantage of multiple prediction begins to appear at 18 months, especially for girls, and by 24 months multiple R's to childhood IQ between 3½ and 10 years are between 0.60 and 0.80.

Specific Items and Abilities

Perhaps the total score on the infant test is too general and includes some items that predict very well but whose contribution to the total score is obscured by the predominance of irrelevant items.

The most celebrated example of this possibility concerns the tendency of infants in the 1st year of life to vocalize during the test situation. Specifically, the age at which an infant first displays certain types of vocalization during the test situation was found to correlate as high as 0.74 with verbal IQ at age 26 years, but this was true only for females (Cameron et al., 1967). Similar results, though less dramatic, have been found by Moore (1967) in London and by McCall et al. (1972) for the Fels data. Other specific clusters of items have been found to predict later IQ as well or better than total test scores, but the level and consistency of prediction does not rival that of the vocalization factor (Anderson, 1939; Fillmore, 1936; McCall et al., 1972, 1977). More generally, there is a tendency for prediction to later IQ to occur when the infant test becomes more verbal in character (McCall et al., 1972, 1977). Therefore, while the items on infant tests appear to have more predictive potential than the total score would indicate, only vocalization in the 1st year of life for females has provided really sizeable predictive coefficients.

Conclusion

Although prediction to later IQ may be increased somewhat at certain ages by separating the sexes, combining the infant test with a measure of socioeconomic class, and/or focusing on specific items rather than the total score, the conclusion that infant tests do not typically reveal highly stable individual differences within the first 18 months or from infancy to later IQ is inescapable.

Some have taken this conclusion to mean that infant tests are not useful assessments and have relatively little validity. Such a position testifies to the American psychologist's penchant for longitudinal prediction as a preferred research strategy and even as a criterion for evaluating the utility and validity of infant assessment techniques. Indeed, one of the first questions developmental psychologists ask about a measurement (and unfortunately, it is often the only question posed) is whether it correlates with some later behavior, and failing this test the measurement is deemed essentially useless or invalid. But, as discussed above, stability of individual differences is only one domain of inquiry; the developmental function is another. Moreover, prediction is a curious criterion for developmentalists to impose on a measure. Since "development" implies change (Wohlwill, 1973), why should those who study change restrict themselves to measurements that yield individual differences that do not change or develop over age? There is wisdom in the claim that a measure can have contemporary validity and utility without predictive significance. Physicians find an infant's birth weight a useful index of contemporary developmental status despite the fact that it does not predict later weight in normal populations. Similarly, infant mental test scores may reflect current status without predictive significance, and it seems counterproductive to deify a criterion that is essentially nondevelopmental in character (McCall, 1977).

The Heritability of Individual Differences in Infant Test Performance

The heritability of mental test behavior has been a topic of some controversy with respect to infant testing as well as child and adult IQs, and portions of this literature have been reviewed recently (Honzik, 1976; McCall, 1976; Scarr-Salapatek, 1976).

It will be helpful to distinguish between the general level at which an infant scores and the pattern of developmental change in score profile over age. If a child has been repeatedly assessed throughout infancy, the average of all the child's scores represents the *general level* of performance. In contrast, if those scores are plotted as a function of age, the developmental profile of spurts and lags in relative performance constitutes the *developmental pattern* (or *profile contour*). Conceptually, general level and pattern are potentially independent of one another (though they may not be so in situ; McCall et al., 1973). For example, infant A could have developmental quotients of 120, 110, 120 at three successive ages, while infant B scores 90, 80, 90. Infants A and B have different levels but the same developmental pattern. Conversely, infant C could produce marks of 90, 100, 110, while infant D records 110, 100, 90. Infants C and D have the same general level but different developmental patterns.

Parent-Child Similarity in General Level

Mothers and fathers each necessarily share 50% of their genes with their children. To what extent are the mental test performances of parents and their children similar?

Casler (1976) studied 151 infants raised in an orphanage who were administered the Gesell at 2, 9, 15, 21, and 27 months. The Binet IQ of their natural mothers was correlated with each of the four Gesell subtests (motor, language, adaptation, personal-social) separately for males and females at each age. There were some significant relationships, despite the fact that the natural mother played no role in rearing these children, but the correlations were modest (maximum $r = 0.31$). There was some association between natural mother's IQ and Gesell performance at 2 months (r's for all subtests for males but only for language for females), but since these r's did not persist to 9 or 15 months they may reflect prenatal variables (nutrition, medical care, etc.) that were correlated both with 2-month performance as well as with maternal IQ. The observation of relations between biological mother's IQ and language performance at 21 and 27 months for girls and personal-social behavior at 21 to 27 months for boys is more favorable to a direct genetic hypothesis. The fact that the kinship correlations were specific to different abilities for the two sexes implies that analyses based either on total scores and/or computed on combined-sex samples, both of which have been predominant strategies in the past, may yield ambiguous results.

Casler's results for adopted children have the advantage of separating environmental factors associated with child-rearing from those associated with genes and prenatal and birth circumstances, but they do so at the cost of an enormous difference in the assessment instruments administered to infants (the Gesell) and parents (the adult Stanford-Binet). An alternative strategy is to correlate infant test performance in the child with the infant test performance of the parent assessed by the same test *when that parent was an infant* ("same age" correlations). This strategy equates assessment instrument and age at testing; but since the parent eventually bears and rears the child, genetic circumstances are not isolated from any salient aspects of child-rearing. The latter disadvantage may not be terribly serious, because one would have to assume that the infant test administered to the parent as an infant correlates with later child-rearing practices. Considering the low correlations between infant test scores and later IQ as well as between infant scores and parent education and socioeconomic class (McCall et al., 1972), this assumption may not be implausible.

Table 20–5 presents the parent-child correlations in mental performance from the Berkeley Growth Study (top of table; Eichorn, 1969) and from the Fels Longitudinal Study (bottom of table; McCall et al., 1973). In the column labeled "Same Age" appear the correlations between parent assessed as an infant with essentially the same test as was administered to the infant at the age specified. Therefore, the figure −0.31 reflects the correlation between the parent's California Preschool score (the precursor of the Bayley) assessed when that future parent was 6 months of age with his or her child's 6-month Bayley score. The column at the right, "Parent at Age 17," gives the correlation between the parent's Stanford-Binet score assessed at 17 years of age with the child's Bayley infant test at each of the five ages. These data indicate essentially no relationship during the first 2 years of life for either the same-age or parent-at-age-17 correlations, despite the fact that these parents not only contributed half the child's genes but also reared these children. Even at 24 and 36 months, an age period when correlations between parent education or socioeconomic status and child test performance first begin to appear (McCall et al., 1972), the correlations are modest.

Same-age and adult-parent correlations with child IQ scores from the Fels Longitudinal Study are given at the bottom of Table 20–5. These data are for Stanford-Binet performance in both parent and child assessed during childhood (e.g., 28–126 months), not infancy. It is well known that the contemporary correlation between parent education and IQ approaches asymptote during this period (Honzik, 1957; Jensen, 1969, McCall et al., 1972), and the correlations between parent-as-an-adult and child Binet IQ performance generally hover around the theoretical genetic maximum of 0.50. However, the same-age correlations are considerably smaller.

Table 20-5. Parent-Child Correlations for Mental Performance from the Berkeley Growth and Fels Studies

Age (Months)	Same Age	Parent at Age 17
Infancy[a]		
6	−0.21	−0.05
12	−0.06	0.03
18	0.04	−0.05
24	0.28	0.13
36	0.29	0.35
Childhood (28–126 Months)[b]		
mother-daughter	0.38	0.53
mother-son	0.04	0.31
father-daughter	0.14	0.45
father-son	0.22	0.57

[a]Bayley scores in infancy, Stanford-Binet scores in adulthood, Berkeley Growth Study, Eichorn (1969).
[b]Stanford-Binet scores, Fels Longitudinal Study, McCall et al. (1973).

In sum, these data do not reveal a substantial genetic influence on individual differences in parent-child pairs in mental test performance prior to the age of 2, either when the parent is assessed as an adult with the Binet or as an infant with essentially the same test as was given the child. Parent-infant correlations are substantially smaller than parent-child r's. Moreover, in childhood when the adult parent-child IQ correlation is known to be approximately 0.50–0.60, the same-age, same-test parent-child correlations run between 0.04 and 0.38, presumably indicating that environmental factors enhance adult-parent and/or diminish same-age parent-child relationships.

Sibling Similarity in General Level

On the average, siblings share one-half their genes, and therefore might be expected to show some similarity in individual differences in mental test performance during infancy under a genetic hypothesis. The available data are skimpy but consistent in suggesting only modest sibling relationships. For example, McCall (1972a) found the similarity in general level for Gesell performance averaged over 6- and 12-month assessments to be 0.24 for a sample of 142 sibling pairs. When general level reflected the average of performance at 6, 12, 18, and 24 months, the sibling similarity was 0.40. The higher value presumably reflects the greater stability of a mean based on four rather than on two assessments. Nichols and Broman (1974) correlated sibling performance on the Bayley at 8 months of age for Blacks and whites as well as same- and opposite-sex sibling pairs. The correlations ranged between 0.16 and 0.22. Therefore, same-age sibling correlations in the first 2 years of life are approximately 0.20 for a single assessment, although the similarity for general level can increase if tests given during the first 2 years of life are averaged. Since the median correlation for siblings reared together on a single child or adult IQ testing is 0.55 (Jensen, 1969), sibling correlations are considerably smaller for infant tests than for child or adult IQ.

Similarity of Twins in General Level

The most direct approach to the demonstration of genetic similarity in mental test performance typically employs twins. In one of the first reports, Freedman and Keller (1963) demonstrated greater similarity in Bayley mental and motor performance over monthly assessments during the 1st year for identical (monozygotic, MZ) than for fraternal (dizygotic, DZ) twins. Werner (1973) found concordance within a pair was highest for vegetative functions (feeding, sleeping behaviors), somewhat less for mental and motor behaviors, and least for assessments of extraversion/intraversion. However, there were only five MZs and four DZs (and three undetermined) pairs in her sample.

Two investigators attempted to assess the heritability of specific behaviors reflected on infant tests during the first 3 years. Matheny (1975) selected 20 items from the Bayley Infant Scale that were judged comparable to classes of behaviors typically assessed on Piaget-inspired developmental scales (e.g., prehension, object permanence, means/ends, space, and imitation). Greater within-pair concordance for MZ versus DZ twins from the Louisville Twin Study was found for some of these scales at some ages, but the percent of difference between MZ and DZ within-pair concordance was not very large. For example, MZs were 13.7% more concordant on prehension at 3 to 6 months, 16.4% on object permanence at 9 months, 12.5% for sound localization at 3 months, and 13.3% on imitation at 12 months. Over all 20 items the average concordance was 0.818 for MZs versus 0.711 for DZs, a difference of 10.8% relative to the difference of 50% in genetic overlap within pairs of MZs versus DZs.

Wilson and his colleagues have concluded from several studies of the Louisville Twin sample that infant mental development as reflected on the Bayley Infant Scale is largely a product of the child's "genetic blueprint." A summary of these data (Wilson, 1974; Wilson and Harpring, 1972) is presented in Table 20-6. The within-pair correlations calculated separately for MZs and DZs are at the left; the maximum heritability, estimated by taking two times the difference between the MZ and DZ correlations (Falconer, 1960), is at the right. This maximum estimate of heritability assumes that *all* differences between the within-pair similarity of MZ versus DZ pairs, regardless of the actual determinants, are associated with genetic circumstances. Since this is a debatable assumption when assessing the heritability of behavioral characteristics, these data should be treated as estimates of the upper limit of heritability. For the present discussion we will concentrate on the column labeled "Single Age," which reflects the maximum heritability assessed separately at each of the ages listed in the table.

The maximum heritability estimates at single ages show rather unsystematic variation between 3 and 72 months, and they average approximately 0.32 (taking the larger of the two values at 18 and 24 months). Interestingly, under certain assumptions the heritability of a characteristic cannot exceed two times the sibling correlation (Falconer, 1960); and because single-age sibling correlations are approximately 0.20, the estimated maximum heritability derived from siblings is 0.40, approximately that found for twins. Such a value is considerably smaller than the heritability of approximately 0.70 attributable to IQ scores for children and adults (Jensen, 1969). Moreover, because these maximum heritability estimates of 0.30 to 0.40 for infants accord all differential similarity within pairs to genetic circumstances, such data do not compel the conclusion that performance on a mental assessment during the first few years of life is mostly governed by genetic circumstances.

Table 20-6. Within-Pair Correlations and Maximum Heritabilities for General Level and Profile Contour from 3 Months to 6 Years for the Louisville Twin Study

Age (Months)	Within-Pair r's		Maximum Heritability	
	MZ	DZ	Single age	Developmental pattern
3[a]	0.84	0.67	.34	
6[a]	0.82	0.74	.16	
9[a]	0.81	0.69	.24	} 48[a]
12[a]	0.82	0.61	.42	} 14[a]
18	0.76[a]; 0.82[b]	0.72[a]; 0.65[b]	.08[a]; .34[b]	} 56[b]
24	0.87[a]; 0.82[b]	0.75[a]; 0.71[b]	.24[a]; .22[b]	
36[b]	0.89	0.79	.20	} 60[a]
48[b]	0.81	0.64	.34	} 82[b]
60[b]	0.81	0.62	.38	} 10[b]
72	0.85	0.59	.52	

[a] Data from Wilson and Harpring (1972).
[b] Data from Wilson (1974).

Developmental Pattern

Since performance on one test or the average score on several tests is potentially independent of the pattern of scores over age, one can also inquire whether individual differences
in the developmental pattern of test scores across age show heritability. McCall (McCall,
1970, 1972a, b; McCall et al., 1973) has compared the developmental profiles of mental
test performance of siblings versus matched unrelated control pairs at 6 and 12 months, 18
and 24 months, 6 to 24 months, 42 to 66 months, 74 to 132 months, and 42 to 132
months. In no case was the developmental pattern of rises and falls in mental test performance more similar among siblings than among unrelated children either matched for sex,
year of birth, and parental education or matched only for sex and year of birth. For
example, the intraclass correlation for profile contour of scores at 6, 12, 18, and 24
months was 0.11 for siblings and 0.06 for matched, unrelated control children. Since there
was greater similarity among siblings than matched unrelated pairs for general level of
performance (0.40 vs. −0.06), the sibling data seem to indicate greater genetic influence
on general level than on developmental pattern.

The Louisville Twin Study appears to give the opposite impression. The rightmost
column of Table 20-6 presents the maximum heritability estimates for developmental
pattern for various combinations of ages. Wilson prefers to analyze subsets of adjacent
ages rather than larger age spans in order to maximize the number of subjects for any
single comparison, choosing not to fill in missing data, as does McCall. One can see that
maximum heritability estimates vary considerably depending on the age span selected.
Thus, maximum heritability estimates for changes between 12 and 18 months and between
60 and 72 months are quite small, whereas the estimate for developmental pattern between
36 and 72 months is rather substantial.

Issues of Interpretation

How should these correlations be interpreted? Both Wilson's methodological approach
(McCall, 1972b; McCall et al., 1973; see Wilson's rebuttal, 1973) and conclusions
(McCall, 1976b; McCall et al., 1973; Scarr-Salapatek, 1976; Wachs, 1972) have been
debated. Ignoring a number of the more technical issues, a few points merit discussion.
Wilson prefers not to publish heritability estimates. The estimation of heritability makes
several assumptions about which there is considerable debate, and Wilson feels that
simple within-pair correlations are more straightforward. However, claims for heritability
rest on the difference between the within-pair correlations for MZs versus DZs, and not
upon the absolute size of either of these correlations alone. Of course, Wilson demonstrates that there is a significant difference between MZs and DZs, but significance tests do
not provide information on the magnitude of the genetic effect which is the issue being
debated. Heritability estimates do accomplish this purpose.

If the correlations within pairs for MZs and DZs predominantly reflect the genetic
similarity of these individuals, then why is it that the correlations for DZ twins are so
much higher than for nontwin siblings and for parent-child pairs, the members of which
also share 50% of their genes? Whereas Wilson finds an average correlation of 0.68 for
DZ twins across ages (from Table 20-6), data reviewed above indicate sibling correlations
of approximately 0.20 for a single assessment. Parent-child correlations are essentially
zero until age 2; after age 2 they are typically less than 0.30 when measured at the same

age and approximately 0.50 when the parent is assessed as an adult. Even the theoretical genetic maximum for DZs should be only 0.50, not 0.68. If genetics were the only contributor, within-pair similarity should be roughly equivalent for DZs, nontwin siblings, and parent-child pairs. From this standpoint, the sibling and parent-child correlations appear too low, which suggests that nongenetic factors are contributing to within-pair differences. In contrast, the DZ correlations appear too high, suggesting that nongenetic factors are contributing to their similarity. Indeed, some of the same environmental aspects could be cited as potential factors in both possibilities—the greater similarity of prenatal environment of twins relative to siblings, the fact that twins are tested on the same or nearly the same day whereas siblings may be tested years apart, and so on. In any case, the correlations for DZ twins in the Louisville Twin Study suggest the operation of environmental circumstances that promote within-pair similarity, perhaps for both DZs and MZs.

Another factor in interpreting the MZ-DZ results pertains to the fact that severe retardation is both more frequent and more likely concordant within MZ twin pairs than within DZ twins. Nichols and Broman (1974) showed that when twin pairs having at least one severely retarded member were eliminated from the Collaborative Perinatal Study sample, the within-pair correlation at 8 months for MZs was reduced from 0.84 (which was comparable to Wilson's MZ correlation of 0.81) to 0.55. In contrast, the within-pair correlation for DZ twins was unchanged at 0.55 (somewhat lower than Wilson's 0.69 at 9 months). Therefore, when pairs having severe retardation were eliminated, the within-pair correlation for MZs was identical to that of DZs—heritability was zero! Wilson and Matheny (1976) subsequently eliminated subject pairs having severe retardation from the Louisville sample but found MZs to remain more similar than DZ twins (0.81 vs. 0.62).

Conclusions

With respect to single-age assessments, there appears to be some evidence for greater similarity in infant test score as a function of genetic similarity, but even maximum estimates of heritability based on MZ versus DZ twins, siblings, and parent-child pairs do not exceed approximately 0.44 (the maximum of maximum estimates). Therefore, the heritability for single infant test scores is considerably less than the heritability for child and adult IQ performance. When individual differences in developmental profile contour are considered, the data are less convergent, there being no evidence for heritability from sibling comparisons but positive evidence from MZ versus DZ twin comparisons. However, the estimate of heritability for developmental pattern depends markedly on the age span involved, and estimates can range from as low as 0.10 to as high as 0.82. Moreover, twins may be more similar to one another than a strictly genetic position would prescribe, thus implicating nongenetic circumstances in determining both general level and developmental pattern.

Environmental Factors in Infant Test Performance

Most research relating environmental factors to infant test performance has relied on global indices of parental education and socioeconomic status, but recently there have been attempts to relate more specific attributes of the home and parental behavior to contemporary as well as future mental test performance.

SES and Later IQ

As indicated above, SES predicts later IQ better than do the infant tests during the first 18 months of life; thereafter, not only does the infant test begin to predict but it apparently reflects variability not directly associated with SES because the multiple correlations of infant test and SES exceed the coefficients for either variable alone (Ireton et al., 1970; Hindley and Munro, 1970; McCall et al., 1972). There is a transition of some sort beginning at 18 to 24 months.

Although social class does not appear to combine with infant test performance to predict later IQ among essentially normal samples in the first 18 months of life, these two factors have a joint salience in predicting later IQ in risk populations. Specifically, infants who score quite low on the test in the 1st year of life can apparently recover if they come from middle- and upper-class homes. However, an infant who scores very poorly during the 1st year of life and who also resides in an impoverished home is far more likely to remain below average some years later (Drillien, 1964; Knobloch and Pasamanick, 1967; Sameroff and Chandler, 1975; Scarr-Salapatek and Williams, 1973; Werner et al., 1967; Willerman et al., 1970). The assumption is that the potential debilitation produced by prematurity and by other adverse pre- and perinatal circumstances can be overcome in a matter of 1 to 3 years through commerce with an adequate or rich environment, but if that environment is not advantageous the deleterious effects may persist through childhood.

SES and Contemporary Infant Test Performance

Two recent reviews of the literature on the correlation between parental socioeconomic status and contemporary mental test performance (Golden & Birns, 1976; McCall et al., 1972) agree that there is no global relationship until 18 to 24 months (Bayley, 1933; Golden and Birns, 1968; Golden et al., 1971; Honzik, 1963; Kagan & Moss, 1959; MacRae, 1955; Willerman et al., 1970). The results across a wide range of literature indicate essentially zero-order correlations prior to 18 months, the beginning of modest correlations (e.g., 0.20–0.30) between 18 and 24 months, followed by a rather sharp rise to asymptotic levels (e.g., approximately 0.50) shortly thereafter. Studies differ with respect to the age at which the relationship spurts and whether the relationship occurs earlier for girls than for boys. Again, there is a transition point beginning at approximately 18 to 24 months.

Parental education and socioeconomic status are frequently taken as gross indices of environmental variables; but they also correlate with genetic and prenatal biological factors. For example, Beckwith (1971) observed no significant relationship between rearing mothers' socioeconomic status and Cattell test performance for 8.7- and 10-month infants adopted at 5 to 10 days of life, but she did find a relationship for biological mother's socioeconomic status (though it is unlikely that these two associations were significantly different from one another). More impressive, however, is Honzik's (1957) finding that the correlation between biological mothers' intellectual achievement and adopted children's IQ performance increased between 2 and 5 years of age in the same manner as the correlation between rearing parents' SES and infant/childhood test performance. Therefore, it is not clear what functional variables are implied by the gross indices of parental education and SES, but genetic and prenatal factors cannot be glibly dismissed as was once commonplace. Moreover, whatever causal factors accompany these indices, they begin to influence individual differences in infant test performance at approximately

18 to 24 months, the age at which symbolic relational thought and language beyond simple vocabulary emerge.

Information Available in the Home

Recently, several investigators have probed more deeply into the specific, perhaps functional, attributes of the environment in search of correlates of individual differences in mental test performance that might suggest developmental processes and causal relations. One common finding suggests a relationship between the amount and variety of objects and experiences available in the home—the amount of information in the infant's environment—and contemporary and future test performance. For example, the visual experiences, internal decor, and colorfulness of the home was related to 7-month Uzgiris-Hunt test (Piaget) performance (Wachs et al., 1971); and the presence of a variety of play objects, especially responsive toys, correlated with contemporary and future test performance from 5 months to 3 years of age (Baldwin et al., 1945; Bradley and Caldwell, 1976; Elardo et al., 1975; Moore, 1968; Wachs, 1976; Yarrow et al., 1972). Of course, the infant and toddler must be able to explore this varied environment, so it is not surprising to find correlates between "freedom to explore" and test performance (Baldwin et al., 1945; Beckwith, 1971; Wachs, 1976).

However, the infant must not be inundated with raw stimulation—there needs to be a moderate signal-to-noise ratio. Several investigators (Bradley and Caldwell, 1976; Elardo et al., 1975; Wachs, 1976; Wachs et al., 1971) noted negative relationships between Bayley and Uzgiris-Hunt test performance on the one hand and intense auditory and social stimulation as well as lack of orderliness of the home on the other. Presumably, over-stimulation implies a low signal-to-noise ratio that renders salient stimuli indistinct from ambient levels and may even lead to the infant "tuning out" the environment in a manner analogous to "learned helplessness."

Verbal Model and Encouragement

While the variety of toys and experiences relates to test performance throughout infancy, one might expect ratings of the adequacy of verbal stimulation and the verbal responsivity of the parent to display their highest correlations with mental test performance in the 2nd year, especially the 18-to-24-month period when the child and the mental tests become more verbal in nature. Several reports are consistent with this hypothesis (Beckwith, 1971; Elardo et al., 1975; Wachs, 1976; Wachs et al., 1971), and Beckwith's observations were made on adopted infants which presumably minimizes covariation between maternal verbal skill and her genetic contribution to the infant.

Social Factors

Another theme running through this literature is the relevance of the social relationship between parent and child, although the nature of the social factor seems to be slightly different for males and females. Stimulated by Mueller and Lucas' (1976) cognitive analysis of peer-peer relations, McCall (McCall, 1976; McCall et al., 1972; McCall et al., 1977) has viewed the presence of social factors in mental development as reasonable, not only because enriching experiences are provided by parents to a helpless infant but because the fundamental transition between 1 and 3 years of life involves the decentering of thought, its release from the bondage of action, and its expression in language to serve social functions.

Several studies implicate the closeness of parent-child relations in individual differences in mental performance, and some (but not all) report higher correlations for males. For example, at Fels, Baldwin et al. (1945) found changes in Gesell performance during infancy related to the emotional warmth of, and the acceleratory methods used by, the parents. Bayley and Schaefer (1964) observed that infant males in the Berkeley Growth Study whose mothers evaluated them positively, expressed affection, and permitted some degree of autonomy were described as happy, positive, and calm infants who earned below-average scores on the Bayley during the 1st year but jumped to rather high IQs later. Somewhat comparable findings emerged from the Berkeley Child Guidance Study sample for which Honzik (1967, 1972) reports that the rating of the closeness of the mother-son relationship at 21 months displayed increasingly higher levels of correlation with boys' mental test scores (e.g., $r = 0.48$ for IQ at 9 years), and there was still a relationship with IQ at 40 years of age (Honzik, 1972). Similarly, in London, Moore (1968) found the correlation between the emotional atmosphere of the home and the example and encouragement of the parent to display increasing correlations with IQ between 3 and 8 years.

Yarrow et al. (1972) studied upper-middle-class Black 5-month infants and related a priori clusters of Bayley items to an assessment of the social and physical aspects of the home environment. The variety of social stimulation (e.g., play, encouragement of motor acts, range of affect displayed by parents, and number of different physical settings in which social relations occurred) had the most correlates with Bayley item clusters (r's as high as 0.48). The social stimulation variables correlated most highly with Bayley items in which the infant reached for objects (a cluster which Yarrow et al. termed "goal orientation") and with items indicating Piagetian secondary circular responses.

Using a new inventory of home stimulation now called HOME, Caldwell et al. (1966) and Elardo et al. (1975) rated "maternal involvement" including the sociability and affection of the parent. At 12 months, this variable correlated 0.22 with contemporary Bayley performance but 0.47 with 3-year Binet. Maternal involvement at 24 months correlated O.55 with 3-year Binet. Further, children who recorded at least 21-point increases in test performance between 6 months and 3 years had more involved mothers than did children who either decreased or remained approximately the same in test performance (Bradley and Caldwell, 1976). Wachs (1976) modified the HOME scale and presented results for a highly diverse sample of 15- to 24-month infants that apparently limit the benefits of social experience. Negative correlations were observed between too many people in the environment and social overstimulation on the one hand and scores on the Uzgiris-Hunt subscales of Schemes for Relating Objects and Objects in Space on the other.

Two studies of adoptive children are important for their presumed ability to separate the effects of experience from genetic contributions. Beckwith (1971) investigated correlates of Cattell performance at 8.7 and 10 months of age in white, middle-class infants adopted at 5 to 10 days of age. Once again, the social experience of infants (e.g., the number of visitors, the number of adult playmates, the number of times taken out, etc.) was the only variable to correlate with Cattell performance ($r = 0.57$). Yarrow (1963) studied 40 adopted children administered the Cattell at 6 months and found that the highest correlations with mental test performance were for ratings of stimulus adaptation ($r = 0.85$), achievement stimulation ($r = 0.72$), and social stimulation ($r = 0.65$). Moreover, several of these 6-month ratings correlated with 10-year WISC scores, but mainly for males (Yarrow et al., 1973).

These data are rather consistent in implicating the closeness of the relationship, the presence of affection, and the degree of encouragement for intellectual accomplishment as correlates of individual differences in concurrent and future mental test performance, especially for males. In the case of females, the social factor tends to be mediated by the child's own social behavior. For example, Bayley and Schaefer (1964) correlated both child and maternal behaviors with the mental test scores of the Berkeley Growth Study subjects between 10 and 36 months. Socially responsive, active, happy, and positively responding girls had high concurrent mental test scores, and the mothers of high-scoring girls were described as emotionally involved, affectionate, sociable, and reluctant to use punishment and fear as disciplinary tactics. Analyzing the individual items of the mental tests, McCall et al. (1977) observed more cross-age consistency in social dispositions for females than for males. Girls who were either affable, extroverted, and frolicky or who were more serious but attentive, obedient, and imitative of the examiner tended to have higher test scores. Stability of individual differences in social behavior between 1 and 3 years has also been described by Wilson et al. (1971) and Werner (1973) for twins, and by Emmerich (1964) for nontwin nursery school children, although no major sex differences were emphasized by these investigators.

Matheny et al. (1974) noted that higher scoring twin females between 6 and 24 months were more oriented to the examiner, cooperative, and positive in emotional tone, but these traits did not predict later test scores as they did in the Berkeley protocols. Finally, taking social pleasure in the tasks of the mental exam at 18 and 24 months was correlated with concurrent performance as well as 3-year Binet scores, the latter predictive correlation remaining even after contemporary test performance was partialed out (Birns and Golden, 1972).

The above data (see also Haviland, 1976; Yarrow and Pedersen, 1976) seem persuasive that social/emotional/personality factors are related to mental test performance, especially between 1 and 3 years of age. While maternal involvement, affection, and encouragement in intellectual pursuits is associated with high scores for males, these maternal characteristics are meshed with the child's own affable, extroverted, or socially attentive dispositions in predicting contemporary and future mental test performance for girls. The adoption studies, assuming no selective matching between biological and adoptive parent, suggest that some of these factors are not epiphenomena of genetic similarity between parent and child, but it is still possible that these social variables are mediated by alternative factors and actually play no significant causal role in mental development (see below).

Information and Influencing

There appear to be two major themes underlying the environmental correlates of individual differences in mental performance reviewed above. The first reflects the amount and variety of stimulus information available to the infant as well as its discriminability. This class of variables includes the amount and variety of stimulus events, the varied experiences that accompany social relations, the provision of appropriate and varied play materials, the freedom to explore the environment, and the orderliness of the physical and temporal environment. The second theme relates to the child's potential for influencing the environment, both inanimate and animate. Thus, there are relationships with the number of responsive toys, the involvement of the parent with the child, and the responsivity of the parent. Moreover, the verbal character of the home environment, which serves both the information and influencing themes, begins to relate to mental test performance between 15 and 24 months of age—the same age that the child becomes verbal, the test becomes verbal, the child's test scores relate to general measures of socioeconomic class, and the child's test scores predict later IQ.

Methodological Caution

Every researcher is well aware that correlation does not necessarily demonstrate causation—two variables can be functionally unrelated but nevertheless correlated, perhaps through their relationship with a third variable. But the temptation to infer causality is strong, especially when a good rationale or theory exists to explain or justify a causal relation. If upper-middle-class parents keep their 1-year-old's shoes highly polished while lower-class parents do not, we do not suspect that highly polished shoes at 1 year causes a child to score higher on the Stanford-Binet at 3 years despite the correlation between them. However, if upper-middle-class parents provide more varied and responsive toys, a higher signal-to-noise ratio, a more intimate social relationship with their children, and a better verbal model, we are more easily seduced into believing that these attributes promote—that is, causally influence—intellectual development and produce higher childhood IQs. However, it is just as possible for a third variable to mediate these relationships as it is for the highly polished shoe example. For instance, the third variable could be genes—parents who have genes for high IQ may be more likely to provide such experiences for their youngsters as well as produce children with high IQs—the early experiences might be functionally irrelevant to childhood IQ. Presumably, the studies of adopted children (Beckwith, 1971; Yarrow, 1963; Yarrow et al., 1973) minimize this possibility for the specific variables examined.

Consider another possibility. Suppose parental language modeling and encouragement have a causal impact on 2- to 5-year IQ; however, parents who will be good language models later may also buy their 6- to 18-month infants a great variety of responsive toys, live in homes with high signal-to-noise ratios, and develop more intimate social relations with their children. These latter variables will show predictive relations to later IQ, but actually they might have no causal sway on childhood performance.

Such an argument is not totally implausible. First, one would expect many variables that correlate with contemporary as well as subsequent IQ to be intercorrelated to a certain extent. Second, several studies recounted above reveal that parental behavior displayed at 6 or 12 months actually correlates more highly with mental test performance 1 and 2 years later than with contemporary infant test performance. This could be interpreted as a genuine sleeper effect; on the other hand, the correlation between biological parents' intellectual behavior and their adopted child's IQ also increases with age, presumably signifying an increasing genetic relationship which may underlie both the nonadopted child's higher IQ performance as well as their natural/rearing parents' early attempts at stimulation. Similarly, low contemporary, but high predictive correlations may also suggest that a third variable, a parental behavior highly related to early stimulation but not to early test performance, is actually producing higher childhood IQ.

It will not be easy to eliminate all third-variable possibilities. For example, a cross-lag design might be explored. Suppose the "forward" correlation between parental behavior at 6 months and IQ at age 3 years is greater than the "backward" correlation between that same parental behavior at 3 years and mental test performance at 6 months. The inference would be that early parental behavior may have caused later IQ because the correlation in that direction is higher than in the reverse direction. Unfortunately, the interpretation of cross-lag results depends on having relatively equivalent test-retest correlations for each of the two variables—parental behavior and mental test performance (Wohlwill, 1973). Since 6-month mental test score does not correlate highly with IQ at 3 years, the interpretation of the cross-lag correlation in this case would require a similarly low correlation between the parental behaviors.

This entire section on environmental factors has been rooted in the stability of individual differences, an approach that completely ignores changes in the developmental function. That is, all children improve enormously in their mental ability between 6 months and 3 years, for example, yet the methodological strategies described above only consider a child's relative deviation from the group mean at 6 months and 3 years (and the same can be said with respect to the parent behavior). All the skills and information acquired by all children during this interval are neglected by this approach. Relying solely on the individual-difference orientation is rather like asking why one giant sequoia tree is 30 feet taller than another while ignoring how both came to be over 300 feet tall in the first place.

CONTINUITY AND DISCONTINUITY IN DEVELOPMENTAL FUNCTION

Up to this point, only evidence regarding the stability of individual differences has been reviewed; the nature of the developmental function has not been discussed. Given the concept of a constant "intelligence" and the convenient practice of scaling intelligence test scores to have the same mean and standard deviation at every age, it was hardly necessary to ask about increases or decreases in "amount of intelligence." Mental age has largely been ignored in favor of IQ. I feel it is time to pay more attention to the issue of developmental function in early mental development and to integrate it with the individual difference literature.

The leading student of the developmental function for mental skills in infancy is Jean Piaget. His theory of sensorimotor development is widely known through his own writings (e.g., Piaget, 1952) and those of others (e.g., Flavell, 1963; Ginsburg and Opper, 1969; Hunt, 1961). It will not be reviewed again here. Rather, this section will describe more recent research on the developmental function that has been inspired by or interpreted in the light of Piaget's theory.

Instability as a Clue to Discontinuity

Until recently, the empirical approach to the study of mental development taken by most American psychologists has been irrelevant to the position held by the leading theoretical spokesman—Piaget. To Piaget, correlations between mental performance at one age and performance at another are simply irrelevant to the major developmental activity transpiring during infancy. This is because Piaget emphasizes the developmental function—the ontogenetic sequence in which various skills emerge in essentially all members of the species. He is not particularly concerned with individual differences about that species-typical developmental function. But, one could hypothesize that individual differences should be more stable within a stage than across a stage boundary. That is, while individual differences and developmental function are potentially independent, in actuality, ages of relative instability in individual differences may also signify a discontinuity in the developmental function.

Points of Instability in the Berkeley Growth Study

Although the data were not collected for this purpose, McCall et al. (1977) examined the pattern of cross-age correlations among the first principal components at each of 25 ages from 1 month to 5 years for the Berkeley Growth Study subjects who were given the California First Year and California Pre-school tests (the forerunners of the Bayley). The pattern of cross-age correlations revealed relative breaks in the stability of individual differences at 8, 13, and 21 months of age. That is, instead of there being a progressive increase and consistency in the cross-age correlations from one age to the next, occasional dips in the size of the cross-age correlation occurred for both males and females at approximately the same ages—8, 13, and 21 months.

Not only was the stability of individual differences interrupted but there were concurrent transformations in the fundamental character of the developmental function (i.e., the item composition of the first principal components) at these same ages. This joint occurrence of instability and discontinuity at 8, 13, and 21 months was interpreted to define a stage boundary, and the age of onset and the underlying cognitive feature of the resulting four stages was remarkably similar to those derived by Uzgiris (1976) using Piaget-inspired test items, a different sample, a contrasting conceptual orientation, and a different methodology.

Corroboration Across Method and Sample

Having formulated the hypothesis that stages are delimited at approximately 8, 13, and 21 months, other methods and other data were examined to see if breaks in the stability pattern could be observed at these same points. Bayley's (1933) cross-age correlations for the total score on the California tests (as opposed to the first principal component used by McCall et al., 1977) separated by 1, 2, 3, or 4 to 9 months were divided into those that resided totally within a stage versus those that covered a period of the same length but straddled one stage boundary. Note at the top of Table 20-7 that the correlations across a stage boundary are always smaller than within a stage, although the differences are quite small when the age span is only a few months (this might be expected if individuals cross the stage boundary at different chronological ages). However, notice that as the age span increases, the correlation within a stage remains at essentially the same level—the customary decline in correlation with longer age spans does not occur when that span remains within a stage. In contrast, there is a decline with increasing interval length when it straddles a stage boundary.

Comparable data from Wilson and Harpring (1972) on the Louisville twins is presented at the bottom of Table 20-7. Here the intervals are longer and the comparisons at 3 and 9 months somewhat more persuasive in indicating that longitudinal correlations are lower the more stage boundaries they straddle.

Qualitative Changes in Developmental Function

McCall (1976; McCall et al., 1977) proposed that although the predominant character of mental performance changes from stage to stage, mental behavior at every age serves two

Table 20-7. Average Bayley Test Score Correlations Across Various Age Spans as a Function of Whether or Not Those Spans Are Within a Stage or Cut Across a Stage Boundary at 8, 13, or 21 Months of Age

Bayley (1933)[a]		Age Span in Months			
		1	2	3	4–9
Within a stage		.84	.75	.82	.82
Across 1 stage boundary		.80	.74	.77	.68

Wilson & Harpring (1972)[b]			Age span in Months		
	3	6	9	12	15
Within a stage	.52				
Across 1 stage boundary	.45	.39	.37		
Across 2 stage boundaries			.29	.28	.20

[a] Averages of 2 to 6 correlations. Data from 1–4 months have been omitted since reliability and cross-age rs are known to be low for this period for reasons irrelevant to this comparison.
[b] Averages of 1 to 4 correlations for members of twin pairs.
From McCall et al. (1977), reprinted with permission.

functions—the acquisition of information and the disposition of the organism to influence the inanimate and animate environment, the latter notion being similar to White's (1959) concept of effectance. These authors integrated their results from the Fels (McCall et al., 1972) and Berkeley data (McCall et al., 1977), with those which Uzgiris (1976) derived from her longitudinal data and Piaget's theory. A brief description of their hypothesized stages follows.

Newborn

Stage I covers the first two months of life, during which the infant primarily exercises endogenous, structural behavioral dispositions, and selective but basically responsive attention to certain aspects of the environment. Age-to-age correlations of mental test performance are essentially zero until approximately age two.

Subjectivity

Stage II stretches from approximately 2 to 7-8 months and represents an amalgamation of Piaget's stages II and III. Basically, the world is known by and is indistinguishable from the infant's perceptual-motor and physical action with it. This is complete subjectivity because, in a sense, objects are what the infant does with them. Therefore, the infant acquires information by exploratory behavior, especially that which produces some obvious perceptual consequence.

Separation of Means from Ends

The major cognitive event hypothesized to occur at approximately 8 months defining the onset of stage III is the separation of means from ends. Now infants distinguish between objects and their actions, but they still rely on active commerce with the object as a means of knowing it. Separation of means and ends permits more systematic and goal-oriented-appearing exploration as well as the stimulus generalization of previously learned schemes. Primitive imitation of behaviors similar to those in the infant's repertoire is also made possible now that the behavior of other people is separated from the behavior of the observing infant.

Entity-Entity Relations

At approximately 13 months, stage IV marks the onset of complete sensorimotor decentering. The infant can appreciate the independence of entities in the world and understand that they carry with them their own properties, including their potential to be independent dynamic forces in the environment. It is only now that one object can be seen in relation to another without the infant having to act upon these entities, an ability McCall et al. (1977) call entity-entity relations. This cognition enhances information acquisition and influencing by permitting consensual vocabulary, a skill requiring the infant to relate a verbal entity agreed upon by society with a specific object. It also allows the infant to insightfully associate one geometric form with another and to group objects according to similarities in their physical characteristics (e.g., Nelson, 1973; Ricciuti, 1965). Finally, the infant can now imitate totally new behaviors not previously seen and not currently in the response repertoire.

Symbolic Relationships

At approximately 21 months, stage V emerges. The child is capable of drawing symbolic relationships between entities in which one or more of the entities as well as the relationship itself may be symbolically coded. For example, the child may understand locative prepositions in which a relationship between two objects is communicated in the symbolic form of a verbal code. Sequences of actions can be remembered and imitated, and serious creative two-word utterances are possible. McCall et al. (1977), McCall (in press), and Uzgiris (1976) present this position in more detail and with supporting evidence.

Implications

The importance of the above approach is that it distinguishes between stability-instability in individual differences and continuity-discontinuity in developmental function. While these are two potentially independent spheres of development, McCall et al.'s (1977) analysis of the Berkeley data suggests that relative breaks in both realms occur at the same ages.

Methodological Implications

This orientation emphasizes an epigenetic step-function conception of mental development characterized by an ordered sequence of emergent skills that permit certain behaviors to become manifest. If the determinants of performance in one stage are different from those governing behavior in another stage, then one might expect one set of environmental variables to correlate with performance during one stage but a different set to correlate at another. But separating the functional from the nonfunctional variables will be difficult: noncausal variables might nevertheless display contemporary and/or predictive correlations with mental test performance because of their relationship with members of the changing set of environmental variables that do have causal implications. But even more methodologically challenging is the distinct possibility that mental development evolves in a total step-wise manner: the attainment of discrete skills might permit certain mental and social behaviors to emerge, but there may be no correlation of individual differences in the level of performance of these diverse behaviors. The salient question for the display of behavior Y is whether skill X has or has not developed—more or less of X might not relate to more or less of Y. If such is the case, we will not make much progress in understanding mental development if we continue to rely on simple correlational procedures, especially when dealing with questions of continuity-discontinuity of developmental function.

Relationships to other Behaviors

McCall and his colleagues (McCall et al., 1977; McCall, in press) have proposed that there may be relationships between the stages of mental development and the emergence of social and language milestones. For example, they have attempted to relate their mental stages to the onset of stranger- and separation-anxiety. Not only is it necessary for infants to distinguish between themselves and another human for stranger- and separation-distress to occur, but at 8 months the infant still needs to act in order to know the world. Therefore, it is response uncertainty in the face of a now independent-acting entity that may produce these social distresses. With respect to language, they submit that the child must be able to cognize entity-entity relations apart from direct physical action with those entities (i.e., their stage IV, approximately 13 months) before consensual vocabulary is possible, and that serious creative two-word utterances must await their stage V, symbolic relations (approximately 21 months).

It would appear that the study of mental development is considerably more complex than observing stability in a single concept called "intelligence." Rather, infancy is a period of enormous metamorphoses in the predominant character of mental behavior and fluctuations in the stability of individual differences in mental performance. If we are to take Piaget's epigenetic conception of mental development seriously, then we must abandon our insistence on stability as the criterion for the validity and utility of developmental measures, maintain the distinction between individual differences and developmental function, and open our thoughts, methods, and statistical approaches to include the variety of possible transitions that could characterize developmental functions (Buss & Royce, 1975; Flavell, 1972; Maccoby, 1969; McCall et al., 1977; Van den Daele, 1969, 1974; Wohlwill, 1973).

TOWARD AN INTEGRATION OF INDIVIDUAL DIFFERENCES AND DEVELOPMENTAL FUNCTION IN THE ONTOGENY OF INFANT MENTAL PERFORMANCE

Ultimately, a comprehensive theory of infant mental development must deal with individual differences as well as developmental function. I believe the schism between these two approaches has lasted too long and has inhibited progress in our understanding of mental development. In addition, the nature-nurture issue is not a question of "either-or" but one of "how," lest we forget Anastasi's (1958) cogent admonition. Despite the fact that all estimates of heritability rely on individual differences and ignore species-typical developmental functions, a comprehensive theory must deal with the heredity-environment issue as it applies to both spheres of interest. McCall (in press) has proffered a beginning on such a theory; for the present purpose, it is appropriate only to consider one possible framework for such an endeavor.

Canalization

Scarr-Salapatek (1976) has called the attention of infant researchers to the concept of canalization. *Canalization* implies a species-typical developmental path, called a *creod*, which nearly all members of the species tend to follow. Environmental inputs are necessary for development to proceed along the creod, but such environmental inputs tend to be available to all members of the species. Species-typical development occurs along the relatively fixed creod *as long as species-typical environmental circumstances predominate*. Therefore, the utility of the concept of canalization depends on the breadth of experiences and circumstances that define species-typical environments and the extent to which individuals will return to the creod after periods of exposure to atypical circumstances.

I propose that mental development is strongly canalized early in life, especially through 18 to 24 months, and slowly becomes less strongly canalized thereafter. This implies that early in infancy even severe but temporary circumstances will not have permanent effects of substantial magnitude on mental development. That is, while moderately severe perinatal events (e.g., prematurity, malnutrition, perinatal anoxia, etc.) will exert a contemporary effect on mental performance, their consequences will not likely be permanent if the infant is returned to an adequate environment. Moreover, while specific attempts by parents to stimulate their infants may have contemporary functional effects on mental test performance, they will not have enduring consequences if the infant is returned to a nonadvantageous environment.

Once 18 months is reached, everything does not abruptly change—it only begins to change. I believe that 18 to 24 months marks the beginning of serious symbolic relational thought (see previous section), both verbal and nonverbal, and that it is no accident that this age signals the start of correlations between infant mental test scores on the one hand and scores on the highly verbal childhood IQ tests, gross measures of parental socioeconomic class, and parental language and insistence on verbal communication and thought on the other. Moreover, behaviors that typify mental performance prior to this age are ultimately accomplished by all infants exposed to a species-typical environment. In contrast, language may represent the first skill to emerge for which one person will ultimately reach levels of performance far higher than another, despite the fact that both experienced environments that, although different, were within the realm of species-typical. In short, canalization slowly begins to weaken at 18 to 24 months of age, and individual differences in experience within species-typical environments and in genetic heritage slowly begin to have a differential effect.

This conception of development is partly illustrated in Figure 20-1. The heavy line represents the developmental function, which is highly canalized at first and somewhat less so thereafter. For example, the small lines about the main function do not show any consistency in relative rank-ordering from age to age during the early years; however, once abilities emerge which can display asymptotic differences between species members all reared in species-typical environments (symbolized by the switch from dashed to solid lines surrounding the main function), relative rank-ordering in behavior from age to age is apparent. However, a large part of this stability (especially those below the mean) may be attributed to the temporal stability of environments plus genetic heritage and not to the permanent effects of an earlier environmental experience.

Canalization and the Evidence

Early Adverse Circumstances

Scarr-Salapatek (1976) has reviewed literature pertaining to canalization, and Honzik (1976) and Hunt (1976) have summarized the impact of early major biological adversity. These authors point out that the effects of nutritional deprivation, prematurity, anoxia, and other neonatal risk factors produce contemporary depression in infant test scores; but if these infants are subsequently reared in adequate environments, the effects of these early circumstances are barely visible by 3 and essentially absent by 6 years of life. However, as emphasized above, if these infants are reared in markedly atypical homes (e.g., desperate poverty), the effects of these early conditions may persist.

Cross-Age Stability

The canalization position, coupled with an epigenetic stage conception of the developmental function, explain why there is relatively modest stability in mental test performance before 18 months. Presumably, individual differences about a highly canalized species-typical developmental function simply are not very stable or important for future development, even when the future is only a few months distant (especially if a stage boundary is crossed). Moreover, heritabilities, being calculated on these relatively inconsequential individual differences, also can be expected to be modest, both with respect to general level and profile contour, despite the fact that the species-typical developmental function (i.e., creod) is predominantly under genetic/maturational control given species-typical environments.

Heredity and Environment

Given this conception of development, what are the roles of heredity and environment? How is it possible for genetic and environmental factors *both* to have minor correlations with mental performance before 18 to 24 months and then *both* to have increasing correlations thereafter? The answer lies in understanding what heritability means and what it does not mean. Since heritability estimates must rely on individual differences, they are essentially irrelevant to the possible genetic-maturational control of a species-typical developmental function. Thus, a developmental progression of stages through which each individual passes—the creod in the present conception—may be thoroughly rooted in the organism's innate biology nurtured by species-typical environmental factors, but conventional procedures for estimating heritability would not reflect such a fact. Rather, these techniques reveal whether individual differences in the rate of developmental progress or the magnitude of the behavior characteristic of a given stage correlate with genetic heritage, but they do not comment on the creod itself. As discussed above, there appears to be some heritability for such individual differences, but prior to 18 to 24 months the levels of heritability are modest and substantially less than later in childhood. This observation meshes with the strong canalization notion in which individual differences about the species-typical creod represent minor and temporary deflections from the developmental path common to each infant.

However, at 18 to 24 months individual differences in mental performance begin to show correlations with both genetic and environmental factors, and these correlations increase until approximately 5 to 6 years (Honzik, 1957; McCall et al., 1972). These relationships signify the weakening of canalization as the rudiments of abilities emerge which ultimately may not characterize all members of the species. Therefore, while all infants (save those with serious mental deficiency) acquire the basic elements of a verbal language, some children will achieve levels of verbal fluency, facility, and reasoning which other children will never attain. Fundamentally, the process of development of these *species-atypical* skills requires some natural genetic endowment and an appropriate nurturing environment, just as was the case for species-typical attributes. But, whereas species-typical behaviors are highly canalized, prone to self-righting after deviations from the creod, and have individual differences that are temporary and relatively inconsequential for later mental performance, species-atypical behaviors are less strongly canalized, are less prone to self-righting, and have individual differences that are more likely to persist as long as appropriate genetic and environmental support is available. The result is that genetic and environmental correlates of individual differences in mental performance emerge and increase after 18 to 24 months. Both genetic and environmental correlates are likely (and likely to be mutually intercorrelated) because both are necessary for a trait to develop. The joint contribution of genetic and environmental factors implies that environmental (or genetic) correlations with mental performance might be quite high without obviating similarly high correlations with genetic (or environmental) circumstances.

Permanence of Environmental Effects

Individual differences on IQ tests administered after the age of 6 are among the most stable of any behavioral characteristic yet measured. This fact encouraged the belief that intellectually stimulating events transpiring between approximately 2 and 6 years of age have relatively permanent effects on mental performance. In its boldest form, this notion constitutes a type of critical period between 2 and 6 years, before and after which stimulating experiences have less impact. Occasionally, we have even acted (e.g., Head Start) on the premise that a brief dose of intellectual experience during this period will inoculate a child against most subsequent exposures to mentally depressing circumstances.

In my opinion, this notion has been overplayed. From the standpoint of the present conceptualization, the infant does become more plastic in the face of conventional enrichment experiences after 18 to 24 months. However, the changing nature of the developmental function implies that mental development, especially in infancy, is a dynamic and changing process that requires a changing set of specific circumstances to sustain its progress. One-shot enrichments should lose their impact as the child progresses from one stage to the next. When long-term effects of early stimulation are observed, they may not be the result of a permanent imprint on the infant per se. Rather, the effects may persist because an appropriately changing and enriching environment has been maintained since that initial positive experience. I submit that the stability in IQ performance after age 6 may not be the result of accumulated experience and natural endowment consolidated into some enduring mature intelligence, but rather the consequence of two facts: (1) major transformations in the fundamental nature of mental ability occur less frequently after the

5- to 7-year period (Gruen and Doherty, 1976; White, 1965), and (2) the nature and availability of the environment required to nurture mental growth remains fairly stable after age 6 for the typical child. Presumably, if the environment changed drastically and appropriately, so would mental performance, even after age 6.

By the same token, one would not expect early poor environments to lock a child into a low IQ unless the environment remained inferior thereafter. The major reversal of rural Guatemalan children from depressed performance at 1 year of age to essentially average ability on several basic mental faculties by mid-childhood (Kagan and Klein, 1973) may illustrate this point. Also, despite the high cross-age correlations for childhood IQ, McCall and his colleagues (McCall, 1970; McCall et al., 1973) reported that middle-class American subjects in the Fels sample displayed an average IQ range of 28.5 points between 2½ and 17 years of age, 1 in 7 demonstrated IQ shifts of 40 points or more (typically at 5–7 and at 10–11 years), and such patterns were simple linear and quadratic progressions which were apparently not random error nor under profound genetic control (i.e., not shared by siblings). Mental growth and change is probably not finished by age 6.

I would invoke essentially this same argument to deal with one finding in the literature that appears to contradict the canalization position. Several studies report that parental and environmental characteristics measured during infancy correlate more highly with IQ later in childhood than with contemporary infant mental test performance. One interpretation is that such early events indeed dispose the infant toward higher test performance later. If this were true, then if one group of infants were given the salient experience at 12 months, another group was not so treated, and *all environmental circumstances were identical for the two groups until age 3*, then the stimulated group would have a higher average IQ at 3 years than the controls. No such study has been done to my knowledge, and I personally believe that the results would not support the indelible role of most infant experiences. Rather, my interpretation of such naturalistic predictive correlations is that parents who provide appropriate stimulation at age 3 are also different from other parents when their children are infants. This different behavior during infancy may be correlated with contemporary and future mental test performance, but it may not be directly causal. If such parental behavior is in turn correlated with later parental behavior that does produce changes in mental performance, the parental behavior with infants will predict later child IQ. Since the infant is more plastic later and individual differences more meaningful, the predictive correlation could be higher than the contemporary correlation—and all the while the parental behavior during infancy be noncausal. Thus, it is the continuing environmental nurturance of mental behavior that is operating, not isolated injections of stimulation that permanently vaccinate a child for intellectual superiority or inferiority.

Summary

A full understanding of the canalization concept as applied here requires one to distinguish between developmental function and individual differences. It is quite possible for the developmental function—the average performance of individuals at each age—to be highly governed by maturational, biological, and genetic circumstances, yet there may be no stability of individual differences across age or with environmental or genetic circumstances. However, as canalization progressively weakens, environmental and genetic correlates increase even in samples of children all reared in species-typical environments. Longitudinal stability of individual differences may increase, not because environmental and genetic factors cast fixed individual developmental trajectories but because the salient environmental and genetic factors typically do not change substantially for most individuals who nevertheless remain potentially malleable in the face of major reversals in these factors, were such changes to occur.

EPILOGUE

This entire chapter is based upon longitudinal research; indeed, Wohlwill (1973) has argued that developmental study of almost any attribute requires a longitudinal approach. However, many longitudinal studies have been maligned for their failure to separate birth year, measurement year, and age, and for their lack of controls for repeated testing and sample attrition. For the most part, these have been valid potential concerns, but McCall (1977) has argued that effects of these confoundings have been blown out of proportion and improperly generalized to the point where the "proper" longitudinal study is beyond the means and time commitment of our discipline. Any kind of longitudinal research requires some assumptions regarding the roles of age, year of birth, and year of measurement (as well as repeated testing and sample attrition), but which assumptions are made depends upon the specific research questions and situation. For example, there is no evidence indicating that stability-instability in individual differences within or across age is altered by secular changes, repeated testing, and certain types of sample attrition (McCall, 1977). And do we really need a control for secular artifacts when describing the sequence of Piaget's sensorimotor stages—is there a decade when symbolic relations develop before means-ends differentiation? The longitudinal approach is the life-blood of developmental psychology (Wohlwill, 1973); we cannot study ontogenetic change within individuals without it. Therefore, while it should never be applied willy-nilly and without relevant control groups, neither should there be dogmatism about which assumptions should be made and which control groups should be run regardless of the specific research question and pertinent literature.

BIBLIOGRAPHY

Anastasi, A. Heredity, environment, and the question "how?" *Psychological Review,* 1958, **65,** 197–208.

Anderson, J. E. The limitations of infant and preschool tests in the measurement of intelligence. *The Journal of Psychology,* 1939, **8,** 351–379.

Baldwin, A. L., Kalhorn, J., and Breese, F. H. Patterns of parent behavior. *Psychological Monographs,* 1945, **58** (whole No. 268).

Bayley, N. Mental growth during the first three years: A developmental study of 61 children by repeated tests. *Genetic Psychology Monographs,* 1933, **14,** 1–92.

Bayley, N. Some increasing parent-child similarities during the growth of children. *Journal of Educational Psychology,* 1954, **45,** 1–21.

Bayley, N. Development of mental abilities. In P. H. Mussen (ed.), *Carmichael's Manual of Child Psychology,* Vol. 1. New York, 1970, 1163–1209.

Bayley, N., and Schaefer, E. S. Correlations of maternal and child behaviors with development of mental ability: Data from the Berkeley Growth Study. *Monographs of the Society for Research in Child Development,* 1964, **29** (97).

Beckwith, L. Relationships between attributes of mothers and their infants' IQ scores. *Child Development,* 1971, **42,** 1083–1097.

Birns, B., and Golden, M. Prediction of intellectual performance at 3 years from infant tests and personality measures. *Merrill-Palmer Quarterly,* 1972, **18**, 53–58.

Bloom, B. S. *Stability and Change in Human Characteristics.* New York: Wiley, 1964.

Bradley, R. H., and Caldwell, B. M. Early home environment and changes in mental test performance in children from 6 to 30 months. *Developmental Psychology,* 1976, **12**, 93–97.

Brooks, J., and Weinraub, M. A history of infant intelligence testing. In M. Lewis (ed.), *Origins of Intelligence.* New York: Plenum, 1976, 19–58.

Buss, A. R., and Royce, J. R. Ontogenetic change in cognitive structure from a multivariate perspective. *Developmental Psychology,* 1975, **11**, 87–101.

Caldwell, B. M., Heider, J., and Kaplan, B. The inventory of home stimulation. Paper presented at the meetings of the American Psychological Association, New York, September 1966.

Cameron, J., Livson, N., and Bayley, N. Infant vocalizations and their relationship to mature intelligence. *Science,* 1967, **157**, 331–333.

Casati, I., and Lézine, I. *Les Étapes de l'Intelligence Sensori-motrice.* Paris: Les Éditions du Centre de Psychologie Appliquée, 1968.

Casler, L. Maternal intelligence and institutionalized children's developmental quotients: A correlational study. *Developmental Psychology,* 1976, **12**, 64–67.

Cattell, P. *The measurement of intelligence in infants and young children.* New York: Science Press, 1940. (Reprinted by The Psychological Corporation, 1960.)

Cavanaugh, M. C., Cohen, I., Dunphy, D., Ringwell, E. A., and Goldberg, I. D. Prediction from the Cattell Infant Intelligence Scale. *Journal of Consulting Psychology,* 1957, **21**, 33–37.

Corman, H. H., and Escalona, S. K. Stages of sensorimotor development: A replication study. *Merrill-Palmer Quarterly,* 1969, **15**, 351–361.

Drillien, C. M. *The Growth and Development of the Prematurely Born Infant.* Baltimore: Williams & Wilkins, 1964.

Eichorn, D. H. Developmental parallels in the growth of parents and their children. Presidential Address, Division 7, APA, September 1969.

Elardo, R., Bradley, R., and Caldwell, B. M. The relation of infants' home environments to mental test performance from six to thirty-six months: A longitudinal analysis. *Child Development,* 1975, **46**, 71–76.

Emmerich, W. Continuity and stability in early social development. *Child Development,* 1964, **35**, 311–332.

Erickson, M. T. The predictive validity of the Cattell Infant Intelligence Scales for young mentally retarded children. *American Journal of Mental Deficiency,* 1968, **72**, 728–733.

Escalona, S. K., & Moriarty, A. Prediction of school-age intelligence from infant tests. *Child Development,* 1961, **32**, 597–605.

Falconer, D. S. *Introduction to Quantitative Genetics.* New York: Ronald Press, 1960.

Fillmore, E. A. Iowa tests for young children. *University of Iowa Studies in Child Welfare,* 1936, **11**, 1–58.

Fish, B. The detection of schizophrenia in infancy: A preliminary report. *Journal of Nervous and Mental Disease,* 1957, **125**, 1–24.

Fish, B. Involvement of the central nervous system in infants with schizophrenia. *AMA Archives of Neurology,* 1960, **2**, 115–121.

Fish, B., Shapiro, F., Halpern, F., and Wile, R. The prediction of schizophrenia in infancy: III. A ten year follow-up report of neurological and psychological development. *American Journal of Psychiatry,* 1965, **121**, 768–775.

Flavell, J. H. *The Developmental Psychology of Jean Piaget.* New York: Van Nostrand, 1963.

Flavell, J. H. An analysis of cognitive-developmental sequences. *Genetic Psychology Monographs,* 1972, **86**, 279–350.

Freedman, D. G., and Keller, B. Inheritance of behavior in infants. *Science,* 1963, **140**, 196–198.

Ginsburg, H., and Opper, S. *Piaget's Theory of Intellectual Development: An Introduction.* Englewood Cliffs, N.J.: Prentice-Hall, 1969.

Goffeney, B., Henderson, N. B., and Butler, B. V. Negro-white, male-female eight-month developmental scores compared with seven-year WISC and Bender test scores. *Child Development,* 1971, **42**, 595–604.

Golden, M., and Birns, B. Social class and cognitive development in infancy. *Merrill-Palmer Quarterly,* 1968, **14**, 139–149.

Golden, M., and Birns, B. Social class and infant intelligence. In M. Lewis (ed.), *Origins of Intelligence.* New York: Plenum, 1976, 299–351.

Golden, M., Birns, B., Bridger, W., and Moss, A. Social class differentiation in cognitive development among black preschool children. *Child Development,* 1971, **42**, 37–45.

Gruen, G. E., and Doherty, J. A constructivist view of a major developmental shift in early childhood. In I. C. Uzgiris and F. Weizmann (eds.), *The Structuring of Experience.* New York: Plenum, 1976, 297–318.

Haviland, J. Looking smart: The relationship between affect and intelligence in infancy. In M. Lewis (ed.), *Origins of Intelligence.* New York: Plenum, 1976, 353–377.

Hindley, C. B. Stability and change in abilities up to five years: Group trends. *Journal of Child Psychology and Psychiatry,* 1965, **6**, 85–99.

Hindley, C. B., and Munro, J. A. A factor analytic study of the abilities of infants, and predictions of later ability. Paper presented at the Symposium on Behavioral Testing of Neonates and Longitudinal Correlations, London, April 1970.

Honzik, M. P. Developmental studies of parent-child resemblance in intelligence. *Child Development,* 1957, **28**, 215–228.

Honzik, M. P. A sex difference in the age of onset of the parent-child resemblance in intelligence. *Journal of Educational Psychology,* 1963, **54**, 231–237.

Honzik, M. P. Environmental correlates of mental growth: Prediction from the family setting at 21 months. *Child Development,* 1967, **38**, 337–364.

Honzik, M. P. Intellectual abilities at age 40 in relation to the early family environment. In F. J. Monks, W. W. Hartup, and J. de Wit (eds.), *Determinants of Behavioral Development.* New York: Academic, 1972.

Honzik, M. P. Value and limitations of infant tests: An overview. In M. Lewis (ed.), *Origins of Intelligence.* New York: Plenum, 1976, 59–95.

Honzik, M. P., Macfarlane, J. W., and Allen, L. The stability of mental test performance between two and eighteen years. *Journal of Experimental Education,* 1948, **18**, 309–324.

Hunt, J. McV. *Intelligence and Experience.* New York: Ronald, 1961.

Hunt, J. V. Environmental risk in fetal and neonatal life and measured infant intelligence. In M. Lewis (ed.), *Origins of Intelligence.* New York: Plenum, 1976, 223–258.

Hunt, J. V., and Bayley, N. Explorations into patterns of mental development and prediction from the Bayley scales of infant development. In J. P. Hill (ed.), *Minnesota Symposia on Child Psychology,* Vol. 5, 1971, 52–71.

Illingworth, R. S. The predictive value of developmental tests in the first year with special reference to the diagnosis of mental subnormality. *Journal of Child Psychology and Psychiatry,* 1961, **2**, 210–215.

Illingworth, R. S., and Birch, L. B. The diagnosis of mental retardation in infancy: A follow-up study. *Archives of Diseases in Childhood,* 1959, **34**, 269–273.

Ireton, H., Thwing, E., and Gravem, H. Infant mental development and neurological status, family socioeconomic status, and intelligence at age four. *Child Development,* 1970, **41**, 937–946.

Jensen, A. R. How much can we boost IQ and scholastic achievement? *Harvard Educational Review,* 1969, 39, **1**.

Kagan, J., and Klein, R. E. Cross-cultural perspectives in early development. *American Psychologist,* 1973, **28**, 947.

Kagan, J., and Moss, H. A. Parental correlates of child's IQ and height: A cross-validation of the Berkeley Growth Study results. *Child Development,* 1959, **30**, 325–332.

Kangas, J., Butler, B. V., and Goffeney, B. Relationship between preschool intelligence, maternal intelligence, and infant behavior. Second Scientific Session, Collaborative Study on Cerebral Palsy Mental Retardation, and Other Neurological and Sensory Disorders of Infancy and Childhood, U.S. Department of Health, Education, and Welfare, Public Health Service, March 1966, Pt. 2, 91–102.

King, W., and Seegmiller, B. Performance of 14–22-month-old black, first-born male infants on two tests of cognitive development: The Bayley Scales and The Infant Psychological Development Scale. *Developmental Psychology,* 1973, **8**, 317–326.

Klackenberg-Larsson, I., and Stensson, J. Data on the mental development during the first five years. In "The development of children in a Swedish urban community: A prospective longitudinal study." *Acta Paediatrica Scandinavica,* Suppl. 187, IV. Stockholm: Almqvist and Wiksell, 1968.

Knobloch, H., and Pasamanick, B. An evaluation of the consistency and predictive value of the 40-week Gesell developmental schedule. *Psychiatric Research Reports of the American Psychiatric Association,* 1960, **13**, 10–13.

Knobloch, H., and Pasamanick, B. Predicting intellectual potential in infancy. *American Journal of Diseases of Children,* 1963, **106**, 43–51.

Knobloch, H., and Pasamanick, B. Prediction from the assessment of neuromotor and intellectual status in infancy. In J. Zubin and G. A. Jervis (eds.), *Psychopathology of Mental Development.* New York: Grune & Stratton, 1967, 387–400.

Knobloch, H., Rider, R., Harper, P., and Pasamanick, B. Neuropsychiatric sequelae of prematurity: A longitudinal study. *Journal of the American Medical Association,* 1956, **161**, 581–585.

Kopp, C. B., Sigman, M., and Parmelee, A. H. Longitudinal study of sensorimotor development. *Developmental Psychology,* 1974, **10**, 687–695.

Lewis, M., and McGurk, H. Evaluation of infant intelligence. *Science,* 1972, **178**, 1174–1177.

Maccoby, E. E. Tracing individuality within age-related change. Paper presented at the meetings of The Society for Research in Child Development, Santa Monica, California, March 1969.

MacRae, J. N. Retests of children given tests as infants. *Journal of Genetic Psychology,* 1955, **87**, 111–119.

Matheny, A. P., Jr. Twins: Concordance for Piagetian-equivalent items derived from the Bayley mental test. *Developmental Psychology,* 1975, **11**, 224–227.

Matheny, A. P., Dolan, A. B., and Wilson, R. S. Bayley's infant behavior record: Relations between behaviors and mental test scores. *Developmental Psychology,* 1974, **10**, 696–702.

McCall, R. B. IQ pattern over age: Comparisons among siblings and parent-child pairs. *Science,* 1970, **170**, 644–648.

McCall, R. B. Similarity in IQ profile among related pairs: Infancy and childhood. *Proceedings* of the American Psychological Association meeting, Honolulu, 1972a, 79–80.

McCall, R. B. Similarity in developmental profile among related pairs of human infants. *Science,* 1972b, **178**, 1004–1005.

McCall, R. B. Toward an epigenetic conception of mental development in the first three years of life. In M. Lewis (ed.), *Origins of Intelligence.* New York: Plenum, 1976, 97–122.

McCall, R. B. Challenges to a science of developmental psychology. *Child Development,* 1977, **48**, 333–344.

McCall, R. B., Appelbaum, M., and Hogarty, P. S. Developmental changes in mental performance. *Monographs of the Society for Research in Child Development,* 1973, **38** (150).

McCall, R. B., Hogarty, P. S., and Hurlburt, N. Transitions in infant sensorimotor development and the prediction of childhood IQ. *American Psychologist,* 1972, **27,** 728–748.

McCall, R. B., Eichorn, D. H., and Hogarty, P. S. Transitions in early mental development. *Monographs of the Society for Research in Child Development,* 1977, **42,** (171).

McCall, R. B. Qualitative transitions in behavioral development in the first three years of life. In M. H. Bornstein and W. Kessen, (eds.), *Psychological Development from Infancy.* New York: Erlbaum, in press.

Moore, T. Language and intelligence: A longitudinal study of the first eight years. Part I. Patterns of development in boys and girls. *Human Development,* 1967, **10,** 88–106.

Moore, T. Language and intelligence: A longitudinal study of the first eight years. Part II. Environmental correlates of mental growth. *Human Development,* 1968, **11,** 1–24.

Mueller, E., & Lucas, T. A developmental analysis of peer interaction among toddlers. In M. Lewis and L. Rosenblum (eds.), *Peer Relations and Friendship.* New York: Wiley, 1976, 223–257.

Nelson, K. Some evidence for the cognitive primacy of categorization and its functional equivalence. *Merrill-Palmer Quarterly,* 1973, **17,** 21–39.

Nelson, V. L., and Richards, T. W. Studies in mental development: III. Performance of twelve-months-old children on the Gesell schedule, and its predictive value for mental status at two and three years. *Journal of Genetic Psychology,* 1939, **54,** 181–191.

Nichols, P. L., and Broman, S. H. Familial resemblances in infant mental development. *Developmental Psychology,* 1974, **10,** 442–446.

Piaget, J. *The Origins of Intelligence in Children.* New York: International Universities, 1952.

Ricciuti, H. N. Object grouping and selective ordering behavior in infants 12 to 24 months old. *Merrill-Palmer Quarterly,* 1965, **11,** 129–148.

Rutter, M. Psychological development—Predictions from infancy. *Journal of Child Psychology and Psychiatry,* 1970, **11,** 49–62.

Sameroff, A. J., and Chandler, M. J. Reproductive risk and the continuum of caretaking casualty. In F. D. Horowitz (ed.), *Review of Child Development Research,* Vol. 4. Chicago: University of Chicago, 1975, 187–249.

Scarr-Salapatek, S. An evolutionary perspective on infant intelligence: Species patterns and individual variations. In M. Lewis (ed.), *Origins of Intelligence.* New York: Plenum, 1976, 165–197.

Scarr-Salapatek, S., and Williams, M. L. The effects of early stimulation on low-birth-weight infants. *Child Development,* 1973, **44,** 94.

Skodak, M., and Skeels, H. M. A final follow-up study of 100 adopted children. *Journal of Genetic Psychology,* 1949, **75,** 85–125.

Starr, R. H. Cognitive development in infancy. *Merrill-Palmer Quarterly,* 1971, **17,** 179–223.

Stechler, G. A longitudinal follow-up of neonatal apnea. *Child Development,* 1964, **35,** 333–348.

Stott, L. H., and Ball, R. S. Infant and preschool mental tests: Review and evaluation. *Monographs of the Society for Research in Child Development,* 1965, **30** (101).

Thomas, H. Psychological assessment instruments for use with human infants. *Merrill-Palmer Quarterly,* 1970, **16,** 179–224.

Uzgiris, I. C. Patterns of cognitive development in infancy. *Merrill-Palmer Quarterly,* 1973, **19,** 181–204.

Uzgiris, I. C. Organization of sensorimotor intelligence. In M. Lewis (ed.), *Origins of Intelligence.* New York: Plenum, 1976, 123–163.

Uzgiris, I. C., and Hunt, J. McV. *Assessment in Infancy: Ordinal Scales of Psychological Development.* Urbana: University of Illinois, 1975.

Van den Daele, L. D. Qualitative models in developmental analysis. *Developmental Psychology,* 1969, **1**, 303–310.

Van den Daele, L. D. Intrastructure and transition in developmental analysis. *Human Development,* 1974, **17**, 1–23.

Wachs, T. D. Technical comment. *Science,* 1972, **178**, 1005.

Wachs, T. D. Utilization of a Piagetian approach in the investigation of early experience effects: A research strategy and some illustrative data. *Merrill-Palmer Quarterly,* 1976, **22**, 11–30.

Wachs, T. D., Uzgiris, I. C., and Hunt, J. McV. Cognitive development in infants of different age levels and from different environmental backgrounds: An explanatory investigation. *Merrill-Palmer Quarterly,* 1971, **17**, 283–318.

Werner, E. E. From birth to latency: Behavioral differences in a multiracial group of twins. *Child Development,* 1973, **44**, 438–444.

Werner, E. E., and Bayley, N. The reliability of Bayley's revised scale of mental and motor development during the first year of life. *Child Development,* 1966, **37**, 39–50.

Werner, E. E., Honzik, M. P., and Smith, R. S. Prediction of intelligence and achievement at 10 years from 20 months pediatric and psychologic examinations. *Child Development,* 1968, **39**, 1063–1075.

Werner, E., Simonian, K., Bierman, J. M., and French, F. E. Cumulative affect of perinatal complications and deprived environment on physical, intellectual, and social development of preschool children. *Pediatrics,* 1967, **39**, 480–505.

White, R. W. Motivation reconsidered: The concept of competence. *Psychological Review,* 1959, **66**, 297–333.

White, S. H. Evidence for a hierarchical arrangement of learning processes. In L. P. Lipsitt and C. C. Spiker (eds.), *Advances in Child Development and Behavior,* Vol. 2. New York: Academic, 1965, 187–220.

Willerman, L., Broman, S. H., and Fiedler, M. Infant development, preschool IQ, and social class. *Child Development,* 1970, **41**, 69–77.

Wilson, R. S. Testing infant intelligence. *Science,* 1973, **182**, 734–737.

Wilson, R. S. Twins: Mental development in the preschool years. *Developmental Psychology,* 1974, **10**, 580–588.

Wilson, R. S., Brown, A. M., and Matheny, A. P., Jr. Emergence and persistence of behavioral differences in twins. *Child Development,* 1971, **42**, 1381–1398.

Wilson, R. S., and Harpring, E. B. Mental and motor development in infant twins. *Developmental Psychology,* 1972, **7**, 277–287.

Wilson, R. S., and Matheny, A. P., Jr. Retardation and twin concordance in infant mental development: A reassessment. *Behavior Genetics,* 1976, **6**, 353–358.

Wohlwill, J. F. *The Study of Behavioral Development.* New York: Academic, 1973.

Yarrow, L. J. Research in dimensions of early maternal care. *Merrill-Palmer Quarterly,* 1963, **9**, 101–114.

Yarrow, L. J., Goodwin, M. S., Manheimer, H., and Milowe, I. D. Infancy experiences and cognitive and personality development at ten years. In L. J. Stone, H. T. Smith, and L. B. Murphy (eds.), *The Competent Infant: Research and Commentary.* New York: Basic Books, 1973, 1274–1281.

Yarrow, L. J., and Pedersen, F. A. The interplay between cognition and motivation in infancy. In M. Lewis (ed.), *Origins of Intelligence.* New York: Plenum, 1976, 379–399.

Yarrow, L. J., Rubenstein, J. L., Pedersen, F. A., and Jankowski, J. J. Dimensions of early stimulation and their differential effects on infant development. *Merrill-Palmer Quarterly,* 1972, **18**, 205–218.

CHAPTER 21

Developmental Designs for Infancy Research[1]

Stephen W. Porges

Unique research designs are necessary to assess the rapidly changing behavioral and biological systems of developing organisms. To avoid the difficulties in sampling and the statistical complexities associated with the measurement of change, most infancy research has opted for the static designs that have been generally used in experimental psychology. Developmental functions that describe the relationship between response systems and age typically have not been adequately described by the predominant experimental designs. The application of techniques capable of identifying and describing developmental functions and the variables affecting them is the methodological challenge posed to developmental psychology.

Methodological problems associated with measuring change as a function of time may be historically traced to the pre-Socratic philosophy of Heraclitus. The doctrine of constant flux, attributed to Heraclitus, precluded the possibility of assessing the *same* person or subject twice. This is often conceptually presented by the statement that an individual could not step into the same river twice. This problem is also manifested in the attempts to assess ontogenetic change—the paradox that one could never test the *same* subject twice.

Not all infancy research depends upon adequate methods of evaluating behavioral change. The content justification and theoretical rationale for various areas of infancy research differ. Although all research on human development may be intricately related to some global theory of development, many researchers justify their work based upon much less demanding expectations. Research may be justified by an intrinsic interest in whether or not infants perform specific behaviors such as orienting or conditioning. This rationale necessitates few assumptions and has limited inferential value for developmental theory, since it does not necessarily relate the infant's behavior to behavior at other points on the time dimension. Other infancy research is defined by the study of psychological phenomena which have parallels later in life, and by the study of learning or conditioning across various ages to identify specific antecedent behavior which will be predictive of behavior later in life. This research investigates infant behavior to identify specific events or patterns of response which will aid in the prediction of later behavior and perhaps contribute to the development of intervention techniques.

The chapter will stress the methodology of studying infant behavior within a developmental approach with emphasis on description and explanation of developmental functions. Thus, the designs described in this chapter, although chosen for their possible application in infancy research, might be applicable throughout the life span. The chapter

[1]The preparation of this chapter was supported, in part, by Research Scientist Development Award K02-MH-0054 from the National Institute of Mental Health and by grant NE-G-00-3-0013 from the National Institute of Education.

is structured to identify and describe problems related to identifying equivalent stimulus situations and behaviors necessary for developmental comparisons, to emphasize the problems associated with using analysis of variance designs to study patterns of early infant behavior, and to identify alternative methods that can be used to evaluate change over time.

EQUIVALENCE

Inherent in developmental psychology are problems that are currently addressed by cross-cultural and comparative research. These problems have often been neglected by infancy researchers. For example, the equivalence of verbal responses, a serious problem when age comparisons are made, is similar to the problem of linguistic equivalence faced in cross-cultural research. Similarly, the functional equivalence of response and antecedent stimulus conditions commonly addressed by comparative psychologists (Bitterman, 1960) is often neglected in developmental research.

Most published attempts to investigate the development of psychological processes have been characterized by testing various age groups, identifying group differences within a specific response system, and then inferring from the age-related differences in the response system a developmental function characterizing a psychological process as a function of age. Utilizing this strategy, observed age-related influences on a specific response system are used to infer changes in a specific psychological process. This inferential approach may portray inappropriate relationships since differences may also be a function of age-related changes in the response system, perhaps independent of the psychological process. For example, GSR conditioning is often assessed as a function of age (e.g., Morrow et al., 1969). However, magnitude and frequency of electrodermal responses may differ as a function of age independent of conditionability. The electrodermal reactivity of the human changes developmentally and this may not be paralleling a change in conditionability. Thus, the identification of age differences in GSR with either a longitudinal or cross-sectional design would be inadequate for drawing inference to age-related changes in conditionability.

Physiological responses have often been used as a means of tapping into the organism during its preverbal stages of development. Inherent in this technique is a series of assumptions: first, that physiological responses are reliable indicators of psychological processes; second, that the physiological response that has been identified as a reliable indicator of psychological responses in older verbal individuals reflects the same psychological processes in the young child; third, that maturation selectively influences the physiological response components which parallel developmental changes in psychological processing.

Although faulty, violations of the above assumptions may not result in a serious problem if the investigator is merely looking for response indicators to various stimulus situations. Thus, a response in any direction in the cardiovascular system (i.e., heart-rate deceleration, heart-rate acceleration, or changes in heart-rate variability) of any reliable magnitude could only be interpreted to reflect the subject's detection of the stimulus and not as a function of an affective property of stimulus. However, if the investigator is interested in interpreting the differences among responses to a class of stimuli at a various stage of maturation, any characteristic other than response occurrence would be uninterpretable.

Since heart-rate responses are commonly used to assess psychological processes during infancy, it is important to understand their physiological determinants. The neural control of the heart is mediated through the autonomic nervous system. Structurally, the autonomic nervous system may be divided into two antagonistic subsystems—the parasympathetic and the sympathetic. Although not totally consistent with the physiology of cardiac innervation, the heart-rate responses that have often been used to monitor developmental shifts in cognitive activity have been simplistically mapped into these systems—heart-rate acceleration resulting from the excitatory sympathetic influences and heart-rate deceleration resulting from the inhibitory parasympathetic influences (bidirectional responses could actually be the result of either excitation or inhibition within either the sympathetic or parasympathetic system). Developmentally, in response to simple physical stimuli (e.g., auditory signals) there is a shift in the primary direction of the heart-rate response from acceleration to deceleration (Graham et al., 1970). In spite of the developmental influences on the autonomic nervous system, responses in newborn infants, who primarily accelerate, have been interpreted to be responding with a protective-defensive system while the older infants, who decelerate, have been interpreted to be attending or orienting to the stimulus (i.e., cardiac orienting; Graham and Jackson, 1974). This simplistic discussion of cognitive correlates of heart-rate responses is complicated by information regarding the differential development of components of the autonomic nervous system. For example, the developmental function of parasympathetic influences on the heart-rate response exhibits a slower rate of maturation than the sympathetic influences.

If the developmental shift in parasympathetic influences on the heart-rate responses is reliable, then the directionality of the heart-rate response which is dependent upon the maturation of the autonomic nervous system may not always reflect the same psychological properties (e.g., acceleration associated with startle or defense and deceleration associated with orienting or attention). However, if the shift in the autonomic nervous system from sympathetic to parasympathetic dominance actually parallels a psychological shift from defensive to orienting behavior, then the directionality of the heart-rate response may be used as an important indicator of psychological activity. The testing of this last suggestion is extremely difficult since it would necessitate behavioral validation in an organism whose limited-response repertoire has encouraged the use of psychophysiological paradigms.

Although the directionality of the heart-rate response is critical to theoretical models of orienting and attention (Graham and Clifton, 1966), it is still possible to detect reliable responses without attributing complex psychological transduction of the stimulus. If concern is limited to detection, then it may be possible to assess perceptual thresholds or to detect responses contingent on the pairing of stimuli such as in a classical conditioning paradigm (Clifton, 1974; Porges, 1974; Stamps and Porges, 1975).

The selection of an optimum measure to study development necessitates that it not be affected by the equivalence problems associated with variation in situations and age. A good measure should be capable of assessing changes in specific psychological processes across different laboratory conditions and age periods. Moreover, a good measure should be sensitive to intra-individual variations associated with state and stimulus manipulations as well as reflecting stable individual differences. If a measure has these characteristics, then observed age-related differences might reflect developmental changes in specific psychological processes.

Multivariate statistical procedures may lend another approach to the problem of equivalence. The multitrait-multimethod matrix technique (Campbell and Fiske, 1959) has been of considerable interest to psychologists because it provides information on the *convergent* (confirmation by independent measurement procedures) and *discriminant* (separation of one trait from another) validity of theoretical constructs (i.e., traits). This technique may be of interest to researchers of infant behavior. For example, to measure an infant's reactivity, one might use three measures of the infant's response to changes in stimulation: one, a subjective measure of the mother's judgment; two, an objective measure of a physiological response; and three, an objective measure of a behavioral response. Despite the differences in these response dimensions, each measure, in principle, is simply another demonstration of the infant's reactivity and should, therefore, tend to give fairly consistent results. If the results are consistent (high correlations among measures), convergent validity is demonstrated. The emphasis on different methods of measurement represents an attempt to insure that the correlations among variables represent commonality with the underlying trait rather than consistencies due to similarities of testing methods. This example may be viewed as an attempt to utilize convergent measurement to functionally deal with equivalent psychological processes.

An infant's attentiveness may also be evaluated using the measures of mother's judgment, and physiological and behavioral measures of the infant. Discriminant validity would be demonstrated if it could be shown that the trait (i.e., factor score) underlying the reactivity was distinctly different from the trait underlying the attentiveness measures. The possibility exists for modifying and applying the multitrait-multimethod matrix technique to identify, independent of development, equivalent psychological processes, which are often reflected in maturationally dependent responses.

DESIGN

Basic Developmental Designs

The basic ontogenetic question is often formulated as behavior being a function of time, $B = f(T)$ (Baltes and Goulet, 1970). This question is generally answered by repeatedly testing the same subject (i.e., longitudinal design) or by simultaneously testing groups of subjects who are representative of different stages of development (i.e., cross-sectional design).

If one wants to perform cross-sectional investigations purely to understand *age differences* at one testing time, there are two major problems: One is obtaining comparable samples of subjects at different age levels; and the second is insuring that the measures mean the same thing at different ages. Comparable samples may be selected by randomization or matching. The problem of response or measurement equivalence may be handled by selecting measures that have been previously assessed as being equivalent across ages. Besides identifying age differences, a second reason for performing cross-sectional studies is to estimate the normal developmental sequences of specific behavior. However, cross-sectional studies have often been misleading and may result in the generation of hypotheses which are inappropriate since cross-sectional data may not accurately match observed developmental changes. Many of these discrepancies have been found to be a function of historical or cultural influences. This has resulted in strong interest in the cross-sequential or cohort design which attempts to separate the historical from the maturational influences (Schaie, 1965).

Longitudinal designs, when feasible, have four advantages over cross-sectional studies: First, they permit a direct analysis of within-subject age changes. Second, they encounter less severe problems with respect to the sampling of subjects. Third, they allow the use of more powerful statistical methods. A purely longitudinal study offers a within-subjects design in which the error term consists of the interaction of subjects and age levels rather than the pooled variance of individual differences. This advantage is particularly large when the repeated measures correlate substantially from age to age as is the case with most measures that are investigated. Fourth, they are not influenced by birth-cohort effects, since group differences in a cross-sectional design could be attributed to cohort effects as well as age differences.

Unfortunately, there are also many criticisms against longitudinal designs. First, is the concern with practice effects? This may be handled by alternate forms of the tests or by actually assessing repeated testing effects over short periods of time. If there are no practice effects at the time of retesting, they are not likely to occur in testing once a year and less frequently. Second, is the often-violated assumption of homogeneity of variance across repeated testing sessions? Statistical methods have been developed to handle data when the assumption is violated. The methods generally employed have ranged from the conservative correction factor described by Greenhouse and Geisser (1959), which reduces the degrees of freedom, to the multivariate tests, which do not make the homogeniety of variance assumption (Davidson, 1972). These methods will be more thoroughly described later in this chapter. Third, is the problem of attrition from one age to another? This greatly affects the inferential power of the longitudinal study since the attrition rate may not be random but correlated with antecedent measurements. Fourth, is the theoretical consideration that longitudinal studies confound the genetically programmed unfolding of behavior by having cumulative effects as a function of repeated experimental interventions? Fifth, longitudinal studies take an excessive period of time to collect data resulting in the experimenter aging with his subjects and being committed to specific designs and measurement instruments over the duration of study. Sixth, changes in performance found in longitudinal studies could be attributable to factors associated with time of testing which are independent of age or interactive with age.

Because of the shortcomings of cross-sectional and longitudinal studies for the estimation of developmental processes, it might be useful to employ designs that combine some of the best features of both approaches. Schaie (1975) introduced additional factors into the equation $B = f(T)$. He expressed behavioral performance as a function of three factors, $P = f(A,C,T)$. In this equation, A refers to chronological age of the subject, C refers to the birth cohort to which the subject belongs, and T refers to the time of testing. Schaie proposed a general developmental model for conducting developmental research, which provides the opportunity to examine the influences of each of these three components on performance. Schaie believed that this model would permit a scheme for both descriptive data collection and explanatory data analysis. His model generates three different sequential research designs which permit chronological age, birth cohort, and time of measurement to be simultaneously varied, two at a time. According to Schaie, developmental explanation would be possible because the three factors in his model could be associated with distinct sources of developmental change: age effects to maturational influences; cohort effects to genetic and/or environmental determinants; and time-of-testing effect to cultural factors.

An antecedent of Schaie's method is found in Bell's convergence method (1953). Bell proposed a similar alternate sampling procedure (replacing longitudinal or cross-sectional designs) to reduce some of the difficulties associated with longitudinal sampling. By assessing performance differences across sets of cohorts matched on chronological age, Bell was able to assess whether his estimate of a longitudinal function derived from the convergence method accurately overlapped with the actual longitudinal function. There is a major difference between the Bell and Schaie methods. Bell attempted to estimate the longitudinal function and implicitly assumed that the longitudinal approach was the method of choice when the purpose of the research was to describe development. Schaie, however, attempted to partition the variance of behavioral performance in developmental research into components that might be attributed to chronological age, time of testing, and cohort membership.

A recent publication (Baltes et al., 1976) argues that the three components in the Schaie model are not independent of each other and that their unconfounding is not possible. It is this confounding of factors that limits the explanatory properties of the model. Schaie and Baltes (1975), in a summary of their respective views, agree that it is important to distinguish between the use of sequential strategies (consisting of successions of either cross-sectional and/or longitudinal studies) as a descriptive method to identify developmental change and the use of Schaie's model in explanatory data analysis to develop a theoretical model of development. In summary, the Schaie model may permit the descriptive identification of developmental change in a changing historical and cultural environment, but researchers may disagree on its contribution to an explanatory developmental theory.

Analysis of Variance and Infancy Research

Many studies of infant behavior have been analyzed with the analysis of variance. By selecting this analysis technique, the researcher makes a series of assumptions regarding his data which may limit the scope of the research questions which may be answered. Thus, by using the analysis of variance design, the researcher implicitly accepts a biased view of development.

To be more explicit, the analysis of variance design is closely associated with hypothesis testing. This implies that in developmental research most analysis of variance designs are capable of answering questions regarding group (in cross-sectional designs) or age (time of testing in longitudinal designs) differences. However, a basic research question underlying much of developmental psychology concerns the formulation of an adequate description of a developmental function (e.g., changes in memory as a function of maturation). The traditional analysis of variance design may not be the most sensitive procedure to assess developmental functions since the analysis evolved from agricultural research primarily concerned with identifying differences in the yield of different plots. The second part of this chapter will discuss techniques that might be applicable to the description of developmental change. This section will continue with examples of designs and techniques used to answer questions that can be formulated in questions about *differences*.

Statistical Properties of Analysis of Variance Designs

Aside from the inferential problems associated with the application of analysis of variance designs to developmental research there are some basic statistical problems. Statistically, there are few serious violations if the measurement of change involves the use of independent groups (cross-sectional design). In this case, the assumption of zero covariance should be easily met (i.e., no correlation between the values of randomly selected subjects in different groups). The assumptions of homogeneity of variance and normality of distribution do not provide real problems since statisticians have shown that failure to meet these assumptions usually has minimal effects on F-tests (Box, 1954; Hays, 1963).

If repeated measurement procedures are used (longitudinal design), there is usually some correlation among treatment measurements (nonzero covariance). However, if the covariance is constant from one treatment measurement to the next and equal within-treatment variances are present, then univariate analysis procedures are appropriate (Gaito and Wiley, 1963). Thus, if independent groups (cross-sectional) are used to assess developmental effects or if there are both equal variance and constant covariance at the various times of measurement in a repeated-measures design (longitudinal), the univariate analysis of variance is an appropriate statistical procedure. Unfortunately, this is usually not the case, since most longitudinal studies generate sequential data which are characterized by both unequal variance and changing covariance.

Techniques to Adjust Violations of Assumptions Underlying the Analysis of Variance

Univariate analyses of variance involve the partitioning of the variance within the experiment into a number of *statistically independent* components. Hypotheses related to these components are then evaluated by F-tests. The univariate hypotheses specify that the experimental data represent random samples drawn independently from the same normal population which by definition may have only one variance. Thus, the assumption of zero covariance, normality of distribution, and homogeneity of variance logically follow and are necessary to justify the use of univariant procedures. In contrast, multivariate analyses of variance procedures are concerned with sampling from a number of normal distributions which need not have the zero-covariance and equal-variance assumptions for testing hypotheses (Anderson, 1958).

It has been argued that when there is a moderate correlation between the subjects' scores on the repeated measurements, and the variance of the scores on each repeated measure is not equal, the probability levels of the various F-ratios are generally distorted. Violation of the assumption of homogeneous population variances and covariances generally cause the usual F-test to be positively biased, resulting in an increased probability of type I error (Box, 1954; Winer, 1971).

If the variance-covariance matrices have characteristics of equal variance and zero or constant covariance, univariate analysis procedures provide an exact test of the hypothesis. Since this is not the representative case in developmental research, some correction must be made to adjust the bias in the analysis. An approximate conservative test for the case in which the variances and covariances are heterogeneous has been proposed by Greenhouse and Geisser (1959). The test is negatively biased and the experimenter will err in the direction of not rejecting the null hypothesis when it is false (type II error). This conservative test is obtained by multiplying the conventional degrees of freedom by ϵ. If the variances are homogeneous and the covariances are homogeneous, $\epsilon =$ 1. As heterogeneity increases, ϵ decreases until at the lower bound of ϵ the repeated measures do not contribute to the degrees of freedom. Computation procedures for a conservative F test are identical to those of conventional F test except that different degrees of freedom are used. If the effects are significant, with ϵ assumed to equal its lower bound, there is no need to proceed further because an exact test would also be significant. If, however, the conservative tests are not significant, the conventional F tests in which ϵ is assumed to equal one should be performed. If the tests, using conventional degrees of freedom, are also insignificant, the experimenter can decide not to reject the null hypothesis. If, however, the conventional test is significant but the conservative test is insignificant, an exact test such as Hotelling T^2 statistic can be used to test the hypothesis that the treatment effects are equal to zero (see Kirk, 1968).

An alternative solution is to estimate the value of ϵ from the sample variance-covariance matrix and adjust the degrees of freedom accordingly (Greenhouse and Geisser, 1959). This procedure more closely approximates the F distribution than either the usual F test or the conservative test described above. For a more thorough discussion of the calculation of ϵ and of a comparison of univariate and multivariate tests in repeated-measures experiments see Davidson (1972).

THE SOLOMON AND LESSAC FOUR-GROUP DESIGN: A SPECIALIZED DESIGN FOR DEVELOPMENTAL RESEARCH

Many infancy researchers focus on intervention effects. Their concern is often directed at assessing the detrimental or facilatory influences of environmental manipulations, such as education and nutrition, on development. To deal with assessing interventions many developmental psychologists have used two major experimental strategies: (1) the isolation or deprivation experiment, and (2) the intervention or enrichment experiment. In the isolation experiment, one group is isolated from or deprived of specified stimulus events. Another group, the control group, is exposed to normal conditions. The two groups may be matched closely for genetic attributes in animal studies or socioeconomic status in human studies. After the intervention, both groups are tested on a psychological or behavioral dimension. Differences in performance are generally interpreted as a function of the deterioration of capacities of the isolated subjects. This interpretation assumes that the subjects had the capacity for normal behavior prior to isolation, but that during isolation the capacity was impeded.

Enrichment studies have also been conducted with a similar two-group design. By comparing the enrichment treatment with a normal control, inference is often made regarding the facilitory influences of the enrichment treatment on rate of development. However, the possibility exists that the capacity being tested may have deteriorated in the normal control group over the course of the experimental period, while the enrichment group did not change. Because the outcome of the traditional two-group design is usually assessed in terms of differences, it is impossible to distinguish whether the differences are a function of deterioration in the control or enhancement in the enrichment treated subjects.

According to Solomon and Lessac (1968) there is an experimental design that is capable of directly testing the deterioration and enrichment hypotheses. This design will enable the assessment of the interaction of preexperimental testing with the experimental treatment and allow the experimenter to make a decision regarding the cause of any identified differences between the treated subjects (deprivation or enrichment) and normal subjects. This design is a four-group design (see Solomon, 1949), and according to Solomon and Lessac it is the minimum design required to perform an adequate developmental study comparing either deprived or enriched subjects with control subjects.

The four-group design has two treated groups and two normal control groups. Two groups, one prior to experimental treatment and one prior to control treatment, receive pretesting to estimate the subjects' capacities at the start of the experiment. The other two groups, an experimental group and a control group, are not pretested. This creates a factorial design; two treatments (control and experimental) and two pretest conditions (pretest and no pretest). A sample of the design adapted from Solomon and Lessac is illustrated in Table 21-1.

This design enables a pretest of performance of groups I and III to make a statistical inference about the initial performance levels of groups II and IV (the groups from the traditional two-group design). The combined means of groups I and III on the pretest is the best estimate of what the performances of groups II and IV would have been on a pretest. The effects of the experimental treatment of group II can be estimated by being compared with group IV on the post-test performance without being contaminated by the pretesting procedures. Of course, this design assumes that the groups have been carefully matched. In studies with animal subjects this may be done by assigning littermates to each of the four groups; in studies with human subjects matching is more difficult.

The main advantages of the four-group design are that it increases the possibility of detecting developmental phenomena and that it enables a quantitative rather than a relative interpretation regarding the developmental shift. The four-group design may allow an assessment of the influence of intervention, extremely important in a theoretical justification of much of infancy research.

Applicability of the four-group design to developmental research is limited. If the subjects in groups I and III (the only groups being pretested) are incapable of performing in the pretest, the result is a two-group experiment. This may occur when the behaviors being assessed following intervention are not in the behavioral repertoire of the subjects at the time of pretesting. If this is the case, it is impossible to know if the capacity unmeasurable during a pretest and presumably emerging during the treatment period has deteriorated, remained static, or developed further in the experimental group relative to the normal control group. Solomon and Lessac have emphasized that the four-group design is adequate only for the case in which there is one type of identifiable treatment difference between experimental and normal control groups.

There are situations in comparative research with animals in which the testing procedure involves sacrificing the animal. An example would be the effects of experience on brain development. In this situation, it is impossible to assess the cortical development in the same animal during both the pre- and post-test conditions. In this type of research, developmental phenomena are often experimentally confounded with intervention effects. For example, infant rats may be separated into two groups, one an enrichment treatment and the other a normal control. After a prolonged treatment period, the animals are sacrificed and the cortex examined. The differences between the groups are assumed to be

Table 21-1. Experimental Events

	Pretest	Experimental Treatment	Post-Test
Experimental Groups			
Group I	✓	✓	✓
Group II		✓	✓
Control Groups			
Group III	✓		✓
Group IV			✓

a function of facilitory effects of the enrichment treatment. This interpretation may be misleading, since we have no idea about the cortical development prior to treatment. However, if a matched group of littermates were tested prior to the treatment, an estimate of the developmental shift might be made.

Summary

There are advantages and disadvantages of the basic analysis of variance research designs. The selection of an analysis technique limits the research questions that may be answered. If the questions asked are related to developmental differences, the analysis of variance design may be appropriate. Regardless of whether the research has utilized univariate or multivariate measures, the research designs discussed in this section have only been capable of treating developmental change in terms of static measurements.

From the preceding sections in this chapter, it would appear that developmental psychology has evolved into a discipline more concerned with identifying age-related differences than in describing developmental functions. Wohlwill (1970a) has discussed the status of age as a concept in developmental psychology. He has expressed a dissatis-- faction with the widespread tendency to consider age as an independent variable, comparable to other *manipulations*, and to study *differences* rather than describing developmental functions. Wohlwill (1970b) suggests that the study of changes in behavior as a function of age is analogous to the study of other changes in behavior which occur along a temporal dimension. Thus, the age variable should not be interpreted as an independent variable but as a *dimension* along which changes in a dependent variable may be studied. The following sections will deal with a more dynamic approach to describe developmental functions.

Developmental Psychology: The Psychology of Change

When articles are reviewed for the major journals in developmental psychology the editors generally ask the reviewers to evaluate the article's contribution toward an understanding of human development. Unfortunately, since most articles have been dependent upon the designs discussed earlier in this chapter, they are only capable of reporting differences among age groups and are not capable of producing any synthesis or insight regarding the development of psychological processes. One underlying goal of developmental research should be to describe development and not merely to identify age differences. However, since the developmental psychologist has often adopted and statistically employed an independent group's analysis of variance design, he has only been able to answer the question, "Do the age groups differ?" Developmental psychologists should pose the more basic question, "How may the functional relationship between maturation and psychological processes be described?"

Developmental functions characteristic of behavioral and physiological activity may often be described by a curve representing a series of successive observations (e.g., body weight, size of vocabulary). These curves may be described by a mathematical function (e.g., growth and decay functions of populations). Moreover, behaviors and physiological activity may at times be related to rhythmic cyclicity (e.g., seasonal cycles of activity, menstrual cyclicity). This rhythmicity might be described in terms of the frequency and amplitude of the behavior. Often, however, actual behavior observed by infancy researchers may be a combination of both a curve and a rhythmicity component; the rhythmicity component may be superimposed on the curve. We may observe this combination in daily activity cycles which may be superimposed on a curve describing the developmental increase in total number of hours awake.

It logically follows that two statistical techniques might be employed to answer developmental questions. One is to utilize curve-fitting techniques (i.e., regression techniques) to describe patterns of a developmental function. The goal of this approach is to empirically determine the general form underlying the developmental function of an observable response parameter. The emphasis of this approach is descriptive, not hypothesis-testing. The experimenter is no longer asking whether groups differ in performance as a function of age, but is now attempting to determine the *form* of the age function to infer the underlying developmental process. The second is to utilize time-series statistics. Time-series statistics may be used as a stochastic or deterministic technique to describe the cyclicity in spontaneous behavioral or physiological patterns or as an evaluative technique to assess intervention influences.

Trends

The typical procedures for handling longitudinal data in an ordinary analysis of variance may yield a significant *effect* of age reflecting differences among the various testing sessions. A more appropriate goal of developmental research, rather than testing hypotheses related to age *differences*, might be to take the approach of constructing descriptions of the form of various developmental functions. By applying a regression approach to the traditional analysis of variance procedures, the resulting analysis trends (Kirk, 1968; Winer, 1971) might produce a good approximation to the form of the developmental function.

Tests for trend are motivated by two concerns: theoretical predictions and descriptions of nature. In the first case we may want to know whether or not the function exhibits a particular shape that is critical for our theory. In the second case the trend analysis is post hoc and we are looking for the simplest function that will adequately describe the data. Developmental psychologists are often interested in the shape or the form of the function relating values of a dependent variable and time of measurement. In infancy research, it is often assumed that a developmental function will be continuous over the entire time span investigated in the study. It may then be unimportant to test differences among contiguous means, because the main concern is in the overall relationship between the elapsing of time and the dependent variable. An analysis of the shape of a function, or trend analysis, is dictated when research questions focus on the *ups and downs* of a function. If the trend reflected in the data is important for answering the research questions, then a trend analysis is most appropriate.

Trend analysis is especially helpful in the description of longitudinal data. Suppose that we have conducted a longitudinal study measuring physiological reactivity to auditory stimuli. In this hypothetical study, heart-rate responses have been evaluated during monthly tests in the 1st year of life. How might we describe these data? We would probably not be satisfied with a description that said the following: The magnitude of the response is greater in month 2 than month 1 and continued to increase through month 7 and then dropped in a monotonic fashion until month 12 when the response magnitude returned to the approximate magnitude of month 1. This statement might accurately describe the graph of the data. However, many psychologists may want to say more than to just report the functional relationships among the data points. They may be more interested in speculating about the basic processes underlying these relationships.

The analysis of trends provides a procedure for the assessment of the strength of the various fluctuations observed and provides information regarding the generalized form (linear, quadratic, cubic, quartic, etc.) that the underlying developmental function might take. A linear function, the least complex trend, is a curve that either rises or drops at the same rate between any two points (i.e., a straight line). If the linear function actually represents the developmental trend, we could devise a relatively simple explanation of physiological reactivity—a theory in which there is a single process changing at a constant rate with time. Unfortunately, the linear function often does not fit the data. There are situations, such as in the above hypothetical study, in which the curve exhibits a consistent rise and then a consistent drop. The function described by this single reversal of direction, a rise followed by a drop, is a quadratic function.

At times, when the best fit for the shape of the curve can not be accounted for by either a linear function (a constant downward or upward trend) or a quadratic function (a rise and fall), higher-order components containing more than two reversals might be used. A curve that has two reversals of slope contains a cubic component; three reversals, a quartic component; four reversals, a quintic component. As the number of slope reversals increases, the complexity of the theoretical interpretations increases considerably. Most existing developmental or infancy theories make linear (constant growth and improvement) or quadratic (a growth phase and a deterioration phase, e.g., life-span approach) predictions.

There are several limitations of the analysis of trend. First, our knowledge about the underlying developmental function comes from the sampling rate we have selected for the experiment. Would the same underlying trend be suggested if the time between observations were shorter or longer? Second, the shape of the function might be different before and after the period of time sampled in the experiment. Third, the analysis is based upon the assumption that the polynomial is the appropriate mathematical function to describe a set of data. In some experiments, certain phenomena are better described by an exponential function or by a logarithmic function.

In developmental research, at least during a stage of theory-construction and model-building, rather than an hypothesis-testing approach, it may be more appropriate to be descriptive by estimating a theoretical function of the parameter being investigated. A trend analysis may be viewed as an example of a descriptive curve-fitting procedure. When applied to developmental data, the analysis may be useful in empirically estimating the shape of an underlying developmental function (linear, quadratic, cubic, quartic, quintic, etc.).

Time-Series

If one surveys the major psychological journals, there are very few articles that have utilized time-series statistics to describe developmental functions. Time-series statistics, however, have been used to describe physiological response patterns (Porges, 1976a) and as a technique to evaluate the effectiveness of an intervention in behavior modification or clinical psychotherapy (Glass et al., 1975). This appears to be ironic since most observations in developmental research are made at discrete, equally spaced intervals of time. When this type of series of equally spaced observations is obtained, various time-series models may be applied which may be capable of describing behavior, forecasting future values, and assessing intervention influences.

An important advantage of the time-series design is that it offers both a technique to describe changing behavioral patterns and to evaluate intervention or treatment effects.

The time-series designs provide a methodology appropriate to the complexity of the serial effects of interventions and of the historical antecedents characteristic of developmental data. However, the logical application of time-series statistics to the study of developmental phenomena has been neglected. There are two main reasons for encouraging the use of time-series designs: the first is feasibility, since many developmental phenomena are not amenable to experimental control; the second is the type of data, since by their very nature, developmental data are sequential, repeated measures.

Two dimensions may be used to describe time-series models: (1) the predictability of the behavior, which will be either stochastic (probabilistic) or deterministic (totally predictable), and (2) the stationarity of the behavior (whether or not the time-related trends of the behavior remain in equilibrium about a constant mean). Since there may be many unknown factors influencing behavioral development, it may not be possible to describe developmental processes with a deterministic model. The two most appropriate time-series models for describing development are forecasting models, which may be used to predict future behavior based upon antecedent observations, and spectral models, which may decompose behavioral patterns into rhythmic cycles of various periodicities.

The concept of using a mathematical model to describe behavior is based upon disciplines such as engineering and economics (Box and Jenkins, 1970). In these disciplines, it has been possible to derive models based on physical laws which have enabled predictions of some time-dependent behavior or activity. If these models were applied to infancy research we might be able to predict the number of words a child might speak at various ages. If an exact calculation were possible, such a model would be entirely *deterministic*. Unfortunately, there are no behavioral phenomena in the domain of infancy research that are totally deterministic. In many problems related to infant development, we have to consider a time-dependent phenomenon in which there are many unknown factors and for which it is not possible to write a deterministic model that allows exact calculation of the future behavior. Nevertheless, it may be possible to derive a mathematical model that can be used to calculate, within a statistically defined confidence interval, the *probability* of a future event. Such a probability model is called a stochastic model and will be the only type of model applicable to the research needs of developmental psychologists.

Spectral Analysis

For a series of at least 100 continuous observations, a method called spectral analysis may be used (Granger and Hataneka, 1964). Spectral analysis views a time-series as a complex wave pattern composed of weighted simple waves. The spectral analysis decomposes the total variance of the time-series into basic frequencies. The spectral distribution function of a time-series has peak values at frequency bands which contribute significantly to oscillations in the series. Spectral models have been used to identify the dominant frequencies in brain waves or to forecast future values of a series (e.g., forecasting shifts in climate) to obtain a causal inference when lead indicators always precede a specific event (i.e., correlated sequential activity), and perhaps most relevant to developmental psychology, to develop and construct theory by conceptualizing an active changing process.

Spectral analyses have been used to describe physiological activity, both spontaneously and in response to a change in stimulation. By comparing the composition of the spectrum before and after the stimulus, the effectiveness of the stimulus in eliciting a response may be assessed. Thus, spectral analysis may be used both as a technique to describe process and also as a technique to test hypotheses. In developmental psychology, if the data exhibit patterns of oscillations, it might be logical and feasible to describe patterns of behavior within specific segments of the life span in terms of a spectral distribution function.

Quasi-Experimental Designs

Campbell and Stanley (1966) have assembled a variety of quasi-experimental time-series designs which may be used to evaluate the effect of interventions on developmental phenomena. Quasi-experimental designs are rooted in conditions where there is no possibility of manipulating the experimental stimulus and no control through matching and randomization over competing stimuli. These designs attempt to approximate the logic of the laboratory. This logic includes three components: (1) the observation of a variation in an independent variable, (2) the observed covariation between the change in an independent variable and change in some other variable, and (3) an assessment that the statistical confidence of the observed covariation between two variables is a nonspurious covariation by examining rival hypotheses.

These unintrusive or quasi-experimental designs may be used to evaluate developmental change. In all these designs, the data are manipulated by the experimenter to render an interpretation of a specific hypothesis as being more plausible than other rival hypotheses. For a more elaborate discussion of these quasi-experimental designs read Campbell and Stanley (1966) or Caporaso and Roos (1973), and for a discussion of rival and plausible hypotheses read Rozelle and Campbell (1969).

Interrupted and Multiple Time-Series Designs

One class of quasi-experimental designs, the interrupted time-series model, is concerned with evaluating the effect of interventions. The interrupted time-series experiment is typical of much of the classical 19th-century experimentation to the physical sciences. It is typified by observations for extended periods before and after a major change in experimental conditions. These designs may be adapted for evaluating interventions on developmental phenomena. Before describing these designs, it is important to identify some of the problems associated with the statistical analyses of intervention influences.

Researchers often apply t-tests to pre- and post-intervention data. This method (and the essentially similar analysis of variance) may be inappropriate for certain series of data for at least two reasons. First, the attribution of an effect to an intervention is not simply a matter of comparing pre- and post-intervention *means*. For example, it is possible to have a time-series that drifts steadily upward but shows neither change in level nor in direction coincident with an intervention. This series will show different pre- and post-intervention means. A significant t-test between the pre- and post-means would be irrelevant. Similarly, an effective intervention that changes the upward drift of a series to a downward drift (in a triangular pattern) would yield a nonsignificant t-statistic. Second, inferential techniques based upon the assumption of independent data cannot safely be applied to time-series data that typically show dependence among observations. Gottman (1973) has addressed himself to these problems and has developed an appropriate statistic capable of testing intervention effects on both slope and level changes. This statistic takes into account the autoregressive properties of the specific time-series.

Campbell and Stanley (1966) and Glass et al. (1975) have presented numerous time-series designs. Three of these designs appear to be appropriate for testing hypotheses regarding treatment influences during early development and will be described below. The multiple time-series design (Campbell and Stanley, 1966) consists of a series of observations for an experimental group and control group. Within the series of observations, as illustrated below, a specific manipulation or intervention is presented to the experimental group.

0 0 0 0X0 0 0 0 — experimental group
0 0 0 0 0 0 0 0 — control group
0: observations; X: intervention

If the observations are viewed over a relatively long period of time, this type of design would control for maturation. The control group would give the experimenter a baseline to evaluate normal maturational shifts independent of an intervention. The critical comparison in applying this design to developmental research is to compare the normal developmental trend of a response (control group) to the behavior of the group receiving the intervention effects.

Time-series statistics offer a unique way of dealing with the problems associated with stimulus and response equivalence. The response patterns of various age groups could be assessed to the same stimulus condition or the response patterns of various age groups could be assessed to different functionally equivalent stimulus conditions. Response equivalence might be evaluated by the multiple-group–single-intervention design (Glass et al., 1975). This design is characterized by the intervention of one treatment into the separate time-series being observed on two or more groups. This design, as illustrated below, parallels the traditional cross-sectional approach and represents an attempt to deal with the generalizability of an intervention effect (i.e., testing the equivalence of the manipulation for the multiple groups). This design could be modified by observing a control group paralleling each age group receiving the intervention. The design permits an examination of the developmental typology of phases or periods which may be differentially sensitive to a specific intervention.

0 0 0 0X0 0 0 0 — age group I
0 0 0 0 0 0 0 0 — age group I, control
0 0 0 0X0 0 0 0 — age group II
0 0 0 0 0 0 0 0 — age group II, control

The multiple-group–multiple-intervention design (Glass et al., 1975) appears to be an appropriate technique for assessing functional equivalence among different age groups to different stimulus conditions. This design is analogous to the multiple-group–single-intervention design with the exception that different interventions occur in the separate groups. Like the earlier time-series designs discussed, a variation could include control groups not receiving the intervention. This design, as illustrated below, might be capable of assessing whether the different stimulus conditions result in similar response patterns (i.e., functional equivalence).

0 0 0 0X0 0 0 0 — age group I
0 0 0 0 0 0 0 0 — age group I, control
0 0 0 0Y0 0 0 0 — age group II
0 0 0 0 0 0 0 0 — age group II, control

X: intervention for age group I
Y: intervention for age group II

The subject-selection problems encountered in time-series designs are similar to the problems associated with cross-sectional research. Actually, the multiple-group–multiple-intervention and the multiple-group–single-intervention designs may be viewed as a combination of both cross-sectional and longitudinal approaches in that they may be composed of age-related groups (cross-sectional) and that they may assess responses across a prolonged period of time (longitudinal). The greater the number of observations, the easier it is to generalize and project (forecast) a developmental function for a specific phenomenon.

Change-Detection Model

The change-detection model and the integrated moving average model are similar to the interrupted time-series model. These models are alternatives to assess change in situations in which traditional statistical tests of significance can be seriously affected by serial correlation (repeated-measurements covariance). The integrated moving average model (Box and Jenkins, 1970) has some unique properties. In this model, if the sequential observations of a variable are subjected to periodic random shocks, a proportion of the energy of this disruption will be absorbed into the level of the series. Also, a property of this model is that the further away from an event in time, the less the behavior is a function of the event. The integrated moving average model has been successfully applied when the changes that occur have no tendency to return to some permanent stable level. Since the observations of behavior during early development are nonstationary, never reaching a permanent stable level, the integrated moving average model might be appropriate.

The change-detection model (Jones et al., 1969) is based upon the assumption that the prestimulus data tend to be stable, unlike the integrated moving average model. This model assumes stationarity. The parameters of the model are estimated from the pre-stimulus data. The difference between the predicted and observed values is divided by an estimated standard deviation from the prestimulus data, giving an approximate t-statistic. This time-series model has been applied to physiologic data to detect responses in a newborn to auditory stimuli (Jones et al., 1969). In this study, a stationary model was assumed for the periods before stimulation. The objective was to detect any deviations from the stationary structure of the prestimulus periods. The limitation of this model is that it may assess only short-term transient effects because it assumes that the process will return to a steady state, characteristic of stationary process. This model has also been generalized to the multivariate case (Jones et al., 1970).

Operant Design

The operant design is very similar to the interrupted time-series models. It relies on a behavior deviating from a stable baseline following the shaping procedure. When a return to baseline and then the reconfirmation of the intervention are added it is labeled an A-B-A-B design and assesses the experiment's control over the behavior. The A-B-A-B design assumes that the series would have remained at stable baseline level in the absence of the intervention. This assumption is tested when the treatment (i.e., reinforcement) is removed and the untreated subject is observed to see if he returns to baseline level. Glass et al. (1975) argue that this assumption is perhaps too stringent, since many behaviors do not have a stable baseline level and are *nonstationary* processes. In these cases, the intervention might be effective even if the process did not return to baseline level when the intervention was removed.

Many operant and developmental psychologists may be unaware of an obvious similarity in technique between behavior modification and the study of various developmental phenomena. The application of operant procedures to behavior modification implies powerful assumptions regarding the programmatic sequence in which behaviors are shaped to reach the target behavior. Operant psychology, like developmental psychology, is dependent upon the observation, description, and measurement of changes in behavior over time. In order to select the behavioral sequence to be shaped, the operant psychologist is left with two options: (1) to systematically observe behavior and to decompose what appears to be normal (representative of the population) behavior into a series of elements which when combined through shaping procedures should result in the target behavior, or (2) to systematically observe the developmental sequence of a behavior and to shape behavior in accordance with this developmental framework.

The first option is dependent upon three points: (1) the practitioner's ability to decompose behavior into elements, (2) the representativeness of the selected elements (i.e., were the elements derived from observing behavior which was both normal and representative), and (3) the assumption that the sequencing (sequential shaping) represents an efficient and functional strategy.

The second option presents another venue for developing an efficient sequence for shaping behavior. It may be possible that through the observation of the development of a specific behavior, an efficient procedure of modifying behavior might be developed. This procedure might reach the developmentally mature target behavior through the normal *developmental* sequence rather than through a *decomposition* of the target behavior. The above discussion suggests that operant psychology may be rooted in the parametric description of behavioral development. Thus, the operant psychologist may be dependent upon descriptive statistics before he begins his research and upon more complex time-series statistics to evaluate his intervention.

Cross-Lag Panel

Often we are interested in asking whether two variables *(X* and *Y)* are causally interrelated. In research, there is often a tendency to choose one of two causal hypotheses: *X* causes *Y,* or *Y* causes *X.* In specific situations, it may be possible that both these hypotheses are partially correct. The social interactions between mother and infant might form a typical example of mutual causality; the mother's behavior influences the infant and the infant's behavior influences the mother. The cross-lag panel design might be appropriate for this type of research, since it has the capacity to evaluate between the relative causal hypotheses (i.e., the direction of causation).

Correlations are involved in this analysis between two variables *(X* and *Y)* measured at two points in time *(t_1* and *t_2).* The basic design is illustrated in Figure 21-1. Six correlations may be generated describing the relationship between the two variables (all lines in Fig. 21-1 represent correlational coefficients). Causal inference is derived from the two lagged diagonal correlations *($rX_{t1}Y_{t2}$* and *$rY_{t1}X_{t2}$).* The name of the design, the cross-lag design, is derived from the emphasis on these two correlations. If the preponderant causal structure is from *X* to *Y,* the correlation between *X_{t1}* and *Y_{t2}* should be greater than the correlation between *Y_{t1}* and *X_{t2}.* The model implies that the following assumptions, which if not consistent with the observed behavior, may cause inferential problems: The assumption that the synchronous correlations *($rX_{t1}Y_{t1}$* and *$rX_{t2}Y_{t2}$)* are smaller than the lagged correlations *($rX_{t1}Y_{t2}$* and *$rY_{t1}X_{t2}$);* the assumption that the time lag is equal for both

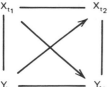

Fig. 21-1.   Cross-lag Panel Design.

variables; the assumption that the mutual influences between the two variables are attenuated from one point in time to the next; and the assumption that influences on X and Y, other than their mutual interaction, are constant from one point in time to the next. Roos (1973) presents a more thorough discussion of these assumptions and of the application of the design.

Directional Correlation

Infancy researchers are often interested in assessing the relationship between two behaviors over time. One might find examples in the relationship between frequency of verbalizations and smiling or the relationship between nutrition and learning. The relationship between two variables sampled over time from the same subject can be statistically described by correlational techniques. However, the traditional product-moment correlation may be insensitive to certain shifts in behaviors; it is possible to have a very low product-moment correlation between two behaviors that are always shifting direction in parallel if the magnitude of the shifts are independent. A statistic labeled the *directional correlation coefficient* (Strahan, 1971) is capable of assessing the tendency of two variables to change value in the same direction from one sampling occasion to the next. If increases in variable X are accompanied by increases in variable Y and decreases in X by decreases in Y, there is a positive directional correlation between variables X and Y. If the measures in variable Y are accompanied by decreases in variable Y, there is a negative directional correlation.

The procedure to calculate the coefficient may be described by taking a set of X and Y values recorded on n successive occasions. The values of each sampling occasion are then compared with the values of the immediately preceding occasion. A plus score is given when the direction of X is the same as Y (both variables increase or both decrease), a minus score when the direction of X is opposite that of Y (one variable increases, the other decreases), and a zero when either or both variables remain unchanged. The coefficient of directional correlation may then be defined as

$$d = \frac{p - m}{p + m}$$

where p is the number of pluses and m the number of minuses. As in other correlational statistics, d ranges from -1 to $+1$. When the association of the two variables is linear or monotonic the directional correlation will approximate product-moment or rank-order correlations. However, if directional characteristics of the relationship between two behaviors is of interest, the d coefficient is the only adequate measure. Strahan (1973) has extended the directional correlation coefficient (d) from the bivariate to the multivariate case. The coefficient of multiple directional correlation (D) measures the overall degree to which k variables change values in the same direction from one sampling occasion to the next.

CONCLUSION

The preceding sections of this chapter sampled research designs applicable to the study of infant development. In developmental research, the selection of a legitimate research question and an acceptable experimental design are dependent upon the philosophical constraints associated with the conceptual view of man accepted by the researcher. This concluding section will attempt to describe the sequential dependencies of research-related operations to which the experimenter is committed once he has tacitly accepted a specific conceptual view of man.

According to Kuhn (1962), the quest for scientific knowledge has resulted in the production of paradigms that are in conflict. By conflict he means that they represent different and irreconcilable world views. Various scientific communities form around these world views, each with only one acceptable paradigm. This results in a different set of criteria for valid scientific questions; what one community accepts as a legitimate research question, the other community might reject as being *unscientific*. Each community has its own research goals, and by accepting a restricted subset of research questions they become insulated from important problems that may not be reducible to their favored paradigm. In spite of these constraints, paradigms are important in organizing scientific knowledge. In the absence of a paradigm, all facts would seem equally relevant, systematic (i.e., programmatic) research would not exist, and communication of scientific knowledge, which is dependent upon the shared language of a specific paradigm, would be greatly limited.

In two very readable papers, Reese and Overton (1970) and Overton and Reese (1973) address the problem of how different world views influence the study of human development. They describe how two radically irreconcilable world views have influenced the nature of psychological inquiry and the conceptualization of developmental influences. These two world views are associated with two families of psychological theory: one family is formulated within the context of a mechanistic view of man; the other family is formulated within the context of the organismic view of man.

The basic metaphor of man within the mechanistic view is that of a machine. Reese and Overton (1970) have classified developmental theorists such as Bijou and Baer (1961) and Sears (Sears et al., 1965) in a family of theories formulated within the context of the mechanistic world hypothesis. The mechanistic view portrays man as a machine composed of discrete elements operating along quantifiable spatial and temporal dimensions. The view is a derivative of the English Empiricists (e.g., Locke, Berkeley, Hume) and has been manifested in American Behaviorism and other modified stimulus-response (S-R) models. Within the mechanistic view, psychology is modeled upon classical Newtonian physics. This model is consistent with hierarchical theories in which laws are deductions from a small set of basic principles—for example, laws of learning. Given a mechanistic model, prediction of activity is in principle possible if complete knowledge of the machine is known. This model is susceptible to quantification, and functional equations may be constructed to exhibit the relationship among the elements of the ''machine.'' The mechanistic model characterizes man, like other parts of the universal machine, as inherently at rest.

In contrast, the basic metaphor of man within the organismic view is that of a spontaneously active, organized "living" system. Reese and Overton (1970) have included Piaget (1970), Erikson (1950), and Werner (1948) in the family of theories formulated within the context of the organismic world hypothesis. The organismic view portrays man as being inherently and spontaneously active—a view of man as the source of acts, rather than as the collection of acts initiated by external forces. This view is a derivative of the synthetic continental philosophy which emphasized an unfolding and synthesis of the organisms. The source of the view is often attributed to Leibnitz, who postulated that the essence of substance was activity rather than static elementary particles (i.e., mechanistic model). Within the organismic view, man is an organized entity, a configuration of parts which gain their meaning and their function from the whole. The research goal of this approach is directed at identifying the principles of organization and the hierarchic integration of the active continuously changing system. This model is consistent with concatenated or pattern theories in which laws form a network of relations constituting a pattern. Quantification poses a different problem for the organismic model. Since the whole is dynamic rather than static, and knowledge of its parts does not yield information regarding its organization, a strictly predictive and quantitative universe is impossible.

The reader may find himself labeling, as Kuhn would have predicted, one approach unscientific and rejecting it. The reader should be very careful, since rejection of a given model may restrict exposure to important scientific knowledge. It is important to realize that models are not "truthful" representations of the universe. Models can not be assessed as being true or false, but only as being more or less useful. In general, a model may aid the experimenter with theoretical organization and interpretation of data. However, it should become obvious that in addition to being an aid for understanding the data, a model causes the experimenter to see data with a specific focus (see Porges, 1976b) and to impose a specific research methodology.

It is easy to follow the transition from the British Empiricists to American Behaviorism and from Liebnitzian philosophy to the cognitive system described by Piaget. The implication of these two trends on developmental methodology is not self-evident but may be clarified by understanding the treatment of developmental influences within each model.

For the behaviorist, a view that shares the mechanistic model, developmental research, merely refers to change over time. Developmental theories for the behaviorist are merely extentions of general behavioristic theories; for example, learning theories deal with performance change over seconds, minutes, and days while developmental learning theories deal with performance change over weeks, months, and years. A characteristic of this approach is that age is often viewed as causal. However, age reduces to time and time by itself can cause nothing. As Wohlwill has suggested (1970a,b), time is a dimension along which other dependent variables may be sampled; time is an indexing variable and not a causal variable. The mechanistic approach actually requires the identification of the causal variables correlated with age. This is consistent with the English philosopher, G. D. Broad (1959), who stated that the position in the time dimension has no physical consequence.

It is true that, if I go out without my overcoat at 2 a.m., I shall probably catch cold; whilst, if I do so at 2 p.m., I shall probably take no harm. But this difference is never ascribed to the mere difference in date, but to the fact that different conditions of temperature and dampness will be contemporary with my two expeditions.

For the family of theories that are derived from the organismic world view, developmental research is concerned with studying changes in organization. These changes in organization may not be directly observable. Development is not an empirical concept but a theoretical concept. Changes in organization are not explainable by material (i.e., mechanistic) causes, although these causes may inhibit or facilitate change (e.g., sensory deprivation, malnutrition). Development may then be viewed as a cause for observed changes in behavior.

The two-world-view conflict is not always clear-cut. There are eclectic models which include more than one world view. However, the connotation of the concept of development will often force the investigator to select a specific methodology. There is a primary difference in the treatment of development by the two world views. Most researchers who share the mechanistic view, approach age related changes as if age served a causal function in the ontogeny of behavior. In contrast, the organismic view does not directly investigate age effects but uses the concept of development as an explanation for changes in cognitive organization inferred from behavior. In the organismic model, the identification of age-related differences is not a legitimate research question. However, the investigation of differences in behavior as a function of various degrees of cognitive organization (e.g., preoperational and concrete operational) would be. An organismic view would be interested in the description of a developmental function to estimate the subject's changing organization of behavior, not to estimate yearly differences in behavior.

Since the mechanistic view is reductionistic and views the universe with an additive model, it is not surprising that most developmental psychologists who share this view also select analysis of variance designs for their research. Analysis of variance designs are based upon the assumption that the variance of a dependent variable may be partitioned into causal independent components. The ideas expressed by Wohlwill (1970a, b) should be a clear warning that chronological age is a biotic variable which is not amenable to procedures such as random assignment or replication. Thus, researchers should be cautious about interpreting significant age effects.

If the investigator finds his research question consistent with the organismic world view, he may find himself searching for techniques to describe the organization of a dynamic system. In attempting to do this, he may use descriptive terms such as *order, sequence, integration, organization,* or *interrelationship,* and he may use spectral analysis or trend analysis. Spectral analysis might be employed to identify the individual differences in the integration of various behaviors or physiological response systems (i.e., organization of the nervous system). Porges (1976a) has applied spectral analyses to investigate the possibility of defective integration in the nervous systems of hyperactive children. Many researchers use this technique when they search for rhythmic generators in the nervous system by applying spectral analysis to EEG data. Since most developmental investigators are not involved in physiological research, a more relevant example might be the spectral analysis of rhythmic motor activity or even the rhythmicity exhibited in play behavior.

Most individuals who share the organismic world view may not have the time or the computer resources to use spectral analysis and, moreover, their research questions may not be amenable to the spectral paradigm. These individuals may be investigating behavior that does exhibit changes over time, and they might want to describe a function to infer the organizational shifts in an underlying process. For these investigators, trend analysis might be applicable.

The number of points of data collected, the period of time elapsed during data collection, and the investigator's specific research question will dictate which measure of change will be employed. If the number of observations are few, it will preclude the possibility of using a spectral analysis. However, the pattern of change could be described by a polynomial in an analysis of trends (i.e., curve-fitting techniques). When research questions and feasibility of research resources dictate a comparison among various age periods regarding the influences of any specific manipulation, the family of multiple-time-series designs appears appropriate. Moreover, with slight variations, these designs could evaluate the influence of repeated interventions or manipulations within each experimental group. Thus, it is possible to develop time-series designs which parallel the general cross-section, longitudinal, and cross-sequential approaches.

Both the curve-fitting approach and the time-series approach have numerous advantages. The advantage that curve-fitting (e.g., analysis of trends) has over traditional analysis of variance designs is that it deals with the question of describing a developmental function rather than the identification of age-group differences. The advantage that time-series analysis has over the static approaches which dominate developmental psychology is that it is capable of more precisely separating the influences of situational or interventional variables from the trends associated with normal development.

The reader should note that the few techniques presented in this chapter are merely examples of statistical techniques that are available for dealing with the dimension of time. Techniques such as Tucker's (1963) three-mode factor analysis, path-analysis, and nonparametric sequential techniques are other examples which might find application in the study of infant development. Developmental psychology should not be plagued by the problem that "one cannot test the same subject twice," but should address itself to the description of basic developmental functions in a changing organism. The infancy researcher should face the challenge of identifying important behavioral patterns and describing their developmental function in order to contribute needed information regarding the rapidly changing infant.

BIBLIOGRAPHY

Anderson, T.W. *Introduction to Multivariate Statistical Analysis*. New York: Wiley, 1958.

Baltes, P.B., Cornelius, S.W., and Nesselroade, J.R. Cohort effects in developmental psychology: Theoretical and methodological perspectives prepared for *Minnesota Symposium on Child Psychology*. Collins, W. A. (ed.). Vol. II, Minneapolis: Institute of Child Development, University of Minnesota, October, 1976.

Baltes, P.B. and Goulet, L.R. Status and issues of a life-span developmental psychology. In L.R. Goulet and P.B. Baltes (eds.), *Life-Span Developmental Psychology: Research and Theory*. New York: Academic, 1970, 3–21.

Bell, R.Q. Convergence: An accelerated longitudinal approach. *Child Development*, 1953, **24**, 145–152.

Bijou, S.W. and Baer, D.M. (eds.) *Child Development I: A Systematic and Empirical Theory*. New York: Appleton-Century-Crofts, 1961.

Bitterman, M.E. Toward a comparative psychology of learning. *American Psychologist*, 1960, **15**, 704–712.

Box, G.E.P. Some theorems on quadratic forms applied in the study of analysis of variance problems. *Annals of Mathematical Statistics*, 1954, **25**, 290–302.

Box, G.E.P. and Jenkins, G.M. *Time Series Analysis: Forecasting and Control*. San Francisco: Holden-Day, 1970.

Broad, C.D. *Scientific Thought*. Paterson, N.J.: Littlefield, Adams, 1959.

Campbell, D.T. and Fiske, D.W. Convergent and discriminant validation by multitrait-multimethod matrix. *Psychological Bulletin,* 1959, **56**, 81–105.

Campbell, D.T. and Stanley, J.C. *Experimental and Quasi-experimental Designs for Research.* Chicago: Rand McNally, 1966.

Caporaso, J.A. and Ross, L.L., Jr. (eds.) *Quasi-experimental Approaches: Testing Theory and Evaluating Policy.* Evanston: Northwestern University, 1973.

Clifton, R.K. Cardiac conditioning and orienting in the infant. In P.O. Obrist, A.H. Black, J. Brener and L.V. Dicara (eds.), *Cardiovascular Psychophysiology,* Chicago: Aldine, 1974, 479–504.

Davidson, M.L. Univariate versus multivariate tests in repeated-measures experiments. *Psychological Bulletin,* 1972, **77**, 446–452.

Erikson, E. *Childhood and Society.* New York: Norton, 1950.

Gaito, J. and Wiley, D.E. Univariate analysis of variance procedures in the measurement of change. In C.W. Harris (ed.) *Problems in Measuring Change,* Madison: University of Wisconsin, 1963, 60–84.

Glass, G.V., Willson, V.L., and Gottman, J.M. *Design and Analysis of Time-series Experiments.* Boulder: Colorado Associated University, 1975.

Gottman, J.M. N-of-one and N-of-two research in psychotherapy. *Psychological Bulletin,* 1973, **80**, 93–105.

Graham, F.K., Berg, K.M., Berg, W.K., Jackson, J.C., Hatton, H.M. and Kantrowitz, S.R. Cardiac orienting response as a function of age. *Psychonomic Science,* 1970, **19**, 363–365.

Graham, F.K. and Clifton, R.K. Heart rate change as a component of the orienting response. *Psychological Bulletin,* 1966, **65**, 305–320.

Graham, F.K. and Jackson, J.C. Arousal systems and infant heart rate responses. In H.W. Reese and L.P. Lipsitt (eds.), *Advances in Child Development and Behavior.* New York: Academic, 1970.

Granger, C.W.J. and Hatanaka, M. *Spectral Analysis of Economic Time Series.* Princeton: Princeton University, 1964.

Greenhouse, S.W. and Geisser, S. On methods in the analysis of profile data. *Psychometrika,* 1959, **24**, 95–111.

Hays, W.L. *Statistics for Psychologists.* New York: Holt, 1963.

Jones, R.H., Crowell, D.H. and Kapuniai, L.E. Change detection model for serially correlated data. *Psychological Bulletin,* 1969, **71**, 352.

Jones, R.H., Crowell, D.H. and Kapuniai, L.E. Change detection for serially correlated multivariate data. *Biometrics,* 1970, **26**, 269–280.

Kirk, R.E. *Experimental Design: Procedures for the Behavioral Sciences.* Belmont, California: Brooks/Cole, 1968.

Kuhn, T.S. *The Structure of Scientific Revolutions.* Chicago: University of Chicago, 1962.

Morrow, M.C., Boring, F.W., Keough, T.E. and Haesly, R.R. Differential GSR conditioning as a function of age. *Developmental Psychology,* 1969, **1**, 229–302.

Overton, W.F. and Reese, H.W. Models of development: Methodological implications. In J.R. Nesselroade and H.W. Reese (eds.), *Life-span Developmental Psychology: Methodological Issues.* New York: Academic, 1973.

Piaget, J. Piaget's theory. In P.H. Mussen (ed.), *Carmichael's Manual of Child Psychology.* New York: Wiley, 1970, 703–732.

Porges, S.W. Heart rate indices of newborn attentional responsivity. *Merrill-Palmer Quarterly,* 1974, **20** (4), 231–254.

Porges, S.W. Cohort effects and apparent secular trends in infant research. In R. F. Reigel and J.A. Meacham (eds.), *The Developing Individual in a Changing World, Vol. II: Social and Environmental Issues*. Chicago: Aldine, 1976, 687–695.

Porges, S.W. Peripheral and neurochemical parallels of psychopathology: A psychophysiological model relating autonomic imbalance in hyperactivity, psychopathy, and autism. In H.W. Reese (ed.), *Advances in Child Development and Behavior*, Vol. II. New York: Academic, 1976, 36–65.

Roos, L.L., Jr. Panels, rotation, and events. In J.A. Caporaso and L.L. Roos, Jr. (eds.), *Quasi-experimental Approaches: Testing Theory and Evaluating Policy*. Evanston, Illinois: Northwestern University, 1973.

Rees, H.W. and Overton, W.F. Models of development and theories of development. In L.R. Goulet and P.B. Baltes (eds.), *Life-span Developmental Psychology: Theory and Research*. New York: Academic, 1970, 116–145.

Rozelle, R.M. and Campbell, D.T. More plausible rival hypothesis in the cross-lagged panel correlation technique. *Psychological Bulletin, 1969, **71**, 74–80.

Schaie, K.W. A general model for the study of developmental problems. *Psychological Bulletin, 1965, **64**, 92–107.

Schaie, K.W. and Baltes, P.B. On sequential strategies in developmental research: Description or explanation? *Human Development, 1975, **18**, 384–390.

Sears, R.R., Rau, L. and Alpert, R. *Identification and Child Rearing*. Stanford, California: Stanford University, 1965.

Solomon, R.L. An extension of control group design. *Psychological Bulletin, 1949, **46**, 137–150.

Solomon, R.L. and Lessac, M.S. A control group design for experimental studies of developmental processes. *Psychological Bulletin, **70**, 145–150.

Stamps, L.E. and Porges, S.W. Heart rate conditioning in newborn infants: Relationships among conditionability, heart rate variability and sex. *Developmental Psychology, 1975, **11**, 424.

Strahan, R. A coefficient of directional correlation for time-series analysis. *Psychological Bulletin, 1971, **76**, 211–214.

Strahan, R. A generalized directional coefficient for multiple time-series analysis. *Multivariate Behavioral Research, 1973, **8**, 109–116.

Tucker, L.E. Implications of factor analysis of three-mode matrices for measurement of change. In C.W. Harris (ed.), *Problems in Measuring Change*. Madison: University of Wisconsin, 1964, 122–137.

Werner, H. *Comparative Psychology of Mental Development*. New York: International Universities, 1948.

Winer, B.J. *Statistical Principles in Experimental Design*. New York: McGraw-Hill, 1971.

Wohlwill, J.F. Methodology and research strategy in the study of developmental change. In L.R. Goulet and P.B. Baltes (cds.), *Life-span Developmental Psychology: Research and Theory*. New York: Academic, 1970, 149–191.

Wohlwill, J.F. The age variable in psychological research. *Psychological Review, 1971, **77**, 49–64.

PART FIVE

Clinical Issues, Applications and Interventions

CHAPTER 22

Conceptual Issues in Infancy Research[1]

Anneliese F. Korner

Over the last 20 years, and at an accelerated rate during the last 5 years, infancy research has become one of the most popular and prolific fields of psychological research. This area of investigation is by no means a unified field of research. It consists of many sub-branches, each encompassing different goals and concerns and each relying on different conceptual frameworks.

THE DIFFERENT BRANCHES OF INFANCY RESEARCH[2]

One of the largest branches of infancy research concerns itself primarily with *environmental influences* which act upon child development. This branch in itself contains many subsidiary research foci. For example, there is a large literature on the *effects of institutionalization* and of *maternal deprivation and separation* on the child's development. In the case of institutionalization the effects are usually the product of a mixture of maternal deprivation and separation and of the drab inanimate environment commonly prevailing in institutions. This mixture of environmental factors is usually so confounded that the effects of each are difficult to estimate. (For a critical review of the conceptual issues involved in this type of research see Casler, 1961, and Yarrow, 1961.)

Also dealing with environmental influences are the studies of the effects of differences in *parental handling* on the child's development. Included in this area of differing child care practices are studies of the differential effects of breast or bottle feeding, early or late weaning or toilet training, authoritarian, democratic, or laissez-faire caretaking practices, and so on (e.g. Davis et al., 1948; Heinstein, 1963; Sears et al., 1957).

Allied to this branch of infancy research are the many studies of *maternal or parental attitudes* and the effects these may have on the child. It is noteworthy that even this subbranch of research on environmental influences comprises conceptually diverse issues which are, however, frequently not differentiated in practice. Research on parental attitudes comprises studies of parental feelings toward their children, the parents' self-perception of how they are dealing with their children, and the parents' child-rearing philosophies which often are merely an abstraction of how they would wish to deal with their children. All too frequently these three aspects of parental attitudes are considered

[1]Preparation of this chapter was supported by The Grant Foundation and by Public Health Service grant HD-03591 from the National Institute of Child Health and Human Development. The contents of parts of this chapter were presented at a Conference on Methodological Issues in Studying Bidirectional Influences in Mother-Infant Interactions, April 13–15, 1975, Boulder, Colorado. Leon J. Yarrow, Chairman.
[2]The references cited in this chapter are illustrative rather than comprehensive.

synonymous and, even more erroneously, are often equated with what parents actually do with their children. Each of these aspects of parental attitudes and actions originate from different layers within the parental personality. These layers are not necessarily highly intercorrelated and are therefore not interchangeable. It is important therefore to conceptually distinguish between these different parental influences because, only by making such distinctions, will it be possible to differentiate which parental influences have the greatest impact on the child's development.

In recent years, a reverse influence between parent and child has been postulated— namely, that the *infant's characteristics exert an influence on parental attitudes and behavior* (e.g. Bell, 1968; Brazelton, 1961; Korner, 1965, 1971, 1974a; Thoman, 1975). This hypothesis and the concepts underlying it have generated considerable research, some of which is represented in this volume. The conceptual issues pertaining to this branch of infancy research will be discussed in greater detail later in this chapter.

An integral part, but not limited to the area of infant-to-parent influence, is the whole field of *individual differences* among infants. This field of research not only comprises the assessment of the infant's attributes that affect the parent but it also includes the study of the infant's characteristic ways of experiencing the world (e.g. Benjamin, 1961; Escalona, 1968; Korner, 1971) as well as the persistence of individual differences, either in direct or derivative form, into later development (e.g. Escalona and Heider, 1959; Korner, 1971; Thomas et al., 1963). The conceptual issues pertaining to this area of research will also be discussed in greater detail later in this chapter.

At this time, one of the most widely investigated areas of research is that of *parent-infant interaction*. Ideally, the focus of this type of research is neither on the parent nor on the child but on the process occurring between the two. In practice, more often than not, observers each focus their attention on one partner, and an attempt is made in later data analysis to synchronize the contributions of each. Mathematical models and schemes of dealing with the voluminous and highly complex data usually generated by this type of research are just beginning to emerge (e.g. Bakeman and Brown, 1977; Stern, 1974; Thomas and Martin, 1976). Related to this area of research are the great number of studies investigating the *mother-infant relationship*. This includes the studies of *mother-infant attachment* pioneered by Bowlby (1958) and by Ainsworth (1964) and the studies of mother-infant bonding (e.g., Klaus et al., 1972).

Another branch of infancy research deals with the *infant's capabilities,* and this branch again has several subdivisions. Some researchers study the infant's abilities primarily to document what the brain is capable of doing at any given stage of human development; others have primarily applied concerns dealing with the range of infant responsiveness to various stimuli which might be utilized to enhance the infant's care and education. Not long ago, it was thought that the newborn, for example, could neither see nor hear to any great extent. Recent research with neonates has definitely disproven this notion. Newborns not only are able to visually fixate on objects from a certain distance, they are able to pursue moving stimuli when they are in the right state (e.g. Barten et al., 1971; Korner, 1970; Wolff and White, 1965). More remarkably, newborns show preferences among visual stimuli as judged by their consistently longer fixations of certain configurations as compared with others (e.g. Fantz, 1963; Haith, 1969; Hershenson et al., 1965). Fantz, for example, found that infants less than 48 h old looked significantly longer at a picture with the stimulus configurations of a human face than at any other visual stimulus. Discriminating auditory responsiveness in newborns has also been demonstrated in carefully controlled studies by Eisenberg (1965), with infants being most responsive to sounds within the human speech range. Infants are also highly responsive to touch or tactile stimulation (e.g. Casler, 1961) and even more so to vestibular-proprioceptive stimulation (Korner and Thoman, 1970, 1972; Gregg et al., 1976). There has been considerable debate in the literature about the extent to which newborns are capable of learning through conditioning (e.g. Sameroff, 1971). In evolutionary terms, it is of interest that the newborn seems to be most capable of responding to those stimuli emanating from the very person on whose care his survival is most dependent—namely, his mother. (For a further elaboration of this topic see Korner, 1973).

Predicated on the infant's capabilities and the range of stimuli to which he is responsive is the branch of infancy research that deals with the effects of *early stimulation* and *early intervention*. Again, this branch of infancy research is subdivided, this time on the basis of the research model used by different investigators. Some investigators are primarily interested in enriching the environment to encourage early learning or to optimize child care and education within a framework of normal infant development. By contrast, an increasing number of intervention studies are based on a deficiency model; these studies aim to provide compensatory stimulation to infants who are deprived of a normal environment. For example, ghetto children and premature infants have been the target of many such intervention studies (e.g. Cornell and Gottfried, 1976; Hasselmeyer, 1963; Weikart, 1971). Some of the intervention studies with premature infants have focused on compensatory types of stimulation which are ontogenetically most relevant to the preterm infant's level of neurophysiological development (Barnard, 1972; Korner et al., 1975; Neal, 1967) and which are highly prevalent in utero (Korner et al., 1975).

Still another branch of infancy research focuses on the ontogeny of the developmental process itself. This branch of infancy research deals with the *invariance of developmental acquisitions through time*. Piaget's (1936) investigations of the invariance of the sensorimotor stages is one of the foremost examples of this type of research. Other examples are, of course, those research studies dealing with infant intelligence and the sensorimotor acquisitions as these change and proliferate with development (e.g. Bayley, 1955; Gesell and Amatruda, 1947). In the sphere of affective development, stages of early psychosexual development, as postulated by Erikson (1950), are another example of invariant developmental sequences.

Tied to the branch of infancy research that deals with the invariance of developmental acquisitions is the field of research dealing with the *changing requirements of care with development*. This is one of the sparsest areas of research in spite of its great practical importance. While there are published reports that address themselves to the antecedents and consequences of parental actions and attitudes on the later development of the child, there is very little solid information about how the care requirements should change with the infant's growth and development. In practice, principles of childrearing as dictated by the developmental changes in the child are largely based on conviction, intuition, or on inferential reasoning from the findings of cross-sectional studies rather than on solid evidence from longitudinal work.

For example, most investigators, clinicians, and educators will agree that parental behavior should be contingent on the infant's needs and the behavioral cues the infant provides. Few investigators have addressed themselves in a systematic way to the question of whether the quality of parental contingent behavior should change as the infant grows older, and if so, in what way. For instance, prompt sensing of a newborn's needs and instantaneous action in response to these needs seems to be a most relevant form of parental contingent behavior at the newborn's stage of development. Shortly after birth, the infant is confronting the task of functioning independently from the mother's body for the first time, and a symbiotic type of interaction between mother and child may actually ease this difficult task. If, on the other hand, a symbiotic type of interaction is perpetuated through the 1st year of life and beyond, as done by some mothers who consider this type of contingent behavior the hallmark of good mothering, such interaction can become a major obstacle to developmental progress. In particular, this kind of symbiotic interaction will delay the infant's sense of separateness and his awareness that there are laws external to himself. This example illustrates that the quality of parental contingent behaviors needs to be appropriate to the changing developmental requirements of the child. The important issue thus is to study the essential changes in mutual stimulus regulation between parent and child which are necessary to promote optimal growth at any given stage of development. Studies of this kind would not only delineate the normal sequence of the changing requirements in the developing mother-infant relationship—they would, at the same time, highlight when this sequence falters and when this relationship begins to be at risk.

One of the few studies that addressed itself to the changing requirements of contingent maternal behavior as development proceeds is that by Sander (1962) entitled "Issues of Early Mother-Child Interaction." The sequence of the infant's changing needs was empirically derived from a longitudinal study headed by Pavenstedt (1962). It is of interest that in Sander's conceptual framework several of his "issues" correspond closely in time with some of Piaget's (1936) stages of sensorimotor development. It seems likely that Sander's "issues" and Piaget's stages touch on factors inherent in the maturational process and may point to important turning points both in the infant's development and in the mother-infant interaction. This implies that the appropriateness of the mother's response to her infant may largely be a function of his neurophysiological maturation, and when she fails to tune in to these changes within the infant she is apt to interfere with his development.

The Conflicting Aims of Some of the Branches of Infancy Research

The division of infancy research into the branches outlined above is, of course, a conceptual one only, and may appear arbitrary or artificial, particularly when one considers studying the infant as a whole. Yet, it should be pointed out that the aims of each of the branches differ and that not infrequently the variables of interest for one branch of infancy research may constitute major interfering variables which confound the results of another branch. Individual differences, for example, which are the primary focus of some studies, are frequently a major obstacle to finding clear-cut results in other types of studies. With infants varying widely in response to a given situation, it is difficult to establish what the general impact is of a certain environment, parental attitude, or intervention. A good case in point is Schaffer's (1966) study of the effects of hospitalization on infants less than 8 months old. Schaffer found that inactive infants were more likely to be adversely affected by the stress of a hospitalization experience than were active infants. Because of the wide variation of response among infants, it is also frequently difficult to establish the generality of a developmental law, the age-specificity of certain skills, or the invariance of sequential developmental acquisitions. In experimental studies testing the effects of different treatments, individual differences often overshadow group differences and obscure the effects of the intervention. In studies of mother-infant interaction the problem is compounded in that individual differences both in the mother and the child frequently obscure the generality of the antecedents and the consequences of the interaction. By contrast, in studies of individual differences, the variation between infants often is not large enough to reliably differentiate among them. Also, environmental, situational, or internal factors such as variations in the infant's state frequently interfere with the expression of stable, self-consistent individual differences. These are just a few illustrations of how the different aims of some of the branches of infancy research conflict and how the crucial variables of one branch can become the obstacles of another.

Methodological approaches to the different issues in infancy research should, of course, be appropriate to the questions asked. Each question has its own optimal level of precision with regard to the data needed to answer it. Flexibility in approach rather than adherence to any given methodological technique is essential. Not infrequently, investigators use the most sophisticated and complex methods of approach, when actually this may not be the most elegant and parsimonious way of approaching a particular question. For example, a distinction should be made in implementing the study of the mother-infant *interaction* and that of the mother-infant *relationship*. Obviously, these two types of studies are not identical, though frequently they are treated as such, with the methods optimal for the study of one being used to approach the other. In the study of the mother-infant interaction, capturing the contemporaneous, contingent, sequential mother and infant behaviors is obviously the method of choice. Stern (1971), for example, studied mutual gazing and gaze aversion between mother and child. In order to capture these split-second events, it was imperative to study microscopically the sequential interactions between the mother-infant pair. If, on the other hand, one were to ask the question as to what infant characteristics evoke what kinds of maternal feelings, assessing this question by studying the contemporaneous interactions between mother and child may be an approach of "overkill" which may not be conducive to best answering the question. It is always the questions posed that should dictate the methods to be used, and not the reverse. The first task of the investigator should always be to define his or her questions and the conceptual issues underlying these. Obviously, these questions should be nontrivial and should address themselves to important issues in the field of child development. Relevant here is a remark made by Reg Bromiley (as quoted by Hebb, 1974): "What's not worth doing is not worth doing well." It is thus most important to first define meaningful questions and then to implement their study in the most elegant and parsimonious ways by using flexibly the wide array of methodological approaches available in the field.

CONCEPTUAL ISSUES IN MEASURING INFANT CHARACTERISTICS

Since many of the chapters in this volume deal with infant characteristics which affect the mother-infant interaction as well as the infant's later development, some of the conceptual issues underlying these topics will be presented here. This section will thus address itself to a discussion of those infant variables that may be the most relevant ones in the mother-infant interaction and those that hold promise to exert a persistent influence through development. Some of the methodological issues intrinsic to the measurement of these variables will also be presented.

In discussing the choice of the most relevant variables, I shall limit myself to those infant characteristics that are most apt to evoke maternal interventions and also those that may express aspects of the infant's basic neurophysiologic make-up. To some extent, differences in CNS functioning do, of course, feed into the characteristics infants present to their caregivers. I shall begin with illustrations of relevant infant characteristics that are likely to evoke mother-infant interactions. The intrinsic problems in measuring these characteristics are less complex than those involved in measuring the infant's sensory regulatory processes, which are likely to be the substrate of the more enduring reaction patterns. Conceptually, it is of interest that the very variables that are the most relevant for the mother-infant interaction are also the ones that pose the greatest obstacles to the reliable measurement of the infant's sensory regulatory processes. Specifically, it is the infant's states and his birth circumstances that feed most strongly into the beginning mother-infant relationship. By contrast, in the assessment of the various aspects of the infant's sensory regulatory processes, these are the very intervening variables that most confound the results.

Newborn Characteristics Likely to Affect Parental Response

In the first postnatal weeks, the mother's interactions with her baby and her ministrations are largely in the service of buffering his level of arousal. In a sense, she acts as a shield, or like an external stimulus barrier in regulating the infant's sensory input and his motor responses. Her task, in other words, is one of regulating the infant's states in the broadest sense of that concept. Her success is determined in large part in how well she synchronizes her action with the needs of her infant, particularly in and around the feeding situation. The infant's well-being in turn, will be a source of maternal pleasure, self-confidence, and self-esteem. If she is fortunate, she will have a pliable, predictable, responsive newborn. His very nature will be a source of self-esteem. A recent study by Duchowny (1974) pointedly illustrated this fact. Duchowny related the results of Brazelton (1973) assessments made on the 3rd day of the infant's life to ratings of the mother's self-image in the maternal role derived from interviews with the mothers when the infant was one month old. He found correlations ranging from 0.63 to 0.83 between high maternal self-esteem and degrees of infant alertness shortly after birth. The highest correlations, interestingly enough, were not between high maternal self-image and the baby's visual behaviors, which involved activities *he* engaged in, but with his auditory responsiveness. A mother thus may feel more rewarded if a baby is responsive to what *she* is apt to do, which, in this case, meant her talking to him.

Differential irritability as expressed by infant crying is one of the most crucial variables in the earliest mother-infant interactions. Since crying is a potent and usually aversive stimulus to the mother, infant crying more or less predictably evokes interaction with the mother. It is thus the infant who commonly initiated the interaction in the earliest weeks of life. Moss and Robson's (1968) evidence on the sequence of mother-infant interaction, revolving around the infant's crying, strongly supports this impression. During two 6-h observation periods at 1 month, it was the infant who initiated roughly four out of five interactions. The young infant may thus be viewed, in part at least, as the determiner of how much stimulation he receives.

Not only does the differential irritability among infants have an effect on his caregiver, the differential soothability among infants does as well. The parents' capability in soothing their infant is one of the cardinal challenges they face in the infant's earliest weeks of life, and their success or failure cannot help but leave an impact on their self-esteem as parents and on the beginning parent-infant bond. Several studies, notably by Birns et al. (1966), Bridger and Birns (1963), and Korner and Thoman (1972) have shown that newborns differ significantly from each other in how soothable they are. In our study (Korner and Thoman, 1972) in which we simulated common maternal soothing techniques, we found that infants not only differed significantly from each other in how soothable they were ($p < 0.001$), but also in how long they remained soothed after completion of the soothing intervention ($p < 0.001$).

Infants who present state characteristics that are not readily changed by maternal efforts present a special challenge to the beginning mother-infant interaction. Brazelton (1962) and Prechtl (1963) described some extreme cases in which unremitting crying, unconsolability, and hypo- and/or hypertonicity and inaccessibility to maternal interventions resulted in maternal depression or rejection. In particular, Brazelton described several infants who, during the first postnatal weeks, showed a very narrow range of states. This turned out to be a very ominous sign for their later development, as several of these infants were later diagnosed as children with atypical development. Brazelton gave a detailed description of one of these infants who essentially was capable of only two states. The infant appeared to be in deep sleep during which his muscle tone was poor, he was difficult to rouse, and impervious to any stimulation. In the second state this infant screamed continuously, was hyperactive, and hypersensitive to any stimulation. Nothing could calm him except restraint and swaddling, which immediately made him revert back to the first state of inaccessible, stupor-like behavior. A neurological examination revealed no abnormalities. The later development of this child was very uneven. The narrow range of this child's states persisted at least until pre-school age, at which time his coping mechanisms were limited to either screaming or withdrawing into a state in which he seemed to neither hear nor see. From the start the mother of this child felt ''rejected'' by the infant and overwhelmed by the task of mothering, for she was unable to do anything to comfort him in his agitated state and was unable to reach him in his state of withdrawal.

While this type of case is very uncommon, difficult and unconsolable infants have heavily contributed to the literature on battered children. The statistics on battered children point to the prevalence of unrewarding, difficult babies among those who become victims of child abuse, sometimes even at the hands of different sets of caregivers. Premature infants whose incidence in the population is between 7 and 10% percent are represented among battered children at the rate of between 23 and 40%, depending on the study quoted (Klein and Stern, 1971; Sameroff and Chandler, 1975). The usual combination of low socioeconomic background, early maternal deprivation, and an unrewarding, difficult child so deplete the mother's resources and self-esteem that the likelihood of child abuse increases with each new crisis, which frequently is an acute illness on the part of the child. It is the maternal depletion and helplessness in dealing adequately with her child's heightened demands which usually take the form of excessive crying, that tips the balance in the already precarious mother-infant relationship.

Turning to conceptual issues, the most relevant infant characteristics to be measured in the parent-infant interaction, whether within normal limits or otherwise, are those that are infant state related. This means not only the frequency and the duration of certain states but also their predictability and alterability. Thus the frequency and duration of the infant's crying, his fussiness, his readiness to be and to remain soothed, the duration of his sleep, his ease of responding with alertness and later with a smile, all feed into the mother-infant relationship. Equally important is the regularity or predictability of the infant's sleep patterns or, for that matter, of his hunger, for these factors may make the difference between a mother's opportunity to replenish her resources by having some time to herself and her losing all sense of separateness.

Methodologically, the measurement of most of these variables is relatively straightforward, provided a large enough sample of the infant's behavior is observed so as to capture a reliable picture of the infant's characteristics (Kraemer and Korner, 1976). Even the baby's prenatal or birth history, or the drugs that have been passed along to him, are not confounding variables, because the effects of these aspects of his history feed directly into what the baby presents to the mother.

Infant Characteristics that May Influence Later Development

Students of individual differences who have studied behavioral differences among neonates and young infants with an eye on the influence that these differences may exert on later development have faced a task that is much more difficult and complex than was originally anticipated (e.g. Bell et al., 1971; Birns, 1965; Birns et al., 1969; Escalona, 1968; Escalona and Heider, 1959; Honzig, 1964; Kagan, 1971; Kagan and Moss, 1962; Korner, 1964, 1971, 1973, 1974b; Korner and Grobstein, 1967; Thomas et al., 1963, 1968). Depending on the different investigators' conceptual framework and the variables studied, the relation between early and later characteristics has ranged from showing some promise to being modest to poor. Sameroff (1975), in addressing himself to this problem in a recent paper entitled "Early Influences on Development: Fact or Fancy?," pointed out that early deviance and even gross insults such as perinatal anoxia will find expression in later deviance only when coupled with poor socioeconomic and familial factors. While one may rejoice in the knowledge that the human organism is resilient and has many self-righting or compensating resources, it is these and other factors that make prediction of developmental outcomes from early assessments of infant characteristics exceedingly difficult. Not only are the correlations between early and later assessments frequently not significant, there are studies like Bell et al.'s (1971) which suggest that certain variables such as the intensity of reaction may be reversed between two points in development. This lack of correspondence and these transformations in development, in my view at least, do not signify that there is no meaningful continuity in development and that early infant characteristics have no influence on the quality and substance of his later attributes. To a large extent, it may simply mean that conceptually we have not approached the task with sufficient clarity, that frequently we may not have chosen the optimal variables to study this problem, and in those instances when we did, we may not have implemented the study of these variables with sufficient methodological sophistication. It is striking, for example, that in spite of the frequently low correlations between the *behaviors* at various points in development, that there exists in most individuals a continuity of a sense of self throughout development. It is equally striking that we readily recognize in others whom we know well a continuity of reaction patterns.

Conceptually, Piaget's (1936) sensorimotor theory of development can help us understand what may go into developmental transformations. Piaget speaks of inborn schemata which, through repetition and alimentation, change and proliferate into new schemata which are related, but not identical, to their precursors. Feeding into the new schemata are a great variety of interacting internal and environmental influences. At a minimum, the new schemata, and the developmental transformations these express, are the product of four different types of influences, which, depending on the circumstances, interact with each other to a greater or lesser degree. One such influence lies in those infant characteristics that are an expression of his basic neurophysiological make-up. Differences in neurophysiologic functioning, particularly those relating to sensory threshold levels and the precursors of the regulatory mechanisms for dealing with overstimulation are, in my view, apt to have the most long-range influence on development, either in direct, derivative, or reverse form. These differences, although modifiable to some extent by experience, are apt to feed strongly into the style, the tempo, and the intensity of reaction, attributes that are likely to persist and to color the manner in which a child will approach and master each new developmental acquisition. These differences will also strongly feed into the development and choice of later cognitive, defensive, and characterological attributes, an individual's preferred coping styles, and what are commonly considered temperamental differences.

Another influence that is related to the infant's basic make-up is his way of subjectively experiencing the world around him (Benjamin, 1961). His own characteristics will color to a large extent how he will experience and perceive his mother and his father and the universal childhood events which are part and parcel of his growing up. For example, depending on his blood sugar regulation, the intensity of his reactions, his ablity to delay, his resources for diverting himself or for self-comforting, his reaction to hunger or to weaning will differ, no matter what the caregiver contributes to this situation. The infant's subjective experience and perception of events are, I believe, a most important influence on his development. It may be the repeated and subjective self-experience that is most instrumental in the development of the continuity of a sense of self. While an infant's way of experiencing himself and the world around him is apt to have a profound impact on his development, this influence is extremely difficult, if not impossible, to investigate in preverbal children.

A third influence is the impact of the infant's characteristics on the mother-infant interaction and relationship. Particularly in the first postnatal weeks it wll be the degree to which a mother can sense and tune in to the behavioral individuality of her baby and can modify her responses that will determine the relative synchrony and mutuality achieved by the mother-infant pair. Such synchrony is an aid to the infant's achievement of homeostasis and to a sense of well-being and, eventually, to a growing feeling of effectance, brought about by a sense that his actions and needs have an impact on his environment. Such synchrony (or asynchrony) of interaction will, of course, in turn affect in a self-perpetuating way subsequent attempts at mutual regulation.

A fourth influence on developmental outcome is the influence of environmental factors which are independent of those evoked by the infant's characteristics. These encompass the parents' personalities, their needs, their child-rearing philosophy and practices, their internal expectations of parenthood, the models they provide for identification, the family's socioeconomic conditions, and many other aspects of family circumstances. Also included here are the environmental influences that impinge upon a child through differences in experience that are a function of his sex, race, and ordinal position.

With all these interacting influences, it is really not surprising that prediction between early infant characteristics and developmental outcomes is inherently fraught with difficulties—for singly, none of these influences is sufficient to shape or to explain developmental outcomes. This is particularly true for the average expectable child in an average expectable environment because developmental outcomes in these cases are apt to express a successful amalgamation between the child's original tendencies and his environmental influences. This is perhaps less true in populations that are at risk by definition of either the child's or the parent's inherent limitations in flexibility or capacity for change. Possibly, in the children of these families whose development is apt to be in greater jeopardy, it may be somewhat easier to trace the influence of the infant's original tendencies on developmental outcome. In the light of this, it is perhaps not too surprising that a number of the investigators who have studied the effects of early individual differences on development are, or have been, clinicians interested in the origins of disturbed development.

If then one wants to study individual differences at birth that may have an impact on later development, which variables are apt to be conceptually the most promising of payoff? In my view, they are variables dealing with the manifestations of an infant's basic neurophysiologic make-up as expressed in the range and limits of sensory stimulation which feel syntonic to him. Particularly promising may be those variables that deal with the balance between an individual's sensory threshold levels and his integrative capacities, for these may represent an important substrate of what eventually will become temperamental differences. It is this balance that, from the first days, will strongly influence how much stimulation a given baby needs, and how much he can tolerate, to function optimally. It is also this balance that contributes to the degree to which novelty, change, complexity, and intensity of stimulation are experienced as syntonic and to what extent coping strategies need to be erected designed to manage excessive excitation through sifting, damping, or tuning out incoming stimuli.

Not much is known about optimal levels of stimulation, as these relate to individual differences in CNS functioning. A few researchers have concerned themselves with this question in adults. Helson (1964) addressed himself to this issue in his adaptation-level theory; Fiske and Maddi (1961) and Frankenhaeuser and Johansson (1974), among others, studied the psychophysiological consequences of understimulation and overstimulation. Toffler's (1970) *Future Shock* and Lipowski's (1970) work on the disruptive effects of stimulus overload deal with this issue in a societal framework, implying that evolutionary changes in CNS functioning may be required for coping with modern society. In the realm of pathology, Ludwig and Stark (1973) showed that chronic schizophrenics maintain relative homeostasis only within a very narrow range of sensory input. Within normal populations there certainly must exist wide variations in this range. Were we to develop the means to discover even approximations of this range in the newborn, we would not only get a handle on the optimal stimulation requirements for each child, but we would become better predictors of later temperamental and characterological differences, at least for those individuals who hold extreme positions within this range.

What are then some of the relevant variables if one wishes to study the range of a newborn's sensory responsiveness and his limits in regulating excitation? They are sensory thresholds, latency, intensity or amplitudes, spread and inhibition of response, rate of recovery, and habituation. Each and every one of these measures is strongly influenced by the minutest state fluctuations, and they are, of course, also affected by long and difficult labors, mode of delivery, and by the drugs used in obstetric management.

Let us begin with habituation. Obviously, if an individual has great difficulty in tuning out any of the vast array of stimuli that impinge upon him, he may readily become subject to disruptive overstimulation. The question is, can we measure habituation in the neonate? Many investigators feel that habituation can be assessed in the newborn, but others emphatically deny this. Hutt et al. (1969), for example, argue that what some consider habituation is frequently merely the manifestation of subtle changes in state. Neurophysiologists such as Brazier (1962) claim that, since the neonate functions largely at a subcortical level, the decline in his responsiveness with repeated stimulation is a function of adaptation rather than habituation, the latter being a cortical phenomenon. If we assume that adaptation to various types of stimulation can be measured reliably in the neonate and that he is reasonably self-consistent in this behavior, does this mean that we are measuring a precursor to his later capability for habituation? If we are, this would be an important accomplishment. But no one has looked into this important problem, to my knowledge.

Only a few investigators have attempted to measure sensory thresholds in newborns. Bell et al. (1971) found reasonable self-consistency in ascending tactile thresholds, using an eastesiometer. Lipsitt and Levy (1959) studied ascending electrotactual thresholds and found significant self-consistency. In our laboratory we attempted to establish ascending auditory thresholds with the help of an artificial larynx, which was electronically altered so as to emit sound at will in 5-db increments, ranging from 43 to 88 db at the infant's exposed ear. The reason we used a modified artificial larynx was because it emits a speechlike noise band and harmonics, which Eisenberg (1965) found most suitable for eliciting responses in neonates. The sound was delivered when the baby was in irregular sleep without REMs, with mock trials interspersed to evaluate the rate of false-positive responses. In our pilot work, we found that some infants were highly self-consistent in when they began to respond, not only from one interfeed period to the next but also on two consecutive days. The reason why we gave up on this study, for the moment at least, is because, with our rigorous requirements for a comparable prestimulus state, it frequently took us an entire day to get six reliable threshold determinations. Sometimes we failed to obtain even four.

Psychophysiological techniques such as evoked potential, GSR, or heart-rate changes can, of course, also be used in sensory threshold determinations. While these techniques are capable of yielding very precise information, this approach does not circumvent the thorny problem of controlling for minute changes in state. Without such control, the threshold levels obtained through these methodological approaches are no more reliable than the ones reflected in overt behavioral responses.

Perhaps, for practical purposes, it may be more fruitful to approach the problem of sensory responsiveness in a less psychophysical way. It is of interest, for example, that the Brazelton (1973) alertness clusters dealing with visual and auditory responsiveness both to animate and inanimate stimuli are some of the most robust measures of the Scale (e.g. Horowitz et al. 1973). Also Birns (1965) and Korner (1970) independently found significant correlations between visual pursuit and auditory responsiveness in newborns. Also, Barton et al. (1971) found high self-consistency over 2 days in visual pursuit in neonates. While it is possible to obtain these consistencies by strictly controlling for prestimulus state, these results tell us nothing about an individual's sensory responsiveness across states. Since in real life we are exposed to sensory stimuli at all times, it would be important to systematically investigate whether sensory sensitivity is a unified trait which cuts across states.

Except for the psychophysiological approach mentioned above, in all the illustrations given, sensory responsiveness was measured by motor response. Perhaps, measuring motor activity as such would tap some of the integrative mechanisms operating in individual differences in dealing with sensory input and in managing excitation. Differences in activity level certainly are easier to measure than differences in sensory thresholds. There is considerable evidence in the literature suggesting that the stimulation requirements differ markedly for individuals who are at either extreme of the activity continuum. For example, there is Pavlov's (1927) classical description of the temperamental differences among dogs, the extremes of which required totally different handling for conditioning to be effective. One extreme reacted quickly to every stimulus, was vivacious and exuberant in response to new situations, and easily became overactive. To condition this kind of dog, stimulation had to be varied continuously. At the other extreme, some of Pavlov's dogs responded to every new and unfamiliar stimulus by cowering to the floor or by inhibiting his movements. This kind of dog was extremely slow in getting used to new surroundings, but, once familiar, he became an excellent subject for conditioning.

Escalona (1963) contrasted the development of very active babies who relied heavily on total-body activation with that of inactive infants whose motions involve mostly small body segments. She found that the pattern of experience differed greatly for these children and that the stimulus requirements to bring out the optimal functioning of these infants differed markedly. Meili-Dworetzki (1959) made very similar observations. The fact that we are dealing here with fairly stable reaction patterns is also suggested by Yarrow's (1964) discussion of four longitudinal studies (The Berkeley Growth Study, The California Guidance Study, The Fels Study of Human Development and the Menninger Coping Study). Yarrow stated that "the one dimension of personality in which there was a high degree of continuity in all four studies—is a physiological psychological characteristic, [namely] the level of energy expenditure."

In the light of the above considerations, we are currently attempting to study individual differences in what may be a gross expression of differences in CNS functioning by monitoring the quality, quantity, and distribution of infant motor output. To reliably assess motor output, we developed an electronic monitor which, for an indefinite period of time, records both the infant's movements and his crying (Korner et al., 1974a). Our system has all the capabilities of Sander and Julia's (1966) original activity monitor for measuring the effects of various types of caregiving activities on the motility and crying of the neonate. Conceptually speaking, it is of interest that our primary aim in developing this monitor was quite the opposite of Sander and Julia's purposes. Since we wished to study individual differences or differing organismic characteristics of the infants, we aimed to obtain an activity measure that was *minimally* affected by environmental factors and by differential caregiving. We thus built a system that separated out total, crying, and noncrying activity. It was reasoned that, by getting a measure of noncrying activity, the activity scores obtained in standard hospital nurseries would not be confounded with how irritable the baby is, and his activity scores at home would not be confounded by the relative promptness with which the mother attends him. Our first study with this monitor confirmed our hypothesis—namely that the *total* activity scores were very much confounded by how irritable a baby was (Korner et al., 1974b). The correlation between total activity and time spent crying was 0.62, while for the noncrying activity scores the correlation was not significant. This study also showed that by using noncrying activity scores we could fairly well capture a baby's characteristic activity output for the day in one interfeed period. The noncrying activity scores for one interfeed period correlated 0.69 with the total day's output, and by the time three interfeed periods were recorded, that correlation rose to 0.91.

We are using this monitor for many different studies, such as a study of the ontogeny of rest-activity cycles in premature infants from 28 weeks' gestation on; a study of the regulatory influences of labor on infant activation and arousal; and a study of drug and circumcision effects. But before all, we are collecting normative data on a large sample of neonates because we want to study what may be some of the precursors of individual differences in motorically regulating excitation. For one, we are getting a measure of total activation, and of crying and noncrying activity. We are also assessing the infants' capacity or inability for motor inhibition through integrated data which very clearly show the length of the infants' rest and activity cycles. Furthermore, we are obtaining a measure of the intensity of the babies' motor activity, for our monitor differentiates between several amplitudes of motions. Some day, we will follow up the most and least active, the perpetually restless and the most and least vigorous babies to determine what kinds of individuals they became. This is predicated on the hypothesis that these *extreme cases* would have a better chance to show persistence of their original tendencies or derivatives of these tendencies since such persistence may largely depend on the strength of the original tendencies. I would postulate that on follow-up the infants with the most extreme scores in the above activity measures may not only show meaningful differences in developmental outcomes as compared with infants in the average ranges, but that many of these children will have posed special challenges to their parents.

SUMMARY

Infancy research consists of many different branches which are briefly described in this chapter. Each branch encompasses different goals and relies on a different conceptual framework. At times, the aims of one branch of infancy research conflict with those of another in that the variables of crucial interest for one branch may become the major interfering variables for another. A typical example of this problem is the conflict between the branch of infancy research that primarily aims to assess individual differences among infants and those studies that attempt to establish invariant developmental laws, or the generality of a given treatment. Individual differences frequently are a major obstacle in finding general developmental trends among infants and they thus often confound the results of studies aiming to establish such trends.

Since a large part of this volume deals with the infant characteristics that affect the mother-infant interaction as well as the infant's later development, some of the conceptual issues underlying these branches of infancy research are presented in greater detail in this chapter. The infant characteristics that most affect the beginning mother-infant interaction and relationship are, among others, the infants' relative irritability, soothability, predict-ability, and alertness and responsiveness. Conceptually speaking, the infant characteris-tics that have the greatest impact on the beginning parent-infant interaction are primarily those that are infant state-related. Even the baby's prenatal or birth history, or the drugs that have been passed along to him, are not confounding variables in the study of the mother-infant interaction because the effects of these aspects of his history feed directly into what the baby presents to the mother by way of his state behavior.

By contrast, the variables that are most relevant for the study of the mother-infant interaction are the very ones that most interfere with the reliable measurement of those variables that are apt to influence the infant's enduring reaction patterns. Conceptually, the variables that are apt to hold the greatest promise for influencing enduring reaction patterns are the expressions of individual differences in CNS functioning. Particularly promising may be those variables that deal with the balance between the individual's sensory threshold levels and his integrative capacities. These factors may express the range and limits of sensory stimulation which feel syntonic to the individual and may represent the anlage for what eventually will become preferred coping strategies and temperamental differences. In the neonate, the relevant variables for studying the individu-al's range of sensory responsivity and the limits in regulating excitation are sensory thresholds, latency, intensity or amplitudes, spread and inhibition of response, rate of recovery, and habituation. Each and every one of these measures is strongly influenced by the minutest state fluctuations, and they are, of course, also affected by long and difficult labors, mode of delivery, and by the drugs used in obstetric management.

Throughout the chapter, examples are given of this and other investigators' research to illustrate the conceptual issues involved in the different branches of infancy research.

BIBLIOGRAPHY

Ainsworth, M. Patterns of attachment behavior shown by the infant in interaction with his mother. *Merrill-Palmer Quarterly*, 1964, **10**, 51–58.

Bakeman, R., and Brown, J. V. Behavioral dialogues: An approach to the assessment of mother-infant interaction. *Child Development*, 1977, **48**, 195–203.

Barnard, K. E. *The Effect of Stimulation on the Duration and Amount of Sleep and Wakefulness in the Premature Infant*. Ann Arbor, Mich.: University Microfilms, 1972.

Barten, S., Birns, B., and Ronch, J. Individual differences in the visual pursuit behavior of neonates. *Child Development*, 1971, **42**, 313–319.

Bayley, N. On the growth of intelligence. *American Psychologist*, 1955, **10**, 805–818.

Bell, R. Q. A reinterpretation of the direction of effects in studies of socialization. *Psychological Review*, 1968, **75**, 81–95.

Bell, R. Q., Weller, G. M., and Waldrop, M. F. Newborn and preschooler: Organization of behavior and relations between periods. *Monographs of the Society for Research in Child Development*, 1971, **36** (1–2; ser. 142).

Benjamin, J. D. The innate and the experiential in development. In H. W. Brosin (ed.), *Lectures on Experimental Psychiatry*. Pittsburgh: University of Pittsburgh, 1961, 19–42.

Birns, B. Individual differences in human neonates' responses to stimulation. *Child Development*, 1965, **36**, 249–256.

Birns, B., Barten, S., and Bridger, W. H. Individual differences in temperamental characteristics of infants. *Transactions of the New York Academy of Sciences*, 1969, **31** (ser. II; 8), 1071–1082.

Birns, B., Blank, M., and Bridger, W. H. The effectiveness of various soothing techniques on human neonates. *Psychosomatic Medicine*, 1966, **28**, 316–322.

Bowlby, J. The nature of the child's tie to his mother. *International Journal of Psychoanalysis*, 1958, **39**, 350–373.

Brazelton, T. B. Psychophysiologic reactions in the neonate. I. The value of observation of the neonate. *The Journal of Pediatrics*, 1961, **58**, 508–512.

Brazelton, T. B. Observations of the neonate. *Journal of Child Psychiatry*, 1962, **1** (1), 38–58.

Brazelton, T. B. *Neonatal Behavioral Assessments Scale*. Clinics in Developmental Medicine, No. 50, Spastics International Medical Publications. Philadelphia: Lippincott, 1973.

Brazier, M. Discussion during Symposium on Research in Infancy in Early Childhood. *Journal of Child Psychiatry*, 1962, **1** (1), 96–97.

Bridger, W. H., and Birns, B. Neonates' behavioral and autonomic responses to stress during soothing. *Recent Advances in Biological Psychiatry*, 1963, **5**, 1–6.

Casler, L. Maternal deprivation: A critical review of the literature. *Monographs of the Society for Research in Child Development*, 1961, **26** (2; ser. 80).

Cornell, E. H., and Gottfried, A. W. Intervention with premature human infants. *Child Development*, 1976, **47**, 32–39.

Duchowny, M. S. Interactional influence of infant characteristics and post-partun maternal self-image. Paper presented at the American Psychological Association 82nd Annual Convention, New Orleans, August 30, 1974.

Eisenberg, R. B. Auditory behavior in the human neonate: I. Methodologic problems and the logical design of research procedures. *Journal of Auditory Research*, 1965, 815, 159–177.

Erikson, E. H. The theory of infantile sexuality. *Childhood and Society*. New York: Norton, 1950, 44–92.

Escalona, S. K. Patterns of infantile experience and the developmental process. *The Psychoanalytic Study of the Child*, 1963, **18**, 197–244.

Escalona, S. K. *The Roots of Individuality*. Chicago: Aldine, 1968.

Escalona, S. K., and Heider, G. M. *Prediction and Outcome: A Study in Child Development*. New York: Basic Books, 1959.

Fantz, R. L. Pattern vision in newborn infants. *Science,* 1963, **140**, 296–297.

Fiske, D. W., and Maddi, S. R. A conceptual framework. In D. Fiske and S. Maddi (eds.), *Functions of Varied Experience*. Homewood, Ill.: Dorsey, 1961, 11–56.

Frankenhaeuser, M., and Johansson, G. On the psychophysiological consequences of under-stimulation and over-stimulation. *Reports from the Psychological Laboratories of the University of Stockholm,* 1974, Suppl. 25.

Gesell, A., and Amatruda, C. S. *Developmental Diagnosis*. New York: Harper, 1947.

Gregg, C. L., Haffner, M. E., and Korner, A. F. The relative efficacy of vestibular-proprioceptive stimulation and the upright position in enhancing visual pursuit in neonates. *Child Development,* 1976, **47**, 309–314.

Haith, M. M. Infrared television recording and measurement of ocular behavior in the human infant. *American Psychologist,* 1969, **24**, 279–283.

Hasselmeyer, E. G. *Handling and Premature Infant Behavior*. Ann Arbor, Mich.: University Microfilms, 1963.

Hebb, D. O. What psychology is about. *American Psychologist,* 1974, **29**, 71–79.

Heinstein, M. I. Behavioral correlates of breast-bottle regimes under varying parent-infant relationships. *Monographs of the Society of Research in Child Development,* 1963, **28** (4; ser. 88).

Helson, H. *Adaptation-Level Theory*. New York: Harper & Row, 1964.

Hershenson, M., Munsinger, H., and Kessen, W. Preference for shapes of intermediate variability in the newborn human. *Science,* 1965, **147**, 630–631.

Honzig, M. P. Personality consistency and change: Some comments on papers by Bayley, Macfarlane, Moss and Kagan, and Murphy. *Vita Humana,* 1964, **7**, 139–142.

Horowitz, F. D., Aleksandrowicz, M., Ashton, L. J., Tims, S., McCloskey, K., Culp, R., and Gallas, II. American and Uruguayan infants: Reliabilities, maternal drug histories and population differences using the Brazelton Scale. Paper presented at the meeting of the Society for Research and Development, Philadelphia, 1973.

Hutt, S. J., Lenard, H. G., and Prechtl, H. F. R. Psychophysiological studies in newborn infants. *Advances in Child Development and Behavior,* 1969, **4**, 127–172.

Kagan, J. *Change and Continuity in Infancy*. New York: Wiley, 1971.

Kagan, J., and Moss, H. A. *Birth to Maturity*. New York: Wiley, 1962.

Klaus, M., Jerauld, R., Kreger, N., McAlpine, W., Steffa, M., and Kennell, J. Maternal attachment: Importance of the first postpartum days. *New England Journal of Medicine,* 1972, **286**, 460–463.

Klein, M., and Stern, L. Low birthweight and the battered child syndrome. *American Journal of Diseases of Children,* 1971, **122**, 15–18.

Korner, A. F. Some hypotheses regarding the significance of individual differences at birth for later development. *The Psychoanalytic Study of the Child,* 1964, **19**, 58–72.

Korner, A. F. Mother-child interaction: One- or two-way street? *Social Work,* 1965, **10** (3), 47–51.

Korner, A. F. Visual alertness in neonates: Individual differences and their correlates. *Perceptual and Motor Skills,* 1970, **31**, 499–509.

Korner, A. F. Individual differences at birth: Implications for early experience and later development. *American Journal of Orthopsychiatry,* 1971, **41** (4), 608–619.

Korner, A. F. Early stimulation and maternal care as related to infant capabilities and individual differences. *Early Child Development and Care,* 1973, **2**, 307–327.

Korner, A. F. The effect of the infant's state, level of arousal, sex and ontogenetic stage on the caregiver. In M. Lewis and L. A. Rosenblum (eds.), *The Origins of Behavior: The Effect of the Child on the Caregiver.* New York: Wiley, 1974a, 105–121.

Korner, A. F. Individual differences at birth: Implications for child care practices. In R. Gross and A. Solnit (eds.), *The Infant at Risk.* Miami: Symposia Specialists, 1974b, 51–62.

Korner, A. F., and Grobstein, R. Individual differences at birth: Implications for mother-infant relationship and later development. *Journal of the American Academy of Child Psychiatry,* 1967, **6** (4), 676–690.

Korner, A. F., and Thoman, E. Visual alertness in neonates as evoked by maternal care. *Journal of Experimental Child Psychology,* 1970, **10**, 67–78.

Korner, A. F., and Thoman, E. B. Relative efficacy of contact and vestibular stimulation on soothing neonates. *Child Development,* 1972, **43** (2), 443–453.

Korner, A. F., Thoman, E. B., and Glick, J. H. A system for monitoring crying and non-crying, large, medium and small neonatal movements. *Child Development,* 1974a, **45**, 946–952.

Korner, A. F., Kraemer, H. C., Haffner, M. E., and Cosper, L. Effects of waterbed flotation on premature infants: A pilot study. *Pediatrics,* 1975, **56**, 361–367.

Korner, A. F., Kraemer, H. C., Haffner, M. E., and Thoman, E. B. Characteristics of crying and non-crying activity in normal full-term newborns. *Child Development,* 1974b, **45**, 953–958.

Kraemer, H. C., and Korner, A. F. Statistical alternatives in assessing reliability, self-consistency, and individual differences for quantative measures: Application to behavioral measures of neonates. *Psychological Bulletin,* 1976, **83** (5), 914–921.

Lipowski, Z. J. The conflict of Buridan's Ass or some dilemmas of affluence: The theory of attractive stimulus overload. *American Journal of Psychiatry,* 1970, **127** (3), 273–279.

Lipsitt, L. P., and Levy, N. Electrotactual threshold in the human neonate. *Child Development,* 1959, **30**, 547–554.

Ludwig, A. M., and Stark, L. H. Schizophrenia, sensory deprivation, and sensory overload. *The Journal of Nervous and Mental Disease,* 1973, **157** (3), 210–216.

Meili-Dworetzki, G. Lust und Angst. Regulative Momente in der Personlichkeitsentwicklung zweier Brüder. *Beitrage zur Genetischen Charakterologie,* 1959, No. 3. Bern: Hans Huber.

Moss, H. A., and Robson, K. The role of protest behavior in the development of mother-infant attachment. Paper presented at the meeting of the American Psychological Association, San Francisco, 1968.

Neal, M. V. *The Relationship between a Regimen of Vestibular Stimulation and the Developmental Behavior of the Premature Infant.* Ann Arbor, Mich.: University Microfilms, 1967.

Pavenstedt, E. Opening comments: Symposium on research and infancy and early childhood. *Journal of Child Psychiatry,* 1962, **1** (1), 138–140.

Pavlov, I. (1927) *Conditioned Reflexes.* New York: Dover, 1960.

Piaget, J. The Origins of Intelligence in Children, 1936. Published in translated form by International University Press, New York, 1952.

Prechtl, H. F. R. The mother-child interaction in babies with minimal brain damage. In B. M. Foss (ed.), *Determinants of Infant Behavior,* Vol. II. London: Methuen, 1963, 53–59.

Sameroff, A. J. Can conditioned responses be established in the newborn infant? *Developmental Psychology,* 1971, **5**, 1–12.

Sameroff, A. J. Early influences on development: Fact or fancy? *Merrill-Palmer Quarterly,* 1975, **21** (4), 267–294.

Sameroff, A. J., and Chandler, M. Reproductive risk and the continuum of caretaking casualty. In F. D. Horowitz, M. Hetherington, S. Scarr-Salapatek, and G. Siegel (eds.), *Review of Child Development Research,* Vol. 4. Chicago: University of Chicago, 1975, 187–244.

Sander, L. W. Issues in early mother-child interaction. *Journal of Child Psychiatry,* 1962, **1**, 141–166.

Sander, L. W., and Julia, H. L. Continuous interactional monitoring in the neonate. *Psychosomatic Medicine,* 1966, **28** (6), 822–835.

Schaffer, H. R. Activity level as a constitutional determinant of infantile reaction to deprivation. *Child Development,* 1966, **37**, 595–602.

Sears, R. R., Maccoby, E. E., and Levin, H. *Patterns of Child Rearing.* Evanston: Row Peterson, 1957.

Stern, D. N. A micro-analysis of mother-infant interaction: Behavior regulating social contact between a mother and her 3½-month-old twins. *Journal of Child Psychiatry,* 1971, **10**, 501–517.

Stern, D. N. Mother and infant at play: the dyadic interaction involving facial, vocal and gaze behaviors. In M. Lewis and L. A. Rosenblum (Eds.) The Origins of Behavior. The Effect of the Child on the Caregiver. New York: Wiley, 1974, 187–213.

Thoman, E. Role of the infant in early transfer of information. *Biological Psychiatry,* 1975, **10**, 161–169.

Thomas, A., Chess, S., Birch, H. G., Hertzig, M. E., and Korn, S. *Behavioral Individuality in Early Childhood.* New York: New York Universities, 1963.

Thomas, A., Chess, S., and Birch, H. G. *Temperament and Behavior Disorders in Children.* New York: New York Universities, 1968.

Thomas, E. A. C., and Martin, J. A. Analyses of parent-infant interaction. *Psychological Review,* 1976, **83** (2), 141–156.

Toffler, A. *Future Shock.* New York: Random, 1970.

Weikart, D. P. Early childhood special education for intellectually subnormal and/or culturally different children. Presented at a Conference of the National Leadership Institute in Early Child Development in Washington, D.C., October 1971.

Wolff, P. H., and White, B. L. Visual pursuit and attention in young infants. *Journal of Child Psychiatry,* 1965, **4**, 473–484.

Yarrow, L. J. Maternal deprivation: Toward an empirical and conceptual re-evaluation. *Psychological Bulletin,* 1961, **58** (6), 459–490.

Yarrow, L. J. Personality consistency and change: An overview of some conceptual and methodological issues. *Vita Humana,* 1963, **7** (2), 67–72.

CHAPTER 23

Parent-Infant Bonding[1]

John H. Kennell
Diana K. Voos
Marshall H. Klaus

Investigators from many disciplines have elaborated the process by which the human infant becomes attached to his mother. They have described the disastrous effects of long-term maternal separation on all aspects of the infant's development: motor, cognitive and emotional. Observations of these effects by Bowlby (1958) and Spitz (1945), and especially those by Anna Freud (1965) of children evacuated from London, have dramatically altered infant care throughout the world. These fundamental studies of infants produced major alterations in the care of children in pediatric hospitals. In the 1940s parents were allowed to visit their hospitalized children for only one or two hours a week. Presently the majority of pediatric units allow unlimited parental visiting and encourage parents to live-in with their young children, thus acknowledging the lifeline effect of the child's attachment to the parent. In the last 10 years interest in attachment in the opposite direction has developed.

PARENT-TO-INFANT ATTACHMENT

In this chapter we will discuss the process by which a parent becomes attached to his/her infant. Most of the richness and beauty of life comes from the close relationship that each individual has with a small number of other human beings—his or her parents, siblings, children and a small group of close friends. Much of the joy and sorrow of life revolves around attachments or affectional relationships: making them, breaking them, preparing for them, and adjusting to their loss. The bond between a mother and father and their newborn infant is one of these very special attachments. Perhaps the parent's attachment to a child is the strongest bond in the human species. The power of this attachment is so great that it enables the mother and father to make the unusual sacrifices necessary for the care of their infant. Early in life the infant becomes attached to one individual, most often it is the mother. This original mother-infant bond is the wellspring for all the infant's subsequent attachments and is the relationship through which the child develops a sense of himself. Throughout his lifetime the strength and character of this attachment will influence the quality of all future bonds to other individuals.

[1]We acknowledge the generous support of the Grant Foundation, the Educational Foundation of America, Maternal and Child Health Grant MC-R-390337, NIH 72-C-202, and the Research Corporation, without which our work would not have been possible.

Observations of mothers and their infants immediately after delivery suggest this is a period of heightened sensitivity for the mother during which she interacts with her newborn infant and begins to form a specific attachment to it. An attachment can be defined as a unique emotional relationship between two people which endures over time and distance. Although it is difficult to define operationally this enduring relationship, we believe that behaviors such as fondling, kissing, cuddling, and prolonged gazing are indicators of attachment that serve to maintain contact with and show affection to a particular individual. Although it is early in our understanding of maternal attachment to describe its dimensions precisely, the qualities of interest, attentiveness, commitment, and protectiveness can be seen as defining the pole of optimal attachment while disinterest, neglect, indiscriminate attention, abandonment, failure to protect, nurture, or interact are at the other pole.

PROBLEMS OF ATTACHMENT

Disturbances of mother-to-infant attachment are often evident after prolonged separations in the neonatal period due to prematurity, low birthweight, or illness. In our clinical experiences, we have noted that a number of mothers who have been separated from their infants are hesitant and awkward when they begin to care for their babies. When the separation is especially prolonged, mothers report that sometimes they forget for a few moments that they even have a baby. At the present time, in premature units where parent-infant contact is encouraged and parents are allowed to participate in the care of their infants, a majority of mothers report that the baby did not seem like her own until she had full responsibility for its care at home for 1 to 3 days. Even after this time at home we have often heard a mother say that although she is fond of her baby, for moments she still thinks of it as belonging to someone else—the nurses or physicians—rather than to her.

An extreme distortion of mother-to-infant attachment is evident in the mother of a child who is battered or the mother of an infant with no organic disease who has failed to thrive at home but who gains weight easily when his needs are more adequately met by another caretaker. Because prematurity and low birthweight often lead to prolonged mother-infant separation, these children are often at risk. Any stress that causes the expectant mother to feel unloved or unsupported, or concerned about her health or the health of her child, may delay preparation for the infant and retard the formation of an affectional bond. Margaret Lynch (1975) has identified six factors that were greatly overrepresented in the history of abused children compared to their unabused siblings. These were an abnormal pregnancy, abnormal labor or delivery, neonatal separation, other separations, in the first 6 months of life, illnesses in the infant during his 1st year, and illnesses in the mother during the infant's 1st year of life. Other studies as well have indicated that prematurely born children constitute a disproportionately large number of both battered children (23–31%) and those with "failure-to-thrive" syndrome (Table 23-1; Klaus and Kennell, 1976). Lynch concluded that "treatment of parents during the pregnancy, the perinatal period, and early infancy may well be fruitful in the prevention of child abuse" and, we add, other serious behavioral disturbances as well.

Relatively mild illness in the newborn appears to have an adverse effect on the relationship between mother and infant. Almost two decades ago the clinical observations of Rose et al. (1960) and Kennell and Rolnick (1960) suggested that affectional ties are easily disturbed and may be permanently altered during the immediate postpartum period.

Table 23-1.   Effect of Separation (Many Days) on Battery and Failure to Thrive Without Organic Cause.

	Authors	N	Number Separated from Mother	Percentage Separated
Failure to Thrive	Ambuel and Harris (1963)	100	27 prematures	27
	Shaheen, Alexander, Turskowsky, and Barbero, (1968)	44	16 prematures	36
	Evans, Reinhart, and Sullop	40	9 prematures	22.5
	Elmer and Gregg (1967)	20	6 prematures	30
	Skinner and Castle (1969)	78	10 prematures	13
Battering	Klein and Stern (1971)	51	12 low-birthweight infants	23.5
	Oliver, Cox, Taylor (1974)	38	8 prematures	21

From Klaus and Kennell (1976).

Mothers are often separated from their infants during the first hours after delivery because of minor neonatal problems such as mild jaundice, slow feeding, and the need for incubator care in the first 24 h due to mild respiratory distress. Behavior in these mothers is often disturbed with overprotectiveness and excessive concern during the 1st year of the baby's life or longer, even though the infant's problems are completely resolved before discharge from the hospital. Andrew Whiten (1975) has recently reported differences in the behavior of both mothers and infants separated for similar mild problems (in which infants were first touched in a mean of 2 days and discharged from the special care unit in a mean of 5 days), when compared to healthy dyads who were not separated. Note that two factors were involved—an illness and a separation. Significant differences in the mothers' and infants' behavior were observed in the following 2 months. Six months after delivery the mothers showed significant differences in the way they presented toys to their infants. Whiten states that "we cannot continue to assume that so long as the average mother really wants her baby, short periods of separation or minor perinatal complications will not result in a mother-infant relationship less successful than those not subject to such disturbances."

MATERNAL SENSITIVE PERIOD (ANIMALS)

The length of the sensitive period varies in different animal species. For example, Klopfer (1971) has shown that if a mother goat is separated from her kid immediately after birth for just over an hour she will often refuse to accept and nurse it, butting and kicking it away when it is returned so that it would perish if there were no intervention. However, if the mother and kid are together for just the first 5 min after birth and then separated for an equal period, the mother will immediately recognize and accept her kid when it is brought to her. The process can occur at a later time, although it will often be more difficult and take longer to achieve. Hersher et al. (1963) found that if drastic measures were taken to keep a mother goat in a small enclosure with her kid, starting within the first 12 h after delivery, maternal attachment could still be achieved but with much more difficulty. The process, which takes only a few minutes immediately after delivery, took an average of 10 days once the sensitive period had passed.

Rosenblatt and Lehrman (1963) studied the effects of mother-infant separation on the maternal behavior of laboratory rats. An important characteristic of the mother rat is that she will behave maternally to pups other than her own. Under certain conditions alien pups elicit her maternal care. This permitted experimentation in reeliciting maternal behavior by introducing new pups ("test pups") for short periods to observe the reactions of mothers who had been separated from their own pups for various periods of time.

Rosenblatt and Lehrman found that separation of mother and infant laboratory rats is debilitating, especially if it occurs immediately after delivery. When separation occurred immediately after the pups were born and lasted for at least 4 days, all test pups introduced to the deprived mother died within 5 days. When the separation lasted only 2 days, half the pups died within the first 5 days. In each case, separation sharply decreased maternal responses to the test pups. New pups allowed to live permanently with the deprived mothers reelicited her nursing, nest-building, and retrieving behaviors for a short time, but eventually maternal behavior fell to a low level. If mothers were allowed as few as 3 days after delivery in which to establish maternal behavior patterns before they were separated from their pups, the mothers were much more likely to respond appropriately to new pups even after 4 days without them.

HUMAN MATERNAL SENSITIVE PERIOD

To investigate the importance of the first few minutes and hours of human maternal-infant contact, 10 studies have been conducted in which the time of first contact between a mother and neonate were varied. The model for a number of these was a study of 28 primiparous mothers and their normal full-term infants in which half of the mothers were given their nude babies in bed for 1 h in the first 2 h after delivery and for an extra 5 h on each of the next 3 days of life (Kennell et al., 1974). The other 14 mothers received the care that is routine in most hospitals in the United States: a glimpse of the baby at birth, brief contact for identification at 6 to 8 h and then visits of 20 to 30 min for feedings every 4 h. The two groups were matched for age, marital, and socioeconomic status of the mothers, and sex and weight of the infants. Women were randomly assigned to a group; all were given the same explanation of the study and were not aware that there were differences in mother-infant contact in the first 3 days. Those making the observations in this and the follow-up studies did not know to which group the subjects belonged.

When the mothers and babies returned to the hospital at 1 month, there were significant differences between the two groups. During a stressful physical examination, the "early-contact" mothers usually stood near their infants and watched, and they soothed their crying infants significantly more, and during feeding engaged in more eye-to-eye contact and fondling. Early-contact mothers were also more reluctant to leave their infants with someone else than were mothers not given the early and extended contact experience. Figure 23-1 shows the difference between the early- and late-contact groups in *en face* and fondling during a filmed feeding in which the first 600 frames, at 1 frame/sec, were analyzed for 25 separate items showing *en face* and close contact. *En face* is the position defined by Robson (1967) which occurs when the mother's face is rotated so that her eyes and those of the infant meet fully in the same vertical plane of rotation. On the left of Figure 23-2 is a representation of the early-contact mothers' feeding style and on the right is that of the late-contact group. At 1 year, the two groups were again significantly different. The early-contact mothers spent a greater percentage of time assisting the

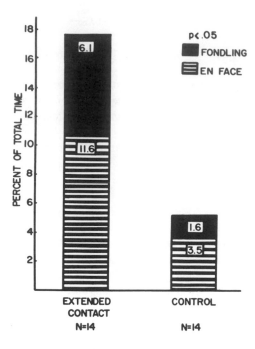

[From Klaus, M.H., et al. Maternal attachment: Importance of the first post-partum days. *New England Journal of Medicine* 1972, **286**.]

Figure 23-1. *Filmed feeding analysis at 1 month, showing the percentage of en face and fondling times in mothers given extended contact with their infants and in the control group.*

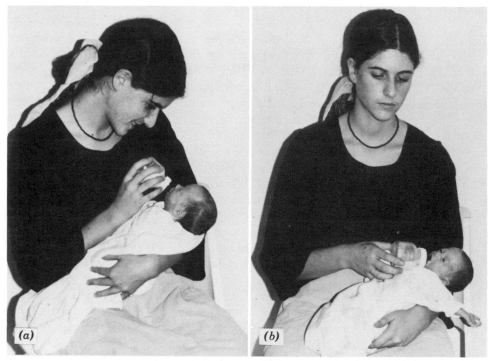

[From Klaus & Kennell, 1.]

Figure 23-2. *A posed mother showing two different caretaking positions:* **(a)** *Infant is held in close contact (mother's body touching infant's), mother is looking at infant* **en face,** *bottle is perpendicular to the mouth, and milk is in the tip of the nipple.* **(b)** *Infant's trunk is held away from mother. Mother is looking at infant, but not* **en face,** *and the bottle is not perpendicular to the mouth.*

physician while he examined their babies and soothing the infants when they cried (Kennell et al., 1974).

We wondered if just a few mothers in one or both groups had accounted for the persistence and consistency of the differences over the span of 11 months. However, the ranking of the mothers within each of the two groups showed no significant correlation for the measures at the 1-month and 1-year examinations.

At 2 years five mothers were selected at random from each group, and the linguistic behaviors of the two groups while speaking to their children were compared (Table 23-2; Ringler et al., 1975). The early-contact mothers used twice as many questions, more words per proposition, fewer content words, more adjectives, and fewer commands than did the controls. These findings suggest that an extra 16 h of contact in the first 3 days of life appear to have affected maternal behavior for 2 years.

Since this study began, there have been nine others that follow the same model of providing either early or late contact for parents and their full-term infants, then measuring the outcome effects on the mother or the infant (Table 23-3). Several of the studies have shown significant increases in the length of breastfeeding in mothers who had early contact with their infants.

In one study, Winters (1973) allowed six mothers to suckle their infants shortly after birth. This group was compared to another group of six mothers who did not have contact with their babies until 16 h after delivery. The mothers in both groups had originally expressed their intention to breastfeed and none discontinued breastfeeding due to physical problems. All six mothers who had nursed their infants on the delivery table were still breastfeeding 2 months later, whereas only one mother in the late contact group was still nursing her baby at that time.

Sousa et al. (1974) recently compared the success of breastfeeding during the first 2 months of life in two groups of 100 women who delivered normal full-term babies in a 20-bed maternity ward in Brazil. In the study group, the infant was put to the breast immediately after birth, and continuous contact between the mother and baby was sustained during the lying-in period by placing the baby's cot beside his mother's bed. The control group had the traditional contact with their infants—a glimpse shortly after birth and, starting 12 to 14 h after birth, subsequent visits of approximately 30 min every 3 h, seven times a day. These babies were otherwise cared for in a separate nursery. Successful

Table 23-2. Characteristics of Mother-to-Child Speech at 2 Years

	2 Years	
	Extended Contact	Control
Number of words per proposition	4.62[a]	3.66
Mean utterance length	3.9	3.1
Percentage of		
Adjectives/all words	16.00[b]	12.00
Content words/all words	48.00	62.00[b]
Questions/sentences	41.00[a]	19.00
Imperatives/sentences	43.00	74.00[a]
Statements/sentences	16.00	6.00

From Ringler et al., 1975.
[a]$p<0.05$
[b]$p<0.02$

Table 23-3.   Early Contact and Significant Outcome Variables

Study	Pairs (N)	Evaluation Time	Mother	Infant
Social Security Guatemala	40	1 Yr.	Breastfeeding	Weight gain; Infections
Roosevelt I Guatemala	60	1 Yr.		Infections
Roosevelt II Guatemala	68	9 Mo.	Breastfeeding	Infections
Winters U.S.A.	12	2 Mo.	Breastfeeding	
Sousa Brazil	200	2 Mo.	Breastfeeding	
Hales Guatemala	19	12 Hrs.	Behavior	
Hales Guatemala	60	36 Hrs.	Behavior	
DeChateau Sweden	40	36 Hrs.	Behavior	
Cleveland	28	1 Mo.	Behavior	
		1 Yr.	Behavior	
		2 Yr.	Speech	
Lind Sweden		2 Mo.	Paternal involvement	

breastfeeding was defined as no complementary feedings other than tea, water, or small amounts of fruit juice until the baby was 2 months old. At 2 months, 77% of the early-contact mothers were successfully breastfeeding, in contrast to only 27% of the control mothers. A feature in the design of this particular study which limits the interpretation of the findings in terms of the effects of early contact is that during the experimental period a special nurse was working in the unit to encourage breastfeeding.

In two studies in Guatemala breastfeeding was increased in the group of mothers who had 45 min of skin-to-skin contact with their newborn infants in contrast to the late-contact groups with contact at 12 or 24 h. The early-contact group fed their babies an average of 92 days longer in one study (Social Security Hospital) and 50 days longer in another (Roosevelt II). In a third study (Roosevelt I), where the matching of mothers' socioeconomic status and birthweights of infants was imperfect, different results were obtained (Table 23-4). Studies of mothers and infants in Guatemala have also shown increases in weight gain and decreases in infection in the infants as a function of early contact.

Mothers and infants of higher socioeconomic background have been studied by de Chateau (1976) in Sweden to determine the effects of early contact. The early-contact mothers were given their babies nude, skin to skin, as soon as possible after birth for the first 30 min of life and then both groups of mothers had their wrapped babies for the next 90 min. Three months later twice as many of the early skin-to-skin contact mothers were breastfeeding (58% vs. 26%) and they continued to breastfeed almost 2 months longer than the controls. Home observations were made when the infants were 3 months old. The mothers who had early contact spent significantly more time looking *en face* and kissing their infants, while control mothers cleaned their infants more often. Furthermore, infants

Table 23-4. Breastfeeding Days During the 1st Year (Mean)

Hospital	Control	Experimental
Roosevelt I	274	173 $p<0.01$
Roosevelt II[a]	109	159 $p<0.1$
Social Security	104	196 $p<0.05$

From Sousa, R., Kennell, J.H., Klaus, M., and Urrutia, J.J. The effect of early mother-infant contact on breastfeeding, infection, and growth. In *Breast Feeding and the Mother*. Ciba Foundation Symposium 45 (new Series), 1977.
[a] 9 months.

of early-contact mothers cried less, and smiled and laughed significantly more than the controls.

In the United States, the predominant tendency of fathers to avoid caretaking involvement with their newborns has been considered a cultural sex-role phenomenon. However, studies of father-infant interaction suggest that fathers can become attached to their infants in the early period following delivery if they are allowed contact with them. Lind et al. (1973) found that paternal caregiving in the first 3 months of life was increased in Sweden when the father was asked to undress his infant twice and to establish eye-to-eye contact with him for 1 h during the first 3 days of life.

Studies of the effects of rooming-in at the maternity hospital have also indicated the importance of the early postnatal period. When rooming-in was inaugurated a number of years ago, it was found that breastfeeding increased from 35 to 58.5% (McBryde, 1951). Phone calls to physicians from anxious mothers during the first 2 weeks after discharge decreased by 90%. In Sweden mothers who had been randomly assigned to rooming-in arrangements felt more confident in infant caretaking and thought that they would need less help in caring for their babies at home than the mothers who had not had the rooming-in experience. These mothers also were more sensitive to their infants' cries (Greenberg et al., 1973). This suggests that close continuous contact of mother and infant after birth may encourage more relaxed maternal behavior.

Two additional studies which also support the hypothesis that early contact enhances the attachment of mother and infant were conducted at Stanford (Leifer et al., 1972) and at Case Western Reserve Universities in premature intensive care nurseries. The mothers studied in these two investigations are distinctly different from the mothers of healthy, full-term infants described in the previous studies. The mothers in the premature studies were difficult to match according to the many variables that might have affected their mothering. The infants were also often critically ill, so the mothers began to mourn their anticipated loss. This anticipatory grief hindered the attachment process once the infant began to recover and grow. There was another major difference in these two studies: the "early-contact" group often did not actually have contact with their infants until as late as 5 days after delivery. At the time of these studies it was the usual practice throughout the country to allow parents to have only visual contact with their premature infants in the glass-enclosed nursery. They were unable to touch, hear, or help with their care until just before the infant was ready to be discharged from the hospital. The hypothesis for these studies was that if human mothers are affected by this period of separation, then one would expect to see altered maternal attachment during the first weeks or months of the infant's life, and therefore differences in the infant's development would become evident as the child grows.

In these investigations, half the mothers were allowed into the nursery within the first 5 days after delivery and the other half were permitted into the nursery after 3 weeks. All the parents in the Stanford study were interviewed seven times while their infants were in the nursery. Both groups thus received some kind of special attention, whereas in the study at Case Western Reserve, statements to parents were limited.

Significant differences between the early- and late-contact groups were found in the Case Western Reserve study. At the time of discharge, early-contact mothers looked at their infants more during a filmed feeding, and mothers of girl babies in the early-contact group held them close to their bodies for a greater percentage of time than the late-contact mothers of girls. When the children were 42 months old, the early-contact children scored significantly higher on the Stanford Binet IQ than the late-contact children (mean IQ 99 vs. 85). A significant correlation (correlation coefficient = 0.71) was found between the IQ at 42 months and the amount of time mothers looked at their babies during the 1-month filmed feeding. This also supports our hypothesis that early contact affects aspects of the mother's behavior which may influence the child's later development.

At 1 month the late-contact mothers in the Stanford study showed no significant differences in attachment behavior to their premature infants from those mothers who had early contact. However, five mothers and fathers subsequently were divorced in the late-contact group—as opposed to one divorce in the early-contact parents. Two infants in the late-contact group were given up for adoption even though all the mothers intended to keep their babies when they entered the study.

These two studies of early and late contact with premature infants indicate that the sooner a mother is allowed to interact with her infant, the firmer the resulting bond.

TIMING OF THE SENSITIVE PERIOD

These studies suggest that it is the very early postpartum period that is especially significant for the development of parental attachment. To explore the timing of the sensitive period, Hales et al. (1977) studied 60 primiparous mothers in Guatemala. Twenty experimental mothers had early skin-to-skin contact with their infants and 20 mothers had no contact before 12 h, as in the previously mentioned studies. A third group of 20 mothers received the same 45 min of skin-to-skin contact as the experimentals, but it was delayed until 12 h after birth. Observations of maternal behavior in all three groups at 36 h showed that the mothers who had the 45 min of extra contact immediately after delivery exhibited significantly more affectionate behavior, *en face,* looking at the baby, talking to the baby, fondling, kissing, and smiling at the baby than those mothers with either delayed extra contact or no extra contact. Thus, some time during the first 12 h the potency of the initial mother-infant contact diminishes.

Our interest in the first few minutes of mother-infant interaction immediately after birth led us to investigate the behavior of mothers and their infants who were delivered at home. We have studied videotapes and 8-mm films of home deliveries and have had lengthy discussions with a midwife (Lang, 1972) who has made naturalistic observations of many home deliveries in the area around Santa Cruz, California. In contrast to the woman who delivers in the hospital, the woman who gives birth at home appears to be in control of the process. She is an active participant in her labor and delivery, rather than a passive patient.

Since the restraints and restrictions of hospital traditions are absent in a home delivery,

OBSERVATIONS OF MOTHERS AND INFANTS

36 HOURS AFTER DELIVERY

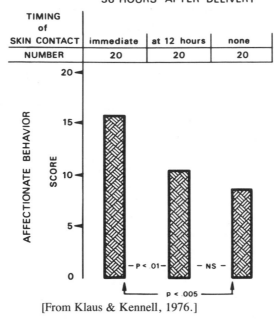

TIMING of SKIN CONTACT	immediate	at 12 hours	none
NUMBER	20	20	20

[From Klaus & Kennell, 1976.]

Figure 23-3. Scores of attachment (which included en face, *looking at the baby, talking to the baby, fondling, caressing, smiling at the infant) observed at 36 h after delivery in three groups of mothers, two of which received their infant skin-to-skin at either 45 min of age or 12 h.*

we were interested in the characteristics of the mother's interactions with her newly born child. Many mothers delivered in the hands and knees position. A few minutes after birth, but before delivery of the placenta, the mothers turned and picked up their infants, after assuming the *en face* position. The mothers appeared to be in a state of ecstacy, which was shared by the friends and relatives who had observed the delivery. Throughout the process these observers had offered encouragement and support to the mother, and in the first 15 to 20 min following delivery they were very attracted to the infant.

This supports the observations of Eibl-Eibesfeldt (1971), who emphasized the unique characteristics of the human infant, such as the large forehead and small face, large eyes, chubby cheeks, small mouth, and unequal bodily proportions, which attract not only the mother and father, but all those present, to the infant. Most of the fathers and mothers in the home deliveries speak to their infants in a higher-pitched voice than they normally use.

Lang observed that the infant quiets when handed to the mother. The mother usually rubs the baby's skin with her fingertips in a gentle stroking motion, starting with the baby's face. Then, before the delivery of the placenta, the baby is put to the breast. Nursing usually does not occur at this time, however, the infant usually just licks the mother's nipple for a prolonged period.

Condon and Sander (1974) have observed that at birth the normal neonate has a complex interaction system in which the organization of his motor behavior can be entrained by and synchronized with adult speech (whether it be English or Chinese). Their work and our observations suggest that this synchronization of visual, tactile, and auditory interactions between mother and infant may begin immediately after birth.

Recent information about the states and capabilities of newborn infants has contributed to our understanding of why the period immediately after birth is so important to the parent. Wolff (1959) described the six separate states of consciousness in the infant, which range from deep sleep (state 1) to screaming (state 6). Desmond et al. (1966) observed that the newborn is in state 4 for a period that lasts from 45 to 60 min immediately after birth. In this state, the infant is alert and active, his eyes are wide open, and he is able to follow objects with his eyes and head. After this period, the infant falls deeply asleep for 3 to 4 h. The infant's early responsiveness to his environment and ability to interact with his parents makes this period optimal for the formation of affectional bonds.

We hypothesize that during this early sensitive period a series of reciprocal interactions begins between the mother and infant which bind them together and insures the further development of attachment. The infant elicits behaviors from the mother which are satisfying to him, and the mother elicits behaviors from the infant which are rewarding to the mother. These interactions occur on many levels—behavioral and physical. When the infant cries, his mother usually comes near and picks the baby up. The baby often quiets, opens his eyes, and will look at the mother and follow her with his eyes. During a feeding the mother may initiate the interaction. She may gently stroke the infant's cheek, eliciting the rooting reflex which brings his mouth in contact with his mother's nipple. Nursing is pleasurable to both the mother and infant, and it stimulates the secretion of oxytocin which causes the mother's uterus to rhythmically contract. Simultaneously the infant receives immunoglobulins and experiences T and B lymphocytes in the breastmilk, which, recent evidence suggests, may line part of the intestinal epithelium, providing protection against the enteric pathogens for which the baby receives little transplacental protection. Because the maternal and infant behaviors complement each other, the probability that interaction will occur is increased. These behaviors seem to be specific and programmed to initiate the process that bonds mother and infant in a sustained reciprocal rhythm.

Although individual infants differ in their capacity to receive and shut out stimuli, as well as their ability to exhibit behaviors to which the environment can respond, we wonder whether some of these individual differences described in later infancy might be the result of whether the mother is permitted early or late contact. We believe that mothers and infants are optimally prepared to start the amazing synchronization of their behaviors in the first few minutes of life.

Twenty-five years ago, when changes in visiting policies in childrens' hospitals were originally suggested, many nurses and physicians felt that children's wards would become unmanageable, the children would be distressed, and their health would suffer. Although now all agree that the change to unrestricted visiting and parental living-in has been extremely important to the overall health of the child as well as his family, the change did not come easily. Pediatricians, nurses, and others who have observed the change have seen that the sensitivity and ingenuity of parents often results in much better care for a child than could be provided by professionals alone.

We now enter an era in which it will be necessary to closely review each of our traditional procedures and techniques for the birth of a baby. It will be necessary for those responsible for the care of mothers and infants to evaluate hospital procedures that interfere with early and sustained mother-infant contact and consider introducing practices that promote a mother's immediate interaction with her infant and help her to appreciate his wide range of sensory and motor responses. In every hospital, keeping parents and infant together should be the rule, not the exception.

BIBLIOGRAPHY

Bowlby, J. The nature of the child's tie to his mother. *International Journal of Psychoanalysis*, 1958, **39**, 350–373.

Condon, W. S., and Sander, L. W. Neonatal movement is synchronized with adult speech: Interactional participation and language acquisition. *Science* (Wash., D.C.), 1974, **183**, 99–101.

de Chateau, P. Neonatal care routines: Influences on maternal and infant behavior and on breastfeeding (thesis). Umea University (Sweden) Medical Dissertations, N.S. No. 20, 1976.

Desmond, M. M., Rudolph, A. J., and Phitaksphraiwan, P. The transitional care nursery: A mechanism of a preventive medicine. *Pediatric Clinics of North America,* 1966, **13**, 651–668.

Eibl-Eibesfeldt, I. *Love and Hate*. New York: Holt, Rinehart & Winston, 1971.

Freud, A. *Normality and Pathology in Childhood: Assessments of Development*. New York: International Universities, 1965.

Greenberg, M., Rosenberg, I., and Lind, J. First mothers rooming-in with their newborns: Its impact upon the mother. *American Journal of Orthopsychiatry* 1973, **43**, 783–788.

Hales, D., Lozoff, B., Sosa, R., and Kennell, J. Defining the limits of the sensitive period. *Developmental Medicine and Child Neurology,* 1977, **19**, 454.

Hersher, L., Richmond, J. B., and Moore, A. V. Modifiability of the critical period for the development of maternal behavior in sheep and goats. *Behavior,* 1963, **20**, 311–320.

Kennell, J. H., Jerauld, R., Wolfe, H., Chesler, D., Kreger, N. C., McAlpine, W., Steffa, N., and Klaus, M. H. Maternal behavior one year after early and extended post-partum contact. *Developmental Medicine and Child Neurology*, 1974, **16**, 172–179.

Kennell, J. H., and Rolnick, A. Discussing problems in newborn babies with their parents. *Pediatrics*, 1960, **26**, 832–838.

Klaus, M. H., and Kennell, J. H. *Maternal-Infant Bonding: The Impact of Early Separation or Loss on Family Development*. St. Louis: Mosby, 1976.

Klopfer, P. Mother love: What turns it on? *American Scientist*, 1971, **59**, 404–407.

Lang, R. *Birth Book*. Ben Lomond, Scotland: Genesis, 1972.

Leifer, A., Leiderman, P., Barnett, C., and Williams, J. Effects of mother-infant separation on maternal attachment behavior. *Child Development* 1972, **43**, 1203–1218.

Lind, J., Vuorenkoski, V., and Wasz-Höckert, O. In N. Morris (ed.). *Psychosomatic Medicine in Obstetrics and Gynaecology*. Basel: Karger, 1973.

Lynch, M. A. Ill-health and child abuse. Lancet, August 16, 1975.

McBryde, A. Compulsory rooming-in in the ward and private newborn service at Duke Hospital. *Journal of the American Medical Association*, 1951, **145**, 625.

Ringler, N. M., Kennell, J. H., Jarvella, R., Navojosky, B. J., and Klaus, M. H. Mother to child speech at 2 years—Effect of early postnatal contact. *Behavioral Pediatrics*, 1975, **86**, 141–144.

Ringler, N. M., Trause, M. A., and Klaus, M. H. Mother's speech to her two-year old, its effect on speech and language comprehension at 5 years. *Pediatric Research*, 1976, **10**, 307.

Robson, K. The role of eye-to-eye contact in maternal-infant attachment. *Journal of Child Psychology and Psychiatry and Allied Disciplines*, 1967, **8**, 13–25.

Rose, J., Boggs, T., Jr., and Alderstein, A. The evidence for a syndrome of "mothering disability" consequent to threats to the survival of neonates: a design for hypothesis testing including prevention in a prospective study. *American Journal of Diseases of Children*, 1960, **100**, 776–777.

Rosenblatt, J. S., and Lehrman, D. In H. R. Rheingold (ed.). *Maternal Behavior in Mammals*. New York: Wiley, 1963.

Sousa, P. L. R., Barros, F. C., Gazalle, R. V., Begéres, R. M., Pinheiro, G. N., Menezea, S. T., and Arruda, L. A. Attachment and Lactation, Fifteenth International Congress of Pediatrics, Buenos Aires, October 3, 1974.

Spitz, R. Hospitalism: An inquiry into the genesis of psychiatric conditions in early childhood. *Psychoanalytic Study of the Child*, 1945, **1**, 53–74.

Whiten, A. Post-natal separation and mother-infant interaction. Paper presented at International Society for the Study of Behavioural Development. 3rd Biennial Conference, Guildford, England, 1975.

Winters, M. The relationship of time of initial feeding to success of breastfeeding. Unpublished master's thesis, University of Washington, 1973.

Wolff, P. H. Observations on newborn infants. *Psychosomatic Medicine,* 1959, **21**, 110–118.

CHAPTER 24

Vulnerability and Risk in Early Childhood[1]

Albert J. Solnit
Sally Provence

There is an increasing literature on the concepts of vulnerability and at-risk conditions in early childhood (Coleman et al., 1953; Green and Solnit, 1964; Anthony, 1969, 1974a; Garmezy, 1972, 1974). This focus is the logical outcome of our broadened understanding of the nature-nurture interactional continuum. As our capability of collecting and reducing systematic observational data in early childhood has become more sophisticated, we have been encouraged to compare such findings with biological findings made possible by improved technical methods for describing and measuring neurophysiological, endocrine, and neuropharmacological changes in the human child and adult suffering from severe psychosomatic and psychiatric disorders (Cohen, 1974). Being able to think simultaneously of the mother-child interactional behavior (Klaus and Kennell, 1976; Winnicott, 1957) and of the biological aspects of behavioral change and deficit has enabled us to look at nature without overlooking nurture, and conversely at nurture without overlooking nature. Thus, it is valid to assume that the human infant is so helpless that he will die if there is not an adult to care for him; and at the same time, without contradiction, to say, ". . . now we have come to see the young infant as an active, striving being who elicits and modulates stimulation and has an effect on his environment" [Yarrow, Chapter 28].

In the human myths of vulnerability and invulnerability that of the warrior, Achilles, has much to tell.[2] When Achilles' mother, Thetis, learned of the fatal destiny that had been predicted for her son, she tried to immunize him against this fate by plunging him into the river Styx at birth. His entire body, except for the heel by which his mother held him, was thus rendered invulnerable. When Achilles was 9, the seer, Calchas, prophesied that he would conquer Troy, but would also meet his death there. His resourceful mother disguised him as a girl, but the deception was revealed by Odysseus, and he was inducted into the military forces. Achilles died at Troy when his vulnerable heel was pierced by an arrow.

The attachment to his mother was not strong enough to ward off the fates, to insulate and immunize him from the arrows of destiny. Thus, vulnerabilities, even those cast up by the gods, can act as a magnet for threatening forces and reactions in the environment.

Another instance of this mythology is contained in the orthodox Jewish custom of attempting to deceive the fates, in this case, the angel of death. The sick or vulnerable

[1]Based in part on The Second Mary Susan Brubaker Memorial Lecture, University of Connecticut School of Social Work, Hartford, April 26, 1976, and The First Ernst Dreyfuss Memorial Lecture, Michael Reese Hospital and Medical Center, Department of Pediatrics and Center for the Dysfunctioning Child, Chicago, July 15, 1977.
[2]*Larousse Encyclopedia of Mythology*. New York: Prometheus, 1959.

child is given an additional secret name to deceive the angel of death, once that shadow has fallen on the child. When the angel of death appears, he or she will not recognize the sick or vulnerable child because of the "new" name. The additional name also may convey a wish or "immunizing" effect by its content, which can refer to the wish that the child should have a long life or be healthy or strong.

Mythology and religious or superstitious customs can give expression to the magnetic effect that vulnerability has in being more likely to attract environmental reactions that promote defeat and dependency than to evoke responses of mastery.

A disease ecologist, Jacques May, has provided us with a striking analogy regarding risk and vulnerability (Anthony, 1974b). Imagine three dolls, one made of glass, one of plastic, and one of steel. Each is hit with exactly the same force, using the same hammer. The glass one was shattered into a thousand pieces; the plastic one was dented with a permanent scar, but remained intact; and the steel one emitted a beautiful sound. Our environment's hammer appears to shatter more frequently than it makes a beautiful sound.

In a recent paper (Solnit, 1974), we formulated a subtitle that emphasizes the goal and power of continuity, "Care for your children as you wish them to care for your grandchildren." This goal implies that there is some consensus about what we wish our children to become, further suggesting that we can have substantial agreement about the concepts of health, vulnerability, resilience, and at-risk conditions in childhood. These agreements are based on the following: Health is characterized by a progression of maturation and development in the mental and emotional spheres as well as in the physical sphere. When there is a failure of developmental progress that is more than transient, ideally the expert observer would detect it before the deviation has created its own complications. Of course, if the child and parents start off with the child poorly or incompletely equipped, or with the parents unable to respond with competence and affection to a healthy child, the vulnerability of the child or the at-risk environment created by the parents may set up a deviant or impaired development that has its own momentum and pattern.

Thus, vulnerability refers particularly to the weaknesses, deficits, or defects of the child, whereas risks refer to the interaction of the environment and the child. For example, a premature infant is vulnerable and usually the environment is a risky one because most hospitals have no program for keeping mother and premature child close together. The work of Leiderman and Seashore (1975) supports the view that vulnerability and risk to mother and premature infant are greatly lessened when the hospital and its personnel facilitate early contact and support the mother in taking care of her infant in the nursery. The work of Klaus and Kennell (1976) has also demonstrated that a mother who is deprived of contacting and caring for her child in the newborn period is a vulnerable mother. Thus, the child (e.g., prematurely) may also be vulnerable, or if the child is well and the mother is not able to begin the bonding immediately after birth, the mother's vulnerability becomes the child's at-risk environment.

As Lois Barclay Murphy has put it in her recent publication, *Vulnerability, Coping and Growth from Infancy to Adolescence* (1976), "Few are so robust as to be free from some zone of vulnerability . . . Most children have a checkerboard of strengths and weaknesses, or an 'Achilles heel' or a cluster of tendencies that interact in such a way as to produce one or another pattern of vulnerability as well as strength."

Healthy development is not a straight-line affair, but is characterized by advances, plateaus, and temporary regressions. For example, rapid advances are often associated with the advent of a new phase of development (latency, adolescence) which is usually preceded by transient regressions. It is as though the developmental push forward is prepared for and aided by a regressive "resting" behavior from which emerges the mobilization of developmental energies and capacities.

In the first months of life, the child's psychic functioning is not sufficiently differentiated to separate it from his physiologic functioning. Spitz (1951), in particular, in the psychological literature emphasized this state of affairs. Hartmann's (1958) concepts of the "average expectable environment" and of the preadaptive ego equipment are consistent with and provide the basis for his assertion that the human infant acquires much of his adaptive capability through the guidance of and identification with his parents.

Born helpless, an infant develops and grows in a social setting which, in order for him to survive, requires that an adult provides nurture, regulatory and filtering functions, and expectations that are the basis for socializing the child into a particular human community. The infant's helplessness becomes a powerful stimulus that evokes the nurturing care and protection of the adult who is becoming a parent. As the child matures and as earlier care is associated with the child's developmental progress, the parents find satisfaction and fulfillment that evoke the continuity of affectionate care of the child by the ordinary devoted parents (Winnicott, 1957), who gradually and intuitively enable the child to become more active in mastering daily and developmental tasks. Thus the child's competence emerges from this mutuality of parent-child relationship (Erikson, 1964). How successfully he develops this competence is largely based on the care provided him by parental adults and older siblings, themselves a family unit, who to one degree or another are representatives of that community. Erikson (1964) has put it well:

While far removed from any measure of mastery over the physical world [the newborn] is endowed with an appearance and with responses which appeal to the attending adults' tenderness and make them wish to attend to his needs . . . and which in making adults care, stimulate their active caretaking . . . Defenseless as babies are, they have mothers at their command, families to protect the mothers, societies to support the structure of families and traditions to give a cultural continuity to systems of child care and training. All this is necessary for the human infant to evolve humanly, for his environment must provide that outer continuity which permits the child to develop his capacities in distinct steps and to unify them.

We further assume that under the crucial impact of these early environmental influences, that biological and social factors are uniquely combined in and mediated by the individual child to form his particular personality. This mediating capacity is itself a product of the child's biologic makeup and environmental experiences. The hypothetical agency that is responsible for mediating and integrating is the ego. The parent is the auxiliary ego until the child's ego capabilities are able to take over these mediating, regulating functions. With the ongoing development of the ego, the child perceives, registers, stores, and reacts to the patterns of his experiences and needs in a manner that normatively enables him to develop a useful memory and to differentiate his social environment from his internal or mental representations and experiences.

This capacity for differentiating an inner psychic life from his or her social experience enables the child to develop other capacities that are essential for mental and social development. Included in these later developments—starting in infancy but becoming crystallized in later life—are the maturing capacities for thinking logically, remembering selectively, and for finding those alternate pathways that lead to gratification, problem-solving, and adaptation. These are discernible consequences of the child's gradually dawning capacities, after infancy, to harness his instinctual energies for learning, for expressing his ideas, and for developing his repertoire of affects—including humor, sadness, joy, and concern (empathy).

Another approach is based on the concept of risks. If the environment is chaotic, overstimulating, disorganized, or lacking in nurture, the risk of retarded or deviant development will be high. For example, children born out of wedlock or born into families disorganized by poverty or psychopathology are more likely to become deviant. When it is recognized that the environment is likely to cause deviant or stunted development, anticipatory interventions should be mobilized to supplement or correct the child's experiential deficits and distortions (Provence et al., 1977). On the other hand, if the child is born into an average expectable environment but is vulnerable because of a biological or constitutional disadvantage, then special guidance with educational and rehabilitative assistance may be necessary (Zigler et al., 1968). For example, a child who is very premature and has a congenital defect or suffers from an inherited metabolic disorder will be vulnerable, the high risk stemming from his biological equipment rather than from the environment. Our assumption is that healthy development will be threatened if either the child's environment or his equipment is disadvantageous.

In outlining the criteria for healthy psychological development, we view social development as a composite of psychological, emotional, and intellectual capabilities. Perceptual, motoric, emotional, and intellectual functioning are assessed in a social context.

From the beginning of life, biological vulnerability is the bedrock of what becomes psychological vulnerability. Another major source of risk for the young child is characterized by what interferes with the parents' capacities to nurture the child while gaining sufficient satisfaction, immediate or deferred, to facilitate their own sense of fulfillment so necessary for maintaining their development as an adult. We can, therefore, speak of parenthood as a phase of development (Benedek, 1959; Erikson, 1959; Bibring et al., 1961; Naylor, 1970).

Interactional experiences between babies and their parents become a pattern that can be viewed in its parts or as a whole in terms of developmental processes in the child and in the adult. Following the traditional medical pathological model, we have learned a great deal about vulnerability and the concept of "at risk" by observing and intervening as best we could when the conditions are severely deviant as in the battered child syndrome or where a child has a significant physical handicap, as in very young deaf infants. All the same, one cannot think of young children without thinking about their parents. Vulnerability and at-risk environments are parts of the whole; you cannot estimate vulnerability without knowing the risks.

The weaknesses and intolerances of the infant often serve as a magnet and magnifier for environmental actions and reactions, for parental perceptions of and responses to the baby (Ritvo et al., 1963). Included in this focus are vital past experiences that influence parental behavior and that tend to utilize the newborn and young infant as a screen on which past feelings and attitudes, often inappropriate ones, are projected onto the baby and distort the current reality of infant and parent. Such adult behavior is not only inappropriate for the child but tends to promote the repetition and continuation of the adult's deviant behavior.

What starts out for the child as a weakness or vulnerability may be magnified and elaborated by the parents' responses either because the parents lack resources or because the parents transfer inappropriate past attitudes or expectations onto the child (Coleman et al., 1953; Solnit and Kris, 1967). For example, the child may be experienced unconsciously as a rivalrous sibling or as a tyrannical parent, despite the reality of the infant's needs and behavior. Conversely, in many of these instances, the child's vulnerabilities activate potential resources within the parents. The child's deficit becomes a challenge to which such parents respond by helping the child to gradually overcome a congenital deficit or vulnerability, enabling the child, often with the help of special services in the community, to optimize his or her development. These assets of the parents, or what could be termed their autonomous ego functions, serve as a counterbalance to the vulnerable tendencies in the same child.

Thus, the child who is weak, handicapped, or deficient in strength and balance of capacities and equipment may evoke the sensitive, extra attention of a competent parent in which the disadvantageous start becomes a challenge that is well met. In these instances, the challenge leads to mastery. From a potential defeat in early functioning, a victorious and exuberant progression of development can result. Usually, these are the quiet cases that we do not see or hear about.

The following cases illustrate many of these formulations:

Jonathan B. was referred to our clinic for evaluation at the age of 15 months by his pediatrician because of delayed language and motor development. He was the first-born child of parents in their thirties who had come to this country about 6 months prior to Jonathan's birth.

Many weeks were required during the evaluation period before a reasonably clear picture unfolded, the high points of which are as follows: Jonathan, a full-term infant in good condition as a newborn, was characterized by his parents as being a responsive but quiet and entirely satisfactory infant. His mother, a shy and constricted woman, attended to his bodily needs but found no special pleasure in holding or cuddling her baby and usually spent several hours each day reading or listening to music.

The atmosphere appears to have been rather low-keyed, not unpleasant, but apparently somewhat impoverished in regard to those experiences that can be expected to be particularly supportive of an infant's development. The father, attentive to his wife and child when he was at home, traveled a great deal in his business. Things appeared to have gone reasonably well, however, until Jonathan was around 3 months old, when he was discovered to have a congenital dislocation of one hip. After several consultations, Jonathan was placed in a cast which was large and bulky enough that it substantially interfered with his mother's ability to handle him in her usual way. This occurrence also revived some hidden but significant anxieties in each parent about other ways in which their child might not be normal.

Over the period from 3 to 15 months, their attitudes toward fears about and behavior with Jonathan became a complicated mix of anxious concern, positive feelings, and anger, the latter frequently being expressed toward the series of physicians they consulted, each of whom they felt in some way failed them. Jonathan was so inactive and inhibited in all of the usual ways in which an infant of 15 months directs himself to the outside world of people and of objects that only after a period of work with him was it possible for us to determine his basically normal intellectual potential.

Over a 3-month period he improved in a manner that permitted us to reassure his parents about his capacities. At the same time, however, it was extremely difficult to get the parents to be involved in that aspect of the work with them that we believed to be of such importance for Jonathan's personality development. After a 3-month period they terminated the twice-weekly contacts with us, saying that they could carry on quite nicely alone and needed nothing further from us.

Quite recently, they were willing to come in for a follow-up visit at our request. Jonathan had continued to progress but was far from a robust, psychologically healthy child. Meanwhile the mother had become pregnant again. Both parents expressed themselves as quite satisfied about Jonathan. They were not available to further intervention at this time. Jonathan remains a vulnerable child in a far from ideal situation. His passivity tends to evoke responses—that is, avoidance of contact—that discourage mastery, and in this way the environmental risks are potentiated rather than mitigated.

Tommy J., age 4, was referred by his nursery school teacher who was concerned about a kind of anxious irritability he manifested in the school setting. While he was obviously an intelligent child, he often seemed fearful and inhibited, and could not use the setting as comfortably nor as constructively as most of his peers. His relationships to the other children were characterized by both imperiousness and anxious compliance.

Tommy's parents accepted the referral for evaluation because they had begun to fear that he would not do well in public school. Over the period of the evaluation it was possible to reconstruct what appeared to have been particularly important influences in the child's development.

He was the first boy in the family and was born prematurely after his mother had had a spontaneous abortion and a stillborn baby. He was a 4½-lb infant who did well in the newborn nursery, and the medical staff never considered him in any real danger. He was discharged home weighing slightly over 5 lb at the age of 3 weeks and after his mother had visited the nursery to feed him during the last week of his hospital stay. His two older sisters, ages 7 and 4 at the time of his birth, were doing well.

In spite of the physician's attempt to reassure her, Mrs. J., and to a large extent her husband, considered the baby very fragile and treated him with a kind of anxious tenderness which was only minimally modified as he grew into a physically sturdy child. As the first boy grandchild in a rather large extended family, he was highly valued by everyone. The parents' fear of losing him was the basis of an anxiety that disturbed their otherwise comfortable and sensible attitudes toward child care, and their consequent behavior was a major determinant of the clinical picture, what has been referred to as the "vulnerable child syndrome" (Green and Solnit, 1964). Tommy's prematurity evoked separation from his mother for the first 2 weeks of life, which delayed an attachment (Klaus and Kennell, 1976). In this case, the mother's anxious feeling that Tommy was fragile created an expectation that promoted anxiety and a sense of fragility. The anxious expectation became a self-fulfilling prophesy—the "fates" had so decreed it. They accepted recommendations for a period of treatment for the child, which of course involved them as well.

Laura D. was referred to us at age 2 as an incorrigible child. Her excellent pediatrician had helped the parents as much as he felt able to and had carefully investigated Laura's physical situation but felt the problem was beyond him. The parents complained that their 2-year-old was a study in opposites—that at times she was loving and lovable, at others aggressive, prone to tantrums and in their terms "spiteful." To complicate the matter, she had recurrent bouts of diarrhea, which raised parental anxiety but during which she was more easily managed. Her mother felt a greater closeness to her at those times than she usually did otherwise.

Laura was an extremely bright 2-year-old who quickly reassured us about the intactness of her central nervous system and her ability to exert greater control over her behavior and to interact with others in a more calm and focused way under favorable conditions. However, it was also clear that she already had a substantial stake as a participant in the atmosphere of excitement and fighting which characterized the relationship of each parent with her and with one another.

The complexity of the case became increasingly apparent and the situation so difficult to understand and to influence that we admitted her to the pediatric research unit of our hospital. The parents were with her a good deal and were invited to live in with Laura as their other obligations permitted. A careful study revealed that her gastrointestinal symptom was a psychophysiologic problem. We also had an opportunity to understand more about what went on between Laura and her parents. We continued to interview them to gain further understanding of their personalities and their relationships to each other. One of the more important influences appeared to be that Laura's father felt displaced by the child in that the considerable amount of support and attention which he needed, and which his wife was obviously willing and able to give prior to Laura's birth, he felt was lost to him after the immediate glow of new fatherhood had dimmed.

The mother, coming from a family in which there was considerable psychopathology, felt torn between her husband and her child and was unable to cope with this situation. The parents often reminisced about what they described as an almost idyllic period of 2 years prior to Laura's birth. Nonetheless, the mother felt strongly committed to her child and, within the limits of his own personality, so was Laura's father.

A period of very careful and painstaking work was required before the plan emerged for a period of treatment for child and parents. The parents viewed this as a period during which they could work on their marital conflicts as well as how to modify their reactions to their daughter's provocative behavior.

DISCUSSION

The above case summaries emphasize that a vulnerable child at birth encounters common tendencies or patterned responses by parents, especially the mother, when the infant's weakness or deficiency appears at birth. In such circumstances parents frequently respond with depressive reactions, defensively and with resentment. They often feel defective, helpless, and hopeless. Parents are often vulnerable when a child is being born because their preparation for the labor and delivery is associated with a rapid, intense review of their past and with the effort to anticipate what lies ahead. The birth of the baby and the parents' contact with their child completes the preparation for parenthood and the parent-child relationship (Anthony and Benedek, 1970). This psychological preparation for parenthood, most intense for the first child, but significantly unique and essential for each subsequent child, is completed or has its last phase after the child is born and there have been the first interactions between parents and child. This preparation, in its final phase, completes the working through of the discrepancies between the fantasies about each child and the realities of each child. The fantasies are both positive and negative, touching upon both the idealized child (preferred sex, complexion, height, temperament, etc.) and the feared child (tyrannical, weak, passive, defective, retarded, grotesque, etc.).

For example, a mother suffering from a depressive reaction in the postpartum period or concerned with marital conflicts may not provide appropriate stimulation and nurturance to a passive child, and a pattern of pseudoretardation may unfold (Coleman and Provence, 1957). In a sense the vulnerable mother is at risk, and if she feels rejected by her child's passivity or by an actual deficiency, a vicious resonance is set into motion—the mother feels rejected and is unable to work patiently and hopefully with her child. A more active child can provide such a mother with more evidence of her competence and can keep her busy enough to ward off transient depressive reactions.

The child with a vulnerability has a narrower range of resources available to extract adequate development-promoting experiences from the environment. Whereas a relatively invulnerable child can make do with a wide range of responses, stimuli, expectations, and satisfaction-frustration options, vulnerability in childhood can be defined by the child's need for more specific growth-promoting experiences. The vulnerable child is not as resilient or resourceful an extractor of development-promoting experiences, lacking the degree of autonomous ego functions (Hartmann, 1958) and adaptive responses that the less vulnerable child brings to life experiences. In fact, one way to conceptualize the child's healthy equipment and functioning is by how well he or she can respond to a limited parental repertoire of stimulation, affection, protection, and nurturant care. Thus, when a child thrives, even though the mother is mildly depressed and feels exhausted, in a situation where father, grandparents, and others fill in for the mother, we assume that the child was able to extract what it needed to activate a healthy development. When the child is vulnerable; he or she needs a human social and physical environment that can elicit healthy development from the nonvulnerable elements of the child's physical-psychological makeup, while gradually compensating for and transforming the weakness into adequate functioning—that is, mastery of vulnerability with a low-risk, resourceful mothering environment.

These general terms can be more specifically illustrated by problems such as hyperactivity, perceptual sensitivity, minor congenital defects of the limbs, a tendency toward irritability, paroxysmal nocturnal fussiness, or relatively poor tolerances for certain foods. Mild to moderate eczema fits into this category, as does a repeated regurgitation of food. The way the parents and doctor respond can determine whether it is a mild or severe burden on the child's development.

We agree with a recent comment (Korsch, 1977): ". . . the one recommendation . . . for families who appear to be at high risk or in trouble is to give them maximal access to available services, to interpret these services to them, and then to allow the particular family or group to select discriminantly the kind of help for which they feel ready and are able to accept."

Although generalizations can be inferred in connection with differing environments or classes of vulnerability, clinical standards avoid the pitfalls of such generalizations by focusing on the individual child and his or her specific environment (parents, family, community, etc.). Psychoanalytic theory brings an organizing and enriching influence to these observations because of its formulations regarding object relationships and the implications of its assumptions about autonomous ego functions. With these theoretical assumptions, vulnerability, at-risk environments, deprivation, trauma, resilience, and mutual adaptation can be more systematically understood.

BIBLIOGRAPHY

Anthony, E. J. A clinical evaluation of children with psychotic parents. *American Journal of Psychiatry,* 1969, **126** (2), 177–184.

Anthony, E. J. Introduction: The syndrome of the psychologically vulnerable child. In E. J. Anthony and C. Koupernik (eds.), *The Child in His Family: Children at Psychiatric Risk.* Year Book of the International Association for Child Psychiatry and Allied Professions, Vol. 3. New York: Wiley, 1974a 3–10.

Anthony, E. J. A risk-vulnerability intervention model for children of psychotic parents. In E. J. Anthony and C. Koupernik (eds.), *The Child in His Family: Children at Psychiatric Risk.*

Year Book of the International Association for Child Psychiatry and Allied Professions, Vol. 3. New York: Wiley, 1974b, 100.

Anthony, E. J., and Benedek, T. (eds.). *Parenthood and Its Psychology and Psychopathology.* Boston: Little Brown, 1970.

Benedek, T. Parenthood as a developmental phase. *Journal of the American Psychoanalytic Association,* 1959, **7**, 389.

Bibring, G. L., Dwyer, T. F., Huntington, D. S. and Valenstein, A. F. A study of the psychological processes in pregnancy and of the earliest mother-child relationship. 1. Some propositions and comments. *The Psychoanalytic Study of the Child,* Vol. 16. New York: International Universities, 1961, 9.

Cohen, D. J. Competence and biology: Methodology in studies of infants, twins, psychosomatic disease, and psychosis. In E. J. Anthony and C. Koupernik (eds.), *The Child in His Family: Children at Psychiatric Risk.* Year Book of the International Association for Child Psychiatry and Allied Professions, Vol. 3. New York: Wiley, 1974, 361–394.

Coleman, R., Kris, E. and Provence, S. The study of variations of early parental attitudes. *The Psychoanalytic Study of the Child,* Vol. 8. New York: International Universities, 1953, 20–47.

Coleman, R., and Provence, S. Environmental retardation (hospitalism) in infants living in families. *Pediatrics,* 1957, **19** (2).

Erikson, E. H. Identity and the life cycle. *Psychological Issues,* Vol. 1. New York: International Universities, 1959, 97.

Erikson, E. H. Human strength and the cycle of generation. In *Insight and Responsibility.* New York: Norton, 1964, 113.

Garmezy, N. Models of etiology for the study of children who are at risk for schizophrenia. In M. Roff, L. Robins, and M. M. Pollack (eds.), *Life History Research in Psychopathology,* Vol. 11. Minneapolis: University of Minnesota, 1972, 9–23.

Garmezy, N. The study of competence in children at risk for severe psychopathology. In E. J. Anthony and C. Koupernik (eds.), *The Child in His Family: Children at Psychiatric Risk.* Year Book of the International Association for Child Psychiatry and Allied Professions, Vol. 3. New York: Wiley, 1974, 77–97.

Garmezy, N., and Nuechterlein, K. H. Vulnerable and invulnerable children: The fact and fiction of competence and disadvantage. *American Journal of Orthopsychiatry,* 1972, **77** (abstract).

Green, M., and Solnit, A. J. Reactions to the threatened loss of a child: A vulnerable child syndrome. Pediatric Management of the Dying Child, Part III. *Pediatrics,* 1964, **34** (1), 58–66.

Hartmann, H. *Ego Psychology and the Problem of Adaptation.* New York: International Universities, 1958.

Klaus, M. H., and Kennell, J. H. *Maternal-Infant Bonding.* St. Louis: Mosby, 1976.

Korsch, B. The answer is no. *Pediatrics* (Neonatology Supplement), June 1977, 1064.

Leidermann, P. H., and Seashore, M. J. Mother-infant neonatal separation: Some delayed consequences. Ciba Foundation Symposium 33, *Parent-Infant Interaction.* Amsterdam: ASP, 1975, 213–239.

Murphy, L. B. *Vulnerability, Coping and Growth from Infancy to Adolescence.* New Haven, Yale University, 1976.

Naylor, A. Some determinants of parent-infant relationships. In *What We Can Learn from Infants.* Washington, D.C.: National Association for the Education of Young Children, 1970.

Provence, S., Naylor, A., and Patterson, J. *The Challenge of Daycare.* New Haven: Yale University, 1977.

Ritvo, S., McCollum, A. T., Omwake, E., Provence, S., and Solnit, A. J. Some relations of constitution, environment, and personality as observed in a longitudinal study of child development: Case report. In A. J. Solnit and S. Provence (eds.), *Modern Perspectives in Child Development*. New York: International Universities, 1963, 107–143.

Solnit, A. J., and Kris, M. Trauma and infantile neurosis—A longitudinal perspective. In *Psychic Trauma*. New York: Basic Books, 1967, 176–220.

Solnit, A. J. A summing up of the Dakar conference. In E. J. Anthony and C. Koupernik (eds.), *The Child in His Family: Children at Psychiatric Risk*. Year Book of the International Association for Child Psychiatry and Allied Professions, Vol. 3. New York: Wiley, 1974, 405.

Spitz, R. A. The psychogenic diseases of infancy: An attempt at their etiologic classification. *The Psychoanalytic Study of the Child*, Vol. 6. New York: International Universities, 1951, 255–275.

Winnicott, D. W. *Mother and Child*. New York: Basic Books, 1957, vii, 3–115.

Zigler, E., Balla, D. and Butterfield, E. C. A longitudinal investigation of the relationship between preinstitutional social deprivation and social motivation in institutionalized retardates. *Journal of Personality and Social Psychology*, 1968, **10** (4), 255.

CHAPTER 25

Effects of Maternal Drinking on Neonatal Morphology and State Regulation[1]

Henry L. Rosett[2]
Louis W. Sander[3]

HISTORICAL SURVEY

Identification of the fetal alcohol syndrome, a pattern of growth deficiency, developmental delay, and physical malformations occurring in infants born to women with severe, chronic alcoholism, has revived interest in the effects of maternal drinking on offspring. The belief that parental consumption of alcohol could have adverse effects on the health of offspring has a long history. The potential danger was probably recognized in classic times when both Carthage and Sparta had laws prohibiting the use of alcohol by newly married couples in order to prevent conception during intoxication. Burton (1906), in 1621, cited Aristotle's *Problemata,* "foolish, drunken or hair-brain women for the most part bring forth children like unto themselves, *morosos et languidos.*"

From 1720 to 1750, England lifted traditional restrictions on distillation; cheap gin flooded the country, creating the "gin epidemic" (Warner and Rosett, 1975). In 1726, the College of Physicians petitioned Parliament for control of the distilling trade, calling gin a "cause of weak, feeble and distempered children." During these years birth rates dropped, and there was a sharp rise in the mortality of children under five years of age (Morris, 1759). Throughout the 19th century, there are medical observations of offspring of alcoholics with a high frequency of mental retardation, epilepsy, stillbirths, and infant deaths. These findings were utilized by religious temperance leaders to prove that the sins of parents could be visited on children for several generations.

In 1899, William Sullivan, physician to a Liverpool prison, published a careful study of 600 offspring of 120 alcoholic women. He also located 28 nondrinking female relatives of the alcoholic women and found that the infant mortality and stillborn rate was 2½ times higher in the alcoholics' children than in the comparison population. Sullivan also observed that several alcoholic women who had infants with severe and often fatal complica-

[1]The investigation of neonatal state regulation was primarily supported by the National Council on Alcoholism, but was an extension of research supported in part by NIAAA Grant AA02446-01, the William T. Grant Foundation, the Massachusetts Developmental Disabilities Council, the U.S. Brewers Association, and both University Hospital and Boston City Hospital General Research Support Awards.
[2]Dr. Rosett was supported by ADAMHA Career Teacher Awards #T01DA00031 (NIDA) and PHSAA07008 (NIAAA).
[3]Dr. Sander is supported by Research Scientist Award #5K5MH205-09

tions later bore healthy children when, because of imprisonment, they were forced to abstain from alcohol during pregnancy.

In the American and British medical literature, interest in the effects of alcohol on offspring declined after 1920, following the institution of Prohibition. The early research in this field was criticized by Haggard and Jellinek in 1942. They felt that while damage to the reproductive organs had been observed in chronic alcoholics, there was no evidence of damage to the human germ cells. The observations of a higher incidence of retardation and epilepsy in the offspring of alcoholics, they believed, could be explained by the fact that "while alcohol does not make bad stock, many alcoholics come from bad stock." They recognized the detrimental influence of poor nutrition in the alcoholic mother and the disturbance of home life created by parental alcoholism, but did not differentiate between genetic damage and possible intrauterine effects of alcohol.

The French and German literature continued to report much higher frequencies of neurologic disorders together with delays in growth and development in the offspring of alcoholic parents (Heuyer et al., 1957; Christiaens et al., 1960).

DESCRIPTION OF THE FETAL ALCOHOL SYNDROME (FAS)

In 1968, Lemoine et al. described 127 offspring from 69 French families in which there was chronic alcoholism. In 29, both parents were alcoholics; in 25, only the mother; and in 15, only the father. The role of maternal alcoholism was considered to be essential for development of abnormalities. Twenty-five of these children had malformations—five cleft palates, three micropthalmia, six limb malformations, seven congenital heart disease, and four visceral anomalies. Their facial profile was characteristic, including a protruding forehead, sunken nasal bridge, short upturned nose, retracted upper lip, receding chin, and deformed ears. Many were hyperactive with delayed psychomotor and language development. When they reached school age, they had difficulty sustaining an activity for a period of time, and developed behavior problems. Intellectual retardation with an average IQ of 70 was described. (No data on the types of tests administered, ages of children examined, or range of scores were presented.) This paper was published in 1968, but was not cited in the English language literature until 1975, after the Seattle group study, described below, had independently described the fetal alcohol syndrome (FAS). The close similarity between the syndromes described independently by two research groups studying very different populations is a strong confirmation of the validity of their observations.

In America awareness of this problem was stimulated in 1970 by observations by Ulleland et al. at the University of Washington in Seattle. After noticing that six infants who failed to thrive had mothers who were chronic alcoholics, a retrospective review of clinic records was made to identify all undergrown infants during an 18-month period. Clinic personnel were also asked to identify known alcoholics or any women who were intoxicated in the morning when seen at prenatal clinics or home visits. Eleven women alcoholics were identified; 10 of their 12 children were small for gestational age. These 10 infants were tested with the Gesell or Denver developmental scales; five had retarded development, and three were borderline, even when their score was corrected for prematurity. Eight of these infants failed to grow, with weight and head circumference remaining below the third percentile. Six of the eight were receiving adequate diets at home, while two infants who were poorly fed at home failed to grow normally when hospitalized.

Subsequently, these eight infants were examined by the dysmorphologists Jones and Smith, who recognized a syndrome in four of them. An additional seven infants were located who showed features of the syndrome. Subsequently, it was discovered that all of their mothers were chronic alcoholics (Jones and Smith, 1973; Jones et al., 1973). Components of the FAS include prenatal and postnatal growth deficiency, microcephaly, and fine motor dysfunction. Facial characteristics include short palpebral fissures with associated micropthalmia, midfacial hypoplasia, and epicanthal folds. In the limbs, abnormal palmar creases and minor joint anomalies have been observed. Cardiac defects, anomalies of the external genitalia, small hemangiomas, and minor ear anomalies have also been observed in a significant number of these children. The Seattle group subsequently reported observations on a total of 41 patients demonstrating this syndrome, all born to severely chronic alcoholic women who drank heavily throughout their pregnancy (Hanson et al., 1976). They also evaluated five children whose mothers were alcoholic throughout pregnancy, but whose physical features did not clearly classify them as having the FAS, suggesting the possibility of a wide range of outcomes.

Streissguth (1976) reported on the intellectual development and motor performance of 12 offspring of chronic alcoholic women referred to the dysmorphology clinic at the University of Washington. All except one child were in the borderline or retarded range of intelligence. In general, children with the clear features of FAS were the most retarded, while those who were mildly affected physically appeared less impaired mentally. Since only malformed children are referred to dysmorphologists, children of chronically alcoholic mothers who demonstrated neither signs of the FAS nor retarded development would have been less likely to have been seen; therefore, these researchers would tend to be pessimistic about prognosis. The more severely retarded children did not respond to an enriched environment in foster homes or infant-stimulation programs. Socioeconomic status is one of many confounding factors; children of welfare parents were the most severely retarded. Three children from middle-class homes were less retarded and did not show the disorganized or hyperactive behavior seen in the less privileged group. These differences may be due to differences in genetic endowment, greater resources of the home, or a combination of prenatal and postnatal factors.

The initial publications from Seattle identifying and describing the FAS stimulated many case reports from around the world (cited in Ferrier et al., 1973; Palmer et al., 1975; Saule, 1974; Tenbrinck and Buchin, 1975; Barry and O'Nuallain, 1975; Root et al., 1975; Christoffel and Salafsky, 1975; Manzke and Grosse, 1975; Reinhold et al., 1975; Loiodice et al., 1975; Mulvihill and Yeager, 1976; Mulvihill et al., 1976; Bierich et al., 1976; Ijaiya et al., 1976; Hall and Orenstein, 1974; Noonan, 197; Tze et al., 1976; Pierog et al., 1977). The variability in the pattern of defects may be related to different patterns of chronic alcohol use at different stages of pregnancy, as well as such issues as the maximum blood alcohol concentration, binge drinking versus relatively steady-state alcohol levels, type of beverage, cigarette smoking, general nutritional status, and so on. There may be genetic differences in the susceptibility of the dysmorphogenic influence of alcohol. There are several reports of dizygotic twins with discordant teratogenically induced anomalies. Differences in rate of development may make different fetuses susceptible to teratogens at different times. Differences in placental and fetal vasculature may also affect growth rates.

Detailed consideration of the FAS in this handbook is presented as an effect of the psychoactive drug most widely consumed in our society. The FAS may also be viewed as a model of a developmental abnormality in which a multiplicity of determinants interact at various stages of the developmental sequence. In humans it is difficult to separate interacting elements. It is hard to find many pregnant women who drink heavily and yet are well nourished, are nonsmokers, receive the best prenatal care, and live in a low-stress environment. Early prospective studies have had methodological limitations (Jones et al., 1974; Kaminski et al., 1976; Mau and Netter, 1974). Ongoing prospective studies at the University of Washington (Streissguth et al., 1977), Loma Linda University (Kuzma and Phillip, 1977), and Boston City Hospital (Ouelette et al., 1977) are aimed at identifying the contribution of each of these components. More understanding of the interaction of these factors can be gained by a review of animal experiments, the effects of ethanol on human maternal and placental metabolism and physiology, and the resultant effects on the fetus and infant. Each of these issues will now be considered.

ANIMAL MODELS OF THE FAS

Development of animal models of the effect of alcohol in offspring has been necessitated by ethical issues in human experimentation, as well as in the inherent difficulty in separating the multiple variables involved in clinical studies. In 1894, Féré exposed hen's eggs to alcohol vapors before incubation. Ethanol, which penetrated the eggshell, produced a broad range of abnormalities. Similar effects were obtained by Stockard (1910) using fish and chicken eggs. Anomalies of the eyes were most common, followed by abnormal development of the CNS. Experiments with mammals were stimulated by the demonstration by Nicloux (1899, 1900) that alcohol crossed the placenta and could be demonstrated in the fetus of the guinea pig, dog, and woman at concentrations close to that in the maternal circulation.

For a review of the effects of alcohol on animal growth and reproduction, including a tabular comparison of 33 experimental regimens, see Wallgren and Barry (1970).

The many conflicting observations in the early literature can be related to species differences, as well as to the amount of alcohol administered, route of administration, stage of pregnancy when alcohol was introduced, and lack of paired feeding (matching food intake of the control animal with the amounts consumed by the experimental animal). Refinements in recent experimental designs have overcome some of these problems.

Chernoff (1975) administered alcohol orally via an all-liquid diet to two females from highly inbred strains of mice which differed in ethanol preference, alcohol dehydrogenase activity, and ethanol sleep times. Blood alcohol levels were maintained in a range from 73 to 398 mg/100 ml for at least 30 days before mating. Females were sacrificed on day 18 and the uterine contents examined. Fetal resorptions increased with increasing ethanol concentrations. The dose-response curve suggests that the strain with the lower ADH activity was more sensitive to ethanol than the strain with the greater metabolic capacity. There was a definite growth deficiency due to ethanol; beyond a point this deficiency was fatal. Fetuses were sectioned, and anomalies affecting the skeleton, brain, heart, and eyes were observed. The pattern of growth deficiency together with ocular, neural, cardiac, and skeletal anomalies was similar to that of the FAS in humans.

Randall et al. (1977) also administered a liquid diet with 25% of total daily calories supplied by ethanol to mice but only administered it from gestation day 5 through gestation day 10. Blood alcohol levels ranged between 70 and 120 mg/100 ml. A pair-fed control group was treated similarly except that sucrose substituted isocalorically for ethanol. Gravid females were sacrificed on gestation day 19. The alcohol-fed group implanted a larger number of ova, but twice as many of their fetuses were resorbed compared to the control group. The increase in resorptions decreased litter size so that the average number of fetuses and fetal weight were similar between groups. Fifteen of the 16 experimental litters had at least one malformed fetus; of the 29 control litters, only five had a malformed fetus. In the ethanol-fed group, limb anomalies included syndactyly, adactyly, and ectrodactyly of the forelimbs. In the ethanol group cardiovascular anomalies included abnormalities of both the major branches of the aorta and vena caval system, as well as intracardiac anomalies such as atresia of the mitral valve and interventricular septal defects. Urogenital anomalies included hydronephrosis and/or hydroureter. Head anomalies included exencephaly, hydrocephalus, anopthalmia, and micropthalmia. These anomalies are analagous to those reported in the children of alcoholic mothers.

Behavioral Effects On Animal Offspring

There are many inconsistencies and contradictions in the literature on the effects of ethanol during pregnancy on the behavior of rat offspring. Several reasons for this become clear when the methodologies of different researchers are compared (Table 25-1). Different results may be explained by a number of variables, including (1) types of behavior examined and tests used to observe this behavior, (2) differences in developmental stage during pregnancy and lactation at which ethanol exposure takes place, (3) differences in quantity of cthanol administered to the subjects, (4) nutritional differences between experimental animals and controls (e.g., only three used pair-feeding), and (5) possible differences between various breeds of rats.

While animal experiments offer the potential for controlling many of the uncertaintics that necessarily exist in collecting data from humans, such as the precise amount of alcohol, date of ingestion, blood alcohol concentration, and genetic characteristics, the literature contains many inconsistencies. Often these are due to differences in technique. The route of administration may be oral by means of a liquid diet with a proportion of the total calories supplied by ethanol, or by ethanol and water as the only source of liquid. Intraperitoneal injection of ethanol may have direct effects on the ovaries and uterus. There also is considerable variation between researchers in terms of the time period selected for administration of ethanol. Some feed it to the mother throughout her pregnancy; others select a few critical days during embryonic development. Some continue the ethanol through lactation; others stop it at birth. Timing is critical in terms of producing morphologic abnormalities during specific growth periods. In rats, pups fail to grow if alcohol is administered to the mother while nursing. This effect is probably secondary to its inhibiting action on the release of oxytocin, essential for milk ejection. Poor growth also may be related to altered maternal behavior or aversion of the offspring to ethanol-contaminated milk. Collard and Chen (1973) found that mouse pups weighed less than their controls at weaning when alcohol was injected into the nursing mother. When litters were raised in alcohol vapor chambers, pups weighed more at weaning and at 7 weeks of age than did controls, presumably due to additional calories from the inhaled ethanol.

Control animals should be pair-fed and receive the same number of calories as the experimental animals. The all-liquid diet, with the experimental animals receiving carbohydrate in the form of ethanol and the pair-fed control animals in the form of sucrose, seems to be the model closest to human alcoholism.

Despite methodologic differences, offspring exposed to ethanol in utero and during lactation, generally show hyperactivity, impaired learning, and greater alcohol prefer-

Table 25-1.   Effects of Ethanol in utero on Animal Offspring Behavior

Authors	Breed	Ethanol (E) Dates [a] & Dose	Pair-Fed	Test Results and Significance
Bond and Digiusto (1976)	Wistar	Days 0–21 6.5% E at 14 g/kg/day	No	Tested in an open field box on 45–50 days, the E-fed had greater ambulation (<0.05), greater hind-leg support (<0.05), but NSD in defecation. At 65–70 days, the E-fed had greater consumption of E up to 6% (<0.05), but for 7% and 8% there was NSD.
Branchey and Friedhoff (1976)	Not given	Days 10–21 Metrecal and E at 12 g/kg/day	Yes	At 23 days, in an open field box, E-fed pups had greater ambulation (<0.25), but hind-leg support and defecation had NSD.
Shaywitz et al. (1977)	Not given	Days 2–51 Sustacal and E (35% of calories)	No	E-fed were more active on days 12 and 19 (<0.001), but not on day 26 (<0.05). E-fed were impaired in learning in the T-maze on day 21 and in shuttle box at 27 and 33 days (significance not given).
Abel (1974)	Sprague Dawley	Days 21–35 10% E ad lib.	No	E-fed pups slept less (<0.05) after receiving 4 g/kg I.P.E. on the 21st day.
Abel (1975)	Sprague Dawley	Days 21–35 8.5% E	Yes	E-fed females ambulated and defecated less (<0.05) than control females. NSD in physical contact or hind-leg support.
Auroux and Dehaupas (1970)	Wistar	Days 0–42 15% E at 105 ml/kg/day	No	At 1½ months, E-fed needed fewer trials to be conditioned in a shuttle box (<0.0001), but there was NSD in the number conditioned.
Auroux (1973)	Wistar	Days (−) 100–21 18 ml of 15% E	Yes	At 1½ months, E-fed males performed worse than their controls (<0.02). Other tests had NSD.
Martin et al. (1976)	Sprague Dawley	AGN [b]: Days 0–42 AN [c]: Days 21–42 1000 mg/kg/d I.P. AGN also had 20% E	Yes	AGN and AN moved less on day 15 (<0.00005), but fewer had open eyes on day 16 (<0.0005). AGN had poorest discrimination of contingencies on punishment schedule.

[a] For this column only, day 0=conception, day 21=delivery, and day 42 starts weaning.
[b] AGN: Alcohol during gestation and nursing.
[c] AN: Alcohol during nursing only.

ences. It has been suggested (Bond and Digiusto, 1976; Shaywitz et al., 1977; Yanai and Ginsburg, 1976) that hyperactivity, which abates with maturation, and cognitive difficulties, which persist, also characterize hyperactive and minimal brain damaged (MBD) children. Evidence linking some cases of MBD to parental alcoholism will be considered in the section on long-term effects.

MECHANISMS OF ETHANOL'S EFFECT ON THE MATERNAL-PLACENTAL-FETAL SYSTEM

Ethanol has the potential to cause a greater variety of metabolic and physiologic disturbances adversely affecting fetal development than any other commonly ingested substance. While the mother, placenta, and fetus interact as a dynamic system, it is helpful to consider the effects of alcohol in terms of mechanisms that directly affect the fetus, and those that have their primary effects on maternal metabolism and physiology and the several maternal risk factors associated with heavy drinking.

Direct Effects of Ethanol on Fetal Physiology and Metabolism

In 1900, Nicloux demonstrated that alcohol ingested by the mother crossed the placenta and reached the fetus in concentrations similar to that found in the maternal circulation. Placental transfer and tissue distribution has been studied employing ethanol labeled with radioactive carbon in the pregnant mouse (Akesson, 1974), hamster, and monkey (Ho et al., 1972). Radioactivity was shown to distribute very quickly throughout the fetal body.

Acute Effects

The use of intravenous ethanol to prevent premature labor served to stimulate research on the acute effects of alcohol on the fetus and the mother close to term (Fuchs et al., 1967). Ethanol inhibits release of oxytocin by the pituitary at concentrations equivalent to blood levels used to arrest premature labor (Fuchs, 1966). There is no effect on the uterine muscle itself (Wagner and Fuchs, 1968; Wilson et al., 1969). Because of the immaturity of fetal hepatic enzymes, the fetal blood alcohol concentration falls at only half the rate of the mother (Seppälä et al., 1971; Waltman and Iniquez, 1972).

The effect of ethanol infusion on maternal and fetal acid-base balance was investigated in pregnant ewes by Mann et al. (1975a). An initial fetal metabolic acidosis and later a mixed acidosis were observed during the alcohol infusion; this worsened during the postinfusion period. Fetal EEG showed a decrease in amplitude and a slowing of the dominant rhythm as the blood alcohol concentration increased (Mann et al., 1975b). The EEG became isoelectric on occasion during the postinfusion period associated with severe fetal acidosis. Fetal cerebral uptake oxygen was unaffected, while the cerebral uptake of glucose and the glucose-oxygen utilization ratio was significantly increased. Horiguchi et al. (1975) carried out similar investigations with pregnant rhesus monkeys. The maternal respiratory rate was decreased and there was increase in the fetal heart rate, and a fetal acidosis. They concluded that intravenous infusion of ethanol in doses sufficient to suppress labor may be hazardous because the fetus becomes progressively asphyxiated.

These experimental studies probably are directly applicable to understanding the physiologic changes in the human fetus when the mother engages in binge drinking. Repeated episodes of severe acidosis and hypoxia may be important factors in the impaired neurologic functioning of the FAS babies. Other dangers of acute alcohol ingestion just prior to anesthesia are related to the acidity and volume of maternal gastric secretion stimulated by the alcohol. Subsequent anesthesia has been associated with aspirations of a highly acid secretion followed by pneumonitis (Greenhouse et al., 1969).

Effects on Fetal Metabolism

The most fundamental effects of ethanol are on cellular metabolism. The concentration of alcohol and the duration of exposure determine whether it is a rapidly metabolized nutrient or a toxic agent. At low concentrations, passive permeability of normal resting cell and capillary membranes are not influenced by ethanol. However, there is a significant effect at concentrations of $0.1\ M$ or less on membrane enzyme systems which employ energy derived from the cleavage of ATP to transport Na+ to the outside of the cell and K+ to the inside. The variable effects of alcohol on mitochondrial membranes with alteration of permeability and swelling have been reviewed by Kalant (1971). Cedarbaum et al. (1975) demonstrated that chronic ethanol ingestion is associated with striking ultrastructural changes in the mitochondria, as well as by persistent impairment of mitochondrial oxidation of fatty acids to carbon dioxide.

Alcohol has profound effects on carbohydrate, lipid, and protein metabolism in the adult (Lundquist, 1975). Rawat (1976) studied rates of protein synthesis by livers of fetal and neonatal rats born to mothers who had consumed ethanol during pregnancy. Rates of incorporation of labeled leucine into hepatic proteins was significantly lower in the offspring of the ethanol-fed rats compared with the control group. Maternal ethanol consumption resulted in a decrease in hepatic total RNA content, the RNA/DNA ratio, and the ribosomal protein content of the fetal liver. Inhibition of protein synthesis could be directly related to the retarded growth of the offspring of alcoholic mothers.

Effects on the Developing CNS

Exposure of the fetal CNS to moderate or high concentrations of ethanol probably has different effects at different stages of development. Malformations at the earliest stages of embryonic growth are probably incompatible with life. The only published report of autopsy findings in a FAS child was presented by Jones and Smith (1973). The brain of this 1300-g premature infant weighed only 140 g. Histologic examination disclosed extensive developmental anomalies. Disorientation of both neuronal and glial elements, as well as the incomplete development of the brain, indicated that the teratogenic effect must have occurred before 80 days' gestation.

A neuropathological study of seven brains from offspring exposed in utero to high concentrations of alcohol has been reported (Clarren et al., 1977). Characteristic malformations, termed leptomeningeal neuroglial heterotopias, result from neuronal and glial migratory failure, and were observed in five of the seven brains. These brain lesions were found in some infants who did not show other morphologic features of the FAS. The most critical period for teratogenesis in the human CNS appears to be within the first 85 days of gestation.

Ethanol affects the CNS via multiple mechanisms. At low concentrations, ethanol has its primary effect on the neuronal membrane; active transport of sodium and potassium across the membrane is impaired (Kalant, 1971). Thiamine, pyridoxine, and folic acid, as well as calcium, magnesium, and zinc, all essential for CNS enzymes, frequently are depleted due to the malnutrition and diuresis associated with chronic alcohol ingestion (Vitale and Coffey, 1971; Flink, 1971). Alcohol effects on the metabolism and development of the fetal CNS has been investigated directly in rats and mice. In the rat, the brain at the time of delivery is at a developmental stage comparable to that of the human brain during the third trimester. This must be taken into account in extrapolating from animal to human studies. Bauer-Moffett and Altman (1975) studied morphologic effects on the developing cerebellar cortex of rat pups who inhaled ethanol vapor from days 3 to 20 after birth. Ethanol exposure during this period of cerebellar neurogenesis produced great reductions of cerebellar tissue nearly twice that observed in parts of the rat pup brain that had developed prior to birth.

Rosman and Malone (1976) maintained pregnant rats on isocaloric liquid diets containing 10%, 21%, and 36% ethanol. Fetal loss was 100% when the mother was on the highest level diet, and 60% on the diets containing less ethanol. Pups were sacrificed between postnatal days 12 and 28. Starting at day 24, brains of the experimental animals, as compared with pair-fed controls, showed delayed myelination affecting all fiber tracts.

Tewari et al. (1975) investigated the effects of chronic ethanol ingestion on brain RNA metabolism in mature mice. Changes in RNA metabolism were due to an alteration in the transcription and/or the processing of RNA in the nucleus (Tewari and Noble, 1975).

Rawat (1975a) studied effects of long-term ethanol consumption by pregnant rats on the incorporation of ^{14}C-leucine into fetal and neonatal brain ribosomes. He found a 30% decrease in the rate of ^{14}C-leucine incorporation by the fetal cerebral ribosomes while neonatal rats suckling on ethanol-fed mothers showed about 60% decrease as compared to the control group.

Impaired learning, observed in animal behavior experiments as well as in psychological evaluation of FAS children, may be related to altered RNA metabolism. Increased motor activity, another behavioral manifestation observed in animals exposed to ethanol in utero, may be due to an alteration in neurohumorol amine metabolism. Ethanol affects uptake, storage, and release of serotonin, catecholamines, acetylcholine, and gamma-aminobutyric acid (Feldstein, 1971). Branchey and Friedhoff (1976) found that the activity of tyrosine hydroxylase, a rate-limiting enzyme in catecholamine biosynthesis, was increased at 1, 2, and 3 weeks of age in the caudates of rat pups exposed to ethanol in utero. They also observed increased activity in littermates at 23 days. Rawat (1975b) studied the influence of prolonged ethanol consumption by pregnant and lactating rats on the activities of several neurotransmitters together with the activities of the enzymes in fetal and neonatal brains. An increase in the cerebral content of GABA was found in both fetal and suckling neonates' brains. Glutamate, serotonin, and norepinephrine were also increased while acetylcholine was decreased in the suckling neonates but was unchanged in the fetuses. Disruption of the metabolism of neurotransmitters may have long-term effects on the developing organization of the fetal CNS.

At the cellular level, alterations of the membrane of the neurone and or neurotransmitters interferes with proper synaptic transduction. Heavy alcohol consumption alters physiologic functions in many areas of the CNS, and sleep disturbances are common (Williams and Salamy, 1973). Polygraphic studies of sleep have revealed marked disruption of the quantitative composition of rapid-eye-movement (REM) and slow-wave sleep (SWS), together with instability or fragmentation of the circadian rhythm of 24-h cycles and the ultradian rhythms (shorter cycles occurring periodically). In adult alcoholics, continued disturbance of sleep rhythms persists months after abstinence has been established. This knowledge prompted investigation of sleep disturbances in newborns exposed to alcohol in utero (Sander et al., 1977; Rosett et al., 1977). These will be discussed below in our review of Boston City Hospital investigations.

Effects of Alcohol on Maternal Metabolism and Physiology

Chronic heavy alcohol consumption adversely affects almost every organ system in the body. Nonspecific risk factors for the pregnancy are associated with disease of the liver and other parts of the gastrointestinal system, the cardiovascular system, the hematopoietic system, as well as the body's defense mechanisms against infectious disease (Seixas et al., 1975). Alcohol-induced metabolic disturbances in the mother, such as alcohol hypoglycemia, alcohol ketoacidosis, alterations in lactate, uric acid, and lipid metabolism, or changes in the metabolism of individual amino acids probably all have effects on the fetus.

Withdrawal Syndrome

Acute alcohol withdrawal syndromes have been described in newborn infants delivered by severely alcoholic mothers (Nichols, 1967; Pierog et al., 1977; Schaefer, 1962). If a woman undergoes an unmodified alcohol withdrawal syndrome in mid-pregnancy, the fetus might be subjected to major metabolic and physiologic disturbances. Two patients who had been consuming over a quart of vodka a day were withdrawn during the second trimester on the Boston City Hospital Obstetrical Service. Chlordiazapoxide was utilized for 1 week to modify withdrawal symptoms. No adverse effects were detected by monitoring fetal heart rate or on careful neurologic examination in the newborn nursery (Rosett et al., 1977).

Mineral Deficiencies

Deficiencies of magnesium, zinc, and calcium occur in chronic alcoholism as a consequence of increased urinary excretion, loss due to vomiting and diarrhea, and inadequate intake (Flink, 1971). A 100% increase in urinary excretion of calcium and a 167% increase in magnesium excretion have been observed to begin within 20 min of the ingestion of 30 cm^3 of ethanol by normal volunteers and to continue for about 2 h. Magnesium has an important role in fetal development since it stabilizes DNA, RNA, and binds RNA to the ribosome, and also is involved in the activating and transfer system of all amino acids. Zinc is needed for a number of enzymes including carbonic anhydrase and alcohol dehydrogenase, and is also necessary for RNA metabolism and DNA synthesis. Pre-school children consuming diets deficient in zinc had many more height, weight, and head-circumference measurements below the third percentile (Hambridge et al., 1976). Recently, the low zinc content of certain infant diets has been shown to be growth-limiting (Walravens and Hambridge, 1975).

Vitamin Metabolism

Chronic alcoholics have multiple disturbances of vitamin metabolism; dietary intake often is poor, intestinal absorption impaired, storage limited by hepatic damage, and urinary loss of water-soluable vitamins may be elevated (Vitale and Coffey, 1971). In a study of 120 indigent or low-income adult patients admitted to a general hospital, 59% had a significant reduction in circulating levels of two or more vitamins. The most common deficiency was of folate, measured by the serum folate level. Ethanol causes impaired intestinal absorption of folic acid. When body stores are decreased and dietary intake is poor, ethanol may act as a weak folate antagonist (Sullivan and Herbert, 1964). Folate antagonists have been shown to cause fetal resorption, stillbirths, and congenital malformations in the rat, and there have been reports suggesting that human fetal malformations may result from dietary deficiency of folate (Sullivan, 1967; Lindenbaum, 1974).

Thiamine deficiency, frequently seen in chronic alcoholics, is due to decreased dietary intake during drinking episodes, impaired absorption, and possibly also acute liver injury, which lowers the response to administered thiamine (Vitale and Coffey, 1971). Magnesium deficiency concomitant with thiamine deficiency may interfere with response to thiamine. CNS lesions produced by experimental thiamine deficiency are comparable to those observed in the Wernicke-Korsakoff syndrome. The effects of thiamine pyridoxine and folate deficiency on the developing fetal nervous system should be investigated.

Effects on Endocrine Function

Stokes (1974) reviewed alcohol-endocrine interrelationships and stressed the importance of differentiating effects of ethanol on the anterior pituitary, its trophic hormones, their hypothalmic releasing factors, and the target glands. He found evidence of effects of alcohol on adrenal medullary function and thyroid function, but little systematic data on the effects of alcohol on gonadal function. Recently, information about the effects of alcohol administration on sex-hormone metabolism in normal men has been acquired (Gordon et al., 1976). No data on corresponding sex-hormone changes in women have been published. A link has been demonstrated between exposure to female sex hormones early in pregnancy and cardiovascular malformation (Heinonen et al., 1977). Heavy-drinking women with chronic liver disease might endogenously produce hormones which alter fetal cardiovascular and genital development.

Hypothalmic-pituitary function in four children ages 9 to 15 born to an alcoholic woman were studied in order to determine if hormonal abnormalities account for FAS aberrant growth patterns (Root et al., 1975). Biochemical and endocrine studies were all within normal limits. In another study of five FAS children, growth-hormone and somatomedin levels were found to be normal (Tze et al., 1976).

Effects on the Placenta

Placental growth and function may be affected by chronic alcohol use, but this problem has received little direct study. Kaminski et al. (1976) compared the mean weight of the placentas from 236 women who consumed over 1½ ounces of absolute alcohol per day with 4074 who drank less than that amount. Heavier drinkers had placentas that weighed 22 g less than the lighter drinkers. This difference attained statistical significance ($p <$ 0.01). However, the clinical significance of this small difference is unclear. Ethanol may have detrimental effects on transfer mechanisms that transport a variety of essential nutrients across placental membranes (Longo, 1972). These also may be impaired by carbon monoxide from cigarette smoke, as well as dietary deficiencies (Longo, 1977).

ASSOCIATED RISK FACTORS

Heavy drinking is often associated with other variables which contribute to reproductive risk, such as nutritional deficiency, heavy smoking, use of other drugs, and emotional stress. Each of these associated factors has been extensively studied; only brief reference to some of the more recent reviews will be cited here.

Nutrition

The relationship between alcoholism and malnutrition has been reviewed by Hillman (1974). Alcohol and vitamin metabolism have been reviewed by Vitalie and Coffey (1971). The clinical stereotype of the malnourished alcoholic has been questioned by Neville et al. (1968), who studied 34 alcoholics on a research ward and found no significant differences between alcoholics and normal controls in terms of the mean excretion of vitamin metabolites. At the Boston City Hospital Prenatal Clinic, few patients' diets met the minimum daily requirements of the National Research Council (Rosett et al.,

1976). Heavy-drinking women did not ingest significantly poorer diets than the abstinent women. However, utilization may be impaired by the effects of alcohol on intestinal absorption, liver function, urinary excretion of vitamins and trace minerals, disturbances of intermediate metabolism, and gastrointestinal disturbances such as vomiting and diarrhea. Fetuses of women with depleted nutrient stores may be more vulnerable to the added effects of alcohol.

Naeye et al. (1973) have considered the effects of maternal nutrition on the human fetus and presented evidence that undernutrition has its greatest effect on fetal growth in late gestation. Dobbing (1974) emphasized that two growth spurts represent critical periods of vulnerability for the development of the human brain. In humans, the first period of vulnerability is between the 12th and 18th gestational week, the period of greatest neuronal multiplication. Neuronal multiplication is probably largely over early in the second trimester. The late spurt of brain growth begins during the third trimester and continues during the first 18 months of life. During this time there is an explosive increase in dendritic complexity with establishment of synaptic connections. This component may be as important in the development of brain function as is the neuronal cell number. Growth restriction during only the first part of the brain growth spurt period may not be sufficient to produce lasting brain-cell deficit. Rebound growth after birth may compensate if birth releases the infant from factors such as intrauterine ethanol exposure, which may have been disrupting normal growth processes.

Smoking

The association between heavy drinking and heavy cigarette smoking, which has been repeatedly observed (U.S. DHEW, 1973) is confirmed by current epidemiologic data coming from Boston, Seattle, and Loma Linda. There is an extensive literature consistently establishing that smoking mothers have more low-birthweight infants. An increase in neonatal mortality rate or congenital anomalies have not yet been reported. Among the many studies relating smoking and low birthweight in these offspring, none took into account that smoking itself was associated with heavier alcohol use, which could have contributed a significant portion of the variance. However, Longo's (1977) recent review seems to establish the adverse effects of carbon monoxide from cigarettes on the fetus.

Other Drugs

The use of other drugs, such as heroin, methadone, LSD, barbiturates, and dilantin, has also been associated with a higher incidence of low-birthweight infants and increased perinatal mortality (Rothstein and Gould, 1974). Heavier drinkers are more likely to have tried other drugs in the past; however, in the Boston City Hospital Prenatal Clinic study, only 4% of the total group reported currently using drugs other than alcohol (Rosett et al., 1976). In the Loma Linda study, 6% reported illicit drug use (Kuzma and Phillip, 1977). In both populations, drugs were used by women with low, moderate, and high alcohol intake. Total abstainers from alcohol also avoided illicit drugs.

Caffeine

Heavy coffee consumption is often associated with heavy alcohol use and smoking (Mau and Netter, 1974). While there have been animal studies of caffeine as a teratogen, the dosages employed range from the equivalent of 40 cups of coffee to 100 cups per day (Mulvihill, 1973). No human malformations have been attributed to caffeine. This may be because man is protected by a rapid metabolism of caffeine, with only 1% excreted unchanged.

Disulfiram

Disulfiram (Antabuse), which may be useful as an adjunct to the treatment of alcoholism, should only be prescribed during pregnancy when probable benefits outweigh risks. Risks for the fetus could be anticipated, since it inhibits several enzymes, including aldehyde dehydrogenase, needed for oxidation of acetaldehyde, and dopamine betahydroxylase, which catalyzes the conversion of dopamine to norepinephrine (Truitt and Walsh, 1974).

Paternal Drinking

The possibility that heavy alcohol consumption by the male can cause genetic damage has been the subject of speculation for over 200 years. The mutagenic role of ethanol in male mice was studied by administering ethanol in a dose of 1.24 g/kg by gastric tube to male mice for 3 consecutive days (Badr and Badr, 1975). Females mated 4 to 13 days after treatment of the male with alcohol had a two- to fourfold increase in the number of dead implants found.

The effects of ethanol on spermatogonal cells has been directly investigated by giving rats a nutritionally adequate diet containing 10% ethanol as the only supply of liquid for 70 days (Kohila et al., 1976). Testicular tissue was directly examined for the frequency of aberrations such as chromosome breaks, chromotid breaks, and chromotid gaps. There were no significant differences between the experimental and control groups. Subsequently, the experiment was repeated with male rats who received a thiamine deficient diet together with ethanol, but this did not lead to any significant increase in the frequency of chromosomal aberrations (Halkka and Erikkson, 1977).

Ethanol has no damaging effects on human chromosomes in vitro (Obe et al., 1977). However, chromosomes of alcoholics show a significant increase in aberrations. One possible reason may be an inhibition of cellular RNA synthesis which impedes cellular repair in vivo.

Maternal Psychological Stress

Emotional stress has been demonstrated to be related to perinatal complications (Sameroff and Chandler, 1975). Differences have not been found between various psychiatric diagnostic groups; however, when psychiatric patients are divided on dimension of chronicity, those with the greatest number of psychiatric contacts in hospitalizations had infants with the most perinatal complications. Heavy-drinking women frequently use alcohol to relieve symptoms of chronic anxiety and depression. Emotional stress data should be reexamined in terms of alcohol and other drug use, including tranquilizers, by the patients with the more severe and chronic diagnoses.

Sameroff and Chandler (1975) emphasize the importance of viewing the continuum between prenatal and newborn care. A number of studies of failure to thrive describe the infants as being irritable, difficult to manage, unappealing, having fussy eating habits, poor food intake, and frequent regurgitations. Traditionally, these symptoms were interpreted as the result of parental neglect. These characteristics may be part of the etiology of parental neglect, rather than the consequence of poor mothering.

There are almost no case studies of the management of the pregnant chronic alcoholic patient in literature. One report of the successful cooperation of the psychiatrist and obstetrician following a patient jointly seemed to have been successful in enabling an alcoholic mother who had a potential for psychosis to successfully deal with the stress of pregnancy and also control her alcohol use (Silber et al., 1960). The dire consequences of fragmentation of medical care is illustrated in another case report of a 37-year-old alcoholic woman who had a ruptured uterus at 32 weeks, which was not managed properly, resulting in her death (Jewett, 1976).

RESEARCH AT THE BOSTON CITY HOSPITAL

The Boston City Hospital (BCH) pilot study was initiated in May 1974 (Rosett et al., 1976). Each year about 1700 women deliver at this municipal hospital, which serves a high-risk, inner-city population. About one-third chooses to receive prenatal care at the BCH prenatal clinic; the others are patients of several affiliated neighborhood health centers. At the time of registration at the BCH prenatal clinic, women were asked to participate voluntarily in a 15-min structured interview designed to determine the volume and variability of alcohol intake, use of drugs, smoking and nutritional status, and demographic data. Cahalan et al.'s (1969) "Volume Variability Index" was used to evaluate alcohol consumption. Heavy drinkers were defined according to Cahalan's criteria for "high-volume high-maximum": they consumed at least five or six drinks on some occasions with a minimum average of 1½ drinks per day. Moderate drinkers included all women who drank more than once a month, but did not meet the criteria for heavy drinkers. Rare drinkers used alcohol less than once a month, and never consumed five or six drinks on any occasion.

Voluntary cooperation was obtained from 633 of 685 women, a 92% rate of participation (Ouellette et al., 1977). Of these 633 women, 58 (9%) were heavy drinkers (42 of the 58 heavy-drinking women delivered in time to be included in the data analysis of 322 neonates to be described below); 249 (39%) were moderate drinkers; and 326 (52%) were rare drinkers. The heavy drinkers consumed an average of 5.8 ounces of absolute alcohol per day; 31% of them drank between 8 and 16 ounces of absolute alcohol per day; their mean dose was estimated at 2.2 g of absolute alcohol per kilogram per day. This is the equivalent of the daily consumption of 13 ounces of 86-proof whisky by a 132-lb woman.

Heavy drinking women had social characteristics comparable to the total sample population with a few significant differences. Heavy drinkers were significantly older, 25.7 years versus 22.8 years ($p < 0.001$). Fewer were married or living with the father of the baby. Heavy-drinking women, being older, were more apt to have had other children, but did not report a greater number of previous miscarriages, abortions, or stillbirths. Most of the women interviewed were poorly nourished, but diets reported by the heavy-drinking women were not significantly different from the diets of the total clinic population. Heavy drinking is associated with heavy smoking. Sixty percent of the heavy drinkers smoked a pack or more a day, in contrast to 15% of the rare drinkers ($p < 0.001$). Fewer than 4% of the women used psychoactive drugs during pregnancy.

Different patterns of alcohol use have been found in women of various ethnic and socioeconomic groups. Little et al. (1976) interviewed 162 obstetrical patients in a health-maintenance organization serving a middle-class population. Seven percent were drinking over an ounce of absolute alcohol per day before pregnancy, but only 2% in early pregnancy and 2% in late pregnancy. The decrease in alcohol consumption during the first trimester was also paralleled by a decrease in heavy coffee consumption during pregnancy. This observation of decreasing alcohol consumption during the course of pregnancy had also been made on some women interviewed at Boston City Hospital. However, at Boston City Hospital, which serves a low-income group, 9% of women were drinking heavily early in pregnancy. They more often sustain their level of consumption throughout pregnancy. A wide spectrum of perinatal risk factors, including malnutrition, poor housing, and general stress, have been observed in this multiproblem group. It is likely that maternal drinking during pregnancy will interact with the other risk factors and compound the adverse effects on the fetus. Therefore, it is important to collect information on drinking practices and living conditions from many different socioeconomic and cultural groups, so that the specific effects of the alcohol on offspring can be disentangled from the social and environmental matrix in which the baby develops.

Detailed pediatric, neurologic, and developmental examinations were administered in the newborn nursery to 322 offspring of women who had participated in the survey (Ouellette et al., 1977). These were conducted by a pediatric neurologist who had no prior knowledge of the mothers' drinking history nor any details of the pregnancy and delivery. These 322 newborns examined represented 94% of the live births at Boston City Hospital to the women who had participated in the prenatal clinic survey as of June 1, 1976.

The relationship between the mothers' drinking classification at the time of prenatal clinic registration and the independent evaluation of the newborn examination of 322 infants is shown in Table 25-2. In comparison with the offspring of moderate- and rare-drinking women, offspring of the heavy-drinking women showed significantly more growth retardation in length, weight, and head circumference. Congenital malformations were significantly more frequent among infants born to heavy-drinking women. Components of the FAS were observed but the complete syndrome was not seen in any individual. Of the 42 heavy-drinking women, 15 had been able to abstain or significantly reduce alcohol intake before the third trimester and maintain this until term (Rosett et al., 1978). Ten of the 15 infants born to these women were diagnosed as normal, as compared with only 3 of the 27 whose mothers continued heavy drinking ($p < 0.001$) (Table 25-3). Methods of therapeutic intervention will be discussed in the section on prevention.

Sander et al. (1977) and Rosett et al. (1977) investigated newborn offspring drawn from the Boston City Hospital study in an effort to determine the extent to which the distribution of sleep substages in the newborn are affected by exposure to high blood alcohol concentrations during fetal life. Sleep and awake status were observed for a 24-h period on the 3rd day of life by means of a continuous nonintrusive bassinet sleep monitor, as well

Table 25-2.   Relationship Between Infant's Clinical Status and Mother's Drinking Classification

Infants' Clinical Status Total Number of Subjects=322	Drinking Classification at Prenatal Clinic Registration					
	Rare $N=152$		Moderate $N=128$		Heavy $N=42$	
Any abnormality	35%	(53/152)	36%	(46/128)	71%	(30/42)
Congenital anomalies	8%	(13/152)	14%	(18/128)	29%	(12/42)
Growth abnormalities	17%	(26/152)	18%	(23/128)	53%	(22/42)
Jittery	10%	(15/152)	11%	(14/128)	29%	(12/42)

Table 25-3. Relationship Between Clinical Status of Offspring of Heavy-Drinking Women and Change in Alcohol Consumption Before Third Trimester

Infants' Clinical Status	Abstinent or Reduced Drinking	Continued Heavy Drinking
Total Number of Subjects=42	$N=15$	$N=27$
Any abnormality	33% (5/15)	92% (25/27)
Congenital anomalies	7% (1/15)	41% (11/27)
Growth abnormalities	27% (4/15)	66% (18/27)
Jittery	13% (2/15)	41% (11/27)

as by standard sleep polygraphy for one interfeed interval on that same day. Measures of infant state obtained from the bassinet sleep monitor have a high correlation with standard polygraphic determination of REM and nonREM states. The 24-h record provides an indication of the characteristics of around-the-clock state distributions, their night or day occurrence, their durations and within-day variations—characteristics that the new mother will have to cope with in making the decisions on which her caregiving interventions will be based. Fourteen babies from the BCH study of mothers with a mean alcoholic intake of 5.16 ounces (SD 2.95) of absolute alcohol composed group A. They were compared with group S, 8 infants of mothers who had consumed a mean of 6.23 ounces (SD 5.25) of alcohol during the first trimester but were able to abstain or markedly reduce alcohol intake during the second trimester and maintain this through delivery, and with 9 infants of mothers whose alcohol consumption during pregnancy was classified as rare or abstinent, group C.

Infants whose mothers continued heavy drinking (group A) slept significantly less than infants in group S, and less than control subjects, although the latter also slept somewhat less than group S subjects. The magnitude of the variables of group S infants fell closer to those of the group C offspring than to those of group A, at times on one side and at times on the other side. This may be a result of the small number of infants in these groups. All three groups spent the same percentage of time in active (62%), quiet (21%), and indeterminate (17%) sleep states. Mean quiet sleep cycle length also in this investigation (60 min ±3) was not different for the three groups, indicating that the regulatory disturbance may not affect the ontogeny of the basic rest/activity cycle.

In regard to qualitative aspects of sleep, the group A infants consistently experienced the most fragmented sleep with many interruptions in both active and quiet sleep states, rarely cycling from one quiet state to another without awakening.

The effects on the newborn of an interaction of heavy smoking plus heavy drinking is currently under investigation by research groups. In this sample, smoking of at least a half-pack of cigarettes per day was engaged in by 19 of the 22 heavy-drinking women in groups A and S, and by seven of the nine control mothers. While this population had few nonsmokers, there was sufficient variance in the amount smoked to produce a significant correlation between increased maternal smoking and an increase in the total sleep time, as well as with a decreased intervention time. Such a finding can be accounted for in our current understanding of the frequent association of heavy smoking and heavy drinking, inasmuch as withdrawal from the stimulant effects of nicotine upon the CNS may produce depression and counter the excitation due to withdrawal from the CNS-depressant effects of alcohol. However, the carbon monoxide and other components of cigarette smoke also are detrimental to fetal health and may act synergistically with alcohol. (Longo, 1972, 1977).

The importance of examining characteristics of newborn state regulation in such infants stems from the extent to which infant state determines the ease or difficulty of the mother's caregiving task. Infants' states along the sleep-awake continuum, which are unpredictable, or difficult to define or interpret, or which are affected in an unpredictable way by caregiving intervention, can create difficulty for any mother. However, for the mother already coping with a stressful interpersonal existence, or having relatively meager personal reserves for adapting to new situations (which may be the case for the woman with relatively high alcoholic intake), the presence of a deviant sleep-awake state regulation in her newborn may initiate a vicious circle. Failure to reach a comfortable adaptation with such infant over the first week or so of life can contribute further to lowered self-esteem and a sense of failure as a caregiver.

The task of defining effects of maternal alcohol consumption during pregnancy on the newborn infant's regulation of its states on the sleep-arousal continuum involves all the difficulties already reviewed in defining the relation of alcohol intake to the appearance of a fetal alcohol syndrome. Heavy-drinking pregnant women who are from a large urban inner-city population such as that sampled in the BCH study are subject to a variety of additional complicating factors. The isolation of effects of alcohol per se from all the other influences on fetal development requires the matching of the control sample on a wide range of variables which are most difficult to assess—for example, maternal stress during pregnancy; subtle physical, genetic, or nutritional factors; effects of associated heavy smoking; other drugs and medications, and so on. The BCH researchers encountered a wider range of state regulatory variation in the offspring of nondrinking mothers of such an inner-city sample than is encountered in samples drawn from higher socioeconomic levels. Mothers who can take advantage of preventive programs which facilitate their reducing alcohol intake or abstaining constitute a sample probably different in a great many ways from those who cannot respond to such interventions. Absence of maternal response to such programs provides an additional indication of risk for subsequent developmental casualty.

A variety of methods are used in assessing infant capacity for regulation of states and of response to stimuli. The significance of findings using the different methods must be evaluated. Although BCH investigators routinely made observations on the 3rd day of life, other investigators have reported their data from the 1st and 2nd days. Furthermore, samples of 1 or 2 h of sleep are difficult to interpret in relation to 24-h records. The persistent effects of analgesic and anesthetic medication given during labor and delivery over the first few days of life are well known. There is much investigative work ahead to separate out acute effects of alcohol withdrawal on newborn state regulation from effects of high maternal alcohol intake during the first trimester of pregnancy. Differentiation of acute postnatal effects from more chronic and enduring disturbances of basic regulatory mechanisms will require data extending over the first 14 to 21 days of postnatal life at least, and possibly extending to many months. Disruptions of quiet sleep in adults being withdrawn from alcohol have been shown to persist for many months (Gross et al., 1975). An approach to the problem from the point of view of regulation of states around the clock offers not only a means of investigating acute versus chronic effects but also a means for assessing the progress of the initial infant-mother adaptation in pairs who are "at risk," as well as for assessing the effectiveness of intervention programs aimed at facilitating the initial adaptation.

Recently, the BCH observations obtained on the 3rd day of life by employing the monitoring bassinet were compared with data from Seattle obtained on the 1st day of life by systematic naturalistic observations (Landesman-Dwyer et al., 1978). Their 124 subjects were selected on the basis of patterns of maternal drinking among 1500 women from a wide range of backgrounds. Most of their heavy-drinking group consumed less alcohol than did the heavy drinkers at BCH. They reported that infants exposed to the greatest amount of alcohol spent more time with their eyes open, had a lower level of body activity, but no differences in REM sleep.

Acute withdrawal symptoms are described as usually associated with infant irritability, tremors, hyperactivity of sensory mechanisms, increased restlessness, muscle tone, and respiratory rate (Pierog et al., 1977). As described above, the BCH bassinet monitor data are entirely consistent with these findings, but go somewhat further in identifying the deviance in sleep state regulation, especially with quality of REM and quiet substages in basic rest-activity cycling during sleep. Present work is directed toward differentiating effects of high alcohol intake later in the pregnancy from possible specific effects of high alcohol intake during the first trimester on developmental disturbances of sleep state regulation. This will be a step toward answering the question of whether or not these particular disturbances will then be the ones which tend to persist postnatally.

EFFECTS OF ALCOHOL IN UTERO UPON LATER DEVELOPMENT

Observations to date on the later development of children born to heavy-drinking mothers have been fragmentary. The most systematic were reported by Streissguth (1976), who tested 12 children referred to the dysmorphology clinic of the University of Washington because of their unusual appearance and/or their mothers' history of alcoholism. Three between the ages (years-months) of 1-02 and 2-10 were evaluated with the Bayley infant scales of mental development; four, between 3-04 and 5-10 with the Stanford Binet intelligence scale; and two, ages 6-09 and 9-05 with the WISC. The lowest IQ was 45, the highest 105. Eight could be considered retarded according to standards set forth by the American Association on Mental Deficiency, and three were in the borderline range. Only one, with questionable physical signs of the FAS and the stimulation of a middle-class home environment, was able to function in a regular school classroom.

Jones et al. (1974) also reported on the IQ difference between 18 children of alcoholic mothers and controls matched on many variables, including socioeconomic status, who had been tested at ages 4 and 7 as part of the Perinatal Collaborative Study of 55,000 pregnancies sponsored by the National Institute of Neurological Diseases and Stroke. At age 4, the offspring of the alcoholic mothers achieved a mean score of 88 on the Stanford Binet, compared with the control groups score of 96 (not significantly different). At age 7, the FAS children scored an average of 81 on the WISC, compared with 95 by the controls ($p < 0.01$). Seventy-five percent of the offspring of chronic alcoholic women scored in the borderline to moderately retarded range, compared to 22% of the matched controls. It is not possible to generalize from this small sample since the prospective research design did not include systematic histories of alcohol use. The 18 mothers who were identified probably were the most conspicuous, and undoubtedly their children were handicapped by a combination of multiple constitutional and environmental factors which contribute to impaired intellectual development.

Lemoine et al. (1968) described developmental problems observed among 127 offspring of alcoholic parents. The children were hyperactive, psychomotor development was retarded, and they were slow in almost all subjects in school. IQ was reported to be in the neighborhood of 70, but no information was given about ages when tested and instruments used. These 127 children were from 69 families; in 29, both parents were alcoholic, while in 25 only the mother, and in 15 only the father. While the authors state that the role of maternal alcoholism is essential, they failed to present data on the extent of maternal drinking in those families where only the father was alcoholic. The criteria used to diagnose alcoholism were not specified. Alcoholism in housewives frequently is underdiagnosed; their drinking is often hidden at home, and the family may conceal it further by a conspiracy of silence. In terms of effect on the fetus, the diagnosis "alcoholism" is less relevant than is the maximum blood alcohol concentrations at critical developmental times. In order to evaluate this, quantity, frequency, and variability of consumption should be evaluated at various stages of pregnancy.

Several different types of observations support parental alcoholism as one factor in the hyperactive child syndrome. Clinical observations of children of alcoholics are consistent with behavioral observations of offspring of animals fed alcohol during pregnancy (Shaywitz et al., 1976). Rat pups born to mothers fed alcohol are often hyperactive and demonstrate impairment on learning tasks. The hyperactivity decreases by 4W but the cognitive defect persists. Parents of hyperactive children have also been surveyed. Morrison and Stewart (1971) diagnosed alcoholism in 5 mothers and 20 fathers of 59 hyperactive children as compared with 10 fathers of 41 controls. In a similar study, Cantwell (1972) diagnosed alcoholism in 4 mothers and 15 fathers of 50 hyperactive children compared with 7 fathers of 5 controls. Goodwin et al. (1975) found that of 133 adult male adoptees, 4 were alcoholics. Among the alcoholics 50% reported hyperactivity during their childhood, compared with 15% of the nonalcoholic men.

In adult alcoholics, EEG abnormalities have been identified up to 6 months after controlled withdrawal and sustained abstinence. Disturbances in the infants' CNS might persist as long. If so, the earliest adaptation negotiated between these infants and their mothers would be distorted. Defects in the infants' physiologic control mechanisms would interact with the alcoholic mothers' behavioral pathology. Early malfunction of state regulation may cause later impairment of the self-regulation of mood, affect, and activity.

The literature on the offspring of alcoholics has recently been reviewed by comparing studies conducted with groups of subjects ranging in age from infancy through grade school, adolescence, and adulthood (El-Guebaly and Offord, 1977). Children of alcoholics appeared to be at higher risk for a variety of psychological and social problems. However, the various studies were criticized as lacking controls, which take into account age, sex, education, socioeconomic class, and family disorganization; data collection with examiners "blind" to the subjects' family background; and clear definitions of alcoholism and drinking problems. The authors also complained about the ambiguity of causal links, "for instance, poverty, family disorganization, alcoholism and antisocial behavior occur together, but whether they are etiologically related [and if so, how] has not been determined."

It seems unlikely that such complex interactions will ever be explained by a linear model of cause and effect. Systems theory, which utilizes concepts of reciprocal interaction and feedback, seems to better conceptualize interactions between the infant, the caregivers, and the multiple variables in the environment. The several factors that interact to determine the condition of the neonate born to a mother who drank heavily during pregnancy demonstrates the complexity of such systems.

STRATEGIES FOR PREVENTION

A pilot program focused on reduction of alcohol use during pregnancy has been initiated at Boston City Hospital Prenatal Clinic. All women who report moderate or heavy alcohol use at the registration survey are informed that excessive drinking may be harmful to their unborn child (Rosett et al., 1977, 1978). Heavy-drinking women are encouraged to meet with the project psychiatrist, who urges them to participate in counselling sessions, conducted in the prenatal clinic, and scheduled to coincide with their routine appointments. Pregnant women are motivated to reduce heavy drinking when potential hazards are explained.

Ten of 14 women who received counselling reported abstinence or a significant reduction of alcohol consumption during the third trimester. Among the 10 women who responded to counselling were three who had been drinking over 1 quart of vodka/day. They were withdrawn from alcohol on an inpatient basis and received continued support from staff. Five other women who received prenatal care at Neighborhood Health Centers were able to reduce alcohol use with the assistance of the Center staff. The 15 newborns of those heavy-drinking women who were able to abstain or reduce alcohol intake during the third trimester demonstrated fewer abnormalities at birth than those 28 mothers who had continued heavy drinking ($p < 0.001$).

Heavy drinking was associated with a continuum of perinatal risk factors including heavy smoking, use of other drugs, and emotional stress. Reduction of alcohol use frequently facilitated improvement in the entire milieu with multiple benefits for the offspring. Women who sustained the counselling relationship were also more likely to have any obstetrical problems diagnosed and treated. Conversely, women who rejected health advice concerning alcohol probably were less likely to follow prenatal instructions about nutrition and matters of hygiene.

Pregnancy presents an opportunity for identification, treatment, and prevention of alcohol-related problems.

1. *Identification.* Heavy drinking women share many characteristics with moderate and abstinent women from similar socioeconomic backgrounds. The differentiating feature is the extent of alcohol use, which can only be determined by a careful history. Therefore, it is imperative that obstetricians, pediatricians, nurses, and social workers ask directly and objectively for a thorough drinking history.

2. *Education.* The training of obstetricians, nurses, and other clinic staff requires more than mere presentation of didactic information. Staff attitudes began to change when they saw that many heavy drinking women, who could only be identified by a complete drinking history, were able to reduce alcohol consumption. When several severely alcoholic women responded to counselling and subsequently had healthy infants, enthusiasm for the efforts increased. Education also involved increased community awareness of the effects of drinking on pregnancy. During the second year of the Boston City Hospital program, many patients reported that they had already heard of the survey and had reduced alcohol use at the suggestions of friends who had attended the clinic. Other methods of educating the public include mass media campaigns comparable to the March of Dimes "Be good to your baby before it is born," or the curriculum, "Will Our Children Be Healthy?"

3. *Treatment*. Identification and treatment of heavy drinking during pregnancy may be more successful because of an increased health concern as well as a need for assistance with new social and emotional demands. Most mothers are strongly motivated by their concern for the health of their unborn child. Many are confronted with a variety of psychological and social difficulties, intensified by the normal crisis related to pregnancy. Confusion about sexual anatomy and the details of the birth process were alleviated through an educational approach. A diagram of the placental circulation helped explain how alcohol reached the fetus; the possible adverse effects of alcohol and other drugs were discussed. Similar information was presented in childbirth classes, but heavy-drinking patients responded best to individual instruction. Support and practical help in dealing with difficult life situations was provided through liaison with obstetricians, public health nurses, social services, and alcoholism treatment agencies. Several women could not reduce their alcohol use until they received this direct assistance. In many instances, members of the regular clinic staff have sufficient skills to provide supportive counselling focused on reduction of alcohol use. Heavy-drinking pregnant women who do not respond promptly should be referred to specialized treatment programs. Programs should be developed which initiate therapy with heavy-drinking women during pregnancy and continue to assist them with their alcohol problem as well as the tasks of motherhood. A supportive and educational approach dealing with parenting and continuing through the first years of life also helps stabilize the drinking problems. If specific defects in neonatal state regulation are identified, unique caretaking procedures might be developed. For example, mothers of infants with sleep-cycle disturbances may be helped in reading cues of state and identifying these specific state characteristics of their infants. For newborns with poorly developed circadian rhythms, caretaking contingent to infant state change and the establishing of familiar and consistent frameworks within which transitions to sleep can be effected may increase predictability for the mother of the infant's state regulation.

Research on Prevention

Epidemiologic research should be designed to provide data needed for development of prevention programs. Careful attention to information on changes in individual drinking patterns during pregnancy may help explain why some offspring of alcoholic women escape damage. Binges should be described as carefully as possible in terms of the types and amounts of alcohol ingested, duration of drinking, and precise stage of the pregnancy. Development of affected offspring should be followed as long as possible so that parents can have more facts about prognosis for different components of the FAS. Educational programs for teenagers should present facts about the FAS together with information on the changes in drinking patterns among adolescents (Demone and Wechsler, 1976).

The development of more specific prevention techniques could be facilitated by therapeutic trials using animal models of the FAS. For example, supplementary vitamins and minerals could be fed to a group of pregnant animals consuming alcohol, a group in whom alcohol was discontinued in mid-pregnancy, and an abstinent control population. Determination of the benefits of specific nutritional or pharmacologic interventions can be obtained with more precision from animal trials than human trials, where ethical issues and variations of life style confound results.

The prognosis for FAS infants has been pessimistic. However, this has developed from observations of the most severely affected offspring of chronic alcoholic women (Streissguth, 1976). Multiple compounding risk factors frequently exist. Initial experience with infants born to women able to abstain or significantly reduce alcohol use in mid-pregnancy suggest that rebound growth and physiologic adaptation can occur in some instances and compensate for early disruption (Rosett et al., 1978).

Long-term follow-up of children impaired by perinatal risk factors such as anoxia and prematurity suggests that in the less severely damaged infants a facilitating environment can effect relatively normal developmental outcomes (Sameroff and Chandler, 1975). Deviant development may result from severe insult to the organism's integrative mechanism or severe familial or social abnormalities, which can prevent the restoration of normal growth processes. Prevention approaches must be developed to effect early identification and reduction of alcohol use by heavy-drinking pregnant women. Particular techniques may be more effective in different settings with various ethnic and socioeconomic groups. Improvement of social supports during pregnancy and assistance with caregiving should be provided to help parents with children who overtax their emotional resources.

BIBLIOGRAPHY

Abel, E. L. Alcohol ingestion in lactating rats: effects on mothers and offspring. *Archives Internationales des Pharmacodynamie et de Therapie*, 1974, **210**, 121–127.

Abel, E. L. Emotionality in offspring of rats fed alcohol while nursing. *Quarterly Journal of Studies on Alcohol,* 1975, **36**, 654–658.

Akesson, C. Autoradiographic studies on the distribution of ^{14}C-2-ethanol and its non-volatile metabolites in the pregnant mouse. *Archives Internationales des Pharmacodynamie et de Therapie,* 1974, **209**, 296–304.

Auroux, M. Influence, chez le rat, de la nutrition de la mere sur le developpement tardif du systeme nerveux central de la progeniture. (Influence on the rat of the mother's nutrition on the late development of the central nervous system of the offspring.) *Compte Rende des Sceances de la Societe de Biologie Paris,* 1973, **167**, 626–629.

Auroux, M., and Dehaupas, M. Influence de la nutrition de la mere sur le developpement tardif du systeme nerveux central de la progeniture. (The influence of the mother's nutrition on the late development of the central nervous system of the offspring.) *Compte Rende des Sceances de la Societe de Biologie Paris,* 1970, **164**, 1432–1436.

Badr, F. M., and Badr, R. S. Induction of dominant lethal mutation in male mice by ethyl alcohol. *Nature*, 1975, **253**, 134–136.

Barry, R. G. G., and O'Nuallain, S. Foetal alcoholism. *Irish Journal of Medical Science,* 1975, **144**, 286–288.

Bauer-Moffett, C., and Altman, J. Ethanol-induced reductions in cerebellar growth of infant rats. *Experimental Neurology,* 1975, **48**, 378–382.

Bierich, J. R., Majewski, F., Michaelis, R., and Tillner, I. Über das embryo-fetal Alkoholsyndrom. (On the embryo-fetal alcohol syndrome.) *European Journal of Pediatrics,* 1976, **121**, 155–177.

Bond, N. W., and Digiusto, E. L. Effects of prenatal alcohol consumption on open-field behavior and alcohol preference in rats. *Psychopharmacology*, 1976, **46**, 163–168.

Branchey, L., and Friedhoff, A. J. Biochemical and behavioral changes in rats exposed to ethanol in utero. *Annals of the New York Academy of Science*, 1976, **273**, 328–330.

Burton, R. (''Democritus Junior'') The anatomy of melancholy. *Causes of Melancholy,* Vol. 1, Pt. I, Sec. 2. London: Tegg, 1906 (Orig. 1621).

Cahalan, D., Cissen, H., and Crossley, H. M. *American Drinking Practices: A National Study of Drinking Behavior and Attitudes*. New Brunswick, N.J.: Rutgers Center for Alcohol Studies, 1969.

Cantwell, D. P. Psychiatric illness in the families of hyperactive children. *Archives of General Psychiatry,* 1972, **27**, 414–417.

Cedarbaum, A. I., Lieber, C. S., Beattie, D. S., and Rubin, E. Effect of chronic ethanol ingestion of fatty acid oxidation of hepatic mitochondria. *Journal of Biological Chemistry,* 1975, **250**, 5122–5129.

Chernoff, G. A mouse model of the fetal alcohol syndrome. *Teratology*, 1975, **11**, 14A.

Christiaens, L., Mizon, J. P., and Delmarle, G. Sur la descendance des alcooliques. (On the offspring of alcoholics.) *Annales de Pediatrie (Paris)*, 1960, **36**, 257–262.

Christoffel, K. K., and Salafsky, I. Fetal alcohol syndrome in dizygotic twins. *Journal of Pediatrics,* 1975, **87**, 963–967.

Clarren, S. K., Alvord, E. C., Sumi, S. M., and Streissguth, A. P. Brain malformation in offspring exposed to alcohol in utero. National Council on Alcoholism Scientific Meeting, San Diego, May 1977. Abstract 1:158 in *Alcoholism: Clinical and Experimental Research*, 1977.

Collard, M. E., and Chen, C. S. Effect of ethanol on growth of neonate mice as a function of modes of ethanol administration. *Quarterly Journal of Studies on Alcohol*, 1973, **34**, 1323–1326.

Demone, J. W., Jr., and Wechsler, H. Changing drinking patterns of adolescents during the last decade. In M. Greenblatt and M. Schuckit (eds.), *Alcoholism Problems in Women and Children*. New York: Grune & Stratton, 1976.

Dobbing, J. The later growth of the brain and its vulnerability. *Pediatrics*, 1974, **53**, 2–6.

El-Guebaly, N., and Offord, D. R. The offspring of alcoholics: a critical review. *American Journal of Psychiatry*, 1977, **134**, 357–365.

Feldstein, A. Effect of ethanol on neurohumoral amine metabolism. In H. Kissen and H. Begleiter (eds.), *The Biology of Alcoholism, Vol. 1. Biochemistry*. New York: Plenum, 1971, 127–159.

Féré, C. Présentation de poulets vivants provenant d'oeufs ayant subi des injections d'alcool ethylique dans l'albumen. (Presentation of living chicks from eggs which had undergone ethanol injections in the albumen.) *Compte Rende des Seances de la Societe de Biologie Paris*, 1894, **46**, 646.

Ferrier, P. E., Nicod, I., and Ferrier, S. Fetal alcohol syndrome. *Lancet*, 1973, **2**, 1496.

Flink, E. B. Mineral metabolism in alcoholismm In H. Kissen and H. Begleiter (eds.), *The Biology of Alcoholism,* Vol. 1. *Biochemistry*. New York: Plenum, 1971, 377–395.

Fuchs, A. R. The inhibitory effect of ethanol on the release of oxytocin during parturition in the rabbit. *Journal of Endocrinology*, 1966, **35**, 125–134.

Fuchs, F., Fuchs, A. R., Poblete, V. F., Jr., and Risk, A. Effect of alcohol on threatened premature labor. *American Journal of Obstetrics and Gynecology,* 1967, **99**, 627–637.

Goodwin, D. W., Schulsinger, F., Hermansen, L., Guxe, S. B., and Winokur, G. Alcoholism and the hyperactive child syndrome. *Journal of Nervous and Mental Disease*, 1975, **160**, 349–353.

Gordon, G. G., Altman, K., Southren, A. L., Rubin, E., and Lieber, C. S. Effect of alcohol (ethanol) administration on sex hormone metabolism in normal men. *New England Journal of Medicine,* 1976, **295**, 793–836.

Greenhouse, B. S., Hook, R., and Hehre, F. W. Aspiration pneumonia following intravenous administration of alcohol during labor. *Journal of the American Medical Association,* 1969, **210**, 2393–2395.

Gross, M. M., Hastey, J. M., Lewis, E., and Young, N. Slow wave sleep and carry-over of functional tolerance and physical dependence in alcoholics. In M. M. Gross (ed.), *Alcohol Intoxication and Withdrawal Experimental Studies,* Vol. II. *Advances in Experimental Medicine and Biology* (Vol. 59). New York: Plenum, 1975.

Haggard, H. W., and Jellinek, E. M. *Alcohol Explored.* Garden City, N.J.: Doubleday, 1942.

Halkka, O., and Erikkson, K. The effects of chronic ethanol consumption on goniomitosis in the rat. In M. M. Gross (ed.), *Alcohol Intoxication and Withdrawal: Experimental Studies,* Vol. Ill. New York: Plenum, 1977, 1–6.

Hall, B. D., and Orenstein, W. A. Noonan's phenotype in an offspring of an alcoholic mother. *Lancet*, 1974, **1**, 680–681.

Hambridge, K. M., Walravens, P. A., Brown, R. M., Webster, J., White, S., Anthony, M., and Roth, M. L. Zinc nutrition of preschool children in the Denver Head Start program. *American Journal of Clinical Nutrition,* 1976, **29**, 734–738.

Hanson, J. W., Jones, K. L., and Smith, D. W. Fetal alcohol syndrome, experience with 41 patients. *Journal of the American Medical Association,* 1976, **235**, 1458–1460.

Heinonen, O. P., Slone, D., Monson, R. R., Hook, E. B., and Shapiro, S. Cardiovascular birth defects and antenatal exposure to female sex hormones. *New England Journal of Medicine*, 1977, **296**, 67–70.

Heuyer, O., Mises, R., and Dereux, J. F. La descendance des alcooliques. (The offspring of alcoholics.) *La Presse Medicale* 1957, **29**, 657–658.

Hillman, R. W. Alcoholism and malnutrition. In H. Kissen and H. Begleiter (eds.), *The Biology of Alcohol,* Vol. 3. *Clinical Pathology.* New York: Plenum, 1974, 513–581.

Ho, B. T., Fritchie, G. E., Indanpaan-Heikkila, J. E., and McIsaac, W. M. Placental transfer and tissue distribution of ethanol-1-^{14}C: A radioautographic study in monkeys and hamsters. *Quarterly Journal of Studies on Alcohol,* 1972 **33**, 485–493.

Horiguchi, T., Suzuki, K., Comas-Urrutia, A. C., Mueller-Heubach, E., Boyer-Milic, A. M., Baratz, R. A., Morishima, H. O., James, L. S., and Adamsons, K. Effect of ethanol upon uterine activity and fetal acid-base state of the rhesus monkey. *American Journal of Obstetrics and Gynecology,* 1975, **122**, 910–917.

Ijaiya, K., Schwenk, A., and Gladtke, E. Fetals Alkoholsyndrom. (Fetal alcohol syndrome.) *Deutsch Medizinsche Wochenschrift* 1976, **101**, 1563–1568.

Jewett, J. F. Alcoholism and ruptured uterus. *New England Journal of Medicine,* 1976, **294**, 335–336.

Jones, K. L., and Smith, D. W. Recognition of the fetal alcohol syndrome in early infancy. *Lancet,* 1973, **2**, 999–1001.

Jones, K. L., Smith, D. W., Streissguth, A. P., and Myrianthopoulos, N. C. Outcome in offspring of chronic alcoholic women. *Lancet,* 1974, **1**, 1076–1078.

Jones, K. L., Smith, D. W., Ulleland, C. N., and Streissguth, A. P. Pattern of malformation in offspring of chronic alcoholic mothers. *Lancet*, 1973, **1**, 1267–1271.

Kalant, H. Absorption, diffusion, distribution, and elimination of ethanol: Effects on biological membranes. In B. Kissin and H. Begleiter. (eds.), *The Biology of Alcoholism*, Vol. 1. *Biochemistry.* New York: Plenum, 1971, 1–62.

Kaminski, M., Rumeau-Rouquette, C., and Schwartz, D. Consommation d'alcool chez les femmes enceintes et issue de la grossesse. (Alcohol consumption among pregnant women and outcome of pregnancy.) *Rev Epidem et Santé Publ*, 1976, **24**, 27–40.

Kohila, T., Erikkson, K., and Halkka, O. Goniomitosis in rats subjected to ethanol. *Medical Biology*, 1976, **54**, 150–151.

Kuzma, J. W., and Phillip, R. L. Characteristics of drinking and non-drinking mothers. Presented at the NIAAA Fetal Alcohol Syndrome Workshop, San Diego, February 1977.

Landesman-Dwyer, S., Keller, L. S., and Streissguth, A. P. Naturalistic observations of newborns: Effects of maternal alcohol intake. Presented at the National Council on Alcohol meeting, San Diego, May 1977.

Lemoine, P., Haronsseau, H., Borteryu, J.-P., and Menuet, J.-C. Les enfants de parents alcooliques: Anomalies observées à propos de 127 cas. (Children of alcoholic parents: Anomalies observed in 127 cases.) *Ouest Medical*, 1968, **25**, 476–482.

Little, R. E., Schultz, F. A., and Mandell, W. Drinking during pregnancy. *Quarterly Journal of Studies on Alcohol*, 1976, **37**, 375–379.

Lindenbaum, J. Hematologic effects of alcohol. In H. Kissen and H. Begleiter (eds.), *The Biology of Alcohol*, Vol. 3. *Clinical Pathology*. New York: Plenum, 1974, 461–480.

Loiodice, G., Fortuna, G., Guidetti, A., Ria, N., and D'Elia, R. Considerazioni cliniche intorno a due casi di malformazioni congenite in bambine nati da madri affette de alcolismo cronico. (Clinical notes on two cases of congenital deformity in children born of chronic alcoholic mothers.) *Minerva Pediatrica*, 1975, **27**, 1891–1893.

Longo, L. D. Disorders of placental transer. In N. Assali and C. R. Brinkman (eds.), *Pathophysiology of Gestation*, Vol. II. New York: Academic, 1972.

Longo, L. D. The biologic effects of carbon monoxide on the pregnant woman, fetus, and newborn infant. *American Journal of Obstetrics and Gynecology*, 1977, 129, 69–103.

Lundquist, F. Interference of ethanol in cellular metabolism. *Annals of the New York Academy of Science*, 1975, **252**, 11–20.

Mann, L. I., Bhakthavathsalan, A., Lui, M., and Makowski, P. Placental transport of alcohol and its effect on maternal and fetal acid-base balance. *American Journal of Obstetrics and Gynecology*, 1975a, **122**, 837–844,

Mann, L. I., Bhakthavathsalan, A., Liu, M., and Makowski, P. Effect of alcohol on fetal cerebral function and metabolism. *American Journal of Obstetrics and Gynecology*, 1975b, **122**, 845–851.

Manzke, H., and Grosse, F. R. Inkomplettes und komplettes Des Alkohol syndrom: Bei drei Kindern einer Trinkerin. (Incomplete and complete alcohol syndrome: Three children of a drinker.) *Medizinische Welt*, 1975, **26**, 709–712.

Martin, J. C., Martin, D. C., Sigman, P., and Redow, B. Offspring survival, development, and operant performance following maternal ethanol consumption. *Developmental Psychobiology*, 1976.

Mau, G., and Netter, P. Kaffee und Alkoholkonsum—Riskfaktoren in der Schwangerschaft? (Are coffee and alcohol consumption risk factors in pregnancy?) *Geburtshilfe und Frauenheilkunde*, 1974, **34**, 1018–1022.

Morris, C. A collection of the yearly bills of mortality from 1657 to 1758 inclusive. To which are subjoined . . . III. Observations on the past growth and present state of the city of London. Reprinted from the edition printed at London in 1751. London: Millar, 1759.

Morrison, J. R., and Stewart, M. A. A family study of the hyperactive child syndrome. *Biological Psychiatry*, 1971, **3**, 189–195.

Mulvihill, J. J. Caffeine as teratogen and mutagen. *Teratology* 1973, **8**, 69–72.

Mulvihill, J. J., Klimas, J. T., Stokes, D. C., and Risemberg, H. M. Fetal alcohol syndrome: seven new cases. *American Journal of Obstetrics and Gynecology*, 1976, **125**, 937–941.

Mulvihill, J. J., and Yeager, A. M. Fetal alcohol syndrome. *Teratology*, 1976, **13**, 345–348.

Naeye, R. L., Blanc, W., and Paul, C. Effects of maternal nutrition on the human fetus. *Pediatrics*, 1973, **52**, 494–503.

Neville, J. N., Samson, G., and Olson, R. E. Nutritional status of alcoholics. *American Journal of Clinical Nutrition*, 1968, **21**, 1329–1340.

Nichols, M. M. Acute alcohol withdrawal syndrome in a newborn. *American Journal of Diseases of Children*, 1967, **113**, 714–715.

Nicloux, M. Sur le passage de l'alcool ingéré de la mère au foetus, en particulier chez la femme. (Passage of alcohol ingested by the mother to the fetus.) *Compte Rende de Seances de la Societe de Biologie Paris*, 1899, **51**, 980–982.

Nicloux, M. Passage de l'alcool ingéré de la mère au foetus et passage de l'alcool ingéré dans le lait, en particulier chez la femme. (Passage of alcohol, ingested by the mother, to the fetus, and passage of alcohol, ingested in milk.) *Obstétrique*, 1900, **5**, 97–132.

Noonan, J. A. Congenital heart disease in the fetal alcohol syndrome. *American Journal of Cardiology*, 1976, **37**, 160.

Obe, G., Jurgen-Ristow, H., and Herha, J. Chromosomal damage by alcohol in vitro and in vivo. In M. M. Gross (ed.), *Alcohol Intoxication and withdrawal: Experimental Studies*, Vol. III. New York: Plenum, 1977, 47–70.

Ouellette, E. M., Rosett, H. L., Rosman, N. P., and Weiner, L. Adverse effects on offspring of maternal alcohol abuse during pregnancy. *New England Journal of Medicine*, 1977, 297, 528–530.

Palmer, H. P., Ouellette, E. M., Warner, L., and Leichtman, S. R. Congenital malformations in offspring of a chronic alcoholic mother. *Pediatrics*, 1975, **53**, 490–494.

Pierog, S., Chandavasu, O., and Wexler, I. Withdrawal symptoms in infants with the fetal alcohol syndrome. *Journal of Pediatrics*, 1977, **90**, 630–633.

Randall, C. L., Taylor, W. J., and Walker, D. W. Ethanol-induced malformations in mice. *Alcoholism: Clinical and Experimental Research*, 1977, 1, 219–224.

Rawat, A. Ribosomal protein synthesis in the fetal and neonatal rat brain as influenced by maternal ethanol consumption. *Research Communications in Chemical Pathology and Pharmacology*, 1975a, **12**, 723–732.

Rawat, A. Effects of maternal ethanol consumption on the fetal and neonatal cerebral neurotransmitters. In K. O., Lindros and C. J. P. Erikkson (eds.), *The Role of Acetaldehyde in the Actions of Ethanol, Satellite Symposium, 6th International Congress of Pharmacology, Helsinki, 1975*. The Finnish Foundation for Alcohol Studies, 1975b, **23**, 159–176.

Rawat, A. K. Effect of maternal ethanol consumption on fetal hepatic metabolism in the rat. *Annals of the New York Academy of Science*, 1976, **273**, 175–187.

Reinhold, L., Hütteroth, H., and Schulte-Wisserman, H. Das fetale Alkohol-Syndrom: Fallbericht über 2 Geschwister. (The fetal alcohol syndrome: Case of two siblings.) *Muenchener Medizinische Wochenschrift*, 1975, **117**, 1731–1734.

Root, A. W., Reiter, E. O., Andriola, M., and Duckett, G. Hypothalmic pituitary function in the fetal alcohol syndrome. *Journal of Pediatrics*, 1975, **87**, 585–587.

Rosett, H. L., Ouellette, E. M., and Weiner, L. A pilot prospective study of the fetal alcohol syndrome at the Boston City Hospital, Part I: Maternal drinking. *Annals of the New York Academy of Science*, 1976, **273**, 123–129.

Rosett, H. L., Ouellette, E. M., Weiner, L., and Owens, E. The prenatal clinic: A site for alcoholism prevention and treatment. In F. A. Seixas (ed.), *Currents in Alcoholism*, Vol. 1. New York: Grune & Stratton, 1977, 419–430.

Rosett, H. L., Ouellette, E. M., Weiner, L., and Owens, E. Therapy of heavy drinking during pregnancy. *Obstetrics and Gynecology*, 1978, 51, 41–46.

Rosett, H. L., Snyder, P., Sander, L. W., Lee, A., Cook, P., Weiner, L., and Gould, J. Effects of alcohol in utero on neonatal state regulation. Presented at the National Council on Alcoholism meeting, San Diego, May 1977.

Rosman, N. P., and Malone, M. J. An experimental study of the fetal alcohol syndrome. Abstracts of meeting of American Academy of Neurology, Monterey, Calif., November 1976.

Rothstein, P., and Gould, J. B. Born with a habit: Infants of drug-addicted mothers. *Pediatric Clinics of North America*, 1974, **21**, 307–321.

Sameroff, A. J., and Chandler, M. J. Reproductive risk and the continuum of caretaking casualty. In F. D. Horowitz et al. (eds.), *Review of Child Development Research*, Vol. IV. Chicago: University of Chicago, 1975, 187–243.

Sander, L. W., Snyder, P. A., Rosett, H. L., Lee, A., Gould, J. B., and Ouellette, E. M. Effects of alcohol intake during pregnancy in newborn state regulation. *Alcoholism: Clinical and Experimental Research*, 1977, **1**, 233–241.

Saule, H. Fetales Alkohol-Syndrom: Ein Fallbericht. (Fetal alcohol syndrome: One case.) *Klinische Paediatrie*, 1974, **186**, 452–455.

Schaefer, O. Alcohol withdrawal syndrome in a newborn infant of a Yukon indian mother. *Canadian Medical Association Journal*, 1962, **87**, 1333–1334.

Seixas, F. A., Williams, K., and Eggleston, S., eds. Medical consequences of alcoholism. *Annals of the New York Academy of Science*, 1975, **252**, 399.

Seppälä, M., Räihä, N. C. R., and Tamminen, V. Ethanol elimination in a mother and her premature twins. *Lancet*, 1971, **1**, 1188–1189.

Shaywitz, B. A., Klopper, J. H., and Gordon, J. W. A syndrome resembling minimal brain dysfunction (MBD) in rat pups born to alcoholic mothers. Presented at the meeting of the Society for Pediatric Research, 1976.

Silber, A., Gottschalk, W., and Sarnoff, C. Alcoholism in pregnancy. *Psychiatric Quarterly*, 1960, **34**, 461–471.

Stokes, P. E. Alcohol-endocrine interrelationships. In H. Kissen and H. Begleiter (eds.), *The Biology of Alcohol*, Vol. 1. *Biochemistry*. New York: Plenum, 1971, 397–436.

Streissguth, A. P. Psychologic handicaps in children with fetal alcohol syndrome. Work in progress on alcoholism. *Annals of the New York Academy of Science*, 1976, **273**, 140–145.

Streissguth, A. P., Martin, J. C., and Martin, D. C. Research design and assessment of alcohol consumption during pregnancy. Presented at the NIAAA Fetal Alcohol Workshop, San Diego, February 1977.

Stockard, C. R. Influence of alcohol and other anaesthetics on embryonic development. *American Journal of Anatomy*, 1910, **10**, 369–392.

Sullivan, L. W. Folates in human nutrition. *Newer Methods of Nutritional Biochemistry*, Vol. III. New York: Academic, 1967, 365–406.

Sullivan, L. W., and Herbert, V. Suppression of hematopoiesis by ethanol. *Journal of Clinical Investigation*, 1964, **43**, 2048–2062.

Sullivan, W. C. A note on the influence of maternal inebriety on the offspring. *Journal of Mental Science*, 1899, **45**, 489–503.

Tenbrinck, M. S., and Buchin, S. Y. Fetal alcohol syndrome: Report of a case. *Journal of the American Medical Association*, 1975, **232**, 1144–1147.

Tewari, S., Fleming, E. W., and Noble, E. P. Alterations in brain RNA metabolism following chronic ethanol ingestion. *Journal of Neurochemistry*, 1975, **24**, 561–569.

Tewari, S., and Noble, E. P. Chronic ethanol ingestion by rodents: effects on brain RNA. In M. A. Rothschild, M. Oratz, and S. S. Schreiber (eds.), *Alcohol and Abnormal Protein Biosynthesis: Biochemical and Clinical*. New York: Pergamon, 1975, 421–448.

Truitt, E. B., and Walsh, M. J. The role of acetaldehyde in the actions of ethanol. In H. Kissen and H. Begleiter (eds.), *The Biology of Alcohol*, Vol. 1. *Biochemistry*. New York: Plenum, 1971, 161–195.

Tze, W. J., Friesen, H. G., and MacLeod, P. M. Growth hormone response in fetal alcohol syndrome. *Archives of Disease in Childhood*, 1976, **51**, 703–706.

Ulleland, C., Wennberg, R. P., Igo, R. P., and Smith, N. J. The offspring of alcoholic mothers. *Pediatric Research*, 1970, **4**, 474.

United States Department of Health, Education, and Welfare. The health consequences of smoking. January 1973. DHEW, Publ. No. (HSM) 73–8704.

Vitale, J. J., and Coffey, J. Alcohol and vitamin metabolism. In H. Kissen and H. Begleiter (eds.), *The Biology of Alcoholism*, Vol. 1. *Biochemistry*. New York: Plenum, 1971, 327–352.

Wagner, G., and Fuchs, A. R. Effect of ethanol on uterine activity during suckling in post-partum women. *Acta Endocrinologica* (Copenhagen), 1968, **58**, 133–141.

Wallgren, H., and Barry, H. *Actions of Alcohol*. Amsterdam: Elsevier, 1970.

Walravens, P. A., and Hambridge, K. M. Growth of infants fed a zinc supplemented formula. *Pediatric Research*, 1975, **9**, 310.

Waltman, R., and Iniquez, E. S. Placental transfer of ethanol and its elimination at term. *Obstetrics and Gynecology*, 1972, **40**, 180–185.

Warner, R., and Rosett, H. The effects of drinking on offspring: an historical survey of the American and British literature. *Quarterly Journal of Studies on Alcohol*, 1975, **36**, 1395–1420.

"Will Our Children Be Healthy?" A curriculum for high school students, under development at Education Development Center, School and Society Programs, Newton, Mass. Funded by the National Foundation/March of Dimes. Ruth MacDonald, Project Director.

Williams, H. L., and Salamy, A. Alcohol and sleep. In H. Kissen and H. Begleiter (eds.), *The Biology of Alcoholism*, Vol. 2. *Physiology and Behavior*. New York: Plenum, 1973, 436–483.

Wilson, K. H., Landesman, R., Fuchs, A. R., and Fuchs, F. The effect of ehtyl alcohol on isolated human myometrium. *American Journal of Obstetrics and Gynecology*, 1969, **104**, 436–439.

Yanai, J., and Ginsburg, B. E. Audiogenic seizures in mice whose parents drank alcohol. *Quarterly Journal of Studies on Alcohol*, 1976, **37**, 1564–1571.

CHAPTER 26

Supportive Programs for Infants and Parents

Dorothy S. Huntington

The programs to be discussed combine knowledge from clinical and developmental psychology, set in the context of social science theory. The chapter focuses on the interaction between parent and child in their own particular social setting. Converting theoretical understandings and findings from the research literature into something directly useful and applicable to parents and children is always one goal.

THE CURRENT SCENE

The following sign in the window of a Washington toy shop reflects the changing "advice to parents" over the past 60 years:

1910—Spank them.
1920—Deprive them.
1930—Ignore them.
1940—Reason with them.
1950—Love them.
1960—Spank them lovingly.
1970—The hell with them!

The anger expressed in the 1970 attitude may be seen as a cover-up or prelude to the despair and depression parents feel when they have lost confidence in their ability to succeed as parents. [Group for Advancement of Psychiatry, 1973]

What is there in our nation's attitudes to families and infants that has proven so damaging to the confidence of parents? Indeed, what has been happening to family structure in general that has been changing our approach to the care and education of infants?

Until recently, and indeed, amazingly recently, infants did not play a large part in the life of a family. It was difficult to allow oneself to care about an infant, when in all likelihood the baby would not survive. The wastage of infant life came close to a massacre of innocents in the 18th century. In England, there was a mortality of about 75% before age 2 amongst the population in general, and the probability of an even higher mortality among the infants of the poor (Caulfield, 1931). But we need not go so far back. In New York State the death rate among children under 2 years of age, averaged for the years 1909–1912, was 87.4 per thousand, while in the institutions of that state during the same time period, the death rate was 422.5 per thousand—42% of these normal, healthy children failed to reach their second birthday; for the foundlings the rate of death was 64.4% (Bremmer, 1971, p. 840).

The concern for children in the United States is a recent phenomenon. In 1915, the country was in the midst of a great debate on the scope of governmental responsibility to protect the health of children through the control of child labor. This was an extremely controversial proposal:

Profit incentives of an uncontrolled market system and the God-given rights of parents to determine the fate of their children combined to return small children to the mills and mines of a rapidly expanding industrial economy.

Poor families, whatever their rights, of course had no choice. Economic pressures were so great that child labor was a necessary slow way of death in order to stave off more immediate and certain ways. A bitterly fought amendment to the constitution would have defined the responsibility of government to protect the health and well being of children against the crushing abuses of child labor. But the amendment lost—and government's role for the protection of children did not become fixed until enactment of reform measures in the early 1930's. At that time concern for children was considerably abetted by concern for their elders who were competing in a tight job market. [Miller, 1975]

In 1915 Lillian Wald wrote in behalf of those who wished to establish a Children's Bureau:

Sympathy and support came from every part of the country, from Maine to California and from every section of society. The national sense of humor was aroused by the grim fact that whereas the federal government concerned itself with the conservation of material wealth, mines and forests, hogs and lobsters, and long since established bureaus that supply information concerning them, citizens who desired instruction and guidance for the conservation and protection of the children of the nation had no responsible governmental body to which to appeal.

Public responsibility for the welfare of children was not easily established. Senators railed against '. . . long haired men and short haired women . . .' snooping around the mills—the owners did not like it. [Miller, 1975]

SOCIAL FORCES

Priorities of concern have been shaped in the past by economic forces. What are the broad social changes occurring now that will require reshaping of social policies?

There have been enormous changes in families (1) in the increase in single-parent families, particularly via divorce, (2) in the increase in adolescent parents, and (3) in the increase in the number of working mothers. Families are under stress now in a way that has never before been experienced—psychologic, social, economic, and reality instability that affects in crucial ways the development of the infants within those families. The theme of "running scared"—a feeling of disarray and hopelessness—is rampant.

Society has not kept pace with the trends, and there are no support systems to take up where traditional childcaring and nurturing leave off. The net effect of the changes means

a progressive fragmentation of the family and the isolation both of the child and of those primarily responsible for his care and development. The fact that such disruptive processes are taking place on a national scale and are occurring most rapidly for families with young children clearly poses questions about their consequences for the welfare and development of the young. . . .

The most important fact about the American family today is the fact of rapid and radical change. The American family is significantly different from what it was only a quarter of a century ago. [Bronfenbrenner, 1973]

Since 1970, the number of children whose mothers were in the labor force has risen sharply: in 1976, 46% of children under age 18 had mothers in the labor force, up from 39% in 1970. Among pre-school children, the proportion whose mothers worked rose from 29 to 37% between 1970 and 1976. The birth rate has dropped sharply since 1970, and the number of children in families has declined 6% (to 61.7 million), yet the number of children with working mothers has risen by 10% (to 28.2 million).[1] The continuing long-term rise in the labor force participation of married women, both with and without children; the briskly declining birth rate; and an increase in the number of families headed by women, largely due to the escalating divorce rate—these factors have changed the American family in ways that have immediate impact on infants and young children.

Consider that one of every three children under the age of 3 has a working mother, and consider the system of family support that mothers need to retain their sanity, and do not have. Think also about the changes in the mental health system that are required—changes that have also not taken place.

Although the great majority of children are in two-parent families, the number and proportion are constantly sliding downward. The precipitous decrease in the birth rate and the increasing number of children affected by divorce and separation now account for the fact that one child in every five is living in a single-parent family.

During 1976, there were 1,077,000 divorces; this was 51,000 higher than the divorce total in 1975, and more than twice the number a decade ago. The 1976 divorce rate was 5.0 per 1000 population, an increase of more than 4% over 1975. This represents the 10th consecutive annual increase in the divorce rate. The 1976 rate was twice the rate in 1965 and 1966 (2.5 per 1000). The 1976 marriage rate was 9.9 per 1000 population, lower than the rate for any year since 1967.[2]

The age of the mothers involved is falling: 617,000 babies were born in 1973 to adolescent mothers—one baby of every five born in the United States has a mother who was under age 19.[3] The fertility rate—the number of live births per 1000 women—is now higher for girls ages 15 thru 19 than it is for women 30 to 34.

Increasing responsibility is thus falling on increasingly younger mothers. At the same time, there has been a breakdown of community, neighborhood, and extended-family supports, and a rise in the number of father-absent homes:

In some segments of the society, the resulting pressures appear to be mounting beyond the point of endurance. For example, the growing number of divorces is now accompanied by a new phenomenon; the unwillingness of either parent to take custody of the child. And in more and more families, the woman is fleeing without waiting for the mechanism of a legal or even agreed upon separation.

Systematic data are at hand, however, to document an increase in a more gruesome trend, the killing of infants under one year of age—this is the age group for which the figures are growing at the fastest rate. Infanticide has been increasing since 1957. Although the number of infant homocides accounted for only 2.2% of the total homocides in 1964, the rate of 5.4 deaths per 100,000 population was higher than that for all persons aged 55 years and over. [Bronfenbrenner, 1973]

The 1974 rate of 5.5 deaths per 100,000 under the age of 1 year continues that trend:

This seems to be a reflection of the desperation in which young mothers are placed today. Child abuse statistics point to a similar situation, in which the most severe injuries are inflicted not by

[1]U.S. Dept. of Labor, Office of Information *News,* USDL 77–165, Feb. 25, 1977.
[2]Monthly Vital Statistics Report, National Center for Health Statistics, DHEW, March 8, 1977.
[3]National Center for Health Statistics, January 30, 1975.

drunken fathers, not by babysitters, but by young mothers in single parent families. What one sees is a growing trend toward alienation of children and families in this country. [Bronfenbrenner, 1973]

We must look at children in their social context and intervene by changing social systems—and the mental health system in its broadest ramifications is one of the most important of our social systems for *supporting* families before they break down.

NEW UNDERSTANDING OF INFANT DEVELOPMENT

With this as a background, let us turn now to consider infants, starting with developmental issues. Our attitudes and understandings about infants have changed enormously in the last 15 to 20 years, and most particularly in the area of the importance of the sense of competence and effectiveness in coping with life—in the areas of motivation and self-esteem.

During the first half of the 20th century, the infant was generally considered to be a passive organism who was the object of forces which determined development; maturational forces, psychosexual drives; or environmental shaping. During this period, there was extensive research about what infants normally do in the course of development. These studies helped to chart the normal developmental sequence, but they did not experimentally analyze what infants *can* do when provided with appropriate opportunities, (nor did they really look at individual differences in infants). Aside from numerous studies of neonatal behavior, experimental work with infants was limited. Although the importance of the opening years was recognized, many of the theoretical constructs about infant development were based upon clinical interviews with adults concerning their childhood and on parents' retrospective accounts of infant-care practices.

In the last 15 years there has been an explosion of infant research of all kinds, and our knowledge continues to expand at a rapid rate. Recently developed methods and equipment have enabled us to test some of the limits of infant capacities, permitting a remarkably different view of the infant to emerge. In comparison with the theoretically constructed infant who was passive, helpless and shaped primarily by experience, the 'real world' infant has come to be viewed as skilled, active and socially influential. In short, he or she is competent

and able to have enormous impact on his family (Appleton et al., 1975). Thus, in order to be most effective in the field of infant mental health, we must bring together findings of three crucial fields—infant development research, child- and family-oriented clinical psychology, and the social psychology of networks and supportive systems.

We now know that what happens to infants and their families has an impact on lifelong prevention of disability and the positive development of competence. The idea that what a baby does is important, and that what an adult does with an infant is equally important, is unfortunately difficult to convey in a way that has any meaningful impact on caregiving practices. Babies learn from the moment of birth (and indeed, before birth); babies actively seek stimulation from the moment of birth; babies are much "smarter" than we had thought. The development of competence in very young children can be related from the earliest months onward to their interactions with their caregivers (Watts et al., 1974; Clarke-Stewart, 1973; White and Watts, 1973; Yarrow et al., 1972).

We now stress the change in concept from the infant as totally helpless, to the infant as an active, perceiving, learning, and information-organizing individual—one from whom we have a great deal to learn, and who demands and requires a great deal of listening *to*.

There have been many such changes in emphasis in our knowledge of infant development. Some of those that are most significant for mental health professionals are as follows:

1. The importance of *individual differences* and individuality in development, responsiveness, sensitivity, ease of soothing, activity level, adequacy of controls, physiologic smoothness, persistence, level of attention, quieting, consolability, and so on.

2. The relationship of what the child is at birth to the development of coping styles and what he becomes later within the limits and with the shaping of parental expectations. Hypotheses relate level of sensory sensitivity, impulse control, level of autonomic reactivity, drive level, and quality of developmental balance to outcome.

3. The crucial role of motivation: the sense of helplessness versus positive attachment as a cognitive and emotional organizing function; the importance to future development of self-image, self-confidence, independence, freedom to try new activities, the enjoyment of mastery of new tasks. The incitement to learning—the lifelong incentive to know more about the world—versus failure, avoidance, apathy, and lack of curiosity. Self-esteem, competence, and the ability to learn—an expectation that what you do will affect the environment—form the basis of the ability to cope with the world.

4. The importance of the structural characteristics: persistence, organization and sequence orientation, goal directedness, ease of making transitions, tempo, and so on.

5. Effects of mild or major anoxia, prematurity, medications, and so on—the issue of intactness of the organism and major as well as minor developmental disabilities and ways of processing information.

6. The importance of attention and learning at a much earlier age than heretofore assumed.

7. The importance of the sense of trust—being able to accept and ask for help appropriately—cooperativeness, responsiveness to requests, ability to communicate needs; curiosity and creativity.

8. The importance of the adult
   a. as a figure for identification—learning how to cope, how to handle feelings, how to approach and solve problems, how to think and explore, how to deal with others, how to respect and accept and value differences and similarities in other children and adults.
   b. as people who *care* about you, who show you that the balance of rewards is greater than disappointments, who show you you are someone special and who show you, by and large, that the world is an interesting and even exciting place to be; as someone you can *trust*.
   c. as figures who radiate a sense that the child can learn and is expected to learn, in the broadest sense. Enthusiasm and positive expectations are infectious.

9. Effect of social and physical environment: need for appropriate stimulation, opportunity and encouragement to learn, relative consistency, contingent responsiveness, and so on. Also the importance of the parents' coping styles: satisfying the child's needs; models for identification with competence, positive reinforcement; expressing approval of the child; lack of disruptive or gratuitous hostility to the child; verbal give and take; using reasons for obedience, and training the child for self-discipline.

10. Effect of extreme conditions—institutions, serial foster homes, severe abuse and neglect, severe emotional or social poverty as reflected in distortions of adult-child interaction.

11. The relationship of cognitive development to environment; learning is not simply a matter of acquiring cognitive skills—the true test of intelligence is *not* how much we know how to do, but how we behave when we do not know what to do (Holt, 1964).

12. The importance of the entire social network: the economy, the interpersonal support system, housing, jobs, medical care, and so on.

INDIVIDUAL DIFFERENCES

There is increasing evidence that vulnerable babies—babies who later will show minor neurologic handicaps, educational and learning disabilities—are identifiable early on. Prechtl and Beintema (1964) of Holland have developed a neurological examination to be administered in the 2nd week of life which identifies children who are likely to have learning and behavior disorders at a later age. In the United States, the collaborative perinatal research project has identified neonatal factors that correlate with poor development at ages four and seven.

Beyond this, the classic work of Drillien (1964) in Scotland has shown the direct relationship between neonatal neurologic status, social class—meaning environmental factors in upbringing—and outcome at age 7. Kessner (1973) has repeated the observations of the relationship between prenatal care, birth weight, and subsequent development.

Beyond the issue of minimal neurologic symptoms are the wide range of personality characteristics that may predict behavior disorders: high and low activity, low regularity, low adaptability, high intensity, persistence, and distractibility (Thomas et al., 1968).

Graham et al. (1973) also see temperamental characteristics as predictors of behavior disorders in children:

It appears that particular adverse temperamental characteristics render the child more vulnerable to the adverse effects of family discord and other "stress" factors. This might occur, for example, with low malleability (or poor adaptability, in the New York study). In addition, certain adverse temperamental characteristics (perhaps marked irregularity) may make it more difficult for parents to deal with the transient disturbances that commonly accompany stressful experiences.

Accordingly, what in another child might be a passing problem of little consequence becomes a more persistent and more handicapping disorder. The effects of adverse temperamental characteristics on other people are also likely to be influential. The very difficult infant (e.g., the highly irregular, unadaptable child with preponderantly negative mood) may be more likely to elicit critical feelings from his mother and more liable to generate discord between his parents. Similarly, parents are sure to be intolerant when difficulties arise later in such unattractive or less lovable children.

Adverse temperamental characteristics are not necessarily genetically determined, fixed, and immutable; they are an important genetic component but environmental influences play a part:

Certain so-called temperamental characteristics can be reliably identified and some of these are predictive of the later development of psychiatric disorder . . . the clinician should be aware that a growing body of evidence supports the notion that a child, by virtue of his personality structure, requires handling geared to his individuality if he is to stand the best chance of avoiding the development of psychiatric disorder. [Graham et al., 1973]

Anneliese Korner (1971) has shown how individual differences at birth affect mother-infant interaction. There are many implications in this for child care—the adult must respond flexibly to the child's individual requirements.

We are thus forever looking for *the* method to raise children, to educate, to cure. . . . In working with parents, it is important that we stress not only their crucial influence on their children's development, but also that we free them to see, to hear, to tune in and to trust their own intuition in dealing differentially with what their children present as *separate* individuals.

Innate differences among babies may make for differences in early experience, both subjective and real. By presenting the caregiver with differences in organismic organization, the infant heavily contributes to the unfolding of the parent/infant relationship and to the kind of mothering that will be required. Some of these differences may contain the seeds of the variations in style with which different children approach and master some of the developmental milestones (Korner, 1974).

For example, there are major implications for the parent/child interaction in the differential rate of crying or the ease of consolability and comfort, leading to differential degrees of self-confidence on the part of the mother tied up with her effectiveness in comforting her baby. The point to be made is that few new mothers realize that it is not only her skill and her devotion that make her a more or less effective mother, but it is also the infants' makeup that is a strong contributory factor.

Extreme irritability and unconsolability on the infant's part can have devastating effects on the early mother-infant relationship. Depression, feelings of helplessness, and rejecting attitudes among mothers are very common under these circumstances, all contributing further to the difficulties.

Teaching parents about infants' skin sensitivities, or difficulties in making transitions, or individual differences in a dozen different spheres, truly makes a difference in terms of informed parenting. You do not teach about *pathology*—it is simply difference, but difference that may contribute substantially to the ease or difficulty in the parent-child relationship.

Of vital importance also in terms of parent-infant programs is the crucial role of motivation. As Yarrow et al. (1972) comment,

One striking finding of this study is the extent to which these functions (cognitive-motivational) seem to be amenable to environmental influences in early infancy. These results support Provence and Lipton's (1961) impressions that motivational functions may be more vulnerable to depriving institutional environments than are specific emerging skills.

Motivation and the expressions of this motivation to assimilate, to learn, and to master the environment may be viewed as an early expression of a competence or an effectance motive (White, 1959):

The importance of these relationships lies in their convergence with a number of theoretical formulations based primarily on laboratory studies. Lewis and Goldberg (1969) have formulated a "generalized expectancy model," emphasizing the role of contingent mother-infant interaction in the development of the child's belief that he can affect his environment, that he can bring about reinforcement by his actions. Watson (1966) speaks of "contingency awareness" as a precondition for later learning. The common thread in these formulations is the active, information processing organism, initiating transactions with the environment and in turn being influenced by these transactions. [Yarrow et al., 1972]

The infant's orientation to objects and people becomes part of a feedback system:

These behaviors become part of a system of reciprocal interactions which may characterize a given infant's transactions with the environment over a long period of time. This orientation to the world may be a more consistent and more significant characteristic of the young infant than any specific cognitive ability. We might speculate that the infant's orientation to his environment adds to the continuity of his experiences. If this is so, then the fact that these aspects of functioning seem to be related to identifiable aspects of the environment during the first six months may have great significance not only for developmental theory, but for intervention programs as well. [Yarrow et al., 1972]

The convergence of all of these data is extremely important at this time. Birns and Golden (1972) have shown clearly that pleasure in problem-solving facilitates cognitive development:

The amount of pleasure manifested by 18 and 24 month old infants on the Cattell and Piaget Object Scales was predictive of their later intellectual performance on the Stanford-Binet at three years of age. The data on the 18 month longitudinal sample is of particular interest in regard to the issue of whether there is continuity or discontinuity between sensori-motor and verbal periods. We had hypothesized that while there may be discontinuity between perceptual motor development and later problem solving ability on the verbal level, reflected in the generally low correlations between infant test scores and later measures of intelligence such as the Stanford-Binet, there may be continuity in terms of certain personality traits related to both pre-verbal and verbal intelligence. The fact that the 18 month Cattell and Piaget Object Scale scores did not correlate with the 36 month Binet scores, whereas Pleasure in Task was significantly correlated with performance on both the Cattell at 18 months and the Binet at three years of age tends to support our hypothesis.

Whether one uses Robert White's (1963) expression of competence motivation, or Buhler's (1918) expression of function pleasure, or Ives Hendrick's (1943) pleasure in mastery, the concepts appear to be very similar. In recent years, Phyllis Levenstein (1969) has shown a significant correlation between IQ gains and the amount of pleasure children manifested on problem-solving tasks.

Is pleasure in problem-solving modified by experience? We can clearly say yes to this. Are there critical periods when the behavior is most susceptible to environmental influences? Here we really do not know the answer. What kinds of parental behaviors foster or inhibit pleasure in problem-solving? This must be spelled out on the basis of further research and observation.

We must also give up the idea that parenting skills, attitudes, and practices come naturally, *or* are based solely on unconscious processes, and move more to an understanding of the effect that the qualities of the infant have on caregiving habits, and the effect that social supports and knowledge have on parenting skills.

SUPPORTING PARENTAL STRENGTHS AND COPING ABILITIES

The general issue here is that we *must* do *functional* assessments of infants—careful explications of their strengths as well as their weaknesses in a broad spectrum of functions, rather than doing diagnostic labeling only. And we *must* teach parents and infants.

There are inherent limitations in an emphasis on *weakness or pathology*—the negative approach. A far more fruitful approach involves thinking explicitly about concepts of strengths and learning and coping skills—in infants and parents. The differences in implications of these two models—pathology versus normality—are major for actual programs that may be developed in mental health settings. Not everything that happens leads to trauma; it is far more useful to think in terms of mastery. People really do, within broad limits, play the role assigned to them. If we expect them to be traumatized, passive, and dependent—"sick"—they probably will act that way, and suffer the consequences in terms of loss of self-esteem. If we anticipate that they will be responsive, responsible, and coping, then they probably will be that also. An elitist position requires that the "downtrodden" be dependent on the elite. Is this what we really want to encourage?

Promotive work in the mental health system implies (1) giving supports through life crises such as divorce, significant object loss, and so on; (2) getting to many people through "rap" sessions for new parents—teaching about *infant characteristics;* (3) teaching about affectivity, persistence, levels of attention, sensitivity, activity, quieting and consolability, initiation of explorations, and so on; and (4) working with parents' feelings about child-bearing and child-rearing as an economic liability; about the downgrading of the sense of personal worth derived from parenthood; on information on child development, on effects of unemployment, other stresses, and so on.

We need to take a larger view of mental health issues—*promotive mental health* and *family mental health*; all this can be seen as part of a proactive and promotive system. Those are unusual words in this context, so let me define them. "Proactive" involves "moving forward or ahead of," *acting first* rather than waiting for something to happen and then reacting. "Promoting" means furthering the growth of something. So in essence, a proactive and promotive system supports strengths, is concerned with health, and supplies the encouragement for the use of healthy coping mechanisms, rather than waiting for the system to break down and develop symptoms, then treating the symptoms!

The philosophy of promotive medicine goes beyond the goal of protecting people's health and preventing harm or disease. . . . For thousands of years medicine has had two primary orientations: curing disease and preventing disease. Actually these are but two aspects of a single orientation disease orientation. The focus is on disease and its causes. The object is, through therapeutics, to cure the disease or, through hygiene, to keep it away. Health and disease have been regarded as polar opposites with health being the absence of disease. Both curative and preventive medicine are based on theories of disease. They are not mutually exclusive, dualistic, entities. Health is a form of behavior. . . . Healthy responses will be life enhancing. Promotive medicine seeks to promote healthy, positive, adaptive responses. [Hoke, 1968]

How can we reinforce patterns of healthy behavior and thereby increase the probability of their occurrence even in the presence of disease or disability? "To do so may require two complimentary professions—the disease profession and the health profession."

Within the formulation of a promotive and proactive system, a primary issue is, What motivates health? We know already that positive self-esteem—the basic belief in one's self-worth and value to the world, however personally defined—is what moves people to positive, constructive responses. Thus supporting and increasing self-esteem and respect become the key issues for infant, parent, staff, and community programs. A program that makes its living dealing only with the casualties of social systems will soon lose its viability.

It should be proactive rather than reactive, adhering to a fundamental tenet of public health that no condition is ever prevented by treating the victims of the condition itself (Iscoe, 1974).

One crucial element within this system is the dropping of the *blame model* of child development—everything that goes wrong is *not* the mother's fault because she is hostile and rejecting. That model has been around for a long time. Soranus of Ephesus, in the 2nd century A.D., asked why many Roman children had twisted limbs, and replied to his own question:

The truth of the matter lies in inexperience with regard to rearing children; for women in the city have not so great a love for their children as to have regard to every particular as the women of purely Greek stock do [Ruhrah, 1925]

The major need in terms of families with young children seems to be material on education for parenthood; preparing for effective parenthood is an extremely complex task. There seems to be an amazing lack of information among young parents today of the social, emotional, educational, and health needs of children and of the role of parents in fostering a child's development. Parents seem ill prepared to meet the problems encountered in rearing children. The problem of teenage parents is also a particularly acute one.

Parents know very little about children and their problems, particularly infants and toddlers; parents simply do not know where to turn for help and information. Parents will respond to programs if they are treated with respect as individual human beings, and if they are integrally involved in the program. Parents need to be helped to cope with their problems, and they learn best from each other. We must stress the absolute necessity of designing programs to strengthen the competence and sense of effectiveness in the adults involved, to utilize and enhance the already existent social coping skills rather than treating everyone as patients, and to accomplish this within a framework of understanding and responding to the personal and social problems that affect family life and care of infants. Work must involve assessing with the families what the problems are and what they want; the concept of doing *with* people rather than doing *to* them must be the constant guide.

APPLIED PROGRAMS

The programs in the Child and Family Services of the Peninsula Hospital Community Mental Health Center are based on the assumption that services which are family supportive in the broadest sense will promote mental health by strengthening parental and child coping skills. We have tried to broaden our conceptualization of human behaviors, and view symptoms as evidence of social and family system failures, as well as purely intrapsychic events. We try to avoid the danger of the "symptoms-have-a-unitary-cause" approach, and stress the need for greater complexity in conceptualizing individual differences and psychological, social, and economic pressures and realities.

The outreach to the community involves principles of enhancement of family strengths before any member of the family is identified as having a specific, well-defined, psychological difficulty. The programs are oriented toward strengthening children's coping and adaptive skills, enhancing parenting skills and self-esteem, and helping parents to become more positively involved in the rearing of their children. Parents are helped in understanding children's physical, social, emotional, and intellectual needs; their child's specific individual differences and variations, strengths and vulnerabilities; and how any particular child's needs may best be met within the context of family needs and desires. At the same time, emphasis is placed on the factors that add stress and strain to a parent's role as an adult in his own right and in his role as parent. Services are then oriented toward helping the parent cope with these personal, social, and economic stresses in ways that are most positive for himself or herself and for the child. The family itself, then, becomes the "clinical unit."

This approach involves an array of progams, for there are many different types of children and families involved. Techniques vary in the entire spectrum from community organization with special groups, to sharing knowledge about child development through a lecture series, to rap sessions with parents about specific topics, to preventive work with a family in a situational crisis such as divorce, to intensive personal support and psychotherapy for an overwhelmed family already showing symptoms.

We feel that it is crucial to identify the social and individual stress situations that are impacting on the families in our community, and thus work within a social-system model to reduce the stresses and enhance the strengths. Important in a social-systems approach is the coordination of programs throughout an area in order to share ideas and avoid both overlap and gaps in programs. Early identification of developmental lags or deviations within the children is also extremely important since this early identification shapes the form of early intervention with both child and family to promote the use of strengths and prevent further disability.

It is difficult to change from the disease model to the health model within the community, in the professional sphere, and in terms of payment, since fees for service are rarely paid for promotive services. It is also of extreme importance to pay attention to individual differences and to be highly flexible in programming. We stress constantly the need for a comprehensive social-systems analysis of problems, rather than a simplified "cause-leads-to-symptom" model, which has worked so poorly in the past. There must also be support for a nonelitist position: self-help groups, community education programs, and the like may prove eventually to be just as valuable as extremely expensive individual psychotherapy.

The programs applicable to parents and young children at the Community Mental Health Center may be divided into six different types:

1. *Community organization,* which involves working with the different groups within our catchment area to discuss with them what their needs are and what kinds of support systems would best help them. For example, we work with the Spanish-speaking families, with the Samoan families, with single-parent families, or those with developmentally disabled children. We also have a Citizens Advisory Committee Family Services Task Force that surveys the community in relation to its needs.

2. *Interagency collaboration* on issues such as developmental assessment within the Early and Periodic Screening, Diagnosis and Treatment program. The emphasis here is on developing networks throughout the community rather than supplying all the services ourselves.

3. *Mental health education,* which involves courses, workshops and discussion groups for parents in the community, as well as a weekly parent communication center, a drop-in, open group discussion where parents talk freely about their concerns about parenting and family life. The workshops cover such topics as surviving as a single parent; issues common in divorce situations; early child development (new knowledge about infants and young children); what is important about their development and how to enhance their psychological growth; and assertiveness skills (skill training for greater effectiveness in personal relationships).

4. *Case and program consultation* to public health nurses and others working with a wide spectrum of families with infants and young children; to the infant day-care program of the Friends to Teen Age Parent Program; to the Pediatric Services within the Hospital; to community day care and nursery programs.

5. *Training and continuing education* to diverse groups within the community: graduate students and community groups and organizations dealing with infants and young children (particularly infant programs involved with school-age parent programs).

6. *Combined community service, promotive and preventive programs* such as
   a. a parent-infant development program for parents with babies from birth through 2 years. Diagnoses and infant assessments are carried out in the context of developing appropriate parent-infant intervention programs, and in helping parents to know fully the attributes of their infants. This work is carried out both individually and in group.
   b. home visit/intervention—a program for families with young children who are unable to attend sessions at the Center, whose primary need is for information about child-rearing techniques, and special developmental programs for their children.
   c. therapeutic group for abusing parents—a special program utilizing the skills of the occupational therapist who runs a craft group for these parents, with the focus on developing appropriate skills such as control, delay, greater frustration tolerance, increased self-esteem and decreased social isolation. There is also a therapeutic group for the abused children whose parents are in these sessions.
   d. emergency services for young children and families are provided by the Crisis Intervention Team, available 24 h/day via the Hospital Emergency Room.
   e. the Developmental Nursery serves families and young children: assessments of child and family functioning, and appropriate treatment, are carried out in the group setting. Parents are involved in the sessions along with their children; they observe the interactions through a one-way mirror. By sharing anxieties and concerns with other parents and with professional staff, by observing and discussing how the teacher interacts with the children and the children with each other, parents are guided in their learning. They also are involved in group discussions about child-rearing issues with a psychologist who is present while the parents observe their children. The parents also frequently join the young children for interaction sessions during the group. The families and young children seen have a wide variety of concerns: foster parents; adoptive parents; normal children whose parents are anxious about them because they do not know normal developmental stages in children ("all" 2-year-olds have tantrums in supermarkets); children going through family crises such as divorce, death, a recent move, and so on; children with special problems such as information-processing difficulties or very early language disabilities.
   f. direct services for families and children with already clear-cut and serious behavioral and emotional problems. Failure-to-thrive infants, and infants

and young children with developmental dysfunctions of a wide variety are worked with, in the context of the entire family unit.

Parents are viewed as competent individuals who have something important to offer each other and their babies. Instead of working with parents as though they were incompetent, or psychologically sick, we see families as having strengths and competencies that need to be mobilized.

Our techniques and approaches involve "tuning in" to individual differences and needs, strengthening ego/cognitive mechanisms, information processing, alternatives for action, planning, sharing, converting inappropriate action or affect into words, developing controls, basic skills in coping with life (be it the infant or adult world), increasing positive motivation to connect with people and to learn, and developing supportive networks. We attempt to enhance people's self-esteem as parents. We teach about infants and young children. We deal with real-life situations of divorce, surviving as a single parent, unemployment, or culture shock. It is not necessary to be "sick" to get into the system. We are directed toward facilitating growth, with an emphasis on competencies, not weaknesses.

What we offer parents and young children essentially, then, is

- New behaviors for interacting with their child; models for identification
- New understandings and awareness of their child's needs and individual differences
- Education about children and parenting in general; opportunities to learn
- Socialization (breakdown of isolation), relationships with other parents (awareness that they are not alone), sharing of feelings, fantasies, and techniques
- Development of inner controls rather than acting out (for the abusing parents in particular); development of the ability to verbalize feelings and to use those verbalizations to enhance the relationship with the child
- Enhanced self-esteem; enhanced self-image as a successful parent
- Release of (or from) guilt about the child's behavior; ability to set and follow limits
- Ability to identify with the child's feelings and fantasies
- Establishing an empathic, sympathetic, stable relationship—showing that someone cares; helping to withstand or change the sense of despair, of hopelessness, and helplessness of having a dysfunctional child or an overwhelming reality situation; accepting the anger and anxiety

We are in the first stages of deliberate conceptualization of programs that will prevent the development of pathology, that will emphasize and enhance strengths rather than reward and enhance weaknesses. It is a sad system indeed that will pay attention to a child or family only after a problem develops.

There is at this time the prospect of innovation based on deliberate social awareness rather than on last-minute necessity. This approach, oriented toward the future, gives us the time needed to develop those services which our technological society so sorely lacks and so desperately demands. We need to examine carefully preventive and interventive programs that support the fullest growth and development of families. We must consider the needs of the family network, and the realities of family existence that shape the direction of an infant's growth, that determine his or her particular life style.

BIBLIOGRAPHY

Appleton, T., Clifton, R., and Goldberg, S. Behavioral competence in infancy. In F. D. Horowitz (ed.). *Review of Child Development Research:* Vol. 4. Chicago: University of Chicago, 1975, 102–103.

Birns, B., and Golden, M. Prediction of intellectual performance at three years from infant tests and personality measures. *Merrill-Palmer Quarterly,* 1972, **18**, 53–58.

Bremmer, R. H. (ed.). *Children and Youth in America.* Volume II: 1866–1932, Parts 7 and 8. Cambridge, Mass.: Harvard University, 1971.

Bronfenbrenner, U. Statement from the hearings before the Sub-committee on Children and Youth of the Committee on Labor and Public Welfare. United States Senate, September 24, 25, and 26, 1973. "American Families; Trends and Pressures, 1973."

Bronfenbrenner, U. Address at the American Orthopsychiatric Association, March 1975.

Buhler, K. *Die Geistige Entwicklung des Kindes.* Jena, East Germany: Fisher, 1918.

Caulfield, E. *The Infant Welfare Movement in the Eighteenth Century.* New York: Hoeber, 1931.

Clarke-Stewart, K. A. Interactions between mothers and their young children: Characteristics and consequences. *Monographs of the Society for Research in Child Development.* 1973, **38** (153).

Drillien, C. *The Growth and Development of the Prematurely Born Infant.* Edinburgh: Livingstone, 1964.

Graham, P., Rutter, M., and George, S. Temperamental characteristics as predictors of behavior disorders in children. *American Journal of Orthopsychiatry,* 1973, **43**, 328–339.

Group for the Advancement of Psychiatry. *The Joys and Sorrows of Parenthood.* 1973, **8** (May), No. 84.

Hendrick, I. The discussion of the "instinct to master." *Psychoanalytic Quarterly,* 1943, **12**, 561–565.

Hoke, B. Promotive medicine and the phenomenon of health. *Archives of Environmental Health,* 1968, **16**, 269–278.

Hoke, B. Healths and healthing: Beyond disease and dysfunctional environments. *Ekistics 220,* 1974, March, 169–172.

Holt, J. *How Children Fail.* New York: Pitman, 1964.

Iscoe, I. Community psychology and the competent community. *American Psychologist,* 1974, **29**, 607–613.

Kessner, D. *Infant Death: An Analysis by Maternal Risk and Health Care.* Contrasts in Health Status, Vol. I. Washington, D.C.: Institute of Medicine, National Academy of Sciences, 1973.

Korner, A. Individual differences at birth: Implications for early experience and later development. *American Journal of Orthopsychiatry,* 1971, **41**, 608–619.

Korner, A. Individual differences at birth: Implications for child care practices. In D. Bergsma (ed.), *The Infant at Risk.* New York: Intercontinental Medical, 1974. Birth Defects—the National Foundation March of Dimes, Vol. 10, No. 2, 1974.

Levenstein, Phyllis. Individual variation among pre-schoolers in a cognitive intervention program in low income families. Paper presented at the Council for Exceptional Children, Conference on Early Childhood Education, New Orleans, December 1969.

Lewis, M., and Goldberg, S. Perceptual-cognitive development in infancy: A generalized expectancy model as a function of the mother-infant interaction. *Merrill-Palmer Quarterly,* 19, **15**, 81–100.

Miller, C. A. Health care of children and youth in America. *American Journal of Public Health,* 1975, **65**, 353–362.

Prechtl, H., and Beintema, D. *The Neurological Examination of the Full Term Newborn Infant.* Clinics in Developmental Medicine, No. 12. London: Spastics Society, Heinemann, 1964.

Provence, S., and Lipton, R. *Infants in Institutions.* New York: International Universities, 1961.

Ruhrah, J. *Pediatrics of the Past.* New York: Hoeber, 1925, 5.

Thomas, A., Chess, S., and Birch, H. *Temperament and Behavior Disorders in Children.* New York: New York University, 1968.

Watson, J. The development and generalization of contingency awareness in early infancy: Some hypotheses. *Merrill-Palmer Quarterly,* 1966, **12**, 123–135.

Watts, J., Halfar, C., and Chan, I. Environment, experience and intellectual development of young children in home care. *American Journal of Orthopsychiatry,* 1974, **44**, 773–781.

White, B. L., and Watts, J. C. *Experience and Environment: Major Influences on the Development of the Young Child.* Vol. I, Englewood Cliffs, New Jersey: Prentice-Hall 1973.

White, R. Motivation reconsidered: The concept of competence. *Psychological Review,* 1959, **66**, 297–323.

White, R. Ego and reality in psychoanalytic theory. *Psychological Issues,* **3** (3), Monogr. 11. New York: International Universities, 1963.

Yarrow, L., Rubenstein, J. L., Pedersen, F. A., and Jankowski, J. J. Dimensions of early stimulation and their differential effects on infant development. *Merrill-Palmer Quarterly,* 1972, **18** (3), 205–218.

CHAPTER 27

Early Intervention Programs[1,2]

E. Kuno Beller

Several major forces have influenced the growing interest in intervention programs for infants. Group care for infants outside the family has existed for centuries. Institutions, such as orphanages and homes for neglected children, which have existed for a long time, have been of considerable concern to society and to human service professions but have attracted interest as an unfortunate necessity with unfortunate consequences for its inhabitants. The function of such programs has been strictly custodial, since society considered infants as basically helpless. The child was considered the possession and the responsibility of the biological parent and the nuclear family that brought it into the world. The role of adult society, be that parent or homes for children, was considered to be one of protection with major emphasis on satisfying the biological needs and carrying out elementary socialization tasks related to biological needs of the infant.

The influence of social philosophers throughout the centuries like John Locke, Jean-Jaque Rousseau, and Charles Darwin did not make its impact on programs for infants until the middle of the 20th century. Locke realized the importance of experience and environmental influences on the infant and young child not only toward socialization but also toward the acquisition of knowledge and learning. Rousseau broke new ground by considering the infant not only an immature adult who is directed by innate instincts and abilities but a developing organism in its own right that is capable to function as a busy, active, and successful explorer of his environment. Although Darwin was concerned primarily with the importance of the infant as a link in the evolution of man, he emphasized the importance of studying and understanding the infant for the development of such human traits as conscience and morality.

These views were known among the educated members of society and became a reality in university laboratories and experimental education movements. For example, Locke's ideas had a great influence on the work of Watson and Skinner, while the thoughts of Rousseau greatly influenced the work of Pestalozzi, Froebel, and Montessori. Darwin exerted his influence most clearly in the work and thinking of Sigmund Freud, who elevated infancy and psychosexual development as cornerstones of his developmental theory. Darwin also profoundly influenced the thinking of Piaget in his concept of adaptation while Rousseau paved the way for Piaget's theory of sensorimotor development. With Piaget the infant emerged as a highly active organism fully partaking in the shaping of his destiny, while ego-psychology in psychoanalysis gradually replaced the conception of the

---

[1] This chapter deals only with intervention programs for children up to 3 years of age.
[2] Barbara Mollenhauer and Ruth Hubbell have greatly contributed to this chapter by searching out, gathering, and making available essential source materials.

child as a battleground between instinctual forces and environmental pressures with a conception of the infant as an active organism. Erikson translated the traditional psychosexual stages into a viable, culturally relevant conception of infant development, in which autonomy and initiative were assigned central roles in infant development.

Against this background of the history of ideas, orphanages and fondling homes were exposed as destructive influences on the development of infants by Goldfarb (1943) and Spitz (1945). The dramatic outcome of these studies was the finding that early care not only affected the health and biological development but also the cognitive development of children. At the time, findings of another pair of investigators demonstrated that individualized care of biologically and mentally disadvantaged children could prevent and reverse their course of development (Skeels and Dye 1939; Skeels, 1966).

The result of these early findings, immediately following the second world war, had dramatic effects on group care of infants. Many fondling homes were either closed or the care changed from being extremely impersonal and detached to being more personal—individualized with an emphasis on stability of the caregiving environment. At the other extreme, all group care for infants, including supplementary care such as infant day care, was equated with the devastating environment of orphanages such as those studied by Spitz (1945). This mentality has been strongly reinforced by the work of Bowlby (1951), the work of Spitz (1950) on stranger anxiety, and the work of Ainsworth (1964) on attachment and separation anxiety. Even Harlow's (1958) work on early attachment and separation effects in monkeys and the work of ethologists on imprinting (Lorenz, 1952; Tinbergen 1951; Hess, 1959) were used as evidence for the existence of innate unlearned attachment needs of newborn organisms in animals and man alike, with detrimental lasting and irreversible effects if this early attachment is disrupted.

The comprehensive reviews of evidence on effects of separation, group care, or multiple mothering by Casler (1961) and Yarrow (1963) began to provide a much-needed perspective for the prevailing views on mother-infant attachment, separation, and group care of infants. Rheingold's (1956) work with infants in institutions also contributed to a change in this respect. Different, almost opposite, influence was exerted by a series of investigations which pointed toward the adverse effects of early overly intensive ties between mother and child in the form of overprotection and maternal control (Levy, 1943) and overdependence of the child on his caregiver (Beller, 1959). Conversely the work of Watson (1957) and Winterbottom (1958) pointed to the importance of early nurturance and autonomy-granting as well as encouragement of independence for the later development of children. While these investigators further strengthened the importance of experience in infancy for the child's later development, they paved the way for a more constructive and positive view of child care and early education outside the close ties between mother and infant. The tide began to turn and investigators of early care and human development became more concerned with the potential of human organism from infancy on and the conditions that might enhance such development. Piaget (1952) and Erikson (1963) signaled these changes theoretically in the fields of developmental psychology. Researchers turned their attention full force to the autonomous capacities of the developing infant (Wolf, 1966; Bruner, 1968; Korner, 1971; Kagan, 1972) and to the active participant role of the infant in the socialization process (Bell, 1968; Osofsky, 1971, 1974; Beller, 1973).

These different interests and perspectives about infants and their development profoundly influenced the goals and the methods of early intervention programs discussed in this chapter. However, the direct impetus for the establishment of such programs came from political and historical changes in contemporary society. The emancipation of women and the crisis of the traditional nuclear family made the exclusive care of infants and young children both a hazard and an impossibility. The need for supplementary care in the case of families in which both parents work, of professional women, and of single parents became a necessity. Group and family day care for infants and young children grew rapidly as a result of these changes. The question was no longer whether such forms of early programs should exist or not but how to make them function to facilitate optimal development of the infants they served as an extension rather than replacement of the family.

Another major impetus for the initiation of early intervention programs came from the War on Poverty, an official policy of the U.S. government during the 1960s. Part of the concern of this attempt to modify poverty as an illness of our society was to improve the opportunities and capacities of children to benefit from educational institutions in our society. It became clear that children from poor families were ill equipped to benefit from the educational programs of public schools by the time they entered first grade. A massive attempt was undertaken to correct this deficit by offering pre-school to all children and particularly the poor in the form of Headstart. Headstart in essence was a correction of what middle-class and educated parents had known for many years, as nursery school which was available to children from 3 years of age onwards as a private institution, sometimes attached as a laboratory school to departments of education at universities. Bloom (1964) and Hunt (1964) provided the conceptual framework to justify early intervention programs not only for children of pre-school age but for infants as well. Pioneers of early intervention programs, such as Caldwell (1964) and Keister (1970), formulated their evaluative efforts of such programs as an investigation of the hypothesis that their programs of infant day-care were not harmful and damaging to their infants because these infants were separated from the protection of their biological mothers and nuclear families. As new intervention programs were initiated their goal was to contribute toward the development of infants, both in and outside the home.

In our discussion of early intervention programs, the concern with both the frailties and capacities, the dependency and autonomy of the developing infant, will fall into perspective.

HOME-BASED PARENT-ORIENTED PROGRAMS

The Florida Parent Education Program, directed by I. J. Gordon (Gordon, 1969, 1972; Gordon and Guinagh, 1974; Guinagh and Gordon, 1976), is one of the pioneer parent-oriented educational programs for infants. Major goals of the program were to enhance intellectual and personality development of the child, and to produce changes in the mother's self-esteem and in her conviction that she could affect what happened to her and her child. An important feature of this program has been the use of paraprofessionals. Women from the community were trained to function as educators, and received a 5-week intensive training program which concentrated on principles of child development, skills in interviewing, techniques of recording information, and specific exercises or games to be played with infants which had to be taught to the mothers.

Gordon attempted to build his instructional program on Piaget's concepts of development. Thus, early games were constructed to be sensorimotor, manipulative, and exploratory—that is, letting the baby pick up objects while describing to him what he is doing, the way things feel, and so on. At later stages games had specific reference to more "preoperational" activities, such as the development of object permanence. For example, an object is attached to a string and hidden from view, requiring the baby to pull the string to bring the object into view; or an object is partly, and later fully, hidden under a blanket while the baby is watching and then the child is asked to find it.

Each mother was visited once a week. The parent educator demonstrated the activities that the mother was to carry out with her infant. The tasks were concretely and specifically spelled out in detail. However, the parent educator was instructed to emphasize to the mother the importance of treating the tasks as games and fun. Parent educators were instructed to test each infant on task competence before demonstrating to the mother how the task was to be performed. An attempt was made to make clear to the mother that the actual sequence of tasks depended on the individual child, and if a task was failed it should be broken down into simpler components.

The subjects of the study were indigent mothers; their babies have been born between June 15, 1966, and September 30, 1967, at a public health center for small town and rural families in central Florida. Although Gordon started with 276 mother-infant pairs, attrition reduced this number and resulted in a final sample of 193 mother-infant pairs. Mothers were randomly assigned to experimental or control groups. The activity with all experimental mothers was the same but the timing of the instructional program was varied for different experimental groups. Each parent educator worked with approximately 10 families. The initial year of the parent education program was an engineering effort to develop a delivery system and create a set of materials for the parent to teach the child. In the second year of the program, half the original experimental group was randomly assigned as a new control group. In the third year of the project, half of the children in each group were randomly assigned to the experimental and half to a control group. New families were also recruited.

All of the intervention had been of a home-visit nature, on a roughly once-a-week schedule. When the children turned 2, a group experience was added to the home-learning centers, or backyard centers, five children at a time, for 4-h a week in two 2-h periods. These were homes of mothers in the project and were a mixture of urban homes in a housing project in the Gainesville area and rural homes around the 12-county area. The mother who lived in the home was employed as an aide to the backyard center director who was the parent educator. Each parent educator still worked with 10 mothers and 10 children; she met groups of children twice a week in the center while continuing to meet with the mothers on a once-a-week basis. New 2-year-olds who had not been in the study were added so that the effect of starting the program at age 2 could be assessed. This created seven treatment groups.

Group 1 received treatment during the first 3 years of life, group 2 during the first 2 years, group 3 during the 1st year only, group 4 during the 2nd year only, group 5 during the 2nd and 3rd years, group 6 during the 3rd year only, and group 7 during the 1st and 3rd years. Group 8 was a no-treatment control group.

Although the intervention program ended when the children were 3, assessment of the children and the parents on the child's 4th, 5th, and 6th birthday continued.

Gordon collected a large set of data on the mothers and the children. The data on the mothers were based on the Parent-Educator Weekly Report, the Rotter Social Reaction Inventory, the Markle-Voice Language Assessment, estimate of mothers' expectance, the Mother How I See Myself Scale, and a final observational report. The data on the child included the Parent-Educator Weekly Report, final observational reports, tests of performance, the Goldman Race Awareness Test, and the Griffith and Bayley Infant Scales.

Apparently the collection and analyses of data were carried out and reported in parts by different associates and students who participated in this large research program.

One major finding in Gordon's study was that at the end of the 1st year of life, experimental infants were slightly but significantly ahead of control infants on total scores of the Griffith Mental Development Scales. When the children were retested at 24 months of age with Bayley Scales of Infant Development, no significant differences were found between any groups. However, while at 21 months of age experimental infants did not differ significantly from control infants on Bayley items, a later comparison at 27 months yielded significant differences on the same scores in favor of the experimental infants. In a later progress report, Gordon (1972) presented findings of a follow-up study of all his experimental and control groups when the children passed their 4th birthday. At that time 192 children were in eight different groups. His findings at that time were based on three measures: the Stanford Binet Test, the Peabody Picture Vocabulary Test, and the Leiter International Performance Scale. Gordon found stronger and more consistent effects of his experimental intervention than he had found in his earlier assessments. The largest and most significant effects on all three tests occurred in children who received intervention for 2 or 3 consecutive years. Children who received intervention only during the 3rd year of life performed better than control children on the Stanford Binet and Leiter scales, although these differences did not reach statistical significance consistently. Discontinuous intervention during the 1st and 3rd years of life and intervention during only the 2nd year had no positive effects.

At age 6, 3 years after the last intervention, comparisons based on Stanford Binet testing yielded essentially the same findings as were reported for age-4 testing.

Gordon resumed following up the children in 1976. The outcome of that analysis has been reported by Guinagh and Gordon (1976). The sample changed both because of attrition and because several groups were dropped from continued follow-up. Three groups ($n = 32$) who received treatment for 2 and 3 years consecutively during the first 3 years of life, the Home Learning Center group—that is, children who received 1 year of treatment from 2 to 3 ($n = 38$)—and control children ($n = 21$) were retained for follow-up. Attrition amounted to 42% for the first group, 24% for the second group, and 59% for the control group. Gordon dropped three groups of children who received less than 2 years of discontinuous treatment because the sizes of each of these groups were too small and for certain reasons they could not be combined into one larger group. No significant differences were found for IQ scores of dropped and retained children at ages 2, 3, and 6. Thus, in spite of attrition, the sample retained for follow-up was considered representative of both the original group and those who were measured at age 6 in his latest follow-up.

Gordon limited himself to an analysis of available achievement test data based on the Metropolitan Achievement Test, the Stanford Achievement Test, and the Comprehensive Test of Basic Skills. Since these tests were not comparable, the results on the three tests could not be combined except for Total Reading and Total Mathematic. Gordon analyzed only the scores on the Metropolitan Achievement Test except for Total Mathematic and Total Reading. An analysis of these scores of third grade age yielded significant differences between the group that received 2 or 3 years of intervention and the control group for Reading, Math-Concepts, and Math Problem Solving. The Home Learning Center group, which received 1 year intervention between 2 and 3 years of age, was generally superior to the control children but not significantly.

The investigators also analyzed differences between intervention and control groups with regard to children's placement in special classes for Educable and Trainable Mentally

Retarded, Specific Learning Disability, Emotionally Retarded, and referrals for discipline problems and psychological help. These comparisons were made between pooled groups of all children who received intervention and control children. Significant differences were found in assignment to special classes for Educable and Trainable Mentally Retarded children. More of the control children than of the intervention children were assigned to such classes. No significant differences were found between the two groups with regard to referrals for discipline problems and for psychological help.

An attempt was made to investigate the predictive value of early IQ scores to assignment to special education classes. Neither the Bayley nor the Stanford Binet scores predicted significantly or appreciably placement in special education classes.

A classroom behavior inventory was used by 90 teachers in 30 schools containing experimental and control pupils to investigate whether experimental children exhibited more positive social behavior and more positive task-oriented behavior than control children. No significant differences were found and the hypotheses of superiority on part of experimental children was not confirmed. The investigators also used Schaefer's Teacher Report of Parents' Behavior in order to determine whether parents of experimental children exhibited more interest in their child's progress in school than parents of control children. This analysis yielded no significant differences although the investigators report that, according to Schaefer, this instrument had no known reliability or validity.

One can conclude that prolonged and continuous intervention of 2 to 3 years during the first 3 years of life produced prolonged effects on intellectual and academic performances in school over a period of 6 or 7 years after the termination of intervention. Attempts to find prolonged effects of intervention on the children's social, emotional, and motivational adjustment in school could not be demonstrated. Similarly, no significant differences were found on parental variables between experimental and control groups. Thus, major lasting effects of this intervention could be demonstrated on the intellectual and academic achievement of the children. No such effects were demonstrated on socioemotional adjustment of children and on the parents of these children.

Gordon and his associates found a multitude of relationships between specific maternal behaviors and performance of infants on a variety of measures. For example, Gordon found sizable correlations between verbal interaction scores of mothers and infant baby scores at age 2 for the group that received home visits the 2nd year only. Correlations between maternal verbal scores and the child's performance on the Bayley Mental Scale and the child's task-orientation behavior during the test ranged from $+ 0.52$ to $+ 0.64$ ($n = 15$). Analyses of data carried out by Herman (1971) showed that maternal behavior correlated significantly with the performance of 31 infants on the Bayley Motor ($r = 0.41$) and Mental ($r = 0.31$) Scales. Herman also reported that mothers of high-scoring boys on both mental and motor scales engaged in significantly more positive verbal behavior than did mothers of low-scoring boys and of high-scoring girls. Scott and Lally (1969) report significant sex differences in the infants' response to the program. For example, trained males performed significantly better than untrained males on the hearing subtest of the Griffith Mental Development Scales. Trained female infants scored significantly higher than untrained female infants on all but the performance subtest. Thus, it seems that female infants benefitted more consistently from the training program than did male infants. Gordon also reported some interesting findings with regard to effects of the education program on the mothers. Mothers for whom pre- and post-information was obtained moved toward greater internal control of a reinforcement orientation. These mothers reported that they now felt greater control and more influence over what was happening in their own lives than they did when they entered the project. However, this change was significant only for mothers trained as parent educators while the majority of mothers who had not been trained as parent educators continued to evidence orientation toward external control.

The Verbal-Interaction Program

The mother-child home program was developed and carried out under the direction of Levenstein and Sunley (1968), Levenstein (1970,1971), Levenstein and Levenstein (1971), and Madden et al. (1977). The program's major assumption was that the principal cognitive element missing from the early experience of many children vulnerable to educational disadvantage was a sufficient amount of verbal interaction in the family, centered on perceptually rich and ordered stimuli, embedded in the affective matrix of the child's most enduring relationships, especially that with his mother. A major goal of this program was to help low-income families to assume the same function of education that the middle-class parent carries out informally in raising her children. The immediate goal of the educational program was to increase conversation and communication between mother and child by using toys and books. The long-term goal was to help the mother become more effective in guiding the cognitive and intellectual growth of her child. Levenstein selected social workers rather than educators or psychologists to carry out the educational program. She believed that the social worker's background provided the most appropriate values and skills for the intervention program she conceptualized. The major function of the educator was to help the mother to become the effective educator. A set of verbal interaction stimulation material (VISM) was selected and used as a major vehicle for the educational intervention. The toys were such that they did not lend themselves to solitary play by the child but needed interaction with someone else for full enjoyment and learning. Mother-child interactions which were demonstrated by the home visitor emphasized the following points: giving information by describing the label, form, color and size of the object; describing toy manipulations such as building and matching; eliciting responses from the child through questions; describing the social interaction; encouraging reflections through questions; encouraging divergence by rewarding independence and curiosity; getting the child interested in books by eliciting verbalizations about illustrations and rewarding the child for his comments; and building the child's self-esteem through frequent positive reinforcements in the form of verbal support and helping. During the early sessions the social worker interacted with the child more than the mother but gradually drew the mother into the activitiies. During the later sessions the home visitor attempted to shift interaction between adult and child entirely to the mother. This course was indicated because of Levenstein's conviction that the mother is the key person who must serve as the principal agent for helping a child acquire language and other cognitive skills. To get the mother to assume this role the visitor emphasized the need for the mother to play and carry out demonstrated interaction with the child between sessions. Family counseling was added to the toy-demonstration program as an additional activity. This was possible because the toy demonstrators were social workers.

The general hypothesis was that the verbal-intellectual competence of lower-class children would rise as a result of the program. A subhypothesis was that increases in intellectual achievement would be greater among 2-year-old children than among 3-year-old children because of the beginning symbolic language development at that age.

Initially, 54 children, 20 to 43 months of age and drawn from housing projects for low-income families on Long Island, New York, served as subjects. Eighty percent of the subjects were Black. Children in the experimental and control groups were equated on social class on the basis of the Hollingshead Index.

The average level of father's education was below high school graduation, from mid-ninth to mid-eleventh grades. Most fathers in the sample were in low-status occupations: unemployed, unskilled, or semi-skilled. Two-thirds of the fathers in the total sample were living in the home. The average level of mother's education was a little higher than that of fathers and ranged from ninth to eleventh grade. About one-third of the mothers in the total sample were receiving welfare aid.

Thirty-three families in the experimental group received two ½-h visits weekly for a period of 7 months. One control group, consisting of nine subjects, received weekly visits from a social worker who carried out the interview with the mother without providing verbal stimulation for the child. To control for the effect of leaving VISM with the mothers in the experimental group, the control mothers received toys other than VISM. Three other control groups received initial and post-tests without any intervening home visits. These three control groups consisted of 19 2- and 3-year-old and 10 4-year-old children recruited in 1967 and a sample of 30 6-year-old children added in 1972. The children all received the Cattell Infant Scales, the Stanford-Binet, and the Peabody Vocabulary Test at the beginning and end of the program. The Peabody Picture Vocabulary Test was also given to the mothers of the infants at the onset and end of the study.

Unfortunately, Levenstein's readiness to explore a good many variations of her program without a reported overall plan for these variations made it very difficult to be precise about sample sizes and about main and interacting effects of different treatments.

The mothers' IQs did not show significant changes. Although there was some indication of mothers' positive attitudes toward the program, no significant differences were found in the kinds of major life events and in the incidence of mothers' employment. A further finding reported by Levenstein was that the training of low-income high-school-educated aides to function as educators lowered the effectiveness of the program significantly as compared with results achieved with social workers in the 1st year of the study.

The investigator correlated 50 background variables with the IQ data of children. Out of 200 correlations, approximately 18 were significant. The investigators do not report relationships between background variables and effect of treatment. For that reason, the findings reported are not discussed here.

Levenstein found that experimental children manifested a gain of 17 points on the Cattell and Stanford-Binet Scales, which was significantly greater than comparable gains of 1 and 2 points by the control groups. The experimental group also manifested a gain of 12 points on the Peabody Picture Vocabulary Test, which was significantly greater than a 4-point loss of the first control group but not significantly different from a 4.7-point gain of the second control group. The second hypothesis—namely, a differential gain between 2- and 3-year-old children—was not supported by the data.

Levenstein introduced a number of variations which showed gains both during the 1st and 2nd year of her program. For example, one group, which received the full program for 1 year plus a 2nd year of some stimulation materials, retained an average of 16 out of 19 IQ points. Another group, which had only 1 year of the intervention, retained half the original 17-point gain when tested in first grade. Still another group of subjects who had received only home visits for the 1st year and then had a year of full program maintained an IQ gain of 13 points into the first grade. Follow-up data for the first control group, which consisted of visitors who left toys in the home, showed a 10-point increase in IQ during the year following the experimental program and a significant increase of 18 IQ points when tested 30 months after the original pretest.

The picture that seems to have emerged from the finding during the first 5 years of Levenstein's study was that the control groups, which include either regular home visits and leaving toys, or leaving VISM only, manifest either immediate or delayed significant gains. This left only those control groups that received neither home visits nor toys as the ones that manifested no significant gain either after the 8-month period or after 30 months following the initial testing.

To investigate the prolonged effect of her early intervention, Levenstein is continuing to follow up the children into elementary school. Follow-up data on intellectual functioning were assessed by means of the Stanford Binet Intelligence Scale for children through kindergarten and the Wechsler Intelligence Scale for Children (WISC) in and beyond first grade. Follow-up findings were reported most recently for children at a mean group age nearest to 5 and for those children who had reached the third grade during the year of 1975. Adjustments were made for test revisions of the Stanford-Binet but no adjustments could be made for changes of the WISC. Eighty-four percent of the children originally enrolled were available for follow-up testing. Differences between groups that received 2 years of treatment, 1 year of treatment, and no treatment were statistically significant. The data presented by the investigators do not permit a statement about specific effects of length of treatment or type of treatment (Madden et al., 1977). However, the prolonged effect of this intervention in early childhood, though variable, remains significant with regard to IQ measures on the Stanford-Binet and WISC through kindergarten and third grade. Thus, one must conclude that the length of treatment and specific technique of home visit or even the choice of specific toys were less important for their prolonged effect on IQ changes through kindergarten and third grade than the range of opportunities for stimulation provided systematically by this program.

Levenstein reports significant differences between experimental and control children on Wide Range Reading Achievement test scores during the third grade. Although the experimental children were appreciably superior to the control children on some scores, such as arithmetic, these differences did not reach statistical significance.

Levenstein did report a few findings based on a prolonged effect of their intervention on social and emotional adjustment of the children during the second and third grade of elementary school. Teachers were asked to rate children on an instrument called the "Child's Behavior Traits Inventory." The teachers did not know whether the children whom they were asked to rate belonged to an experimental or to a control group. Levenstein found that mean scores of her 2-year treated groups were significantly higher on social and emotional competence than for children from the untreated comparison group.

One of the most fruitful explorations that Levenstein undertook was to divide children into high and low gainers and compare the behaviors of these children during the home visits. The home visitors reported a higher incident among high gainers of asking and answering questions, initiating conversation, cooperating with toy demonstrator, and playing with the toys. With these findings the effects of the program on the child and the child's response emerge still more clearly while the effects of the program on the main target—that is, the mother—remain unclear.

A doubt was raised concerning the short-term efficacy of this model of intervention by the outcome of a field experiment which these investigators carried out between 1973 and 1975. Fifty-one mother-child pairs were assigned randomly to treated and control conditions; 19 treated and 16 untreated dyads remained after the 2-year intervention. Although the treated children obtained a higher average Stanford-Binet Score of 104.8 than the control children, who obtained the score of 100.9, the difference tested by covariance analysis failed to reach statistical significance. Although the authors plan to follow up these children for the study of prolonged effects, these short-range findings introduced a note of caution. However, Levenstein has replicated her intervention in a variety of ways, and results have been overwhelmingly positive. Not only did she replicate her own interventions, but a number of other interventions were involved in repeating the mother-child program. By 1972, eight of the programs reported an average IQ gain of 11 points after the first year of intervention and several of these programs reported a second year average IQ gain of 15 points. This leaves little doubt as to the validity of generalizing positive effects of the toy demonstrator intervention with mothers on infants' intellectual development.

DARCEE Infant Programs

A third set of programs, the DARCEE Infant Programs, were primarily parent-oriented. These programs were intervention studies with mothers of infants conducted at the Demonstration and Research Center for Early Education of the John F. Kennedy Center for Research on Education and Human Development at the George Peabody College, under the direction of Forester et al. (1971) and of Gray (1977). Although the program of Forester et al. was concerned with the physical and psychological growth and development of the infant, its overriding goal was to enable the parents to become a more effective educational change agent. The program focused on the parent rather than the child because of the conviction that the parent is the most available sustaining agent to turn the home-visit program into a lasting experience. To accomplish the goal of making the parent an effective educational change agent, an attempt was made to get the parent to take increasing initiative in planning for her child. To implement this, a further subgoal was to help the parent develop better coping skills in her daily life experiences. It was hoped that such a broad approach would increase her ability to guide and shape the child's behavior rather than merely cope with it from moment to moment.

With regard to procedure and techniques, one home visitor worked directly in each home for at least 1 h per visit for a maximum of 24 or 32 visits. Overall guiding principles for carrying out the procedure in the home were (1) to focus on the parent rather than the child, (2) not to exclude any family member from lessons during the home visit in order to promote rapport and spread the benefit of the experience to other members of the family, and (3) to employ materials that are easily available by making use of discarded objects around the home—for example, plastic containers and coffee cans. Great stress was placed on encouraging the parent to use positive reinforcement, because it is believed that most lower-class parents are convinced of the validity of punishment as the most effective way to change a child's behavior. Beyond these general guidelines the approach to each home was highly individualized. Cultural as well as individual differences received a great deal of attention.

The implementation phase included six sessions or six cycles of home visits from April to November 1970. One-week evaluation and planning activities preceded each of the six sessions. Foci and procedures over the six sessions changed in the following ways: in the first session, initial visits focused on physical care, while social and cognitive components of basic routines were pointed out to the mother. Information regarding infant growth and development was offered to the parents. During the next session emphasis was placed on improving the mother's ability to observe and record the baby's progress and development, and to construct suggested play materials. The mother's observations were directed toward such events as teething, the appearance of new infant vocalizations, verbalizations, and other behaviors. During the third session mothers were encouraged to carry out between-visit activities with the infant and to select appropriate toys or playthings. The home visitor dealt to a considerable extent with the need for rewarding, reinforcing, disciplining, and gaining the infant's attention. During the fourth session the home visitor systematically fostered the increasing involvement of the mother in the content of activities. During the fifth session each mother was asked to verbalize to the home visitor some of the things she had observed, such as motor development, new behavior, the infant's responses to discipline and toilet training, eating habits, social habits, environmental change, materials they had made, provision of new playthings, and father involvement. During the sixth and final session the home visitor reviewed the project with the mother and outlined expectations the mother may have had for the child after 18 months of age.

The subjects in the study were 20 white and Black mothers from low-income homes recruited from well-baby clinics. The infants were between 7 and 9 months of age. An equal number of mother-infant dyads were in comparison groups.

The Bayley Scales of Infant Development, the Griffith Mental Development Scales, and the Uzgiris-Hunt Scales were the three major instruments used in the evaluation of the program's effectiveness. All these scales were administered individually, prior to the onset of the training program and again at the end of the program. The interval between pre- and post-testing was 8 months. The maternal behaviors were observed during testing. The homes were rated using the Caldwell Inventory of Home Stimulation. Data have been made available only of pre-post changes on all the infants' measures (Forester et al., 1971). The experimental infants exceeded the control infants on their performance on the mental scales of the Bayley and on the locomotion and performance scales of the Griffith. Although the focus of the study was on the education of the parent as a change agent for the child, findings obtained on the parent have not yet been made available.

A second DARCEE program is being carried out by Gray (1976). This program shares the basic goals of the one just reported but introduces several variations with regard to parent training. The program encompasses three experimental groups and one control group: (1) the extensive home-visiting treatment, (2) the materials-only treatment, (3) the mother-pairs treatment, and (4) a nonintervention control group. The first program—namely, the extensive home-visiting treatment—involves once-a-week 1 h home visits over a period of a year by a trained home visitor. Gray describes in some detail the qualifications of the home visitor, which include an ability to relate well with low-income families and to act as a model for the mother, serving both as a friend and confidante. For that reason, older women are preferred. The home visitor is also expected to function as a partner without being judgmental or acting as a superior. Teaching or training is carried out through demonstration and showing rather than telling the mother what to do. The home visitor is expected to assume a supporting role which is implemented through an abundance of positive reinforcement. The supervisors, however, are at least college graduates, with the concentration in child development.

The goals for the child are spelled out in detail in this program. Among these is a growing ability to control immediate impulses, to share with others, and to persist toward a goal. Another goal for the child is to create a positive self-concept and trust in others. As a result the child is expected to become more independent and to develop intrinsic motivation. The theoretical basis of the program is an Eriksonian orientation. The first three stages of development—namely, trust, autonomy, and initiative—are stressed. Language development is stressed in order to develop communication skills.

Two aspects of the teaching strategy of the mother are stressed: she must be helped to adjust the environment and her own behavior to the temperament and state of the child and she must provide stimulation to create an optimal discrepancy between the child's level of skill and expectancy and the task or stimulation. Such teaching strategies are designed to be optimal for the development of motivation to learn and for the development of self-confidence and initiative. Consistent application of appropriate limits and explanation for these limits, providing the child with alternatives in case of failure and undesirable behavior, were encouraged to facilitate the development of inner controls and initiatives rather than shame.

The mother-pairs treatment is basically the same as the extensive home treatment. The only difference is that the mothers are paired. For example, the visitor meets one day a week with mother A and her children along with mother B's children. This gives the children the benefit of seeing the home visitor twice a week and also gives the mothers a little time to themselves once a week. Another objective of this particular program is to provide the mother with some training and experience as a family day-care worker. For that reason workshops are offered to the mother, and if she is interested the staff helps the mother to obtain a license as a family day-care worker. In other words, professional training is an important aspect of this program.

The third program—namely, materials-only treatment—involves no specific adaption to the individual home or family. The home visitor is recruited on a volunteer basis and is trained through workshops. Home visitors are not permitted to remain working in the same family throughout the program. Materials are kept the same as in the extensive home-visiting group. The function of the home visitor is limited to instructing the mother in construction and use of play materials, and in providing her with books and puzzles for use with her children. The mother is also given a stenopad to record activities and make entries of the infant's development.

The investigator has reported the first results of one of the three programs—namely, of the extensive home-visiting program (and the control group). Scores on the maternal teaching strategy showed that mothers in the control group used more physical directions in teaching their children while mothers in the extensive home-visiting group used cue-labels significantly more often.

Children from the experimental group exceeded children from the control group on Bayley Mental Scales scores and on Stanford Binet scores. The samples for the younger group were small ($- 5$ and $n = 4$) and the difference of 11 points in favor of the experimental children approached significance. The samples of the older children were larger ($n = 19$, $n = 14$) and the difference of a 10-point superiority of the experimental children on the second post-test was statistically significant. Experimental children were also found to be significantly superior to control children on a receptive language test. However, comparisons on the Gillmor Basic Concept Test showed no significant differences between experimental and control children. The Slossen intelligence test was used to compare pre-school siblings in the experimental and control families. It failed to support the hypothesis of vertical dissemination of the intervention program from younger siblings in the program to older siblings not in the program. It is interesting to note in this context that the same investigator, Susan Gray, found successful vertical dissemination of her intervention in an earlier study from older siblings in the program to younger siblings not in that program.

Gray (1977) found some evidence for the effectiveness of the extensive (but not of the materials only) home visit program, as measured by Caldwell's HOME test, when this program was compared with the control group 9, 19 and 31 months after primary intervention. Both programs changed effectively Maternal Teaching Strategies by reducing the use of physical direction and increasing the use of cue labels more in the two intervention groups than in the control groups.

The Ypsilanti Infant Education Project

The Ypsilanti project began operation in 1968 (Lambie et al., 1974). The goal of the program was to assist parents in realizing their individual potential as teachers of their children. The study aimed at changing the self-concepts of mothers to think of themselves as capable teachers of their children and to change their behaviors so as to provide opportunities to the children to develop through active experimentation. For the children, the program intended to facilitate merging skills during the sensorimotor period of development.

The intervention program consisted of three different conditions. The first condition, which made up the experimental treatment over a 16-month period, consisted of weekly home visits of 60- to 90-min duration from professionally trained staff. The home visitors introduced a formally organized set of infant activities and a curriculum which was closely associated with Piaget's sensorimotor period. The parent was encouraged in observing and in interpreting the child's behavior in order to apply the activities appropriately to the child's level of functioning. The emphasis was on helping the mother to develop her own individual child-rearing activities rather than impose preconceived strategies. Mothers were reinforced for taking the initiative and assuming responsibility as the child's teacher. The home visitor tried to offer a model in the use of supportive language and to encourage initiative.

The second program condition was called the contrast treatment. The frequency and length of home visits were the same as those for the experimental group. The staff in this program consisted of college students and teacher aids who had some experience with young children. The home visitors in this group introduced informal intuitive play activities rather than highly planned activities. The emphasis was to be on gross and fine motor skills. The investigators report that there was a serious breakdown of relations between the student home visitors and the families, which resulted in a disruption of this program. In order to continue the program, women from the community were hired to complete service to this group. The investigators comment that the experience for most of these families was probably more negative than positive. The third condition, the control group, consisted of no treatment with only periodic testing. In contrast to the second condition the parents from the control group responded with considerable interest in the visits and interpreted their contact as intervention. For these reasons the investigators considered this control group as a minimal-treatment rather than a nontreatment group.

Eighty-eight infants were initially recruited for the study. The families were mostly lower-class Black families. Subjects were assigned randomly to each of the three conditions. The attrition was approximately 20%. The original sample of 88 children was reduced to 65 by the end of the project because of sample attrition. All analyses reported were based on the sample of 65 children who were considered to have completed the program: experimental children ($n = 22$), control children ($n = 22$), and contrast children ($n = 21$). The study had three cohorts. The infants entering the program in cohort 1 were 3 months of age; in cohort 2, 7 months of age; and in cohort 3, 11 months of age. The children were tested at 4-month intervals four times after the initial testing. One year after completion of the program children were retested on the Stanford Binet. Thus the ages of the children at the end of the program were on the average 19, 23, and 27 months in the three cohorts, and on post-testing 31, 35, and 39 months.

Three instruments were used to assess the impact of the program on the mothers: the Verbal Interaction Record, the Mothers' Observation Check-list, and the Ypsilanti Picture Sorting Inventory. The Verbal Interaction Record was applied during one period in which the mother attempted to elicit verbalization from her child and during a second period during which the mother attempted to teach the child a block task. On this test the mothers received positive scores for supportive verbal expressions and negative scores for imperatives, negatives, and restrictions. Experimental mothers scored significantly higher on positive scores than mothers in the contrast and control groups and thereby provided evidence for the impact of the program on the mothers. Moreover, the mothers' scores on the Verbal Interaction Record correlated positively and significantly with infant scores on the Bayley Mental Scales ($r = 0.32$) and the Language Scales ($r = 0.28$).

The Mothers' Observation Check-list, which was applied during the administration of the Bayley Scales, yielded superior scores for experimental mothers, followed by control mothers, followed by contrast-group mothers. Significant differences were found between both experimental and control mothers when compared with contrast-group mothers. However, the investigators questioned the reliability of the instrument.

The Ypsilanti Picture Sorting Inventory was developed by the Infant Project Staff to attempt to measure the mothers' perception of child development in general and her expectations of her own child in particular. This sorting inventory did not reveal clear differences among the mothers from the three treatment groups in their perceptions of and expectations for child development.

The major measure of the infants' cognitive functioning was based on the Bayley Scales of Infant Development. Experimental children consistently outperformed control children, who consistently outperformed children from the contrast group. However, only the comparison between the experimental and contrast children was significant. One year after the program terminated comparisons based on the Stanford Binet Intelligence Scale yielded the same picture—that is, experimental outperformed controls, who outperformed contrast children; none of the comparisons reached significance. When all cognitive tests were combined a repeated measure analysis yielded significant program effects, with infants in the experimental group scoring significantly higher on the average than children in either the contrast or control group. Thus, there was some evidence of a significant impact of the program on the cognitive development of the children.

Children in the experimental group received higher language scores at the end of treatment than control children, who in turn received higher scores than contrast children. Although the experimental group was substantially superior to the control children, only comparisons between experimental and contrast children were significant. The investigators offer an additional piece of evidence for the impact of the program on language development. The Bayley Mental Scales at entry predicted generally a performance on the language scale at the end of the project. This relationship was absent in the experimental children. Since the experimental children tended to score high on the language scale at the end of the program regardless of their entering cognitive ability, this was interpreted as a major positive effect of the program.

The Bayley Motor Scores yielded no significant difference between the three treatment groups. The only evidence of socioemotional development was based on the Bayley Infant Behavior Record filled out by the testers at the end of administrating the Bayley Mental and Motor Scales and by physicians following pediatric examinations. Experimental children were judged to be more responsive to persons and more imaginative in their play with materials. However, these differences are discounted by the investigators because they were two among many comparisons, all of which, with the exception of these two, failed to reach significance.

Lally

Lally (1971) has investigated the impact of a home-visit program that started during the mother's pregnancy and continued until 6 months after the infant was born. Paraprofessional home visitors designated as child-development trainers disseminated information necessary for the growth and development of the fetus and young infant. During the prenatal phase, weekly home visits were designed to aid the expectant mother to understand her own nutritional needs and to prepare her for the arrival of her new infant. The home visitor helped each mother select adequate food for her baby. After the infant was born, the child-development trainer continued to help the mother in the area of infant feeding but also began to introduce cognitive-stimulation exercises which the mother would later practice with her child. The exercises oriented toward the development of object permanence—the development of a concept that an object exists independently of the child's own actions—were activities such as peek-a-boo, following of moving toy objects, and finding hidden toys. Other areas of exercise dealt with the use of objects as instruments in attaining goals, with ways of acting on objects, with forming a distinction between act and external result, with developing the concept of space, with developing the sense organs, and with developing gestural imitation, as well as verbal learning.

The Infant Intervention Program for infants 6 months or older was composed of two groups of mothers, those who entered the program during pregnancy and continued to receive home instruction for 6 months following birth and those who entered when their infants were approximately 6 months old. Data were reported for infants of 23 mothers in the intervention groups and the 35 infants of mothers who entered the program when their infants were 6 months old. All mothers were from Black lower-class families. Seventy-seven percent of the mothers were unmarried; none had a high-school diploma. The vast majority of mothers were under 30 years and living with their parents when their infants were born.

At 6 months of age, when entering the Infant Intervention Program, all children were tested by means of the Cattell Infant Intelligence Scale. The children from the home-visit program had an average IQ score of 114 while the infants who had no prior home visit had an average IQ score of 104. The difference between the two groups was statistically significant. While this is only a first report of the findings, it is important because it offers results from an educational program—the home-visit program—which went further back than any other program in the history of the child's development.

HOME-BASED CHILD-ORIENTED PROGRAMS

One of the earliest child-oriented programs for infants from underprivileged families was carried out by Schaefer (1968, 1972). A major goal of Schaefer's program was to promote intellectual development of lower-class children through a program of tutoring infants in the acquisition of verbal skills and language development. Home tutoring was offered to experimental subjects between 15 and 36 months of age 1 h a day, 5 days a week. The reasons for selecting this particular age period for language intervention came from evidence in the literature that sensorimotor functioning does not predict later (verbal) intelligence and that this period is marked by rapid language growth. Sixty-four male infants were selected by a door-to-door canvass in two lower-class neighborhoods. The children were all pretested on the Bayley Scales of Infant Development 1 month prior to the onset of the study. No significant differences were found between the children assigned to the control and experimental groups. However, comparisons between the groups revealed small differences favoring the controls on family variables that might be expected to influence the child's intellectual development. To minimize bias in family attachment to tutors and to achieve continuity of the tutoring experience, tutors were rotated to different subjects.

College graduates were trained to function as tutors. The program emphasized verbal stimulation, the provision of varied experiences, and the development of positive relationships with the infant. Tutors were encouraged to interact informally with infants and to instruct when the opportunity arose. For instance, a puzzle was presented to a child when he could be interested in it. Children were never pressed to play with the puzzle. The puzzle was first presented intact. The object depicted in the puzzle was named and the child was asked to touch the object and repeat the name. Later the tutor presented the puzzle intact, named the presented object, took one puzzle piece out, showed it to the child, had the child touch it, described his actions, and put the piece back in place (with assistance, if necessary). Verbalizations elicited and describing actions were used as a supplementary technique—for example, "Push it in," "Boom, it went in," "Where is the head?"

In order to assess the effectiveness of the program, the Bayley Scales were used at 14 and 21 months, the Stanford-Binet Test at 27 and 36 months, a Preposition Test, the Peabody Picture Vocabulary Test, and the Johns Hopkins Perceptual Test, and ratings of task-oriented behavior during testing at 36 months. After the baseline testing at 14 months, the infants were retested at 21, 27, and 36 months. In order to assess the effect of home factors on the intellectual and emotional development of infants, Schaefer obtained measures of the mothers' attitudes toward their infants.

Schaefer found significant differences between his experimental control infants at the end of intervention—that is, at 36 months of age after intervention terminated. Although the differences were in favor of experimental subjects, these differences were due more to a decline in performance on the part of the control infants than an increase on the part of experimental subjects—that is, the IQs of the experimental subjects at the ages of 14 and 36 months was 106 and 106, respectively, while the IQs at 14 and 36 months for the control subjects was 109 and 89, respectively. This trend continued until first grade, when after repeated annual testing the IQ scores were 101 for experimental and 97 for control children. Thus, the decline for experimental children from original testing was 5 points, while control children evidenced a 12-point drop over the same period of 5 years.

Significant correlations were found between maternal attitudes toward the infants and measures of the children's cognitive and emotional functioning. Negative maternal attitudes such as withdrawal, punishment, irritability, hostile involvement and detachment, and low verbal expressiveness assessed at 16, 30, and 36 months yielded correlations of -0.38, -0.34, and -0.40 with the infant Stanford-Binet score at 36 months of age.

Comparable median correlations between maternal attitude and scores on the Johns Hopkins Perception Test at 36 months of age were -0.36, -0.48, and -0.56. Correlations between maternal attitude and the Infant's performance on the Preposition Test at 36 months were of the same magnitude, except that low verbal expressiveness on the mother's part correlated most highly with this test at 36 months—that is, -0.60 and -0.53. Maternal attitudes were uncorrelated with scores on the Peabody Picture Vocabulary Test.

Turning to measures of noncognitive behavior, maternal attitudes correlated significantly with task orientation. Negative maternal attitudes yielded a median correlation of 0.42 with the child's emotional functioning at 36 months of age—that is, hostility, belligerence, negativism, and irritability. The same child measures correlated quite highly with the child's task orientation (median $r = -0.65$). Finally, median correlations between the child's emotional functioning at 36 months and performance on the Stanford-Binet, the Johns Hopkins Perception Test, and the Preposit Test were -0.55, -0.61, and -0.39, respectively. Thus, although this study was carried out to investigate primarily the effect of educational tutoring in language and concept-formation on the child's intellectual development, it yielded a series of impressive relationships of maternal attitudes to socioemotional and cognitive functioning of infants. As a result of these findings, Schaefer has become convinced that a comprehensive approach to the study of early childhood education is more necessary than the employment of isolated educational techniques with the child.

The goal of another child-oriented program carried out by Painter (1969) was to accelerate the spontaneous development of deprived infants and prevent anticipated cognitive and language deficits. Half of 20 children, 8 to 24 months of age, were assigned to a control group and the other half to an experimental group. The latter received an hour of structured tutoring in their homes 5 days a week for a period of 1 year. In contrast to Schaefer's tutors, the tutors in this study came from a variety of educational backgrounds and were put to work after a week of intensive training which was continued throughout the study. The program emphasized language and conceptual development. Both training aspects were highly structured. In language training each child was presented with (1) beginning language, (2) elaborative language, (3) the breaking down of "giant word units," and (4) the encouragement of internal dialogue. In conceptual training, the concepts of (1) body image, (2) space, (3) number, (4) time, and (5) categorical classification were emphasized. Some examples of activities used were dramatic play, rhymes, songs, imitation of tutor's speech, whispering solutions to problem-solving tasks, mirror games where the child labeled his body parts, and resting games. Language development was encouraged in all activities.

Scores of experimental and control infants did not differ at the onset of the program on the Cattell Infant Test, but at the end of the tutoring period the experimental group achieved an average of 10 Stanford-Binet IQ points above the control group. Painter included other tests such as the Illinois Test of Psycholinguistic Abilities, the Merrill-Palmer Scales, and various items from other tests, and found that her experimental subjects performed better than the control subjects on 25 of the 26 variables measured, with eight of these attaining statistical significance.

In contrast to Schaefer, Painter did not attempt to measure the infants' home environment nor to discover relationships between the home and the infants' emotional and intellectual development. It is therefore not surprising to find Painter conclude from her tutorial program that infants are not only capable of serious work for at least 1 h a day but that infants might benefit even more from group programs away from home free of the problems encountered in tutorial programs at home. In sharp contrast to Painter, Schaefer concluded that successful and lasting educational programs for infants must include their families.

CENTER-BASED CHILD-ORIENTED PROGRAMS

A third child-oriented program was carried out under the direction of Palmer (1968, 1969, 1972, 1976). The goals of the program were to determine whether intellectual training early in life has demonstrable effects on children's ability to perform in the first grade, whether one age or another is more responsive to the program, whether duration of the effects varies with the age at which training takes place, and, finally, whether the program would counteract the educational disadvantage of deprived lower-class Black children in their cognitive development.

There were 120 2-year-olds, 120 3-year-olds, and 70 control children in this program. The 310 subjects in the original sample were selected from 1500 birth records of Black male children born in the Harlem and Sydenham Hospital in Manhattan between August and December 1964. The subject pool was established with those children who met the following criteria: over 5 lb at birth, mother with no history of syphilis or drug addiction, both parents self-described as Negro, both parents spoke English as a first language, and no serious illnesses between birth and 24 months of age. The 310 subjects were drawn from that pool to meet a predetermined distribution by social class. That distribution specified more lower class in each relevant cell than middle class because it was assumed attrition would be greatest for the former. The children were randomly assigned to two experimental programs and one control program. The experimental program consisted of a highly structured, intensive concept-training curriculum while the other consisted of a less formalized discovery program.

Each child had regular appointments every week for two 1-h sessions, staggered with at least 1 day intervening. Parents were encouraged to attend at least the first six sessions, to be present while the child adapted to the Center, and to provide the opportunity for them to see and hear what activities their child would be engaged in. After the first six sessions, parents could attend when they desired, and if anything occurred in the training session they wanted explained, they were free to inquire of instructors and other staff personnel.

In the concept-training program the tutors talked more, followed a specific assignment plan with the children, and employed sequences of training presenting increasingly more difficult concepts to the children. Each task was carefully defined in relation to concept, series, stage, and level. "Concepts" referred to bipolar dimensions of the child's environment believed to be essential for subsequent complex learning (i.e., up and down, in and out, hard and soft, etc.) "Series" referred to several related concepts which could be ordered into one training series, as with sensory tactile concepts where stage 1 is wet and dry, stage 2 is hard and soft, and so on. "Stages" were defined as sequences of training—for example, for the development of form concepts, simple trial-and-error puzzle work was employed in stage 1, while visual discrimination and more complex trial-and-error work was used in stage 2.

"Level" referred to arbitrarily defined strata of relative complexity across training series. The trainers for the concept group presented each concept in the same four steps: (1) demonstrate and label actions related to the concept; (2) have the child perform an action related to the concept; (3) have the child perform such an action at the educator's demand in a choice situation to determine the child's knowledge of the concept; and (4) ask the child to label objects appropriately while the educator performed a task related to the concept.

In the discovery group the tutors gave the same amount of individual attention during the instructional period but left the child to his own initiative for selecting activities. Although the same materials were available during the teaching periods and possible activities with the toys listed as in the more structured program, the instructor refrained from labeling and direct teaching. A list of toys used in the concept-training groups was posted weekly so that the same toys could be used from week to week in the discovery group. Procedures were suggested to the instructors of the discovery group for involving reluctant discovery children who did not take initiative in selecting their own activities. For example, the teacher was instructed to take out the puzzle and the pieces and hand them to the child, but to go no further. With regard to the use of Play Dough, the instructor was encouraged to open the box, take out one can of dough, and show the child how it could be molded. Blocks are a third example. The instructor was instructed to take out some blocks, informing the child that he was going to play with blocks, build a tower or a house and label it, without asking the child to use the blocks. The same group of instructors rotated in both programs and changed approximately every 3 weeks.

Early results indicated significant superiority of experimental subjects over control subjects on a number of measures of intellectual functioning both at the end of the 8-month experimental program and 1 year after the program ended. However, differences between the two experimental groups—that is, concept training versus discovery training—were minimal. After training, the experimental groups performed better than the control group on such tests as the Stanford-Binet Intelligence Test, language comprehension, perceptual discrimination, motor behavior, delayed reaction, and persistence at a boring task. When retested a year later the experimental groups maintained their superiority on all but four of the assessment measures. A comparison between the two experimental groups yielded significant superiority of the concept-training group only on a few measures—for example, the concept-familiarity index, which is highly loaded with items taught in the curriculum, motor performance, ability to follow instructions in sequence, and simple form discrimination. Palmer interpreted the comparable outcome of the concept-training and discovery groups as follows: (1) the 2-year-old is highly capable of learning a great deal with only 2 hours per week of instruction, but (2) what he is taught is not so important as the conditions under which he is taught, specifically, the nature of the adult-child relationship. In a later progress report, Palmer (1972) presented findings of follow-up testing of his experimental and control children at age 4 years, 8 months. The initial findings were essentially upheld on the battery as a whole. Middle-class children at that point definitely outperformed lower-class children. At that point, Palmer interpreted some trends in his findings as indicating that the discovery program might be more effective for younger children, while concept training might be more effective in older children—that is, children 3 years or older.

Palmer has recently resumed following his subjects (Palmer 1976). He has been able to retrieve for post-testing approximately 50% of his experimental subjects and 40% of his control subjects. The majority of these subjects had been tested on the Metropolitan Achievement Test while they were in the third and fourth grade and on the Stanford Achievement Test while they were in the fifth grade. By 1976 these subjects received Wechsler IQ Tests, administered by the staff of the project.

The results for the IQ testing were unequivocally positive. After a 10-year period the findings were the same as earlier, only stronger than they had been when the children had been tested at age 4 years, 8 months. Again both experimental groups were superior to the control groups but do not differ from one another. Time of training made no difference, and middle-class children were superior to both lower-class children and control children. When the Wechsler scales were broken down into verbal and performance scales, the analysis showed that the performance scale-measures contributed most to the differences between experimental and control children. While the difference between the type of training groups was not significant on the Wechsler Performance Scale Scores, the concept-training group, as earlier, was most superior to control children on these performance measures. It will be remembered that the concept-training group was originally superior to the discovery group on motor performance, ability to following instructions in sequence, and form discrimination. All of these skills are more emphasized on the Wechsler Performance Scales than on the Verbal Scales and may account for the fact that the prolonged and sustained effect of this concept-training program emerged most clearly on the Performance Scales of the Wechsler Test and not on the Verbal Scales.

The outcome of the analysis of the performance on the reading test is also positive, although less conclusive at this point in time. Unfortunately the school system changed tests so that the children were tested in the third and fourth grades with the Metropolitan Achievement Test but in the fifth grade with the Stanford Achievement Test. Thus the findings vary both as a function of age tested and as a function of the test used. This, however, does not destroy some uniformity in the findings. Both experimental groups were superior to the control group in the third and fourth grades and the concept-training group was superior to the control group in the fifth grade, although none of the differences were significant.

Palmer reasoned that his control group was affected by the Hawthorn effect, by repeated testing experiences, and by contact with the research staff. For these reasons he decided to select a new comparison group from the schools in which his subjects were enrolled in the fifth grade. The subjects of this new group were selected to be of the same social class background as his follow-up sample. This carefully selected group was more than 20 times as large as any of the original groups. Comparisons between the experimental groups and the comparison group failed to yield significant differences when each group was compared with one another. However, when comparisons were made on the basis of a number of children exceeding the norm on each of the two tests, significant differences emerged between several groups and the comparison group. Although there were still no differences between type and time of training and between each of these two conditions and the control group, significant differences emerged in that both the concept-training group and the group trained earlier were consistently superior in their performance to the children in the comparison group. Palmer makes a series of cautionary

statements concerning this tentative but promising finding, which resulted from the introduction of the new large comparison group. The study will continue with attempts to
retrieve more of the original subjects and to use a wider range, as well as more differentiated measures of cognitive and socioemotional development.

A major goal of pioneer group infant programs was to demonstrate that an infant will
not be harmed by spending some of his time away from his mother and home. This
explicit and often repeated objective was necessary because of the much-publicized
findings of mental and physical growth retardation of infants cared for in orphanages
(Goldfarb, 1943; Spitz 1945) These findings have led to public decrees and decisions to
eliminate infant group care wherever and whenever possible. Thus, it was necessary for
such pioneers as Caldwell and Richmond (1964) and Keister (1970) to formulate, as one
of the basic objectives of their undertaking, that group care for infants will not have
damaging effects on the infant when his development is compared to infants reared at
home. A second related objective was that educational group programs for infants will
provide supplemental services, not substitute mothering, and will support the parent-child
relationship in whatever way possible. The other objectives, especially with regard to
furthering the child's development, did not differ from those described for tutorial programs earlier in this chapter.

Caldwell's educational program and teaching techniques were dictated largely by two
concerns: first, with separating the child from his mother, and second, with the accepted
notion that infants benefit from a continued stable relationship with a nurturant adult.
Thus, careful safeguards were taken to insure that every child accepted into the program
maintained a continuing relationship with members of his own family so that he would
not experience identity confusion or question the relative status of family members and
educators in his life. Care was taken to provide the infants, especially those between 6 and
18 months, with organized routines similar to those they experienced at home. For the
youngest group an attempt was made to assign most of the care for a given child to the
same staff member throughout the day and week.

Special emphasis was placed on having the same person attend basic physical needs
such as feeding, putting the child to sleep, being there when the child awakened, and so
on. This emphasis required a ratio of approximately one adult to four infants. Beyond
object constancy there was also concern to provide concentrated individual contact between infant and adult by giving individual attention to each infant for at least 15 to 30 min
each day in the form of holding him, rocking him, taking him for a walk, playing
structured learning games, and so on. Regarding educational experiences, each daily
schedule contained some activities that were carefully planned by the teaching staff and
others that involved completely free selection of activity and expression of interest by the
children. As a result, alternating opportunities were provided for child and teacher in each
choice of activities and materials—reading books, labeling objects, playing sensory games,
and playing group games. An attempt was made to match teaching activities and experiences to the child's current level of cognitive organization as determined both by tests and
systematic observations of each child. Other concerns in the teaching program were to
minimize unnecessary restriction on early exploratory attempts—for example keeping
toys within the infant's reach or removing obstacles to exploration as much as possible.
In order to optimize the infant's perception and awareness of his surrounding objects,
furniture was occasionally moved to maintain the child's perceptual alertness to his
environment.

The groups consisted of 10 infants between 6 and 18 months of age and 15 infants between 18 and 36 months of age. Although the children were separated into age groups, the age separation was never rigid; and during each day planned opportunities were provided for contact between older and younger children. Attendance in the program varied from half days to full days, 5 days a week. Caldwell and Richmond (1964) have provided a careful chart for educational activities and routines in an infant nursery.

Finally, in order to maintain continuity between home and nursery, parent involvement included a brief orientation to infant development, monthly conferences with the staff, and social work as needed by the family. Volunteer positions in the center were offered to mothers as an opportunity to observe the staff as they cared for very young children, as well as an opportunity for the staff to learn about the mother-child relationships.

A comparison of mother-child attachment patterns in children attending the nursery and children reared at home revealed that children 30 to 36 months of age, following 1 year or more of participation in the program, did not differ significantly from comparably home-reared children (Caldwell et al., 1968). Age of entry in the program was not related to rated level of personal and social adjustment. These findings were interpreted by Caldwell as demonstrating that there was no negative effect associated with entering the nursery at an early age.

Caldwell (1970a) compared 23 infants who had received their primary care from their mothers and 18 infants who had attended the Children's Center between 12 and 30 months on their performance on the Cattell Infant Intelligence Scales. Although the home-reared infants were significantly superior at 12 months of age, the Center infants were slightly, but significantly, ahead at 30 months of age. The changed positions of the two groups were due to a decline in the Developmental Quotients of the home-reared infants and a simultaneous rise of Center-reared infants during the 18-month period between the first and second testing.

Caldwell also found that gains were not related to the child's sex, his ethnic background, or age at which he entered the program. At a later point Caldwell (1970b) compared children who entered the program before and after 3 years of age. Children who entered the program between 12 and 24 months of age ($n = 86$) showed an average gain of 14 points following approximately 2 years in the program. Children who entered the program after 3 years of age ($n = 22$) showed an average gain of 18 points following a year and a half in the program. Again, Caldwell failed to find a relationship between age of intervention and gain in IQ. Moreover, she also found that length of the program—that is, having entered the program a year earlier—did not result in superior performance on IQ tests.

Another study was carried out by Honig and Brill (1970) on 12-month-old infants who had participated in the program started by Caldwell and Richmond described above. This study investigated effects on the development of cognitive functions as defined by Piaget and measured by means of Piagetian Infancy Scales, specially constructed for the purpose of this study.

The sample consisted of 32 1-year-old Black infants from lower-class families. The 16 experimental infants attended either a morning or afternoon enrichment program for 6 months at the Syracuse University Children's Center. The 16 control group infants received no intervention.

The experimental infants performed significantly better on Piagetian Infancy Scales than the control infants. A more detailed analysis, however, revealed that the experimental infants performed significantly better only on two of the six Piagetian Scales, one of which was Object Permanence involving behavior such as finding an object after successive visible displacements and following an object through a series of increasingly invisible displacements. The second scale on which the experimental infants were significantly superior to the control infants dealt with developing means for achieving desired environmental ends. Specifically, this task involved the using of a stick to obtain a distant object. The particular contribution of this study was that it marked the beginning of the use of assessment procedures which fit into a theoretical system of cognitive development rather than the usual IQ assessment, which most other investigators working with very young infants have been forced to employ. The advantage of using the former is that it makes it possible to relate specific elements of the educational program to specific outcome variables in a systematic and theoretically meaningful way.

Keister (1970) also reported findings of no significant differences between children attending infant day-care and home-reared children. Saunders (1972) investigated the effects of infants attending the Keister Program on IQ and several socioemotional measures, such as fear of strangers, emotional upset related to eating and sleeping, and exploratory behavior. Saunders matched 12 pairs of infants aged 3 to 13 months and three pairs of infants aged 13 to 24 months for comparisons between children attending the Keister Program and control infants who had not attended any day-care center. The infants were matched on sex, race, parents' educational background and age, and birth order. Saunders found no significant differences on any of the measures mentioned between the infants attending the Keister Programs and the control infants.

Robinson and Robinson (1971) evaluated effects of the early Frank Porter Graham Child Development Center Infant Daycare Program. A comparison of 17 intervention and 11 control infants tested repeatedly with the Bayley Developmental Scales from 6 to 18 months yielded a significant difference in favor of the program children on the mental scales of the Bayley Developmental Test. It is interesting to note that the changes over time showed the same pattern that other investigators, such as Schaefer and Caldwell described earlier, have reported—namely, that the difference between experimental and control children was due in large part to a selective decline with age in the control infants. Comparisons of 4-year-old children who entered the program at 2 years of age yielded significant gains over control children. The investigators report that the most dramatic differences between these program and control children occurred among Black children. For example, Black children at the Center obtained a mean Stanford Binet of approximately 120, as opposed to the control Black children's mean IQ of approximately 86.

Finally, after Caldwell's and Saunders' studies of mother-child attachment in infants attending day-care and in home-reared infants, three other studies investigated effects of infant day-care on attachment and separation reactions in children. Kearsley et al. (1975) studied separation reactions in 24 day-care and 28 home-reared infants in a controlled experimental situation at 2-months intervals from 3½ and 13½ months of age and then again at 20 months of age. No differences were found between day-care and home-reared infants, and significant age differences were the same in both groups of infants.

Blehar (1974) investigated separation reactions in four groups of 10 2- and 3-year-old children, half of whom attended day-care while the other half were home-reared. Separation reactions were studied in an experimental control situation 4 months after the children entered day-care. Blehar found a strong interaction effect between age and day-care versus non-day-care. Children who entered day-care at 2 years of age did not differ in their separation reaction from home-reared 2-year-old children. Among the 4-year-olds separation reactions were significantly higher in the children attending day-care than in the non-day-care children. These findings could not be replicated in a study of 20 day-care children, carried out by Ragazin (1975). In terms of age differences, Ragazin's findings were opposite to those of Blehar in the same experimental situation. As in the case of home-reared children reported by other investigators, Ragazin found a higher incidence of separation reactions in 2-year-old than in 3-year-old children. In an analysis of separation reactions during arrival and reunion in the naturalistic day-care situation, Ragazin found no age differences between 2- and 3-year-olds.

Thus, we find that of five studies investigating effects of infant day-care on attachment and separation reactions, four studies show no differences between infants attending day-care and home-reared children. The fifth study, by Blehar, yielded equivocal findings which could not be replicated by Ragazin. Thus, the weight of the evidence clearly suggests that separation anxiety is not affected by infant day-care intervention, at least when the conditions of care are reasonably approximated for children attending day-care and children being reared exclusively at home.

CENTER-BASED PARENT-ORIENTED PROGRAMS

The next program to be discussed is a 2-year educational group intervention program with mothers by Karnes (1969) and Teska et al. (1970). A major goal of this program was to forestall developmental deficiencies characteristic of disadvantaged children at 3 and 4 years of age by training mothers of infants to be the primary intervention agent. Mothers were met weekly in groups and provided with a sequential education program. The mothers were helped to produce their own toys—for example, cutting out magazine pictures which the infant identified by naming and pointing, pasting these pictures in a scrapbook, and then occasionally reading the book to the infant. Other activities involved nested cans, snap beads, interlocking cubes of clay, and a form box with masonite shapes in various colors and sizes. Mothers were told to instruct their infants only when the infants were attentive. When the child did not want to carry out the activities the mother was instructed to put the toys away and wait until later. Activities were sequenced throughout the 2-year period. For example, matching skills acquired in object motor games during the 1st year were incorporated into classification activities during the 2nd year. Form perception introduced during the 1st year with the form box and the masonite shapes was reinforced the 2nd year with masonite templates.

A portion of each meeting was devoted to discussion which emphasized the need for a positive working relationship between mother and child and frequent use of positive reinforcement. An attempt was made to foster a sense of dignity and worth in the mother through the development of self-help capabilities, both in the family and in the community at large, and by discussions on birth control, community involvement, and so on. The mothers were divided into two groups and met weekly over a 7-month period for the 1st year and weekly over an 8-month period during the 2nd year. The staff workers made one or more monthly home visits to the experimental mothers.

The experimental group consisted of 20 mothers recruited primarily by community and staff referrals. Fifteen of these 20 mothers continued to the end of the 2nd year. Fourteen of the 15 mothers were Black. The average age of the infants at the onset of the program was 15 months. None of the experimental children had attended a day-care center prior to or during the 2-year study. The control group consisted of 15 infants who were selected from a larger study and matched with the experimental group on the basis of socioeconomic status, educational level, and size of family.

Comparisons between experimental and control groups were based on post-testing only. The Stanford-Binet and the Illinois Test of Psycholinguistic Abilities were used as measures. The children were approximately 38 months of age at the time of post-testing. The children who received intervention significantly exceeded the control-group children on the Stanford-Binet and on the Illinois Test of Psycholinguistic Abilities. A comparison of the experimental children with their older siblings showed that the experimental group exceeded their siblings on both the Stanford-Binet and on the Illinois Test of Psycholinguistic Abilities. Karnes points out that it is difficult to single out the component that might have been responsible for the improved functioning of the experimental children. Since the control-group mothers received no attention during the same period that the experimental mothers were in the training program, it is possible that some of the effects may have been due to the increased attention the mothers received and gave to their infants and some to the special activities and techniques that were devised for the experimental mother-infant pairs.

CENTER-BASED PARENT CHILD ORIENTED PROGRAMS

The Milwaukee Model*

One of the most ambitious mother-infant intervention programs was undertaken by Heber and Garber (1975). The overall goal of this study was to use family intervention in order to prevent cultural familial mental retardation. Heber undertook his study with 40 Black high-risk families in which the mothers had a Wechsler Adult Intelligence Scale IQ under 80 and a newborn infant. The program started when the infants were 3 months of age and continued until the children were 6 years old.

The goals of the program were to prepare mothers for employment opportunities and to improve their homemaking as well as child-rearing skills. For the children the goal was to provide an extremely intensive program which in conjunction with the maternal intervention program would enable them to develop normally so that they were ready to enter school at the age of 6 like children from nonretarded parents.

The program for the mother consisted of adult-education classes, which were to prepare the mothers for occupational training at a later point. The program emphasized basic skills of reading and arithmetic. Classes were conducted 5 days a week for 1 month before phase 2, the job training, was initiated. In phase 2 the mothers received vocational training 3 days a week for 6 months. To increase the effectiveness of this training each mother was paired with an experienced employee. Vocational training aimed at such professional positions as nursing assistant and dietary aid. Each day of training also included group counseling sessions for the mothers. A number of fathers (the exact number is not given) became actively involved in the program.

The infant program started for infants between 3 and 6 months of age. It was carried out on a 5-days-a-week basis during 12 months of the year. Although there were common elements with regard to the cognitive, language, and social curriculum, the program was adapted to individual children. All children received their learning activities in small steps

---

* The validity of Heber's findings have been questioned (Page, 1975). The major problems surrounding the study at present are that Heber has failed to respond to the request for raw data and technical details of the study. In the view of this writer the available material in published form is impressive even if Heber has been insufficiently careful in various phases of his work. The decision of this writer to report the study in spite of the serious criticism leveled at its validity is based on the hope that Heber will subject his data to public examination which will put his findings in proper perspective scientifically. However, caution is indicated in the evaluation of any conclusion drawn from Heber's reported study.

with an abundance of positive reinforcement, feedback, and support. The curriculum content concentrated on such aspects as perceptual, motor, cognitive, language, and socioemotional functioning.

The staff of the educational programs consisted of a director, a curriculum coordinator, a teacher supervisor, a parent supervisor, and a number of teachers. The teachers were for the most part para-professionals. Teacher-training programs that were carried out consisted of formal instruction, on-the-job training, and annual seminars.

Once a child entered the center program the relationship between teacher and child remained on a one-to-one basis, with each teacher caring consistently for the same infant. At the age of 15 months, two infants shared two teachers. At about 18 months all the same-age children were grouped together with three teachers in a transition program. The pre-school program began when the infants were about 20 months old. The nursery rooms were constructed to provide security, as well as opportunity for exploring novel objects. Novelty, however, was introduced gradually by presenting familiar objects in slightly different contexts. As the children developed concepts for classification, opportunities were created for them to use these concepts in problem-solving situations. Once the children entered pre-school the classrooms were constructed in such a way that each room contained three learning centers: one for language, one for reading, and one for solving problems. Each classroom also had an open area that was used for large group learning experiences and child-directed activities. Every child visited every teacher in her interest area. Learning periods were carefully planned and sequenced throughout the day. As already indicated, great care was taken to provide each child with many small-step success experiences.

Of the 40 families selected by Heber, half were assigned to the experimental and half to the control group. Heber has thus far reported only one situation in which maternal behavior was measured to assess the impact of the program on the mother. A Hess and Shipman situation for measuring maternal behavior was used. The mother was instructed to tell the child a story based on a picture, to teach a child a block-sorting task, and to copy three designs on a toy Etch-A-Sketch.

The first finding from this situation was that experimental dyads transmitted more information than control dyads. However, the source of this difference was not the mother but the child. Experimental children supplied more information verbally and initiated more verbal communication than did the control children. The experimental children structured the interaction either by questioning or teaching the mother. This qualitatively and quantitatively different behavior of the experimental children accounted for the faster and more successful problem-solving of the experimental children. These are the only data that have been reported so far on the impact of 6 years of working intensively with the mothers.

Extensive data have been reported on the physical and intellectual development of the children. With regard to physical development extensive data of medical, dental, and physical development from birth to 6 years of age showed no difference between experimental and control children.[3] The extensive data of intellectual functioning and learning reported by Heber for the children can only be highlighted and summarized here. Heber compared experimental and control children with regard to the centrality of various cues in problem-solving. He found that responding to position rather than to form and color, which is a developmentally more primitive response, characterized the control children much more than the experimental children. For example, during the 3rd year of life none

---

[3]This finding has been challenged by Page (1975).

of the control children demonstrated preferential responses to color and form, whereas 55% of the experimental children gave such evidence. This difference was maintained up to the 6th year of age. By contrast, when the children were between ages 5 and 6, only 20% of the experimentals showed position response as compared to nearly two-thirds of the control children. With regard to perseveration on problem-solving, between 50% and two-thirds of the control children gave such evidence compared to between 15 and 20% of the experimental children.

Measures of language development also yielded a striking difference between experimental and control children. At the age of 3 years children's replies were analyzed for omissions, substitutions, and additions. The experimental children were superior to control children on these measures at ages 3 and 4. On a test of grammatical comprehension (such as active and passive voices) the experimental group performed significantly superior to control children at all age levels tested—3, 4, and 5. In grammatical comprehension the experimental children were at least 1 year ahead of the control children. The Illinois Test of Psycholinguistic Abilities was administered at 51 months of age. The experimental group performed at a level equivalent to the test norms for children age 63 months while the control group performed at the 45-month level. There was an 18-month gap in favor of experimental children in psycholinguistic development.

With regard to IQ changes, the outcome of repeated testing from 6 to 22 months on the Gesell Scale showed that scores were roughly comparable for experimental and control children up to 14 months, with performance of all scales slightly in advance of test norms. At 22 months performance of experimental children was clearly accelerated, while control group performance was slightly at or below norms for the Gesell test. Seventeen of the experimental children and 18 of the original control children were available for testing at 66 months. Further data based on the Cattell and Binet Test Scores from 24 to 66 months yielded striking differences in the development of control and experimental children. The experimental group obtained an IQ of 122, while control children obtained an IQ of 91.

Heber also reported comparisons between IQ scores of siblings of children in the study between 36 and 66 months of age. The IQ scores of slightly older siblings of the experimental subjects received a mean IQ score of 79, which was similar to the mean IQ score of 77 obtained for siblings of the control children and to the mean IQ score of 83 obtained for control subjects. The mean IQ of the experimental subjects of the same age was 118.

Two conclusions can be drawn from these findings. The impact of the experimental program on the children has been striking and dramatic. However, both the data from the mother-child interaction study and the comparisons of the siblings of the experimental subjects with the experimental subjects show that the program did not affect the maternal functioning to an extent that it could be held responsible for the changes in the experimental children. Neither the maternal behavior in the mother-child interaction situation nor her effect on the slightly older sibling of the experimental child give any evidence of improved educational role-functioning of experimental mothers.

It is hoped that data were gathered on the social and emotional development of these children and will be analyzed and published at a later point.

PARENT-CHILD CENTERS

The Office of Economic Opportunity funded 36 community controlled parent-child centers in various parts of the United States in 1967. These centers were designed to provide services to low-income families of children under 3 years of age. The services were intended to be comprehensive, including health care, social services, and educational services. Some of these centers provided both center-based and home-visiting programs, others provided only center-based programs, while still others provided only home-visiting programs which emphasized education of the parents as the most salient way of improving child care and early childhood education.

Out of these centers emerged a small number of parent-child development centers that were to function as a national experiment in parent education and program replication (Robinson, 1975). The primary goal of three centers to be described here remained, as originally intended, to provide educational opportunities and supportive services for low-income families with children under 3 years of age. The three centers selected for this purpose are located in Birmingham, New Orleans and Houston.

Each of the three centers was to develop its own model of parent-infant education and to carry out both the development of the model and the evaluation of the effectiveness of its program over a 5-year period from 1970 to 1975. After successful completion of these two phases—that is, program development and evaluation—the experiment was to enter its second phase, which was to consist of replication of each of the models in other sites of the country. Apparently, the models met these criteria and the replication experiment was started in 1975 under the management organization of Bank Street College of Education in New York City.

Each of the centers have published information about goals, procedures, sampling, and at least initial findings of the evaluation of their effectiveness. The present discussion will limit itself to a presentation of these aspects of the three programs.

The three programs share certain common features but also differ in important ways. The common features can be summarized as follows: The programs focus on the mother-child and peer interaction during the first 3 years of a child's life. The mother is viewed as a primary target of the program because she is considered the most influential agent in the child's development. Every program offers a broad range of services to the families including health and social services, education about child development, knowledge of community resources, and other topics which will help the adults in the family, especially mothers, to become competent in various aspects of their lifes. Every program is inter-disciplinary. Development of the content of the program and of its staff are considered a central effort of each program. Although the staff is interdisciplinary and diversified, each program is concerned with selecting staff from the same culture and ethnic background as the participating families. In order to meet scientific criteria for evaluation of effective-ness, participants in each program were assigned randomly to program or control groups. The population of participating mothers and children was restricted to normal mothers with regard to their physical health and intellectual capacity and to children who were judged to be free of debilitating impairments or chronic illness at birth.

Important differences between the three centers can be summarized as follows: the ethnic backgrounds of the families served by each model; the location of the program—center-based or home-based; the relative concentration on mother and child; the age of the child at the time of entering the program; and the educational process. Two of the centers were sponsored by the Department of Psychology at universities and the third by a community agency.

The Houston Model

The major goal of this model is to increase such parental behaviors as warmth, autonomy-granting techniques, and encouragement of verbal skills. The goals for the child are the enhancement not only of cognitive abilities but also of self-esteem and emotional adjustment.

When the program child is 1 year of age the family is enrolled in a home program. Mother and child are visited in their home weekly for a year by a specially trained bilingual teacher who concentrates on attempting to help the mother become a more effective teacher of her child. The teacher involves the mother in interactions with her child on various tasks and builds upon the mother's strength by reinforcing them. The mother is encouraged to take on increasingly the role of the child's teacher while the home visitor takes on the role of the mother's consultant, sharing her knowledge of research and practice with the mother. The home-visitor attempts to help the mother examine critically her educational objectives for her child and the appropriateness of her child-rearing methods, (e.g., spanking, which occurs frequently in lower-class families) to reach such objectives. Alternative ways of reaching educational objectives are examined together by the home-visitor and the mother.

During the 1st year the entire family is encouraged to participate in workshops. About 10 families participate together in weekend workshops, which afford the opportunity to fathers, mothers, and children of various ages to interact together and separately, strengthening their skills of communication and decision-making.

During the 2nd year, when the child is 2 years of age, the program shifts to an in-center program. Mother and child attend together at first four and later two mornings a week. The separate program for mothers offers an opportunity for improving her child-development role and her home-management skills. Fathers and mothers attend biweekly evening discussions on topics related to home management and community issues. Micro-teaching is used as an important method for developing mother-child interaction. The videotapes are viewed by the mothers individually and by mothers as a group to foster objectivity, social insight, and communication.

Since this program serves Mexican-American parents, there is a strong emphasis on bilingual and bicultural needs of the families. Both the Spanish and English languages are cultivated. The children are offered sequenced toy activities in their home during the 1st year of the program, while the emphasis shifts toward language and concept training during the 2nd-year nursery program in the center.

The staff consists of both professionals and para-professionals with a predominance of Mexican-American backgrounds. A good deal of time is spent on planning, preparation, and scheduling. In-service training and attendance as well as participation in meetings of professional organizations are used to foster staff development.

The sample consists each year of a cohort of about 80 experimental and control subjects. About 80 experimental families are involved in the program at any one time, with another 80 in a control group receiving medical examination only.

This discussion of results is based on two reports (1973 and 1975) which offer results of analysis for cohorts 1, 4, and 5, but not 2 and 3.

The evaluation of the program concentrated on changes in mother-child interactions, in the home as a learning environment, and in the cognitive development of the children.

A structured situation was used to measure maternal behavior. Experimental mothers manifested significantly more change than control mothers in affection, praising the child, granting autonomy, using more reason and less criticism, and encouraging the child to verbalize.

Significant differences were found in greater change of the home as a learning environment in experimental families than control families, as measured by Caldwell's Home Inventory. The greatest differences were found in the "parent's provision of appropriate play-materials" and "the organization of the environment for the child."

The intellectual functioning of children changed significantly more in 1st- and 2nd-year experimental than in control subjects. Intellectual functioning was measured in 1st-year children—that is, the younger children—by the Bayley Mental Development Scales and in 2nd-year children by Stanford-Binet Scales. Changes on the Palmer Concept Index were significantly greater in experimental than control children for two cohorts but failed to yield such differences on two other cohorts. However, in no instance did the control children show a greater change than the experimental children.

In conclusion, in its evaluative phase this program has produced most evidence concerning its effect on parental functioning, particularly maternal behavior, and on the home as a learning environment. Unfortunately the impact of the program on the children has been assessed or reported to this point only for IQ change. The impact of the program on both parents and children has been appreciable and statistically significant in most of the reported comparisons between experimental and control groups.

The Birmingham Model

A major goal with regard to the mothers was to increase the mothers' active participation in the mothering role and to increase her facilitation of the child's use of materials. The program also attempted to change the mother's attitude toward herself and her competence in managing her daily life. To this end the program attempted to increase the mother's skills in obtaining and evaluating information, in planning her daily activities, expanding her social interactions, and increasing her communication skills. With regard to the children, major goals were to achieve greater self-sufficiency, social maturity through the development of language competence, intellectual abilities, and social abilities.

A unique aspect of this program is its reliance on learning through teaching or on the mother as a participating teacher. Teaching is used as a learning experience. All the teaching of children in this program is done by mothers, offering them an opportunity to practice what they learned and develop competence in themselves as teachers. A small professional staff offers in-service training for the more experienced mothers and continues consultation as they learn through practice. The program is entirely center-based and is organized into nurseries based on the age of the children: under 6 months of age, 6 to 18 months of age, and 18 to 36 months of age.

In nursery 1 the mother remains with her infant in the nursery. This arrangement is intended to strengthen the attachment and trust between infant and mother. The activities for the infants are orienting to and exploring sensory stimuli. Nursery 2 includes a wider age range—from 6 to 18 months—and therefore offers more modeling for younger children from older peers. This arrangement also offers mothers of younger children experience with older children. Mothers stay with their own children together in nursery 2 until they reach 12 months of age. At that point the mother moves out, entering a sequence of activities designed for the development of maternal and adult functioning, although she continues to visit her children daily. The 12-month-old child is expected to become more independent via secondary attachments that have been formed to other mothers. In nursery 2 activities are designed to increase the child's responsiveness to his environment, his manipulation skills, and his verbal control.

In nursery 3 children are taught by mothers other than their own. Again the older children are expected to function as models for the younger ones. The curriculum stresses self-awareness, development of skills, and concept development.

Depending on the mothers' interest and abilities and on Center needs, mothers are offered one of five different roles which they can assume: Participating Mother, Senior Participating Mother, Model Mother 1, Model Mother 2, and Senior Model Mother. The Participating Mother role extends into nursery 2. It consists of learning new mother-child transactions and in developing new transactions with other adults. Following her separation from her child, the mother is ready to change roles and titles. As a Senior Participating Mother she attends the center 5 half-days, developing skills in interviewing, planning, and teaching. After her apprenticeship, the Senior Participating Mother may change into Model Mother 1. In that role she works 5 days a week, 8 h each day. She may work in a nursery of her choice primarily with individual mothers. After at least 3 months of such experience the mother may change to serve in the fourth role of Model Mother 2. In that role both her pay and her responsibility increase. She now works with groups of mothers and mother-child pairs. In her fifth and highest role as Senior Model Mother, which is reserved only for exceptional Model Mother 2s, during the final 3 to 6 months in the program, the mother may carry out special tasks such as using videotape equipment or carrying out health-care education. Mothers are offered classes which enable them to obtain General Education Degrees or Red Cross certification. Certain services, such as dental and health care, lunch and breakfast, and health counseling, are made available to all mothers to decrease stress and facilitate change.

The findings of effects of the intervention are based on approximately 60 mother-child pairs over a period of 2 years of the program. Effects of the program on mothers were evaluated in terms of changes in information, in attitudes, and in behavior. With regard to increased functional information, it was found that more program mothers than control mothers obtained General Education Degrees and Red Cross first-aid certification. Changes in attitudes were assessed by means of the Parental Attitudes Research Instrument over the first 2 years of the program. Ten scales indicated more favorable change in program mothers than control mothers, while none of the scales indicated a greater change in the favorable direction for control mothers. Program mothers became more flexible and tolerant with regard to socialization and maturation pressure, less critical of their husbands, less power-oriented in relation to their parental role and their children, and less rigid and repressive in their attitudes toward nonsocial behavior and feelings in their children. With regard to changes in their behavior, mothers gave evidence of becoming more independent by moving out of the homes of their extended family into their own homes and making more use of community resources; they became less dependent on welfare enrollment than control mothers. In response to their work in the program for children, mothers exhibited higher incidents of social responsiveness and sensitivity to their children in play situations and in response to the child's reaction to brief separation.

Longitudinal data collected on the children yielded significantly higher increases in program children than in control children. This was found for infants from 4 to 22 months of age over a period of 18 months. Longitudinal data for older children assessed by means of the Stanford-Binet Test showed an increase in program children and a decrease in control children. The difference between the groups was statistically significant. Descriptive differences are reported with regard to exploratory and interactional behavior of program infants when compared with control infants. Vocalizing and smiling behavior occurred more frequently in program than in control infants. Duration of play with free available toys and talking while playing was also constantly higher in program infants. Program infants also manifested more age-appropriate attachment in separation behavior than control children—that is, program children between 7 and 12 months of age manifested greater search and protest behavior while program children around 24 months of age demonstrated greater tolerance of brief separations than control children.

To judge by the early results from this program, it appears that the careful planning of its sponsors and concentration on specific cognitive and socioemotional behaviors in parents and children are yielding promising results. The assessment of occupational, educational, and social changes in the parents, as well as intellectual and socioemotional changes in children, deserves special attention.

The New Orleans Model

The major goals and desired effects of the educational efforts for parents of this model were spelled out in considerable detail. The program aimed at giving parents an informational base about child development. It thereby hoped to change the parents' attitudes toward their child and their child-rearing practices in the direction of being both more supportive and more stimulating. The program worked toward developing parental capacities as teachers and parental attitudes toward a more active role in arranging their child's learning environment. The goals for children were broadly defined as increasing their emotional, social, and intellectual development as a direct result of changes brought about in their parents.

The program was primarily center-based. Home-visit mothers made biweekly home visits of about an hour each. Mothers and their infants came to the center two mornings a week for 3 h each. The program for mothers consisted of two components: child development and parent development. The child-development component was broken down into child-development discussion groups and a parent-child laboratory. Both were attended on the same program day. The child-development discussion group was designed to give mothers basic information on child development. It was led by a parent educator with a small group of 10 to 15 mothers. The program focused both on the content of development and on how the environment is to be structured to facilitate development. The laboratory was designed to allow parents to practice what they had learned. The laboratories were divided into three age groups: 2 months to 1 year, 1 to 2 years, and 2 to 3 years. There was also a pre-school program for siblings of the target child. These laboratories were staffed by parent educators. The child-development discussion groups and the laboratory were closely coordinated with one another. The parent-development component consisted of three content areas: maternal and child health education, social development education, and parent activities and home resources education.

The teaching techniques used with mothers encompassed modeling, demonstration, role-playing, group discussion, and direct teaching. Micro-teaching with the videotapes was employed to give the mother an opportunity to examine critically what she was doing. Games and puzzles were used to increase language skills. Most of the materials were developed by the staff and were sequenced to increase in difficulty as the mother's skill increased. Day-by-day suggestions for interacting with the child and a system for recording the child's behavior were supplied.

The staff consisted of a professional director, a registered nurse, an educational coordinator, and a social worker. Fourteen para-professional staff members were chosen from the same ethnic background as the participating mothers. Staff engaged in general staff meetings and in service training meetings, in addition to weekly discussions, preparation, scheduling, and so on. Staff also participated in meetings of professional organizations.

The population served consisted of 65 to 70 urban Black families. The mothers ranged from 17 to 35 years of age and children were enrolled from 2 months on. Parents were expected to stay in the program for 2 years. Three waves were taken into the program. The first two waves included 20 mothers, while the third wave included 25 to 30 mothers. Random assignment to control and experimental group was used in waves 2 and 3, while wave 1 was designated at a pilot group.

Evidence for the impact of the program on mothers was as follows: Measures were taken of mother-child interactions in unstructured observations in the center waiting room and at home. Data were available of these observations for waves 1 and 3 at 4 months, 12 months, and 24 months of approximately 10 mother-child pairs per group. At the 2-year testing the experimental group of wave 1 was found to be significantly more sensitive and accepting than control group mothers. At 12 months, wave 3 experimental mothers were found to be significantly more sensitive, accepting, and cooperative than wave 3 control group mothers. A second dimension of mother-child interaction dealt with the amount of language used by the mother. No significant differences were found between experimental and control mothers on this dimension. The third dimension dealt with length of utterances mothers expressed in their interaction with children. Experimental mothers from wave 1 expressed significantly longer sentences than control mothers from wave 1 at 2 years' testing time. The fourth dimension dealt with the amount of encouragement the mother gave to her child. Both wave 1 and wave 3 experimental mothers exceeded control mothers in this dimension, but the difference reached significance only for wave 3 mothers in their interaction with their 12-month-old infants. However, wave 1 experimental mothers exceeded wave 1 control mothers significantly in the more frequent use of positive language as a tool to alter the child's environment and differentiate objects in the environment while interacting with their 2-year-old children. This difference only approached significance in wave 3 mothers' use of language with their 12-month-old children. However, with regard to the general use of positive maternal techniques—that is, facilitating a child's perceived goal, positive reinforcement and affection rather than restriction, punishment, and other forms of negative reinforcement—wave 3 experimental mothers exceeded wave 3 control mothers significantly, while this difference only approached significance in the same direction in wave 1 mothers.

These findings suggest that length of experience of individual mothers with the program and accumulated experience of the program had the same effect on maternal behavior. Unfortunately, age of child remains confounded and its interaction with length of experience is as yet unclear in the reported findings. These are important dimensions, and it is hoped that their role in program effect will be clarified.

With regard to the program's effect on children it was found that experimental children from both waves 1 and 3 exceeded control children on sensorimotor competence measured by the Uzgiris-Hunt Scales. However, only program children of wave 1 exceeded their control peers on only one of the psychomotor scales of the Bayley Test. None of the other comparisons pointed toward significant effects of the program intervention. In conclusion, the findings point toward positive effects of this model on both parental and child behavior.

A PROGRAM COMPONENT STUDY

Positive effects of group-intervention programs for disadvantaged infants have been reported repeatedly. In these programs a vast portion of exerted effort has gone into stimulating the cognitive development of infants and assessing the effect of such stimulation on changes in IQ as well as in achievement skills. A number of important variables have not received the attention they deserve in these studies. One of the areas that has not received sufficient attention is variations in the style and technique of care and education and the relationships of such variations to socioemotional development of children. The realization of this gap has been a major reason for the undertaking of a study by the present writer (Beller et al., 1977). This study investigated two major areas of group intervention or infant day care for lower-class disadvantaged children under age 3. They were effects of age and social class grouping in infant day care on (1) adult-child and peer interaction and (2) developmental changes in trust and persistence, as well as in intellectual functioning of infants. Age and social-class grouping have been chosen as control variables because of the importance from educational planning, while trust and persistence have been selected as dependent measures because of their implication for socialization and for the development of achievement motivation and performance. Thus the major goal of the study was to investigate specific factors in early group-intervention programs for infants which might affect social interactions in the program and changes in socioemotional development of participating infants.

The trust and persistence study was carried out on 60 24-month-old lower-class, predominantly Black, infants participating in 10 infant day-care centers in Philadelphia and New York City. Four types of age and social-class grouping (i.e., mixed and homogeneous) were represented by these 10 centers. The children were pre- and post-tested for change over a period from 8- to 12-months' attendance in the day-care centers. Attrition was 40%, so that only 36 of the original 60 children were available for post-testing at the age of 36 months. Analysis of IQ scores and scores on trust and persistence in pretesting between dropouts and remaining subjects yielded no significant differences. For that reason the remaining sample was considered to be representative of the sample originally selected on the basis of matching subjects on age and sex.

Intellectual level was measured with the Bayley Infant Development Scales and with the Stanford-Binet Intelligence Test. Both trust and persistence were measured in structured situations. The trust situation consisted of a series of playful interactions between the infants and an unfamiliar person. The persistence situation consisted of five tasks of varying difficulty with extrinsic and intrinsic rewards. The scoring for both variables was carried out by trained observers in predetermined time samples behind one-way-vision screens. Because of unequal ns in cells, a modified analysis of covariants was used to determine pre-post change. The analysis yielded the following results: Children from a heterogeneous age grouping showed significantly greater increases of positive affect in the trust situation than children from a homogeneous age grouping. Children from a mixed social class grouping showed a significantly greater decrease in mistrust—that is, negative affect—and in uncooperative behavior when compared with children who had attended homogeneous all-lower-class infant day-care centers. The measure of body tension yielded no significant differences. Thus, heterogeneous age grouping and heterogeneous social-class grouping emerged as main effects in 1 year's experience of infant group day care on the development of trust in lower-class 2- to 3-year-old children.

The effects of age and social-class grouping on the development of task-oriented persistence were also significant in this group of children. Children adapted differently to solvable tasks with intrinsic rewards than to insolvable tasks with extrinsic rewards. Children from heterogeneous social class groups showed greater increase of persistence in task-oriented behavior when the task was solvable and offered intrinsic rewards. However, when confronted with an insolvable task of getting a candy out of a jar, which the children found could only be solved by the experimenter, the children from heterogeneous social class groups persisted less and withdrew earlier on repeated exposure (1 year later) than children from the all-lower-class group.

Mixed age grouping also had a positive effect on the development of persistence in these lower-class 2- to 3-year-old children. Children from the mixed age groups sought more direct help from the adult on the post-test of the insolvable task, whereas children from all-lower-class homogeneous age groups resorted to more indirect and less effective ways of seeking help during the task—that is, by glancing at the adult and manifested an increase in emotional involvement while perseverating in trying to get the candy out of the jar. Children from mixed age groups increased significantly more on intelligence tests than did children from homogeneous age groups.

An intensive observational study was carried out between pre- and post-testing in 8 of the 10 day-care centers in which the trust and persistence study was carried out. This was done to provide an empirical basis for the investigated changes in trust and persistence in children from intervention programs with different compositions of age and social class grouping. The subjects for this study were 80 2- and 3-year-old children (20 to 28 months and 32 to 40 months, respectively) from 14 classrooms cared for by 28 caregivers.

All observations were made in the child's normal day-care classroom in the morning, in a low-structured situation of free play and in a semistructured situation of organized activity or work. The observations were carried out by trained observers speaking into hand-held tape recorders while following the target-child to be close enough for hearing verbalizations and seeing gestures. An interaction category system was used to observe approach actions, in-contact actions, and terminating actions. Each subject was observed for five 2-min periods on 2 different days in each of the two situations. The dictated tapes were content-analyzed on the basis of 77 coding categories.

In addition to these 2-min time-sampling interactional observations, ratings were carried out separately by observers on two ½-h time samples on 2 different days in the same two situations as those in which the more detailed observations were carried out. Twenty rating scales were used for observation for the second data-collection, encompassing caregiver interaction with all children in her group. The interactional direct observations described earlier focused on the target child and its interactions with the adult caregiver and with peers. The teacher-rating scales dealt with educational techniques and social as well as emotional behaviors of the caregivers in their interactions with the children.

For present purposes the major findings from that observational study will only be summarized. The interactional observational study yielded the following statistically significant differences between heterogeneous and homogeneous groupings. Caregivers in heterogeneous social class groups were more facilitative toward their children and made more suggestions, while their children expressed needs more assertively and accepted adult initiations more readily than children in homogeneous (lower) social class groups. Adult caregivers in homogeneous lower social class groupings were more nonresponsive to children's expressed needs and requests, while their children were more passive-dependent in their interactive behavior with the adult caregiver. Adult caregivers in the heterogeneous age groups were more nurturant and employed modeling more often as a technique of teaching. The reciprocity of adult-child interaction emerged most clearly in the groups that were heterogeneous both with regard to age and social class. Both caregivers and children were responsive to each other's requests in this grouping, and children were least disruptive during organized play with one another.

The major findings from the analysis of the rating scale data obtained in ½-h observations of caregivers' interactions with all children were as follows: Caregivers in heterogeneous social class groups interacted more verbally, spent more time with their children in educational activities, and were more individual rather than group-oriented in their educational contacts with children. In contrast, caregivers in homogeneous social class groups spent more time in custodial care, exercised more direct control over their children, especially with regard to the use of materials, were more critical, and were more intrusive in their interactions with their children than caregivers in heterogeneous social class groups. A similar difference was found between heterogeneous and homogeneous age groups. Caregivers in heterogeneous age groups spent less time in custodial care and were less intrusive in their interactions with their children.

It can be seen from these findings from the two parallel studies in the same four environments that the observational study provided the empirical basis for interpreting the differential impact of different social class and age grouping on the socioemotional development of 2-year-old children with regard to trust and persistence. The development of trust was significantly greater in environments in which caregivers were most nurturant and responsive to requests of children. Conversely, trust developed least in environments in which the caregivers were nonresponsive to children and children passive-dependent in their reactions to caregivers. Persistence increased most in environments in which caregivers manifested facilitative behaviors, made suggestions to children during organized activities or work, spent more time with educational activities, and were more individual- rather than group-oriented in their contact with children. Conversely, persistence increased significantly less in groups in which caregivers spent more time in custodial activities, controlled children more in their use of material, and were more critical and intrusive.

DISCUSSION AND CONCLUSION

One major question that has prompted the initiation of infant-intervention programs has been whether the decline of cognitive and socioemotional development is the result of adverse experiences in childhood and whether it can be prevented or reversed. The impetus for the pioneer programs of infant day care was to investigate whether the child's separation from his family and his mother for a portion of a day several days a week would have adverse effects on the cognitive and social development of a child. At this point, with regard to intellectual and social development of the children, the evaluation of these programs leaves no doubt that no adverse effects result from the separation that occurs in the course of attending infant day care.

A further finding that emerged from the early intervention programs of Caldwell (1970) and of Robinson and Robinson (1971) was that the separation from the nuclear family or the mother affected neither middle- nor lower-class, neither white or black, children detrimentally. However, most disadvantaged children—that is, lower-class Black children—gained substantially from the infant intervention program.

The issue as to whether prevention referred to a lack of development from earliest infancy or a decline in development was answered by several studies. Schaefer (1972), Caldwell (1970), and Robinson and Robinson (1971) found that the continued superiority of children in the intervention programs was due to a decline in IQ of control children over time in contrast to a lack of decline or continued rise in the IQ of children who had received infant intervention programs. However, the prevention issue has only been barely touched on by the programs reported and reviewed in this chapter. The whole issue of deviant social and emotional development, which is at least as burning and as old as the issue of IQ or cognitive development, has not as yet been directly attacked through infant intervention as a mean of prevention. There is some evidence in this direction, but more as a side-effect than as the outcome of a direct focused effort.

Other major issues addressed by infant intervention programs are whether infants from lower-class educationally deprived families can be stimulated to develop faster and to a higher level than disadvantaged lower-class infants who do not experience such intervention, and whether intervention programs have short-time or lasting, immediate or delayed effects. Repeated evaluation of a number of programs provides very strong evidence for effective stimulation of intellectual development in the lower-class disadvantaged infants. The evidence is very strong for short-range, immediate effects within the first 3 years of life, when children in intervention programs are compared with controls who do not receive intervention or stimulation. The power of the evidence is not only derived from the fact that a number of disparate programs all produced the same effect but from the fact that the method of stimulation was often not closely aligned with the evaluation measure or the outcome measure. In spite of the fact that such a disparity between measures of stimulation and measures of outcome existed, the results are quite uniform in producing hypothesized effects for disadvantaged infants. The care taken in describing the stimulation provided to infants in the various programs discussed in this chapter should make it very evident that there was wide range of diversity in such stimulation from program to program. The fact that the outcome was consistently positive makes the findings under such conditions more impressive.

Effects of variations in the age of onset of treatment, length of treatment, and type of treatment are very difficult to evaluate at the present time. Research efforts to date in the field of infant intervention programs have not been numerous enough to yield accumulated evidence, which would be necessary to answer these questions. Age of intervention and length of intervention during the first 3 years of life are confounded in most instances so that answers to the separate questions are not yet possible. At the present time there is an indication that age of onset is not associated with effectiveness, while length of intervention does seem to be associated with more lasting effectiveness (Caldwell, 1970; Gordon, 1976; Levenstein, 1977).

The evidence concerning the effectiveness of different types of treatment is not yet sufficient to permit critical evaluation or generalization. One of the problems in dealing with this issue is the fact that in most instances type of treatment and amount of attention are confounded. Highly focused treatment is usually associated with more focused, intensive, and frequent attention. Even at that, the differential effect of highly focused and structured treatment versus a more broad-based, less focused treatment emerges only when the outcome measure is very closely tied to the training—for example, sequential problem-solving, involving performance or motor responses (Palmer 1972, 1976). When the transfer of such training to a broader level of cognitive functioning, as IQ tests measure, is considered, differential effects between different treatments disappear (Palmer, 1976). A close coordination between type of treatment and type of outcome measure is, as yet, altogether very rare. So we find for example that one investigator (Gordon, 1976) used a cognitive problem-solving training method involving Piagetian concepts but relied on general IQ tests and later on achievement tests for assessing the effectiveness of his intervention. Several intervention programs used essentially language training and communication as the major intervention method during infancy but measured the effect of their infant intervention on IQ tests, which were a mixture of verbal and performance items (Schaefer 1968; Levenstein 1970). One program used very specific outcome measures but the training was so comprehensive that it was impossible to relate specific type of training to specific outcome (Heber and Garber, 1975). Most infant intervention programs that are not essentially laboratory studies are too broad and comprehensive to justify an analysis of effects of different types of treatment on different types of outcome measures. However, it has been possible to evaluate effects of specific treatment dimensions within programs and measure their effect on specific social and emotional behavior of parents and children. Two approaches have proven fruitful in this respect. When the program focused on specific aspects of the mother-child or caregiver-child interaction and the outcome on the caregiver's or child's behavior was measured, effects of the intervention were found as predicted (Houston Model, Birmingham Model, New Orleans Model-parent-child centers; Gray, 1976). When the emphasis was on the parent or caregiver as the central but general target of the training without specifically formulated effects to be sought, the intervention yielded measurable effects on the children but not on the parent (Gordon, 1976; Levenstein, 1971). In some instances there was a detailed description of the intervention with the parent or the caregiver but no reported attempt of measuring the effect of such intervention on the target (Karnes, 1969; Heber and Garber, 1975).

A second approach to evaluating effects of program components or of specific types of treatment was illustrated in the study carried out by this writer (Beller et al., 1977). Specific aspects of grouping, such as age and social class mix, could be associated with caregiver-child interactions and with specific changes in socioemotional behaviors, such as trust and task persistence.

Another aspect of treatment that can be distinguished among the infant intervention programs that have been discussed is whether the intervention focused on the child or the parent, whether it was home-based or center-based, whether it focused on the individual child or parent, on both together, or in sequence. As far as infant intervention programs are concerned, especially the ones reviewed in the present chapter, it can be said that within the first 3 years of life a focus on the child or the parent, within the home or outside the home, has been equally effective. Even long-range follow-up of the few programs that have begun to report them show no differential effectiveness when length of intervention and time of intervention are controlled between programs (Palmer, 1976; Gordon, 1976; Levenstein, 1977). We shall return to this issue in the context of longitudinal follow-up. The most recent effort has been exerted on intervention programs which attempt to encompass the broader ecology of both infant and parent. This model is exemplified in the Parent Child Development Centers. These centers have been set up with specified treatment methods for parents and children at home and away from home with built-in evaluation over a 5-year period. Because of the successful outcome of these evaluations, replication efforts have been initiated. These centers have begun to publish the results of their evaluations and have contributed both the most comprehensive as well as the most specific evidence concerning the effectiveness of infant intervention programs to date. In the long run, these more complex models addressing the wider ecology of disadvantaged infants may prove to offer an opportunity for more valid investigations of some of the questions raised and discussed so far.

The question of short- versus long-term effects of infant intervention programs is very important and complex. To expect long-term effects of early infant intervention programs with regard to general intellectual performance is predicated on the assumption that cognitive ability is both changeable at an early age and perpetuated in a variety of ways once the change has been set into motion. Indeed, the first returns of the longitudinal investigations of infant interventions have yielded amazing results of persistent effects that have lasted close to a decade from infancy into the school years (Gordon, 1976; Levenstein, 1977; Palmer, 1976).

However, in spite of the persuasiveness of the argument, the evidence does not support the assumption that focusing on the parent as the change agent is responsible for the lasting effect of these infant intervention programs. Since these programs have not been able to attempt to trace the continued ecology of the developing and growing child from the time of infant intervention to the end of childhood, one simply has to conclude that they do not offer supportive evidence for differential effectiveness of focusing on the child or the parent at home or outside the home once length of intervention is controlled. Suggestive evidence exists from several studies (Heber and Garber, 1975; Beller, 1974) that the child plays a very active role in the reciprocal process which is set off by the intervention. Evidence in this direction makes it particularly important that greater emphasis be placed on assessing enduring effects on the motivational and socioemotional variables in the child to better understand the positive changes that have been set into motion by early intervention programs. Particularly important in this respect might be a greater concern with individual histories rather than sole reliance on averages which have value but fail to point up significant processes set off by early intervention programs. Breakdown of samples of children that received early intervention into gainers and losers, lasting changers and lasting nonchangers, might be particularly fruitful in leading to a better understanding as well as planning of early and continued intervention. Several such samples exist in the literature (Beller, 1974; Levenstein, 1977).

Considerable concern has been expressed about the efficacy of intervening prior to 18 months when the child begins to manifest accelerated language development. Existing evidence simply does not support or contradict this hypothesis. However, the view that intervention during the sensorimotor period is of questionable value because measures of intelligence during that period do not have high predictive value for performance on intelligence tests later in life has been advanced with special reference to Piaget. It seems that such a suggestion overlooks a central aspect of Piaget's theory—namely, that practice during the sensorimotor stage prepares the child for further development. It does this by alerting the child—looking in order to see, listening in order to hear. In short, Piaget has shown the way of understanding more fully the role of experience during the first 2 years of life. The fact that we have not yet fully grasped the links between central processes of cognitive development of the first 2 years of life to later phases of development does not justify negating the importance of providing stimulating experience to the infant. There is some evidence that the attitude of the adult environment of children under 2 years of age (Schaefer, 1968; Carew, 1975) and social motivational measures accompanying the Bayley Developmental Scales have more predictive value to later performance on intelligence tests than measures of test performance under age 2. Some of the evidence presented in this chapter (Heber and Garber, 1975) has shown that initiative and assertiveness of the children toward their caregivers was associated with intellectual gains. The present writer (Beller, 1974) has found that autonomous achievement-striving—readiness of disadvantaged children to seek help—was highly predictive of later academic performance. Such evidence points toward greater concern in studying the effects of early intervention programs on process variables, such as motivation to learn, decentering, attention span, assertiveness, and initiative in interaction with and utilization of the adult environment.

A paradox has arisen among some investigators whose early intervention programs have been surprisingly successful in producing long-range effects. When these long-range effects show up very clearly on general intelligence measures, one investigator tends to be almost apologetic, while another indicates that he is not continuing to use intelligence tests intentionally for longitudinal follow-up because a general measure of intelligence is not relevant to specific intervention. The emphasis is placed heavily on specific academic achievement skills and performance in school. Should infant intervention not account for the attitude and motivation to learn, while attainment of specific achievement skill in school is considered the result of the effectiveness of ongoing school experience? Without underestimating the importance of academic skills, one must ask whether they should be considered a more central and lasting factor in a person's enduring capacity to cope with life tasks than general intelligence as measured by an intelligence test.

This great emphasis on achievement skills by investigators who have initiated and conducted infant intervention programs in fact does represent a downward extension of elementary school, not only to pre-school but to infancy. We are again witnessing a historical lag. Elementary schools and high schools in many places have turned away from an emphasis on traditional skill orientation to an open classroom, and alternative schools, which aim at an individualized relationship between teacher and pupil, at stimulating an interest in learning, a capacity to explore independently based on intrinsic motivation rather than on external pressures and rewards. Yet, disadvantaged lower-class infants and pre-schoolers are being made to catch up with what middle-class elementary schools and high schools are turning away from. Intrinsic motivation to learn and ability to concentrate might be the variables to measure, as long-range effects; then the contribution of the child's ability and the contribution of the ongoing school will fall into perspective.

BIBLIOGRAPHY

Ainsworth, M. D. S. Patterns of attachment behaviour shown by the infant in interaction with his mother. *Merrill-Palmer Quarterly*, 1964, **10**, 51–58.

Andrews, S. R., Blumenthal, J. M., Bache III, W. L., and Wiener, G. The New Orleans Model: Parents as early childhood educators. Presented at the Society for Research in Child Development Meeting, Denver, Colorado April 1975.

Bell, R. Q. A reinterpretation of the direction of effects in studies of socialization. *Psychological Review*, 1968, **75**, 84–88.

Beller, E. K. Exploratory studies of dependency. *Transactions of the New York Academy of Science*, 1959, **21**, 414–426.

Beller, E. K. Research on organized programs for early education. In R. Travers (ed.), *Handbook of Research on Teaching*. Chicago: Rand-McNally, 1973.

Beller, E. K. Impact of early education on disadvantaged children. In S. Ryan (ed.), *A Report on Longitudinal Evaluations of Preschool Programs*. Washington, D.C.: Office of Child Development, 1974.

Beller, E. K. Environmental Reciprocity: A Social-Emotional View of Development. In *The Develop-*

ing Individual in a Changing World. Vol. II. Riegel, K. and Meacham, J. (eds.) The Hague Mouton Press, 1976.

Beller, E. K., Litwok, E., and Smolak, L. A study of infant daycare. Final report to the Office of Child Development. Washington, D.C.: USDHEW, 1977.

Blehar, M. C. Anxious attachment and defensive reactions associated with daycare. *Child Development*, 1974, **45**, 683–692.

Bloom, B. S. *Stability and Change in Human Characteristics*. New York: Wiley, 1964.

Bowlby, J. *Maternal Care and Mental Health*. Geneva: World Health Organization, 1951, 198, 199.

Bruner, J. *Processes of Cognitive Growth: Infancy*. Worcester, Mass.: Clark University, 1968.

Caldwell, B., and Richmond, J. B. Programmed day care for the very young child—A preliminary report. *Journal of Marriage and the Family,* 1964, **26**, 481–488.

Caldwell, B. Impact of interest in early cognitive stimulation. Paper presented at the meeting of the National Association for the Education of Young Children, Boston, 1970.

Casler, L. Maternal depriviation: A critical review of the literature. *Monographs of the Society for Research in Child Development,* 1961, **26** (ser. 80, No. 2).

Erikson, E. H. *Childhood and Society,* 2nd ed. New York: Norton, 1963, 97–98, 196–197, 226.

Goldfarb, W., The effects of early institutional care on adolescent personality. *Journal of Experimental Education,* 1943, **12**, 106–129.

Gordon, I. J. Early childhood stimulation through parent education. Final report to the Children's Bureau, Social and Rehabilitation Service, Department of Health, Education and Welfare, Gainesville, Fla., University of Florida, Institute for Development of Human Resources, 1969, ED 038 166.

Gordon, I. J. Infant intervention project: Progress report, 1972.

Gordon, I. J., and Guinagh, B. J. A home learning center approach to early stimulation. Final Report to the National Institute of Mental Health, Project No. R01 MH 16037–01. Gainesville: Institute for Development of Human Resources, University of Florida, 1974.

Gray, S. A report on a home-parent centered intervention program: Home visiting with mothers of toddlers and their siblings. DARCEE, Peabody College, 1976.

Gray, S. The Family-Oriented Home Visiting Program: A Longitudinal Study. Peabody College, 1977.

Guinagh, B. J., and Gordon, I. J. School performance as a function of early stimulation. Final Report to Office of Child Development, 1976.

Harlow, H. F. The nature of love. *American Psychologist,* 1958, **15**, 675–685.

Heber, R., and Garber, H. The Milwaukee Project: A study of the use of family intervention to prevent cultural-familial mental retardation. In B. Z. Friedländer, G. M. Sterrit, and G. E. Kirk (eds.), *Exceptional Infant*. New York: Brunner/Mazel, 1975.

Herman, S. J. The relationship between maternal variable scores and infant performance in a Negro experimental stimulation training population. Ph.D. dissertation, University of Florida. Ann Arbor, Mich.: University Microfilms, 1971, No. 71–16, 791.

Hess, E. H. Imprinting: An effect of early experience. *Science,* 1959b, **130**, 133–141.

Honig, A. S., Brill, S. A comparative analysis of the Piagetian development of twelve month old disadvantaged infants in an enrichment center with others not in such a center. Paper presented at the meeting of the American Psychological Association, Miami, 1970.

Hunt, J. Mc.V. The psychological basis for using preschool as an antidote for cultural deprivation. *Merrill-Palmer Quarterly,* 1964, **10**, 209–248.

Johnson, D. J., Leler, H., Rios, L., Brandt, L., Kahn, A. J., Mazeika, E. Frede, M., and Bisett, B. The Houston Parent-Child Development Center Model: A parent education program for

Mexican-American families. Presented at the 1973 annual meeting of the American Orthopsychiatric Association, New York. In *American Journal of Orthopsychiatry,* 1974, **44**, (1), 121–128.

Kagan, J. Do infants think? *Scientific American,* 1972, **226**, 74–82.

Karnes, M. B. Investigations of classroom and at-home interventions: Research and development program on preschool disadvantaged children. Final report, Bureau No. 5–1181, Bureau of Research, Office of Education, U.S. Department of Health, Education and Welfare, 1969.

Kearsley R. B., Zelazo, P. R., Kagan J., and Hartmann, R. Seperation protest in day care and home reared infants. *Pediatrics,* 1975, **55**, 171–175.

Keister, M. E. *The Good Life for Infants and Toddlers.* Washington, D.C.: National Association for the Education of Young Children, 1970.

Korner, A. F. Individual differences at birth: Implications for early experience and later development. *American Journal of Orthopsychiatry,* 1971, **41** (4), 608–619.

Lambie, D. Z., Bond, I. T., and Weikart, D. P. *Home Teaching with Mothers and Infants.* Ypsilanti, Mich.: High Scope Educational, 1974.

Lasater, T. M., Briggs, J., Malone, P., Gilliom, C. F., and Weisburg, P. The Birmingham Model for Parent Education. Presented at the biennial meeting of the Society for Research in Child Development, Denver, 1975.

Leler, H., Johnson, D. L., Kahn, A. J., Hines, R. P., and Torres, M. The Houston Model for Parent Education Model. Presented at the biennial meeting of the Society for Research in Child Development, Denver, 1975.

Levenstein, P. Mothers as early cognitive trainers: Guiding low income mothers to work with their preschoolers. Paper presented at the meeting of the Society for Research in Child Development, Minneapolis, April 1971.

Levenstein, P., and Levenstein, S. Fostering learning potential in preschoolers. *Social Casework,* 1971, **52**, 74–78.

Levenstein, P., and Sunley, R. M. Aiding cognitive growth in disadvantaged preschoolers: A progress report. Freeport, N.Y.: Mother-Child Home Program, Family Service Association of Nassau County, 1968.

Levy, D. M. *Maternal Overprotection.* New York: Columbia University, 1943b, 54.

Lorenz, K. Z. *King Solomon's Ring: A New Light on Animal Ways.* New York: Crowell, 1952, 204.

Madden, J., Levenstein, P., and Levenstein, S. Longitudinal IQ outcomes of the mother-child home program. Unpublished manuscript, 1977.

Osofsky, J. D. Children's influences upon parental behaviour: An attempt to define the relationship with the use of laboratory tasks. *Genetic Psychology Monographs,* 1971, **83**, 147–169.

Osofsky, J. D., and Danzger, B. Relationships between neonatal characteristics and mother-infant interaction. *Developmental Psychology,* 1974, **10**, 124–130.

Page, E. B. Miracle in Milwaukee: Raising the I.Q. In B. Z. Friedlander, G. M. Sterrit, and G. E. Kirk (eds.), *Exceptional Infant.* New York: Brunner/Mazel, 1975.

Palmer, F. H. Concept training curriculum for children aged two and three years old. Institute for Child Development and Experimental Education, the City University of New York, 1968.

Palmer, F. H. Children under three—Finding ways to stimulate development: II. Some current experiments: Learning at two. *Children,* 1969, **16**, 55–57.

Palmer, F. H. Minimal interaction at age two and three and subsequent intellectual changes. In R. K. Parker (ed.), *The Preschool in Action.* Boston: Allyn & Bacon, 1972, 437–465.

Palmer, F. H. The effects of minimal early intervention on subsequent I.Q. scores and reading achievement. Research Report for the Educational Commission of the States, 1976.

Piaget, J. *The Origins of Intelligence in Children.* New York: International Universities, 1952, 69, 75, 165.

Ragozin, A. Attachment in daycare children: Field and laboratory findings. Presented at the meetings of the Society for Research in Child Development, Denver, 1975.

Rheingold, H. L. The modification of social responsiveness in institutional babies. *Monographs of the Society for Research in Child Development,* 1956, **21**, (Series No. 63).

Robinson, M. E. The parent child development centers: An experiment in R & D strategy. Presented at the biennial meeting of the Society for Research in Child Development, Denver, 1975.

Robinson H. R., and Robinson, N. M. Longitudinal development of very young children in a comprehensive day care program: The first two years. *Child Development,* 1971, **42**, 1673–1683.

Saunders, M. M. Some aspects of the effects of day care on infants' emotional and personality development, ERIC 1972.

Schaefer, E. S. Progress report: Intellectual stimulation of culturally deprived parents. National Institute of Mental Health, 1968.

Schaefer, E. S., and Aaronson, M. Infant education research project: Implementation and implications of the home-tutoring programm In R. K. Parker (ed.), *The Preschool in Action.* Boston: Allyn & Bacon, 1972, 410–436.

Scott, G., and Lally, J. R. A comparison of the scores of trained and untrained environmentally deprived male and female infants on the Griffith's Mental Development Scale. In I. Gordon (ed.), *Reaching the Child through Parent Education, the Florida Approach.* Gainsville, Fla.: University of Florida, Institute for Development of Human Resources, 1969, 57–67.

Skeels, H. M., and Dye, H. B. A study of the effects of differential stimulation on mentally retarded children. *Proceedings of the American Association of Mental Defectives,* 1939, **44**, 114.

Skeels, H. M. Adult status of children with contrasting early life experiences. *Monographs of the Society for Research in Child Development,* 1966, **31** (3, whole No. 105).

Spitz, R. A., Hospitalism. *Psychoanalytic Study of the Child,* 1945, **1**, 53–74.

Spitz, R. A. Anxiety in infancy: A study of its manifestations in the first year of life. *International Journal of Psycho-Analysis,* 1950, **31**, 138–143.

Tinbergen, N. *The Study of Instinct.* London: Oxford University, 1951.

Watson, G. Some personality differences in children related to strict or permissive parental discipline. *Journal of Psychology,* 1957, **44**, 227–249.

Winterbottom, M. R. The relation of need for achievement to learning experiences in independence and mastery. In J. W. Atkinson (ed.), *Motives in Fantasy, Action and Society.* Princeton: Van Nostrand, 1958, 406–407.

Yarrow, L. J. Research in dimensions of early maternal care. Merrill-*Palmer Quarterly,* 1963, **8**, 101–114.

Conclusion

CHAPTER 28

Historical Perspectives and Future Directions in Infant Development[1]

Leon J. Yarrow

Our historical perspectives on infant development are surely a product of our professional rearing and our unique experiences in the field. The issues that we see as important and our view of their historical antecedents are necessarily selective. At the present time there are a number of issues at the forefront of infancy research. No one of these issues is completely new; they have a long history, but the formulations of these problems have evolved. They have become more differentiated and more precise. As researchers have come to recognize human complexity in a multidimensional world, the problems studied have become less academic and more relevant to social policy questions. In the last 20 years the great advances in our knowledge of infant development have contributed to a changed view of the infant. This change has not come about simply by the accumulation of new data; it reflects a willingness to see the young organism in new perspectives, perspectives to which we previously were insensitive or unconsciously closed off. For a long time, we clung tenaciously to the conception of the infant as a helpless, completely dependent organism, little more than a bundle of isolated reflexes; now we have come to see the young infant as an active, striving being who elicits and modulates stimulation and has an effect on its environment. Our theoretical thinking about the infant has also advanced. In the past our conceptualizations consisted of isolated hypotheses only loosely related to each other; now there seems to be some progress toward a more integrated theory of early development.

There are five major issues in infant development which will be addressed in this chapter:

1. The radical change in our view of the infant, from a completely helpless organism to one with many competencies

2. A revision of the concept of early experience and its effects on development

3. The changing perspectives on the special relationship between the infant and caregiver

4. The shift in our view of cognitive development—a change to a more complex and more differentiated view which recognizes the interdependence of emotional, personality, and motivational functions

[1] I am indebted to Dr. Frank Pedersen, Dr. Peter Vietze, and Dr. Robert Klein for their many suggestions and constructive critique.

5. The increasing emphasis on the ecological context of development, on the importance of studying development in the natural environment rather than in contrived experimental situations.

If we look back at the major controversies in the history of infant psychology, it is clear that many of these controversial issues were also the dominant theoretical concerns of the larger field of psychology—for example, the role of early experience, nature-nurture, experimental versus naturalistic contexts for research. Curiously, this was the case despite the fact that for many years child psychology had low status in the discipline. Many of these research issues had political-ideological overtones; they were linked to the concerns of the times and to specific social programs—for example, the development of pre-school education, placement in child care institutions, adoption and foster care policies, intervention programs for disadvantaged children, day care for children of working mothers. Research on these issues had a cyclical course: some were dominant concerns for a number of years, then attention shifted to other issues. Although it would be intellectually satisfying to be able to point to a single cause for the shifting dominance of particular themes, it is probable that there were multiple determinants. The scientific issues with which research in infant development was concerned were never based completely on purely theoretical formulations; they always represented an interplay between conceptual considerations, technological and methodological advances, the social concerns of the time, and the broader philosophical *Zeitgeist*. In the discussion that follows we shall consider each of these themes separately, but with constant awareness of their interrelations. We shall try to describe the interaction among these factors and their influence on research in infant development. Finally, we shall comment upon the implications of research on infants for social policy.

INFANT COMPETENCE

Although the research in the 1930s and 1940s described in great detail the infant's responsiveness to auditory and visual stimuli, responsiveness to people, and learning capacities, there was a stereotype of the infant which persisted despite the evidence. The young infant was still seen as an unaware, unresponsive, essentially helpless organism, buffeted by random stimuli. In the past decade, this view of the infant has changed dramatically. It is now recognized that the infant is much more complex and has many more competencies than were assumed in the past. The infant is seen as an active organism who influences people by eliciting stimulation from caregivers, and who affects the inanimate environment by manipulating objects and obtaining feedback from potentially responsive materials. This view of infant competence has had many important repercussions. One of the more significant of these has been a shift from a dichotomous view of the infant and the environment to one that conceptualizes the infant and environment as an interactive system of mutual influences. The notion of the dynamic interplay between infant and environment would not have evolved had we not recognized these early competencies.

One consequence of this view of infant competence has been a revival of interest in the study of infant temperament. Philosophical discussion of temperamental differences goes back to ancient times, but new attempts to measure infant temperament give promise of throwing light on how these early differences influence the infant's interactions with people and objects in the environment (Brazelton, 1973; Thomas et al., 1963; Berger and

Passingham, 1973). Studies of infant temperament have not established any simple continuity over time in these characteristics; in fact, on some measures like vigor of responsiveness there even seem to be reversals—that is, there is a significant negative relationship between what is apparently the same characteristic at two ages (Bell et al., 1971). On the other hand, some investigators (Rutter et al., 1964) report some predictability of later behavioral difficulties from early reports of infant temperamental characteristics.

Recognition that the very young infant shows competence has led to an uneasiness about our traditional view of competence as indexed simply by intellectual functioning. Increasingly, we are attempting to conceptualize and to measure other aspects of the infant's functioning—persistence on difficult tasks, attempts to secure feedback from objects, goal-directed behavior in practicing emerging skills (White, 1959; Wenar, 1976; Yarrow et al., 1977; Yarrow and Pedersen, 1976), as well as his ability to take the initiative in social interactions and influence his caregivers and siblings (Wenar, 1976). Moreover, inherent in the notion of competence is the idea that cognitive, motivational, and social behaviors are inextricably linked, a view that gives more than token respect to the concept of the whole organism. In our own recent studies we have identified some behaviors at 6 months of age which we think index such important but elusive concepts as goal-directedness (Yarrow et al., 1975b).

The growing commitment to the notion of reciprocal interactions between the infant and his environment is also resulting in a change in approaches to studying the environment. Interactive categories such as mutual regard, contingent response to infant vocalization, and contingent response to the infant's distress signals have been used (Yarrow et al., 1975b). While these categories represent an advance over our earlier unidirectional codes and are useful for answering some kinds of questions, they deal only with the elements of the parent-infant exchange. Strategies for sequential recording of parent-infant interaction overcome, to some extent, the limitations of this type of category and give us more direct information about the process of interaction. Recording instruments such as the Datamyte, which facilitate interactive recording, are increasingly available and should expedite the analysis of interaction. There are, however, many methodological and conceptual problems which need to be recognized and addressed (Yarrow and Anderson, 1978; Bakeman and Brown, 1977) before the potentialities of sequential recording and interactive analysis can be fully realized.

EARLY EXPERIENCE

The role of early experience in later development has been a theme of philosophical discourse since antiquity. This problem, first discussed by Plato, was resurrected at the time of the Enlightenment in the 17th century. It is an intrinsic part of the ancient and never-ending debate on the relative importance of heredity and environment. It is reflected in the intriguing tales of the wolf children and was revived in the sharp controversy on the origins of the intelligence quotient; moreover, it is the background for the long tradition of learning research.

Early experience, like many controversial issues in developmental psychology, has always had ideological overtones. There exist simultaneously apparent ideological contradictions. On the one hand, there is the basic belief that in a democratic society, each individual should have an equal chance. Implicit in this belief is the assumption that everyone begins life with a clean slate on which experience makes its imprint. On the other hand, we know there are great individual differences even at birth, and there is a conviction that each individual's uniqueness should be respected. These views, however, are only contradictory on the surface. In recent years, recognition of differences in functioning associated with inequalities in opportunities for even very young children has resulted in intervention programs to provide special experiences for the "underprivileged." There are sharply contradictory interpretations of the outcomes of these intervention programs. Certainly the findings are not clear-cut and indeed, the same results are open to different interpretations. The equivocal findings of these studies have led to further questioning of the significance of early experience, and the role of heredity and environment. Some investigators see these results as supporting their views of the malleability of the organism; others see them as supporting a genetic interpretation.

Throughout modern history, the environmental and the hereditarian views have been on a perpetual seesaw, one gaining the ascendancy, then the other, with an insistent regularity. Sometimes in the heat of controversy, views have been polarized. Some held the inflexible position that environmental influences were all-important, others, that the genes were completely decisive in determining differences in intelligence or personality. In time, the formulations have become more sophisticated, the variables to be studied have been sharpened, and the designs refined. At present, most researchers acknowledge some contribution from both heredity and environment, with differences in emphasis on the relative importance of one or the other depending in part upon the specific behaviors being studied.

In the early years of the 20th century the role of early experience had its strongest emphasis and most convincing formulation in psychoanalytic theory. On the one hand, it was natural that a doctrine based on the retrospective reconstructions of psychologically troubled individuals might dogmatically attribute overriding importance to the early years and should be essentially pessimistic about the prospects of reversing or undoing the effects. On the other hand, it is curious that a therapeutic system should have been built on such a foundation. It is easy to assume that psychoanalytic theory was *the* major stimulus to research on infancy and the study of the impact of early experiences. But this is too simple a view, for there were many converging influences. The descriptive research on the normative characteristics of infants, which dominated work in the 1920s and 1930s, was significantly influenced by developmental biology as well as the more practical concerns of pediatrics. One can, however, identify a substantial amount of research carried out in the 1940s and 1950s that directly or indirectly was influenced by psychoanalysis. Sears' (1943) monograph reviewing the research evidence for the major psychoanalytic formulations pointed to the tenuous evidence for many of the analytic hypotheses. His careful review of the literature also dramatized the inadequacy of the research—the use of very simple designs to test very complex hypotheses. This review was a stimulus to more thoughtful approaches to studying some of the basic tenets of psychoanalytic theory. The research of Katherine Wolf (1953), John Benjamin (1959, 1963), Sibylle Escalona (1968) and Rene Spitz (Spitz et al., 1970) approached some of these problems from a psychoanalytic perspective, but in a much more sophisticated, though by necessity indirect, way. Recognizing the complexity of the questions posed, they did not attempt to obtain simple answers by a frontal approach, and they never lost sight of the whole child. They were among the earliest investigators with a psychoanalytic orientation who studied early experiences prospectively from infancy rather than retrospectively from the recollections of adults.

One facet of the early experience controversy is the question of its decisiveness—that is, the extent to which experiences early in life have permanent effects. The research in the past quarter of a century does not offer simple support for the extreme claims that early experience is decisive for later development, and that its effects are irreversible. These newer studies, however, like the earlier ones from which conclusions about irreversibility were drawn, also have limitations in basic design and methodology. Therefore, it is no more defensible to dismiss summarily the proposition that early experiences have effects than to accept it. It is likely that experiences early in life affect the young, vulnerable organism and these effects may be pervasive and long-term, but not in the simple sense— that is, that the organism is unalterably damaged or influenced by a single event. Rather, there may be a series of interactions—certain experiences predispose the organism to behave in ways that elicit reinforcing responses. Thus, some events may set in motion a cyclical pattern of interactions. This view seems more reasonable than accepting the inevitability of damage and the impossibility of reversing effects.

It seems clear that there are cumulative effects of traumatic or depriving experiences. The research documents that children who very early experience extreme deprivation which continues into early childhood and sometimes even to adolescence, tend to be damaged. At the same time, there is evidence that those who experience deprived or traumatic experiences in infancy, but are then moved to better environments, do not show gross disturbances or impairments later in life. These data seem to offer evidence for the resiliency of the organism. However, the issue is not so easily resolved. It is not known, for instance, whether those children who experience early trauma or were deprived of adequate stimulation are more vulnerable to disruptive experiences later in life, whether they have a lower threshold for future disturbances. Some psychodynamically oriented clinicians would claim that such is the case, and point to individual examples, but there are no unequivocal research findings on this significant question.

There is no doubt that in calling attention to maternal deprivation and the possibilities of its enduring consequences, Bowlby (1951) articulated the dormant fears and activated the consciences of social workers, psychologists, and psychiatrists. His work led to significant revisions in many social policies, not only with regard to institutionalization but in hospital practices with children and in policies of social agencies regarding the age of adoption. There is no question that most of these revisions were to the benefit of children and their families. They were salutary for research as well. The forceful statement of the issues stimulated research not only on the effects of separation but on attachment and many other issues of early experience.

Not too many years after his influential review, Bowlby recognized the extreme views that had developed as a result of inadequate interpretation of his writings. He cautioned that "some workers who first drew attention to the dangers of maternal deprivation . . . have tended on occasion to overstate their case" (Bowlby et al., 1956).

Certainly the view that any single experience is likely to lead to irreversible damage is a belief that is no longer tenable. For a long time single causes have been rejected as too simplistic. There is recognition that almost any kind of outcome is a product of multiple influences, some of which facilitate or exacerbate the action of a given influence and others which attenuate, modify, or soften its influence. This is a basic and difficult question on which more definitive data are needed. It is especially important to try to understand the process by which several influences act in harmony or in opposition to each other. There are research designs and statistical techniques that allow one to tease out the relative contributions of multiple sources of influence on a variable (Duncan, 1966; Li, 1977). One must, however, have a meaningful conceptual basis for applying these statistical methods and for interpreting the data. One should not use multivariate statistics without at least trying to understand the *process* underlying the relationships among the variables.

We have not always been clear about the criteria on the basis of which to define effects, neither the depth nor the permanence of effects. Perhaps a psychoanalyst, using depth interviews, can find residues of earlier trauma, but outwardly the person may be functioning essentially normally. Should these residues expressed symbolically or in other indirect forms and uncovered only by intensive probing be accepted as evidence for the effects of early experience? Or should we restrict our criteria to unambiguous overt behaviors, or to easily recognizable changes in the child's functioning? At some point, we must be willing to give up asking simple questions on issues such as these and to understand that there can only be partial or relativistic answers; ultimately we may be able to deal with the more complex questions.

The impact of early experience and issues of personality continuity have become linked. They are not identical problems, nor are they completely independent of each other. There are several facets to the problem of continuity. First, there is the question of whether there is simple stability in overt characteristics over time. Second, there is the problem of whether there are predictable transformations in characteristics at later developmental periods. Third, there is the question of whether there are consistencies in how a child is perceived—for example, parents and peers see a persisting core of similarity. Fourth, there is the question of whether there is consistency in structure associated with idiosyncratic perceptions of the environment, through individualized ways of organizing experiences, and through distinctive self-regulatory systems. Finally, there is the question of whether there is stability over time in a person's own self-image.

The assumption that early experience has effects does not rest on the validity of the assumption of a simple consistency in behaviors over time. If we accept an interactional view, it follows that an individual's characteristics at any given time will have a significant influence on his experiences. Even if the organism is changing constantly in the course of development, if there is no simple consistency in personality or intellectual characteristics, the infant is probably seen by his caregiver as having a stable core of individuality. The caregiver's behavior towards the infant may be in response to this more or less stable image, thus resulting in some consistency in the infant's experience.

Research on early experience is being pushed back to earlier periods of development, even to the prenatal period. There are many ramifications. First, there is the question of the impact on the developing fetus of the mother's psychological adaptation during the changing periods of pregnancy. The question becomes one of how the mother's changing emotional states are communicated to the fetus and whether they have any long-term impact. Another question is concerned with the influence of the mother's adjustment during pregnancy on the course of labor and delivery. The third question deals with the effects of variations in the labor and delivery process on the initial adaptation of the neonate and whether there are any long-range effects. And finally, we have the question of how the experiences of the mother and father during pregnancy, labor, and delivery influence both their perceptions of the infant and their parental behavior. These aspects of early experience have generally been ignored until very recently, but there are beginnings of systematic studies with designs that do justice to the complexity of the problem (Sameroff and Chandler, 1975; Shereshefsky and Yarrow, 1973; Wenner et al., 1969; Yarrow et al., 1974).

In the past there has been a tendency to equate early experience with mother-infant interaction. The narrowness of this view is becoming evident. Research on early experience is slowly moving beyond the closed circle of mother and infant to the larger environment, to include the father, siblings, and peers (Parke, Chapter 15; Lamb, 1977; Pedersen et al., 1975). As yet this research represents only a small start in the study of the larger environment of the infant. We are just beginning to develop a conceptual framework in which to formulate research questions regarding the father's influence as a direct stimulus, as an influence mediating the mother's behavior, and as a member of the three-person system: the father-infant-mother triad.

We should not accept either of the extreme positions—that is, that early experience has no impact whatsoever or that it is so decisive that it inevitably structures later behavior so that there can be no modifications by subsequent events. We need more precise questions about the specific conditions under which certain events may have profound effects and the conditions under which the same events may have no or only transient effects. The impact of early experience remains a very vital issue in infant research. The accumulating evidence has answered some questions, but at the same time it has raised many more questions which are both subtle and complex.

ATTACHMENT

A direct offshoot of the findings on maternal deprivation is the research on attachment (Maccoby and Masters, 1970). In the past decade there has been a tremendous amount of research on this issue. The growth of significant interpersonal relationships is clearly one of the most important developments during the 1st year of life, inasmuch as the first relationship is thought to serve as the prototype for all later relationships.

Psychoanalytic theorizing about the development of object relationships is based on the principle of secondary reinforcement in learning theory. The mother or caretaker becomes the infant's first love object—that is, the person toward whom intense positive feelings and dependency develop as a result of associations with the gratification of basic instinctual needs. There are several learning-theory formulations of the conditions underlying the development of dependency on the mother. The one enunciated by Sears et al. (1953) is essentially similar to the psychoanalytic formulation. Another (Gewirtz, 1972), based on operant learning principles, holds that the mother's smiles and vocalizations act as generalized conditioned reinforcers which are contingent on the infant's behavior. In turn, the infant's smiles, vocalizations, and approach movements are strengthened by these contingent responses. Another learning approach (Cairns, 1972) maintains that the mothers's presence by itself is a reinforcer of the infant's response and, conversely, the infant's proximity is a reinforcer of the mother, with the result that conditioning begins soon after birth.

Bowlby (1969) rejected the secondary reinforcement interpretation of the development of "dependency" in favor of an ethological view. He used the term "attachment" to refer to certain built-in behaviors of the infant — for example, smiling, clinging, and following, which elicit nurturance from the mother and maintain the infant in close physical contact with her. These behaviors in time become part of complex feedback systems which regulate the child's subsequent behaviors. The research on attachment, which was stimulated by this formulation, has yielded some important findings (Ainsworth, 1973), but it has been constricted by an almost standardized methodology.

We (Yarrow, 1967, 1972; Yarrow and Pedersen, 1972) have pointed out some of the limitations of the concept of attachment and the simple measures that have been used to study it. Over the past 10 years there have been many studies of simple variations in the infant's response to a stranger in the presence or absence of the mother, of the young child's response to the mother's leaving briefly in an unfamiliar setting, and the child's behavior when "reunited with" the mother. We have suggested that it might be clarifying to view attachment from a developmental perspective as part of a chain of cognitive and social developmental changes. Attachment can be seen as an organizing concept that indexes a broad range of behaviors which extend across a wide developmental time span. It is probably linked closely to other aspects of early social development, beginning with the establishment of boundaries between the self and the environment. In the process of externalizing the environment, the infant develops a rudimentary concept of separateness and learns to discriminate people from inanimate objects. The distinction between animate and inanimate objects is followed by discrimination of the familiar caregiver, usually the mother, from other people. Through exposure to the varied behaviors of the mother in a variety of situations, the infant acquires an elaborated concept of her and develops specific expectations of her. This stage, in turn, is followed by a higher level of relationship with the mother, characterized by the development of trust, a sense of confidence that the mother will be there and will gratify needs for food or comfort.

Viewed from this perspective, further research is needed to delineate sensitively the behaviors that index such diverse but related developments as the recognition of boundaries between one's body and the outside world, the externalization of the environment, the differentiation of human beings from inanimate objects, and discrimination of the familiar caregiver from other people. These behaviors are not simply indexed by fear of strangers; we need measures of the infant's positive responses to familiar persons in order to index the development of a focused relationship with the mother. The development of specific expectations of the mother and the growth of feelings of trust in her are especially difficult concepts to measure in the preverbal infant. Considerable ingenuity will be required to document the overt and subtle behavioral indicators. Moreover, we still know very little about the environmental antecedents of these behaviors. We do not know the extent to which these behaviors and feelings are influenced by maturation and the extent to which they are shaped by the environment. An obvious next step in research is to study how variations in experience are associated with variations in the development of positive behaviors and feelings of affection and trust. We know only in a gross sense that extreme deprivation or insensitive handling come to be associated with deficiencies in these characteristics and eventuate in an apparent inability to establish focused relationships, but we know little about the antecedents of variations in these characteristics within a normal range.

It is likely that these social-developmental characteristics are closely dependent on the attainment of a number of perceptual and cognitive skills. Differentiation of the self from the environment is dependent at least partly on the development of the child's awareness that he can have an effect on the environment. Therefore, study of the infant's exploration and manipulation of objects and attempts to secure feedback from objects in much the way Piaget has described secondary circular behaviors might help in understanding the infant's individuation. The growth of social discrimination is probably tied in with the development of basic perceptual discriminations, not only in the visual and auditory modalities but in the tactile, kinesthetic, and olfactory as well. The development of trust is closely related to the growth of contingency awareness and the capacity for mental representation of objects and persons in their absence—that is, object and person permanence.

The relations between cognitive skills and social development may not be simple unidirectional relationships. It may be that the social-perceptual and cognitive developments do not always precede the social and affective developments. As we have indicated elsewhere, "They may appear concurrently and may simply be different expressions of the same structural changes. In other cases, some cognitive functions, such as object permanence, may be strengthened or consolidated by the formation of social attachments" (Yarrow, 1972, p. 93).

In spite of the tremendous amount of research on attachment, there are no generally acceptable indices of attachment during infancy. Most of the indices are negative behaviors such as withdrawal and crying; researchers have rarely used positive signs of attachment. Studies have been constricted by the paradigms developed in the earliest work on attachment—reactions to strangers and to brief separations. Before we can study the environmental antecedents of variations in focused relationships, we must clarify the concept of attachment and develop more meaningful behavioral indices. We are only beginning to explore some of the substantive problems and methodological issues systematically.

BEYOND COGNITIVE DEVELOPMENT

For some time now a dominant concern of research in infant development has been the growth of cognitive abilities. Even before the stimulus of Piaget, much of developmental research in the first 2 years was concerned with charting the emerging abilities of the infant. With the development of infant tests such as the Bayley and the Cattell Scales of Infant Development, it was thought that this aspect of development could be easily measured. Moreover, as compared to the infant's emotional, personality, or motivational characteristics, it was believed that the intellectual characteristics of the organism had stability and that earlier cognitive functioning was predictive of later intellectual status.

Piaget's first writings appeared in the 1920s, almost at the beginning of scientific research in child development. His observations were either ignored or were superficially assimilated into the then current views of intellectual development. Almost 30 years elapsed before his adaptational view of cognition began to be appreciated. The interconnectedness of motivation, affect, and cognitive functioning was not given serious attention in research until very recently. Piaget's (1936) great contribution to a theory of cognitive development comes from his broad view of cognitive processes. Cognition is not limited to symbolic processes or to the precursors of these processes; it is part of the organism's adaptation to the environment. His descriptions and theoretical discussions of sensorimotor development, primary and secondary circular reactions, and problem-solving behaviors emphasize the interrelatedness of these processes as well as the dynamic interaction between the infant and his environment. Throughout Piaget's writings there is a constant emphasis on the goal-oriented character of behavior. The behaviors he describes are not simple expressions of intellectual abilities—they are expressions of the infant's active striving to act on and to master the environment.

The adaptational viewpoint has also become a significant part of psychoanalytic theory. In psychoanalysis, ego psychology was in its early stages of development at the time of Freud's death. It represented a significant shift from a theory concerned primarily with the origins of pathology to a general theory of behavior, a theory concerned with coping and constructive adaptation. It became a central interest of a number of investigators: Anna

Freud (1966), Hartmann et al. (1946), and Rapaport (1960), among others. Erikson (1959) linked psychoanalysis and developmental psychology. He proposed that the early stages of sensorimotor development, the development of motor skills, and associated manipulation and exploration of objects, eventually lead to a sense of industry, with the child being motivated to engage in behaviors that have significance.

Drawing on psychoanalytic theory, Eriksonian hypotheses, and Piaget's insights, White (1959) affirmed the interdependence of motivation and cognition. He rejected the traditional drive-reduction theory of motivation which viewed all behavior as impelled by the desire to reduce stimulation, and proposed a model that sees the infant as actively seeking and processing stimulation. White contended that the motivation to master and deal competently with the environment is as basic as the physiological drives of hunger and sex.

Hunt (1965) offered a similar alternative to drive-reduction theory, emphasizing that mastery and competent behaviors are self-reinforcing; they lead to an intrinsic motivation to master tasks. He postulated that, almost from birth, the infant is active in attempting to make and maintain visual contact with objects, first with familiar objects, and then, after he adapts to the familiar, he becomes interested in attending to and exploring novel objects. Hunt concludes that "a basic source of motivation is inherent within the organism's informational interaction with its circumstances . . . ."

These theories have been provocative, but there are limited empirical data on this aspect of functioning. The few relevant studies have dealt with some aspect of contingent responsiveness in infancy (Lewis and Goldberg, 1969; Watson, 1966) or with competent behavior in pre-school children (Wenar, 1976; Bronson, 1974). It has been difficult, however, to operationalize the concept and to develop measures of mastery.

In a study of early environmental influences on development we (Yarrow et al., 1972) developed some measures of mastery behavior in 6-month-infants by clustering items on the Bayley Developmental Scales. We found that some of these measures, which we called cognitive-motivational—that is, goal-directedness, reaching and grasping, secondary circular reactions, and problem-solving—were significantly related to a number of environmental variables at 6 months. These measures of the infant's persistent interest in exploring objects and learning about their properties and in securing a response from them were related to the amount of kinesthetic stimulation provided by the mother, to her contingent responsiveness to the infant's distress, and to the variety of social and inanimate stimulation she gave him (Yarrow et al., 1975b).

In a later study, where the primary objective was to develop measures for investigating mastery behavior in 12-month infants, three aspects of mastery motivation were distinguished: persistence in working on difficult tasks, in practicing emerging skills, and in attempting to secure feedback from objects (Yarrow et al., 1977). Some of the same kinds of environmental stimulation (in the first 6 months) as in the earlier study were significantly related to mastery motivation at 12 months: the amount of kinesthetic stimulation, the responsiveness of the mother to the child's signals of distress, and the responsiveness of play materials which were available to the infant (Yarrow, 1977).

Mastery motivation is an area in which further research is needed to develop sensitive and valid indices of this aspect of functioning. After refining the measures, it may be possible to look more closely at the ways in which these aspects of behavior are influenced by experience. Research on mastery is likely to have important implications for developmental theory as well as for intervention programs. Much more is known about the origins of neurosis and the bases for incompetent functioning than about the origins of constructive attempts to handle the environment. The development of the infant's expectation that it can exert some degree of control over the environment is a significant landmark in the growth of a sense of competence and may influence the development of a positive self-concept.

THE ECOLOGICAL PERSPECTIVE ON INFANT DEVELOPMENT

Methods for studying early experience have undergone many changes in the past 50 years; interviews and free observations were replaced for a time by tightly controlled laboratory manipulations and more recently there has been a shift to systematic observations in the home. For a long time, retrospective reports of disturbed individuals were the major source of data. When the distortions of these reports became apparent, prospective studies were initiated. Parents were interviewed about their children's experiences and about their own child-rearing practices. Although verbal report gives important information about parents' conscious perception of their behavior and feelings toward an offspring, it is far from an objective description of the child's experiences. As an alternative to this approach, investigators developed semistructured or experimental situations, focusing on specific parameters of parent and child behaviors (Bishop, 1951); by manipulating variables under carefully controlled conditions, specific hypotheses could be tested.

Experimental situations differ from natural conditions in many significant ways. Laboratory manipulations are usually of short duration and are designed to evoke a limited range of behaviors. The structured laboratory situation may inhibit spontaneous behavior and may elicit different kinds of behaviors from a mother and infant than are evoked in the natural setting. Although much significant information can be obtained about the relations between discrete aspects of maternal behavior and infant response, experimental situations by design do not begin to approximate the total environment in its intricate complexity; they ignore the complex reciprocal interactions of many variables. The information obtained from laboratory findings is limited, and the generalizations that can be made to real-life settings are at best tenuous.

Recognizing the limitations of these artifical situations, investigators began to study child and parent behavior in the natural setting—the home, the school, and the community. Roger Barker (1965), who pioneered in studies of children in their natural environment, contends that psychologists' views of what can be studied are constricted by canons of appropriate methodology. Barker's ecological psychology emphasizes the naive description of observable molar behavior and avoids high-order interpretations of behavior or events. Only relatively recently have mothers and infants been studied in their natural settings, using direct observations (Beckwith, 1971; Clarke-Stewart, 1973; Elardo et al., 1975, 1977; Moss, 1967; Richards and Bernal, 1972; Yarrow, 1963; Yarrow et al., 1975b).

We need methodological studies to clarify a number of issues regarding naturalistic and experimental situations. The broad question is the extent to which findings in contrived situations are similar to findings in natural settings and the points at which they diverge. There are also sampling questions. Whereas the experimental situation may elicit the kind of behaviors in which we are especially interested, in the natural situation it may be difficult to obtain an adequate sample of usual events and behaviors. It is likely that the natural situation may yield very low frequencies of certain experiential categories. Moreover, there may not be a simple monotonic relationship between the frequency or intensity of an event and its impact. In fact there may be critical levels either of frequency or intensity for some environmental events, below or above which they have no observable effects. On the other hand, as Scott and Wertheimer (1962) note in their discussion of experimental and naturalistic methods:

In laboratory studies, the particular functional relationships observed may be in large part a product of the special, artificial conditions of the experiment. such a restriction in generality is likely to be particularly serious in those "hold constant" experiments in which control of extraneous variables artificially places them at levels that would hardly be encountered in the subject's normal activity. A given experiment may show conclusively a relationship between independent and dependent variables, which, however, is demonstrated only under such peculiar circumstances that the result is uninteresting, except as a curiosity. [pp. 95–96]

Aside from sampling problems there is the question of the choice of categories for recording. A microanalytic analysis of a situation may be antithetical to portraying the meaning of the situation. It is difficult to develop objective recording categories that are sufficiently comprehensive to summarize the infant's characteristic experiences and usual responses to these experiences. Descriptive accounts are also selective, both in what is seen and what is recorded. Increasingly, observations are being filmed or videotaped, thus presumably reducing selectivity. Whether videotaping or filming gives the same behavioral cues as live observation is still an unresolved question.

Although we have become aware of these gross and subtle methodological issues, methodological studies are rare. Comparative investigations of the impact of the environment using similar categories in natural and contrived situations are practically nonexistent (Belsky, 1977; Lytton, 1971, 1973; Klein and Durfee, 1977). We are sorely in need of methodological research to gain greater understanding of the distinctive benefits and limitations of experimental and natural situations and to help clarify the similarities and differences in the relationships found in each.

Some proponents of naturalistic investigations maintain that research in the natural situation makes possible generalizations that cannot be made from experimental studies. Laboratory manipulation may permit more precise statements about relations between specific variables and infant outcomes, but as Willems (1969) has pointed out, "unless someone explicitly investigates the phenomenon outside the laboratory the investigator has no basis for knowing whether his statements are important or trivial beyond the conditions of the laboratory." In addition, we need much more descriptive information about the usual, expectable environments of infants, and about the distinctive experiences of an infant, data that can only be obtained by studying the infant in his natural environment.

The arguments for naturalistic observations must be tempered by a recognition that the boundaries between naturalistic and experimental methods are not always sharply defined. There is not a basic discontinuity; naturalistic and experimental are on a continuum. Menzel (1969) indicates that what the experimenter does is begin with a small field of view and zoom out to more molar units and larger contexts, whereas the naturalistic investigator begins with a broad view and zooms in to more molecular phenomena. For some purposes at certain times, the naturalistic approach is preferable; at other times and for other purposes the experimental approach may make more sense.

THE NEW VIEW OF THE INFANT AND ENVIRONMENT: SOME RECENT HISTORICAL ANTECEDENTS

The notion of infant-environment interaction evolved with our growing knowledge of the infant's competence. Research that documented the infant's capabilities and active striving for mastery contributed to this view. But it was not simply this knowledge; researchers and theoreticians were also at a point in time when they were ready to give up the search for simple causal relations between the environment and the child's development and to take a more dynamic view of interaction. This receptivity to an interactionist view has been an important change in the basic orientation to infancy research that has occurred in recent years, one that is still in process; it has not yet been assimilated in the mainstream of theory nor consolidated in the views and methodologies of infant researchers.

This orientation is not a totally new one; it is a theme that has emerged recurrently in the history of psychology. It was articulated and developed systematically by Kurt Lewin (1954) in his dynamic theory of personality, a theory that represented psychological concepts in terms of mathematical topology. A central concept is the psychological environment, a concept that holds that the environment and the person are inextricably interrelated. From this perspective, the objective physical environment has no direct influence on behavior; its influence derives from its meaning to the person. In order to understand the relation between a stimulus and behavior, it is necessary to know how the infant perceives the environment, its idiosyncratic meaning to the young child.

The personal definition of the child's experience is acquiring new force in developmental psychology. Increasingly, we are coming to recognize that objective stimuli defined in terms of their physical properties cannot be seen as simple instigators of behavior; the physical stimulus acquires its distinctive meaning from the organism. It is undoubtedly as true for infants as for older children and adults, but it creates especially difficult problems for infancy research. With the older child one can ask about the meaning of the stimulus to him, but with the young infant we can only make inferences as to its idiosyncratic meaning.

In recent years the concept of the "effective environment" has become part of our thinking about environmental influences (Yarrow and Goodwin, 1965). The effective environment includes those aspects of the environment that have an impact on the infant. Its importance lies in the recognition that not all events have equal impact. One way of dealing with the implicit tautology in this view is to define the effective environment indirectly in relation to the individualized vulnerabilities and sensitivities of the young child. We need to be sensitive to more subtle cues than we have in the past and to make fine differentiations of infant responses to small variations in stimuli in order to obtain indirect evidence of their meaning to the infant. We can also, as we have in studying infant temperament, develop techniques for identifying infant sensitivities to different kinds and intensities of stimuli (Brazelton, 1973; Escalona, 1968; Murphy, 1962). We have to be sensitive to a variety of nonverbal cues, such as approach and withdrawal movements, defensive gestures, intensity of focus on people and objects, and a range of variation in positive and negative responses to people and objects. Moreover, through refinements in neurophysiological recording, we should be able to document how such stimulation is processed.

THE IMPLICATIONS OF RESEARCH IN INFANT DEVELOPMENT FOR PUBLIC POLICIES

Parallelling the enormous research activity and important discoveries in child development in the past 50 years has been a significant growth in public programs to safeguard the health and well-being of the infant and young child. Although they have influenced each other, it has been difficult to see the direct interplay between research findings and public policies and programs. Public policies, of course, are never direct expressions of our findings in child development; they are always tempered by the value systems of the larger culture, the political process, and the particular time when they are being developed. In research on infant development the scientific *Zeitgeist* and social policy issues are never completely independent. The larger society exerts pressures, sometimes subtly and sometimes bluntly, on the research of a particular discipline. Physical and biological scientists in the past have been somewhat insulated from these pressures because in some areas these disciplines have had separate fields dedicated to the interpretation and application of scientific findings. However, in the behavioral sciences, which have no separate engineering profession, those directly engaged in research have, to varying degrees, always been subjected to demands of social relevance.

Throughout the history of scientific child development, interpreters of child research have been alert to the implications of findings for parents and teachers. Certainly John Watson's theories were quickly incorporated into the lore of child rearing in the 1920s. Sometimes findings are prematurely translated into programs and policies. Perhaps our vivid memories of the too facile application of Watsonian principles induced caution in many researchers in trying to apply the results of child development research. There probably is need in child development for what might be comparable to engineers in other fields, to systematically translate the implications of research for public policies for children as well as their more immediate implications for childrearing. There is a body of knowledge obtained in abstract settings that needs to be tested in real situations. It would be desirable if the implications of these findings were explicitly stated and then tested; but, of course, this may not be reasonable ethically.

Translating findings into programs to promote the well-being of children seems, on the surface, to be simple, but when we look at this task closely we realize that it is not so simple. Programs for children can never be literal translations of findings, but must represent the distillation of wisdom that comes about through thoughtful consideration of the data in a broader context of the goals and values of the larger culture. At least in its earlier phases, research workers should be responsible for the first step in drawing implications, since they know the data intimately, both where they come from and what they mean. The individual investigator is likely to have a better feel for how readily the findings can be applied in particular situations. Then the child development engineers might take over.

However, there are few areas of research where investigators feel findings are sufficiently solid to permit one to make definitive statements about applications. It requires filtering a great number of findings through our theoretical lenses and seeing them in relation to other data, some of which may be only peripherally related to the issues with which we are directly concerned. But we can arrive at intelligent guesses and should be reasonably comfortable in evolving courses of action that have implications for prevention, intervention, or effective therapy (Clarke-Stewart, 1977).

Among the findings that we can accept with a fair degree of assurance are the existence of differential sensitivities at different periods of development. These findings have implications for the kinds of stimulation we provide for children at different levels of development. Knowing that there is a greater likelihood that children will respond with distress to separation from their mothers after 6 months has direct practical significance for the timing of the mother's return to work or for moving a child from a foster to an adoptive home. We also have some data that suggest ways to mitigate these reactions, such as sharing caregiving between parents from birth and possibly inoculating the infant against extreme stranger reactions by gradual exposure to substitute caregivers. There is much we do not know about alternative caregiving—for instance, whether there is an upper limit to the number of persons with whom the infant can establish meaningful relationships, even if these persons are sensitive and responsive. We only know from the institutional studies that having many changing caregivers, no one of whom is closely invested in the infant, is likely to impair the child's capacity to establish meaningful relationships.

The growing conviction that early experiences do not inexorably determine the future course of development but that experiences throughout the life cycle may modify or even reverse initially harmful effects has tremendous implications for intervention programs and for our general orientation to therapeutically beneficial experiences throughout life. It suggests that it may be possible to intervene at any point in the developmental cycle. Recognition that the impact of early experience represents an interaction between the environment and the sensitivities of the infant suggests that our recommendations for early child care and for specific interventions must be tailored to the individual child's characteristics.

A current policy issue of high priority is day care. This issue illustrates some of the difficulties in making policy recommendations on the basis of research findings. Although there have been few methodologically sound studies, on the whole, the findings indicate that there are no differences in cognitive development between children who had attended day care centers and those reared exclusively in the home (Bronfenbrenner, 1976). With regard to attachment and emotional development the findings are not consistent across studies. There is evidence (Blehar, 1974) that infants in day care show greater separation anxiety (crying, attempting to follow the mother, decreased exploratory behavior) than children who have not been in day care; other studies find no differences (Caldwell et al., 1970). We are very much in need of follow-up studies of the social and cognitive development of children who have been in day care to determine whether there are any long-term effects. Equally important are studies of variations in forms of day care, such as home day care by a surrogate, group day care in which the mother participates on a part-time basis, and shared day care in which mother and father alternate in assuming responsibility for the child.

The discrepant findings in studies of day care may be due in part to the fact that we have taken the term, day care, and assumed it is a simple homogeneous entity, when in fact there are great variations in the psychological dimensions of day care programs—variations in the kind of stimulation offered the infants, in the ability of teacher-caregivers to individualize their behaviors with children, and in the capacity of the teachers to provide warmth. Moreover, there is great variability in structural characteristics such as staff turnover. These factors, as well as a variety of methodological problems—such as matching control and experimental groups in terms of both the mother-infant attachment prior to day care and the mother-infant relationship after the child is in day care—will have a significant influence on the findings. Even with clear findings, one's values may influence interpretation of similar data. For example, the findings that children who have had day care experience are freer than non-day-care children in expressing direct verbal and physical aggression toward other children and adults has had very different interpretations. In the one case this behavior has been interpreted as being indicative of greater self-assertiveness and less conformity. In another case, similar findings are thought to be symptomatic of generally poor adjustment (Bronfenbrenner, 1976). All of these factors only suggest the complexity of the issues which may inhibit some researchers from making too facile recommendations about social policy issues.

If we look closely at the history of child development research we realize that vacillation and ambivalence about making recommendations for social policy have been characteristic of researchers for a long time. The first organized research institutes were institutes of child welfare. Although a great variety of problems were studied then, problems of society had a significant place in the research pursuits of that time. In the decades that followed, especially in the late 1940s and the early 1950s there was a strong tendency to identify with the physical and biological sciences, an identification associated with veneration of objectivity and to some extent an avoidance of concern about application. During this period, it sometimes seemed as if rats were preferred as research subjects to the too-complex human. During the past 10 years, the professional self-image of the child development researcher seems to be changing. Research in child development has become more deeply involved with the problems of society and the applied aspects of social work, pediatrics, psychiatry, and education. We are becoming less fearful of trying to translate our research findings into socially relevant models that can be used by policy makers and program designers. Moreover, we recognize the value of testing our theoretically based hypotheses in real-life situations. It forces us to revise, polish, and elaborate our theories.

There still remains a strong awareness of the tentative state of our knowledge and some reluctance about drawing implications for programs. Most of our research can only give some suggestive clues or partial answers to the big questions that we ask. Our research paradigms have been simplistic; they deal only with a very few of the many variables operating in complicated life situations. This fact places a special burden on the scientist *not* to be limited to excessively narrow interpretations of findings, but to be more creative in thinking about the implications of findings for programs and policies. There is a sensitive balance between drawing inappropriate conclusions based on one's humanistic or political biases and being sufficiently free to think imaginatively and to draw creative implications from one's data. It demands *both* creativity and restraint in setting up appropriately rigorous research designs, in measuring a few variables, and then making sensible interpretations of these limited findings. But the real test of our creativity comes when we are asked to elaborate on the meaning of these findings for social programs. We need to see our data in the perspective of other findings and theoretical integrations. After viewing them from this perspective, we need the courage to be willing to make broad leaps in suggesting what needs to be done, always recognizing that these recommendations represent the best considered judgment at this point in time. Of course, we must always remain open to drastic revisions as new knowledge is acquired.

It seems clear that, in spite of the dearth of systematic efforts by investigators of infant development to translate their findings for the practitioner, much of the knowledge that we have acquired in developmental research has had both a direct and indirect influence on programs and policies for children. Sometimes this influence has been subtle; our research findings have affected society's view of the child. The gradually accumulating knowledge about the young child that has penetrated into the popular consciousness has influenced individual's and society's feeling towards children and in many ways it has influenced what we do with children.

OVERVIEW

The issues in infant development we have presented are basically variations on a theme. They are elaborations of the question of how the environment interacts with the changing biological organism and how both continue to mutually influence each other. They are questions of how cognitive, social, emotional, and motivational functions emerge, how these characteristics selectively screen and give meaning to experience and in turn are modified by experience. Within this theme there are divergent and contradictory notes. We must accept the biological givens which set limits to the environmental influences which can be apprehended; these organismic characteristics determine not only which environmental events can have impact but the extent of their impact. We must be aware that the specific environmental stimuli which we have isolated for study may have very different effects individually than in concert; the larger patterns of stimulation may have very different meaning than the individual stimuli.

We have seen how many aspects of functioning, which have become separated and, to some extent, isolated for purposes of study, are closely dependent upon and influence each other. For example, our traditional distinction between independent and dependent variables breaks down in thinking of the mother-infant relationship. This close interdependence is evident in cognitive functioning as well. The capacity to make perceptual discriminations is basic to the discrimination of persons; memory and the development of object permanence are necessary for the development of trust in the mother; these same functions influence the capacity to distance oneself from objects and represent them symbolically. Similar interdependencies are found for cognitive and motivational characteristics.

Research in the past half- century has contributed significantly to the mosaic of infant development, and we can expect systematic and serendipitous findings in the future to fill in more pieces of this complex mosaic. In spite of the progress and the mass of data, many of the questions with which the study of infant development began still remained unanswered or unresolved. Consolidation of our gains can probably only come about through an integrative theoretical framework which will point up the inconsistencies, guide the formulation of problems, and suggest future directions.

As our knowledge of infant development increases, our awareness of the complexity of development becomes more deeply entrenched. To study infant development requires a harmonious balance of a number of contradictory characteristics: a sensitivity to minute variations in behavior, an ability to draw tentative conclusions while remaining open to new evidence, a capacity to delay premature closure on issues, and an ability to reconcile these characteristics with a healthy respect for evidence.

BIBLIOGRAPHY

Ainsworth, M. D. S. The development of infant-mother attachment. In B. Caldwell and H. Ricciuti (eds.), *Review of Child Development Research*. Chicago: University of Chicago, 1973.

Bakeman, R., and Brown, J. V. Behavioral dialogues: An approach to the assessment of mother-infant interaction. *Child Development*, 1977, **48**, 195–203.

Barker, R. G. Explorations in ecological psychology. *American Psychologist*, 1965, **20**, 1–14.

Beckwith, L. Relationships between attributes of mothers and their infants' IQ scores. *Child Development*, 1971, **42**, 1083–1097.

Bell, R. Q., Weller, G. M., and Waldrop, M. F. Newborn and Preschooler: Organization of behavior and relations between periods. *Monographs of Society for Research in Child Development*, 1971, **36** (1–2; serial 142).

Belsky, J. Mother-infant interaction at home and in the laboratory: The effect of setting. Paper presented at the meetings of the society for Research in Child Development, New Orleans, March 1977.

Benjamin, J. D. Prediction and psychopathological theory. In L. Jessner and E. Pavenstedt (eds.), *Dynamics of Psychopathology in Childhood*. New York: Grune & Stratton, 1959.

Benjamin, J. D. Further comments on some developmental aspects of anxiety. In H. S. Gaskill (ed.), *Counterpoint*. New York: International Universities, 1963.

Berger, M., and Passingham, R. E. Early experience and other environmental factors: An overview. In H. J. Eysenck (ed.), *Handbook of Abnormal Psychology*, 2nd ed. London: Pitman's, 1973.

Bishop, B. M. Mother-child interaction and the social behavior of children. *Psychological Monographs*, 1951, **65** (11).

Blehar, M. Anxious attachment and defensive reactions associated with day care. *Child Development*, 1974, **45**, 683–692.

Bowlby, J. *Maternal Care and Mental Health*. Geneva: World Health, 1951.

Bowlby, J. *Attachment and Loss: I. Attachment*. New York: Basic Books, 1969.

Bowlby, J., Ainsworth, M., Boston, M., and Rosenbluth, D. The effects of mother-child separation: A follow-up study. *British Journal of Medical Psychology*, 1956, **29**, 211–247.

Brazelton, T. B. *Neonatal Behavioral Assessment Scale*. Philadelphia: Lippincot, 1973.

Bronfenbrenner, U. Research on the effects of day care on child development. *Towards a National Policy for Children and Families*. Washington, D.C.: National Academy of Sciences, 1976, 117–133.

Bronson, W. C. Competence and the growth of personality. In K. J. Connolly and J. S. Bruner (eds.), *The Growth of Competence*. New York: Academic, 1974.

Cairns, R. B. Attachment and dependency: A psychological and social learning synthesis. In J. Gerwirtz (ed.), *Attachment and Dependency*. Washington, D.C.: Winston, Halsted, 1972.

Caldwell, B. M., Wright, C., Honig, A., and Tannenbaum, J. Infant day care and attachment. *American Journal of Orthopsychiatry*, 1970, **40**, 397–412.

Clarke-Stewart, K. A. Interactions between mothers and their young children: Characteristics and consequences. *Monographs of the Society for Research in Child Development*, 1973, **38** (153).

Clarke-Stewart, A. Child care in the family. A review of research and some propositions for policy. New York, Academic Press, 1977.

Duncan, O. D. Path analysis: Sociological examples. *American Journal of Sociology*, 1966, **72**, 1–16.

Elardo, R., Bradley, R., and Caldwell, B. The relation of infants' home environments to mental test performance from six to thirty-six months: A longitudinal analysis. *Child Development*, 1975, **46**, 71–76.

Elardo, R., Bradley, R., and Caldwell, B. A longitudinal study of the relation of infants' home environments to language development at age three. *Child Development*, 1977, **48**, 595–603.

Erikson, E. H. *Identity and the Life Cycle*. New York: International Universities, 1959.

Escalona, S. K. *The Roots of Individuality*. Chicago: Aldine, 1968.

Freud, A. *The Ego and the Mechanisms of Defense*. New York: International Universities, 1966.

Gewirtz, J. Dependency and a distinction in terms of stimulus controls. In J. Gewirtz (ed.), *Attachment and Dependency*. Washington, D.C.: Winston, Halsted, 1972.

Hartmann, H., Kris, E., and Lowenstein, R. N. Comments on the formation of the psychic structure. *Psychoanalytic Study of the Child*, 1946, **2**, 11–38.

Hartmann, H. *Ego Psychology and the Problem of Adaptation*. New York: International Universities, 1939.

Hunt, J. Mc.V. Intrinsic motivation and its role in psychological development. In D. Levine (ed.), *Nebraska Symposium on Motivation*. Lincoln: University of Nebraska, 1965.

Klein, R. P., and Durfee, J. T. Effects of sex and birth order on infant social behavior. *Infant Behavior and Development*, 1978, **1**, 106–117.

Lamb, M. (ed.) *The Role of the Father in Child Development*. New York: Wiley, 1976.

Lewin, K. Behavior and development as a function of the total situation. In L. Carmichael (ed.), *Manual of Child Psychology*. New York: Wiley, 1954.

Lewis, M., and Goldberg, S. Perceptual cognitive development in infancy: A generalized expectancy model as a function of the mother-infant interaction. *Merrill-Palmer Quarterly*, 1969, **15**, 81–100.

Li, C. C. *Path analysis: A primer*. Pacific Grove: Boxwood, 1977.

Lytton, H. Observation studies of parent-child interaction: A methodological review. *Child Development*, 1971, **42**, 651–684.

Lytton, H. Three approaches to the study of parent-child interaction: Ethological, interview and experimental. *Journal of Child Psychology and Psychiatry*, 1973, **14**, 1–17.

Maccoby, E. E., and Masters, J. C. Attachment and dependency. In P. H. Mussen (ed.), *Carmichael's Manual of Child Psychology*. New York: Wiley, 1970.

Menzel, E. W., Jr. Naturalistic and experimental approaches to primate behavior. In E. Willems and H. Raush (eds.), *Naturalistic Viewpoints in Psychological Research*. New York: Holt, Rinehart, & Winston, 1969.

Murphy, L. B. *The Widening World of Childhood*. New York: Basic Books, 1962.

Moss, H. A. Sex, age and state as determinants of mother-infant interaction. *Merrill-Palmer Quarterly*, 1967, **13**, 19–36.

Pedersen, F. A., Yarrow, L. J., and Strain, B. A. Conceptualization of father influences and its implications for an observational methodology. Paper presented at the biennial meeting of the International Society for the Study of Behavioral Development, Guilford, England, July 1975.

Piaget, J. *The Origins of Intelligence in the Child*. New York: International Universities, 1953. (First published 1936.)

Rapaport, D. On the psychoanalytic theory of motivation. In M. R. Jones (ed.), *Nebraska Symposium on Motivation*. Lincoln: University of Nebraska, 1960.

Rheingold, H. L. The effect of environmental stimulation upon social and exploratory behavior in the human infant. In B. M. Foss (ed.), *Determinants of Infant Behavior*. New York: Wiley, 1961.

Richards, M. P. M., and Bernal, J. F. An observational study of mother-infant interaction. In N. B. Jones (ed.), *Ethological Studies of Child Behavior*. London: Cambridge University, 1972.

Rutter M., Birch, H. G., Thomas, A., and Chess, S. Temperamental characteristics in infancy and the later development of behavior disorders. *British Journal of Psychiatry*, 1964, **110**, 651–661.

Sameroff, A. J., and Chandler, M. J. Reproductive risk and the continuum of caretaking casualty. In F. Horowitz, E. M. Hetherington, S. Scarr-Salapatek, and G. Siegel (eds.), *Review of Child Development Research*, Vol. 4. Chicago: University of Chicago, 1975.

Schwarz, J. C., Strickland, R. G., and Krolick, G. Infant day care: Behavioral effects at preschool age. *Developmental Psychology*, 1974, **10**, 502–506.

Scott, W. A., and Wertheimer, M. *Introduction to Psychological Research*. New York: Wiley, 1962.

Sears, R. R. *Survey of Objective Studies of Psychoanalytic Concepts*. New York: Social Science Research, 1943.

Sears, R. R., Whiting, J. W. M., Nowlis, V., and Sears, P. S. Some childrearing antecedents of dependency and aggression in young children. *Genetic Psychology Monographs*, 1953, **47**, 135–234.

Shereshefsky, P. M., and Yarrow, L. J. (Eds.) *Psychological Aspects of a First Pregnancy and Early Postnatal Adaptation.* New York: Raven, 1973.

Spitz, R. A., Emde, R., and Metcalf, D. Further prototypes of ego formation: A working paper from a research project on early development. *Psychoanalytic Study of the Child.* 1970, **25**, 417–441.

Tennes, K., Emde, R., Kisley, A., and Metcalf, D. The stimulus barrier in early infancy: An exploration of some formulations of John Benjamin. *Psychoanalysis and Contemporary Science,* 1972, **1**, 206–234.

Thomas, A., Birch, H., Chess, S., Hertzig, M., and Korn, S. *Behavioral Individuality in Early Childhood.* New York: New York University, 1963.

Thomas, A., Chess, S., and Birch, H. G. *Temperament and Behavior Disorders in Children.* New York: New York University, 1968.

Watson, J. S. The development and generalization of "contingency awareness" in early infancy: Some hypotheses. *Merrill-Palmer Quarterly,* 1966, **12**, 123–135.

Wenar, C. Executive competence in toddlers: A prospective, observational study. *Genetic Psychology Monographs,* 1976, **93**, 189–285.

Wenner, N., Cohen, M., Weigert, E., Kvarnes, R., Ohanesen, E., and Fearing, J. Emotional problems in pregnancy. *Psychiatry,* 1969, **32**, 389–410.

White, R. Motivation reconsidered: The concept of competence. *Psychological Review,* 1959, **66**, 297–333.

Whiting, J. W. M., and Whiting, B. B. Contributions of anthropology to methods of studying child rearing. In P. H. Mussen (ed.), *Handbook of Research Methods in Child Development.* New York: Wiley, 1959.

Willems, E. Planning a rationale for naturalistic research. In E. Willems and H. Raush (eds.), *Naturalistic Viewpoints in Psychological Research.* New York: Holt, Rinehart, & Winston, 1969.

Wolf, K. M. Observations of individual tendencies in the first year of life. In M. J. E. Senn (ed.), *Problems of Infancy and Childhood.* New York: Macy Foundation, 1953.

Yarrow, L. J. Research in dimensions of early maternal care. *Merrill-Palmer Quarterly,* 1963, **9**, 101–114.

Yarrow, L. J. The development of focused relationships in infancy. In J. Hellmuth (ed.), *The Exceptional Infant,* Vol. I. *The Normal Infant.* Seattle: Special Child, 1967.

Yarrow, L. J. Attachment and dependency: A developmental perspective. In J. Gewirtz (ed.), *Attachment and Dependency.* Washington, D.C.: Winston, Halsted, 1972.

Yarrow, L. J. The origins of mastery motivation. Paper presented at the annual meetings of the American Academy of Child Psychiatry, October 1976.

Yarrow, L. J., and Goodwin, M. S. Some conceptual issues in the study of mother-infant interaction. *American Journal of Orthopsychiatry,* 1965, **35**, 473–481.

Yarrow, L. J., Rubenstein, J. L., Pedersen, F. A., and Jankowski, J. J. Dimensions of early stimulation and their differential effects on infant development. *Merrill-Palmer Quarterly,* 1972, **18**, 205–218.

Yarrow, L. J., Soule, B., Standley, K., Duchowny, M., and Copans, S. Parents and infants: An interactive network. Symposium presented at the annual convention of the American Psychological Association, New Orleans, August 1974.

Yarrow, L. J., Klein, R. P., Lomonaco, S., and Morgan, G. Cognitive and motivational development in early childhood. In B. Z. Friedlander, G. M. Sterritt, and G. E. Kirk (eds.), *Exceptional Infant,* Vol. 3. *Assessment and Intervention.* New York: Brunner/Mazel, 1975a.

Yarrow, L. J., Rubenstein, J. L., and Pedersen, F. A. *Infant and Environment: Early Cognitive and Motivational Development.* New York: Hemisphere, Halsted, 1975b.

Yarrow, L. J., and Pedersen, F. A. Interplay between cognition and motivation in infancy. In M. Lewis (ed.), *Origins of Intelligence: Infancy and Early Childhood*. New York: Plenum, 1976.

Yarrow, L. J., Morgan, G. A., Jennings, K. D., Harmon, R. J., and Gaiter, J. L. Conceptualization and measurement of mastery motivation. Unpublished, 1977.

Yarrow, L. J., and Anderson, B. A. Methodological perspectives in observing parent-infant interaction. In E. J. Thoman and V. Dennenberg (eds.), *The origins of the infant's social responsiveness*. Hillside, N.J.: Erlbaum, 1978.

Yarrow, M. R. Problems of method in parent-child research. *Child Development,* 1963, **34,** 215–226.

Author Index

Numbers in *italics* indicate page numbers on which full references appear.

Subject Index